首都

地绿、水清……

右上：春天的北京街头

右下：北京东北郊草皮种植中心

新兴农业发展喜人

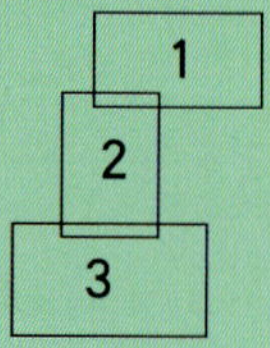

①北京蝴蝶兰繁殖中心
②北京大兴县庞各庄以闻名全国的西瓜，开展观光农业
③大兴县长子营乡的蔬菜基地

工交生产形势良好

左：北京高碑店热电厂机组安装

右：京九铁路配套工程—北京西黄线铁路铺设完工

文化事业
蓬勃发展

北京图书大厦

商品市场
购销两旺

按旧前门火车站原貌修建的商业楼

环保日发放环保布袋

环境保护
深入人心

环保日街头宣传

建设中的首都新航站楼

东四环朝阳桥正在铺设沥青路面

人民共和国

50周年

首都建设项目巡礼

天安门城楼大修

天安门广场整修工程紧张进行

故宫筒子河铺方砖完工

八达岭高速公路投入使用

地铁复八线开始全面铺轨

北京市人

Beijing Talent

每周三、周六、周日定期举行人才交流洽谈会

为人尽其才服务——
神圣崇高的职业
内涵丰富的专业
功德无量的事业
大有作为的产业

北京市人才服务中心是经市委、市政府批准成立，由市委组织部、市人事局共同领导的全市综合性人才市场社会化服务机构。

北京市人才服务中心前身是1984年6月成立的北京市人才交流服务中心。为进一步健全功能，完善组织机构，为发展人才市场提供全方位服务，1993年9月扩建为北京市人才服务中心。

中心主要业务是：

1、开办北京人才市场，建立北京人才信息系统，收集、发布人才供求信息，为各类人才提供就业指导，进行职业介绍。

2、根据政府有关社会保险政策，协助政府主管部门做好流动人员和人事代理单位社会保险基金的筹集、管理、发放工作，做好市级国家机关被辞退公务员管理工作。

3、开展流动人员人事档案管理、因私出国政审以及其它有关工作。

4、开展国际间的人才交流与合作，提供出国留学、就业等咨询服务。

5、开展人才培训工作。

6、开展人才素质测评与考试工作。

7、开展人事代理业务。

8、开发老年人才资源为社会服务。

9、协调指导各区、县人才服务中心的工作。

10、开展市委、市政府交办的其他业务。

才服务中心

Service Centre

◀ 北京市人事档案社会管理中心管理流动人员人事档案，开具相关的各种人事证明办理因私出国政审，承办申报专业技术职务资格等人事管理工作。拥有全国最大的人才档案库。

值得终生奉献的事业

到今年6月21日，市人才中心成立15周年了。我作为中心的创始人之一，看到今天如此蓬勃发展的人才市场感到极大地欣慰。就北京而言，15年前市人才中心成立之日，标志着人才流动开始进入有组织地推动发展之时。当时，人事工作一部分职能由管理转向服务，人才资源的配置由计划转向市场，一切都在刚刚开始。面对强大的旧体制、旧观念，人才中心按照改革发展的方向在相当长的一段时间内为开通航道在艰难探索中破冰前进。15年后的今天，已是千帆竞发，百舸争流，人才市场进入了万紫千红的春天。这是改革开放的硕果，是历史的必然，其中也有我们中心辛勤耕耘的汗水。

15年，是从计划经济转向市场经济发生历史性巨变的15年，市人才中心从成立到尔后的发展壮大，是这一历史时代所发生的深刻社会变化的缩影。在市场经济的推动下，各条战线深化改革，从根本上改善了人才市场培育发展的社会环境。今天，市人才中心已有14个工作部门、200余名工作人员，每年参加中心举办的各种业务活动的人才达40万人次，无论是服务规模还是服务能力，这在15年前都是不可想象的。15年的发展是喜人的，但是，这并不值得骄傲。与发达的市场经济国家相比，我国的市场经济还不成熟，我国的人才市场也同样不成熟。总体上看，人才资源配置的市场化程度还不高，服务还比较粗放，形式比较单一，手段比较落后。人才市场的发展刚刚起了个好头，要做的事情还很多。比如，就业指导、职业咨询业务、信息网络的发展完善，企业经营管理人才市场的机制建设，中国猎头业务的发展、市场价格体系的形成和薪资调查业的发展，人才素质测评的技术开发和市场开发、各种适合市场需要的人才派遣业务、以市场为导向的转换岗位培训、扩大国际人才的交流与合作等等，都是目前相对薄弱而又发展潜力很大的业务。

中国是人力资源大国，又是人才资源相对短缺的发展中国家，另一方面，人才的浪费也确实相当严重地存在着，市场经济给每个人的职业生涯注入了活力，我们的工作牵涉到千家万户，事关社会的发展、国家的兴旺，也事关老百姓安居乐业的生活向往。不论从哪个意义上，我们干的这一行都是值得终生奉献的事业。我常对同事们说，为人才服务，是神圣崇高的职业，是内涵丰富的专业，是功德无量的事业，是大有作为的产业。借市人才中心成立15周年之机，我衷心地期望全体同仁们热爱这项事业，继续竭心尽智，不懈地努力，在这伟大的改革时代，为人才市场这一特殊行业的发展奉献自己的力量。

北京市人才服务中心主任　韩光耀

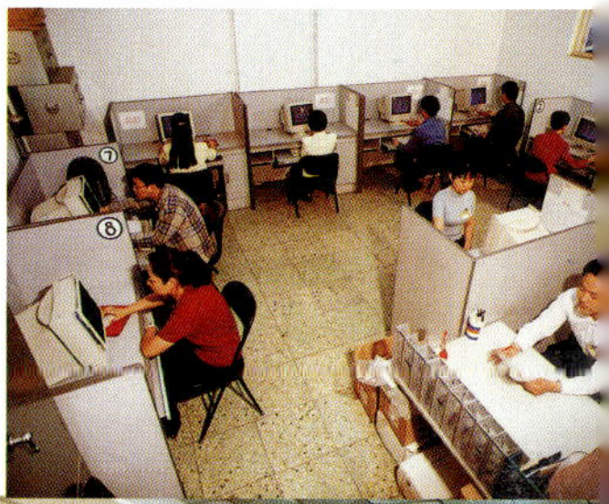

▶用人单位通过计算机信息系统查询各类人才信息

▲ 社会保障部为存档单位和个人提供养老保险、个人提供养老保险、失业保险、医疗保险和住房公积金服务

地址：北京市劳动人民文化宫内
电话：65123374　传真：65232103
邮编：100006
网址：WWW.BJRC.COM
电子邮件：service@bjrc.com

北 京

国安电气总公司

Beijing Guo An Electrical Company

北京国安电气公司创建于1988年6月，系中信国安总公司下属全资子公司，肩负着中信公司开展通信业务的光荣使命。

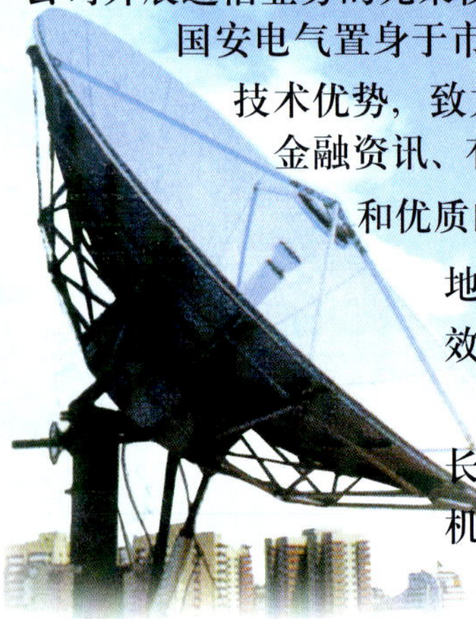

国安电气置身于市场经济的大潮，置根于信息产业的沃土，充分发挥人才、资金和技术优势，致力于拓展以通信业务为核心的主体业务，在卫星通信、移动通信、金融资讯、有线电视、计算机网络系统诸领域，以其先进的设备、合理的价位和优质的服务迅速占领市场，成就卓著。同时，公司还涉足海陆运输、房地产开发、医疗仪器研制等业务领域，取得了良好的经济效益和社会效益。

国安电气的经营活动以北京为中心，辐射全国，在天津、武汉、长沙、西安、沈阳、青岛、张家港、连云港、郑州等地均设立了分支机构，并先后与日本、台湾等国家和地区的公司组建了合资企业。

面向二十一世纪，国安电气总公司的努力方向和奋斗目标是，本着中信“遵纪守法、作风正派、实事求是、开拓创新、谦虚谨慎、团结互助、勤勉奋发、雷厉风行”的精神，继续以通信、信息业为核心，牢固树立科学的经营观念，把电气公司建设成为一个实力雄厚，技术一流，跨地区、跨行业的高科技产业集团。

地址：北京市海淀区海淀南路32号

邮编：100080

电话：62541748　62541923

传真：62541943

莱太花卉®
Flower

北京莱太花卉交易中心是在北京市、朝阳区人民政府的大力支持下，由朝阳区太阳宫乡农工商总公司与北京国朝国有资产运营有限公司联合投资1.24亿元兴建的占地面积为23,000平方米的亚太地区最大的花卉超级市场、批发市场和拍卖市场。

本交易中心直接引进了荷兰的先进技术设施和管理模式，建立了符合中国国情的花卉经营体系，具备了与国际市场接轨的条件。率先在国内采用了花卉超市形式和拍卖交易形式，并率先推行花卉等级标准。本交易中心努力成为全国花卉的高科技示范中心、培训中心、博览中心和信息中心。

本交易中心地处东三环商业旺地，紧邻第三、四使馆区，交通便利，距机场仅16公里。与著名的亮马河商业区仅相距500米，经营中外名优的特色鲜切花、盆花、观叶植物及花卉相关的花土、花肥、花药、图书、园林器械、音像制品等。同时，还具有128K带宽的互联网信息系统（Internet网络）以及银行、保险、通讯、运输等配套机构。

北京莱太花卉有限公司

Beijing Lai Tai Flower & Plant Co., Ltd.

交易中心不仅是消费者满意的大型花卉交易场所，也是北京市内又一个独具特色的旅游观光景点。

①开业典礼②超市一角③展示大厅 ④花卉超市

亚太花卉热忱欢迎国内外朋友光临惠顾

地址：北京市朝阳区麦子店西路9号
邮编：100016
电话：64636554　64636048
传真：64634556
电子信箱：Webmaster@laitai.com
No.9 Maizidian West Road
Chaoyang District Beijing
People's Republic Of China
Post Code:100016
Tel:64636554　64636048
Fax:64634556
E-mail:Webmaster@laitai.com

广东发展银行北京分行

精干的员工队伍

广东发展银行北京分行成立于1997年12月30日，行址位于北京市东城区东单大华路2号。该行以“服务立行、科技兴行、创新求实、稳健经营”为办行宗旨，遵循“以人为本”的企业理念，以“精品银行”为奋斗目标。

为办成具有广发特色的高起点、规范化、现代化的商业银行，向社会提供全方位的金融服务，他们提出要创办“精品银行”，即“精干的员工队伍，精良的技术装备，精简的机构设置，精确的市场定位，精益求精的敬业精神”。

▲ 宽敞明亮的营业大厅

在未来的发展道路上，他们将以科技为支撑，以创新为突破，以稳健经营为保障，以优质服务为基础，努力把北京分行建成现代化、规范化的“精品银行”。

▶ 1998年5月28日，广东发展银行北京分行举办“献爱心”专场演出，李宝光行长（右一）代表该行向中华慈善总会捐款。

北京开关厂

厂长：黄国诚

北京开关厂始建于1952年，系研制和生产高、低压电器、高、低压成套配电装置及核电站控制设备的大型企业，是机械工业统计学会，高压电器行业统计支会会长单位。法人代表黄国诚。企业占地面积19.3万平方米，建筑面积12.4万平方米，厂房面积8.1万平方米，总资产6.523亿元。现有职工2916名，其中工程技术人员约600名，管理人员273名。

北京开关厂在连续5年生产经营以20%以上年均速度增长情况下，1998年完成工业总产值2.8091亿元；产品销售收入为3.8125亿元，包含三产为4.5亿元，实现利税2718万元，含三产为3330万元；承接订货销售额6.5亿元。北开厂在人均工业总产值、人均销售收入、劳产率等经济效益综合指标上名列全国五大开关制造厂前列。1988年至1997年，十年来产值增长了2.8倍；销售收入增长了4.6倍；总资产增长了4.66倍。

企业精神：团结拼搏、志在一流；经营管理思想：坚持全员、全方位、全过程实施99＋“1”＝0的管理。此种管理思想的实质是：坚持以市场为导向、以“零缺陷”严格要求，以“零起点”不断进取，以“零突破”创新发展。

北开是全国机械工业文明单位和北京市双十佳企业，厂长黄国诚同志被授予双十佳厂长、全国五一劳动奖章荣誉称号，北开于1997年获得全国“五一劳动奖状”，1997年机械部、电力部授予本厂“全国电站服务优秀奖牌”，北京市质量管理协会授予“用户满意企业”。

地址：北京市朝阳区关东店12号
邮编：100020
电话：65025779

北京市京工服装工业集团公司

北京市京工服装工业集团公司（其前身系北京市服装工业公司）成立于1961年，在中国服装制造业名列前矛，并获最佳企业形象AAA级。

北京市京工服装工业集团公司拥有“雷蒙牌”、“天坛牌”、“坦博牌”、“伊里兰牌”、“枫叶牌”等一批荣获国优和国家金牌、银牌奖的名优产品，有较完善的设计、生产、科研、教学、检测体系，服装产品种类齐全，设备先进，技术精湛，年服装生产能力1000万件。

北京市京工服装工业集团公司有自营进出口权，出口服装畅销三十多个国家和地区在国内外市场享有较高声誉，是全国重要生产出口服装的基地之一。

北京市京工服装工业集团公司生产经营的产品有：梭织衬衫、毛呢服装、童装、风雨衣和加克衫、羽绒制品、软料时装、职业服、室内纺织装饰用品等。

北京市京工服装工业集团公司还经营服装面料、辅料、服饰用品、服装专用设备，及服装技术咨询、技术服务，货物仓储。

北京市京工服装工业集团公司以向科工商贸全方位发展为经营战略，以质量第一、用户至上、重合同、守信誉为经营宗旨。欢迎各界朋友前来订购内销服装，洽谈进出口业务和合资合作等项目，愿竭诚为国内外朋友提供优质服务。

地　　址：北京市宣武区珠市口西大街20号

邮政编码：100050

传　　真：63014979　电报挂号:6528

北京泰跃房地产开发有限责任公司成立于1995年7月，公司注册资本1000万元人民币。
公司成立至今，始终坚持严谨敬业的经营理念，致力于优质住宅的开发建设。公司凭借扎实的专业底蕴、严格的管理体制以及翔实细致的市场调研，最先出色的开发建设了海淀区“怡秀园”公寓。98年又进一步推出了占地5.45公顷，总建筑面积22万平方米的“太月园”小区。展望未来，公司将一如既往，不断从实践中总结宝贵经验，为提高人民居住品质不遗余力、诚挚服务！
北京泰跃房地产开发有限责任公司
TOPEAK
地址：北京市海淀区
白石桥路40号
邮编：100081
电话：62173281

罡正节能

北京市罡正节能工

北京市罡正节能工程研究所主要从事节能技术的研究、节能产品的生产制造和节能工程的开发。现主要产品有：BRV03、BRV10、BRV20、BRW30、BRW302、BRW50、BRW503、BRW80、BRW805、BRW802、BRW130、BRW1309、BRW1307等许多型号板式换热器系列，单板换热面积：0.033、0.10、0.23、0.325、0.22、0.513、0.33、0.82、0.54、0.265、1.337、0.946、0.75m^2。我所还生产节能热交换机组，以满足市场需求。经国家产品质量监督检验测试中心检验我所生产的板式换热器产品为合格产品，并由该中心评定为一级品。我所生产的板式热交换

系列器系列产品自1997年11月起，由
机械工业部换热器产品质量监督检验
测试中心实施监制。我所生产的板式
热交换系列器系列产品自1989年起
至96年连续被北京市经委、北京市节
能办定为重点推广项目之一。并在北
京市优秀节能技术产品成果展评会上
荣获二等奖，第六界中国新技术新产
品博览会获银奖，中国国际技术产品
展览会荣获金奖。95年获得机械工业
部发放的节能机电产品标志。产品销
往全国各地，多次在国内招标项目中
中标，并出口伊朗等国家和地区，广
泛应用于化工、石油、食品、冶金、机
械、轻工、电力、造纸、矿山、医药、
集中供热等工业部门中。欢迎来人来
函联系业务。

程研究所

也址：北京市西三环中路十三号
沂长：陈继增
电话：(010)68458187 68456633 68464997
专真：(010)68254572
邮政编码：100036

所长：陈继增

罡正节能

附：伊朗锌冶炼厂项目／合同号CHMC(92)068／产品号PP03-13-1～3

河南温县淀粉厂／合同号WSS31.1／项目号C1-510～512.507.522

江西万年珍珠营养保健饮料厂／合同号NC-95002L3-IFBb-D／项目号CNTCA-NC94025

裕龙大酒店

裕龙大酒店是三星级旅游涉外饭店，它位于航天桥西侧风景秀丽的京密引水渠河畔。裕龙大酒店地理位置适中，交通便利，距首都机场39公里，西客站3.5公里，建筑面积3万平方米，主楼20层，具有现代建筑风格。

裕龙大酒店有宽敞幽雅的单人间、双人标准间、套间、豪华套间370套。

裕龙大酒店有大小餐厅17个，可同时接待1000人用餐，有独具风味的粤、鲁、川、上海菜系。裕龙大酒店设有多功能厅、会议室、酒吧、咖啡厅和豪华康乐城，配套设施齐全，裕龙大酒店价格优惠，收费合理。是您开会、旅游、商务、住宿休闲娱乐的理想场所。

裕龙大酒店服务人员经过专业培训，保证为您提供优质服务。

欢迎各界朋友光临

电　　话：68415588
预订电话:68413106　68413111　68425704
传　　真:68413108
地　　址:中国北京海淀区阜城路40号
邮　　编:100036

北京统计年鉴

BEIJING STATISTICAL YEARBOOK

1999

北 京 市 统 计 局 编

COMPILED BY BEIJING

MUNICIPAL STATISTICAL BUREAU

中国统计出版社

CHINA STATISTICAL PUBLISHING HOUSE

(京)新登字 041 号

图书馆版编目（CIP）数据

北京统计年鉴 1999：中英文对照/北京市统计局编

北京：中国统计出版社，1999.6

ISBN 7－5037－2967－8/C・1637

Ⅰ.北… Ⅱ.北… Ⅲ.统计资料 － 北京 －1999－ 年鉴 － 汉、英 Ⅳ.C832.1－54

中国版本图书馆 CIP 数据核字（99）第 17670 号

中国统计出版社出版

Pubished by China Statistical Publishing House

(中国・北京三里河月坛南街 75 号 100826)

(75 Yuetan Nanjie, Sanlihe, Beijing 100826, P. R. Ching)

北京理工大学印刷厂印刷

*

787×1092 毫米 16 开本 42.5 印张 24 彩页 150 万字

1999 年 6 月第 1 版 1999 年 6 月第 1 次印刷

印数：1－4000 册

*

定价：280 元

《北京统计年鉴》编辑委员会

Editorial Board and Staff

编 辑 说 明

1.《北京统计年鉴》是一部按年连续出版的大型统计资料书。本书通过大量的统计数据，真实地记录了北京市一年来社会经济和科技等方面的发展变化情况，是国内外各界人士了解北京认识北京的重要资料工具书。

2.《北京统计年鉴——1999》为全部中英文对照版；并配有电子版统计年鉴，具备制图和快速查询的功能，而且可通过转换键实现中英文切换，以增强图书版统计年鉴的功能，满足各方面读者的爱好和习惯，紧跟当前电子信息化的步伐。内容上增加了投入产出表，文化产业资料，服务业企业财务指标，并完善了重点行业财务状况统计。为了便于读者查阅，每个细目编排了主要指标提要和指标解释。

3. 年鉴全书分为两部分——统计公报和统计图表，第一部分登载了北京市 1998 年国民经济和社会发展统计公报及北京市社会商业普查公报；第二部分分综合，人口，劳动力和工资，固定资产投资及房地产，农业和农村经济，工业，能源、原材料消费和库存，建筑业，交通运输、邮电通信业，批发零售贸易及餐饮业，对外经济贸易、旅游业，金融、保险，物价，教育，卫生、体育，城市公用事业，人民生活，社会福利、政法及其他，服务业，区县资料等 21 个细目。另外，还在附录部分中分列了北京市自改革开放以来的主要经济数据，各类市场情况，开发区情况和世界各国及香港、澳门资料等。

4. 本年鉴的资料来源大部分来自年度统计报表，部分来自抽样调查；世界各国及香港、澳门资料来自国家统计局。

5. 本年鉴对以前发表的统计资料重新进行了核实，相应地调整了部分数据。读者在使用历史数据时，如数据有出入，请以本年鉴为准。

6. 1997 年 10 月北京市行政区划中通县改为通洲区，本年鉴中已作出相应调整，顺义县于 1998 年 4 月改为顺义区，本年鉴未作调整，请读者使用时注意。

7. 本年鉴采用的国民经济行业分类是按照中华人民共和国国家标准《国民经济行业分类和代码》划分的；经济类型是按照 1992 年 10 月 20 日国家统计局、国家工商行政管理局颁布的《关于经济类型划分的暂行规定》划分的；登记注册类型是按照 1998 年 9 月 2 日国家统计局、国家工商行政管理局合发的《关于划分企业登记注册类型的规定》划分的；使用的度量单位均采用国际统一的标准计量单位。

8. 各表分组数相加与总计数略有差额，因四舍五入之故。

9. 本年鉴使用的符号说明：“...”表示数据不足该表最小单位数；“空格”表示该项指标数据不详或没有数据；“#”表示其中项。

Preface

1.Beijing Statistical Yearbook is a regular large-scale statistical reference book published yearly.With a vast amount of statistical data, the book can keep you abreast of new developments in Beijing on various aspects, including society, science and technology, etc. It is really an important and efficient reference book for people of various circles in and outside China to know and understand Beijing.

2.Based on the original style, Beijing Statistical Yearbook 1998 is a radical revision of its predecessor.

- To support the opening to outside of Beijing and meet the foreigners' needs for their business and investment in Beijing, Beijing Statistical Yearbook 1998 is published in complete Chinese-English edition.
- To meet various interests and habits of users and reinforce the functions of the yearbook, Beijing Statistical Yearbook 1998 has its electronic edition published simultaneously, With additional functions like charting, quick search, shift between Chinese and English in search by Shift key, etc.
- The content is enriched by additions on the historical data of main indicators in the resent two decades, input / output sheet , statistics for cultural industry and financial indicators on service enterprises.
- For the convenience of consulting, outline and explanatory of main indicators are added to every chapter.

3.The yearbook has two parts:Statistical Communique and Statistical Graph, The first part consists of Statistical Communique on 1998 Economic and Social Development of Beijing, Communique on the Commercial Census in Beijing ; The second part consists of all the 21 chapters concerning General Survey, Population, Labor Force and Wage, Investment in Fixed Assets and Real Estate, Agriculture and Rural Economy, Industry, Energy, Materials Consumption and Storage, Construction, Transportation, Posts and Communications, Wholesale, Retail and Catering, Foreign Economy, Trade and Tourism, Finance and Insurance, Price, Education and Culture, Health and Sports, Municipal Public Utilities, People' s Livelihood, Social Welfare, Politics, Law and Others, Services, General Survey of Districts and Counties, etc. You can find also in the second part as the content of appendix that the main economic data from 1978 to 1998, conditions of various markets and Beijing Development Zone, data of countries and territories, HongKong and Macao, etc.

4.Most of the data in this yearbook sources are from annual statistical reports, a small part sources from sample survey, data of countries and territories, HongKong and Macao from State Statistical Bureau.

5.Some of the published data are changed in this yearbook according to our checking, therefore, date in this yearbook are reliable whenever you find different data in other publications.

6.Your attention please on that the Tongzhou County in this yearbook has been changed to Tongzhou District according to the new administrative divisions of October 1997, but Shunyi County has not been changed to Shunyi District because of the new administrative divisions on April 1998-not the whole conditions in year.

7.The classification of national economy in this yearbook is in line with state standard Classification and Code of National Economy by Sector of the People' s Republic of China.The classification of ownership is in line with The Temporary Provisions on Classification of Owenership issued by State Statistical Bureau and State Administrative Bureau for Industry and Commerce.The classification of registered type is in line with The Provisions on classification of Registered Type of Enterprises issued by State Statistical Bureau and State Administrative Bureau for Industry and Commerce.The units of weights and measures adopted in the yearbook are all international standard units of weights and measures.

8.Sum of numbers of each group may be not equal to the total because of rounding up.

9.Special symbols in this yearbook: "…" indicates the amount is too small to be recorded in the table; "blank space" indicates missing case; " # " indicates an item(indicator)among the previous one.

目　　录
CONTENTS

文章选编
ARTICLES

统计图表
STATISTICAL GRAPH AND CHART
综合
GENERAL SURVEY

人口

POPULATION

劳动力和工资

LABOR FORCE AND WAGE

固定资产投资及房地产业

INVESTMENT IN FIXED ASSETS AND REAL ESTATE

农业及农村经济

AGRICULTURE AND RURAL ECONOMY

主要统计指标提要及统计图

SUMMARY OF MAIN STATISTICAL INDICATORS AND GRAPH

能源生产与消费

PRODUCTION AND CONSUMPTION OF ENERGY

教育、文化

EDUCATION AND CULTURE

科 技

SCIENCE AND TECHNOLOGY

附录 2：各类开发区资料

APPENDIX 2：VARIOUS DEVELOPMENT ZONES

附录 3：各类市场情况

APPENDIX 3：VARIOUS MARKETS

1999

文章选编

ARTICLES

北京市统计局
1998年国民经济和社会发展统计公报

1999年2月2日

1998年，在中共北京市委、市人民政府的领导下，全市各项工作以党的十五大精神为指导，认真贯彻落实党中央、国务院的各项方针政策，努力克服亚洲金融危机和国内需求不足等因素带来的不利影响，积极扩大内需，努力开拓国内外市场，完成了全年经济增长9%的目标。各项社会事业全面进步，城乡人民生活水平继续提高。但经济发展中的旧有矛盾特别是结构调整进展缓慢，低效问题仍很突出，经济增长质量有待提高。

一、综合经济

社会总供给：初步统计，全市实现国内生产总值2009.9亿元，按可比价格计算，比上年同期增长9.7%，实现了年初市人代会通过的经济增长9%的奋斗目标。全市总体经济形势趋好，经济运行的稳定性增强，波动幅度明显小于上年。人均国内生产总值达到18423元，提前两年实现了比1980年翻两番的目标。

产业发展的“三二一”格局进一步强化，第三产业继续领先增长。全年第三产业实现增加值1132.1亿元，增长10.5%，比全市经济增速高0.8个百分点；占国内生产总值的比重达到56.3%，比上年提高1.8个百分点。第二产业实现增加值790.8亿元，增长9.6%，比上年增速提高1.5个百分点。第一产业发展保持稳定。全年第一产业实现增加值达87亿元，增长1.8%，比上年增速提高0.8个百分点。

社会总需求：扩大内需政策效应明显，投资、消费、出口三大需求全面上升，对经济增长产生重要影响。其中：

投资需求：以扩大内需为契机，全市固定资产投资在经历两年的低速增长后迅速回升。全年完成全社会固定资产投资1115.3亿元，比上年增长16%，增速提高6.4个百分点，其中地方完成投资732.3亿元，增长18.6%，提高12.8个百分点。这是1995年全市经济实现“软着陆”后，投资增长最快的一年。基本建设投资415.6亿元，更新改造投资252.4亿元，房地产开发投资377.4亿元，分别增长11%、31.7%和14.2%。固定资产投资向基础设施和住宅建设倾斜，其比重分别达到30%和25.8%，比上年提高6.1和1个百分点。

消费需求：以消费品零售额为代表的国内消费增长较快，实际增幅再创新高。在物价持续走低的形势下，全年实现社会消费品零售额1167.2亿元，增长11%，扣除价格因素后实际增长12.9%，实际增幅比上年提高3.3个百分点，这是1985年以来全市零售额实际增幅最高的一年，有力地拉动了经济的增长。其中用类商品保持旺销态势，全年实现销售额570.3亿元，增长15.9%；吃类商品实现销售额423.6亿元，增长8.4%；穿类商品销售平稳，全年实现销售额144.8亿元，增长2.3%。

外贸出口：虽然受到亚洲金融危机的影响，但全市外贸出口仍保持增势，增幅高于全国。据海关统计，全市完成进出口总值305.2亿美元，比上年增长0.4%，其中出口总值105.2亿美元，同比增长9.5%；地方完成出口28.3亿美元，增长14.7%。从地方出口结构看，工业制成品出口总值26.36亿美元，增长16.3%，占出口总值的93.2%，比上年提高1.3个百分点，初级产品出口下降3.5%；国有企业出口领先增长，全年出口15.24亿美元，增长20.5%，比三资企业出口增幅高 11.4 个百分点。

物价： 全年物价水平始终呈低位运行状况，商品零售价格指数自改革开放以来，首次出现负增长。商品零售价格指数为 98.3%，消费价格指数为 102.4%。物价改革稳步推进，年内先后调整了普通高校学费标准、民用自来水、出租车等价格，理顺了部分商品、服务项目的比价关系。

宏观经济效益： 宏观经济效益有所改善。每百元固定资产投资创造国内生产总值 180.3 元。全社会劳动生产率为 30770 元/人，比上年增长 10.2%。其中，第一产业 12464 元/人，增长 2.2%；第二产业 31356 元/人，增长 12%；第三产业 34182 元/人，增长 9.4%。

地方财政收入继续保持快速增长。全市地方财政收入 227.3 亿元，为预算的 107.8%，按可比口径计算，比上年增长 20.0%；财政支出 281.1 亿元，为预算的 109.0%，按可比口径计算，增长 14.9%。

二、行业发展

农业： 农业生产稳定。粮食总产量 239.2 万吨，增长 0.7%；畜牧业呈现较快增长，肉类总产量达 44.9 万吨，比上年增长 11.4%；菜、蛋、奶、果生产基本保持稳定。新兴农业发展喜人。据调查，年末设施农业实现总收入 9.7 亿元，比上年增长 18.3%；籽种农业实现总收入 7.72 亿元，增长 26.5%；特种养殖和种植业实现总收入 10.2 亿元，增长 50%；家庭养殖业实现总收入 31.1 亿元，增长 75.7%；农业出口供货额 7 亿元，增长 28.4%。农业机械化水平继续提高。年末农业机械总动力达到 415.5 万千瓦；农村用电量 27.5 亿千瓦小时，比上年增长 9.6%。

工业： 全年实现增加值 614 亿元，比上年增长 9.1%,其中年销售收入在 500 万元及以上企业实现增加值 540 亿元，增长 10.5%。重工业在投资的带动下快速回升。全年完成增加值 364.1 亿元，比上年增长 12.7%；轻工业完成 175.9 亿元，比上年增长 6.1%。非国有工业和小型工业高速发展。全市非国有工业企业全年完成增加值 265.5 亿元，增长 17.5%，高于国有工业增速 14.2 个百分点；小型工业完成增加值 261.8 亿元，增长 17.6%；高于大中型工业增速 14.8 个百分点。高新技术产业渐成主导。全年高新技术产业实现增加值 138.7 亿元，比上年增长 11.2%；高新技术产业增加值占国内生产总值的比重为 6.9%，占全市工业增加值的比重达到 22.6%，对全市工业增长的贡献率达到 54.6%，比上年提高 15.2 个百分点。工业经济效益仍在低水平上徘徊。工业经济效益综合指数为 91.9%，比上年下降 4.7 个百分点；实现利税 144.9 亿元，比上年增长 5.9%。

建筑业： 全市建筑业在投资的拉动下，施工生产规模迅速扩大。全年实现增加值 176.8 亿元，按可比价格计算，增长 12.4%，增速比上年提高 7.3 个百分点，占全市经济的比重由上年的 8.3% 提高到 8.8%；全年施工面积 6496 万平方米，比上年增长 11.6%，竣工面积 1821.5 万平方米，比上年增长 12.0%。工程质量又有提高。全市工程优良品率达 45%，比上年提高 2.2 个百分点。经济效益明显改善。全年实现利润总额 12 亿元，全员劳动生产率达 7.5 万元/人，均增长 15.4 %。

交通运输业： 全年实现增加值 64.6 亿元,比上年增长 4.9%。货物运输量 32185.3 万吨，比上年略有下降；旅客运输量 12175.2 万人次，比上年增长 17.4%。各种交通运输形式在竞争中发展。公路运输发挥方便快速、四通八达的优势，客运增长较快；铁路通过提速、增开夕发朝至列车、提高服务质量等手段重新吸引了大批乘客；航空则以其速度的优势适应人们不断加快的生活节奏。三种运输方式分别占货运量的 86.66%、13.27%、0.07%和客运量的 52.5%、41.3%、6.2%。

邮电通信业： 全年实现增加值 92.0 亿元,比上年增长 22.0%。随着社会经济发展和科学技术水平的提高，全市邮电通信业持续高速发展。邮电业务总量达到 127.8 亿元，增长 37.7%。发送报刊 14.06 亿件，杂志 5385 万份，特快专递 630 万件，分别增长 7. 6%、4.8%和 35.2%。全市交换机容量达686万门，比上年增长25.6%。全市电话普及率达到48部/百人，比上年增加9.5部；市区电话普及率达到69部/百人，比上年增加13部；年末移动电话用户达到116.7万户，当年新增50万户。此外，电子信箱、电视会议、传真存储转发及公众信息网迅猛发展。

国内贸易业：全年批发和零售贸易、餐饮业实现增加值207.8亿元,比上年增长4.5%。全年社会商业商品购进总额2047亿元，比上年增长5.5%；商品销售总额2125.5亿元，下降5.6%。商业效益状况不佳。全市1799户大中型批发零售贸易业累计实现商品销售收入127.8亿元，比上年下降6%；利税总额44.1亿元，下降27.9%；销售利税率3.45%，比上年下降1.1个百分点。

金融、保险业：全年实现增加值271.95亿元，比上年增长8.62%。金融机构认真贯彻中央金融政策，加强监管，改进服务，保持金融平稳运行。全市金融机构存款余额6666.8亿元，比年初增加1263.2亿元，比上年增长45%；全市贷款余额3326.6亿元，比年初增加610.8亿元，增长20.2%，较好地支持了首都经济的发展。全年累计回笼现金70.7亿元，创历史最好水平。

证券市场平稳发展。全年证券交易机构交易额10241.5亿元，比上年增长29.1%，股票交易额3426.37亿元，下降12.2%，全年国债交易额1219.8亿元，增长87%。

保险业继续发展。全年完成国内外保险业务收入84.3亿元，比上年增长2.5%，其中，人寿保险业实现保费收入60.2亿元，下降2.4%。全年保险理赔总额18.0亿元，增长27.8%；综合赔付率21.4%，比上年上升4.2个百分点。

房地产业：全年实现增加值68.1亿元，比上年增长55.8%。房地产业随着国家房改政策的出台逐渐升温。房地产施工面积3499.1万平方米，比上年增长21.6%；竣工面积842.8万平方米，比上年增长 23.5%。商品房销售大幅增长。全年销售商品房409.1万平方米,增长40.6%,其中销售商品住宅376.8万平方米,比上年增长47.1%；商品房销售额216亿元,增长31.6%,其中商品住宅销售额181.4亿元，比上年增长29.2%。年末房地产空置面积334.2万平方米，比上年末增加35.9万平方米，其中住宅空置262.4万平方米，比上年末增加3.5万平方米。

三、城市建设

城市基础设施建设：基础设施投资力度加大。全市完成基础设施投资317.8亿元，比上年增长45.6%，是北京历史上基础设施投资规模最大的一年。

重点工程建设进展顺利。市政府根据首都城市发展的需要和可能，经科学论证，严格筛选，年初确定了67项重大建设项目，目前这些重大项目已完成投资247.3亿元。首都图书大厦、首都医科大学教学科研楼、小营世纪村住宅小区、国际金融大厦、首都师范大学文科教学楼、北京戏曲学校排演场、北京工业大学经贸楼、中国评剧院剧场等10项程已经建成。

城市道路建设日新月异。年末全市道路总长度达到3800公里，道路面积4200万平方米，分别比上年增长4.5%和3.4%。具有国际水准的八达岭高速公路二期工程建成通车；平安大街改扩建、地铁复八线等工程正按计划进行。

城市公用事业：公共交通能力增强。年末，全市公共交通运营车辆达到7524辆，比上年增加278辆。运营线路总长度9384公里，增加927公里；新辟公共电汽车线路26条，调整延长线路26条。城市公共交通共运送乘客46.63亿人次,其中公共电汽车运送乘客35.7亿人次,占76.6%；地铁4.63亿人次，占9.9%；出租汽车6.3亿人次，占13.5%。

全年新增天然气用户超过26.6万户，其中为提高燃气质量而置换天然气的用户达到19.9万户。年末，全市集中供热采暖面积突破3800万平方米。全年用电总量为276.2亿千瓦小时。全年售水量超过8.2亿吨。

城市环境保护与绿化：市政府将防治大气污染作为工作重点，加大治理力度，并决定公布空气质量周报。据全年空气质量周报显示，大气环境质量不容乐观。全年空气污染指数 4 级以上的 23 周，占全年的 42.2%，空气质量 3 级的有 21 周，占全年的 40.4%。为此经国务院批准，决定采取控制北京大气污染 18 项紧急措施，主要包括控制煤烟型污染、控制机动车污染和控制扬尘污染三个方面的内容。各级政府和有关部门认真落实紧急措施，到年末改装的天然气、液化石油气公交车可达 515 辆；强制报废了 1.4 万辆尾气严重超标和超期服役的"面的"；出动 10 万人次，取缔露天烧烤 4000 多个；道路机扫面积扩大到 74%,喷雾压尘面积达到 1000 万平方米；积极推广使用低硫低灰优质煤和清洁燃料。由于采取了综合防治措施，初步控制了污染加重的趋势。

积极开展植树绿化工作。全年完成绿化面积 538 公顷，年末全市城近郊区公共绿地面积达 4945 公顷，人均占有公共绿地 8.18 平方米；城市绿化覆盖率 34.9%，比上年提高了 0.26 个百分点。新建改建公园 7 处。

四、对外开放

利用外资：全市新批外商投资企业 651 家，合同总金额 62.4 亿美元，合同外资金额 41 亿美元，比上年分别增长 71.2%和 1.4 倍。利用外资大项目增加。项目平均吸收外资 629 万美元，比上年净增 416 万美元。利用外资逐步向第三产业、第一产业倾斜。第三产业新批外资企业 296 家，占新批项目总数的 45.5%，比上年提高 11.5 个百分点；合同外资金额 28.8 亿美元，比上年净增 19 亿美元，比重为 70.3%；第一产业利用外资项目和合同外资金额也比上年有所增长，项目数占总项目数 3.6%，合同外资金额比重为 0.7%，比上年分别增加了 1.3 个和 0.3 个百分点。年末，全球最大 500 家跨国公司已有 151 家来京投资。欧美国家投资大幅度增长，新批欧盟国家合同外资 5.1 亿美元，比上年增长 1 倍；新批美国合同外资 4.1 亿美元，比上年增长 2.2 倍。实际利用外资保持较快增长速度。全年完成 28.7 亿美元，其中外商直接投资额 20.7 亿美元，增长 29.6%；非投资性对外借款 5.7 亿美元，下降 12.0%。

对外承包工程和劳务合作：全年新签合同额 2.85 亿美元，比上年下降 19.98%；完成营业额 4.58 亿美元，增长 54.62%。年末在外人数 3645 人，增长 16.98%。

旅游：全市旅游业克服亚洲金融危机的影响，实现了国际旅游收入稳中有升，国内旅游收入持续增长。全年接待海外旅游者 220.1 万人次，比上年下降 4.2%；全年旅游外汇收入 23.8 亿美元，比上年增长 6%；海外游客人均日消费 216.5 美元，比上年增长 4.3%。全市接待国内旅游者 8731 万人次，总花费 424.5 亿元，比上年增长 8.4%，其中外地来京游客 5780 万人次，增长 5.1%，外地游客在京花费 393.2 亿元，增长 8.2%。全市宾馆饭店客房出租率为 55%。旅游功能进一步完善，我市被国家旅游局首批评为 "中国优秀旅游城市"。

开发区：全市开发区、试验区和工业小区发展较快。全年新招商企业 965 家，累计入区企业达 9228 家，其中，新投产企业 612 家，比上年增加 323 家，累计达 7851 家。共完成固定资产投资 65.9 亿元，比上年增长 10.2%；实现增加值 214 亿元，比上年增长 25.3%，占全市国内生产总值的比重为 10.6%，比上年增加 1.1 个百分点；对全市经济增长贡献率达 21.6%。北京新技术产业开发试验区经济继续保持快速增长。技工贸总收入完成 492.2 亿元，比上年增长 29.9%；工业总产值 245.4 亿元，比上年增长 28.4%；实现工业增加值 71.3 亿元，比上年增长 15.7%，对全市工业的贡献率达 28.1%。北京经济技术开发区初步形成了现代化工业群体。累计完成招商 294 家，项目总投资 137 亿元，其中：三资企业 128 家，总投资 122.3 亿元；投产开业企业 85 家，实现工业增加值 7.2 亿元，比上年增长 81.8%。

五、社会事业

科学技术：全市从事科技活动人员 28.1 万人，比上年增长 2.9%。科技活动经费支出 191.7

亿元，增长 14.8%，其中研究与发展经费支出 52.3 亿元，增长 19.4%，占国内生产总值比重为 2.6%。全市技术市场签定合同 20724 项，合同金额达 81.6 亿元，其中技术交易额 73.9 亿元，分别比上年增长 49.5%、50.2%和 53.7%。全市申请专利 6321 项，与上年持平；专利授权 3800 项，比上年增长 14.2%。

教育：全面推进中小学素质教育，小学毕业生免试就近升入初中的改革全部到位。高等学校进行了管理体制改革，接收了中央划转在京的 11 所学校及 21 所成人高等学校；积极调整高等学校专业结构，调整前北京地区共有 502 个专业，现在减为 249 个。大力发展高等职业教育，形成了以六所大学郊区分校为基地，其他普通高等学校、成人高等学校部分专业为补充的高等职业教育网络。全市全年招收研究生 1.6 万人，普通高校本科生和大专生 6.2 万人，中等职业技术教育 10.3 万人，普通教育 30.8 万人，成人教育 10.4 万人。向社会输送各类高等教育人才 6 万人，中等专业技术人才 7.2 万人，成人教育 9.9 万人。

文化：年初北京电视台通过“上星”转播，使卫星广播电视节目覆盖全部北京地区，全市共架设光缆 3285 公里，新增覆盖用户 50 万户，累计近 150 万户。群众文化活动广泛开展，夏日文化广场、文化科技下乡活动深受群众欢迎。出版了大量优秀图书，其中 25 部获得市级以上奖励。文物保护工作受到全社会广泛重视，天坛、颐和园被联合国列入世界文化遗产。

卫生：通过调整诊所、精简人员、加强管理，卫生机构改革初见成效。全市共有医疗卫生机构 5723 个，比上年减少 854 个，拥有医院床位 6.3 万张，比上年增加 0.1 万张，拥有卫生技术人员 11.6 万人，比上年减少 3315 人，平均每千人拥有卫生技术人员 10.63 人。大力推进社区服务，全市城近郊区共建社区卫生服务站 162 个，覆盖 62%的居委会和 48%的居民。各级各类医院认真落实“总量控制，结构调整”的医药费用改革方案，医药费用增长过快势头得到控制，按可比口径计算，全年共为国家和企业减少支出 10.9 亿元。

体育：全民健身运动蓬勃发展。全市已有 139 处公共体育场馆面向社会公众开放，平均每月接待 100 万人次，比上年增加 30 万人次。竞技体育取得佳绩。在第 13 届亚运会上，我市有 57 名运动员参赛，共获奖牌 45 块，其中金牌 28 块，银牌 9 块，铜牌 8 块。

六、人民生活

人口：据人口抽样调查统计，全市人口出生率 6‰，人口死亡率为 5.3‰，人口自然增长率 0.7‰，比上年下降 1.2 个千分点。年末在京居住半年以上常住人口 1245.6 万人，比上年增加 5.6 万人，据公安部门统计，年末户籍人口为 1091.5 万人。

就业：全市再就业工程取得进展。全年下岗职工 16.96 万人，其中 10.21 万人实现了再就业，下岗职工再就业率 60.2%；富余人员分流安置率为 72.9%。年末城镇失业登记 2.95 万人，登记失业率 0.66%。社会保障制度改革稳步推进。全市养老保险统筹覆盖面为 95%，失业保险统筹覆盖面为 94%，地方企业大病医疗统筹覆盖面为 85.2%，分别比上年增加 12.6 个、9.7 个和 12.2 个百分点。

居民收入：全市职工平均工资 12300 元，比上年增长 11.6%，扣除价格因素，实际增长 9%。全市城镇居民人均可支配收入 8472 元，比上年增长 8.4%，扣除价格因素，实际增长 5.9%；人均消费性支出为 6970.8 元，比上年同期增长 6.7%。消费结构日趋合理，城镇居民恩格尔系数为 41.1%，比 1997 年降低 2.6 个百分点。农民人均纯收入 4029 元，扣除价格因素，实际增长 6.7%。

居民储蓄：城乡居民储蓄余额 2287.2 亿元，比年初增加 312 亿元，增长 19.3%，其中城镇居民储蓄存款余额达 2063.2 亿元，比年初增加 292.4 亿元；农村居民储蓄存款余额达 224 亿元，比年初增加 19.6 亿元。

居民住房：住宅建设快速发展。全市全年完成住宅投资 273[illegible]比上年增长 21.1%，住宅竣工面积 1090.6 万平方米，比上年增长 9.4%，其中普通住宅[illegible]1004.5 万平方米，增长 22.9%。居住条件不断改善。城镇居民人均住房使用面积达到 14.8[illegible]米，比上年增长 3.5%。农村居民人均生活用房面积 27.6 平方米，比上年增长 0.7%。市政府[illegible]立的 19 片共 568 万平方米经济适用住房建设项目，已陆续开工。

附 1 公报注释:

1、本公报数据为初步统计数。

2、本公报中所涉及的增加值和全社会劳动生产率，绝对数均按当年价格计算，增长速度均按可比价格计算。

附 2 统计表:

指标名称	单 位	1998年	1998年为1997年%
主要农副产品产量			
粮食总产量	万吨	239.2	100.7
蔬菜总产量	万吨	406.1	99.0
肉类总产量	万吨	44.9	111.4
鲜蛋总产量	万吨	17.9	75.2
牛奶总产量	万吨	22.7	102.3
淡水鱼总产量	万吨	7.7	100.0
出栏猪	万头	374.8	106.0
主要产品产量			
生铁	万吨	751.5	100.6
钢	万吨	803.2	100.2
成品钢材	万吨	676.1	103.4
原煤	万吨	989.5	99.6
发电量	亿千瓦小时	144.5	98.6
化肥 （折纯）	万吨	11.3	94.8
水泥	万吨	762	114.9
乙烯	万吨	57	98.2
越野汽车	万辆	2.7	65.5
微型计算机	万部	160.9	139.8
彩电	万部	11.1	28.5
程控交换机	万线	772.2	166.9
房间空调器	万台	39.5	334.8
白酒	万吨	9.9	117.9
啤酒	万吨	117.2	102.1
无酒精饮料	万吨	30.1	99.6
货物运输量			
铁路	万吨	4271.9	90.0
公路	万吨	27892.0	95.0
民航	万吨	21.42	112.4
旅客运输量			
铁路	万人次	5031.8	104.6
公路	万人次	6390.0	130.4
民航	万人次	753.43	115.3
商品零售价格指数(以上年为100)		**98.3**	
居民消费价格指数(以上年为100)		**102.4**	
食品类		97.1	
衣着类		105.9	
家庭设备及用品		97.5	
医疗保健		108.6	
交通和通讯工具类		99.0	
娱乐教育文化用品类		97.8	
居住		104.7	
服务项目		121.3	

STATISTICAL COMMUNIQUE ON THE 1998 NATIONAL ECONOMIC AND SOCIAL DEVELOPMENT OF BEIJING

February 2, 1999

Led by the municipal Party committee and government, the people of Beijing adopted the gist of the 15th National Congress of the Communist Party of China as the guiding ideology in all work, conscientiously implemented all policies of the Party Central Committee and the State Council, tried to overcome unfavorable factors of Asian financial crisis and inadequate domestic demand, actively expanded domestic demand, made great efforts to exploit foreign and domestic market and achieved the goal of 9 percent economic growth in 1998. All social causes made overall progress and the living standard of urban and rural residents continued to rise. However, former contradictions in the economic development especially structural adjustment progressed slowly, the problem of poor efficiency still existed and the quality of economic growth had to be raised urgently.

I. Comprehensive Economy

Total social supply: According to primary statistics, the city's gross domestic product (GDP) accomplished in 1998 reached 200.99 billion yuan, a growth of 9.7 percent over the previous year at comparable prices. The economic growth rate of 9 percent set by the municipal people's congress at the beginning of the year had been accomplished. The city's general economic situation showed a tendency to improve, and economic operation had great stability and fluctuated less frequently than that of the previous year. The per capita GDP amounted to 18,423 yuan, achieving the goal of quadrupling that of 1980 two years ahead of the schedule.

The pattern was further strengthened that the service sector contributed the most, the secondary industry the second most and the primary industry the third most to the city's economic development. The service sector continued to take the lead in the growth. Its annual added value came to 113.21 billion yuan, up 10.5 percent over the previous year and 0.8 percentage points more than the city's economic growth rate; the proportion of the service sector in the GDP reached 56.3 percent, 1.8 percentage points more than in 1997. The added value accomplished by the secondary industry attained 79.08 billion yuan, up 9.6 percent and 1.5 percentage points more than the growth rate of the previous year. The primary industry developed steadily. Its added value of the whole year amounted to 8.7 billion yuan, an increase of 1.8 percent over the previous year and 0.8 percentage points more than the growth rate of the previous year.

Total social demand: The policies to expand domestic demand were effective. The demand of investment, consumption and export rose in an all-round way, exerting important influence on the economic growth.

Investment demand: At the turning point of expanding domestic demand, a large group of major projects quickened their step of construction and fixed investments of the city rapidly picked up after two years of slow growth. The total social fixed investments accomplished annually reached 111.53 billion yuan, a growth of 16 percent over the previous year and an increase of 6.4 percentage points; of which, 73.23 billion yuan was the investment accomplished locally, a growth of 18.6 percent and an increase of 12.8 percentage points. The year 1998 was the one with the fastest investment growth after the "Soft Landing" of the city's economy in 1995. The city's investment in capital construction was 41.56 billion yuan; investment in modification was 25.24 billion yuan; real estate development was 37.74 billion yuan, up 11 percent、31.7 percent and 14.2 percent. The fixed investments favored the infrastructure construction and residential buildings, accounting for 30 percent and 25.8 percent, up 6.1 percentage points and 1 percentage points respectively.

Consumption demand: Represented by retail sales of consumer goods, the domestic consumption grew relatively rapidly and its actual growth range set a new record once more. Under the situations of low prices, retail sales of social consumer goods accomplished annually amounted to 116.72 billion yuan, up 11 percent. After deducting the price factor, sales actually rose 12.9 percent and the actual growth range was 3.3 percentage points high than that of the previous year. The year 1998 saw the highest actual growth range of retail sales in the city since 1985, which had spurred the economic growth. Articles for use sold well and accomplished a sales volume of 57.03 billion yuan, up 15.9 percent; food accomplished a sales volume of 42.36 billion yuan, up 8.4 percent; and clothes sold steadily and accomplished a sales volume of 14.48 billion yuan, up 2.3 percent.

Foreign trade exports: Although the city's foreign trade export was affected by the Asian financial crisis, it still kept rising and its growth range was higher than the national one. According to the statistics from the Customs, the city accomplished gross import and export of 30.52 billion US dollars, up 0.4 percent over the previous year; of which, 10.52 billion US dollars were gross export, up 9.5 percent; the export accomplished locally was 2.83 billion US dollars, up 14.7 percent. In export structure, the gross export of manufactured products reached 2.636 billion US dollars, increasing by 16.3 percent and accounting for 93.2 percent of export volume, a rise of 1.3 percentage points. The proportion of the export of primary products decreased by 3.5 percent. State-owned enterprises took the lead in raising the export and achieved export of 1.524 billion US dollars annually, up 20.5 percent over the previous year and 11.4 percentage points more than that of foreign-funded enterprises.

Prices: The prices of 1998 always fluctuated at the low level and the retail price index had negative growth for the first time since reform and opening. The annual retail price index was 98.3 percent and the consumption price index was 102.4 percent. The reform of prices progressed steadily. The tuition standards of regular colleges and universities, charges of city water, gas and taxi had been adjusted and the price parities between some commodities and service had been rationalized.

Macro-economic efficiency: Macro-economic efficiency was bettered. Every a hundred-yuan of fixed investments produced 180.3 yuan of GDP. The total social production rate was 30,770 yuan per capita, up 10.2 percent over the previous year. Of which, the production rate in the primary industry was 12,464 yuan per capita, up 2.2 percent; the secondary industry 31,356 yuan per capita, up 12 percent and the service sector 34,182 yuan per capita, up 9.4 percent.

The local revenue kept growing rapidly. The city's local revenue attained 22.73 billion yuan, accounting for 107.8 percent of budget and increasing by 20.0 at comparable prices percent against the previous year. The financial expenditure reached 28.11 billion yuan, accounting for 109.0 percent and increasing by 14.9 percent at comparable prices.

II. Trade Development

Agriculture: The agricultural production steadily grew, Animal husbandry developed at a rationally moderate speed. The total output of meat and grain came to 449,000 tons and 2.392 million tons, an increase of 11.4 percent and 0.7 percent respectively. The production of vegetables, eggs and milk remained basically stable. New agriculture development made progress. According to a survey, facility agriculture achieved a total income of 970 million yuan annually, 18.3 percent more than that of the previous year; Seed agriculture achieved a total income of 772 million yuan annually, 26.5 percent high than that of the previous year; Special cultivation and farm production achieved a total income of 1.02 billion yuan annually, up 50 percent; Household cultivation achieved a total income of 3.11 billion yuan annually, up 75.7 percent; Agricultural products export order volume reached 700 million yuan, up 28.4 percent. The level of agricultural mechanization kept rising. The total power of agricultural machinery had reached 4.155 million kilowatts by the end of 1998. The amount of electricity consumed in the countryside attained 2.75 billion kilowatt-hours, an increase of 9.6 percent over the previous year.

Industry: The added value accomplished by industry annually was 61.4 billion yuan, up 9.1 percent over the previous year. The industrial enterprises with more than 5 million yuan achieved the added value of 54 billion yuan, up 10.5 percent. Driven by investment, the heavy industry quickly picked up and accomplished the added value of 36.41 billion yuan annually, up 12.7 percent over the previous year. The light industry achieved 17.59 billion yuan annually, up 6.1 percent over the previous year. Non-state-owned industry and small industry developed swiftly. In 1998, the city's non-state-owned industrial enterprises accomplished the added value of 26.55 billion yuan, up 17.5 percent over the previous year, and 14.2 percentage points more than the city's industrial growth rate. Small enterprises accomplished the added value of 26.18 billion yuan, up 17.6 percent, and 14.8 percentage points more than the large and medium industrial growth rate. The new high technology industry gradually took the lead and accomplished the added value of 13.87 billion yuan annually, up 11.2 percent over the previous year. The added value accomplished by the new high technology accounted for 6.9 percent of GDP and 22.6 percent of the city's industrial added value. The proportion of its contribution to the city's industrial growth reached 54.6 percent, an increase of 15.2 percentage points over the previous year. Industrial economic efficiency stayed at the low level. Industrial economic efficiency complex index was 91.9 percent, a decrease of 4.7 percentage points over the previous year. Profit and tax accomplished reached 14.49 billion yuan, Up 5.9 percent over the previous year.

Construction: In 1998, driven by investment, the construction sector was further expended. The added value accomplished by construction annually reached 17.68 billion yuan, up 12.4 percent at comparable prices and 7.3 percentage points more than the growth rate of the previous year, Its proportion in the city's economy grew from 8.3 percent of 1997 to 8.8 percent of 1998. The floor space under construction accomplished annually reached 64.96 million square meters, up 11.6 percent over the previous year; the floor space completed attained 18.215 million square meters, up 12 percent over the previous year. The quality of engineering was further improved. The fine rate of the city's engineering reached 45 percent, 2.2 percentage points more than that of the previous year. Economic efficiency was enhanced distinctly. The total amount of profit accomplished annually reached 1.2 billion yuan, up 15.4 percent; the overall labor productivity 75,000 yuan per capita, up 15.4 percent.

Transportation: The added value accomplished by transportation annually reached 6.46 billion yuan, up 4.9 percent over the previous year. The volume of goods delivery came to 321.853 million tons, decreased a little with the previous year; the volume of passenger delivery 121.752 million times person, up 17.4 percent over the previous year. All transportation modes developed in competition. Road transportation grew relatively quickly by giving play to convenience and swiftness; railway attracted a large number of passengers by speeding up, improving service quality and adding trains which set off in the evening and arrive in the morning; aviation won the favor of more and more passengers with its advantage of high speed. Three transportation modes accounted for 86.66 percent, 13.27 percent and 0.07 percent of volume of goods transported and 52.5 percent, 41.3 percent and 6.2 percent of volume of passenger transport respectively.

Posts and telecommunications: With the social and economic development and the enhancement of scientific and technological standard, the city's post and telecommunications continued to develop at a high speed. The added value accomplished by post and telecommunications reached 9.20 billion yuan, up 22 percent over the previous year. The total volume of post and telecommunications service attained 12.78 billion yuan, up 37.7 percent. Newspapers and periodicals delivered reached 1.406 billion, magazine 53.85 million and the express mail 6.3 million. Up 7.6 percent, 4.8 percent and 35.2 percent respectively. The city's capacity of switchboard amounted to 6.86 million gates, up 25.6 percent over the same period of 1997. Every 100 residents owned 48 telephone sets, a growth of 9.5 sets over the previous year; of which, 69 sets were in urban districts, a growth of 13 sets. The number of subscribers of mobile telephones had come to 1.167 million by the end of the year, an increase of 500,000 in 1998. Furthermore, electronic mail, television conference, fax storage and retransmission as well as public information network developed swiftly and vigorously.

Domestic trade: The added value accomplished by wholesale and retail trade and catering trade reached 20.78 billion yuan, up 4.5 percent over the previous year. The annual total purchase volume of social commercial commodities attained 204.7 billion yuan, up 5.5 percent over the previous year; the gross sales of commodities 212.55 billion yuan, down 5.6 percent. Commercial efficiency was not good. The annual sales income of commodities amounted to 12.78 billion yuan, up 6 percent over the previous year; the total volume of profit and tax 4.41 billion yuan, down 27.9 percent; the profit and tax rate of sales 3.45 percent, a down 1.1 percentage points over the previous year.

Finance and insurance: Financial institutions conscientiously implemented the financial policies formulated by the central government, strengthened supervision, improved service and kept the stable operation of finance. The added value accomplished annually was 27.195 billion yuan, up 8.62 percent over the previous year. Savings in the financial institutions totaled 666.68 billion yuan, 126.32 billion yuan more than that of the beginning of the year and 45 percent increase compared with the previous year. Net loans were 332.66 billion yuan, increasing by 20.2 percent to 61.08 billion yuan over the beginning of the year. Financial institutions had supported the capital's economic development. The currency withdrawn from circulation totaled 7.07 billion yuan, setting the all-time highs.

Securities market developed steadily. The annual turnover of securities exchanges reached 1024.15 billion yuan, up 29.1 percent over the previous year. The turnover on the stock exchange attained 342.64 billion yuan, down 12.2 percent. All government loans sold well. The national debt sold annually totaled 121.98 billion yuan, up 87 percent.

Insurance business kept developing. The income earned at home and abroad in 1998 was 8.43 billion yuan, 2.5 percent over the previous year. Of which, life insurance premium received in 1998 totaled 6.02 billion yuan, down 2.4 percent. The total sum from compensation was 1.8 billion yuan, up 27.8 percent. The rate of comprehensive compensation was 21.4 percent, up 4.2 percentage points over the previous year.

Real estate: With the implementation of the state housing reform policies, the market of real estate was thriving. The added value accomplished annually attained 6.81 billion yuan, up 55.8 percent over the previous year. The floor space under construction reached 34.991 million square meters, up 21.6 percent over the previous year. The floor space completed attained 8.428 million square meters, up 23.5 percent over the previous year. The commercial buildings sold annually amounted to 4.091 million square meters (floorage), up 40.6 percent; of which, 3.768 million square meters were commercial residential buildings, up 47.1 percent. The annual sales volume of commercial buildings reached 21.6 billion yuan, up 31.6 percent; of which, 18.14 billion yuan was the sales volume of commercial residential buildings, up 29.2 percent. By the end of 1998, the vacant space of real estate was 3.342 million square meters, 359,000 square meters more than that of the end of the previous year; of which, 2.624 million square meters were vacant residential buildings, 35,000 square meters more than that of the end of the previous year.

III. Urban Construction

Urban infrastructure construction: Investment in infrastructure was intensified, whose scale had been the largest in the history of Beijing. The city's investment in infrastructure totaled 31.78 billion yuan, up 45.6 percent over the previous year.

Major construction projects progressed successfully. After scientific demonstration and strict screening, the municipal government set 67 major projects according to the demand and possibilities of the capital's urban development. At present, these major construction projects progressed smoothly. The investment accomplished annually reached 24.73 billion yuan. The 10 projects such as Capital Book Mansion, the Teaching and Scientific Research Building of the Capital Medical Sciences University and Xiaoying Century Village Residential District, International Financial Mansion, the Teaching Building of Liberal Arts at the Capital Normal University, and the rehearsal ground of Beijing Opera School had been completed.

The city's road construction changed with each passing day. By the end of 1998, the total length of the city's roads reached 3800 kilometers and the total area of roads attained 42 million square meters, up 4.5 percent and 3.4 percent over the end of 1997 respectively. The second-phase project of Badaling Expressway with international standard was open to traffic. The projects of the Ping'an Avenue transformation and expansion and the Xidan-Bawangfen Line of the subway progressed as planned, and the transformation of the second and third ring roads were fully carried out.

Urban public utilities: The capacity of public transport was intensified. By the end of the year, the number of vehicles for public transport reached 7524, 278 more than that of the end of 1997. The total length of transportation lines exceeded 9384 kilometers, a growth of 927 kilometers. During the year, 26 new public transportation lines were put into use and 26 lines were adjusted and extended. The number of passengers transported was 4.663 billion, of which, 3.57 billion were transported by buses and trolley-buses, accounting for 76.6 percent of the passengers; 463 million were transported by subways, accounting for 9.9 percent of the passengers; 630 million were transported by taxis, accounting for 13.5 percent of the passengers.

In the year, more than 266,000 households had been newly supplied with gas; of which, 199,000 were households which changed gas to improve the quality of gas. By the end of the year, the city's concentrated heat-supply area exceeded 38 million square meters. The annual total amount of power consumption was 27.62 billion kilowatt-hours and the annual total amount of water sold was 820 million tons.

Urban environmental protection: To strengthen the supervision of environmental protection, the municipal government decides to publish air quality weekly report. The city's air quality weekly report showed that the city's environmental quality was not optimistic. In the year, there were 23 weeks with above four-grade air quality, accounting for 42.2 percent of the whole year; 21 weeks with three-grade air quality, accounting for 40.4 percent of the whole year. Therefore, ratified by state council the municipal Party committee and government adopted 18 emergency measures to prevent and control air pollution, which mainly included three aspects: the control of pollution caused by smoke from burning coal, motor vehicles and rising dust. As many as 515 vehicles for public transport had been modified by gas or liquefied petroleum gas by the end of 1998. 14,000 cabs whose tail gas failed to meet the standard were scrapped by force. 10,000 persontimes were organized to outlaw 4,000 barbecue sites. Area of roads swept by machine came to 74 percent of the all. Spraying areas reached 10 million square meters. High grade coal and cleaner fuel were encouraged to use widely. Through intensifing the improvement of urban environment in a comprehensive way, the upward tendency of air pollution was controlled preliminary.

The work of afforestation had been developed actively and the green area accomplished annually reached 538 hectare. By the end of 1998, the afforested area in public places of urban districts covered 4,945 hectare, 8.18 square meters per capita; 34.9 percent of the city was covered by greenery, an increase of 0.26 percentage points over the previous year. Seven parks had been newly built.

IV. Opening to the Outside World

Introducing foreign investment: The city had newly authorized 651 foreign-funded enterprises. The total amount of contract money reached 6.24 billion US dollars and the amount of contract foreign capital 4.1 billion US dollars, up 71.2 percent and 1.4 times over the previous year respectively. The number of large projects using foreign investment grew and the projects absorbed the foreign capital of 6.29 million US dollars on average, a new increase of 4.16 million US dollars over the previous year. The industrial structure utilizing foreign capital gradually favored the service sector and the primary industry. The foreign-funded enterprises newly authorized in the service sector came to 296, a growth of 11.5 percentage points over the previous year and accounting for 45.5 percent of the total number of newly authorized projects; the amount of contract foreign capital attained 2.88 billion US dollars, a net increase of 1.9 billion US dollars over the previous year and accounting for 70.3 percent. The number of projects introducing foreign investment in the primary industry and the amount of contract foreign capital also grew compared with the previous year. The number of projects accounted for 3.6 percent of the total number and the amount of contract foreign capital 0.7 percent of the total amount of contract foreign capital, an increase of 1.3 percentage points and 0.3 percentage points over the previous year respectively. By the end of the year, 151 of the 500 largest transnational corporations in the world had invested in Beijing. The investment from European and American countries rose greatly. The amount of newly authorized contract foreign capital from the European Communities totaled 510 million US dollars, 1 times more than the previous year; the amount of newly authorized contract foreign capital from the United States attained 410 million US dollars, up 2.2 times; The actual use of foreign investment kept growing swiftly and accomplished 2.87 billion US dollars in the year, of which, the amount of direct foreign investment reached 2.07 billion US dollars, up 29.6 percent; non-investment foreign loans totaled 570 million US dollars, down 12 percent.

Contracting foreign projects and cooperative labor service: The amount of newly signed contracts in the year totaled 285 million US dollars, down 19.98 percent over the previous year; The turnover accomplished reached 458 million US dollars, up 54.62 percent. 3645 persons offering labor service were sent abroad, up 16.98 percent.

Tourism: The city's tourism overcame the influence imposed by the Asian financial crisis. The income of international tourism rose and domestic travel kept growing. The city received 2.201 million overseas tourists in the year, down 4.2 percent over the previous year. The foreign currency earnings of tourism reached 2.38 billion US dollars, up 6 percent over the previous year; the per capita consumption of overseas tourists was 216.5 US dollars every day, up 4.3 percent over the previous year. The number of domestic tourist to Beijing reached 87.31 million, these tourists spent 42.45 billion yuan in Beijing, up 8.4 percent, of which, the city received 57.8 million travelers from other places of China, up 5.1 percent. These Chinese travelers spent 39.32 billion yuan in Beijing, up 8.2 percent. 55 percent of the city's guest rooms of hotels were taken. The tourist function was further perfected. The city ranked among the first group of "Excellent Tourist Cities of China."

Development zones: During the year, 965 new enterprises landed in the city's development zones, experimental zones and industrial zones (hereinafter referred to as "the three zones"), bringing the total number of enterprises in the three zones to 9228. 612 new enterprises went into operation, increasing 323 over the previous year and bringing the total number of new enterprises to 7851. The total fixed investments accomplished reached 6.59 billion yuan, up 10.2 percent over the previous year; The added value realized rose 25.3 percent to 21.4 billion yuan, accounting for 10.6 percent of Beijing's GDP, increasing 1.1 percentage points over the previous year and contributing 21.6 percent to the city's economic growth. The economy of Beijing New Technology Industry Development and Experiment Zone continued to develop at a faster speed. The total income achieved by technology, industry and trade reached 49.22 billion yuan, up 29.9 percent over the previous year; the total value of industrial output (current price) attained 24.54 billion yuan, up 28.4 percent over the previous year; the added value accomplished by industry came to 7.13 billion yuan, increasing by 15.7 percent over the previous year and contributing more than 28.1 percent to the city's industry. The modern industrial enterprises were established in the Beijing economy and technology development zone. The total number of enterprises in the zones came to 294, and the amount of contract investment was 13.7 billion yuan of which, 128 was foreign-founded enterprises and the amount of investment was 12.23 billion yuan; 85 enterprises was put into use, The added value accomplished by industry was 720 million yuan up 81.8 percent over the previous year.

V. Social Undertaking

Science and technology: In the city, 281,000 people participated in scientific and technological activities, up 2.9 percent over the previous year. The expenditure on scientific and technological activities totaled 19.17 billion yuan, up 14.8 percent. Of which, 5.23 billion yuan was the expenditure on research and development, up 19.4 percent and accounting for 2.6 percent of GDP. On the city's technological market, 20724 contracts were signed and the amount of contract reached 8.16 billion yuan including 7.39 billion yuan of technological trade volume, increasing by 49.5 percent, 50.2 percent and 53.7 percent over the previous year respectively. In the city, 6321 patents were applied, balanced with the previous year; and 3800 patents were authorized, up 14.2 percent .

Education: The quality education was promoted at middle and primary schools in an all-round way. The reform that primary school graduates went to junior middle schools in the neighborhood without examination had been successfully carried out. Colleges and universities underwent the reform of administrative system and accepted 11 schools under departments dismissed or integrated and 21 institutions of adult higher education. The specialty structure of colleges and universities was adjusted and the scope of disciplines widened. After the adjustment, the number of disciplines in Beijing had been reduced from 502 to 249. The development of higher vocational education was intensified. A higher vocational education network was formed, which took the branch schools in the suburbs of six colleges and universities as its base, and some specialties of other institutions of regular higher education and institutions of adult higher education as its supplement. The city enrolled 16,000 graduate students, 62,000 undergraduates, 103,000 students for secondary specialized education, 308,000 for regular education and 104,000 for adult education in the year. 60,000 college and university students, 72,000 students from secondary specialized schools and 99,000 graduates from adult education institutions had completed their study and entered society.

Culture: At the beginning of the year, Beijing Television Station made the television cover all population through the satellite relay. The optical cable erected in the city totaled 3,285 kilometers and 500,000 families were newly covered, and the total number came to 1.5 million families. The mass cultural activities were widely developed, and the activities of Summer Cultural Square and sending culture, science and technology to the countryside were well received by the people. A large number of excellent books were published, 25 of which won the prizes above the municipal level. The work of preserving cultural relics attracted wide social attention, and the Temple of Heaven and the Summer Palace were listed in the world cultural heritage by the United Nations.

Health: Through adjustment, the number of clinics and medical workers were decreased. The medical management was better. The reform of facilities of medical care and public health made new achievements. The city had 5723 facilities of medical care and public health, decrease 854 of the previous year. The hospitals possessed 63,000 beds, 1000 beds more than previous year; 116,000 professional medical workers, decreased 3,315 of the previous year; and 10.63 per 1,000 persons. The community medical service stations built in the city's urban and near-urban areas totaled 162, covered 62 percent of neighborhood committees and 48 percent of residents, All hospitals conscientiously carried out the medical charge reform program of "control in total amount and adjustment in structure" so that the rapid growth of medicine expenditure had been controlled, The city's medical expenditure decreased 1.09 billion yuan more than the previous year.

Sports: The nationwide body-building activities grew vigorously. A total of 139 stadiums and gymnasiums were open to the public and received one million every month on average, 300,000 people more than that of the previous year. Great achievements were made in athletics. On the 13th Asian Games, 57 athletes from Beijing won 28 gold medals, 9 sliver medals and 8 bronze medals.

VI. Life of the People

Population: According to the census sample, the city's human fertility was 0.6 percent, human mortality 0.53 percent and natural population growth rate 0.07 percent, a decrease of 0.12 percentage points over the previous year. By the end of 1998, the permanent resident population (having lived in Beijing for more than half a year) reached 12.456 million, 56,000 more than that of the previous year. According to the statistics from the public security department, the registered population was 10.915 million by the end of the year.

Employment: New progress was made in the re-employment project. There were 169,600 laid-off workers in the year, 102,100 of whom were reemployed, and the reemployment rate of laid-off workers was 60.2 percent. 72.9 percent of surplus personnel were settled. By the end of the year, 29,500 people were registered unemployed and the urban registered unemployment rate was 0.66 percent. The reform of social security system progressed steadily. The city's pool of endowment insurance, unemployment insurance and medical treatment of serious illness of local enterprises covered 95 percent, 94 percent and 85.2 percent respectively, 12.6 percentage points, 9.7 percentage points and 12.2 percentage points more than that of the previous year.

Resident income: The annual average per capita salary of the city's employees was 12,300 yuan, up 11.6 percent over the previous year. Deducting the price factor, the actual growth was 9 percent. The annual per capita disposable income of urban residents was 8,472 yuan, up 8.4 percent over the previous year. Eliminating the price factor, the actual growth was 5.9 percent. The per capita nonproductive expenditure was 6,970.8 yuan, up 6.7 percent over the same period of the previous year. The consumption structure was getting rational. The Engel index of urban residents was 41.1 percent, a decrease of 2.6 percentage points over 1997. The per capita net income of farmers reached 4,029 yuan. Eliminating the price factor, the actual growth was 6.7 percent.

Savings of urban and rural residents: The savings of urban and rural residents reached 228.72 billion yuan, 31.2 billion yuan more than that of the beginning of the year and a growth of 19.3 percent. Of which, 206.32 billion yuan was the savings of urban residents and increased 29.24 billion yuan from the beginning of the year; 22.4 billion yuan belonged to rural residents and increased 1.96 billion yuan as compared to the beginning of the year.

Urban and rural residence: The city's annual investment in residential buildings totaled 27.37

billion yuan, up 21.1 percent over the previous year. The floor space completed reached 10.906 million square meters, up 9.4 percent over the previous year of which, residence was 10.045 million square meters, up 22.9 percent. The per capita floorage of urban residents attained 14.86 square meters, up 3.5 percent over the previous year. The per capita living area of rural residents amounted to 27.6 square meters, up 0.7 percent over the previous year. The municipal government set the construction projects to build 5.68 million square meters economical and practical residential buildings in 19 places, which had gradually started.

Appendix 1: Notes

a) All data in this communique are primary statistical data.

b) Added value index, overall production rate absolute value involved in this communique are calculated according to the price of the year, and the growth rate is calculated by comparable prices.

Appendix 2: Statistical Chart

Indicator	Unit	1998	1998 as % of 1997
Output of Major Farm and By-Products			
Grain	(10000 tons)	239.2	100.7
Vegetable	(10000 tons)	406.1	99.0
Meat	(10000 tons)	44.9	111.4
Fresh Eggs	(10000 tons)	17.9	75.2
Cow Milk	(10000 tons)	22.7	102.3
Fresh-water Fish	(10000 tons)	7.7	100.0
Slaughtered Hogs	(10000 heads)	374.8	106.0
Output of Major Products			
Pig Iron	(10000 tons)	751.5	100.6
Steel	(10000 tons)	803.2	100.2
Steel Products	(10000 tons)	676.1	103.4
Coal	(10000 tons)	989.5	99.6
Electricity	(100 million kwh)	144.5	98.6
Fertilizer(pure)	(10000 tons)	11.3	94.8
Cement	(10000 tons)	762.0	114.9
Ethlene	(10000 tons)	57.0	98.2
Cross-country Motor Vehicles	(10000)	2.7	65.5
Micro-computer	(10000)	160.9	139.8
Color TV Set	(10000)	11.1	28.5
Program Control Telephone	(10000 lines)	772.2	166.9
Exchange	(10000)	39.5	334.8
HouseAir Conditioner	(10000 tons)	9.9	117.9
Liquor			
Beer	(10000 tons)	117.2	102.1
Soft Drinks	(10000 tons)	30.1	99.6
Performance of Various Means of Transportation			
Freight Traffic			
Railway	(10000 tons)	4271.9	90.0
Highway	(10000 tons)	27892.0	95.0
Civil Aviation	(10000 tons)	21.42	112.4
Passengers Traffic			
Railway	(10000 person.times)	5031.8	104.6
Highway	(10000 person.times)	6390.0	130.4
Civil Aviation	(10000 person.times)	753.43	115.3
Retail Price Indices (preceding year=100)	**(%)**	**98.3**	
Residents Consumer Price Indices (preceding year=100)	**(%)**	**102.4**	
Foods		97.1	
Clothing		105.9	
Household Facilities		97.5	
Medicine and Medical Services		108.6	
Means of Transportation and Communications		99.0	
Recreation, Education and Culture Articles		97.8	
Residence		104.7	
Services		121.3	

北京市社会商业普查公报

北京市社会商业普查办公室

(1999年5月11日)

根据北京市人民政府办公厅“关于开展北京市社会商业普查工作的通知”(京政办发［1998］50号)的要求，从1998年下半年开始的全市社会商业普查工作在市、区、县各级政府的领导下，在中央和市属各业务主管部门的大力支持下，在各机关、企事业单位和个体工商户的积极配合下，经过各级普查机构及全体普查工作人员的辛勤努力，全市普查资料的登记、上报、审核、汇总工作已经完成，现将普查的主要成果公布如下：

一、基本概况

1、商业机构

截止到1998年底，全市共有批发零售贸易业、餐饮业法人单位和产业活动单位、有商品销售活动的非商业企业、各类商品交易市场以及个体户(以下简称商业机构)257411个，比1987年增长1.4倍，年均增长8.4%。

商业机构情况

项　目	单位数(个)	零售额(亿元)
合计	**257411**	**1195.2**
1.商业企业	31140	704.5
批发贸易业	11357	139.9
零售贸易业	16079	510.2
餐饮业	3704	54.4
2.非商业企业	9069	160.2
居民服务、旅馆业	4276	18.5
制造业	1019	40.2
其他	3774	101.5
3.各类商品交易市场	943	87.5
4.个体户	216259	243.0

2、商业营业网点

截止到1998年底，全市零售贸易业、餐饮业和居民服务业营业网点241261个，比1987年增长1.3倍，年均增长8%。其中零售贸易业营业网点180510个，增长1.6倍，占全部营业网点的74.8%；餐饮业28754个，居民服务业31997个，分别增长2倍和34.7%，占全部营业网点的11.9%和13.3%。

3、社会消费品零售额

1998年，消费品市场活跃兴旺，全年实现社会消费品零售额1195.2亿元，比1987年增长5.8倍，年均增长19%。对国民经济的发展起到了重要的促进作用。

从消费结构看，用类商品占全部消费品零售额的比重明显提高，吃、穿类商品比重有所下降。1998年，吃、穿、用消费品零售额分别实现347.9亿元、145.5亿元和664.9亿元，比1987年分别增长3.8倍、4.7倍和7.9倍。用类商品比重达到55.6%，比1987年提高13.1个百分点，吃、穿类商品比重分别为29.1%和12.2%，下降13.7和2.9个百分点。

4、商品购、销、存总额

1998年，全市消费品市场货源充足，品种齐全，全年批发零售贸易业商品购进总额为2750.9

亿元，比 1987 年增长 9.4 倍，年均增长 23.7%；商品销售总额为 2837 亿元，比 1987 年增长 8.7 倍，年均增长 23%。从商品销售量看，一批新型家电产品和美化生活的商品旺销，带动消费品市场销售更加活跃。

批发零售贸易业主要商品销售量

项　目	单　位	市内销售量
各种服装	万　件	5514
皮鞋	万　双	671
黄金饰品	亿　元	11.3
彩电	万　台	49.1
录相机	万　台	5.1
影碟机	万　台	36.1
家用电冰箱	万　台	24.7
家用洗衣机	万　台	28.0
房间空调器	万　台	30.4
组合音像	万　台	6.4
摄像机	万　台	1.5
微型计算机	万　台	6.9

二、商业分布

1、按地域划分：城近郊区在网点建设和实现零售额上占有绝对优势。截止到 1998 年底，城近郊区共有各类商业机构 162662 个，当年实现的消费品零售额 991.5 亿元，分别占全市商业机构和社会消费品零售额的 63.2%和 83%。

商业机构区域分布情况

项　目	单位数(个)	比重(%)	零售额(亿元)	比重(%)
合计	**257411**	**100.0**	**1195.2**	**100.0**
城近郊区	162662	63.2	991.5	83.0
远 郊 区	48321	18.8	114.6	9.6
各　县	46428	18.0	89.1	7.4

2、按地理位置划分：三环路以内集中了全市主要的商业机构。在城市规划区域内，三环路以内各类商业机构(不含个体)19966 个，全年实现消费品零售额 513.1 亿元，占全市社会消费品零售额的 42.9%。

商业机构地理位置分布情况

项　目	单位数(个)	比重(%)	零售额(亿元)	比重(%)
合计	**41152**	**100.0**	**952.2**	**100.0**
二环路以内	10479	25.5	227.4	23.9
二环路至三环路	9487	23.0	285.7	30.0
三环路至四环路	8263	20.1	241.7	25.4
四环路以外卫星城	4978	12.1	97.0	10.2
四环路以外(不含卫星城)	7945	19.3	100.4	10.5

三、商业结构

1、按企业经济类型划分：多种经济成分并存，非公有经济快速发展。1998 年，在全市社会消费品零售额中，国有、集体经济实现的零售额为 576.3 亿元，占全市社会消费品零售额的 48.2%，比 1987 年的 91.5%下降了 43.3 个百分点；而私营经济、股份制经济、外商投资经济、港澳台投资经济和个体经济等其他经济得到了长足的发展，实现零售额 618.9 亿元，占零售额的比重为 51.8%。

商业机构经济类型分布情况

项　目	单位数(个)	比重(%)	零售额(亿元)	比重(%)
合计	**257411**	**100.0**	**1195.2**	**100.0**
国有经济	12472	4.8	344.8	28.8
集体经济	16036	6.2	231.5	19.4
私营经济	5137	2.0	37.7	3.2
个体经济	216259	84.0	243.0	20.3
联营经济	553	0.2	28.8	2.4
股份制经济	5544	2.2	214.8	18.0
外商投资经济	757	0.3	59.9	5.0
港澳台投资经济	513	0.2	25.6	2.1
其他经济	140	0.1	9.1	0.8

2、按行业划分：传统单一的批发零售贸易业在市场所占的份额逐渐缩小。1998 年，全市批发零售贸易业实现消费品零售额 865.7 亿元，占全市社会消费品零售额的 72.4%，比 1987 年下降 6.9 个百分点；餐饮业零售额 81.8 亿元，占 6.8%，比 1987 年增加 0.8 个百分点；制造业零售额 63.8 亿元，占 5.3%，比 1987 年下降 1.5 个百分点；其他行业零售额 183.9 亿元，占 15.4%，比 1987 年增加 7.6 个百分点。

3、按隶属关系划分：在中央商业企业中，集中了全市主要的大型批发贸易企业，1998 年实现的商品销售总额占到全市批发零售贸易业的 36.2%。在地方商业企业中，集中了全市主要的大中型零售贸易企业，1998 年地方各类商业机构实现消费品零售额 609.6 亿元(不含个体)，占全市社会消费品零售额的 51%。

商业机构隶属关系分布情况

项　目	单位数(个)	比重(%)	零售额(亿元)	比重(%)
合　计	**257411**	**100.0**	**1195.2**	**100.0**
中　央	4641	1.8	137.2	11.5
地　方	240380	93.4	852.6	71.3
市　属	6584	2.6	249.8	20.9
区县及以下	17537	6.8	359.8	30.1
个　体	216259	84.0	243.0	20.3
其　他	12390	4.8	205.4	17.2

4、按大中小型企业划分：大型商业企业是我市商业发展的主力军。大型商业企业由于资金雄厚、企业规模大、竞争能力强，在市场经济中起着主导作用。1998 年，全市大型商业企业 322 个，其中商品销售总额超过 10 亿元的批发企业有 33 家，商品销售总额超过 1 亿元的零售企业有 105 家，营业收入超过 1000 万元的餐饮企业有 92 家；大型商业企业实现消费品零售额 355.1 亿元，占全市社会消费品零售额 29.7%，充分显示了大型商业企业的实力。

商业企业规模分布情况

项　目	单位数(个)	比重(%)	零售额(亿元)	比重(%)
合　计	**31140**	**100.0**	**704.5**	**100.0**
大　型	322	1.0	355.1	50.4
中　型	2767	8.9	252.9	35.9
小　型	28051	90.1	96.5	13.7

5、按经营业态划分：在零售贸易业中，超级市场、便利店、专卖店、仓储式商场已遍布全市。1987 年以前，我市零售贸易业业态基本上局限于综合性百货商店和副食店，1987 年以后，各种形式的商业业态得到了全面发展，截止到 1998 年底，全市超级市场、便利店、专卖店和仓储式商场达 3510 个，实现消费品零售额 78.9 亿元，占零售贸易企业零售额的 15.5%

零售贸易业经营业态分布情况

项　　目	单位数(个)	比重(%)	零售额(亿元)	比重(%)
合计	**16079**	**100.0**	**510.2**	**100.0**
百货商店	1977	12.3	251.6	49.3
超级市场	159	1.0	24.0	4.7
专业店	4580	28.4	102.8	20.2
专卖店	642	4.0	12.1	2.4
便利店	2651	16.5	20.1	3.9
仓储式商场	58	0.4	22.7	4.4
其他	6012	37.4	76.9	15.1

四、商业设施

现代化商业设施发展迅速，购物环境大为改善。截止到 1998 年底，全市商业企业各类房屋建筑面积 2427 万平方米，营业面积 1342 万平方米，仓库面积 768 万平方米，拥有机动车 3.5 万辆，其中生产经营用 2.4 万辆，占机动车拥有量的 68.6%。全市商业企业商业信息化累计投资总额达 14.6 亿元，其中硬件设备投资额为 10 亿元。零售商业企业中有 357 家拥有中央空调、156 家拥有电动扶梯、356 家拥有 POS 系统、109 家拥有 MIS 系统、180 家拥有电子监控系统等现代化设施。

五、各类商品交易市场

各类商品交易市场迅速发展，新型市场不断涌现。截止到 1998 年底，全市各类商品交易市场 943 家，占地面积为 965.2 万平方米，成交额 540 亿元。其中占地面积超过 1 万平方米的市场有 207 家，面积达 801.4 万平方米，占全市各类商品交易市场占地总面积的 83%。成交额超亿元的大型商品交易市场 77 家，成交额 439.2 亿元，占全市商品交易市场成交额的 81.3%。建材装饰品交易市场、机动车辆交易市场、家具市场等一批专业市场以其专业性强、价格低廉、购物方便而受到消费者的喜爱，从无到有，从少到多，发展迅速。

各类商品交易市场情况

项　　目	单位数(个)	成交额(亿元)
合计	**943**	**540.4**
农副产品市场	637	326
工业品市场	163	86
家具市场	22	7.1
建材市场	47	21
机动车市场	4	89.3
其他市场	70	11

普查结果表明，我市社会商业迅速发展，已初步形成服务功能配套、流通渠道畅通、各种经济形式并存、整体效益较好的产业群体。对完善首都的城市功能方便城乡居民生活、促进工农业生产发展等发挥了积极的作用，是第三产业重要的支柱行业之一，在推进首都现代化建设，满足人民不断增长的物质文化需求等方面发挥了巨大的作用。

注：北京市第一次商业普查是1987年进行的，因此，本次普查资料均与1987年对比。

COMMUNIQUE ON THE COMMERCIAL CENSUS IN BEIJING

May 11 , 1999

According to the General Office of Beijing Municipal Government's instruction on the commercial census in Beijing, the commercial census in Beijing was conducted in the second half year of 1998. Under the leadership of municipal government, district and county government, with the support of related units and self-employed households, and great efforts of thousands of census working staff, the works on the stage of interviewing, quality check and summary have been smoothly completed.

The summarized data are as follows:

I. General Situation

1. Commercial Operating Units

By the end of 1998, the number of commercial operating units in the whole city totaled 257, 411, 1.4 times more than that of 1978 and the average annual rate of growth was 8.4 percent. The commercial operating units include the institutional units and establishments of wholesale, retail trade and catering, non-commercial enterprises engaged in sales, all commodities trade markets and self-employed households.

Table 1. The General Situation of Commercial Operating Units

Item	Number of Units(unit)	Retail Sales (100 million yuan)
Total	**257411**	**1195.2**
1.Commercial Eterprises	31140	704.5
Wholesale Trade	11357	139.9
Retail Sales Trade	16079	510.2
Catering	3704	54.4
2.Non-commercial Enterprises	9069	160.2
Residential Services,Hotels	4276	18.5
Manufacture	1019	40.2
Others	3774	101.5
3.All Commodities Trade Market	943	87.5
4.Self-employed Households	216259	243.0

2. Commercial Operating Outlets

By the end of 1998, the number of operating outlets of retail sales trade, catering and residential services totaled 241261, 1.3 times that of 1987 and the average annual rate of growth was 8 percent. Among them, 180510 were retail trade outlets, 1.6 times that of 1987 and accounting for 74.8 percent of the total outlets; 28754 were catering outlets and 31997 were residential services outlets, 2 times and 34.7 percent that of 1987 respectively; accounting for 11.9 percent and 13.3 percent respectively.

3. Retail Sales of Social Consumer Goods

The year 1998 saw a prosperous market with retail sales of social consumer goods amounted 119.52 billion yuan and up 5.8 times that of 1987, and the average annual rate of growth was 19 percent. It became the driving force behind the development of national economy.

Viewing from the structure of consumption, the percentage of daily use articles to the total retail sales of social consumer goods was obvious improved, but the percentage of food and clothes was down. In 1998, the retail sales of social consumer goods of food, clothes and daily use articles increased 3.8 times, 4.7 times and 7.9 times that of 1987 to reach 34.79 billion yuan, 14.55 billion yuan and 66.49 billion yuan respectively. The percentage of daily use articles to the total retail sales of social consumer goods accounted 55.6 percent, and up 13.1 percent over that of 1987; food accounted 29.1 percent and clothes accounted 12.2 percent, and down 13.7 percent and 2.9 percent respectively.

4. Purchases, Sales and Inventory

In 1998, the supply of consumer market was rich and variety. The total purchases of goods by wholesale and retail trade was 275.09 billion yuan, up 9.4 times that of 1987, and the average annual rate of growth was 23.7 percent; total sales was 283.7 billion yuan, up 8.7 times that of 1987, and the average annual rate of growth was 23 percent.

Viewing from the volume of sales, a batch of new type of household electric articles was sold well and enliven the consumer market.

Table 2 The Volume of Sales by Wholesale and Retail Sale Trade

Item	Unit	Sales in City
All Garments	10,000 pieces	5514
Leather Shoe	10,000 pair	671
Gold Ornament	100 million yuan	11.3
Color TV Set	10,000 sets	49.1
Recorder	10,000 sets	5.1
Video CD	10,000 sets	36.1
Refrigerator	10,000 sets	24.7
Washing-machine	10,000 sets	28.0
Air conditioner	10,000 sets	30.4
Hi-Fi	10,000 sets	6.4
Pickup Camera	10,000 sets	1.5
Micro Computer	10,000 sets	6.9

II. Geographical Distribution

Regarding geographical distribution, the number of outlets and the retail sales of social consumer goods of city proper and near-suburbs were important priority to the others. By the end of 1998, there were162,662 commercial operating units in city proper and near-suburbs, the retail sales of social consumer goods was accomplished 99.15 billion yuan and accounted for 63.2 percent and 83 percent of the total respectively.

Table 3 Geographical Distribution of Commercial Operating Units

Item	Number of Units(unit)	Proportion(%)	Retail Sales(100 million yuan)	Proportion(%)
Total	**257411**	**100.0**	**1195.2**	**100.0**
City Proper,Near Suburbs	162662	63.2	991.5	83.0
Outer Suburbs	48321	18.8	114.6	9.6
Counties	46428	18.0	89.1	7.4

The commercial operating units were distributed mainly inside of the third-ring road and amounted to 19,966(not included self-employed households); accomplished the retail sales of social consumer goods 51.31 billion yuan and accounted for 42.9 percent of the total.

Table 4 Geographical Distribution of Commercial Operating Units

Item	Number of Units(unit)	Proportion(%)	Retail Sales(100 million yuan)	Proportion(%)
Total	**41152**	**100.0**	**952.2**	**100.0**
Inside of Two-Ring Road	10479	25.5	227.4	23.9
Two-Three Ring Road	9487	23.0	285.7	30.0
Three-Four Ring Road	8263	20.1	241.7	25.4
Satellite Town Outside of Four-Ring Road	4978	12.1	97.0	10.2
Outside of Four-Ring Road (Not Included Satellite Town)	7945	19.3	100.4	10.5

III. Structure of Commerce

1. Classified by Types of Ownership

The economic pattern with public ownership and collective ownership as the principal part and other economic ownership sharing the development has formed. Non-public ownership economy developed rapidly. Among the total retail sales of social consumer goods, 57.63 billion yuan was accomplished by state-owned and collective-owned commercial operating units, accounted for 48.2 percent of the total and down 43.3 percentage point from 91.5 percent of 1987; 61.89 billion yuan was accomplished by the other economic pattern and accounted for 51.8%.

Table 5 The Commercial Operating Units Classified by Types of Ownership

Item	Number of Units(unit)	Proportion(%)	Retail Sales(100 million yuan)	Proportion(%)
Total	**257411**	**100.0**	**1195.2**	**100.0**
State-Owned	12472	4.8	344.8	28.8
Collective-Owned	16036	6.2	231.5	19.4
Private-Owned	5137	2.0	37.7	3.2
Individuals	216259	84.0	243.0	20.3
Joint-Owned	553	0.2	28.8	2.4
Share Holding	5544	2.2	214.8	18.0
Foreign Funded	757	0.3	59.9	5.0
HongKong,Macao, Taiwan Funded	513	0.2	25.6	2.1
Others	140	0.1	9.1	0.8

2. Classified by Types of Sector

The market shared by the traditional sole sector, the wholesale, retail trade sector was gradually shrunk and the shared by other sectors were increased. In 1998, 86.57 billion yuan of retail sales of social consumer goods was accomplished by the wholesale and retail trade and accounted 72.4 percent of the total, down 6.9 percentage point over that of 1987; 8.18 billion yuan by catering, accounted for 6.8 percent, up 0.8 percentage point over the 1987; 6.38 billion yuan by manufacture and accounted for 5.3 percent, down 1.5 percentage point over the 1987; 18.39 billion yuan by the other sectors, accounted for 15.4 percent and up 7.6 percentage point over the 1987.

3. Classified by Types of Administration Level

The major large commercial wholesale enterprises were distributed mainly in the central commercial enterprises and its sales of 1998 accounted for 36.2. percent of the wholesale and retail sale trade. The major large and medium commercial retail enterprises were distributed mainly in the local commercial enterprises. The retail sales of social consumer goods accomplished by local commercial operating units accounted for 51 percent of the total with 60.96 billion yuan.

Table 6 The Commercial Operating Units Classified by Administration Level

Item	Number of Units(unit)	Proportion(%)	Retail Sales(100 million yuan)	Proportion(%)
Total	**257411**	**100.0**	**1195.2**	**100.0**
Central	4641	1.8	137.2	11.5
Local	240380	93.4	852.6	71.3
Municipal	6584	2.6	249.8	20.9
Below District and County	17537	6.8	359.8	30.1
Individuals	216259	84.0	243.0	20.3
Others	12390	4.8	205.4	17.2

4. Classified by Types of Enterprises Size

The large commercial enterprises play important role in the city's commercial development with their solid capital and strong competition. In 1998, there are 322 large commercial enterprises in the city, among them, 33 are the wholesale enterprises with the sales surpassing 1 billion yuan; 105 are the retail enterprises with the sales surpassing 100 million yuan and 92 are catering enterprises with business income surpassing 10 million. They accomplished the retail sales of social consumer goods 35.51 billion yuan and accounted 29.7 percent of the total.

Table 7 Composition of Commercial Enterprises by Operating Size

Item	Number of Units(unit)	Proportion(%)	Retail Sales(100 million yuan)	Proportion(%)
Total	**31140**	**100.0**	**704.5**	**100.0**
Large	322	1.0	355.1	50.4
Medium	2767	8.9	252.9	35.9
Small	28051	90.1	96.5	13.7

5. Classified by Types of Operating Mode

The retail trade was mainly confined to comprehensive department stores before 1978. Since reform and opening, there has been presented the various commercial operating modes and distributed in the whole city. By the end of 1998, the number of supermarket, convenient shop, monopoly shop and store market totaled 3510, with the retail sales of social consumer 7.89 billion yuan and accounted for 15.5 percent of the retail sale trade.

Table 8 Retail Sale Trade Classified by Operating Mode

Item	Number of Units(unit)	Proportion(%)	Retail Sales(100 million yuan)	Proportion(%)
Total	**16079**	**100.0**	**510.2**	**100.0**
Department Store	1977	12.3	251.6	49.3
Supermarket	159	1.0	24.0	4.7
Specialized Shop	4580	28.4	102.8	20.2
Monopoly Shop	642	4.0	12.1	2.4
Convenient Shop	2651	16.5	20.1	3.9
Store Market	58	0.4	22.7	4.4
Others	6012	37.4	76.9	15.1

IV. Commercial Equipment

The modern commercial equipment was developed rapidly and the environment of shopping was improved. By the end of 1998, the housing area (construction area) of commercial enterprises was 24.27 million square meters, the operating area was 13.42 million square meters and the storehouse area was 7.68 million square meters. There were 35,000 motor vehicles, among them, 24,000 were used for operating and accounted for 68.6 percent of the total. The city's investment in commercial enterprise automation was 1.46 billion yuan, among them, the investment in hardware was 1 billion yuan. 357 retail trade enterprises have central air conditioning; 156 enterprises have escalator; 356 enterprises have POS system; 109 enterprises have MIS system and 180 enterprises have electric monitor system and etc.

V. All Commodities Trade Markets

All commodities trade markets development rapidly, and the new type of markets present continuously. By the end of 1998, the city have 943 all commodities trade markets with the volume of business 54 billion yuan, among them, 207 trade markets, with areas surpassing 10,000 square meters, occupy areas of 8.014 million square meters and accounted for 83 percent of the total. The number of large trade markets with volume business surpassing 100 million yuan amounted to 77 and accounted for 81.3 percent of the total with the volume of business of 43.92 billion yuan. A batch of special trade markets, such as the construction materials trade market, furniture trade markets and motor vehicle trade markets were acclaimed by residents with its convenient to the public and low price and developed rapidly.

Table 9 General Situation of All Commodity Trade Markets

Item	Number of Units	Value of Business(100 million yuan)
Total	**943**	**540.4**
Farm and Sideline Products Markets	637	326
Industrial Products Markets	163	86
Furniture Markets	22	7.1
Construction Materials Markets	47	21
Motor Vehicle Markets	4	89.3
Others	70	11

The result of survey showed that the city's commerce developed rapidly. The enterprises, with consorted service function, circulation channel smoothly, various economic pattern co-exiting and good efficient, have preliminary been formulated. The city's commerce also promoted the development of industry and farming, made life convenient to the public, became one of the pillar sector in tertiary industry and took great effect in pushing capital's modernization construction and with meeting the growing needs of material culture.

Notes:

The first commercial census in Beijing was conducted in1987, so the data in this communique was contrasted with that for 1987.

1999

统计图表

STATISTICAL GRAPH AND CHART

综 合

GENERAL SURVEY

地方财政收入占国内生产总值比重（1978-1998）

Ratio of Local Financial Revenue to Gross Domestic Product

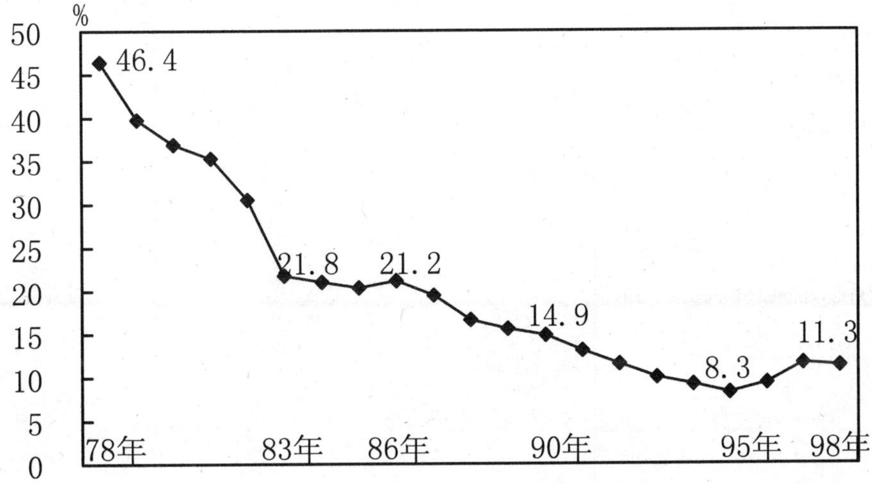

	1998	1997	1998年为1997年% 1998 as % of 1997
国内生产总值（亿元） Gross domestic product (100 million yuan)	2011.3	1810.1	109.8
地方财政收入（亿元） Local financial revenue (100 million yuan)	227.3	189.4	120.0

1998年国内生产总值构成（%）

Compsition of GDP(%)

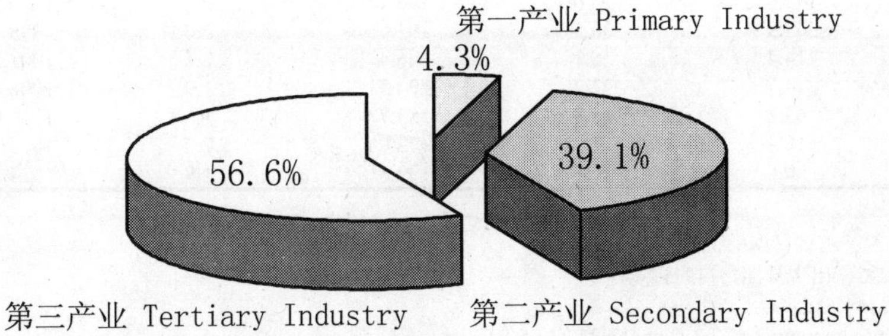

1-1 土 地 面 积
LAND AREA

项 目 Item		范 围 Scope		面 积 (平方公里) Area (sq.km)	比 重 (%) Proportion (%)
全 市	**Total**			**16807.8**	**100**
城 区	City Proper	东城区、西城区、崇文区、宣武区	Dongcheng,Xicheng, Chongwen,Xuanwu	87.1	0.5
近郊区	Near Suburbs	朝阳区、丰台区、石景山区、海淀区	Chaoyang,Fengtai, Shijingshan,Haidian	1282.8	7.6
远郊区	Outer Suburbs	门头沟区、房山区通州区	Mentougou,Fangshan Tongzhou	4105.0	24.4
各 县	Counties	昌平县、顺义县、大兴县、平谷县怀柔县、密云县延庆县	Changping,Shunyi, Daxing,Pinggu Huairou,Miyun Yanqing	11332.9	67.4
规划市区	**Programmed Scope of the City**	东：定福庄 南：南苑 西：石景山 北：清河	East：Dingfuzhuang South：Nanyuan West：Shijingshan North：Qinghe	**1041.0**	**6.2**
市区中心地区	Central Part of the City	边缘大体在四环路内外	The edge is roughly around the Fourth ring road	289.8	1.7
建成区	Completed Part			488.3	2.9
三环路以内	Within The Third Ring Road			158.0	0.9

附：全市平原面积6390.3平方公里，占38%。山区面积10417.5平方公里，占62%。

Appendix：Area of plain is 6390.3 sq.km,as 38% of total.Area of mountain is 10147.5 sq.km,as 62% of total.

注：1.规划市区、市中心地区面积是1992年重新修订北京市城市总体规划后确定的数字。

2.建成区面积是市规划院根据1989年航空遥感照射资料重新计算的。

a) Figures on area of programmed scope of the city and central part of the city were in line with revised overall plan of Beijing in 1992.

b) Figure of completed part was recalculated according to data of air remote sensing irradiation by Beijing Planning Institution.

1-2 气 象
METEOROLOGY

月 份 Month	降水量(毫米) Precitation (mm)	平均气温(℃) Average Tem-preture (℃)	日照时数(时) Hours of Sun-shine (hour)	平均风速(米／秒) Average Wind Speed (mile／second)	平均气压(百帕) Average Pressure (100 pa)	大风日数(日) Days of Strong Wind (day)
全 年 Total	**731.7**	**13.1**	**2420.7**	**2.3**	**1012.5**	**10**
1	1.3	-3.9	174.4	2.6	1024.8	1
2	26.3	2.4	194.3	2.8	1021.5	1
3	4.3	7.6	207.8	2.8	1017.8	2
4	54.7	15.0	175.8	2.6	1009.8	
5	61.5	19.9	272.7	2.6	1008.3	
6	142.9	23.6	196.1	2.6	1000.9	
7	247.9	26.5	193.0	2.0	998.8	2
8	114.4	25.1	246.4	2.1	1002.5	1
9	4.7	22.2	204.7	1.9	1008.4	
10	61.8	14.8	183.7	1.8	1015.0	
11	11.3	4.0	172.0	2.0	1017.9	2
12	0.6	0.1	199.8	1.9	1024.1	1

附：1.无霜期199天。

2.年极端最高气温37.2℃，出现日期6月27,28日。

3.年极端最低气温-14.2℃，出现日期1月19日。

a) Annual forst-free period is 199 days.

b) Annual utmost highest air tempreture is 37.2℃,on the 27th,28th of June.

c) Annual utmost lowst air tempreture is -14.2℃,on the 19th of January.

1-3 行 政 区 划
ADMINISTRATIVE DIVISIONS

单位：个 (unit)

地区	Region	镇 Town	乡 Township	街道办事处 Urban Sub-district Office	居民委员会 Neighborhood Committee	村民委员会 Village Committee
全　市	Total	**105**	**120**	**134**	**5649**	**4032**
城　区	**City Propers**			**35**	**1525**	
东城区	Dongcheng			10	412	
西城区	Xicheng			10	515	
崇文区	Chongwen			7	246	
宣武区	Xuanwu			8	352	
近郊区	**Near Suburbs**	**1**	**35**	**69**	**3244**	**342**
朝阳区	Chaoyang		19	26	1223	170
丰台区	Fengtai		6	16	696	81
石景山区	Shijingshan			10	283	11
海淀区	Haidian	1	10	17	1042	80
远郊区	**Outer Suburbs**	**38**	**28**	**30**	**562**	**1548**
门头沟区	Mentougou	7	3	5	208	181
房山区	Fangshan	11	13	10	175	463
通州区	Tongzhou	8	12	6	149	481
各　县	**Counties**	**66**	**57**		**318**	**2142**
昌平县	Changping	17	6		124	313
顺义县	Shunyi	12		9	30	423
大兴县	Daxing	9	18		44	547
平谷县	Pinggu	10	11		34	273
怀柔县	Huairou	10	5		31	287
密云县	Miyun	12	7		60	346
延庆县	Yanqing	8	10		25	376

1-4 全部法人单位数(按所在地分)
TOTAL INSTITUTIONAL UNITS(BY REGION)

单位：个 (unit)

地区	Region	合计 Total	# 中央单位 Central Entities	# 市属单位 City Entities	# 区县属单位 of District and County
全　市	**Total**	**86805**	**10815**	**12402**	**16805**
城　区	**City Proper**	**21991**	**4274**	**4295**	**4134**
东城区	Dongcheng	6673	1401	1148	945
西城区	Xicheng	7677	2216	1413	1183
崇文区	Chongwen	3167	223	727	1089
宣武区	Xuanwu	4474	434	1007	917
近郊区	**Near Suburbs**	**40369**	**5872**	**6756**	**5478**
朝阳区	Chaoyang	15885	1653	3268	1365
丰台区	Fengtai	8062	925	1312	908
石景山区	Shijingshan	2234	178	263	1128
海淀区	Haidian	14188	3116	1913	2077
远郊区	**Outer Suburbs**	**8611**	**305**	**494**	**2325**
门头沟区	Mentougou	1734	37	83	594
房山区	Fangshan	2973	170	131	745
通州区	Tongzhou	3904	98	280	986
各　县	**Counties**	**15834**	**364**	**857**	**4868**
昌平县	Changping	3076	114	304	827
顺义县	Shunyi	2778	25	100	920
大兴县	Daxing	4211	117	301	964
平谷县	Pinggu	1376	15	26	506
怀柔县	Huairou	1651	34	37	628
密云县	Miyun	1418	36	38	499
延庆县	Yanqing	1324	23	51	524

1-5 全部法人、产业活动单位数(按所在地分)

TOTAL INSTITUTIONAL UNITS AND ESTABLISHMENTS(BY REGION)

单位：个 (unit)

地区	Region	法人单位数 合计 Institutional Units	单产业法人 Single Sector	多产业法人 Multi-sector	多产业法人单位的产业活动单位数 Establishments of Multi-sector Institutional Units
全市	**Total**	**86805**	**83408**	**3397**	**16422**
城区	City Proper	**21991**	**21072**	**919**	**4664**
东城区	Dongcheng	6673	6444	229	1196
西城区	Xicheng	7677	7297	380	2034
崇文区	Chongwen	3167	3046	121	595
宣武区	Xuanwu	4474	4285	189	839
近郊区	**Near Suburbs**	**40369**	**38957**	**1412**	**6786**
朝阳区	Chaoyang	15885	15116	769	3223
丰台区	Fengtai	8062	7835	227	1385
石景山区	Shijingshan	2234	2125	109	552
海淀区	Haidian	14188	13881	307	1626
远郊区	**Outer Suburbs**	**8611**	**8174**	**437**	**2211**
门头沟区	Mentougou	1734	1580	154	749
房山区	Fangshan	2973	2837	136	738
通州区	Tongzhou	3904	3757	147	724
各县	**Counties**	**15834**	**15205**	**629**	**2693**
昌平县	Changping	3076	2899	177	803
顺义县	Shunyi	2778	2729	49	159
大兴县	Daxing	4211	4049	162	588
平谷县	Pinggu	1376	1330	46	283
怀柔县	Huairou	1651	1570	81	391
密云县	Miyun	1418	1357	61	191
延庆县	Yanqing	1324	1271	53	278

注：多产业法人单位的产业活动单位因为有68个在外区县，在本市有16354个。

Note：Establishments of multi-sector institutional units of city totaled 16354, because 68 are out of districts and counties.

1-6 全部法人、产业活动单位数
TOTAL INSTITUTIONAL UNITS AND ESTABLISHMENTS

单位：个 (unit)

项目 Item		法人单位数 合计 Institutional Units	单产业法人 Single Sector	多产业法人 Multi-sector	多产业法人单位的产业活动单位数 Establishments of Multi-sector Institutional Units
总　计	**Total**	**86805**	**83408**	**3397**	**16422**
按登记注册类型分	**Grouped by Registered Type**				
内资经济	Domestic Investment Economy	81992	78635	3357	16220
国有经济	State-owned	25022	23189	1833	10301
集体经济	Collective-owned	28859	28161	698	5196
股份合作企业	Share Holding Cooperative	3712	3681	31	114
联营经济	Joint-owned	1020	999	21	89
国有独资公司	State-owned Funded Company	203	189	14	51
其他有限责任公司	Other Limited-Liability Company	4660	4620	40	167
股份有限公司	Share Holding Company	1079	1050	29	171
私营经济	Private-owned	8377	8349	28	125
其　他	Others	9060	8397	663	6
港澳台商投资经济	Hongkong,Macao and Taiwan Funded	1992	1976	16	55
与港澳台商合资经营	Joint Venture with Hongkong, Macao and Taiwan	1431	1420	11	34
与港澳台商合作经营	Cooperative with Hongkong, Macao and Taiwan	168	166	2	4
港、澳、台商独资经济	Hongkong,Macao and Taiwan Funded	364	362	2	6
港澳台商投资股份有限公司	Hongkong,Macao and Taiwan Share Holding Company	29	28	1	11
外商投资经济	Foreign Funded	2821	2797	24	147
中外合资经营	Chinese-Foreign Joint Venture	1805	1786	19	130
中外合作经营	Chinese-Foreign Cooperative	207	205	2	6
外资(独资)经济	Foreign Funded	790	787	3	11
外商投资股份有限公司	Foreign Share Holding Company	19	19		
按单位类别分	**Grouped by Type of Units**				
农　业	Agriculture	679	645	34	274
工　业	Industry	18994	18613	381	1585
建筑业	Construction	3145	3000	145	664
运输邮电业	Transportation,Posts and Telecommunications	566	520	46	307
批发零售贸易及餐饮业	Wholesale, Retail and Catering	24890	23831	1059	7511
服务业	Services	19817	19354	463	3392
行政事业及其他	Administrative Units, Institutions and Others	18714	17445	1269	2689
按隶属关系分	**Grouped by Administrative Relationship**				
中央属	Central	10815	10384	431	2035
市　属	City	12402	11600	802	3575
区县属	Districts and Counties	16805	15676	1129	6431
街道属	Subdistrict	4623	4477	146	1411
镇　属	Town	3586	3505	81	394
乡　属	Township	3626	3533	93	357
居委会属	Neighborhood Committee	3896	3514	382	837
村委会属	Village Committee	11867	11633	234	957
其　他	Others	19185	19086	99	425
按地理位置分	**Grouped by Geographic Position**				
二环路以内	Within the Second Ring	16072	15430	642	3303
二环路至三环路	the Second-third Ring Road	17518	16842	676	3202
三环路至四环路	the Third-Fourth Ring Road	14404	13924	480	2192
四环路以外	Beyond the Fourth Ring Road	38811	37212	1599	7725
按执行会计制度分	**Grouped by Accounting System Executed**				
企　业	Enterprises	68590	66435	2155	11782
事　业	Institutions	7607	7098	509	2486
机　关	Organizations	1501	1437	64	198
其　他	Others	9107	8438	669	1956

1-7 企业法人单位数
ENTERPRISE INSTITUTIONAL UNITS

单位：个 (unit)

项目	Item	法人单位合计 Institutional Unit
总计	Total	68590
城区	City Proper	17666
东城区	Dongcheng	5430
西城区	Xicheng	6028
崇文区	Chongwen	2550
宣武区	Xuanwu	3658
近郊区	Near Suburbs	34140
朝阳区	Chaoyang	13515
丰台区	Fengtai	6750
石景山区	Shijingshan	1705
海淀区	Haidian	12170
远郊区	Outer Suburbs	6012
门头沟区	Mentougou	1083
房山区	Fangshan	1988
通州区	Tongzhou	2941
各县	Counties	10772
昌平县	Changping	2233
顺义县	Shunyi	1989
大兴县	Daxing	3192
平谷县	Pinggu	790
怀柔县	Huairou	1176
密云县	Miyun	763
延庆县	Yanqing	629
按营业状况分	Grouped by Business	
营业	Going on	63905
停业	Closed	2697
筹建	Preparation	1197
当年撤销	Recall in this Year	346
其他	Others	443
按开业时间分	Grouped by Set up Time	
1949年以前	Before 1949	577
1950-1965		1835
1966-1979		2236
1980-1989		12134
1990年以后	After 1990	51808
按企业规模分	Grouped by Size	
大型	Large	614
中型	Medium	2781
小型	Small	44069
按登记注册类型分	Grouped by Type of Enterprises Registered	

项目	Item	法人单位合计 Institutional Unit
内资企业	Domestic Investment Enterprises	63787
国有企业	State-owned	16559
集体企业	Collective-owned	28156
股份合作企业	Share Holding Cooperative	3707
联营企业	Joint-owned	1017
国有独资公司	State-owned Funded Company	201
其他有限责任公司	Other Limited-Liability Company	4659
股份有限公司	Share Holding Company	1079
私营企业	Private	8333
其他内资企业	Others	76
港澳台商投资企业	Hongkong,Macao and Taiwan Funded	1989
与港澳台商合资经营企业	Joint Venture with Hongkong,Maocao and Taiwan	1431
与港澳台商合作经营企业	Cooperative with Hongkong,Macao and Taiwan	167
港、澳、台商独资企业	Hongkong,Macao and Taiwan Funded	362
港澳台商投资股份有限公司	Hongkong,Macao and Taiwan Share Holding Company	29
外商投资企业	Foreign Funded	2814
中外合资经营企业	Chinese-Foreign Joint Venture	1805
中外合作经营企业	Chinese-Foreign Cooperative	204
外资(独资)企业	Foreign Funded	786
外商投资股份有限公司	Foreign Share Holding Company	19
按地理位置分	Grouped by Location	
二环路以内	Within the Second Ring Road	13069
二环路至三环路	Between the Second-third Ring Road	14513
三环路至四环路	Between the Third-Fourth Ring Road	12327
四环路以外	Beyond the Fourth Ring Road the Three-Four Ring Road	28681
按控股情况分	Grouped by Share Holding Conditions	
# 国有绝对控股	State-owned Relative Holding	16758
# 国有相对控股	State-owned Absolute Holding	1232

1-8 国民经济各行业法人和产业活动单位数(按行业分)
INSTITUTIONAL UNITS AND ESTABLISHMENTS(BY SECTOR)

单位：个 (unit)

行业	Sector	法人单位数 合计 Institutional Units	单产业法人 Single Sector	多产业法人 Multi-sector	多产业法人单位的产业活动单位数 Establishments of Multi-sector Institutional Units
合计	**Total**	**86805**	**83408**	**3397**	**16422**
农业	Agriculture	325	312	13	129
林业	Forestry	60	47	13	26
畜牧业	Animal Husbandry	324	304	20	122
渔业	Fishery	48	47	1	12
农、林、牧、渔服务业	FFAF Services	510	486	24	100
煤炭采选业	Coal Mining and Dressing	186	183	3	66
石油和天然气开采业	Petroleum and Natural Gas Extraction	1	1		
黑色金属矿采选业	Ferrous Metals Mining and Dressing	21	20	1	5
有色金属矿采选业	Nonferrous Metals Mining and Dressing	16	16		3
非金属矿采选业	Nonmetal Minerals Mining and Dressing	270	267	3	21
其他矿采选业	Other Minerals Mining and Dressing	2	2		
食品加工业	Food Processing	545	537	8	56
食品制造业	Food Making	633	625	8	59
饮料制造业	Beverage Production	242	240	2	9
烟草制造业	Tobacco Processing	3	3		
纺织业	Textile Industry	521	506	15	52
服装及其他纤维制品制造业	Garments and Other Fiber Products	942	915	27	87
皮革、毛皮、羽绒及其制品业	Leather,Furs,Down and Related Products	177	173	4	11
木材加工及竹、藤、棕、革制品业	Timber Processing,Bamboo, Cane,Palm Fiber and Straw Products	243	241	2	21
家具制造业	Furniture Manufacturing	529	524	5	26
造纸及纸制品业	Papermaking and Paper Products	506	505	1	11
印刷业、记录媒介的复制	Printing and Record Medium Reproduced	981	963	18	58
文教体育用品制造业	Stationery,Education and Sports Goods	227	222	5	9
石油加工及炼焦业	Petroleum Processing and Coking Products	100	97	3	5
化学原料及化学制品制造业	Raw Chemical Materials and Chemical Products	1278	1264	14	70
医药制造业	Medical and Pharmaceutical Products	223	219	4	20
化学纤维制造业	Chemical Fibers	45	45		

1-8 续表 1 continued

单位：个 (unit)

行业	Sector	法人单位数 合 计 Institutional Units	单产业法人 Single Sector	多产业法人 Multi sector	多产业法人单位的产业活动单位数 Establishments of Multi-sector Institutional Units
橡胶制品业	Rubber Products	132	124	8	14
塑料制品业	Plastic Products	726	716	10	42
非金属矿物制品业	Nonmetal Mineral Products	1725	1702	23	116
黑色金属冶炼及压延加工业	Smelting and Processing of Ferrous Metals	77	72	5	34
有色金属冶炼及压延加工业	Smelting and Processing of Nonferrous Metals	146	143	3	7
金属制品业	Metal Products	2235	2214	21	133
普通机械制造业	Ordinary Machinery	1241	1218	23	94
专业设备制造业	Special Purpose Equipment	956	920	36	115
交通运输设备制造业	Transportation Equipment	1331	1286	45	207
武器弹药制造业	Weapons and Ammunition	9	5	4	4
电气机械及器材制造业	Electric Equipment and Machinery	889	862	27	65
电子及通信设备制造业	Electronic and Telecommunication	724	711	13	30
仪器仪表及文化办公用机械制造业	Instruments,Meters,Cultural and Official Machinery	438	431	7	25
其他制造业	Other Manufacturing	588	560	28	92
电力、蒸汽、热水的生产和供应业	Electricity,Steam,Hot Water Production and Supply	65	62	3	16
煤气生产和供应业	Gas Production and Supply	9	8	1	1
自来水的生产和供应业	Tap Water Production and Supply	12	11	1	1
土木工程建筑业	Civil Engineering	1412	1303	109	484
线路、管道和设备安装业	Circuit,Pipelines and Equipment Installation	731	703	28	96
装修装饰业	Buildings Decoration	1002	994	8	84
地质勘查业	Geological Prospecting	54	51	3	3
水利管理业	Water Conservancy	196	178	18	28
铁路运输业	Railway Transport	22	19	3	85
公路运输业	Highway Transport	422	383	39	158
管道运输业	Pipeline Transport	2	2		
水上运输业	Water Way Transport	10	10		
航空运输业	Air Transport	20	20		
交通运输辅助业	Transport Supporting and Auxiliary Services	225	220	5	32
其他交通运输业	Other Transport	19	19		3
仓储业	Storage	206	200	6	22
邮电通信业	Posts and Telecommunications	85	81	4	62
食品、饮料、烟草和家庭用品批发业	Wholesale of Food, Beverage,Tabacoo and Household Goods	4949	4737	212	686

1-8 续表 2 continued

单位：个 (unit)

行业 Sector		法人单位数 合计 Institutional Units	单产业法人 Single Sector	多产业法人 Multi-sector	多产业法人单位的产业活动单位数 Establishments of Multi-sector Institutional Units
能源、材料和机械电子设备批发业	Wholesale of Energy, Materials and Electronic Equipment	4727	4597	130	537
其他批发业	Other Wholesale	775	754	21	64
零售业	Retail	11722	11116	606	5040
商业经纪与代理业	Commercial Brokerage and Agencies	69	67	2	5
餐饮业	Catering	2717	2627	90	1184
金融业	Banking	594	436	158	1106
保险业	Insurance	54	54		
房地产开发与经营业	Real Estate Development and Operation	600	581	19	60
房地产管理业	Real Estate Management	742	716	26	72
房地产代理与经纪业	Real Estate Brokerage and Agency	90	90		2
公共服务业	Public Services	1278	1218	60	186
居民服务业	Resident Services	1531	1459	72	946
旅馆业	Hotels	1623	1575	48	430
租赁服务业	Leasing	329	324	5	47
旅游业	Tourism	301	296	5	30
娱乐服务业	Recreation	269	263	6	45
信息、咨询服务业	Information and Consultancy Services	4507	4482	25	110
计算机应用服务业	Computer Application Services	1592	1587	5	18
其他社会服务业	Other Social Services	1153	1126	27	144
卫　生	Health	633	620	13	49
体　育	Sports	107	99	8	19
社会福利保障业	Social Welfare	160	156	4	17
教　育	Education	2843	2581	262	1459
文化艺术业	Culture and Arts	945	904	41	76
广播电影电视业	Radio,Film,Television	159	153	6	12
科学研究业	Scientific Research	538	510	28	52
综合技术服务业	Polytechnical Services	4922	4888	34	104
国家机关	Government Organs	1589	1511	78	104
政党机关	Party Organs	110	110		
社会团体	Social Bodies	469	458	11	18
基层群众自治组织	Masses Autonomous Body	8959	8297	662	664
其他行业	Other Sectors	1082	1024	58	105

1-9 国民经济主要指标
MAJOR INDICTORS FOR NATIONAL ECONOMY

项目	Item	1998	1997	1998年为1997年% 1998 as % of 1997
人口	Population			
年底常住人口 (万人)	Year-end Permanent Residents (10000 persons)	1091.5	1085.5	100.6
劳动力	**Labor Force (10000 persons)**			
从业人员 (万人)	Employment (10000 persons)	622.2	655.8	94.9
# 职工人数 (万人)	Staff and Workers (10000 persons)	450.1	465.3	96.7
国内生产总值 (亿元)	**Gross Domestic Product (100 million yuan)**	**2011.3**	**1810.1**	**111.1**
工农业总产值 (1990年不变价,亿元)	**Gross Output Value of Industry and Agriculture(at 1990 constant prices, 100 million yuan)**	**2054.2**	**1751.1**	**117.3**
全社会固定资产投资 (亿元)	**Total Investment in Fixed Asstes (100 million yuan)**	**1115.3**	**961.2**	**116.0**
# 固定资产投资 (亿元)	Investment in Fixed Assets	682.9	582.1	117.3
# 基本建设投资 (亿元)	Capital Construction	415.5	374.3	111.0
更新改造投资 (亿元)	Innocation	252.4	191.2	132.0
房地产开发投资 (亿元)	Real Estate Development	377.4	330.3	114.3
财政	**Finance**			
财政收入 (亿元)	Revenue (100 million yuan)	262.0	209.9	124.8
财政支出 (亿元)	Expenditures (100 million yuan)	307.8	262.2	117.4
物价	**Price Indices**			
居民消费价格总指数 (%)	Consumer Price Index (%)	102.4	105.3	
商品零售价格总指数 (%)	Retail Price Index (%)	98.3	103.8	
职工工资	**Wages of Staff and Workers**			
职工工资总额 (亿元)	Total Wages (100 million yuan)	558.2	514.8	108.4
职工平均工资 (元)	Average Wage (yuan)	12285.0	11019.0	111.5
居民消费水平 (元)	**Per Capita Consumption (yuan)**	**5178.0**	**4557.0**	**113.6**
非农业居民 (元)	Non-Agricultural (yuan)	6240.0	5524.0	113.0
农业居民 (元)	Agricultural (yuan)	3032.0	2661.0	113.9
农村经济	**Rural Economy**			
农林牧渔业总产值 (1990年不变价,亿元)	Gross Output Value of Farming,Forestry,Animal Husbandry and Fishery (at 1990 constant prices,100 million yuan)	93.5	90.4	103.4
乡镇集体企业数 (个)	Number of Township and Village Enterprises (unit)	15711.0	16080.0	97.7
乡镇企业从业人数 (万人)	Employment of Township and Village Enterprises (10000 persons)	73.7	78.2	94.2
乡镇企业总收入 (亿元)	Total Revenue of Township and Village Enterprises (100 million yuan)	574.7	542.8	105.9
工业	**Industry**			
工业总产值(1990年不变价,不含个体工业,亿元)	Gross Output Value (at 1990 constant prices,excluding individual industry, 100 million yuan)	1926.7	1628.0	118.3
轻工业 (亿元)	Light Industry (100 million yuan)	539.4	527.8	102.2
重工业 (亿元)	Heavy Industry (100 million yuan)	1387.4	1100.2	126.1
独立核算工业企业全员劳动生产率(按增加值计算,元/人)	Overall Labor Productivity of Enterprises with Independent Accounting System (according to added value,yuan/person)	35130.0	28220.0	124.5

注：本表的发展速度按可比口径计算。(续表同)

Note：Development Indices are calculated at constant prices.(the continued tables are the same)

1-9 续表 1 continued

项 目 Item		1998	1997	1998年为1997年% 1998 as % of 1997
独立核算工业企业主要财务指标	Major Financial Indicators for Enterprises with Independent Accounting System			
固定资产原价 (亿元)	Original Value of Fixed Assets (100 million yuan)	2221.3	1850.3	120.1
利润和税金总额 (亿元)	Total Pre-tax Profits (100 million yuan)	161.7	140.5	115.1
运输邮电	**Transportation,Posts and Telecommunications**			
货物周转量 (亿吨公里)	Freight Ton-Kilometers (100 milliom ton-km)	284.7	312.7	91.0
铁路	Railways	195.3	226.3	86.3
公路	Highways	78.3	76.9	101.8
民航	Civil Aviation	11.0	9.5	116.4
管道	Pipelines	0.03	0.04	75.0
旅客周转量 (亿人公里)	Passenger-Kilometers (100 milliom passenger-km)	242.0	215.4	112.3
铁路	Railways	50.6	47.8	106.0
公路	Highways	30.5	26.1	116.8
民航	Civil Aviation	161.0	141.5	113.7
邮电业务总量 (万元)	Business Volume of Posts and Telecommunication Services (10000 yuan)	1290966.5	930136.7	138.8
全市电话交换机总容量 (万门)	Total Capacity of Telephone Exchanges (10000 lines)	686.8	546.4	125.7
商 业	**Commerce**			
社会消费品零售额 (亿元)	Total Retail Sales of Consumer Goods (100 million yuan)	1195.2	1051.5	113.7
批发零售贸易业	Wholesale and Retail	865.7	709.4	122.0
餐饮业	Catering	81.8	72.5	112.8
其他	Others	247.7	269.6	91.9
商业、饮食业、服务业营业点 (万个)	Outlets of Commerce,Catering and Services (10000)	24.1	26.2	92.0
# 商业	Commerce	18.1	20.1	90.0
饮食业	Catering	2.9	3.0	96.7
服务业	Services	3.2	3.2	100.0
对外经济贸易和旅游	**Foreign Economy,Trade and Tourism**			
进出口总额 (亿美元)	Total Import and Export (USD100million)	65.1	57.8	112.6
进口额	Total Imports	36.8	33.1	111.2
出口额	Total Exports	28.3	24.7	114.6
新批三资企业数 (个)	Number of Foreign-funded Enterprises	656.0	809.0	81.1

1-9 续表 2 continued

项目 Item		1998	1997	1998年为1997年% 1998 as % of 1997
协议外资金额 (亿美元)	Total Amount of Foreign Capital in the Signed Agreements (USD 100 million)	41.1	18.5	222.2
实际利用外资 (亿美元)	Total Amount of Foreign Capital Actually Used (USD 100 million)	28.7	25.9	110.8
# 外商直接投资	Foreign Direct Investments	20.6	15.9	129.6
接待入境旅游人数 (万人)	Number of International Tourists (10000 persons)	220.1	229.8	95.8
金融保险	**Banking and Insurance**			
银行贷款增加额 (亿元)	Adding Deposits of Banks (100 million yuan)	610.8	489.7	124.7
城乡居民储蓄存款余额 (亿元)	Saving Deposits of Urban and Rural Residents (100 million yuan)	2287.2	1975.3	115.8
城镇 (亿元)	Urban (100 million yuan)	2063.2	1770.9	116.5
农村 (亿元)	Rural (100 million yuan)	224.0	204.4	109.6
保险公司保险费收入 (亿元)	Premiums Income of Insurance Companies (100 million yuan)	84.3	84.6	99.6
教育	**Education**			
毕业生数 (万人)	Number of Graduates (10000 persons)	49.1	46.2	106.3
研究生 (人)	Postgraduates (person)	11045.0	8369.0	132.0
高等学校 (万人)	Institutions of Higher Education (10000 persons)	4.9	5.0	98.0
中等职业技术教育 (万人)	Secondary Vocational Technical Education (10000 persons)	7.2	6.0	120.0
普通中学 (万人)	Regular Secondary School (10000 persons)	21.3	20.5	103.9
小学 (万人)	Primary Schools (10000 persons)	15.6	14.6	106.8
文化	**Culture**			
公共图书馆藏书 (万册)	Collection of Public Libraries (10000 copies)	2848.0	2789.0	102.1
艺术剧团国内演出场次 (场)	Times of Domestic Performance of Art Troupes (time)	8105.0	8426.0	96.2
科技	**Science and Technology**			
科技人员 (万人)	Personnel (10000 persons)	132.2	113.7	116.3
卫生	**Health**			
医院病床数 (万张)	Hospitals Beds (10000)	6.3	6.2	101.6
卫生技术人员数 (万人)	Medical Technical Personnel (10000 persons)	11.6	11.9	97.5
# 中西医生 (万人)	Doctors of Traditional Chinese Medicine and Western Medicine (10000 persons)	5.2	5.5	94.5
护师(士) (万人)	Senior and Junior Nurses (10000 persons)	3.9	3.9	100.0
城市公用事业	**Urban Public Utilities**			
用电量 (亿千瓦时)	Electricity Consumption (100 million kwh)	276.2	263.6	104.8
自来水销售量 (亿吨)	Sales of Tap Water (100 million tons)	7.6	7.9	96.2
居民燃气用户 (万户)	Households of Access to Gas (10000)	247.3	235.9	104.8
城市公共交通客运量 (亿人次)	Passengers Carried of City Public Transport (100 million person.times)	41.9	39.1	107.2
城市大型立交桥 (座)	Large Flyovers (unit)	138	140	98.6
城市绿化覆盖率 (%)	Coverage Rate of Urban Green Area (%)	35.57	34.22	
城市居民人均住房使用面积 (平方米)	Per Capita Using Space of Rooms of Urban Residents (sq.m)	14.96	14.36	104.2
农村居民人均住房面积 (平方米)	Per Capita Floor Space of Rooms of Rural Residents (sq.m)	27.60	27.39	100.8

1-10 国民经济主要指标比例关系

PERCENTAGE OF MAIN NATIONAL ECONOMIC INDICATORS

项目 Item	绝对值(万元) Value(10000 yuan)		构成(%) Composition(%)	
	1998	1997	1998	1997
全市从业人员 (人) Total Employment (person)	**6221565**	**6558142**	**100**	**100**
第一产业 Primary Industry	714503	701056	11.5	10.7
第二产业 Secondary Industry	2259949	2576202	36.3	39.3
第三产业 Tertiary Industry	3247113	3280884	52.2	50.0
国内生产总值 Gross Domestic Product	**20113100**	**18100900**	**100**	**100**
第一产业 Primary Industry	865600	848500	4.3	4.7
第二产业 Secondary Industry	7868500	7385600	39.1	40.8
第三产业 Tertiary Industry	11379000	9866800	56.6	54.5
固定资产投资 Investment in Fixed Assets	**6829237**	**5820764**	**100**	**100**
生产性 Production	3640529	3043271	53.3	52.3
非生产性 Non-Production	3188708	2777493	46.7	47.7
# 住宅 Residence	1060692	932743	15.5	15.9
固定资产投资拨贷款 Allocations and Loans on Investment in Fixed Assets	**6693722**	**5875251**	**100**	**100**
国家预算内投资 State Budgetary Appropriation	938629	828522	14.0	14.1
国内贷款 Domestic Loans	1084327	897504	16.2	15.3
利用外资 Foreign Capital	412267	512668	6.2	8.7
债券 Bonds	158300		2.4	
自筹资金 Self-raised Funds	3829243	3223577	57.2	54.9
# 股票 Stocks	33445	4507	0.5	0.1
其他资金 Other Capital	270956	412980	4.0	7.0
工农业总产值(现价) Gross Output Value of Industry and Agriculture(at current prices)	**22036374**	**21346907**	**100**	**100**
工业 Industry	20270235	19638338	92.0	92.0
农业 Agriculture	1766139	1708569	8.0	8.0
工业总产值(现价) Gross Output Value of Industry (at current prices)	**19919611**	**19251950**	**100**	**100**
轻工业 Light Indutry	6120157	6468667	30.7	33.6
重工业 Heavy Industry	13799453	12783283	69.3	66.4
农林牧渔业总产值(现价) Gross Output Value of Farming, Forestry,Animal Husbandry and Fishery(at current prices)	**1766139**	**1708569**	**100**	**100**
种植业 Farming	891630	869772	50.5	50.9
林业 Forestry	32302	28630	1.8	1.7
牧业 Animal Husbandry	766338	748049	43.4	43.8
渔业 Fishery	75868	62118	4.3	3.6
货运量 (万吨) Freight Traffic (10000 tons)	**30127.5**	**32349.7**	**100**	**100**
铁路 Railways	2562.5	2883.3	8.5	8.9
公路 Highways	27490.0	29360.0	91.2	90.8
民航 Civil Aviation	22.4	19.0	0.1	0.1
管道 Pipelines	51.6	87.4	0.2	0.3
客运量 (万人) Passenger Traffic (10000 persons)	**12419.4**	**10383.8**	**100**	**100**
铁路 Railways	4953.3	4828.8	39.9	46.5
公路 Highways	6704.0	4902.0	54.0	47.2
民航 Civil Aviation	762.1	653.0	6.1	6.3
社会消费品零售总额 Retail Sales of Consumer Goods	**11952118**	**10515342**	**100**	**100**
批发零售贸易业 Wholesale and Retail	8657131	7094362	72.4	67.5
餐饮业 Catering	818162	724889	6.8	6.3
制造业 Manufacturing	637469	563239	5.3	5.4
其他 Others	1839356	2132852	15.4	20.3
农民对非农民 Peasants Saling to Non-Peasants	89463	1393255	0.7	13.3
地方财政收入相当于国内生产总值的比例 (%) The Proportion of Local Financial Revenue in Gross Domestic Product (%)	**13.0**	**11.6**		
地方基建支出占地方财政收入的比例 (%) The Proportion of Local Capital Construction Expenditures in Local Financial Revenue (%)	**12.4**	**11.9**		

1-11 按经济类型分国民经济主要指标比例关系
PERCENTAGE OF MAIN NATIONAL ECONOMIC INDICATORS BY OWNERSHIP

项目	Item	绝对值 Value		构成(%) Composition(%)	
		1998	1997	1998	1997
全市从业人员 (人)	**Total Employment (person)**	**6221565**	**6558142**	**100**	**100**
国 有	State-Owned	3080645	3546956	49.5	54.1
集 体	Collective Owned	509986	684998	8.2	10.5
其 他	Others	840916	543489	13.5	8.3
城镇个体、私营	Urban Individuals	200722	212088	3.2	3.2
农村劳动者	Rural Labor Force	1589296	1570611	25.5	24.0
固定资产投资 (万元)	**Investment in Fixed Assets (10000 yuan)**	**6829237**	**5820764**	**100**	**100**
国 有	State-Owned	5924236	4734588	86.7	81.3
集 体	Collective Owned	119613	116452	1.8	2.0
联 营	Joint Owned	19757	7942	0.3	0.1
股份有限公司	Share Holding Company	54083	21284	0.8	0.4
中外合资经营	Chinese-foreign Joint Venture	289461	635980	4.2	10.9
中外合作经营	Chinses-foreign Cooperative	33138	103814	0.5	1.8
外商独资	Foreign Enterprises	10730	32239	0.2	0.6
与港澳台合资经营	Joint Venture with HongKong, Macao and Taiwan	196402	78651	2.9	1.4
与港澳台合作经营	Cooperative from HongKong,Macao and Taiwan	108825	41291	1.6	0.7
港澳台独资	HongKong,Macao and Taiwan Enterprises	7863	26113	0.1	0.5
其他经济	Others	13490	9935	0.2	0.2
工业总产值 不含个体工业, 现价,万元)	**Gross Output Value of Industry (excluding individual industry, at current prices,10000 yuan)**	**19919611**	**19251950**	**100**	**100**
国 有	State-Owned	8634587	9600424	43.3	49.9
集 体	Collective Owned	3011353	3299733	15.1	17.1
私 营	Private	32972	61402	0.2	0.3
联 营	Joint Owned	274056	223587	1.4	1.2
股份制	Share Holding	1852929	650654	9.3	3.4
中外合资经营企业	Chinese-foreign Joint Venture	4500746	3944461	22.6	20.5
中外合作经营企业	Chinses-foreign Cooperative	68663	136822	0.3	0.7
外商独资企业	Foreign Enterprises	286846	177881	1.4	0.9
与港澳台合资经营	Joint Venture with HongKong, Macao and Taiwan	1102666	1025676	5.5	5.3
与港澳台合作经营	Cooperative from HongKong,Macao and Taiwan	25593	14849	0.13	0.08
港澳台独资	HongKong,Macao and Taiwan Enterprises	128992	108806	0.6	0.6
其他经济	Others	208	7656	0.001	0.04
建筑业总产值 (万元)	**Gross Output Value of Construction (10000 yuan)**	**6246618**	**5192363**	**100**	**100**
国 有	State-Owned	3323586	3509050	53.2	67.6
集 体	Collective Owned	1390342	1277938	22.3	24.6
私 营	Private	26873	2508.9	0.43	0.05
联 营	Joint Owned	26560.8	1713.4	0.43	0.03
股份制	Share Holding	1249403	219971.6	20.0	4.2
外商投资经营	Foreign Funded	131916.2	115232.4	2.1	2.2
港澳台投资经营	HongKong,Macao and Taiwan Funded	95078.2	65150.5	1.5	1.3
其他经济	Others	2858.8	798.6	0.05	0.02
社会消费品零售额 (万元)	**Retail Sales Consumer Goods (10000 yuan)**	**11952118**	**10515342**	**100**	**100**
国 有	State-Owned	3447559	3688052	28.8	35.1
集 体	Collective Owned	2314640	2478622	19.4	23.6
私营经济	Private	377490	66570	3.2	0.6
个体经济	Individuals	2430042	2364454	20.3	22.5
联营经济	Joint Owned	288264	311815	2.4	3.0
股份制经济	Share Holding	2148256	940565	18.0	8.9
外商投资经济	Foreign Funded	599036	377779	5.0	3.6
港澳台投资经济	HongKong,Macao and Taiwan Funded	255809	144020	2.1	1.4
其他经济	Others	91022	143465	0.8	1.4

1-12 北 京 一 日
A DAY IN BEIJING

项 目	Item	1998	1997
生产量	**Output**		
国内生产总值(当年价格) (万元)	Gross Domestic Product(at current prices) (10000 yuan)	55104.4	49591.5
工业总产值(当年价格) (万元)	Gross Output Value of Industry(at current prices) (10000 yuan)	55534.9	53803.7
原 煤 (吨)	Coal (ton)	27108.5	27719.4
发电量 (万千瓦时)	Electricity (10000 kwh)	4292.1	4011.8
钢 (吨)	Steel (ton)	22006.1	21964.3
农业总产值(当年价格) (万元)	Gross Output Value of Agriculture (at current prices) (10000 yuan)	4838.7	4681.0
建筑业总产值 (万元)	Gross Output Value of Construction (10000 yuan)	17114.0	14349.8
新建住宅竣工面积 (万平方米)	Floor Space of New Residence Completed (10000 sq.m)	3.0	2.7
货运量(包括管道) (万吨)	Freight Traffic(including pipelines) (10000 tons)	82.5	88.6
客运量 (万人)	Passenger Traffic (10000 persons)	34.0	28.5
社会消费品零售总额 (万元)	Retail Sales of Consumer Goods (10000 yuan)	32745.5	28809.2
海关出口额 (万美元)	Exports (USD 10000)	775.1	675.4
财政收入 (万元)	Financial Revenue (10000 yuan)	7178.3	5750.8
旅游收入 (万美元)	Tourism Revenue (USD 10000)	653.2	615.9
消费量	**Consumption**		
粮 食 (吨)	Grain (ton)	5939.2	9388.8
猪 肉 (吨)	Pork (ton)	672.2	902.8
牛羊肉 (吨)	Beef and Mutton (ton)	278.7	413.1
鲜 蛋 (吨)	Fresh Eggs (ton)	260.3	341.5
水产品 (吨)	Aquatic Products (ton)	738.2	716.5
食用植物油 (吨)	Edible Vegetable Oil (ton)	807.8	1184.9
鲜 菜 (吨)	Fresh Vegetable (ton)	11932.3	13242.0
生活用水(自来水厂) (万吨)	Residential Use of Tap Water (10000 tons)	156.3	153.3
其 他	**Others**		
市内公共交通客运量 (万人次)	Urban Passenger Traffic (10000 person.times)	1147.5	1071.7
接待旅游人数 (人)	Tourists Received (person)	6030.0	6296.0
邮寄函件 (万件)	Mail Delivery (10000)	139.1	150.3
拍发公众电报 (万份)	Telegrams (10000)	0.2	0.3
城乡居民储蓄存款 (万元)	Saving Deposit of Urban and Rural Residents (10000 yuan)	8545.9	7350.2
出生人口 (人)	Birth Population (person)	183.3	208.2
死亡人口 (人)	Death Population (person)	206.2	183.4
结婚对数 (对)	Marriage (couple)	231.9	228.6
离婚对数 (对)	Divorce (couple)	64.9	61.0

1-13 平均每人主要社会经济活动
MAJOR ECONOMIC INDICATORS PER CAPITA

项目	Item	1998	1997	1998年为1997年% 1998 as % of 1997
国内生产总值(当年价格) (元)	**Gross Domestic Product (at current prices) (yuan)**	**18478.0**	**16735.0**	**110.4**
工农业总产值(1990年不变价) (元)	**Gross Output Value of Industry and Agriculture(at 1990 constant prices) (yuan)**	**18871.9**	**16131.7**	**117.0**
财政收入 (元)	**Financial Revenue (yuan)**	**2407.0**	**1940.7**	**124.0**
房屋建筑竣工面积 (平方米)	**Floor Space of Building Completed (sq.m)**	**1.7**	**1.5**	**113.3**
# 新建住宅 (平方米)	New Residence (sq.m)	1.0	0.9	108.7
工　业	**Industry**			
工业总产值(1990年不变价) (元)	Gross Output Value of Industry (at 1990 constant prices,yuan)	18012.8	15353.9	117.3
主要工业产品产量	Output of Major Products			
布 (米)	Cloth (meter)	19.6	23.3	84.1
电视机(百人) (台)	Television(100 persons) (unit)	1.1	3.8	28.9
原　煤 (千克)	Coal (kg)	909.0	935.4	97.2
发电量 (千瓦时)	Electricity (kwh)	1439.2	1353.8	106.3
钢 (千克)	Steel (kg)	737.9	741.2	99.6
农　业	**Agriculture**			
农业总产值(1990年不变价) (元)	Gross Output Value of Agriculture (at 1990 constant prices,yuan)	859.1	835.9	102.8
主要农产品产量	Output of Major Products			
粮　食 (千克)	Grain (kg)	219.8	219.6	100.1
肉　类 (千克)	Meat (kg)	41.3	37.2	111.0
鲜　蛋 (千克)	Fresh Eggs (kg)	16.4	22.0	74.5
鲜　菜 (千克)	Fresh Vegetable (kg)	373.1	379.3	98.4
水产品 (千克)	Aquatic Products (kg)	7.0	7.1	98.6
牛　奶 (千克)	Milk (kg)	20.9	20.5	102.0
干鲜果 (千克)	Dry and Fresh Fruit (kg)	51.6	48.6	106.2
商　业	**Commerce**			
社会消费品零售总额 (元)	Retail Sales of Consumer Goods (yuan)	10980.4	9722.0	112.9
# 吃的商品	Food	3196.0	3602.8	88.7
穿的商品	Clothing	1336.7	1299.7	102.8
用的商品	Daily Used Articles	6108.2	4550.2	134.2
主要消费品零售量	Retail Sales of Major Consumer Goods in Quantity			
粮　食 (千克)	Grain (kg)	109.8	215.4	51.0
食用植物油 (千克)	Edible Vegetable Oil (kg)	25.1	31.4	79.9
猪　肉 (千克)	Pork (kg)	20.2	30.0	67.3
鲜　蛋 (千克)	Fresh Eggs (kg)	8.7	11.5	75.7
水产品 (千克)	Aquatic Products (kg)	15.4	24.1	63.9
棉　布 (米)	Cotton Cloth (meter)	0.46	0.47	97.9
邮　电	**Posts and Telecommunications**			
邮寄函件 (件)	Mail Delivery (unit)	46.6	50.2	92.8
城市公用事业	**Urban Public Utilities**			
日生活用水量 (千克)	Daily Residential Use of Water (kg)	238.2	229.0	104.0
城市居民居住面积 (平方米)	Living Space of Urban Residents (sq.m)	10.03	9.66	103.8
平均每千人拥有公共交通车辆 (辆)	Possession of Public Traffic Vehicles Per 1000 Persons (unit)	0.99	0.97	102.1
乘坐公共电汽车次数 (次)	Times of Riding in Bus or Trolley (time)	342.2	320.5	106.8
公共绿地面积 (平方米)	Public Green Areas (sq.m)	9.0	7.8	115.0
卫　生	**Health**			
平均每千人拥有医生 (人)	Number of Doctors Per 1000 Persons (person)	4.76	5.06	94.1
平均每千人拥有医院床位 (张)	Number of Beds Per 1000 Persons (unit)	6.13	6.06	101.2
人民生活	**Pepople's Livelihood**			
职工年平均工资 (元)	Annual Average Wage (yuan)	12285.0	11019.0	111.5
居民家庭可支配收入 (元)	Annual Discretionary Income of Urban Residence (yuan)	8472.0	7813.1	108.4
农民家庭纯收入 (元)	Annual Net Income of Rural Residence (yuan)	4028.9	3762.4	107.1
城乡居民储蓄存款余额 (元)	Savings Deposit of Urban and Rural Residents (yuan)	20954.5	18196.8	115.2
城镇居民	Urban	28120.3	24504.0	114.8
农村居民	Rural	6260.5	5632.7	111.1

1-14 总 产 出
TOTAL OUTPUT

单位：万元　　　　(10000 yuan)

项目	Item	1998	1997	1998年为1997年% 1998 as % of 1997
总　计	**Total**	**65985000**	**58391500**	**114.6**
第一产业	Primary Industry	1766100	1708600	102.7
第二产业	Secondary Industry	30757600	28170000	113.0
工　业	Industry	24197500	22919600	110.3
建筑业	Construction	6560100	5250400	128.3
第三产业	Tertiary Industry	33461300	28512900	117.9
# 交通运输、仓储及邮电业	Transportation,Storage, Posts and Telecommunications	4442500	4053100	108.7
批发和零售贸易、餐饮业	Wholesale,Retail and Catering	3910300	3464700	111.0

注：绝对数按现价计算，发展速度按可比价格计算(下同)。

Note：The data in terms of value are calculated at current prices,while the related indices are calculated at comparable prices.(The following table is the same.)

1-15 国 民 生 产 总 值
GROSS NATIONAL PRODUCT

单位：万元　　　　(10000 yuan)

项目	Item	1998	1997	1998年为1997年% 1998 as % of 1997	构成(%) Composition(%) 1998	1997
国民生产总值	**Gross National Product**	**20117700**	**18104900**	**109.8**		
国内生产总值	**Gross Domestic Product**	**20113100**	**18100900**	**109.8**	**100**	**100**
第一产业	**Primary Industry**	**865600**	**848500**	**101.5**	**4.3**	**4.7**
第二产业	**Secondary Industry**	**7868500**	**7385600**	**109.6**	**39.1**	**40.8**
工　业	Industry	6106600	5883600	108.7	30.4	32.5
建筑业	Construction	1761900	1502000	114.2	8.7	8.3
第三产业	**Tertiary Industry**	**11379000**	**9866800**	**110.8**	**56.6**	**54.5**
农林牧渔服务业	FFAF Services	19400	18700	103.2	0.1	0.1
地质勘探业、水利管理业	Geological Prospecting and Water Conservancy	45000	34000	131.3	0.2	0.2
交通运输、仓储及邮电业	Transportation,Storage, Posts and Telecommunications	1544500	1357900	110.0	7.7	7.5
批发和零售贸易、餐饮业	Wholesale,Retail and Catering	2073300	2024500	104.0	10.3	11.2
金融保险业	Banking and Insurance	2776400	2468700	109.4	13.8	13.6
房地产业	Real Estate	682500	412400	161.3	3.4	2.3
社会服务业	Social Services	1357900	1224900	101.0	6.8	6.8
卫生、体育、社会福利事业	Health,Sports and Social Welfare	305800	290600	102.4	1.5	1.6
教育、文艺、广播电影电视事业	Education,Culture,Art,Radio,Film and Television	1106700	774900	129.8	5.5	4.3
科学研究和综合技术服务业	Scientific Research and Polytechnical Services	808300	667100	112.2	4.0	3.7
国家政党机关、社会团体	Government Organs,Party Organs and Social Bodies	518300	490200	102.1	2.6	2.7
其他	Others	140900	102900	125.6	0.7	0.6
国外(地区)净要素收入	**Net Income of Essential Factor from Foreign Country(Territory)**	**4600**	**4000**	**105.0**		
人均国内生产总值　(元)	**Per Capita Gross Domestic Products　(yuan)**	**18478**	**16735**	**113.0**		

1-16 国内生产总值构成项目
COMPOSITION OF GROSS DOMESTIC PRODUCT

单位：万元 (10000 yuan)

项目	Item	增加值 Added Value	劳动者报酬 Remuneration for Labors	固定资产折旧 Depreciation of Fixed Asset	生产税净额 Net Taxes on Production	营业盈余 Operating Surplus
国内生产总值	**Gross Domestic Product**	**20113100**	**9799000**	**3849400**	**2740700**	**3724000**
第一产业	**Primary Industry**	**865600**	**528000**	**69800**	**22500**	**245300**
第二产业	**Secondary Industry**	**7868500**	**4267700**	**1548900**	**1648500**	**403400**
工　业	Industry	6106600	3035800	1425600	1414300	230900
建筑业	Construction	1761900	1231900	123300	234200	172500
第三产业	**Tertiary Industry**	**11379000**	**5003300**	**2230700**	**1069700**	**3075300**
农林牧渔服务业	FFAF Services	19400	17700	3200	500	-2000
地质勘探业、水利管理业	Geological Prospecting and Water Conservancy	45000	22000	15900	3400	3700
交通运输、仓储及邮电业	Transportation,Storage, Posts and Telecommunications	1544500	491100	594900	153800	304700
批发和零售贸易、餐饮业	Wholesale,Retail and Catering	2073300	1216300	381400	261600	214000
金融保险业	Banking and Insurance	2776400	173600	95400	297100	2210300
房地产业	Real Estate	682500	172500	255000	145900	109100
社会服务业	Social Services	1357900	974300	378500	69100	-64000
卫生、体育、社会福利事业	Health,Sports and Social Welfare	305800	246700	46300	3200	9600
教育、文艺、广播电影电视事业	Education,Culture,Art,Radio,Film and Television	1106700	715000	150800	65500	175400
科学研究和综合技术服务业	Scientific Research and Polytechnical Services	808300	501800	178100	55400	73000
国家政党机关、社会团体	Government Organs,Party Organs and Social Bodies	518300	400000	107000	7100	4200
其他	Others	140900	72300	24200	7100	37300

1-17 按支出法计算的国内生产总值
GROSS DOMESTIC PRODUCTS CALCULATED WITH EXPENDITURE APPROACH

单位：万元 (10000 yuan)

项目	Item	1998	1997	1998年为1997年% 1998 as % of 1997
国内生产总值	**Gross Domestic Product**	**20463100**	**18709300**	**110.7**
最终消费	Final Consumption	8098200	7033600	109.6
居民总消费	Residential Consumption	5636200	4928800	109.7
农业居民	Agricultural	1092600	972500	108.3
非农业居民	Non-Agricultural	4543600	3956300	110.1
政府消费	Government Consumption	2462000	2104800	109.3
资本形成总额	Total Capital Formation	13964000	12286500	112.6
固定资产形成总额	Completed Fixed Assets	11719000	10017300	115.8
存货增加	Changes in Stock	2245000	2269200	100.6
货物和服务净出口	Net Export of Products and Services	-1599100	-610800	

1-18 居 民 总 消 费 水 平
CONSUMPTION LEVEL OF RESIDENTS

单位：元 (yuan)

项目	Item	1998	1997	1998年为1997年% 1998 as % of 1997
全市居民总消费水平	**Consumption Level of all Residents**	**5178**	**4557**	**113.6**
农业居民	Agricultural	3032	2661	114.0
非农业居民	Non-Agricultural	6240	5524	113.0
农业居民与非农业居民对比 (以农业居民为100)	**Ratio of Consumption of Agricultural to Non-Agricultural (Agricultural=100)**	**1:2.1**	**1:2.1**	

1-19 最 终 消 费
FINAL CONSUMPTION

单位：万元 (10000 yuan)

项目	Item	1998	1997	1998年为1997年% 1998 as % of 1997
最终消费	**Final Consumption**	**8098200**	**7033600**	**109.6**
居民消费	**Resident Consumption**	**5636200**	**4928800**	**109.7**
农业居民	Agricultural	1092600	972500	108.3
自给性消费	Self-sufficiency	61500	56400	106.9
商品性消费	Commodity	657600	596100	108.2
文化生活及服务性消费	Culture and Services	230000	192600	105.7
住房及水电消费	Residence,Water and Electricity	143500	127400	111.7
# 住房消费	Residence	77800	49600	155.6
非农业居民	Non-Agricultural	4543600	3956300	110.1
商品性消费	Commodity	2774300	2769400	99.7
文化生活及服务性消费	Culture and Services	1458800	989100	119.9
住房及水电消费	Residence,Water and Electricity	310500	197800	155.4
# 住房消费	Residence	201200	98900	201.8
政府消费	**Government Consumption**	**2462000**	**2104800**	**109.3**

1-20 主要社会经济效益指标
MAJOR ECONOMIC EFFICIENCY INDICATORS

项目	Item	1998	1997
社会劳动生产率 (当年价格) (元/人)	**Overall Labor Productivity(at current prices) (yuan/person)**	**32328**	**27601**
第一产业 (元/人)	Primary Industry (yuan/person)	12106	12103
第二产业 (元/人)	Secondary Industry (yuan/person)	34816	28669
第三产业 (元/人)	Tertiary Industry (yuan/person)	35045	30074
每百元总投资新增国内生产总值 (元)	**Incremental GDP Per 100 yuan Investment (yuan)**	**14.4**	**15.8**
总产出中间投入率 (%)	**Intermediate Input/Total Output (%)**	**69.5**	**69.0**
第一产业 (%)	Primary Industry (%)	51.0	50.3
第二产业 (%)	Secondary Industry (%)	74.4	73.8
第三产业 (%)	Tertiary Industry (%)	66.0	65.4
增加值率 (%)	**GDP/Total Output (%)**	**30.5**	**31.0**
第一产业 (%)	Primary Industry (%)	49.0	49.7
第二产业 (%)	Secondary Industry (%)	25.6	26.2
第三产业 (%)	Tertiary Industry (%)	34.0	34.6

1-21 1997 年资产负债表

单位：亿元

项目	Item	非金融部门 Non-banking 使用 Use	非金融部门 Non-banking 来源 Source	金融部门 Banking 使用 Use	金融部门 Banking 来源 Source
非金融资产	**Non-financial Assets**	**6397.88**		**255.18**	
固定资产	Fixed Assets	3914.7		125.95	
固定资产净值	Net Value	2733		104.58	
固定资产原值	Original Value	3960.34		135.86	
减：累计折旧	Substract：Accumulative Depreciation	1227.34		31.28	
在建工程	Projects under Construction	1181.7		21.37	
固定资产清理	Liquidation Fixed Assets				
待处理固定资产净损失	Net Lossing of Fixed Assets Unsettled				
存货	Inventories	1876.78		50.86	
产成品和商品库存	Finished Products and Commodity Stock	212.72			
其他资产	Others	606.4		78.37	
无形资产	Intangible Assets	148.22		47.51	
金融资产与负债	**Financial Assets and Liabilities**	**3508.81**	**5078.45**	**2554.73**	**5457.43**
国内金融资产与负债	Domestic Financial Assets and Liabilities	3506.36	4764.96	2554.73	5457.43
通　货	Currency	29.01		0.77	
存　款	Deposits	2956.34			5397.66
短期存款	Short-term	2107.33			2750.74
# 财政存款	Financial				38.16
长期存款	Long-term	849.01			2646.92
贷　款	Loans		2488.23	2536.18	
短期贷款	Short-term		1922.37	1967.75	
# 财政借款	Financial				
长期贷款	Long-term		565.86	568.43	
股票及其他股权	Stock and Other Stock Ownership	492.76	2273.98		
证　券(不含股票)	Securities(excluding stock)	21.6	2.75	17.78	
短期证券	Short-term	2.77		2.67	
# 政府债券	Government	2.77		2.67	
长期证券	Long-term	18.83	2.75	15.11	
# 政府债券	Government	17.89		15.11	
保险准备金	Premium Reserve	6.65			59.77
其　他	Others				
国外金融资产与负债	Foreign Financial Assets and Liabilities	2.45	313.49		
短期资本	Short-term Capital				
长期资本	Long-term Capital	2.45	313.49		
资产负债差额	**Balance of Assets and Liabilities**		**4828.24**		**-2647.52**

1997 BALANCE SHEET

(100 million yuan)

政府部门 Government		住户部门 Private		国外 Foreign		合计 Total	
使用 Use	来源 Source	使用 Use	来源 Source	使用 Use	来源 Source	使用 Use	来源 Source
1143.83		**2681.77**				**10478.66**	
1065.81		2613.76				7720.22	
854.8		2613.76				6306.14	
917.07		3520.47				8533.74	
62.27		906.71				2227.6	
211.01						1414.08	
60.87		56.01				2044.52	
						212.72	
17.15		12				713.92	
						195.73	
2086.54	**488.79**	**2728.91**	**0.97**	**471.7**	**2.45**	**11350.69**	**11350.69**
2086.54	488.79	2728.91	0.97	158.21		11034.75	11034.75
11.02		281.8				322.6	322.6
466.05		1975.27				5397.66	5397.66
350.61		292.8				2750.74	2750.74
38.16						38.16	38.16
115.44		1682.47				2646.92	2646.92
	46.98		0.97			2536.18	2536.18
	44.41		0.97			1967.75	1967.75
	2.57					568.43	568.43
1587.9		35.11		158.21		2273.98	2273.98
21.57	441.81	383.61				444.56	444.56
3.29	87.04	78.31				87.04	87.04
3.29	87.04	78.31				87.04	87.04
18.28	354.77	305.3				357.52	357.52
18.28	354.77	303.49				354.77	354.77
		53.12				59.77	59.77
				313.49	2.45	315.94	315.94
				313.49	2.45	315.94	315.94
	2741.58		**5409.71**		**469.25**		**10478.66**

1-22 1997 年 6 个部门投入产出表(按当年生产者价格计算)

INPUT/OUTPUT SHEET OF SIX BRANCHES IN 1997 (AT CURRENT PRODUCER PRICES)

单位：万元 (10000 yuan)

投入 Input		产出 Output →	农业 Agriculture	工业 Industry	建筑业 Construction	交通运输、仓储及邮电业 Trans,Storage and Telecommunications	批发和零售贸易餐饮业 Wholesale,Retail Sales and Catering	其他服务部门 Other Services	中间使用合计 Total Intermediate Use
中间投入 Intermediate Input	农业	Agriculture	325224	627668	1	3	76582	12324	1041800
	工业	Industry	268570	12098192	2810659	1036237	622360	3710905	20546923
	建筑业	Construction	362	12516	747	10316	14441	294718	333099
	交通运输、仓储及邮电业	Transportation,Storage and Telecommunications	25946	939016	260156	340437	154348	1017856	2737758
	批发和零售贸易、餐饮业	Wholesale,Retail Sales and Catering	137296	1412145	358729	169656	95567	672186	2845578
	其他服务部门	Other Services	87129	1922857	512832	561321	578261	6196067	9858467
	中间投入	Intermediate Input	844527	17012394	3943123	2117969	1541558	11904055	37363625
增加值 Value Added	固定资产折旧	Depreciation of Fixed Assets	78743	968089	89160	608121	219907	2031674	3995694
	劳动者报酬	Remuneration of Labors	479493	3228265	1172725	935401	1058831	6624673	13499387
	生产税净额	Net Taxes on Production	27979	1547457	215285	252354	366494	907722	3317290
	营业盈余	Earning Surplus	277828	234256	62048	-152578	277911	1145273	1844737
	增加值	Value Added	864042	5978066	1539218	1643297	1923142	10709342	22657107
	总投入	**Total Input**	**1708569**	**22990460**	**5482341**	**3761266**	**3464700**	**22613397**	**60020733**

投入 Input		产出 Output →	城镇居民消费 Consumption of Urban Residents	农村居民消费 Consumption of Rural Residents	政府消费 Government Consumption	固定资产形成 Fixed Assets Formation	库存增加 Changes of Inventory	净调出 Net Moving Out	净出口 Net Export	总产出 Total Output
中间投入 Intermediate Input	农业	Agriculture	562754	198147		41848	50622	-166822	-19781	1708569
	工业	Industry	4241410	807302		3632949	2080781	-7736736	-582170	22990460
	建筑业	Construction				5254605		-172219	66856	5482341
	交通运输、仓储及邮电业	Transportation,Storage and Telecommunications	193181	25370		40014	62782	145544	556618	3761266
	批发和零售贸易、餐饮业	Wholesale,Retail Sales and Catering	1166431	221458		170926	404676	-1555690	211320	3464700
	其他服务部门	Other Services	1850635	267829	3454781	232682	176	5690897	1257930	22613397
	中间投入	Intermediate Input	8014412	1520106	3454781	9373024	2599037	-3795026	1490773	60020733

1-23 1997年6个部门直接消耗系数表
DIRECT CONSUMPTION COEFFICIENT OF SIX BRANCHES IN 1997

产出 Output / 投入 Input		农业 Agriculture	工业 Industry	建筑业 Construction	交通运输、仓储及邮电业 Trans,Storage and Telecommunications	批发和零售贸易餐饮业 Wholesale,Retail Sales and Catering	其他服务部门 Other Services
农业	Agriculture	0.190	0.027			0.022	0.001
工业	Industry	0.157	0.526	0.513	0.276	0.180	0.164
建筑业	Construction		0.001		0.003	0.004	0.013
交通运输、仓储及邮电业	Transportation,Storage and Telecommunications	0.015	0.041	0.047	0.091	0.045	0.045
批发和零售贸易、餐饮业	Wholesale,Retail Sales and Catering	0.080	0.061	0.065	0.045	0.028	0.030
其他服务部门	Other Services	0.051	0.084	0.094	0.149	0.167	0.274

1-24 1997年6个部门完全消耗系数表
COMPLETE CONSUMPTION COEFFICIENT OF SIX BRANCHES IN 1997

产出 Output / 投入 Input		农业 Agriculture	工业 Industry	建筑业 Construction	交通运输、仓储及邮电业 Trans,Storage and Telecommunications	批发和零售贸易餐饮业 Wholesale,Retail Sales and Catering	其他服务部门 Other Services
农业	Agriculture	0.259	0.087	0.052	0.033	0.051	0.026
工业	Industry	0.588	1.416	1.382	0.874	0.617	0.651
建筑业	Construction	0.004	0.007	0.007	0.009	0.010	0.021
交通运输、仓储及邮电业	Transportation,Storage and Telecommunications	0.065	0.137	0.142	0.164	0.099	0.110
批发和零售贸易、餐饮业	Wholesale,Retail Sales and Catering	0.151	0.177	0.177	0.124	0.087	0.096
其他服务部门	Other Services	0.205	0.354	0.362	0.372	0.346	0.501

1-25 1997年6个部门分配系数表
DISTRIBUTION COEFFICIENT OF SIX BRANCHES IN 1997

产出 Output 投入 Input		农业 Agriculture	工业 Industry	建筑业 Construction	交通运输、仓储及邮电业 Trans,Storage and Telecommunications	批发和零售贸易餐饮业 Wholesale,Retail Sales and Catering	其他服务部门 Other Services	城镇居民消费 Consumption of Urban Residents
农业	Agriculture	0.190	0.367			0.045	0.007	0.329
工业	Industry	0.012	0.526	0.122	0.045	0.027	0.161	0.184
建筑业	Construction		0.002		0.002	0.003	0.054	
交通运输、仓储及邮电业	Transportation,Storage and Telecommunications	0.007	0.250	0.069	0.091	0.041	0.271	0.051
批发和零售贸易、餐饮业	Wholesale,Retail Sales and Catering	0.040	0.408	0.104	0.049	0.028	0.194	0.337
其他服务部门	Other Services	0.004	0.085	0.023	0.025	0.026	0.274	0.082

产出 Output 投入 Input		农村居民消费 Consumption of Rural Residents	政府消费 Government Consumption	固定资产形成 Fixed Assets Formation	库存增加 Changes of Inventory	净调出 Net Moving Out	净出口 Net Export	总产出 Total Output
农业	Agriculture	0.116		0.024	0.030	-0.098	-0.012	1.000
工业	Industry	0.035		0.158	0.091	-0.337	-0.025	1.000
建筑业	Construction			0.958		-0.031	0.012	1.000
交通运输、仓储及邮电业	Transportation,Storage and Telecommunications	0.007		0.011	0.017	0.039	0.148	1.000
批发和零售贸易、餐饮业	Wholesale,Retail Sales and Catering	0.064		0.049	0.117	-0.449	0.061	1.000
其他服务部门	Other Services	0.012	0.153	0.010		0.252	0.056	1.000

1-26 1997 年国民经济总体帐户
OVERALL ACCOUNT OF NATIONAL ECONOMY OF 1997
1-26-1 生产帐户
PRODUCTION ACCOUNT

单位：亿元 (100 million yuan)

劳动者报酬	Remuneration for Labors	867.5	总产出	Total Output	5839.2
工资及工资性收入	Wages	827.8	减：中间消耗	Substract：Intermediate Consumption	4029.1
单位社会保险付款	Organization Insurance	39.7			
生产税净额	Net Taxes on Production	300.3			
生产税	Production Tax	355.0			
减：生产补贴	Substract：Production Subsidy	54.8			
亏损补贴	Lossing Subsidy	44.9			
价格补贴	Price Subsidy	9.9			
固定资产折旧	Depreciation of Fixed Assets	304.3			
营业盈余	Earnings Surplus	338.1			
增加值分配	**Distribution of Value Added**	**1810.1**	**增加值**	**Value Added**	**1810.1**

1-26-2 收入分配及支出帐户
INCOME DISTRIBUTION AND EXPENDITURE ACCOUNT

单位：亿元 (100 million yuan)

财产收入支付	Payment for Property Right	1189.4	营业盈余	Earnings Surplus	338.1
利息支出	Interest	1189.4	固定资产折旧	Depreciation of Fixed Asset	304.3
红利支出	Dividend Payment		财产收入	Property Income	1400.8
土地租金支出	Land Rental		利息收入	Interest Income	1298.5
其他支出	Other Expenditures		红利收入	Dividend Income	102.3
经常转移支出	Current Payment	373.0	土地租金收入	Land Rental Income	
收入税支出	Income Taxes	73.1	其他收入	Other Income	
财政经常性拨款支出	Fiscal Current Allocation	161.9	劳动者报酬	Remuneration for Labors	867.5
社会保险付款支出	Social Insurance Payment	39.7	工资及工资性收入	Wages	827.8
社会补助支出	Social Subsidy	2.7	单位社会保险付款	Organization Insurance	39.7
其他经常转移支出	Other Current Expenditure	95.6	生产税净额	Net Taxes on Production	300.3
可支配总收入	Total Disposable Income	2072.1	生产税	Production Tax	355.0
最终消费	Final Consumption	703.4	减：生产补贴	Substract：Production Subsidy	54.8
居民消费	Private Consumption	492.9	亏损补贴	Lossing Subsidy	44.9
政府消费	Government Consumption	210.5	价格补贴	Price Subsidy	9.9
总储蓄	Total Savings	1368.7	经常转移收入	Current Income	423.5
			收入税收入	Income Tax	73.1
			财政经常性拨款收入	Fiscal Current Allocation	162.7
			社会保险付款收入	Social Insurance Payment	39.7
			社会补助收入	Social Subsidy Income	52.3
			其他经常转移收入	Other Current Income	95.7
支出和总储蓄	**Expenditure and Total Savings**	**3634.4**	**收入**	**Income**	**3634.4**

1-26-3 资　本　帐　户
CAPITAL ACCOUNT

单位：亿元　　(100 million yuan)

资本运用	Capital Use		资本筹集	Capital Source	
固定资产形成总额	Fixed Asset Formation	1001.7	总储蓄	Total Savings	1368.7
存货增加	Changes of Inventory	226.9	资本转移收入净额	Net Flow of Capital	
其他非金融资产获得减处置	Net Incremental Non-financial Assets		资本转移收入	Inflow of Capital	40.1
资金余缺	Surplus or Shortage of Capital	140.1	投资性补助收入	Investment-subsidy	40.1
统计误差	Statistical Error	286.8	其他资本转移收入	Other Capital	
			减：资本转移支出	Substract：Capitalchange Expenditure	40.1
			投资性补助支出	Investment-subsidy	40.1
			其他资本转移支出	Other Capital-change Expenditure	
资本运用	**Capital Use**	**1368.7**	**资本筹集**	**Capital Source**	**1368.7**

1-26-4 金　融　帐　户
BANKING ACCOUNT

单位：亿元　　(100 million yuan)

国内金融交易	Domestic Banking Business	2206.4	国内金融交易	Domestic Banking Business	1749.7
通货	Currency	85.6	通货	Currency	
存款	Deposits	1197.2	存款	Deposits	1177.9
短期存款	Short-term	503.4	短期存款	Short-term	503.4
长期存款	Long-term	693.7	长期存款	Long-term	674.5
贷款	Loans	842.2	贷款	Loans	918.4
短期贷款	Short-term	460.0	短期贷款	Short-term	460.0
长期贷款	Long-term	382.2	长期贷款	Long-term	458.4
证券(不含股票)	Securities(excluding stock)	128.5	证券(不含股票)	Securities(excluding stock)	128.5
短期证券	Short-term		短期证券	Short-term	
长期证券	Long-term	128.5	长期证券	Long-term	128.5
股票及其他股权	Stock and Other Stock Ownership	41.6	股票及其他股权	Stock and Other Stock Ownership	41.6
保险准备金	Premium Reserve		保险准备金	Premium Reserve	
其他金融资产	Other Financial Assets	-88.8	其他负债	Other Liabilities	-516.7
国际资本往来	International Capital Movement	-34.1	国际资本往来	International Capital Movement	-4.3
短期资本	Short-term	-26.1	短期资本	Short-term	-0.5
长期资本	Long-term	-8.0	长期资本	Long-term	-3.8
国际储备资产	International Reserves		资金余缺	Surplus or Shortage of Capital	426.9
金融资产净增额	**Net Increase of Banking Capital**	**2172.3**	**负债净增额与资金余缺**	**Net Increase of Liability and Surplus or Shortage of Capital**	**2172.3**

1-26-5 期 末 资 产 负 债 帐 户
YEAR-END BALANCE ACCOUNT

单位：亿元 (100 million yuan)

非金融资产	Non-financial Assets	10478.7	负债	Liabilities	11025.6
固定资产	Fixed Assets	7720.2	国内金融资产	Domestic Financial Assets and Liabilities	10712.2
存货	Inventories	2044.5	通货	Currency	
其他非金融资产	Others	713.9	存款	Deposits	5397.7
金融资产	Financial Assets	10879.0	短期存款	Short-term	2750.7
国内金融资产	Domestic Financial Assets and Liabilities	10876.5	长期存款	Long-term	2646.9
通货	Currency	322.6	贷款	Loans	2536.2
存款	Deposits	5397.7	短期贷款	Short-term	1967.8
短期存款	Short-term	2750.7	长期贷款	Long-term	568.4
长期存款	Long-term	2646.9	证券(不含股票)	Securities(excluding stock)	444.6
			短期证券	Short-term	87.0
贷款	Loans	2536.2	长期证券	Long-term	357.5
短期贷款	Short-term	1967.8			
长期贷款	Long-term	568.4	股票及其他股权	Stock and Other Stock Ownership	2274.0
证券(不含股票)	Securities(excluding stock)	444.6	保险准备金	Premium Reserve	59.8
短期证券	Short-term	87.0	其他负债	Other Liabilities	
长期证券	Long-term	357.5	国外金融负债	Foreign Financial Liabilities	313.5
股票及其他股权	Stock and Other Stock Ownership	2115.8	短期负债	Short-term	
保险准备金	Premium Reserve	59.8	长期负债	Long-term	313.5
其他金融资产	Other Financial Assets				
国外金融资产	Foreign Financial Assets	2.5			
短期资本	Short-term Capital				
长期资本	Long-term Capital	2.5			
储备资产	Reserves		资产负债差额	Balance of Assets and Liabilities	10332.0
资　产	**Assets**	**21357.7**	**负债与资产负债差额**	**Liabilities and Balance of Assets and Liabilities**	**21357.7**

1-27 地方财政收入
LOCAL FINANCIAL REVENUE

项目	Item	绝对数(万元) Value(10000 yuan) 1998	1997	1998年为1997年% 1998 as % of 1997	构成(%) Composition(%) 1998	1997
总计	**Total**	**2620068**	**2099055**	**124.8**	**100.0**	**100.0**
一般预算财政收入合计	**General Budgetary Financial Revenue**	**2273313**	**1893913**	**120.0**	**86.8**	**90.2**
# 增值税	Increased Value Tax	375807	326680	115.0	14.3	15.6
营业税	Operating Tax	1129996	975355	115.9	43.1	46.5
个人所得税	Private Income Tax	364938	287625	126.9	13.9	13.7
城市维护建设税	City Maintenance Tax	120054	127442	94.2	4.6	6.1
固定资产投资方向调节税	Adjusting Tax of Investment in Fixed Assets	51374	42577	120.7	2.0	2.0
农牧业税和耕地占用税类	Tax for Farming and Animal Husbandry and Cultivated Land Occupation	45187	23653	191.0	1.7	1.1
企业所得税类	Enterprise Income Tax	269813	221616	121.7	10.3	10.6
国有资产经营收益	Operating Income of State-owned Assets	611	-262	-233.2		
国有企业计划亏损补贴类	Losing Subsidies of Planning of State-owned Enterprises	-631097	-632628	99.8	-24.1	-30.1
企业所得税退税类	Returned Tax of Income Tax of Enterprises	-66276	-33157	199.9	-2.5	-1.6
罚没收入、行政性收费	Forfeit and Administrative Fee	91825	61539	149.2	3.5	2.9
基金预算收入合计	**Total Fund Budgetary Income**	**346755**	**205142**	**169.0**	**13.2**	**9.8**

注：财政收入的发展速度按可比口径计算。

Note：The Indices of financial revenue are calculated at comparable prices.

1-28 地方财政支出
LOCAL FINANCIAL EXPENDITURE

项目 Item		绝对数(万元) Value(10000 yuan) 1998	1997	1998年为1997年% 1998 as % of 1997	构成(%) Composition(%) 1998	1997
总计	**Total**	**3078329**	**2621984**	**117.4**	**100.0**	**100.0**
一般预算财政支出	**General Budgetary Financial Expenditure**	**2810718**	**2445761**	**114.9**	**91.3**	**93.3**
#基本建设支出类	Capital Construction	326077	248948	131.0	10.6	9.5
企业挖潜改造资金类	Innovation Funds of Enterprises	193348	151722	127.4	6.3	5.8
简易建筑费类	Simple Construction	1632	1443	113.1	0.1	0.1
地质勘探费类	Geological Prospecting		70			
科技三项费用类	Science and Technology Promotion	22105	20216	109.3	0.7	0.8
流动资金类	Circulating Funds	9889	13798	71.7	0.3	0.5
农林水气等部门事业费类	Agriculture,Forestry, Water Conservancy and Meteorology	33129	27305	121.3	1.1	1.0
支援农村生产支出类	Supporting Agricultural Production	57680	53245	108.3	1.9	2.0
城市维护费类	City Maintenance	129914	107551	120.8	4.2	4.1
工业交通等部门的事业费类	Fees of Industrial and Transportation Departments	12120	12605	96.2	0.4	0.5
文化事业费类	Fees of Culture	21294	16987	125.4	0.7	0.6
教育事业费	Fees of Education	414950	375753	110.4	13.5	14.3
卫生经费类	Funds of Health	204056	165907	123.0	6.6	6.3
科学事业费类	Science	41118	37386	110.0	1.3	1.4
行政管理费类	Government Administration	137347	113484	121.0	4.5	4.3
公检法支出类	Public Security Agency,Procuratorial Agency and Court of Justice	218024	194473	112.1	7.1	7.4
抚恤和社会福利救济费类	Pensions and Relief Funds for Social Welfare	65477	57448	114.0	2.1	2.2
政策性补贴支出类	Policy Subsidies	139032	139182	99.9	4.5	5.3
基金支出合计	**Funds Expenditure**	**267611**	**176223**	**151.9**	**8.7**	**6.7**

注：财政支出发展速度按可比口径计算。

Note: The Indices of financial expenditure are calculated at comparable prices.

主要统计指标解释

国内生产总值 是按市场价格计算的国内生产总值的简称。它是一个国家（地区）所有常住单位在一定时期内生产活动的最终成果。国内生产总值有三种表现形式，即价值形态、收入形态和产品形态。从价值形态看，它是所有常住单位在一定时期内所生产的全部货物和服务价值超过同期投入的全部非固定资产货物和服务价值的差额，即所有常住单位的增加值之和；从收入形态看，它是所有常住单位在一定时期内所创造并分配给常住单位和非常住单位的初次分配收入之和；从产品形态看，它是最终使用的货物和服务减去进口货物和服务。在实际核算中，国内生产总值的三种表现形态表现为三种计算方法，即生产法、收入法和支出法。三种方法分别从不同的方面反映国内生产总值及其构成。

三次产业 根据社会生产活动历史发展的顺序对产业结构的划分，产品直接取自自然界的部门称为第一产业，对初级产品进行再加工的部门成为第二产业。为生产和消费提供各种服务的部门称为第三产业。它是世界上通用的产业结构分类，但各国的划分不尽一致。我国的三次产业划分是：

第一产业：农业（包括种植业、林业、牧业和渔业）。

第二产业：工业（包括采掘工业、制造业、自来水、电力、蒸汽、热水、煤气）和建筑业。

第三产业：除第一、第二产业以外的其他各业。由于第三产业包括的行业多、范围广，根据我国的实际情况第三产业可分为两大部分：一是流通部分，二是服务部分。具体又可分为四个层次：

第一层次：流通部门，包括交通运输业、邮电通讯业、商业、饮食业、物资供销业和仓储业。

第二层次：为生产和生活服务的部门，包括金融、保险业、地质普查业、房地产业、公用事业，居民服务业，咨询服务业和综合技术服务业，农、林、牧、渔、水利服务业和水利业，公路、内河（湖）航道养护业等。

第三层次：为提高科学文化水平和居民素质服务的部门，包括教育、文化、广播电视，科学研究、卫生、体育和社会福利事业。

第四层次：为社会公共需要服务的部门，包括国家机关、社会团体，以及军队和警察等。

可比价格 指在不同时期的价值指标对比时，扣除了价格变动的因素，以确切反映物量的变化。按可比价格计算有两种方法：一种是直接用产量乘某一年的不变价格计算；另一种是用价格指数换算。

不变价格 指用同类产品的年平均价格作为固定价格，来计算各年产品价值。按不变价格计算的产品价值消除了价格变动因素，不同时期对比可以反映生产的发展速度。新中国成立后，随着工农业产品价格水平的变化，国家统计局先后五次制定了全国统一的工业产品不变价格和农业产品不变价格，从 1952 年到 1957 年使用 1952 年工（农）业产品不变价格，从 1957 年到 1971 年使用 1957 年不变价格，从 1971 年到 1981 年使用 1970 年不变价格，从 1981 年到 1990 年使用 1980 年不变价格，从 1990 年开始使用 1990 年不变价格。

支出法国内生产总值 指一个国家（或地区）所有常住单位在一定时期内用于最终消费、资本形成总额，以及货物和服务的净出口总额，它反映本期生产的国内生产总值的使用构成。

最终消费 指常住单位在一定时期内对于货物和服务的全部最终消费支出，也就是常住单位为满足物质、文化和精神生活的需要，从本国经济领土和国外购买的货物和服务的支出。它不包括非常住单位在本国经济领土内的消费支出。最终消费分为居民消费和政府消费。

（一）居民消费：指常住住户在一定时期内对于货物和服务的全部最终消费支出。居民关于货物的最终消费支出在货物的所有权发生变化时记录，关于服务的最终支出在服务提供的时候记录。居民消费支出按市场价格计算，即按居民支付的购买者价格计算，货物的购买价格是购买者取得交货所支付的价格，它包括购买者支付的运输和商业费用。居民支出除了直接以货币形式购买的货物和服务的消费支出外，还包括以其他方式获得的货物和服务的消费支出，即所谓的虚拟消费支出。居民虚拟消费支出包括如下几种类型：单位以实物报酬及实物转移的形式提供给劳动者的货物和服务；住户生产并由本住户消费了的货物和服务，其中自有住房服务；金融机构提供的金融媒介服务；保险公司提供的保险服务。

（二）政府消费 指政府部门为全社会提供的公共服务的消费支出和免费或以较低的价格向居民住户提供的货物和服务的净支出，前者等于政府服务的产出价值减去政府单位所获得的经营收入的价值，政府服务的产出价值等于它的经常性业务支出加上固定资产折旧；后者等于政府部门向居民住户提供的货物和服务的市场价值减去向居民住户收取的价值。

资本形成总额 指常住单位在一定时期内获得减去处置的固定资产和存货的净值，包括固定资产形成总额和存货增加两项。

（一）固定资产形成总额　指常住单位在一定时期内购置、转入和自产自用的固定资产价值，扣除固定资产的销售和转出后的价值 。可分为有形固定资产形成总额和无形固定资产形成总额。有形固定资产形成总额包括一定时期内完成的建筑工程、安装工程和设备工器具购置（减处置）价值，以及土地改良、新增役、种、奶、毛、娱乐用牲畜和新增经济林木价值。无形固定资产形成总额包括矿藏的勘探、计算机软件、娱乐和文学艺术品原件等获得减处置。

（二）存货增加　指常住单位在一定时期内存货实物量变动的市场价值即期末价值减期初价值的差额。存货增加可以是正值，也可以是负值，正值表示存货上升，负值表示存货下降。它包括生产单位购进的原材料、燃料和储备物资等存货，以及生产单位生产的产成品、在制品和半成品等存货。

货物和服务净出口　指货物和服务出口减货物和服务进口的差额。出口包括常住单位向非常住单位出售或无偿转让的各种货物和服务的价值；进口包括常住单位从非常住单位购买或无偿得到的各种货物和服务的价值。由于服务活动的提供与使用同时发生，因此服务的进出口业务并不发生出入境现象，一般把常住单位从国外得到的服务作为进口，非常住单位从本国得到的服务作为出口。货物的出口和进口都按离岸价格计算。

净出口　指出口与进口的差额。出口包括常住单位向非常住单位出售或无偿转让的各种货物和服务的总值；进口包括常住单位从非常住单位购买或无偿得到的各种货物和服务的总值。由于服务活动提供与使用同时发生，因此服务的进出口业务并不发生出入境现象，应把常住单位从国外得到的服务作为进口，反之，非常住单位从我国得到的服务作为出口。

劳动者报酬　劳动者报酬是指劳动者因从事生产活动所获得的全部报酬。它包括劳动者获得的各种形式工资、奖金和津贴，既包括货币形式的，也包括实物形式的，它还包括劳动者所享受的公费医疗和医药卫生费、上下班交通补贴和单位支付的社会保险费等。单位支付的社会保险费，就是单位直接支付给负责社会保险的政府单位（一般指劳动部门）的社会保险金或为本单位职工离退休、发生死亡、伤残、医疗保险等而支付的保险费。对于个体经济来说，其所有者所获得的劳动报酬和经营利润不易区分，这两部分统一作为劳动者报酬处理。

生产税净额　指生产税减生产补贴后的差额。生产税指政府对生产单位生产、销售和从事经营活动以及因从事生产活动使用某些生产要素，如固定资产、土地、劳动力所征收的各种税、附加费和规费。具体包括销售税金及附加、增值税、管理费中开支的各种税、应交纳的养路费、排污费和水电费附加、烟酒专卖上缴政府的专项收入等。生产补贴与生产税相反，是政府对生产单位的单方面收入转移，因此视为负生产税处理，包括政策亏损补贴、粮食系统价格补贴、外贸企业出口退税收入等。

固定资产折旧　指一定时期内为弥补固定资产损耗按照核定的固定资产折旧率提取的固定资产折旧，或按国民经济核算统一规定的折旧率虚拟计算的固定资产折旧。它反映了固定资产在当期生产中的转移价值。各种类型企业和企业化管理的事业单位的固定资产折旧指实际计提并计入成本费用中的折旧费；不计提折旧的单位，如政府机关、非企业化管理的事业单位和居民住房的固定资产折旧则是按照统一规定的折旧率和固定资产原值计算的虚拟折旧。原则上，固定资产折旧应按固定资产的重置价值来计算，但是我国目前尚不具备对全社会固定资产进行重估价的基础，所以暂时只能采用上述方法来计算。

营业盈余　指常住单位创造的增加值扣除劳动者报酬、生产税净额和固定资产折旧后的余额。它相当于企业的经营利润加上生产补贴，但要扣除从利润中开支的工资和福利以及从税后利润中提取的公益金等。

登记注册类型　以在工商行政管理机关登记注册的各类企业为划分对象。行政机关、事业单位和社会团体及其他经济组织参照执行。

国有企业　指企业全部资产归国家所有，并按国家有关法律规定登记注册的非公司制的经济组织。不包括有限责任公司中的国有独资公司。

集体企业　指企业资产归集体所有，并按国家有关法律规定登记注册的经济组织。

股份合作企业　指以合作制为基础，由企业职工共同出资入股，吸收一定比例的社会资产投资组建，实行自主经营、自负盈亏，共同劳动，民主管理，按劳分配与按股分红相结合的一种集体经济组织。

联营企业　指两个及两个以上相同或不同所有制的企业法人或事业单位法人，按自愿、平等、互利的原则，共同投资组成的经济组织。包括国有联营、集体联营、国有与集体联营和其他联营企业。

有限责任公司　指根据国家有关法律规定登记注册，由两个以上，五十个以下的股东共同出资，公司以其全部资产对其债务承担责任的经济组织。包括国有独资公司以及其他有限责任公司。

股份有限公司 指根据国家有关法律规定登记注册，其全部注册资本由等额股份构成并通过发行股票筹集资本的经济组织。

私营企业 指由自然人投资设立或由自然人控股，以雇佣劳动为基础的盈利性经济组织。包括按照有关法律、条例规定登记注册的私营独资企业、私营合伙企业、私营有限责任公司和私营股份有限公司。

其他企业 指上述单位之外的其他内资经济组织。

港、澳、台商投资企业 指港澳台地区投资者依照中华人民共和国有关涉外经济的法律、法规，以合资、合作、独资、股份有限公司的形式在内地设立的企业。凡其中港澳台股本占公司注册资本比例小于25%的，属于内资企业中的股份有限公司。

外商投资企业 指外国企业或外国人依照中华人民共和国有关涉外经济的法律、法规，以合资、合作、独资、股份有限公司的形式在中国内地投资设立的企业。凡其中外资股本占公司注册资本比例小于25%的，属于内资企业中的股份有限公司。

Explanatory Notes On Main Statistical Indicators

Gross Domestic Product refers to gross domestic product calculated at market prices, which is the final products of all resident units in a country （or region）during a certain period of time. Gross domestic product is expressed in three different forms, i. e. value added, income, and products respectively. The form of value added refers to the total value of all products and services produced by all resident units during a certain period of time minus total value of input of non-fixed assets materials and services, or the summation of the value added by each of the resident units; the form of income refers to the total income created by each resident unit and distributed Primarily to all resident and non-resident units; the form of products refers to the total of final goods and services minus imports of goods and services. In the practice of national accounting, gross domestic product is calculated with three approaches, i. e. product approach, income approach, and expenditure approach respectively to reflect gross domestic product and its composition from different aspects.

Three Industries An industry structure classified according to the historical evolution of economic activity. Primary industry refers to extraction of natural resources ; secondary industry involves processing of primary products; and tertiary industry provides various kinds of services for production and consumption. The classification is universal although it varies to some extent form country to country. Each industry in China comprises:

Primary industry: Agriculture（including farming, forestry, animal husbandry, and fishery）.

Secondary industry: Industry（including mining and quarrying, manufacturing , water supply, electricity generation and supply, steam, hot water, gas）and Construction .

Tertiary industry: all other industries not included in primary or secondary industry.

Due to the fact that tertiary industry involves in a large variety of industries in China, it is divided into two groups: circulation groups, and service groups and further into four levels:

The first level: Circulation department, including transportation, posts and telecommunications, commerce, catering, material distribution, and storage.

The second level: Service department providing production and consumption services, including banking, insurance, geological survey, real estates, public utilities, service for residents, consulting service, and comprehensive technical services, and service for agriculture, forestry, animal husbandry, fishery, water conservancy, and maintenance of roads and inland water ways, etc.

The third level: Service department for upgrading scientific, educational and cultural level of the people, including education , culture, broadcasting , television, scientific research, public health, sports, and social welfare, etc.

The fourth level: Department providing public goods, including government organs, social organizations, armies, and policemen.

Comparable Prices are applied when comparing indicators of value over time to reflect accurately the changes in real term. Two methods are used for calculating comparable price indicators: 1. Multiplying the output of products by their constant prices of a certain year; 2. Conversion of the data in current prices by relevant price index.

Constant Prices refers to the average price of a given product in a certain year, which is used for comparison of output value over time. As the output value at constant prices removes the factor of price changes, it reflects the trend of production development over time. Since 1949, with the changes in general price level, the State Statistical Bureau has issued nationally unified constant prices five times: the 1952 constant prices for 1952-1957; the 1957 constant prices for 1958-1970; the 1970 constant prices for 1971-1981; the 1980 constant prices for 1981-1990; and the 1990 constant prices have been used since 1991.

GDP Calculated with Expenditure Approach refers to total expenditure on final consumption, total capital formation and net export of goods and services by resident units of a country in a certain period of time. It reflects the composition of GDP by its uses.

Final Consumption refers to the total expenditure of resident units on final consumption of goods and services in a certain period, namely the expenditure of the resident units on goods and services from domestic economic territory and abroad to meet the needs of material, cultural and spiritual life. It excludes the consumption expenditure of non-resident units in the economic territory of the country. The final consumption is classified into private consumption and government consumption.

(1) Private consumption refers to the total expenditure of households on the final consumption of goods and services in a certain period of time. The expenditure of households on final consumption of goods is recorded when the change of the ownership of goods happens. The expenditure of residents on the final consumption of services is recorded when the services is provided. The expenditure of private consumption is calculated at market prices, namely the purchasers' prices which the households pay; the purchasers' prices of goods are the prices the households pay when they obtain the goods, including the transport and commercial expenses paid by the households. In addition to the expenditure on consumption of goods and services with cash, there are other expenditures on goods and services obtained in other ways, i. e. the so-called fictitious expenditure on consumption, is also included in the expenditure of private consumption. The fictitious expenditure of private consumption includes the following cases: (a) the goods and services provided to private by the units as remuneration or benefit; (b) consumption of self-produced goods and services, in which the services refer only to the services provided by the residential buildings owned by the households; (c) the financial intermediary services provided by the financial institutions; (d) the insurance services provided by the insurance companies.

(2) Government consumption refers to the expenditure on the consumption of the public services provided by the government to the whole society and the net expenditure on the goods and services provided by the government to the households free charge or at lower prices. The former equals to the actual output value of the government services minus the value of operating income obtained by the government department. (The output value of the government services equals to its current operating expenditure plus the depreciation of its fixed assets). The latter equals to the market value of the goods and services provided by the government to the households minus the value received by the government from the households.

Total Capital Formation refers to the net amount of that the fixed assets and inventory acquired minus those disposed, including the net incremental fixed assets and the net incremental inventory.

(1) Net incremental fixed assets refers to the value of fixed assets purchased, transferred in and self-produced by the resident units deducting the value of fixed assets sold and transferred out in a certain period. It can be classified into net incremental tangible assets and net incremental intangible assets. The net incremental tangible assets include the value of the construction projects, installation projects completed and the equipment, apparatus and instruments purchased as well as the value of land improved, the incremental value of draught animals, breeding stock, milk, wool and recreational animals and the economic forest in a certain period. The net incremental intangible assets includes the prospecting of minerals, the acquisition of computer softwares, the originals of recreational, literary and art works minus the disposal of them.

(2) Net incremental inventory refers to the market value of the change in inventory in a certain period, i.e, the difference of inventory value between the beginning and the end of the period. The net incremental inventory can be positive or negative. A positive value indicates the net increase in inventory while a negative value indicates the net decrease in inventory. The inventory includes the raw materials, fuels and reserve materials purchased by the production units as well as the inventory of finished products, semi-finished products, work-in-progress, etc.

Net Export of Goods and Services refers to the difference between the exports and the imports of goods and services. The exports include the value of various goods and services sold or voluntary transferred by the resident units to the non-resident units. The imports include the value of various goods and services purchased or gratuitously acquired by the resident units from the non-resident units. Because the provision and the use of services happen simultaneously, the import and export of services are not necessarily to cross the border of a country. The services received by the resident units from abroad are usually regarded as imports while the services received by non-resident units are usually regarded as exports. The exports and imports of goods are calculated at FOB.

Laborers' Remuneration refers to all the incomes earned by the laborers from their productive activities, which include wages, bonuses and allowances the laborers received in various forms, including incomes in money and in kind. It also includes the free medical services and the medicine subsidies provided to the laborers as well as traffic subsidies and social insurance fee paid by the laborers' working units for them. The social insurance fee paid by the laborers' working units refers to the social insurance fee paid directly by the working units to the government department (usually the department of labor) or the insurance fee paid by the enterprises and institutions for the retirement, death, and medical injury treatment of the staff and workers. For the individual economy, since the laborers' remuneration is not easily distinguished from the operating profit, both are treated as laborers' remuneration.

Net Taxes on Production refers to the difference between the taxes and the subsidies on production. The taxes on production refers to the various taxes, extra charges and fees levied on the production units on their production, sale and business activities as well as on some factors in production, such as fixed assets, land and labor force. In detail,, they include sales tax and extra charges, value added tax, various taxes paid from overhead, road toll, sewage charges, extra charges on water and electric power consumed, special revenue turned over to the government by the monopolized trade of tobacco and liquor, etc. In contrast to the taxes on production , the subsidies on production is an unilateral revenue transfer from the government to the production units and is therefore treated as the negative taxes on production. They include subsidies on the loss due to implementation of government policies, price subsidies to the grain institutions, foreign trade corporations' export rebates, etc.

Depreciation of Fixed Assets refers to the depreciation of fixed assets drawn in accordance with the stipulated depreciation rate for the purpose of compensating the wear loss of the fixed assets, or the depreciation of fixed assets calculated in a fictitious way in accordance with the stipulated unified depreciation rate in the national economic accounting system. It reflects the transferred value of the fixed assets in the production of the current period. The depreciation of fixed assets in various enterprises and institutions managed as enterprises refers to the depreciation expenses actually drawn and recorded as cost. In the units which do not draw the depreciation expenses, such as government organs, institutions not managed as enterprises as well as the houses of residents, the depreciation of fixed assets is the fictitious depreciation, which is calculated in accordance with the stipulated unified depreciation rate. In principle, the depreciation of fixed assets should be calculated on the basis of the re-purchased value of the fixed assets. However, it is not feasible to re-evaluate all the fixed assets in China. Therefore, the above-mentioned methods are temporarily adopted at present.

Operating Surplus refers to the net value of that the value added created by the resident units deducting the laborers' remuneration, net taxes on production and the depreciation of fixed assets. It is equivalent to the business profit of the enterprises plus subsidies on production , but the wages and welfare expenses paid from the profits and the public welfare fund drawn from the post-tax profits should be deducted.

Registered Type refers to type that all kinds of enterprises registered in administrative organ of industry and commerce. And registered type of government organs, party organs, institutions, social bodies and other economic organizations will be in light of the above.

State-owned Enterprises refers to non-company economic organizations with enterprises' assets owned by the state and registered according to related laws of the state, exclude state-owned sole-funds company of limited-liability company.

Collective-owned Enterprises refers to economic organizations with enterprises' assets owned by collectives and registered according to related laws of the state.

Share Holding Cooperative Enterprises refers to collective-owned economic organizations founded on bases of cooperative system and funded by shares of staff and workers and social assets in a certain proportion. They carry out rules of voluntary, equality, personal responsibility for profit and loss, working together, democratic management, combine distribution according to work with sharing profits according to shares.

Joint Enterprises refers to economic organizations funded by two or above institutional units with same or different ownership on the basis of voluntary, equality and mutual benefit , include state-owned joint, collective-owned joint, state-collective joint and other joint enterprises.

Limited-liability Company refers to economic organizations funded by two-fifty shareholders and registered according to related laws of the state, include state-owned sole-funds company and other limited-liability companies.

Share Holding Company refers to economic organizations registered according to related laws of the state and their total capital composed with same quota shares and collected by issuing shares.

Private Owned Enterprises refers to profit-making economic organizations founded on bases of wage labor and funded or share held by personnel, include sole-funded enterprises, cooperative enterprises, limited-liability company and share holding company registered according to related laws of the state.

Other Enterprises refers to other domestic investment economic organizations excluding the above.

Hongkong,Macao and Taiwan Funded Enterprises refers to enterprises established by entrepreneurs from Hongkong, Macao and Taiwan within the territory of mainland China according to related economic laws and regulations of the People's Republic of China in forms of joint ventures, cooperative sole-funded and share holding company. And those proportion of shares capital of Hongkong, Macao and Taiwan in registered capital less than 25% will be part of share holding company of domestic invested enterprises.

Foreign Funded Enterprises refers to enterprises established by foreign entrepreneurs within the territory of mainland China according to related economic laws and regulations of the People's Republic of China in forms of joint ventures, cooperative sole-funded and share holding company. And those proportion of foreign shares capital in registered capital less than 25% will be part of share holding company of domestic invested enterprises.

人 口
POPULATION

人口自然增长率(1978-1998)
Natural Growth Rate of Population

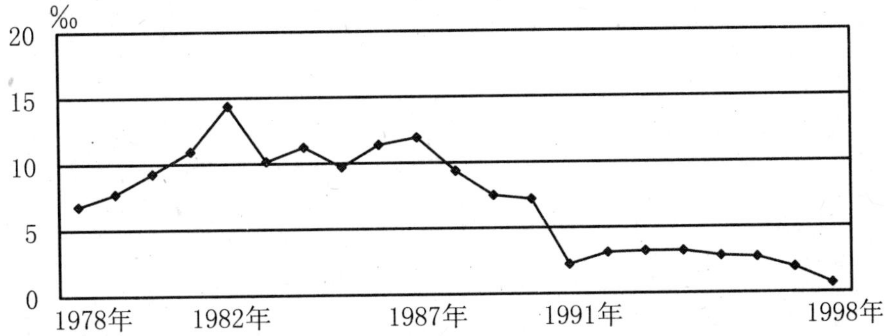

	1998	1978	1998年为1978年% 1998 as % of 1978
常住人口 （万人） Permanent Population(10000 persons)	1091.5	849.7	128.5
人口密度 （人/平方公里） Population Density(person/sq.km)	647	506	127.9
暂住人口 （万人） Temporary Population(10000 persons)	131.9	21.8	605.0

总人口　Total Population

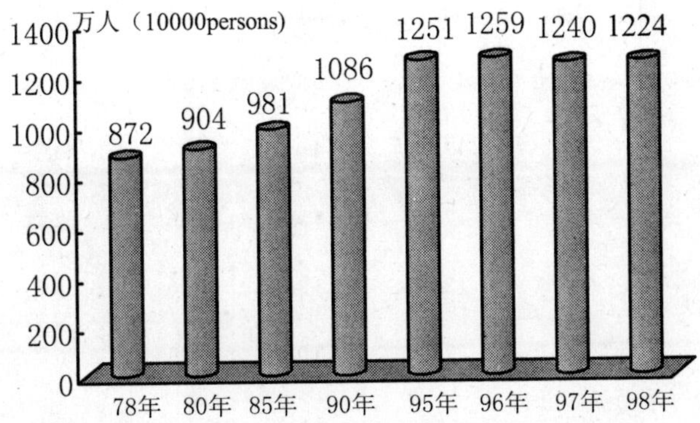

2-1 户数及人口数(户籍统计)
NUMBER OF HOUSEHOLDS AND POPULATION(REGISTERED STATISTICS)

地区 Region		总人口(万人) Total Population (10000 persons)	户数(万户) Households(10000 households)			常住人口(万人) Permanent Residents(10000 persons)			暂住人口(万人) Temporary Residents (10000 persons)
			合计 Total	非农业户 Non-Agricultural	农业户 Agricultural	合计 Total	非农业户 Non-Agricultural	农业户 Agricultural	
全市	**Total**	**1223.4**	**383.4**	**259.2**	**124.2**	**1091.5**	**733.7**	**357.8**	**131.9**
城区	**City Proper**	**265.1**	**87.2**	**87.2**	**...**	**240.9**	**240.9**	**...**	**24.2**
东城区	Dongcheng	70.0	23.4	23.4		63.3	63.3		6.7
西城区	Xicheng	86.9	28.1	28.1	...	79.2	79.2	...	7.7
崇文区	Chongwen	46.2	15.7	15.7	...	42.0	42.0	...	4.2
宣武区	Xuanwu	62.0	20.0	20.0	...	56.4	56.4	...	5.6
近郊区	**Near Suburbs**	**493.3**	**141.9**	**121.7**	**20.2**	**410.9**	**362.0**	**48.9**	**82.4**
朝阳区	Chaoyang	174.9	53.1	44.7	8.4	146.4	126.9	19.5	28.5
丰台区	Fengtai	101.0	29.2	23.4	5.8	79.5	64.7	14.8	21.5
石景山区	Shijingshan	39.9	11.0	10.3	0.7	32.4	30.8	1.6	7.5
海淀区	Haidian	177.5	48.6	43.3	5.3	152.6	139.6	13.0	24.9
远郊区	**Outer Suburbs**	**166.5**	**56.0**	**22.2**	**33.8**	**157.5**	**58.6**	**98.9**	**9.0**
门头沟区	Mentougou	25.9	8.8	5.6	3.2	23.5	15.0	8.5	2.4
房山区	Fangshan	78.0	25.0	9.1	15.9	74.4	26.0	48.4	3.6
通州区	Tongzhou	62.6	22.2	7.5	14.7	59.6	17.6	42.0	3.0
各县	**Counties**	**298.5**	**98.3**	**28.1**	**70.2**	**282.2**	**72.2**	**210**	**16.3**
昌平县	Changping	46.0	15.1	6.3	8.8	41.9	16.6	25.3	4.1
顺义县	Shunyi	57.0	17.7	4.0	13.7	53.7	10.3	43.4	3.3
大兴县	Daxing	57.3	17.1	5.5	11.6	52.1	14.4	37.7	5.2
平谷县	Pinggu	39.7	12.9	3.3	9.6	38.9	8.9	30.0	0.8
怀柔县	Huairou	28.0	9.9	3.0	6.9	26.2	7.5	18.7	1.8
密云县	Miyun	43.2	15.5	3.6	11.9	42.5	8.9	33.6	0.7
延庆县	Yanqing	27.3	10.1	2.4	7.7	26.9	5.6	21.3	0.4

2-2 人 口 密 度 (户籍统计)
POPULATION DENSITY(REGISTERED STATISTICS)

地区	Region	常住人口 (万人) Permanent (10000 persons)	土地面积 (平方公里) Land Area (sq.km)	人口密度 (人/平方公里) Population Density (person/sq.km)
全市	**Total**	**1091.5**	**16807.8**	**647**
城区	**City Proper**	**240.9**	**87.1**	**27358**
市中心最稠密街道	The Densest Streets			
天坛街道	Tiantan Street	6.9	1.3	52918
椿树街道	Chunshu Street	5.0	1.0	50026
崇文门街道	Chongwenmen Street	4.8	1.1	43623
前门街道	Qianmen Street	4.8	1.1	43280
大栅栏街道	Dashanlan Street	5.5	1.3	42181
东城区	Dongcheng	63.3	24.7	25609
西城区	Xicheng	79.2	30.0	26387
崇文区	Chongwen	42.0	15.9	26449
宣武区	Xuanwu	56.4	16.5	32620
近郊区	**Near Suburbs**	**410.9**	**1282.8**	**3196**
朝阳区	Chaoyang	146.4	470.8	3110
丰台区	Fengtai	79.5	304.2	2612
石景山区	Shijingshan	32.4	81.8	3842
海淀区	Haidian	152.6	426.0	3582
远郊区	**Outer Suburbs**	**157.5**	**4068.0**	**387**
门头沟区	Mentougou	23.5	1331.3	176
房山区	Fangshan	74.4	1866.7	399
通州区	Tongzhou	59.6	870.0	685
各县	**Counties**	**282.2**	**11369.9**	**248**
昌平县	Changping	41.9	1430.0	293
顺义县	Shunyi	53.7	980.0	548
大兴县	Daxing	52.1	1012.0	515
平谷县	Pinggu	38.9	1075.0	362
怀柔县	Huairou	26.2	2557.3	102
密云县	Miyun	42.5	2335.6	182
延庆县	Yanqing	26.9	1980.0	136

2-3 常住人口性别构成及性别比（户籍统计）
SEX COMPOSITION AND SEX RATIO OF PERMANENT RESIDENTS (REGISTERED STATISTICS)

地区	Region	常住人口(万人) Permanent Residents(10000 persons) 合计 Total	男 Male	女 Female	性别比(女=100) Sex Ratio (female=100)
全市	**Total**	**1091.5**	**552.6**	**538.9**	**102.6**
城区	**City Proper**	**240.9**	**121.6**	**119.3**	**102.0**
东城区	Dongcheng	63.3	31.6	31.7	99.5
西城区	Xicheng	79.2	39.7	39.5	100.6
崇文区	Chongwen	42.0	21.0	21.0	100.0
宣武区	Xuanwu	56.4	29.3	27.1	108.4
近郊区	**Near Suburbs**	**410.9**	**210.5**	**200.4**	**105.1**
朝阳区	Chaoyang	146.4	74.6	71.8	103.9
丰台区	Fengtai	79.5	40.5	39.0	103.6
石景山区	Shijingshan	32.4	17.1	15.3	111.8
海淀区	Haidian	152.6	78.3	74.3	105.5
远郊区	**Outer Suburbs**	**157.5**	**79.2**	**78.3**	**101.1**
门头沟区	Mentougou	23.5	12.3	11.2	109.5
房山区	Fangshan	74.4	37.5	36.9	101.5
通州区	Tongzhou	59.6	29.4	30.2	97.3
各县	**Counties**	**282.2**	**141.3**	**140.9**	**100.3**
昌平县	Changping	41.9	20.9	21.0	99.5
顺义县	Shunyi	53.7	26.4	27.3	97.0
大兴县	Daxing	52.1	26.1	26.0	100.2
平谷县	Pinggu	38.9	19.5	19.4	100.3
怀柔县	Huairou	26.2	13.3	12.9	103.5
密云县	Miyun	42.5	21.4	21.1	101.5
延庆县	Yanqing	26.9	13.7	13.2	103.5

2-4 户籍人口自然变动人数 (户籍统计)
NATURAL CHANGE OF OF REGISTERED POPULATION(REGISTERED STATISTICS)

单位:人 (person)

地区 Region		出生人数 Number of Birth		死亡人数 Number of Death		自然增加人数 Number of Natural Growth	
		1998	1997	1998	1997	1998	1997
全 市	**Total**	**66892**	**75976**	**75247**	**66926**	**-8355**	**9050**
城 区	**City Proper**	**8838**	**11047**	**19148**	**15334**	**-10310**	**-4287**
东城区	Dongcheng	2472	3059	4538	3942	-2066	-883
西城区	Xicheng	3085	3981	5687	5037	-2602	-1056
崇文区	Chongwen	1326	1771	3897	2652	-2571	-881
宣武区	Xuanwu	1955	2236	5026	3703	-3071	-1467
近郊区	**Near Suburbs**	**20042**	**24137**	**25184**	**20307**	**-5142**	**3830**
朝阳区	Chaoyang	6911	8625	8652	7925	-1741	700
丰台区	Fengtai	4146	5118	6678	4148	-2532	970
石景山区	Shijingshan	1522	1796	2239	1655	-717	141
海淀区	Haidian	7463	8598	7615	6579	-152	2019
远郊区	**Outer Suburbs**	**13130**	**13212**	**11432**	**11487**	**1698**	**1725**
门头沟区	Mentougou	1590	1875	2431	1906	-841	-31
房山区	Fangshan	6345	6507	5064	5203	1281	1304
通州区	Tongzhou	5195	4830	3937	4378	1258	452
各 县	**Counties**	**24882**	**27580**	**19483**	**19798**	**5399**	**7782**
昌平县	Changping	2969	3578	3670	3154	-701	424
顺义县	Shunyi	4197	4522	4373	4041	-176	481
大兴县	Daxing	5510	4965	3387	3591	2123	1374
平谷县	Pinggu	3462	4540	2162	2582	1300	1958
怀柔县	Huairou	2739	2763	2239	1667	500	1096
密云县	Miyun	3561	4478	1739	2932	1822	1546
延庆县	Yanqing	2444	2734	1913	1831	531	903

2-5 人　口　变　动 (户籍统计)
POPULATION CHANGE(REGISTERED STATISTICS)

单位:人 (person)

项　目	Item	1998	1997
自然变动	**Natural Change**		
自然增加	Natural Increase	-8355	9050
非农业人口	Non-agricultural Population	-12121	4003
农业人口	Agricultural Population	3766	5047
出生	Birth	66892	75976
非农业人口	Non-agricultural Population	33542	40308
农业人口	Agricultural Population	33350	35668
死亡	Death	75247	66926
非农业人口	Non-agricultural Population	45663	36305
农业人口	Agricultural Population	29584	30621
机械变动	**Non-natural Change**		
机械增加	Non-natural Increase	57609	63206
非农业人口	Non-agricultural Population	49817	57625
农业人口	Agricultural Population	7792	5581
市外迁入	Move in from outside	102840	105700
非农业人口	Non-agricultural Population	90648	96336
农业人口	Agricultural Population	12192	9364
迁往市外	Move out	45231	42494
非农业人口	Non-agricultural Population	40831	38711
农业人口	Agricultural Population	4400	3783

2-6 1998年人口实际自然变动情况
ACTUAL NATURAL CHANGE OF POPULATION

项　目	Item	常住人口 Permanent Residents
自然变动人数(人)	**Natural Change of Population** (person)	
出生人数	Number of Birth	74556
死亡人数	Number of Death	65858
自然增加人数	Natural Increase of Population	8698
自然变动率 (‰)	**Natural Growth Rate** (‰)	
出生率	Birth Rate	6.0
死亡率	Death Rate	5.3
自然增长率	Natural Growth Rate	0.7

注：本表"常住人口"栏中数字为1998年人口变动情况抽样调查推算数字。

Note：Data in column"Permanent Residents" are estimated through sample survey on population change in 1998.

2-7 家 庭 户 规 模 (人口变动情况抽样调查资料)

FAMILY SIZE(DATA FROM SAMPLE SURVEY ON POPULATION CHANGE)

地 区	Region	家庭总户数 (户) Total Number of Households (household)	家庭户规模所占比重(%) Percentage of Various Sized Family(%)				
			一人户 One Person	二人户 Two Persons	三人户 Three Persons	四人户 Four Persons	五人及以上户 Five Persons and above
全 市	**Total**	**22669**	**9.92**	**20.76**	**42.94**	**15.86**	**10.52**
城 区	**City Proper**	**6192**	**11.42**	**23.98**	**41.80**	**13.16**	**9.64**
东城区	Dongcheng	1450	9.66	24.41	40.28	13.65	12.00
西城区	Xicheng	1987	11.42	24.06	44.49	11.93	8.10
崇文区	Chongwen	1179	14.25	24.34	40.20	13.57	7.64
宣武区	Xuanwu	1576	10.91	23.22	40.99	13.96	10.92
近郊区	**Near Suburbs**	**9228**	**9.31**	**21.18**	**47.66**	**13.42**	**8.43**
朝阳区	Chaoyang	3488	11.44	24.42	44.47	12.30	7.37
丰台区	Fengtai	1698	9.72	23.44	50.00	10.83	6.01
石景山区	Shijingshan	1037	1.64	9.74	59.40	17.36	11.86
海淀区	Haidian	3005	9.25	20.10	45.99	14.81	9.85
远郊区	**Outer Suburbs**	**2283**	**15.07**	**20.45**	**40.17**	**14.50**	**9.81**
门头沟区	Mentougou	529	30.06	22.69	25.14	17.01	5.10
房山区	Fangshan	993	12.89	21.15	43.81	11.98	10.17
通州区	Tongzhou	761	7.49	18.00	45.86	16.03	12.62
各 县	**Counties**	**4966**	**6.83**	**16.07**	**36.89**	**24.40**	**15.81**
昌平县	Changping	680	3.24	13.38	26.47	29.26	27.65
顺义县	Shunyi	1224	6.62	14.54	31.29	28.02	19.53
大兴县	Daxing	1118	8.14	16.55	36.58	25.04	13.69
平谷县	Pinggu	400	5.50	14.50	22.00	30.75	27.25
怀柔县	Huairou	573	5.41	19.90	44.15	19.20	11.34
密云县	Miyun	489	15.95	19.02	40.49	19.02	5.52
延庆县	Yanqing	482	2.90	16.39	66.60	13.28	0.83

2-8 年龄组人口数 (人口变动情况抽样调查资料)

POPULATION GROUP BY AGE(DATA FROM SAMPLE SURVEY ON POPULATION CHANGE)

项目	Item	1998年被抽样人口 Sample Data of 1998		1997年人口抽样调查各年龄组占总人口比重(%) Percentage in Year 1997 (%)
		抽样人口数(人) Number of Persons Sampled (person)	年龄组人口占总人口比重(%) Percentage (%)	
总计	**Total**	**71486**	**100.0**	**100.0**
# 法定婚龄 男(22岁以上)	Legal Marry Age: Male (age 22 and above)	26863	37.6	37.2
女(20岁以上)	Female (age 20 and above)	27058	37.9	38.1
育龄妇女(15-49岁)	Women of Child-bearing Age (age15-49)	21329	29.8	29.6
不满周岁婴儿(0岁)	Below Age 1	381	0.5	0.8
学龄前儿童(1-6岁)	Age 1-6	3128	4.4	4.6
小学学龄组(7-12岁)	Age 7-12	5892	8.2	8.1
初中学龄组(13-15岁)	Age 13-15	2929	4.1	4.8
劳动年龄组	Of Labor Age	47591	66.6	65.1
男(16-59岁)	Male(age 16-59)	25126	35.2	33.9
女(16-54岁)	Female(age 16-54)	22465	31.4	31.2
超过劳动年龄组	Over Labor Age	11565	16.2	16.6
男(60岁以上)	Male(age 60 and above)	4926	6.9	6.8
女(55岁以上)	Female(age 55 and above)	6639	9.3	9.8

2-9 人口年龄构成及性别比 (人口变动情况抽样调查资料)

AGE COMPOSITION AND SEX RATIO OF POPULATION(DATA FROM SAMPLE SURVEY ON POPULATION CHANGE)

年龄组 Age Group	抽样人口数(人) Number of Persons Sampled (person)			占抽样人口数的比重(%) Percentage(%)			性别比 (女=100) Sex Ratio (Female=100)
	合计 Total	男 Male	女 Female	合计 Total	男 Male	女 Female	
总计 Total	**71486**	**36417**	**35069**	**100**	**50.94**	**49.06**	**103.84**
0-4	2295	1191	1104	3.21	1.67	1.54	107.88
5-9	3857	2004	1853	5.39	2.80	2.59	108.15
10-14	5096	2615	2481	7.13	3.66	3.47	105.40
15-19	5178	2605	2573	7.24	3.64	3.60	101.24
20-24	4769	2597	2172	6.67	3.63	3.04	119.57
25-29	5930	2974	2956	8.30	4.16	4.14	100.61
30-34	6540	3302	3238	9.15	4.62	4.53	101.98
35-39	7755	3963	3792	10.84	5.54	5.30	104.51
40-44	7643	3866	3777	10.69	5.41	5.28	102.36
45-49	5836	3015	2821	8.17	4.22	3.95	106.88
50-54	3562	1899	1663	4.99	2.66	2.33	114.19
55-59	3014	1460	1554	4.21	2.04	2.17	93.95
60-64	3575	1748	1827	5.01	2.45	2.56	95.68
65-69	2798	1438	1360	3.91	2.01	1.90	105.74
70-74	1867	915	952	2.61	1.28	1.33	96.11
75-79	996	492	504	1.40	0.69	0.71	97.62
80-84	514	218	296	0.71	0.30	0.41	73.65
85-89	197	90	107	0.28	0.13	0.15	84.11
90岁及以上 90 and above	64	25	39	0.09	0.03	0.06	64.10

2-10 劳动年龄人口抚养系数（人口变动抽样调查资料）
DEPENDENCY RATIO(DATA FROM SAMPLE SURVEY ON POPULATION CHANGE)

单位：%　　　　(%)

地区	Region	总抚养系数 Total Dependency Ratio	抚养老年人口系数 Of the Old	抚养少儿人口系数 Of Children
全　市	**Total**	**32.87**	**11.96**	**20.91**
城　区	City Proper	30.81	14.84	15.97
近郊区	Near Suburbs	30.25	10.80	19.45
远郊区	Outer Suburbs	32.98	11.11	21.87
各　县	Counties	40.21	10.53	29.68

2-11 育龄妇女分年龄、孩次的生育状况（人口变动情况抽样调查资料）
FERTILITY OF WOMEN ON CHILDBEARING AGE BY AGE OF MOTHER AND BIRTH ORDER (DATA FROM SAMPLE SURVEY ON POPULATION CHANGE)

单位：人，‰　　　　(person, ‰)

年龄 Age	平均育龄妇女人数 Average Number of Women on Childbearing Age	出生人数 Number of Birth	生育率 Fertility Rate	第一孩 1st Birth		第二孩 2nd Birth	
				出生数 Birth	生育率 Fertility	出生数 Birth	生育率 Fertility
总　计 Total	**21256**	**381**	**17.92**	**355**	**16.70**	**26**	**1.22**
15-19	2554	1	0.39	1	0.39		0.00
20-24	2203	64	29.06	63	28.60	1	0.45
25-29	2997	227	75.74	216	72.07	11	3.67
30-34	3483	66	18.95	58	16.65	8	2.30
35-39	3622	17	4.69	12	3.31	5	1.38
40-44	3737	6	1.61	5	1.34	1	0.27
45-49	2662						

2-12 计 划 生 育 状 况
FAMILY PLANNING

项目		Item		1998	1997	1998年比1997年增、减 1998 compared with 1997
全 市		**Total**				
计划生育状况		Family Planning Status				
计划内生育	(人)	Within Plan	(person)	74193	80479	-6286
计划生育率	(%)	Family Planning Rate	(%)	98.68	98.91	-0.23
已婚有生育条件的育龄妇女人数	(人)	Number of Married Women of Childbearing Age	(person)	2260899	2284309	-23410
实际采取节育措施人数	(人)	Number of Women Controlled Birth	(person)	2018799	2053266	-34467
独生子女领证率	(%)	Acceptance Rate of Only-child Certificate	(%)	64.82	63.54	1.28
城 市		**City**				
计划生育率	(%)	Planned Birth Rate	(%)	99.77	99.76	0.01
已婚有生育条件的育龄妇女人数	(人)	Number of Married Women of Childbearing Age	(person)	1370604	1391298	-20694
实际采取节育措施人数	(人)	Number of Women Controlled Birth	(person)	1200284	1221489	-21205
独生子女领证率	(%)	Acceptance Rate of Only-child Certificate	(%)	79.43	78.04	1.39
农 村		**Rural**				
计划生育率	(%)	Planned Birth Rate	(%)	97.36	97.93	-0.57
已婚有生育条件的育龄妇女人数	(人)	Number of Married Women of Childbearing Age	(person)	890295	893011	-2716
实际采取节育措施人数	(人)	Number of Women Controlled Birth	(person)	818515	831777	-13262
独生子女领证率	(%)	Acceptance Rate of Only-child Certificate	(%)	42.34	40.95	1.39

资料来源：北京市计划生育委员会。
Data source：Beijing Birth Control Committee.

主要统计指标解释

人口数 指一定时点、一定地区范围内有生命的个人的总和。年度统计的年末人口数是指每年 12 月 31 日 24 时的人口数。

出生率 指在一定时期内（通常为一年）出生人数与同期平均人数(或期中之数)的比率，一般用千分率表示。计算公式：

$$出生率=\frac{年出生人数}{年平均人数}\times 1000‰$$

出生人数是指活产，即脱离母体时（不管怀孕月数），有过呼吸或其他生命现象的活婴儿总和。

年平均人数是年初、年底人口数的平均数，也可用年中人口数代替。

死亡率 指在一定时期内（通常为一年）一定地区的死亡人数与同期平均人数（或期中人数）之比，一般用千分率表示。计算公式：

$$死亡率=\frac{年死亡人数}{年平均人数}\times 1000‰$$

人口自然增长率 指在一定时期内（通常为一年）人口自然增加数（出生人数减死亡人数）与该时期内平均人数（或期中人数）之比，一般用千分率表示。计算公式：

$$人口自然增长率 = \frac{本年出生人数—本年死亡人数}{年平均人数}\times 1000‰$$

人口自然增长率=人口出生率—人口死亡率

Explanatory Notes On Main Statistical Indicators

Total Population refers to the total number of people alive at a certain point of time within a given area. Year-end total population is that at 24:00 on 31st of December.

Birth Rate refers to the ratio of the number of births to the average population during a certion period of time (usually a year), which is often expressed in ‰. The following formula is used:

$$\text{Birth Rate} = \frac{\text{Number of Birth}}{\text{Average Population}}\times 1000‰$$

Number of Birth refers to live births, i. e. the births when babies had showed any vital phenomena regardless of the length of prcgnancy.

Average Population is the average of population at the beginning of a year and that at the end of the year. Sometimes it is substituted for with the mid-year population.

Death Rate refers to the ratio of the number of deaths to the average population （or mid-year population）during a certain period of time (usually one year), which is often expressed in ‰. The following formula is used:

$$\text{Death Rate} = \frac{\text{Number of Deaths}}{\text{Average Population}}\times 1000‰$$

Natural Growth Rate of Population refers to the ratio of the natural increase in population （number of births minus number of deaths ）in a certain period of time （usually a year）to the average population （or mid-year population）of the same period, which is often expressed in ‰. The following formulas are applied:

$$\text{Natural Growth Rate of Population} = \frac{\text{Number of Births} - \text{Number of Deaths}}{\text{Average Population}}\times 1000‰$$

Natural Growth Rate of Population = Birth Rate – Death Rate

1999

劳动力和工资

LABOR FORCE AND WAGE

职工平均工资（1978-1998）

Average Wage for Staff and Workers(1978-1998)

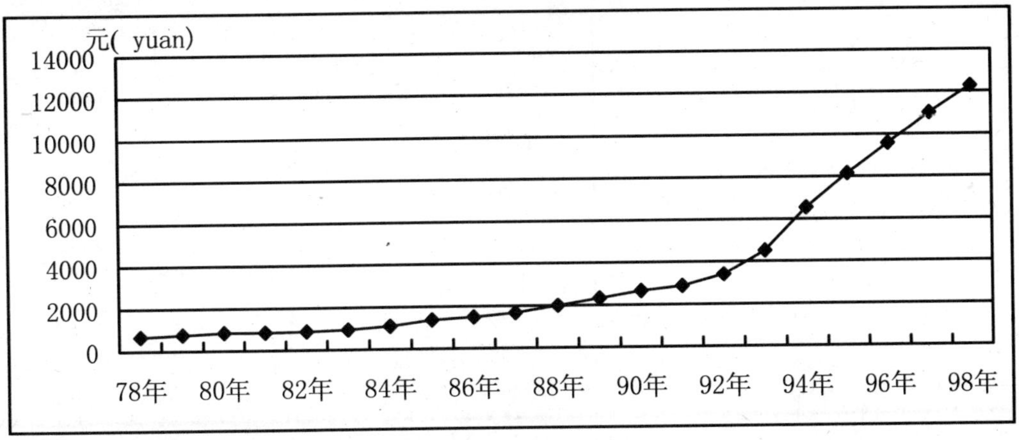

	1998	1997
职工人数（万人） Number of Staff and Workers(10000 persons)	450.1	465.3
职工工资总额（万元） Total Wages of Staff and Workers(10000 yuan)	5581851	5147632
职工平均工资（元） Average Wage for Staff and Workres(yuan)	12285	11019

职工平均工资（按经济类型分）

Average Wage for Staff and Workers(Grouped by Ownership)

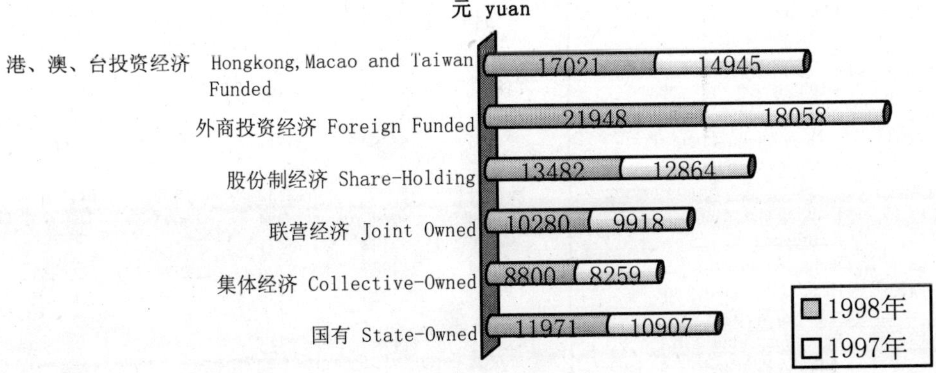

3-1 全市从业人员(产业、部类分)
EMPLOYMENT BY INDUSTRY AND SECTOR

项目	Item	1998 合计 Total	1998 城市 Urban	1998 农村 Rural	1997 合计 Total	1997 城市 Urban	1997 农村 Rural
人数(人)	**Number of Persons (person)**	**6221565**	**4632269**	**1589296**	**6558142**	**4987531**	**1570611**
按产业分	**Grouped by Industry**						
第一产业	Primary Industry	714503	35037	679466	701056	45771	655285
第二产业	Secondary Industry	2259949	1722123	537826	2576202	2017679	558523
第三产业	Tertiary Industry	3247113	2875109	372004	3280884	2924081	356803
按部类分	**Grouped by Sector**						
物质生产部门	Material Production	3318679	1981903	1336776	3631859	2305445	1326414
非物质生产部门	Nonmaterial Production	2902886	2650366	252520	2922289	2678092	244197
构成(%)	**Composition (%)**	**100**	**100**	**100**	**100**	**100**	**100**
按产业分	**Grouped by Industry**						
第一产业	Primary Industry	11.5	0.8	42.8	10.7	0.9	41.7
第二产业	Secondary Industry	36.3	37.2	33.8	39.3	40.5	35.6
第三产业	Tertiary Industry	52.2	62.0	23.4	50	58.6	22.7
按部类分	**Grouped by Sector**						
物质生产部门	Material Production Sectors	53.3	42.8	84.1	55.4	46.3	84.5
非物质生产部门	Nonmaterial Production Sectors	46.7	57.2	15.9	44.6	53.7	15.5

注：根据国家统计局的规定，1998年对从业人员进行口径调整。下同。

Note: According to the rules of State Statistical Bureau, standard counted of employment is adjusted from 1998. (the followings are the same)

3-2 全市从业人员(按经济类型分)
EMPLOYMENT BY OWNERSHIP

单位：人 (person)

行业	Sector	合计 Total	国有经济 State-Owned	集体经济 Collective-Owned	其他经济 Others	城镇个体私营劳动者 Urban Individuals and Private Owned	农村劳动者 Rural Labors
总计	**Total**	**6221565**	**3080645**	**509986**	**840916**	**200722**	**1589296**
农、林、牧、渔业	Farming,Forestry,Animal Husbandry and Fishery	714503	29529	788	4330	390	679466
采掘业	Excavation	38565	32818	676		50	5021
制造业	Manufacturing	1505229	624327	134348	318769	17521	410264
电力、煤气及水的生产和供应业	Electricity,Gas,Water Production and Supply	42251	40956	627	451		217
建筑业	Construction	673904	332629	130765	85809	2377	122324
地质勘查业水利管理业	Geological Prospecting and Water Conservancy	16956	16527	198	8		223
交通运输、仓储及邮电通信业	Transportation,Storage,Post and Telecommunication	327271	183894	11295	7154	5667	119261
批发和零售贸易餐饮业	Wholesale,Retail and Catering	888251	259007	112132	151592	144746	220774
金融、保险业	Banking and Insurance	73434	49647	7784	16003		
房地产业	Real Estate	94256	52142	3471	38188		455
社会服务业	Social Services	592284	334987	58706	148974	23293	26324
卫生体育和社会福利业	Health Care,Sports and Social Welfare	137673	127098	9276	1133		166
教育、文化艺术和广播电影电视业	Education,Culture,Art, Radio,Film and Television	432405	419787	7326	4329		963
科学研究和综合技术服务业	Scientific Research and Polytechnical Services	303609	223834	23187	56462		126
国家机关、政党机关和社会团体	Government Organs,Party Organs and Social Bodies	309517	309328	101	88		
其他行业	Others	71457	44135	9306	7626	6678	3712

3-3 城镇单位从业人员年末人数
YEAR-END EMPLOYMENT IN URBAN UNITS

单位：人 (person)

项目	Item	从业人员 Total Employees	在岗职工 Staff and Workers at their Posts	聘用留用的离退休人员 Retired and VCSR Engaged and Kept on	聘用的外籍及港澳台方人员 Personnel of Foreign,Hong-kong,Macao and Taiwan	人事档案关系保留在原单位人员 Personnel Organization-al Affiliation Reserved
总计	**Total**	**4431547**	**4187600**	**109679**	**4618**	**129650**
按登记注册类型分	**Grouped by Registered Type**					
内资经济	Domestic Investment Economy	4088977	3882265	98351	552	107809
国有经济	State-owned	3080645	2984179	50869	397	45200
集体经济	Collective-owned	509986	456658	28431	30	24867
联营经济	Joint-owned	51882	47166	1538	11	3167
股份有限公司	Share Holding Company	184683	165869	6344	49	12421
有限责任公司	Limited-Liability Company	191056	167515	7301	40	16200
股份合作企业	Share Holding Cooperative	69009	59516	3750	25	5718
其他经济	Others	1716	1362	118		236
外商投资经济	Foreign Funded	211764	192738	4475	2849	11702
港、澳、台商投资经济	Hongkong,Macao and Taiwan Funded	130806	112597	6853	1217	10139
按隶属关系分	**Grouped by Administrative Relationship**					
# 中央	Central	1354789	1287125	32954	1033	33677
地方	Local	2771133	2635709	62097	1988	71339
按行业分	**Grouped by Sector**					
农、林、牧、渔业	Farming,Forestry,Animal Husbandry and Fishery	34647	34428	101	22	96
# 农业	Farming	4663	4609	15	5	34
采掘业	Excavation	33494	33417	75		2
制造业	Manufacturing	1077444	1038093	17233	1236	20882
电力、煤气及水的生产和供应业	Electricity,Gas,Water Production and Supply	42034	41467	325		242
建筑业	Construction	549203	525946	13162	97	9998
地质勘查业水利管理业	Geological Prospecting and Water Conservancy	16733	16559	162		12
交通运输、仓储及邮电通信业	Transportation,Storage,Posts and Telecommunications Services	202343	192892	1504	48	7899
# 交通运输业	Transportation	143169	138662	614	41	3852
邮电通信业	Posts and Telecommunications Services	48197	43428	822		3947
批发和零售贸易餐饮业	Wholesale, Retail and Catering	522731	483474	15435	357	23465
# 批发业	Wholesale	200629	184348	7125	72	9084
零售业	Retail	254192	236388	7119	86	10599
餐饮业	Catering	64467	59385	1138	193	3751
金融、保险业	Banking and Insurance	73434	71533	1131	191	579
房地产业	Real Estate	93801	83622	5184	301	4694
社会服务业	Social Services	542667	485145	23808	1324	32390
# 公共服务业	Public Services	165092	156100	2661	5	6326
居民服务业	Residents Services	28789	23825	3274	34	1656
旅馆业	Hotels	123014	109696	5971	414	6933
卫生体育和社会福利业	Health Care,Sports and Social Welfare	137507	134721	2225	75	486
# 卫生	Health Care	124765	122517	1980	25	243
体育	Sports	8346	7930	178	13	225
教育、文化艺术和广播电影电视业	Education,Culture,Art, Radio,Film and Television	431442	415699	9580	406	5757
教育	Education	338906	329908	6829	291	1878
文化艺术业	Culture and Art	73106	68423	2171	62	2450
广播电影电视业	Radio,Film and Television	19430	17368	580	53	1429
科学研究和综合技术服务业	Scientific Research and Polytechnical Services	303483	268887	15825	317	18454
科学研究业	Scientific Research	140428	135782	4256	13	377
综合技术服务业	Polytechnical Services	163055	133105	11569	304	18077
国家机关、政党机关和社会团体	Government Organs,Party Organs and Social Bodies	309517	305769	2734		1014
其他行业	Others	61067	55948	1195	244	3680

注：城镇单位从业人员年末人数与报国家统计局劳动工资年报口径一致，不含城镇个体企业、私营企业、农村从业人员。

Note:Data in this table is in accordance to the annual bulletin of labors and wages reported to state statistical bureau,not include urban individuals, private and rural employees.

3-4 职　工　人　数
NUMBER OF STAFF AND WORKERS

单位：人 (person)

项　目	Item	1998	1997	1998年为1997年% 1998 as % of 1997
总　计	**Total**	**4500635**	**4653489**	**96.7**
按经济类型分	**Grouped by Ownership**			
国有经济	State-Owned	3216576	3486553	92.3
集体经济	Collective-Owned	508146	650206	78.2
联营经济	Joint Owned	57379	30464	188.4
股份制经济	Share Holding	402930	183558	219.5
外商投资经济	Foreign Funded	198379	202297	98.1
港、澳、台投资经济	Hongkong,Macao and Taiwan Funded	115861	95730	121.0
其他经济	Others	1364	4681	29.1
按隶属关系分	**Grouped by Administrative Relationship**			
# 中央	Central	1322242	1353397	97.7
地方	Local	2911922	3021429	96.4
按行业分	**Grouped by Sector**			
农、林、牧、渔业	Farming,Forestry,Animal Husbandry and Fishery	37302	54244	68.8
# 农业	Farming	5122	19011	26.9
采掘业	Excavation	36030	40719	88.5
制造业	Manufacturing	1215468	1270767	95.6
电力、煤气及水的生产和供应业	Electricity,Gas,Water Production and Supply	41697	42123	99.0
建筑业	Construction	561489	607954	92.4
地质勘查业水利管理业	Geological Prospecting and Water Conservancy	16743	15700	106.6
交通运输、仓储及邮电通信业	Transportation,Storage,Posts and Telecommunications Services	200397	209627	95.6
# 交通运输业	Transportation	144469	157122	91.9
邮电通信业	Posts and Telecommunications Services	43456	45777	94.9
批发和零售贸易餐饮业	Wholesale, Retail and Catering	531295	554083	95.9
# 批发业	Wholesale	205731	241041	85.4
零售业	Retail	260898	255421	102.1
餐饮业	Catering	61266	55492	110.4
金融、保险业	Banking and Insurance	71650	73928	96.9
房地产业	Real Estate	85530	68851	124.2
社会服务业	Social Services	504239	484895	104.0
# 公共服务业	Public Services	160148	161071	99.4
居民服务业	Residents Services	25573	34329	74.5
旅馆业	Hotels	113701	112811	100.8
卫生体育和社会福利业	Health Care,Sports and Social Welfare	135152	135412	99.8
# 卫生	Health Care	122825	122886	100.0
体育	Sports	8021	7982	100.5
教育、文化艺术和广播电影电视业	Education,Culture,Art, Radio,Film and Television	418926	421614	99.4
教育	Education	332246	335765	99.0
文化艺术业	Culture and Art	69238	67026	103.3
广播电影电视业	Radio,Film and Television	17442	18823	92.7
科学研究和综合技术服务业	Scientific Research and Polytechnical Services	272683	286919	95.0
科学研究业	Scientific Research	138213	172247	80.2
综合技术服务业	Polytechnical Services	134470	114672	117.3
国家机关、政党机关和社会团体	Government Organs,Party Organs and Social Bodies	313810	324848	96.6
其他行业	Others	58224	61805	94.2

3-4 续表 continued continued

单位：人 (person)

项目 Item		1998
总计	**Total**	**4500635**
按登记注册类型分	**Grouped by Registered Type**	
内资经济	Domestic Investment Economy	4186395
国有经济	State-owned	3216576
集体经济	Collective-owned	508146
联营经济	Joint-owned	57379
股份有限公司	Share Holding Company	169231
有限责任公司	Limited-Liability Company	172839
股份合作企业	Share Holding Cooperative	60860
其他经济	Others	1364
外商投资经济	Foreign Funded	198379
港、澳、台商投资经济	Hongkong,Macao and Taiwan Funded	115861

3-5 职工人数增减情况(国有经济)

CHANGES IN NUMBER OF STAFF AND WORKERS(STATE-OWNED)

单位：人 (person)

项目 Item		1998			1997		
		合计 Total	#中央单位 Central	#地方单位 Local	合计 Total	#中央单位 Central	#地方单位 Local
净增人数	**Net Increase**	**-157026**	**-44497**	**-140890**	**-73421**	**-7973**	**-63395**
增加人数	**Number of Persons Increased**	**641668**	**185011**	**357327**	**255055**	**100508**	**150132**
从农村招收	Recruited from Rural Area	249624	72837	144126	98615	42611	54173
从城镇招收	Recruited from Urban Area	62693	13248	27110	18166	6917	9957
录用的退伍军人	Employment of Demobilized Soldiers	4827	1335	3040	1940	936	969
录用大中专技校毕业生	Employment of Graduate	69095	22398	40953	28518	11814	16484
不在岗职工重新上岗	Personnel Rework after off their posts	10009	2073	6902			
调入人数	Job Changes	123659	36387	74759	83168	32121	50223
# 市外调入	from Outside Beijing	14306	8380	3745	3625	1124	1984
其他	Others	121761	36733	60137	24648	6109	18326
减少人数	**Number of Persons Decreased**	**798694**	**229508**	**498217**	**328476**	**108481**	**213527**
离休退休退职	Retire and Quit	98920	38362	58540	56004	15057	40861
开除除名辞退	Discharge	126105	65588	45843	51297	36204	14410
终止解除合同	Contract Expiration	232259	33634	168397	84133	19146	60443
在岗职工无岗	Personnel at their posts but have no work	88643	14699	73332			
调出人数	Job Changes	137912	39042	85368	103537	30070	72559
# 调往市外	to Outside Beijing	11411	2238	2950	7717	3234	4251
其他	Others	114855	38183	66737	33505	8004	25254

3-6 城镇新增就业人数

INCREMENTAL IN URBAN AREA

单位：人 (person)

项目 Item		1998	1997	1998年为1997年% 1998 as % of 1997
总计	**Total**	**105270**	**116373**	**90.5**
国有经济	State-Owned Economy	59604	70585	84.4
集体经济	Collective-Owned Economy	8455	11900	71.1
其他经济	Other	37211	33888	109.8

3-7 国民经济各行业职工人数（按隶属关系、登记注册类型分）

单位：人

行业	Sector	全市 Total	# 在岗职工中女性 Female at their posts	比重(%) Proportion(%)
总计	**Total**	**4500635**	**1590115**	**35.3**
农、林、牧、渔业	**Farming,Forestry,Animal Husbandry and Fishery**	**37302**	**13245**	**35.5**
# 农、林、牧、渔服务业	FFAF Services	8734	2907	33.3
采掘业	**Excavation**	**36030**	**7353**	**20.4**
制造业	**Manufacturing**	**1215468**	**412967**	**34.0**
食品加工业	Food Processing	25863	7939	30.7
食品制造业	Food Making	34958	15084	43.1
饮料制造业	Beverage Manufacturing	27570	9611	34.9
烟草制造业	Tobacco Processing	1059	445	42.0
纺织业	Textile Industry	61563	31712	51.5
服装及其他纤维制品制造业	Garments and Other FiberProducts	43722	26753	61.2
皮革、毛皮、羽绒及其制品业	Leather,Furs,Down and Related Products	10444	3276	31.4
木材加工及竹、藤、棕、革制品业	Timber Processing,Bamboo,Cane, Palm Fiber and Straw Products	5778	1854	32.1
家具制造业	Furniture Manufacturing	8268	2379	28.8
造纸及纸制品业	Papermaking and Paper Products	12650	4321	34.2
印刷业、记录媒介的复制	Printing and Record Medium Reproduced	43892	20078	45.7
文教体育用品制造业	Stationery,Education and Sports Goods	10809	4243	39.3
石油加工及炼焦业	Petroleum Processing and Coking Products	49076	14433	29.4
化学原料及化学制品制造业	Raw Chemical Materials and Chemical Products	55793	18792	33.7
医药制造业	Medical and Pharmaceutical Products	26277	12784	48.7
化学纤维制造业	Chemical Fibers	7466	2492	33.4
橡胶制品业	Rubber Products	13468	4550	33.8
塑料制品业	Plastic Products	22375	7547	33.7
非金属矿物制品业	Nonmetal Mineral Products	77843	20968	26.9
黑色金属冶炼及压延加工业	Smelting and Pressing Ferrous Metals	166830	38937	23.3
有色金属冶炼及压延加工业	Smelting and Pressing of Non-ferrous Metals	4863	1269	26.1
金属制品业	Metal Products	35233	10129	28.7
普通机械制造业	Ordinary Machinery	75351	21988	29.2
专业设备制造业	Special Purpose Equipment	70974	21892	30.8
交通运输设备制造业	Transportation Equipment	117178	32590	27.8
武器弹药制造业	Weapons and Ammunition	12831	3771	29.4
电气机械及器材制造业	Electric Equipment and Machine	59856	21625	36.1
电子及通信设备制造业	Electronic and Telecommunication	82177	31719	38.6
仪器仪表及文化办公用机械制造业	Instruments,Meters,Cultural and Official Machinery	30519	11920	39.1
其他制造业	Other Manufacturing	20782	7866	37.9
电力、煤气及水的生产和供应业	**Electricity,Gas and Water Production and Supply**	**41697**	**13678**	**32.8**
电力、蒸气、热水的生产和供应业	Electricity,Steam and Hot Water Production and Supply	27049	7963	29.4
煤气生产和供应业	Gas Production and Supply	8280	3325	40.2
自来水的生产和供应业	Water Production and Supply	6368	2390	37.5
建筑业	**Construction**	**561489**	**76635**	**13.6**
土木工程建筑业	Civil Engineering	453953	60905	13.4
线路、管道和设备安装业	Pipeline and Equipment Installation	77737	12564	16.2
建筑物的装修装饰业	Building Completion	29799	3166	10.6
地质勘查业、水利管理业	**Geological Prospecting and Water Conservancy**	**16743**	**3876**	**23.2**
地质勘查业	Geological Prospecting	6057	1624	26.8
水利管理业	Water Conservancy	10686	2252	21.1

NUMBER OF STAFF AND WORKERS BY SECTOR
(BY ADMINISTRATIVE RELATIONSHIP AND REGISTERED TYPE)

(person)

# 中 央 Central	# 地 方 Local	国有经济 State-Owned	# 中 央 Central	# 地 方 Local	集体经济 Collective-Owned	其他经济 Others
1322242	**2911922**	**3216576**	**1167848**	**2025507**	**508146**	**775913**
1574	**35600**	**32284**	**1310**	**30974**	**759**	**4259**
1151	7513	8173	1146	7027	488	73
117	**35913**	**35353**	**117**	**35236**	**677**	
191186	**989974**	**734147**	**165107**	**569040**	**160091**	**321230**
621	24145	16423	167	16256	645	8795
531	31702	17233	188	17045	2429	15296
245	26742	14107	39	14068	1723	11740
16	1043	1043		1043	16	
134	61087	36677	16	36661	6107	18779
1889	38088	10472	1723	8749	13050	20200
74	9634	5043		5043	3006	2395
749	4515	4038	655	3383	710	1030
887	5067	2336	529	1807	1826	4106
357	11735	7978	256	7722	1805	2867
25197	17692	32957	23292	9665	6360	4575
176	10128	5729	47	5682	2847	2233
46633	2371	47064	46367	697	416	1596
1166	53542	24532	370	24162	3443	27818
1936	23159	17308	1844	15464	1136	7833
7	7397	4728	7	4721	117	2621
548	12881	9504	139	9365	2872	1092
901	20931	8985	361	8624	4573	8817
3140	72407	30258	2370	27888	11710	35875
102	166708	159681		159681	1025	6124
36	4744	2825	28	2797	978	1060
3579	29284	13773	1640	12133	11870	9590
9315	65094	48655	5154	43501	12599	14097
11947	56823	38918	10723	28195	12238	19818
49887	65367	69689	43530	26159	15651	31838
12831		12831	12831			
4435	53043	33567	3505	30062	15589	10700
7298	72536	34870	4178	30692	8996	38311
5525	24124	17981	4897	13084	4972	7566
1024	17985	4942	251	4691	11382	4458
11999	**29698**	**40740**	**11353**	**29387**	**503**	**454**
11969	15080	26122	11353	14769	503	424
30	8250	8250		8250		30
	6368	6368		6368		
182119	**323404**	**358217**	**144140**	**206625**	**120614**	**82658**
144210	274805	312820	128398	177381	83129	58004
32748	37885	38043	13199	24657	28811	10883
5161	10714	7354	2543	4587	8674	13771
6225	**10510**	**16541**	**6225**	**10316**	**194**	**8**
5332	717	6049	5332	717		8
893	9793	10492	893	9599	194	

3-7 续表 1 continued

单位：人

行业	Sector	全市 Total	# 在岗职工中女性 Female at their posts	比重(%) Proportion(%)
交通运输、仓储及邮电通信业	**Transportation,Storage,Posts and Telecommunications**	**200397**	**56436**	**28.2**
铁路运输业	Railway	64851	12294	19.0
公路运输业	Highway	31536	8471	26.9
管道运输业	Pipeline			
航空运输业	Airway	12493	4399	35.2
交通运输辅助业	Transportation Subsidiary	35589	8217	23.1
仓储业	Storage	12472	3403	27.3
邮电通信业	Posts and Telecommunications	43456	19652	45.2
批发和零售贸易餐饮业	**Wholesale,Retail and Catering**	**531295**	**246634**	**46.4**
批发业	Wholesale	205731	73805	35.9
零售业	Retail	260898	140094	53.7
商业经纪与代理业	Commercial Management and Agency	3400	1135	33.4
餐饮业	Catering	61266	31600	51.6
金融、保险业	**Banking and Insurance**	**71650**	**36588**	**51.1**
金融业	Banking	66333	34277	51.7
保险业	Insurance	5317	2311	43.5
房地产业	**Real Estate**	**85530**	**29120**	**34.0**
房地产开发与经营业	Real Estate Development	31036	10069	32.4
房地产管理业	Real Estate Management	53413	18620	34.9
房地产代理与经纪业	Real Estate Brokerage and Agency	1081	431	39.9
社会服务业	**Social Services**	**504239**	**184716**	**36.6**
公共设施服务业	Public Utilities	160148	61758	38.6
# 市内公共交通业	Public Transportation in City	100368	39659	39.5
# 市内公共汽电车业	Public Bus and Trolleybus	57763	29892	51.7
园林绿化业	Gardens Afforest	18229	7706	42.3
环境卫生业	Environmental Sanitation	24277	8740	36.0
市政工程管理业	Municipal Engineering Management	8428	2332	27.7
居民服务业	Residential Services	25573	10631	41.6
旅馆业	Hotels	113701	55661	49.0
租赁服务业	Leasing	4880	1570	32.2
旅游业	Tourism	12174	4835	39.7
娱乐服务业	Recreation	9364	4772	51.0
信息、咨询服务业	Information and Consultancy Services	60281	22437	37.2
# 广告业	Advertisement	9324	3677	39.4
咨询服务业	Consultancy Services	7394	3086	41.7
计算机应用服务业	Computer Application Services	30319	10529	34.7
其他社会服务业	Other Social Services	87799	12523	14.3
# 市场管理服务业	Market Management Services	17663	5129	29.0
卫生、体育和社会福利业	**Health Care,Sports and Social Welfare**	**135152**	**84638**	**62.6**
卫生	Health Care	122825	79942	65.1
体育	Sports	8021	2531	31.6
社会福利	Social Welfare	4306	2165	50.3
教育、文化艺术及广播电影电视业	**Education,Culture and Arts, Radio, Film and Television**	**418926**	**211545**	**50.5**
教育	Education	332246	177954	53.6
高等教育	Higher Education	114790	49072	42.7
普通高等教育	Ordinary Higher Education	102604	43225	42.1
成人高等教育	Adult Higher Education	12186	5847	48.0

3-7 续表 2 continued

(person)

# 中 央 Central	# 地 方 Local	国有经济 State-Owned	# 中 央 Central	# 地 方 Local	集体经济 Collective-Owned	其他经济 Others
134133	**63768**	**182536**	**130019**	**52394**	**11333**	**6528**
64594	257	64851	64594	257		
1683	29585	22008	1516	20492	8780	748
12365		11335	11335			1158
12682	22256	32899	11078	21698	608	2082
1602	10729	10897	1329	9568	1310	265
41207	941	40546	40167	379	635	2275
71143	**382211**	**281590**	**52214**	**225735**	**112267**	**137438**
45472	131725	124367	38299	84262	45982	35382
16536	213287	133792	9088	123607	55585	71521
2865	427	3186	2773	413	14	200
6270	36772	20245	2054	17453	10686	30335
66980	**2994**	**48896**	**47496**	**1133**	**7810**	**14944**
62079	2578	45752	44352	1133	7810	12771
4901	416	3144	3144			2173
12890	**60962**	**50339**	**6242**	**43823**	**3202**	**31989**
3907	23983	18483	2760	15687	934	11619
8956	36285	31213	3445	27520	2202	19998
27	694	643	27	616	66	372
103278	**341352**	**330676**	**72009**	**249576**	**50137**	**123426**
5622	151401	143620	3297	140190	7329	9199
3356	95563	90911	2320	88468	4568	4889
	57763	57756		57756	7	
342	17806	17088	340	16748	203	938
199	23841	22493	47	22446	372	1412
51	8184	7818		7818	176	434
3868	17505	11604	1764	9799	9172	4797
40673	61128	59171	25327	27167	8708	45822
1559	2032	2136	970	1166	821	1923
6820	5140	10618	6642	3969	305	1251
1149	4808	1536	129	1367	483	7345
22173	16526	22054	16553	5326	8582	29645
2448	2294	2353	1558	775	2073	4898
1832	4551	2248	1246	1002	412	4734
5976	18504	9292	4920	4372	4355	16672
15438	64308	70645	12407	56220	10382	6772
167	17276	16375	157	16218	364	924
41790	**92790**	**125235**	**41414**	**83821**	**9028**	**889**
38765	83702	113835	38553	75282	8738	252
2914	4961	7478	2771	4707	60	483
111	4127	3922	90	3832	230	154
163928	**252664**	**409601**	**162911**	**246685**	**6470**	**2855**
99109	232099	324984	98637	226347	6133	1129
87425	27167	114339	87172	27167	63	388
80550	22054	102604	80550	22054		
6875	5113	11735	6622	5113	63	388

3-7 续表 3 continued

单位：人

行业	Sector	全市 Total	# 在岗职工中女性 Female at their posts	比重(%) Proportion(%)
中等教育	Secondary School Education	109282	59892	54.8
中等专业学校	Specialized Secondary Schools	14370	7406	51.5
普通中学	Regular Secondary Schools	75725	42708	56.4
农业、职业中学	Agricultural and Vocational Schools	12481	6692	53.6
技工学校	Technical Schools	2761	1168	42.3
成人中等学校	Adult Secondary Schools	3536	1770	50.1
工读学校	Schools for Juvenile Delinquents	409	148	36.2
初等教育	Primary Education	78746	51908	65.9
小学校	Primary Schools	78678	51846	65.9
成人初等学校	Adult Primary Schools	68	62	91.2
学前教育	Preschool Education	11837	9993	84.4
特殊教育	Special Education	931	650	69.8
其他教育	Other Education	16660	6439	38.6
文化艺术业	Culture and Arts	69238	27854	40.2
艺术	Arts	10723	3701	34.5
出版	Publication	38114	15826	41.5
文物保护	Protection of Historical Relics	5129	2090	40.7
图书馆	Library	3112	1836	59.0
档案馆	Archives	1067	540	50.6
群众文化	Mass Culture	3779	1555	41.1
新闻	News	4402	1494	33.9
文化艺术经纪与代理业	Cultural Art Brokerage	944	347	36.8
其他文化艺术业	Other Cultural Art	1968	465	23.6
广播电影电视业	Radio,Film and Television	17442	5737	32.9
广播	Radio	5137	2101	40.9
电影	Film	5736	2155	37.6
电视	Television	6569	1481	22.5
科学研究和综合技术服务	**Scientific Research and Polytechnical Services**	**272683**	**94174**	**34.5**
科学研究业	Scientific Research	138213	50472	36.5
自然科学研究	Natural Science Research	90598	32970	36.4
社会科学研究	Social Science Research	7819	2843	36.4
其他科学研究	Other Scientific Research	39796	14659	36.8
综合技术服务业	Polytechnical Services	134470	43702	32.5
气象	Atmospheric	2410	860	35.7
地震	Seismology	1310	448	34.2
测绘	Surveying and Mapping	1702	538	31.6
技术监督	Technology Supervisor	8542	2978	34.9
海洋环境	Sea and Ocean Environments	337	7	2.1
环境保护	Environmental Protection	1569	538	34.3
技术推广和科技交流服务业	Technology Promotion and Exchange Services	13784	4790	34.8
工程设计业	Engineering Design	30660	11053	36.1
其他综合技术服务业	Other Polytechnical Services	74156	22490	30.3
国家机关、政党机关和社会团体	**Government Organs,Party Organs and Social Bodies**	**313810**	**98776**	**31.5**
国家机关	Government Organs	292294	90800	31.1
政党机关	Party Organs	11374	3701	32.5
社会团体	Social Bodies	10142	4275	42.2
其他行业	**Other Sectors**	**58224**	**19734**	**33.9**

3-7 续表 4 continued

(person)

# 中 央 Central	# 地 方 Local	国有经济 State-Owned	# 中 央 Central	# 地 方 Local	集体经济 Collective-Owned	其他经济 Others
4373	104562	107016	4277	102739	2022	244
1102	13222	14010	1102	12908	314	46
2709	72735	74079	2707	71372	1453	193
8	12473	12481	8	12473		
217	2544	2632	217	2415	129	
293	3223	3405	199	3206	126	5
44	365	409	44	365		
838	77695	78533	838	77695		213
838	77627	78465	838	77627		213
	68	68		68		
1790	10047	9437	1790	7647	2400	
155	757	912	155	757	19	
4528	11871	14747	4405	10342	1629	284
52717	15410	67539	52294	15240	270	1429
6920	3752	10454	6793	3656	72	197
34345	3646	37718	34083	3635	108	288
3132	1885	4998	3132	1866		131
2081	1031	3112	2081	1031		
687	380	1067	687	380		
327	3409	3733	327	3406	3	43
4366	36	4402	4366	36		
249	546	782	241	541	14	148
610	725	1273	584	689	73	622
12102	5155	17078	11980	5098	67	297
4058	1079	5137	4058	1079		
3648	1941	5490	3601	1889	36	210
4396	2135	6451	4321	2130	31	87
175277	**85158**	**211916**	**170381**	**40601**	**18630**	**42137**
124551	12764	137965	124551	12559	119	129
81070	9464	90352	81070	9261	117	129
7370	449	7819	7370	449		
36111	2851	39794	36111	2849	2	
50726	72394	73951	45830	28042	18511	42008
2342	68	2410	2342	68		
1246	64	1310	1246	64		
692	1010	1638	692	946	64	
4661	3760	8207	4636	3571	88	247
337		337	337			
288	1040	961	244	717	195	413
3823	6813	6508	2943	3527	2379	4897
22254	7061	26774	21161	5613	1309	2577
15083	52578	25806	12229	13536	14476	33874
130804	**182016**	**313672**	**130698**	**181996**	**76**	**62**
115563	175753	292294	115563	175753		
7206	4168	11374	7206	4168		
8035	2095	10004	7929	2075	76	62
28799	**22908**	**44833**	**26212**	**18165**	**6355**	**7036**

3-8 国民经济各行业在岗职工人数(按用工期限分)

单位：人

行业	Sector	全市 Total	长期职工 Permanent Workers	临时职工 Temporary Workers
总计	**Total**	**4187600**	**3568189**	**619411**
农、林、牧、渔业	**Farming,Forestry,Animal Husbandry and Fishery**	**34428**	**28770**	**5658**
#农、林、牧、渔服务业	FFAF Services	8530	7870	660
采掘业	**Excavation**	**33417**	**32175**	**1242**
制造业	**Manufacturing**	**1038093**	**956443**	**81650**
食品加工业	Food Processing	20703	16720	3983
食品制造业	Food Making	29901	25414	4487
饮料制造业	Beverage Manufacturing	25950	22300	3650
烟草制造业	Tobacco Processing	1044	998	46
纺织业	Textile Industry	48435	45665	2770
服装及其他纤维制品制造业	Garments and Other Fiber Products	36083	28474	7609
皮革、毛皮、羽绒及其制品业	Leather,Furs,Down and Related Products	6315	5377	938
木材加工及竹、藤、棕、革制品业	Timber Processing,Bamboo,Cane, Palm Fiber and Straw Products	4758	4169	589
家具制造业	Furniture Manufacturing	7871	5564	2307
造纸及纸制品业	Papermaking and Paper Products	9764	8514	1250
印刷业、记录媒介的复制	Printing and Record Medium Reproduced	41058	37577	3481
文教体育用品制造业	Stationery,Education and Sports Goods	8513	7681	832
石油加工及炼焦业	Petroleum Processing and Coking Products	40941	40445	496
化学原料及化学制品制造业	Raw Chemical Materials and Chemical Products	49722	46894	2828
医药制造业	Medical and Pharmaceutical Products	24757	23187	1570
化学纤维制造业	Chemical Fibers	5078	4922	156
橡胶制品业	Rubber Products	10824	9165	1659
塑料制品业	Plastic Products	16434	13451	2983
非金属矿物制品业	Nonmetal Mineral Products	69080	60328	8752
黑色金属冶炼及压延加工业	Smelting and Pressing Ferrous Metals	147139	146399	740
有色金属冶炼及压延加工业	Smelting and Pressing of Nonferrous Metals	4023	3597	426
金属制品业	Metal Products	29339	24377	4962
普通机械制造业	Ordinary Machinery	61922	59355	2567
专业设备制造业	Special Purpose Equipment	63404	59381	4023
交通运输设备制造业	Transportation Equipment	102944	99305	3639
武器弹药制造业	Weapons and Ammunition	11244	11194	50
电气机械及器材制造业	Electric Equipment and Machine	48470	43930	4540
电子及通信设备制造业	Electronic and Telecommunication	71889	66335	5554
仪器仪表及文化办公用机械制造业	Instruments,Meters,Cultural and Official Machinery	25183	23364	1819
其他制造业	Other Manufacturing	15305	12361	2944
电力、煤气及水的生产和供应业	**Electricity,Gas and Water Production and Supply**	**41467**	**39815**	**1652**
电力、蒸气、热水的生产和供应业	Electricity,Steam and Hot Water Production and Supply	26965	25539	1426
煤气生产和供应业	Gas Production and Supply	8270	8246	24
自来水的生产和供应业	Water Production and Supply	6232	6030	202
建筑业	**Construction**	**525946**	**324327**	**201619**
土木工程建筑业	Civil Engineering	421015	259692	161323
线路、管道和设备安装业	Pipeline and Equipment Installation	75483	51498	23985
建筑物的装修装饰业	Building Completion	29448	13137	16311
地质勘查业、水利管理业	**Geological Prospecting and Water Conservancy**	**16559**	**13401**	**3158**

STAFF AND WORKERS AT THEIR POSTS IN DIFFERENT TRADES (BY TYPE OF STAFF AND WORKERS)

(person)

# 全市国有经济 Total State-Owned Economy	长期职工 Permanent Workers	临时职工 Temporary Workers	# 地方国有经济 Local State-Owned Economy	长期职工 Permanent Workers	临时职工 Temporary Workers
2984179	**2646903**	**337276**	**1826626**	**1648397**	**178229**
29417	**24331**	**5086**	**28129**	**23110**	**5019**
7971	7451	520	6841	6349	492
32741	**32044**	**697**	**32624**	**31927**	**697**
612135	**589609**	**22526**	**466289**	**447436**	**18853**
11816	10773	1043	11649	10637	1012
12496	11321	1175	12311	11281	1030
13533	11961	1572	13496	11924	1572
1028	996	32	1028	996	32
28775	28540	235	28759	28524	235
8336	7053	1283	6912	5908	1004
2205	2194	11	2205	2194	11
3220	2983	237	2704	2467	237
2147	1886	261	1618	1394	224
5540	5188	352	5284	5006	278
30760	28782	1978	9045	8101	944
4296	4169	127	4249	4125	124
38966	38958	8	591	586	5
20373	19514	859	20003	19189	814
16132	15341	791	14377	13879	498
2751	2712	39	2744	2705	39
7397	6885	512	7268	6758	510
5899	5191	708	5538	4891	647
25831	22627	3204	23466	20709	2757
140496	140165	331	140496	140165	331
2118	1937	181	2090	1922	168
10896	9677	1219	9523	8588	935
38323	37480	843	33581	32831	750
33197	32380	817	23428	22730	698
61413	60268	1145	22174	21443	731
11244	11194	50			
26008	24910	1098	22701	21660	1041
29423	27674	1749	25501	23826	1675
14021	13652	369	10304	9990	314
3495	3198	297	3244	3007	237
40520	**38914**	**1606**	**29174**	**27893**	**1281**
26048	24644	1404	14702	13623	1079
8240	8240		8240	8240	
6232	6030	202	6232	6030	202
325106	**225512**	**99594**	**178476**	**146898**	**31578**
281648	189475	92173	150874	122512	28362
36268	32647	3621	23169	21970	1199
7190	3390	3800	4433	2416	2017
16358	**13257**	**3101**	**10227**	**7426**	**2801**

3-8 续表 1 continued

单位：人

行业	Sector	全市 Total	长期职工 Permanent Workers	临时职工 Temporary Workers
地质勘查业	Geological Prospecting	5949	5657	292
水利管理业	Water Conservancy	10610	7744	2866
交通运输、仓储及邮电通信业	**Transportation,Storage,Posts and Telecommunications**	**192892**	**171168**	**21724**
铁路运输业	Railway	63622	63432	190
公路运输业	Highway	27165	24294	2871
航空运输业	Airway	12492	10705	1787
交通运输辅助业	Transportation Subsidiary	35383	22188	13195
仓储业	Storage	10802	10134	668
邮电通信业	Posts and Telecommunications	43428	40415	3013
批发和零售贸易餐饮业	**Wholesale,Retail and Catering**	**483474**	**412955**	**70519**
批发业	Wholesale	184348	161693	22655
零售业	Retail	236388	212323	24065
商业经纪与代理业	Commercial Management and Agency	3353	3207	146
餐饮业	Catering	59385	35732	23653
金融、保险业	**Banking and Insurance**	**71533**	**67632**	**3901**
金融业	Banking	66216	62657	3559
保险业	Insurance	5317	4975	342
房地产业	**Real Estate**	**83622**	**66658**	**16964**
房地产开发与经营业	Real Estate Development	30434	25240	5194
房地产管理业	Real Estate Management	52111	40544	11567
房地产代理与经纪业	Real Estate Brokerage and Agency	1077	874	203
社会服务业	**Social Services**	**485145**	**376905**	**108240**
公共设施服务业	Public Utilities	156100	140979	15121
# 市内公共交通业	Public Transportation in City	96856	92962	3894
# 市内公共汽电车业	Public Bus and Trolleybus	55908	55385	523
园林绿化业	Gardens Afforest	17941	15393	2548
环境卫生业	Environmental Sanitation	24212	19193	5019
市政工程管理业	Municipal Engineering Management	8299	7468	831
居民服务业	Residential Services	23825	16457	7368
旅馆业	Hotels	109696	88576	21120
租赁服务业	Leasing	4483	2993	1490
旅游业	Tourism	11953	10329	1624
娱乐服务业	Recreation	9310	5750	3560
信息、咨询服务业	Information and Consultancy Services	59461	46985	12476
# 广告业	Advertisement	9267	7113	2154
咨询服务业	Consultancy Services	7373	6537	836
计算机应用服务业	Computer Application Services	30084	26416	3668
其他社会服务业	Other Social Services	80233	38420	41813
# 市场管理服务业	Market Management Services	11243	9600	1643
卫生、体育和社会福利业	**Health Care,Sports and Social Welfare**	**134721**	**124376**	**10345**
卫生	Health Care	122517	113999	8518
体育	Sports	7930	6964	966
社会福利保障业	Social Welfare	4274	3413	861
教育、文化艺术及广播电影电视业	**Education,Culture and Arts, Radio, Film and Television**	**415699**	**382957**	**32742**
教育	Education	329908	305018	24890
高等教育	Higher Education	114293	103196	11097
普通高等教育	Ordinary Higher Education	102196	92526	9670
成人高等教育	Adult Higher Education	12097	10670	1427

3-8 续表 2 continued

(person)

# 全市国有经济 Total State-Owned Economy	长期职工 Permanent Workers	临时职工 Temporary Workers	# 地方国有经济 Local State-Owned Economy	长期职工 Permanent Workers	临时职工 Temporary Workers
5941	5649	292	703	666	37
10417	7608	2809	9524	6760	2764
176295	**156899**	**19396**	**47846**	**33494**	**14352**
63622	63432	190	257	245	12
18722	16666	2056	17435	15419	2016
11335	9651	1684			
32706	19963	12743	21639	9720	11919
9392	9025	367	8138	7889	249
40518	38162	2356	377	221	156
248879	**228164**	**20715**	**194335**	**178634**	**15701**
110035	102078	7957	71050	65341	5709
116890	108717	8173	106860	100110	6750
3141	3037	104	404	348	56
18813	14332	4481	16021	12835	3186
48829	**46494**	**2335**	**1122**	**1082**	**40**
45685	43632	2053	1122	1082	40
3144	2862	282			
49280	**41146**	**8134**	**42842**	**35890**	**6952**
17950	15490	2460	15218	12973	2245
30689	25104	5585	27010	22392	4618
641	552	89	614	525	89
315860	**247313**	**68547**	**235574**	**190794**	**44780**
139860	129526	10334	136461	126618	9843
87569	85257	2312	85152	83138	2014
55901	55378	523	55901	55378	523
16806	14524	2282	16471	14282	2189
22428	18729	3699	22381	18682	3699
7789	6984	805	7789	6984	805
10603	8591	2012	8801	7080	1721
56778	42906	13872	25094	21000	4094
1750	1319	431	780	607	173
10411	8908	1503	3826	3059	767
1505	1027	478	1337	885	452
21801	17483	4318	5231	4449	782
2313	1944	369	756	601	155
2243	2037	206	1002	880	122
9169	8527	642	4322	3851	471
63983	29026	34957	49722	23245	26477
9965	8499	1466	9808	8360	1448
124876	**115664**	**9212**	**83569**	**77773**	**5796**
113592	105827	7765	75078	70357	4721
7387	6610	777	4680	4275	405
3897	3227	670	3811	3141	670
406659	**375270**	**31389**	**244507**	**227226**	**17281**
322922	298959	23963	224711	210047	14664
113842	102769	11073	27024	24082	2942
102196	92526	9670	21971	19530	2441
11646	10243	1403	5053	4552	501

3-8 续表 3 continued

单位：人

行业	Sector	全市 Total	长期职工 Permanent Workers	临时职工 Temporary Workers
中等教育	Secondary School Education	108320	101918	6402
中等专业学校	Specialized Secondary Schools	14286	13175	1111
普通中学	Regular Secondary Schools	75007	71511	3496
农业、职业中学	Agricultural and Vocational Schools	12346	11014	1332
技工学校	Technical Schools	2751	2523	228
成人中等学校	Adult Secondary Schools	3528	3305	223
工读学校	Schools for Juvenile Delinquents	402	390	12
初等教育	Primary Education	78365	74885	3480
小学校	Primary Schools	78297	74817	3480
成人初等学校	Adult Primary Schools	68	68	
学前教育	Preschool Education	11507	10582	925
特殊教育	Special Education	931	870	61
其他教育	Other Education	16492	13567	2925
文化艺术业	Culture and Arts	68423	62020	6403
艺术	Arts	10458	9601	857
出版	Publication	37866	34447	3419
文物保护	Protection of Historical Relics	5122	4449	673
图书馆	Library	3099	2913	186
档案馆	Archives	1063	983	80
群众文化	Mass Culture	3529	3150	379
新闻	News	4402	4100	302
文化艺术经纪与代理业	Cultural Art Brokerage	927	723	204
其他文化艺术业	Other Cultural Art	1957	1654	303
广播电影电视业	Radio,Film and Television	17368	15919	1449
广播	Radio	5136	4844	292
电影	Film	5664	4954	710
电视	Television	6568	6121	447
科学研究和综合技术服务	**Scientific Research and Polytechnical Services**	**268887**	**243709**	**25178**
科学研究业	Scientific Research	135782	129604	6178
自然科学研究	Natural Science Research	88645	85034	3611
社会科学研究	Social Science Research	7786	7505	281
其他科学研究	Other Scientific Research	39351	37065	2286
综合技术服务业	Polytechnical Services	133105	114105	19000
气象	Atmospheric	2406	2305	101
地震	Seismology	1310	1276	34
测绘	Surveying and Mapping	1647	1584	63
技术监督	Technology Supervisor	8451	7720	731
海洋环境	Sea and Ocean Environments	337	334	3
环境保护	Environmental Protection	1557	1359	198
技术推广和科技交流服务业	Technology Promotion and Exchange Services	13494	11780	1714
工程设计业	Engineering Design	30449	28961	1488
其他综合技术服务业	Other Polytechnical Services	73454	58786	14668
国家机关、政党机关和社会团体	**Government Organs,Party Organs and Social Bodies**	**305769**	**275766**	**30003**
国家机关	Government Organs	284328	255538	28790
政党机关	Party Organs	11371	10648	723
社会团体	Social Bodies	10070	9580	490
其他行业	**Other Sectors**	**55948**	**51132**	**4816**

3-8 续表 4 continued

(person)

# 全市国有经济 Total State-Owned Economy	长期职工 Permanent Workers	临时职工 Temporary Workers	# 地方国有经济 Local State-Owned Economy	长期职工 Permanent Workers	临时职工 Temporary Workers
106061	99875	6186	101834	95961	5873
13933	12847	1086	12831	11776	1055
73361	70023	3338	70695	67618	3077
12346	11014	1332	12338	11006	1332
2622	2424	198	2409	2211	198
3397	3177	220	3203	3004	199
402	390	12	358	346	12
78152	74764	3388	77325	73957	3368
78084	74696	3388	77257	73889	3368
68	68		68	68	
9353	8604	749	7571	6898	673
912	851	61	757	696	61
14602	12096	2506	10200	8453	1747
66731	60680	6051	14753	12955	1798
10189	9386	803	3499	3271	228
37470	34124	3346	3583	3082	501
4991	4345	646	1860	1528	332
3099	2913	186	1027	927	100
1063	983	80	380	354	26
3484	3105	379	3157	2789	368
4402	4100	302	36	36	
765	593	172	524	354	170
1268	1131	137	687	614	73
17006	15631	1375	5043	4224	819
5136	4844	292	1079	935	144
5419	4763	656	1834	1518	316
6451	6024	427	2130	1771	359
208563	**197168**	**11395**	**39228**	**35172**	**4056**
135534	129377	6157	11726	11030	696
88399	84809	3590	8603	7998	605
7786	7505	281	431	415	16
39349	37063	2286	2692	2617	75
73029	67791	5238	27502	24142	3360
2406	2305	101	68	61	7
1310	1276	34	64	63	1
1583	1535	48	934	892	42
8116	7445	671	3536	3072	464
337	334	3			
949	825	124	710	588	122
6301	5852	449	3353	3143	210
26606	25751	855	5557	5307	250
25421	22468	2953	13280	11016	2264
305644	**275646**	**29998**	**175941**	**168366**	**7575**
284328	255538	28790	169720	162377	7343
11371	10648	723	4165	4019	146
9945	9460	485	2056	1970	86
43017	**39472**	**3545**	**16743**	**15276**	**1467**

3-9 职 工 工 资 总 额

TOTAL WAGES OF STAFF AND WORKERS

单位：万元 (10000 yuan)

项 目	Item	1998	1997	1998年为1997年% 1998 as % of 1997
总 计	**Total**	**5581851**	**5147632**	**108.4**
按经济类型分	**Grouped by Ownership**			
国有经济	State-Owned	3919010	3835676	102.2
集体经济	Collective-Owned	450010	537736	83.7
联营经济	Joint Owned	59308	30488	194.5
股份制经济	Share Holding	517908	221353	234.0
外商投资经济	Foreign Funded	434192	363311	119.5
港、澳、台投资经济	Hongkong,Macao and Taiwan Funded	199885	142272	140.5
其他经济	Others	1537	16796	9.2
按隶属关系分	**Grouped by Administrative Relationship**			
# 中央	Central	1830990	1654680	110.7
地方	Local	3367399	3186585	105.7
按行业分	**Grouped by Sector**			
农、林、牧、渔业	Farming,Forestry,Animal Husbandry and Fishery	31434	39256	80.1
# 农业	Farming	3533	11589	30.5
采掘业	Excavation	36945	42694	86.5
制造业	Manufacturing	1316529	1291802	101.9
电力、煤气及水的生产和供应业	Electricity,Gas,Water Production and Supply	63888	57538	111.0
建筑业	Construction	619696	614406	100.9
地质勘查业水利管理业	Geological Prospecting and Water Conservancy	19407	14517	133.7
交通运输、仓储及邮电通信业	Transportation,Storage,Posts and Telecommunications Services	265270	253052	104.8
# 交通运输业	Transportation	180924	183712	98.5
邮电通信业	Posts and Telecommunications Services	71188	62691	113.6
批发和零售贸易餐饮业	Wholesale, Retail and Catering	609684	582863	104.6
# 批发业	Wholesale	259880	265060	98.0
零售业	Retail	271635	254431	106.8
餐饮业	Catering	71228	59927	118.9
金融、保险业	Banking and Insurance	152731	137432	111.1
房地产业	Real Estate	132545	102651	129.1
社会服务业	Social Services	717604	613902	116.9
# 居民服务业	Residents Services	25463	29718	85.7
旅馆业	Hotels	159184	142275	111.9
卫生体育和社会福利业	Health Care,Sports and Social Welfare	197004	157944	124.7
# 卫生	Health Care	179542	142983	125.6
体育	Sports	12379	10434	118.6
教育、文化艺术和广播电影电视业	Education,Culture,Art, Radio,Film and Television	542418	466968	116.2
教育	Education	405330	356632	113.7
文化艺术业	Culture and Art	101611	81809	124.2
广播电影电视业	Radio,Film and Television	35476	28526	124.4
科学研究和综合技术服务业	Scientific Research and Polytechnical Services	384399	340656	112.8
科学研究业	Scientific Research	184310	196900	93.6
综合技术服务业	Polytechnical Services	200089	143756	139.2
国家机关、政党机关和社会团体	Government Organs,Party Organs and Social Bodies	387520	343219	112.9
其他行业	Others	104779	88732	118.1

3-9 续表 continued

单位：万元 (10000 yuan)

项目	Item	1998
总　计	**Total**	**5581851**
按登记注册类型分	**Grouped by Registered Type**	
内资经济	Domestic Investment Economy	4947772
国有经济	State-owned	3919010
集体经济	Collective-owned	450010
联营经济	Joint-owned	59308
股份有限公司	Share Holding Company	234898
有限责任公司	Limited-Liability Company	229306
股份合作企业	Share Holding Cooperative	53703
其他经济	Others	1537
外商投资经济	Foreign Funded	434192
港、澳、台商投资经济	Hongkong,Macao and Taiwan Funded	199885

3-10 职 工 平 均 工 资
AVERAGE WAGE OF STAFF AND WORKERS

单位：元 (yuan)

项目	Item	1998	1997	1998年为1997年% 1998 as % of 1997
总计	**Total**	**12285**	**11019**	**111.5**
按经济类型分	**Grouped by Ownership**			
国有经济	State-Owned	11971	10907	109.8
集体经济	Collective-Owned	8800	8259	106.6
联营经济	Joint Owned	10280	9918	103.6
股份制经济	Share Holding	13482	12864	104.8
外商投资经济	Foreign Funded	21948	18058	121.5
港、澳、台投资经济	Hongkong,Macao and Taiwan Funded	17021	14945	113.9
其他经济	Others	10773	37094	29.0
按隶属关系分	**Grouped by Administrative Relationship**			
# 中央	Central	13671	12144	112.6
地方	Local	11441	10455	109.4
按行业分	**Grouped by Sector**			
农、林、牧、渔业	Farming,Forestry,Animal Husbandry and Fishery	8254	7054	117.0
# 农业	Farming	7054	6099	115.7
采掘业	Excavation	9714	10261	94.7
制造业	Manufacturing	10602	9964	106.4
电力、煤气及水的生产和供应业	Electricity,Gas,Water Production and Supply	15076	13365	112.8
建筑业	Construction	10777	10111	106.6
地质勘查业水利管理业	Geological Prospecting and Water Conservancy	11668	9550	122.2
交通运输、仓储及邮电通信业	Transportation,Storage,Posts and Telecommunications Services	13183	12173	108.3
# 交通运输业	Transportation	12443	11661	106.7
邮电通信业	Posts and Telecommunications Services	16639	14423	115.4
批发和零售贸易餐饮业	Wholesale, Retail and Catering	11329	10418	108.7
# 批发业	Wholesale	12462	10750	115.9
零售业	Retail	10260	9946	103.2
餐饮业	Catering	11618	10889	106.7
金融、保险业	Banking and Insurance	21718	19017	114.2
房地产业	Real Estate	16311	15355	106.2
社会服务业	Social Services	14280	12802	111.5
# 居民服务业	Residents Services	10058	8720	115.3
旅馆业	Hotels	13750	12531	109.7
卫生体育和社会福利业	Health Care,Sports and Social Welfare	14616	11709	124.8
# 卫生	Health Care	14654	11692	125.3
体育	Sports	15412	12901	119.5
教育、文化艺术和广播电影电视业	Education,Culture,Art, Radio,Film and Television	12959	11126	116.5
教育	Education	12207	10668	114.4
文化艺术业	Culture and Art	14720	12264	120.0
广播电影电视业	Radio,Film and Television	20262	15254	132.8
科学研究和综合技术服务业	Scientific Research and Polytechnical Services	14133	11844	119.3
科学研究业	Scientific Research	13052	11202	116.5
综合技术服务业	Polytechnical Services	15300	12852	119.0
国家机关、政党机关和社会团体	Government Organs,Party Organs and Social Bodies	12301	10698	115.0
其他行业	Others	18073	14139	127.8

3-10 续表 continued

单位：元 (yuan)

项目	Item	1998
总 计	**Total**	**12285**
按登记注册类型分	**Grouped by Registered Type**	
内资经济	Domestic Investment Economy	
国有经济	State-owned	11971
集体经济	Collective-owned	8800
联营经济	Joint-owned	10280
股份有限公司	Share Holding Company	14559
有限责任公司	Limited-Liability Company	13873
股份合作企业	Share Holding Cooperative	9336
其他经济	Others	10773
外商投资经济	Foreign Funded	21948
港、澳、台商投资经济	Hongkong,Macao and Taiwan Funded	17021

3-11 国民经济各行业职工工资总额及平均工资

行业	Sector	工资总额 (万元) Total Wages (10000 yuan)	# 中央 Central	# 地方 Local	国有经济 State-Owned
总计	**Total**	**5581851**	**1830990**	**3367399**	**3919010**
农、林、牧、渔业	**Farming,Forestry,Animal Husbandry and Fishery**	**31434**	**2180**	**29084**	**27304**
# 农、林、牧、渔服务业	FFAF Services	9563	1790	7655	9090
采掘业	**Excavation**	**36945**	**345**	**36600**	**36643**
制造业	**Manufacturing**	**1316529**	**233825**	**1041936**	**742973**
食品加工业	Food Processing	23559	877	21086	12166
食品制造业	Food Making	40015	564	36109	14731
饮料制造业	Beverage Manufacturing	29325	269	27779	11867
烟草制造业	Tobacco Processing	2204	13	2191	2191
纺织业	Textile Industry	51770	100	51389	31522
服装及其他纤维制品制造业	Garments and Other Fiber Products	33764	1786	27677	8075
皮革、毛皮、羽绒及其制品业	Leather,Furs,Down and Related Products	7034	189	6058	2964
木材加工及竹、藤、棕、革制品业	Timber Processing,Bamboo,Cane, Palm Fiber and Straw Products	4888	675	3831	3716
家具制造业	Furniture Manufacturing	7576	720	4480	1883
造纸及纸制品业	Papermaking and Paper Products	11960	427	11006	6111
印刷业、记录媒介的复制	Printing and Record Medium Reproduced	51263	31754	18159	38442
文教体育用品制造业	Stationery,Education and Sports Goods	10356	489	9313	5873
石油加工及炼焦业	Petroleum Processing and Coking Products	65371	63012	2297	63153
化学原料及化学制品制造业	Raw Chemical Materials and Chemical Products	64521	1779	61705	20235
医药制造业	Medical and Pharmaceutical Products	32946	3068	28575	19990
化学纤维制造业	Chemical Fibers	4747	6	4688	2450
橡胶制品业	Rubber Products	10404	611	9761	7652
塑料制品业	Plastic Products	17281	966	15833	6481
非金属矿物制品业	Nonmetal Mineral Products	79706	3121	74350	26795
黑色金属冶炼及压延加工业	Smelting and Pressing Ferrous Metals	186944	66	186867	178885
有色金属冶炼及压延加工业	Smelting and Pressing of Non-ferrous Metals	4718	27	4620	2482
金属制品业	Metal Products	28060	3060	22933	10259
普通机械制造业	Ordinary Machinery	68529	11826	55485	40308
专业设备制造业	Special Purpose Equipment	77477	13953	59473	37771
交通运输设备制造业	Transportation Equipment	124628	55609	67297	70751
武器弹药制造业	Weapons and Ammunition	11816	11816		11816
电气机械及器材制造业	Electric Equipment and Machine	58545	4787	51499	32059
电子及通信设备制造业	Electronic and Telecommunication	136760	14591	118221	50197
仪器仪表及文化办公用机械制造业	Instruments,Meters,Cultural and Official Machinery	52122	6576	44155	17889
其他制造业	Other Manufacturing	18240	1087	15096	4258
电力、煤气及水的生产和供应业	**Electricity,Gas and Water Production and Supply**	**63888**	**20984**	**42904**	**62410**
电力、蒸气、热水的生产和供应业	Electricity,Steam and Hot Water Production and Supply	43708	20952	22756	42262
煤气生产和供应业	Gas Production and Supply	11455	32	11423	11423
自来水的生产和供应业	Water Production and Supply	8725		8725	8725
建筑业	**Construction**	**619696**	**194617**	**369818**	**402899**
土木工程建筑业	Civil Engineering	479632	139848	303685	330232
线路、管道和设备安装业	Pipeline and Equipment Installation	110111	48640	54556	64211
建筑物的装修装饰业	Building Completion	29953	6129	11577	8456
地质勘查业、水利管理业	**Geological Prospecting and Water Conservancy**	**19407**	**7195**	**12204**	**19266**
地质勘查业	Geological Prospecting	7222	5782	1432	7214
水利管理业	Water Conservancy	12185	1413	10772	12052

TOTAL WAGES AND AVERAGE WAGE OF STAFF AND WORKERS BY DIFFERENT TRADES OF NATIONAL ECONOMY

				平均工资			
# 中 央 Central	# 地 方 Local	集体经济 Collective-Owned	其他经济 Others	(元) Average Wage (yuan)	国有经济 State-Owned	集体经济 Collective-Owned	其他经济 Others
1576796	**2295101**	**450010**	**1212831**	**12285**	**11971**	**8800**	**15989**
1908	**25396**	**537**	**3593**	**8254**	**8276**	**6783**	**8357**
1783	7307	349	125	10972	11178	6794	17536
345	**36299**	**301**		**9714**	**9793**	**4917**	
192299	**550673**	**117301**	**456256**	**10602**	**9852**	**7112**	**14137**
354	11813	472	10920	8603	6830	7288	12234
118	14614	1439	23845	11040	8177	5588	15231
50	11817	1690	15768	10480	8414	9699	12992
	2191	13		20639	20770	10011	
14	31508	3149	17100	7997	8085	4858	8874
1552	6523	7061	18628	7482	7553	5077	9075
	2964	1857	2213	6524	5774	6069	8547
563	3153	374	798	8239	8821	5207	7968
389	1494	1346	4347	9107	7986	7338	10533
283	5827	1075	4775	9312	7680	5886	15603
28980	9462	5285	7536	11624	11565	8214	17023
82	5791	1889	2594	9383	9971	6586	11384
62621	532	482	1737	13207	13301	11689	10822
337	19898	3012	41275	11320	8030	8500	14608
2959	17031	1072	11884	12262	11045	9256	15612
6	2444	58	2239	6172	5011	4944	8342
153	7499	1672	1079	7461	7669	5783	10042
320	6161	3019	7781	7871	6954	6424	9805
2432	24364	7574	45337	10136	8797	6323	12523
	178885	918	7141	11079	11077	8704	11529
23	2459	898	1338	9239	8049	9260	12707
1396	8863	7908	9892	7852	7255	6569	10350
5663	34645	8929	19292	8799	7970	7060	13161
12075	25697	11837	27869	10735	9489	9174	14317
44980	25771	10987	42891	10271	9786	6719	13119
11816				9040	9040		
3769	28290	11102	15384	9464	9193	6912	14083
5682	44515	9864	76698	16582	14046	10699	20443
5382	12508	4371	29862	16628	9358	8478	42219
303	3956	7949	6034	8732	8462	6843	14227
20026	**42384**	**834**	**644**	**15076**	**15058**	**16982**	**14605**
20026	22236	834	612	15712	15707	16982	14572
	11423		32	14005	14002		15264
	8725			13673	13673		
154094	**231891**	**110620**	**106177**	**10777**	**10553**	**9527**	**13767**
123562	190271	72364	77036	10397	10164	8850	14094
27011	36887	31528	14372	12791	13057	11983	13562
3521	4733	6727	14770	10851	10982	8372	12443
7195	**12071**	**133**	**8**	**11668**	**11705**	**8026**	**10250**
5782	1432		8	11600	11601		10250
1413	10639	133		11709	11769	8026	

3-11 续表 1 continued

行业	Sector	工资总额 (万元) Total Wages (10000 yuan)	# 中央 Central	# 地方 Local	国有经济 State-Owned
交通运输、仓储及邮电通信业	**Transportation,Storage,Posts and Telecommunications**	**265270**	**198903**	**62650**	**240411**
铁路运输业	Railway	83202	82989	213	83202
公路运输业	Highway	27362	2733	24074	18258
航空运输业	Airway	19932	19654		16716
交通运输辅助业	Transportation Subsidiary	50427	22655	26532	44215
仓储业	Storage	13157	2079	10817	11565
邮电通信业	Posts and Telecommunications	71188	68793	1013	66454
批发和零售贸易餐饮业	**Wholesale,Retail and Catering**	**609684**	**135279**	**395663**	**341708**
批发业	Wholesale	259880	95336	134834	175758
零售业	Retail	271635	23018	218497	138721
商业经纪与代理业	Commercial Management and Agency	6942	6168	584	6623
餐饮业	Catering	71228	10756	41748	20606
金融、保险业	**Banking and Insurance**	**152731**	**134214**	**8167**	**94529**
金融业	Banking	142150	124527	7273	90190
保险业	Insurance	10581	9687	894	4339
房地产业	**Real Estate**	**132545**	**22006**	**94104**	**69880**
房地产开发与经营业	Real Estate Development	62724	7360	48655	30965
房地产管理业	Real Estate Management	68017	14615	44120	37776
房地产代理与经纪业	Real Estate Brokerage and Agency	1803	31	1330	1140
社会服务业	**Social Services**	**717604**	**147899**	**440151**	**418445**
公共设施服务业	Public Utilities	239712	6792	202060	208280
# 市内公共交通业	Public Transportation in City	155372	3082	122877	132734
# 市内公共汽电车业	Public Bus and Trolleybus	82509		82509	82502
园林绿化业	Gardens Afforest	24770	265	24425	23336
环境卫生业	Environmental Sanitation	35625	394	35055	33902
市政工程管理业	Municipal Engineering Management	13067	99	12854	12094
居民服务业	Residential Services	25463	4733	17267	13303
旅馆业	Hotels	159184	58461	87385	66811
租赁服务业	Leasing	5790	2433	1779	2259
旅游业	Tourism	17163	10739	6260	15157
娱乐服务业	Recreation	12627	2127	6787	1860
信息、咨询服务业	Information and Consultancy Services	110299	36898	25501	33402
# 广告业	Advertisement	13286	4581	3055	3732
咨询服务业	Consultancy Services	17405	4965	10191	4863
计算机应用服务业	Computer Application Services	59229	8936	37306	14844
其他社会服务业	Other Social Services	88136	16779	55807	62530
# 市场管理服务业	Market Management Services	25046	180	24694	24227
卫生、体育和社会福利业	**Health Care,Sports and Social Welfare**	**197004**	**67277**	**128976**	**184961**
卫生	Health Care	179542	62296	116624	168754
体育	Sports	12379	4877	7402	11615
社会服务保障业	Social Welfare	5083	104	4950	4593
教育、文化艺术及广播电影电视业	**Education,Culture and Arts, Radio, Film and Television**	**542418**	**222679**	**316396**	**531105**
教育	Education	405330	122373	281294	396931
高等教育	Higher Education	140833	106813	33844	140405
普通高等教育	Ordinary Higher Education	126118	98722	27396	126118
成人高等教育	Adult Higher Education	14715	8091	6448	14287

3-11 续表 2 continued

# 中 央 Central	# 地 方 Local	集体经济 Collective-Owned	其他经济 Others	平均工资 (元) Average Wage (yuan)	国有经济 State-Owned	集体经济 Collective-Owned	其他经济 Others
187398	**52749**	**10255**	**14603**	**13183**	**13123**	**8573**	**24090**
82989	213			12676	12676		
1528	16730	7772	1332	8220	7832	8298	21772
16716			3216	16130	14893		28388
18327	25624	680	5532	14782	14082	10728	26584
1755	9811	1065	527	10087	10095	8073	19674
66083	371	739	3995	16639	16542	11491	20301
105002	**232967**	**94397**	**173579**	**11329**	**11822**	**8242**	**12899**
83874	90255	41420	42701	12462	13707	8763	12921
13221	124121	44191	88723	10260	10097	7777	12577
6053	570	14	305	19653	19935	9172	15652
1854	18021	8773	41849	11618	10250	8418	13594
92090	**2066**	**6073**	**52129**	**21718**	**19616**	**7803**	**36324**
87751	2066	6073	45887	21798	19936	7803	37647
4339			6241	20698	14710		28869
9918	**59512**	**3382**	**59283**	**16311**	**14403**	**11153**	**19953**
5020	25821	948	30812	20709	17222	11687	26798
4868	32581	2324	27918	13618	12629	10792	15613
29	1110	110	553	17558	18179	16194	16664
92653	**303433**	**61067**	**238092**	**14280**	**12632**	**11916**	**19837**
3178	190966	21677	9756	14663	14160	28391	11135
2008	116598	17868	4769	15066	14181	38810	9682
	82502	8		13699	13699	10821	
261	23074	166	1268	12843	12782	7330	15790
65	33837	313	1410	14691	15214	5862	9843
	12094	356	616	15365	15242	19346	16004
2262	11009	7476	4684	10058	11470	7973	10791
29278	31036	7525	84849	13750	11095	8463	18183
1429	831	649	2881	12348	10764	8541	15746
10450	4700	269	1738	13587	13713	8115	13926
149	1691	445	10322	14107	11393	8587	15179
25269	7892	9229	67668	19238	15269	11017	24988
2553	1160	2110	7444	14469	15576	10393	15652
2879	1984	780	11762	25101	22388	19958	26909
7243	7594	4656	39729	20212	15746	10668	25610
13396	47714	9142	16464	10362	9435	8314	21143
173	24054	261	559	14790	15282	7445	7641
66655	**118307**	**10350**	**1693**	**14616**	**14799**	**11523**	**20719**
62108	106646	10193	595	14654	14857	11694	27153
4465	7150	39	726	15412	15454	6422	15917
81	4512	118	372	12014	11825	5745	26218
220749	**310351**	**6723**	**4590**	**12959**	**12984**	**9806**	**17173**
121433	275498	6320	2079	12207	12231	9731	20205
106561	33844	56	372	12222	12228	9571	10579
98722	27396			12247	12247		
7839	6448	56	372	12009	12064	9571	10579

3-11 续表 3 continued

行业 Sector		工资总额 (万元) Total Wages (10000 yuan)	# 中央 Central	# 地方 Local	国有经济 State-Owned
中等教育	Secondary School Education	139993	6528	132783	137219
中等专业学校	Specialized Secondary Schools	16815	1229	15548	16464
普通中学	Regular Secondary Schools	98529	4506	93418	96439
农业、职业中学	Agricultural and Vocational Schools	16144	10	16112	16121
技工学校	Technical Schools	3464	357	3107	3322
成人中等学校	Adult Secondary Schools	4457	361	4079	4287
工读学校	Schools for Juvenile Delinquents	585	65	520	585
初等教育	Primary Education	89468	1315	87716	89031
小学校	Primary Schools	89394	1315	87642	88957
成人初等学校	Adult Primary Schools	74		74	74
学前教育	Preschool Education	13637	2246	11392	11370
特殊教育	Special Education	1068	127	924	1051
其他教育	Other Education	20332	5344	14636	17855
文化艺术业	Culture and Arts	101611	75570	24682	99394
艺术	Arts	12223	7546	4630	11991
出版	Publication	62925	53063	9652	62115
文物保护	Protection of Historical Relics	6521	3959	2378	6313
图书馆	Library	3831	2695	1136	3831
档案馆	Archives	1267	737	530	1267
群众文化	Mass Culture	4512	393	4094	4485
新闻	News	5372	5318	54	5372
文化艺术经纪与代理业	Cultural Art Brokerage	1895	1015	737	1746
其他文化艺术业	Other Cultural Art	3065	845	1470	2274
广播电影电视业	Radio,Film and Television	35476	24736	10420	34780
广播	Radio	7682	5154	2528	7682
电影	Film	6846	4519	2139	6528
电视	Television	20949	15063	5753	20570
科学研究和综合技术服务	**Scientific Research and Polytechical Services**	**384399**	**246547**	**124264**	**295145**
科学研究业	Scientific Research	184310	166829	16337	183890
自然科学研究	Natural Science Research	121893	110005	11843	121477
社会科学研究	Social Science Research	8085	7477	608	8085
其他科学研究	Other Scientific Research	54332	49347	3887	54328
综合技术服务业	Polytechnical Services	200089	79718	107927	111255
气象	Atmospheric	3220	2988	232	3220
地震	Seismology	1449	1366	83	1449
测绘	Surveying and Mapping	2547	700	1847	2486
技术监督	Technology Supervisor	12346	6869	5295	11792
海洋环境	Sea and Ocean Environments	308	308		308
环境保护	Environmental Protection	2222	306	1668	1464
技术推广和科技交流服务业	Technology Promotion and Exchange Services	18802	5666	9235	7857
工程设计业	Engineering Design	51420	36348	13589	44803
其他综合技术服务业	Other Polytechnical Services	107776	25168	75979	37876
国家机关、政党机关和社会团体	**Government Organs,Party Organs and Social Bodies**	**387520**	**149038**	**237304**	**387383**
国家机关	Government Organs	361516	131385	228988	361516
政党机关	Party Organs	12949	7491	5458	12949
社会团体	Social Bodies	13054	10162	2858	12918
其他行业	**Other Sectors**	**104779**	**48003**	**27176**	**63949**

3-11 续表 4 continued

				平均工资			
# 中 央 Central	# 地 方 Local	集体经济 Collective-Owned	其他经济 Others	(元) Average Wage (yuan)	国有经济 State-Owned	集体经济 Collective-Owned	其他经济 Others
6188	131032	2022	752	12952	12968	9947	30804
1229	15235	313	38	11998	12055	10017	8293
4297	92142	1401	689	13116	13128	9555	35696
10	16112		22	13152	13134		
357	2966	142		12564	12642	10971	
230	4057	167	2	12699	12688	13289	4850
65	520			14266	14266		
1315	87716		437	11303	11279		20416
1315	87642		437	11304	11279		20416
	74			10879	10879		
2246	9124	2267		11533	12102	9330	
127	924	17		11594	11648	9006	
4996	12859	1958	518	12083	12186	10018	23660
74849	24540	291	1926	14720	14751	9824	14258
7431	4556	51	182	11311	11370	6418	9975
52478	9637	181	629	16592	16560	14482	21686
3959	2354		208	12892	12807		16147
2695	1136			12254	12254		
737	530			12198	12198		
393	4093	1	25	11798	11838	4062	7816
5318	54			12146	12146		
1012	733	5	144	22090	23816	3971	12898
827	1447	53	738	15549	17642	6931	12179
24467	10313	111	585	20262	20279	17147	19970
5154	2528			14669	14669		
4485	2042	32	286	11726	11661	8804	14031
14828	5742	80	299	32559	32568	27504	33581
235501	**58432**	**17910**	**71345**	**14133**	**13694**	**10427**	**18167**
166829	15940	88	332	13052	13044	7492	28602
110005	11449	85	332	13153	13141	7316	28602
7477	608			10233	10233		
49437	3883	4		13371	13371	17717	
68672	42492	17821	71013	15300	14921	10447	18136
2988	232			13246	13246		
1366	83			10951	10951		
700	1786	61		14816	14995	9949	
6757	5035	99	454	14455	14338	11431	19756
308				9271	9271		
250	1214	172	586	14161	15205	9582	13727
4062	3729	2221	8724	13948	11762	10050	19005
33493	11310	1443	5174	16374	16315	10261	20403
18748	19103	13826	56075	15402	14860	10542	17874
148943	**237297**	**68**	**69**	**12301**	**12302**	**8662**	**11513**
131385	228988			12320	12320		
7491	5458			11191	11191		
10067	2851	68	69	13025	13068	8662	11513
42020	**21273**	**10060**	**30770**	**18073**	**14212**	**15248**	**48206**

3-12 分地区职工人数、平均工资
NUMBER OF STAFF AND WORKERS,AVERAGE WAGE BY REGION

地区	Region	职工人数(人) Staff and Workers (person) 1998	1997	平均工资(元) Average Wage (yuan) 1998	1997
全市	**Total**	**4500635**	**4653489**	**12285**	**11019**
城区	**City Proper**	**1440433**	**1463325**	**13155**	**11806**
东城区	Dongcheng	437364	448899	13462	11883
西城区	Xicheng	580036	572939	13970	12599
崇文区	Chongwen	142699	153174	11432	9952
宣武区	Xuanwu	280334	288313	11908	11126
近郊区	**Near Suburbs**	**2289480**	**2377452**	**12523**	**11205**
朝阳区	Chaoyang	874995	852858	13203	11963
丰台区	Fengtai	382792	398247	10074	9172
石景山区	Shijingshan	296310	318507	10380	10153
海淀区	Haidian	735383	807840	13840	11811
远郊区	**Outer Suburbs**	**290431**	**324339**	**10223**	**10202**
门头沟区	Mentougou	74420	83407	9329	9056
房山区	Fangshan	130831	139688	11764	10855
通州区	Tongzhou	85180	101244	8644	7805
各县	**Counties**	**478470**	**487392**	**9202**	**8160**
昌平县	Changping	116822	122820	8549	7970
顺义县	Shunyi	75817	77257	9274	7996
大兴县	Daxing	108901	102360	10459	9310
平谷县	Pinggu	49464	55010	8027	7248
怀柔县	Huairou	42445	43420	9770	8925
密云县	Miyun	49014	50002	8823	7790
延庆县	Yanqing	36007	36523	8867	7981
外地	**Nonlocal**	**1821**	**981**	**11702**	**7096**

注：由于口径调整，1997年数字与1998年年鉴不一致。

Note: As standard counted is adjusted,data of 1997 is different from that of "1998 Beijing Statistical Yearbook".

主要统计指标解释

从业人员 指从事一定社会劳动并取得劳动报酬或经营收入的人员。包括：（1）全部职工（2）再就业的离退休人员（3）私营业主（4）个体户主（5）私营和个体从业人员（6）乡镇企业从业人员（7）农村从业人员（8）其他从业人员（包括民办教师、宗教职业者、现役军人等）

这一指标反映了一定时期内全部劳动力资源的实际利用情况，是研究我国基本国情国力的重要指标。

职工 指在国有经济、城镇集体经济、联营经济、股份合作经济、股份有限公司、有限责任公司、外商和港、澳、台商投资经济、其他经济及其附属机构工作，并由其支付工资的各类人员。

职工工资总额 指各单位在一定时期内直接支付给本单位全部职工的劳动报酬总额。

工资总额的计算原则应以直接支付给职工的全部劳动报酬为根据。各单位支付给职工的劳动报酬以及其他根据有关规定支付的工资，不论是计入成本的还是不计入成本的，不论是按国家规定列入计征奖金税项目的，还是未列入计征奖金税项目的，不论是以货币形式支付的还是以实物形式支付的，均包括在工资总额内。

职工平均工资 指企业、事业、机关单位的职工在一定时期内平均每人所得的货币工资额。它表明一定时期职工工资收入的高低程度，是反映职工工资水平的主要指标。计算公式为：

$$\text{职工平均工资}=\frac{\text{报告期实际支付的全部职工工资总额}}{\text{报告期全部职工平均人数}}$$

Explanatory Notes On Main Statistical Indicators

Employment refers to the persons who are engaged in social labor and receive payment or earn business income, including:（1）all staff and workers,（2）re-employed retirees ,（3）owners of private enterprises,（4）owners of individual business,（5）employed persons in private enterprises and individual business,（6）employed persons in the township and village enterprises,（7）employed persons in agriculture,（8）other employed persons （including teachers in the schools run by the local people , people engaged in religious profession and the servicemen, etc.）.

This indicator reflects the actual utilization of total labor force during a certain period of time and is often used for the research on China's economic affairs and national power.

Staff and Workers refer to the persons who work in （and receive payment therefrom）enterprises and institutions of state-owned,collective-owned,share holding cooperative,share holding company,limited-liability company, and foreign, HongKong, Macao, Taiwan funded, and other types of ownership and their affiliated units.

Total Wages of Staff and Workers refer to the total remuneration payment to staff and workers in various units during a certain period of time.

The calculation of total wages is based on the total remuneration payment to the staff and workers. Therefore, all the wages and salaries and other payments to staff and workers are included in the total wages regardless of their sources, categories, and forms（in kind or cash）.

Average Wage of Staff and Workers refers to the average wage in money terms per employed person during a certain period of time for staff and workers in enterprises, institutions and government agencies, which reflects the general level of wage income during a certain period of time, and is calculated as follows:

$$\text{Average Wage of Staff and Workers} = \frac{\text{Total Wages of Staff and Workers}}{\text{Average Number of Staff and Workers}}$$

1999

固定资产投资及房地产业

INVESTMENT IN FIXED ASSETS AND REAL ESTATE

城市基础设施投资占固定资产投资比重(1978-1998)

tio of Municipal Infrastructure Investment to Total Investment in Fixed Assets

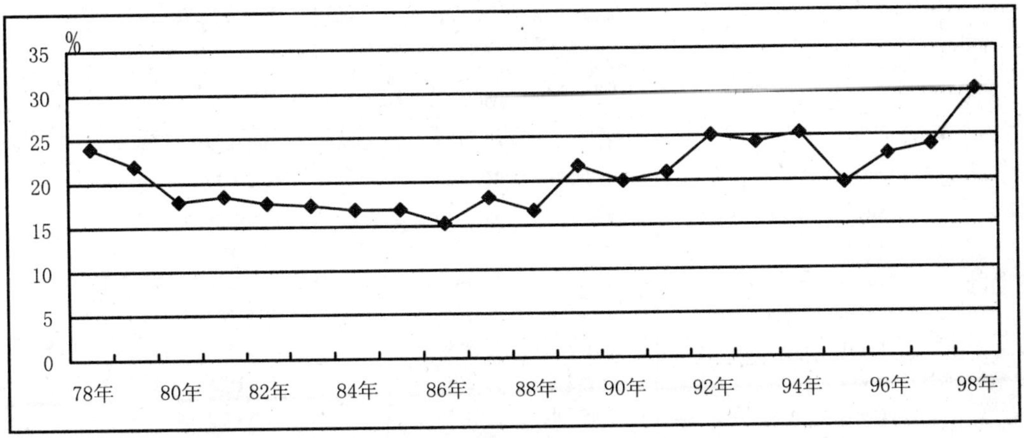

单位:亿元(100 million yuan)

	1998	1997
全社会固定资产投资额 Investment in Fixed Assets	1115.3	961.2
基本建设 Capital Construction	415.5	374.3
更新改造 Innovation	252.4	191.2
房地产开发 Real Estate Development	377.4	330.3

房屋建筑每平方米造价（元）

Cost Per SQ.M OF Buildings(yuan)

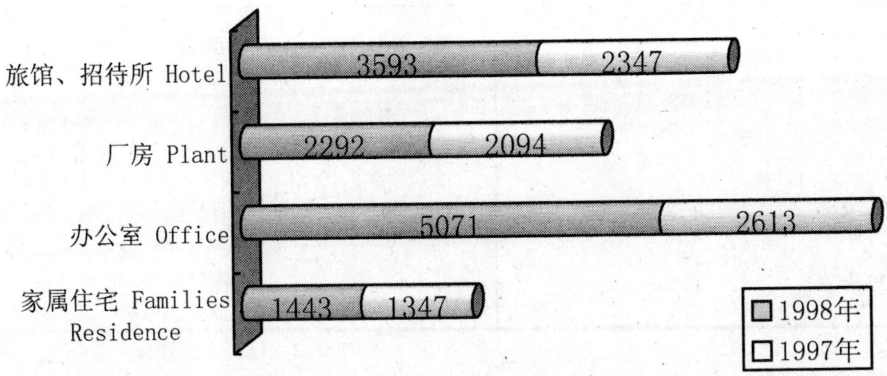

4-1 全社会固定资产投资额
TOTAL INVESTMENT IN FIXED ASSETS

单位：万元 (10000 yuan)

项目	Item	1998 合计 Total	1998 #国有 State-Owned	1998 #集体 Collective Owned	1997 合计 Total	1997 #国有 State-Owned	1997 #集体 Collective Owned
投资总额	**Total**	**11153389**	**6984015**	**664612**	**9611680**	**6057079**	**546687**
#地　方	Local	7324091	3673924	656390	6174979	3161798	532943
固定资产投资	Investment in Fixed Assets	6829237	5924236	119613	5820764	4734588	116452
#地方	Local	3319283	2702660	119613	2693004	1926408	116452
基本建设投资	Capital Construction	4155182	3541432		3743212	2941258	
中央	Central	2506556	2237446		2233708	1930241	
地方	Local	1648626	1303986		1509504	1011017	
更新改造措施	Innovation	2524288	2352650		1911525	1743755	
中央	Central	1003398	984130		894052	877939	
地方	Local	1520890	1368520		1017473	865816	
其他投资	Others	149767	30154	119613	166027	49575	116452
房地产开发	Real Estate Development	3773996	996642	105604	3303366	1272297	32191
#地方	Local	3478327	927067	102117	3022486	1208726	22978
零星固定资产建造及购置	Building and Purchase of Odd Fixed Assets	78921	63137	15784	63137	50194	12943
农村集体投资	Rural Collective Investment	423611		423611	385101		385101
城乡私人建房投资	Buildings Construction by Individuals	47624			39312		
城镇	Urban	22672			18519		
乡村	Rural	24952			20793		

4-2 产业投资及比重
INVESTMENT AND PERCENTAGE BY INDUSTRY

项目	Item	投资额(万元) Investment(10000 yuan) 1998	投资额(万元) Investment(10000 yuan) 1997	比重(%) Percentage(%) 1998	比重(%) Percentage(%) 1997
总　　计	**Total**	**6829237**	**5820764**	**100**	**100**
第一产业	Primary Industry	15226	9067	0.2	0.2
第二产业	Secondary Industry	2017281	2011328	29.5	34.5
第三产业	Tertiary Industry	4796730	3800369	70.3	65.3

注：本表不含房地产投资。

Note：Data of this table exclude investment in real estate.

4-3 全市固定资产投资额
INVESTMENT IN FIXED ASSETS OF THE CITY

单位：万元 (10000 yuan)

项目 Item		1998			1997		
		合计 Total	# 基本建设 Capital Construction	# 更新改造 Technical Updating and Transformation	合计 Total	# 基本建设 Capital Construction	# 更新改造 Technical Updating and Transformation
投资额	**Total**	**6829237**	**4155182**	**2524288**	**5820764**	**3743212**	**1911525**
按构成分	**Grouped by Use of Fund**						
建筑安装工程	Construction and Installation	3761993	2601851	1053450	3382014	2338565	907650
设备工器具购置	Purchases of Equipments and Instruments	1576605	718836	837479	1424563	708094	707618
其他	Others	1490639	834495	633359	1014187	696553	296257
按用途分	**Grouped by User**						
农林牧渔业用	Farming,Forestry, Animal Husbandry and Fishery	2037	1435	602	7650	1202	6022
工业、建筑业用	Industry,Construction	1682749	1011303	632775	1708969	1066145	609138
商业、运输邮电业用	Commerce,Transportation,Posts and Tele communications	1955743	684538	1243951	1326652	484355	778955
住宅	Residence	1060692	843968	162075	932743	722037	160596
其他	Others	2128016	1613938	484885	1844750	1469473	356814
更新改造投资按用途分	**Grouped by Effect of Investment in Innovation**						
增产	Increase Production	206871		206871	309357		309357
节约能源	Economize on Energy	21062		21062	18774		18774
其他节约	Other Economy	933		933	4580		4580
增加品种	Increase Varieties	67400		67400	62946		62946
提高产品质量	Improve Quality of Products	36358		36358	42797		42797
三废治理	Deal with the Three Wastes	51681		51681	51099		51099
其他	Others	2139983		2139983	1421972		1421972
按建设性质分	**Grouped by Feature of Construction**						
新建	New Construction	1638524	1196701	437531	1441386	1250778	180134
改建和扩建	Replacement and Expanding	4483048	2559533	1822482	3776620	2124370	1550027
单纯建造生活设施	Living Installation	535909	363517	131870	409480	295146	67271
迁建和恢复	Movement and Recovery	103155	32235	67990	112685	68648	38373
单纯购置设备	Purchase of Equipment	68601	3196	64415	80593	4270	75720

4-3 续表1 continued

单位：万元 (10000 yuan)

项目 Item		1998 合计 Total	1998 # 基本建设 Capital Construction	1998 # 更新改造 Technical Updating and Transformation	1997 合计 Total	1997 # 基本建设 Capital Construction	1997 # 更新改造 Technical Updating and Transformation
按建设项目规模分	**Grouped by Size of Construction Projects**						
基本建设大中型项目	Large and Medium Projects of Capital Construction	826628	826628		724958	724958	
基本建设小型项目	Small Projects of Capital Construction	3325358	3325358		3013984	3013984	
更新改造限额以上项目	Projects of Technical Updating and Transformation above the Limits	1281211		1281211	779148		779148
更新改造限额以下项目	Projects of Technical Updating and Transformation below the Limits	1178662		1178662	1056657		1056657
其他	Others	217378	3196	64415	246017	4270	75720
按经济类型分	**Grouped by Ownership**						
国有经济	State-Owned	5924236	3541432	2352650	4734588	2941258	1743755
集体经济	Collective Owned	119613			116452		
联营经济	Joint Owned	19757	15634	4123	7945	7945	
股份有限公司	Share Holding Company	54083	29250	24833	21284	15553	5731
有限责任公司	Limited-Liability Company	51666	17211	34455	12472	10456	2016
中外合资经营	Joint Venture	289461	216064	73397	635980	557593	78387
中外合作经营	Cooperative	33138	33138		103814	101239	2575
外资企业	Foreign Enterprises	10703	10703		32239	32239	
港澳台与大陆合资经营	Joint Venture with Hongkong,Macao and Taiwan	196402	168139	28263	78651	2933	75718
港澳台与大陆合作经营	Cooperative Enterprises with HongKong Macao and Taiwan	108825	106520	2305	41291	38366	2925
港澳台独资企业	Hongkong,Macao and Taiwan Enterprises	7863	7863		26113	26113	
其他经济	Others	13490	9228	4262	9935	9517	418

注：本表及以下各表包括基本建设、更新改造和其他投资，不含房地产开发投资。

Note：This table and its followings include capital constrution,technical updating and transformation and other investment,exclude real estate development investment.

4-3 续表2 continued

单位：万元 (10000 yuan)

项目	Item	合计 Total	# 基本建设 Capital Construction	# 更新改造 Technical Updating and Transformation
投资额	**Total**	**6829237**	**4155182**	**2524288**
按企业登记注册类型分	**Grouped by Type of Enterprises Registered**			
内资企业	Domestic Investment Enterprises	6182845	3612755	2420323
国有企业	State-Owned	5924236	3541432	2352650
集体企业	Collective Owned	119613		
联营企业	Joint Owned	19757	15634	4123
股份合作企业	Share Holding Cooperative	9008	9008	
股份有限公司	Share Holding Company	54083	29250	24833
有限责任公司	Limited-Liability Company	51666	17211	34455
其他企业	Others	4482	220	4262
港澳台商投资企业	Hongkong,Macao and Taiwan Funded Enterprises	313090	282522	30568
港澳台合资经营	Joint Venture	196402	168139	28263
港澳台合作经营	Cooperative	108825	106520	2305
港澳台商独资企业	Hongkong,Macao and Taiwan Enterprises	7863	7863	
港澳台商投资股份有限公司	Hongkong,Macao and Taiwan Funded Share Holing Company			
外商投资企业	Foreign Funded Enterprises	333302	259905	73397
中外合资经营	Joint Venture	289371	215974	73397
中外合作经营	Cooperative	33138	33138	
外资(独资)企业	Foreign Enterprises	10703	10703	
外商投资股份有限公司	Foreign Funded Share Holding Company	90	90	

4-4 地方固定资产投资额
LOCAL INVESTMENT IN FIXED ASSETS

单位：万元 (10000 yuan)

项 目 Item		1998 合 计 Total	1998 # 基本建设 Capital Construction	1998 # 更新改造 Technical Updating and Transformation	1997 合 计 Total	1997 # 基本建设 Capital Construction	1997 # 更新改造 Technical Updating and Transformation
投 资 额	**Total**	**3319283**	**1648626**	**1520890**	**2693004**	**1509504**	**1017473**
按构成分	**Grouped by Use of Fund**						
建筑安装工程	Construction and Installation	1922198	1034985	780521	1601608	897536	568273
设备工器具购置	Purchases of Equipments and Instruments	404721	182455	201976	570779	304517	257411
其他	Others	992364	431186	538393	520617	307451	191789
按用途分	**Grouped by User**						
农林牧渔业用	Farming,Forestry, Animal Husbandry and Fishery	2037	1435	602	7650	1202	6022
工业、建筑业用	Industry,Construction	879966	462130	379165	1027617	644284	349647
商业、运输邮电业用	Commerce,Transportation,Posts and Tele communications	683937	115700	540983	406173	124799	218032
住宅	Residence	486580	289902	142029	438869	260649	128110
其他	Others	1266763	779459	458111	812695	478570	315662
更新改造投资按用途分	**Grouped by Effect of Investment in Innovation**						
增产	Increase Production	144143		144143	130105		130105
节约能源	Economize on Energy	17690		17690	17795		17795
其他节约	Other Economy	883		883	3379		3379
增加品种	Increase Varieties	38037		38037	59258		59258
提高产品质量	Improve Quality of Products	27850		27850	32285		32285
三废治理	Deal with the Three Wastes	39129		39129	42502		42502
其他	Others	1253158		1253158	732149		732149
按建设性质分	**Grouped by Feature of Construction**						
新建	New Construction	1150287	708564	437431	855743	665135	180134
改建和扩建	Replacement and Expanding	1712959	759073	852853	1419920	657907	659790
单纯建造生活设施	Living Installation	332444	163757	128165	235989	121655	67271
迁建和恢复	Movement and Recovery	88027	17107	67990	108495	64458	38373
单纯购置设备	Purchase of Equipment	35566	125	34451	72857	349	71905

4-4 续表1 continued

单位：万元 (10000 yuan)

项目	Item	1998 合计 Total	1998 # 基本建设 Capital Construction	1998 # 更新改造 Technical Updating and Transformation	1997 合计 Total	1997 # 基本建设 Capital Construction	1997 # 更新改造 Technical Updating and Transformation
按建设项目规模分	**Grouped by Size of Construction Projects**						
基本建设大中型项目	Large and Medium Projects of Capital Construction	263356	263356		145648	145648	
基本建设小型项目	Small Projects of Capital Construction	1385145	1385145		1363507	1363507	
更新改造限额以上项目	Projects of Technical Updating and Transformation above the Limits	1093462		1093462	594440		594440
更新改造限额以下项目	Projects of Technical Updating and Transformation below the Limits	392977		392977	351128		351128
其他	Others	184343	125	34451	238281	349	71905
按经济类型分	**Grouped by Ownership**						
国有经济	State-Owned	2702660	1303986	1368520	1926408	1011017	865816
集体经济	Collective Owned	119613			116452		
联营经济	Joint Owned	14927	10804	4123	7945	7945	
股份有限公司	Share Holding Company	48719	29250	19469	16095	15553	542
有限责任公司	Limited-Liability Company	38815	13589	25226	12253	10237	2016
中外合资经营	Joint Venture	164286	95564	68722	420674	353211	67463
中外合作经营	Cooperative	13475	13475		40972	38397	2575
外资企业	Foreign Enterprises	10703	10703		32239	32239	
港澳台与大陆合资经营	Joint Venture with Hongkong,Macao and Taiwan	158858	130595	28263	78651	2933	75718
港澳台与大陆合作经营	Cooperative Enterprises with HongKong Macao and Taiwan	25874	23569	2305	5267	2342	2925
港澳台独资企业	Hongkong,Macao and Taiwan Enterprises	7863	7863		26113	26113	
其他经济	Others	13490	9228	4262	9935	9517	418

4-4 续表2 continued

单位：万元 (10000 yuan)

项目	Item	合计 Total	# 基本建设 Capital Construction	# 更新改造 Technical Updating and Transformation
投资额	**Total**	**3319283**	**1648626**	**1520890**
按企业登记注册类型分	**Grouped by Type of Enterprises Registered**			
内资企业	Domestic Investment Enterprises	2938224	1366857	1421600
国有企业	State-Owned	2702660	1303986	1368520
集体企业	Collective Owned	119613		
联营企业	Joint Owned	14927	10804	4123
股份合作企业	Share Holding Cooperative	9008	9008	
股份有限公司	Share Holding Company	48719	29250	19469
有限责任公司	Limited-Liability Company	38815	13589	25226
其他企业	Others	4482	220	4262
港澳台商投资企业	Hongkong,Macao and Taiwan Funded Enterprises	192595	162027	30568
港澳台合资经营	Joint Venture	158858	130595	28263
港澳台合作经营	Cooperative	25874	23569	2305
港澳台商独资企业	Hongkong,Macao and Taiwan Enterprises	7863	7863	
港澳台商投资股份有限公司	Hongkong,Macao and Taiwan Funded Share Holing Company			
外商投资企业	Foreign Funded Enterprises	188464	119742	68722
中外合资经营	Joint Venture	164196	95474	68722
中外合作经营	Cooperative	13475	13475	
外资(独资)企业	Foreign Enterprises	10703	10703	
外商投资股份有限公司	Foreign Funded Share Holding Company	90	90	

4-5 固定资产投资财务拨贷款额

FINANCIAL ALLOCATIONS AND LOANS FOR INVESTMENT IN FIXED ASSETS

单位：万元 (10000 yuan)

项目	Item	1998			1997		
		合计 Total	# 基本建设 Capital Construction	# 更新改造 Technical Updating and Transformation	合计 Total	# 基本建设 Capital Construction	# 更新改造 Technical Updating and Transformation
上年结余资金	**Balance of Last Year**	**870327**	**630079**	**223560**	**728813**	**499869**	**219065**
本年拨款贷款	**Allocations and Loans in this Year**	**6693722**	**4261228**	**2288422**	**5875251**	**3903193**	**1809178**
国家预算内资金	State Budgetary Appropriation	938629	866744	71885	828522	778226	50219
国内贷款	Domestic Loans	1084327	586527	490266	897504	611921	277548
债　券	Bonds	158300	58500	96800			
利用外资	Foreign Capital	412267	368558	43709	512668	442653	68095
自筹资金	Self-raised Funds	3829243	2210699	1497554	3223577	1781315	1311510
# 股票	Stocks	33445	10555	22890	4507	4387	120
其他资金	Others	270956	170200	88208	412980	289078	101806

4-6 地方固定资产投资财务拨贷款额

FINANCIAL ALLOCATIONS AND LOANS FOR LOCAL INVESTMENT IN FIXED ASSETS

单位：万元 (10000 yuan)

项目	Item	1998			1997		
		合计 Total	# 基本建设 Capital Construction	# 更新改造 Technical Updating and Transformation	合计 Total	# 基本建设 Capital Construction	# 更新改造 Technical Updating and Transformation
上年结余资金	**Balance of Last Year**	**507213**	**281241**	**209284**	**403583**	**232615**	**161089**
本年拨款贷款	**Allocations and Loans in this Year**	**3125718**	**1594941**	**1386705**	**2772515**	**1637805**	**971830**
国家预算内资金	State Budgetary Appropriation	150522	81055	69467	83822	43895	39850
国内贷款	Domestic Loans	699271	328889	362848	556354	380557	167762
债　券	Bonds	144300	44500	96800			
利用外资	Foreign Capital	202024	172457	29567	330546	261037	67589
自筹资金	Self-raised Funds	1708746	844496	743260	1481532	728912	621868
# 股票	Stocks	33445	10555	22890	4507	4387	120
其他资金	Others	220855	123544	84763	320261	223404	74761

4-7 城市基础设施投资额
MUNICIPAL INFRASTRUCTURE INVESTMENT

项目	Item	投资额（万元） Investment(10000 yuan) 全市 Total	# 地方 Local	比重（%） Proportion(%) 全市 Total	# 地方 Local
全市总计	**Total**	**3203920**	**1545711**	**100**	**100**
能源	**Energy**	**851386**	**334018**	**26.6**	**21.6**
电力	Electricity	542050	24682	17.0	1.6
供热	Heat	141766	141766	4.4	9.2
供气	Gas	67217	67217	2.1	4.3
供水	Water	100353	100353	3.1	6.5
公共服务业	**Public Services**	**624141**	**624141**	**19.5**	**40.4**
市内公共交通	Public Traffic	244211	244211	7.6	15.8
# 市内公交电汽车	Buses and Trolleys	32794	32794	1.0	2.1
出租汽车	Taxies	11410	11410	0.4	0.7
园林绿化	Parks and Green Areas	29528	29528	0.9	1.9
环境卫生	Environmental Sanitation	19355	19355	0.6	1.3
市政工程管理	Municipal Construction	331047	331047	10.4	21.4
其他公共服务业	Others				
交通运输	**Transportation**	**802013**	**436504**	**25.0**	**28.2**
铁路	Railway	79556		2.5	
公路	Highway	421232	421232	13.1	27.2
管道运输	Pipeline				
航空	Aviation				
其他	Others	301225	15272	9.4	1.0
邮政电信	**Posts and Telecommunications**	**774849**		**24.2**	
邮政	Posts	18199		0.6	
电信	Telecommunications	756650		23.6	
其他	**Others**	**151531**	**151048**	**4.7**	**9.8**
水利	Water Conservancy	141573	141573	4.4	9.2
环境保护	Environmental Protection	125	125	...	...
其他	Others	9833	9350	0.3	0.6

4-8 能源及交通投资额
INVESTMENT IN ENERGY AND TRANSPORTATION

单位：万元 (10000 yuan)

项目	Item	全市 Total 1998	全市 Total 1997	#地方 Local 1998	#地方 Local 1997
全市固定资产投资总额	**Investment in Fixed Assets of the City**	**6829237**	**5820764**	**3319283**	**2693004**
# 能源、交通投资额	Investment in Energy and Transportation	2660138	2066871	711610	460399
占全市投资额比重 (%)	Proportion (%)	39.0	35.5	21.4	17.1
能源投资额	Investment in Energy	961932	933304	256810	301178
占全市投资额比重(%)	Proportion (%)	14.1	16.0	7.7	11.2
运输、邮电投资额	Investment in Transportation, Posts and Telecommunications	1698206	1133567	454800	159221
占全市投资额比重(%)	Proportion (%)	24.9	19.5	13.7	5.9
在能源投资中	**Of the Investment in Energy**				
煤(国家统配煤矿)	Coal(State Collieries)	5197	9165	5197	9165
电(公用电厂及小水电)	Electricity(Public Power Plants and Hydropower Stations)	577305	537106	30762	100472
油品(炼油厂原油加工)	Oil Products(Crude Oil Processing of Refinery)	162485	205330	3906	9838
燃料气(液化石油气、焦炉煤气)	Fuel Gas(Liquefied Petroleum Gas,Gas)	72200	77073	72200	77073
热气(公用局)	Heat(Public Utilities Bureau)	144745	104630	144745	104630
在运输投资中	**Of Investment in Transportation**				
铁路	Railway	107309	95884		
公路	Highway	432313	118766	432043	118766
航空	Aviation	20649	27105		
邮政、电信	Posts and Telecommunications	827231	638551	3703	2933
其他交通运输	Other Transportation	310704	253261	19054	37522

4-9 施工及投入生产(或交付使用)的项目数
NUMBER OF PROJECTS UNDER CONSTRUCTION AND PRODUCTION (OR PUT INTO OPERATION)

单位：个 (unit)

项目	Item	全市 Total 1998	全市 Total 1997	#地方 Local 1998	#地方 Local 1997
全市施工项目	**Total Projects under Construction**	**3213**	**3234**	**1675**	**1730**
# 本年新开工	Begin Construction this Year	1658	1633	779	804
全部竣工投产项目	Total Projects Completed	1607	1552	801	793
建设项目投产率 (%)	the Projects under Construction as a Percentage of Total Projects (%)	50.0	48.0	47.8	45.8
基本建设施工项目	**Capital Construction Projects**	**1260**	**1246**	**713**	**697**
# 本年新开工	Begin Construction this Year	456	460	319	316
全部竣工投产项目	Total Projects Completed	415	377	294	263
建设项目投产率 (%)	the Projects under Construction as a Percentage of Total Projects (%)	32.9	30.3	41.2	37.7
更新改造措施施工项目	**Projects of Innovation and Replacement**	**1812**	**1837**	**821**	**882**
# 本年新开工	Begin Construction this Year	1136	1097	394	412
全部竣工投产项目	Total Projects Completed	1109	1104	424	459
建设项目投产率 (%)	the Projects under Construction as a Percentage of Total Projects (%)	61.2	60.1	51.6	52.0
其他投资施工项目	**Other Projects under Construction**	**141**	**151**	**141**	**151**
# 本年新开工	Begin Construction this Year	66	76	66	76
全部竣工投产项目	Total Projects Completed	83	71	83	71
建设项目投产率 (%)	the Projects under Construction as a Percentage of Total Projects (%)	58.9	47.0	58.9	47.0

4-10 全市固定资产投资额及新增固定资产（按行业分）

TOTAL INVESTMENT IN FIXED ASSETS AND INCREMENTAL FIXED ASSETS (BY SECTOR)

单位：万元 (10000 yuan)

行业	Item	投资额 Investment			新增固定资产 Incremental Fixed Assets		
		合计 Total	中央 Central	地方 Local	合计 Total	中央 Central	地方 Local
总计	**Total**	**6829237**	**3509954**	**3319283**	**4771142**	**2736861**	**2034281**
农、林、牧、渔业	**Farming,Forestry,Animal Husbandry and Fishery**	**19854**	**6600**	**13254**	**14991**		**14991**
农业	Farming	8184		8184	7634		7634
林业	Forestry	2577		2577	2827		2827
渔业	Fishery	4465	4100	365	2144		2144
海洋渔业	Sea Fishery	4100	4100				
淡水渔业	Freshwater Fishery	365		365	2144		2144
农、林、牧、渔服务业	FFAF Services	4628	2500	2128	2386		2386
采掘业	**Excavation**	**27044**		**27044**	**1899**		**1899**
煤炭采选业	Coal Mining and Dressing	5197		5197	1064		1064
黑色金属矿采选业	Ferrous Metals Mining and Dressing	20739		20739			
铁矿采选业	Iron Mining and Dressing	20739		20739			
非金属矿采选业	Nonmetal Minerals Mining and Dressing	1108		1108	835		835
土砂石开采业	Sand and Stone Mining and Dressing	873		873	835		835
其他非金属矿采选业	Others	235		235			
制造业	**Manufacturing**	**1003652**	**348919**	**654733**	**910496**	**290430**	**620066**
食品加工业	Food Processing	6993		6993	15194		15194
粮食及饲料加工业	Grain and Feed	3781		3781	9266		9266
植物油加工业	Vegetable Oil	403		403	383		383
屠宰及肉类蛋类加工业	Butcher, Meat and Egg	2700		2700	4513		4513
盐加工业	Salt	109		109	1032		1032
食品制造业	Food Making	20800		20800	14801		14801
糕点、糖果制造业	Pastry and Candy	346		346	158		158
发酵制品业	Ferments	19809		19809	14533		14533
调味品制造业	Flavorings	645		645	110		110
其他食品制造业	Other Foods	21983		21983	990		990
饮料制造业	Beverage Production	660		660	990		990
酒精及饮料酒制造业	Alcohol and Beverage Wine	21323		21323			
软饮料制造业	Soft Drink	21643		21643	7392		7392
纺织业	Textile Industry	10230		10230	5939		5939
棉纺织业	Cotton Textile	1501		1501	778		778
毛纺织业	Woolen Textile	9212		9212	245		245
针织品业	Knitting Textile	700		700	430		430
其他纺织业	Others	11824		11824	16235		16235
服装及其他纤维制品制造业	Garments and Other Fiber Products	11708		11708	16119		16119
服装制造业	Garment Industry	116		116	116		116
皮革、毛皮、羽绒及其制品业	Leather,Furs,Down and Related Products	1192		1192	379		379
制革业	Leather Making	518		518	86		86
皮革制品制造业	Leathers and Related Products	674		674	293		293
木材加工及竹、藤、棕、草制品业	Timber Processing,Bamboo, Cane,Palm Fiber and Straw Products	6926	930	5996	50	50	
锯材、木片加工业	Timber and Wood Piece Processing	930	930		50	50	
人造板制造业	Artificial Board Manufacturing	5996		5996			

4-10 续表1 continued

单位：万元 (10000 yuan)

行业	Item	投资额 Investment			新增固定资产 Incremental Fixed Assets		
		合计 Total	中央 Central	地方 Local	合计 Total	中央 Central	地方 Local
家具制造业	Furniture Industry	11649		11649	4617		4617
木制家具制造业	Wooden Furniture	6446		6446	1595		1595
金属家具制造业	Metal Furniture	5203		5203	3022		3022
造纸及纸制品业	Papermaking and Paper Products	5257		5257	3569		3569
纸浆制造业	Paper Pulp	1000		1000			
纸制品业	Paper Products	4257		4257	3569		3569
印刷业、记录媒介的复制	Printing and Record Medium Reproduced	34722	17342	17380	43149	25770	17379
印刷业	Printing	33796	16416	17380	43149	25770	17379
记录媒介的复制	Record Medium Reproduced	926	926				
文教体育用品制造业	Stationery,Education and Sports Goods	4340		4340	1304		1304
文化用品制造业	Cultural Goods	1264		1264	699		699
乐器及其他文娱用品制造业	Music Instruments and Other Stationery Goods	3076		3076	605		605
石油加工及炼焦业	Petroleum Processing and Coking Products	162485	158579	3906	159705	149919	9786
原油加工业	Petroleum Processing	150370	150370		143425	143425	
石油制品业	Petroleum Products	11021	8209	2812	16160	6494	9666
炼焦业	Coking Products	1094		1094	120		120
化学原料及化学制品制造业	Raw Chemical Materials and Chemical Products	158877	69639	89238	78846	19998	58848
基本化学原料制造业	Elementary Raw Chemical Materials	209		209	100		100
化学肥料制造业	Chemical Fertilizer	9168		9168	9982		9982
有机化学产品制造业	Organic Chemical Products	73053	17804	55249	49749	13013	36736
合成材料制造业	Synthetic Materials	52828	51835	993	6985	6985	
专用化学产品制造业	Special Purpose Chemical Products	18853		18853	640		640
日用化学产品制造业	Daily Use Chemical Products	4766		4766	11390		11390
医药制造业	Medical and Pharmaceutical Products	28052	4350	23702	9733	4849	4884
化学药品制剂制造业	Original Chemical Medicine	21651	1370	20281	1170	1170	
中药材及中成药加工	Raw Material and Products of Chinese Medicine	1622	733	889	2570		2570
动物药品制造业	Animal Medicine	385		385	562		562
生物制品业	Biological Products	4394	2247	2147	5431	3679	1752
化学纤维制造业	Chemical Fiber Manufacturing	2217	2217		2417	2417	
合成纤维制造业	Synthetic Fibers	2217	2217		2417	2417	
橡胶制品业	Rubber Products	16155	2565	13590	25384	2565	22819
轮胎制造业	Tire Manufacturing	11843	2565	9278	21984	2565	19419
日用橡胶制品业	Daily-use Products	4262		4262	3400		3400
其他橡胶制品业	Other Rubber Products	50		50			
塑料制品业	Plastic Products	3530	50	3480	3679	50	3629
塑料薄膜制造业	Plastic Film	567		567	567		567
塑料包装箱及容器制造业	Plastic Cases and Container	745		745	2656		2656
其他塑料制品业	Other Plastic Products	2218	50	2168	456	50	406
非金属矿物制品业	Nonmetal Mineral Products	44635	28682	15953	42243	29533	12710
水泥制造业	Cement Manufacturing	1315		1315	836		836

4-10 续表2 continued

单位：万元 (10000 yuan)

行业	Item	投资额 Investment 合计 Total	中央 Central	地方 Local	新增固定资产 Incremental Fixed Assets 合计 Total	中央 Central	地方 Local
水泥制品和石棉水泥制品业	Cement and Asbestos Products	4278	1741	2537	5299	2351	2948
砖瓦、石灰和轻质建筑材料制造业	Brick,Tile and Light Construction Material	31203	26941	4262	28418	27182	1236
玻璃及玻璃制品业	Glass and Glass Products	4340		4340	4292		4292
陶瓷制品业	Ceramics Products	3046		3046	3046		3046
耐火材料制品业	Refractory Products	352		352	352		352
其他类未包括的非金属矿物制品业	Other Nonmetal Mineral Products	101		101			
黑色金属冶炼及压延加工业	Smelting and Pressing of Ferrous Metals	32144		32144	20758		20758
炼铁业	Iron-smelting	4259		4259			
炼钢业	Steel-smelting	717		717			
钢压延加工业	Steel Pressing	27168		27168	20758		20758
有色金属冶炼及压延加工业	Smelting and Pressing of Nonferrous Metals	1050		1050	800		800
有色金属压延加工业	Nonferrous Metals Pressing	1050		1050	800		800
金属制品业	Metal Products	13372		13372	12101		12101
金属结构制造业	Metal Structure	150		150			
铸铁管制造业	Tube of Cast Iron	182		182	249		249
工具制造业	Tools Manufacturing	295		295			
集装箱和金属包装物品制造业	Container and Metal Cover Manufacturing	4394		4394	1955		1955
建筑用金属制品业	Products for Construction Use	6989		6989	8235		8235
日用金属制品业	Daily Metal Products	582		582	882		882
其他金属制品业	Other Products	780		780	780		780
普通机械制造业	Ordinary Machine-building	21899	3050	18849	24788	2630	22158
锅炉及原动机制造业	Boiler and Motive Machine	6243		6243	3848		3848
金属加工机械制造业	Metal Processing Machine	7830	3050	4780	6564	2630	3934
通用设备制造业	Universal Equipment	970		970	1747		1747
轴承、阀门制造业	Bearing and Valve	823		823	1945		1945
其他通用零部件制造业	Other Universal Components and Parts	5533		5533	10184		10184
其他普通机械制造业	Other Ordinary Machine-building	500		500	500		500
专用设备制造业	Special Purpose Equipment Building	38424	10554	27870	35100	7817	27283
机电工业专用设备制造业	Equipment for Engine and Electricity	7303	6966	337	4268	4209	59
石化及其他工业专用设备制造业	Equipment for Petroleum and Other Sector of Industry	9278	3588	5690	5730	3608	2122
轻纺工业专用设备制造业	Equipment for Light and Textile Industry	11043		11043	15603		15603
农、林、牧、渔,水利业机械制造业	Machines for Farming,Forestry,Animal Husbandry,Fishing and Irrigation	2808		2808	52		52
医疗器械制造业	Medical Machines	4391		4391	4615		4615
其他专用设备制造业	Other Special Purpose Equipment	3601		3601	4832		4832
交通运输设备制造业	Transportation Equipment Manufacturing	91218	36507	54711	83577	24347	59230
铁路运输设备制造业	Railway Transportation Equipment	18124	7558	10566	8745	5370	3375
汽车制造业	Motor Vehicles	40195		40195	47442		47442
航空航天器制造业	Aviation and Spaceflight Equipment	20265	20265		6516	6516	
交通运输设备修理业	Transportation Equipment Repairing	12634	8684	3950	20874	12461	8413

4-10 续表3 continued

单位：万元 (10000 yuan)

行业	Item	投资额 Investment 合计 Total	中央 Central	地方 Local	新增固定资产 Incremental Fixed Assets 合计 Total	中央 Central	地方 Local
电气机械及器材制造业	Electric Equipment and Appliances Manufacturing	16915		16915	9718		9718
电机制造业	Generator	64		64	462		462
输配电及控制设备制造业	Electricity Transmit,Distribution and Control Equipment	6530		6530	854		854
电工器材制造业	Electrical Appliances	5206		5206	5206		5206
日用电器制造业	Daily Use Electrical Appliances	2920		2920	2486		2486
照明器具制造业	Lighting Equipment and Products	710		710	710		710
其他电气机械制造业	Other Electronic Machines	1485		1485			
电子及通信设备制造业	Electronic and Telecommunication Equipment	159627	3536	156091	227757	3240	224517
通信设备制造业	Telecommunication Equipment	26847	3236	23611	29004	3240	25764
广播电视设备制造业	Radio and Television Equipment	75		75			
电子计算机制造业	Computer	6672	300	6372	8546		8546
电子器件制造业	Electronic Device	99839		99839	141655		141655
电子元件制造业	Electronic Cell	19655		19655	44957		44957
日用电子器具制造业	Daily Use Electronic Appliances	2184		2184	2195		2195
其他电子设备制造业	Other Electronic Machines	4355		4355	1400		1400
仪器仪表及文化、办公用机械制造业	Instruments,Meters,Cultural and Official Machinery	24427	19	24408	7338		7338
通用仪器仪表制造	General Instruments and Meters	10895	19	10876	6854		6854
电子测量仪器制造业	Electronic Survey Instrument	1522		1522	484		484
计量器具制造业	Measuring Implements	12010		12010			
其他制造业	Other Manufacturing	30887	490	30397	42117	490	41627
工艺美术品制造业	Art Products Manufacturing	22706		22706	29527		29527
日用杂品制造业	Daily Use Groceries	2901		2901	5310		5310
其他生产、生活用品制造业	Others	5280	490	4790	7280	490	6790
电力、煤气及水的生产和供应业	**Electricity,Gas and Water Production and Supply**	**895303**	**546543**	**348760**	**772142**	**590543**	**181599**
电力、蒸气、热水的生产和供应业	Electricity,Steam and Hot Water Production and Supply	722050	546543	175507	626593	590543	36050
电力生产业	Electricity Production	257649	251569	6080	551565	550690	875
电力供应业	Electricity Supply	319656	294974	24682	60847	39853	20994
蒸气、热水生产和供应业	Steam and Hot Water Production and Supply	144745		144745	14181		14181
煤气生产和供应业	Gas Production and Supply	72200		72200	89790		89790
煤气生产业	Gas Production	3954		3954	6122		6122
煤气供应业	Gas Supply	68246		68246	83668		83668
自来水的生产和供应业	Water Production and Supply	101053		101053	55759		55759
自来水生产业	Water Production	89302		89302	41278		41278
自来水供应业	Water Supply	11751		11751	14481		14481
建筑业	**Construction**	**91282**	**37179**	**54103**	**56140**	**19851**	**36289**
土木工程建筑业	Civil Engineering Construction	86791	34583	52208	52568	18943	33625
房屋建筑业	Building Construction	81062	30277	50785	46341	14347	31994
铁路、公路、遂道、桥梁建筑业	Railways,Highways,Tunnels and Bridges Construction	4206	4206		4596	4596	
堤坝、电站、码头建筑业	Dikes and Dams,Power Station and Wharves	1029		1029	431		431
其他土木工程建筑业	Other Civil Engineering Construction	494	100	394	1200		1200
线路、管道和设备安装业	Line and Equipments Installation	4491	2596	1895	3572	908	2664

4-10 续表4 continued

单位：万元 (10000 yuan)

行业	Item	投资额 Investment 合计 Total	中央 Central	地方 Local	新增固定资产 Incremental Fixed Assets 合计 Total	中央 Central	地方 Local
线路、管道安装业	Line Installation	2288	2288		600	600	
设备安装业	Equipment Installation	2203	308	1895	2972	308	2664
地质勘查业、水利管理业	**Geological Prospecting and Water Conservancy**	**168027**	**15004**	**153023**	**19769**	**7046**	**12723**
地质勘查业	Geological Prospecting	4159	3153	1006	11332	7046	4286
矿产地质勘查业	Minerals Prospecting	2183	1477	706	6720	5034	1686
工程地质勘察设计业	Engineering Geological Prospecting and Design	512	212	300	2812	212	2600
地球物理和地球化学勘察业	Geophysical and Geochemical Prospecting	1464	1464		1800	1800	
水利管理业	Water Conservancy	163868	11851	152017	8437		8437
交通运输、仓储及邮电通信业	**Transportation,Storage,Posts and Telecommunications**	**1742581**	**1261002**	**481579**	**889878**	**630796**	**259082**
铁路运输业	Railways	107309	107309		97450	97450	
公路运输业	Highways	432313	270	432043	215088		215088
汽车运输业	Motor Vehicles	432313	270	432043	215088		215088
航空运输业	Aviations	20649	20649		8189	8189	
航空客货运输业	Passenger and Freight Transportation	20649	20649		8189	8189	
交通运输辅助业	Logistic Support for Transportation	310704	291650	19054	24406	10341	14065
公路管理及养护业	Highway Management and Maintenance	16054		16054	14065		14065
机场及航空运输辅助业	Airport and Logistics of Aviation	291650	291650		10341	10341	
其他类未包括的交通运输辅助业	Other Logistics for Transportation	3000		3000			
仓储业	Storage	44375	17596	26779	45271	15342	29929
邮电通信业	Posts and Telecommunications	827231	823528	3703	499474	499474	
邮政业	Posts	19388	19388		12677	12677	
电信业	Telecommunications	803164	803164		485911	485911	
批发和零售贸易餐饮业	**Wholesale,Retail and Catering**	**178665**	**59499**	**119166**	**240557**	**92183**	**148374**
食品、饮料、烟草和家庭用品批发业	Wholesale of Food,Beverage, Tabacco and Family Use Goods	24944	215	24729	13806	215	13591
食品、饮料、烟草批发业	Food,Beverage and Tabacco	9880		9880	6823		6823
棉麻土畜产品批发业	Cotton,Fiber,Local and Animal Products	268		268			
纺织品、服装和鞋帽批发业	Textile,Garments,Shoes and Hats	4940		4940	3409		3409
日用百货批发业	Daily Use Goods	7680		7680	1010		1010
日用杂品批发业	Daily Use Groceries	103		103	103		103
五金交电化工批发业	Hardware,Electrical Appliance and Chemical	1668		1668	1796		1796
药品及医疗器械批发业	Medicine and Medical Appliance	405	215	190	665	215	450
能源、材料、机械和电子设备批发业	Wholesale of Energy,Materials Machine and Electronic Equipment	37252	10713	26539	69284	39510	29774
能源批发业	Energy	10079		10079	15091		15091
化工材料批发业	Chemical Materials	2137		2137	1050		1050
建筑材料批发业	Building Materials	10447	4830	5617	41042	27923	13119
金属材料批发业	Ferrous Materials	6349	4780	1569	514		514
机械、电子设备批发业	Machine and Electronic Equipment	1103	1103		11587	11587	
汽车、摩托车及零配件批发业	Automobile,Motorcycle and Spares and Fittings	5137		5137			
再生物资回收批发业	Recovery of Reclaimed Materials	2000		2000			
其他批发业	Other Wholesales	22155	21346	809	1847	860	987
图书报刊批发业	Books,Newspapers and Magazines	190	190		860	860	

4-10 续表5 continued

单位：万元 (10000 yuan)

行业	Item	投资额 Investment 合计 Total	中央 Central	地方 Local	新增固定资产 Incremental Fixed Assets 合计 Total	中央 Central	地方 Local
农业生产资料批发业	Agricultural Capital Goods	475	5	470	160		160
其他类未包括的批发	Others	21490	21151	339	827		827
零售业	Retail	85320	21225	64095	148673	51598	97075
食品、饮料和烟草零售业	Food,Beverage and Tabacco	865		865	38374		38374
日用百货零售业	Daily Use Goods	69004	21195	47809	69035	51598	17437
纺织品、服装和鞋帽零售业	Textile,Garments,Shoes and Hats	475		475			
五金交电化工零售业	Hardware,Electrical Appliance and Chemical	1160		1130	2450		2450
药品及医疗器械零售业	Medicine and Medical Appliances	300		300	300		300
图书报刊零售业	Books,Newspapers and Magazines	12086		12086	36814		36814
其他零售业	Others	1430		1430	1700		1700
商业经纪与代理业	Business Agencies	6858	6000	858			
餐饮业	Catering	2136		2136	6947		6947
正餐	Dinner	1677		1677	525		525
其他餐饮业	Others	459		459	6422		6422
金融、保险业	**Banking and Insurance**	**103471**	**102721**	**750**	**181828**	**181528**	**300**
金融业	Banking	100661	99911	750	178818	178518	300
中央银行	Central Bank	14787	14787				
商业银行	Commercial Bank	85124	85124		178518	178518	
信用合作社	Credit Cooperative	750		750	300		300
保险业	Insurance	2810	2810		3010	3010	
房地产业	**Real Estate**	**48454**	**7553**	**40901**	**29716**		**29716**
房地产管理业	Management	47572	7553	40019	27053		27053
房地产代理与经纪业	Brokerage and Agencies	882		882	2663		2663
社会服务业	**Social Services**	**862369**	**95073**	**767296**	**373470**	**159493**	**213977**
公共服务业	Public Services	650541		650541	118634		118634
市内公共交通业	Urban Public Traffic	267980		267980	56898		56898
园林绿化业	Gardens Afforest	34004		34004	3819		3819
环境卫生业	Environmental Sanitation	20109		20109	32020		32020
市政工程管理业	Municipal Engineering Mana- gement	326192		326192	25669		25669
居民服务业	Personal Services	10317	375	9942	8368	95	8273
沐浴业	Bath	1346		1346			
殡葬业	Funeral and Interment Services	7743		7743	5767		5767
其他居民服务业	Others	853		853	2506		2506
旅馆业	Hotels	76737	4740	71997	55963		55963
租赁服务业	Rentals	33882	32059	1823	119372	117549	1823
旅游业	Tourism	14373	1384	12989	2173	749	1424
娱乐服务业	'Recreation	3849		3849			
信息、咨询服务业	Information and Consultancy	17416	8634	8782	20100		20100
广告业	Advertisement	197		197	197		197
咨询服务业	Consultancy Services	4500		4500	19000		19000
其他类未包括的信息咨询服务业	Others	12719	8634	4085	903		903
计算机应用服务业	Computer Application	5484	583	4901	653	653	
软件开发咨询业	Software Development Consultancy	5484	583	4901	653	653	
其他社会服务业	Other Social Services	49770	47298	2472	48207	40447	7760
市场管理服务业	Market Management	9754	9754		34018	34018	
其他类未包括的社会服务业	Others	40016	37544	2472	14189	6429	7760
卫生体育和社会福利业	**Health Care,Sports and Social Welfare**	**93918**	**45919**	**47999**	**62101**	**25188**	**36913**
卫生	Health Care	85906	44641	41265	56023	25188	30835

4-10 续表6 continued

单位：万元 (10000 yuan)

行业	Item	投资额 Investment 合计 Total	中央 Central	地方 Local	新增固定资产 Incremental Fixed Assets 合计 Total	中央 Central	地方 Local
医院	Hospitals	69269	31240	38029	46495	18408	28087
疗养院	Sanitariums	3048	2515	533	4411	3878	533
妇幼保健所(站)	Maternity and Child Care Institutions	2606		2606	2215		2215
药品检验所(室)	Medicines and Chemical Reagents Test Labs	81	81		2255	2255	
其他医院	Other Hospitals	10697	10600	97			
体育	Sports	7310	1278	6032	4399		4399
社会福利保障业	Social Welfare and Securation	702		702	1679		1679
社会福利业	Social Welfare	702		702	1679		1679
教育、文化艺术及广播电影电视业	**Education,Culture and Arts, Radio,Film and Television**	**499010**	**333931**	**165079**	**392671**	**279538**	**113133**
教育	Education	367869	233063	134806	300859	206358	94501
高等教育	Higher Education	259717	213297	46420	223739	181324	42415
中等教育	Secondary School Education	69673	10291	59382	39117	11099	28018
初等教育	Primary Education	5676	485	5191	5504	500	5004
特殊教育	Special Education	288		288			
其他教育	Other Education	32515	8990	23525	32499	13435	19064
文化艺术业	Culture and Arts	98881	73104	25777	42325	25129	17196
艺术	Arts	16871	8604	8267	12957	12197	760
出版	Publication	21081	18061	3020	17345	12545	4800
文物保护	Preservation of Culture Relics	2032	1849	183			
图书馆	Libraries	5060	359	4701	57	57	
档案馆	Archives	45		45	908		908
群众文化	Mass Culture	5868		5868	10389		10389
新闻	News	24199	24199				
其他文化艺术业	Others	23725	20032	3693	669	330	339
广播电影电视业	Radio,Film and Television	32260	27764	4496	49487	48051	1436
广播	Radio	15407	13697	1710	38166	38166	
电影	Film	7086	6486	600	9322	8722	600
电视	Television	9767	7581	2186	1999	1163	836
科学研究和综合技术服务业	**Scientific Research and Polytechnical Services**	**220960**	**171011**	**49949**	**198106**	**161672**	**36434**
科学研究业	Scientific Research	169175	153475	15700	153298	136197	17101
自然科学研究	Natural Science	134315	125670	8645	136499	122652	13847
社会科学研究	Social Science	4205	4205		145	145	
其他科学研究	Others	30655	23600	7055	16654	13400	3254
综合技术服务业	Polytechnical Services	51785	17536	34249	44808	25475	19333
气象	Meteorology	2917	2917		1707	1707	
测绘	Mapping	1479		1479	3031		3031
环境保护	Enviromental Protection	125		125	125		125
技术推广和科技交流服务业	Technology Spreading and Scientific Technical Exchanges	2293	41	2252	3598		3598
工程设计业	Engineering Design	15166	14404	762	24530	23768	762
其他综合技术服务业	Others	29631		29631	11817		11817
国家机关、政党机关和社会团体	**Government Agencies,Party Agencies and Social Organizations**	**652431**	**442953**	**209478**	**420257**	**287067**	**133190**
国家机关	Government Agencies	535711	332443	203268	317186	193612	123574
政党机关	Party Agencies	86227	86227		91559	91559	
社会团体	Social Organizations	30493	24283	6210	11512	1896	9616
其他行业	**Other Sectors**	**222216**	**36047**	**186169**	**207121**	**11526**	**195595**
企业管理机构	Administrative Organs of Enterprises	99724	23271	76453	121645	3864	117781
其他类未包括的行业	Others	122492	12776	109716	85476	7662	77814

4-11 全市基本建设投资额及新增固定资产(按行业分)

TOTAL INVESTMENT IN CAPITAL CONSTRUCTION AND INCREMENTAL FIXED ASSETS (BY SECTOR)

单位：万元 (10000 yuan)

行业	Item	投资额 Investment 合计 Total	中央 Central	地方 Local	新增固定资产 Incremental Fixed Assets 合计 Total	中央 Central	地方 Local
总计	**Total**	**4155182**	**2506556**	**1648626**	**3000077**	**1918932**	**1081145**
农、林、牧、渔业	**Farming,Forestry,Animal Husbandry and Fishery**	**15857**	**6600**	**9257**	**10336**		**10336**
农业	Farming	5720		5720	4897		4897
林业	Forestry	2247		2247	2827		2827
渔业	Fishery	4427	4100	327	2144		2144
海洋渔业	Sea Fishery	4100	4100				
淡水渔业	Freshwater Fishery	327		327	2144		2144
农、林、牧、渔服务业	FFAF Services	3463	2500	963	468		468
采掘业	**Excavation**	**6416**		**6416**			
黑色金属矿采选业	Ferrous Metals Mining and Dressing	6416		6416			
铁矿采选业	Iron Mining and Dressing	6416		6416			
制造业	**Manufacturing**	**518775**	**237171**	**281604**	**364719**	**91472**	**273247**
食品加工业	Food Processing	4505		4505	7643		7643
粮食及饲料加工业	Grain and Feed	2895		2895	3597		3597
屠宰及肉类蛋类加工业	Butcher, Meat and Egg	1501		1501	3014		3014
其他食品加工业	Others	109		109	1032		1032
食品制造业	Food Making	8793		8793	8723		8723
糕点、糖果制造业	Pastry and Candy	228		228	158		158
乳制品制造业	Dairy Products	8565		8565	8565		8565
饮料制造业	Beverage Production	21883		21883	990		990
酒精及饮料酒制造业	Alcohol and Beverage Wine	560		560	990		990
软饮料制造业	Soft Drinking	21323		21323			
纺织业	Textile Industry	8743		8743			
棉纺织业	Cotton Textile	1400		1400			
针织品业	Knitting Textile	7343		7343			
服装及其他纤维制品制造业	Garments and Other Fiber Products	9836		9836	6569		6569
服装制造业	Garment Industry	9836		9836	6569		6569
木材加工及竹、藤、棕、草制品业	Timber Processing,Bamboo, Cane,Palm Fiber and Straw Products	3484	930	2554	50	50	
锯材、木片加工业	Timber and Wood Piece Processing	930	930		50	50	
人造板制造业	Artificial Board Manufacturing	2554		2554			
家具制造业	Furniture Industry	6166		6166	1595		1595
木制家具制造业	Wooden Furniture	6166		6166	1595		1595
造纸及纸制品业	Papermaking and Paper Products	2073		2073	385		385
纸浆制造业	Paper Pulp	1000		1000			
纸制品业	Paper Products	1073		1073	385		385
印刷业、记录媒介的复制	Printing and Record Medium Reproduced	26280	13250	13030	21431	21431	
印刷业	Printing	25354	12324	13030	21431	21431	
记录媒介的复制	Record Medium Reproduced	926	926				
文教体育用品制造业	Stationery,Education and Sports Goods	860		860	250		250

4-11 续表1 continued

单位：万元 (10000 yuan)

行业	Item	投资额 Investment 合计 Total	中央 Central	地方 Local	新增固定资产 Incremental Fixed Assets 合计 Total	中央 Central	地方 Local
乐器及其他文娱用品制造业	Music Instruments and Other Stationery Goods	860		860	250		250
石油加工及炼焦业	Petroleum Processing and Coking Products	122301	122072	229	25673	24602	1071
原油加工业	Petroleum Processing	118960	118960		20790	20790	
石油制品业	Petroleum Products	3341	3112	229	4883	3812	1071
化学原料及化学制品制造业	Raw Chemical Materials and Chemical Products	49111	44500	4611	4848		4848
有机化学产品制造业	Organic Chemical Products	980		980			
合成材料制造业	Synthetic Materials	44500	44500				
日用化学产品制造业	Daily Use Chemical Products	3631		3631	4848		4848
医药制造业	Medical and Pharmaceutical Products	24718	3150	21568	5027	3065	1962
化学药品制剂制造业	Original Chemical Medicine	20651	1370	19281	1170	1170	
中药材及中成药加工	Raw Material and Products of Chinese Medicine	973	733	240	210		210
生物制品业	Biological Products	3094	1047	2047	3647	1895	1752
橡胶制品业	Rubber Products	430		430	380		380
轮胎制造业	Tire Manufacturing	380		380	380		380
其他橡胶制品业	Other Rubber Products	50		50			
塑料制品业	Plastic Products	745		745	2656		2656
塑料包装箱及容器制造业	Plastic Cases and Container	745		745	2656		2656
非金属矿物制品业	Nonmetal Mineral Products	8475	3800	4675	8917	4651	4266
水泥制品和石棉水泥制品业	Cement and Asbestos Products	4278	1741	2537	5299	2351	2948
砖瓦、石灰和轻质建筑材料制造业	Brick,Tile and Light Construction Material	3825	2059	1766	3266	2300	966
玻璃及玻璃制品业	Glass and Glass Products	20		20			
耐火材料制品	Refractory Products	352		352	352		352
黑色金属冶炼及压延加工业	Smelting and Pressing of Ferrous Metals	4259		4259			
炼铁业	Iron-smelting	4259		4259			
有色金属冶炼及压延加工业	Smelting and Pressing of Nonferrous Metals	800		800	800		800
有色金属压延加工业	Pressing of Nonferrous Metals	800		800	800		800
金属制品业	Metal Products	800		800	950		950
金属结构制造业	Metal Structure	150		150			
建筑用金属制品业	Products for Construct Use	68		68	68		68
日用金属制品业	Daily Metal Products	582		582	882		882
普通机械制造业	Ordinary Machine-building	12123	3050	9073	18172	2630	15542
锅炉及原动机制造业	Boiler and Motive Machine	3437		3437	3046		3046
金属加工机械制造业	Metal Processing Machine	3410	3050	360	2710	2630	80
轴承、阀门制造业	Bearing and Valve	362		362	1807		1807
其他通用零部件制造业	Other Universal Components and Parts	4414		4414	10109		10109
其他普通机械制造业	Other Ordinary Machinebuilding	500		500	500		500
专用设备制造业	Special Purpose Equipment Building	8753	3961	4792	1872	611	1261
机电工业专用设备制造业	Equipment for Engine and Electricity	3787	3787		417	417	
石化及其他专用设备制造业	Equipment for Petroleum and Other Sector of Industry	922	174	748	194	194	
轻纺工业专用设备制造业	Equipment for Light and Textile Industry	349		349	349		349

4-11 续表2 continued

单位：万元 (10000 yuan)

行业	Item	投资额 Investment 合计 Total	中央 Central	地方 Local	新增固定资产 Incremental Fixed Assets 合计 Total	中央 Central	地方 Local
农、林、牧、渔,水利业机械制造业	Machines for Farming,Forestry,Animal Husbandry,Fishing and Irrigation	2500		2500			
医疗器械制造业	Medical Machines	985		985	912		912
其他专用设备制造业	Other Special Purpose Equipment	210		210			
交通运输设备制造业	Transportation Equipment Manufacturing	30369	28023	2346	18378	13947	4431
铁路运输设备制造业	Railway Transportation Equipment	4464	4464		4465	4465	
汽车制造业	Motor Vehicles	350		350	1204		1204
航空航天器制造业	Aviation and Spaceflight Equipment	20265	20265		6516	6516	
交通运输设备修理业	Transportation Equipment Repairing	5290	3294	1996	6193	2966	3227
电气机械及器材制造业	Electric Equipment and Appliances Manufacturing	9310		9310	4933		4933
输配电及控制设备制造业	Electricity Transmit,Distribution and Control Equipment	4600		4600	223		223
电工器材制造业	Electrical Appliances	4000		4000	4000		4000
照明器具制造业	Lighting Equipments and Products	710		710	710		710
电子及通信设备制造业	Electronic and Telecommunication Equipment	120855	3536	117319	191453	3240	188213
通信设备制造业	Telecommunication Equipment	16131	3236	12895	22941	3240	19701
电子计算机制造业	Computer	4489	300	4189			
电子器件制造业	Electronic Device	93552		93552	137600		137600
电子元件制造业	Electronic Cell	2628		2628	29812		29812
其他电子设备制造业	Other Electronic Machines	4055		4055	1100		1100
仪器仪表及文化、办公用机械制造业	Instruments,Meters,Cultural and Official Machinery	12803		12803	1679		1679
通用仪器仪表制造	General Instruments and Meters	793		793	1679		1679
计量器具制造业	Measuring Implements	12010		12010			
其他制造业	Other Manufacturing	9891	490	9401	14590	490	14100
工艺美术品制造业	Art Products	1710		1710	2000		2000
日用杂品制造业	Daily Use Groceries	2901		2901	5310		5310
其他生产、生活用品制造业	Others	5280	490	4790	7280	490	6790
电力、煤气及水的生产和供应业	**Electricity,Gas and Water Production and Supply**	**671163**	**418652**	**252511**	**587583**	**464287**	**123296**
电力、蒸气、热水的生产和供应业	Electricity,Steam and Hot Water Production and Supply	547654	418652	129002	485281	464287	20994
电力生产业	Electricity Production	127440	127440		429553	429553	
电力供应业	Electricity Supply	315894	291212	24682	55728	34734	20994
蒸气、热水生产和供应业	Steam and Hot Water Production and Supply	104320		104320			
煤气生产和供应业	Gas Production and Supply	35245		35245	71085		71085
煤气生产业	Gas Production	3000		3000	2122		2122
煤气供应业	Gas Supply	32245		32245	68963		68963
自来水的生产和供应业	Water Production and Supply	88264		88264	31217		31217
自来水生产业	Water Production	76681		76681	18017		18017
自来水供应业	Water Supply	11583		11583	13200		13200

4-11 续表3 continued

单位：万元 (10000 yuan)

行业	Item	投资额 Investment 合计 Total	中央 Central	地方 Local	新增固定资产 Incremental Fixed Assets 合计 Total	中央 Central	地方 Local
建筑业	**Construction**	**79794**	**31948**	**47846**	**46118**	**14830**	**31288**
土木工程建筑业	Civil Engineering Construction	75303	29352	45951	42546	13922	28624
房屋建筑业	Building Construction	71207	25256	45951	37950	9326	28624
铁路、公路、遂道、桥梁建筑业	Railways,Highways,Tunnels and Bridges Construction	3996	3996		4596	4596	
其他土木工程建筑业	Others	100	100				
线路、管道和设备安装业	Line and Equipment Installation	4491	2596	1895	3572	908	2664
线路、管道安装业	Line Installation	2288	2288		600	600	
设备安装业	Equipment Installation	2203	308	1895	2972	308	2664
地质勘查业、水利管理业	**Geological Prospecting and Water Conservancy**	**16270**	**15004**	**1266**	**11862**	**7046**	**4816**
地质勘查业	Geological Prospecting	4159	3153	1006	11332	7046	4286
矿产地质勘查业	Minerals Prospecting	2183	1477	706	6720	5034	1686
工程地质勘察设计业	Engineering Geological Prospecting and Design	512	212	300	2812	212	2600
地球物理和地球化学勘察业	Geophysical and Geochemical Prospecting	1464	1464		1800	1800	
水利管理业	Water Conservancy	12111	11851	260	530		530
交通运输、仓储及邮电通信业	**Transportation,Storage,Posts and Telecommunications**	**553192**	**521698**	**31494**	**180351**	**155221**	**25130**
铁路运输业	Railways	89752	89752		88119	88119	
公路运输业	Highways	4529	270	4259	1060		1060
汽车运输业	Motor Vehicles	4529	270	4259	1060		1060
航空运输业	Aviations	15772	15772		3312	3312	
航空客货运输业	Passenger and Freight Transportation	15772	15772		3312	3312	
交通运输辅助业	Logistic Support for Transportation	287224	286621	603	6377	6077	300
公路管理及养护业	Highway Management and Maintenance	603		603	300		300
机场及航空运输辅助业	Airport and Logistics of Aviation	286621	286621		6077	6077	
仓储业	Storage	25683	2754	22929	23770		23770
邮电通信业	Posts and Telecommunications	130232	126529	3703	57713	57713	
邮政业	Posts	19273	19273		12482	12482	
电信业	Telecommunications	106280	106280		44345	44345	
批发和零售贸易餐饮业	**Wholesale,Retail and Catering**	**123920**	**59499**	**64421**	**202532**	**92183**	**110349**
食品、饮料、烟草和家庭用品批发业	Wholesale of Food,Beverage, Tabacco and Family Use Goods	21533	215	21318	12080	215	11865
食品、饮料、烟草批发业	Food,Beverage and Tabacco	8410		8410	5200		5200
棉麻土畜产品批发业	Cotton,Fiber,Local and Animal Products	268		268			
纺织品、服装和鞋帽批发业	Textile,Garments,Shoes and Hats	4940		4940	3409		3409
日用百货批发业	Daily Use Goods	5842		5842	1010		1010
五金交电化工批发业	Hardware,Electrical Appliance and Chemical	1668		1668	1796		1796
药品及医疗器械批发业	Medicine and Medical Appliance	405	215	190	665	215	450
能源、材料、机械和电子设备批发业	Wholesale of Energy,Materials Machine and Electronic Equipment	17346	10713	6633	50699	39510	11189
能源批发业	Energy	105		105	335		335
化工材料批发业	Chemical Materials	1397		1397			
建筑材料批发业	Building Materials	8392	4830	3562	38263	27923	10340
金属材料批发业	Ferrous Materials	6349	4780	1569	514		514
机械、电子设备批发业	Machine and Electronic Equipment	1103	1103		11587	11587	

4-11 续表4 continued

单位：万元 (10000 yuan)

行业	Item	投资额 Investment 合计 Total	中央 Central	地方 Local	新增固定资产 Incremental Fixed Assets 合计 Total	中央 Central	地方 Local
其他批发业	Others	21626	21346	280	1140	860	280
图书报刊批发业	Books,Newspapers and Magazines	190	190		860	860	
农业生产资料批发业	Agricultural Capital Goods	165	5	160	160		160
其他类未包括的批发	Others	21271	21151	120	120		120
零售业	Retail	55398	21225	34173	131791	51598	80193
食品、饮料和烟草零售业	Food,Beverage and Tabacco	775		775	38004		38004
日用百货零售业	Daily Use Goods	40222	21195	19027	52718	51598	1120
五金交电化工零售业	Hardware,Electrical Appliance and Chemical	780	30	750	2450		2450
药品及医疗器械零售业	Medicine and Medical Machine	300		300	300		300
图书报刊零售业	Books,Newspapers and Magazines	12086		12086	36814		36814
其他零售业	Others	1235		1235	1505		1505
商业经纪与代理业	Business Agencies	6000	6000				
餐饮业	Catering	2017		2017	6822		6822
正餐	Dinner	1558		1558	400		400
其他餐饮业	Others	459		459	6422		6422
金融、保险业	**Banking and Insurance**	**102411**	**102411**		**181218**	**181218**	
金融业	Banking	99911	99911		178518	178518	
中央银行	Central Bank	14787	14787				
商业银行	Commercial Bank	85124	85124		178518	178518	
保险业	Insurance	2500	2500		2700	2700	
房地产业	**Real Estate**	**32079**	**7553**	**24526**	**16002**		**16002**
房地产管理业	Management	31197	7553	23644	13339		13339
房地产代理与经纪业	Brokerage and Agencies	882		882	2663		2663
社会服务业	**Social Services**	**518628**	**94221**	**424407**	**267815**	**158851**	**108964**
公共服务业	Public Services	340134		340134	45319		45319
市内公共交通业	Urban Public Traffic	199127		199127	3973		3973
园林绿化业	Gardens Afforest	28796		28796	3289		3289
环境卫生业	Environmental Sanitation	19909		19909	31820		31820
市政工程管理业	Municipal Engineering Management	90202		90202	6165		6165
居民服务业	Personal Services	9942		9942	8273		8273
沐浴业	Bath	1346		1346			
殡葬业	Funeral and Interment Services	7743		7743	5767		5767
其他居民服务业	Others	853		853	2506		2506
旅馆业	Hotels	48770	4740	44030	35254		35254
租赁服务业	Rentals	32059	32059		117549	117549	
旅游业	Tourism	14277	1384	12893	1867	749	1118
娱乐服务业	Recreation	3849		3849			
信息、咨询服务业	Information and Consultancy	16492	8634	7858	19000		19000
咨询服务业	Consultancy Services	4500		4500	19000		19000
其他类未包括的信息咨询服务业	Others	11992	8634	3358			
计算机应用服务业	Computer Application	5007	106	4901	106	106	
软件开发咨询业	Software Development Consultancy	5007	106	4901	106	106	
其他社会服务业	Other Social Services	48098	47298	800	40447	40447	
市场管理服务业	Market Management	9754	9754		34018	34018	
其他类未包括的社会服务业	Others	38344	37544	800	6429	6429	
卫生体育和社会福利业	**Health Care,Sports and Social Welfare**	**90379**	**43994**	**46385**	**59481**	**24081**	**35400**
卫生	Health Care	82367	42716	39651	53403	24081	29322
医院	Hospitals	65730	29315	36415	43875	17301	26574

4-11 续表5 continued

单位：万元 (10000 yuan)

行业	Item	投资额 Investment 合计 Total	中央 Central	地方 Local	新增固定资产 Incremental Fixed Assets 合计 Total	中央 Central	地方 Local
疗养院	Sanitariums	3048	2515	533	4411	3878	533
妇幼保健所(站)	Maternity and Child Care Institutions	2606		2606	2215		2215
药品检验所(室)	Medicines and Chemical Reagents Test Labs	81	81		2255	2255	
其他医院	Other Hospitals	10697	10600	97			
体育	Sports	7310	1278	6032	4399		4399
社会福利保障业	Social Welfare and Securation	702		702	1679		1679
社会福利业	Social Welfare	702		702	1679		1679
教育、文化艺术及广播电影电视业	**Education,Culture and Arts, Radio,Film and Television**	**482842**	**326981**	**155861**	**380756**	**278588**	**102168**
教育	Education	359300	232113	127187	289871	205408	84463
高等教育	Higher Education	259517	213097	46420	223539	181124	42415
中等教育	Secondary School Education	66284	9541	56743	36733	10349	26384
初等教育	Primary Education	5664	485	5179	5504	500	5004
特殊教育	Special Education	288		288			
其他教育	Other Education	27547	8990	18557	24095	13435	10660
文化艺术业	Culture and Arts	91882	67104	24778	41998	25129	16869
艺术	Arts	16871	8604	8267	12957	12197	760
出版	Publication	21081	18061	3020	17345	12545	4800
文物保护	Preservation of Culture Relics	2032	1849	183			
图书馆	Libraries	4954	359	4595	57	57	
档案馆	Archives	45		45	908		908
群众文化	Mass Culture	5868		5868	10389		10389
新闻	News	24199	24199				
其他文化艺术业	Others	16832	14032	2800	342	330	12
广播电影电视业	Radio,Film and Television	31660	27764	3896	48887	48051	836
广播	Radio	15407	13697	1710	38166	38166	
电影	Film	6486	6486		8722	8722	
电视	Television	9767	7581	2186	1999	1163	836
科学研究和综合技术服务业	**Scientific Research and Polytechnical Services**	**209777**	**166847**	**42930**	**191812**	**157243**	**34569**
科学研究业	Scientific Research	164250	149761	14489	147766	131768	15998
自然科学研究	Natural Science	129605	121956	7649	131182	118223	12959
社会科学研究	Social Science	4205	4205		145	145	
其他科学研究	Others	30440	23600	6840	16439	13400	3039
综合技术服务业	Polytechnical Services	45527	17086	28441	44046	25475	18571
气象	Meteorologe	2467	2467		1707	1707	
测绘	Mapping	1479		1479	3031		3031
环境保护	Enviromental Protection	125		125	125		125
技术推广和科技交流服务业	Technology Spreading and Scientific Technical Exchanges	2293	41	2252	3598		3598
工程设计业	Engineering Design	14404	14404		23768	23768	
其他综合技术服务业	Others	24585		24585	11817		11817
国家机关、政党机关和社会团体	**Government Agencies,Party Agencies and Social Organizations**	**628755**	**440574**	**188181**	**397216**	**284163**	**113053**
国家机关	Government Agencies	517399	330667	186732	300075	191311	108764
政党机关	Party Agencies	85624	85624		90956	90956	
社会团体	Social Organizations	25732	24283	1449	6185	1896	4289
其他行业	**Other Sectors**	**104924**	**33403**	**71521**	**102276**	**9749**	**92527**
企业管理机构	Administrative Organs of Enterprises	51599	20627	30972	59404	2087	57317
其他类未包括的行业	Others	53325	12776	40549	42872	7662	35210

4-12 全市更新改造投资额及新增固定资产(按行业分)

TOTAL INVESTMENT IN INNOVATION AND INCREMENTAL FIXED ASSETS (BY SECTOR)

单位：万元 (10000 yuan)

行业	Item	投资额 Investment 合计 Total	中央 Central	地方 Local	新增固定资产 Incremental Fixed Assets 合计 Total	中央 Central	地方 Local
总计	**Total**	**2524288**	**1003398**	**1520890**	**1616523**	**817929**	**798594**
农、林、牧、渔业	**Farming,Forestry,Animal Husbandry and Fishery**	**3377**		**3377**	**3612**		**3612**
农业	Farming	2464		2464	2737		2737
林业	Forestry	330		330			
渔业	Fishery	38		38			
淡水渔业	Freshwater Fishery	38		38			
农、林、牧、渔服务业	FFAF Services	545		545	875		875
采掘业	**Excavation**	**5455**		**5455**	**1737**		**1737**
煤炭采选业	Coal Mining and Dressing	4347		4347	902		902
非金属矿采选业	Nonmetal Minerals Mining and Dressing	1108		1108	835		835
土砂石开采业	Sand and Stone Mining and Dressing	873		873	835		835
化学矿采选业	Chemical Minerals Mining and Dressing	235		235			
制造业	**Manufacturing**	**440503**	**111748**	**328755**	**492951**	**198958**	**293993**
食品加工业	Food Processing	2488		2488	7551		7551
粮食及饲料加工业	Grain and Feed	886		886	5669		5669
植物油加工业	Vegetable Oil	403		403	383		383
屠宰及肉类蛋类加工业	Butcher, Meat and Egg	1199		1199	1499		1499
食品制造业	Food Making	12007		12007	6078		6078
糕点、糖果制造业	Pastry and Candy	118		118			
乳制品制造业	Dairy Products	11244		11244	5968		5968
调味品制造业	Flavourings	645		645	110		110
饮料制造业	Beverage Production	100		100			
酒精及饮料酒制造业	Alcohol and Beverage Wine	100		100			
纺织业	Textile Industry	10460		10460	6962		6962
棉纺织业	Cotton Textile	8810		8810	5939		5939
毛纺织业	Woolen Textile	678		678	778		778
针织品业	Knitting Textile	972		972	245		245
皮革、毛皮、羽绒及其制品业	Leather,Furs,Down and Related Products	518		518	86		86
制革业	Leather Making	518		518	86		86
木材加工及竹、藤、棕、草制品业	Timber Processing,Bamboo, Cane,Palm Fiber and Straw Produts	3442		3442			
人造板制造业	Artificial Board	3442		3442			
家具制造业	Furniture Industry	5203		5203	3022		3022
金属家具制造业	Metal Furniture	5203		5203	3022		3022
造纸及纸制品业	Papermaking and Paper Products	3184		3184	3184		3184
纸制品业	Paper Products	3184		3184	3184		3184

4-12 续表1 continued

单位：万元 (10000 yuan)

行业	Item	投资额 Investment 合计 Total	中央 Central	地方 Local	新增固定资产 Incremental Fixed Assets 合计 Total	中央 Central	地方 Local
印刷业、记录媒介的复制	Printing and Record Medium Reproduced	6640	4092	2548	21718	4339	17379
印刷业	Printing	6640	4092	2548	21718	4339	17379
文教体育用品制造业	Stationery,Education and Sports Goods	3480		3480	1054		1054
文化用品制造业	Cultural Goods	1264		1264	699		699
乐器及其他文娱用品制造业	Music Instruments and Other Stationery Goods	2216		2216	355		355
石油加工及炼焦业	Petroleum Processing and Coking Products	40184	36507	3677	134032	125317	8715
原油加工业	Petroleum Processing	31410	31410		122635	122635	
石油制品业	Petroleum Products	7680	5097	2583	11277	2682	8595
炼焦业	Coking Products	1094		1094	120		120
化学原料及化学制品制造业	Raw Chemical Materials and Chemical Products	109601	25139	84462	72804	19998	52806
基本化学原料制造业	Elementary Raw Chemical Materials	174		174			
化学肥料制造业	Chemical Fertilizer	9168		9168	9982		9982
有机化学产品制造业	Organic Chemical Products	71943	17804	54139	48655	13013	35642
合成材料制造业	Synthetic Materials	8328	7335	993	6985	6985	
专用化学产品制造业	Special Purpose Chemical Products	18853		18853	640		640
日用化学产品制造业	Daily Use Chemical Products	1135		1135	6542		6542
医药制造业	Medical and Pharmaceutical Products	3334	1200	2134	4706	1784	2922
化学药品制剂制造业	Original Chemical Medicine	1000		1000			
中药材及中成药加工	Raw Material and Products of Chinese Medicine	649		649	2360		2360
动物药品制造业	Animal Medicine	385		385	562		562
生物制品业	Biological Products	1300	1200	100	1784	1784	
化学纤维制造业	Chemical Fiber Manufacturing	2217	2217		2417	2417	
合成纤维制造业	Synthetic Fibers	2217	2217		2417	2417	
橡胶制品业	Rubber Products	15725	2565	13160	25004	2565	22439
轮胎制造业	Tire Manufacturing	11463	2565	8898	21604	2565	19039
日用橡胶制品业	Dailyuse Products	4262		4262	3400		3400
塑料制品业	Plastic Products	2785	50	2735	1023	50	973
塑料薄膜制造业	Plastic Film	567		567	567		567
其他塑料制品业	Other Plastic Products	2218	50	2168	456	50	406
非金属矿物制品业	Nonmetal Mineral Products	32489	24882	7607	32058	24882	7176
水泥制造业	Cement Manufacturing	620		620	680		680
砖瓦、石灰和轻质建筑材料制造业	Brick,Tile and Light Construction Material	27378	24882	2496	25152	24882	270
玻璃及玻璃制品业	Glass and Glass Products	1344		1344	3180		3180
陶瓷制品业	Ceramics Products	3046		3046	3046		3046
其他类未包括的非金属矿物制品业	Other Nonmetal Mineral Products	101		101			
黑色金属冶炼及压延加工业	Smelting and Pressing of Ferrous Metals	27885		27885	20758		20758
炼钢业	Steel-smelting	717		717			
钢压延加工业	Steel Pressing	27168		27168	20758		20758
有色金属冶炼及压延加工业	Smelting and Pressing of Nonferrous Metals	250		250			
有色金属压延加工业	Nonferrous Metals Pressing	250		250			
金属制品业	Metal Products	12572		12572	11151		11151

4-12 续表2 continued

单位：万元 (10000 yuan)

行业	Item	投资额 Investment 合计 Total	中央 Central	地方 Local	新增固定资产 Incremental Fixed Assets 合计 Total	中央 Central	地方 Local
铸铁管制造业	Tube of Cast Iron	182		182	249		249
工具制造业	Tools Manufacturing	295		295			
集装箱和金属包装物品制造业	Container and Metal Cover Manufacturing	4394		4394	1955		1955
建筑用金属制品业	Products for Construct Use	6921		6921	8167		8167
其他金属制品业	Others	780		780	780		780
普通机械制造业	Ordinary Machine-building	9279		9279	5089		5089
锅炉及原动机制造业	Boiler and Motive Machine	2656		2656	352		352
金属加工机械制造业	Metal Processing Machine	4420		4420	3854		3854
通用设备制造业	Universal Equipment	623		623	670		670
轴承、阀门制造业	Bearing and Valve	461		461	138		138
其他通用零部件制造业	Other Universal Components and Parts	1119		1119	75		75
专用设备制造业	Special Purpose Equipment Building	27561	6593	20968	28928	7206	21722
机电工业专用设备制造业	Equipment for Engine and Electricity	3516	3179	337	3851	3792	59
石化及其他工业专用设备制造业	Equipment for Petroleum and Other Sector of Industry	8356	3414	4942	5536	3414	2122
轻纺工业专用设备制造业	Equipment for Light and Textile Industry	10694		10694	15254		15254
农、林、牧、渔,水利业机械制造业	Machines for Farming,Forestry,Animal Husbandry,Fishing and Irrigation	308		308	52		52
医疗器械制造业	Medical Machines	3406		3406	3703		3703
其他专用设备制造业	Other Special Purpose Equipment	1281		1281	532		532
交通运输设备制造业	Transportation Equipment Manufacturing	57477	8484	48993	61827	10400	51427
铁路运输设备制造业	Railway Transportation Equipment	13660	3094	10566	4280	905	3375
汽车制造业	Motor Vehicles	36473		36473	42866		42866
交通运输设备修理业	Transportation Equipment Repairing	7344	5390	1954	14681	9495	5186
电气机械及器材制造业	Electric Equipment and Appliances Manufacturing	5900		5900	4167		4167
输配电及控制设备制造业	Electricity Transmit,Distribution and Control Equipment	1774		1774	475		475
电工器材制造业	Electrical Appliances	1206		1206	1206		1206
日用电器制造业	Daily Use Electrical Appliances	2920		2920	2486		2486
电子及通信设备制造业	Electronic and Telecommunication Equipment	36986		36986	33811		33811

4-12 续表3 continued

单位：万元 (10000 yuan)

行业	Item	投资额 Investment 合计 Total	中央 Central	地方 Local	新增固定资产 Incremental Fixed Assets 合计 Total	中央 Central	地方 Local
通信设备制造业	Telecommunication Equipment	10715		10715	4855		4855
广播电视设备制造业	Radio and Television Equipment	75		75			
电子计算机制造业	Computer	2183		2183	8546		8546
电子器件制造业	Electronic Device	6287		6287	4055		4055
电子元件制造业	Electronic Cell	15542		15542	14160		14160
日用电子器具制造业	Daily Use Electronic Appliances	2184		2184	2195		2195
仪器仪表及文化、办公用机械制造业	Instruments,Meters,Cultural and Official Machinery	5293	19	5274	2078		2078
通用仪器仪表制造	General Instruments and Meters	5175	19	5156	2078		2078
电子测量仪器制造业	Electronic Survey Instrument	118		118			
其他制造业	Other Manufacturing	3443		3443	3443		3443
工艺美术品制造业	Art Products Manufacturing	3443		3443	3443		3443
电力、煤气及水的生产和供应业	**Electricity,Gas and Water Production and Supply**	**224140**	**127891**	**96249**	**184559**	**126256**	**58303**
电力、蒸气、热水的生产和供应业	Electricity,Steam and Hot Water Production and Supply	174396	127891	46505	141312	126256	15056
电力生产业	Electricity Production	130209	124129	6080	122012	121137	875
电力供应业	Electricity Supply	3762	3762		5119	5119	
蒸气、热水生产和供应业	Steam and Hot Water Production and Supply	40425		40425	14181		14181
煤气生产和供应业	Gas Production and Supply	36955		36955	18705		18705
煤气生产业	Gas Production	954		954	4000		4000
煤气供应业	Gas Supply	36001		36001	14705		14705
自来水的生产和供应业	Water Production and Supply	12789		12789	24542		24542
自来水生产业	Water Production	12621		12621	23261		23261
自来水供应业	Water Supply	168		168	1281		1281
建筑业	**Construction**	**8794**	**5231**	**3563**	**8792**	**5021**	**3771**
土木工程建筑业	Civil Engineering Construction	8794	5231	3563	8792	5021	3771
房屋建筑业	Building Construction	7161	5021	2140	7161	5021	2140
铁路、公路、遂道、桥梁建筑业	Railways,Highways,Tunnels and Bridges Construction	210	210				
堤坝、电站、码头建筑业	Dikes and Dams,Power Station and Wharves	1029		1029	431		431
其他土木工程建筑业	Other Civil Engineering Construction	394		394	1200		1200
地质勘查业、水利管理业	**Geological Prospecting and Water Conservancy**	**151757**		**151757**	**7907**		**7907**
水利管理业	Water Conservancy	151757		151757	7907		7907
交通运输、仓储及邮电通信业	**Transportation,Storage,Posts and Telecommunications**	**1173012**	**739304**	**433708**	**695731**	**475575**	**220156**
铁路运输业	Railways	17557	17557		9331	9331	
公路运输业	Highways	426758		426758	213002		213002
汽车运输业	Motor Vehicles	426758		426758	213002		213002

4-12 续表4 continued

单位：万元 (10000 yuan)

行业	Item	投资额 Investment 合计 Total	中央 Central	地方 Local	新增固定资产 Incremental Fixed Assets 合计 Total	中央 Central	地方 Local
航空运输业	Aviations	4877	4877		4877	4877	
航空客货运输业	Passenger and Freight Transportation	4877	4877		4877	4877	
交通运输辅助业	Logistic Support for Transportation	8769	5029	3740	5350	4264	1086
公路管理及养护业	Highway Management and Maintenance	740		740	1086		1086
机场及航空运输辅助业	Airport and Logistics of Aviation	5029	5029		4264	4264	
其他类未包括的交通运输辅助业	Other Logistics for Transportation	3000		3000			
仓储业	Storage	18052	14842	3210	21410	15342	6068
邮电通信业	Posts and Telecommunications	696999	696999		441761	441761	
邮政业	Posts	115	115		195	195	
电信业	Telecommunications	696884	696884		441566	441566	
批发和零售贸易餐饮业	**Wholesale,Retail and Catering**	**46339**		**46339**	**36935**		**36935**
食品、饮料、烟草和家庭用品批发业	Wholesale of Food,Beverage, Tabacco and Family Use Goods	1373		1373	1726		1726
食品、饮料、烟草批发业	Food,Beverage and Tabacco	1270		1270	1623		1623
日用杂品批发业	Daily Use Groceries	103		103	103		103
能源、材料、机械和电子设备批发业	Wholesale of Energy,Materials Machine and Electronic Equipment	17672		17672	18106		18106
能源批发业	Energy	9940		9940	14277		14277
化工材料批发业	Chemical Materials	740		740	1050		1050
建筑材料批发业	Building Materials	1855		1855	2779		2779
汽车、摩托车及零配件批发业	Automobile,Motorcycle and Spares and Fittings	5137		5137			
其他批发业	Other Wholesales	219		219	707		707
其他类未包括的批发业	Others	219		219	707		707
零售业	Retail	27006		27006	16271		16271
食品、饮料和烟草零售业	Food,Beverage and Tabacco	90		90	370		370
日用百货零售业	Daily Use Goods	26322		26322	15782		15782
纺织品、服装和鞋帽零售业	Textile,Garments,Shoes and Hats	475		475			
其他零售业	Others	119		119	119		119
餐饮业	Catering	69		69	125		125
正餐	Dinner	69		69	125		125
金融、保险业	**Banking and Insurance**	**310**	**310**		**310**	**310**	
保险业	Insurance	310	310		310	310	
房地产业	**Real Estate**	**4867**		**4867**	**4597**		**4597**
房地产管理业	Management	4867		4867	4597		4597

4-12 续表5 continued

单位：万元 (10000 yuan)

行业	Item	投资额 Investment 合计 Total	中央 Central	地方 Local	新增固定资产 Incremental Fixed Assets 合计 Total	中央 Central	地方 Local
社会服务业	**Social Services**	**341925**	**852**	**341073**	**97895**	**642**	**97253**
公共服务业	Public Services	310407		310407	73315		73315
市内公共交通业	Urban Public Traffic	68853		68853	52925		52925
园林绿化业	Gardens Afforest	5208		5208	530		530
环境卫生业	Environmental Sanitation	200		200	200		200
市政工程管理业	Municipal Engineering Management	235990		235990	19504		19504
居民服务业	Personal Services	375	375		95	95	
旅馆业	Hotels	27823		27823	20709		20709
租赁服务业	Rentals	1823		1823	1823		1823
旅游业	Tourism	96		96	306		306
信息、咨询服务业	Information and Consultancy	924		924	1100		1100
广告业	Advertisement	197		197	197		197
其他类未包括的信息咨询服务业	Others	727		727	903		903
计算机应用服务业	Computer Application	477	477		547	547	
软件开发咨询业	Software Development Consultancy	477	477		547	547	
卫生体育和社会福利业	**Health Care,Sports and Social Welfare**	**2651**	**1925**	**726**	**1282**	**1107**	**175**
卫生	Health Care	2651	1925	726	1282	1107	175
医院	Hospitals	2651	1925	726	1282	1107	175
教育、文化艺术及广播电影电视业	**Education,Culture and Arts, Radio,Film and Television**	**14918**	**6950**	**7968**	**7455**	**950**	**6505**
教育	Education	7319	950	6369	6528	950	5578
高等教育	Higher Education	200	200		200	200	
中等教育	Secondary School Education	3089	750	2339	2024	750	1274
初等教育	Primary Education	12		12			
其他教育	Other Education	4018		4018	4304		4304
文化艺术业	Culture and Arts	6999	6000	999	327		327
图书馆	Libraries	106		106			
其他文化艺术业	Others	6893	6000	893	327		327
广播电影电视业	Radio,Film and Television	600		600	600		600
电影	Film	600		600	600		600
科学研究和综合技术服务业	**Scientific Research and Polytechnical Services**	**8007**	**4164**	**3843**	**6294**	**4429**	**1865**
科学研究业	Scientific Research	4925	3714	1211	5532	4429	1103
自然科学研究	Natural Science	4710	3714	996	5317	4429	888
其他科学研究	Others	215		215	215		215
综合技术服务业	Polytechnical Services	3082	450	2632	762		762
气象	Meteorology	450	450				
工程设计业	Engineering Design	762		762	762		762
其他综合技术服务业	Others	1870		1870			
国家机关、政党机关和社会团体	**Government Agencies,Party Agencies and Social Organizations**	**18915**	**2379**	**16536**	**17714**	**2904**	**14810**
国家机关	Government Agencies	18312	1776	16536	17111	2301	14810
政党机关	Party Agencies	603	603		603	603	
其他行业	**Other Sectors**	**79318**	**2644**	**76674**	**48752**	**1777**	**46975**
企业管理机构	Administrative Organs of Enterprises	15377	2644	12733	13750	1777	11973
其他类未包括的行业	Others	63941		63941	35002		35002

4-13 新增生产能力(或效益)
INCREMENTAL PRODUCTION CAPACITY(OR BENEFIT)

能力名称	Item	合计 Total	# 国有 State-Owned	# 集体 Collective Owned
催化重整设备 (万吨/年)	Catalytic Equipment (10000 tons/year)	200	200	
油罐容量 (万立方米)	Capacity of Oil Tank (10000 cu.m)	0.61		
冷加工钢材 (万吨/年)	Cold Steel Products (10000 tons/year)	1	1	
火力发电 (万千瓦)	Thermal Power (10000 kw)	46.5		
输电线路长度 (11万伏及以上,公里)	Length of Transmit Electricity Line (over 11,0000 volts,km)	3.5	3.5	
合成氨 (吨/年)	Synthetic Ammonia (ton/year)	40000	40000	
化学药制剂 (吨/年)	Chemicals Preparation (ton/year)	14	2	
中成药 (吨/年)	Chinese Medicine (ton/year)	800	800	
金属切削机床制造 (台/年)	Metal-Cutting Machine (unit/year)	400	400	
载货汽车制造 (辆/年)	Production of Cargo Truck (unit/year)	40000		
彩色显像管 (万只/年)	Tricolor Tube (10000/year)	90		
大中规模半导体集成电路 (万块/年)	Large-medium Semiconductor Integrated Circuit (10000/year)	12000		
肉加工品 (吨/年)	Meat Products (ton/year)	14000		
奶　粉 (吨/年)	Milk Powder (ton/year)	4000		
其他乳制品 (吨/年)	Other Dairy Products (ton/year)	98250	7000	
机制纸及纸板 (万吨/年)	Machine-made Paper and Paperboard (10000 tons/year)	0.3	0.3	
合成洗涤剂 (吨/年)	Synthetic Detergents (ton/year)	30000	30000	
皮　鞋 (万双/年)	Leather Shoes (10000 pairs/year)	3		3
塑料制品 (万吨/年)	Plastic Products (10000 tons/year)	1.45	1.45	
载货汽车购置 (辆)	Purchase of Cargo Truck (unit)	171	127	36
载客汽车购置 (辆)	Purchase of Coach (unit)	668	663	1
小汽车购置 (辆)	Purchase of Car (unit)	1858	1846	2
其他汽车购置 (辆)	Purchase of Other Motor Vehicles (unit)	63	45	
增建铁路第二线交付运营里程 (公里)	Mileage put into Operation of the Second Line of Railway Increased Built (km)	3.7	3.7	
新建公路 (公里)	Highway New Built (km)	30.7	30.7	
# 高速公路	Expressway	30.7	30.7	

4-13 续表 continued

能力名称 Item				合计 Total	# 国有 State-Owned	# 集体 Collective Owned
改建公路	(公里)	Reconstructed Highways	(km)	50.65	50.65	
新建独立公路桥梁	(延长米)	Absolute Highway and Bridge New Built		749	749	
	(座)		(extension meter,unit)	2	2	
市内电话自动交换机	(门)	Local Telephone Exchange	(line)	1277852	1267852	
粮食仓库	(万公斤)	Grain Storehouse	(10000 kg)	24517	24517	
	(平方米)		(sq.m)	60609	60609	
商业饮食服务网点	(处)	Commercial and Food Service Outlets	(unit)	65	55	4
	(平方米)		(sq.m)	453553	272124	11120
高等院校：学生席位	(个)	Institutions of Higher Education: Student Seats	(unit)	4096	4096	
建筑面积	(平方米)	Floor Space	(sq.m)	55194	55194	
中等院校：学生席位	(个)	Secondary Schools: Student Seats	(unit)	5680	5680	
建筑面积	(平方米)	Floor Space	(sq.m)	42056	42056	
小学校：学生席位	(个)	Primary Schools: Student Seats	(unit)	8800	8800	
建筑面积	(平方米)	Floor Space	(sq.m)	39780	39780	
其他学校：学生席位	(个)	Other Schools: Student Seats	(unit)	4710	4590	120
建筑面积	(平方米)	Floor Space	(sq.m)	40683	39298	1385
文化馆	(平方米)	Cultural Center	(sq.m)	9431	9431	
医院病床	(张)	Hospital Beds	(unit)	2605	2485	120
疗养院、所病床	(张)	Beds of Sanitariums	(unit)	400	400	
宾馆旅馆招待所客房数	(间)	Guest Rooms of Hotels	(room)	839	314	134
	(平方米)		(sq.m)	43437	13822	10000
城市自来水供水能力	(万吨/日)	Urban Tap Water Supplying Capacity	(10000 tons/day)	37	37	
城市自来水管道长度	(公里)	Length of City Tap Water Pipelines	(km)	11	11	
城市煤气生产能力	(万立方米/日)	Production Capacity of City Gas	(10000 cu.m/day)	60	60	
城市公共交通车辆购置	(辆)	Purchase of Public Traffic Vehicles	(unit)	18	18	
城市道路扩建长度	(公里)	Expanded Length of Highways	(km)	4.42	4.42	
城市道路扩建面积	(万平方米)	Expanded Area of Highways	(10000 sq.m)	34.82	34.82	
城市排水管道铺设长度	(公里)	Length of Paved Drainage Pipeline	(km)	1.2	1.2	
城市污水处理能力	(万吨/日)	Disposal Capability of City Sewage	(10000 tons/day)	0.07	0.07	
城市永久性桥梁	(座)	Perpetual Bridges	(unit)	5	5	

4-14 房屋建筑施工及竣工面积
FLOOR SPACE OF BUILDINGS UNDER CONSTRUCTION AND COMPLETED

单位：万平方米 (10000 sq.m)

项目	Item	1998	1997	占竣工面积(%) Proportion in Floor Space Completed(%) 1998	1997
施工总面积	**Floor Space of Buildings under Construction**	**6496.1**	**5819.4**		
竣工总面积	**Floor Space of Buildings Completed**	**1821.5**	**1625.7**	**100**	**100**
在竣工总面积中:	**Of the Floor Space Completed:**				
按用途分	**Grouped by Use**				
#厂房	Plant	97.0	68.0	5.3	4.2
仓库	Storehouse	17.4	25.6	1.0	1.6
办公室	Office	103.2	79.4	5.7	4.9
家属住宅	Families Residence	974.7	817.4	53.5	50.3
单身宿舍	Benchelor Quarters	27.0	25.4	1.5	1.6
教育用房	Education	71.4	58.0	3.9	3.6
科研用房	Scientific Research	25.7	29.6	1.4	1.8
医疗用房	Medical	17.4	10.9	1.0	0.7
商业营业用房	Commerce	122.7	80.3	6.7	4.9
礼堂、俱乐部	Assembly Hall and Club	3.0	3.5	0.2	0.2
影剧院	Theater and Cinema	1.2		0.1	
托儿所、幼儿园	Nursery and Kindergarten	4.0	4.5	0.2	0.3
旅馆、招待所	Hotel	5.5	6.6	0.3	0.4
按隶属关系分	**Grouped by Administrative Relationship**				
中央	Central	439.7	462.6	24.1	28.4
地方	Local	539.0	480.8	29.6	29.6
#国有	State-Owned	412.0	346.3	22.6	21.3
集体	Collective Owned	59.1	90.2	3.2	5.5
房地产开发企业	Comprehensive Development	842.8	682.3	46.3	42.0
按地区分	**Grouped by Region**				
城区	City Propers	367.3	285.1	20.2	17.5
近郊区	Near Suburbs	1087.6	1035.4	59.7	63.7
远郊区	Outer Suburbs	366.6	305.2	20.1	18.8

4-15 房屋建筑每平方米造价
COST PER SQ.M OF BUILDINGS

单位：元 (yuan)

项目	Item	1998	1997	1998年比1997年增(+)减(-) Increase or Decrease
平均造价	**Average Cost**	**2126**	**1857**	**269**
厂房	Plant	2292	2094	198
仓库	Storehouse	1353	1174	179
办公室	Office	5071	2613	2458
家属住宅	Families Residence	1443	1347	96
单身宿舍	Benchelor Quarters	1392	1479	-87
教育用房	Education	1955	1911	44
科研用房	Scientific Research	1997	2654	-657
医疗用房	Medical	2157	1725	432
商业营业用房	Commerce	3182	2473	709
礼堂、俱乐部	Assembly Hall and Club	2578	3907	-1329
影剧院	Theater and Cinema	2792		2792
托儿所、幼儿园	Nursery and Kindergarten	1634	1291	343
旅馆、招待所	Hotel	3593	2347	1246

4-16 基本建设大中型项目一览表

单位：万元

建设项目名称 Construction Project	建设地址 Address	国民经济行业 Sector	隶属关系 Administrative Relationship	建设性质 Type of Construction	建设阶段 Stage	开工年月 Beginning Time	投产年月 Operating Time	计划总投资 Total Investment
总计								**4312661**
中国农业大学211工程	北京	普通高等教育	中央	扩建	施工	199612		4100
北京西客站	北京	铁路运输业	中央	新建	收尾	199301		400000
天桥剧场翻扩建工程	北京	艺术	中央	扩建	施工	199611		19800
中央台业务楼	北京	广播	中央	新建	施工	199212		48012
中国国际广播中心	北京	广播	中央	新建	施工	199209	199807	37823
国家教委电教大楼	北京	国家机关	中央	新建	施工	199009		20070
北京科技大学211工程	北京	普通高等教育	中央	扩建	施工	199706		7280
清华大学211工程	北京	普通高等教育	中央	扩建	施工	199611		47034
北京大学211工程	北京	普通高等教育	中央	扩建	施工	199510		53194
中国人民大学211工程	北京	普通高等教育	中央	扩建	施工	199406		8858
中国医科院北京协和医院	北京	综合医院	中央	扩建	施工	199003		59386
北京医科大学211工程	北京	普通高等教育	中央	扩建	施工	199609		3150
中国地质大学(北京)211工程	北京	普通高等教育	中央	扩建	筹建			558
中国石油大学(北京)211工程	北京	普通高等教育	中央	扩建	施工	199601		8454
北京理工大学211工程	北京	普通高等教育	中央	扩建	施工	199612		51901
北京微电子所	北京	自然科学研究	中央	新建	施工	199603		46600
北京航空航天大学211工程	北京	普通高等教育	中央	扩建	施工	199703		8811
现代文学馆一期工程	北京	其他文化艺术业	中央	新建	施工	199801		15000
北京燕山石化(集团)有限公司 丁基橡胶	北京	合成橡胶制造业	中央	扩建	施工	199711		109977
首都机场航站区扩建	北京	机场及航空运输辅助业	中央	扩建	施工	199510		918412
北京炼焦化学厂 两段炉	北京	煤气生产业	市属	扩建	施工	199309		31431
北京首钢矿业公司 水厂铁矿扩建	北京	铁矿采选业	市属	扩建	施工	198612		299406
NEC日电工程技术升级	北京	集成电路制造业	市属	扩建	施工	199606		105000
米非司酮扩产项目	北京	化学药品制剂制造业	市属	扩建	施工	199706		5413
北京销区中心库	北京	仓储业	市属	新建	施工	199410		15000
第九水厂二期	北京	自来水生产业	市属	扩建	施工	199012	199807	212257
陕北天然气进京市内工程	北京	煤气供应业	市属	新建	施工	199604		355439
北京地铁复兴门--八王坟	北京	轨道交通业	市属	新建	施工	198805		757174
华能北京热电厂	北京	火力发电业	中央	新建	施工	199404		663121

LARGE AND MEDIUM PROJECTS OF CAPITAL CONSTRUCTION

(10000 yuan)

本年计划投资 Planning Investment of this Year	自年初累计完成投资 Accumulative Investment Since Year-Beginning	# 建筑工程 Construction	# 安装工程 Installation	# 设备购置 Purchase of Equipments	本年新增固定资产 Incremental Fixed Assets	年初累计资金来源合计 Accumulative Fund Source Since Year-Beginning	建筑规模和新增生产能力(或效益) Construction Size and Incremental Productive Capital(or Benefit): 名称 Item	计算单位 Counting Unit	建设规模 Size	新增能力累计 Accumulative Incremental Capacity	# 本年 of this Year
966896	**826628**	**275963**	**57563**	**282738**	**663034**	**726141**					
2338	2338			2338	2338						
62968	58879	52005	157	2412	58879	62968	新建铁路主线正线交付运营里程	公里	29	29	
							电气化铁路主线正线交付运营里程	公里	32	32	
							商业饮食服务网点	处	1	1	
								平方米	68000	68000	
							城市自来水管道长度	公里	22	22	
							城市供热能力:蒸汽	吨/小时	315	315	
							城市道路扩建长度	公里	6	6	
							城市道路扩建面积	万平方米	36	36	
							城市排水管道铺设长度	公里	46	46	
							城市永久性桥梁	座	4	4	
4500	4253	2400		326		4500					
1501	5721	2930	434	2156		1501					
263	263	263			38086						
1094	1090	1037				1096					
1900	1819	1330				1619					
6006	6006	4330		1625	249	6902					
10866	10784	9186		1575	3161	10866					
1869	1629	1488			2783	1879					
6976	2377	1578				6976	医院病床	张	841	841	
1571	1571			1571	1571	1571					
558	558			558	558	558					
2168	2168			2168	2168	2168					
13960	12764	10663		1402	3565	12764	高等院校:学生席位	个	2000		
							建筑面积	平方米	38130		
3635	3635	3635			6963	2835					
2830	2830	933		1897	1897	2830					
13000	6946	4013		124		5000	小汽车购置	辆	1	1	1
44500	44500	5188	7163	20685		44500	合成橡胶	吨/年	30000		
275500	280131	87542	21008	138675		257425	候机楼	座	1		
								平方米	268000		
3000	3000	2122	185	437	2122	413	城市煤气生产能力	万立方米/日	60	60	60
7350	6416	791		3195		6416	铁矿石原矿开采	万吨/年	1050		
							铁矿石成品矿	万吨/年	305		
45814	17303		1384	15919	9657	17303	大中规模半导体集成电路	万块/年	3000	3000	
3000	3900	2000	470	1200		3170	中成药	吨/年	800		
4500	8952	2283		6460	14684	4461	粮食仓库	万公斤	6200	6200	6200
								平方米	4298	4298	4298
57	57	57			18017		城市自来水供水能力	万吨/日	50	50	
							城市自来水管道长度	公里	104	102	
117172	32245	10179	868	4110	68963	60394	天然气管输	公里	204		
								亿立方米/年	10		
198000	191483	63132	8480	10110		141000					
130000	113010	6878	17414	63795	427373	65026	火力发电	万千瓦	65	47	47

4-17 国家及北京市重点工程一览表

单位：万元

建设项目名称 Construction Project	国民经济行业 Sector	隶属关系 Administrative Relationship	建设性质 Type of Construction	建设阶段 Stage	开工年月 Beginning Time	投产年月 Operating Time	计划总投资 Total Investment
一.重大项目							**10001614**
1.市政基础设施项目							**4355848**
地铁"复---八"线工程	轨道交通	市属	新建	施工	198805		757174
八达岭高速公路二期工程	汽车运输	市属	新建	施工	199701	199812	200000
东四环工程(高速公路联络线)	汽车运输	市属	新建	施工	199805		287200
平安大街建设工程	市政管理	市属	扩建	施工	199802		270291
菜市口南大街道路工程	市政管理	区属	扩建	施工	199807		145000
南闹市口打通工程	市政管理	市属	新建	施工	199805		76000
陕甘宁天然气进京市内工程	煤气供应	市属	新建	施工	199604		355439
高碑店热电厂市内供热管网工程	蒸气热水	市属	新建	施工	199404		331791
双榆树供热厂及供热管网工程	蒸气热水	市属	新建	施工	199412		134440
第九水厂三期及分钟寺调蓄水厂工程	自来水生产	市属	扩建	施工	199710		268978
高碑店北京热电厂（华能）	火力发电	中央	新建	施工	199404		663121
北京供电城网"9950"工程	电力供应	市属	扩建	施工	199512		493788
电信及广播通讯工程	电信业	中央	扩建	施工	199505		103815
高碑店污水处理厂二期工程	市政管理	市属	扩建	施工	199711		90000
水系综合整治及故宫护城河改造工程	水利管理	市属	改建	施工	199804		160000
北京市垃圾处理工程	环境卫生业	区属	新建	施工	199802		18811
2.大型公建和社会事业及公用设施项目							**4417024**
首都机场航站区扩建	航空运输	中央	扩建	施工	199510		918412
北京公共交通运营调度指挥中心	市内公共交通	市属	新建	施工	199802		9500
"八一"大楼	国家机关	中央	新建	施工	199703		45300
东方广场	房地产开发	区属	新建	施工	199409		1618500
首都时代广场	房地产开发	区属	新建	施工	199511		235200
国际金融大厦	金融业	市属	新建	施工	199612		160000
航华科贸中心	房地产开发	中央	新建	施工	199505		240345
国贸中心二期工程	旅馆业	中央	扩建	施工	199612		51190
中国银行总行大厦	金融业	中央	新建	施工	199608		120000
北京站改造	市政管理	区属	改建	施工	199808		6000
北京远洋大厦	房地产开发	市属	新建	施工	199708		193221
北京饭店改造	旅馆业	市属	改建	施工	199808		38800
嘉里中心	房地产开发	市属	新建	施工	199510		228306
华润大厦	房地产开发	市属	新建	施工	199705		86103
中国评剧院剧场	艺术	市属	新建	施工	199703		4845
北京戏曲学校排演场综合楼	中等专业学校	市属	扩建	施工	199711		19942
中国建筑文化中心	其它文化艺术	中央	新建	施工	199705		34000
中国现代文学馆一期工程	其它文化艺术	中央	新建	施工	199801		15000
首都图书大厦	图书报刊零售	市属	新建	施工	199312	199808	32000
首都图书馆新馆	图书馆	市属	新建	施工	199712		20000
中国紫檀博物馆	文物保护	中央	新建	施工	199803		15200
西单文化广场	房地产开发	区属	新建	施工	199804		54000
玉渊潭南门广场(中华世纪坛)	房地产开发	区属	新建	筹建			19000
朝阳公园	园林绿化业	区属	扩建	施工	199803		18500
中华民族园二期工程	旅游业	区属	扩建	施工	199712		30000
北京海洋馆	园林绿化业	市属	新建	施工	199510		77190
北京植物园展览温室	园林绿化业	市属	扩建	施工	199806		20000
北京大学理科群楼1#、2#	普通高教	中央	扩建	施工	199710		21834
首都经贸大学图书馆	普通高教	市属	扩建	施工	199712		2998
北京工业大学信息工程楼、经管楼	普通高教	市属	扩建	施工	199502		2310
首都师范大学文科教学楼	普通高教	市属	扩建	施工	199610		3760
北京联合大学图书馆	普通高教	市属	扩建	施工	199712		2300
首都医科大学科研楼	普通高教	市属	扩建	施工	199308	199812	13332
中国戏曲学院迁建工程	普通高教	中央	迁建	施工	199804		37489
中国科技馆二期工程	其它文化艺术	中央	扩建	施工	199802		10867
妇婴保健中心	妇婴保健	市属	新建	施工	199509		6580
佑安医院病房手术楼	专科医院	市属	扩建	施工	199610		5000
3.住宅开发项目							**1228748**
望京A5住宅区	房地产开发	市属	单建	施工	199503		358357
小营世纪住宅村	房地产开发	市属	单建	施工	199512	199806	95400
育新花园住宅区二期工程	房地产开发	市属	单建	施工	199709		35000

MAJOR PROJECTS OF STATE AND BEIJING

(10000 yuan)

本年计划投资 Planning Investment of this Year	自年初累计完成投资 Accumulative Investment Since Year-Beginning	# 建筑工程 Construction	# 安装工程 Installation	# 设备、工器具购置 Purchase of Equipments and Implements	本年新增固定资产 Incremental Fixed Assets	本年资金来源 Fund Source of this Year	建筑规模和新增生产能力(或效益) Construction Size and Incremental Productive Capital(or Benefit)				
							名称 Item	计算单位 Counting Unit	建设规模 Size	新增能力累计 Accumulative Incremental Capacity	# 本年 of this Year
2943935	2473301	1294320	88770	320242	893699	2450214					
1627481	**1298221**	**552930**	**45633**	**130793**	**782733**	**1083763**					
198000	191483	63132	8480	10110		141000	地铁	公里	13.50	1.81	
130000	105539	97048			204161	109950	高速路	公里	30.70	30.70	30.70
144000	169000	70184				143500	高速路	公里	15.00		
161000	132190	33757				68000	城市道路	公里	7.00		
105572	82908	4500				77908	城市道路	公里	2.10		
1479	1479	596				1479	城市道路	公里	0.86		
117172	32245	10179	868	4110	68963	60394	天然气管	公里	204.00		
105088	63213	29643				86042	供热	兆瓦/小时	500.00		
50835	40420	15717	1679	6292		16844	供热水	兆瓦/小时	348.00		
126585	81838	53662	556	1740	13200	52142	自来水	万吨/日	50.00		
130000	113010	6878	17414	63795	427373	65026	火力发电	万千瓦	65.00	46.50	46.50
113872	111330	52707	15936	32751	60286	83660	变电设备	万千伏安	165.80	63.00	63.00
45647	45647	44544		3	8350	35928	交换机	万门	160.00		
60727	32220	18777	500	9792	3400	46560	污水处理	万吨/日	50.00		
125000	87073	45777				84000					
12504	8626	5829	200	2200		11330					
1150638	**1026769**	**618587**	**42853**	**188134**	**46751**	**1134618**					
275500	280131	87542	21008	138675		257425	候机楼	平方米	268000.00		
8900	5662	4610				11980					
42670	42670	42670				25000					
233000	193831	168115		129		187093					
51545	51545	49658				187093					
89057	74235	8956	8143	620		53584					
64046	18550	14439	259	2381		52107					
39840	33622	33622				39840					
58500	47204	33469	2269	6573		74837					
3000	6000	5958				6000					
29500	27306	19066				29500					
8000	4850	3700		900		4850					
65830	65830	13804	7259	36919	191	70059					
31484	31484	31193				18915					
500	4845	4845									
3880	4089	3857				3964					
7150	9390	7635				7150					
13000	6946	4013		124		5000					
2000	12033	8588	237	757	36814	6725					
5000	4435	4154				5900					
10000	1789	839				1789					
20000	28409	11566				12165					
1900	1719	425		12	12	1900					
12267	2100	300		72	72	6767					
9000	11925	11202				7446					
13710	13152	6738	3451		123	14448					
12000	9757	8549		412		13802					
8232	8135	8130				8135					
2998	1706	947		66		2950					
1725	1440	1440				1700					
1610	1907	1907				1610					
1950	1265	1229		4		1950					
1542	1584	1178	10	52	9539	1614	席位	个	3400.00	3400.00	2900.00
8000	7168	6000		75							
8520	5814	4944				7020					
2482	2342	1409	217	363		2400	病床	张	300.00		
2300	1899	1890				1900	病床	张	700.00		
165816	**148311**	**122803**	**284**	**1315**	**64215**	**231833**					
8960	15001	14765				39941					
600	1597	1597				1597					
17724	10934	10244				33656					

4-17 续表

单位：万元

建设项目名称 Construction Project	国民经济行业 Sector	隶属关系 Administrative Relationship	建设性质 Type of Construction	建设阶段 Stage	开工年月 Beginning Time	投产年月 Operating Time	计划总投资 Total Investment
梅源住宅小区	科学研究	中央	单建	施工	199711		6540
力鸿花园住宅区	房地产开发	市属	单建	施工	199512		45498
燕化星城住宅区	企业管理机构	中央	单建	施工	199503		150000
牛街危改住宅区一期工程	房地产开发	市属	单建	施工	199804		200000
平渊里危改住宅区	房地产开发	市属	单建	施工	199512		90000
东花市二期危改住宅区工程	房地产开发	市属	单建	施工	199208		83700
小黄庄危改住宅区	房地产开发	市属	单建	施工	198810		39247
沙子口危改住宅小区	房地产开发	市属	单建	施工	199612		41000
马家堡安居小区	房地产开发	市属	单建	施工	199511		16000
采石路安居小区东区	房地产开发	市属	单建	施工	199511		23000
望京K4区安居小区	房地产开发	市属	单建	施工	199512		45000
二.国家及北京市重点工程							**3338376**
1.国家重点							**1766419**
北京大学"211"工程	普通高教	中央	扩建	施工	199510		53194
清华大学"211"工程	普通高教	中央	扩建	施工	199611		47034
中国人民大学"211"工程	普通高教	中央	扩建	施工	199406		8858
北京航空航天大学"211"工程	普通高教	中央	扩建	施工	199703		8811
北京理工大学"211"工程	普通高教	中央	扩建	施工	199612		51901
中国农业大学"211"工程	普通高教	中央	扩建	施工	199612		4100
北京医科大学"211"工程	普通高教	中央	扩建	施工	199609		3150
中国地质大学"211"工程	普通高教	中央	单购				558
北京科技大学"211"工程	普通高教	中央	扩建	施工	199706		7280
高碑店北京热电厂（华能）	火力发电	中央	新建	施工	199404		663121
首都机场航站区扩建	航空运输	中央	扩建	施工	199510		918412
2.北京市重点工程							**1571957**
危旧房改造	房地产管理	市属	改建	施工			
安居工程	房地产管理	市属	单建	施工			
松下彩管三期工程	电真空器件	市属	扩建	施工	199610		287400
三菱四通集成电路	集成电路制造	其他	新建	施工	199703	199811	83300
市委党校改造工程	其他教育	市属	扩建	施工	199712		3400
公安局"9111"工程	国家机关	市属	新建	筹建			
监所建设	国家机关	区属	扩建	施工	199708		8100
政法管理干部学院教学用房	成人高教	市属	扩建	施工	198912		6908
第二中级法院	国家机关	市属	新建	施工	199812		8500
北京销区中心库	仓储业	市属	新建	施工	199410		15000
北京第一热电厂技改工程	火力发电	中央	扩建	施工	199612		352382
化工三厂搬迁	化学试剂	市属	迁建	筹建			46253
电子城	其他行业	市属	新建	施工	199801		25400
高校开发望京花园一期	房地产开发	市属	新建	施工	199706		168100
北京联合大学机械工程学院实习工厂	高等教育	市属	扩建	筹建			9600
北京十二中迁建	中等教育	区属	迁建	筹建			
通州区妇幼保健院	妇幼保健	区属	迁建	施工	199806		1200
三台山危险品仓库迁建	仓储业	市属	迁建	筹建			6000
北京六里桥长途客运主枢纽	汽车运输业	市属	新建	筹建			20000
变电站工程	电力供应	中央	扩建	施工	199412		39586
电话局工程	电信业	中央	新建	施工			36359
南部城区污水截流工程	市政管理	市属	新建	施工	199209		90000
通惠河整治工程	水利管理	市属	扩建	施工	199702		76824
密云水库加固工程	水利管理	市属	改建	施工	199707		45270
西翠路道路及雨污水	市政管理	市属	新建	施工	199807		2000
西便门至菜园街道路	市政管理	市属	新建	施工	199712		900
石景山给水厂	自来水生产	区属	新建	施工	199805		12000
北京经济技术开发区基础设施	房地产开发	市属	新建	施工	199204		90482
郊区河道整治	水利管理	市属	改建	施工	199510		16393
青塔住宅小区二期工程	房地产开发	市属	单建	筹建			20000
北京农产品批发市场	零售批发贸易	市属	新建	施工	199410		30600
东北旺望儿山住宅小区	房地产开发	区属	单建	筹建			14000
北京市机动车驾驶员法规培训学校	其他教育	市属	新建	筹建			3000
地铁古城车辆段	轨道交通	市属	扩建	施工	199606		51000
公交站点建设	市内公共交通	市属	新建	筹建			
市委政法委党校	其他教育	市属	扩建	筹建			2000

continued

(10000 yuan)

本年计划投资 Planning Investment of this Year	自年初累计完成投资 Accumulative Investment Since Year-Beginning	# 建筑工程 Construction	# 安装工程 Installation	# 设备、工器具购置 Purchase of Equipments and Implements	本年新增固定资产 Incremental Fixed Assets	本年资金来源 Fund Source of this Year	建筑规模和新增生产能力(或效益) Construction Size and Incremental Productive Capital(or Benefit)				
							名称 Item	计算单位 Counting Unit	建设规模 Size	新增能力累计 Accumulative Incremental Capacity	# 本年 of this Year
3405	3405	3405			500	3930					
22000	10417	9752	75	350	45498	29454					
31491	31491	30621			12633	31700					
30230	15260	6755				30230					
9170	11639	9106			5584	8411					
1360	14832	11916				13147					
1600	3784	3320				200					
10000	8000	6856	200	944		8000					
4376	4376	3225				4538					
6155	6155	1849	9	21		12351					
18745	11420	9392				14678					
1358221	**1418553**	**249693**	**79313**	**334649**	**709086**	**1575781**					
447398	**433440**	**122350**	**38422**	**213436**	**440495**	**361440**					
10866	10784	9186		1575	3161	10866					
6006	6006	4330		1625	249	6902					
1869	1629	1488			2783	1879					
2830	2830	933		1897	1897	2830					
13960	12764	10663		1402	3565	12764					
2338	2338			2338	2338	0					
1571	1571			1571	1571	1571					
558	558			558	558	558					
1900	1819	1330				1619					
130000	113010	6878	17414	63795	424373	65026	火力发电	万千瓦	65	46.5	46.5
275500	280131	87542	21008	138675		257425	候机楼	平方米	268000		
916202	**985113**	**127343**	**40891**	**121213**	**268591**	**1214341**					
495427	627413					885111	建筑面积	万平方米	620.46		
20259	20299	2034	960	17305	78043	20299	彩管	万只	380.0	90.0	90.0
55950	55950	3950	15000	30600	49900	28525					
1831	2570	2467		103		1831					
3780	3780	3780				1682					
1640	2233	1670	121	404		2380					
1531	2323	343				0					
4500	8952	2283		6460	14684	4461	粮食仓库	万公斤	6200.0		
127100	112168	9436	20422	62807	108400	97636	火力发电	万千瓦/年	40.0		
4300	333					6000					
11680	12317	11122				15789					
33724	15835	15130				33656					
1802	1802	50		223	223	4515					
						0					
587	590	486				627	病床	张	251.0		
2000	320					420					
2000	469					2000					
14468	13656	8054	3672	1327	15985	13656	变电设备	万千伏安	108.0	52.0	52.0
13400	13400	9423				12400					
12036	6138	4638				8500					
27500	22611	12546	70			27500					
17000	26494	22012	188	102		17000					
1250	1923	1519				1923	城市道路	公里	2.5	1.9	1.9
500	500	500				500					
10468	4669	1950	192	727		4055	供水	万吨/日	5.0	5.0	5.0
24374	4299	1670	236	100		4598					
8743	8706	6802	5	147		7091					
9852	6243	1353		23	1356	3570					
8500	9120	4125	25	885		8616					

4-18 新建住宅竣工面积

FLOOR SPACE OF NEW RESIDENCE COMPLETED

单位：万平方米 (10000 sq.m)

项目	Item	1949-1998 合计 Total	1949-1998 1998	占新建住宅面积(%) Proportion in Floor Space of New Residence(%) 合计 Total	占新建住宅面积(%) Proportion in Floor Space of New Residence(%) 1998
总计	**Total**	**15431.8**	**1093.1**	**100**	**100**
平房	Singal-storey House	806.8	7.3	5.2	0.7
楼房	Storied Building	14625.0	1085.8	94.8	99.3
二～三层	2-3 Stories	877.1	27.2	5.7	2.5
四～五层	4-5 Stories	3120.0	57.3	20.2	5.2
六～八层	6-8 Stories	6709.5	495.4	43.5	45.3
九层以上	Over 9 Stories	3918.4	505.9	25.4	46.3
在总计中：	**Of Total:**				
城区	City Proper	2601.5	141.8	16.9	12.9
近郊区	Near Suburb	10236.3	703.5	66.3	64.4
远郊区	Outer Suburb	2594.0	247.8	16.8	22.7

4-19 农村集体及城乡私人建房面积

FLOOR SPACE OF BUILDINGS CONSTRUCTED BY RURAL COLLECTED-OWNED UNITS,URBAN AND RURAL INDIVIDUALS

单位：万平方米、间 (10000 sq.m,room)

项目	Item	1998年建成房屋面积 Floor Space of Buildings in 1998	#住宅面积 Floor Space of Residence	#住宅间数 Rooms of Residence	1997年建成房屋面积 Floor Space of Buildings in 1997	#住宅面积 Floor Space of Residence	#住宅间数 Rooms of Residence
总计	**Total**	**354.3**	**211.7**	**176416**	**333.8**	**201.2**	**167667**
农村集体建房	Rural Collective-Owned Units	268.8	131.9	109917	253.6	124.3	103583
城镇私人建房	Urban Individuals	35.2	31.3	26083	34.7	32.9	27417
农村私人建房	Rural Individuals	50.3	48.5	40416	45.5	44.0	36667

4-20 房地产开发企业基本情况
BASIC INFORMATION OF REAL ESTATE COMPANIES

项目 Item		企业单位个数（个） Number of Companies (unit)	资本金合计（万元） Total Capital (10000 yuan)	资产总计（万元） Total Assets (10000 yuan)	年末职工人数（人） Staff and Workers (year-end) (person)
总计	**Total**	**585**	**4653220**	**23317511**	**34629**
按企业登记注册类型分	**Grouped by Type of Enterprises Registered**				
内资企业	Domestic Investment Enterprises	362	1719697	12940499	22805
国有企业	State-Owned	226	779804	7583449	14660
集体企业	Collective Owned	18	29049	368304	1160
联营企业	Joint Owned	5	16115	241011	188
股份合作企业	Share Holding Cooperative	4	9450	169690	185
股份有限公司	Share Holding Company	27	632704	856425	2252
有限责任公司	Limited-Liability Company	81	250675	3714924	4351
其他企业	Others	1	1900	6696	9
港澳台商投资企业	Hongkong,Macao and Taiwan Funded Enterprises	154	1938024	7247838	7574
港澳台合资经营	Joint Venture	72	704274	2546506	3730
港澳台合作经营	Cooperative	72	959934	4247114	3402
港澳台商独资企业	Hongkong,Macao and Taiwan Enterprises	2	11464	60301	119
港澳台商投资股份有限公司	Hongkong,Macao and Taiwan Funded Share Holing Company	8	262352	393917	323
外商投资企业	Foreign Funded Enterprises	69	995499	3129174	4250
中外合资经营	Joint Venture	30	405785	1412389	2029
中外合作经营	Cooperative	38	459714	1126603	1976
外资(独资)企业	Foreign Enterprises				
外商投资股份有限公司	Foreign Funded Share Holding Company	1	130000	590182	245
按隶属关系分	**Grouped by Administrative Relationship**				
中央单位	Central	73	460285	2357278	4076
地方单位	Local	512	4192935	20960233	30553
按资质等级分	**Grouped by Grade**				
一级	First-grade	33	463219	6157636	7317
二级	Second-grade	51	278884	1738223	3008
三级	Third-grade	31	142788	1182011	2118
四级	Fourth-grade				
五级	Fifth-grade	14	125485	757194	1761
无级	No-grade	435	3367893	12310975	18969
兼营	Part-time Operating	21	274951	1171472	1456
按营业状况分	**Grouped by Business Condition**				
营业	Going on	527	4197736	21552953	33444
停业	Closed down	11	70280	57753	81
筹建	Preparing to Establish	30	323565	1322197	680
当年撤消	Cancel in this Year				
其他	Others	17	61639	384608	424

4-21 房地产开发企业开发情况

BUSINESS OF REAL ESTATE DEVELOPMENT ENTERPRISES

单位：万元,平方米 (10000 yuan,sq.m)

项目	Item	全市合计 Total	# 国有企业 State-Owned	# 三资企业 Foreign Funded	按隶属关系分 Grouped by Administrative Relationship 中央单位 Central Unit	地方单位 Local Unit
计划总投资	Total Planned Investment	29796113	9495701	11868640	1964420	27831693
自开始建设至本年度累计完成投资	Accumulative Investment up to the End of This Year	14185961	3517836	7341067	1129763	13056198
本年完成投资合计	Investment in This Year	3773996	996642	1858831	295669	3478327
# 商品房建设投资	Commercial House	2814395	643676	1521786	193468	2620927
土地开发投资	Land Development	227038	83384	42577	1240	225798
土地购置费	Purchase of Land	283768	58417	151701	35655	248113
本年完成投资按用途分	Grouped by Purpose of Investment in This Year					
住宅	Residence	1679818	528428	603744	140231	1539587
办公楼	Office	785201	76629	643900	93469	691732
商业营业用房	Commerce	360755	71120	233342	19119	341636
其他	Others	948222	320465	377845	42850	905372
本年土地开发	Land Development in The Year					
完成开发土地面积	Area of Development Completed	1949882	1121282	310199	71888	1877994
开发土地面积	Area of Land Development	4018074	1173061	290177	59020	3959054
购置土地面积	Area of Land Purchasing	1975387	699500	372687	250354	1725033
房屋建筑施工和竣工面积	Floor Space of Buildings under Construction or Completed					
施工面积	Floor Space of Buildings under Construction	34990608	11973588	12135086	2568073	32422535
# 住宅	Residence	21071849	8084932	4459727	1415952	19655897
竣工面积	Floor Space of Buildings Completed	8428074	3525685	1887126	686861	7741213
# 住宅	Residence	5887122	2655227	882770	386922	5500200
销售面积	Floor Space of Buildings Sold	4091953	1875173	701698	152905	3939048
# 住宅	Residence	3769896	1788720	558793	129817	3640079

主要统计指标解释

全社会固定资产投资　固定资产投资是全社会固定资产再生产的主要手段。通过建造和购置固定资产的活动，国民经济不断采用先进技术装备，建立新兴部门，进一步调整经济结构和生产力的地区分布，增强经济实力，为改善人民物质文化生活创造物质条件。这对我国的社会主义现代化建设具有重要意义。

全社会固定资产投资包括国有经济单位投资、城乡集体经济单位投资、其他各种经济类型的单位投资和城乡居民个人投资。按照我国现行计划管理体制，全社会固定资产投资总额分为基本建设、更新改造、房地产开发投资和其他固定资产投资四个部分；城乡集体经济单位投资包括城镇集体所有制单位投资和农村集体所有制单位投资；其他各种登记注册类型单位投资包括联营经济、股份制经济、中外合资经营、中外合作经营、外资、与大陆合资经营、与大陆合作经营、港澳台独资及其他经济的单位投资。城乡居民个人投资包括城市、县城、镇、工矿区所辖范围内的个人建房和农村个人建房及购买生产性固定资产的投资。

基本建设投资　基本建设是企业、事业、行政单位以扩大生产能力或工程效益为主要目的的新建、扩建工程及有关工作。包括（1）列入中央和各级地方本年基本建设计划的建设项目，以及虽未列入本年基本建设计划，但使用以前年度基建计划内结转投资（包括利用基建设备材料）在本年继续施工的建设项目；（2）本年基本建设计划内投资与更新改造计划内投资结合安排的新建项目和新增生产能力（或工程效益）达到大中型项目标准的扩建项目，以及为改变生产力布局而进行的全厂性迁建项目；（3）国有单位既未列入基建计划，也未列入更新改造计划的总投资在 50 万元以上的新建、扩建、恢复项目和为改变生产力布局而进行的全厂性迁建项目，以及行政、事业单位增建业务用房和行政单位增建生活福利设施的项目。

更新改造投资　更新改造是指企业、事业单位对原有设施进行固定资产更新和技术改造，以及相配套的工程和有关工作（不包括大修理和维护工程）。包括：（1）列入中央和各级地方本年更新改造计划的项目和虽未列入本年更新改造计划，但使用上年更新改造计划内结转的投资在本年继续施工的项目；（2）本年更新改造计划内投资与基本建设计划内投资结合安排的对企、事业单位原有设施进行技术改造或更新的项目，和增建主要生产车间、分厂等其新增生产能力（或工程效益）未达到大中型项目标准的项目，以及由于城市环境保护和安全生产的需要而进行的迁建项目；（3）国有企、事业单位既未列入基建计划也未列入更新改造计划，总投资在 50 万元以上的属于改建或更新改造性质的项目，以及由于城市环境保护和安全生产的需要而进行的迁建工程。

房地产开发投资　包括各种经济类型的房地产开发公司、商品房建设公司及其他房地产开发单位统一开发的包括统代建、拆迁还建的住宅、厂房、仓库、饭店、宾馆、度假村、写字楼、办公楼等房屋建筑物和配套的服务设施、土地开发工程，如道路、给水、排水、供电、供热、通讯、平整场地等基础设施工程的投资。包括非房地产企业实际从事房地产开发或经营活动，不包括单纯的土地交易活动。

其他固定资产投资　全社会固定资产投资中未列入基本建设、更新改造和房地产开发投资的建造和购置固定资产的活动。包括：

1. 国有单位按规定不纳入基本建设计划和更新改造管理计划，计划总投资在 50 万元及以上的以下工程：（1）用油田维护费和石油开发基金进行的油田维护和开发工程；（2）煤炭、铁矿、森工等采掘采伐业用维简费进行的开拓延伸工程；（3）交通部门用公路养路费对原有公路、桥梁进行改建的工程；（4）商业部门用简易建筑费建造的仓库工程。

2. 集体经济单位固定资产投资：包括城镇集体经济单位计划总投资在 50 万元及以上建造和购置固定资产的项目;农村集体经济单位计划总投资在 5 万元及以上建造和购置固定资产的项目。

3. 联营经济、股份制经济、外商投资经济、港澳台投资经济及其它登记注册类型的企、事业单位建造和购置固定资产计划总投资在 50 万元及以上的、未列入基本建设和更新改造计划的项目。

4. 城镇和工矿区私人建房投资和农村个人投资。城镇和工矿区私人建房包括市、县城、镇、工矿区所辖范围内的全部私人建房，不论其房主是否系本地的常住户口均应包括；农村个人投资包括农村个人建房及购置生产性固定资产的投资。

固定资产投资的资金来源　根据固定资产投资的资金来源不同，分为上年末结余资金、本年资金来源小计和各项应付款。其中本年资金来源小计又分为国家预算内资金、国内贷款、股票、债券、利用外资、自筹资金和其他资金来源七种：

1. 国家预算内资金　指国家预算、地方财政、主管部门和国家专业投资公司拨给或委托银行贷给建设单位的基本建设拨款和中央基本建设基金，拨给企业单位的更新改造拨款，以及中央财政安排的专项拨款中用于基本建设的基金。

2. 国内贷款　指报告期企、事业单位向银行及非银行金融机构借入的用于固定资产投资的各种国内借款。国内贷款包括：银行利用自有资金及吸收的存款发放的贷款、上级主管部门拨入的国内贷款、国家专项贷款（包括煤代油贷款、劳改煤矿专项贷款等），地方财政专项资金安排的贷款、国内储备贷款、周转贷款等。

3. 股票　是股份制企业通过发行股票筹集到的，用于固定资产投资的资金。

4. 证券　是企业（公司）或金融机构通过发行各种证券筹集到的用于固定资产投资的资金，包括由银行代理国家专业投资公司发行的重点企业证券和重点建设证券。

5. 利用外资　指报告期收到的用于固定资产投资的国外资金，包括统借统还、自借自还的国外贷款，中外合资项目中的外资，以及无偿捐赠等。其中，国家统借统还的外资，是指由我国政府出面同外国政府、团体或金融组织签定贷款协议、并负责偿还本息的国外贷款。

6. 自筹资金　指建设单位报告期收到的，用于进行固定资产投资的上级主管部门、地方和本单位自筹资金。

7. 其他资金来源　指报告期收到的除以上各种拨款、借款、自筹资金之外，其他用于固定资产投资的资金。

固定资产投资按国民经济行业分　建设项目归哪个行业，按其建成投产后的主要产品或主要用途及社会经济活动性质来确定。基本建设按建设项目划分国民经济行业，更新改造、国有经济单位其他固定资产投资及城镇集体投资根据整个企业、事业单位所属的行业来划分。一般情况下，一个建设项目或一个企业、事业单位只能属于一种国民经济行业。为了更准确地反映国民经济各行业之间的比例关系，联合企业（总厂）所属分厂属于不同行业的，原则上按分厂划分行业。

固定资产投资按建设性质分　建设项目的性质一般分为新建、扩建、改建、单纯建造生活设施、迁建、恢复、单纯购置。基本建设按建设项目划分建设性质，更新改造、国有经济单位其他固定资产投资及城镇集体投资按整个企业、事业单位的建设情况确定建设性质。

1. 新建　一般是指从无到有、"平地起家"的新开始建设单位。有的单位原有基础很小，经过建设后其新增加的固定资产价值超过原有固定资产价值（原值）三倍以上的也算新建。

2. 扩建　一般是指为扩大原有产品的生产能力，在厂内或其他地点增建主要生产车间（或主要工程）、独立的生产线或总厂之下的分厂的企业；事业单位和行政单位在原单位增建业务用房（如学校增建教学用房、医院增建门诊部或病床用房、行政机关增建办公楼等）也作为扩建。

3. 改建　一般是指现有企业、事业单位为了技术进步，提高产品质量，增加花色品种，促进产品升级换代、降低消耗和成本，加强资源综合利用和三废治理、劳保安全等，采用新技术、新工艺、新设备、新材料等对现有设施、工艺条件进行技术改造或更新（包括相应配套的辅助性生产、生活福利设施）。有的企业为充分发挥现有生产能力，进行填平补齐而增建不增加本单位主要产品生产能力的车间等，也属于改建。

4. 单纯建造生活设施　是指企、事业及行政单位在不扩建、改建生产性工程和业务用房的情况下，单纯建造职工住宅、托儿所、子弟学校、医务室、浴室、食堂等生活福利设施。

固定资产投资按用途分　固定资产投资按工程的用途分为农林牧渔业用、工业建筑业用、商业运输邮电业用、住宅和其他四部分，是研究不同用途的固定资产投资之间比例关系的重要指标。基本建设投资、国有经济单位其他固定资产投资及城镇集体投资的用途按单项工程确定，现有企业、事业单位更新改造投资的用途按更新改造项目确定。

固定资产投资按构成分　固定资产投资活动按其工作内容和实现方式分为建筑安装工程，设备、工具、器具购置，其他费用三个部分。

1. 建筑安装工程（建安工作量）　指各种房屋、建筑物的建造工程和各种设备、装置的安装工程。包括各种房屋建造工程，各种用途设备基础和各种工业窑炉的砌筑工程；为施工而进行的各种准备工作和临时工程以及完工后的清理工作等；铁路、道路的铺设，矿井的开凿及石油管道的架设等；水利工程；防空地下建筑等特殊工程；以及各种机械设备的安装工程；为测定安装工程质量，对设备进行的试行工作。在安装工程中，不包括被安装设备本身的价值。

2. 设备、工具、器具购置　指购置或自制达到固定资产标准的设备、工具、器具的价值，固定资产的标准按财务部门规定。新建单位、扩建单位的新建车间按照设计和计划要求购置或自制的全部设备、工具、器具，不论是否达到固定资产标准均计入"设备、工具、器具购置"中。

3. 其他费用　指除建筑安装工程和设备、工具、器具购置以外的投资完成额。它包括两种性质的费用，一种是属于增加固定资产的费用，主要有：建设单位管理费，土地、青苗等补偿费和安置补助费、勘察设计费，研究试验费、农林单位牲畜购置费、各种经济林木的营造费、办公和生活家具、器具购置费、引进技术和进口设备项目的其他费用、联合试运转费等；一种是属于不增加固定资产的费用，主要有：施工机械转移费、生产职工培训费、农业开荒费用及报废工程损失费等。

施工项目　指报告期内曾进行建筑或安装工程施工活动的建设项目。包括报告期内新开工项目、报告期以前开工跨入报告期继续施工的项目以及报告期施工过并在报告期内全部建成投产或停缓建的项目。

新增生产能力　指通过固定资产投资活动而增加的设计能力或工程效益，它是用实物形态表示的固定资产投资的成果。新增生产能力的计算，是以能独立发挥生产能力或效益的单项工程（或项目）为对象。当单项工程（或项目）建成，经有关部门鉴定合格，正式移交投入生产，即可计算新增生产能力。

新增生产能力或工程效益有以下几种表现形式：

1. 以建设项目或单位工程建成后的年产能力表示。如煤炭开采、石油开采等。

2. 以建设项目或单项工程建成后处理原料的能力表示。如选矿工程的处理矿石能力，洗煤厂年洗原煤能力等。

3. 以新增的主要设备数量或容量表示。如棉纺锭枚数，发电机组容量等。

4. 以建筑物容积、容量、面积或长度表示。如水库容量、铁路公路里程等。

新增生产能力的数量一般按设计能力计算。设计能力是指设计文件中规定的在正常情况下能够达到的生产能力，而不论投产后的实际产量如何。以设备数量、建筑物容积、面积、长度等表示的新增生产能力（或效益），则按建成的实际数量计算。

城市基础设施投资　城市基础设施包括第二产业中的电力、煤气及水的生产和供应业；第三产业中的水利业、铁路运输、公路运输、管道运输、航空运输、邮电通信、公共服务和环境保护等。

房屋施工面积　房屋建筑面积是从房屋外墙线算起的各层平面面积的总和，包括房屋结构（如柱、墙）占用的面积和地下室面积。多层建筑按各自然层面积总和计算，包括房屋内的楼隔层，突出墙面的眺望间、门斗、有柱雨罩的面积。不包括突出墙面结构的构件、艺术装饰等所占的面积，如台阶等。凹阳台、挑阳台按其水平投影面积一半计算建筑面积。

房屋竣工面积　指在报告期内房屋建筑按照设计要求已全部完工，达到住人和使用条件，经验收鉴定合格，正式移交使用单位的建筑面积。

房屋面积竣工率　指一定时期内房屋竣工面积占同期房屋施工面积的比率。它是从房屋建筑施工速度的角度反映投资效果和建筑业经济效益的指标。

新增固定资产　指通过投资活动所形成的新的固定资产价值。包括已经建成投入生产或交付使用的工程价值和达到固定资产标准的设备、工具、器具的价值及有关应摊入的费用。它是以价值形式表示的固定资产投资成果的综合性指标，可以综合反映不同时期、不同部门、不同地区的固定资产投资成果。

建设项目投产率　指一定时期内全部建成投产项目个数占同期正式施工项目个数的比率。它是从建设项目建设速度的角度反映投资效果的指标。

Explanatory Notes On Main Statistical Indicators

Total investment in fixed assets: Investment in fixed assets is essential for reproduction of fixed assets. By means of construction and purchase of fixed assets, more advanced technologies and equipments are adopted in the national economy, and new sectors are established, which promote the adjustment of economic structure and the regional distribution of production and enhance the economic strengths so as to provide the material conditions for improving people's livelihood. This is significant for speeding up the socialist modernization in China.

Total investment in fixed assets includes the investment by the state-owned units, the investment by the urban and rural collective units, the investment by the units of other registered types and the investment by the individuals in the urban and rural areas. According to China's current planning administration system, the aggregate investment in fixed assets is classified into the following four categories: investment in capital construction, investment in replacement & innovation, investment in real estates development and other aspects of fixed assets. The investment by the urban and rural collective units includes the investment by the urban collective units and the investment by the rural collective units. The investment by the units of other types of ownership includes the investment by the joint-owned business, share-holding business, Sino-foreign joint venture, Sino-foreign cooperative business, business with exclusive foreign investment, Mainland-Hong Kong or Mainland-Macao or Mainland-Taiwan joint business, Mainland -Hong Kong or Mainland-Macao or Mainland-Taiwan cooperative business, and business with exclusive investment of Hong Kong or Macao or Taiwan. The investment by the individuals in the urban and rural areas includes the investment in personal house building in the areas under the jurisdiction of city, county, town and village as well as the investment in purchase of productive fixed assets in the rural areas.

Investment in Capital Construction: Capital construction refers to the new construction projects or extension projects and the related work of the enterprises, institutions or administrative units mainly for the purpose of expanding production capacity or improving project efficiency. It includes: (1) Projects listed in the capital construction plan of the central government and the local governments at various levels in current year as well as the on-going projects from previous years' plan of capital construction and carried forward the investment to this year (including the equipments and materials kept in stock of the capital construction); (2) New construction projects arranged in both the plan of capital construction and the plan of replacement & innovation; Extension projects with the newly increased production capacity (or project efficiency) up to the standard of a large and medium-sized project; and the projects of moving the whole factory to a new site so as to improve the distribution of productive forces; (3)New construction projects, extension projects or restoration projects with the total investment more than 500 thousand RMB by the state-owned units, though listed neither in the plan of capital construction nor in the plan of replacement & innovation; the projects in the state-owned units of moving the whole factory to a new site so as to improve the distribution of productive forces; and the projects of additional business houses by the administrative units and institutions and welfare facilities by the administrative units.

Investment in Replacement & Innovation: Replacement & innovation refers to the renewal or technological upgrade of the original fixed assets by the enterprises and institutions as well as the corresponding supplementary projects and works (excluding major overhaul and maintenance). It includes: (1) Projects listed in the replacement & innovation plan of the central government and the local governments at various levels in current year as well as the on-going projects from previous years replacement & innovation plan with the investment carried forward to this year; (2) Replacement or innovation projects arranged both in the plan of replacement & innovation and in the plan of capital construction; Extension projects (main workshops or a branch of the factory) with the newly increased production capacity (or project efficiency) below the standard of a large and medium-sized project; and the projects of moving the whole factory to a new site so as to meet the requirements of urban environmental protection or safe production; (3) Replacement or innovation projects with the total investment more than 500 thousand RMB by the state-owned units, though listed neither in the plan of capital construction nor in the plan of replacement & innovation; Projects in state-owned units of moving a whole factory to new site so as to meet the requirements of urban environmental protection or safe production.

Investment in Real Estate Development includes the investment by the real estate development companies, commercial buildings construction companies and other real estate development units of various types of ownership in the construction of buildings, such as residential buildings, factory buildings, warehouses, hotels, guesthouses, holiday villages, office buildings, and the complementary service facilities and land development projects, such as road, water supply, water drainage, power supply, heating, telecommunications, land leveling and other infrastructures. It covers the activities of the non-real estate companies in real estate development or management, but excludes the activities in simple land transactions.

Other Investment in Fixed Assets refers to the construction and purchases of fixed assets not listed in the government plan of investment in capital construction or replacement & innovation or real estate development, which includes:

1. The following projects of the state-owned units with the total investment at 500 thousand RMB and above, which are not listed in the government plan of capital construction or replacement & innovation: (1) Projects of oil fields maintenance and exploitation with the oil fields maintenance funds and petroleum development funds; (2) Opening and extending projects with the maintenance funds in coal, ore and other mining enterprises and logging enterprises; (3) Reconstruction of the original highways and bridges with the highway maintenance funds in the department of communications; (4) Construction of warehouses with the funds of simple construction in the commercial department.

2. The investment in fixed assets of collective units refers to the urban collective units with the planned total investment at 500 thousand yuan and above and rural collective units with the planned total investment at 50 thousand yuan and above, including the construction and purchases of fixed assets. .

3. The construction and purchases of fixed assets by the enterprises or institutions of various ownership with the planned total investment at 500 thousand yuan and above, which are not included in the government plan of capital construction or replacement & innovation.

4. The private investment in house construction in the urban areas and industrial and mining areas as well as the

individual investment in the rural areas. The private house construction in the urban areas and industrial and mining areas includes all the private house construction under the jurisdiction of cities, counties, towns and industrial and mining areas, no matter whether the owner of the house is registered as the permanent resident in the locality. The individual investment in the rural areas includes the investment in house construction and purchase of productive fixed assets by the individuals in the rural areas. The individual investment in fixed assets in the rural areas is estimated by the Rural Socio-economic Survey Organization, SSB on the basis of the data collected by the sample survey.

Sources of Funds for Investment in Fixed Assets are classified into: (a) balance of funds brought forward from the previous year, (b)subtotaled sources of funds in this year and (c)various payable funds. The subtotaled sources of funds in this year is further divided into seven categories: state budgetary appropriation, domestic loans, stocks, bonds, foreign investment, self-raised funds, and others.

(I) State budgetary appropriation includes: (1) the central capital construction fund and the appropriation for capital construction, which are appropriated to or entrusted the banks to lend to the construction enterprises by state budget, local finance, responsible department and state specialized investment companies; (2) the appropriations to enterprises for replacement or innovation; (3) the special appropriation for capital construction, which is arranged in the central government finance.

(II) Domestic loans refer to various funds borrowed by enterprises and institutions from banks and non-bank financial institutions during the reference period for the purpose of investment in fixed assets. Domestic loans include loans issued by bands from their self-owned funds and deposit, loans appropriated by higher responsible authorities, special loans by government (including loan for replacing petroleum with coal, special loan for reform-through-labour coal mines) , loans arranged by local government from special funds, domestic reserve loan, and working loan, etc..

(III) Stocks refer to funds raised by share holding enterprises through issuing stocks for the purpose of investment in fixed assets.

(IV)Bonds refer to funds raised by enterprises (companies)or financial institutions through issuing various bonds for the purpose of investment in fixed assets, The bonds include Key Enterprise Bond and Key Construction Program Bonds issued by the banks on behalf of the state specialized investment companies.

(V) Foreign Investment refers to foreign funds received during the reference period for the purpose of investment in fixed assets, including foreign funds borrowed and managed by the government, by individual units, foreign fund in joint venture program, and grants and donations, etc.. Foreign funds borrowed and managed by the government refer to foreign loan borrowed by the government from foreign government, organizations, or financial institutions under official agreements and the government is responsible for the repayment of the principal and the interests.

(VI) Self-raised funds refer to funds received by construction enterprises from their higher responsible authorities, local governments, and internal financing for the purpose of investment in fixed assets during the reference period.

(VII) Other sources refer to funds received during the reference period which are not included in the above-mentioned sources.

Investment in Fixed Assets by Sector The classification of construction projects by sector is determined by the major products or the purpose of the projects when they are put into use, and by the nature of their social economic activities. The investment in capital construction is classified according to construction projects, while investment in replacement & innovation, other investment by state-owned units and urban collective units are classified according to the sector which the whole enterprise or institution belongs to. In general, one project or one enterprise or institution can only belong to one sector. In order to reflect more accurately the proportions among various sectors, the branch factories of integrated complex are classified into different sectors according to their economic activities.

Investment in Fixed Assets by Type of Construction The investment projects in general can be classified into new construction, expansion, reconstruction, building living construction, moving away, purchasing and restoration. For capital construction the type of construction is determined by the project. For investment in replacement & innovation and for other investment by state-owned and collective-owned units, the type of construction is determined by the enterprise or the institution. (1) New construction in general refers to newly constructed units; some of expansions are also considered as new constructions in the case that the value of the original fixed assets is quite small, and the value of increased fixed assets exceeds the original ones over three times,.

(2) Expansion refers to construction of new major production workshop or independent production line within a factory or in other locations, or construction branch of a factory so as to increase the production capacity of the original products. Newly constructed business houses in institutions and administrative organizations (such as the newly constructed teaching buildings in schools, clinics or bed building in hospitals, and office buildings in administrative organizations, etc.) are classified as expansions.

(3) Reconstruction refers to technical upgrade and renewal of the existing equipment and technical conditions undertaken by enterprises and institutions for the purposes of technological advancement, improvement in product quality, enlarging variety of products, promoting new generation of products, reducing productive consumption and cost, promoting comprehensive utilization of resources, strengthening treatment of waste gas, wastewater and solid wastes, and safety in production, etc. through application of new technologies and techniques, use of new equipment and new materials (including accessory facilities for production or for living and welfare purposes). Construction of new workshops for easing the bottleneck limits rather than increasing production capacity is also considered as reconstruction.

(4) Building living construction refers to Building welfare constructions such as residence,kingdergarden,sch ools,clinics,canteens and so on for staff and workers with no expansion,reconstruting productive projects and busi ness buildings.

Investment in Fixed Assets by Industry can be classified into four fields, i. e. construction for FFAF; industry and construction; commerce,transportation,posts and telecommunications; residence and others, which reflects important proportions of investment among different industries. The industry of the investment in capital construction, other investment in fixed assets by state-owned units and urban collective units is determined according to the individual projects. The industry of the investment in replacement & innovation by enterprises and institutions is determined according to the relevant projects.

Investment in Fixed Assets by Composition refers to the three major parts of investment activities, i. e. construction and installation, purchase of equipment and instrument, and other expenses.

(1) Construction and installation (work load of construction and installation) refers to the construction of various houses and buildings and installation of various kinds of equipment and instruments, including construction of various houses, equipment foundations and industrial kilns and stoves, preparation in advance and clearing up afterwards for project construction, pavement of railways and roads, drilling of mines and putting up of oil pipes, construction for water conservancy, underground constructions for air defense and other special projects, installation of various machinery equipment, trial running for testing the quality of installation. The value of equipment installed is not included in the value of installation projects.

(2) Purchase of equipment and instruments refers to the total value of equipment, tools, and vessels purchased or self-produced which come up to standards for fixed assets. Equipment, tools and vessels purchased or self-produced for new workshops by newly established or expanded units are categorized as "purchase of equipment and instruments" no matter whether they come up to the standards for fixed assets or not.

(3) Other expenses refers to investment excluded in above items, which consist of two categories: one results in the increase of fixed assets, including administration expenses of construction units, compensation for the loss of land and young crops, subsidies for moving, and expenses on geological prospecting and designing, research and testing, purchase of animals by agricultural and forestry units, planting and operating of various economic forest, purchase of office and home furniture, purchase of instruments and vessels, introduction of technology and imports of equipment, and joint trial running; the other does not result in the increase of fixed assets, including expenses on transportation of construction machines, training of staff and workers , opening up waste land, and loss of discarded projects.

Projects under Construction refer to projects having construction and installation activities undertaken in the reference period, including projects started in the reference period, or continued from previous period, or completed and put into production or suspended in the reference period.

Newly Increased Production Capacity refers to the increase of designed capacity and project efficiency through investment in fixed assets, which reflects the accomplishment of investment in fixed assets in kind. The statistics of newly increased production capacity is based on individual project with possibility of operating independently. A project is counted as newly increased production capacity when it is completed and checked and accepted and put into use.

The newly increased production capacity and project efficiency are usually expressed in one of the following terms:

(1) annual production capacity , such as extraction of coal and petroleum;

(2) raw material processing capacity, such as ore dressing capacity of ore dressing projects, the dressing, capacity of a coal washer;

(3) number or capacity of major equipment increased, such as the number of cotton spindles increased and the capacity of generating sets increased;

(4) physical measures of construction, such as volume, capacity, area, and length, for instance, the capacity of reservoirs, the length of railways or highways.

Newly increased production capacity in terms of quantity is calculated at designed capacity in general, which refers to the production capacity of a project under normal conditions supposed in construction documents regardless of the actual output.

Investment in urban infrastructure facilities include the production and supply of electricity, gas and tap water in the secondary industry and water conservancy, railway transportation, highway transportation, pipeline transportation, air transportation, posts and telecommunications, public services, environmental protection in the tertiary industry.

Floor Space of Buildings under Construction refers to total floor space in each story of buildings calculated from the outside line of building walls, including the space occupied by constructions like pillars or walls and basements. The floor space of space of multi-story building is the totaled floor·space of each story, including area occupied by separating walls, watching rooms, doorways, and pillars, excluding protruding wall structures, artistic decoration, etc. (for example, flight of steps) . The space of porch and balcony is counted by half of the projection area.

Floor Space of Buildings Completed refers to the total floor space of the completed buildings, which have met the designed using or living conditions, passed the check and accepted by the users in the reference period.

Percentage of Floor Space of Buildings Completed refers to the ratio of the floor space of buildings completed to the floor space of buildings under construction in the same period, which reflects the investment result and economic efficiency of the construction industry from the point of the construction speed.

Incremental Fixed Assets refer to the newly increased value of fixed assets through investment, including the value of projects completed and put into use, the value of equipment, tool and vessels considered as fixed assets as well as the relevant expenses accounted as investment in fixed assets. This is a comprehensive indicator of investment in fixed assets, reflecting the achievements of investment in fixed assets in given periods, given sectors or given regions.

Rate of Construction Projects Put into Use refers to the ratio of the number of construction projects completed and put into use to the number of projects under construction in the same period, which reflects the investment efficiency from the point of the construction speed.

1999

农业及农村经济

AGRICULTURE AND RURAL ECONOMY

1998年主要农作物、农产品产量(万吨)

Yield of Major Farm Crops and Farm Products (10000ton)

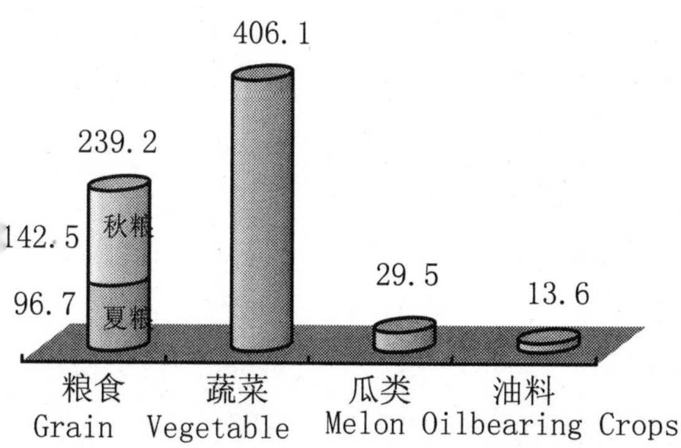

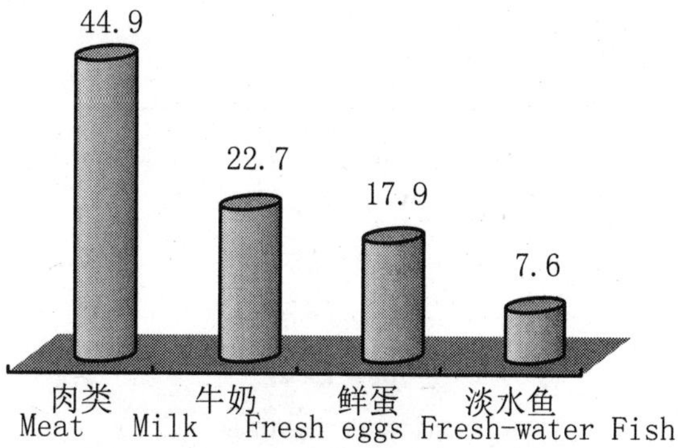

1998年乡镇企业主要产品产量占全市的比重

Major Products Output of Town and Township Enterprises and Their Proportion in Total of the City

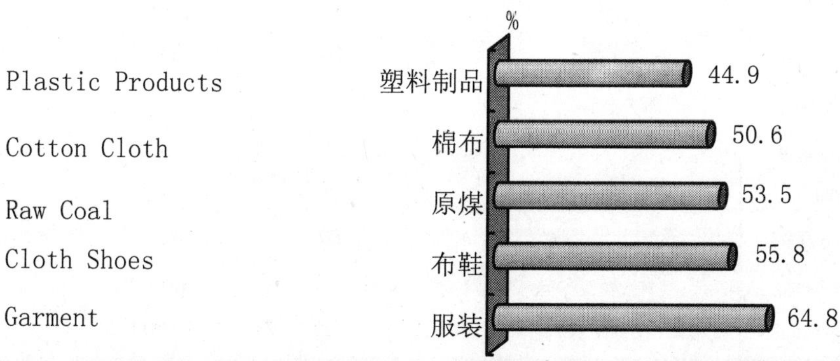

5-1 农村基层组织情况
BASIC RURAL UNITS

项目 Item			1998	1997	1998年为1997年% 1998 as % of 1997
乡镇政府个数	**(个) Number of Township and Town Government**	**(unit)**	**246**	**254**	**96.9**
乡政府	(个) Township Government	(unit)	126	139	90.6
镇政府	(个) Town Government	(unit)	120	115	104.3
村民委员会个数	**(个) Village Committees**	**(unit)**	**4044**	**4071**	**99.3**
乡村户数	**(户) Households**	**(household)**	**1259368**	**1246380**	**101.0**
乡村人口	**(人) Rural Population**	**(person)**	**3644265**	**3653138**	**99.8**
男	(人) Male	(person)	1753050	1757161	99.8
女	(人) Female	(person)	1891215	1898977	99.6

注：乡政府、镇政府个数含有农村的街道办事处和区县政府派出的管理机构。

Note：Township and town government contains rural subdistrict offices,district and county government agencies.

5-2 郊区县基层组织情况
BASIC UNITS IN SUBURBS AND COUNTIES

单位：个 (unit)

项目	Item	乡政府 Township Government	镇政府 Town Government	村民委员会 Village Committee	乡村户数 (户) Rural Household (household)	乡村人口 (人) Rural Population (person)
全市	**Total**	**126**	**120**	**4044**	**1259368**	**3644265**
朝阳区	Chaoyang	24		170	88722	211888
丰台区	Fengtai	6		81	58300	152609
石景山区	Shijingshan	1		12	6273	15588
海淀区	Haidian	10	1	80	58305	151740
门头沟区	Mentougou	3	9	186	34673	92622
房山区	Fangshan	13	15	463	161079	488196
通州区	Tongzhou	12	10	482	151411	425254
昌平县	Changping	6	17	313	87888	249221
顺义县	Shunyi		19	427	136172	431388
大兴县	Daxing	18	9	547	114292	378618
平谷县	Pinggu	11	10	275	97815	309415
怀柔县	Huairou	5	10	287	70495	190325
密云县	Miyun	7	12	347	117708	332269
延庆县	Yanqing	10	8	374	75935	215132

5-3 农 村 劳 动 力
RURAL LABOR FORCE

单位：人 (person)

项目	Item	1998	1997	构成(%) Composition(%)	
				1998	1997
农村劳动力	**Rural Social Labor Force**	**1610221**	**1611713**	**100**	**100**
# 种植业	Planting	564893	556435	35.1	34.5
林 业	Forestry	40783	42026	2.5	2.6
牧 业	Animal Husbandry	60951	44056	3.8	2.7
渔 业	Fishery	10658	10805	0.7	0.7
农村工业	Industry	366347	394420	22.8	24.5
乡镇工业	Township and Town Industry	144573	163713	9.0	10.2
村及村以下工业	Industry at Village Level and Below	221774	230707	13.8	14.3
农村建筑业	Construction	117744	107765	7.3	6.7
农村运输业	Transportation	101562	92418	6.3	5.7
农村商业、饮食业	Commerce and Catering	87219	73057	5.4	4.5

5-4 郊 区 县 农 村 劳 动 力
RURAL LABOR FORCE IN SUBURBS AND COUNTIES

单位：人 (person)

项目	Item	劳动力 Labor Force		# 种植业劳动力 Labor Force of Planting	
		1998	1997	1998	1997
全 市	**Total**	**1610221**	**1611713**	**564893**	**556435**
朝阳区	Chaoyang	92615	87641	15629	15600
丰台区	Fengtai	70258	70855	15603	15742
石景山区	Shijingshan	7729	8212	736	627
海淀区	Haidian	57154	56277	9375	9913
门头沟区	Mentougou	45530	44593	10237	10468
房山区	Fangshan	217501	223286	68081	69481
通州区	Tongzhou	183317	181392	70083	68448
昌平县	Changping	102781	104089	32798	28873
顺义县	Shunyi	1873978	191123	45238	45958
大兴县	Daxing	179112	179723	114804	112059
平谷县	Pinggu	139513	139337	62818	59648
怀柔县	Huairou	81135	79461	24636	21967
密云县	Miyun	156927	155867	54679	55955
延庆县	Yanqing	88671	89857	40176	41696

5-5 郊区国内生产总值
GROSS DOMESTIC PRODUCT OF SUBURBS

单位：万元 (10000 yuan)

项目	Item	1998	1997	1998年为1997年% 1998 as % of 1997	构成(%) Composition(%) 1998	1997
总计	**Total**	**4466070.5**	**4146742.2**	**107.7**	**100**	**100**
第一产业	**Primary Industry**	**865618.7**	**848494.8**	**102.0**	**19.4**	**20.5**
第二产业	**Secondary Industry**	**1809374.5**	**1691008.8**	**107.0**	**40.5**	**40.8**
# 工业	Industry	1374344.9	1308946.8	105.0	30.8	31.6
第三产业	**Tertiary Industry**	**1791077.3**	**1607238.6**	**111.4**	**40.1**	**38.7**
农林牧渔服务业	Services of FFAF	18677.3	23829.6	78.4	0.4	0.6
地质勘查及水利管理业	Geographic Prospect and Water Conservancy	5307.5	4845.5	109.5	0.1	0.1
交通运输、仓储及邮电通信业	Transportation,Storge, Posts and Telecommunications	246807.7	242534.3	101.8	5.5	5.8
批发零售贸易及餐饮业	Wholesales,Retail Sales and Catering	363963.8	343712.5	105.9	8.1	8.3
金融保险业	Banking and Insurance	244422.8	247926.5	98.6	5.5	6.0
房地产业	Real Estate	191272.9	173824.4	110.0	4.3	4.2
社会服务业	Social Services	332543.5	195779.9	169.9	7.4	4.7
卫生、体育及社会福利事业	Health,Sports and Social Welfares	44666.5	44599.2	100.2	1.0	1.1
教育、文化及广播电影电视业	Education,Culture, Radio,Film and Television	119626.3	114262.1	104.7	2.7	2.8
科学研究及综合技术服务业	Scientific Research and Polytechnic Services	19256.1	11838.5	162.7	0.4	0.3
国家机关、党政机关及社会团体	Government Organs, Party Organs and Social Bodies	110233.9	112614.7	97.9	2.5	2.7
其他行业	Others	94299.0	91471.1	103.1	2.1	2.2

注："郊区国内生产总值"统计口径：近郊区为乡及乡以下农村部分；远郊区（县）为县及县以下所属部分。(下表同)

Note: Gross domestic product of near suburbs is that produced by units of rural area at townships level and below,and that of outer suburbs and counties is produced by units at counties level and below.(the following is the same)

5-6 郊区国内生产总值构成项目
COMPOSITION OF GROSS DOMESTIC PRODUCT OF SUBURBS

单位：万元 (10000 yuan)

项目	Item	增加值 Added Value	劳动者报酬 Remuneration for Labors	固定资产折旧 Depreciation on Fixed Assets	生产税净额 Net Taxes on Production	营业盈余 Operating Surplus
总计	**Total**	**4466070.5**	**2252816.9**	**466924.7**	**712173.8**	**1034155.1**
第一产业	**Primary Industry**	**865618.7**	**527993.1**	**22531.3**	**69751.9**	**245342.4**
第二产业	**Secondary Industry**	**1809374.5**	**902975.8**	**308718.6**	**298825.4**	**298854.7**
# 工业	Industry	1374344.9	649866.4	257474.7	260807.4	206196.4
第三产业	**Tertiary Industry**	**1791077.3**	**821848.0**	**135674.8**	**343596.5**	**489958.0**
农林牧渔服务业	Services of FFAF	18677.3	12956.1	477.8	2302.2	2941.2
地质勘查及水利管理业	Geographic Prospect and Water Conservancy	5307.5	3574.5	284.2	1507.4	-58.6
交通运输、仓储及邮电通信业	Transportation,Storge, Posts and Telecommunications	246807.7	118683.7	19696.0	48107.7	60320.3
批发零售贸易及餐饮业	Wholesales,Retail Sales and Catering	363963.8	194138.4	33102.3	41510.2	95212.9
金融保险业	Banking and Insurance	244422.8	25800.0	19490.2	12686.1	186446.5
房地产业	Real Estate	191272.9	23932.0	13946.8	139199.7	14194.4
社会服务业	Social Services	332543.5	170151.7	41565.7	44181.5	76644.6
卫生、体育及社会福利事业	Health,Sports and Social Welfares	44666.5	37692.2	60.3	4611.4	2302.6
教育、文化及广播电影电视业	Education,Culture, Radio,Film and Television	119626.3	99815.1	1085.1	14864.5	3861.6
科学研究及综合技术服务业	Scientific Research and Polytechnic Services	19256.1	6646.9	1474.0	5293.1	5842.1
国家机关、党政机关及社会团体	Government Organs, Party Organs and Social Bodies	110233.9	83385.6	507.1	14615.7	11725.5
其他行业	Others	94299.0	45071.8	3985.3	14717.0	30524.9

5-7 农村固定资产结构
CONSTRUCTURE OF RURAL FIXED ASSETS

单位：万元 (10000 yuan)

项目	Item	合计 Total	乡级所有 at Township Level	村及村以下所有 at Village Level and Below	农户所有 of Peasant Household
年末固定资产原值	**Original Value of Fixed Assets (year-end)**	**7390968**	**1688166**	**1906468**	**3796334**
农林牧渔业固定资产	Fixed Assets for Farming, Forestry,Animal Husbandry and Fishery	799149	133709	506296	159144
# 生产用房屋及建筑物	Buildings for Production	348225	55717	231965	60542
役畜及产品畜	Draught Animals and Commodity Animals	34242	4250	13823	16168
大中型铁木农具	Large and Medium Wood and Iron Farm Tools	69289	10002	49517	9770
农林牧渔业设备	Machinery for Farming, Forestry,Animal Husbandry and Fishery	214431	25415	121331	67685
工业固定资产	Fixed Assets for Industry	1784863	941550	831341	11972
# 生产用房屋及建筑物	Buildings for Production	652028	310745	334985	6298
生产设备	Machinery for Production	885782	516344	363764	5674
建筑业固定资产	Fixed Assets for Construction	124504	78673	42969	2862
运输业固定资产	Fixed Assets for Transportation	345891	32046	55906	257939
商、饮、服务业固定资产	Fixed Assets for Commerce, Catering and Services	208870	111603	90468	6799
住宅	Residence	3439695	117331	57397	3264967
其他固定资产	Other Fixed Assets	687996	273254	322091	92651

注：本资料为农调队8县75乡抽样调查推算数。集体固定资产规定单位价值200元以上统计，农户为50元以上。

Note：Data in this table are calculated from the sample surveys in 8 counties,75 townships.According to the rules,the data only include the value per unit of fixed assets of those unit value above 200 yuan for collective fixed assets or unit value above 50 yuan for households fixed assets.

5-8 农业总产值
GROSS OUTPUT VALUE OF AGRICULTURE

单位：万元 (10000 yuan)

项目	Item	总产值（1990年不变价格） Gross Output Value(at 1990 constant prices) 1998	1997	1998年为1997年% 1998 as % of 1997	总产值（现价） Gross Output Value(at current prices) 1998	1997	1998年为1997年% 1998 as % of 1997
总计	**Total**	**935164.4**	**904152.5**	**103.4**	**1766138.8**	**1708568.9**	**103.3695**
种植业	**Planting**	**484585.7**	**473578.4**	**102.3**	**891629.8**	**869772.1**	**102.513**
谷物	Cereal	123353	120490.7	102.4	302562.5	304849	99.24996
豆类	Soybeans	3599	3059.8	117.6	8778.8	7840.3	111.9702
经济作物	Cash Crops	5864.9	5930.8	98.9	11405.1	11655.5	97.85166
蔬菜、瓜类	Vegetable and Melon	220061.4	200075.8	110.0	412014.3	370300.4	111.2649
桑、水果	Mulberry and Fruit	82906.9	67886.2	122.1	102787.6	82361.9	124.7999
其他	Others	48800.5	76135.1	64.1	54081.5	92765	58.29947
林业	**Forestry**	**15880.7**	**17817**	**89.1**	**32302.2**	**28630.3**	**112.8252**
牧业	**Animal Husbandry**	**395030.4**	**377670.9**	**104.6**	**766338.4**	**748048.8**	**102.445**
家畜繁殖增重	Weight Increase of Domestic Animals Breeding	178598.2	150227.6	118.9	410361.8	380021.5	107.9838
# 养猪	Hogs	147947.8	121823.5	121.4	341258	320248.3	106.5604
家禽饲养	Poultry Raising	99813.7	88008.4	113.4	169778.6	140046.7	121.23
活的畜禽产品	Live Animal and Poultry Production	111262.6	132838.8	83.8	168175.3	218454.7	76.98406
# 鲜蛋	Fresh Eggs	80471	109351.8	73.6	100528.7	128369.6	78.31192
其他	Others	5355.9	6596.1	81.2	18022.7	9525.9	189.1968
渔业	**Fishery**	**39667.6**	**35086.2**	**113.1**	**75868.4**	**62117.7**	**122.1365**

5-9 农林牧渔业中间消耗

INTERMEDIATE INPUT OF FARMING,FORESTRY,HUSBANDRY AND FISHERY

单位：万元 (10000 yuan)

项目	Item	1998	1997	1998年为1997年% 1998 as % of 1997
农林牧渔业生产中间消耗总计	**Total**	**900520.1**	**860074**	**104.7**
农业中间消耗合计	**Farming**	**376133**	**365162**	**103.0**
种植业中间消耗	Planting	368679.1	355785	103.6
中间物质消耗	Intermediate Material Input	335218.5	322768	103.9
# 用种量	Seeds	44948.1	43922	102.3
肥　料	Fertilizer	103300.8	86902	118.9
农　药	Farm Chemical	13132.2	28954	45.4
对非物质生产部门劳务支出	Services Expenditure to Non-material Production Departments	33460.6	33017	101.3
其他农业中间消耗	Others	7453.9	9377	79.5
中间物质消耗	Intermediate Material Input	6790.1	8328	81.5
对非物质生产部门劳务支出	Services Expenditure to Non-material Production Departments	663.8	1049	63.3
林业中间消耗合计	**Forestry**	**12013.7**	**10716**	**112.1**
中间物质消耗	Intermediate Material Input	11231	9793	114.7
# 农　药	Farm Chemical	757.1	681	111.2
对非物质生产部门劳务支出	Services Expenditure to Non-material Production Departments	782.7	922	84.9
牧业中间消耗合计	**Animal Husbandry**	**469476**	**448877**	**104.6**
中间物质消耗	Intermediate Material Input	455783.2	435708	104.6
# 饲料、饲草	Forage and Forage Grass	411404.3	377847	108.9
对非物质生产部门劳务支出	Services Expenditure to Non-material Production Departments	13692.8	13168.9	104.0
渔业中间消耗合计	**Fishery**	**42897.4**	**35319**	**121.5**
中间物质消耗	Intermediate Material Input	41197.1	33864	121.7
# 饲　料	Forage	30721.7	26774	114.7
对非物质生产部门劳务支出	Services Expenditure to Non-material Production Departments	1700.3	1456	116.8

5-10 耕　地　面　积

AREA UNDER CULTIVATION

项目	Item	面积(公顷) Area (hectare)		构成(%) Composition(%)	
		1998	1997	1998	1997
合　计	**Total**	**341056.7**	**342362.0**	**100**	**100**
按水利状况分	**Grouped by Irrigation Conditions**				
水　田	Irrigated Field	31091.4	30917.2	9.1	9.0
旱　地	Non-irrigated Farmland	309965.3	311444.8	90.9	91.0
# 水浇地	Irrigated Land	253494.1	252505.7	74.3	73.8
# 菜　地	Vegetable Plot	…	…	…	…
按当年使用分	**Grouped by Using in this Year**				
粮食作物	Grain Crops	249346.5	251839.8	73.1	73.6
经济作物	Cash Crops	11634.9	11788.2	3.4	3.4
蔬　菜	Vegetable	42679.1	42469.0	12.5	12.4
其　他	Others	37396.2	36265.0	11.0	10.6

注：本表数字由市土地局提供。

Note: Data of this table are provided by Beijing Municipal Land Bureau.

5-11 国有农场基本情况
BASIC STATISTICS ON STATE-OWNED FARMS

项目		Item		1998	1997	1998年为1997年% 1998 as % of 1997
农场数	(个)	Number of Farms	(unit)	15	16	93.8
年末固定职工	(人)	Number of Full-time Staff(year-end)	(person)	41734	67061	62.2
耕地面积	(公倾)	Cultivated Land	(hectare)	3003	3298	91.1
农业总产值 (1990年不变价,万元)		Gross Output Value of Agriculture (at 1990 constant prices,10000 yuan)		253363	25025	1012.4
工业总产值 (1990年不变价,万元)		Gross Output Value of Industry (at 1990 constant prices,10000 yuan)		115183	120487	95.6
主要农产品产量		Yield of Major Farm Products				
粮食	(吨)	Grain	(ton)	7664	5961	128.6
蔬菜	(吨)	Vegetable	(ton)	1787	2646	67.5
牛奶	(吨)	Milk	(ton)	122662	135585	90.5
# 商品量	(吨)	Commodity	(ton)	119070	131643	90.4
干鲜果品	(吨)	Dry and Fresh Fruit	(ton)	5012	9814	51.1
大中型拖拉机	(台)	Large and Medium Tractors	(unit)	169	242	69.8
小型拖拉机	(台)	Mini-Tractors	(unit)	72	162	44.4
载重汽车	(辆)	Trucks	(unit)	301	655	46.0
销售收入	(万元)	Sales Revenue	(10000 yuan)	369963	395579	93.5
利润	(万元)	Profits	(10000 yuan)	3238	5047	64.2
税金	(万元)	Taxes	(10000 yuan)	8568	11318	75.7

5-12 主要农作物播种面积及产量
SOWN AREAS AND YIELD OF MAJOR FARM CROPS

项目	Item	1998			1997		
		播种面积 (公顷) Sown Areas (hectare)	单产 (公斤/公顷) Unit Yield (kg/hectare)	总产量 (吨) Total Yield (ton)	播种面积 (公顷) Sown Areas (hectare)	单产 (公斤/公顷) Unit Yield (kg/hectare)	总产量 (吨) Total Yield (ton)
粮食	**Grain**	**422659.1**	**5660.6**	**2392472.0**	**424540.8**	**5593.5**	**2374721.0**
按季节分	Grouped by Season						
夏粮	Summer Grain	171275.9	5648.9	967507.0	171390.5	5626.5	964260.0
秋粮	Autumn Grain	251383.1	5668.5	1424965.0	253150.3	5571.6	1410461.0
按品种分	Grouped by Variety						
稻谷	Rice	19430.0	6847.5	13305.5	23171.2	6820.5	158038.0
冬小麦	Winter Wheat	171154.6	5651.1	96721.2	171273.1	5628.0	963925.0
玉米	Corn	207722.7	5904.0	1226395.0	206268.3	5766.0	1189416.0
薯类	Tubers	4955.1	4686.0	23216.0	5219.1	4636.5	24201.0
大豆	Soybean	10237.7	2445.0	25031.0	9318.3	2433.0	22667.0
棉花	**Cotton**	**2103.0**	**854.4**	**1797.0**	**2162.3**	**1039.5**	**2248.0**
油料	**Oil-bearing Crops**	**9652.2**	**2941.4**	**28391.0**	**9993.3**	**2736.0**	**27345.0**
# 花生	Peanuts	9227.5	3010.9	27783.0	9496.4	2827.5	26855.0
蔬菜	**Vegetable**	**90177.7**	**45036.2**	**4061262.0**	**88840.2**	**46182.9**	**4102904.0**
瓜类	**Melon**	**5405.7**	**54494.9**	**294581.0**	**4637.9**	**56175.0**	**260537.0**
# 西瓜	Watermelon	5122.9	55197.0	282767.0	4471.8	56530.5	252794.0

5-13 郊区县粮食、油料占耕地面积
THE PROPORTION OF GRAIN,OIL-BEARING CROPS IN CULTIVATED AREA OF SUBURBS AND COUNTIES

单位：公顷 (hectare)

地区	Region	粮食 Grain 1998	粮食 Grain 1997	1998年为1997年% 1998 as % of 1997	油料 Oil-bearing Crops 1998	油料 Oil-bearing Crops 1997	1998年为1997年% 1998 as % of 1997
全市	**Total**	**249346.5**	**251839.8**	**99.0**	**9093.5**	**9413.1**	**96.6**
朝阳区	Chaoyang	7150.2	7678.7	93.1			
丰台区	Fengtai	2293.2	2469.8	92.9	2.7	10.5	25.7
海淀区	Haidian	5116.3	5433.7	94.2			
门头沟区	Mentougou	3638.3	3597	101.1			
房山区	Fangshan	32038.4	32200.4	99.5	679	817.1	83.1
通州区	Tongzhou	39564.2	39521.3	100.1	449	407.7	110.1
昌平县	Changping	19859.9	20297.8	97.8	15.2	24.1	63.1
顺义县	Shunyi	40309.2	40136.4	100.3	311.3	369.2	84.3
大兴县	Daxing	31485	31422.8	100.2	3242.7	3302.5	98.2
平谷县	Pinggu	14270.8	15608.1	91.4	244.6	281.9	86.8
怀柔县	Huairou	12917.2	12959.3	99.7	642.7	657.5	97.7
密云县	Miyun	16436.3	16342.1	100.6	3439.7	3474.7	99.0
延庆县	Yanqing	24267.5	24172.4	100.4	66.6	67.9	98.1

5-14 郊区县蔬菜、西瓜占耕地面积
THE PROPORTION OF VEGETABLE,WATERMELON IN CULTIVATED AREA OF SUBURBS AND COUNTIES

单位：公顷 (hectare)

地区	Region	蔬菜 Vegetable 1998	蔬菜 Vegetable 1997	1998年为1997年% 1998 as % of 1997	西瓜 Watermelon 1998	西瓜 Watermelon 1997	1998年为1997年% 1998 as % of 1997
全市	**Total**	**42679.0**	**42469.0**	**100.5**	**3515.0**	**3109.7**	**113.0**
朝阳区	Chaoyang	2315.0	2297.0	100.8		1.5	
丰台区	Fengtai	2178.0	2354.2	92.5			
石景山区	Shijingshan	126.7	126.7	100.0			
海淀区	Haidian	1854.0	1919.9	96.6			
门头沟区	Mentougou	436.9	451.9	96.7			
房山区	Fangshan	2341.5	2215.7	105.7	62.3	59.0	105.6
通州区	Tongzhou	6118.9	6118.9	100.0	252.7	222.0	113.8
昌平县	Changping	1447.5	1765.3	82.0	36.4	6.7	543.3
顺义县	Shunyi	7164.0	7348.6	97.5	348.7	286.5	121.7
大兴县	Daxing	9257.8	9173.3	100.9	2606.9	2442.4	106.7
平谷县	Pinggu	2807.0	2740.3	102.4	174.3	74.9	232.7
怀柔县	Huairou	871.6	1106.5	78.8	1.0		
密云县	Miyun	1350.5	1456.8	92.7	24.9	8.5	292.9
延庆县	Yanqing	4408.8	3393.9	129.9	7.8	8.2	95.1

5-15 郊区县粮食、油料播种面积

SOWN AREAS OF GRAIN,OIL-BEARING CROPS IN SUBURBS AND COUNTIES

单位：公顷 (hectare)

地区	Region	粮食 Grain 1998	1997	1998年为1997年% 1998 as % of 1997	油料 Oil-bearing Crops 1998	1997	1998年为1997年% 1998 as % of 1997
全市	**Total**	**422659.1**	**424540.8**	**99.6**	**9652.2**	**9993.3**	**96.6**
朝阳区	Chaoyang	12144.9	12675.3	95.8			
丰台区	Fengtai	3417.4	3630.6	94.1	2.7	10.5	25.7
海淀区	Haidian	5341.2	5906.3	90.4			
门头沟区	Mentougou	4009.1	3914.5	102.4			
房山区	Fangshan	53724.7	53770.1	99.9	680.8	886.4	76.8
通州区	Tongzhou	77477.6	77548.9	99.9	449	407.7	110.1
昌平县	Changping	33813.1	33913.5	99.7	19.1	24.8	77.0
顺义县	Shunyi	77827.9	77793.7	100.0	321.3	369.2	87.0
大兴县	Daxing	56892.2	57013.5	99.8	3647.6	3682.8	99.0
平谷县	Pinggu	26912.7	27457.2	98.0	261.3	282.2	92.6
怀柔县	Huairou	20856.5	20965.4	99.5	646.4	681.7	94.8
密云县	Miyun	25445.3	25326.5	100.5	3547.5	3579.1	99.1
延庆县	Yanqing	24796.0	24625.3	100.7	76.5	68.9	111.0

5-16 郊区县蔬菜、西瓜播种面积

SOWN AREAS OF VEGETABLE,WATERMELON IN SUBURBS AND COUNTIES

单位：公顷 (hectare)

地区	Region	蔬菜 Vegetable 1998	1997	1998年为1997年% 1998 as % of 1997	西瓜 Watermelon 1998	1997	1998年为1997年% 1998 as % of 1997
全市	**Total**	**90177.7**	**88840.2**	**101.5**	**5122.9**	**4471.8**	**114.6**
朝阳区	Chaoyang	4720.0	5092.3	92.7		3.0	
丰台区	Fengtai	4474.0	4717.6	94.8			
石景山区	Shijingshan	258.0	279.6	92.3			
海淀区	Haidian	3556.6	4286.6	83.0			
门头沟区	Mentougou	871.6	905.4	96.3			
房山区	Fangshan	4686.2	4741.3	98.8	62.3	72.3	86.2
通州区	Tongzhou	15257.0	13838.1	110.3	505.5	444.0	113.9
昌平县	Changping	2985.8	3289.9	90.8	38.5	6.9	558.0
顺义县	Shunyi	14485.0	13891.1	104.3	697.3	573.0	121.7
大兴县	Daxing	20775.0	20061.5	103.6	3477.8	3225.8	107.8
平谷县	Pinggu	6747.5	6708.7	100.6	278.3	117.3	237.3
怀柔县	Huairou	1878.0	2096.1	89.6	1.9		
密云县	Miyun	3212.0	3372.0	95.3	48.3	16.0	301.9
延庆县	Yanqing	6271.0	5560.0	112.8	13.0	13.5	96.3

5-17 郊区县粮食、油料总产量

TOTAL YIELD OF GRAIN,OIL-BEARING CROPS IN SUBURBS AND COUNTIES

单位：吨 (ton)

地区	Region	粮食 Grain			油料 Oil-bearing Crops		
		1998	1997	1998年为1997年% 1998 as % of 1997	1998	1997	1998年为1997年% 1998 as % of 1997
全市	**Total**	**2392472**	**2374721**	**100.7**	**28391**	**27345**	**103.8**
朝阳区	Chaoyang	75726	79780	94.9			
丰台区	Fengtai	15289	14352	106.5	3	24	12.5
海淀区	Haidian	34819	37776	92.2			
门头沟区	Mentougou	8784	4503	195.1			
房山区	Fangshan	298006	289638	102.9	1444	1880	76.8
通州区	Tongzhou	500344	501588	99.8	1190	1346	88.4
昌平县	Changping	170506	164468	103.7	78	60	130.0
顺义县	Shunyi	443929	437725	101.4	1280	1163	110.1
大兴县	Daxing	332873	332815	100.0	11512	11463	100.4
平谷县	Pinggu	156311	157874	99.0	579	629	92.1
怀柔县	Huairou	133264	125255	106.4	2616	2363	110.7
密云县	Miyun	129593	110592	117.2	9585	8349	114.8
延庆县	Yanqing	176539	137360	128.5	104	68	152.9

注：粮食产量郊区县之和不等于全市合计。

Note: The sum of yield of grain of suburbs and counties is not equal to the total.

5-18 郊区县蔬菜、西瓜总产量

TOTAL YIELD OF VEGETABLE,WATERMELON IN SUBURBS AND COUNTIES

单位：吨 (ton)

地区	Region	蔬菜 Vegetable			西瓜 Watermelon		
		1998	1997	1998年为1997年% 1998 as % of 1997	1998	1997	1998年为1997年% 1998 as % of 1997
全市	**Total**	**4061262.0**	**4102903.6**	**99.0**	**282767.0**	**252794.0**	**111.9**
朝阳区	Chaoyang	182846.0	216313.0	84.5		180.0	
丰台区	Fengtai	190516.2	191163.0	99.7			
石景山区	Shijingshan	9653.0	10068.0	95.9			
海淀区	Haidian	157836.0	178391.0	88.5			
门头沟区	Mentougou	21293.8	28412.0	74.9			
房山区	Fangshan	202449.0	200103.0	101.2	3657.0	3549.0	103.0
通州区	Tongzhou	753073.3	749612.0	100.5	30781.0	31355.0	98.2
昌平县	Changping	104995.0	124237.5	84.5	981.0	231.0	424.[illegible]
顺义县	Shunyi	839945.7	830444.1	101.1	37633.0	32095.0	117.3
大兴县	Daxing	929425.2	896028.0	103.7	194146.0	177913.0	109.1
平谷县	Pinggu	296576.0	268606.0	110.4	14502.0	6329.0	229.1
怀柔县	Huairou	50341.3	57649.0	87.3	114.0		
密云县	Miyun	161349.0	166298.0	97.0	386.0	590.0	65.4
延庆县	Yanqing	360962.0	355579.0	101.5	567.0	552.0	102.7

注：蔬菜产量郊区县之和不等于全市合计。

Note: The sum of yield of vegetable of suburbs and counties is not equal to the total.

5-19 蔬菜播种面积及产量

SOWN AREAS AND YIELD OF VEGETABLE

项目	Item	播种面积 (公顷) Sown Areas(hectare)		总产量 (吨) Total Yield(ton)	
		1998	1997	1998	1997
合计	**Total**	**90177.7**	**88840.2**	**4061261.5**	**4102903.6**
冬季生产	**Produced in Winter**	**6678.3**	**6459.3**	**297935.6**	**273627.7**
越冬根茬菜小计	**Winter Stubble Vegetable**	**6475.6**	**6544.6**	**200403.3**	**211447.5**
# 菠菜	Spinach	1905.3	1831.3	42876.4	60931.5
芹菜	Celery				
早春风障菜小计	**Early Spring Windbreak Vegetable**	**4346.6**	**4915.1**	**143208.7**	**188545.5**
# 小萝卜	Radish	935.9	1017.2	37395.1	39484.2
小白菜	Chinese Cabbage	470.3	496.3	18965.0	17682.7
小油菜	Rape	864.4	957.6	33703.1	36345.8
春播露地菜小计	**Spring-sown Open-land Vegetable**	**30724.1**	**30573.4**	**1362358.2**	**1363401.1**
# 黄瓜	Cucumber	3625.7	3524.8	182194.3	199478.0
茄子	Aggplant	2758.6	2839.8	124221.2	124490.5
大椒	Chili	1741.5	1811.9	78076.9	78885.0
冬瓜	Wax Guard	743.9	946.4	52281.5	57524.2
西红柿	Tomato	3430	3489.7	192417.4	199125.7
元白菜	Cabbage	3042.7	2934.7	143903.7	131815.5
云架豆	Beans round Trellis	1276.2	1494.8	39412.6	44662.1
老葱	Overgrown Onion	1208.5	1094.4	49239.6	45835.9
大蒜	Garlic	746.3	943.1	27499.6	32006.3
夏播菜小计	**Summer-sown Vegetable**	**14726.9**	**13715.2**	**568769.2**	**500879.0**
# 黄瓜	Cucumber	2840.5	2619.6	119156.8	117555.8
茄子	Aggplant	1472.5	1454.1	71729.1	63260.9
冬瓜	Wax Guard	796.5	795.9	50575.8	42646.2
元白菜	Cabbage	999.3	1044.9	50934.0	48647.2
云架豆	Beans round Trellis	1930.2	1984.8	60972.5	53735.2
秋播菜小计	**Autumn-sown Vegetable**	**27204.1**	**26632.5**	**1485516.7**	**1562519.1**
# 窖白菜	Chinese Cabbage Stored	12550.2	13660.5	806258.5	1040052.5
贩白菜	Chinese Cabbage for Selling	2511.9	2223.2	128387.7	104558.1
菜花	Cauliflower	1190.9	956.8	44588.1	32333.3
各种萝卜	Radish	3447.4	3269.8	156444.2	155869.7
芹菜	Celery	1073.8	911.4	66583.6	52724.7

5-20 郊区县粮食耕地面积单位产量
UNIT YIELD OF GRAIN CULTIVATED AREA IN SUBURBS AND COUNTIES

地区	Region	1998			1997		
		耕地面积 (公顷) Cultivated Areas (hectare)	单产 (公斤/公顷) Unit Yield (kg/hectare)	总产量 (吨) Total Yield (ton)	耕地面积 (公顷) Cultivated Areas (hectare)	单产 (公斤/公顷) Unit Yield (kg/hectare)	总产量 (吨) Total Yield (ton)
全市	**Total**	**249347**	**9595**	**2392472**	**251840**	**9429**	**2374721**
朝阳区	Chaoyang	7150	10590.1	75726	7679	10389	79780
丰台区	Fengtai	2293	6667.1	15289	2470	5811	14352
海淀区	Haidian	5116	6806	34819	5434	6953	37776
门头沟区	Mentougou	3638	2414.3	8784	3597	1253	4503
房山区	Fangshan	32038.4	9301.5	298006	32200	8996	289638
通州区	Tongzhou	39564	12646	500344	39521	12692	501588
昌平县	Changping	19860	8585.4	170506	20298	8103	164468
顺义县	Shunyi	40309	11013	443929	40136	10907	437725
大兴县	Daxing	31485	10572.4	332873	31423	10592	332815
平谷县	Pinggu	14271	10953.2	156311	15608	10115	157874
怀柔县	Huairou	12917	10316.8	133264	12959	9666	125255
密云县	Miyun	16436	7884.6	129593	16342	6768	110592
延庆县	Yanqing	24268	7274.7	176539	24173	5682	137360

5-21 郊区县蔬菜耕地面积单位产量
UNIT YIELD OF VEGETABLE CULTIVATED AREA IN SUBURBS AND COUNTIES

地区	Region	1998			1997		
		耕地面积 (公顷) Cultivated Areas (hectare)	单产 (公斤/公顷) Unit Yield (kg/hectare)	总产量 (吨) Total Yield (ton)	耕地面积 (公顷) Cultivated Areas (hectare)	单产 (公斤/公顷) Unit Yield (kg/hectare)	总产量 (吨) Total Yield (ton)
全市	**Total**	**42679.1**	**95158.1**	**4061262**	**42469.0**	**100612.0**	**4102903.6**
朝阳区	Chaoyang	2315.1	78979.7	182846	2297.0	94377.0	216313.0
丰台区	Fengtai	2178.3	87461	190516.2	2354.2	81200.0	191163.0
石景山区	Shijingshan	126.7	76187.8	9653	126.7	79463.0	10068.0
海淀区	Haidian	1854.1	85128.1	157836	1919.9	92916.0	178391.0
门头沟区	Mentougou	436.9	48738.4	21293.8	451.9	62872.0	28412.0
房山区	Fangshan	2341.5	86461.2	202449	2215.7	90311.0	200103.0
通州区	Tongzhou	6118.9	123073.3	753073.3	6118.9	122507.0	749612.0
昌平县	Changping	1447.5	72535.4	104995	1765.3	70377.0	124237.5
顺义县	Shunyi	7164.3	117240.4	839945.7	7348.6	113007.0	830444.1
大兴县	Daxing	9257.8	100393.7	929425.2	9173.3	97677.0	896028.0
平谷县	Pinggu	2807	105655.9	296576	2740.3	98020.0	268606.0
怀柔县	Huairou	871.6	57757.3	50341.3	1106.5	52100.0	57649.0
密云县	Miyun	1350.5	119473.5	161349	1456.8	114152.0	166298.0
延庆县	Yanqing	4408.9	81871.2	360962	3393.9	104770.0	355579.0

5-22 畜 牧 业 生 产
ANIMALS HUSBANDRY

项 目 Item	1998 合计 Total	1998 #国有集体 State-Owned and Collective-Owned	1997 合计 Total	1997 #国有集体 State-Owned and Collective-Owned	1998年为1997年% 1998 as % of 1997 合计 Total	1998年为1997年% 1998 as % of 1997 #国有集体 State-Owned and Collective-Owned
大牲畜 Large Animals						
年末总头数 (万头) Total(year-end) (10000 heads)	18.5		19.7	5.7	93.9	
# 役 畜 Draught Animals	7.4		6		123.3	
牛 Cattle and Buffaloes	12.5		12.8		97.7	
马 Horses	0.9		1		90.0	
骡 Mules	2.1		2.5		84.0	
驴 Donkeys	3.1		3.3		93.9	
乳 牛 Cows						
年末总头数 (头) Total(year-end) (head)	54514	31240	57907	47146	94.1	66.3
# 成乳牛 Adult Cows	35949		35048		102.6	
牛奶总产量 (万吨) Cow Milk (10000 tons)	22.7	18.4	22.2	18.6	102.3	98.9
肉 牛 Beef Cattle						
全年出栏 (头) Slaughtered Cattle (head)	116127		108868		106.7	
折净肉 (吨) Converted into Beef (ton)	20618.9		19052		108.2	
羊 Sheep and Goats						
全年出栏羊 (万只) Slaughtered Sheep and Goats (10000 heads)	80		70.5		113.5	
折净肉 (吨) Converted into Mutton (ton)	12191		10575		115.3	
年末存栏 (万只) Livestock on Hand (year-end) (10000 heads)	95.8		80.9		118.4	
山 羊 (万只) Goats (10000 heads)	45.2		39.3		115.0	
绵 羊 (万只) Sheep (10000 heads)	50.6		41.6		121.6	
猪 Hogs						
全年出栏肥猪 (万头) Slaughtered Fattened Hogs (10000 heads)	374.8	165.8	353.5	259.3	106.0	63.9
折带骨肉 (万吨) Converted into Pork with Bone (10000 tons)	27.9		24.7		113.0	
折带骨肉 (万吨) Converted into Pork with Bone(10000 tons)			24.5			
年末存栏 (万头) Livestock on Hand (year-end) (10000 heads)	254.5	105.7	241	166.1	105.6	63.6
家 禽 Poultry						
年末存栏 (万只) Livestock on Hand (year-end) (10000 heads)	2810.2		3063.8		91.7	
鸭 Ducks	260.7		223		116.9	
肉 鸡 Chickens	1118.2	527.3	1009.7		110.7	
产蛋鸡 Hens	1431.3	460	1830.1		78.2	
产蛋量 (万吨) Poultry Eggs (10000 tons)	17.9		23.8		75.2	
# 鸡 蛋 (万吨) Eggs (10000 tons)	17.6		23.5		74.9	
年末养兔 (万只) Rabbits(year-end) (10000 heads)	**34.6**		**7.8**		**443.6**	
养 蜂 Bees						
年末养蜂 (万箱) Bees(year-end) (10000 boxes)	4.5		2.7		166.7	
蜂蜜产量 (吨) Honey (ton)	1779.5		894.7		198.9	

5-23 林业及干鲜果品生产
FORESTRY,DRY AND FRESH FRUIT PRODUCTION

项目 Item				1998	1997	1998年为1997年% 1998 as % of 1997
林业生产		**Forestry**				
本年造林面积	(公顷)	Afforestation Area this Year	(hectare)	36874.0	37567.0	98.2
育苗面积	(公顷)	Nursery Garden Area	(hectare)	4410.1	4355.1	101.3
# 本年新育	(公顷)	New Growing this Year	(hectare)	1311.4	1102.9	118.9
果类生产		**Fruit**				
干鲜果总产量	(吨)	Output of Dry and Fresh Fruit	(ton)	561782.0	525838.3	106.8
干　果	(吨)	Dry Fruit	(ton)	20725.0	19053.7	108.8
# 核　桃	(吨)	Walnut	(ton)	7364.0	6439.8	114.4
板　栗	(吨)	Chinese Chestnut	(ton)	8917.0	8024.6	111.1
鲜　果	(吨)	Fresh Fruit	(ton)	541057.0	506784.6	106.8
# 苹　果	(吨)	Apple	(ton)	162930.0	153835.0	105.9
梨	(吨)	Pear	(ton)	105436.0	94535.4	111.5
葡　萄	(吨)	Grape	(ton)	20318.0	18310.4	111.0
柿　子	(吨)	Persimmon	(ton)	40781.0	40204.1	101.4
桃	(吨)	Peach	(ton)	174066.0	166479.9	104.6
年末实有果园面积	**(公顷)**	**Orchard Area(year-end)**	**(hectare)**	**60223.5**	**58808.3**	**102.4**

5-24 水　产　品　生　产
AQUATIC PRODUCTS

项目 Item				1998	1997	1998年为1997年% 1998 as % of 1997
现有水面面积	**(公顷)**	**Area of Water Surface**	**(hectare)**	**24391.6**	**23030.7**	**105.9**
# 已利用水面面积	(公顷)	Utilized Area	(hectare)	23385.6	22175.8	105.5
大水库	(公顷)	Large Reservoir	(hectare)	13853.3	12320.0	112.4
中、小水库	(公顷)	Medium and Small Reservoirs	(hectare)	1631.9	2083.7	78.3
坑　塘	(公顷)	Puddle and Pond	(hectare)	7878.8	8260.1	95.4
# 鱼种池	(公顷)	Fish Fry Pond	(hectare)	1033.9	1053.1	98.2
鱼种生产量	**(万尾)**	**Output of Fish Fry**	**(10000 piece)**	**12887.2**	**14339.1**	**89.9**
放养鱼种	**(万尾)**	**Breeding Fish Fry**	**(10000 piece)**	**15342.7**	**16552.8**	**92.7**
成鱼捕捞量	**(吨)**	**Fish Catched**	**(ton)**	**76366.4**	**76626.0**	**99.7**
# 大水库	(吨)	Large Reservoir	(ton)	3709	3316.7	111.8
中、小水库	(吨)	Medium and Small Reservoirs	(ton)	864.4	818.7	105.6
坑　塘	(吨)	Puddle and Pond	(ton)	71290.8	72109.1	98.9
# 鱼类商品量	(吨)	Commodity Fish	(ton)	63626.2	65798.2	96.7

5-25 主要农产品产量
OUTPUT OF MAJOR FARM PRODUCTS

项目 Item			1998	1997	1998年为1997年% 1998 as % of 1997
蔬菜产量	**(吨) Yield of Vegetable**	**(ton)**	**4061261.5**	**4102903.6**	**99.0**
#特菜	(吨) Special Vegetable	(ton)	128241.4	67970	188.7
干鲜果品产量	**(吨) Yield of Dry and Fresh Fruit**	**(ton)**	**561782**	**525838.3**	**106.8**
#干果产量	(吨) Dry Fruit	(ton)	20725	19053.7	108.8
鲜果产量	(吨) Fresh Fruit	(ton)	541057	506784.6	106.8
肉类总产量	**(吨) Output of Meat**	**(ton)**	**449063**	**402544**	**111.6**
#猪肉	(吨) Pork	(ton)	279283	247184	113.0
牛肉	(吨) Beef	(ton)	20618.9	21164.8	97.4
羊肉	(吨) Mutton	(ton)	12191	10470	116.4
牛奶产量	**(吨) Output of Cow Milk**	**(ton)**	**227073**	**221706**	**102.4**
鲜蛋产量	**(吨) Output of Fresh Eggs**	**(ton)**	**178833.4**	**237721.4**	**75.2**
#鸡蛋	(吨) Eggs	(ton)	175861	234599.8	75.0
鸭蛋	(吨) Duck's Eggs	(ton)	2925.4	3080.6	95.0
淡水鱼产量	**(吨) Output of Fresh-water Fish**	**(ton)**	**76366.4**	**76626**	**99.7**

5-26 郊区县副食品产量
OUTPUT OF NON-STAPLE FOOD IN SUBURBS AND COUNTIES

地区	Region	蔬菜 (吨) Vegetable (ton)	鲜蛋 (吨) Fresh Eggs (ton)	牛奶 (吨) Cow Milk (ton)	干鲜果 (吨) Dry and Fresh Fruit (ton)	成鱼捕捞量 (吨) Adult Fish Catched (ton)	肥猪出栏量 (头) Slaughtered Fattened Hog (head)	蛋鸡存栏量 (万只) Hens on Hand (10000 head)
全市	**Total**	**4061261.5**	**178833.4**	**227073**	**561782**	**76366.4**	**3748097**	**1431.4**
朝阳区	Chaoyang	182846	1584	7498	980	6921.6	304187	13.8
丰台区	Fengtai	109516.2	8213	4578	5814	648.9	100712	51.8
石景山区	Shijingshan	9653	2254	2154	852	40	27558	14.9
海淀区	Haidian	157836	8419	14016	14844	3107.3	170924	40
门头沟区	Mentougou	21293.8	1705	3355	4886	350	38983	14.6
房山区	Fangshan	202449	12962	14151	48027	2027.4	276430	140.3
通州区	Tongzhou	753073.3	14116	34108	30963	11663	394745	130.7
昌平县	Changping	104995	13077	38340	50838	8002.3	273996	86.8
顺义县	Shunyi	839945.7	22789.2	4673.3	41127	16140	1199115	221.7
大兴县	Daxing	929425.2	29220	46273	83413	5208.6	357803	237.5
平谷县	Pinggu	296576	28423	435	146147	14495	228547	212.5
怀柔县	Huairou	50341.3	8625.2	11558.7	46179	1602.7	192098	64
密云县	Miyun	161349	16267	1617	55000	3550	304893	124.1
延庆县	Yanqing	360962	11179	17437	32712	2609.6	132106	78.7

5-27 设施农业面积及产量
AREAS AND OUTPUT OF FACILITY-AGRICULTURE

项目	Item	设施农业面积（亩） Areas of Facility-agriculture (hectare)	设施农业产量（吨） Output of Facility-agriculture (ton)
合计	**Total**	**168566.7**	**895210**
按类型划分	Grouped by Type		
#温室	Hothouse	19285	152814
日光温室	Sunshine-hothouse	18138.5	84307
大棚	Large Shed	43625	269166
中、小棚	Medium and Small Shed	80895.2	350423
阳畦	Sunshine Bed	6623	38500
按品种划分	Grouped by Variety		
#蔬菜	Vegetable	134276.7	770378
花卉	Flowers	2693	2107
瓜类	Melon	29445	122212
果类	Fruits	2120	2570

5-28 农村劳动生产率
RURAL LABOR PRODUCTIVITY

项目	Item	1998	1997	1998年为1997年% 1998 as % of 1997
每一农村劳动力创造产值 (按各业劳动力分别计算)	Output Value Per Labor Force **(calculated separately by sectors)**			
每一农村劳动力创造农村社会总产值 (元)	Rural Gross Output Value Per Labor Force (yuan)	51737	48656	106.3
每一农村劳动力创造农业总产值 (元)	Gross Output Value of Agriculture Per Labor Force (yuan)	26077	26152	99.7
每一农村劳动力创造工业总产值 (元)	Gross Output Value of Industry Per Labor Force (yuan)	104979	95132	110.4
每一农村劳动力创造建筑业总产值 (元)	Gross Output Value of Construction Per Labor Force (yuan)	98608	104118	94.7
每一农村劳动力创造运输业总产值 (元)	Gross Output Value of Transportation Per Labor Force (yuan)	66913	59604	112.3
每一农村劳动力创造商业、饮食业总产值 (元)	Gross Output Value of Commerce and Catering Per Labor Force (yuan)	100686	96958	103.8
每一农业劳动力生产的农产品产量 (按农林牧渔劳动力合计计算)	**Yield of Farm Products Per Labor Force (calculated by total labor force of farming,forestry,animal husbandry and fishery)**			
粮食 (公斤)	Grain (kg)	3532	3635	97.2
油料 (公斤)	Oil-bearing Crops (kg)	42	42	100.0
蔬菜 (公斤)	Vegetable (kg)	5996	6540	91.7
水果 (公斤)	Fruit (kg)	799	776	103.0
猪牛羊肉 (公斤)	Pork,Beef and Mutton (kg)	461	427	108.0
牛奶 (公斤)	Cow Milk (kg)	335	339	98.8
鲜蛋 (公斤)	Fresh Eggs (kg)	264	364	72.5
淡水鱼 (公斤)	Fresh-water Fish (kg)	113	117	96.6

5-29 农 业 生 产 条 件

PRODUCTIVE CONDITIONS OF AGRICULTURE

项目		Item	1998	1997	1998年为1997年% 1998 as % of 1997
主要农业机械拥有量		**Possession of Agricultural Machinery**			
农业机械总动力	(万千瓦)	Total Power of Agricultural Machinery (10000 kw)	415.5	433.2	95.9
大中型拖拉机	(混合台)	Large and Medium Tractors (unit)	12032.0	12088.0	99.5
小型拖拉机	(台)	Mini-Tractors (unit)	30000.0	30000.0	100.0
机引农具	(台)	Towing Farm Machinery (unit)	36800.0	36800.0	100.0
机动喷雾器	(部)	Motorized Sprayer (unit)	127700.0	131900.0	96.8
机动插秧机	(台)	Motorized Rice Transplanter (unit)	378.0	425.0	88.9
联合收割机	(台)	Combine Harvester (unit)	4445.0	4277.0	103.9
机动脱粒机	(台)	Motorized Sheller (unit)	12174.0	12736.0	95.6
米面加工机	(台)	Processing Machine of Rice and Flour (unit)	10586.0	10500.0	100.8
机动挤奶器	(台)	Motorized Milker (unit)	104.0	186.0	55.9
饲料粉碎机	(台)	Fodder Grinder (unit)	5100.0	5600.0	91.1
载重汽车	(辆)	Truck (unit)	18147.0	20729.0	87.5
农业机械作业面积		**Operation Area of Agricultural Machinery**			
机耕面积	(公顷)	Cultivated Area by Machine (hectare)	263570.0	269233.0	97.9
占全部耕地面积比重	(%)	As Percentage of Total (%)	77.3	78.6	98.3
机播面积	(公顷)	Sown Area by Machine (hectare)	339430.0	338566.0	100.3
占播种面积比重	(%)	As Percentage of Sown Area (%)	63.4	63.2	100.3
机收面积	(公顷)	Harvest Area by Machine (hectare)	254620.0	262520.0	97.0
占播种面积比重	(%)	As Percentage of Harvest Area (%)	47.6	49.0	97.1
农村用电量及小水电		**Rural Electricity Consumption and Small Hydropower Station**			
农村用电量	(万千瓦小时)	Rural Electricity Consumption (10000 kwh)	290859.0	301655.0	96.4
# 农业生产用	(万千瓦小时)	For Agricultural Productive Use (10000 kwh)	107992.0	124575.0	86.7
乡镇、村办企业用	(万千瓦小时)	For Township and Village Enterprises Use (10000 kwh)	82831.0	85354.0	97.0
农村小水电站	(处)	Rural Small Hydropower Station	40.0	40.0	100.0
发电量	(万千瓦小时)	Generated Energy (10000 kwh)	2573.3	3806.4	67.6
农田水利		**Irrigation and Water Conservancy**			
排灌用动力机械	(台)	Power-driven Irrigation Machinery(unit)	63200.0	64400.0	98.1
	(万千瓦)	(10000 kwh)	68.4	70.4	97.2
机(电)井	(眼)	Motor-pumped Well (unit)	49385.0	44298.0	111.5
# 已配套	(眼)	Completed Set (unit)		43851.0	0.0
扬水站(固定机电排灌站)	(处)	Pumping Station (unit)	4815.0	4856.0	99.2
有效灌溉面积	(公顷)	Irrigated Areas (hectare)	323000.0	323270.0	99.9
占耕地面积		As Percentage of Cultivated Areas (%)	94.7		
化肥施用量(折纯)		**Consumption of Chemical Fertilizers (converted into Pure)**			
化肥施用量	(吨)	Consumption of Chemical Fertilizers (ton)	192870.9	196528.0	98.1
氮 肥	(吨)	Nitrogenous Fertilizer (ton)	119056.9	123600.0	96.3
磷 肥	(吨)	Phosphate Fertilizer (ton)	10181.1	12429.0	81.9
钾 肥	(吨)	Potash Fertilizer (ton)	3803.0	2817.9	135.0
每公顷耕地施用量	(公斤)	Consumption Per Hectare Cultivated Areas (kg)	566.0	574.0	98.6

注：农村小水电站是指乡村两级小水电实有数。农村用电量为市供电局提供。

Note: Data of rural small hydropower station refer to actual number of small hydropower at township and Village level.Data on consumption of electricity are provided by Beijing Municipal Power Supply Bureau.

5-30 乡镇集体企业各业基本情况
BASIC STATISTICS ON SECTORS OF TOWN AND TOWNSHIP ENTERPRISES

行业 Sector	企业个数（个）Number of Enterprises (unit)		从业人员（人）Employment (person)		总收入（万元）Total Revenue (10000 yuan)		利润总额（万元）Total Profits (10000 yuan)		税金（万元）Taxes (10000 yuan)
	数量 Number	占% Proportion	数量 Number	占% Proportion	数量 Number	占% Proportion	数量 Number	占% Proportion	
合计 Total	**15711**	**100**	**736799**	**100**	**5747286**	**100**	**283459**	**100**	**214553**
农业 Agriculture	397	2.5	11696	1.6	162986	2.8	18358	6.5	2174
工业 Industry	9916	63.0	488337	66.3	3162016	55.0	136071	48.0	134488
交通运输业 Transportation	970	6.2	13813	1.9	108820	1.9	7049	2.5	3454
施工建筑业 Construction	904	5.8	134967	18.3	851476	14.8	45011	15.9	35855
商品流通业 Commerce	2177	13.9	40850	5.5	1022322	17.8	34388	12.1	21084
旅游饮服业 Tourism,Catering and Services	1205	7.7	41103	5.6	321540	5.6	25528	9.0	12686
其他 Others	142	0.9	6033	0.8	118126	2.1	17054	6.0	4812

5-31 乡镇集体企业出口供货情况
GOODS SUPPLIES FOR EXPORT OF TOWN AND TOWNSHIP ENTERPRISES

单位：万元 (10000 yuan)

行业	Sector	出口产品交货总额 Total Amount on Delivery of Exports		直接出口 Direct Export		间接出口 Indirect Export	
		1998	1997	1998	1997	1998	1997
合计	**Total**	**405727**	**394684**	**284529**	**280625**	**121198**	**114059**
化工	Chemical Products	5620	2630	2722	902	2898	1728
机械	Machinery	13945	9516	10180	8051	3765	1465
矿产	Mineral Products	5574	1881	3291	351	2283	1530
轻工	Light Industry	60262	36761	35095	19909	25167	16852
食品	Food	8362	8190	2255	3571	6107	4619
土产	Local Products	1213		1181		32	
畜产	Livestock Products	3751	1301	3615	1301	136	
纺织	Textile	52093	52016	41183	31995	10910	20021
服装	Garment	162969	192003	118336	147445	44633	44558
工艺品	Handicraft	45692	45254	37885	33763	7807	11491
其他	Others	46246	45132	28786	33337	17460	11795

5-32 乡镇企业主要产品产量及占全市的比重
MAJOR PRODUCTS OUTPUT OF TOWN AND TOWNSHIP ENTERPRISES AND THEIR PROPORTION IN TOTAL OF THE CITY

产品名称 Products				1998		1997	
				数量 Output	占全市比重(%) Proportion(%)	数量 Output	占全市比重(%) Proportion(%)
发电量	(万千瓦时)	Generated Energy	(10000 kwh)	3874	0.3	3123	0.2
原煤	(万吨)	Raw Coal	(10000 tons)	529	53.5	545.6	53.9
塑料制品	(吨)	Plastic Products	(ton)	44049	44.9	38282	27.3
泵	(台)	Pump	(unit)	22020	79.7	13524	24.3
暖气片	(万片)	Heating Radiator	(10000 pieces)			34	1.1
水泥	(万吨)	Cement	(10000 tons)	229	30.1	194	27.7
砖	(亿块)	Brick	(100 million pieces)	53.5	100.0	57.4	85.7
石灰	(万吨)	Lime	(10000 tons)	119.7	…	171.6	35.6
水磨石	(万平方米)	Terrazzo	(10000 sq.m)	49.3	…	64.3	64.3
水泥预制构件	(万立方米)	Cement Prefabricated Components	(10000 sq.m)	92.8	82.5	123.1	81.9
棉布	(万米)	Cotton Cloth	(10000 meters)	7223	50.6	7934	44.2
服装	(万件)	Garment	(10000)	7051	64.8	8818	58.8
布鞋	(万双)	Cloth Shoes	(10000 pairs)	298	55.8	531	46.3
白酒	(吨)	White Sprite	(ton)	4344	4.4	3637	4.1
家具	(万件)	Furniture	(10000)	464	…	366	74.3

5-33 郊区县乡镇集体企业主要经济指标
MAIN ECONOMIC INDICATORS FOR TOWN AND TOWNSHIP ENTERPRISES IN SUBURBS AND COUNTIES

地区	Region	企业个数 (个) Number of Enterprises (unit)	从业人员 (人) Employment (person)	总收入 (万元) Total Revenue (10000 yuan)	利润总额 (万元) Total Profits (10000 yuan)	人均利润 (元) Profit Per Capita (yuan)	税金 (万元) Taxes (10000yuan)	# 所得税 (万元) Income Tax (10000 yuan)
全市	**Total**	**15711**	**736799**	**5747286**	**283459**	**3847**	**214553**	**45131**
朝阳区	Chaoyang	1956	92692	714662	25486	2750	28414	6221
丰台区	Fengtai	1469	63843	637843	46540	7289	20590	5618
石景山区	Shijingshan	256	9151	144203	2897	3166	4620	352
海淀区	Haidian	1133	47433	548687	20793	4384	18405	2874
门头沟区	Mentougou	638	18447	105805	4916	2665	3853	648
房山区	Fangshan	1637	97279	621762	26664	2741	24457	4671
通州区	Tongzhou	2823	80252	507618	25960	3235	20473	4136
昌平县	Changping	1101	48067	278073	16988	3534	10732	1761
顺义县	Shunyi	1007	86325	495420	23702	2746	21867	3167
大兴县	Daxing	1427	50566	444039	30459	6024	16260	3617
平谷县	Pinggu	768	49644	325580	15204	3063	10307	2358
怀柔县	Huairou	730	39553	628902	35373	8943	22352	7473
密云县	Miyun	423	31284	152573	2983	953	6774	1179
延庆县	Yanqing	343	22263	142119	5494	2468	5449	1056

5-34 郊区县农村个体、联合体企业主要经济指标

MAIN ECONOMIC INDICATORS FOR RURAL PRIVATE AND JOINT ENTERPRISES IN SUBURBS AND COUNTIES

地区 Region		企业个数 (个) Number of Enterprises (unit)	从业人员 (人) Employment (person)	总收入 (万元) Total Revenue (10000 yuan)	利润总额 (万元) Total Profits (10000 yuan)	人均利润 (元) Profit Per Capita (yuan)	税金 (万元) Taxes (10000 yuan)	# 所得税 (万元) Income Tax (10000 yuan)
全市	**Total**	**62975**	**186959**	**1208616**	**93219**	**4990**	**25104**	**4694**
朝阳区	Chaoyang	8	282	514	51	1809	43	4
丰台区	Fengtai	395	2505	12510	1613	6440	656	103
石景山区	Shijingshan	230	1228	6117	993	8086	537	32
海淀区	Haidian	704	1813	9162	813	4484	342	19
门头沟区	Mentougou	6149	13119	81899	11509	8773	2295	384
房山区	Fangshan	24379	71031	613394	21524	3030	7317	1641
通州区	Tongzhou	7177	22480	103010	23850	10610	2341	707
昌平县	Changping	1827	4168	18156	1398	3354	471	28
顺义县	Shunyi	3717	19639	122381	11214	5710	3017	441
大兴县	Daxing	6055	14771	67971	3447	2333	1797	120
平谷县	Pinggu	1599	5200	11838	1315	2529	347	50
怀柔县	Huairou	1021	1835	9439	1591	8670	450	141
密云县	Miyun	7764	20907	125857	11211	5362	3666	689
延庆县	Yanqing	1950	7981	26368	2690	3371	1825	335

5-35 8县75乡农村劳动力转移情况

STATISTICS ON RURAL LABOR FORCE TRANSFERRING OF THE 75 TOWNSHIPS IN 8 COUNTIES

项目 Item		合计 Total		平原 Plain		山区 Mountain Area	
		数量（人） Number (person)	构成（%） Composition (%)	数量（人） Number (person)	构成（%） Composition (%)	数量（人） Number (person)	构成（%） Composition (%)
调查户劳动力转移人数	**Labor Force Transferring of Household in Surveyed**	**1653**	**100**	**1305**	**100**	**348**	**100**
当年转移的劳动力	**Labor Force Transferred in This Year**	**151**	**9.1**	**94**	**7.2**	**57**	**16.4**
转移劳动力素质情况	**Quality Level of Labor Force Transferring**						
性别构成	Sex Composition						
男劳动力	Male	1029	62.3	801	61.4	228	65.5
# 整劳动力	Full Labor Force	845	51.1	650	49.8	195	54.0
女劳动力	Female	624	37.8	504	38.6	120	34.5
# 整劳动力	Full Labor Force	482	29.2	382	29.7	100	28.7
文化程度	Educational Level						
小学以下文化程度	at Primary School Level and below	114	6.9	88	6.7	26	7.5
初中文化程度	at Junior Middle School Level	909	55.0	722	55.3	187	53.7
中专以上文化程度	at Specialized Secondary School Level and above	554	33.5	428	32.8	126	36.2
大专及以上文化程度	at Junior College Level	76	4.6	67	5.1	9	2.6
接受专业培训情况	Taking Professional Training						
接受专业培训	Trained	877	53.1	674	51.7	203	58.3
未接受专业培训	No Trained	776	46.9	631	48.4	145	41.7
转移劳动力行业分布	**Sector Transfer to**						
农牧渔业	Farming,Animal Husbandry and Fishery	6	0.4	4	0.3	2	0.6
工业	Industry	583	35.3	457	35.0	126	36.2
建筑业	Construction	128	7.7	94	7.2	34	9.8
交通运输业	Transportations,	174	10.5	138	10.6	36	10.3
邮电通讯业	Posts and Telecommunications	20	1.2	14	1.1	6	1.7
商业饮食业	Commerce and Catering	121	7.3	107	8.2	14	4.0
服务业	Services	225	13.6	165	12.7	60	17.2
文教卫生	Culture,Education and Health	118	7.1	98	7.5	20	5.8
其他	Others	278	16.8	228	17.5	50	14.4
转移地域	**Region Transfer To**						
本市内转移	Within Local City	1648	99.7	1301	99.7	347	99.7
转向外省市	To Nonlocal	5	0.3	4	0.3	1	0.3
调查户当年返回农业的劳动力	**Labor Force Back to Agriculture in This Year of Households in Survey**	**1**		**1**			

注：本表是在8个被调查县抽选75个乡(镇)，每个乡(镇)抽选3个村，每村调查1个村民小组。

Note：Sampling of the survey is as following--select 75 townships from 8 counties,select 3 villages from those of townships,and select a villager group from those of villages.

5-36 8县75乡劳动力构成
COMPOSITION OF LABOR FORCE OF THE 75 TOWNSHIPS IN 8 COUNTIES

项目	Item	合计 Total 数量（人）Number (person)	合计 Total 构成（%）Composition (%)	平原 Plain 数量（人）Number (person)	平原 Plain 构成（%）Composition (%)	山区 Mountain Area 数量（人）Number (person)	山区 Mountain Area 构成（%）Composition (%)
调查村整半劳动力	**Full and Half Labor Force in Village Surveyed**	**3578**	**100**	**2716**	**100**	**862**	**100**
按性别分	Grouped by Sex						
男劳动力	Male	1859	52.0	1413	52.0	446	51.7
# 整劳动力	Full Labor Force	1429	40.0	1085	40.0	344	39.9
女劳动力	Female	1719	48.0	1303	48.0	416	48.3
# 整劳动力	Full Labor Force	1153	32.2	853	31.4	300	34.8
按文化程度分	Grouped by Educational Level						
文盲或半文盲	Illiteracy and Half-illiteracy	62	1.7	30	1.1	32	3.7
小学程度	at Primary School Level	433	12.1	289	10.6	144	16.7
初中程度	at Junior Middle School Level	2042	57.1	1592	58.6	450	52.2
中专程度	at Specialized Secondary School	956	26.7	729	26.8	227	26.3
大专及以上程度	at Junior College Level	85	2.4	76	2.8	9	1.0
按是否接受过专业培训分	Grouped by Whether Received Specialized Training						
受过各种专业培训	Received All Kinds of Specialized Training	1417	39.6	1092	40.2	325	37.7
未接受专业培训	Never Received Specialized Training	2161	60.4	1624	59.8	537	62.3

注：本表是在8个被调查县抽选75个乡(镇)，每个乡(镇)抽选3个村，每村调查1个村民小组。

Note：Sampling of the survey is as following--select 75 townships from 8 counties,select 3 villages from those of townships,and select a villager group from those of villages.

5-37 8县75乡平均每人拥有固定资产及投资情况

FIXED ASSETS AND INVESTMENT PER CAPITA OF THE 75 TOWNSHIPS IN 8 COUNTIES

单位：元 (yuan)

项目	Item	合计 Total	乡(镇)所有 Of Township	村组所有 Of Village	农户所有 Of Household
年末拥有固定资产原值	**Original Value of Fixed Assets(year-end)**	**20281.1**	**4632.4**	**5231.4**	**10417.3**
农　业	Agriculture	2192.9	366.9	1389.3	436.7
# 生产用房屋及建筑物	Buildings for Production	955.5	152.9	636.5	166.1
役畜及产品畜	Draught Animals and Commodity Animals	94.0	11.7	37.9	44.4
农林牧渔业机械	Machinery for Farming, Forestry,Animal Husbandry and Fishery	588.4	69.7	332.9	185.7
工　业	Industry	4897.7	2583.7	2281.2	32.9
# 生产用房屋及建筑物	Buildings for Production	1789.2	852.7	919.2	17.3
生产设备	Productive Equipments	2430.6	1416.9	998.2	15.6
建筑业	Construction	341.6	215.9	117.9	7.9
交通运输邮电业	Transportation,Posts and Telecommunications	957.7	92.0	157.9	707.8
商饮服务业	Commerce,Catering and Services	573.1	306.3	248.2	18.7
文教卫生社会福利事业	Culture,Education,Health and Social Welfare	589.6	389.7	199.9	
住　宅	Residence	9438.7	322.0	157.5	8959.2
其　他	Others	1289.7	356.0	679.5	254.2
本年固定资产投资完成额	**Investment in Fixed Assets Completed in this year**	**1703.4**	**703.9**	**459.6**	**539.9**
按资金来源分	Grouped by Source of Funds				
自有资金	One's Own	1365.7	502.6	373.3	489.8
银行信用社贷款	Loan from Bank and Credit Cooperative	149.9	97.8	46.7	5.4
其他来源	Others	187.8	103.5	39.7	44.7
按资金投向分	Grouped by Use of Funds				
农　业	Agriculture	225.5	41.9	99.7	83.9
工　业	Industry	364.3	194.9	158.1	11.3
建筑业	Construction	50.4	38.7	6.7	5.0
其　他	Others	1063.1	428.4	195.1	439.6
# 住　宅	Residence	678.3	255.4	44.0	378.9

5-38 农村经济收入与分配
INCOME AND DISTRIBUTION OF RURAL ECONOMY

单位：万元 (10000 yuan)

项目	Item	1998	1997	1998年为1997年% 1998 as % of 1997
营业收入	**Operation Income**	**10115280.6**	**9234893.3**	**109.5**
农业	Agriculture	705823.1	651027.5	108.4
#粮食	Grain	316289.4	296905.6	106.5
林业	Forestry	91350.1	84983.4	107.5
牧业	Animal Husbandry	531826.9	506276.3	105.0
渔业	Fishery	60441.8	71642.3	84.4
工业	Industry	3588332.7	3451403.2	104.0
交通运输业	Transportation	895605.8	736420.4	121.6
建筑业	Construction	1241911.0	1168239.9	106.3
商业、饮食业	Commerce and Catering	1701188.3	1602109.8	106.2
服务业	Services	700346.4	552054.9	126.9
其他	Others	598454.3	410735.6	145.7
营业成本	**Operation Cost**	**8971404.6**	**7975856.3**	**112.5**
农业	Agriculture	611777.2	501632.4	122.0
#粮食	Grain	217502.5	221027.9	98.4
林业	Forestry	82513.8	70503.1	117.0
牧业	Animal Husbandry	504887.0	446275.4	113.1
渔业	Fishery	55608.5	51769.2	107.4
工业	Industry	3138350.2	2990494.3	104.9
交通运输业	Transportation	819376.2	650546.6	126.0
建筑业	Construction	1101346.4	1013534.3	108.7
商业、饮食业	Commerce and Catering	1574650.3	1444328.5	109.0
服务业	Services	587546.9	441799.7	133.0
其他	Others	495347.9	364972.8	135.7
营业利润	**Operation Profits**	**495906.1**	**627324.9**	**79.1**
利润总额	**Total Profits**	**582196.5**	**706484.8**	**82.4**
税后利润	**Net Profits**	**529998.2**	**658188.3**	**80.5**
可供分配的利润	**Profit to be Divided**	**476848.5**	**591289.4**	**80.6**
未分配利润	**Retained Profits**	**55159.7**	**157595.2**	**35.0**

5-39 郊区规模乡镇发展情况

STATISTICS FOR LARGE SCALE TOWN AND TOWNSHIPS IN SUBURBS AND COUNTIES

乡镇名称 Name	总人口 (人) Population (person)	总劳动力 (人) Labor Force (person)	农村社会总产值 (万元) Rural Gross Output Value (10000 yuan)	乡镇企业个数 (个) Town and Township Enterprises (unit)	乡镇企业总收入 (万元) Total Revenue of Town and Township Enterprises (10000 yuan)	乡镇企业利润总额 (万元) Total Profits of Town and Township Enterprises (10000 yuan)
小红门乡	18119	8346	118686.3	264	103860	2812
十八里店乡	22659	12704	52618	220	56903	1693
南磨房乡	5109	2830	121385	46	133102.5	7117
高碑店乡	11936	6308	68004	320	92011	7599
平房乡	11032	4589	58560.3	156	45365	2155
来广营乡	8169	3700	54226.2	132	47275	631
洼里乡	8080	3558	56634.9	173	55270.4	0
卢沟桥乡	38064	19296	117102	617	242278	21269
花乡	38693	20235	133772	476	238665	15617
南苑乡	26232	15160	66373	438	16002	6580
石景山乡	15588	7729	63196.4	486	144203	2545
四季青乡	49213	15688	79143.3	373	89856	596
玉渊潭乡	9338	6312	56366	172	176295	13171
石楼镇	28232	12136	57879	982	50220.3	2851.3
东营乡	14866	7252	156893	1133	124302	8680
琉璃河地区	24500	11861	89786.7	506	59041	2173
窦店镇	19710	8158	113007.4	1177	126465	5223
交道镇	15079	6681	68404.5	445	63235	2823.6
良乡地区	24840	9562	94328.1	1974	119626.3	9122
阎村镇	24663	10339	94015.5	2189	99941	14875
房山街道	30771	14895	156119.9	2501	245306.4	6471
周口店地区	28270	10390	127010	138	130392	7987
顺义镇	37521	16298	122050.4	132	90091	2704
后沙峪镇	15305	7442	59660.2	452	49380	3492
天竺镇	41506	16833	73013	168	34204	1705
杨镇	19536	8668	64256.6	146	47144	1469.8
北务镇	30078	11770	79339.9	213	36706	3266
张镇	31152	15071	71629.8	546	43084	1804
木林镇	26538	11640	80039.8	66	22257	183.8
北小营镇	22119	9933	70129.5	136	27927	1250
牛山镇	16214	7847	50378.4	368	20700	1150
北石槽镇	34555	13346	59096.3	167	31057	1987
赵全营镇	28647	11445	80458.8	84	38759	2216
马坡乡	22512	10153	70391.7	79	28229	2234
宋庄镇	28996	13511	107348.6	207	87095	3644
牛堡屯镇	24996	12178	52620.2	682	34477	1615
张家湾镇	29274	10653	78057.3	1138	62041.2	4283.7
梨园镇	22809	8202	82688	889	65438	4027
通州城关镇	36229	11440	119341	1259	123988	18854
黄村镇	14982	8083	69956	1319	58030	3852
旧宫镇	11427	2415	60876.1	809	45271.7	2481
西红门镇	8930	3935	79125.7	198	87831	9644
怀柔镇	23364	10376	216549	196	232820	12302
北房镇	15769	7586	57318.8	199	36006	2131
杨宋镇	14972	5040	61214	67	58033	3338
庙城镇	16073	6019	78397.8	129	63334	3703
桥梓镇	18614	7756	91425.6	74	69101	3865
太师屯镇	34191	17263	53433.5	612	32240.1	613
延庆镇	33627	14843	60651.2	45	26000	646

注：规模乡镇是指农村社会总产值达到5亿元的乡镇。

Note：Town and townships refer to those their rural gross output value amount to 500 million yuan.

主要统计指标解释

农业总产值 是以货币表现的农、林、牧、渔业全部产品的总量，它反映一定时期内农业生产总规模和总成果。

农、林、牧、渔业的统计范围包括国有经济各种专业农（农、林、牧、渔）场以及国家各级机关团体学校、部队；集体所有制的乡、镇、村各级办农场；工矿企业经营的农、林、牧、渔业，农村各种经济组织和农户经营的农林牧渔业和农民家庭兼营的商品性工业等。

（1）农业 包括种植业和其他农业。

种植业 包括谷物、豆类、薯类、棉、油料、糖料、麻类、烟叶、蔬菜、药材、瓜类和其他农作物的种植，以及茶园、桑园、果园的生产经营。

其他农业 包括采集野生植物的果实、纤维、树胶、树脂、油料以及柴草、野生药材、菌类等及农民家庭兼营的商品性工业。

（2）林业 包括林木的栽培（不包括茶园、桑园和果园的栽培、管理和收获等活动）、林产品的采集和村及村以下合作经济组织和农户的竹木采伐。

（3）牧业 包括除渔业养殖以外的一切动物饲养和放牧以及野生动物的捕猎和饲养。

（4）渔业 包括水生动物和海藻类植物的养殖和捕捞。

农业总产值的计算方法通常是按农林牧渔业产品及其副产品的产量分别乘以各自单位产品价格求得，少数生产周期较长，当年没有产品或产品产量不易统计的，则采用间接方法匡算其产值，然后将四业产品产值相加即为农业总产值。

1957 年以前的农业总产值中包括了厩肥和农民自给性手工业（如农民自制衣服、鞋、袜，自己从事粮食初步加工等）。1958 年及以后的农业总产值，林业中增加了村及村以下竹木采伐产值；牧业中取消费厩肥产值；副业中取消了农民自给性手工业产值；渔业中增加了海洋捕捞水产品产值。1980 年及以后的农业总产值，在副业中增加了农民家庭兼营工业商品部分的产值。从 1984 年起村及村以下办工业产值划归工业。从 1993 年起，取消副业。将野生动物的捕猎划入牧业，野生植物采集和农民家庭兼营商品性工业划归农业。

耕地面积 指年初可以用来种植农作物、经常进行耕锄的田地，除包括熟地、当年新开荒地、连续撂荒未满三年的耕地和当年的休闲地（轮歇地）外，还包括以种植农作物为主并附带种植桑树、茶树、果树和其他林木的土地，以及沿海、沿湖地区已围垦利用的“海涂”、“湖田 ”等面积。但不包括属于专业性的桑园、茶园、果园、果木苗圃、林地、芦苇地、天然或人工草地面积。

农作物播种面积 指实际播种或移植有农作物的面积。凡是实际种植有农作物的面积，不论种植在耕地上还是种植在非耕地上，均包括在农作物播种面积中。在播种季节基本结束后，因遭灾而重新改种和补种的农作物面积，也包括在内。

有效灌溉面积 指具有一定的水源，地块比较平整，灌溉工程或设备已经配套，在一般年景下当年能够进行正常灌溉的耕地面积。

农业机械总动力 指主要用于农、林、牧、渔业的各种动力机械的动力总和。包括耕作机械、排灌机械、收获机械、农用运输机械、植物保护机械、牧业机械、渔业机械和其他农用机械[内燃机按引擎马力折成瓦（特）计算，电动机按功率折成瓦（特）计算]。不包括专门用于乡、镇、村、组办工业、基本建设、非农业运输、科学实验和教学等非农业生产方面用的动力机械与作业机械。

农林牧渔业劳动力 指直接参加农林牧渔业生产劳动的劳动力。

期初（末）畜禽存栏头（只）数 指本期期初（末）农村各种合作经济组织和国营农场、农民个人、机关、团体、学校、工矿企业、部队等单位以及城镇居民饲养的大牲畜、猪、羊、家禽等禽畜的存栏头（只）数。

乡镇企业 即原来农村人民公社和生产大队两级集体经济举办的社队企业。在农村政社组织管理体制分设以后，除了乡、村合作经济组织办企业外，又出现了部分农民联营或其他形式的合作企业和个体企业。1984 年 3 月确定将这类企业统称“乡镇企业”。

乡镇企业单位一般应拥有固定的组织、生产场所、生产设备和从业人员；有核算制度，承担经济责任和纳税义务；是一个比较稳定的经济实体。

Explanatory Notes On Main Statistical Indicators

Gross Output of Agriculture refers to the total volume of products of farming, forestry, animal husbandry and fishery in value terms, which reflects the total scale and total result of agricultural production during a given period of time.

The statistical coverage of farming, forestry, animal husbandry and fishery are as follows:

In terms of ownership, China's agriculture includes specialized state farms (farming, forestry, animal husbandry and fishery), farms managed by various government organs, organizations, schools, research institutions, and army; farms managed by rural collective organizations at levels of township, town, and village; farming, forestry, animal husbandry, fishery run by mining and industrial enterprises; farming, forestry, animal husbandry and fishery and some commodity industries run by individual farmers.

(1) Farming includes cultivation of farm crops and other agricultural activities .

Cultivation includes the cultivation of grain crops, beans, tubers, cotton, oil-bearing crops, sugar crops, fiber crops, tobacco, vegetables, medicinal herbs, melons and gourds, and cultivation and management of tea plantations, mulberry fields and orchards.

Other agricultural activities includes gathering fruits, fiber, oil, gum and resin of wild plants, firewood and firegrass, wild medicinal herbs, fungus plants, and commodity industries of the rural households.

(2) Forestry refers to planting various kinds of trees (excluding tea plantations, mulberry fields and orchards) , gathering of forest products, and felling of bamboo and trees by villages and other cooperative organizations under villages.

(3) Animal husbandry refers to raising and grazing of all animals except fishery and aquaculture, and hunting and raising of wild animals.

(4) Fishery refers to cultivation and catching of fish and other aquatic animals and cultivation and collection of seaweed and other aquatic plants.

Gross output value of agriculture is obtained by first multiplying the output of each product or by-product by its price, resulting in the output value of each single item. For a small number of products, annual output of which is not available or difficult to get due to the long production/ growing process involved, the output value is estimated through an indirect approach. The sum of output value of all products of farming, forestry, animal husbandry, and fishery is then equal to the gross output value of agriculture.

Prior to 1957, China's gross agricultural output value included barnyard manure and handicraft products for self-consumption (clothes, shoes, stockings, and initial grain processing undertaken by peasants) . Since 1958, felling of bamboo and trees by villages and other cooperative organizations under villages had been added to forestry; value of barnyard manure had been removed from animal husbandry; self-consumed handicrafts had been removed from sideline productions; while the output value of industries run by villages and cooperative organizations under village had been added in sideline productions and the output value of fish catches by motor fishing boats had been added to fishery. Since 1980, the value of handicraft products made for sale by households had been added to sideline productions. Since 1984, industry run by villages and cooperative organizations under villages has been put in the sector of industry. Since 1993, the subdivision of sideline productions has been canceled, and the hunting of wild animals has been classified into animal husbandry, and the gathering of wild plants and commodity industry run by rural households has been put in farming.

Cultivated Area (Area under cultivation) refers to farmland which is plowed constantly for growing crops, including cultivated land, newly cultivated land in the current year, farmland left without cultivation for less than three years and fallow land in the current year, rotation land, farmland for crops but growing also a few fruit trees, mulberry trees and other trees and cultivated seashore land and lake land, etc. The land of mulberry fields, tea plantations, orchards, nurseries of young plants, forestland, reed land, natural and man-made grassland are not included in cultivated land.

Sown Area of Crops refers to area of land sown or transplanted with crops regardless of being in cultivated area or non-cultivated area. Area of land resown after natural disasters is also included in.

Irrigated Area refers to areas that are effectively irrigated, i. e. level land which has water source and complete sets of irrigation facilities and is able to provide adequate water for irrigation under normal conditions.

Total Power of Farm Machinery refers to total mechanical power of machinery used in farming, forestry, animal husbandry, and fishery, including plow, irrigation and drainage, harvesting, transport, plant protection, stock breeding, forestry and fishery. The horsepower of internal combustion engines is converted into watts and the power of electric motors is converted into watts. Machinery employed for non-agricultural industry, construction, transportation, scientific experiments and teaching is excluded.

Labor Force Engaged in Farming, Forestry, Animal Husbandry and Fishery refers to the total labors who are directly engaged in production of farming, forestry, animal husbandry and fishery.

Number of Livestock or Poultry on Hand at the Beginning (or End) of the reference Period refers to the total number of big animals, pigs, sheep, fowls, etc. raised by rural cooperative organizations, army, and urban residents at the beginning (or end) of the reference period.

Township Enterprises refer to enterprises originally run by the collective economies at the people's commune and the production brigade levels. After the rural administrative system reform, besides the enterprises run by townships and villages, farmers' cooperative or other types of cooperative enterprises and private enterprises had appeared in the rural areas. In March 1984, all the aforesaid enterprises were defined as the "township enterprises."

Township Enterprises should have fixed organization, production sites, production equipment and employees, and also have accounting systems, undertake economic responsibilities and pay taxes. So, they are relatively stable economic entities.

工 业

INDUSTRY

工业企业及总产值构成%（不含个体工业）

Composition of Endustrial Enterprises and Their Gross Output Value %(exclude Individual Industry)

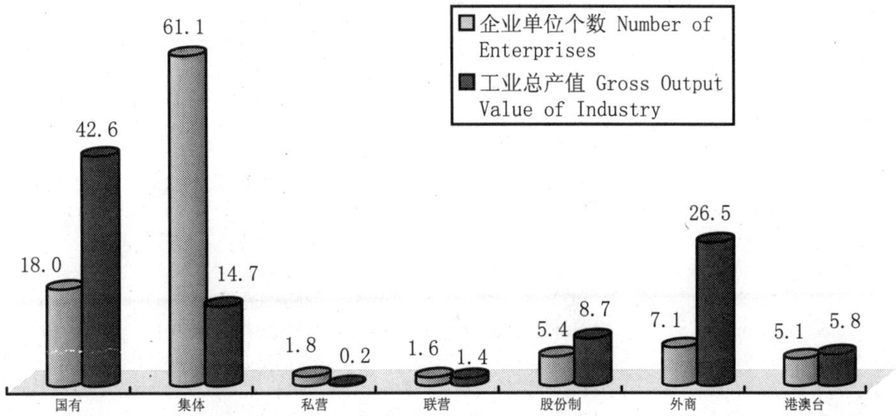

		1998	1997
企业单位数	(个)	30160	37362
Number of Enterprises	(unit)		
工业总产值	(亿元)	1960.7	1660.7
Gross Output Value of Industry(100 million yuan)			

1998年部分工业产品产量

Output of Industry Products

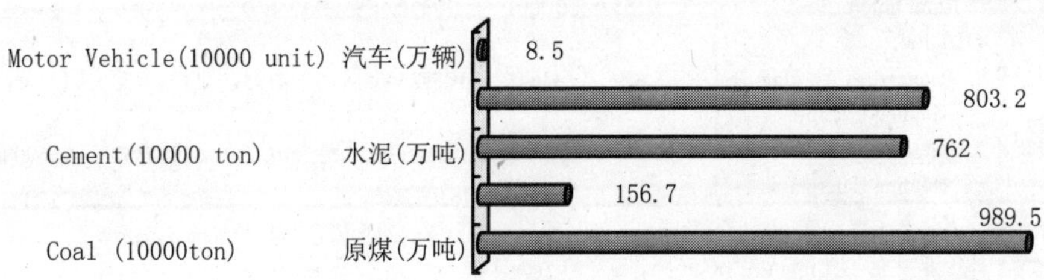

6-1 工业企业单位数和工业总产值、销售产值

NUMBER OF INDUSTRIAL ENTERPRISES，GROSS OUTPUT VALUE AND SALES

单位：万元 (10000 yuan)

项目	Item	企业单位数(个) Number of Enterprises (unit) 1998	1997	工业总产值 Gross Output Value of Industry 1990年不变价 at 1990 constant prices 1998	1997	当年价格 at current prices 1998	1997	销售产值(当年价格) Sales (at current prices)
全市合计(含个体工业)	**The Whole City (include Individual Industry)**	**30160**	**37362**	**19606882**	**16606725**	**20270235**	**19638338**	**19765872**
总计(不含个体工业)	**Total (exclude Individual Industry)**	**18089**	**27530**	**19267723**	**16280051**	**19919611**	**19251950**	**19423973**
在总计中:	**Of Total:**							
中央企业	Central Enterprises	922	1236	7072085	4553806	6400471	5094485	6407943
地方企业	Local Enterprises	17167	26294	12195638	11726245	13519140	14157465	13016030
工业系统	Industry System	1593	1975	5886694	5704389	6386871	6711943	6286200
非工业系统	Non-Industry System	1094	1531	819917	851166	1225320	1521929	1190908
区县工业	ndustry of District and County	13126	21591	4605908	4480339	4977600	5165340	4660581
其他	Others	1354	1197	883119	690351	929349	758253	878341
在总计中:	**Of Total:**							
国有经济	State-owned Enterprise	3253	4334	8205913	7573102	8634587	9600424	8613457
集体经济	Collective-owned Enterprise	11049	18501	2837132	2896638	3011353	3299733	2794851
私营经济	Private Enterprise	322	462	32015	51090	32972	61402	30583
联营经济	Joint-owned Enterprise	284	341	274976	193777	274056	223587	265379
股份制经济	Share Holding Enterpri	979	604	1682413	526486	1852929	650654	1755216
外商投资经济	Foreign Funded Enterprise	1284	1537	5112880	4036675	4856255	4259163	4746114
中外合资经营	Joint Venture	922	1172	4784978	3782915	4500746	3944461	4398546
中外合作经营	Co-operative	55	99	70632	127805	68663	136822	72532
外资企业	Foreign Enterprises	307	266	257271	125956	286846	177881	275037
港澳台投资经济	HongKong,Macao and Taiwan Funded Enterprises	914	1689	1122273	996431	1257251	1149331	1218163
与大陆合资经营	Joint Venture	702	1480	983725	881802	1102666	1025676	1069957
与大陆合作经营	Co-operative	37	22	22532	9489	25593	14849	25584
港澳台独资企业	HongKong,Macao and Taiwan Enterprises	175	187	116016	105140	128992	108806	122622
其他经济	Others	4	62	121	5851	208	7656	208
在总计中:	**Of Total:**							
农村企业	Rural Enterprises	9155	10001	2741020	2126049	2915391	2466223	2701520
在总计中:	**Of Total:**							
国有绝对控股企业	State-owned Absolute Holding Enterprises	2639	3641	10592340	9744195	11230475	12468315	11133701
国有相对控股企业	State-owned Relative Holding Enterpeises	312	122	2690140	730123	2295182	690883	2271092

注：1.本资料除"主要工业产品生产总量"(全社会)及标明者外，均为不含个体的独立核算工业企业统计范围。
2.全市合计(含个体工业)中的不变价工业总产值及销售产值为折算数。

a) Data of this chapter refers to industrial enterprises except individuals with independent accounting system,except the table of "major products output"(refers to total)and items with note.

b) Data of gross output value at constant prices and sales of the whole city(include individual)is that converted.

6-1 续表 1 continued

单位：万元 (10000 yuan)

项目	Item	企业单位数(个) Number of Enterprises (unit)		工业总产值 Gross Output Value of Industry				销售产值(当年价格) Sales (at current prices)
				1990年不变价 at 1990 constant prices		当年价格 at current prices		
		1998	1997	1998	1997	1998	1997	
在总计中：	**Of Total:**							
轻工业	Light Industry	8837	13486	5393576	5278120	6120157	6468667	5907045
以农产品为原料	Using Farm Products as Raw Material	5327	8022	3209874	3326836	4019696	4472476	3862132
以非农产品为原料	Using Non-Farm Products as Raw Material	3510	5464	2183702	1951285	2100461	1996191	2044913
重工业	Heavy Industry	9252	14044	13874148	11001930	13799453	12783283	13516927
采掘工业	Excavation	497	654	122113	140004	199917	229209	189146
原料工业	Raw Material	1162	1834	3104281	3188420	4591597	5196003	4560939
加工工业	Processing	7593	11556	10647755	7673508	9007939	7358072	8766842
在总计中：	**Of Total:**							
大型企业	Large Enterprises	266	215	9312944	6179643	9659578	8283363	9596633
中型企业	Medium Enterprises	268	284	945904	1002705	1182932	1321866	1168827
小型企业	Small Enterprises	17555	27031	9008876	9097703	9077101	9646720	8658513
在总计中：	**Of Total:**							
煤炭采选业	Coal Mining and Dressing	203	222	59908	68306	125821	144912	119946
石油和天然气开采业	Petroleum and Natural Gas Extraction	1	4	155	1047	155	1105	132
黑色金属矿采选业	Ferrous Metals Mining and Dressing	26	22	13888	12065	22220	21155	20808
有色金属矿采选业	Nonferrous Metals Mining and Dressing	19	20	6082	7289	6259	10645	5359
非金属矿采选业	Nonmetal Minerals Mining and Dressing	247	386	41867	42533	45253	50933	42645
其他矿采选业	Other Minerals Mining and Dressing	1	1	213	229	211	279	255
食品加工业	Food Processing	558	905	571689	668993	819264	1080934	797478
食品制造业	Food Making	641	939	333086	359855	464351	508144	441233
饮料制造业	Beverage Production	230	317	484259	451463	603891	624295	599409
烟草加工业	Tobacco Processing	4	3	46449	46490	68203	68335	67905
纺织业	Textile Industry	469	730	411755	461348	470389	555539	444704
服装及其他纤维制品制造业	Garments and Other Fiber Products	876	1259	435354	444884	509911	539385	478025
皮革、毛皮、羽绒及其制品业	Leather,Furs,Down and Related Products	164	254	48443	54522	58672	68770	58814
木材加工及竹藤、棕、草制品业	Timber Processing,Bamboo Cane,Palm Fiber and Straw Products	233	380	41774	41348	46660	48755	44553
家具制造业	Furniture Manufacturing	514	860	142930	138038	148018	150652	138698
造纸及纸制品业	Papermaking and Paper Products	489	831	180851	175221	201040	212905	192353
印刷业，记录媒介的复制	Printing and Record Medium Reproduced	980	1383	324648	302113	422291	388592	410562

6-1 续表 2 continued

单位：万元 (10000 yuan)

项目	Item	企业单位数(个) Number of Enterprises (unit) 1998	1997	工业总产值 Gross Output Value of Industry 1990年不变价 at 1990 constant prices 1998	1997	当年价格 at current prices 1998	1997	销售产值(当年价格) Sales (at current prices)
文教体育用品制造业	Stationery,Educational and Sports Goods	214	351	89792	93323	107609	111970	102408
石油加工及炼焦业	Petroleum Processing and Coking Products	97	176	750125	784448	1142289	1424535	1150173
化学原料及化学制品	Raw Chemical Materials and Chemical Product	1196	1806	1005914	864506	1022599	1045964	980029
医药制造业	Medical and Pharmaceutical Products	220	242	428956	337721	397817	337125	368886
化学纤维制造业	Chemical Fibers	37	51	61158	75720	50169	67089	49586
橡胶制品业	Rubber Products	133	197	143788	154765	122422	136752	122486
塑料制品业	Plastic Products	689	1065	280883	315161	279258	343844	267040
非金属矿物制品	Nonmetal Mineral Products	1674	2590	784915	772437	948051	985239	899190
黑色金属冶炼及压延加工业	Smelting and Pressing of Ferrous Metals	100	132	1113519	1277010	1680659	1993866	1673445
有色金属冶炼及压延加工业	Smelting and Pressing of Nonferrous Metals	134	261	92763	92395	88103	104066	83703
金属制品业	Metal Products	2130	3616	604608	568520	614993	615611	591723
普通机械制造业	Ordinary Machinery Manufacturing	1145	1737	501321	514094	546997	593486	521439
专用设备制造业	Special Purposes Equipment Manufacturing	897	1200	810186	508719	827211	543055	795285
交通运输设备制造业	Transportation Equipment Manufacturing	1296	2048	1050675	1463070	1161437	1630003	1181156
武器弹药制造业	Weapon and Ammunition Manufacturing	10	10	47628	59042	62344	75057	62677
电气机械及器材制造	Electric Equipment and Machinery	848	1302	720118	4292232	710585	603711	663586
电子及通信设备制造	Electronic and Telecommunications	568	751	6800618	3834276	4780540	2856482	4698840
仪器仪表及文化、办公用机械制造	Instruments,Meters, Cultural and official Machine	376	496	347974	310296	339448	302628	323061
其他制造业	Other Manufacturing	574	875	179297	168539	185864	201785	185509
电力、蒸汽、热水的生产和供应业	Electricity,Steam and Hot Water Production and Supply	77	82	252298	239622	726370	717134	726954
煤气生产和供应	Gas Production and Supply	8	10	32132	32777	37750	33550	37750
自来水的生产和供应	Tap Water Production and Supply	11	16	25708	21580	74489	53485	76170

6-1 续表 3 continued

单位：万元 (10000 yuan)

项目	Item	企业单位数(个) Number of Enterprises (unit)	工业总产值 Gross Output Value of Industry: 1990年不变价 at 1990 constant prices	工业总产值 Gross Output Value of Industry: 当年价格 at current prices	销售产值(当年价格) Sales (at current prices)
全市合计(含个体工业)	**The Whole City (include Individual Industry)**	**30160**	**19606882**	**20270235**	**19765872**
总计(不含个体工业)	**Total (exclude Individual Industry)**	**18089**	**19267723**	**19919611**	**19423973**
内资企业	Domestic Investment Enterprises	15891	13032570	13806105	13459696
国有企业	State-Owned	3253	8205913	8634587	8613457
集体企业	Collective Owned	10446	2595723	2752170	2557226
私营企业	Private Owned	849	184157	199641	179980
联营企业	Joint Owned	284	274976	274056	265379
股份合作企业	Share Holding Cooperative	603	241410	259183	237625
股份有限公司	Share Holding Company	157	679439	652427	598747
有限责任公司	Limited-Liability Company	295	850832	1033833	1007073
其他企业	Others	4	121	208	208
港澳台商投资企业	Hongkong,Macao and Taiwan Funded Enterprises	914	1122273	1257251	1218163
港澳台合资经营	Joint Venture	686	974073	1092185	1060847
港澳台合作经营	Cooperative	37	22532	25593	25584
港澳台商独资企业	Hongkong,Macao and Taiwan Enterprises	175	116016	128992	122622
港澳台商投资股份有限公司	Hongkong,Macao and Taiwan Funded Share Holing Company	16	9652	10481	9110
外商投资企业	Foreign Funded Enterprises	1284	5112880	4856255	4746114
中外合资经营	Joint Venture	911	4725495	4441395	4336962
中外合作经营	Cooperative	55	70632	68663	72532
外资(独资)企业	Foreign Enterprises	307	257271	286846	275037
外商投资股份有限公司	Foreign Funded Share Holding Company	11	59483	59352	61584

6-2 主要工业产品生产总量
OUTPUT OF MAIN INDUSTRIAL PRODUCTS

主要工业产品名称		Products		本年生产量 Output in this Year
原　煤	(吨)	Coal	(ton)	9894595
铁矿石成品矿	(吨)	Iron Ore Products	(ton)	6636836
发电量	(万千瓦小时)	Electricity	(10000 kwh)	1566621
火　电	(万千瓦小时)	Thermal Power	(10000 kwh)	1474370
供热量	(万百万千焦)	Heating Supply	(1 billion kjoule)	6625
自来水生产量	(万吨)	Tap Water Production	(10000 tons)	77849
大　米	(吨)	Rice	(ton)	1887
小麦粉	(万吨)	Wheat Flour	(10000 tons)	49
食用植物油	(吨)	Edible Vegetable Oil	(ton)	119733
配混合饲料	(吨)	Concerted and Mixed Feed	(ton)	1808368
乳制品	(吨)	Dairy Products	(ton)	8773
罐　头	(吨)	Canned Food	(ton)	2190
白　酒	(吨)	Liquor	(ton)	99149
啤　酒	(吨)	Beer	(ton)	1172178
软饮料(无酒精)	(吨)	Soft Drinking	(ton)	301095
卷　烟	(箱)	Cigarettes	(case)	166148
合成纤维	(吨)	Synthetic Fiber	(ton)	22117
纱	(吨)	Yarn	(ton)	61298
布	(万米)	Cloth	(10000 m)	21299
# 棉　布	(万米)	Cotton Cloth	(10000 m)	14272
混纺交织布	(万米)	Blend Cloth	(10000 m)	6996
纯化纤布	(万米)	Pure Chemical Fiber Cloth	(10000 m)	30
绒线(毛线)	(吨)	Knitting Wool	(ton)	3944
呢　绒	(万米)	Woolen Piece Goods	(10000 m)	987
丝织品	(万米)	Silk Fabrics	(10000 m)	803
服　装	(万件)	Garments	(10000)	10876
锯　材	(立方米)	Sawn Timber	(cu.m)	21977
人造板	(立方米)	Artificial Wooden Board	(cu.m)	34542
机制纸	(吨)	Machine-made Paper	(ton)	51146
机制纸板	(吨)	Machine-made Paperboard	(ton)	79527
汽　油	(吨)	Gasoline	(ton)	1180581
煤　油	(吨)	Kerosene	(ton)	237
柴　油	(吨)	Diesel Oil	(ton)	1171251
润滑油	(吨)	Lubricating Oil	(ton)	140342
燃料油	(吨)	Fuel Oil	(ton)	1207573
焦　炭	(吨)	Coke	(ton)	4056543
硫酸(折100%)	(吨)	Sulphuric Acid(100%)	(ton)	77507
氢氧化钠(烧碱)(折100%)	(吨)	Caustic Soda(100%)	(ton)	102848
碳化钙(电石)(折 300升／千克)	(吨)	Calcium Carbide(300 liters/kg)	(ton)	8233
合成氨	(吨)	Synthetic Ammonia	(ton)	135378
农用氮、磷、钾化学肥料(折纯)	(吨)	Chemical Fertilizer(pure)	(ton)	112502
乙　烯	(吨)	Ethylene	(ton)	569516
纯　苯	(吨)	Pure Benzene	(ton)	108285
冰醋酸	(吨)	Glacial Acetic Acid	(ton)	9704
油　漆	(吨)	Paint	(ton)	18844
染　料	(吨)	Dyestuff	(ton)	4243
塑料树脂及共聚物	(吨)	Plastic Resin and Copolymer	(ton)	736470
合成橡胶	(吨)	Synthetic Rubber	(ton)	93819
合成纤维单体	(吨)	Synthetic Fiber(Monomer)	(ton)	5654
合成纤维聚合物	(吨)	Synthetic Fiber(Polymerizate)	(ton)	7051
合成洗涤剂	(吨)	Synthetic Detergents	(ton)	62834

6-2 续表 continued

主要工业产品名称		Products		本年生产量 Output in this Year
化学原料药	(吨)	Chemical Raw Medicine	(ton)	2954
轮胎外胎	(条)	Tires	(unit)	2647326
塑料制品	(吨)	Plastic Products	(ton)	98184
# 农业用薄膜	(吨)	Film for Farm Use	(ton)	19195
水 泥	(万吨)	Cement	(10000 tons)	762
平板玻璃	(重量箱)	Plate Glass	(wt.case)	5003130
生 铁	(吨)	Pig Iron	(ton)	7514962
钢	(吨)	Steel	(ton)	8032221
成品钢材	(吨)	Steel Products	(ton)	6760665
# 铁道用钢材	(吨)	For Railway Use	(ton)	634
普通中型钢材	(吨)	Ordinary Rolled-Steel,Medium	(ton)	148426
普通小型钢材	(吨)	Ordinary Rolled-Steel,Small	(ton)	2449017
优质钢型钢材	(吨)	High Quality Section Steel	(ton)	354330
线 材	(吨)	Wire Rod	(ton)	2865270
中厚钢板	(吨)	Medium Steel Plate	(ton)	461478
薄钢板	(吨)	Steel Sheet	(ton)	4414
硅钢片	(吨)	Silicon Steel Sheet	(ton)	1503
钢 带	(吨)	Steel Band	(ton)	342070
焊接钢管	(吨)	Welded Steel Pipe	(ton)	115716
铁合金	(吨)	Ferroalloy	(ton)	37376
铜	(吨)	Copper	(ton)	107
铜加工材	(吨)	Copper Products	(ton)	9254
铝 材	(吨)	Aluminum Products	(ton)	17098
日用精铝制品	(吨)	Daily-use Refined Aluminum Products	(ton)	53
工业锅炉	(台)	Boiler for Industrial Use	(ton)	1645
金属切削机床	(台)	Metal-Cutting Machine	(unit)	1908
# 高精度机床	(台)	High-Precision Machine Tools	(unit)	125
数控机床	(台)	Numerical Control Machine Tools	(unit)	430
大型机床	(台)	Large Machine Tools	(unit)	31
小型拖拉机	(台)	Mini-tractor	(unit)	1757
汽 车	(辆)	Motor Vehicle	(unit)	84826
摩托车	(辆)	Motorcycle	(unit)	10220
发电设备	(千瓦)	Generating Equipment	(kw)	508000
交流电动机	(千瓦)	Alternating Current Electric Motor	(unit)	1497085
家用洗衣机	(台)	Household Washing Machines	(unit)	63653
家用电冰箱	(台)	Household Refrigerators	(unit)	2481
冷冻箱	(台)	Freezer	(unit)	853
电风扇	(台)	Electric Fan	(unit)	52679
房间空气调节器	(台)	House Air Conditioner	(unit)	394766
排油烟机	(台)	Smoke Absorber	(unit)	140
程控交换机	(线)	Program Control Telephone Exchange	(line)	7721683
电子计算机	(部)	Computer	(unit)	1960
微型电子计算机	(部)	Micro-computer	(unit)	1608829
彩色显象管	(只)	Tricolor Tube	(unit)	4159079
半导体集成电路	(万块)	Semiconductor Integrated Circuit	(10000)	6074
彩色电视机	(部)	Color TV Set	(unit)	111277
黑白电视机	(部)	Black-and-white TV Set	(unit)	9358
录相机	(部)	Videocorder	(unit)	825256
收音机	(部)	Radio	(unit)	47300
收录放机	(部)	Recorder	(unit)	895282
组合音响	(部)	Hi-Fi	(unit)	6219
照相机	(台)	Camera	(unit)	1777301
表	(只)	Clock	(unit)	1486441

6-3 全部独立核算工业企业主要经济指标

单位：万元

项 目 Item		企业单位个数(个) Number of Enterprises (unit)	#亏损企业 Loss-making Enterprises	工业总产值(当年价格) Gross Output Value of Industry (at current price)	新产品产值 Value of New Products	工业总产值(1990年不变价格) Gross Output Value of Industry (at 1990 constant prices)	工业增加值(生产法) Added Value of Industry (with production method)
总 计	**Total**	**17069**	**4249**	**19886587**	**3733090**	**19234923**	**6052363**
在总计中:	**Of Total:**						
中央企业	Central Enterprises	834	304	6391864	2296552	7062227	2158162
地方企业	Local Enterprises	16235	3945	13494723	1436538	12172695	3894202
工业系统	Industry System	1379	459	6386871	999604	5886694	1628774
非工业系统	Non-Industry System	872	339	1212685	27242	808756	352432
区县工业	Industry of District and County	12636	2411	4972876	198558	4601184	1637609
其他	Others	1348	736	922292	211135	876062	275387
在总计中:	**Of Total:**						
内资企业	Domestic Investment Enterprises	14890	3114	13773081	3085501	12999769	4314034
国有企业	State-Owned	2604	702	8615543	2413808	8185996	2681731
集体企业	Collective Owned	10116	1820	2751952	93225	2595548	905563
私营企业	Private Owned	847	246	192584	32860	177100	75354
联营企业	Joint Owned	279	65	274056	30398	274976	79625
股份合作企业	Share Holding Cooperative	601	136	259183	26757	241410	90447
股份有限公司	Share Holding Company	156	47	652427	290790	679439	198265
有限责任公司	Limited-Liability Company	283	96	1027129	197662	845180	283068
其他企业	Others	4	2	208		121	-17
港澳台商投资企业	Hongkong,Macao and Taiwan Funded Enterprises	910	495	1257251	60263	1122273	330970
港澳台合资经营	Joint Venture	682	344	1092185	56176	974073	284039
港澳台合作经营	Cooperative	37	23	25593		22532	10288
港澳台商独资企业	Hongkong,Macao and Taiwan Enterprises	175	118	128992	4087	116016	33068
港澳台商投资股份有限公司	Hongkong,Macao and Taiwan Funded Share Holing Company	16	10	10481		9652	3574
外商投资企业	Foreign Funded Enterprises	1269	640	4856255	587326	5112880	1407359
中外合资经营	Joint Venture	898	421	4441395	530682	4725495	1272373
中外合作经营	Cooperative	54	22	68663	6561	70632	23629
外资(独资)企业	Foreign Enterprises	306	190	286846	34415	257271	93246
外商投资股份有限公司	Foreign Funded Share Holding Company	11	7	59352	15668	59483	18111
在总计中:	**Of Total:**						
农村企业	Rural Enterprises	9047	1345	2910667	44586	2736296	955627
在总计中:	**Of Total:**						
国有绝对控股企业	State-owned Absolute Holding Enterprises	2639	785	11225751	3098823	10587616	3438623
国有相对控股企业	State-owned Relative Holding Enterprises	312	132	2295182	131506	2690140	535640
在总计中:	**Of Total:**						
轻工业	Light Industry	8415	2297	6112179	367735	5385552	2028580
以农产品为原料	Using Farm Products as Raw Material	5069	1475	4012639	149806	3202816	1370543
以非农产品为原料	Using Non-Farm Products as Raw Material	3346	822	2099540	217930	2182736	658037
重工业	Heavy Industry	8654	1952	13774408	3365354	13849371	4023783
采掘工业	Excavation	425	63	199917	566	122113	98549
原料工业	Raw Material	1073	243	4591597	199070	3104281	1268213
加工工业	Processing	7156	1646	8982893	3165719	10622978	2657020
在总计中:	**Of Total:**						
大型企业	Large Enterprises	266	83	9659578	2289823	9312944	2863293
中型企业	Medium Enterprises	268	83	1182932	105704	945904	367872
小型企业	Small Enterprises	16535	4083	9044077	1337562	8976075	2821198

MAIN INDICATORS FOR INDUSTRIAL ENTERPRISES WITH INDEPENDENT ACCOUNTING SYSTEM

(10000 yuan)

工业销售产值(当年价格) Sales Value of Industry (at current price)	出口交货值 Delivery Value of Exports	全部从业人员年平均人数(人) Average Number of Employment (person)	工业品自销零售额 Retail Sales of Self-selling Industrial Products	资产负债 Assets and Liabilities: 流动资产合计 Circulating Assets	应收帐款净额 Accounts Receivable	存货 Stock	产成品 Finished Products	流动资产平均余额 Average Balance of Circulating Assets	长期投资 Long-time Investment	固定资产合计 Fixed Assets
19399627	**1437002**	**1671140**	**2105779**	**18022969**	**4281702**	**6137262**	**2271287**	**18191431**	**2293198**	**17672425**
6401677	342630	233522	833037	4334842	1235482	1128948	292638	5018458	405964	5199069
12997951	1094373	1437618	1272742	13688128	3046220	5008314	1978649	13172973	1887235	12473356
6286200	613623	615418	498701	6900754	1791716	2506862	831411	6727698	1438501	7462594
1178671	24431	113817	209135	1304085	273170	437725	198988	1227526	87893	1850047
4655928	404858	658199	460349	3958140	749328	1684215	812252	3773613	281445	2718969
877153	51462	50184	104557	1525148	232007	379512	135999	1444136	79395	441747
13435351	706580	1424571	1832376	12772872	2615955	4525255	1759435	12444016	2162301	14448679
8597135	486325	702501	1120459	8064019	1700592	2650844	860654	7882172	1527619	10699373
2557024	162442	500471	276800	2448723	432579	1080371	558254	2352519	187171	1377377
178792	2535	20809	18436	122753	18502	61453	30224	123158	5640	63523
265379	24123	43958	29844	377506	70867	141089	64414	395758	62084	264061
237625	12327	30616	24851	217679	44661	93630	48099	201743	11227	126893
598747	11219	36116	293132	594041	93984	188525	73473	559069	130227	317653
1000440	7608	90038	68855	948079	254744	309340	124317	929530	238313	1599658
208		62		72	26	4	1	68	20	140
1218163	136911	86666	131016	1241526	281751	473429	202383	1186501	39779	717543
1060847	111916	74968	102528	1071379	252244	398867	172089	1026459	35494	637818
25584	3916	2714	8438	28960	6904	11749	3893	27547	907	23486
122622	20779	8045	19410	129523	20392	57511	23362	122378	1917	48161
9110	301	939	640	11664	2212	5302	3039	10117	1461	8079
4746114	593511	159903	142387	4008571	1383996	1138578	309469	4560914	91118	2506203
4336962	520391	130697	117605	3615516	1279074	1006782	263016	4197098	61698	2185906
72532	8440	4563	6314	61721	18043	23116	8882	56674	5528	56988
275037	47888	16486	8588	251073	61052	79199	26738	225808	21267	184159
61584	16792	8157	9880	80261	25827	29481	10833	81335	2625	79150
2696867	284290	445481	264262	1954937	394244	979668	527038	1854584	89171	1277073
11129048	554097	846250	1480374	10585767	2563938	3428343	1113600	11109852	1899793	13194261
2271092	356281	52657	46502	1391963	506943	406169	125107	1343528	48972	1029749
5904951	683314	679403	568448	5853535	1021802	2137098	1008361	5574675	603528	4482177
3860944	474097	454894	310413	3655997	608297	1315399	607813	3475928	366023	2702335
2044008	209218	224509	258035	2197538	413505	821699	400548	2098746	237505	1779842
13494676	753688	991737	1537331	12169435	3259900	4000164	1262927	12616757	1689671	13190248
189146	31267	59240	35234	222128	88814	37004	23080	214660	17011	187167
4560939	147079	241188	87144	3606017	801745	1070065	270471	3612048	685129	8458832
8744591	575343	691309	1414953	8341290	2369341	2893095	969375	8790049	987530	4544249
9596633	584493	620960	647824	9321038	2290276	2941800	893220	9162107	1534050	12667882
1168827	90664	156250	92263	1295112	296042	472614	198058	1205314	250166	919823
8634168	761845	893930	1365692	7406819	1695383	2722848	1180009	7824010	508982	4084720

6-3 续表 1 continued

单位：万元

项目	Item	资产负债: 固定资产原价合计 Original Value of Fixed Assets	#生产经营用 For Productive Use	累计折旧 Accumulative Depreciation	#本年折旧 Depreciation in this Year	固定资产净值年平均余额 Average Net Value of Fixed Assets	无形资产及递延资产 Intangible and Deferred Assets
总 计	**Total**	**22213387**	**18592939**	**7142947**	**1073575**	**14243427**	**1756331**
在总计中：	**Of Total:**						
中央企业	Central Enterprises	6374794	4992143	2211408	330262	3628614	419148
地方企业	Local Enterprises	15838593	13600795	4931539	743313	10614813	1337183
工业系统	Industry System	9695345	8652486	3387265	422282	6232654	870633
非工业系统	Non-Industry System	2314855	2072557	567250	112539	1644553	80484
区县工业	Industry of District and County	3295527	2458791	853100	168916	2360970	278704
其他	Others	532866	416962	123924	39575	376635	107362
在总计中：	**Of Total:**						
内资企业	Domestic Investment Enterprises	18137100	15081401	6067707	791783	11352165	1284804
国有企业	State-Owned	13621321	11564172	4791521	604539	8243917	757389
集体企业	Collective Owned	1783272	1251269	560318	89027	1159584	104076
私营企业	Private Owned	61802	41661	11050	4099	48057	9507
联营企业	Joint Owned	339313	216266	105819	17495	232402	28546
股份合作企业	Share Holding Cooperative	146030	116337	37809	8738	108211	20301
股份有限公司	Share Holding Company	319991	283255	113325	16052	191138	51057
有限责任公司	Limited-Liability Company	1865224	1608296	447859	51831	1368731	313928
其他企业	Others	147	146	7	2	125	
港澳台商投资企业	Hongkong,Macao and Taiwan Funded Enterprises	896679	725323	212374	50396	685817	98485
港澳台合资经营	Joint Venture	804424	660690	192311	44781	613211	88978
港澳台合作经营	Cooperative	26248	12715	4538	1282	21357	1073
港澳台商独资企业	Hongkong,Macao and Taiwan Enterprises	56852	43860	13591	3823	43789	6981
港澳台商投资股份有限公司	Hongkong,Macao and Taiwan Funded Share Holing Company	9155	8058	1933	509	7461	1453
外商投资企业	Foreign Funded Enterprises	3179608	2786215	862866	231396	2205445	373042
中外合资经营	Joint Venture	2786099	2462108	765199	207336	1939392	314533
中外合作经营	Cooperative	65475	56765	15013	4914	48744	7774
外资(独资)企业	Foreign Enterprises	216684	159419	41275	14937	148715	36699
外商投资股份有限公司	Foreign Funded Share Holding Company	111350	107923	41379	4210	68595	14036
在总计中：	**Of Total:**						
农村企业	Rural Enterprises	1632479	1185715	450174	82534	1162300	88313
在总计中：	**Of Total:**						
国有绝对控股企业	State-owned Absolute Holding Enterprises	16553369	14117790	5605771	724669	10315056	1146983
国有相对控股企业	State-owned Relative Holding Enterprises	1370539	1245860	393288	104268	906653	120649
在总计中：	**Of Total:**						
轻工业	Light Industry	5593890	4442867	1588146	295436	3919393	550795
以农产品为原料	Using Farm Products as Raw Material	3377834	2597214	978709	181534	2341597	293056
以非农产品为原料	Using Non-Farm Products as Raw Material	2216055	1845653	609437	113902	1577796	257739
重工业	Heavy Industry	16619498	14150071	5554802	778139	10324035	1205536
采掘工业	Excavation	255463	178872	81779	8980	163272	11443
原料工业	Raw Material	10579742	9357738	3571086	463755	6434331	564796
加工工业	Processing	5784293	4613461	1901937	305404	3726432	629298
在总计中：	**Of Total:**						
大型企业	Large Enterprises	15958298	13931072	5335772	732471	9941891	1157078
中型企业	Medium Enterprises	1196002	942583	406735	52065	760654	105728
小型企业	Small Enterprises	5059087	3719283	1400440	289039	3540883	493524

6-3 续表 2 continued

(10000 yuan)

		Assets and Liabilities								
#无形资产 Intangible Assets	其他资产 Other Assets	资产总计 Total Assets	流动负债合计 Liquid Liabilities	短期借款 Short-time Loans	长期负债合计 Long-term Liabilities	长期借款 Long-time Loans	负债合计 Total Liabilities	所有者权益 Ownership Interest	实收资本 Contributed Capital	国家资本 State
848717	**383618**	**40129028**	**17221826**	**6286110**	**7362924**	**4617342**	**24839166**	**15289862**	**10129225**	**4680626**
349246	69775	10429283	3630087	967183	3073500	1370322	6897425	3531858	1757894	1429185
499470	313844	29699745	13591740	5318927	4289424	3247021	17941741	11758005	8371331	3251442
213295	48155	16720637	7223714	3149676	3131309	2269377	10370380	6350257	3810782	1664836
45497	26993	3349502	1218268	403947	310484	269527	1534599	1814903	1466379	1128192
171306	126889	7364148	4012207	1395696	712564	595520	4745688	2618460	2275128	379585
69373	111806	2265458	1137550	369607	135066	112597	1291074	974384	819042	78829
496018	107238	30776381	12409587	4575906	6547654	3873097	19163747	11612634	6561397	4067096
358413	17933	21066820	7874755	2928402	4838259	2351541	12903633	8163187	4287671	3500115
48888	67183	4184529	2409718	809432	415669	348370	2838409	1346120	1043062	50462
6738	891	202314	99297	27008	7439	5043	107551	94763	65375	155
8737	678	732876	417742	153099	91701	73896	509574	223302	160931	47167
10013	12461	388562	199576	84822	35147	26164	235431	153131	124261	13003
34087	8552	1101530	347522	125908	40356	27242	389056	712474	336788	78543
29143	-462	3099515	1060893	447235	1119074	1040832	2179996	919520	543174	377653
	2	234	85		11	10	96	138	135	
67484	100258	2197591	1320462	455590	138232	120996	1469372	728219	802392	142873
62743	93898	1927567	1141137	432427	121785	111215	1271436	656131	695150	137592
412	1923	56348	36003	6076	3473	3460	41095	15253	24082	1619
3207	4249	190831	131229	14266	9499	3321	141273	49557	75950	2000
1123	188	22845	12093	2821	3475	2999	15568	7278	7210	1662
285215	176122	7155057	3491778	1254614	677038	623250	4206048	2949009	2765437	470657
242665	143903	6321556	3044584	1170658	592711	544961	3658068	2663488	2351054	461183
6186	11242	143252	60298	14867	13109	12227	73464	69789	67685	9140
22789	17747	510944	296079	41183	65064	63507	377545	133399	275031	125
13576	3231	179304	90817	27906	6154	2555	96971	82333	71668	210
55467	57569	3467063	1914150	726731	293343	240400	2216834	1250229	1065032	56111
440632	61833	26889124	10135412	3904115	6231498	3647548	16563236	10325888	5562219	4039478
99447	43453	2634787	1268218	466808	193955	186199	1474655	1160132	1008251	243069
247469	213068	11703101	5702423	2231373	1332862	1109569	7079453	4623648	3841554	1215570
159439	121818	7139228	3526745	1383141	708850	568157	4273363	2865865	2401720	680949
88030	91250	4563874	2175678	848232	624012	541412	2806090	1757784	1439835	534621
601247	170550	28425927	11519404	4054736	6030062	3507774	17759713	10666214	6287671	3465056
1074	462	438211	178047	58791	73685	55516	251997	186214	109590	68477
187202	21427	13336201	3872720	1570282	4336819	2115887	8394995	4941206	2644820	2225924
412971	148661	14651515	7468636	2425663	1619558	1336372	9112720	5538795	3533261	1170655
525662	114037	24794572	9122543	3677202	5954448	3476099	15288139	9506433	5323447	3277784
30150	31723	2602552	1294134	459233	309856	234181	1606771	995781	769076	421691
292905	237858	12731904	6805150	2149674	1098620	907063	7944255	4787648	4036702	981151

单位：万元

6-3 续表 3 continued

项目	Item	资产负债 Assets and Liabilities 集体资本 Collective	法人资本 Institutional Units	个人资本 Individuals	港澳台资本 Hongkong, Macao and Taiwan	外商资本 Foreign
总计	**Total**	**1052983**	**1982077**	**233965**	**452601**	**1726973**
在总计中：	**Of Total:**					
中央企业	Central Enterprises	20528	110220	10603	22289	165070
地方企业	Local Enterprises	1032455	1871857	223362	430313	1561902
工业系统	Industry System	204021	1196694	44918	67430	632883
非工业系统	Non-Industry System	23782	70490	1129	44221	198565
区县工业	Industry of District and County	774431	446391	110907	214878	348937
其他	Others	30221	158282	66408	103784	381518
在总计中：	**Of Total:**					
内资企业	Domestic Investment Enterprises	893143	1342439	190447	17619	50652
国有企业	State-Owned	35776	729234	17884	2205	2458
集体企业	Collective Owned	749734	157942	39187	14819	30918
私营企业	Private Owned	3539	16876	44271	448	86
联营企业	Joint Owned	51919	60115	1683	48	
股份合作企业	Share Holding Cooperative	25879	63578	19669	3	2130
股份有限公司	Share Holding Company	13149	175383	54764		14950
有限责任公司	Limited-Liability Company	13110	139278	12928	96	110
其他企业	Others	38	35	62		
港澳台商投资企业	Hongkong,Macao and Taiwan Funded Enterprises	78770	163812	15839	345441	55657
港澳台合资经营	Joint Venture	75700	159208	15249	263816	43585
港澳台合作经营	Cooperative	1683	1529		19102	150
港澳台商独资企业	Hongkong,Macao and Taiwan Enterprises	244	971	590	60513	11631
港澳台商投资股份有限公司	Hongkong,Macao and Taiwan Funded Share Holing Company	1143	2104		2010	291
外商投资企业	Foreign Funded Enterprises	81070	475826	27679	89541	1620663
中外合资经营	Joint Venture	76219	436196	21318	41057	1315080
中外合作经营	Cooperative	4692	2700	508	16448	34197
外资(独资)企业	Foreign Enterprises	159	6353	514	32036	235844
外商投资股份有限公司	Foreign Funded Share Holding Company		30576	5340		35542
在总计中：	**Of Total:**					
农村企业	Rural Enterprises	563356	214687	61008	67330	102540
在总计中：	**Of Total:**					
国有绝对控股企业	State-owned Absolute Holding Enterprises	66869	1161026	64472	71182	159191
国有相对控股企业	State-owned Relative Holding Enterprises	21103	188627	633	63898	490921
在总计中：	**Of Total:**					
轻工业	Light Industry	517829	759637	124145	312214	912159
以农产品为原料	Using Farm Products as Raw Material	319058	422521	83590	214185	681417
以非农产品为原料	Using Non-Farm Products as Raw Material	198771	337115	40556	98029	230742
重工业	Heavy Industry	535154	1222441	109820	140387	814814
采掘工业	Excavation	19521	16300	3322	23	1947
原料工业	Raw Material	81733	212781	16455	9213	98712
加工工业	Processing	433900	993359	90043	131151	714154
在总计中：	**Of Total:**					
大型企业	Large Enterprises	88953	990031	50441	70637	845602
中型企业	Medium Enterprises	77331	175293	16598	13074	65089
小型企业	Small Enterprises	886699	816753	166927	368891	816282

6-3 续表 4 continued

(10000 yuan)

损益及分配 Profits,Loss and Distribution										
产品销售收入 Sales Revenue	产品销售成本 Cost of Sales	产品销售费用 Expenses of Sales	产品销售税金及附加 Sales Tax and Extra Charges	产品销售利润 Sales Profits	管理费用 Overhead Cost	税金 Taxes	财产保险费 Premium of Property	劳动待业保险费 Premium for Employment Insurance	财务费用 Financial Expenses	利息支出 Expenses of Interest
20345380	**16697396**	**1026748**	**226805**	**2393910**	**2107802**	**61216**	**23937**	**262516**	**637169**	**584363**
6611757	5329925	380194	79088	822550	591958	9153	8191	55426	158367	151943
13733623	11367471	646554	147717	1571360	1515844	52063	15747	207090	478801	432420
6877913	5767941	237889	54200	817883	832410	30420	9294	175810	298955	294131
1453663	1246351	84252	36764	85776	179156	7274	2056	18730	38035	33887
4462184	3605760	229260	58553	568609	386691	11912	3877	11854	123738	93759
939863	747419	95153	-1800	99091	117587	2457	520	697	18073	10642
14240606	11738794	576655	190012	1734624	1569412	49710	19167	255951	476218	453865
9532486	7821040	390315	161395	1159215	1081931	31766	13639	212153	343888	339202
2517562	2110029	90263	19558	297711	242358	7656	2006	16619	70238	54656
165533	127093	12971	1871	23597	14750	213	113	28	2287	1879
257100	211904	11972	2084	31140	44238	3244	497	5840	12845	11969
212935	168657	13899	1328	29051	20039	519	235	963	8186	7619
604477	488161	24379	2990	88948	49264	2748	346	3760	5896	4317
950287	811690	32830	783	104984	116828	3563	2331	16589	32879	34223
227	220	26	4	-23	6	1				
1226793	1024070	73274	2803	126646	127157	1828	1258	1190	33291	28556
1059783	897046	55425	2579	104733	103008	1614	1032	1007	31859	27585
24266	19283	2373	87	2523	3490	79	28	17	438	360
133288	100379	14502	127	18281	18993	120	187	156	694	359
9456	7363	975	10	1109	1666	15	11	11	301	252
4877981	3934532	376819	33989	532640	411233	9677	3513	5375	127659	101942
4470285	3624148	316406	32798	496934	343155	7671	3232	4649	119864	97326
67156	53343	4376	406	9032	6430	120	44	22	1337	816
279160	208542	48689	602	21327	52127	1648	117	98	2802	72
61379	48499	7348	184	5347	9521	238	119	607	3656	3729
2567823	2139869	98664	16226	313062	177018	5617	1642	1077	63377	46729
12032356	9841376	484847	181995	1523618	1331319	40115	17224	233002	420274	420517
2377924	2045560	149845	10951	171568	146556	3410	1846	3438	55284	44599
6035836	4821035	415470	101455	697355	694411	18956	7961	72597	173975	148044
3980946	3166540	261665	85593	466647	434025	11204	5414	45141	100692	87787
2054891	1654495	153805	15861	230708	260386	7751	2547	27455	73283	60258
14309543	11876361	611278	125350	1696555	1413391	42260	15977	189920	463193	436319
191479	128302	13394	2834	46950	33182	791	90	16157	3225	2695
5290755	4573391	55111	77021	585232	419817	16646	10241	78959	237940	233073
8827309	7174667	542773	45496	1064373	960393	24823	5647	94804	222029	200550
10540258	8637106	522001	146254	1234897	1120437	35295	15159	196723	408534	391082
1106499	886736	47426	41606	130232	167896	6772	2817	30144	37229	35055
8698623	7173554	457321	38945	1028780	819469	19149	5961	35650	191405	158225

6-3 续表 5 continued

单位：万元

项目	Item	损益及分配 Profits,Loss and Distribution 营业利润 Operating Profits	投资收益 Investment Income	补贴收入 Subsidy Income	营业外收入 Out-business Income	营业外支出 Out-business Expenditure	利润总额 Total Profits
总计	**Total**	**34624**	**141627**	**132392**	**245128**	**113476**	**484460**
在总计中：	**Of Total:**						
中央企业	Central Enterprises	243358	55916	5619	33984	25454	339620
地方企业	Local Enterprises	-208734	85710	126772	211143	88022	144840
工业系统	Industry System	-166521	69256	62370	162255	52380	81118
非工业系统	Non-Industry System	-112771	5140	57501	17876	7979	-39649
区县工业	Industry of District and County	85842	7856	6556	25795	18993	114834
其他	Others	-15283	3460	345	5217	8670	-11463
在总计中：	**Of Total:**						
内资企业	Domestic Investment Enterprises	-26688	139093	131877	163625	80101	361877
国有企业	State-Owned	-68970	108820	97640	114184	58307	220217
集体企业	Collective Owned	26439	5338	3526	20243	10505	47179
私营企业	Private Owned	7744	-2	166	391	469	8009
联营企业	Joint Owned	-14196	2972	1446	19409	2975	9187
股份合作企业	Share Holding Cooperative	3775	714	530	1073	843	5285
股份有限公司	Share Holding Company	44386	9148	2453	2744	4228	56453
有限责任公司	Limited-Liability Company	-25838	12104	26115	5580	2775	15574
其他企业	Others	-29			1		-28
港澳台商投资企业	Hongkong,Macao and Taiwan Funded Enterprises	-26992	149	325	11605	4537	-17810
港澳台合资经营	Joint Venture	-24256	147	325	9573	3700	-16776
港澳台合作经营	Cooperative	-1355	2		194	454	-1601
港澳台商独资企业	Hongkong,Macao and Taiwan Enterprises	-578			543	355	87
港澳台商投资股份有限公司	Hongkong,Macao and Taiwan Funded Share Holing Company	-805			1295	27	480
外商投资企业	Foreign Funded Enterprises	88304	2385	190	69898	28838	140393
中外合资经营	Joint Venture	118642	2060	95	67688	25055	170220
中外合作经营	Cooperative	2380			104	447	2043
外资(独资)企业	Foreign Enterprises	-24336	123	18	1956	3372	-23954
外商投资股份有限公司	Foreign Funded Share Holding Company	-8381	202	77	150	-36	-7916
在总计中：	**Of Total:**						
农村企业	Rural Enterprises	81398	2157	2340	11527	7448	92682
在总计中：	**Of Total:**						
国有绝对控股企业	State-owned Absolute Holding Enterprises	4731	130137	126074	181139	72241	403085
国有相对控股企业	State-owned Relative Holding Enterprises	42592	1256	139	17574	8484	54447
在总计中：	**Of Total:**						
轻工业	Light Industry	-52181	35530	31623	80391	39194	62420
以农产品为原料	Using Farm Products as Raw Material	-8498	21766	12556	51408	25163	54957
以非农产品为原料	Using Non-Farm Products as Raw Material	-43683	13764	19067	28982	14031	7463
重工业	Heavy Industry	86805	106097	100768	164737	74282	422040
采掘工业	Excavation	-1752	1196	14914	694	3769	13131
原料工业	Raw Material	-23012	25821	72019	29386	31424	95944
加工工业	Processing	111569	79080	13835	134657	39089	312965
在总计中：	**Of Total:**						
大型企业	Large Enterprises	-79351	113901	114743	153593	68826	262815
中型企业	Medium Enterprises	-33303	4394	2740	20222	8860	-14600
小型企业	Small Enterprises	147278	23332	14909	71313	35789	236245

6-3 续表 6 continued

(10000 yuan)

				工资，福利费，增值税 Wages,Welfares and Added Value Tax					
应交所得税 Income Tax Payable	应付利润 Profits Payable	亏损企业亏损额 Total Loss-ing of Loss-making Enterprises	利税总额 Total Pre-tax Profits	本年应付工资总额 Total Wags Payable	本年应付福利费总额 Total Welfares Payable	本年应交增值税 Added Value Tax	本年进项税额 Tax In-clude in Purchas-ing Cost	本年销项税额 Tax In-clude in Sales Cost	工业中间投入合计 Intermediate Input of Industry
131877	**156386**	**548660**	**1617338**	**1726048**	**284897**	**906073**	**2438456**	**3219859**	**14740297**
37266	38980	49100	672498	349338	60870	253790	887160	1076911	4487492
94611	117406	499560	944841	1376710	224027	652284	1551296	2142948	10252805
39476	62558	194924	475693	730525	122724	340375	834506	1146582	5098472
9208	5466	87524	66058	136331	24304	68943	151690	212830	929196
40147	44136	145491	349465	435126	63117	176078	453109	609183	3511345
5779	5246	71621	53625	74728	13882	66888	111992	174354	713793
91180	69656	228976	1177051	1328188	174072	625162	1795143	2349169	10084209
47342	22614	119737	823114	827395	109730	441502	1213799	1603325	6375314
19960	19856	64865	158838	303537	36565	92101	260425	341639	1938490
2285	1318	3674	15206	15447	1709	5326	17635	21722	122556
1903	5616	4792	21832	34937	5431	10561	30225	38127	204992
1868	1812	4997	15235	21785	3091	8622	21427	28924	177358
10886	16752	8601	82122	37843	5202	22679	110110	130875	476841
6934	1686	22281	60726	87221	12344	44369	141511	184542	788430
1	2	30	-21	24		3	12	15	228
9006	17592	81396	33476	98520	22418	48483	132033	173798	974764
8092	16066	69698	27572	81037	19886	41769	116378	152371	849915
26	4	1958	-547	2661	516	967	2332	3213	16272
619	850	9029	5319	13617	1753	5105	12418	16731	101029
269	672	710	1132	1206	263	642	905	1482	7549
31691	69138	238288	406810	299340	88407	232428	511280	696892	3681324
29981	65086	189041	416286	258545	77847	213268	474517	642998	3382290
281	469	3440	5940	4817	959	3491	6945	10186	48525
1398	3583	37339	-10883	28734	7446	12469	24980	35789	206069
32		8467	-4533	7244	2155	3199	4838	7919	44440
22940	28546	41897	194104	264239	35076	85196	224325	300237	2040236
77537	71412	179705	1139357	1015518	153098	554277	1542354	2031506	8341405
7121	39549	68198	143141	118533	36788	77743	257477	305097	1837285
58011	49943	287259	469829	572657	96295	305954	609110	887258	4389553
41465	35746	197472	347541	372460	64933	206991	393751	582928	2849087
16546	14197	89787	122287	200197	31362	98963	215359	304330	1540466
73866	106443	261400	1147509	1153391	188602	600119	1829346	2332602	10350744
1517	1029	1487	25927	50937	6288	9962	9861	18962	111330
16845	8730	40944	481900	405804	56704	308935	661212	952734	3632319
55504	96684	218969	639683	696649	125611	281222	1158273	1360906	6607095
55030	73349	197434	939600	841851	142965	530531	1316777	1781334	7326816
9870	5692	51699	81606	145877	22246	54600	129074	178136	869660
66977	77344	299527	596132	738320	119686	320942	992604	1260389	6543821

6-4 全部独立核算工业企业主要经济指标(按行业分)

单位：万元

项目	Item	企业单位个数(个) Number of Enterprises (unit)	#亏损企业 Loss-making Enterprises	工业总产值(当年价格) Gross Output Value of Industry (at current price)	新产品产值 Value of New Products	工业总产值(1990年不变价格) Gross Output Value of Industry (at 1990 constant prices)	工业增加值(生产法) Added Value of Industry (with production method)
煤炭采选业	Coal Mining and Dressing	153	19	125821	32	59908	69133
石油和天然气开采业	Petroleum and Natural Gas Extraction	1		155		155	42
黑色金属矿采选业	Ferrous Metals Mining and Processing	21	3	22220		13888	8829
有色金属矿采选业	Nonferrous Metals Mining and Processing	16	4	6259		6082	1914
非金属矿采选业	Nonmetal Minerals Mining and Processing	233	36	45253	534	41867	18575
其他矿采选业	Other Minerals Mining and Processing	1	1	211		213	58
食品加工业	Food Processing	516	164	819264	56847	571689	138841
食品制造业	Food Making	591	207	457294	7522	326028	144619
饮料制造业	Beverage Production	224	87	603891	12961	484259	253217
烟草加工业	Tobacco Processing	4		68203	844	46449	43373
纺织业	Textile Industry	460	145	470389	25545	411755	179558
服装及其他纤维制品制造业	Garments and Other Fiber Products	826	286	509911	13963	435354	162630
皮革、毛皮、羽绒及其制品业	Leather,Furs,Down and Related Products	161	56	58672	5154	48443	20178
木材加工及竹、藤、棕、草制品业	Timber Processing,Bamboo,Cane, Palm Fiber and Straw Products	217	49	46660	836	41774	14966
家具制造业	Furniture Manufacturing	495	102	148018	3150	142930	50900
造纸及纸制品业	Papermaking and Paper Products	481	91	201040	322	180851	68922
印刷业、记录媒介的复制	Printing and Record Medium Reproduced	935	228	422291	2323	324648	202568
文教、体育用品制造	Stationery,Educational and Sports Goods	212	60	107609	8487	89792	39487
石油加工及炼焦业	Petroleum Processing and Coking Products	92	19	1142289	66397	750125	322639
化学原料及化学制品制造业	Raw Chemical Materials and Chemical Products	1148	262	1022599	72543	1005914	260202
医药制造业	Medical and Pharmaceutical Product	200	53	397817	53948	428956	129876
化学纤维制造业	Chemical Fibers	37	14	50169	438	61158	11559
橡胶制品业	Rubber Products	122	25	122422	16744	143788	20624
塑料制品业	Plastic Products	664	186	279258	6760	280883	76611
非金属矿物制品业	Nonmetal Mineral Products	1584	279	945649	45461	783823	318296
黑色金属冶炼及压延加工业	Smelting and Pressing of Ferrous Metals	68	19	1680659	58965	1113519	230977
有色金属冶炼及压延加工业	Smelting and Pressing of Nonferrous Metals	133	29	88103	10508	92763	27539
金属制品业	Metal Products	2037	382	614072	10247	603642	211749
普通机械制造业	Ordinary Machinery Manufacturing	1092	236	546182	52499	500716	180134
专用设备制造业	Special Purposes Equipment Manufacturing	830	229	827211	320766	810186	235886
交通运输设备制造业	Transportation Equipment Manufacturing	1176	309	1153077	291485	1042315	308608
武器弹药制造业	Weapon and Ammunition Manufacture	8	2	62344	22953	47628	13869
电气机械及器材制造	Electric Equipment and Machinery	813	221	707181	142434	716347	216490
电子及通信设备制造	Electronic and Telecommunications	556	174	4770614	2342064	6789807	1376664
仪器仪表及文化、办公用机械制造业	Instruments,Meters,Cultural and Official Machine Manufacturing	363	104	339448	65148	347974	112191
其他制造业	Other Manufacturing	517	154	185726	12164	179159	83371
电力、蒸汽、热水的生产和供应业	Electricity,Steam and Hot Water Production and Supply	63	11	726370	3047	252298	426960
煤气生产和供应业	Gas Production and Supply	8		37750		32132	28784
自来水的生产和供应	Water Production and Supply	11	3	74489		25708	41527

MAIN INDICATORS FOR INDUSTRIAL ENTERPRISES WITH INDEPENDENT ACCOUNTING SYSTEM(BY SECTOR)

(10000 yuan)

工业销售产值(当年价格) Sales Value of Industry (at current price)	出口交货值 Delivery Value of Exports	全部从业人员年平均人数(人) Average Number of Employment (person)	工业品自销零售额 Retail Sales of Self-selling Industrial Products	资产负债 Assets and Liabilities						
				流动资产合计 Circulating Assets	应收帐款净额 Accounts Receivable	存货 Stock	产成品 Finished Products	流动资产平均余额 Average Balance of Circulating Assets	长期投资 Long-time Investment	固定资产合计 Fixed Assets
119946	31121	46339	27984	162163	68103	19720	11791	158130	9607	129476
132		30		164	33	131		28		53
20808		3847	244	28129	12767	10120	5903	28945	1472	24175
5359		676		9220	491	576	328	6233	2980	1982
42645	146	8335	7006	22242	7355	6353	4958	21066	2952	31440
255		13		209	64	103	100	258		41
797478	4222	32478	67514	689547	107303	148241	45611	661897	27706	273308
440045	11667	42310	14127	441985	76675	113445	43037	415088	51146	418448
599409	13906	31445	75792	497295	77540	174549	44299	451559	102589	467540
67905	1930	971		18408	3856	13307	316	18540	1478	34160
444704	181382	88626	11254	479579	79207	233272	127365	441496	49899	375136
478025	201076	100313	29687	428810	73450	207055	122891	418923	24666	229312
58814	19846	13924	8726	108951	16250	40218	21307	108183	10174	50425
44553	2783	9547	5567	60353	11653	35837	18143	60072	3963	40689
138698	15863	23239	33071	134081	19094	72284	32302	125953	4080	68942
192353	6814	24629	10778	179829	44715	57711	29772	179717	24962	147384
410562	758	67704	19266	293527	43177	88619	29660	266571	33912	466250
102408	20714	17730	14785	119020	23210	53507	20807	112647	8140	69012
1150173	10761	41896	9034	681884	182908	192503	60063	708494	69584	1316694
980029	24443	82483	30603	788062	181775	296234	135863	768230	136187	1309552
368886	20719	30817	37452	580293	102317	210335	125916	579973	65760	289581
49586	162	6726	1322	38915	5803	21649	10139	39666	1089	69171
122486	20032	15644	4487	148603	34079	74555	30199	140793	7934	138846
267040	14843	36264	24062	258436	42101	109320	47322	241204	34114	284234
896803	26979	155040	146022	958274	227473	345208	202466	905181	192013	988021
1673445	101046	69431	873	1222231	192506	560423	82167	1194319	350888	2411578
83703	18353	7435	5838	69731	19204	26361	10960	64806	9368	58005
590818	25829	85878	55860	518953	106529	236717	119050	501717	24235	366855
520960	32329	102969	50183	834603	197042	365917	123742	872365	56416	549612
795285	13606	89852	347442	963771	184460	427232	186125	931873	138984	565903
1172796	12841	142433	81106	1202407	297803	508869	122395	1960840	281633	891007
62677	433	12724	25306	93551	29903	35767	6224	84934	13751	116770
660274	40590	76189	63217	912304	258641	326765	139931	854657	63841	463578
4691233	510750	96452	768312	3581668	1202605	867840	220529	3352767	388864	1116285
323061	32039	35133	47249	402855	90662	148125	48772	406751	41377	211251
185402	19019	28088	10438	178836	43952	71384	37511	169823	12138	97485
726954		28867	3	758546	189345	21988	335	796888	38919	2768893
37750		8266	6878	69988	23046	7459	22	65888	4230	371369
76170		6397	64292	85550	4604	7563	2969	74960	2150	459964

6-4 续表 1 continued

单位：万元

项　　目	Item	资产负债: 固定资产原价合计 Original Value of Fixed Assets	# 生产经营用 For Productive Use	累计折旧 Accumulative Depreciation	#本年折旧 Depreciation in this Year	固定资产净值年平均余额 Average Net Value of Fixed Assets	无形资产及递延资产 Intangible and Deferred Assets
煤炭采选业	Coal Mining and Dressing	186473	116626	62441	5912	115567	3894
石油和天然气开采业	Petroleum and Natural Gas Extraction	169		116	18	65	
黑色金属矿采选业	Ferrous Metals Mining and Processing	25726	24839	7248	1321	17135	2319
有色金属矿采选业	Nonferrous Metals Mining and Processing	2301	2248	349	66	1978	1089
非金属矿采选业	Nonmetal Minerals Mining and Processing	40731	35099	11605	1660	28483	4139
其他矿采选业	Other Minerals Mining and Processing	62	60	21	3	43	2
食品加工业	Food Processing	341110	267789	92209	17515	240388	27940
食品制造业	Food Making	510078	364864	127883	29508	373744	43776
饮料制造业	Beverage Production	522290	441221	118416	28089	396230	69489
烟草加工业	Tobacco Processing	40616	37650	10929	1644	30218	407
纺织业	Textile Industry	544259	449292	192845	23443	359401	46669
服装及其他纤维制品制造业	Garments and Other Fiber Products	290907	222189	87379	16262	200470	22498
皮革、毛皮、羽绒及其制品业	Leather,Furs,Down and Related Products	60437	46640	16855	2391	43444	6492
木材加工及竹、藤、棕、草制品业	Timber Processing,Bamboo,Cane, Palm Fiber and Straw Products	48751	32424	11702	1747	99509	5015
家具制造业	Furniture Manufacturing	88059	61410	24282	4927	59682	4553
造纸及纸制品业	Papermaking and Paper Products	163043	130649	39266	7552	115974	25692
印刷业、记录媒介的复制	Printing and Record Medium Reproduced	608045	423778	204785	39622	372702	10839
文教、体育用品制造	Stationery,Educational and Sports Goods	82732	61997	25813	3818	55057	7162
石油加工及炼焦业	Petroleum Processing and Coking Products	2100352	1727846	1006851	114222	875551	85776
化学原料及化学制品制造业	Raw Chemical Materials and Chemical Products	1531624	1309294	388156	46859	1100059	337538
医药制造业	Medical and Pharmaceutical Product	318446	256971	85416	14775	227522	46785
化学纤维制造业	Chemical Fibers	103924	86705	36211	2172	69273	32932
橡胶制品业	Rubber Products	134216	111861	37793	5625	85017	15629
塑料制品业	Plastic Products	361974	260802	90880	17102	273220	45852
非金属矿物制品业	Nonmetal Mineral Products	1183007	965291	336935	58761	832462	125101
黑色金属冶炼及压延加工业	Smelting and Pressing of Ferrous Metals	3299349	3289512	1288608	136296	2024142	70791
有色金属冶炼及压延加工业	Smelting and Pressing of Nonferrous Metals	70897	55441	21651	2918	48181	25230
金属制品业	Metal Products	460032	351648	121758	24995	327364	50545
普通机械制造业	Ordinary Machinery Manufacturing	716732	568429	249886	29387	459894	56192
专用设备制造业	Special Purposes Equipment Manufacturing	708416	541701	258728	27459	439999	40166
交通运输设备制造业	Transportation Equipment Manufacturing	1135566	913625	416499	62441	688131	30820
武器弹药制造业	Weapon and Ammunition Manufacture	148922	69112	42428	3206	107401	3774
电气机械及器材制造	Electric Equipment and Machinery	600293	496757	181791	26758	415039	41296
电子及通信设备制造	Electronic and Telecommunications	1466926	1221813	464145	110607	931667	374672
仪器仪表及文化、办公用机械制造业	Instruments,Meters,Cultural and Official Machine Manufacturing	280716	238790	84334	15960	169189	23439
其他制造业	Other Manufacturing	119212	90003	37962	7363	76522	11559
电力、蒸汽、热水的生产和供应业	Electricity,Steam and Hot Water Production and Supply	2869047	2311864	716163	129958	1771397	55259
煤气生产和供应业	Gas Production and Supply	465128	448433	105096	22396	355030	4
自来水的生产和供应	Water Production and Supply	582819	558268	137516	28820	456279	996

6-4 续表 2 continued

(10000 yuan)

Assets and Liabilities										
#无形资产 Intangible Assets	其他资产 Other Assets	资产总计 Total Assets	流动负债合计 Liquid Liabilities	短期借款 Short-time Loans	长期负债合计 Long-term Liabilities	长期借款 Long-time Loans	负债合计 Total Liabilities	所有者权益 Ownership Interest	实收资本 Contributed Capital	国家资本 State
22	213	305354	125846	37868	52703	42222	178652	126702	68794	60384
		217	97				97	119	3	
		56096	27191	14995	11634	6550	38825	17271	8991	6613
47	2	15273	1757	312	2135	1275	3891	11382	11210	720
1005	248	61020	22933	5556	7213	5469	30308	30712	20581	760
2		252	224	60			224	28	11	
18705	16632	1035133	547540	198591	73947	55463	626289	408845	265696	122390
22107	16213	971567	555269	186467	118513	110643	692177	279391	495308	83071
50788	42440	1179352	448852	198006	92938	78081	543518	635834	415470	133393
		54453	5809	85	1488	1627	7296	47156	39025	38995
11731	5306	956589	564643	308269	146006	129126	715103	241486	246067	28887
9414	7602	712888	417353	142732	45064	35036	464102	248787	256821	14798
1596	539	176581	117883	36810	15664	12807	133899	42682	42356	4813
3644	4196	114217	62476	13439	7728	3978	70214	44003	39849	10867
2207	1605	213261	130863	30306	14073	11391	145531	67730	64329	6947
9464	13977	391843	197664	85958	42324	30258	242628	149216	112456	7463
4842	7805	812332	243630	59379	116328	80818	361721	450611	317228	183254
2989	1388	204722	118961	44939	12160	10749	131951	72771	53015	12535
84587	923	2154861	678283	284378	308756	269571	1169391	985470	517967	512084
52248	12063	2583401	909590	400387	954696	877250	1867098	716303	454561	218615
36577	15721	998140	458371	194275	80044	47024	538771	459369	247538	74229
136	364	142471	52702	25099	81445	80168	134197	8273	29924	2096
1545	319	311330	186731	61087	62520	50520	249440	61890	51016	12980
10523	8129	630765	329642	133764	108509	100979	438739	192025	195237	37321
39285	29612	2293022	983743	322482	434074	375167	1420601	872420	615341	225623
54116	2147	4057635	1560473	798247	542150	23593	2102622	1955012	763398	656057
1064	1056	163389	74787	33220	46273	38205	122766	40623	30591	17681
24407	20460	981048	552012	194321	113337	103191	668204	312843	312310	35396
30006	9380	1506204	816323	276052	202769	173933	1019548	486655	436322	123403
21006	9014	1717839	893835	248341	104568	62856	999961	717878	381710	86780
17250	9961	2416315	1127023	369534	303253	248268	1437289	979026	753220	327431
3723		227846	75697	38488	29449	18333	105146	122700	43841	43784
16519	75146	1556165	963979	424832	145181	116451	1111846	444319	376814	54193
283792	51897	5513386	2834562	956309	556078	489047	3399634	2113752	1105382	427968
15092	9015	687937	342277	104772	44526	30192	387386	300551	186810	58215
3794	2629	302647	160789	40132	26701	18499	189401	113246	92366	16267
13863	6952	3628568	586472	15249	2333957	757844	2920430	708138	469176	427147
		445591	25772	187	10169	6515	35941	409650	292313	291783
622	664	549324	19776	1181	114553	114244	134330	414994	316182	315683

6-4 续表 3 continued

单位：万元

项目	Item	资产负债 Assets and Liabilities 集体资本 Collective	法人资本 Institutional Units	个人资本 Individuals	港澳台资本 Hongkong, Macao and Taiwan	外商资本 Foreign
煤炭采选业	Coal Mining and Dressing	7852	221	337		
石油和天然气开采业	Petroleum and Natural Gas Extraction	3				
黑色金属矿采选业	Ferrous Metals Mining and Processing	2279	4	95		
有色金属矿采选业	Nonferrous Metals Mining and Processing	280	10112	98		
非金属矿采选业	Nonmetal Minerals Mining and Processing	9095	5963	2793	23	1947
其他矿采选业	Other Minerals Mining and Processing	11				
食品加工业	Food Processing	18713	32179	4268	37069	51077
食品制造业	Food Making	18005	24456	6705	77647	285425
饮料制造业	Beverage Production	24942	71797	21951	18462	144926
烟草加工业	Tobacco Processing	31				
纺织业	Textile Industry	53687	117987	4811	21100	19596
服装及其他纤维制品制造业	Garments and Other Fiber Products	86359	62329	11770	17375	64190
皮革、毛皮、羽绒及其制品业	Leather,Furs,Down and Related Products	18308	11229	627	1825	5553
木材加工及竹、藤、棕、草制品业	Timber Processing,Bamboo,Cane, Palm Fiber and Straw Products	7447	13355	2281	2519	3380
家具制造业	Furniture Manufacturing	19525	14488	8833	6398	8137
造纸及纸制品业	Papermaking and Paper Products	23422	31973	12953	4328	32318
印刷业、记录媒介的复制	Printing and Record Medium Reproduced	36715	33075	2888	15302	45992
文教、体育用品制造	Stationery,Educational and Sports Goods	13904	18365	701	3983	3528
石油加工及炼焦业	Petroleum Processing and Coking Products	3190	977	340	210	1165
化学原料及化学制品制造业	Raw Chemical Materials and Chemical Products	45627	106142	16959	13992	53227
医药制造业	Medical and Pharmaceutical Product	15100	76287	13150	14822	53951
化学纤维制造业	Chemical Fibers	2278	24469	148	125	809
橡胶制品业	Rubber Products	7536	22415	118		7967
塑料制品业	Plastic Products	40531	50823	2832	17626	46104
非金属矿物制品业	Nonmetal Mineral Products	104664	153480	11112	17179	103284
黑色金属冶炼及压延加工业	Smelting and Pressing of Ferrous Metals	15666	77797	387		13491
有色金属冶炼及压延加工业	Smelting and Pressing of Nonferrous Metals	6484	1567	766	480	3612
金属制品业	Metal Products	97517	68570	13521	50680	46626
普通机械制造业	Ordinary Machinery Manufacturing	66562	97408	3428	4724	140797
专用设备制造业	Special Purposes Equipment Manufacturing	34244	193185	26291	14662	26549
交通运输设备制造业	Transportation Equipment Manufacturing	83344	226425	11070	17049	87901
武器弹药制造业	Weapon and Ammunition Manufacture	56				
电气机械及器材制造	Electric Equipment and Machinery	76643	137004	22005	26301	60668
电子及通信设备制造	Electronic and Telecommunications	46841	216672	26834	31345	355722
仪器仪表及文化、办公用机械制造业	Instruments,Meters,Cultural and Official Machine Manufacturing	18153	56923	2482	32472	18565
其他制造业	Other Manufacturing	32958	15112	1402	4902	21724
电力、蒸汽、热水的生产和供应业	Electricity,Steam and Hot Water Production and Supply	15013	8272			18744
煤气生产和供应业	Gas Production and Supply		519	11		
自来水的生产和供应	Water Production and Supply		499			

6-4 续表 4 continued

(10000 yuan)

损益及分配 Profits,Loss and Distribution										
产品销售收入 Sales Revenue	产品销售成本 Cost of Sales	产品销售费用 Expenses of Sales	产品销售税金及附加 Sales Tax and Extra Charges	产品销售利润 Sales Profits	管理费用 Overhead Cost	税金 Taxes	财产保险费 Premium of Property	劳动待业保险费 Premium for Employment Insurance	财务费用 Financial Expenses	利息支出 Expenses of Interest
127330	77855	10703	1385	37387	27158	548	59	15532	1481	1258
132	131			1						
20851	14865	855	790	4340	1492	59	19	250	1415	1344
5405	4859	66	4	477	823	1			-193	-291
37506	30349	1770	654	4734	3692	183	11	375	516	378
255	244		1	11	17	1			7	7
812494	735115	23801	690	52890	42720	981	491	2187	14842	14150
476314	354579	82756	964	38016	68650	1589	619	4540	14388	11385
596124	388638	54026	47071	106389	56872	1042	569	3010	11095	8762
66919	32591	227	29015	5086	4437	73	235	441	448	448
433259	389126	11378	1054	31701	51592	1575	793	12081	16358	17045
462305	390372	30596	1147	39690	49753	1228	603	3920	13395	10785
55659	48644	3716	158	3141	10405	340	151	1821	3318	2948
44883	37602	1566	268	5447	6040	130	36	537	1421	1254
140773	117125	6582	867	16199	12773	484	254	539	2953	2463
184029	145257	10571	556	27646	22960	690	337	2420	5927	4255
400106	304707	12201	2440	80758	68617	2364	791	10833	7056	5701
111272	88374	5452	505	16941	16410	458	195	2314	3528	3169
1198877	967754	18403	54218	158502	145173	3907	6873	16799	28232	28056
925958	778757	37184	10954	99064	104235	2521	2527	12538	31322	31580
523243	360989	72199	2334	87721	69462	1206	751	4409	19313	17751
41274	39997	590	133	554	6140	173	168	924	2540	2722
134490	107966	4100	4958	17466	15398	438	207	2637	8235	7689
254452	224009	9945	1053	19445	33137	918	323	3440	15163	10559
884766	724682	31042	5886	123156	106283	3548	1632	13016	30045	26447
2062437	1806723	12885	11092	231737	137821	8749	10	43878	100881	97149
82434	70356	2459	221	9398	7350	194	100	787	2830	2280
532863	448790	20382	2483	61208	54704	2649	446	3555	23126	18995
525772	436185	22454	1531	65602	87113	3348	777	16230	20032	18222
779454	606148	38684	-79	134701	120291	4878	560	13927	21570	20011
1161345	995031	28875	18460	118978	162695	5552	874	23960	43546	40069
64484	50881	855	48	12700	15500	257	81	3479	2529	2542
668870	535861	38172	2412	92405	95982	3035	693	11684	22946	18957
4899806	3965009	337310	7589	589899	384373	3826	1915	15298	85568	76743
353697	287291	74764	6531	-14889	49536	1588	294	6070	5901	5799
153227	110929	19610	985	21702	28919	613	268	3111	3888	3050
948522	822285	316	7511	118410	17713	683	190	2790	72044	71493
111669	131731		445	-20506	11561	406	74	1112	-75	-75
62126	65592	256	472	-4195	10007	983	10	2073	-419	-736

6-4 续表 5 continued

单位：万元

项目	Item	损益及分配 Profits,Loss and Distribution 营业利润 Operating Profits	投资收益 Investment Income	补贴收入 Subsidy Income	营业外收入 Out-business Income	营业外支出 Out-business Expenditure	利润总额 Total Profits
煤炭采选业	Coal Mining and Dressing	-3139	1004	14481	383	3479	11057
石油和天然气开采业	Petroleum and Natural Gas Extraction	1					1
黑色金属矿采选业	Ferrous Metals Mining and Processing	522	-42	43	53	88	488
有色金属矿采选业	Nonferrous Metals Mining and Processing	-151	81	391	25	18	328
非金属矿采选业	Nonmetal Minerals Mining and Processing	1029	153		227	179	1270
其他矿采选业	Other Minerals Mining and Processing	-13			6	5	-13
食品加工业	Food Processing	-2223	1728	5028	1492	1655	5217
食品制造业	Food Making	-41248	2028	167	9201	8502	-37923
饮料制造业	Beverage Production	42307	3003	998	6480	3045	50232
烟草加工业	Tobacco Processing	588			9	83	513
纺织业	Textile Industry	-29692	3308	4857	18169	3404	-6376
服装及其他纤维制品制造业	Garments and Other Fiber Products	-12863	692	352	4106	1312	-9050
皮革、毛皮、羽绒及其制品业	Leather,Furs,Down and Related Products	-4970	-122	27	3558	265	-1294
木材加工及竹、藤、棕、草制品业	Timber Processing,Bamboo,Cane, Palm Fiber and Straw Products	-1892	131	69	974	82	-763
家具制造业	Furniture Manufacturing	2435	625	42	959	817	3538
造纸及纸制品业	Papermaking and Paper Products	1874	4908	194	2003	1923	7236
印刷业、记录媒介的复制	Printing and Record Medium Reproduced	22157	1431	245	4044	1843	26199
文教、体育用品制造	Stationery,Educational and Sports Goods	1648	1269	38	2725	587	5099
石油加工及炼焦业	Petroleum Processing and Coking Products	1806	6188	2206	1230	4770	29680
化学原料及化学制品制造业	Raw Chemical Materials and Chemical Products	-24680	10167	24599	5679	4242	11785
医药制造业	Medical and Pharmaceutical Product	8401	8137	2254	3336	3258	18974
化学纤维制造业	Chemical Fibers	-6867	50	56	864	553	-6447
橡胶制品业	Rubber Products	-1510	133	279	405	564	-2548
塑料制品业	Plastic Products	-26256	219	104	12670	1476	-14132
非金属矿物制品业	Nonmetal Mineral Products	-4309	4542	5307	7073	3584	9608
黑色金属冶炼及压延加工业	Smelting and Pressing of Ferrous Metals	13435	9912	75	17259	15584	25122
有色金属冶炼及压延加工业	Smelting and Pressing of Nonferrous Metals	204	453	634	601	142	1776
金属制品业	Metal Products	-10181	423	343	6490	4198	-6233
普通机械制造业	Ordinary Machinery Manufacturing	-33277	591	725	19437	3636	-15529
专用设备制造业	Special Purposes Equipment Manufacturing	9625	3785	2716	17458	5025	32664
交通运输设备制造业	Transportation Equipment Manufacturing	-77637	12992	1038	39698	6930	-27628
武器弹药制造业	Weapon and Ammunition Manufacture	-934	857	1881	245	725	1333
电气机械及器材制造	Electric Equipment and Machinery	-8304	923	132	10076	2063	3364
电子及通信设备制造	Electronic and Telecommunications	227707	55478	493	35101	15865	306687
仪器仪表及文化、办公用机械制造业	Instruments,Meters,Cultural and Official Machine Manufacturing	3965	3541	193	6161	2714	11406
其他制造业	Other Manufacturing	-657	327	2594	4067	2992	3634
电力、蒸汽、热水的生产和供应业	Electricity,Steam and Hot Water Production and Supply	31197	1976	15934	2640	7687	43901
煤气生产和供应业	Gas Production and Supply	-30310	757	30400	44	41	926
自来水的生产和供应	Water Production and Supply	-13161	-19	13500	180	139	360

6-4 续表 6 continued

(10000 yuan)

				工资，福利费，增值税 Wages,Welfares and Added Value Tax					
应交所得税 Income Tax Payable	应付利润 Profits Payable	亏损企业亏损额 Total Loss-ing of Loss-making Enterprises	利税总额 Total Pre-tax Profits	本年应付工资总额 Total Wags Payable	本年应付福利费总额 Total Welfares Payable	本年应交增值税 Added Value Tax	本年进项税额 Tax In-clude in Purchas-ing Cost	本年销项税额 Tax In-clude in Sales Cost	工业中间投入合计 Intermediate Input of Industry
886	606	220	20467	42399	5466	8025	5923	13632	64713
			19	13		18	12	29	131
188	88	255	2032	3250	260	754	3204	3706	14145
177	71	301	367	420	24	35	36	67	4380
266	264	699	3037	4834	535	1113	643	1502	27791
		13	6	22	3	18	43	26	171
4723	6195	30041	34590	27815	5197	28683	71198	98555	709106
3962	8665	63929	5629	49302	11780	42588	45750	85799	355263
11041	2703	26757	136654	32222	7553	39351	62360	99018	390025
170	2		38421	2305	166	8893	6858	16012	33723
1644	1059	18010	8146	57790	7823	13468	48884	59414	304299
2458	2224	22309	4680	63874	10589	12583	43209	53401	359864
385	812	4015	376	9162	1527	1512	5010	6228	40006
257	214	2454	1237	6923	795	1732	4175	5728	33426
778	2276	4414	9377	19604	1996	4972	13207	17849	102090
2262	878	10619	17139	20647	3222	9347	20956	29696	141465
9541	8873	10415	58083	62333	8664	29444	38678	65514	249167
1251	1830	1889	15017	15612	2281	9413	32593	41728	77535
3346	5582	1103	153382	69149	9643	69484	212216	279424	889134
7698	5441	21613	66612	75428	13107	43873	107323	148689	806270
7377	1845	18485	49335	34971	8305	28027	57131	81821	295968
36	98	6854	-5056	4768	743	1258	5977	6967	39868
274	201	4353	8112	12471	1780	5702	24779	30015	107500
1544	1366	23415	-5104	25247	3608	7975	29316	34069	210622
6970	4948	30494	63878	121485	18219	48384	81991	125990	675737
3914	27	9392	152569	180217	24091	116355	241447	352373	1566037
520	421	1506	3398	6030	939	1401	7594	8756	61965
3472	5103	29342	15502	62194	8856	19252	57596	74641	421575
1442	2922	28546	8175	82434	11541	22173	64502	82985	388221
7783	12267	20883	68170	89126	14560	35585	134997	168973	626910
6989	2328	60743	37921	154975	29965	47089	133054	174968	891558
320	1570	396	1758	12018	1699	377	4929	5157	48852
3538	3295	19663	37011	68759	10759	31235	74842	103424	521926
27648	69038	54439	426986	152807	29850	112710	651071	706048	3506660
2363	1146	5049	28901	54917	16526	10964	36339	44185	238221
1930	1388	6403	14999	23579	3502	10380	13202	22051	112735
4716	225	9001	123934	56479	6291	72522	86299	151015	371932
3	412		6253	11635	1823	4882	11116	15992	13848
6		643	5332	8835	1209	4500		4414	37462

6-5 全部独立核算工业企业主要经济分析指标

单位：%

项　目	Item	企业亏损面 Loss-making Enterprises as % of Total	总资产贡献率 Contribution Rate of Total Assets	资产保值增值率 Changing Rate of Net Assets
总计（不含个体工业）	**Total (exclude individual industry)**	**24.89**	**6.21**	**123.63**
在总计中：	**Of Total:**			
中央企业	Central Enterprises	36.45	8.93	100.29
地方企业	Local Enterprises	24.30	5.25	132.93
工业系统	Industry System	33.28	4.97	118.00
非工业系统	Non-Industry System	38.88	3.29	120.06
区县工业	Industry of District and County	19.08	7.35	172.03
其他	Others	54.60	3.83	226.49
在总计中：	**Of Total:**			
国有企业	State-owned Enterprise	26.96	5.95	103.89
集体企业	Collective-owned Enterprise	17.99	6.24	170.09
私营企业	Private Enterprise	29.04	11.84	225.01
联营企业	Joint-owned Enterprise	23.30	4.98	108.32
股份制企业	Share Holding Enterpri	34.96	5.59	203.12
外商投资企业	Foreign Funded Enterprise	50.43	8.44	148.64
中外合资经营	Joint Venture	46.88	9.53	141.99
中外合作经营	Co-operative	40.74	5.32	137.48
外资企业	Foreign Enterprises	62.09	-3.16	-576.00
港澳台投资企业	HongKong,Macao and Taiwan Funded Enterprises	54.40	3.18	121.40
与大陆合资经营	Joint Venture	51.43	3.18	116.88
与大陆合作经营	Co-operative	62.16	-0.44	279.85
港澳台独资企业	HongKong,Macao and Taiwan Enterprises	67.43	3.64	171.71
其他企业	Others	19.67	5.17	113.53
在总计中：	**Of Total:**			
农村企业	Rural Enterprises	14.84	9.62	230.09
在总计中：	**Of Total:**			
国有绝对控股企业	State-owned Absolute Holding Enterprises	29.75	6.38	111.91
国有相对控股企业	State-owned Relative Holding Enterpeises	42.31	7.91	131.35
在总计中：	**Of Total:**			
轻工业	Light Industry	27.30	6.12	141.62
以农产品为原料	Using Farm Products as Raw Material	29.10	7.14	147.58
以非农产品为原料	Using Non-Farm Products as Raw Material	24.57	4.57	132.87
重工业	Heavy Industry	22.56	6.25	117.18
采掘工业	Excavation	14.82	7.45	135.77
原料工业	Raw Material	22.65	5.68	92.89
加工工业	Processing	23.00	6.79	151.93
在总计中：	**Of Total:**			
大型企业	Large Enterprises	31.20	5.89	109.97
中型企业	Medium Enterprises	30.97	4.69	102.84
小型企业	Small Enterprises	24.69	7.29	173.83

MAIN INDICATORS ON ECONOMIC BENIFIT OF INDUSTRIAL ENTERPRISES WITH INDEPENDENT ACCOUNTING SYSTEM

(%)

资产负债率 Liabilities/ Total Assets	流动资产周转率(次) Turnover Rate of Circulating Assets (time)	成本费用利润率 Total Profits/Total Costs and Expenses	全员劳动生产率(元) Overall Labor Productivity (yuan)	产品销售率 Sales Value/ Gross Output Value	增加值率 Value Added/ Gross Output Value	人均销售收入(元) Sales Revenue Per Capita	流动比率 Circulating Assets/ Liquid Liabilities	速动比率 Quick-circulating Assets/ Liquid Liabilities
61.90	1.12	2.37	35033	97.55	26.28	121746	104.65	69.02
66.14	1.32	5.26	89396	100.15	29.04	283132	119.41	88.31
60.41	1.04	1.03	26202	96.32	24.96	95530	100.71	63.86
62.02	1.02	1.14	25601	98.42	21.86	111760	95.53	60.83
45.82	1.18	-2.56	29952	97.20	25.35	127719	107.04	71.11
64.44	1.18	2.64	24067	93.63	28.98	67794	98.65	56.68
56.99	0.65	-1.17	53081	95.11	25.19	187283	134.07	100.71
61.25	1.21	2.29	36926	99.79	26.65	135694	102.40	68.74
67.83	1.07	1.88	17503	92.92	28.97	50304	101.62	56.78
53.16	1.34	5.10	35028	92.84	34.59	79549	123.62	61.73
69.53	0.65	3.27	17522	96.83	25.30	58488	90.37	56.59
60.84	1.06	4.68	37209	95.01	24.77	119157	110.41	73.53
58.78	1.07	2.89	85135	97.73	25.36	305059	114.80	82.19
57.87	1.07	3.87	94169	97.65	25.05	342034	118.75	85.68
51.28	1.18	3.12	50091	105.63	29.88	147175	102.36	64.02
73.89	1.24	-7.67	54711	95.88	28.81	169332	84.80	58.05
66.86	1.03	-1.42	36940	96.89	23.06	141554	94.02	58.17
65.96	1.03	-1.54	36649	97.13	22.74	141365	93.89	58.93
72.93	0.88	6.26	36668	99.96	35.50	89410	80.44	47.80
74.03	1.09	0.06	39760	95.06	22.78	165678	98.70	54.88
68.96	0.71	3.27	17846	96.40	25.82	58491	90.96	56.35
63.94	1.38	3.74	20750	92.65	29.39	57642	102.13	50.95
61.60	1.08	3.34	39305	99.14	26.21	142184	104.44	70.62
55.97	1.77	2.27	98396	98.95	20.68	451587	109.76	77.73
60.49	1.08	1.02	28882	96.61	28.94	88840	102.65	65.17
59.86	1.15	1.39	29144	96.22	29.79	87514	103.66	66.37
61.48	0.98	0.35	28352	97.36	27.30	91528	101.00	63.24
62.48	1.13	2.94	39246	97.97	25.12	144288	105.64	70.92
57.51	0.89	7.37	16092	94.61	44.85	32323	124.76	103.97
62.95	1.46	1.81	50862	99.33	23.41	219362	93.11	65.48
62.20	1.00	3.52	37178	97.35	25.63	127690	111.68	72.95
61.66	1.15	2.46	44603	99.35	25.36	169741	102.18	69.93
61.74	0.92	-1.28	22774	98.81	26.79	70816	100.08	63.56
62.40	1.11	2.73	30528	95.47	27.25	97308	108.84	68.83

6-6 全部独立核算国有工业企业主要经济指标

单位：万元

项目	Item	企业单位个数（个）Number of Enterprises (unit)	#亏损企业 Loss-making Enterprises	工业总产值（当年价格）Gross Output Value of Industry (at current price)	新产品产值 Value of New Products	工业总产值（1990年不变价格）Gross Output Value of Industry (at 1990 constant prices)	工业增加值（生产法）Added Value of Industry (with production method)
总　计	**Total**	**2604**	**702**	**8615543**	**2413808**	**8185996**	**2681731**
在总计中：	**Of Total:**						
中央企业	Central Enterprises	421	132	4425917	2058786	4980460	1577158
地方企业	Local Enterprises	2183	570	4189626	355022	3205535	1104573
工业系统	Industry System	432	104	2837622	318842	2226447	593952
非工业系统	Non-Industry System	482	205	732853	12974	490366	294960
区县工业	Industry of District and County	1260	258	615532	23206	484046	233947
其他	Others	9	3	3619		4676	1232
在总计中：	**Of Total:**						
轻工业	Light Industry	1290	385	1720228	141214	1315507	643797
以农产品为原料	Using Farm Products as Raw Material	835	267	1178338	45707	780708	490336
以非农产品为原料	Using Non-Farm Products as Raw Material	455	118	541889	95507	534799	153459
重工业	Heavy Industry	1314	317	6895315	2272594	6870489	2037935
采掘工业	Excavation	24	4	103728	534	43676	56726
原料工业	Raw Material	165	37	3310348	86855	2085191	905025
加工工业	Processing	1125	276	3481239	2185205	4741621	1076184
在总计中：	**Of Total:**						
大型企业	Large Enterprises	168	42	6238424	1535061	5960640	1848747
中型企业	Medium Enterprises	174	45	636224	45050	481458	262802
小型企业	Small Enterprises	2262	615	1740895	833697	1743897	570182

MAIN INDICATORS FOR STATE-OWNED INDUSTRIAL ENTERPRISES WITH INDEPENDENT ACCOUNTING SYSTEM

(10000 yuan)

工业销售产值(当年价格) Sales Value of Industry (at current price)	出口交货值 Delivery Value of Exports	全部从业人员年平均人数(人) Average Number of Employment (person)	工业品自销零售额 Retail Sales of Self-selling Industrial Products	资产负债 Assets and Liabilities						
				流动资产合计 Circulating Assets	应收帐款净额 Accounts Receivable	存货 Stock	产成品 Finished Products	流动资产平均余额 Average Balance of Circulating Assets	长期投资 Long-time Investment	固定资产合计 Fixed Assets
8597135	**486325**	**702501**	**1120459**	**8064019**	**1700592**	**2650844**	**860654**	**7882172**	**1527619**	**10699373**
4436683	182903	192613	758559	3073084	768729	789978	216443	3060189	339504	4518898
4160453	303422	509888	361900	4990935	931864	1860866	644211	4821983	1188115	6180476
2834894	281598	353345	147064	3503848	656066	1392943	428401	3412170	1023070	4227620
722885	9510	86032	165474	858756	191013	286469	146392	833509	51704	1476261
599273	12314	69862	49336	490957	72964	178295	66920	441696	108829	474959
3401		649	27	137375	11821	3160	2498	134608	4511	1637
1705308	134139	236329	241056	1917729	265514	708770	344838	1814792	373335	2061165
1168216	98002	153967	110664	1126602	168084	430311	219684	1064288	213443	1092574
537092	36137	82362	130392	791127	97430	278459	125154	750504	159891	968591
6891828	352186	466172	879403	6146290	1435078	1942074	515815	6067380	1154284	8638209
97946	30653	37301	1511	169177	73602	19003	8606	165044	15039	137000
3315644	121593	138391	23100	2610737	549571	756386	135035	2638016	484187	6754458
3478238	199941	290480	854793	3366377	811905	1166685	372174	3264320	655058	1746750
6306246	424795	444356	285141	5726602	1226866	1955284	595917	5653641	1080514	9283068
632577	25227	105641	52249	754089	137080	293074	118793	705747	209741	603948
1658313	36303	152504	783069	1583329	336647	402487	145944	1522784	237364	812357

6-6 续表 1 continued

单位：万元

项目		资产负债					
项目	Item	固定资产原价合计 Original Value of Fixed Assets	# 生产经营用 For Productive Use	累计折旧 Accumulative Depreciation	#本年折旧 Depreciation in this Year	固定资产净值年平均余额 Average Net Value of Fixed Assets	无形资产及递延资产 Intangible and Deferred Assets
总　计	**Total**	**13621321**	**11564172**	**4791521**	**604539**	**8243917**	**757389**
在总计中：	**Of Total:**						
中央企业	Central Enterprises	5564165	4335669	1999204	275594	3097016	350336
地方企业	Local Enterprises	8057156	7228503	2792317	328946	5146901	407053
工业系统	Industry System	5673510	5114383	2190673	220146	3473790	354937
非工业系统	Non-Industry System	1863533	1696384	464578	85462	1305958	26182
区县工业	Industry of District and County	517336	414961	135911	23139	365265	25809
其他	Others	2777	2775	1155	199	1888	126
在总计中：	**Of Total:**						
轻工业	Light Industry	2567711	2077243	805509	114330	1734005	190722
以农产品为原料	Using Farm Products as Raw Material	1355744	1045593	447527	63692	878652	70783
以非农产品为原料	Using Non-Farm Products as Raw Material	1211967	1031650	357982	50638	855353	119939
重工业	Heavy Industry	11053610	9486929	3986012	490209	6509912	566667
采掘工业	Excavation	194344	131002	66982	6661	118219	8131
原料工业	Raw Material	8612455	7668902	3100008	393289	5005140	207012
加工工业	Processing	2246811	1687025	819023	90260	1386553	351524
在总计中：	**Of Total:**						
大型企业	Large Enterprises	11800336	10273189	4201816	523576	7052957	625292
中型企业	Medium Enterprises	796642	620298	278384	31158	502095	70513
小型企业	Small Enterprises	1024344	670684	311321	49805	688865	61585

6-6 续表 2 continued

(10000 yuan)

Assets and Liabilities										
#无形资产 Intangible Assets	其他资产 Other Assets	资产总计 Total Assets	流动负债合计 Liquid Liabilities	短期借款 Short-time Loans	长期负债合计 Long-term Liabilities	长期借款 Long-time Loans	负债合计 Total Liabilities	所有者权益 Ownership Interest	实收资本 Contributed Capital	国家资本 State
358413	**17933**	**21066820**	**7874755**	**2928402**	**4838259**	**2351541**	**12903633**	**8163187**	**4287671**	**3500115**
295395	16227	8298535	2620293	625458	2906929	1216131	5711232	2587303	1211743	1144045
63018	1706	12768285	5254462	2302943	1931329	1135409	7192402	5575884	3075928	2356070
48161	-11655	9097819	4007157	1864116	1607104	884228	5615459	3482360	1691614	1094497
8594	9712	2422614	713808	226345	216483	183931	930635	1491979	1065299	1027237
6205	3650	1104204	470611	182138	94941	66683	570620	533584	262770	178093
57		143649	62886	30345	12802	568	75687	67961	56245	56245
20104	10371	4553321	1909082	829993	710504	575996	2624535	1928786	1173416	818887
9382	3943	2507345	1091889	493214	316454	235870	1412720	1094625	604964	398239
10722	6427	2045976	817193	336779	394050	340126	1211815	834161	568452	420648
338309	7562	16513499	5965673	2098409	4127754	1775545	10279098	6234401	3114255	2681228
	69	329416	130110	45218	66063	48447	196173	133243	81221	66824
105881	-4050	10052344	2764890	1105519	3247125	1093774	6195881	3856463	1878620	1826564
232427	11543	6131739	3070674	947671	814566	633325	3887044	2244695	1154414	787841
332788	-8360	16707603	5754260	2259226	4331512	1968433	10269303	6438300	3176281	2643823
5265	2274	1640564	778822	274220	241705	179365	1021749	618816	453136	363545
20360	24019	2718653	1341673	394956	265042	203742	1612582	1106071	658253	492746

6-6 续表 3 continued

单位：万元

项目 Item		资产负债 Assets and Liabilities 集体资本 Collective	法人资本 Institutional Units	个人资本 Individuals	港澳台资本 Hongkong, Macao and Taiwan	外商资本 Foreign
总计	**Total**	**35776**	**729234**	**17884**	**2205**	**2458**
在总计中:	**Of Total:**					
中央企业	Central Enterprises	807	65769	804	104	215
地方企业	Local Enterprises	34968	663465	17080	2101	2243
工业系统	Industry System	24692	572425			
非工业系统	Non-Industry System	5713	29198	550	484	2119
区县工业	Industry of District and County	4564	61843	16531	1617	124
其他	Others					
在总计中:	**Of Total:**					
轻工业	Light Industry	20118	313365	16828	1975	2243
以农产品为原料	Using Farm Products as Raw Material	14204	174649	16221	1527	124
以非农产品为原料	Using Non-Farm Products as Raw Material	5914	138716	608	448	2119
重工业	Heavy Industry	15658	415869	1056	230	215
采掘工业	Excavation	289	14068	41		
原料工业	Raw Material	646	51238	83	90	
加工工业	Processing	14723	350563	932	140	215
在总计中:	**Of Total:**					
大型企业	Large Enterprises	17352	499544	15562		
中型企业	Medium Enterprises	6169	83422			
小型企业	Small Enterprises	12255	146267	2322	2205	2458

6-6 续表 4 continued

(10000 yuan)

损益及分配 Profits,Loss and Distribution										
产品销售收入 Sales Revenue	产品销售成本 Cost of Sales	产品销售费用 Expenses of Sales	产品销售税金及附加 Sales Tax and Extra Charges	产品销售利润 Sales Profits	管理费用 Overhead Cost	税金 Taxes	财产保险费 Premium of Property	劳动待业保险费 Premium for Employment Insurance	财务费用 Financial Expenses	利息支出 Expenses of Interest
9532486	**7821040**	**390315**	**161395**	**1159215**	**1081931**	**31766**	**13639**	**212153**	**343888**	**339202**
4591448	3645678	265152	68117	612501	478643	7204	7531	53307	131377	128351
4941038	4175362	125163	93278	546715	603287	24563	6109	158846	212511	210851
3462595	2969764	75351	28460	389021	433285	19268	3635	137430	180440	181523
905093	781939	27132	35360	60142	116197	3969	1331	16633	19095	17321
569867	420322	22199	29427	97918	53135	1281	1143	4772	13009	12037
3483	3338	481	32	-367	671	45	1	12	-33	-31
1949653	1539235	85114	73287	251497	279170	9158	3845	55175	58860	58657
1282378	978874	50813	67173	185018	177389	5268	2673	36874	30927	31699
667275	560361	34301	6114	66479	101780	3890	1172	18301	27933	26959
7582833	6281805	305201	88108	907719	802761	22609	9795	156978	285028	280544
106003	63613	10439	1333	30619	26111	616	69	16110	1626	1483
4104047	3554585	27466	72580	449416	305455	13717	7843	66285	199907	199080
3372783	2663608	267297	14195	427683	471196	8275	1883	74584	83495	79981
7178815	5883244	296348	114343	884880	790717	24947	10376	170940	286744	286891
564967	423698	18876	40217	81675	110290	3361	2118	24754	21963	20440
1788704	1514099	75090	6835	192660	180924	3458	1146	16459	35181	31870

6-6 续表 5 continued

单位：万元

项 目 Item		损益及分配 Profits,Loss and Distribution 营业利润 Operating Profits	投资收益 Investment Income	补贴收入 Subsidy Income	营业外收入 Out-business Income	营业外支出 Out-business Expenditure	利润总额 Total Profits
总 计	**Total**	**-68970**	**108820**	**97640**	**114184**	**58307**	**220217**
在总计中：	**Of Total:**						
中央企业	Central Enterprises	91608	51214	2675	14452	17202	165624
地方企业	Local Enterprises	-160577	57606	94965	99732	41105	54593
工业系统	Industry System	-134877	49231	37828	86366	33401	7920
非工业系统	Non-Industry System	-63396	3940	55771	9251	5587	316
区县工业	Industry of District and County	38093	3747	1366	4022	2102	45986
其他	Others	-397	689		94	15	371
在总计中：	**Of Total:**						
轻工业	Light Industry	-14602	29168	25683	38181	12322	68010
以农产品为原料	Using Farm Products as Raw Material	14317	18154	8335	27931	7570	61460
以非农产品为原料	Using Non-Farm Products as Raw Material	-28919	11014	17348	10250	4752	6550
重工业	Heavy Industry	-54368	79652	71957	76004	45986	152207
采掘工业	Excavation	-9420	1108	14444	431	3337	5032
原料工业	Raw Material	-13557	20020	47496	22558	27626	71646
加工工业	Processing	-31391	58524	10018	53015	15023	75529
在总计中：	**Of Total:**						
大型企业	Large Enterprises	-71150	91750	89278	82706	45311	173270
中型企业	Medium Enterprises	-16838	2881	2202	14356	6169	-3546
小型企业	Small Enterprises	19019	14189	6160	17122	6827	50492

6-6 续表 6 continued

(10000 yuan)

				工资，福利费，增值税 Wages,Welfares and Added Value Tax					
应交所得税 Income Tax Payable	应付利润 Profits Payable	亏损企业亏损额 Total Lossing of Loss-making Enterprises	利税总额 Total Pre-tax Profits	本年应付工资总额 Total Wags Payable	本年应付福利费总额 Total Welfares Payable	本年应交增值税 Added Value Tax	本年进项税额 Tax Include in Purchasing Cost	本年销项税额 Tax Include in Sales Cost	工业中间投入合计 Intermediate Input of Industry
47342	**22614**	**119737**	**823114**	**827395**	**109730**	**441502**	**1213799**	**1603325**	**6375314**
20881	13534	26065	420307	250489	32249	186566	641188	793929	3035325
26461	9080	93672	402807	576906	77482	254936	572611	809396	3339989
8376	1904	55054	211885	429110	57896	175505	423698	586193	2419175
7192	654	23816	83426	90823	13143	47750	95419	139781	485643
10207	6467	14670	106956	55788	6367	31543	53164	83167	413128
686	56	133	541	1186	76	138	330	256	2525
25529	12363	44741	242439	206808	28026	101142	196320	289127	1177573
20452	8740	29097	200966	132506	17415	72333	135009	202356	760335
5077	3623	15644	41473	74302	10611	28809	61312	86771	417239
21813	10251	74996	580676	620587	81704	340361	1017479	1314198	5197741
139		410	13492	35183	4874	7127	7596	14457	54129
10725	5700	13732	402154	313733	41992	257928	527985	777201	2663251
10949	4551	60854	165029	271672	34839	75305	481898	522540	2480360
26957	17877	49395	641491	597301	79065	353878	891178	1200945	4743555
6708	734	24452	70567	96256	12521	33896	67567	99249	407318
13677	4003	45891	111055	133838	18145	53728	255054	303132	1224441

6-7 全部独立核算国有工业企业主要经济分析指标

单位：%

项目	Item	企业亏损面 Loss-making Enterprises as % of Total	总资产贡献率 Contribution Rate of Total Assets	资产保值增值率 Changing Rate of Net Assets
总计	**Total**	**26.96**	**5.38**	**89.23**
在总计中：	**Of Total:**			
中央企业	Central Enterprises	31.35	6.91	77.02
地方企业	Local Enterprises	26.11	4.49	96.32
工业系统	Industry System	24.07	3.85	86.58
非工业系统	Non-Industry System	42.53	4.38	109.93
区县工业	Industry of District and County	20.48	11.06	130.48
其他	Others	33.33	0.70	18467.66
在总计中：	**Of Total:**			
轻工业	Light Industry	29.84	6.69	111.67
以农产品为原料	Using Farm Products as Raw Material	31.98	9.53	120.71
以非农产品为原料	Using Non-Farm Products as Raw Material	25.93	3.32	101.68
重工业	Heavy Industry	24.12	5.04	84.01
采掘工业	Excavation	16.67	4.89	110.35
原料工业	Raw Material	22.42	5.64	76.98
加工工业	Processing	24.53	3.99	98.00
在总计中：	**Of Total:**			
大型企业	Large Enterprises	25.00	5.49	89.71
中型企业	Medium Enterprises	25.86	5.26	81.91
小型企业	Small Enterprises	27.19	4.82	90.99

MAIN INDICATORS ON ECONOMIC BENEFIT OF STATE-OWNED INDUSTRIAL ENTERPRISES WITH INDEPENDENT ACCOUNTING SYSTEM

(%)

资产负债率 Liabilities/Total Assets	流动资产周转率(次) Turnover Rate of Circulating Assets (time)	成本费用利润率 Total Profits/Total Costs and Expenses	全员劳动生产率(元) Overall Labor Productivity (yuan)	产品销售率 Sales Value/Gross Output Value	增加值率 Value Added/Gross Output Value	人均销售收入(元) Sales Revenue Per Capita	流动比率 Circulating Assets/Liquid Liabilities	速动比率 Quick-circulating Assets/Liquid Liabilities
61.25	**1.21**	**2.29**	**36929**	**99.79**	**26.65**	**135694**	**102.40**	**68.74**
68.82	1.50	3.66	79205	100.24	30.38	238377	117.28	87.13
56.33	1.02	1.07	20955	99.30	22.65	96904	94.98	59.57
61.72	1.01	0.22	16260	99.90	17.90	97995	87.44	52.68
38.41	1.09	0.03	33163	98.64	34.86	105204	120.31	80.17
51.68	1.29	9.04	32392	97.36	33.17	81570	104.32	66.44
52.69	0.03	8.32	18362	93.98	31.71	53667	218.45	213.43
57.64	1.07	3.47	26350	99.13	32.59	82497	100.45	63.33
56.34	1.20	4.96	26350	99.14	35.94	83289	103.18	63.77
59.23	0.89	0.90	18023	99.11	25.06	81017	96.81	62.74
62.25	1.25	1.98	42287	99.95	25.19	162662	103.03	70.47
59.55	0.64	4.94	14710	94.43	48.12	28418	130.03	115.42
61.64	1.56	1.75	63257	100.16	22.99	296554	94.42	67.07
63.39	1.03	2.17	35837	99.91	26.77	116111	109.63	71.64
61.46	1.27	2.39	40245	101.09	25.39	161555	99.52	65.54
62.28	0.80	-0.62	24064	99.43	35.13	53480	96.82	59.19
59.32	1.17	2.80	36165	95.26	28.01	117289	118.01	88.01

6-8 全部独立核算集体工业企业主要经济指标

单位：万元

项目	Item	企业单位个数(个) Number of Enterprises (unit)	#亏损企业 Loss-making Enterprises	工业总产值(当年价格) Gross Output Value of Industry (at current price)	新产品产值 Value of New Products	工业总产值(1990年不变价格) Gross Output Value of Industry (at 1990 constant prices)	工业增加值(生产法) Added Value of Industry (with production method)
总计	**Total**	**10116**	**1820**	**2751952**	**93225**	**2595548**	**905563**
在总计中：	**Of Total:**						
中央企业	Central Enterprises	193	70	61964	1670	56817	27381
地方企业	Local Enterprises	9923	1750	2689988	91555	2538731	878182
工业系统	Industry System	515	180	160291	8264	156594	44010
非工业系统	Non-Industry System	193	44	30630	2073	28303	12499
区县工业	Industry of District and County	9090	1461	2451601	71943	2301191	808706
其他	Others	125	65	47467	9275	52643	12967
在总计中：	**Of Total:**						
街镇农村企业	Rural Enterprises of Subdistricts and Towns	8344	1247	2112327	22880	1971642	713266
在总计中：	**Of Total:**						
轻工业	Light Industry	4679	869	1280538	17995	1218041	427210
以农产品为原料	Using Farm Products as Raw Material	2694	509	806289	5511	745020	257726
以非农产品为原料	Using Non-Farm Products as Raw Material	1985	360	474249	12484	473021	169484
重工业	Heavy Industry	5437	951	1471414	75230	1377507	478353
采掘工业	Excavation	376	53	87268	2	69575	37865
原料工业	Raw Material	642	121	225149	2199	205195	56773
加工工业	Processing	4419	777	1158997	73029	1102738	383715
在总计中：	**Of Total:**						
大型企业	Large Enterprises	9	5	128641	27358	136003	24496
中型企业	Medium Enterprises	38	18	73358	2076	73111	21613
小型企业	Small Enterprises	10069	1797	2549953	63791	2386435	859454

MAIN INDICATORS FOR COLLECTIVE-OWNED INDUSTRIAL ENTERPRISES WITH INDEPENDENT ACCOUNTING SYSTEM

(10000 yuan)

工业销售产值(当年价格) Sales Value of Industry (at current price)	出口交货值 Delivery Value of Exports	全部从业人员年平均人数(人) Average Number of Employment (person)	工业品自销零售额 Retail Sales of Self-selling Industrial Products	资产负债 Assets and Liabilities 流动资产合计 Circulating Assets	应收帐款净额 Accounts Receivable	存货 Stock	产成品 Finished Products	流动资产平均余额 Average Balance of Circulating Assets	长期投资 Long-time Investment	固定资产合计 Fixed Assets
	162442	**500471**	**276800**	**2448723**	**432579**	**1080371**	**558254**	**2352519**	**187171**	**1377377**
58647		10747	7871	53126	9253	18366	3910	48439	8734	23063
2498377	162442	489724	268928	2395598	423325	1062005	554345	2304079	178437	1354314
157892	13447	60235	20749	299775	51712	130494	67262	297429	40302	199559
28938	58	6453	3162	46382	5181	16774	4381	44287	5499	18005
2264420	148912	418513	241459	1911959	342457	870205	455958	1839035	105304	1112139
47128	25	4523	3558	137482	23975	44532	26744	123329	27333	24612
1961294	132238	365887	196481	1354964	265368	699658	386574	1294472	68403	832915
1209048	126717	230261	97414	1017622	189900	470985	248259	976228	90045	598074
756165	107261	148753	55302	536990	102916	259180	132899	513373	44938	381982
452883	19456	81508	42112	480632	86984	211806	115360	462855	45108	216092
1347976	35725	270210	179386	1431101	242678	609385	309996	1376290	97125	779303
83145	614	20845	32825	49807	14237	16843	13416	46471	1791	43924
206169	5345	28292	25284	170404	34064	75360	38814	159834	11343	141819
1058662	29766	221073	121277	1210890	194377	517183	257766	1169985	83992	593559
105473	5383	12137	17324	402168	51327	93875	35196	386338	41613	155729
67569	8694	17477	5334	95533	15544	43754	21499	90323	9250	92039
2383982	148365	470857	254142	1951022	365708	942742	501559	1875858	136308	1129608

6-8 续表 1 continued

单位：万元

项目 Item		资产负债 固定资产原价合计 Original Value of Fixed Assets	# 生产经营用 For Productive Use	累计折旧 Accumulative Depreciation	#本年折旧 Depreciation in this Year	固定资产净值年平均余额 Average Net Value of Fixed Assets	无形资产及递延资产 Intangible and Deferred Assets
总　计	**Total**	**1783272**	**1251269**	**560318**	**89027**	**1159584**	**104076**
在总计中：	**Of Total:**						
中央企业	Central Enterprises	33853	19438	12364	2674	19844	694
地方企业	Local Enterprises	1749419	1231831	547954	86354	1139740	103382
工业系统	Industry System	247102	176806	95506	10347	145920	20334
非工业系统	Non-Industry System	25413	21147	8660	1538	17929	1452
区县工业	Industry of District and County	1447075	1007374	434827	73641	957801	78244
其他	Others	29828	26505	8961	828	18092	3353
在总计中：	**Of Total:**						
街镇农村企业	Rural Enterprises of Subdistricts and Towns	1106000	777377	340987	58211	748009	40615
在总计中：	**Of Total:**						
轻工业	Light Industry	759168	532134	236843	38210	505971	38436
以农产品为原料	Using Farm Products as Raw Material	490020	340702	150347	25550	330090	19917
以非农产品为原料	Using Non-Farm Products as Raw Material	269148	191432	86496	12660	175881	18518
重工业	Heavy Industry	1024104	719136	323475	50818	653613	65641
采掘工业	Excavation	53698	40767	13464	2136	38993	2247
原料工业	Raw Material	171052	130790	45842	8052	110785	15954
加工工业	Processing	799354	547579	264169	40629	503835	47440
在总计中：	**Of Total:**						
大型企业	Large Enterprises	193493	136453	47672	7414	113222	32260
中型企业	Medium Enterprises	119314	86838	42869	4777	71152	4983
小型企业	Small Enterprises	1470465	1027978	469777	76836	975211	66834

6-8 续表 2 continued

(10000 yuan)

Assets and Liabilities										
#无形资产 Intangible Assets	其他资产 Other Assets	资产总计 Total Assets	流动负债合计 Liquid Liabilities	短期借款 Short-time Loans	长期负债合计 Long-term Liabilities	长期借款 Long-time Loans	负债合计 Total Liabilities	所有者权益 Ownership Interest	实收资本 Contributed Capital	国家资本 State
48888	**67183**	**4184529**	**2409718**	**809432**	**415669**	**348370**	**2838409**	**1346120**	**1043062**	**50462**
194	424	86041	44073	3566	4412	2573	49758	36282	21235	2638
48694	66759	4098489	2365645	805866	411257	345796	2788651	1309838	1021827	47824
3022	1170	561139	314954	84139	61966	48310	378340	182799	150763	3553
542	350	71688	47458	14095	5815	2554	53286	18401	10439	957
43600	25577	3233222	1837290	629601	336870	289320	2184477	1048745	847351	43101
1530	39661	232440	165943	78032	6605	5613	172548	59892	13274	214
21149	18878	2315775	1270810	473098	214225	177442	1491899	823876	660933	31385
13553	51355	1795532	1038691	418812	161005	127885	1206017	589514	446963	22502
6976	5642	989469	542962	222753	100351	81553	648561	340908	277821	10421
6577	45713	806062	495729	196059	60654	46332	557456	248607	169143	12081
35335	15828	2388998	1371027	390620	254664	220485	1632392	756606	596099	27960
432	391	98159	44668	12391	6599	6120	51532	46628	22089	625
13452	1844	341364	194609	74136	48269	42168	244132	97232	86685	8295
21451	13594	1949474	1131750	304093	199797	172197	1336728	612746	487324	19040
21442	44936	676705	428048	133645	87436	83749	515484	161222	92959	3310
1156	309	202114	108440	45169	21798	19969	130238	71876	56907	1369
26290	21938	3305710	1873230	630618	306436	244652	2192688	1113022	893195	45783

单位：万元

6-8 续表 3 continued

项目 Item		资产负债 Assets and Liabilities 集体资本 Collective	法人资本 Institutional Units	个人资本 Individuals	港澳台资本 Hongkong, Macao and Taiwan	外商资本 Foreign
总计	**Total**	**749734**	**157942**	**39187**	**14819**	**30918**
在总计中：	**Of Total:**					
中央企业	Central Enterprises	16728	1866	3		
地方企业	Local Enterprises	733006	156076	39184	14819	30918
工业系统	Industry System	130474	14654	2037	45	
非工业系统	Non-Industry System	8819	451	213		
区县工业	Industry of District and County	583782	138770	36007	14774	30918
其他	Others	9932	2201	928		
在总计中：	**Of Total:**					
街镇农村企业	Rural Enterprises of Subdistricts and Towns	468941	111690	32422	8779	7717
在总计中：	**Of Total:**					
轻工业	Light Industry	327425	64606	19228	7811	5391
以农产品为原料	Using Farm Products as Raw Material	199442	44576	11274	7282	4827
以非农产品为原料	Using Non-Farm Products as Raw Material	127983	20031	7955	528	565
重工业	Heavy Industry	422310	93335	19959	7009	25526
采掘工业	Excavation	17239	1704	2346		176
原料工业	Raw Material	65733	10222	2418		17
加工工业	Processing	339338	81410	15195	7009	25333
在总计中：	**Of Total:**					
大型企业	Large Enterprises	42458	17788	267	5996	23141
中型企业	Medium Enterprises	49499	5992	48		
小型企业	Small Enterprises	657778	134162	38872	8824	7777

6-8 续表 4 continued

(10000 yuan)

损益及分配 Profits,Loss and Distribution										
产品销售收入 Sales Revenue	产品销售成本 Cost of Sales	产品销售费用 Expenses of Sales	产品销售税金及附加 Sales Tax and Extra Charges	产品销售利润 Sales Profits	管理费用 Overhead Cost	税金 Taxes	财产保险费 Premium of Property	劳动待业保险费 Premium for Employment Insurance	财务费用 Financial Expenses	利息支出 Expenses of Interest
2517562	**2110029**	**90263**	**19558**	**297711**	**242358**	**7656**	**2006**	**16619**	**70238**	**54656**
66982	54603	3099	491	8789	9039	134	33	373	33	-32
2450580	2055426	87163	19068	288922	233319	7522	1973	16245	70205	54688
180572	151972	6587	937	21075	55197	2096	548	10771	7648	7320
24490	19583	1655	218	3034	5492	108	35	310	1075	824
2198382	1845225	75305	17716	260134	167387	5303	1378	5034	59803	44903
47136	38647	3616	196	4678	5244	14	12	131	1679	1642
1879843	1573729	62527	12309	231277	127173	4298	1068	1298	46096	35343
1152656	969056	42754	9810	131035	104983	3478	1068	8872	33018	27073
724391	613207	26672	6625	77886	59135	2065	651	3505	20631	17126
428265	355849	16081	3185	53149	45848	1413	417	5367	12387	9947
1364906	1140973	47509	9748	166676	137375	4178	939	7747	37220	27583
77951	58795	2727	1269	15161	6169	173	20	47	1377	1101
211225	181656	4551	878	24140	16807	347	119	387	8897	3992
1075729	900521	40231	7602	127375	114399	3657	799	7313	26945	22491
122413	109778	4945	245	7445	16164	213	72	950	7002	3484
70149	57293	2379	545	9932	15543	414	268	2955	3924	3461
2325000	1942958	82939	18768	280334	210651	7028	1666	12714	59312	47711

6-8 续表 5 continued

单位：万元

项目 Item		营业利润 Operating Profits	投资收益 Investment Income	补贴收入 Subsidy Income	营业外收入 Out-business Income	营业外支出 Out-business Expenditure	利润总额 Total Profits
		损益及分配 Profits,Loss and Distribution					
总　计	**Total**	**26439**	**5338**	**3526**	**20243**	**10505**	**47179**
在总计中：	**Of Total:**						
中央企业	Central Enterprises	520	145		149	467	614
地方企业	Local Enterprises	25919	5193	3526	20093	10038	46566
工业系统	Industry System	-22504	1845	403	8968	1858	-13064
非工业系统	Non-Industry System	872	67	342	407	186	1534
区县工业	Industry of District and County	47984	3250	2780	10614	7857	58493
其他	Others	-432	32		104	138	-398
在总计中：	**Of Total:**						
街镇农村企业	Rural Enterprises of Subdistricts and Towns	64247	1405	1783	8034	5734	71500
在总计中：	**Of Total:**						
轻工业	Light Industry	16314	1762	1697	9833	5011	25276
以农产品为原料	Using Farm Products as Raw Material	10669	198	1351	4995	3121	14562
以非农产品为原料	Using Non-Farm Products as Raw Material	5645	1565	346	4839	1890	10714
重工业	Heavy Industry	10125	3575	1829	10410	5494	21903
采掘工业	Excavation	7619	85	73	250	367	7701
原料工业	Raw Material	-704	66	322	466	435	16
加工工业	Processing	3210	3424	1434	9694	4693	14187
在总计中：	**Of Total:**						
大型企业	Large Enterprises	-10401	1497		1062	579	-8398
中型企业	Medium Enterprises	-6367	1003		1276	519	-4516
小型企业	Small Enterprises	43207	2838	3526	17904	9407	60093

6-8 续表 6 continued

(10000 yuan)

				工资，福利费，增值税 Wages,Welfares and Added Value Tax					
应交所得税 Income Tax Payable	应付利润 Profits Payable	亏损企业亏损额 Total Loss-ing of Loss-making Enterprises	利税总额 Total Pre-tax Profits	本年应付工资总额 Total Wags Payable	本年应付福利费总额 Total Welfares Payable	本年应交增值税 Added Value Tax	本年进项税额 Tax In-clude in Purchas-ing Cost	本年销项税额 Tax In-clude in Sales Cost	工业中间投入合计 Intermediate Input of Industry
19960	**19856**	**64865**	**158838**	**303537**	**36565**	**92101**	**260425**	**341639**	**1938490**
849	267	1839	4332	9340	1421	3227	7143	10052	37810
19112	19589	63027	154508	294197	35144	88874	253281	331587	1900680
612	52	15625	-3311	46030	5787	8816	23624	30955	125097
275	25	893	3211	6536	981	1459	2866	4248	19590
18093	19424	45406	153048	238440	27812	76839	219938	287888	1719734
133	88	1103	1558	3191	564	1760	6853	8496	36260
16510	18668	25639	148338	205163	22716	64529	167657	225519	1463590
8921	8849	25883	75071	132194	16044	39985	116404	152741	893313
5508	5793	16342	45627	82031	9895	24440	72385	95190	573003
3413	3055	9541	29444	50162	6149	15545	44018	57551	320310
11039	11007	38983	83767	171344	20521	52116	144021	188898	1045177
1305	947	956	11666	14897	1274	2696	2212	4343	52099
1328	693	5952	7754	18055	2394	6860	23866	30110	175236
8407	9367	32075	64348	138392	16853	42559	117943	154446	817841
136	2	8854	-4312	9126	1622	3841	28340	31660	107986
370	453	5572	-1201	11862	1566	2770	8476	10949	54515
19454	19402	50440	164351	282550	33377	85490	223609	299030	1775989

6-9 全部独立核算"三资"工业企业主要经济指标

单位：万元

项目	Item	企业单位个数(个) Number of Enterprises (unit)	#亏损企业 Loss-making Enterprises	工业总产值(当年价格) Gross Output Value of Industry (at current price)	新产品产值 Value of New Products	工业总产值(1990年不变价格) Gross Output Value of Industry (at 1990 constant prices)	工业增加值(生产法) Added Value of Industry (with production method)
总　计	**Total**	**2179**	**1135**	**6113506**	**647589**	**6235153**	**1738329**
在总计中：	**Of Total:**						
中央企业	Central Enterprises	168	84	1660712	93180	1812990	463245
地方企业	Local Enterprises	2011	1051	4452794	554409	4422164	1275084
工业系统	Industry System	331	155	2172761	397862	2368116	635186
非工业系统	Non-Industry System	163	82	391996	11050	250895	51647
区县工业	Industry of District and County	948	443	1243258	19077	1197829	382818
其他	Others	569	371	644780	126421	605324	205433
在总计中：	**Of Total:**						
轻工业	Light Industry	1348	729	2474492	170189	2213550	749234
以农产品为原料	Using Farm Products as Raw Material	901	490	1654823	80602	1355112	508349
以非农产品为原料	Using Non-Farm Products as Raw Material	447	239	819668	89588	858438	240884
重工业	Heavy Industry	831	406	3639014	477400	4021603	989095
采掘工业	Excavation	4	2	1057		1531	560
原料工业	Raw Material	98	45	287728	7318	219901	81264
加工工业	Processing	729	359	3350229	470082	3800171	907270
在总计中：	**Of Total:**						
大型企业	Large Enterprises	60	30	2062247	403760	2151959	635119
中型企业	Medium Enterprises	36	16	385205	16784	307991	64490
小型企业	Small Enterprises	2083	1089	3666054	227045	3775204	1038720

MAIN INDICATORS FOR FOREIGN INDUSTRIAL ENTERPRISES WITH INDEPENDENT ACCOUNTING SYSTEM

(10000 yuan)

工业销售产值(当年价格) Sales Value of Industry (at current price)	出口交货值 Delivery Value of Exports	全部从业人员年平均人数(人) Average Number of Employment (person)	工业品自销零售额 Retail Sales of Self-selling Industrial Products	资产负债 Assets and Liabilities						
				流动资产合计 Circulating Assets	应收帐款净额 Accounts Receivable	存货 Stock	产成品 Finished Products	流动资产平均余额 Average Balance of Circulating Assets	长期投资 Long-time Investment	固定资产合计 Fixed Assets
5964277	**730422**	**246569**	**273402**	**5250097**	**1665747**	**1612007**	**511852**	**5747415**	**130897**	**3223746**
1679519	156359	20790	15759	947939	404589	259084	46894	1656708	13070	462905
4284758	574063	225779	257644	4302158	1261159	1352924	464958	4090707	117828	2760841
2111290	290098	83192	51034	1873521	817371	580041	168712	1814388	16756	1243734
372971	14862	15600	24328	344423	68739	108384	41761	297423	29479	325684
1181027	219404	102054	123440	1085820	234892	429643	183905	1016416	35609	859184
619471	49700	24933	58842	998394	140157	234856	70580	962481	35983	332239
2397041	386511	146371	157720	2356227	473729	726915	292549	2245077	88618	1490480
1597043	238731	110604	108392	1702518	286117	507621	194303	1625415	83802	1033763
799998	147779	35767	49328	653708	187612	219294	98247	619662	4815	456718
3567236	343912	100198	115682	2893870	1192018	885092	219303	3502338	42279	1733266
978		146		999	300	446	398	994		3123
288910	14027	14216	20675	222254	70398	55682	21962	222040	1207	250778
3277348	329885	85836	95007	2670617	1121321	828964	196943	3279305	41072	1479366
1984263	128192	54163	55949	1955302	722060	489849	105546	1912024	53702	1445329
384447	51162	20158	27406	350482	119997	98921	37894	323007	16012	160951
3595567	551068	172248	190047	2944313	823690	1023237	368411	3512384	61183	1617466

单位：万元

6-9 续表 1 continued

项目	Item	资产负债 固定资产原价合计 Original Value of Fixed Assets	# 生产经营用 For Productive Use	累计折旧 Accumulative Depreciation	#本年折旧 Depreciation in this Year	固定资产净值年平均余额 Average Net Value of Fixed Assets	无形资产及递延资产 Intangible and Deferred Assets
总　计	**Total**	**4076288**	**3511538**	**1075240**	**281792**	**2891262**	**471527**
在总计中：	**Of Total:**						
中央企业	Central Enterprises	590203	493436	141618	41710	402902	46855
地方企业	Local Enterprises	3486085	3018102	933622	240081	2488361	424672
工业系统	Industry System	1663701	1541042	542471	127848	1093961	173161
非工业系统	Non-Industry System	393606	333536	82981	23846	302249	51565
区县工业	Industry of District and County	1013402	811903	210308	55699	799525	130393
其他	Others	415376	331620	97861	32690	292626	69553
在总计中：	**Of Total:**						
轻工业	Light Industry	1876787	1528465	451433	123960	1390279	260611
以农产品为原料	Using Farm Products as Raw Material	1306207	1030323	324471	82177	965080	182565
以非农产品为原料	Using Non-Farm Products as Raw Material	570580	498143	126962	41783	425199	78047
重工业	Heavy Industry	2199501	1983073	623807	157832	1500983	210916
采掘工业	Excavation	3463	3433	397	66	2948	828
原料工业	Raw Material	293906	264672	68490	17521	210728	53552
加工工业	Processing	1902132	1714968	554920	140245	1287307	156535
在总计中：	**Of Total:**						
大型企业	Large Enterprises	1859208	1734217	551730	138259	1247561	171370
中型企业	Medium Enterprises	206793	178937	60276	13678	139938	26272
小型企业	Small Enterprises	2010287	1598383	463233	129855	1503763	273886

6-9 续表 2 continued

(10000 yuan)

Assets and Liabilities										
#无形资产 Intangible Assets	其他资产 Other Assets	资产总计 Total Assets	流动负债合计 Liquid Liabilities	短期借款 Short-time Loans	长期负债合计 Long-term Liabilities	长期借款 Long-time Loans	负债合计 Total Liabilities	所有者权益 Ownership Interest	实收资本 Contributed Capital	国家资本 State
352699	**276380**	**9352647**	**4812240**	**1710203**	**815270**	**744246**	**5675419**	**3677228**	**3567829**	**613530**
39087	52868	1523636	818660	273270	113624	107973	939696	583940	390764	168313
313612	223512	7829012	3993579	1436933	701646	636273	4735723	3093289	3177065	445217
139036	59373	3366546	1606208	670122	305642	270086	1924588	1441958	1312227	232969
36038	16931	768083	400787	153992	83734	80638	490010	278072	373352	93039
94093	87278	2198284	1278101	426426	218625	199584	1501104	697180	884449	99725
44445	59930	1496099	708483	186393	93645	85965	820021	676078	607037	19484
187079	144532	4340468	2239036	764701	374839	337023	2644978	1695490	1897761	313244
133213	107448	3110095	1605928	547943	261574	230232	1895498	1214598	1335998	234383
53865	37085	1230372	633108	216758	113266	106790	749480	480892	561763	78861
165620	131848	5012180	2573204	945502	440431	407223	3030441	1981738	1670068	300286
626	2	4953	1696	554			1696	3257	3516	
50162	23581	551373	238495	64345	23140	14331	261819	289554	265309	75578
114832	108264	4455854	2333013	880604	417290	392892	2766927	1688927	1401242	224708
142916	79255	3704958	1627794	713254	355800	334735	2011212	1693746	1383383	233517
23041	29058	582775	327572	119572	26869	22661	356000	226775	200420	43256
186742	168067	5064915	2856873	877377	432601	386850	3308208	1756708	1984026	336757

6-9 续表 3 continued

单位：万元

项目 Item		资产负债 Assets and Liabilities				
		集体资本 Collective	法人资本 Institutional Units	个人资本 Individuals	港澳台资本 Hongkong, Macao and Taiwan	外商资本 Foreign
总计	**Total**	**159841**	**639638**	**43518**	**434982**	**1676320**
在总计中：	**Of Total:**					
中央企业	Central Enterprises	2144	33229	38	22185	164855
地方企业	Local Enterprises	157697	606409	43481	412798	1511465
工业系统	Industry System	9336	380784	5658	67385	616096
非工业系统	Non-Industry System	7316	32705	108	43737	196446
区县工业	Industry of District and County	129084	134456	5520	198082	317583
其他	Others	11961	58464	32195	103594	381340
在总计中：	**Of Total:**					
轻工业	Light Industry	117760	227493	35018	301933	902314
以农产品为原料	Using Farm Products as Raw Material	75223	126204	20763	204973	674452
以非农产品为原料	Using Non-Farm Products as Raw Material	42536	101289	14254	96960	227863
重工业	Heavy Industry	42081	412145	8501	133049	774006
采掘工业	Excavation	1685		37	23	1771
原料工业	Raw Material	9567	72346		9123	98695
加工工业	Processing	30829	339799	8463	123903	673540
在总计中：	**Of Total:**					
大型企业	Large Enterprises	2407	261540	13767	64641	807511
中型企业	Medium Enterprises	10080	53165	15757	13074	65089
小型企业	Small Enterprises	147354	324933	13995	357267	803721

6-9 续表 4 continued

(10000 yuan)

损益及分配 Profits,Loss and Distribution										
产品销售收入 Sales Revenue	产品销售成本 Cost of Sales	产品销售费用 Expenses of Sales	产品销售税金及附加 Sales Tax and Extra Charges	产品销售利润 Sales Profits	管理费用 Overhead Cost	税金 Taxes	财产保险费 Premium of Property	劳动待业保险费 Premium for Employment Insurance	财务费用 Financial Expenses	利息支出 Expenses of Interest
6104774	**4958602**	**450093**	**36793**	**659286**	**538390**	**11505**	**4771**	**6565**	**160950**	**130498**
1721185	1454667	99587	8930	158001	81073	1391	441	197	24015	20830
4383589	3503935	350506	27863	501285	457317	10114	4330	6368	136936	109668
2139039	1715387	125436	19654	278562	200518	4761	2343	3642	73808	66097
448582	372105	54380	232	21864	50202	1236	617	1402	16826	14435
1147947	899863	101475	7499	139110	121381	2088	1003	903	36014	24896
648021	516580	69215	477	61749	85216	2030	367	422	10288	4239
2407012	1885076	256235	14873	250828	256559	5126	2315	3753	67587	49356
1658079	1309469	164600	10122	173889	169504	3313	1669	2878	41290	32531
748934	575607	91635	4751	76940	87056	1813	645	875	26297	16824
3697762	3073526	193858	21919	408458	281830	6380	2456	2812	93364	81142
811	591	112		108	116				25	11
288890	238536	7584	202	42568	22083	319	168	215	4899	3882
3408061	2834400	186163	21717	365782	259632	6061	2288	2597	88440	77249
2086393	1670789	180393	25573	209638	169934	3909	1992	2589	72954	57570
385947	330727	24662	629	29930	31304	683	300	460	8674	8581
3632434	2957086	245039	10590	419719	337152	6913	2479	3516	79323	64347

6-9 续表 5 continued

单位：万元

项目 Item		营业利润 Operating Profits	投资收益 Investment Income	补贴收入 Subsidy Income	营业外收入 Out-business Income	营业外支出 Out-business Expenditure	利润总额 Total Profits
		损益及分配 Profits,Loss and Distribution					
总计	**Total**	**61312**	**2534**	**515**	**81503**	**33374**	**122583**
在总计中：	**Of Total:**						
中央企业	Central Enterprises	121003	14	256	18722	7210	133683
地方企业	Local Enterprises	-59692	2520	259	62781	26164	-11100
工业系统	Industry System	17926	170	38	45938	11761	55832
非工业系统	Non-Industry System	-43479	857	5	3318	1896	-40980
区县工业	Industry of District and County	-13389	243	210	9500	7421	-8754
其他	Others	-20750	1251	7	4025	5086	-17197
在总计中：	**Of Total:**						
轻工业	Light Industry	-61576	2394	304	26113	17966	-47631
以农产品为原料	Using Farm Products as Raw Material	-32396	2342	260	16185	13048	-24950
以非农产品为原料	Using Non-Farm Products as Raw Material	-29179	51	44	9928	4918	-22681
重工业	Heavy Industry	122887	140	211	55390	15408	170214
采掘工业	Excavation	-33			9	3	-27
原料工业	Raw Material	16664			2940	2051	17629
加工工业	Processing	106256	140	211	52440	13354	152612
在总计中：	**Of Total:**						
大型企业	Large Enterprises	33402	1903	5	45914	16169	68092
中型企业	Medium Enterprises	-9748	381		2543	592	-7300
小型企业	Small Enterprises	37658	250	510	33045	16613	61791

6-9 续表 6 continued

(10000 yuan)

				工资，福利费，增值税 Wages,Welfares and Added Value Tax					
应交所得税 Income Tax Payable	应付利润 Profits Payable	亏损企业亏损额 Total Lossing of Loss-making Enterprises	利税总额 Total Pre-tax Profits	本年应付工资总额 Total Wags Payable	本年应付福利费总额 Total Welfares Payable	本年应交增值税 Added Value Tax	本年进项税额 Tax Include in Purchasing Cost	本年销项税额 Tax Include in Sales Cost	工业中间投入合计 Intermediate Input of Industry
40697	**86730**	**319684**	**440287**	**397860**	**110825**	**280911**	**643313**	**870690**	**4656088**
10969	12934	20136	197251	76843	25529	54638	206172	231663	1252105
29728	73796	299548	243036	321017	85296	226273	437142	639027	3403983
20191	55108	106768	183039	146507	43290	107553	214180	311235	1645128
1561	4754	61639	-23376	30497	9067	17372	46256	59337	357721
4731	9737	69520	43209	92982	21793	44464	104490	142297	904904
3246	4197	61621	40164	51032	11147	56884	72216	126159	496231
16681	24495	197990	109568	185810	45489	142326	222003	352196	1867584
12507	18205	139051	86236	129948	33345	101064	157441	249915	1247538
4174	6290	58939	23332	55862	12144	41262	64562	102280	620046
24017	62235	121694	330718	212050	65336	138585	421310	518494	2788504
1		33	-11	161	48	16		16	513
397	1133	14676	29261	19477	3965	11430	28036	32134	217894
23618	61102	106984	301468	192411	61324	127139	393275	486345	2570098
19872	49616	121429	216408	128418	47763	122743	221329	325433	1549871
2031	4473	19478	8555	27797	6817	15226	41105	53543	335941
18795	32641	178777	215323	241645	56245	142942	380878	491714	2770276

6-10 地方独立核算大中型工业企业主要经济指标

单位：万元

项目	Item	企业单位个数(个) Number of Enterprises (unit)	#亏损企业 Loss-making Enterprises	工业总产值(当年价格) Gross Output Value of Industry (at current price)	新产品产值 Value of New Products	工业总产值(1990年不变价格) Gross Output Value of Industry (at 1990 constant prices)	工业增加值(生产法) Added Value of Industry (with production method)
总计	**Total**	**434**	**147**	**7062931**	**1065432**	**6162063**	**1838498**
在总计中:	**Of Total:**						
工业系统	Industry System	287	82	5299401	912733	4780393	1282484
非工业系统	Non-Industry System	64	29	761283	5871	485980	230514
区县工业	Industry of District and County	66	26	678965	72365	573771	223492
其他	Others	17	10	323282	74463	321919	102008
在总计中:	**Of Total:**						
内资企业	Domestic Investment Enterprises	348	103	4957316	664290	3981930	1275175
国有企业	State-Owned	256	70	3545497	315685	2693371	889043
集体企业	Collective Owned	46	23	201946	29434	209102	46077
私营企业	Private Owned	1		2763		2348	740
联营企业	Joint Owned	23	4	127173	8473	143343	23991
股份合作企业	Share Holding Cooperative	3		27101	5782	25644	5452
股份有限公司	Share Holding Company	8	2	378279	234688	372617	93477
有限责任公司	Limited-Liability Company	11	4	674558	70229	535504	216396
其他企业	Others						
港澳台商投资企业	Hongkong,Macao and Taiwan Funded Enterprises	23	13	285750	4283	202137	37261
港澳台合资经营	Joint Venture	23	13	285750	4283	202137	37261
港澳台合作经营	Cooperative						
港澳台商独资企业	Hongkong,Macao and Taiwan Enterprises						
港澳台商投资股份有限公司	Hongkong,Macao and Taiwan Funded Share Holing Company						
外商投资企业	Foreign Funded Enterprises	63	31	1819865	396859	1977996	526062
中外合资经营	Joint Venture	52	23	1722991	383125	1888210	490792
中外合作经营	Cooperative	2	1	12670	259	12168	197
外资(独资)企业	Foreign Enterprises	6	4	33564	62	27449	22433
外商投资股份有限公司	Foreign Funded Share Holding Company	3	3	50640	13413	50169	12639
在总计中:	**Of Total:**						
农村企业	Rural Enterprises	15	4	67034	332	57586	17683
在总计中:	**Of Total:**						
轻工业	Light Industry	211	75	2076984	207992	1740130	652660
以农产品为原料	Using Farm Products as Raw Material	130	51	1428038	90139	1033838	477525
以非农产品为原料	Using Non-Farm Products as Raw Material	81	24	648946	117854	706292	175133
重工业	Heavy Industry	223	72	4985947	857440	4421933	1185839
采掘工业	Excavation	8	1	99947		40688	54453
原料工业	Raw Material	32	9	2373744	116043	1721531	438613
加工工业	Processing	183	62	2512257	741397	2659714	692774
在总计中:	**Of Total:**						
大型企业	Large Enterprises	209	73	6063026	969358	5381851	1538134
中型企业	Medium Enterprises	225	74	999906	96073	780212	300365

MAIN INDICATORS FOR LOCAL LARGE AND MEDIUM INDUSTRIAL ENTERPRISES WITH INDEPENDENT ACCOUNTING SYSTEM

(10000 yuan)

工业销售产值(当年价格) Sales Value of Industry (at current price)	出口交货值 Delivery Value of Exports	全部从业人员年平均人数(人) Average Number of Employment (person)	工业品自销零售额 Retail Sales of Self-selling Industrial Products	资产负债 Assets and Liabilities: 流动资产合计 Circulating Assets	应收帐款净额 Accounts Receivable	存货 Stock	产成品 Finished Products	流动资产平均余额 Average Balance of Circulating Assets	长期投资 Long-time Investment	固定资产合计 Fixed Assets
6924881	**482368**	**610394**	**676093**	**8006628**	**1920531**	**2702652**	**884319**	**7718401**	**1547539**	**9031208**
5227653	410888	485474	438615	5729058	1569310	2065528	630918	5582840	1303061	6668904
753568	17030	61207	145715	851399	175937	282805	138304	798269	66698	1551666
650752	44576	58156	81063	723551	91812	232901	81021	673019	127748	580507
292908	9875	5557	10699	702619	83473	121418	34076	664273	50032	230132
4886951	331237	542948	592762	5865102	1139129	2159215	750752	5665615	1477945	7645388
3539403	286797	393587	273939	4120642	784045	1599723	527460	3984048	1076812	5684754
173008	14077	29576	22657	497522	66854	137484	56642	476466	50863	247759
2519		300		1999	130	1623	973	1999		2105
127848	17876	27045	8146	242814	36579	89161	41070	239617	52752	186370
25834		1301	7000	53989	7067	16641	9012	46846	1293	20213
352924	7698	18763	266240	271936	46234	91946	31996	246621	96553	115880
665415	4789	72376	14780	676200	198221	222638	83600	670018	199673	1388306
284026	12023	13670	39714	284298	82362	77317	27555	272769	8812	139418
284026	12023	13670	39714	284298	82362	77317	27555	272769	8812	139418
1753905	139108	53776	43617	1857228	699041	466120	106012	1780017	60782	1246403
1657030	119810	43961	34088	1743764	664935	423332	89464	1670221	34277	1063191
13970	3192	1273	62	12649	4747	6504	2847	14103	5323	14085
27962	1049	1037	5	35479	5578	10457	3478	28909	19457	92641
54943	15058	7505	9463	65336	23781	25827	10222	66784	1725	76487
66615	25242	8765	6768	73861	16364	34020	21080	75912	4795	36293
2056415	207886	199591	247714	2683845	423807	850091	402536	2516796	419775	2271928
1403648	155645	124705	114465	1707268	261182	530363	246054	1603746	252780	1232685
652767	52240	74886	133248	976577	162625	319729	156482	913050	166995	1039243
4868466	274482	410803	428379	5322784	1496724	1852560	481784	5201605	1127765	6759280
94484	30653	36555	364	159945	72834	18823	8455	158898	11621	135581
2356988	107168	128343	38446	1811451	384190	714571	134378	1781628	524019	4317874
2416994	136661	245905	389570	3351388	1039700	1119167	338951	3261079	592125	2305825
5933090	405629	477700	599899	6891278	1665066	2297963	712215	6673125	1313040	8250683
991791	76739	132694	76193	1115350	255465	404688	172104	1045276	234500	780525

6-10 续表 1 continued

单位：万元

项目	Item	资产负债：固定资产原价合计 Original Value of Fixed Assets	# 生产经营用 For Productive Use	累计折旧 Accumulative Depreciation	#本年折旧 Depreciation in this Year	固定资产净值年平均余额 Average Net Value of Fixed Assets	无形资产及递延资产 Intangible and Deferred Assets
总计	**Total**	**11599883**	**10395552**	**3765504**	**508814**	**7616767**	**887648**
在总计中：	**Of Total:**						
工业系统	Industry System	8738304	7853050	3073839	369336	5609805	742954
非工业系统	Non-Industry System	1934933	1781087	468117	89973	1369936	43173
区县工业	Industry of District and County	641632	515882	160870	29264	437490	56345
其他	Others	285013	245533	62679	20240	199536	45176
在总计中：	**Of Total:**						
内资企业	Domestic Investment Enterprises	9807149	8746253	3215505	374291	6404357	719313
国有企业	State-Owned	7438672	6773082	2606882	302546	4715166	356222
集体企业	Collective Owned	312778	223292	90521	12191	184364	37242
私营企业	Private Owned	3498	3498	1487	110	2011	16
联营企业	Joint Owned	244438	148597	76908	12093	167272	16639
股份合作企业	Share Holding Cooperative	17027	13816	4171	879	13687	5177
股份有限公司	Share Holding Company	139055	130157	45337	6223	92056	14813
有限责任公司	Limited-Liability Company	1651681	1453812	390199	40249	1229801	289205
其他企业	Others						
港澳台商投资企业	Hongkong,Macao and Taiwan Funded Enterprises	183770	159571	50312	12914	131465	26400
港澳台合资经营	Joint Venture	183770	159571	50312	12914	131465	26400
港澳台合作经营	Cooperative						
港澳台商独资企业	Hongkong,Macao and Taiwan Enterprises						
港澳台商投资股份有限公司	Hongkong,Macao and Taiwan Funded Share Holing Company						
外商投资企业	Foreign Funded Enterprises	1608964	1489729	499687	121609	1080945	141934
中外合资经营	Joint Venture	1380392	1289529	437988	110023	938001	115430
中外合作经营	Cooperative	19025	18645	6404	1523	13363	2319
外资(独资)企业	Foreign Enterprises	101479	76858	14827	6088	63490	13688
外商投资股份有限公司	Foreign Funded Share Holding Company	108068	104698	40468	3975	66092	10498
在总计中：	**Of Total:**						
农村企业	Rural Enterprises	48023	37513	13833	1927	33490	1478
在总计中：	**Of Total:**						
轻工业	Light Industry	2832955	2447263	819663	136082	1991936	284008
以农产品为原料	Using Farm Products as Raw Material	1520084	1276052	444524	76534	1046271	140608
以非农产品为原料	Using Non-Farm Products as Raw Material	1312871	1171211	375139	59549	945665	143401
重工业	Heavy Industry	8766928	7948290	2945841	372732	5624831	603640
采掘工业	Excavation	192194	128888	66242	6504	116768	7147
原料工业	Raw Material	5604879	5366509	1809986	215499	3668295	379153
加工工业	Processing	2969855	2452893	1069613	150729	1839769	217339
在总计中：	**Of Total:**						
大型企业	Large Enterprises	10604557	9600715	3427981	467887	6979566	786776
中型企业	Medium Enterprises	995326	794837	337524	40927	637201	100871

6-10 续表 2 continued

(10000 yuan)

Assets and Liabilities										
#无形资产 Intangible Assets	其他资产 Other Assets	资产总计 Total Assets	流动负债合计 Liquid Liabilities	短期借款 Short-time Loans	长期负债合计 Long-term Liabilities	长期借款 Long-time Loans	负债合计 Total Liabilities	所有者权益 Ownership Interest	实收资本 Contributed Capital	国家资本 State
232078	**97866**	**19570889**	**8065048**	**3553776**	**3395535**	**2525608**	**11492071**	**8078818**	**4928079**	**2624578**
133883	19605	14463582	6179655	2843721	2931331	2120301	9120390	5343192	2980671	1487941
25245	9398	2522334	708133	273181	244973	217422	956571	1565763	1203596	1015692
35572	8589	1496740	669973	207551	174247	143893	846637	650103	372048	116945
37379	60274	1088233	507287	229324	44985	43992	568473	519760	371766	4000
93707	30338	15738086	6311516	2792266	3037004	2188109	9350831	6387255	3481752	2423083
47391	-13195	11225236	4440114	2056213	1768318	1018275	6210743	5014493	2675292	2080562
22598	45245	878632	536342	178814	109229	103718	645571	233060	149837	4678
		4120	1905	129	1755		3660	460	201	95
270		498574	289289	113850	68757	55610	358046	140528	93250	26244
2175		80672	47465	32025	5556	5400	53021	27651	25959	
8421	82	499264	156645	47931	20198	8236	176843	322421	161660	32873
12851	-1794	2551588	839756	363304	1063191	996870	1902947	648642	375553	278631
21530	32819	491747	290551	125001	22091	20802	316860	174887	180862	52078
21530	32819	491747	290551	125001	22091	20802	316860	174887	180862	52078
116842	34709	3341056	1462981	636509	336440	316696	1824380	1516676	1265466	149416
90973	31209	2987870	1335487	589019	308478	292333	1653163	1334707	1081203	142124
2319		34375	13817	7182	8686	8686	22503	11872	16713	7083
13266	1124	162389	31982	12631	13370	13370	61114	101275	108189	
10284	2376	156421	81695	27677	5905	2307	87600	68821	59361	210
464	753	117180	53503	18614	6132	4357	60570	56610	46390	1319
92575	72938	5732494	2578614	1210979	769576	659225	3370629	2361865	1741930	661398
68215	29637	3362977	1528417	722795	341172	282171	1890476	1472500	1080647	310638
24360	43302	2369517	1050197	488184	428404	377054	1480153	889364	661283	350760
139504	24928	13838395	5486434	2342797	2625959	1866382	8121441	5716954	3186150	1963179
		314293	127274	44668	64928	48368	192202	122091	70173	66587
56031	-2182	7030316	2236177	1121871	1622046	1034842	3858223	3172094	1608570	1511865
83473	27109	6493786	3122984	1176259	938985	783173	4071017	2422769	1507407	384727
204543	68057	17309834	6924790	3132339	3112187	2304871	10065808	7244026	4271584	2307261
27535	29809	2261055	1140258	421437	283348	220736	1426263	834792	656495	317317

6-10 续表 3 continued

单位：万元

项目	Item	资产负债 Assets and Liabilities				
		集体资本 Collective	法人资本 Institutional Units	个人资本 Individuals	港澳台资本 Hongkong, Macao and Taiwan	外商资本 Foreign
总计	**Total**	**166254**	**1138004**	**67038**	**83445**	**848760**
在总计中:	**Of Total:**					
工业系统	Industry System	88879	948841	26232	15927	412851
非工业系统	Non-Industry System	11668	23425		31377	121433
区县工业	Industry of District and County	59700	101996	16622	18248	58536
其他	Others	6007	63742	24184	17893	255940
在总计中:	**Of Total:**					
内资企业	Domestic Investment Enterprises	153767	823299	37515	5996	38091
国有企业	State-Owned	23521	555647	15562		
集体企业	Collective Owned	91926	23780	315	5996	23141
私营企业	Private Owned	5	101			
联营企业	Joint Owned	31825	35181			
股份合作企业	Share Holding Cooperative	3200	22711	47		
股份有限公司	Share Holding Company		92247	21590		14950
有限责任公司	Limited-Liability Company	3290	93632			
其他企业	Others					
港澳台商投资企业	Hongkong,Macao and Taiwan Funded Enterprises	3257	41602	10458	53987	19479
港澳台合资经营	Joint Venture	3257	41602	10458	53987	19479
港澳台合作经营	Cooperative					
港澳台商独资企业	Hongkong,Macao and Taiwan Enterprises					
港澳台商投资股份有限公司	Hongkong,Macao and Taiwan Funded Share Holing Company					
外商投资企业	Foreign Funded Enterprises	9230	273103	19066	23463	791190
中外合资经营	Joint Venture	9230	247638	13726	11463	657023
中外合作经营	Cooperative					9630
外资(独资)企业	Foreign Enterprises				12000	96189
外商投资股份有限公司	Foreign Funded Share Holding Company		25464	5340		28347
在总计中:	**Of Total:**					
农村企业	Rural Enterprises	16255	23027	48	1156	4585
在总计中:	**Of Total:**					
轻工业	Light Industry	89776	411335	40538	56016	482867
以农产品为原料	Using Farm Products as Raw Material	51324	221007	26813	48270	422595
以非农产品为原料	Using Non-Farm Products as Raw Material	38451	190328	13726	7746	60272
重工业	Heavy Industry	76479	726669	26500	27429	365894
采掘工业	Excavation		3586			
原料工业	Raw Material	8107	70636	305		17657
加工工业	Processing	68371	652448	26195	27429	348237
在总计中:	**Of Total:**					
大型企业	Large Enterprises	88953	962928	50441	70637	791365
中型企业	Medium Enterprises	77301	175076	16598	12808	57395

6-10 续表 4 continued

(10000 yuan)

损 益 及 分 配 Profits,Loss and Distribution										
产品销售收入 Sales Revenue					管理费用 Overhead Cost				财务费用 Financial Expenses	
	产品销售成本 Cost of Sales	产品销售费用 Expenses of Sales	产品销售税金及附加 Sales Tax and Extra Charges	产品销售利润 Sales Profits		税金 Taxes	财产保险费 Premium of Property	劳动待业保险费 Premium for Employment Insurance		利息支出 Expenses of Interest
7814194	**6576167**	**271774**	**115452**	**850301**	**849605**	**34912**	**10434**	**173874**	**316830**	**300317**
5817215	4906828	167176	47280	695932	659205	25913	7729	155199	266476	263526
1010193	886005	49148	34711	39830	112757	5752	1545	14548	23712	21762
649508	495596	30521	33060	90331	54292	2911	1136	4091	15544	11030
337278	287738	24930	401	24209	23351	336	24	36	11098	3999
5694281	4847991	139068	95472	611250	672331	30503	8231	170889	239902	236989
4376978	3718506	96683	89114	472175	498751	21648	5174	144199	186684	186543
192495	167014	7324	789	17368	31674	628	340	3905	10926	6945
2153	1755		2	396	144				180	165
129714	116121	3850	1509	8233	29354	2840	380	5133	8851	8767
22325	14545	2791	184	4806	2393	85	18	356	2629	2627
383048	316632	15714	1257	49445	25666	2497	210	2721	3285	2442
587568	513419	12706	2617	58826	84350	2806	2109	14576	27347	29499
286661	257626	12589	686	15759	22653	636	242	53	6440	7068
286661	257626	12589	686	15759	22653	636	242	53	6440	7068
1833252	1470550	120117	19294	223292	154621	3772	1961	2931	70488	56260
1736790	1393893	107217	18715	216965	141590	3353	1791	2313	64913	51683
13489	11124	936	395	1034	1318	8	35	15	524	515
29105	21806	6078		1221	4093	175	18		1504	431
53869	43727	5887	184	4072	7620	235	118	604	3546	3631
66221	52920	6177	129	6996	5243	129	76	1	2035	1526
2341849	1887634	145783	78108	229825	277224	8303	4269	45396	78225	71123
1593051	1264335	89551	72085	166579	174543	4542	2909	27638	43870	40158
748798	623299	56232	6022	63245	102681	3761	1361	17758	34355	30965
5472346	4688533	125991	37345	620477	572381	26609	6164	128478	238605	229194
104125	62032	10339	1318	30435	25594	610	66	16109	1913	1843
2813406	2513179	24883	14446	260898	222370	11743	2993	59412	125085	123414
2554815	2113322	90769	21581	329144	324417	14256	3105	52957	111606	103937
6888409	5835634	229685	74377	748714	717767	28800	7861	151124	282787	267945
925785	740533	42089	41075	101588	131838	6112	2572	22750	34043	32372

6-10 续表 5 continued

单位：万元

项目	Item	营业利润 Operating Profits	投资收益 Investment Income	补贴收入 Subsidy Income	营业外收入 Out-business Income	营业外支出 Out-business Expenditure	利润总额 Total Profits
		损益及分配 Profits,Loss and Distribution					
总计	**Total**	**-193733**	**70885**	**112301**	**159259**	**59527**	**95285**
在总计中:	**Of Total:**						
工业系统	Industry System	-123638	59889	59601	139384	45975	94622
非工业系统	Non-Industry System	-88096	4155	51621	15162	5108	-22440
区县工业	Industry of District and County	25410	4376	1080	3905	1687	33915
其他	Others	-7409	2465		808	6757	-10812
在总计中:	**Of Total:**						
内资企业	Domestic Investment Enterprises	-183495	68601	112296	116120	45317	71150
国有企业	State-Owned	-128799	49332	88976	88104	36197	64572
集体企业	Collective Owned	-16765	2499		2335	1098	-12914
私营企业	Private Owned	72					72
联营企业	Joint Owned	-19541	2520	210	18477	2046	-445
股份合作企业	Share Holding Cooperative	1031	104		319	320	1134
股份有限公司	Share Holding Company	20231	6178	1059	2291	3587	26067
有限责任公司	Limited-Liability Company	-39723	7968	22052	4593	2070	-7336
其他企业	Others						
港澳台商投资企业	Hongkong,Macao and Taiwan Funded Enterprises	-13755	139		1207	978	-13313
港澳台合资经营	Joint Venture	-13755	139		1207	978	-13313
港澳台合作经营	Cooperative						
港澳台商独资企业	Hongkong,Macao and Taiwan Enterprises						
港澳台商投资股份有限公司	Hongkong,Macao and Taiwan Funded Share Holing Company						
外商投资企业	Foreign Funded Enterprises	3518	2145	5	41932	13232	37448
中外合资经营	Joint Venture	16060	1966	5	41700	12615	50197
中外合作经营	Cooperative	-731			4	27	-754
外资(独资)企业	Foreign Enterprises	-4190			79	513	-4623
外商投资股份有限公司	Foreign Funded Share Holding Company	-7622	178		149	78	-7372
在总计中:	**Of Total:**						
农村企业	Rural Enterprises	-325	171		215	216	-141
在总计中:	**Of Total:**						
轻工业	Light Industry	-64244	27253	21188	44974	18398	11966
以农产品为原料	Using Farm Products as Raw Material	-25257	16613	6777	30513	11898	17106
以非农产品为原料	Using Non-Farm Products as Raw Material	-38987	10640	14410	14462	6501	-5140
重工业	Heavy Industry	-129489	43632	91114	114284	41129	83319
采掘工业	Excavation	-9390	1051	14444	406	3342	4975
原料工业	Raw Material	-61832	14516	68751	23222	18449	26419
加工工业	Processing	-58267	28065	7919	90657	19337	51925
在总计中:	**Of Total:**						
大型企业	Large Enterprises	-160854	68159	109561	141131	51857	111314
中型企业	Medium Enterprises	-32879	2726	2740	18128	7670	-16029

6-10 续表 6 continued

(10000 yuan)

				工资，福利费，增值税 Wages,Welfares and Added Value Tax					
应交所得税 Income Tax Payable	应付利润 Profits Payable	亏损企业亏损额 Total Lossing of Loss-making Enterprises	利税总额 Total Pre-tax Profits	本年应付工资总额 Total Wags Payable	本年应付福利费总额 Total Welfares Payable	本年应交增值税 Added Value Tax	本年进项税额 Tax Include in Purchasing Cost	本年销项税额 Tax Include in Sales Cost	工业中间投入合计 Intermediate Input of Industry
49467	**63008**	**227760**	**619807**	**745894**	**124285**	**409070**	**953537**	**1332094**	**5633503**
31028	55463	133581	429457	599150	99783	287555	719413	984617	4304472
6829	2095	48810	59406	84729	14688	47135	111621	152916	577904
10022	5450	17581	100826	50856	7965	33851	82239	114191	489324
1588		27788	30118	11159	1850	40529	40264	80371	261803
30100	11770	93834	447665	624211	83611	281043	719781	982181	3963184
22473	6094	59454	381360	490965	65235	227674	509357	722146	2884128
506	455	14426	-5525	20959	3188	6600	36810	42592	162469
			106	175	25	32	30	33	2055
207	15	2151	5544	21871	2720	4480	18064	20664	107662
177	33		2874	956	251	1556	2655	4212	23205
5048	5174	2877	40784	20526	2388	13460	81839	94862	298262
1689		14926	22522	68759	9804	27241	71027	97673	485403
1279	2145	19805	-4522	15559	3120	8105	37717	43765	256594
1279	2145	19805	-4522	15559	3120	8105	37717	43765	256594
18087	49093	114121	176664	106124	37555	119922	196039	306148	1413725
17483	49072	97441	183637	96016	34144	114725	187643	292733	1346924
10	21	785	323	1087	284	682	1620	2151	13155
594		8522	-2664	2730	1140	1959	2093	4042	13090
		7372	-4632	6290	1987	2556	4683	7223	40557
347	473	1284	1620	6525	1687	1632	4902	6417	50983
22315	9616	110708	229024	190933	32737	138950	257812	385049	1563274
16716	6703	83216	191711	118615	21982	102520	186684	280082	1053033
5599	2913	27492	37311	72318	10755	36429	71128	104967	510242
27151	53393	117052	390785	554961	91548	270121	695725	947046	4070229
62		149	13348	34839	4829	7055	7581	14402	52549
5479	808	13038	196375	254698	35905	155510	326374	475534	2090641
21611	52585	103865	181062	265424	50815	107556	361771	457110	1927039
41035	60837	181681	547402	624566	106328	361711	843726	1178907	4886603
8432	2172	46079	72405	121328	17958	47359	109810	153187	746900

6-11 地方独立核算大中型工业企业主要经济指标(按行业分)

单位：万元

项目	Item	企业单位个数(个) Number of Enterprises (unit)	#亏损企业 Loss-making Enterprises	工业总产值(当年价格) Gross Output Value of Industry (at current price)	新产品产值 Value of New Products	工业总产值(1990年不变价格) Gross Output Value of Industry (at 1990 constant prices)	工业增加值(生产法) Added Value of Industry (with production method)
煤炭采选业	Coal Mining and Dressing	1		86946		33356	50164
黑色金属矿采选业	Ferrous Metals Mining and Processing	3		10477		6158	3435
非金属矿采选业	Nonmetal Minerals Mining and Processing	4	1	2524		1174	853
食品加工业	Food Processing	26	17	429832	50947	293753	52440
食品制造业	Food Making	15	8	84118	1491	53895	18867
饮料制造业	Beverage Production	15	5	353790	12849	242867	161381
纺织业	Textile Industry	22	6	215257	19825	173857	89946
服装及其他纤维制品制造业	Garments and Other Fiber Products	16	5	65035	210	47633	16533
皮革、毛皮、羽绒及其制品业	Leather,Furs,Down and Related Products	4		3508	18	2603	233
木材加工及竹、藤、棕、草制品业	Timber Processing,Bamboo,Cane, Palm Fiber and Straw Products	1	1	3802		2269	687
家具制造业	Furniture Manufacturing	1		3103		3202	326
造纸及纸制品业	Papermaking and Paper Products	7	2	75814		65624	27008
印刷业、记录媒介的复制	Printing and Record Medium Reproduced	16	4	60235		45378	35217
文教、体育用品制造	Stationery,Educational and Sports Goods	7		35785	4925	25572	10994
化学原料及化学制品制造业	Raw Chemical Materials and Chemical Products	23	10	561771	57134	574081	128440
医药制造业	Medical and Pharmaceutical Product	11	3	111404	6917	110347	10724
化学纤维制造业	Chemical Fibers	5	5	29834	393	40818	38
橡胶制品业	Rubber Products	8	4	80381	9403	103672	13999
塑料制品业	Plastic Products	15	6	50401	1384	51089	1257
非金属矿物制品业	Nonmetal Mineral Products	31	8	364968	24683	288731	129516
黑色金属冶炼及压延加工业	Smelting and Pressing of Ferrous Metals	7	3	1637842	58681	1072707	210135
金属制品业	Metal Products	16	5	29745	259	26479	9768
普通机械制造业	Ordinary Machinery Manufacturing	30	9	208058	38855	178333	64439
专用设备制造业	Special Purposes Equipment Manufacturing	28	9	436692	234887	423419	110515
交通运输设备制造业	Transportation Equipment Manufacturing	20	10	478533	264950	423916	88352
电气机械及器材制造	Electric Equipment and Machinery	29	11	278989	104180	303314	66021
电子及通信设备制造	Electronic and Telecommunications	39	10	986868	154187	1314374	307467
仪器仪表及文化、办公用机械制造业	Instruments,Meters,Cultural and Official Machine Manufacturing	14	1	36044	4092	38333	14180
其他制造业	Other Manufacturing	10	4	65136	11238	64762	42942
电力、蒸汽、热水的生产和供应业	Electricity,Steam and Hot Water Production and Supply	3		90138		35297	59928
煤气生产和供应业	Gas Production and Supply	3		36993		31654	28510
自来水的生产和供应	Water Production and Supply	1		67495		22989	38042

MAIN INDICATORS FOR LOCAL LARGE AND MEDIUM INDUSTRIAL ENTERPRISES WITH INDEPENDENT ACCOUNTING SYSTEM(BY SECTOR)

(10000 yuan)

工业销售产值(当年价格) Sales Value of Industry (at current price)	出口交货值 Delivery Value of Exports	全部从业人员年平均人数(人) Average Number of Employment (person)	工业品自销零售额 Retail Sales of Self-selling Industrial Products	资产负债 Assets and Liabilities: 流动资产合计 Circulating Assets	应收帐款净额 Accounts Receivable	存货 Stock	产成品 Finished Products	流动资产平均余额 Average Balance of Circulating Assets	长期投资 Long-time Investment	固定资产合计 Fixed Assets
82173	30653	33921		140239	64057	12627	5984	137600	8995	104963
9800		1542		14385	7590	4918	1330	16298	1472	18081
2512		1092	364	5321	1187	1278	1141	5000	1154	12536
416111	605	10647	11459	490336	59358	86615	23608	474320	19800	123831
76780	126	8078	39	171199	20706	23421	10048	152183	33770	181138
353222	10496	18227	66033	277287	36000	104959	17574	237838	93040	334871
211213	91834	46077	1128	260667	44792	115912	65806	235559	43858	248390
69937	43820	13364	8119	92967	20481	37501	26512	94049	9367	45977
3807	291	4664	453	34917	4981	7179	4606	31006	2559	20015
3176		1763	3000	13812	2418	9484	7082	13983	1225	4800
3971		523	3306	3170	1180	1521	1288	3362	290	2732
74534	1031	5802		101509	25492	23036	12847	104798	23761	69268
58893	602	6937	2728	61510	13925	13435	2978	52180	11214	96801
35572	8370	5983	8904	46694	11844	20554	7863	43512	4709	38862
545731	17086	37949	4866	413446	109748	155989	61848	418883	91739	1055116
109236	9984	14289	21681	288128	46187	129056	89298	273168	28557	150970
30230	155	5012		29352	4235	17738	7591	30488	1069	63797
81937	7495	8589	2790	94843	15977	51906	22446	90853	7257	102352
49076	929	10093	2579	84328	10304	33232	11121	79624	24549	117986
360519	12452	53614	40052	446656	105097	125562	67076	424245	159856	521843
1630400	100064	63861		1126667	179745	547660	74232	1098979	333892	2355321
31896	4621	9083	1640	62174	11655	20111	10984	62181	4831	46551
201771	4675	46726	26342	479822	121570	184959	46319	492629	43559	365796
422849	2718	48024	290745	475117	78393	217603	80993	459127	112410	384229
487984	10991	40847	44208	514144	171128	160228	43347	539365	213304	380208
272036	23951	34270	9920	513947	163429	159276	61358	478749	44700	226812
913205	92619	42844	52691	1365098	484501	351671	89776	1288022	190751	688691
37371	2800	10524	2047	80850	11268	36538	16878	77633	20887	52084
69063	2071	3228	835	53408	25929	12815	7817	50324	3917	33482
92247		7664		86441	33041	2219	255	87732	2494	335905
36993		8147	6878	69705	22947	7330	20	65612	4228	370623
69845		5168	62384	78087	2984	6764	2813	68552	1695	425906

6-11 续表 1 continued

单位：万元

项目	Item	资产负债 固定资产原价合计 Original Value of Fixed Assets	# 生产经营用 For Productive Use	累计折旧 Accumulative Depreciation	#本年折旧 Depreciation in this Year	固定资产净值年平均余额 Average Net Value of Fixed Assets	无形资产及递延资产 Intangible and Deferred Assets
煤炭采选业	Coal Mining and Dressing	159822	98081	57582	5489	94312	2828
黑色金属矿采选业	Ferrous Metals Mining and Processing	16660	16660	4040	846	11188	2236
非金属矿采选业	Nonmetal Minerals Mining and Processing	15712	14146	4620	169	11267	2083
食品加工业	Food Processing	157815	124404	46430	9300	113608	16722
食品制造业	Food Making	213237	175849	52503	11717	150066	20574
饮料制造业	Beverage Production	362767	330605	85295	19217	270345	36464
纺织业	Textile Industry	364665	303548	133656	14785	232913	32633
服装及其他纤维制品制造业	Garments and Other Fiber Products	62397	49111	19817	2534	42468	2861
皮革、毛皮、羽绒及其制品业	Leather,Furs,Down and Related Products	22692	20580	6928	1000	15226	2501
木材加工及竹、藤、棕、草制品业	Timber Processing,Bamboo,Cane, Palm Fiber and Straw Products	8242	5431	3442	291	4968	25
家具制造业	Furniture Manufacturing	3377	2223	1604	64	1780	16
造纸及纸制品业	Papermaking and Paper Products	70406	64342	18394	3157	48607	21835
印刷业、记录煤介的复制	Printing and Record Medium Re-. produced	122811	87492	35363	8683	82159	4723
文教、体育用品制造	Stationery,Educational and Sports Goods	44864	37071	14637	1918	28421	3319
化学原料及化学制品制造业	Raw Chemical Materials and Chemical Products	1256330	1108115	279071	29377	933623	287547
医药制造业	Medical and Pharmaceutical Product	158756	138202	42856	6159	111179	11138
化学纤维制造业	Chemical Fibers	97026	81673	33803	1718	64743	32596
橡胶制品业	Rubber Products	93855	77940	29057	3421	52864	13121
塑料制品业	Plastic Products	155757	91687	43705	4150	112713	32160
非金属矿物制品业	Nonmetal Mineral Products	651749	539754	184095	29929	461938	79154
黑色金属冶炼及压延加工业	Smelting and Pressing of Ferrous Metals	3232094	3228370	1277269	134592	1970600	56385
金属制品业	Metal Products	56008	46807	18384	2654	35794	4728
普通机械制造业	Ordinary Machinery Manufacturing	462781	383649	165744	15690	291536	37521
专用设备制造业	Special Purposes Equipment Manufacturing	468675	379117	175203	13777	288293	14135
交通运输设备制造业	Transportation Equipment Manufacturing	453484	405368	187448	28150	252502	9550
电气机械及器材制造	Electric Equipment and Machinery	322089	268373	119983	15114	203270	22332
电子及通信设备制造	Electronic and Telecommunications	951491	784753	329952	67997	597595	110147
仪器仪表及文化、办公用机械制造业	Instruments,Meters,Cultural and Official Machine Manufacturing	73068	60912	29385	5828	44078	4703
其他制造业	Other Manufacturing	40864	36208	11177	2027	26673	1360
电力、蒸汽、热水的生产和供应业	Electricity,Steam and Hot Water Production and Supply	425878	396305	99109	16926	231238	710
煤气生产和供应业	Gas Production and Supply	464487	448149	104999	22378	354439	
自来水的生产和供应	Water Production and Supply	546413	532760	130387	27411	431880	728

6-11 续表 2 continued

(10000 yuan)

Assets and Liabilities										
#无形资产 Intangible Assets	其他资产 Other Assets	资产总计 Total Assets	流动负债合计 Liquid Liabilities	短期借款 Short-time Loans	长期负债合计 Long-term Liabilities	长期借款 Long-time Loans	负债合计 Total Liabilities	所有者权益 Ownership Interest	实收资本 Contributed Capital	国家资本 State
		257024	109327	34620	50165	40029	159492	97533	60025	60025
		36175	12481	8350	10669	5588	23150	13025	6563	6563
		21094	5466	1698	4094	2751	9560	11533	3586	
13373	10356	661044	341634	96278	30531	20936	375629	285415	139538	69195
8721	3750	410430	181528	108961	59403	55688	257133	153297	275238	37163
30613	2125	743786	238168	117876	38690	29017	277548	466239	275239	96812
4030		585548	333721	213680	118308	110070	452308	133240	121198	14552
	694	151866	71173	20505	9199	5613	80589	71276	55961	3735
		59992	40082	14095	6033	5053	46115	13877	11722	3543
	527	20388	15440	370	742	30	16182	4207	2941	
		6208	3908	1811	725		4632	1576	973	
6972	10950	227323	109376	53320	30073	20603	139448	87874	58706	
2804	864	175111	51662	16578	36427	27227	88089	87022	65087	18768
1588	5	93589	54215	31614	7597	7140	62530	31060	17904	733
17778	421	1848269	572994	282801	895923	836454	1469440	378829	232705	183063
7906	342	479134	269636	127121	42218	13522	311854	167281	76127	25046
	199	127012	44095	21516	80456	79182	124552	2461	23717	959
582		217573	140209	50237	45041	42064	185250	32323	20915	7165
1676		259023	128300	53898	65860	61917	194160	64863	54878	10118
11268	9460	1216970	462622	165883	297950	259479	760613	456357	275942	150092
40062	-2240	3870024	1507414	788251	534903	20247	2042317	1827707	680654	648143
2725	1918	120202	72342	35457	15649	14097	88261	31941	33577	8312
19895	2695	929393	484459	186198	162920	142564	647379	282014	203793	55120
2259	-1188	984703	486859	146591	75132	40491	563088	421616	180828	13411
5550	3272	1120478	485809	207275	125684	102018	611493	508985	369946	127542
6758	39301	847092	522439	262008	88946	67470	611385	235707	165354	10093
43284	13218	2367906	1099041	460654	368657	339387	1475650	892256	534009	157231
1988	654	159178	68613	23670	16786	7433	85399	73778	56228	14893
899	544	92712	45319	6596	8543	7548	53897	38816	27503	5079
710		425551	44918	9700	12572	11710	57489	368061	278626	278626
		444556	25306		10150	6501	35456	409100	291779	291779
621		506416	15490		110544	110544	126034	380382	284828	284828

6-11 续表 3 continued

单位：万元

项目	Item	资产负债 Assets and Liabilities				
		集体资本 Collective	法人资本 Institutional Units	个人资本 Individuals	港澳台资本 Hongkong, Macao and Taiwan	外商资本 Foreign
煤炭采选业	Coal Mining and Dressing					
黑色金属矿采选业	Ferrous Metals Mining and Processing					
非金属矿采选业	Nonmetal Minerals Mining and Processing		3586			
食品加工业	Food Processing	362	11260		25335	33387
食品制造业	Food Making	39	3171		16894	217970
饮料制造业	Beverage Production	4597	47519	15562	1125	109623
纺织业	Textile Industry	11545	91660	745	2361	335
服装及其他纤维制品制造业	Garments and Other Fiber Products	16632	28772			6822
皮革、毛皮、羽绒及其制品业	Leather,Furs,Down and Related Products	4799	3381			
木材加工及竹、藤、棕、草制品业	Timber Processing,Bamboo,Cane, Palm Fiber and Straw Products		2941			
家具制造业	Furniture Manufacturing		973			
造纸及纸制品业	Papermaking and Paper Products	3173	21532	10505		23496
印刷业、记录煤介的复制	Printing and Record Medium Reproduced	2923	10371		2062	30963
文教、体育用品制造	Stationery,Educational and Sports Goods	4058	12806		306	
化学原料及化学制品制造业	Raw Chemical Materials and Chemical Products	3789	31111			14742
医药制造业	Medical and Pharmaceutical Product	6065	30142		850	14023
化学纤维制造业	Chemical Fibers		22758			
橡胶制品业	Rubber Products	3004	10747			
塑料制品业	Plastic Products	7787	30580		697	5697
非金属矿物制品业	Nonmetal Mineral Products	11991	79145	10		34704
黑色金属冶炼及压延加工业	Smelting and Pressing of Ferrous Metals	8107	24099	305		
金属制品业	Metal Products	9224	5771		5893	4378
普通机械制造业	Ordinary Machinery Manufacturing	6801	65908	41		75923
专用设备制造业	Special Purposes Equipment Manufacturing	2100	145317	20000		
交通运输设备制造业	Transportation Equipment Manufacturing	14183	160642	5299	11463	50818
电气机械及器材制造	Electric Equipment and Machinery	22519	96827	13726		22189
电子及通信设备制造	Electronic and Telecommunications	17646	160658	845	5996	191634
仪器仪表及文化、办公用机械制造业	Instruments,Meters,Cultural and Official Machine Manufacturing	474	30891		9971	
其他制造业	Other Manufacturing	4437	5435		493	12059
电力、蒸汽、热水的生产和供应业	Electricity,Steam and Hot Water Production and Supply					
煤气生产和供应业	Gas Production and Supply					
自来水的生产和供应	Water Production and Supply					

6-11 续表 4 continued

(10000 yuan)

损益及分配 Profits,Loss and Distribution										
产品销售收入 Sales Revenue	产品销售成本 Cost of Sales	产品销售费用 Expenses of Sales	产品销售税金及附加 Sales Tax and Extra Charges	产品销售利润 Sales Profits	管理费用 Overhead Cost	税金 Taxes	财产保险费 Premium of Property	劳动待业保险费 Premium for Employment Insurance	财务费用 Financial Expenses	利息支出 Expenses of Interest
90454	52353	10088	859	27155	23282	535	55	15497	1165	1158
11261	7914	236	447	2664	1090	50	9	242	630	566
2410	1765	16	12	617	1222	24	2	370	119	119
432940	405974	5590	119	21257	18177	524	237	1080	5695	5858
124036	94907	28404	231	493	22566	593	316	2428	9526	5991
348118	219928	23773	40842	63575	36401	609	400	2576	5880	4719
203843	185308	4906	576	13053	31789	1130	573	10878	7050	9435
72440	61707	6575	112	3546	9233	286	213	1414	2184	2087
3746	4158	478	2	-891	3285	143	72	1296	1206	1205
2547	2194		16	338	1137	40	5	317	452	451
4037	3384	47	14	592	770	16	15	251	159	159
71666	51652	6761	71	13182	12831	305	206	2276	3013	2007
59643	43743	1007	249	14644	12109	334	177	2194	2564	2121
42983	34952	1596	220	6215	7665	239	121	1630	1963	1867
480321	423164	10371	5182	41604	57347	1840	2102	10431	21118	22829
297478	233393	32349	1038	30698	34805	690	520	3412	13350	12390
28941	28924	354	63	-399	5314	161	166	917	2343	2593
86391	69231	2344	4496	10320	7261	207	127	2316	5679	5674
53605	47867	1778	77	3882	11795	611	127	2668	6711	6642
351102	285353	11826	1678	52245	51789	1713	1241	10379	14513	13799
2037112	1783702	12335	11011	230065	130320	8529		43708	100064	96502
23418	20353	1469	38	1558	5732	454	43	1124	2357	2317
215207	183163	5916	480	25648	43547	2206	548	12595	11188	11018
413741	331273	13627	1562	67279	60806	3904	353	9007	12892	12719
525247	489791	12675	13555	9226	57877	3760	411	7285	21239	19825
274705	219422	14207	987	40088	46046	1293	376	8202	15882	13910
1151183	922172	47518	847	180645	101737	2279	1277	10212	45294	40061
37587	30745	2426	104	4313	8548	297	123	2499	1648	1687
42567	17397	12665	230	12275	9383	146	127	792	878	675
79033	84505	27	517	-6017	10246	554	150	2011	-251	-254
110913	131087		412	-20586	11418	406	74	1112	-85	-85
55677	61087		368	-5778	8251	897		1992	-685	-820

6-11 续表 5 continued

单位：万元

项目	Item	损益及分配 Profits,Loss and Distribution 营业利润 Operating Profits	投资收益 Investment Income	补贴收入 Subsidy Income	营业外收入 Out-business Income	营业外支出 Out-business Expenditure	利润总额 Total Profits
煤炭采选业	Coal Mining and Dressing	-9213	986	14444	309	3280	5053
黑色金属矿采选业	Ferrous Metals Mining and Processing	108	-42		30	24	71
非金属矿采选业	Nonmetal Minerals Mining and Processing	-284	106		67	39	-149
食品加工业	Food Processing	-1291	1641	1952	304	652	1954
食品制造业	Food Making	-30128	1327		3041	4428	-30114
饮料制造业	Beverage Production	24262	2985	48	5194	1902	30710
纺织业	Textile Industry	-20992	3139	4520	15295	2071	397
服装及其他纤维制品制造业	Garments and Other Fiber Products	-2644	424	121	1335	178	-942
皮革、毛皮、羽绒及其制品业	Leather,Furs,Down and Related Products	-3080	28		3082	28	2
木材加工及竹、藤、棕、草制品业	Timber Processing,Bamboo,Cane, Palm Fiber and Straw Products	-1179	120	69		8	-999
家具制造业	Furniture Manufacturing	-29	69		3	43	
造纸及纸制品业	Papermaking and Paper Products	-306	4862	68	1157	1648	4133
印刷业、记录煤介的复制	Printing and Record Medium Reproduced	2532	701		1049	141	4141
文教、体育用品制造	Stationery,Educational and Sports Goods	-405	1231		894	108	1612
化学原料及化学制品制造业	Raw Chemical Materials and Chemical Products	-30037	5267	22991	3534	2605	-907
医药制造业	Medical and Pharmaceutical Product	-9199	5322	340	259	851	-4449
化学纤维制造业	Chemical Fibers	-6824	50	56	693	454	-6478
橡胶制品业	Rubber Products	-1104	128		262	249	-2256
塑料制品业	Plastic Products	-13401	88	58	11313	783	-2766
非金属矿物制品业	Nonmetal Mineral Products	-9255	2083	4153	4677	1347	319
黑色金属冶炼及压延加工业	Smelting and Pressing of Ferrous Metals	16206	9880	57	17183	15473	27878
金属制品业	Metal Products	-4437	68	44	1625	216	-2914
普通机械制造业	Ordinary Machinery Manufacturing	-24374	268	506	15248	2091	-10259
专用设备制造业	Special Purposes Equipment Manufacturing	-1437	3217	2415	13611	3631	13759
交通运输设备制造业	Transportation Equipment Manufacturing	-65894	11142	280	24085	2086	-29770
电气机械及器材制造	Electric Equipment and Machinery	-7299	229	26	6005	1300	-1057
电子及通信设备制造	Electronic and Telecommunications	61344	13556	310	24121	9766	90823
仪器仪表及文化、办公用机械制造业	Instruments,Meters,Cultural and Official Machine Manufacturing	-1778	1017	80	1977	909	388
其他制造业	Other Manufacturing	3792	113	70	2666	2343	4310
电力、蒸汽、热水的生产和供应业	Electricity,Steam and Hot Water Production and Supply	-14821	122	15795	29	720	619
煤气生产和供应业	Gas Production and Supply	-30273	757	30400	44	39	915
自来水的生产和供应	Water Production and Supply	-12918		13500	9	6	584

6-11 续表 6 continued

(10000 yuan)

应交所得税 Income Tax Payable	应付利润 Profits Payable	亏损企业亏损额 Total Loss-ing of Loss-making Enterprises	利税总额 Total Pre-tax Profits	工资，福利费，增值税 Wages,Welfares and Added Value Tax 本年应付工资总额 Total Wags Payable	本年应付福利费总额 Total Welfares Payable	本年应交增值税 Added Value Tax	本年进项税额 Tax In-clude in Purchas-ing Cost	本年销项税额 Tax In-clude in Sales Cost	工业中间投入合计 Intermediate Input of Industry
37			12439	32349	4529	6527	4943	11447	43309
24			899	1653	162	381	2635	2807	7423
1		149	9	838	138	146	2	149	1817
1633	2425	14427	23675	11468	2559	21602	53032	73652	398994
388	1644	35378	-10188	12324	2844	19695	12948	30849	84946
8021	1399	14594	98014	18989	4812	26462	38261	62661	218871
895	200	5341	7998	31188	3427	7025	25682	31370	132336
290		2352	1075	9792	2606	1905	5758	6498	50407
			81	2661	332	77	743	697	3352
		999	-898	1356	156	85	353	437	3200
			208	668	24	194	551	715	2971
1373		7181	8823	8619	1641	4619	8228	12723	53425
1126	897	2915	10043	9356	1653	5653	6953	11931	30671
469	174		3845	5732	854	2013	5600	7547	26804
3213	1598	9624	25295	40495	6504	21020	60430	80800	454351
2730		11779	4901	14649	2527	8312	40471	47089	108992
		6478	-5635	3792	575	780	5024	5700	30576
		2377	5250	6270	842	3010	12066	14971	69392
191		3768	-1270	7298	1057	1419	8476	8936	50563
2291	142	8126	24377	52843	8233	22380	36242	57910	257832
3704	16	5796	154763	177643	23903	115874	237640	348210	1543581
33	21	3015	-1986	8053	1324	890	2924	3618	20867
225	33	11705	-236	38523	5701	9543	30585	38922	153162
4866	6716	10575	32703	47577	7167	17382	96137	113273	343559
813	17	33474	8114	57110	16546	24329	72702	96125	414510
1263	326	5788	15640	33267	4110	15710	31177	45868	228678
14110	46850	29615	131754	66834	13905	40084	119958	151695	719485
181	1	980	2061	8590	1156	1569	3614	4997	23433
1421	139	1325	11439	4874	693	6899	2487	9253	29093
			6435	8816	1182	5299	7832	12726	35509
	412		6194	11542	1816	4867	11057	15924	13350
			5090	7445	1008	4138		4138	33591

6-12 个体经营工业主要指标
MAIN INDICATORS ON INDIVIDUAL ENTERPRISES

单位：万元 (10000 yuan)

项 目 Item		企业单位数(个) Number of Enterprise (unit)	从业人员年末人数(人) Employment (year-end) (person)	工业总产值(当年价格) Gross Output Value of Industry (at current prices)	上缴税金 Taxes Turned Over	自有资金 Self-own Capital
总 计	**Total**	**12071**	**57721**	**350624**	**11379**	**90147**
在总计中：	**Of Total:**					
轻工业	Light Industry	8778	39287	214039	7483	59377
重工业	Heavy Industry	3293	18434	136586	3896	30770
在总计中：	**Of Total:**					
城镇个体工业	Urban Individual Enterprises	2357	4863	12712	443	3253
农村个体工业	Rural Individual Enterprises	9714	52858	337912	10936	86894

6-13 大中型工业企业按销售收入排序
ARRANGING IN SALES REVENUE ORDER OF LARGE AND MEDIUM INDUSTRIAL ENTERPRISES

单位：千元 (1000 yuan)

企业名称 Enterprise	序号 No.	销售收入 Sales Revenue
首钢总公司	1	19260946
联想集团控股公司	2	11143810
北京燕山石油化工(集团)有限公司	3	10886286
中国华北电力集团公司(在京单位)	4	4284808
北京化学工业集团有限责任公司	5	3096934
北京国际交换系统有限公司	6	2915535
北京松下彩色显像管有限公司	7	2787406
北京吉普汽车有限公司	8	2458164
北汽福田车辆股份有限公司	9	1941396
中国北京同仁堂集团公司	10	1908417
北京建筑材料集团有限责任公司	11	1682287
和德集团有限公司	12	1532013
北京燕京啤酒集团公司	13	1337032
北京牡丹电子集团公司	14	1221244
中国惠普有限公司	15	976708
北京矿务局	16	904536
北京京棉集团有限责任公司	17	869567
北京大唐发电股份有限公司	18	848156
北京汽车摩托车联合制造公司	19	744753
北京邮电通信设备厂	20	726479
北京市热力公司	21	723472
中国石化长城高级润滑油公司	22	684439
北京轻型汽车有限公司	23	677061
北京市松下通信设备有限公司	24	671171
北京市石景山热电厂	25	668651
北京首钢宝生带钢厂	26	668135
北京卷烟厂	27	666459
首钢日电电子有限公司	28	633391
北京市顺义区肉类联合加工厂	29	630497
北京六所华科高技术股份有限公司	30	624981
首都航天机械公司	31	602890
北京印钞厂	32	572240
北京可口可乐饮料有限公司	33	569500
北京市自来水公司	34	556765
北京二七车辆厂	35	547590
北京制药厂	36	528465
北京市煤气公司	37	511313
北京松下电子部品有限公司	38	510674
北内集团总公司	39	492097
北京朗讯科技光缆有限公司	40	478082
北京四通集团公司	41	459675
北京重型电机厂	42	452991
北京轮胎厂	43	450601
北京首钢机电有限公司	44	437112

6-13 续表 continued

单位：千元 (1000 yuan)

企业名称 Enterprise	序号 No.	销售收入 Sales Revenue
北京福田车辆股份有限公司怀柔车辆厂	45	432738
北人印刷机械股份有限公司	46	424176
北京巴布科克威尔科克斯有限公司	47	422310
北新建材（集团）有限公司	48	420681
北京市牛栏山酒厂	49	419368
北京北方车辆制造厂	50	413899
北京市天然气公司	51	408668
北京红星酿酒集团公司	52	393321
北京开关厂	53	381247
北京三元食品有限公司	54	372399
北京市汽车修理公司	55	350307
北京无线电厂	56	350263
北京恩布拉科雪花压缩机有限公司	57	342885
北京利乐包包装有限公司	58	334989
北京星海乐器有限责任公司	59	329651
北京博士伦眼镜护理产品有限公司	60	321021
北京四通松下电工有限公司	61	320563
北京电力设备总厂	62	300751
北京市客车总厂	63	296743
北京市宏利钢管厂	64	294802
北京兆维电子(集团)有限责任公司	65	291005
北京煤矿机械厂	66	289879
北京统益油脂有限公司	67	281218
北京广东健力宝饮料有限公司	68	279111
北京南顺油脂有限公司	69	274226
北京玻璃集团公司	70	271842
北京亚洲双合盛五星啤酒有限公司	71	263137
北京统一食品有限公司	72	261453
北京二七机车厂	73	260020
北京艾森绿宝油脂有限公司	74	250236
北京东方电子集团股份有限公司	75	245040
北京化工实验厂	76	244634
北京顺美服装股份有限公司	77	240140
北京市造纸包装工业公司	78	226503
北京金万利油脂有限公司	79	212715
北京天纬油泵油嘴股份有限公司	80	208159
北京市三环毛纺针织集团公司	81	201458
中国迅达电梯有限公司	82	198717
北京染料厂	83	195160
北京爱立信通信系统有限公司	84	193421
北京恒通食品有限公司	85	190130
北京京海集团公司	86	189789
北京市液化石油气公司	87	189146
北京市电机总厂	88	185109
北京东陶有限公司	89	184260
北京第一机床厂	90	182931
北京橡胶一厂	91	180308
北京万东医疗装备公司	92	179628
北京邮电电话设备厂	93	177769
北京市三露厂	94	177622
航卫通用电气医疗系统有限公司	95	173237
北京三环亚太啤酒有限公司	96	173109
北京北化精细化学品有限责任公司	97	173071
北京敬业电工集团	98	169551
北京亚都科技股份有限公司	99	166358
北京合成纤维实验厂(北京华英纶化纤公司)	100	164790

6-14 大中型工业企业按利税总额排序
ARRANGING IN TOTAL PRE-TAX PROFITS OF LARGE AND MEDIUM INDUSTRIAL ENTERPRISES

单位：千元　　　　(1000 yuan)

企业名称 Enterprise	序号 No.	利税总额 Pre-tax Profits
首钢总公司	1	1582952
北京燕山石油化工(集团)有限公司	2	1426337
北京国际交换系统有限公司	3	1071188
北京燕京啤酒集团公司	4	642499
中国华北电力集团公司(在京单位)	5	608418
联想集团控股公司	6	543150
北京卷烟厂	7	384113
北京大唐发电股份有限公司	8	317668
北京邮电通信设备厂	9	294754
和德集团有限公司	10	285136
北京松下彩色显像管有限公司	11	239448
北汽福田车辆股份有限公司	12	183553
北京市牛栏山酒厂	13	173407
北京建筑材料集团有限责任公司	14	149668
北京利乐包包装有限公司	15	145076
北京矿务局	16	124388
北京红星酿酒集团公司	17	124345
中国北京同仁堂集团公司	18	123764
北京印钞厂	19	122874
北京博士伦眼镜护理产品有限公司	20	115970
北人印刷机械股份有限公司	21	108419
北京市石景山热电厂	22	106000
北京吉普汽车有限公司	23	105943
北新建材（集团）有限公司	24	98002
中国惠普有限公司	25	92203
北京可口可乐饮料有限公司	26	88855
北京东方电子集团股份有限公司	27	84788
北京市三露厂	28	82221
北京化学工业集团有限责任公司	29	77072
中国石化长城高级润滑油公司	30	75869
北京市热力公司	31	61228
北京市松下通信设备有限公司	32	56594
北京轮胎厂	33	52655
北京市自来水公司	34	50898
北京东陶有限公司	35	50609
北京三元食品有限公司	36	50178
北京市汽车修理公司	37	48568
北京二七车辆厂	38	48020
北京兆维电子(集团)有限责任公司	39	47877
北京日邦印刷有限公司	40	47068
北京重型电机厂	41	46157
北京市顺义区肉类联合加工厂	42	45177
北京福田车辆股份有限公司怀柔车辆厂	43	39852
北京三环亚太啤酒有限公司	44	38635
北京朗讯科技光缆有限公司	45	38089
北京丽都亚洲啤酒有限公司	46	35857
北京平谷县化工总厂	47	35194
邮电部北京邮票厂	48	34149
北京四通松下电工有限公司	49	33130
北京开关厂	50	31892

6-14 续 表 continued

单位：千元 (1000 yuan)

企业名称 Enterprise	序号 No.	利税总额 Pre-tax Profits
北京市煤气公司	51	31499
北京星海乐器有限责任公司	52	30709
北京京棉集团有限责任公司	53	30418
北京万东医疗装备公司	54	29810
北京统一食品有限公司	55	27528
北京雪莲羊绒有限公司	56	25314
北京亚都科技股份有限公司	57	24595
航卫通用电气医疗系统有限公司	58	23862
北京市天然气公司	59	23288
北京煤矿机械厂	60	23287
北京恩布拉科雪花压缩机有限公司	61	22509
北京广东健力宝饮料有限公司	62	21601
北京巴布科克威尔科克斯有限公司	63	20436
北京玻璃集团公司	64	19933
北京市客车总厂	65	19804
北京日用化学二厂	66	18728
北京轻型汽车有限公司	67	18344
北京轻联包装印刷集团公司	68	18334
北京爱立信通信系统有限公司	69	18227
北京电视配件三厂	70	17682
北京第一机床厂	71	17130
北京制药厂	72	16879
北京北方车辆制造厂	73	16771
北京天纬油泵油嘴股份有限公司	74	16676
北京精工华晖凹印制板有限公司	75	16652
北京汽车摩托车联合制造公司	76	16164
北京市东方罗门哈斯有限公司	77	15878
北京清河毛纺织厂	78	15682
北京制呢厂	79	15202
北京丽源公司	80	15089
新华通讯社印刷厂	81	14886
北京北化精细化学品有限责任公司	82	14198
北京宝岛包装印刷有限公司	83	14051
北人集团公司	84	13983
国营华北光学仪器厂	85	13101
北京威顿玻璃制品有限公司	86	12846
北京电力设备总厂	87	12459
北京辛普劳食品加工有限公司	88	12136
北京正大饲料有限公司	89	10739
北京铁路信号工厂	90	10620
北京无线电厂	91	10582
丰台桥梁工厂	92	10320
北京光华染织厂	93	10134
北京市华都酿酒食品工业公司	94	10132
北京华德液压工业集团有限责任公司	95	10121
北京保温瓶工业公司	96	9909
北京轻联塑料集团公司	97	9713
北京牡丹电子集团公司	98	9706
北京生物制品研究所	99	9485
北京普莱克斯实用气体有限公司	100	9474

6-15 大中型工业企业按总资产贡献率排序
ARRANGING IN RATIO OF PRE-TAX PROFITS TO TOTAL CAPITAL ORDER OF LARGE AND MEDIUM ENTERPRISES

单位：% (%)

企业名称 Enterprise	序号 No.	总资产贡献率 Contribution Rate of Total Assets
北京卷烟厂	1	63
北京利乐包包装有限公司	2	50
北京邮电通信设备厂	3	46
北京日邦印刷有限公司	4	41
北京市牛栏山酒厂	5	37
北汽福田车辆股份有限公司	6	35
北京宝岛包装印刷有限公司	7	35
北京市三露厂	8	34
北京国际交换系统有限公司	9	33
北京红星酿酒集团公司	10	29
北京大唐发电股份有限公司	11	29
北京博士伦眼镜护理产品有限公司	12	28
北京市石景山热电厂	13	28
北京可口可乐饮料有限公司	14	28
北京平谷县化工总厂	15	26
北京燕京啤酒集团公司	16	24
北京福田车辆股份有限公司怀柔车辆厂	17	21
北京东陶有限公司	18	20
北京市顺义区肉类联合加工厂	19	19
北京精工华晖凹印制板有限公司	20	19
北京丽都亚洲啤酒有限公司	21	18
北京市酱油厂	22	18
北京中彩印刷有限公司	23	18
北京统一食品有限公司	24	17
北京晓星容器有限公司	25	17
北京四通松下电工有限公司	26	16
北京朗讯科技光缆有限公司	27	16
北京市松下通信设备有限公司	28	15
北京印钞厂	29	15
北京市酿造六厂	30	15
航卫通用电气医疗系统有限公司	31	14
北京康达电器控制设备集团公司	32	14
北京辛普劳食品加工有限公司	33	14
联想集团控股公司	34	13
北京威顿玻璃制品有限公司	35	13
北京市礼花厂	36	13
中国石化长城高级润滑油公司	37	12
房山区水泥一厂	38	12
北京长城制药厂	39	12
北京二七车辆厂	40	12
北京市东方罗门哈斯有限公司	41	12
新华通讯社印刷厂	42	11
北京电视配件三厂	43	11
北京埃姆毛纺有限公司	44	11
房山区双山水泥集团	45	10
北京市华都酿酒食品工业公司	46	10
国营北京大兴酒厂	47	10
北京市平谷福粮砖厂	48	10
北京三环亚太啤酒有限公司	49	10
北京印刷三厂	50	10

6-15 续 表 continued

单位：% (%)

企业名称 Enterprise	序号 No.	总资产贡献率 Contribution Rate of Total Assets
北人印刷机械股份有限公司	51	10
北京松下彩色显像管有限公司	52	10
北京联合印刷纸器有限公司	53	10
北京市汽车修理公司	54	10
北京三元食品有限公司	55	10
解放军报社印刷厂	56	9
北京市顺义飞达玻璃厂	57	9
北京东方电子集团股份有限公司	58	9
北京光华染织厂	59	9
北京清河毛纺织厂	60	9
北京雪莲羊绒有限公司	61	9
北京星海乐器有限责任公司	62	9
北京轻联包装印刷集团公司	63	9
北京艾森绿宝油脂有限公司	64	9
北京神州摩奇食品饮料有限公司	65	9
北京燕山石油化工(集团)有限公司	66	9
北京凌奇印刷厂	67	8
广播电影电视部设备制造厂	68	8
北新建材（集团）有限公司	69	8
北京亚都科技股份有限公司	70	8
中国惠普有限公司	71	8
北京外文印刷厂	72	8
北京煤矿机械厂	73	8
北京京城汽车车厢总厂	74	8
北京保温瓶工业公司	75	8
北京铁路信号工厂	76	8
平谷县水泥二厂	77	8
北京广东健力宝饮料有限公司	78	8
北京汽车玻璃钢制品总公司	79	8
北京轮胎厂	80	8
北京印刷二厂	81	8
中国北京同仁堂集团公司	82	8
北京轴承厂	83	8
北京大华无线电仪器厂	84	8
北京帆布厂	85	8
北京万东医疗装备公司	86	8
北京联合收割机发展集团	87	8
北京市政汽车改装厂	88	8
北京正大饲料有限公司	89	8
北京双桥制药公司	90	8
邮电部北京邮票厂	91	7
和德集团有限公司	92	7
北京石油 机械厂	93	7
北京市顺义建筑产品总厂	94	7
北京向阳制药厂	95	7
北京北化精细化学品有限责任公司	96	7
北京胶印厂	97	7
北京市京华印刷总厂	98	7
北京人民轴承厂	99	7
北京开关厂	100	7

6-16 大中型工业企业按资产总额排序

ARRANGING IN TOTAL ASSETS OF LARGE AND MEDIUM INDUSTRIAL ENTERPRISES

单位：千元 (1000 yuan)

企业名称 Enterprise	序号 No.	资产总额 Total Assets
首钢总公司	1	36707118
中国华北电力集团公司(在京单位)	2	25981470
北京燕山石油化工(集团)有限公司	3	20232202
北京化学工业集团有限责任公司	4	13712443
联想集团控股公司	5	7418034
北京建筑材料集团有限责任公司	6	6276559
北京市自来水公司	7	5064161
北京国际交换系统有限公司	8	4259528
和德集团有限公司	9	3914226
北京市热力公司	10	3834061
北京燕京啤酒集团公司	11	3436431
北京四通集团公司	12	3105351
北京松下彩色显像管有限公司	13	2928744
北内集团总公司	14	2747682
北京首钢机电有限公司	15	2609309
北京矿务局	16	2570241
北京吉普汽车有限公司	17	2504004
中国北京同仁堂集团公司	18	2216706
首钢日电电子有限公司	19	2034354
北京市煤气公司	20	1925698
北京汽车工业集团总公司	21	1876555
北京汽车摩托车联合制造公司	22	1863025
北京市天然气公司	23	1861296
北京兆维电子(集团)有限责任公司	24	1807148
北京京海集团公司	25	1790993
北京轻型汽车有限公司	26	1716475
北京牡丹电子集团公司	27	1708670
北京市石景山热电厂	28	1681455
北京重型电机厂	29	1632353
北京玻璃集团公司	30	1511771
北新建材（集团）有限公司	31	1501879
首都航天机械公司	32	1476160
北京东方电子集团股份有限公司	33	1443767
北京京棉集团有限责任公司	34	1437023
中国惠普有限公司	35	1375359
北人集团公司	36	1371535
北京轮胎厂	37	1188223
北京首钢宝生带钢厂	38	1173325
北人印刷机械股份有限公司	39	1133375
北汽福田车辆股份有限公司	40	1126609
北京大唐发电股份有限公司	41	1109836
和路雪(中国)有限公司	42	1087270
北京制药厂	43	1041879
北京市造纸包装工业公司	44	1039567
北京雪花电器集团公司	45	1016681
北京亚洲双合盛五星啤酒有限公司	46	945075
北京北方车辆制造厂	47	889365
北京天纬油泵油嘴股份有限公司	48	889156
北京电力设备总厂	49	883526
中国石化长城高级润滑油公司	50	880766

6-16 续 表 continued

单位：千元 (1000 yuan)

企 业 名 称 Enterprise	序 号 No.	资 产 总 额 Total Assets
北京三元食品有限公司	51	835404
北京第一机床厂	52	815632
北京邮电通信设备厂	53	814607
北京印钞厂	54	798904
北京航星机器制造公司	55	759592
北京市平板玻璃集团公司	56	735600
北京市液化石油气公司	57	658570
北京市三环毛纺针织集团公司	58	657940
北京开关厂	59	652283
北京亚都科技股份有限公司	60	642228
北京可口可乐饮料有限公司	61	635367
北京拖拉机公司	62	613501
北京巴布科克威尔科克斯有限公司	63	610919
北京六所华科高技术股份有限公司	64	601811
北京华德液压工业集团有限责任公司	65	588937
北京市宏利钢管厂	66	579964
北京化工实验厂	67	570594
北京万东医疗装备公司	68	567197
北京朗讯科技光缆有限公司	69	565448
北京市汽车修理公司	70	548211
北京市松下通信设备有限公司	71	544994
北京第三制药厂	72	543587
邮电部北京邮票厂	73	542279
北京广播器材厂(七六一厂)	74	541316
北京卷烟厂	75	541201
北京电视设备厂	76	536329
SMC(中国)有限公司	77	532375
北京星海乐器有限责任公司	78	530577
北京恩布拉科雪花压缩机有限公司	79	523341
北京二七机车厂	80	521580
北京市客车总厂	81	518880
北京中策北京啤酒有限公司	82	516115
北京松下电子部品有限公司	83	515992
北京化学纤维厂	84	513796
北京雪莲羊绒有限公司	85	505370
北京红星酿酒集团公司	86	491943
北京二毛纺织集团	87	491229
北京齿轮总厂	88	478747
北京北化精细化学品有限责任公司	89	472995
北京合成纤维实验厂(北京华英纶化纤公司)	90	469397
北京市牛栏山酒厂	91	464885
北京博士伦眼镜护理产品有限公司	92	461309
北京丝绸总厂	93	459356
北京丽源公司	94	458288
拜耳医药保健有限公司	95	454498
东陶机器(北京)有限公司	96	453314
北京起重机器厂	97	441839
北京四通松下电工有限公司	98	439242
北京二七车辆厂	99	436410
丰台桥梁工厂	100	432840

主 要 统 计 指 标 解 释

工业　指从事自然资源的开采，对采掘品和农产品进行加工和再加工的物质生产部门。具体包括：（1）对自然资源的开采，如采矿、晒盐、森林采伐等（但不包括禽兽捕猎和水产捕捞）；（2）对农副产品的加工、再加工，如粮油加工、食品加工、扎花、纺织、制革等；（3）对采掘品的加工、再加工，如炼铁、炼钢、化工生产、石油加工、机器制造、木材加工等，以及电力、自来水、煤气的生产和供应等；（4）对工业品的修理、翻新，如机器设备的修理、交通运输工具（包括小卧车）的修理等。

1984年以前农村的村及村以下办工业归属农业，1984年以后划归工业。

独立核算工业企业　非独立核算工业生产单位　工业企业按其行政和财务是否独立，分为核算工业企业和非独立核算工业生产单位。

独立核算工业企业应同时具备下列三个条件：（1）行政上有独立的组织形式；（2）经济上独立核算、自负盈亏、编制独立的资金平衡表；（3）有权与其他单位签订合同，并在银行社有独立帐户。独立核算工业企业不论是单一性生产或联合性生产的企业，均以整个企业作为一个基层单位进行统计，而不按分厂、车间统计。

非独立核算工业生产单位是指不同时具备独立核算工业企业三个条件，附设与其他企业、事业、机关、团体、学校、科研机构、部队等单位的工业生产单位。非独立核算工业生产单位必须同时具备下列三个条件，才能列入工业统计范围，即：（1）有固定的生产场所和生产设备；（2）有固定的生产工人和学徒在十人以上；（3）一般单位常年生产，季节性生产的单位全年开工时间在三个月以上。

轻工业　指主要提供生活消费品和制作手工工具的工业。按其所使用的原料不同，可分为两大类：（1）以农业为原料的轻工业，是指直接或间接以农产品为基本原料的轻工业。主要包括食品制造、饮料制造、烟草加工、纺织、缝纫、皮革和毛皮制作、造纸以及印刷等工业；（2）以非农产品为原料的轻工业，是指以工业品为原料的轻工业。主要包括文教体育用品、化学药品制造、合成纤维制造、日用化学制品、日用玻璃制品、日用金属制品、手工工具制造、医疗器械制造、文化和办公用机械制造等工业。

重工业　是指为国民经济各部门提供物质技术基础的主要生产资料的工业。按其生产性质和产品用途，可以分为下列三类：（1）采掘（伐）工业，是指对自然资源的开采，包括石油开采、煤炭开采、金属矿开采、非金属矿开采和木材采伐等工业；（2）原材料工业，指向国民经济各部门提供基本材料、动力和燃料的工业。包括金属冶炼及加工、炼焦及焦炭化学、化工原料、水泥、人造板以及电力、石油和煤炭加工等工业；（3）加工工业，是指对工业原材料进行再加工制造的工业。包括装备国民经济各部门的机械设备制造工业、金属结构、水泥制品等工业，以及为农业提供的生产资料如化肥、农药等工业。

根据上述划分原则，修理业中以重工业产品为修理作业对象的划为重工业，反之划为轻工业。

工业总产值　是以货币表现的工业在一定时期内生产的已出售或可供出售工业产品总量，它反映一定时期内工业生产的总规模和总水平。它包括：在本企业内不再进行加工，经检验、包装入库（规定不需包装的产品除外）的成品价值，工业性作业价值，自制半成品、在产品期末初差额价值。工业总产值采用“工厂法”计算，即以工业作业为一个整体，按企业生产活动的最终成果来计算，企业内部不允许重复计算，不能把企业内部各个车间（分厂）生产的成果相加。但在企业之间、行业之间、地区之间存在着重复计算。

轻重工业总产值的划分也是按“工厂法”计算的，即一个工业企业在正常情况下生产的主要产品的性质属于轻工业，则该企业的全部总产值作为轻工业总产值；一个工业企业生产的主要产品的性质属于重工业，则该企业的全部总产值作为重工业总产值。

工业增加值　是指工业行业在报告期内以货币表现的工业生产活动的最终成果。

工业销售产值　是以货币表现的工业企业在一定时期内销售的本企业生产的工业产品产量。包括已销售的成品、半成品价值，对外提供的工业性作业价值和对本单位基本建设部门、生活福利部门等提供的产品和工业性作业及自制设备的价值。已销售的成品、半成品不论是本期生产的、还是上期生产的，只要是本期销售出去的均包括在内。对外提供的工业性作业是指企业按合同对外提供的工业性劳务。企业为本单位基本建设部门、生活福利部门等提供的产品和工业性作业及自制设备也应视同销售，这部分也应作为销售统计。

工业销售产值的计算范围、计算价格和计算方法与工业总产值一致，但两者计算的基础不同，工业销售产值计算的基础是产品销售总量，工业总产值计算的基础是工业产品生产总量。

固定资产原价　指企业在建造、购置、安装、改建、扩建、技术改造某项固定资产时所支出的全部货币总额。它一般包括买价、包装费、运杂费和安装费等。

固定资产净值 是指固定资产原价减去历年已提折旧额后的净值。

新产品 指采用新技术原理、新设计构思、生产的全新产品或在结构、材质、工艺等某一方面比老产品有明显改进，从而显著提高了生产性能或扩大了使用功能的产品。

出口交货值 指工业企业交给外贸部门或自营（委托）出口（包括销往香港、澳门、台湾），用外汇价格结算的批量销售，在国内或边境批量出口的产品价值，还包括外商来样、来料加工、来件装配和补偿贸易等生产的产品价值。

工业品自销零售额 指各种经济类型的制造业生产单位，将本单位生产的产品直接售给居民（包括本企业职工）和社会集团取得的零售额。

工业企业主要财务指标和经济效益指标

1. 资本金合计 是企业在工商行政管理部门登记的注册资金。资本金合计包括国家资本金、法人资本金、个人资本金、外商资本金和集体资本金等。

（1）国家资本金 是指有权代表国家投资的政府部门或者机构以国有资产投入企业形成的资本金。不论企业的资本金是哪个政府部门或机构投入的，只要是以国家资金进行投资的，均作为国家资本金。

（2）法人资本金 是指其他法人单位以其依法可以支配的资产投入企业形成的资本金。

（3）个人资本金 是指社会个人或者企业内部职工以个人合法财产投入企业形成的资本金。

（4）外商资本金 是指外国投资者以及香港、澳门、台湾地区投资者投入企业形成的资本金。

（5）集体资本金 是指集体所有制企业投入企业形成的资本金。

2. 资产合计 指企业拥有或控制的全部资产。包括流动资产、长期投资、固定资产、无形及递延资产、其他长期资产、递延税项等，即为企业资产负债表的资产总计项。

（1）流动资产 指企业可以在一年内或者超过一年的一个生产周期内变现或耗用的资产合计。包括现金及各种存款、短期投资、应收及预付款项、存货等。

（2）固定资产 指企业固定资产净值、固定资产清理、在建工程、待处理固定资产损失所占用的资金合计。

（3）无形资产 指企业长期使用而没有实物形态的资产。包括专利权、非专利技术、商标权、著作权、土地使用权、商誉等。

3. 负债合计 指企业承担并需要偿还的全部债务。包括流动负债和长期负债、递延税项等，即为企业资产负债表的负债合计项。

（1）流动负债 指企业在一年内或者超过一年的营业周期内需要偿还的债务合计，其中包括短期借款、应付及预收款项、应付工资、应交税金和应交利润等。

（2）长期负债 指企业在一年以上或者超过一年的生产周期以上需要偿还的债务合计，其中包括长期借款、应付债务、长期应付款项等。

4. 利税总额 指企业利润总额、产品销售税金及附加和应交增值税之和。

5. 产品销售收入 指企业销售产品的销售收入和提供劳务等主要经营业务取得的业务总额。

6. 产品销售成本 指企业销售产品和提供劳务等主要经营业务的实际成本。

7. 产品销售税金及附加 指企业销售产品和提供工业性劳务等主要经营业务应负担的城市维护建设税、消费税、资源税和教育费附加。

8. 产品销售利润 指企业销售产品和提供工业性劳务等主要经营业务收入扣除其成本、费用、税金后的利润。

9. 利润总额 指企业实现的利润。

10. 所有制者权益 指企业投资人对企业净资产的所有权。企业净资产等于企业全部资产减去全部负债后余额，其中包括投资者对企业的最初投入，以及资本公积金、盈余公积金和未分配利润，对股份制企业即为股东权益。

11. 工业经济效益综合指数 是综合衡量工业经济效益各方面在数量上总体水平的一种特殊相对数，是反映工业经济运行质量的总量指数，是以各项工业经济效益指数实际数值分别除以该项指标的全国标准值并乘以各自权数求得。计算公式：

$$\text{工业经济效益综合指数}=\frac{\text{某项经济效益指标报告期数值}}{\text{该项指标全国标准值}}\times(\text{权数})\div\text{总权数}$$

计算工业经济效益综合指数时，各项经济效益指标的分子、分母应按报告期止累计数（如产品销售收入为报告期止累计产品销售收入）或序时平均数（如平均流动资产为报告期止各月平均流动资产之和除以累计月数）计算。

全国的标准值：是根据“八五”期间全国乡及乡以上工业企业每项指标实际完成数值加权平均计算出来的。

权数：是根据上述各项工业经济效益指标在综合经济效益中的重要程度，由专家调查法确定的。

12. 工业产品销售率　指报告期工业销售产值与同期全部工业总产值之比。计算公式：

$$工业产品销售率（\%）=\frac{报告期现价工业销售产值}{报告期现价工业总产值}\times 100\%$$

13. 工业资金利税率　指报告期已实现的利润、税金总额与同期的资产（流动资产和固定资产净值）之比，反映每单位（通常是每万元）资金所提供的利润税金额。它是考察和评价部门或企业资金运用的经济效益，分析资金投入效果的主要分析指标。计算公式：

$$工业资金利税率（\%）=\frac{报告期累计实现利税总额}{流动资产平均余额+固定资产净值平均余额}\times 100\%$$

14. 工业增加值率　指报告期工业增加值占工业总产值的比重，反映降低中间消耗的经济效益。计算公式：

$$工业增加值率（\%）=\frac{报告期现价工业增加值}{报告期现价工业总产值}\times 100\%$$

15. 工业成本费用利润率　指在一定时期内实现的利润与成本费用之比，是反映工业生产成本及费用投入的经济效益指标，同时也是反映降低成本的经济效益的指标。计算公式：

$$工业成本费用利润率（\%）=\frac{利润总额}{成本费用总额}\times 100\%$$

16. 工业全员劳动生产率　指根据产品的价值量指标计算的平均每一个职工在单位时间内的产品生产量。是考核企业经济活动的重要指标，是企业生产技术水平、经济管理水平、职工技术熟练程度和劳动积极性的综合表现。目前我国的全员劳动生产率是将工业企业的工业增加值除以同一时期全部职工的平均人数来计算的。计算公式：

$$工业全员劳动生产率（元/人）=\frac{工业增加值}{全部职工平均人数}$$

17. 流动资产周转次数　指在一定时期内流动资产完成的周转次数，反映流动资产的周转速度。计算公式：

$$流动资产周转次数（次）=\frac{产品销售收入}{流动资产平均余额}$$

18. 销售收入利税率　指报告期已实现的利润、税金总额（包括利润总额、产品销售税金及附加和应交增值税）占同期全部销售收入的百分比。计算公式：

$$销售收入利税率（\%）=\frac{利税总额}{销售收入}\times 100\%$$

19. 流动比率　是反映企业每百元流动负债中，有多少元流动资产作后盾。计算公式：

$$流动比率=\frac{流动资产总额}{流动负债总额}$$

20. 速动比率　是衡量企业流动资产中可以立即用于偿付流动负债的能力。计算公式：

$$速动比率=\frac{速动资产}{流动负债}$$

注：速动资产是流动资产中流动性相对更强的部分，通常等于现金，短期有价证券与应收款之和。

21. 资产负债率　是反映在企业资产总额中有多少资产是通过借债而得的，也可以用于衡量企业利用债权人提供资金进行经营活动的能力以及企业在清算时保护债权人利益的程度。计算公式：

$$资产负债率 = \frac{负债总额}{资产总额} \times 100\%$$

22. 总资产贡献率 反映企业全部资产的获利能力，是企业经营业绩和管理水平的集中体现，是评价和考核企业盈利能力的核心指标。计算公式为：

$$总资产贡献率 = （利润总额+税金总额+利息支出）\div 平均资产总额 \times \frac{12}{累计月数}$$

其中：税金总额为产品销售税金及附加与应交增值税之和；平均资产总额为期初期末资产总计的算术平均值。

23. 资本保值增值率 反映企业净资产的变动状况，是企业发展能力的集中体现。计算公式为：

资本保值增值率 = 报告期期末所有者权益/上年同期期末所有者权益

Explanatory Notes On Main Statistical Indicators

Industry refers to the physical production concerning extraction of natural resources, processing and reprocessing of minerals and agricultural products: (1) extraction of natural resources, such as mining, salt production, logging (but excluding hunting and fishing); (2) processing and reprocessing of farm and sideline products, such as rice husking, flour milling, wine making, oil pressing, cotton ginning, silk reeling, spinning and weaving, and leather making; (3) manufacturing of industrial products, such as steel making, iron smelting, chemicals production, petroleum processing, machine building, timber processing; production and supply of water, gas and electricity; (4) repairing of industrial products such as the repairing of machine and vehicles for transportation (including cars).

Prior to 1984, the rural industrial run by villages and cooperative organizations under village was classified into agriculture. Since 1984, it has been grouped into industry.

Independent Accounting Industrial Enterprises and Non-Independent Accounting Industrial Production Units are distinct by whether they have independent administration and accounting system.

An independent accounting industrial enterprises should satisfy all the following three conditions: (1) having an independent organization for administration; (2) having independent accounting system and filling independent balance sheets, being responsible for its own profits and losses; (3) being able to sign contracts with outside units and having independent bank accounts. An independent accounting industrial enterprise, no matter it is a single-business company or multi-business corporation, is counted as a basic statistical unit and its branch factories and workshops are no longer counted separately.

A non-independent accounting industrial production units is an industrial production unit with one or more of the three conditions unsatisfied. They usually attach to some enterprises, institutions, government departments, organizations, schools , scientific research institutions, or army units. A non-independent accounting industrial production units become a basic units of industrial statistics only when it can satisfy all the following three conditions: (1) having stable production sites and production equipment; (2) having more than 10 permanent workers and apprentices; (3) operating all-year-round for normal production or more than three months a year for seasonal production.

Light Industry refers to the industry that produces consumer goods and hand tools. Depending on the materials used, it is classified into two categories:

(1) Industries using farm products as raw materials directly or indirectly input farm products as basic raw materials, including the production of foods and beverages, tobacco processing, textile, clothing, fur and leather manufacturing, paper making, printing, etc..

(2) Industries using non-farm products as raw materials input manufactured goods as raw materials, including the manufacture of cultural, educational articles and sports goods, chemicals, synthetic fiber, daily use chemical products, glass products, metal products, hand tools, medical apparatus and instruments, and the manufacturing of cultural and office equipment.

Heavy Industry refers to the industry that produces capital goods. It provides various sectors of the national economy with necessary material and technical basis. According to the nature of production and the use of products, it is classified into three groups:

(1) Mining, quarrying and logging industry refers to the extraction of natural resources, including petroleum, coal,

metal and non-metal ores and logging.

(2) Raw materials industry refers to the industry that provides various sectors of the national economy with raw materials, fuels and power. It includes smelting and processing of metals, coke and coke chemistry, chemical materials and building materials such as cement, plywood, power, petroleum refining and coal dressing, etc..

(3) Manufacturing industry refers to the industry that processes raw materials. It includes machine-building industry that equips sectors of the national economy, industries of metal structure and cement products, industries producing means of agricultural production, such as chemical fertilizers and pesticides.

According to the above principle of classification, the repairing mainly for heavy industry products are classified into heavy industry while these mainly for light industry products are put into light industry.

Gross Industrial Output Value is the total volume of industrial products sold or available for sale in value terms which reflects the total achievements and overall scale of industrial production during a given period. It includes the value of the finished products, which are not to be further processed in the enterprises and have been inspected, packed and put in storage, the value of industrial services rendered to other units and the differences in the value of the semi-finished products and products in process between the beginning and closing of the period. The gross industrial output value is calculated with "factory method". Based on the final products of every enterprise, there is no double calculation within every enterprise. However, double calculation does occur among different enterprises as well as different sectors and different regions.

Gross output value of light and heavy industries is also classified with the "factory" method. Under normal conditions, if the major products of an industrial enterprise belong to light industry products, the gross output value of the enterprise is put into light industry; the same principle apples to the contrary case.

Value Added of Industry refers to the final results of industrial production in money terms during the reference period.

Sales Value of Industry refers to total sales value of products produced by industrial enterprises during a given period, including sales of finished goods, semi-finished products, value of industrial services provided to outside units, value of products, industrial services and self-produced equipment provided for internal capital construction and welfare. Sales of finished goods and semi-finished products in current period are taken into account regardless whether the production is in the same period. Gross output value of industry is based on output of products while sales value of industry is based on sales of products.

Original Value of Fixed Assets refers to the total value of fixed assets calculated at the cost paid for purchase, installation, reconstruction, expansion, innovation and replacement of the fixed assets, which is normally classified into expenses on purchase, package, transportation, and installation.

Net Value of Fixed Assets is obtained by deducting cumulative depreciation over years from the original value of fixed assets.

New Products refers to new products using new technological principal, new designing ideas or be improved than old products in structure, materials or technology, and so improve production performance or exploited using function.

Delivery Value of Exports refers to value of products which delivered to foreign trade department or self exported(including selled to Hongkong, Macao and Taiwan) by industrial enterprises, and batch selled at exchange prices, batch exported within country or at border, also including value of sample from foreigners, materials received processing, scripts received assembling and compensation trade.

Retail Sales of Self-selling Industrial Products refers to retails sales of products which directly selled to residents(including staff and workers of enterprises) and social groups by manufacturing production units of various ownership.

The Main Financial Indexes and Economic Efficiency Indexes of Industrial Enterprises

1. Total Equity Capital refers to capital of an enterprise registered in Administrative Bureau for Industry and Commerce, which includes the state equity capital, the legal entity equity capital, individuals equity capital, foreign equity capital and collective equity capital.

State equity capital refers to the equity capital formed with the state-owned assets input by government departments or organizations that have the right to invest on behalf of the state. As long as the equity capital formed with the state-owned assets, it belongs to state equity capital, regardless which government department or organization the investor is.

Legal entity equity capital refers to the equity capital formed with the legal assets of a company or organization.

Individual equity capital is the equity capital formed with the legal individual assets from outside persons or internal employees.

Foreign equity capital is the equity capital formed with the legal assets from foreign parties, including parties or investors from Hong Kong, Macao and Taiwan.

Collective equity capital is the equity capital formed with the legal assets from collective enterprises.

2. Total Assets refers to all assets owned or controlled by an enterprises, including current assets, long-term investment, fixed assets, intangible assets and deferred assets, other long-term assets, and deferred taxes, etc. The summation of above items is equal to total assets shown in the balance sheet of the enterprise.

(1) current assets (working capital) refer to assets which can be cashed in or consumed in one year or an operating cycle over one year, including cash, all kinds of deposits, short term investment, receivable, advance payment, inventory, etc.

(2) Fixed assets refer to the total net value of fixed assets, clearance of fixed assets, project under construction, fixed assets losses in suspense. These are corporations' fund holdings.

(3) Intangible assets refer to the assets without physical form used by enterprises over a long time, such as patents, know-how, trade marks, copyright, usufruct of land, good-will, etc.

3. Total Liabilities refers to the debts that enterprises are responsible for repayment, including liquid liabilities, long-term liabilities and deferred taxes, etc. Total liabilities correspond to the summation item of liabilities shown in the balance sheets of the enterprises.

(1) Current liabilities refer to enterprises total debt payable within one year or an operating cycle over one year, including short term loans, payables and advance receipts, wages payable, taxes payable and profit payable, etc.

(2)Long-term liabilities refers to total debt payable within an operating cycle of one year or over one year, including long-term loans, long-term debts, long-term payables, etc.

4. Total Value of Profit and Tax (Pre-tax Profits) refers to the sum of the total net profits, products sales tax and surcharges and the value added tax payable of industrial enterprises, namely pre-tax profits.

5. Product Sales Income refers to the total income obtained by an enterprise via selling its products and providing industrial services.

6. Sales Cost of Industrial Products refers to actual cost of the products sold and the industrial services provided, etc.

7. Sales Tax and surcharges of Products refer to the tax of city maintenance and construction, consumption tax, resources tax and extra charges for education, which levied on enterprises providing products and industrial services.

8. Sales Profit of Products refers to the profit earned by the enterprises after deducting cost, charges and taxes from the business income with selling products and providing industrial services.

9. Total Profits refer to the total profits gained by the enterprises.

10. Owners' Equity refers to investors' claim for net assets of the enterprise, which equals to the total assets of the enterprise minus its total liabilities, including the initial capital from investors, capital accumulation fund, surplus accumulation fund and undistributed profit. It is the share holders' equity in share holding companies.

11. Aggregate Index of Industrial Economic Efficiency is a special relative value for comprehensively measuring the overall levels in quantitative terms of the industrial economic efficiency from various aspects. It is also a total quantity index reflecting the economic performance quality of the industry. It is the result of the actual value of the industrial economic efficiency index divided by the national standard value in the same field and then multiplied by the weight. The formula is as follows:

$$\text{Value of an economic deficiency index} = \left(\frac{\text{Aggregate index of industrial economic deficiency (\%)}}{\text{National standard value in the same field}} \times \text{weight}\right)$$

(overall weight)

12. Sales Rate of Industrial Products refers to the ratio of the sales value of industry to the gross industrial output value in the same period. The formula is as follows:

$$\text{Sales Rate of Industrial Products (\%)} = \frac{\text{Sales value of industry}}{\text{Gross industrial output value}} \times 100\%$$

13. Ratio of Profit and Tax to Capital in Industry refers to the ratio of the total realized profits and taxes to total assets (net fixed assets plus working capital), often expressed as pre-tax profit earned per 10000 yuan capital, which reflects the utilization efficiency of the assets and is calculated as follows:

$$\text{Total realized pre-tax profit} = \frac{\text{Ratio of Profit and Tax to Capital in Industry (\%)}}{\text{Average current assets} + \text{Average net value of fixed assets}} \times 100\%$$

14. Value Added Rate of industry refers to the ratio of value added of industry to the gross output value in the same period, which reflects the economic efficiency of productive consumption and is calculated as follows:

$$\text{Value Added Rate of industry (\%)} = \frac{\text{Value Added of Industry}}{\text{Gross industrial Output Value}} \times 100\%$$

15. Ratio of Profits to Total Industrial Costs refers to the ratio of profits realized to the total costs occurred in the same period, which reflects the economic efficiency of input in costs and expenses and is calculated as follows:

$$\text{Ratio of Profits to Total Industrial Costs (\%)} = \frac{\text{Total Profits}}{\text{Total Costs}} \times 100\%$$

16. Overall Labor Productivity of Industrial Enterprises refers to the average output per staff and worker in industrial enterprises in value terms within a given period, which reflects comprehensively the technological level, the management level, the skills and initiatives of the staff or workers. At present, the overall labor productivity is gotten via dividing the value added by the average number of staff and workers of an industrial enterprises in a given period. The formula:

$$\text{Overall Labor Productivity (yuan/person)} = \frac{\text{Value Added of Industry}}{\text{Average Number of Staff and Workers}}$$

17. Current Assets Turnover refers to times of the current assets turnover in a given period, which reflects the speed of the turnover of current assets and is calculated as follows:

$$\text{Current Assets Turnover (time)} = \frac{\text{Product Sales Income}}{\text{Average Balance of Circulating Assets}}$$

18. Ratio of Pre-tax Profits to Sales Revenue refers to the ratio of the total amount of pre-tax profits (including total profits, products sales tax and surcharges as well as the value added tax payable) to the total sales revenue in the same period. The formula is as follows:

$$\text{Ratio of Pre-tax Profits to Sales Revenue (\%)} = \frac{\text{Total Pre-tax Profits}}{\text{Total Sales Revenue}} \times 100\%$$

19. Current Ratio refers to how many times of the current assets can cover the current liabilities. The formula is as follows:

$$\text{Current Ratio} = \frac{\text{Total Current Assets}}{\text{Total Current Liabilities}}$$

20. Quick Ratio reflects to the capability of an enterprise to repay its current liabilities immediately. The equation is as follows:

$$\text{Quick Ratio} = \frac{\text{Total Quick Assets}}{\text{Total Current Liabilities}}$$

Note: Quick Assets is the more liquid part of current assets, usually equals to the sum of cash, short-term securities and receivable.

21. Debt - Asset Ratio refers to the proportion of debts as an enterprise's total assets, which reflects the enterprise's capability in utilizing debts for operation and also to what extent the interest of the creditors be protected at the expiration. The formula:

$$\text{Debt - Asset Ratio} = \frac{\text{Total Debt}}{\text{Total Assets}} \times 100\%$$

22. EBIT to Total Assets reflects the profitability of total assets, depending on performance in various aspects of an enterprise, therefore, became a central indicators for evaluate an enterprise. The formula:

$$\text{EBIT to Total Assets} = \frac{\text{Net profit} + \text{Total tax} + \text{Interest payment}}{\text{Average total Assets}} \times 100\%$$

23. Ratio of Capital Increment and Preservation refers to the change of owner's net assets,and presents corporations' strength.The formula:

$$\text{Capital Increment and Preservation Ratio} = \frac{\text{Owner's Capital of the end of Reference Period}}{\text{Owner's Capital of the previous end of Reference Period}}$$

1999

能源生产与消费

PRODUCTION AND CONSUMPTION OF ENERGY

7-1 能 源 消 费 总 量
TOTAL CONSUMPTION OF ENERGY

单位：万吨标准煤 (10000 tons standard-coal)

项目	Item	1998 数量 Quantity	1998 构成(%) Composition(%)	1997 数量 Quantity	1997 构成(%) Composition(%)
合计	**Total**	**3913.3**	**100**	**3832.7**	**100**
第一产业	Primary Industry	96.2	2.5	95.7	2.5
第二产业	Secondary Industry	2543.5	65.0	2514.1	65.6
# 工业	Industry	2486.1	63.5	2456.8	64.1
第三产业	Tertiary Industry	818.6	20.9	768.8	20.0
# 交通邮电	Transportation,Posts and Telecommunications	233.5	6.0	213.8	5.6
生活消费	Living consumption	455.0	11.6	454.1	11.9
城镇	Urban	303.2	7.7	293.8	7.7
农村	Rural	151.8	3.9	160.3	4.2

注：电力按当年平均火力发电煤耗折算标准煤，其他能源品种均按其当量热值折算标准煤，以下各表同。

Note: Electricity conversed to ton-standard-coal according to average coal consumption from thermal power, other energy other energy conversed to tsd according to calorific value.(the followings are the same.)

7-2 能 源 生 产 量
PRODUCTION VOLUME OF ENERGY

项目		Item		1998	1997	1998年为1997年% 1998 as % of 1997
一次能源	**(吨标煤)**	**Directly Used Energy**	**(ton-standard-coal)**	**738.0**	**754.0**	**97.9**
原煤	(万吨)	Coal	(10000 tons)	989.5	1011.8	97.8
水电	(亿千瓦时)	Water and Electricity	(100 million kwh)	9.2	9.2	100.4
二次能源	**(吨标煤)**	**Indirectly Used Energy**	**(ton-standard-coal)**	**2183.3**	**2234.7**	**97.7**
洗精煤	(万吨)	Clean Coal	(10000 tons)	42.8	42.7	100.3
其他洗煤	(万吨)	Other Clean Coal	(10000 tons)	9.9	13.0	75.7
煤制品	(万吨)	Coal Products	(10000 tons)	28.8	41.1	70.0
焦炭	(万吨)	Coke	(10000 tons)	406.2	399,4	101.7
焦炉煤气	(亿立方米)	Coking Gas	(100 million cu.m)	18.4	18.2	100.8
其他煤气	(亿立方米)	Other Gas	(100 million cu.m)	3.8	3.1	122.9
汽油	(万吨)	Gasoline	(10000 tons)	118.1	127.1	92.9
煤油	(万吨)	Kerosene	(10000 tons)		0.6	
柴油	(万吨)	Diesel Oil	(10000 tons)	117.1	109.2	107.3
燃料油	(万吨)	Fuel Oil	(10000 tons)	120.8	161.7	74.7
液化石油气	(万吨)	Liquefied Petroleum	(10000 tons)	32.7	32.0	102.0
炼厂干气	(万吨)	Gas of Plant	(10000 tons)	7.4	7.5	98.5
其他石油制品	(万吨)	Other Petroleum Products	(10000 tons)	194.6	207.1	93.9
其他焦化产品	(万吨)	Other Coking Products	(10000 tons)	19.7	19.9	99.0
热力	(万百万千焦)	Heat	(100 ten thousand kilo-joules)	7789.2	8067.3	96.6
电力	(亿千瓦时)	Electricity	(100 million kwh)	147.2	137.2	107.3

7-3 工业分行业能源终端消费量(实物量)

项　目	Item	原　煤 (万吨) Coal (10000 tons)	洗精煤 (万吨) Clean Coal (10000 tons)	其他洗煤 (万吨) Other Clean Coal (10000 tons)	焦炭 (万吨) Coke (10000 tons)	焦炉煤气 (亿立方米) Coking Gas (100 million cu.m)	其他煤气 (亿立方米) Other Gas (100 million cu.m)	原　油 (万吨) Crude Oil (10000 tons)
工　业	**Industry**	**686.49**	**28.64**	**4.19**	**474.52**	**9.69**	**2.97**	**25.17**
轻工业	Light Industry	125.67	0.04		0.17	0.08		0.16
重工业	High Industry	560.82	28.60	4.19	474.35	9.61	2.97	25.01
采掘业	**Excavation**	**8.78**						
煤炭采选业	Coal Mining and Dressing	8.24						
石油和天然气开采	Petroleum and Natural Gas Extraction							
黑色金属矿采选业	Ferrous Metals Mining and Dressing	0.32						
有色金属矿采选业	Nonferrous Metals Mining and Dressing							
非金属矿采选业	Nonmetal Minerals Mining and Dressing	0.22						
其他矿采选业	Other Minerals Mining and Dressing							
木材及竹材采运业	Timber and Bamboo Cutting and Shipping							
制造业	**Manufacturing**	**660.33**	**28.64**	**4.19**	**474.52**	**9.63**	**2.97**	**24.95**
食品加工业	Food Processing	9.33						
食品制造业	Food Making	17.19				0.03		0.16
饮料制造业	Beverage Production	33.19						
烟草加工业	Tobacco Processing	1.37						
纺织业	Textile Industry	18.12	0.04			0.02		
服装及其他纤维制品制造业	Garments and Other Fiber Products	7.89						
皮革、毛皮、羽绒及其制品业	Leather,Furs,Down and Related Products	2.09						
木材加工及竹、藤、棕、草制品业	Timber Processing,Bamboo,Cane,Palm Fiber and Straw Products	1.91						
家具制造业	Furniture Manufacturing	2.44						
造纸及纸制品业	Papermaking and Paper Products	6.36						
印刷业、记录媒介的复制	Printing and Record Medium Reproduced	9.06				0.01		
文教体育用品制造业	Stationery,Educational and Sports Goods	1.08			0.18			
石油加工及炼焦业	Petroleum Proçessing and Coking Products	1.95						
化学原料及化学制品制造业	Raw Chemical Materials and Chemical Products	61.81			21.15	3.48	2.92	24.76
医药制造业	Medical and Pharmaceutical Products	9.84				0.01		
化学纤维制造业	Chemical Fibers	4.66						
橡胶制品业	Rubber Products	9.70						
塑料制品业	Plastic Products	6.64						
非金属矿物制品业	Nonmetal Mineral Products	203.66			1.29	0.31		0.03
黑色金属冶炼及压延加工业	Smelting and Pressing of Ferrous Metals	168.08	28.60	4.19	447.94	5.47		
有色金属冶炼及压延加工业	Smelting and Pressing of Nonferrous Metals	1.37			0.12			
金属制品业	Metal Products	5.24			1.08	0.06		
普通机械制造业	Ordinary Machinery	13.32			1.87	0.10		
专用设备制造业	Special Purpose Equipment	11.53			0.25	0.03		
交通运输设备制造业	Transportation Equipment	26.44			0.49	0.05		
武器弹药制造业	Weapon and Ammunition	4.68						
电气机械及器材制造	Electric Equipment and Machinery	9.80			0.14	0.04		
电子及通信设备制造	Electronic and Telecommunications	6.24				0.02	0.05	
仪器仪表及文化、办公用机械制造业	Instruments,Meters,Cultural and Official Machinery	2.98			0.01			
其他制造业	Other Manufacturing	2.36						
电力、煤气及水的生产和供应业	**Electricity,Gas and Water Production and Supply**	**17.38**				**0.06**		**0.22**
电力、蒸汽、热水的生产和供应业	Electricity,Steam and Hot Water Production and Supply	16.18				0.01		0.22
煤气生产和供应业	Gas Production and Supply					0.05		
自来水的生产和供应	Water Production and Supply	1.20						

ENERGY TERMINAL CONSUMPTION IN KIND OF INDUSTRY BY SECTOR

汽油 (万吨) Gasoline (10000 tons)	煤油 (万吨) Kerosene (10000 tons)	柴油 (万吨) Diesel Fuel Oil (10000 tons)	燃料油 (万吨) Fuel Oil (10000 tons)	液化石油气 (万吨) Liquefied Petroleum (10000ton)	炼厂干气 (万吨) Net Gas of Plant (10000 tons)	天然气 (亿立方米) Natural Gas (100 million cu.m)	其他石油制品 (万吨) Other Petroleum Products (10000 tons)	其他焦化产品 (万吨) Other Coking Product (10000 tons)	热力 (万百万千焦) Heat (1 billion kilo-joule)	电力 (亿千瓦时) Electricity (100 million kwh)	能源合计 (万吨标准煤) Total (10000 standard-coal)
11.46	**0.41**	**11.27**	**48.12**	**7.16**	**2.11**	**0.25**	**182.88**	**20.48**	**5110.30**	**157.68**	**2351**
3.52	0.07	1.45	0.20	0.15		0.04	0.02		492.49	14.15	164.62
7.94	0.34	9.82	47.92	7.01	2.11	0.21	182.86	20.48	4617.81	143.53	2186.42
0.23		0.73								2.59	16.33
0.16		0.19								1.91	12.77
0.03		0.11								0.51	2.16
										0.02	0.06
0.04		0.15								0.15	0.93
		0.28									0.41
10.59	0.41	10.31	45.98	6.78	2.11	0.25	182.88	20.48	4957.19	127.15	2216.19
0.51							0.02			1.43	12.18
0.59		0.74	0.16	0.12					52.88	1.17	20.92
0.49		0.10							31.19	1.96	31.98
0.01										0.04	1.11
0.34	0.01	0.11		0.01					263.55	3.53	35.7
0.35		0.08							1.95	0.81	9
0.05										0.11	1.92
0.05		0.01								0.14	1.89
0.15		0.02							0.89	0.26	2.88
0.19	0.05	0.04		0.01					2.47	1.04	8.51
0.41	0.02	0.02				0.04			28.16	1.45	13.6
0.14		0.01							9.25	0.17	2.09
0.42		0.43	7.15	6.33	2.11		182.56		2397.73	14.27	424.35
0.58		0.31	7.45	0.01		0.06	0.29	10.96	653.06	14.83	227.12
0.19		0.03	0.04						42.78	1.05	12.55
0.03									58.48	0.92	8.68
0.17		0.02	0.40						0.25	0.88	10.65
0.22		0.08	0.04	0.01					0.25	1.20	9.23
1.19	0.27	2.02	5.56	0.11		0.06			39.08	11.21	199.5
0.71	0.01	4.32	24.38	0.14				9.52	993.57	55.19	1039.59
0.06		0.19							4.82	0.57	3.64
0.64		0.23	0.08							2.01	13.29
0.54	0.02	0.27							116.04	2.20	24.87
0.49	0.01	0.52				0.04			44.43	1.98	18.94
0.97	0.02	0.37	0.60				0.01		151.63	3.24	39.02
0.06		0.10	0.02			0.02			5.86	0.35	5.24
0.50		0.13	0.07	0.01		0.01			32.13	1.36	14.27
0.34		0.12	0.03	0.03		0.02			8.94	2.93	15.88
0.13		0.02							16.91	0.62	5.07
0.07		0.02							0.89	0.23	2.59
0.64		0.23	2.14	0.38					153.11	27.94	118.48
0.36		0.21	2.14						153.11	25.29	107.28
0.19				0.37						0.18	1.81
0.09		0.02		0.01						2.47	9.4

7-4 分 品 种 能 源 消 费 量
ENERGY CONSUMPTION BY CATEGORY

项 目		Item		1998	1997	1998年为1997年% 1998 as % of 1997
煤 炭	(万吨)	Coal	(10000 tons)	2677.7	2621.8	102.1
焦 炭	(万吨)	Coke	(10000 tons)	482.5	480.2	100.5
焦炉煤气	(亿立方米)	Coking Gas	(100 million cu.m)	16.6	16.7	99.9
其他煤气	(亿立方米)	Other Gas	(100 million cu.m)	3.0	3.1	95.8
原 油	(万吨)	Crude Oil	(10000 tons)	643.0	689.5	93.3
汽 油	(万吨)	Gasoline	(10000 tons)	82.3	71.2	115.6
煤 油	(万吨)	Kerosene	(10000 tons)	91.3	88.6	103.0
柴 油	(万吨)	Diesel Oil	(10000 tons)	64.5	52.4	123.3
燃料油	(万吨)	Fuel Oil	(10000 tons)	154.7	198.1	78.1
液化石油气	(万吨)	Liquefied Petroleum	(10000 tons)	25.9	26.9	96.3
炼厂干气	(万吨)	Gas of Plant	(10000 tons)	7.4	7.5	98.5
天然气	(亿立方米)	Natural Gas	(100 million cu.m)	3.2	1.6	196.3
其他石油制品	(万吨)	Other Petroleum Products	(10000 tons)	185.9	193.4	96.1
其他焦化产品	(万吨)	Other Coking Products	(10000 tons)	20.5	21.2	96.8
热 力	(万百万千焦)	Heat	(100 ten thousand kilo-joules)	7789.2	7911.1	98.5
电 力	(亿千瓦时)	Electricity	(100 million kwh)	291.5	277.8	104.9

7-5 平均每万元国内生产总值能源消费量
ENERGY CONSUMPTION PER 10000 YUAN GROSS DOMESTIC PRODUCT

项 目		Item		1998	1997
能源总消费量	**(吨标煤/万元)**	**Total**	**(ton standard-coal/10000 yuan)**	**1.95**	**2.12**
煤 炭	(吨/万元)	Coal	(ton/10000 yuan)	1.33	1.45
电 力	(万千瓦时/万元)	Electricity	(10000 kwh/10000 yuan)	0.15	0.15
石 油	(吨/万元)	Petroleum	(ton/10000 yuan)	0.32	0.37

7-6 人 均 生 活 用 能 量
LIVING CONSUMPTION OF ENERGY PER CAPITA

项 目		Item		1998	1997
人均生活用能量	**(千克标准煤)**	**Living Consumption Per Capita**	**(kg standard-coal)**	**416.8**	**418.3**
煤 炭	(千克)	Coal	(kg)	289.3	318.2
电 力	(千瓦时)	Electricity	(kwh)	269.4	243.8
液化石油气	(千克)	Liquefied Petroleum	(kg)	14.1	14
天然气	(立方米)	Natural Gas	(cu.m)	11.4	7.5
煤 气	(立方米)	Gas	(cu.m)	25.3	29.7

主要统计指标解释

能源总消费量 指报告期内社会各行业和居民生活所消费的各种能源数量，是观察本地区能源消费水平、构成和发展速度的总量指标，能源总消费量包括终端能源消费量、加工转换损失量和损失量三部分。

一次能源生产量 指报告期内生产一次能源的企业将自然界现存的能源资源经过开采而产出的合格产品，主要包括原煤、原油、天然气、水电等。

二次能源生产量 指报告期内将一次能源经过各种加工转换设备生产出的另一种形式的各种合格的能源产品。如火电、热力、洗煤、焦碳、各种石油制品、焦炉煤气、城市煤气等。

工业终端消费量 又称最终消费量。它反映报告期内工业企业作为原料、燃料和动力消费的能源及其去向。它们的消费过程体现了能源消费的终止。不包括加工转换投入量、加工转换损失量和损失量。

平均每万元国内生产总值能源消费量 能源总消费量或分品种能源消费量与国内生产总值之比。

人均生活用能量 指用于生活消费的各种能源数量与人口总数之比。

Explanatory Notes On Main Statistical Indicators

Total Energy Consumption refers to the total consumption of all sectors and households in a given period. It is a comprehensive indicator to show the scale, composition and trend of energy consumption of some region. The total energy consumption can be divided into three parts: Final Energy Consumption, Loss During the Process of Energy Conversion and Loss.

Production Volume of Directly-use Energy refers to qualified products through excavation and production from energy source in stock of nature , mainly include coal, crude oil, natural gas, water and electricity and so on.

Production Volume of Indirectly-use Energy refers to qualified energy products in another form through pressing and changing-over from directly-use energy, such as thermal power, heat, clean coal, coke, petroleum products, coking gas, city gas and so on.

Terminal Consumption of Industry named final consumption, too. It reports energy consumped as raw materials, fuels and power by industrial enterprises and the direction that has gone. The process of consumption reflects the end of energy consumption, exclude input in pressing and changing-over, loss in pressing and changing-over and loss.

Energy Consumption Per 10000 yuan GDP refers to ratio of total consumption or consumption put into different categories to Gross Domestic Product(GDP).

Living Consumption of Energy Per Capita refers to ratio of living consumption to total population.

1999

建筑业

CONSTRUCTION

全市建筑施工企业主要经济指标
Main Economic Indicators on Construction Enterprises

		1998	1997
企业单位数 Number of Enterprises	（个） (unit)	1511	1358
建筑业总产值 Gross Output Value of Construction	（万元） (10000 yuan)	6268097	5237663
年末从业人员 Number of Employment(year-end)	（人） (person)	758438	810799
劳动生产率 Overall Labor Productivity	（元/人） (yuan/person)	73620	64376

1998年独立核算建筑施工企业工程质量
Projects Quality of Construction Enterprises with Independent Accounting System

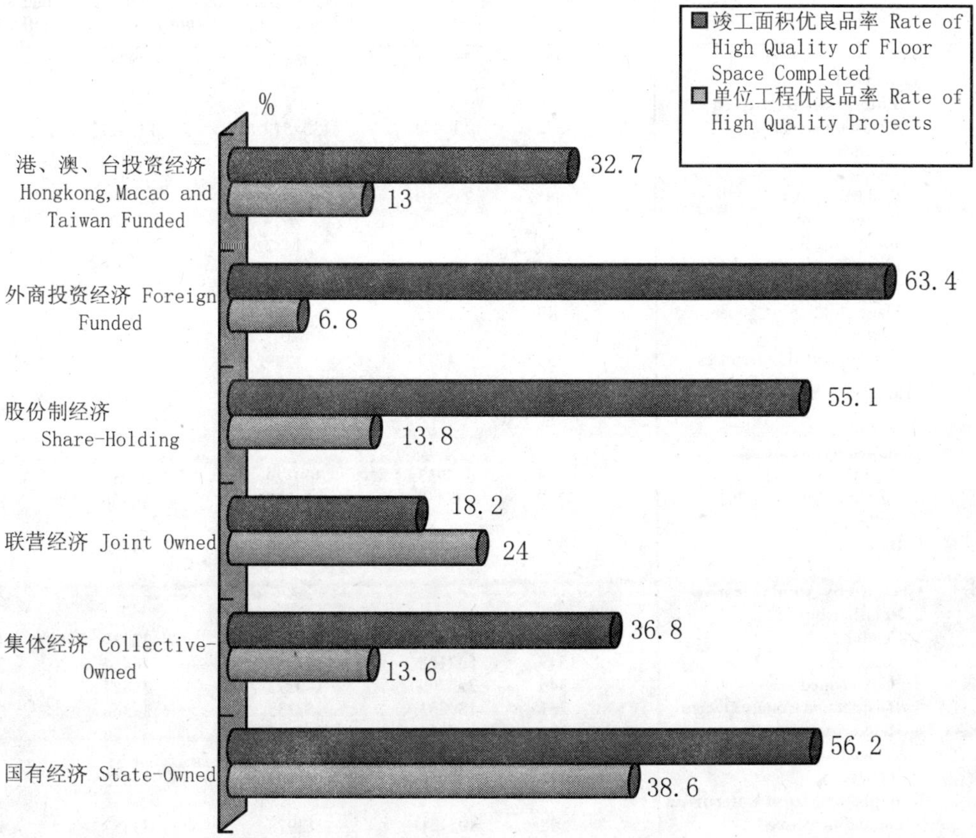

8-1 全市建筑施工企业主要经济指标
MAIN ECONOMIC INDICATORS ON CONSTRUCTION ENTERPRISES

项目 Item		全市总计 Total	独立核算建筑施工企业 Construction Enterprises with Independent Accounting System	#大中型企业 Large and Medium Enterprises	建筑业活动单位 Construction Units
企业单位数 (个)	Number of Enterprises (unit)	1511	1482	222	29
建筑业总产值 (万元)	Gross Output Value of Construction (10000 yuan)	6268097	6246618	4869777	21479
自有机械设备年末总台数 (台)	Number of Machinery and Equipment Owned(year-end) (unit)	150113	149384	100142	729
自有机械设备年末总功率 (千瓦)	Total Power of Machinery and Equipment Owned(year-end) (kw)	3155449	3139612	2414674	15837
年末从业人数 (人)	Number of Employment(year-end) (person)	758438	755591	512945	2847
劳动生产率 (元／人)	Overall Labor Productivity (yuan/person)	73620	73644	82551	6718

8-2 独立核算建筑施工企业基本情况
BASIC STATISTICS FOR CONSTRUCTION ENTERPRISES WITH INDEPENDENT ACCOUNTING SYSTEM

项目	Item	企业单位数(个) Number of Enterprises (unit)	年末从业人员(人) Employment (year-end) (person)	年末自有机械设备 Machinery and Equipment Owned(year-end)		
				净值(万元) Net Value (10000 yuan)	总台数(台) Total Number (unit)	总功率(千瓦) Total Power (kw)
总计	**Total**	**1482**	**755591**	**345575**	**149384**	**3139612**
按企业登记注册类型分	**Grouped by Type of Enterprises Registered**					
内资企业	Domestic Investment Enterprises	1352	738550	338519	143422	3097565
国有企业	State-owned	402	389237	185824	68444	1751540
集体企业	Collective-owned	685	245219	84156	57100	892629
私营企业	Private Business	57	5686	2699	800	7486
联营企业	Joint-owned	16	3005	1482	1028	7258
股份有限公司	Share Holding Company	31	30170	30297	4185	169511
有限责任公司	Limited-Liability Company	118	53649	30114	8613	232433
股份合作企业	Share Holding Cooperative	40	11045	3755	3170	36132
其他企业	Others	3	539	192	82	576
外商投资企业	Foreign Funded Enterprises	50	4777	3289	2753	18001
港澳台商投资企业	HongKong,Macao and Taiwan Funded	80	12264	3767	3209	24046
按行业类别分	**Grouped by Sector**					
土木工程	Civil Engineering	873	643953	300329	123258	2707735
线路、管道和设备安装	Line and equipment Installation	237	77440	36327	16386	339721
建筑物的装修装饰业	Building Decoration	372	34198	8919	9740	92156
按隶属关系分	**Grouped by Administrative Relationship**					
中央	Central	233	218463	97813	32930	1013481
地方	Local	1249	537128	247762	116454	2126131
市属	City Owned	346	252799	140273	45827	1040072
区县属	District and County Owned	261	139261	57355	37366	620672
街道	Subdistrict Owned	96	17366	5292	5186	62357
镇	Town Owned	123	36734	21048	11020	165903
其他	Others	423	90968	23794	17055	237127
按企业规模分	**Grouped by Size of Enterprises**					
大型	Large Enterprises	98	405121	213978	73357	1942151
中型	Medium Enterprises	124	107824	56713	26785	472523
小型	Small Enterprises	1260	242646	74884	49242	724938

8-3 独立核算建筑施工企业总产值和劳动生产率

GROSS OUTPUT VALUE AND LABOR PRODUCTIVITY OF CONSTRUCTION ENTERPRISES WITH INDEPENDENT ACCOUNTING SYSTEM

项 目	Item	总 产 值 (万元) Gross Output Value (10000 yuan)		劳动生产率(元/人) Overall Labor Productivity (yuan/person)	
		1998	1997	1998	1997
总 计	**Total**	**6246617.6**	**5192362.8**	**73644**	**64633**
按经济类型分	**Grouped by Ownership**				
国有经济	State-owned	3323585.9	3509049.7	75341	68735
集体经济	Collective-owned	1390341.7	1277937.7	55097	51155
私营经济	Private	26873.0	2508.9	56730	45287
联营经济	Joint-owned	26560.8	1713.4	69897	33795
股份制经济	Share Holding Enterprise	1249403.0	219971.6	100501	89631
外商投资经济	Foreign Funded Enterprises	131916.2	115232.4	122508	112741
港澳台投资经济	Honkong,Macao and Taiwan Funded	95078.2	65150.5	93969	93019
其他经济	Others	2858.8	798.6	28906	41165
按行业类别分	**Grouped by Sector**				
土木工程	Civil Engineering	5178611.8	4344056.6	71716	62871
线路、管道和设备安装	Line and Equipment Installation	797516.8	662215.2	86928	75981
建筑物的装修装饰业	Building Decoration	270489.0	186091	78695	73670
按隶属关系分	**Grouped by Administrative Relationship**				
中 央	Central	2049461.7	1829965.6	85446	76174
地 方	Local	4197155.9	3362397.2	68992	59709
市 属	City Owned	2396764.9	2003218.4	80003	67973
区县属	District and County Owned	944131.8	810650.4	59598	50458
街 道	Subdistrict Owned	73282.1	76681.3	42579	41180
镇	Town Owned	248300.7	119200.7	49671	45094
其 他	Others	534676.4	352646.4	64297	56238
按企业规模分	**Grouped by Size of Enterprises**				
大 型	Large Enterprises	4053311.8	3627845	86107	70381
中 型	Medium Enterprises	816465.6	301432	68508	68778
小 型	Small Enterprises	1376840.2	1263085.8	53303	51749

8-3 续表 continued

项 目	Item	总 产 值 (万元) Gross Output Value (10000 yuan)	劳动生产率(元/人) Overall Labor Productivity (yuan/person)
总 计	**Total**	**6246617.6**	**73644**
按企业登记注册类型分	**Grouped by Type of Enterprises Registered**		
内资企业	Domestic Investment Enterprises	6019623.2	72760
国有企业	State-Owned	3323585.9	75341
集体企业	Collective Owned	1390341.7	55097
私营企业	Private	26873.0	56730
联营企业	Joint Owned	26560.8	69897
股份有限公司	Share Holding Company	572431.1	111040
有限责任公司	Limited-Liability Company	524404.2	95997
股份合作企业	Share Holding Cooperative	152567.7	84115
其他企业	Others	2858.8	28906
外商投资企业	Foreign Funded	131916.2	122508
港、澳、台商投资企业	Hongkong,Macao and Taiwan Funded	95078.2	93969

8-4 独立核算建筑施工企业竣工率

RATIO OF COMPLETED OF CONSTRUCTION INDEPENDENT ACCOUNTING SYSTEM

单位：%　　(%)

项目	Item	产值竣工率 Ratio of Output Value Completed to Total		面积竣工率 Ratio of Floor Space of Building Completed	
		1998	1997	1998	1997
总计	**Total**	**67.7**	**70.6**	**34.1**	**36.5**
按经济类型分	**Grouped by Ownership**				
国有经济	State-owned	71.1	71.2	32.4	32.9
集体经济	Collective-owned	68.8	71.0	43.7	46.2
私营经济	Private	88.3	77.4	47.6	19.1
联营经济	Joint-owned	58.2	37.8	56.1	50.5
股份制经济	Share Holding Enterprise	55.9	72.1	24.9	26.4
外商投资经济	Foreign Funded Enterprises	87.5	45.9	62.6	34.2
港澳台投资经济	Honkong,Macao and Taiwan Funded	56.7	67.0	19.3	18.4
其他经济	Others	98.9	38.5	100.0	100.0
按行业类别分	**Grouped by Sector**				
土木工程	Civil Engineering	66.8	72.4	34.0	36.1
线路、管道和设备安装	Line and Equipment Installation	73.4	59.8	54.1	57.5
建筑物的装修装饰业	Building Decoration	67.9	65.3		61.0
按隶属关系分	**Grouped by Administrative Relationship**				
中　央	Central	69.2	69.0	32.5	32.2
地　方	Local	67.0	71.4	34.7	38.2
市　属	City Owned	68.1	72.1	27.7	31.9
区县属	District and County Owned	60.4	69.9	40.0	46.6
街　道	Subdistrict Owned	67.1	85.7	45.2	42.4
镇	Town Owned	67.4	81.3	48.4	50.4
其　他	Others	73.5	64.4	48.4	40.8
按企业规模分	**Grouped by Size of Enterprises**				
大　型	Large Enterprises	66.8	70.8	30.0	32.8
中　型	Medium Enterprises	65.9	63.4	37.2	31.2
小　型	Small Enterprises	71.6	71.7	49.5	49.7

8-4 续表 continued

单位：%　　(%)

项目	Item	产值竣工率 Ratio of Output Value Completed to Total	面积竣工率 Ratio of Floor Space of Building Completed
总计	**Total**	**67.7**	**34.1**
按企业登记注册类型分	**Grouped by Type of Enterprises Registered**		
内资企业	Domestic Investment Enterprises	67.5	33.9
国有企业	State-Owned	71.1	32.4
集体企业	Collective Owned	68.8	43.7
私营企业	Private	88.3	47.6
联营企业	Joint Owned	58.2	56.1
股份有限公司	Share Holding Company	48.3	21.7
有限责任公司	Limited-Liability Company	63.6	25.4
股份合作企业	Share Holding Cooperative	57.8	37.0
其他企业	Others	98.9	100.0
外商投资企业	Foreign Funded	87.5	62.6
港、澳、台商投资企业	Hongkong,Macao and Taiwan Funded	56.7	19.3

8-5 独立核算建筑施工企业工程质量
PROJECTS QUALITY OF CONSTRUCTION ENTERPRISES WITH INDEPENDENT ACCOUNTING SYSTEM

单位：%　　　　(%)

项　目	Item	单位工程优良品率 Rate of High Quality Project		竣工面积优良品率 Rate of High Quality of Floor Space Completed	
		1998	1997	1998	1997
总　计	**Total**	**21.4**	**19.8**	**48.9**	**42.8**
按经济类型分	**Grouped by Ownership**				
国有经济	State-owned	38.6	33.0	56.2	54.0
集体经济	Collective-owned	13.6	13.8	36.8	25.5
私营经济	Private	28.1	8.6	23.8	
联营经济	Joint-owned	24.0	100.0	18.2	98.2
股份制经济	Share Holding Enterprises	16.7	8.7	52.9	43.0
外商投资经济	Foreign Funded Enterprises	6.8	6.9	63.4	21.3
港澳台投资经济	Honkong,Macao and Taiwan Funded	13.0	10.5	32.7	5.0
按行业类别分	**Grouped by Sector**				
土木工程	Civil Engineering	26.7	24.6	49.1	43.5
线路、管道和设备安装	Line and Equipment Installation	16.1	15.7	13.7	24.6
建筑物的装修装饰业	Building Decoration		9.8		15.0
按隶属关系分	**Grouped by Administrative Relationship**				
中　央	Central	43.3	26.9	62.3	60.8
地　方	Local	14.3	14.1	44.3	36.7
市　属	City Owned	26.0	19.1	57.5	54.1
区县属	District and County Owned	14.9	9.3	33.1	18.5
街　道	Subdistrict Owned	11.4	8.9	27.3	10.4
镇	Town Owned	14.5	18.6	22.1	23.8
其　他	Others	7.5	13.3	47.1	39.3
按企业规模分	**Grouped by Size of Enterprises**				
大　型	Large Enterprises	41.1	34.5	62.2	51.7
中　型	Medium Enterprises	21.0	27.7	47.1	35.7
小　型	Small Enterprises	14.3	12.1	14.2	25.7

8-5 续表 continued

单位：%　　　　(%)

项　目	Item	单位工程优良品率 Rate of High Quality Project	竣工面积优良品率 Rate of High Quality of Floor Space Completed
总　计	**Total**	**21.4**	**48.9**
按企业登记注册类型分	**Grouped by Type of Enterprises Registered**		
内资企业	Domestic Investment Enterprises	21.6	48.6
国有企业	State-Owned	38.6	56.2
集体企业	Collective Owned	13.6	36.8
私营企业	Private	28.1	23.8
联营企业	Joint Owned	24.0	18.2
股份有限公司	Share Holding Company	13.8	55.1
有限责任公司	Limited-Liability Company	34.9	54.8
股份合作企业	Share Holding Cooperative	10.0	40.6
外商投资企业	Foreign Funded	6.8	63.4
港、澳、台商投资企业	Hongkong,Macao and Taiwan Funded	13.0	32.7

8-6 独立核算建筑施工企业主要财务指标

单位：万元

项目	Item	资产总计 Total Assets	流动资产合计 Total Circulating Assets	#货币资金 Cash	#应收帐款 Accounts Receivable	#存货 Stock
总计	**Total**	**8710909**	**6971441**	**975562**	**2152966**	**2075964**
按企业登记注册类型分	**Grouped by Type of Enterprises Registered**					
内资企业	Domestic Investment	8450935	6745676	922492	2112753	2021448
国有企业	State-Owned	5708984	4553650	624008	1443092	1335554
集体企业	Collective Owned	1361238	1086543	203366	218765	423140
私营企业	Private	32018	22427	4072	7924	5894
联营企业	Joint Owned	27382	20648	4313	5782	4030
股份有限公司	Share Holding Company	440128	382108	40453	146346	125391
有限责任公司	Limited-Liability Company	758397	591898	30644	259983	97519
股份合作企业	Share Holding Cooper-tive	121129	87105	15054	30558	29573
其他企业	Others	1659	1297	582	303	347
外商投资企业	Foreign Funded	129770	112354	31714	17741	26943
港、澳、台商投资企业	Hongkong,Macao and Taiwan Funded	130205	113411	21356	22474	27573
按行业类别分	**Grouped by Sector**					
土木工程	Civil Engineering	7146024	5696270	709808	1874583	1688767
线路、管道和设备安装	Line and Equipment Ins-tallation	1218193	993527	211936	215049	307561
建筑物的装修装饰业	Building Decoration	346691	281644	53818	63334	79635
按隶属关系分	**Grouped by Adminis-trative Relationship**					
中央	Central	2911301	2278453	392750	774177	435899
地方	Local	5799608	4692988	582812	1378789	1640065
市属	City Owned	4162154	3425069	368828	1071731	1149931
区县属	District and County Owned	823218	632672	98730	159841	250719
街道	Subdistrict Owned	96044	80061	15013	11434	32891
镇	Town Owned	207063	152807	20713	50512	56864
其他	Others	511128	402380	79528	85271	149661
按企业规模分	**Grouped by Size of Enterprises**					
大型	Large Enterprises	5934828	4709036	579177	1615880	1328661
中型	Medium Enterprises	1099283	903986	124407	269472	301705
小型	Small Enterprises	1676797	1358419	271978	267614	445598

MAIN FINANCIAL INDICATORS ON CONSTRUCTION ENTERPRISES WITH INDEPENDENT ACCOUNTING SYSTEM

(10000 yuan)

#在建工程 under Construction	长期投资 Long-term Investment	固定资产合计 Total Fixed Assets	固定资产原价合计 Original Value of Fixed Assets	#生产经营用 for Production Use	累计折旧 Accumulative Depreciation	#本年折旧 of this Year	专项工程 Special Projects	无形及递延资产合计 Intangible and Deffered Assets	#无形资产 Intangible
904192	**429233**	**1022521**	**1543265**	**1010762**	**539767**	**95964**	**141241**	**56478**	**39573**
877499	426456	1000987	1510774	990065	528642	92617	140322	51344	35339
479309	310015	656695	1013775	642332	367935	62852	98259	30988	22344
219443	35816	207159	282789	185387	81289	17089	15915	5950	1894
1134	2710	6308	7341	5135	1173	606	154	156	19
2897	972	4264	5342	4445	1183	269	508	48	17
94737	7807	43126	68040	52650	25355	5353	2426	1257	72
59904	63564	65164	109955	87289	46387	5155	20200	11617	9795
20075	5484	18006	23162	12523	5215	1285	2860	1318	1198
	88	265	370	304	105	8		10	
10531	938	11543	16410	10194	4876	1638	509	1337	1029
16161	1839	9991	16081	10502	6248	1709	411	3797	3205
677505	376049	836355	1264992	833063	443160	77351	113687	46505	33897
186636	43967	146602	225913	147046	82282	14387	23226	4778	2693
40050	9217	39565	52360	30653	14325	4226	4328	5195	2984
256033	142977	399028	617333	399038	227323	39693	53150	19958	12844
648159	286256	623492	925931	611724	312444	56271	88091	36520	26729
374735	242042	362977	575631	378973	215591	34717	59238	21270	19144
136713	20316	130472	177916	113669	49542	10987	18262	10800	6087
20384	2556	11293	17068	14423	6410	1290	570	774	338
30362	4837	43480	56974	35675	15411	2550	2199	729	200
85966	16505	75271	98342	68983	25491	6726	7822	2947	960
471335	358969	663673	1029550	678440	376234	64945	107223	37920	30751
190425	27593	127672	191609	132378	66445	11489	21023	7439	3318
242432	42672	231176	322106	199944	97088	19530	12995	11119	5505

8-6 续表1 continued

单位：万元

项目	Item	其他资产合计 Other Assets	负债合计 Total Liability	流动负债合计 Total Circulating Liability	#短期借款 Short-term Loans	#应付帐款 Accounts Payable
总计	**Total**	**89960**	**6931441**	**6657715**	**820976**	**1577565**
按企业登记注册类型分	**Grouped by Type of Enterprises Registered**					
内资企业	Domestic Investment	86115	6776372	6507670	801372	1552481
国有企业	State-Owned	59366	4731837	4505648	481754	1093292
集体企业	Collective Owned	9832	954386	937170	90942	180444
私营企业	Private Owned	264	21954	21017	1824	3505
联营企业	Joint Owned	941	18604	18205	6890	2858
股份有限公司	Share Holding Company	3403	361597	359033	95218	74417
有限责任公司	Limited-Liability Company	5953	599043	578103	112367	179280
股份合作企业	Share Holding Cooperative	6356	88147	87690	12358	18628
其他企业	Others		804	804	19	57
港澳台商投资企业	Hongkong,Macao and Taiwan Funded Enterprises	757	68865	67829	9900	10970
外商投资企业	Foreign Funded Enterprises	3088	86204	82216	9705	14114
按行业类别分	**Grouped by Sector**					
土木工程	Civil Engineering	77144	5713376	5500904	758331	1369854
线路、管道和设备安装	Line and Equipment Installation	6073	1000788	944519	35411	169283
建筑物的装修装饰业	Building Decoration	6743	217277	212292	27234	38428
按隶属关系分	**Grouped by Administrative Relationship**					
中央	Central	17724	2389582	2253712	246221	542777
地方	Local	72236	4541859	4404002	574755	1034788
市属	City Owned	51538	3441890	3329487	431306	779096
区县属	District and County Owned	10693	569457	557061	77706	164306
街道	Subdistrict Owned	791	71226	70466	1334	7554
镇	Town Owned	3012	129197	125981	27483	33465
其他	Others	6203	330089	321008	36927	50367
按企业规模分	**Grouped by Size of Enterprises**					
大型	Large Enterprises	57995	4863581	4641209	596058	1148504
中型	Medium Enterprises	11571	893460	870397	82166	202238
小型	Small Enterprises	20393	1174400	1146109	142752	226823

8-6 续表2 continued

(10000 yuan)

长期负债合计 Total Long-term Liability	#长期借款 Long-term Loans	所有者权益合计 Ownership Interest	实收资本 Contri-buted Capital	国家资本 State	集体资本 Collective	法人资本 Institution-nai Units	个人资本 Individuals	港澳台资本 Hongkong, Macao and Taiwan	外商资本 Foreign	工程结算收入 Revenue of Settlement of Projects
273726	**92359**	**1779468**	**1155899**	**550875**	**249654**	**281649**	**26513**	**28710**	**18499**	**5793141**
268703	88182	1674562	1060169	539394	242977	251503	26294			5575142
226189	75625	977147	611474	477075		134399				3284943
17216	10280	406852	253576		218632	34731	213			1155290
938	938	10064	10631			4314	6316			21905
399	323	8778	11391	4692	6056	643				21686
2564	520	78531	40073	17453	2660	16781	3179			532513
20940	125	159353	108852	40174	1561	54999	12118			443265
457	371	32982	23324		14068	4788	4468			114120
		855	848			848				1420
1036	685	61340	59225	9251	4419	17038	218	28298		92932
3988	3493	43566	36507	2230	2259	13108		411	18499	125069
212472	55914	1432649	902641	482954	201994	197938	7545	7113	5097	4762559
56269	33775	217405	126052	39154	30837	46589	4952	3250	1269	756850
4985	2670	129414	127207	28766	16823	37123	14016	18346	12133	273733
135869	56033	521719	318786	244937	15218	46075	2363	7643	2550	1997644
137857	36326	1257748	837114	305938	234436	235574	24150	21067	15949	3795497
112402	19822	720264	459445	243758	25613	166410	4837	10044	8783	2317115
12396	6443	253761	178555	56537	93700	22294	1136	1980	2910	732811
760	367	24818	19298		16638	1772	222	156	510	75066
3216	1721	77866	50777	40	43873	6780	18	66		203143
9082	7974	181039	129039	5603	54612	38320	17936	8821	3747	467363
222371	67484	1071248	611687	370308	72930	161440	4968	698	1344	3712982
23063	6785	205824	149569	63454	44942	34201	3649	1485	1839	781955
28292	18090	502397	394643	117113	131782	86008	17896	26527	15316	1298204

8-6 续表3 continued

单位：万元

项目 Item		工程结算成本 Cost of Settlement of Projects	工程结算税金及附加 Tax and Extra Charges of Settlement of Projects	工程结算利润 Profits of Settlement of Projects	其他业务收入 Revenue of Other Business	其他业务利润 Profits of Other Business
总计	**Total**	**5002905**	**172717**	**617519**	**397617**	**65789**
按企业登记注册类型分	**Grouped by Type of Enterprises Registered**					
内资企业	Domestic Investment	4819783	166326	589033	394947	65177
国有企业	State-Owned	2859444	95034	330464	359552	54625
集体企业	Collective Owned	994777	37134	123380	16389	7339
私营企业	Private Owned	17942	707	3256	151	63
联营企业	Joint Owned	18856	669	2161	344	216
股份有限公司	Share Holding Company	453021	15323	64169	3866	78
有限责任公司	Limited-Liability Company	376401	13407	53457	14392	2753
股份合作企业	Share Holding Cooperative	98096	4005	12019	253	103
其他企业	Others	1246	47	127		
港澳台商投资企业	Hongkong,Macao and Taiwan Funded Enterprises	79242	2667	11023	2278	279
外商投资企业	Foreign Funded Enterprises	103881	3723	17465	393	333
按行业类别分	**Grouped by Sector**					
土木工程	Civil Engineering	4127300	143411	491848	345187	58201
线路、管道和设备安装	Line and Equipment Installation	645363	20697	90789	46058	5648
建筑物的装修装饰业	Building Decoration	230242	8609	34882	6371	1939
按隶属关系分	**Grouped by Administrative Relationship**					
中　央	Central	1755234	56261	186149	107295	12383
地　方	Local	3247671	116455	431370	290321	53406
市　属	City Owned	1974098	69105	273911	267756	43756
区县属	District and County Owned	634673	23754	74384	10599	5034
街　道	Subdistrict Owned	63435	2392	9239	2945	846
镇	Town Owned	171354	6876	24913	2415	1818
其　他	Others	404112	14329	48923	6607	1952
按企业规模分	**Grouped by Size of Enterprises**					
大　型	Large Enterprises	3217803	108471	386708	351838	49022
中　型	Medium Enterprises	676751	24576	80629	21686	9817
小　型	Small Enterprises	1108351	39671	150183	24093	6950

8-6 续表4 continued

(10000 yuan)

管理费用 Overhead Cost	# 税金 Taxes	# 财产保险费 Premium of Property	# 劳动待业保险费 Premium for Employment	财务费用 Financial Expense	# 利息支出 Interest Expenditure	营业利润 Operating Profits	投资收益 Investment Income	营业外收入 Out-business Income	营业外支出 Out-business Expenditure	利润总额 Total Profits
497019	**9518**	**1676**	**49649**	**51986**	**46993**	**134304**	**10417**	**20430**	**17821**	**123744**
473914	9152	1541	49408	51932	46508	128364	10047	20201	17638	117716
299106	3645	995	40996	29629	28095	56354	8408	15845	14213	45362
81720	4473	359	1198	5142	2333	43857	1130	3042	2176	45073
2949	46	7	12	33	1	338	9	3	29	357
1714	69	5	273	84	-23	578		16	39	548
35406	375	46	2179	7424	6929	21417	251	272	459	21503
46318	451	118	4716	8720	8479	1172	239	828	628	110
6569	93	11	34	901	695	4652	10	195	94	4767
132				-1	-1	-4				-4
11430	158	55	158	153	176	-281	348	107	86	-189
11675	209	80	83	-99	311	6221	22	122	99	6217
388824	7898	1283	36544	49696	44271	111530	8590	17266	15338	98753
74573	1291	249	12478	790	1553	21075	1713	2364	2009	22843
33622	329	145	626	1501	1169	1698	114	800	474	2148
154272	1579	300	17901	15287	12704	28974	2567	4366	6593	25133
342747	7939	1377	31748	36699	34289	105329	7850	16064	11229	98611
231482	3102	824	29407	28002	30133	58183	6365	12464	7804	51040
58122	3754	329	2055	4085	1933	17211	277	2047	2409	16441
8507	92	50	203	-24	-46	1603	53	128	109	1694
10618	332	40	6	3001	1304	13112	557	163	224	13016
34019	659	134	78	1635	965	15220	598	1261	683	16421
314425	6836	794	40155	44890	42270	76416	8434	13286	9273	68342
61935	646	246	6191	4334	2843	24177	904	3509	5756	19876
120659	2037	637	3302	2763	1880	33711	1078	3635	2793	35526

8-6 续表5 continued

单位：万元

项目	Item	应交所得税 Income Tax Payable	转作奖金的利润 Profits Distributed as Bonus	提取盈余公积 Surplus Accumulation Funds Drawn	应付利润 Profits Payable	# 已分配股利 Divided Payment
总计	**Total**	**39576**	**9802**	**28314**	**16282**	**1002**
按企业登记注册类型分	**Grouped by Type of Enterprises Registered**					
内资企业	Domestic Investment	38389	9672	27773	12705	166
国有企业	State-Owned	13866	6057	18144	1964	-148
集体企业	Collective Owned	13381	3433	6602	8339	172
私营企业	Private Owned	171	4	45	11	5
联营企业	Joint Owned	114	80	119	89	
股份有限公司	Share Holding Company	6846	6	1260	329	89
有限责任公司	Limited-Liability Company	2505	48	1197	1875	17
股份合作企业	Share Holding Cooperative	1506	44	406	98	31
其他企业	Others					
港澳台商投资企业	Hongkong,Macao and Taiwan Funded Enterprises	538	29	232	826	199
外商投资企业	Foreign Funded Enterprises	650	103	309	2751	638
按行业类别分	**Grouped by Sector**					
土木工程	Civil Engineering	30580	8953	22372	10612	588
线路、管道和设备安装	Line and Equipment Installation	7042	703	5113	3814	209
建筑物的装修装饰业	Building Decoration	1954	146	829	1856	206
按隶属关系分	**Grouped by Administrative Relationship**					
中央	Central	8773	2956	7206	1912	-106
地方	Local	30803	6846	21108	14371	1108
市属	City Owned	16919	3482	13915	5342	345
区县属	District and County Owned	5372	1104	2514	2152	-22
街道	Subdistrict Owned	635	202	365	225	20
镇	Town Owned	2678	1058	1973	1621	
其他	Others	5199	999	2342	5030	766
按企业规模分	**Grouped by Size of Enterprises**					
大型	Large Enterprises	22683	6526	17546	5904	
中型	Medium Enterprises	5265	692	4259	2437	590
小型	Small Enterprises	11628	2585	6509	7941	412

8-6 续表6 continued

(10000 yuan)

未分配利润 Profits Undistributed	本年应付工资总额 Total Wages Payable in the Year	# 主营业务应付工资 Wage Payable of Major Business	本年应付福利费总额 Welfares Payable in the Year	# 主营业务应付福利费 of Major Business	建筑业增加值 Value Added of Construction	流动比率(%) Circulating Assets/Liquid Liabilities(%)	速动比率(%) Quick-circulating Assets/Liquid Lia-bilities(%)	资产负债率(%) Liabilities/Total Assets(%)	存货周转率(%) Turnover Rate of Stock(%)	资本金利润率(%) Profits/Capital(%)
45361	**825741**	**752230**	**82379**	**73432**	**1771029**	**1.05**	**0.74**	**0.80**	**2.54**	**0.11**
42279	811737	738992	80133	71378	1716906	1.04	0.73	0.80	2.51	0.11
-960	465147	425770	51120	46131	1004892	1.01	0.71	0.83	2.22	0.07
25884	223319	204071	16337	14648	401993	1.16	0.71	0.70	2.50	0.18
39	2930	2712	247	224	7563	1.07	0.79	0.69	4.14	0.03
72	1739	1631	648	628	5699	1.13	0.91	0.68	5.08	0.05
14560	52864	50426	5263	4953	142778	1.06	0.72	0.82	3.88	0.54
-1921	50013	46645	4537	4041	127871	1.02	0.86	0.79	4.42	
4607	15479	7491	1950	722	25650	0.99	0.66	0.73	4.16	0.20
-2	246	246	31	31	460	1.61	1.18	0.48	7.18	
-1041	6651	6159	1128	1041	22912	1.67	1.27	0.53	3.14	
4124	7353	7079	1117	1013	31210	1.37	1.04	0.66	4.57	0.17
39315	659317	603919	66216	59578	1420550	1.04	0.73	0.80	2.57	0.11
8735	103007	86585	13305	11223	237451	1.05	0.73	0.82	2.24	0.18
-2689	63417	61725	2858	2632	113028	1.33	0.95	0.63	3.21	0.02
6386	256242	229798	25704	22875	554257	1.01	0.82	0.82	4.11	0.08
38975	569499	522431	56675	50558	1216772	1.07	0.69	0.78	2.11	0.12
9175	311186	286792	35451	31993	729027	1.03	0.68	0.83	1.79	0.11
15851	105834	95302	12692	11210	221446	1.14	0.69	0.69	2.84	0.09
305	54517	49797	1185	927	63940	1.14	0.67	0.74	1.97	0.09
6676	36141	33074	2385	2042	69793	1.21	0.76	0.62	3.18	0.26
6968	61822	57466	4961	4385	132565	1.25	0.79	0.65	3.17	0.13
20898	519762	475860	54540	48572	1131546	1.01	0.73	0.82	2.52	0.11
8746	98272	90864	10804	9881	224276	1.04	0.69	0.81	2.40	0.13
15717	207706	185506	17035	14979	415207	1.19	0.80	0.70	2.72	0.09

8-7 全市建筑施工企业利税总额前50名
THE FIRST FIFTY PLACES OF TOTAL PRE-TAX PROFITS OF CONSTRUCTION ENTERPRISES

单位：千元 (1000 yuan)

名 次 No.	企 业 名 称 Enterprise	利 税 总 额 Total Pre-tax Profits
1	中国建筑第一工程局第四建筑公司	97333
2	北京韩村河建筑集团总公司	75308
3	交通部第一公路工程总公司	67573
4	北京市第五城市建设工程公司	66781
5	北京城建集团二公司	64725
6	北京市第一城市建设工程公司	62688
7	北京市第四城市建设工程公司	62575
8	铁道部第十六工程局	52060
9	北京怀柔建筑企业集团总公司	51751
10	北京市朝阳田华建筑集团公司	47115
11	北京市第六建筑工程公司	45284
12	北京市房山区建筑企业集团总公司	44164
13	北京市第三建筑工程公司	42526
14	北京中铁建筑工程公司	40470
15	中国建筑一局(集团)有限公司	40000
16	北京市第一建筑工程公司	39957
17	北京市第三城市建设工程公司	38327
18	北京市第五建筑工程公司	37955
19	中国人民解放军总后工程总队	36770
20	中建第一工程局第五建筑公司	35523
21	北京市城建道桥工程公司	32431
22	中国建筑第二局第一建筑工程公司	30642
23	北京市第二建筑工程公司	28926
24	中国建筑二局第三建筑公司	28005
25	北京住宅开发建设集团总公司	27802
26	房山建工企业集团总公司	26510
27	北京市第三市政工程公司	26173
28	北京建雄建筑集团	25574
29	北京市第五住宅建筑工程公司	25246
30	北京市路明路灯工程安装处	24996
31	北京中北华宇建筑工程公司	24800
32	北京市第七建筑工程公司	24563
33	北京城建亚泰工程公司	24460
34	北京市平谷县建筑工程总公司	24197
35	中建建筑承包公司	23681
36	北京市第三住宅建筑工程公司	23437
37	北京市城市建设工程安装公司	22122
38	北京长城贝尔芬格伯格建筑工程有限公司	21509
39	北京市第七城市建设工程公司	20734
40	北京铁路工程总公司	20331
41	北京恒基建筑工程有限公司	19457
42	中国建筑第一工程局第二建筑公司	18986
43	北京市合力电信集团	18522
44	北京市第四市政工程公司	17958
45	北京顺义建筑企业集团公司	17636
46	北京市房山城乡建筑企业集团总公司	16350
47	北京市第六住宅建筑工程公司	15898
48	北京市第一住宅建筑工程公司	15669
49	北京燕山石油化工公司建筑安装工程公司	15558
50	北京市第二住宅建筑工程公司	15326

8-8 外埠进京施工单位主要指标
MAIN INDICATORS ON NON-LOCAL CONSTRUCTION UNITS IN BEIJING

项目		Item		1998	1997
单位个数	(个)	Number of Units	(unit)	187	175
职工人数	(万人)	Number of Staff and Workers	(10000 persons)	5.1	4.9
施工产值	(亿元)	Output Value of Construction	(100 million yuan)	25.9	22.3
施工面积	(万平方米)	Floor Space of Buildings under Construction	(10000 sq.m)	349.1	372.3
竣工面积	(万平方米)	Floor Space of Buildings Completed	(10000 sq.m)	120.8	125.1

8-9 北京市违法建筑情况调查汇总表
COLLECTING LIST OF SURVEY ON ILLEGAL CONSTRUCTION OF BEIJING

项目	Item	面积总计(平方米) Total Floor Space (sq.m)	楼房 Storied Building		平房 Singal-storey House	
			幢数(幢) Number (unit)	建筑面积(平方米) Floor Space (sq.m)	间数(间) Rooms (room)	建筑面积(平方米) Floor Space (sq.m)
合计	**Total**	**7337965**	**2397**	**1288141**	**361519**	**6049824**
按所在地类别	**By Type of Location**					
主干道	Main Lines	1172838	401	268821	45221	904017
次干道	Secondary Lines	672205	178	120535	28678	551670
支路	Branch Lines	701579	323	234399	22096	467180
街巷(胡同)	Street(Lane)	1522010	476	156772	106669	1365238
小区(楼群)	Residential Districts	571755	87	28037	44296	543718
# 1985年后新建小区	New Buildings Built after 1985	156249	49	12678	9928	143571
单位大院	Residential Districts of Units	696563	239	71782	29624	624781
公园、风景区	Parks and Scenic Spots	118471	18	41337	3887	77134
水源保护区	Protection Area of Water Source	42313	12	11664	3169	30649
城乡结合部	Combination Area of Urban and Rural Areas	1840231	663	354794	77879	1485437
按区域	**By Geographic Position**					
二环路以内	within the Second Ring Road	389691	437	51649	25980	338042
二环路外至三环路内	the Second-third Ring Road	1417250	328	182030	94450	1235220
三环路外至四环路内	the Third-fourth Ring Road	1990720	992	543325	77896	1447395
四环路以外	Beyond the Fourth Rind Road	3540304	640	511137	163193	3029167
按隶属关系	**By Administrative Relationship**					
中央	Central	512657	136	81243	20292	431414
市	City	817029	267	102606	34069	714423
区	District	711619	309	133497	29556	578122
街道	Street	257585	75	13254	16719	244331
镇	Town	54297	2	388	2800	53909
乡	Township	1032392	157	192953	36474	839439
居委会	Neighborhood Committee	82819	5	1679	7114	81140
村	Village	2379176	408	643701	83452	1735475
其他	Others	1490391	1038	118820	131043	1371571

主 要 统 计 指 标 解 释

建筑业统计单位 指从事房屋、构筑物建造和设备安装活动的生产单位。根据不同的组织方式，建筑业统计的调查单位可分为法人建筑业企业和附营建筑施工单位。法人建筑业企业是指专门组织的独立核算的法人建筑业企业。它应同时具备的条件是：（1）依法成立，有自己的名称、组织机构和场所，能够承担民事责任；（2）独立拥有和使用资产，承担负债，有权与其他单位签订合同；（3）独立核算盈亏，能够编制资产负债表。附营建筑施工单位是指建筑业以外行业的企业、事业单位为完成本单位固定资产建造任务而自行组织的建筑施工单位。它应同时具备的条件是：（1）具有一个场所，从事或主要从事建筑安装活动；（2）单独组织生产经营活动；（3）在企业内部单独核算收支。

建筑业总产值（即自行完成施工产值） 指建筑业企业或附营建筑施工单位自行完成的按工程进度计算的建筑安装生产总值。建筑业产值包括：

（1）建筑工程产值 指列入建筑工程预算内的各种工程价值。

（2）设备安装工程产值 指设备安装工程价值。

（3）房屋、构筑物修理产值 指房屋构筑物修理所完成的价值，但不包括被修理房屋、构筑物本身的价值和生产设备的修理价值。

（4）非标准设备制造产值 指加工制造没有定型的、非标准的生产设备的加工费和原材料价值，不论是现场还是附属加工厂为本单位承建工程制造的非标准设备的价值，都应计算产值。

自有机械设备年末总台数 指归本企业（或单位）所有，属于本企业固定资产的生产性机械设备年末总台数。包括施工机械、生产设备、运输设备以及其他设备。

自有机械设备年末总功率 指本企业（或单位）自有施工机械、生产设备、运输设备以及其他设备等列为在册固定资产的生产性机械设备年末总功率，按设定能力或查定能力计算。包括机械本身的动力和为该机械服务的单独动力设备，如电动机等。计算单位用千瓦，动力换算可按 1 马力=0.735 千瓦折合成千瓦数。电焊机、变压器、锅炉不计算动力。

企业总收入 指与企业生产经营直接有关的各项收入，包括工程结算收入和其他业务收入，即：

企业总收入=工程结算收入+其他业务收入

Explanatory Notes On Main Statistical Indicators

Statistical Unit of Construction refers to the establishment engaged in the construction of buildings and structures or the installation of equipment. Depending upon the way of organization, they can be divided into two categories: corporate construction enterprises and affiliated construction units,. A corporate construction enterprise is a legal entity with independent accounting system, especially set up to undertake construction activities. It should meet the following three conditions:(1)being set up in line with relevant legal basis, having its full name, organization and location, and capable of taking civil liabilities; (2) independently possessing and using its assets and assuming its liabilities, and entitled to sign contracts with other institutions; and (3) making independent accounts of its profits and losses, and capable of compiling its own balance sheet. On the other hand, the affiliated construction units are subsidiary constructing units that are established by enterprises or institutions in other industries to take construction projects to build up their fixed assets. They should also meet three conditions: (1)engaged exclusively or mainly in construction and installation activities with a stable sits; (2)organizing independently their production/management; and (3)with independent accounting capability in the enterprises to which they are attached.

Gross Output Value of Construction (Output Value of Projects Under Construction) refers to the gross output value of construction and installation projects that are undertaken by construction enterprises or affiliated constructing units, calculated in line with the planned schedule. It includes:

(1) Output value of construction projects, which is the value of projects covered by the project budgets;

(2) Output value of installation projects, which is the value of the installation of equipment;

(3) Output value of repair of buildings and structures, which is the value created through the repairs, exclude the value of buildings or structures being repaired or the value of the repair of production equipment;

(4) Output value of manufactured non-standard equipment, that is the value of non-standard production equipment (including raw materials and manufacturing cost)made for the construction project, irrespective of whether the equipment is manufactured on the construction site or in subsidiary workshops.

Total Number of Self-Owned Machinery at Year End refers to the number of machines and equipment owned by the enterprises(or units) , and listed as the fixed assets of the enterprises(or units)by the end of the year, including machinery and equipment for construction, production, transportation and other purposes.

Total Power of Self-Owned Machinery at Year End refers to the total power of machines and equipment owned by the enterprises (or units) , and listed as the fixed assets of the enterprises (or units) by the end of the year, including machines and equipment for construction, production, transportation and other purposes. The power of the machinery is calculated on basis of the designed or verified capacity, covering the power of the machinery/equipment and the separate power equipment serving the machinery/equipment (such as electric motors) , but excluding welders, transformers and boilers. The unit used for the calculation of power is kilowatt, with horsepower converted to kilowatt by 1 horsepower = 0.735 kilowatt.

Total Revenue of Enterprises refers to the sum of income from production and operation of enterprises, including income from settlement of projects and other operational income, namely:

Total Revenue of Enterprises = Income from Settlement of Projects + Other Operation Income

交通运输、邮电通信业

TRANSPORTATION，POSTS AND TELECOMMUNICATIONS

社会客货运总量（换算周转量）
Passenger and Freight Traffic(converted into turnover volume)

单位：万吨公里 （10000 tn-km）

	1998	1997	1998年为1997年% 1998 as % of 1997
铁路 Railway	2458156	2740812	89.7
公路 Highway	813696	795310	102.3
民航 Civil Aviation	217548	227848	95.5
管道 Pipeline	343	431	79.6

邮电业务总量
Posts and Telecommunications Services

Public Telephones (unit)
Local Telephone (10000 subscriber)
Public Telegrams (10000 pcs)
Magazines (10000 copies)
Newspaper (10000 copies)

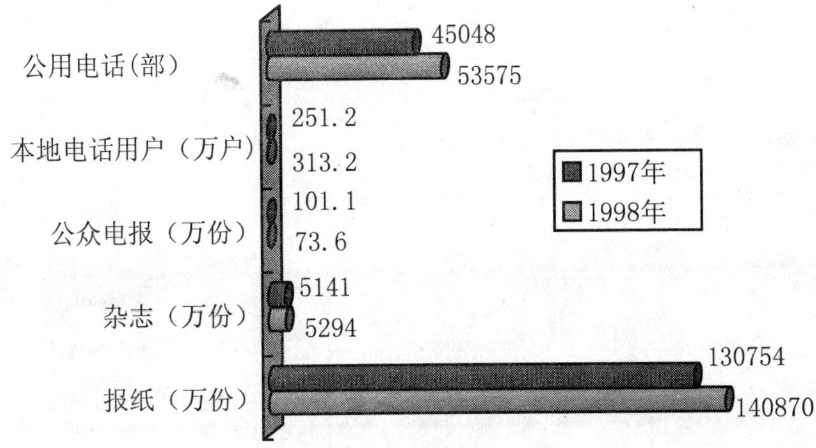

9-1 社 会 客 货 运 总 量 (换算周转量)
PASSENGER AND FREIGHT TRAFFIC(CONVERTED INTO TURNOVER VOLUME)

项 目 Item		1998	1997	1998年为1997年% 1998 as % of 1997	构 成(%) Composition(%)	
					1998	1997
运输总量(万吨公里) Total	**(10000 tn-km)**	**3489742.0**	**3764400.7**	**92.7**	**100**	**100**
铁路	Railway	2458156.0	2740811.8	89.7	70.44	72.81
公路	Highway	813696.0	795310.4	102.3	23.32	21.13
# 交通运输系统	Transportation System	52009.9	53348.4	97.5	1.49	1.4
民航	Civil Aviation	217547.5	227847.7	95.5	6.23	6.05
管道	Pipeline	342.7	430.8	79.6	0.01	0.01

9-2 社会货物运输量及周转量
FREIGHT TRAFFIC AND TON-KILOMETERS

项 目 Item		1998	1997	1998年为1997年% 1998 as % of 1997	构 成(%) Composition(%)	
					1998	1997
货运总量 (万吨)	**Freight Traffic (10000 tn)**	**30127.5**	**32349.7**	**93.1**	**100**	**100**
铁路	Railway	2562.5	2883.3	88.9	8.51	8.91
公路	Highway	27490.0	29360.0	93.6	91.25	90.76
交通运输系统	Transportation System	688.0	880.0	78.2	2.28	2.72
非交通运输系统	Non-transportation System	26802.0	28480.0	94.1	88.96	88.04
民航	Civil Aviation	22.4	19.0	117.7	0.07	0.06
管道	Pipeline	51.6	87.4	59.1	0.17	0.27
货物周转总量 (万吨公里)	**Freight Ton-Kilometers (10000 tn-km)**	**2846652.2**	**3127394.5**	**91.0**	**100**	**100**
铁路	Railway	1952602.4	2263274.0	86.3	68.59	72.37
公路	Highway	783237.0	769190.0	101.8	27.51	24.6
交通运输系统	Transportation System	32085.0	36982.0	86.8	1.13	1.19
非交通运输系统	Non-transportation System	751152.0	732208.0	102.6	26.39	23.41
民航	Civil Aviation	110470.5	94499.7	116.9	3.88	3.02
管道	Pipeline	342.7	430.8	79.6	0.01	0.01

9-3 运 输 线 路
TRANSPORTATION ROUTES

项 目 Item		条 数 (条) Routes(unit)		长 度 (公里) Length(km)	
		1998	1997	1998	1997
铁 路	Railway	26	26	1817.2	1817.2
公 路	Highway	2647	2616	12498.0	12084.0
民 航	Civil Aviation	168	168		
其中: 国航	Air China	134	130		
新华	Xinhua	34	38		
管 道	Pipeline	8	8	28.8	28.8

注：民航包括国际航空公司,新华航空公司。

Note：Data of civil aviation include those of Air China and China Xinhua Airlines.

9-4 铁路运输量及主要技术经济指标(铁路分局范围)
RAILWAY TRAFFIC AND MAIN ECONOMIC AND TECHNICAL INDICATORS (WITHIN RAILWAY BUREAU BRANCH)

项 目 Item		1998	1997	1998 年为 1997 年 % 1998 as % of 1997
营业里程 (公里)	Length of Railways in Operation (km)	1817.2	1817.2	100.0
旅客发送量 (万人)	Passengers Dispatched (10000 persons)	4953.3	4828.8	102.6
旅客周转量 (万人公里)	Passenger-Kilometers (10000 passenger-km)	1071241.0	1024732.0	104.5
货物发送量 (万吨)	Freight Dispatched (10000 tons)	4256.3	4748.4	89.6
货物到达量 (万吨)	Freight Arrived (10000 tons)	7216.9	7848.0	92.0
货物周转量 (万吨公里)	Freight Ton-Kilometers (10000 ton-km)	4506860.0	5225177.6	86.3
货物平均净载重 (吨)	Average Net Load of Freight (ton)	55.8	56.0	99.6
平均日装车数 (辆)	Daily Average Number of Freight Car Loaded (car)	2089.0	2322.0	90.0
平均日卸车数 (辆)	Daily Average Number of Freight Car Unloaded (car)	3553.0	3859.0	92.0
货车周转时间 (天)	Turnover Time of Freight Train	1.8	1.4	127.7
蒸汽机车万吨公里耗煤 (公斤)	Coal Consumption of Steam Locomotives Per 10000 Ton-km (kg)		422.9	
内燃机万吨公里耗油 (公斤)	Oil Consumption of Diesel Locomotives Per 10000 Ton-km (kg)	29.2	29.2	100.0

9-5 全社会客、货运输量及周转量
PASSENGER AND FREIGHT TRAFFIC AND TURNOVER VOLUME

项目 Item		1998	1997	1998年为1997年% 1998 as % of 1997	构成(%) Composition(%) 1998	1997
旅客运输量	**(万人) Passenger Traffic (10000 persons)**	**12419.4**	**10383.8**	**119.6**	**100**	**100**
铁路	Railway	4953.3	4828.8	102.6	39.89	46.51
公路	Highway	6704.0	4902.0	136.8	53.98	47.2
民航	Civil Aviation	762.1	653.0	116.7	6.13	6.29
旅客周转量	**(万人公里) Passenger-Kilometers (10000 passenger-km)**	**2419786.9**	**2154186.2**	**112.3**	**100**	**100**
铁路	Railway	505553.8	477537.8	105.9	20.89	22.17
公路	Highway	304592.0	261204.0	116.6	12.59	12.13
民航	Civil Aviation	1609641.1	1415444.5	113.7	66.53	65.7
货运量	**(万吨) Freight Traffic (10000 tons)**	**30127.5**	**32349.7**	**93.1**	**100**	**100**
铁路	Railway	2562.5	2883.3	88.9	8.51	8.91
公路	Highway	27490.0	29360.0	93.6	91.25	90.76
民航	Civil Aviation	22.4	19.0	117.7	0.07	0.06
管道	Pipeline	51.6	87.4	59.1	0.17	0.27
货物周转量	**(万吨公里) Freight Ton-Kilometers (10000 ton-km)**	**2846652.2**	**3127394.5**	**91.0**	**100**	**100**
铁路	Railway	1952602.0	2263274.0	86.3	68.59	72.37
公路	Highway	783237.0	769190.0	101.8	27.51	24.6
民航	Civil Aviation	110470.5	94499.7	116.9	3.88	3.02
管道	Pipeline	342.7	430.8	79.6	0.01	0.01

9-6 公路、民航、邮电主要技术经济指标
MAIN TECHNICAL AND ECONOMIC INDICATORS OF HIGHWAY,CIVIL AVIATION, POSTS AND TELECOMMUNICATIONS

项目 Item		1998	1997	1998年为1997年% 1998 as % of 1997
公路货运	**Highway Freight Traffic**			
货车百吨公里耗汽油	Petroleum Consumption of Trucks Per 100 Ton-km (liter)	6.7	6.7	100
货车百吨公里耗柴油	Diesel Consumption of Trucks Per 100 Ton-km (liter)	4.5	4.5	100
货车车吨日产量	Average Daily Tonnage of Trucks (ton-km)	46.8	40	115
货车完好率	Intact Rate of Trucks (%)			
民　航	**Civil Aviation**			
每吨公里耗航空油	Aviation-oil Consumption Per Kilometer (kg)	0.4	0.378	105
邮　电	**Posts and Telecommunications**			
总包邮件延误率	Lossing Rate of Mails (‰)			
总包邮件损失	Loss of Parcels (piece)	126	16	
电报发报逾限率	Rate of Delayed Delivery of Telegrams (%)	0.03		

注：民航包括国际航空公司,新华航空公司。

Note：Data of civil aviation include those of Air China and China Xinhua Airlines.

9-7 邮电业务总量
POSTS AND TELECOMMUNICATIONS SERVICES

项目 Item				1998	1997	1998年为1997年% 1998 as % of 1997
邮电业务量	**(万元)**	**Sales Revenue of Posts and Telecommunications**	**(10000 yuan)**	**1290966.5**	**930136.7**	**138.8**
邮电业务总量		**Sales Volume of Posts and Telecommunications**				
函件	(万件)	Letters	(10000 pcs)	50762.0	54687.0	92.8
包件	(万件)	Parcels	(10000 pcs)	438.0	362.0	121.0
汇票	(万件)	Postal Money Order	(10000)	869.0	844.0	103.0
报纸累计	(万份)	Newspaper	(10000 copies)	140870.0	130754.0	107.7
杂志累计	(万份)	Magazines	(10000 copies)	5294.0	5141.0	103.0
公众电报	(万份)	Public Telegrams	(10000 pcs)	73.6	101.1	72.8
用户电报	(万次)	Telex	(10000 times)	125.0	99.5	125.6
长途电话	(万次)	Long-Distance Calls	(10000 times)	70375.8	54690.2	128.7
本地电话用户	(户)	Local Telephone Subscribers	(subscriber)	3132642.0	2512032.0	124.7
公用电话	(部)	Public Telephone	(unit)	53575.0	45048.0	118.9

注：本地电话用户包括市内电话用户和农村电话用户，以后农村电话指标不再单独反映。

Note：Data of local telephone subscribers included urban and rural areas,and rural telephones won't be reported separately any more.

9-8 邮电局、所及邮路
POSTS AND TELECOMMUNICATIONS OFFICES AND POSTAL ROUTES

单位：公里 (km)

项目 Item				1998	1997	1998年为1997年% 1998 as % of 1997	结构(%) Composition(%)	
							1998	1997
邮电局所	**(处)**	**Number of Posts and Telecommunications Offices**	**(unit)**	**728**	**701**	**103.9**		
邮路单程总长度		**Length of Postal Route**		**101715**	**96788**	**105.1**	**100**	**100**
航空邮路		Air Routes		48987	48669	100.7	48.16	50.28
铁路邮路		Railway Routes		19844	19127	103.7	19.51	19.76
自办汽车邮路		Highway Routes		31094	27410	113.4	30.57	28.32
其　他		Others		1790	1582	113.1	1.76	1.64
农村投递线路单程长度		**Length of Rural Delivery Routes**		**...**	**...**			

9-9 邮电局、所地区分布
POSTS AND TELECOMMUNICATIONS OFFICES BY REGION

地区	Region	邮电局、所 Posts and Telecommunications Offices		# 设在农村 In Rural Areas	
		1998	1997	1998	1997
全市	**Total**	**728**	**701**	**265**	**264**
城区	City Proper	**386**	**371**		
东城区	Dongcheng	38	43		
西城区	Xicheng	42	41		
崇文区	Chongwen	10	19		
宣武区	Xuanwu	20	14		
近郊区	**Near Suburbs**	**276**	**254**		
朝阳区	Chaoyang	116	98		
丰台区	Fengtai	40	38		
石景山区	Shijingshan	13	15		
海淀区	Haidian	107	103		
远郊区	**Outer Suburbs**	**135**	**132**	**104**	**104**
门头沟区	Mentougou	20	19	13	13
房山区	Fangshan	68	68	56	56
通州区	Tongzhou	47	45	35	35
各县	**Counties**	**207**	**198**	**161**	**160**
昌平县	Changping	40	40	35	36
顺义县	Shunyi	31	30	23	23
大兴县	Daxing	40	36	30	28
平谷县	Pinggu	23	22	16	16
怀柔县	Huairou	25	24	21	20
密云县	Miyun	25	24	19	19
延庆县	Yanqing	23	22	17	18

9-10 各种车辆
VARIOUS VEHICLES

单位：辆 (unit)

项目	Item	1998	1997	1998年为1997年% 1998 as % of 1997	构成(%) Composition(%)	
					1998	1997
机动车	**Motor Vehicles**	**1163338**	**1019042**	**114.2**	**100**	**100**
汽车	Automobiles	890141	775946	114.7	76.52	76.1
货车	Trucks	196068	198090	99.0	16.85	19.4
#大货	Heavy Trucks	56550	66845	84.6	4.86	6.6
客车	Coaches	690344	574452	120.2	59.34	56.4
#小客车	Small Coaches	670217	554545	120.9	57.6	54.4
特种车	Special Purpose Vehicles	3729	3404	109.6	0.32	0.3
机动脚踏车(摩托车)	Motorcycles	272612	242483	112.4	23.43	23.8
#轻便	Light	115992	104663	110.8	9.97	10.3
电车	Trolleys	585	613	95.4	0.05	0.1
私人机动车	**Private Automobiles**	**697707**	**540565**	**129.1**		
非机动车	**Nonmotor Vehicles**	**10002620**	**9852190**	**101.5**	**100**	**100**
自行车	Bicycles	9404252	9071116	103.7	94.0	92.1
三轮车	Tricycles	598368	781074	76.6	6.0	7.9

主 要 统 计 指 标 解 释

铁路营业里程 又称营业长度，指办理客货运输业务的铁路正线总长度。凡是全线或部分建成双线及以上的线路，以第一线的实际长度计算；复线、站线、段管线、岔线和特殊用途线以及不计算运费的联络线都不计算营业里程。铁路营业里程是反映铁路运输业基础设施发展水平的重要指标，也是计算客货周转量、运输密度和机车车辆运用效率等指标的基础资料。

货（客）运量 指在一定时期内，各种运输工具实际运送的货物（旅客）数量。是反映运输业为国民经济和人民生活服务的数量指标，也是制定和检查运输生产计划，研究运输发展规模和速度的重要指标。货运按吨计算，客运按人计算。货物不论运输距离长短，货物类别，均按实际重量统计；旅客不论行程远近或票价多少，均按一人一次作为客运量统计。半价票、小孩票也按一人统计。

货物（旅客）周转量 指在一定时期内，由各种运输工具运送的货物（旅客）数量与其相应运输距离的乘积之总和，是反映运输业生产总成果的重要指标，也是编制和检查运输生产计划，计算运输效率、劳动生产率以及核算运输单位主要基础资料。通常以吨公里和人公里为计算单位。计算货物周转量通常按发出站与到达站之间的最短距离，也就是计费距离计算。

邮电业务总量 指以货币表现的邮电部门用于传递信息和提供其他邮电服务的总数量。它综合反映了一定时期邮电工作的总成果，是研究邮电业务量构成和发展趋势的重要指标。根据邮电管理体制不同，分为中央国营业务总量和地方国营业务总量。它用各种邮电分类业务量，如函件件数、电报份数、长话张数、市内电话和农村电话的年均户数、订销报刊累计份数等，分别乘以相应的平均单价（不变价），加总后再加上出租电路和设备的收入、代用户维护电话交换机和线路等设备的收入、其他业务收入求得。

Explanatory Notes On Main Statistical Indicators

Length of Railways in Operation refers to the total length of the trunk line for passenger and freight transportation. The calculation is based on the actual length of the first line if the line has a full or partial double track or more tracks, excluding double tracks, station sidings, tracks under the charge of stations, branch lines, specialpurpose lines and the non-payable connecting lines. The length of railways in operation is an important indicator to show the development of the infrastructure for the railway transport, and also the essential data to calculate volume of passenger freight , traffic density and utilization of the locomotives and carriages.

Freight （Passenger）Traffic refers to the volume of freight （passenger）transported with various means. Freight transport is calculated in tons and passenger traffic is calculated in the number of persons. Despite the type of freight and traveling distance, the freight traffic is calculated by weight. Similarly, the passenger traffic is calculated by person regardless he/she travels with a half-price ticket or a child ticket or an adults ticket or how long his/her trip is. The freight （passenger）traffic provides a quantitative measure to show how the transport industry serves the national economy and people, and is also an important indicator for planning the transport industry and for studying the development scale and speed of the transport industry.

Freight Ton-kilometers（Passenger -kilometers）refer to the sum of the products of the volume of transported cargo（passengers）multiplying by the transport distance, usually using ton-kilometer and passenger-kilometers as units for measurement. Normally , the shortest distance between the departure station and the destination station(I. e., the payable distance）is the bases to calculate the freight ton-kilometers. This is an important indicator to show the total results of the transport industry, to prepare and examine the transport plan and to measure the efficiency, the labour productivity and the unit cost of transport.

Business Volume of Posts and Telecommunications refers to the total value of the information delivered and other posts and telecommunications services provided by the posts and telecommunications departments for the customers. It is derived by first multiplying the business volume of different types, such as number of letters, telegrams, long distance calls., city and rural telephone subscribers and accumulated number of newspapers and journals subscribed and sold, etc. by their respective average unit price（fixed price）, and then adding these products together, and then plus the income from the rent of line and equipment, the income from maintenance of telephone exchanges and lines, and the income from other business operations. The business volume of posts and telecommunication indicates the total achievements made by the posts and telecommunications department during a given period of time in a comprehensive way, and is an important indicator to study the composition and development of the posts and telecommunications business.

1999

批发零售贸易业和餐饮业

WHOLESALE, RETAIL AND CATERING

社会消费品零售额（1978-1998）
Total Retail Sales of Consumer Goods

(100 million yuan)

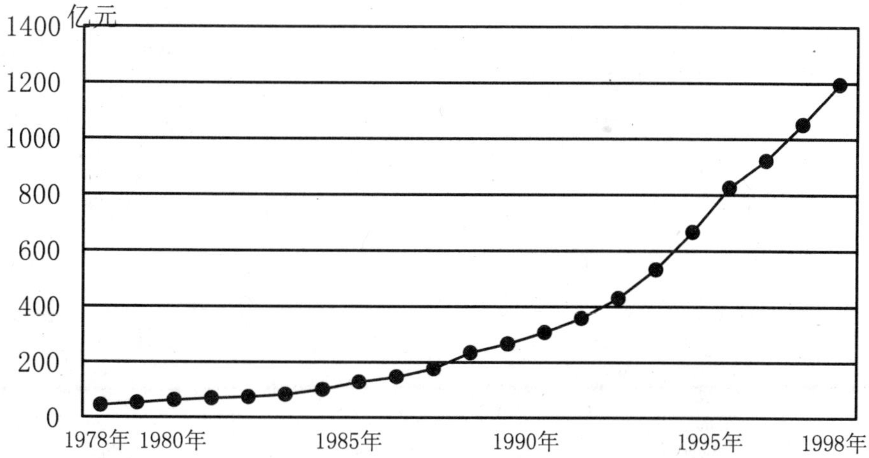

	1998	1997	1998年为1997年% 1998 as % of 1997
社会消费品零售额 （亿元） Total Retail Sales of Consumer Goods (100 million yuan)	1195.2	1051.5	113.7

构成(%)　　Composition(%)

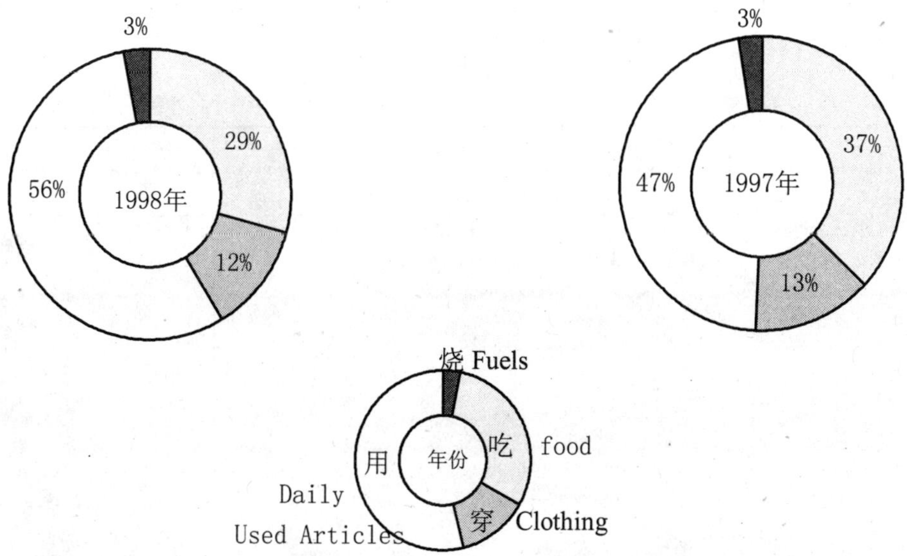

10-1 社会消费品零售额
TOTAL RETAIL SALES OF CONSUMER GOODS

单位：万元 (10000 yuan)

项目	Item	1998	1997	1998年为1997年% 1998 as % of 1997
社会消费品零售额	**Total**	**11952118**	**10515342**	**113.7**
按用途分	**Grouped by Purpose**			
吃的商品	Food	3478850	3896781	
穿的商品	Clothing	1454982	1405779	
用的商品	Daily Used Articles	6648774	4921483	
烧的商品	Fuels	369512	291299	
按地区分	**Grouped by Region**			
市的零售额	City	9525197	8083257	117.8
县的零售额	Counties	770409	881814	87.4
县以下零售额	Below County Level	1656512	1550271	106.9
按行业分	**Grouped by Sectors**			
批发零售贸易业	Wholesale and Retail Trade	8657131	7094362	122.0
餐饮业	Catering	818162	724889	112.9
制造业	Manufacturing	637469	563239	113.2
其他	Others	1839356	2132852	86.2
# 农民对非农民	Peasant to Non-peasant	89463	1393255	6.4
按经济类型分	**Grouped by Type Ownership**			
国有经济	State-owned	3447559	3688052	93.5
集体经济	Collective-owned	2314640	2478622	93.4
私营经济	Private Owned	377490	66570	567.1
个体经济	Individuals	2430042	2364454	102.8
联营经济	Joint Owned	288264	311815	92.4
股份制经济	Share Holding	2148256	940565	228.4
外商投资经济	Foreign Funded	599036	377779	158.6
港澳台投资经济	Hongkong,Macao and Taiwan Funded	255809	144020	177.6
其他经济	Others	91022	143465	63.4

注：1998年数字为商业普查数字。
Note: Data of 1998 is that from commerce survey.

10-1 续表 continued

单位：万元 (10000 yuan)

项目	Item	1998
社会消费品零售额	**Total**	**11952118**
按企业登记注册类型分	**Grouped by Type of Enterprises Registered**	
内资企业	Domestic Investment Enterprises	11097273
国有企业	State-Owned	3447559
集体企业	Collective Owned	2314640
私营企业	Private Owned	377490
联营企业	Joint Owned	288264
股份合作企业	Share Holding Cooperative	352140
股份有限公司	Share Holding Company	795913
有限责任公司	Limited-Liability Company	1000203
其他企业	Others	2521064
港澳台商投资企业	Hongkong,Macao and Taiwan Funded Enterprises	255809
外商投资企业	Foreign Funded Enterprises	599036

10-2 各区县消费品零售额

RETAIL SALES OF CONSUMER GOODS IN DISTRICTS AND COUNTIES

单位：万元 (10000 yuan)

地区	Region	合计 Total	按用途分 Grouped by Purpose			
			吃的商品 Food	穿的商品 Clothing	用的商品 Daily Used Articles	烧的商品 Fuels
全　市	**Total**	**9355796**	**2809962**	**1058582**	**5230151**	**257101**
城　区	**City Proper**	**2462610**	**793702**	**378837**	**1275323**	**14748**
东城区	Dongcheng	706419	271561	101142	327852	5864
西城区	Xicheng	974557	267432	185988	517994	3143
崇文区	Chongwen	357645	117083	50765	187129	2668
宣武区	Xuanwu	423989	137626	40942	242348	3073
近郊区	**Near Suburbs**	**4778791**	**1176702**	**391555**	**3103199**	**107335**
朝阳区	Chaoyang	1483969	348733	227047	851798	56391
丰台区	Fengtai	599632	249481	42115	284436	23600
石景山区	Shijingshan	306219	160954	14069	124027	7169
海淀区	Haidian	2388971	417534	108324	1842938	20175
远郊区	**Outer Suburbs**	**875713**	**332132**	**94960**	**400326**	**48295**
门头沟区	Mentougou	143717	63138	4392	71347	4840
房山区	Fangshan	412075	107829	67668	199008	37570
通州区	Tongzhou	319921	161165	22900	129971	5885
各　县	**Counties**	**1238682**	**507426**	**193230**	**451303**	**86723**
昌平县	Changping	158686	62788	17072	66214	12612
顺义县	Shunyi	301749	112808	45729	111827	31385
大兴县	Daxing	237173	119370	27244	76544	14015
平谷县	Pinggu	121959	39911	30856	40289	10903
怀柔县	Huairou	128162	35962	23407	63162	5631
密云县	Miyun	135258	74889	16082	38226	6061
延庆县	Yanqing	155695	61698	32840	55041	6116

注：本表中区县商业企业为中央属及区县属口径。

Note: Data of this table refers to that of central units,districts and counties.

10-3 社会批发零售贸易业商品购、销、存总值
TOTAL PURCHASES,SALES AND INVENTORY IN WHOLESALE AND RETAIL

单位：万元 (10000 yuan)

项　　目	Item	1998	1997	1998年为1997年% 1998 as % of 1997
商品购进总额	**Total Purchases of Goods**	**26521113**	**22602490**	**117.3**
市内纯购进	In the City	11577465	9431271	122.8
市外购进	From Outside	10084294	9402035	107.3
进　口	Import	4859354	3769184	128.9
商品销售总额	**Total Sales**	**27239511**	**24688972**	**110.3**
市内纯销售	In the City	16793976	16459354	102.0
市外销售	To Outside	3575296	3138538	113.9
出　口	Export	6870239	5091080	134.9
年末库存	**Inventory(year-end)**	**5729750**	**4609289**	**124.3**

10-4 批发零售贸易业商品购、销、存总值
PURCHASES,SALES AND INVENTORY IN WHOLESALE AND RETAIL

单位：万元 (10000 yuan)

项　　目	Item	1998	1997	1998年为1997年% 1998 as % of 1997
商品购进总额	**Total Purchases of Goods**	**21904768**	**17327294**	**126.4**
市内纯购进	In the City	8656702	5787124	149.6
市外购进	From Outside	8388712	7770986	107.9
进　口	Import	4859354	3769184	128.9
商品销售总额	**Total Sales**	**22623166**	**19413776**	**116.5**
市内纯销售	In the City	12177631	11184158	108.9
市外销售	To Outside	3575296	3138538	113.9
出　口	Export	6870239	5091080	134.9
年末库存	**Inventory(year-end)**	**5729750**	**4609289**	**124.3**

10-5 商委各局大中型批发零售贸易业商品购、销、存总值

PURCHASES,SALES AND INVENTORY OF LARGE AND MEDIUM WHOLESALE AND RETAIL TRADES OF COMMERCIAL COMMITTEE

单位：千元 (1000 yuan)

项目	Item	亿商集团公司 Yishang Group	食品工贸集团 Food Industry and Commerce Group	粮食局 Grain Bureau	饮食服务总公司 Catering Services Company	石油总公司 Petroluem Company	供销社 Supply and Marketing Cooperative	旅游商品公司 Tourism Commodity Company
商品购进总额	**Total Purchases**	**2499953**	**2987661**	**1951900**	**27122**	**3349114**	**1717345**	**1527114**
从生产者购进	From Producers	1301776	740539	7099	25765	1155984	1086033	731935
# 农副产品	Farm and Sideline Products		31134	7099			341280	3188
市外购进	From Outside	810587	338305			195523	707263	272413
从批发零售贸易业购进	From Wholesalers and Retailers	1185123	1821015	1636240	1357	2193130	566036	792273
# 市外购进	From Outside	526582	420049	138015		266375	18169	91764
进口额	Import			308561			64858	2913
其他	Others	13054	426107				418	-7
商品销售总额	**Total Sales**	**2712077**	**3273190**	**1442035**	**68841**	**3615083**	**1948709**	**1989439**
对生产经营单位销售额	To Producers	314774	213243	71387		1190481	374082	
# 生产资料销售	Capital Goods	88		10		21867	19843	
市外销售	To Outside	26938	16666			58400	50520	
对批发零售贸易业批发	To Wholesalers and Retailers	1841823	2874909	1281125		2152690	1076229	394831
# 市外批发	From Outside	142309	245039	116423		71735	195424	20096
出口额	Export		476					27
对居民的商品零售额	To Residents	409736	180864	79166	68841	20446	402845	1476268
对集团的商品零售额	To Organizations	145744	3698	10357		251466	95553	118313
年末库存	**Inventory(year-end)**	**599092**	**551881**	**3004478**	**9595**	**90775**	**314045**	**206111**

项目	Item	烟草专卖局 Tabacco Monopoly Bureau	百货大楼股份公司 Department Store Building	西单商场股份有限公司 Xidan Market Ltd	东安集团 Dongan Group	友谊商店股份有限公司 Friendship Market Ltd	盐业公司 Salt Industry Company
商品购进总额	**Total Purchases**	**3267631**	**1049743**	**1690561**	**1551000**	**112899**	**30871**
从生产者购进	From Producers	745570	505865	1140281	1050950	62113	30871
# 农副产品	Farm and Sideline Products	745570		233			
市外购进	From Outside	7010	280150	429195	550544	30717	30871
从批发零售贸易业购进	From Wholesalers and Retailers	2519079	529865	550260	500050	50736	
# 市外购进	From Outside	1783228	11160	55599	95853	9741	
进口额	Import		14013				
其他	Others	2982		20		50	
商品销售总额	**Total Sales**	**3660759**	**1330043**	**1959471**	**1888271**	**174434**	**66644**
对生产经营单位销售额	To Producers		50530	180319		30	25911
# 生产资料销售	Capital Goods						
市外销售	To Outside		15630	69064		30	
对批发零售贸易业批发	To Wholesalers and Retailers	3440201	438990	357813	18364	20649	39869
# 市外批发	From Outside	1139057	7520	8479	3235	3195	
出口额	Export		80643				
对居民的商品零售额	To Residents	219708	673540	1392573	1777718	151565	488
对集团的商品零售额	To Organizations	850	86340	28766	92189	2190	376
年末库存	**Inventory(year-end)**	**302221**	**73607**	**86023**	**97702**	**39666**	**5905**

10-6 大中型批发零售贸易业商品购、销、存总值(按行政区划分)
PURCHASES,SALES AND INVENTORY LARGE AND MEDIUM WHOLESALE AND RETAIL TRADES(BY ADMINISTRATIVE REGION)

单位：千元 (1000 yuan)

项目	Item	东城 Dong-cheng	西城 Xicheng	崇文 Chongwen	宣武 Xuanwu	朝阳 Chaoyang	丰台 Fengtai	石景山 Shijing-shan	海淀 Haidian
商品购进总额	**Total Purchases**	**38101980**	**88290442**	**8761435**	**17766216**	**39154459**	**13678477**	**3295458**	**26297214**
从生产者购进	From Producers	26491641	30872385	5905046	10630129	23843881	7002328	1751215	13895458
# 农副产品	Farm and Sideline Products	413294	94835	72637	72422	197701	156146	3232	257395
市外购进	From Outside	17488300	8380782	1749691	7327378	11401993	1201749	386578	4224321
从批发零售贸易业购进	From Wholesalers and Retailers	7109494	20664755	2374700	6011445	11602517	4569797	1520902	9881268
# 市外购进	From Outside	1698798	12093635	472789	1387815	3733209	660116	57386	2950922
进口额	Import	4323664	36661614	347210	1037504	3390305	87008		2215931
其他	Others	177181	91688	134479	87138	317756	2019344	23341	304557
商品销售总额	**Total Sales**	**41558475**	**71549202**	**10132680**	**18851528**	**49026145**	**14654836**	**3299765**	**29300709**
对生产经营单位销售额	To Producers	10116744	14386353	1318891	7450610	12295637	7665335	1184315	10385727
# 生产资料销售	Capital Goods	8704	54332	7	189009	67087	3969		9657
市外销售	To Outside	5715134	5768650	51385	3192890	4373535	145298	63937	1354889
对批发零售贸易业批发	To Wholesalers and Retailers	6334001	14912353	4459220	7136535	11419284	2626990	732854	7820885
# 市外批发	From Outside	1235180	3482763	446916	3039382	2582176	228692	814	967368
出口额	Export	19240534	32810231	728148	532434	12936885	210807		1568639
对居民的商品零售额	To Residents	4588790	7726844	2041317	2983749	9222211	3105713	1059549	7497614
对集团的商品零售额	To Organizations	1278406	1713421	1585104	748200	3152128	1045991	323047	2027844
年末库存	**Inventory(year-end)**	**4817904**	**19525431**	**1977254**	**6135392**	**7817754**	**1615186**	**766505**	**3116859**

10-6 续表 continued

单位：千元 (1000 yuan)

项目 Item		门头沟 Mentou-gou	房山 Fang-shan	昌平 Chang-ping	顺义 Shunyi	通州 Tong-zhou	大兴 Daxing	平谷 Pinggu	怀柔 Huairou	密云 Miyun	延庆 Yanqing
商品购进总额	**Total Purchases**	**426968**	**2874613**	**1714221**	**2470784**	**1145095**	**1882164**	**446279**	**980449**	**721032**	**406168**
从生产者购进	From Producers	90304	2034235	776390	1059374	522320	1193167	284122	308525	244460	112351
# 农副产品	Farm and Sideline Products	799	32857	156697	131608	5889	40548	21997	16031	54857	1097
市外购进	From Outside	11924	33945	163029	191913	78662	383999	36355	100887	89938	67386
从批发零售贸易业购进	From Wholesalers and Retailers	320561	775720	937279	1408493	570976	663368	161635	668882	376111	293148
# 市外购进	From Outside	8757	75683	196903	308575	90683	134585	13884	38292	55016	30762
进口额	Import		31834				25283			97173	
其　他	Others	16103	32824	552	2917	51799	346	522	3042	3288	669
商品销售总额	**Total Sales**	**548335**	**3054125**	**1875645**	**2714115**	**1263854**	**2317363**	**758758**	**1269818**	**824332**	**466757**
对生产经营单位销售额	To Producers	64443	925410	555247	488477	235204	736814	51032	201149	155750	47813
# 生产资料销售	Capital Goods	343	24350	73424	88960	31886	105494	27530	29975	60470	7996
市外销售	To Outside	19285	66079	1604	1882	1083	6208	2950	1810	6018	547
对批发零售贸易业批发	To Wholesalers and Retailers	105011	966785	677050	888324	361081	828946	381438	404854	413168	169394
# 市外批发	From Outside	3508	86767	36164	49655	32670	19665	7747	64444	89872	15450
出口额	Export		100333		3094	102666	11		10998	38076	
对居民的商品零售额	To Residents	345372	811214	524324	998070	434635	579298	199542	582755	166723	218388
对集团的商品零售额	To Organizations	33509	250383	119024	336150	130268	172294	126746	70062	50615	31162
年末库存	**Inventory(year-end)**	**53127**	**270660**	**217294**	**434073**	**455497**	**238683**	**88499**	**140151**	**123549**	**43871**

10-7 批发零售贸易企业商品分类销售库存

SALES AND INVENTORY BY CATEGORY IN WHOLESALE AND RETAIL TRADES

单位：千元 (1000 yuan)

项目	Item	合计 Total			# 大型企业 Large Enterprises		
		商品总销售 Total Sales	# 零售额 Retail	年末库存 Inventory (year-end)	商品总销售 Total Sales	# 零售额 Retail	年末库存 Inventory (year-end)
合计	**Total**	**283702931**	**65011416**	**57297497**	**166292429**	**32415548**	**33131065**
食品、饮料、烟酒类	Food,Beverage,Tabacco and Liquor	37040111	11296159	8381822	20250682	5753452	5096313
针、纺织品类	Knitwear	9069724	2079632	1545798	5421618	1299111	657938
服装、鞋帽类	Garments,Shoes and Hats	14523132	8137146	1849638	9908030	6294486	649140
化妆品类	Cosmetics	3145873	1445777	409659	1887326	1079532	168643
钟表、眼镜类	Clocks,Watches and Glasses	1332635	765519	243201	804890	485006	83959
日用品类	Articles for Daily Use	6187333	3680687	949084	3152687	2308264	369473
五金、电工器具类	Hardware and Electrical Appliances	3088133	1135459	884198	449258	239873	73958
生活电器类	Household Appliances	9291003	5289624	1727068	5239442	3262004	859636
音像器材类	Sound-video Equipment	3304429	2179150	517457	2035620	1596615	254538
自行车、摩托车类	Bicycles and Motorcycles	980308	524063	231053	288345	219950	37658
体育、娱乐用品类	Recreation and Sports Articles	1781537	957480	318270	729027	521781	75563
文化、办公用品类	Culture and Office Articles	6318800	2325269	1074941	857838	707399	87706
金银珠宝类	Jewelry	2522397	1384782	672645	1877159	1103507	354136
家具类	Furniture	1180365	807025	171674	278124	236238	36925
中西药品类	Medicines	9228830	5148303	2060469	3424310	2317238	646992
书报、杂志类	Book and Newspaper	3932105	1394380	1085622	2189468	341558	346546
汽车类	Automobiles	14217230	5875941	2410424	7801046	3021539	1074622
建筑材料类	Building Materials	4804214	1002521	1353993	503593	36368	233165
木材类	Timber	935928	44248	203348	295773	89	43789
化工材料及制品类	Chemical Materials and Products	19289433	456599	2672172	12257235	23756	1691992
黑色金属材料类	Ferrous Metal Materials	20324409	391031	2652630	11026471	64339	1254955
有色金属材料类	Nonferrous Metal Materials	4499270	78467	703179	2526684		438497
机电设备及零件类	Mechanical and Electrical Instruments	48160480	1458469	6480744	37080844	47619	4012166
煤炭及制品类	Coal and Coal Products	11421977	586446	302383	9735567		627
石油及制品类	Petroleum and Related Products	16862981	2559882	606043	10976790	326971	103678
种子饲料类	Seeds and Forage	4512358	34636	1137720	3123419		943623
棉麻、土畜产品类	Cotton,Flax,Local and Animal Products	2270545	10285	11790201	1138322	160	11580311
再生资源类	Reclaimed Source	272794	11771	58280	46109		4477
其他类	Others	23204597	3950665	4803781	10986752	1128693	1950039
# 生活消费品	Consumer Goods	1182036	431646	138447	752914	217400	45417

10-7 续表 continued

单位：千元 (1000 yuan)

项目	Item	# 中型企业 Medium Enterprises 商品总销售 Total Sales	# 零售额 Retail	年末库存 Inventory (year-end)	# 小型企业 Small Enterprises 商品总销售 Total Sales	# 零售额 Retail	年末库存 Inventory (year-end)
合计	**Total**	**87174013**	**23864914**	**14706624**	**30236489**	**8730954**	**9459808**
食品、饮料、烟酒类	Food,Beverage,Tabacco and Liquor	13294267	4413732	2364422	3495162	1128975	921087
针、纺织品类	Knitwear	2843849	566334	525944	804257	214187	361916
服装、鞋帽类	Garments,Shoes and Hats	3807466	1506779	770931	807636	335881	429567
化妆品类	Cosmetics	969651	299798	158463	288896	66447	82553
钟表、眼镜类	Clocks,Watches and Glasses	350771	233039	114073	176974	47474	45169
日用品类	Articles for Daily Use	2145424	1051568	294462	889222	320855	285149
五金、电工器具类	Hardware and Electrical Appliances	1136640	430257	226979	1502235	465329	583261
生活电器类	Household Appliances	3201130	1621435	547237	850431	406185	320195
音像器材类	Sound-video Equipment	1018344	464045	153334	250465	118490	109585
自行车、摩托车类	Bicycles and Motorcycles	545394	208875	142952	146569	95238	50443
体育、娱乐用品类	Recreation and Sports Articles	819360	337443	122539	233150	98256	120168
文化、办公用品类	Culture and Office Articles	3892340	1098461	583929	1568622	519409	403306
金银珠宝类	Jewelry	551914	243999	242728	93324	37276	75781
家具类	Furniture	735483	459955	57994	166758	110832	76755
中西药品类	Medicines	5206851	2566155	1198315	597669	264910	215162
书报、杂志类	Book and Newspaper	1455997	875151	611608	286640	177671	127468
汽车类	Automobiles	5146635	2336007	741715	1269549	518393	594087
建筑材料类	Building Materials	2109765	337172	291687	2190856	628981	829141
木材类	Timber	464334	15696	88176	175821	28463	71383
化工材料及制品类	Chemical Materials and Products	5103741	202824	621042	1928457	230019	359138
黑色金属材料类	Ferrous Metal Materials	7213726	160036	837819	2084212	166656	559856
有色金属材料类	Nonferrous Metal Materials	1503066	40766	153519	469520	37701	111163
机电设备及零件类	Mechanical and Electrical Instruments	7401401	821899	1504313	3678235	588951	964265
煤炭及制品类	Coal and Coal Products	1203641	435953	181584	482769	150493	120172
石油及制品类	Petroleum and Related Products	4625805	1495109	308096	1260386	737802	194269
种子饲料类	Seeds and Forage	1134450	414	110420	254489	34222	83677
棉麻、土畜产品类	Cotton,Flax,Local and Animal Products	1030807	3282	183685	101416	6843	26205
再生资源类	Reclaimed Source	103605	133	24557	123080	11638	29246
其他类	Others	8158156	1638597	1544101	4059689	1183375	1309641
# 生活消费品	Consumer Goods	296251	157168	38248	132871	57078	54782

10-8 社会农副产品购进、销售、库存数量
PURCHASES,SALES AND INVENTORY OF FARM AND SIDELINE PRODUCTS

单位：百公斤 (100 kg)

项目 Item		从生产者购进 Purchase from Producers	市外购进 Purchase from Outside	商品总销售 Total Sales	# 对生产经营单位销售 To Producer	# 出口 Export	# 零售量 Retail Sales	年末库存 Inventory (year-end)
粮食	Grain	13422881	13670845	33631210	6161042	3561322	11955861	27390205
食用植物油	Edible Vegetable Oil	3158500	1066244	7310986	220948		2727606	1153429
猪和猪肉	Hog and Pork	2054677	763331	3042283	253379	81058	2200301	179834
牛和牛肉	Oxes and Beef	553211	96592	600148	4720	54929	499808	53319
羊和羊肉	Goat,Sheep and Mutton	500565	78587	591884	1199	1997	511691	78765
家禽	Poultry	694870	314454	643016	11227	259172	353115	214896
鲜蛋	Fresh Eggs	997810	1066	1001702	1019		949182	8824
鲜菜	Fresh Vegetable	43807266	276608	44006409	31889	113231	43520856	21993
水产品	Aquatic Products	2871855	478374	3331568	1017263	356285	1677057	203472
鲜瓜果	Fresh Melon and Fruit	9217507	1106534	9274788	10533	26249	7556283	13151

10-9 大中型批发零售贸易企业商品购进、销售、库存数量
PURCHASES,SALES AND INVENTORY VOLUME BY LARGE AND MEDIUM WHOLESALERS AND RETAILERS

项目 Item	从生产者购进 Purchase from Producers	市外购进 Purchase from Outside	商品总销售 Total Sales	# 对生产经营单位销售 To Producer	# 出口 Export	# 零售量 Retail Sales	年末库存 Inventory (year-end)
粮食 (百公斤)Grain (100 kg)	2317280	12735178	21064968	2914871	5350728	2678032	26060459
食用植物油 (百公斤)Edible Vegetable Oil (100 kg)	1144266	970544	4986446	226203	178353	796880	1081908
猪和猪肉 (百公斤)Hog and Pork (100 kg)	451567	708692	1421268	52337	123577	775909	162788
牛和牛肉 (百公斤)Cattle and Beef (100 kg)	74963	85526	121813	526	1163	34452	50136
羊和羊肉 (百公斤)Goat,Sheep and Mutton (100 kg)	20874	75820	110947	8405	513	32983	77586
家禽 (百公斤)Poultry (100 kg)	416838	308279	359980	5	1791	89161	208501
鲜蛋 (百公斤)Fresh Eggs (100 kg)	31510	75	36299		446	25472	2420
鲜菜 (百公斤)Fresh Vegetable (100 kg)	467948	205238	643692	537	30740	259127	15544
鲜瓜果 (百公斤)Fresh Melon and Fruit (100 kg)	1713396	1095799	1756365		88	84813	8773
水产品 (百公斤)Aquatic Product (100 kg)	1224131	459488	1660442	1514	1001307	47603	176628
盐 (百公斤)Salt (100 kg)	883085	868149	335531		96676	123479	136042
食糖 (百公斤)Sugar (100 kg)	1489728	1478913	4969187	81473	983834	119200	1596641
卷烟 (箱)Cigarettes (case)	1092633	1903415	4020304	802678	84701	200517	279551
酒 (百公斤)Alcoholic Beverage (100 kg)	643183	183755	1244485	35851	10576	328087	98849
茶叶 (百公斤)Tea (100 kg)	274787	258666	288780	17	121	37178	21947
棉花 (百公斤)Cotton (100 kg)	13039	3302397	369082	310251	346703	486	6455827
布 (百米)Cloth (100 m)	3261820	2778974	5802556	39943	736437	103803	805774
# 棉布 (百米) Cotton Cloth (100 m)	1459408	1290320	1474143	23866	158754	49517	399763
呢绒 (百米)Wool Fabric (100 m)	43109	24857	64280	432	5707	17282	29527
绸缎 (百米)Silk and Satin (100 m)	82669	86348	124629	415	3318	23094	23742
各种服装 (百件)All Garments (100 pieces)	1473009	512445	1953757	6360	22447	461517	188106

10-9 续表 1 continued

项目 Item	从生产者购进 Purchase from Producers	市外购进 Purchase from Outside	商品总销售 Total Sales	# 对生产经营单位销售 To Producer	# 出口 Export	# 零售量 Retail Sales	年末库存 Inventory (year-end)
# 针织内衣裤 Knitted Underwear	415828	114280	559638	12	1737	129393	67918
鞋 (百双) Shoe (100 pairs)	305819	87362	403058	335	47	130237	73790
# 皮鞋 Leather Shoe	38568	20945	70700	325	40	57289	30258
毛线 (百公斤) Knitting Wool (100 kg)	5659	1657	9165	3	1507	6831	6810
手表 (百个) Watches (100)	5990	3649	11471	557	40	10349	3205
黄金饰品 (千元) Gold Ornament (1000 yuan)	1186751	565946	1612785	95839	100322	1000263	410015
照相机 (台) Cameras (set)	164814	146499	370406	14369	14079	252129	65930
自行车 (辆) Bicycle (unit)	168322	134879	304517	116	25623	195134	44694
电视机 (台) TV Sets (set)	817232	480395	1214267	141655	6876	486344	272754
# 彩色电视机 Color TV Set	808072	473561	1084346	141655	6876	473119	265497
# 25寸及以上 25 inches and above	519656	299163	665979	98757	2586	296726	157861
录音机 (台) Recorders (set)	126890	100867	372122	152		283672	38821
# 组合音响 Hi-Fi	40850	29608	85052	12280	148	57191	15228
摄像机 (架) Pickup Camera (set)	3815	11133	19792	561		15015	2461
录相机 (台) Video-corders (set)	22599	18491	53294	300	47	43608	13559
影碟机 (台) Video CD (set)	299910	210317	543032	12020	6243	344296	61181
# 进口影碟机 Import	5602	23125	32727	400		17348	4018
家用电风扇 (台) Electrical Fans (unit)	141817	99882	350576	675	2910	275688	137956
家用电冰箱 (台) Refrigerators (unit)	178186	164840	381587	5801	474	240510	48469
家用洗衣机 (台) Washing Machine (unit)	374627	323496	349389	3652	2560	271020	85058
房间空调器 (台) Air Conditioners (unit)	236364	212170	374421	15886	27880	216066	46532
微波炉 (台) Microwave Oven (unit)	191807	165667	343450	8726	878	235284	39018
热水淋浴器 (台) Showers (unit)	126047	121020	236422	437	955	201289	47552

10-9 续表 2 continued

项 目 Item	从生产者购进 Purchase from Producers	市外购进 Purchase from Outside	商品总销售 Total Sales	# 对生产经营单位销售 To Producer	# 出口 Export	# 零售量 Retail Sales	年末库存 Inventory (year-end)
冰　柜 (台) Ice Cabinet (unit)	32269	25328	57677	294	125	42307	13981
吸尘器 (台) Dust Catcher (unit)	27322	37386	74775	3414	83	53247	14801
抽油烟机 (台) Range Hoods (unit)	67746	43960	153343	232	348	143164	10883
电饭锅 (个) Electric Rice Cooker (unit)	172409	141474	366460	712	4941	231312	95251
微型计算机 (台) Micro Computers (unit)	65667	84159	110545	3002	39917	12502	23182
普通电话机 (部) Telephones (unit)	242580	23838	335871	3160	189608	119581	37839
移动电话机 (部) Mobilphone (unit)	1400333	624126	1506050	656453	714924	54873	121339
寻呼机 (部) BP (unit)	1363264	436406	1472521	390913	1022773	29051	118900
煤　炭 (吨) Coal (ton)	35033012	32322473	36397750	971802	2346225	2143193	1029772
木　材 (立方米) Timber (cu.m)	147600	67110	345374	51552	125706	406	79116
汽　油 (吨) Gasoline (ton)	1196388	587417	2332559	72840	510926	477270	136824
柴　油 (吨) Diesel Oil (ton)	444781	187742	1305206	36216	796570	123096	71382
煤　油 (吨) Kerosene (ton)	918762	914465	933772	1711	928813	367	31472
硫　酸 (吨) Sulphuric Acid (ton)	5433	5227	5258	11	3619	2	50
纯　碱 (吨) Soda (ton)	5656	4939	6116	4530	5773	103	546
烧　碱 (吨) Ashcaustic Soda (ton)	4443	2952	6558	2860	367	20	210
橡　胶 (吨) Rubber (ton)	78175	158278	194904	31321	138614		25637
化学肥料 (吨) Chemical Fertilizer (ton)	788587	662718	2195676	169201	1592120	27621	196363
农用塑料薄膜 (吨) Agricultural Plastic Film (ton)	3649	1412	4871	383	1882	218	839
化学农药 (吨) Farm Chemical (ton)	86465	92830	165423	138273	89705	3946	12988
钢　材 (吨) Steel Products (ton)	3951733	2102209	5381707	1291820	2470224	127165	756211
铜 (吨) Copper (ton)	49734	30474	55078	16648	39236	831	6210
铝 (吨) Aluminum (ton)	198854	22715	102226	5319	42025	1543	105882
铅 (吨) Lead (ton)	1427	708	1539	121	390	230	282
锌 (吨) Zinc (ton)	7880	1950	15363	727	2292	877	360
锡 (吨) Tin (ton)	642	180	4020	77	3871	26	153
铜　材 (吨) Copper Products (ton)	40720	53884	15010	13102	13784	45	707
铝　材 (吨) Aluminum Products (ton)	3617	3861	4163	203	3369	422	1117
水　泥 (吨) Cement (ton)	1812934	742084	1864872	179573	1221175	93059	412216
汽　车 (辆) Automobile (unit)	91638	104199	188440	21580	24549	96710	36753
# 小轿车 Cars	23584	42969	50450	1896	3188	24779	14123
摩托车 (辆) Motorcycle (unit)	86852	66854	95237	3690	1023	59568	11500
拖拉机 (台) Tractors (unit)	801	572	1861	16	77	271	279

10-10 重点零售商业企业主要经济指标

单位：万元

项 目 Item	商品销售收入 Sales Revenue		利税总额 Total Profits		人均销售额 Sales Value Per Capita	
	1998	1997	1998	1997	1998	1997
百货类						
西单商场股份有限公司	147317	154524	17662	15827	46.3	47.8
城乡贸易中心股份有限公司	112308	156034	16114	17134	55.2	69.6
赛特购物中心	66667	70769	8723	9978	62.4	63.6
北京燕莎友谊商城有限公司	89820	87623	11479	13537	46.0	41.9
百货大楼	113935	131168	10729	16572	32.8	35.7
北京百盛轻工发展有限公司	47274	43036	6135	5547	54.8	51.2
北辰购物中心	60819	13681	4652	707	72.6	16.0
北京市西单购物中心	45478	54615	4746	5419	45.0	47.7
北京贵友大厦有限公司	46235	49524	4000	6485	56.0	57.8
北京市菜市口百货有限责任公司	33212	31185	3838	3460	77.8	71.7
北京市复兴商业城	43297	44688	3437	3672	48.3	45.2
双安商场	84271	85053	3965	4025	40.6	36.5
北京蓝岛大厦	99846	110142	7563	8555	32.5	34.6
西单赛特商城有限责任公司	26096	26906	1714	827	52.5	42.6
北京东安集团公司长安商场	43558	68856	1717	4524	21.6	30.8
翠微大厦	61274		2668		22.4	
东安市场	34480		1399		28.0	
北京市宣武区国华商场有限公司	15882	15674	1613	1660	43.2	42.0
西单商场顺义联营大楼	17839	20965	1003	1208	24.0	29.9
北京市天桥百货商场	18340	25042	4543	3395	15.6	21.7
北京市超音波公司	24089	21519	826	692	70.4	83.7
北京天元和平商业大厦	23044	17622	2193	1352	20.2	21.1
北京市亿客隆商城	37515	32081	1276	945	19.1	16.9
白广路百货商场	11267	11708	761	943	49.2	45.6
中贸联万客隆商业有限公司	56770		130		77.2	
北京华奥商厦	14768	16367	1019	1285	20.4	27.0
北京市西直门外百货商场	20250	9960	509	732	36.0	20.4
北京兴城商厦	21033	22825	686		17.8	32.4
北京星座商厦	19790	24515	739	925	19.4	19.7
北京华普商厦	17723		670		25.0	
北京方庄中心股份有限公司	14017	14036	1344	1317	23.2	22.3
北京市地百商贸股份有限公司	13082	18154	683	1604	24.5	31.2
金伦股份有限公司	22680	30795	745	2401	19.7	23.4
北京燕莎望京购物中心	26677	26730	156		31.9	31.8
北京市新街口百货商场	12798	14538	436	876	25.5	28.1
北京市朝阳商业大楼	10062	11121	486	556	32.3	35.6
北京友谊商店	14365	18997	1144	1255	10.6	12.7
华联商厦	57174	63036			77.0	68.1
利生体育用品服务中心	12635	12220	965	1340	15.7	1.1
北京市成文厚账簿卡片公司	4653	4697	495	740	41.9	48.4

MAIN ECONOMIC INDICATORS FOR MAJOR RETAIL ENTERPRISES

(10000 yuan)

人均创利税 Pre-tax Per Capita		销售利税率(%) Ratio of Pre-tax to Sales Revenue(%)		存货周转率(%) Turnover Rate of Stock(%)	
1998	1997	1998	1997	1998	1997
5.5	4.9	12.0	10.2	2036.7	2864.4
7.9	7.6	14.3	11.0	981.2	712.3
8.2	9.0	13.1	14.1	844.6	489.4
5.9	6.5	12.8	15.4	790.9	857.7
3.1	4.5	9.4	12.6	1329.7	936.2
7.1	6.6	13.0	12.9	1455.7	1847.6
5.6	0.8	7.6	5.2	1519.6	1031.4
4.7	4.7	10.4	9.9	1360.8	2014.1
4.8	7.6	8.7	13.1	1178.8	2090.4
9.0	8.0	11.6	11.1	1427.2	2149.0
3.8	3.7	7.9	8.2	2917.0	2223.1
1.9	1.7	4.7	4.7	1254.4	1393.7
2.5	2.7	7.6	7.8	529.4	3673.8
3.4	1.3	6.6	3.1	2438.5	1859.2
0.9	2.0	3.9	6.6	3868.3	7255.1
1.0		4.4		649.1	
1.1		4.1		2282.6	
4.4	4.5	10.2	10.6	652.3	669.6
1.3	1.7	5.6	5.8	8469.9	29614.5
3.9	2.9	24.8	13.6	488.1	668.1
2.4	2.7	3.4	3.2	339.8	361.5
1.9	1.6	9.5	7.7		
0.7	0.5	3.4	2.9	649.6	703.1
3.3	3.7	6.8	8.1	1917.2	1749.3
0.2		0.2		1876.9	
1.4	2.1	6.9	7.9	743.3	1074.2
0.9	1.5	2.5	7.3	1219.7	1259.4
0.6		3.3		984.2	800.5
0.7	0.7	3.7	3.8	681.1	635.2
0.9		3.8		658.1	
2.2	2.1	9.6	9.4		757.5
1.3	2.8	5.2	8.8	738.5	1070.1
0.6	1.8	3.3	7.8	508.3	579.9
0.2		0.6		1555.2	2007.8
0.9	1.7	3.4	6.0	982.6	1601.3
1.6	1.8	4.8	5.0	1116.3	668.4
0.8	0.8	8.0	6.6	265.5	355.2
				546.1	1055.3
1.2	0.1	7.6	11.0		
4.5	7.6	10.6	15.8	217.6	192.4

10-10 续表 1 continued

单位：万元

项　　目 Item	商品销售收入 Sales Revenue		利税总额 Total Profits		人均销售额 Sales Value Per Capita	
	1998	1997	1998	1997	1998	1997
天元百货商场	4063	3713	608	577	8.8	8.9
昌平县新世纪商城	11662	10409	501	359	18.8	16.6
北京市西四电器公司	3050	3348	274	301	32.1	35.6
当代商城实业公司	44613	52374		2306	27.1	29.5
北京丰台百货商场	10498	12407	332	473	14.2	16.2
雪银大厦	14658	20107	432	729	16.0	21.6
华光商厦	6968	9149	423	618	17.4	24.1
北京市朝阳区新蕾百货商场	5882	8508	299	197	23.6	23.9
北京市劲松百货商场	8178	10111	346	372	16.4	20.4
北京世都百货有限责任公司	21092	17062			31.9	28.2
顺义国泰商业大厦	12157	17976	249	439	19.9	22.9
北京市朝阳区万惠商场	8915	9488	297	387	15.8	22.4
北京市海淀金五星商业大厦	9948	8984	272	231	21.9	20.7
北京市门头沟区百货商场	2877	2938	366	138	8.6	9.4
麒麟大厦	11471		356		9.6	
北京市京北大世界商贸集团	14309	12745			18.3	12.7
北京中商西友大厦有限公司	12535	12692			18.2	16.6
北京市崇文区光明百货商场	6467	8578	227	310	15.0	19.9
怀柔百货大楼股份有限公司	8688	6835	94	128	27.4	19.8
北京市隆福大厦	19704	15496		143	8.8	6.7
隆华购物中心	13572		1		29.3	
北京市昌平商业大厦	6075	6357	200	204	16.3	15.9
北京鑫帝大厦	9689	16226	261	467	11.7	19.0
北京万方商城	10867	12850	24	81	17.5	15.8
北京银岛商厦有限责任公司	3882	3874	292	363	9.9	10.6
北京东高地百货商场	3528	4281	182	225	15.6	18.9
北京海升商厦	10289	7524			37.6	19.5
北京前门商业大厦	9911	12848	195	356	14.5	15.1
朝阳区团结湖百货商场	4105	4594	106	206	18.8	21.1
前门文化体育用品公司	1910	2385	107	194	9.1	11.4
万通新世纪商城	4351	6925			27.2	13.9
北京市菜市口文化用品商店	1101	1455	118	209	11.6	15.5
北京市百货公司第一商场	3253	3173	56	192	14.6	13.6
三环毛纺织集团三友商场	4501	6750	126	184	10.2	14.5
北京市鼓楼电器公司	3761	5577	27	113	18.9	26.8
西城区三里河百货商场	1189	1967	75	137	5.6	8.9
北京市新汇奥尼尔皮衣店	219	1396	39	132	11.5	26.3
北京市西直门五金批发商店	2045	2421	65	128	15.4	17.2
北京市内联升鞋店	1473	1583	108	92	7.9	8.3
海蓝云天购物商城	7523				11.5	
北京丝绸商店	1365	1389	65	122	12.0	12.1
北京元隆丝绸股份有限公司	1258	1142	90	90	8.4	6.8

10-10 续表 2 continued

(10000 yuan)

人均创利税 Pre-tax Per Capita		销售利税率(%) Ratio of Pre-tax to Sales Revenue(%)		存货周转率(%) Turnover Rate of Stock(%)	
1998	1997	1998	1997	1998	1997
1.3	1.4	15.0	15.5	1629.4	1530.1
0.8	0.6	4.3	3.4	278.2	294.1
2.9	3.2	9.0	9.0	1507.5	560.1
	1.3		4.4	252.8	369.0
0.4	0.6	3.2	3.8	1863.9	2200.2
0.5	0.8	2.9	3.6		5109.5
1.1	1.6	6.1	6.8	573.1	812.1
1.2	0.6	5.1	2.3	618.2	526.0
0.7	0.8	4.2	3.7	709.0	574.7
				447.0	315.0
0.4	0.6	2.0	2.4	559.4	829.3
0.5	0.9	3.3	4.1	802.6	649.5
0.6	0.5	2.7	2.6	494.6	411.4
1.1	0.4	12.7	4.7	1079.7	1050.8
0.3		3.1		310.7	
				634.2	357.8
				1144.0	5931.6
0.5	0.7	3.5	3.6	581.8	747.5
0.3	0.4	1.1	1.9	649.3	509.1
	0.1		0.9	509.5	1028.3
				270.2	
0.5	0.5	3.3	3.2	540.0	362.0
0.3	0.5	2.7	2.9	447.2	493.3
	0.1	0.2	0.6	804.4	532.0
0.7	1.0	7.5	9.4	401.6	300.9
0.8	1.0	5.2	5.3	574.0	561.0
				568.4	505.3
0.3	0.4	2.0	2.8	288.7	311.9
0.5	0.9	2.6	4.5	716.8	454.1
0.5	0.9	5.6	8.1	3997.3	1966.7
				1244.0	721.4
1.2	2.2	10.7	14.4	625.4	668.9
0.3	0.8	1.7	6.1	1911.2	3828.6
0.3	0.4	2.8	2.7	327.6	449.9
0.1	0.5	0.7	2.0	670.2	1512.7
0.4	0.6	6.3	7.0	1813.0	868.9
2.1	2.5	17.8	9.5	571.9	1196.9
0.5	0.9	3.2	5.3	413.2	396.9
0.6	0.5	7.3	5.8	224.3	173.8
				332.6	
0.6	1.1	4.8	8.8	258.5	303.7
0.6	0.5	7.2	7.9	106.3	79.7

10-10 续表 3 continued

单位：万元

项　　目 Item	商品销售收入 Sales Revenue		利税总额 Total Profits		人均销售额 Sales Value Per Capita	
	1998	1997	1998	1997	1998	1997
北京市交电公司金源商城	2016	2556			7.5	8.4
北京市西四商场	1274	2213		117	6.0	10.0
密云县鼓楼商场	4495	5175		45	5.9	6.1
和平门百货商场	777	1163	25	75	8.0	11.7
北京密云燕赛购物中心	1918	2199		38	6.2	6.6
延庆县百货大楼	1361	1507	41	49	7.9	9.4
正阳商城	1191	1915	42	43	6.6	8.8
北京蓝枫叶商厦	3451	10932			8.1	14.7
好友世界商场有限责任公司	188	736	40		1.8	5.3
新时代妇女儿童用品公司	560	1200			2.6	5.1
海淀区永定路百货商场	531	4500	36	108	0.0	18.7
天元商业大楼	1158	5080		655	3.6	8.7
怀柔商业大厦	568	1224		20	3.0	5.3
北京前门妇女服装店	310	676			2.6	3.1
房山购物中心	279	511			3.1	5.1
威地亚商贸有限责任公司	219	1902			4.1	5.9
北京市平谷银座购物中心	244	769			0.7	2.2
北京市平谷县商业大厦	75	785			3.8	4.2
天元妇女儿童用品商城	78	1418			0.1	3.6
副食类						
北京稻香村食品集团	48113	38369	7692	6519	39.9	36.6
奥之光茶叶公司	3272	2518	566	463	26.0	30.7
崇文门菜市场	23053	12306	1567	1424	15.6	30.9
北京市朝阳区燕丰商场	11195	12066	487	566	29.5	31.8
北京市海淀区北太平庄商场	9180	8644	528	519	21.9	18.8
白广路商业大楼	3312	3560	136	197	23.7	24.6
北京市西城和平门菜市场	2819	2989	211	226	18.9	19.2
东城区奥之光银龙商贸公司	2488	2236	225	164	5.4	10.1
北京市桂香村食品中心	2710	3797	177	453	6.4	8.8
北京市海淀区海淀菜市场	3126	4320	112	135	11.6	14.4
北京市新街口购物中心	2321	3271	97	301	9.1	12.8
北京市西城区京沪食品商场	1584	2367	115	188	9.3	13.4
北京博兰特北大地副食商场	1523	1662	84	79	10.7	10.9
东城区奥之光宝龙商贸公司	1534	1268	124	120	5.6	8.2
西四万方超市	2874	3080	19	180	11.0	11.7
碧泉食品店	1409	1472	50	43	27.6	19.1
北京市石景山区北里菜市场	1783	1259	10		11.4	8.2
宣武区西珠市口副食店	1013	1237	61	61	8.0	9.4
宣武门副食商场	1284	1369	5	39	15.5	16.1
北京市东城奥之光富龙商贸公司	909	1267	28	184	4.4	5.9
宣武区菜市口菜市场	670	678	3	28	12.2	12.3
东城区奥之光裕龙商贸公司	873	1249		36	2.9	6.8
王府井食品商场	441	1783		330	2.5	10.0

10-10 续表 4 continued

(10000 yuan)

人均创利税 Pre-tax Per Capita		销售利税率(%) Ratio of Pre-tax to Sales Revenue(%)		存货周转率(%) Turnover Rate of Stock(%)	
1998	1997	1998	1997	1998	1997
				2340.8	1316.0
	0.5		5.3	6362.5	4008.9
	0.1		0.9	381.7	440.1
0.3	0.8	3.2	6.4	802.6	869.5
	0.1		1.7	744.5	888.5
0.2	0.3	3.0	3.3	492.3	573.7
0.2	0.2	3.5	2.2	445.7	770.2
				144.7	316.7
0.4		21.3			283.5
				834.0	718.1
	0.4	6.8	2.4		2044.1
	1.1		12.9	212.9	
	0.1		1.6	168.9	274.3
				221.2	385.2
				70.8	182.0
				58.2	182.0
				23.5	198.8
6.4	6.2	16.0	17.0	2578.4	2544.4
4.5	5.6	17.3	18.4	812.6	581.7
1.1	3.6	6.8	11.6		
1.3	1.5	4.4	4.7	817.9	935.6
1.3	1.1	5.8	6.0	1257.3	1981.7
1.0	1.4	4.1	5.5	1627.4	1218.4
1.4	1.4	7.5	7.6	1269.2	1396.0
0.5	0.7	9.0	7.3	2679.7	2916.9
0.4	1.1	6.5	11.9	71033.3	4729.5
0.4	0.5	3.6	3.1	1708.6	1555.2
0.4	1.2	4.2	9.2	7219.2	4676.4
0.7	1.1	7.3	7.9	807.9	857.2
0.6	0.5	5.5	4.8	6961.1	12545.5
0.5	0.8	8.1	9.5	625.1	502.5
0.1	0.7	0.7	5.8		
1.0	0.6	3.5	2.9	811.2	2164.4
0.1		0.6		1206.9	1190.0
0.5	0.5	6.0	4.9	1163.2	2197.7
0.1	0.5	0.4	2.8	9750.0	4485.2
0.1	0.9	3.1	14.5	3518.2	1452.7
0.1	0.5	0.4	4.1	5209.1	3105.6
	0.2		2.9	1082.1	1685.2
	1.8		18.5	281.1	769.5

10-11 商委各局大中型批发零售贸易业财务状况

单位：千元

企业名称 Enterprise	商品销售收入 Sales Revenue	商品销售收入净额 Net Value of Sales Revenue	商品销售成本 Sales Cost	经营费用 Operating Expense	商品销售税金及附加 Sales Tax and Extra Charges	商品销售利润 After-tax Profits	主营业务利润 Profits from Major Business
亿商集团公司	2267472	2267366	2068675	96894	4677	97120	97123
食品工贸集团	2208857	2208629	2000783	139160	5095	63591	63638
粮食局	1159710	1159710	1159402	258633	1667	-259992	-250671
石油总公司	3089861	3089861	2856583	99088	3382	130808	130813
供销社	1468020	1466283	1333427	88838	4801	39217	39217
旅游商品公司	1726720	1704848	1368949	107075	2106	226718	226787
烟草专卖局	3240224	3240224	2900429	55792	2401	281602	281602
百货大楼股份公司	1143145	1143145	1003184	50891	3810	85260	85260
西单商场股份有限公司	1682396	1682396	1428650	63759	4455	185532	185532
东安集团	1655027	1655027	1345546	145718	9503	154260	154260
友谊商店股份有限公司	124741	124741	90367	14610	687	19077	19077
盐业公司	57079	57079	32114	7308	409	17248	17248

FINANCIAL INDICATORS FOR LARGE AND MEDIUM WHOLESALERS AND RETAILERS OF COMMERCIAL COMMISSION

(1000 yuan)

其他业务利润 Profits from Other Business	管理费用 Overhead Cost	财务费用 Financial Expense	利润总额 Total Profits	应付工资 Wages Payable	资产总计 Total Assets	流动资产合计 Total Circulating Assets	固定资产合计 Total Fixed Assets	流动负债合计 Total Liquid Liability	长期负债合计 Total Long-term Liability	实收资本 Total Capital
58055	131920	37506	-8934	84811	2128012	1187080	761263	1352420	291461	360875
31977	95403	38588	14687	60744	1810538	1349889	348273	1427576	97071	283329
12615	76946	690304	-4193	28152	10617230	9674867	496945	9188467	605372	385503
18303	97164	33011	23793	42295	1371626	576653	280297	842558	12497	339980
83403	104311	26013	3001	59237	963449	600199	283057	703202	39742	185269
6783	207445	7300	25792	85128	596938	404541	142444	376314	45905	169527
5744	33541	35812	219442	10714	775120	675845	90686	608081	1499	81999
10032	89107	-34080	53159	56971	2200257	1329121	382590	615250	27061	357248
12636	98118	1660	100783	64649	1332787	401822	612711	282254	29000	448224
8597	149916	9466	11474	105325	1656062	499727	471732	797541	62519	445654
8170	23343	1437	4462	17614	160204	90845	68866	64983		83770
5	13225	2488	1536	5673	91375	64900	21475	44514	6552	13811

10-12 大中型批发零售贸易业财务状况

单位：千元

项目	Item	流动资产 合计 Total Circulating Assets	#货币资金 Cash	#应收帐款 Accounts Receivable	#存货 Stock	长期投资 Long-term Investment
合计	**Total**	**178010644**	**26056695**	**44330427**	**47528626**	**27385357**
按企业登记注册类型分	**Grouped by Type of Enterprises Registered**					
内资企业	Domestic Investment	176859399	25502656	44209595	47209154	27382657
国有企业	State-Owned	138243486	21019423	39682889	29202681	23782937
集体企业	Collective Owned	18085807	1246606	1102135	12566933	457557
私营企业	Private Owned	1131550	159855	163366	569812	13703
联营企业	Joint Owned	3853147	316087	376357	1439093	90540
股份合作企业	Share Holding Cooperative	1196898	156438	69905	523856	105232
股份有限公司	Share Holding Company	4927444	889805	377331	1054505	1302176
有限责任公司	Limited-Liability Company	9415174	1712234	2437596	1848605	1630512
其他企业	Others	5893	2208	16	3669	
港澳台商投资企业	Hongkong,Macao and Taiwan Funded Enterprises	219417	68188	13693	93972	100
外商投资企业	Foreign Funded Enterprises	931828	485851	107139	225500	2600
按国民经济行业分	**Grouped by Sectors**					
批发业	Wholesale	178010644	26056695	44330427	47528626	27385357
食品饮料烟草和家庭用品批发业	Food,Beverage,Tabacoo and Family Use Goods	56514865	5446698	9086614	26244137	6147101
食品饮料烟草批发业	Food,Beverage and Tabacco	26135586	2628558	4423595	11495200	3355632
棉麻、土畜产品批发业	Cotton,Flax,Local and Animal Products	14863015	785899	986785	10617660	1433161
纺织品、服装和鞋帽批发业	Textile,Garments,Shoes and Hats	6530360	978020	1759139	1267579	558584
日用百货批发业	Daily Use Goods	1981637	179862	413593	729035	109439
日用杂品批发业	Grocery	243706	45116	46336	75451	13309
五金交电化工批发业	Hardware,Electrical Appliance and Chemic	2869863	363647	706789	733658	348757
药品及医疗器械批发业	Medicine and Medical Appliance	3890698	465596	750377	1325554	328219
能源、材料和机械电子设备批发业	Energy,Materials,Machinery and Electronic Equipments	71748873	12363611	24133823	10258383	14027403
能源批发业	Energy	10462397	2596513	3629211	568035	2275154
化工材料批发业	Chemical Materials	6097922	1205585	1821429	1119717	1566033
木材批发业	Timbers	832559	109830	252848	155152	248415
建筑材料批发业	Building Materials	1533344	181086	409606	276604	163591
矿产品批发业	Mineral Products	837529	206091	281421	206523	44239
金属材料批发业	Metal Materials	28149555	3650879	9700392	3192610	6471207
机械、电子设备批发业	Machinery and Electronic Equipments	17784972	3278607	6937768	3246041	2418808
汽车摩托车及零配件批发业	Spares and Fittings of Automobile and Motorcycle	5607076	1072994	1033595	1438415	692375
再生物资回收批发业	Recovery of Reclaimed Materials	443519	62026	67553	55286	147581
其他批发业	Others	31029127	4856087	9838893	4784153	4465393
工艺美术品批发业	Handicrafts	796054	81959	172784	148372	168903
图书报刊批发业	Books,Newspaper and Magazines	1462578	295579	303564	446298	133368
农业生产资料批发业	Agricultural Capital Goods	5735455	582199	1486564	1021542	613191
其他类未包括的批发	Others	23035040	3896350	7875981	3167941	3549931
零售业	Retail	18717779	3390299	1271097	6241953	2745460
食品、饮料和烟草零售业	Food,Beverage and Tabacco	2658521	587187	94619	882749	72371
日用百货零售业	Daily Use Goods	9534719	1603425	361948	2611821	1916128
纺织品、服装和鞋帽零售业	Textile,Garments,Shoes and Hats	962314	63610	61628	399351	31051
日用杂品零售业	Grocery	111754	20535	5589	60623	5028
五金交电化工零售业	Hardware,Electrical Appliance and Chemical	1485573	275413	193760	722803	79261
药品及医疗器械零售业	Medicine and Medical Appliance	459901	102171	68821	198014	21208
图书报刊零售业	Books,Newspaper and Magazines	447010	124810	57323	235168	101078
其他零售业	Others	3057987	613148	427409	1131424	519335
按规模划分	**Grouped by Size**					
大型企业	Large Enterprises	115890680	15955249	27809521	34962193	18405011
中型企业	Medium Enterprises	62119964	10101446	16520906	12566433	8980346

FINANCIAL INDICATORS FOR LARGE AND MEDIUM WHOLESALERS AND RETAILERS

(1000 yuan)

固定资产合计 Total Fixed Assets	固定资产原价合计 Original Value of Fixed Assets	# 生产经营用 for Production Use	累计折旧 Accumulative Depreciation	#本年折旧 of this Year	无形及递延资产合计 Intangible and Deffered Assets	#无形资产 Intangible	其他资产合计 Other Assets	资产合计 Total Assets	流动负债合计 Total Circulating Liability
28338780	**27933411**	**16892416**	**5736931**	**1186538**	**3865289**	**1769522**	**22450977**	**260051047**	**155715120**
27274919	27251729	16262746	5610418	1145383	3217947	1204622	22334568	257069490	154339113
19392152	19321917	11971615	4145020	786820	1885382	714585	1647241	184951198	119660890
2472936	2588602	1183448	539065	112256	389556	63624	20237334	41643190	16269594
86663	112507	73382	27297	11469	22511	228	29891	1284318	1001153
863981	1086178	944479	234616	78139	287189	210399	122115	5216972	3986655
318251	314850	131365	47689	14042	63042	49601	3846	1687269	1047609
2689794	2423920	1255939	357608	74764	259061	105089	131840	9310315	3638337
1450757	1403205	701968	258958	67733	311206	61096	162301	12969950	8729012
385	550	550	165	160				6278	5863
90428	132647	110166	47813	8699	16208	7258	10222	336375	182124
973433	549035	519504	78700	32456	631134	557642	106187	2645182	1193883
28338780	27933411	16892416	5736931	1186538	3865289	1769522	22450977	260051047	155715120
4828978	4840036	3032416	1193464	201457	344450	184802	20618960	88454354	48570126
2239915	2256163	1134341	639391	77516	108841	43386	238050	32078024	22003441
814534	816969	765639	99683	45974	52493	17905	20114024	37277227	13171803
467657	387401	259746	88052	19883	54016	.48525		7610617	6072052
237697	315725	160460	97212	16423	21359	13029	38457	2388589	2018367
48814	64304	26458	15605	2500	76		1599	307504	272222
420931	370075	233743	73403	12070	71456	32134	145041	3856048	2207581
599430	629399	452029	180118	27091	36209	29823	81789	4936345	2824660
8660100	8334298	4581880	1844490	347962	684952	421359	1339737	96461065	66055283
1910466	2222736	1693694	602398	113324	112012	81536	130032	14910061	8668876
564288	509013	320996	118929	27410	47573	23833	3759	8279575	5790633
28937	35287	28818	6351	1027	9633	6083		1119544	761941
316963	390757	142925	78363	11674	44452	24506	1424	2059774	1583261
30364	40895	38676	10631	2194	1773		3083	916988	686329
2637499	2057877	1206219	472423	62970	177542	126281	905737	38341540	27504343
2732932	2535738	859815	421344	95883	105052	68743	248935	23290699	14960535
399217	487233	270165	114210	30940	179862	84103	26454	6904984	5700482
39434	54762	18572	19841	2540	7053	6254	313	637900	398883
3386175	3547463	2255956	603718	178624	298819	123212	26272	39205786	21010203
222172	253761	31601	32341	3980	5708	5305	1	1192838	1172416
371629	377770	159273	97978	9889	13122	11635	1809	1982506	1063100
446822	501183	341601	105783	29018	85804	82323	1760	6883032	5136678
2345552	2414749	1723481	367616	135737	194185	23949	22702	29147410	13638009
11463527	11211614	7022164	2095259	458495	2537068	1040149	466008	35929842	20079508
1776330	2125353	1444759	438560	74201	369167	180491	38184	4914573	3189182
7855553	7147658	4279015	1166867	273249	1812608	800168	231816	21350824	10849389
233169	245209	181376	66239	12486	77848	7398	18988	1323370	934758
31142	36856	28164	11508	2009	2577		50	150551	91012
255704	307067	228977	80374	20975	36020	8845	12025	1868583	1299742
117352	133717	117776	34067	8315	31174	10716	1373	631008	435156
183744	226168	200042	53685	10577	16782	5779	10665	759279	408792
1010533	989586	542055	243959	56683	190892	26752	152907	4931654	2871477
16973335	16066176	10420239	2852333	695303	2665154	1326165	20977262	174911442	98285637
11365445	11867235	6472177	2884598	491235	1200135	443357	1473715	85139605	57429483

10-12 续表 1 continued

单位：千元

项目	Item	#短期借款 Short-term Loans	#应付帐款 Accounts Payable	长期负债合计 Total Long-term Liability	#长期借款 Long-term Loans	负债合计 Total Liabili-ties
合计	**Total**	**69305480**	**27366905**	**44859536**	**40806939**	**200574656**
按企业登记注册类型分	**Grouped by Type of Enterprises Registered**					
内资企业	Domestic Investment	69018630	25679074	44655691	40630616	198994804
国有企业	State-Owned	48888606	20317718	20695991	17380745	140356881
集体企业	Collective Owned	13991718	1967974	22512370	22322115	38781964
私营企业	Private Owned	139932	338158	27521	24798	1028674
联营企业	Joint Owned	1213657	122744	63728	56797	4050383
股份合作企业	Share Holding Cooperative	158533	285736	145805	77276	1193414
股份有限公司	Share Holding Company	1540521	844429	422278	248279	4060615
有限责任公司	Limited-Liability Company	3085663	1802286	787998	520606	9517010
其他企业	Others		29			5863
港澳台商投资企业	Hongkong,Macao and Taiwan Funded Enterprises	94950	34197	7635	7145	189759
外商投资企业	Foreign Funded Enterprises	191900	548938	196210	169178	1390093
按国民经济行业分	**Grouped by Sectors**					
批发业	Wholesale	69305480	27366905	44859536	40806939	200574656
食品饮料烟草和家庭用品批发业	Food,Beverage,Tabacoo and Family Use Goods	31819197	5532153	26958634	24685464	75528760
食品饮料烟草批发业	Food,Beverage and Tabacco	13184533	1640926	3626077	2365067	25629518
棉麻、土畜产品批发业	Cotton,Flax,Local and Animal Products	13690687	665574	21897628	22047780	35069431
纺织品、服装和鞋帽批发业	Textile,Garments,Shoes and Hats	2715657	1033041	70107	31427	6142159
日用百货批发业	Daily Use Goods	801147	608279	115501	31723	2133868
日用杂品批发业	Grocery	112659	83142	2429		274651
五金交电化工批发业	Hardware,Electrical Appliance and Chemic	658865	372718	337836	175390	2545417
药品及医疗器械批发业	Medicine and Medical Appliance	655649	1128473	909056	34077	3733716
能源、材料和机械、电子设备批发业	Energy,Materials,Machinery and Electronic Equipments	24243047	13454004	7075113	6027077	73130396
能源批发业	Energy	2254844	3510168	788648	522369	9457524
化工材料批发业	Chemical Materials	2117135	975271	307280	252009	6097913
木材批发业	Timbers	374354	81760	99631	98694	861572
建筑材料批发业	Building Materials	466126	360776	43199	17929	1626460
矿产品批发业	Mineral Products	348311	142788	234881	223910	921210
金属材料批发业	Metal Materials	10251202	4338742	1602958	1407402	29107301
机械、电子设备批发业	Machinery and Electronic Equipments	5080545	2953253	3659285	3276948	18619820
汽车摩托车及零配件批发业	Spares and Fittings of Automobile and Motorcycle	3085290	1064483	336901	227816	6037383
再生物资回收批发业	Recovery of Reclaimed Materials	265240	26763	2330		401213
其他批发业	Others	6990648	3189507	8624127	8516442	29634330
工艺美术品批发业	Handicrafts	1019858	39670	-31		1172385
图书报刊批发业	Books,Newspaper and Magazines	109739	348893	51973	7323	1115073
农业生产资料批发业	Agricultural Capital Goods	1818749	943732	277435	257914	5414113
其他类未包括的批发	Others	4042302	1857212	8294750	8251205	21932759
零售业	Retail	6252588	5191241	2201662	1577956	22281170
食品、饮料和烟草零售业	Food,Beverage and Tabacco	671325	740974	354905	199830	3544087
日用百货零售业	Daily Use Goods	4220903	2402336	1279467	1008962	12128856
纺织品、服装和鞋帽零售业	Textile,Garments,Shoes and Hats	253398	374689	87334	76472	1022092
日用杂品零售业	Grocery	10004	46339	2455	362	93467
五金交电化工零售业	Hardware,Electrical Appliance and Chemical	284624	468108	54075	23696	1353817
药品及医疗器械零售业	Medicine and Medical Appliance	48471	201670	22770	14584	457926
图书报刊零售业	Books,Newspaper and Magazines	34997	183544	4572		413364
其他零售业	Others	728866	773581	396084	254050	3267561
按规模划分	**Grouped by Size**					
大型企业	Large Enterprises	45582994	16270881	37281993	35339728	135567630
中型企业	Medium Enterprises	23722486	11096024	7577543	5467211	65007026

10-12 续表 2 continued

(1000 yuan)

所有者权益合计 Ownership Interest	# 实收资本 Proceeds of Capital	#国家资本 State	#集体资本 Collective	#法人资本 Institutional Units	#个人资本 Individual	#港澳台资本 Hongkong, Macao and Taiwan	#外商资本 Foreign	资本公积 Accumulation Capital	商品销售收入 Sales Revenue
59476391	**31539631**	**22150649**	**1693705**	**5998517**	**1018083**	**92713**	**585964**	**8870841**	**188558402**
58074686	30263276	21869538	1689125	5679530	1018083		7000	8707928	185073635
44594317	21847292	20199369	36848	1583120	27955			6060129	129744674
2861226	2108720	163517	1536398	354716	54089			228867	16358781
255644	282219	2303	14885	120988	144043			22634	4567919
1166589	965240	407924	22603	525628	2085		7000	31056	5805988
493855	453928	141374	16829	154926	140799			38381	2587639
5249700	2116657	428470	7900	1156402	523885			2243652	9470281
3452940	2488720	526581	53162	1783750	125227			83209	16454391
415	500		500						83962
146616	118822	6013	3123	45823		62613	1250	-292	772947
1255089	1157533	275098	1457	273164		30100	577714	163205	2711820
59476391	31539631	22150649	1693705	5998517	1018083	92713	585964	8870841	188558402
12925594	6231072	5149651	272642	708871	96680	2610	618	1370009	47201356
6448506	3002100	2662036	102025	232972	4449		618	1134474	20459688
2207796	944110	795130	71467	77513				32381	3257536
1468458	840856	679185	5053	139794	16824			29041	9333835
254721	270879	172541	18369	51342	26017	2610		27444	3451730
32853	49843	29627	16013	2725	1478			12153	558194
1310631	633328	397676	28578	162099	44975			30061	4151879
1202629	489956	413456	31137	42426	2937			104455	5988494
23330669	13344713	10743336	254382	2194352	147899	3000	1744	2872893	76333894
5452537	2778410	1926966	59593	781473	10378			544133	16937289
2181662	1591181	1498559	48312	42130	2180			128509	7905103
257972	213461	210956		1505	1000			17580	739801
433314	222585	155937	6026	32803	27819			104808	1634170
-4222	52596	51907		321	368			31275	664645
9234239	4980957	4052194	79584	825883	23296			1466212	24522038
4670879	2418143	2100749	19026	268770	24854	3000	1744	385171	16231317
867601	994204	681578	20975	233647	58004			193859	7233783
236687	93176	64490	20866	7820				1346	465748
9571456	3281197	2868188	174477	226311	9821	100	2300	1232470	17569609
20453	90246	90246						21485	1284092
867433	365307	352965		12342				121328	2447308
1468919	649448	398870	144789	103593	2196			68376	6128428
7214651	2176196	2026107	29688	110376	7625	100	2300	1021281	7709781
13648672	8682649	3389474	992204	2868983	763683	87003	581302	3395469	47453543
1370486	897630	454936	129867	184617	18530		109680	202417	7800328
9221968	5542659	2064209	349725	2073765	562764	34638	457558	2883806	23129003
301278	291231	52188	96984	103861	37648	550		35173	1120063
57084	33353	708	29369	1500	1776			1272	245722
514766	364925	84532	148590	84213	40590		7000	54120	3673789
173082	78673	35108	8797	19132	4530	11106		13301	1439427
345915	229490	66614	3200	159056	620			26810	737632
1664093	1244688	631179	225672	242839	97225	40709	7064	178570	9307579
39343812	17899686	13302799	292245	3186225	519290	34638	564489	6084380	115605335
20132579	13639945	8847850	1401460	2812292	498793	58075	21475	2786461	72953067

10-12 续表 3 continued

单位：千元

项目	Item	销售折扣与折让 Sales Discount	商品销售收入净额 Net Value of Sales Revenue	商品销售成本 Sales Cost	经营费用 Operating Expense	# 运杂及装卸费 Traffic Related Expense	商品销售税金及附加 Sales Tax and Extra Charges
合计	**Total**	**1745109**	**186813293**	**169114148**	**8701064**	**1335396**	**363934**
按企业登记注册类型分	**Grouped by Type of Enterprises Registered**						
内资企业	Domestic Investment	1721784	183351851	166233818	8419905	1330604	360666
国有企业	State-Owned	1667961	128076713	116124480	5856553	1128495	228235
集体企业	Collective Owned	12154	16346627	14712424	846632	73306	46235
私营企业	Private Owned	1188	4566731	4195948	224647	16976	6168
联营企业	Joint Owned	18174	5787814	5217245	211317	19982	12570
股份合作企业	Share Holding Cooperative	2063	2585576	2336507	150848	7921	4710
股份有限公司	Share Holding Company	17463	9452818	8267884	452168	7221	37143
有限责任公司	Limited-Liability Company	2781	16451610	15297404	676522	76703	25604
其他企业	Others		83962	81926	1218		1
港澳台商投资企业	Hongkong,Macao and Taiwan Funded Enterprises	1562	771385	649990	50779	1005	1076
外商投资企业	Foreign Funded Enterprises	21763	2690057	2230340	230380	3787	2192
按国民经济行业分	**Grouped by Sectors**						
批发业	Wholesale	1745109	186813293	169114148	8701064	1335396	363934
食品饮料烟草和家庭用品批发业	Food,Beverage,Tabacoo and Family Use Goods	34361	47166995	43605666	1809815	306011	50146
食品饮料烟草批发业	Food,Beverage and Tabacco	3742	20455946	19220401	759966	122478	23105
棉麻、土畜产品批发业	Cotton,Flax,Local and Animal Products		3257536	3099914	130224	41134	1570
纺织品、服装和鞋帽批发业	Textile,Garments,Shoes and Hats	1154	9332681	8395462	312343	72645	3017
日用百货批发业	Daily Use Goods	1059	3450671	3118173	159367	13867	6430
日用杂品批发业	Grocery	3	558191	470444	47724	8720	574
五金交电化工批发业	Hardware,Electrical Appliance and Chemic	1838	4150041	3996666	119363	28876	5849
药品及医疗器械批发业	Medicine and Medical Appliance	26565	5961929	5304606	280828	18291	9601
能源、材料和机械电子设备批发业	Energy,Materials,Machinery and Electronic Equipments	1103145	75230749	70657736	2405123	761602	87395
能源批发业	Energy		16937289	15378680	777065	233653	38711
化工材料批发业	Chemical Materials	518	7904585	7528031	224556	140803	7138
木材批发业	Timbers		739801	664720	86788	20055	365
建筑材料批发业	Building Materials	19	1634151	1486575	76557	10276	2584
矿产品批发业	Mineral Products		664645	549772	99736	77569	1402
金属材料批发业	Metal Materials	1075415	23446623	22266556	656164	176192	18400
机械、电子设备批发业	Machinery and Electronic Equipments	25717	16205600	15232811	337162	80179	13202
汽车摩托车及零配件批发业	Spares and Fittings of Automobile and Motorcycle	1476	7232307	7118981	125874	14864	4384
再生物资回收批发业	Recovery of Reclaimed Materials		465748	431610	21221	8011	1209
其他批发业	Others	501836	17067773	14123037	1019580	161315	52076
工艺美术品批发业	Handicrafts		1284092	1172991	42217	7625	1237
图书报刊批发业	Books,Newspaper and Magazines	497991	1949317	1572298	147426	17804	4258
农业生产资料批发业	Agricultural Capital Goods		6128428	5674166	215737	43397	10260
其他类未包括的批发	Others	3845	7705936	5703582	614200	92489	36321
零售业	Retail	105767	47347776	40727709	3466546	106468	174317
食品、饮料和烟草零售业	Food,Beverage and Tabacco	14022	7786306	6821655	730875	21364	24385
日用百货零售业	Daily Use Goods	60338	23068665	19248183	1771255	32662	103920
纺织品、服装和鞋帽零售业	Textile,Garments,Shoes and Hats	906	1119157	877943	166753	3806	6238
日用杂品零售业	Grocery	145	245577	204354	18411	1708	777
五金交电化工零售业	Hardware,Electrical Appliance and Chemical	52	3673737	3291975	210722	12576	11902
药品及医疗器械零售业	Medicine and Medical Appliance	5772	1433655	1203382	98608	3598	3956
图书报刊零售业	Books,Newspaper and Magazines	22388	715244	522608	93595	2291	2802
其他零售业	Others	2144	9305435	8557609	376327	28463	20337
按规模划分	**Grouped by Size**						
大型企业	Large Enterprises	1578711	114026624	102653765	5077083	860137	219883
中型企业	Medium Enterprises	166398	72786669	66460383	3623981	475259	144051

10-12 续表 4 continued

(1000 yuan)

商品销售利润 Sales Profits	代购代销收入 Revenue from Agency Activity	主营业务利润 Profits of Major Business	其他业务利润 Profits of Other Business	管理费用 Overhead Expense	#税金 Taxes	#财产保险费 Premium of Property	#劳动待业保险 Premium for Employment	财务费用 Financial Expense	#利息支出 Interest Expenditure	营业利润 Operating Profits
8634147	**1029598**	**9663745**	**2081895**	**7992514**	**251278**	**76439**	**610339**	**3817289**	**3750982**	**8579**
8337462	1028928	9366390	2073257	7661576	232577	74518	608184	3812149	3748597	39935
5867445	972503	6839948	1452901	5191691	169000	55510	468070	3355071	3274212	-201240
741336	3586	744922	181075	761355	24335	5784	54629	187620	187022	-12247
139968	406	140374	12649	139319	2057	1121	3610	3764	1870	11167
346682	71	346753	18371	290311	3745	1835	12155	60854	58839	14386
93511	1542	95053	17142	101150	953	524	8002	10392	9947	-6204
695623	3	695626	154539	526553	20597	6218	38117	12050	59419	317203
452080	50817	502897	236580	650285	11880	3506	23594	182408	157288	-83045
817		817		912	10	20	7	-10		-85
69540	118	69658	263	43261	585	301	80	1914	1798	23474
227145	552	227697	8375	287677	18116	1620	2075	3226	587	-54830
8634147	1029598	9663745	2081895	7992514	251278	76439	610339	3817289	3750982	8579
1701368	155260	1856628	442218	1652750	51910	15162	101525	1507596	1437305	-851885
452474	52986	505460	274801	577183	24996	7960	41606	942876	975474	-731338
25828	18982	44810	35026	163059	7785	1490	18188	129084	123454	-204201
621859	45090	666949	31458	289244	10615	1043	6042	259259	164078	149437
166701	8522	175223	33054	153645	2526	1823	8105	61948	60130	-9553
39449	396	39845	2456	33892	475	73	2155	15552	14182	-7143
28163	23970	52133	45199	130119	1778	749	8779	47841	50097	-80624
366894	5314	372208	20224	305608	3735	2024	16650	51036	49890	31537
2080495	646103	2726598	659437	2267193	90706	23000	138243	1493495	1458908	-332594
742833	240848	983681	-23571	545424	9743	10663	32162	154916	113289	261384
144860	65216	210076	88504	168829	5175	2384	8451	178306	182018	-40246
-12072	913	-11159	4579	28899	310	154	1380	39059	36231	-74708
68435	1349	69784	29211	85353	5257	685	3319	28722	27828	-30348
13735	22913	36648	486	16216	102		1201	15243	13846	5675
505503	127883	633386	323478	632466	40228	2867	40110	584498	574090	-229150
622425	178787	801212	152992	624794	21076	4875	40610	362170	377418	-16498
-16932	8194	-8738	62710	136833	7722	959	6032	117823	126952	-200321
11708		11708	21048	28379	1093	413	4978	12758	7236	-8382
1873080	221423	2094503	211089	801003	24441	6456	37592	491940	473555	1014960
67647	1844	69491	17049	58128	1419	25	10194	67204	68857	-38792
225335	-13603	211732	27341	114966	1468	486	7692	-2348	-2516	126453
228265	116257	344522	67668	151727	2940	678	8297	79966	92069	180497
1351833	116925	1468758	99031	476182	18614	5267	11409	347118	315145	746802
2979204	6812	2986016	769151	3271568	84221	31821	332979	324258	381214	178098
209391	475	209866	177508	414778	25479	5936	103365	48390	43156	-76457
1945307	2372	1947679	386677	1959474	37126	18725	156859	192044	261517	194303
68223	555	68778	31234	134676	5422	911	10393	15769	14255	-50430
22035		22035	9054	22957	2337	178	2668	1526	1434	6607
159138	679	159817	22748	166657	3249	1000	13765	12280	13600	5038
127709	2039	129748	6178	100428	2313	582	12846	3213	2978	31890
96239	8	96247	16565	84402	1524	782	15248	-311	32	29365
351162	684	351846	119187	388196	6771	3707	17835	51347	44242	37782
6075893	613617	6689510	1034963	4014973	151068	41199	262832	2351450	2436710	1384950
2558254	415981	2974235	1046932	3977541	100210	35240	347507	1465839	1314272	-1376371

10-12 续表 5 continued

单位：千元

项目	Item	投资收益 Investment Income	补贴收入 Subsidy Income	营业外收入 Out-business Income	营业外支出 Out-business Expenditure	利润总额 Total Profits	应交所得税 Income Tax Payable
合计	**Total**	**1380334**	**1585593**	**714532**	**437246**	**3398403**	**1273791**
按企业登记注册类型分	**Grouped by Type of Enterprises Registered**						
内资企业	Domestic Investment	1380334	1584526	709741	433105	3428042	1259209
国有企业	State-Owned	1215826	1461546	572874	336287	2835312	956257
集体企业	Collective Owned	21941	114094	86946	42796	184180	94597
私营企业	Private Owned	709	2388	2697	1865	15760	25921
联营企业	Joint Owned	4277	-57	5233	2445	21405	27487
股份合作企业	Share Holding Cooperative	8324	96	7872	1388	8763	3848
股份有限公司	Share Holding Company	91679		8970	20701	397405	84773
有限责任公司	Limited-Liability Company	37578	6459	25149	27623	-34698	66326
其他企业	Others					-85	
港澳台商投资企业	Hongkong,Macao and Taiwan Funded Enterprises			194	281	23387	5012
外商投资企业	Foreign Funded Enterprises		1067	4597	3860	-53026	9570
按国民经济行业分	**Grouped by Sectors**						
批发业	Wholesale	1380334	1585593	714532	437246	3398403	1273791
食品饮料烟草和家庭用品批发业	Food,Beverage,Tabacoo and Family Use Goods	274563	1311600	177591	86351	805670	341341
食品饮料烟草批发业	Food,Beverage and Tabacco	122055	1166923	80633	33815	607960	149756
棉麻、土畜产品批发业	Cotton,Flax,Local and Animal Products	41754	125584	56624	12283	11151	31759
纺织品、服装和鞋帽批发业	Textile,Garments,Shoes and Hats	7962	18228	11116	15303	134654	93832
日用百货批发业	Daily Use Goods	1470		5675	1643	-349	18720
日用杂品批发业	Grocery	-51		3622	1421	-4993	3866
五金交电化工批发业	Hardware,Electrical Appliance and Chemic	25565	465	14278	8033	-46394	15082
药品及医疗器械批发业	Medicine and Medical Appliance	75808	400	5643	13853	103641	28326
能源、材料和机械电子设备批发业	Energy,Materials,Machinery and Electronic Equipments	782568	134087	288250	187700	781337	212983
能源批发业	Energy	336834	101991	23685	15724	736750	51788
化工材料批发业	Chemical Materials	46151	43158	10738	15345	44936	18708
木材批发业	Timbers	1115		55783	4261	-22159	3297
建筑材料批发业	Building Materials	4229		3724	2009	-6140	8379
矿产品批发业	Mineral Products	744		214	325	6317	4367
金属材料批发业	Metal Materials	221701	4483	33077	128574	-51110	27081
机械、电子设备批发业	Machinery and Electronic Equipmenst	131771	-78648	156092	19088	175214	85248
汽车摩托车及零配件批发业	Spares and Fittings of Automobile and Motorcycle	36638	59065	2274	2230	-104031	13787
再生物资回收批发业	Recovery of Reclaimed Materials	3385	4038	2663	144	1560	328
其他批发业	Others	177636	28428	29576	47542	1243654	431998
工艺美术品批发业	Handicrafts	1275		3498	3892	-37848	3024
图书报刊批发业	Books,Newspaper and Magazines	4601	952	872	6087	124530	51380
农业生产资料批发业	Agricultural Capital Goods	41031	27410	5434	19627	260584	80251
其他类未包括的批发	Others	130729	66	19772	17936	896388	297343
零售业	Retail	145567	111478	219115	115653	567742	287469
食品、饮料和烟草零售业	Food,Beverage and Tabacco	25759	98647	48712	9810	88591	51396
日用百货零售业	Daily Use Goods	87731	1481	110411	66657	347832	154539
纺织品、服装和鞋帽零售业	Textile,Garments,Shoes and Hats	2632	2518	6828	20100	-54893	1835
日用杂品零售业	Grocery	121	10	1120	875	6985	1851
五金交电化工零售业	Hardware,Electrical Appliance and Chemical	13411	2	19579	2202	36540	11699
药品及医疗器械零售业	Medicine and Medical Appliance	1998		7002	7580	33311	10885
图书报刊零售业	Books,Newspaper and Magazines	525	198	1000	722	30372	12521
其他零售业	Others	13390	8622	24463	7707	79004	42743
按规模划分	**Grouped by Size**						
大型企业	Large Enterprises	619189	993695	328231	252145	3132704	923562
中型企业	Medium Enterprises	761145	591898	386301	185101	265699	350229

10-12 续表 6 continued

(1000 yuan)

转作奖金的利润 Profits Distributed as Bonus	提取盈余公积 Surplus Accumulation Funds Drawn	应付利润 Profits Payable	# 已分配股利 Divided Payment	本年应付工资总额 Total Wages Payable in the Year	# 主营业务应付工资 Wage Payable of Major Business	本年应付福利费总额 Welfares Payable in the Year	# 主营业务应付福利费 of Major Business	本年应交增值税 Value Added Payable in the Year	本年进项税额 Tax included in Purchasing Cost	本年销项税额 Tax included in Sales Value
29767	**1469276**	**1127050**	**-26203**	**3646180**	**3001158**	**578946**	**462104**	**-379560**	**22858175**	**22320299**
29767	1469276	1125670	-27161	3506392	2930779	531031	439633	-460054	22396084	21740851
3103	1279363	997145	-43659	2238813	1915022	359244	301531	267963	13701512	13767864
15916	104185	33458	-631	426782	320728	68275	58034	-1025245	3370714	2365293
689	1324	675		75289	59732	7539	5861	16029	750402	761912
793	9616	28850	264	109074	107470	11265	10884	54210	689078	746398
16	1808	3346	9	71164	62158	11937	10672	25357	368302	391234
	48246	21449	5312	346593	259220	41939	26922	146235	1576067	1733503
9250	24734	40832	11629	238357	206129	30788	25729	55375	1928659	1963275
		-85	-85	320	320	44		22	11350	11372
		1357	958	30071	22540	15322	11659	10751	108146	118938
		23		109717	47839	32593	10812	69743	353945	460510
29767	1469276	1127050	-26203	3646180	3001158	578946	462104	-379560	22858175	22320299
5000	522814	317724	-4746	553895	496646	92092	79273	-1451735	6615539	5087642
3149	292253	188623		209441	189328	43448	40810	69180	2037945	2178308
	50268	9373		32697	28382	6106	1119	-1383903	1548537	253076
179	106280	102754		77196	70019	12150	10981	-262109	983016	509584
530	3390	-2390	-4606	54457	47441	5140	3951	20744	514859	545170
140	540	3639		13247	12953	2048	2007	3396	51402	27383
225	2573	800	-408	61370	56104	8605	7947	26336	652637	683410
777	67510	14925	268	105487	92419	14595	12458	74621	827143	890711
2730	446701	562872	-33107	666781	558110	119033	95922	134289	8611475	8589742
14	25909	454450	-36866	138389	128966	24169	21951	185254	1060317	1252768
	55930	40556		50340	42425	8518	7392	1797	1178702	1123823
	18686	3329		5221	4239	860	379	5315	47161	52476
1389	3229	2139		38962	26545	8619	4453	16043	211590	231181
	3	15		9377	5451	1337	632	3704	32806	36261
296	183466	15270	700	196745	153626	28421	21605	-29000	3155808	3034307
676	92144	44862	2941	176086	160593	36951	32411	-80449	1795684	1699724
355	66871	1967	118	36653	26094	7878	5281	24916	1060115	1082915
	463	284		15008	10171	2280	1818	6709	69292	76287
2209	240409	110585		219653	169370	37567	30126	51962	927030	974335
2146	3291			24139	19373	6983	6016	1451	21096	19971
	50242	16664		62830	46625	8832	6508	40176	174793	216063
63	9833			34059	31642	4894	4441	2875	126340	126673
	177043	93921		98625	71730	16858	13161	7460	604801	611628
19828	259352	135869	11650	2205851	1777032	330254	256783	885924	6704131	7668580
10631	84732	9497	797	475904	438848	73000	67155	169714	979666	1154627
3791	117294	80678	10504	1197288	902455	186770	128511	506432	3358936	3927214
55	2879	1348		93479	80133	11513	10705	17466	141394	161639
	1065	-220	-444	13863	10342	1820	1501	6989	34317	41341
1363	15572	5025	-24	97746	69382	12242	10712	38116	516714	557126
4	17361	2809	-33	67154	63674	11396	10410	40784	198109	238985
	4752	13922		61168	58875	9297	8913	20714	66191	87748
3984	15697	22810	850	199249	153323	24216	18876	85709	1408804	1499900
18157	927361	786205	9471	1690842	1338875	277000	208613	-572540	13752598	13000121
11610	541915	340845	-35674	1955338	1662283	301946	253491	192980	9105577	9320178

10-13 大中型餐饮业财务状况

单位：千元

项目	Item	合计 Total	按登记注册类型分 国有企业 State-Owned	集体企业 Collective Owned	私营企业 Private Owned	联营企业 Joint-Owned	股份有限公司 Share Holding Company
流动资产合计	Total Circulating Assets	2018985	538890	158914	53021	39578	94502
# 货币资金	Cash	675739	254984	47194	9740	10092	34509
应收帐款	Accounts Receivable	212306	21856	38158	2958	4856	3299
存　货	Inventory	219852	33608	22835	9999	7772	2108
长期投资	Long-term Investment	344892	61939	16967	1037	260	5590
固定资产合计	Total Fixed Assets	2103687	602811	112704	91310	42587	130450
固定资产原价合计	Total Original Value of Fixed Assets	2651317	684401	153699	93038	47069	158509
# 生产经营用	For Production and Business Use	2110759	534247	88706	80388	24160	158499
累计折旧	Accumulative Depreciation	662111	163140	46507	6354	10396	28541
# 本年折旧	of this Year	162873	34059	15230	3967	1424	4466
无形及递延资产合计	Total Intangible and Deffered Assets	692023	123409	65138	58513	5811	16600
# 无形资产	Intangible Assets	115305	10563	1958	601		4456
其他资产合计	Other Assets	243606	3634	2353	4321	175	861
资产合计	Total Assets	5403193	1330683	356076	208202	88411	248003
流动负债合计	Total Liquid Liabilities	2857664	642322	209982	164147	68013	53515
# 短期借款	Short-term Loans	592670	52777	42734	12000	13756	15000
应付帐款	Payment Payable	502875	38930	69775	43029	14111	9554
长期负债合计	Total Long-term Liabilities	503848	88399	21081	2337	2	35846
# 长期借款	Long-term Loans	419671	62164	12483			35846
负债合计	Total Liabilities	3361512	730721	231063	166484	68015	89361
所有者权益合计	Total Ownership Interest	2041681	599962	125013	41718	20396	158642
# 实收资本	Capital Stock	2288632	377174	202809	91070	36362	105710
# 国家资本	State	600246	346542	11237	70	9121	
集体资本	Collective	216154	4031	127162	12903	9044	
法人资本	Institutional Units	563659	21421	61396	30680	17435	102560
个人资本	Individual	103626	2322	3014	47417	762	3150
港澳台资本	Honkong,Macao and Taiwan	353958	2858				
外商资本	Foreign	450989					
资本公积	Accumulation Capital	247685	103057	5558	6303	15979	32219
营业收入	Business Revenue	4403466	910091	430888	177087	79058	145814
营业成本	Business Cost	2102534	436335	241858	99350	37892	53585
营业费用	Business Expenses	1590777	321937	130416	72313	30480	44075
营业税金及附加	Business Tax and Extra Charges	222690	48654	22310	9946	4111	7814
主营业务利润	Profits of Major Business	487465	103165	36304	-4522	6575	40340
其他业务利润	Profits of Other Business	3069	1944	-495	-32		
管理费用	Overhead Expenses	634873	110923	63370	33989	8116	16320
# 税　金	Taxes	13419	4339	2832	151	326	563
财产保险费	Premium of Property	8200	1175	1129	185	84	356
劳动待业保险费	Premium for Employment	50732	40388	619	1	1549	4513
财务费用	Financial Expenses	58255	-3529	3957	1532	3824	-1052
# 利息支出	Interest Expenditure	29951	-4010	3440	961	-32	-1322
营业利润	Operating Profits	-201070	-1968	-34416	-40077	-5365	25072
投资收益	Investment Income	12365	7605	-622			1469
补贴收入	Subsidy Income	-1269	2				
营业外收入	Out-business Income	29646	9367	1321	873	155	269
营业外支出	Out-business Expenditure	22732	3147	1085	587	74	398
利润总额	Total Profits	-170313	14224	-32147	-39680	-5274	26421
应交所得税	Income Tax Payable	68587	15692	1401	372	1811	8732
转作奖金的利润	Profits Distributed as Bonus	1371	67	233		502	
提取盈余公积	Surplus Accumulation Funds Drawn	34599	23051	629	37	12	4890
应付利润	Profits Payable	64904	1579	1955	213	1790	9622
# 已分配股利	Divided Payment	10116	-48				6293
本年应付工资总额	Total Wages Payable of this Year	550356	155139	54252	18334	12241	19708
# 主营业务应付工资	of Major Business	482360	144075	45071	12211	11785	19708
本年应付福利费总额	Total Welfares Payable of this Year	85767	19532	5344	1413	1233	2618
# 主营业务应付福利费	of Major Business	67499	17539	4457	931	1221	2618

FINANCIAL INDICATORS FOR LARGE AND MEDIUM CATERING TRADES

(1000 yuan)

By Registered Type					按行业划分 By Sectors			按规模划分 By Size	
有限责任公司 Limited-liabilities	股份合作企业 Share Holding Cooperative	其它企业 Others	港澳台商投资企业 Hongkon,Macao, Taiwan Funded	外商投资企业 Foreign Funded	正餐 Dinner	快餐 Fast Food	其他餐饮业 Others	大型企业 Large	中型企业 Medium
107288	56515	1112	468129	501036	1637056	357083	24846	1261394	757591
24747	7594	343	96504	190032	560696	98630	16413	420274	255465
18789	10584		36765	75041	194243	17554	509	118152	94154
19880	11064	768	47489	64329	166651	52101	1100	124200	95652
116005	4666		37611	100817	341325	3167	400	316266	28626
74628	29086	725	199914	819472	1529902	568583	5202	1349904	753783
79801	37425	725	325014	1071636	1917836	725140	8341	1713556	937761
63056	20318		264588	876797	1504330	601083	5346	1482506	628253
12981	8339		125277	260576	500331	158641	3139	403090	259021
5974	2248		22489	73016	102467	59740	666	106299	56574
55689	26408		173894	166561	477908	214022	93	396377	295646
6579	71		75622	15455	43522	71783		90111	25194
9798	1661		76940	143863	186028	56892	686	136629	106977
363408	118336	1837	956488	1731749	4172219	1199747	31227	3460570	1942623
180799	94049	2512	599292	843033	2247939	604285	5440	1782546	1075118
32968	30141		112477	280817	365368	227130	172	431838	160832
50302	19409	2512	77297	177956	389330	111715	1830	299317	203558
63543	9076		54466	229098	460602	41938	1308	196228	307620
36973	725		54087	217393	393515	26156		149822	269849
244342	103125	2512	653758	1072131	2708541	646223	6748	1978774	1382738
119066	15211	-675	302730	659618	1463678	553524	24479	1481796	559885
91150	50915	380	566263	766799	1706363	552552	29717	1344503	944129
32583			65598	135095	511486	86260	2500	315712	284534
2260	8824	380	12951	38599	204789	11365		67093	149061
23111	31800		176870	98386	380771	179638	3250	388725	174934
33196	10291		1474	2000	100350	3276		30187	73439
			277184	73916	236516	93475	23967	210758	143200
			32186	418803	272451	178538		332028	118961
35731	2718		6495	39625	216866	31005	-186	154912	92773
312332	135029	2626	479183	1731358	3204522	1185734	13210	2969220	1434246
171673	86475	1821	200453	773092	1540553	554613	7368	1376062	726472
121615	38532	386	233083	597940	1139027	446099	5651	1027139	563638
15487	5077	144	23442	85705	164250	57928	512	147616	75074
3557	4945	275	22205	274621	360692	127094	-321	418403	69062
61			1543	48	1493	1576		1652	1417
35067	13243	410	94117	259318	523131	110210	1532	376658	258215
671	18		1467	3052	10681	2734	4	7178	6241
967	9		1415	2880	5526	2668	6	5301	2899
1382	171		1369	740	47938	2794		32136	18596
7498	2844		11616	31565	50493	7787	-25	30847	27408
6534	2454		765	21161	23352	6607	-8	9846	20105
-38902	-8950	-135	-77159	-19170	-207170	7928	-1828	16878	-217948
3640			29	244	12336		29	10266	2099
				-1271	2	-1271		-1271	2
1587	372		3471	12231	17520	12117	9	21200	8446
576	181		1862	14822	9697	12930	105	17067	5665
-34445	-10934	-135	-70659	-17684	-174948	6530	-1895	37624	-207937
1803	647		3944	34185	49394	19006	187	61688	6899
			426	143	1371			1130	241
4765	17		260	938	33988	611		27474	7125
1002	233		3881	44629	32206	32318	380	57232	7672
	55		-128	3944	10116			10253	-137
38850	15173	208	76800	159651	452652	94776	2928	314906	235450
34130	13743	208	65924	135505	388167	91908	2285	285814	196546
3856	1160		19269	31342	67241	17504	1022	54225	31542
3147	1105		17391	19090	50147	16425	927	42912	24587

10-14 商业、饮食业、服务业经营机构及人员
OPERATING UNITS AND PERSONNEL OF COMMERCE,CATERING AND SERVICES

项目 Item		经营机构(个) Operating Units (unit)		人员(人) Personnel (person)	
		1998	1997	1998	1997
总计	**Total**	**252618**	**262367**	**1250212**	**1422874**
商业	Commerce	191867	200755	827218	1005324
批发	Wholesale	11357	19663	269237	376142
零售	Retail	180510	181092	557981	629182
饮食业	Catering	28754	29562	192694	179814
服务业	Services	31997	32050	230300	237736

10-15 商业、饮食业、服务业营业网点及人员(按所有制形式分)
OUTLETS AND PERSONNEL OF COMMERCE,CATERING AND SERVICES (BY OWNERSHIP)

单位：个、人 (unit,person)

项目 Item		合计 Total	国有 State-owned	集体 Collective-owned	个体 Individuals	其他 Others
营业网点	**Outlets**	**241261**	**7867**	**9767**	**216259**	**7368**
人员	**Personnel**	**980975**	**262953**	**157346**	**347600**	**213076**
商业	Commerce					
零售网点	Retail Outlets	180510	5155	6359	163488	5508
人员	Personnel	557981	140128	91745	216757	109351
饮食业	Catering					
营业网点	Outlets	28754	992	1649	25050	1063
人员	Personnel	192694	27032	27698	94620	43344
服务业	Services					
营业网点	Outlets	31997	1720	1759	27721	797
人员	Personnel	230300	95793	37903	36223	60381

10-16 批发业网点及人员

OUTLETS AND PERSONNEL OF WHOLESALE

单位：个、人 (unit,person)

项目	Item	网点 Outlets	人员 Personnel
总计	**Total**	**11357**	**269237**
食品、饮料、烟草批发业	Food,Beverage and Tabacco	1466	45258
棉、麻、土畜产品批发业	Cotton,Fiber,Local and Livestock Products	53	2308
纺织品、服装和鞋帽批发业	Textile Products,Garments,Shoes and Hats	670	14309
日用百货批发业	Daily Use Goods	1011	18778
日用杂品批发业	Daily Use Groceries	124	2999
五金、交电、化工批发业	Hardware,Electrical Appliances and Chemical	1765	28564
药品及医疗器械批发业	Medicines and Medical Appliances	349	12829
工艺美术品批发业	Handicraft Articles	101	3060
图书报刊批发业	Books,Newspapers and Magazines	62	3842
农业生产资料批发业	Agricultural Capital Goods	174	4718
其他批发业	Others	5582	132572

10-17 商业零售网点及人员

OUTLETS AND PERSONNEL OF RETAIL

单位：个、人 (unit,person)

项目	Item	网点 Outlets	人员 Personnel
总计	**Total**	**180510**	**557981**
食品、饮料、烟草零售业	Food,Beverage and Tabacco	48222	122801
日用百货零售业	Daily Use Goods	29110	207103
纺织品、服装和鞋帽零售业	Textile Products,Garments,Shoes and Hats	18729	37497
日用杂品零售业	Daily Use Groceries	3469	8011
五金、交电、化工零售业	Hardware,Electrical Appliances and Chemical	23927	61104
药品及医疗器械零售业	Medicines and Medical Appliances	5254	14583
图书报刊零售业	Books,Newspapers and Magazines	4749	12402
其他零售业	Others	47050	94480

10-18 饮食业营业网点及人员

OUTLETS AND PERSONNEL OF CATERING

单位：个、人 (unit,person)

项目	Item	网点 Outlets	人员 Personnel
总计	**Total**	**28754**	**192694**
正餐	Dinner	24345	162643
快餐	Fast Food	2515	25344
其他	Others	1894	4707

10-19 服务业营业网点及人员
OUTLETS AND PERSONNEL OF SERVICES

单位：个、人　　(unit,person)

项目	Item	网点 Outlets	人员 Personnel
总计	**Total**	**31997**	**230300**
理发及美容化妆业	Services of Haircut,Beauty and Making-up	2596	4110
沐浴业	Bath Service	962	4846
洗染业	Cleaning and Dyeing	1353	3499
摄影及扩印业	Photography and Large-printing	2406	5894
日用品修理业	Repairs of Daily Use Articles	12807	18140
其他居民服务业	Other Residential Services	9177	28133
旅馆业	Hotels	2696	157176

10-20 个体工商业户数及人数
OUTLETS AND PERSONNEL OF SELF-EMPLOYMENT BUSINESS

单位：个、人　　(unit,person)

项目 Item		1998			1997		
		全市 Total	城镇 Urban	农村 Rural	全市 Total	城镇 Urban	农村 Rural
总户数	**Total Outlets**	**246294**	**108329**	**137965**	**247377**	**106947**	**140430**
总人数	**Total Persons**	**346550**	**155037**	**191513**	**347896**	**154237**	**193659**
农林牧渔业							
Farming,Forestry,Animal	户数 Units	1131	36	1095	1319	29	1290
Husbandry and Fishery	人数 Persons	1519	60	1459	1564	48	1516
工业	户数 Units	16254	4513	11741	16820	4710	12110
Industry	人数 Persons	33339	7018	26321	34412	7169	27243
建筑业	户数 Units	700	220	480	779	237	542
Construction	人数 Persons	2272	500	1772	2825	544	2281
交通运输业	户数 Units	20594	4939	15655	22236	5155	17081
Transportation	人数 Persons	22690	5419	17271	24716	5740	18976
商业	户数 Units	154214	73046	81168	154405	72152	82253
Commerce	人数 Persons	188288	91188	97100	190024	92049	97975
饮食业	户数 Units	24263	12411	11852	24143	12333	11810
Catering	人数 Persons	60328	33377	26951	58244	32194	26050
服务业	户数 Units	15222	6962	8260	13599	6036	7563
Services	人数 Persons	21416	10637	10779	18716	8905	9811
修理业	户数 Units	12557	5953	6604	13175	6026	7149
Repairs	人数 Persons	14876	6515	8361	16115	7218	8897
其他行业	户数 Units	1359	249	1110	901	269	632
Others	人数 Persons	1822	323	1499	1280	370	910

主要统计指标解释

社会消费品零售额 指各种经济类型的批发零售贸易业、餐饮业、制造业及其他业对城乡居民、社会集团的消费品零售额。这个指标反映通过各种商品流通渠道向居民和社会集团供应的生活消费品以满足他们生活需要，是研究人民生活、社会消费品购买力、货币流通等问题的重要指标。社会消费品零售额包括：（1）售给城乡居民作为生活用的商品和修建房屋用的建筑材料；（2）售给机关、团体、学校、部队、企业、事业单位的职工食堂和旅店（招待所）附设专门供本店旅客食用、不对外营业的食堂的各种食品、饮料；企业、单位和国营农场直接售给本单位职工和职工食堂的自己生产的产品；（3）售给部队、战士生活用的粮食、副食品、衣着品、日用品、燃料；（4）售给来华的外国人、华侨、港澳台同胞的消费品；（5）居民自费购买的中、西药品、中药材及医疗用品；（6）报社、出版社直接给居民和社会集团的报纸、图书、杂志、集邮公司出售的新、旧纪念邮票、特种邮票、首日封、集邮册、集邮工具等；（7）旧货寄售商店自购、自销部分的商品；（8）煤气公司、液化石油气站售给居民和社会团体的煤气灶具和罐装液化石油气；（9）农民售给非农业居民和社会团体的商品。不包括售给国民经济各部门企业、事业单位（包括国有经济的农场）生产经营用的各种原材料、燃料、设备、工具等和售给批发零售贸易业、餐饮业作为转卖用的商品、旧货寄售商店受托寄售卖出的商品、服务业的营业收入、邮局出售邮票的收入、自来水、电力、煤气生产（供应）单位的产品供应收入，也不包括农民之间的商品销售。

批发零售贸易业商品购、销、存总额 指以各种经济类型的批发、零售贸易业（不包括个体）为总体的商品购、销、存。

商品购进总额 指从本企业（单位）以外的单位和个人购进（包括从国外直接购进）作为转卖或加工后转卖的商品。这个指标反映批发零售贸易业从国内、国外市场上购进商品的总量。商品购进总额包括：（1）从工农业生产者购进的商品；（2）从出版社、报社的发行部门购进的图书、杂志和报纸；（3）从各种经济类型的批发零售贸易企业（单位）购进的商品，如从机关、团体、企业、单位购进的剩余物资，从餐饮业、服务业购进的商品，从海关、市场管理部门购进的缉私和没收的商品，从居民收购的废旧商品等；（5）从国（境）外直接进口的商品。不包括企业（单位）为自身经营用，和未通过买卖行为而收入的商品以及销售退回、商品升溢等。

商品销售总额 指对本企业（单位）以外的单位和个人出售（包括对国（境）外直接出口）的商品。这个指标反映批发零售贸易业在国内市场上销售商品以及出口商品的总量。商品销售总额包括：（1）售给城乡居民和社会集团消费用的商品；（2）售给工业、农业、建筑业、运输邮电业、批发零售贸易业、餐饮业、服务业等作为生产、经营使用的商品；（3）售给批发零售贸易业作为转卖或加工后转卖的商品；（4）对国（境）外直接出口的商品。不包括：出售本企业（单位）自用的废旧包装用品，为通过买卖行为付出的商品，经本单位介绍，由买卖双方直接结算，本单位只收取手续费的业务，购货退出的商品以及商品损耗和损失等。

年末库存 指年末各种经济类型的批发零售贸易企业（单位）已取得所有权的商品。它反映各地区、各批发零售企业（单位）的库存情况，和对市场商品供应的保证程度。年末库存包括：（1）存放在批发零售贸易经营单位（如门市部、批发站、经营处）仓库、货场、货柜和货架中的商品；（2）挑选、整理、包装中的商品；（3）已计入购进而尚未运到本单位的商品，即发货单或银行承兑凭证已到而货未到部分；（4）寄放他处的商品，如因购货方拒绝承付而暂时存放在购货方的商品和已办完加工成品收回手续而未提回的商品；（5）委托其他单位代销（未作销售或调出）尚未售出的商品；（6）代其他单位购进尚未交付的商品。不包括所有权不属于本单位的商品、拨付除批发零售贸易业以外的其他行业所属独立核算加工等加工生产尚未收回成品的商品、代国家物资储备部门保管的商品等。年末库存总额计算方法是：农副产品采购单位按购进价计算，批发单位按进货价计算，零售单位按什么价格核算就按什么价格计算。

Explanatory Notes On Main Statistical Indicators

Total Retail Sales of Consumer Goods refer to the sum of retail sales of consumer goods to urban and rural residents and social groups by the establishments in wholesale, retail, catering, manufacturing and other industries of various ownerships. This indicator is used to show the supply of consumers goods through various channels to households and institutions to meet their demands, and is therefore very important for the study of the issues on people's livelihood , on the purchasing power of consumer goods and on the circulation of money. The retail sales of consumer goods include: (1) commodities sold to urban and rural residents for residential use and building materials sold to them for the construction or repair of houses; (2) food and Beverage sold to canteens of institutions, enterprises, schools, military units and to canteens of hotels that only serve their guests, and commodities produced by enterprises, institutions or state farms and sold directly to their employees or their canteens; (3) grain and non-staple food, clothing, daily articles and fuels sold to military and soldiers; (4) consumer goods sold to foreigners, overseas Chinese and Chinese compatriots from Taiwan, Hong Kong and Macao during their stay in the mainland of China; (5) Chinese and western medicines, herbs and medical facilities purchased by residents; (6) newspapers, books and magazines directly sold to residents and social groups by publishers, new and old commemorative stamps, special stamps, first-day envelope, stamp albums and other stamp-collection articles sold by stamp companies; (7) consumer goods purchased and then sold by second-hand shops; (8) stoves and other heating facilities and liquefied gas sold by gas companies to households and institutions; and (9) commodities sold by farmers to non-agricultural residents and social groups. But sales like followings are not included in total retail sales of consumer goods: (1) raw materials, fuels, equipment, tools sold to enterprises, institutions and state farms for production purpose; (2) commodities sold to trade establishments for re-selling; (3) commissioned sales at second-hand shops; (4) operational income of various services; (5) stamps sold at post offices; (6) income of water, power, gas production and supply establishments from the supply of their products; (7) and sales of commodities among farmers.

Purchase, Sales and Stock of Commodities by Wholesalers and Retailers refer to the purchase, sales and stock of commodities by wholesale and retail establishments of different ownership (excluding individual sellers) .

Total Purchases of Commodities refer to the purchases of commodities by the establishments from other establishments or individuals (including direct import from abroad) for the purpose of re-selling, with or without further processing of the commodities purchased. This indicator is used to show the total value of purchases of commodities by wholesale and retail establishments from domestic and overseas markets. The total purchases include: (1) agricultural and industrial products purchased from producers; (2) books, magazines and newspapers purchased from distribution departments of the publishers; (3) commodities purchased from wholesale and retail establishments of various ownership; (4) commodities purchased from other units, such as surplus materials purchased from government agencies, enterprises or institutions, commodities purchased · from catering and service establishments, confiscated goods purchased from customs authorities or market management agencies, second-hand goods and wastes purchased from residents; and (5) commodities directly imported from abroad. Excluded are commodities purchased by establishments (units) for use in their own business operation, commodities obtained without buying or selling procedures, rejected commodities, etc.

Total Sales of Commodities refer to selling of commodities by the establishments to other establishments and individuals (including direct export) . This indicator is used to show the total value of sales of commodities at domestic markets and export, The total sales include: (1) commodities sold to urban and rural residents and social groups for final consumption; (2) commodities sold to establishments in industry, agriculture, construction, transportation, post and telecommunications, wholesale and retail trades, catering and public utility for productive consumption; (3) commodities sold to wholesale and retail establishments for re-selling, with or without further processing; and (4) commodities for direct export to other countries. Excluded are sales of self-used waste packaging materials, commodities transferred without buying or selling procedures, commission income from brokerage in transactions whose settlement is directly handled by buyers and sellers, rejected commodities in the purchase, loss in commodities, etc.

Commodity Stock at Year-end refers to total commodities possessed by wholesale and retail enterprises (units) of various ownership, which reflects the inventory level of various wholesale and retail enterprises and the potential for market supply. It includes: (1) Commodities put in storage, garages, counters, and shelves of operating units (such as stores, wholesale centers, and operating offices) of wholesale and retail enterprises; (2) commodities in the process of selecting, sorting, and packing ; (3) commodities not arrived but recorded as purchase in the account, i. e. Commodities not arrived but payment receipts for the commodities from the sellers or the banks arrived; (4) specially deposited commodities, for instance, commodities in the hold of purchasers temporarily due to the refusal of payment and commodities not taken back after going through the formalities; (5) commodities entrusted to other units to sell but not sold yet; (6) commodities purchased for other units but not delivered yet. Commodities not included as stock are those not owned by the enterprise (units) , those allocated to financially independent factories rather than wholesale and retail enterprises for processing but not taken back yet, and finally those put in stock by wholesale and retail enterprises on behalf of the state material reserves units. In the calculation of the value of commodities stock at the end of period, the value is calculated at purchasing prices for agricultural goods purchasing units and wholesale units, and at the market prices for retail units.

1999

对外经济贸易、旅游

FOREIGN ECONOMY，TRADE AND TOURISM

进出口构成
Compsition of Imports and Exports

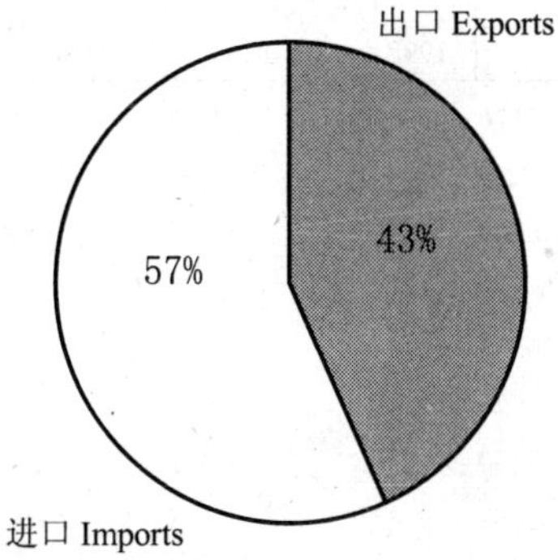

出口构成
Compsition of Exports

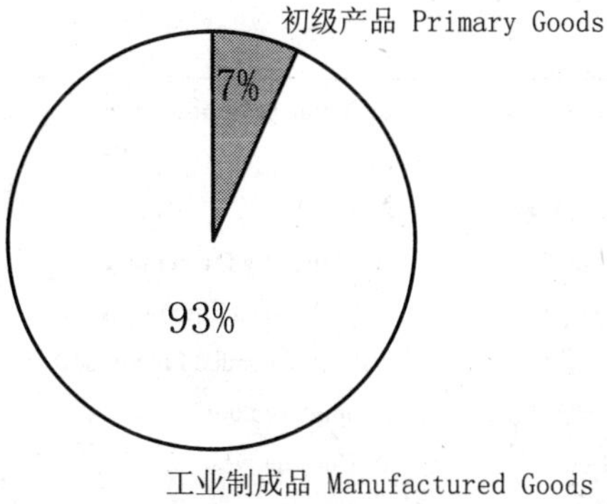

亿美元(100 million USD)	1998	1997	1998年为1997年% 1998 as % of 1997
进出口总额 Total Value of Imports and Exports	65.1	57.8	112.6
出口 Exports	28.3	24.7	114.7
进口 Imports	36.8	33.1	111.0

接待旅游人数(1978-1998) Tourists

(10000 person times)

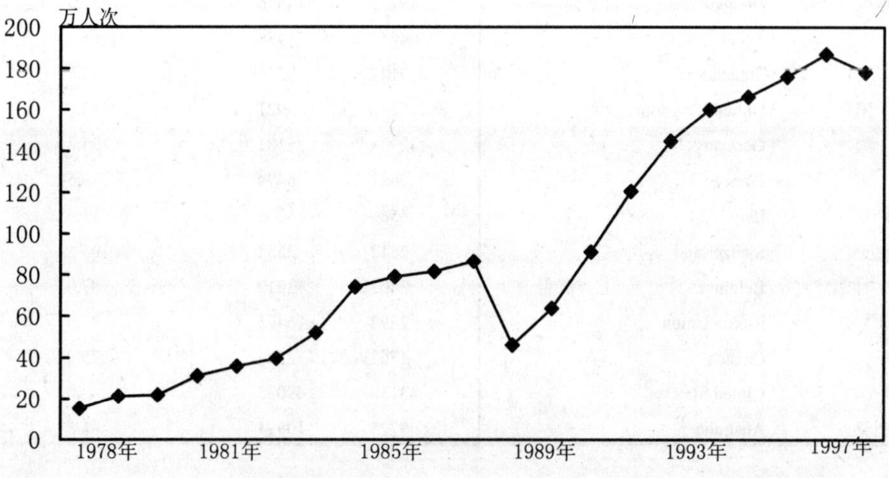

11-1 海关进出口贸易总额
TOTAL VALUE OF IMPORTS AND EXPORTS AT CUSTOMS

项目	Item	金额(万美元) Value (USD 10000) 1998	1997	1998年为1997年% 1998 as % of 1997	构成(%) Composition(%) 1998	1997
进出口总额	**Total Value of Imports and Exports**	**650536**	**577576**	**112.6**		
出口总额	**Exports**	**282896**	**246503**	**114.7**	**100**	**100**
按经济类型分	**Grouped by Ownership**					
国有企业	State-owned Enterprises	152402	126378	120.5	53.9	51.3
外商投资企业	Foreign Funded Enterprises	126273	115677	109.1	44.6	46.9
中外合资	Joint Venture	105989	97450	108.7	37.4	39.5
中外合作	Cooperative	2203	2667	82.7	0.8	1.1
外商独资	Foreign Enterprises	18081	15560	116.2	6.4	6.3
集体企业	Collective-owned Enterprises	4116	4364	94.4	1.5	1.8
其他	Others	105	84	124.8	...	...
按国别(地区)分	**Grouped by Country(Region)**					
# 香港地区	Hongkong	49131	40858	120.2	17.4	16.6
澳门地区	Macao	63	103	60.5	...	...
日本	Japan	67337	72012	93.6	23.8	29.2
新加坡	Singapore	6343	6656	95.3	2.2	2.7
英国	United Kingdom	4190	4775	88.0	1.5	1.9
德国	Germany	10363	9452	109.6	3.7	3.8
法国	France	2658	1816	146.3	0.9	0.7
意大利	Italy	4012	4270	94.0	1.4	1.7
瑞士	Switzerland	923	726	127.1	0.3	0.3
波兰	Poland	1760	1160	151.8	0.6	0.5
俄罗斯联邦	Russia Union	20975	6245	335.8	7.4	2.5
埃及	Egypt	498	290	171.7	0.2	0.1
加拿大	Canada	3161	297	6.3	1.1	0.1
美国	United States	39491	31824	124.0	14.0	12.9
澳大利亚	Australia	4731	4363	108.4	1.7	1.8
进口总额	**Imports**	**367640**	**331073**	**111.0**	**100**	**100**
# 香港地区	Hongkong	19172	14416	132.9	5.2	4.4
日本	Japan	64656	74488	86.8	17.6	22.5
新加坡	Singapore	9147	6276	145.7	2.5	1.9
英国	United Kingdom	5232	3921	133.4	1.4	1.2
德国	Germany	32938	26181	125.8	9.0	7.9
法国	France	5081	6474	78.5	1.4	2
意大利	Italy	5586	5002	111.6	1.5	1.5
瑞士	Switzerland	2612	2532	103.1	0.7	0.8
比利时	Belgium	3407	3919	87.0	0.9	1.2
俄罗斯联邦	Russia Union	2392	6471	37.0	0.7	2
加拿大	Canada	1762	2324	75.9	0.5	0.7
美国	United States	43154	49037	88.0	11.7	14.8
澳大利亚	Australia	9725	10991	88.5	2.6	3.3

11-2 海关进出口商品类别及构成

VALUE AND COMPOSITION OF IMPORTS AND EXPORTS AT CUSTOMS BY CATEGORY OF COMMODITIES

项目	Item	金额(万美元) Value (USD 10000)		构成(%) Composition(%)	
		1998	1997	1998	1997
出口总额	**Exports**	**282896**	**246503**	**100**	**100**
初级产品	**Primary Goods**	**19302**	**20019**	**6.8**	**8.1**
食品及主要供食用的活动物	Food and Lively Animals Chiefly for Food	12416	12150	4.4	4.9
饮料及烟草	Beverage and Tabacco	599	521	0.2	0.2
非食用原料（燃料除外）	Non-edible Raw Materials(excluding Fuel)	3838	5512	1.4	2.3
矿物燃料、润滑油及有关原料	Mineral Fuels,Lubricants and Related Materials	2318	1721	0.8	0.7
动植物油、脂及蜡	Animal and Vegetable Oils,Fats and Waxes	131	115	...	...
工业制成品	**Manufactured Goods**	**263594**	**226484**	**93.2**	**91.9**
化学品及有关产品	Chemicals and Related Products	9446	10355	3.3	4.2
按原料分类的制成品	Finished Products Grouped by Materials	50822	51109	18.0	20.7
机械及运输设备	Machinery and Transport Equipment	86890	70357	30.7	28.6
杂项制品	Miscellaneous Products	116380	94624	41.2	38.4
未分类商品	Products Not Classified	56	39	...	...
进口总额	**Imports**	**367640**	**331073**	**100**	**100**
初级产品	**Primary Goods**	**43161**	**40444**	**11.7**	**12.2**
食品及主要供食用的活动物	Food and Lively Animals Chiefly for Food	10913	10930	3.0	3.3
饮料及烟草	Beverage and Tabacco	864	561	0.2	0.1
非食用原料（燃料除外）	Non-edible Raw Materials(excluding Fuel)	23872	24489	6.5	7.4
矿物燃料、润滑油及有关原料	Mineral Fuels,Lubricants and Related Materials	769	2550	0.2	0.8
动植物油、脂及蜡	Animal and Vegetable Oils,Fats and Waxes	6743	1914	1.8	0.6
工业制成品	**Manufactured Goods**	**324479**	**290629**	**88.3**	**87.8**
化学品及有关产品	Chemicals and Related Products	19028	18275	5.2	5.5
按原料分类的制成品	Finished Products Grouped by Materials	45418	55023	12.4	16.6
机械及运输设备	Machinery and Transport Equipment	235271	196013	64.0	59.2
杂项制品	Miscellaneous Products	24451	21015	6.7	6.4
未分类商品	Products Not Classified	311	303	...	0.1

11-3 进 出 口 商 品 检 验
TEST OF IMPORTS AND EXPORTS COMMODITIES

项目 Item			1998	1997	1998年为1997年% 1998 as % of 1997
进口商品检验	Imports				
批　数　(批)	Batches	(batch)	2058	1606	128.1
金　额　(万美元)	Value	(USD 10000)	70105	50061	140.0
# 不合格商品	Substandard				
批　数　(批)	Batches	(batch)	396	403	98.3
金　额　(万美元)	Value	(USD 10000)	1523	1720	88.5
出口商品检验	Exports				
批　数　(批)	Batches	(batch)	33718	30389	110.9
金　额　(万美元)	Value	(USD 10000)	93235	86621	107.6
# 不合格商品	Substandard				
批　数　(批)	Batches	(batch)	107	108	99.1

11-4 海关主要商品出口量
MAJOR EXPORTS COMMODITIES IN VOLUME(CUSTOMS STATISTICS)

品名 Item	1998	1997	品名 Item	1998	1997
食用油籽 (万吨) Edible Oil Seeds (10000 tons)	1	1	铅笔 (吨) (Pencils) (ton)	660	862
冻鸡 (吨) Frozen Chicken (ton)	18917	12650	洗衣粉 (吨) Detergents (ton)	53	54
蔬菜 (万吨) Vegetable (10000 tons)	1	1	彩色电视机 (万美元) Color TV Sets (USD 10000)	22	54
干鲜果 (万吨) Dry and Fresh Fruit (10000tons)		1	收录机 (万台) Recorders (10000)	17	24
栗子 (吨) Chestnuts (ton)	4414	2842	照相机 (万架)	94	123
罐头 (吨) Canned Food (ton)		279	自行车 (万辆) Bicycle (10000)	80	40
啤酒 (万升) Beer (10000 l)	592	608	地毯 (万平方米) Carpets (10000 sq.m)	68	114
中成药 (万美元) Chinese Medicines (USD 10000)	762	934	首饰 (万美元) Jewelry (USD10000)	8045	4039
棉纱 (吨) Cotton Yarn (ton)	5310	3279	玻璃制品 (万美元) Glass Ware (USD 10000)	752	791
棉布 (万米) Cotton Cloth (10000 m)	10510	9727	石蜡 (万美元) Paraffin Wax (USD 10000)	635	543
真丝绸缎 (万米) Silk and Satins (10000 m)	1070	1349	钢材 (万美元) Rolled-steel (USD 10000)	3620	7626
手表 (万只) Watches (10000)	64	62	铜材 (吨) Copper Products (ton)	586	838
服装及衣着附件 (万美元) Garments (USD 10000)	75787	61706	铝材 (吨) Aluminum Products (ton)	182	502
皮鞋 (万双) Leather Shoes (10000 pairs)	384	259	机床 (万台) Machine Tools (10000)	256	414
胶或塑料底布鞋 (万双) Cloth Shoes with Outer Soles of Rubber or Artificial Plastic Materials (10000 pairs)	887	994	汽车 (辆) Motor Vehicle (unit)	363	328

11-5 海关主要商品进口量
MAJOR IMPORTS COMMODITIES IN VOLUME(CUSTOMS STATISTICS)

品名 Item	1998	1997	品名 Item	1998	1997
食糖 (万吨) Sugar (10000 tons)	1	1	复印机 (台) Duplicators (unit)	109	147
谷物及谷物粉 (万吨) Cereal and Cereal Powder (10000tons)	1	8	食品加工机械 (万美元) Food Processing Machine (USD 10000)	1011	1485
纺织用合成纤维 (万吨) Synthetic Fibers Suitable for Spin-ning (10000 tons)	2		聚乙烯 (吨) Polyethylene (ton)	14408	4001
合成纤维纱线 (吨) Synthetic Fibers, Continuous Filament and Yarn (ton)	338	1314	聚丙烯 (吨) Polypropylene (ton)	1491	1590
羊毛及羊毛条 (吨) Wool and Wool Top (ton)	15056	6826	聚苯乙烯及共聚物 (吨) Polystyrene and Copolymer (ton)	3557	1136
肥料 (万吨) Fertilizers (10000 tons)		14	钢材 (万吨) Rolled-steel (10000 tons)	5	14
纸及纸板 (万吨) Paper and Paper-board (10000 tons)	3	3	铝材 (吨) Aluminum Products (ton)	12741	8256
空气调节器 (台) Air Conditioners (unit)	293	975	机床 (台) Machine Tools (unit)	477	846
家用电冰箱 (台) Refrigerator (unit)	28	40	汽车 (辆) Motor Vehicle (unit)	1008	1300
彩色电视机 (台) Color TV Set (unit)	1937	666	成套数字式数据处理设备 (台) Complete Sets of Digital Data Process-ing Equipment (unit)	5208	2097
收录机 (万台) Recorders (10000)		2	成套数字式中央处理机 (台) Complete Sets of Digital Central Processing (unit)	3960	145
电视摄像机 (台) Television Camera (unit)	127	2122			

11-6 利用外资签约情况
UTILIZATION OF FOREIGN CAPITAL

项目 Item		合同数(个) Number of Contracts (unit)		合同外资金额(万美元) Contracted Foreign Capital(USD 10000)	
		1998	1997	1998	1997
合计	**Total**	**656**	**798**	**410567.2**	**171532.2**
对外借款	Foreign Loans	5	8	890.0	3429.0
外商直接投资	Direct Foreign Investments	651	790	409677.2	168103.2
合资经营	Joint Venture	344	471	61426.3	79284.7
合作经营	Cooperative Operation	104	92	232524.0	42624.0
独资经营	Foreign Enterprises	201	227	105952.1	46194.5
股份制	Share Holding	2		9774.9	

注：1.外商投资企业投资性借款作为外商直接投资统计，对外借款中不再重复统计。

2.合资经营项目合同外资金额为项目注册资本乘以外商出资比例。

a) Loans for investment of foreign funded enterprises are counted as foreign direct investment and not counted in foreign loans any more.

b) Contracted foreign capital of joint venture projects are counted from registered capital multiplied proportion of foreign investment.

11-7 外商投资企业签约情况
STATISTICS ON CONTRACTS OF FOREIGN FUNDED ENTERPRISES

项目	Item	项目数（个）Number of Contracts (unit) 1998	1997	合同总金额（万美元）Total Value of Contracts(USD 10000) 1998	1997	# 外资金额 Foreign Capital 1998	1997
合　计	**Total**	**651**	**790**	**624008.2**	**364446.1**	**409677.2**	**168103.2**
按投资方式分	**Grouped by Investment Manner**						
合资经营	Joint Venture	344	471	173877.7	195595.6	61426.3	79284.7
合作经营	Cooperative Operation	104	92	307899.1	110093.9	232523.9	42624.0
独资经营	Foreign Funded Enterprises	201	227	115756.5	58756.6	105952.1	46194.5
股份制	Share Holding	2		26474.9		9774.9	
按三次产业分	**Grouped by Three Industry**						
第一产业	Primary Industry	23	18	5171.6	783.5	2885.0	576.2
第二产业	Secondary Industry	332	504	185433.7	143572.3	119086.9	70162.3
第三产业	Tertiary Industry	296	268	433402.9	220090.3	287705.3	97364.8
按客商国别(地区)分	**Grouped by Country(Region) of Foreign Partner**						
# 日　本	Japan	53	68	28529.4	40991.8	21066.7	22372.0
美　国	United States	120	124	86139.2	27831.6	41297.2	12982.8
香港地区	Hongkong	176	235	345262.8	125883.5	250018.6	46055.1
澳大利亚	Australia	15	19	7344.3	2018.3	3247.2	1491.4
法　国	France	16	16	14173.0	10101.1	11705.5	5405.7
新加坡	Singapore	23	36	6778.7	12078.5	5005.5	4381.5
加拿大	Canada	15	29	3770.8	2653.9	2800.9	1943.4
德　国	Germany	15	21	18385.6	11146.5	24989.3	8427.8
西班牙	Spain	1	2	192.2	50.0	113.7	38.0
台　湾	Taiwan	55	66	6763.9	5467.1	4063.9	2959.4
瑞　典	Sweden	4	1	5361.9	100.0	1915.6	70.0
泰　国	Thailand	3	5	4382.9	680.5	2105.2	445.3
比利时	Belgium	4		290.0		119.3	
丹　麦	Denmark	1	3	235.0	3400.0	180.0	3371.0
韩　国	Korea	40	58	2290.7	4671.7	1492.8	2845.5
俄罗斯	Russia	1		100.0		49.0	

注：合资企业外资金额是以项目注册资本乘以外商出资比例。

Note: Foreign capital of joint venture are counted from registered capital multiplied proportion of foreign investment.

11-8 外商投资企业生产经营情况

STATISTICS ON PRODUCTION AND BUSINESS OF FOREIGN ENTERPRISES

单位：万元 (10000 yuan)

项目	Item	销售营业收入 Business Revenue 1998	1997	利润总额 Total Profits 1998	1997	交纳税金总额 Taxes 1998	1997
合计	**Total**	**7387798**	**6687748**	**-142558**	**7909**	**521210**	**418395**
按投资方式分	**Grouped by Investment Manner**						
合资经营	Joint Venture	6340849	6078973	-46950	65072	443245	383388
合作经营	Cooperative Operation	314520	207672	-26465	-15995	32541	20597
独资经营	Foreign Funded Enterprises	732429	401103	-69143	-41168	45424	14410
按行业分	**Grouped by Sector**						
农林牧渔水利业	Farming,Forestry,Animal Husbandry,Fishery and Water Conservancy	98713	104550	-5421	2548	309	1149
工业	Industry	5161669	5074738	-78256	-36574	362661	293638
运输邮电业	Transportation,Post and Telecommunications	17906	21083	-2950	781	488	519
商业饮食业	Commerce and Catering Services	421640	330069	-15864	6796	24556	15716
居民服务业	Residential Services	530949	567328	-51097	28663	45726	49291
其他行业	Others	1156921	589980	11029	5695	87470	58082
按客商国别(地区)分	**Grouped by Country (Region) of Foreign Partner**						
# 香港地区	Hongkong	2568491	2511057	-135576	-33074	145688	97094
澳门地区	Macao	30780	29569	-804	-1	476	577
台湾地区	Taiwan	311526	259567	-14029	-9513	14359	10281
朝鲜民主主义人民共和国	Democratic People's Republic of Korea	9964	2383	-1260	-582	116	38
日本	Japan	1072942	1028521	-45124	27036	65820	58256
泰国	Thailand	216399	145804	2392	3253	4671	1294
新加坡	Singapore	300397	207837	53414	4979	17278	8711
印度尼西亚	Indinesia	960	2910	-955	-601	98	191
法国	France	93823	91131	-7079	-3641	6639	5483
意大利	Italy	13255	8527	-391	-2311	261	105
荷兰	The Holland	161135	99062	-19446	-12842	8951	7050
瑞典	Sweden	71278	82281	8311	10529	8446	8385
西班牙	Spain	1851	1958	-1361	-1696	80	27
美国	United States	1292377	1250078	-51490	-20491	110741	107149
德国	Germany	458472	324722	81029	50162	81277	64491
丹麦	Denmark	6987	24559	-2567	6879	1259	4210
菲律宾	Philippines	24149	17117	-11223	-1967	4076	3681
澳大利亚	Australia	44179	54999	-14486	-11423	1639	1978
新西兰	New Zealand	4217	3760	-688	119	95	193
韩国	Korea	114265	110537	-12045	-12215	5553	3866
英国	United Kingdom	151577	145214	31717	33767	14808	18017
瑞士	Switzerland	67189	28443	-2741	-2905	6344	2428
奥地利	Austria	2949	1825	-234	-217	136	72
加拿大	Canada	46944	31937	-3625	-7291	1672	1739

11-9 外商投资企业利用外资情况

UTILIZATION OF FOREIGN CAPITAL OF FOREIGN FUNDED ENTERPRISES

单位：万美元 (USD 10000)

项　目	Item	实际利用外资额 Amount of Foreign Capital Actually Used	客商实际投资 Auctual Foreign Investment	企业对外借款投资 Foreign Loans for Investment
合　计	**Total**	**206414.9**	**181221.4**	**25193.5**
按投资方式分	**Grouped by Investment Manner**			
合资经营	Joint Venture	80725.7	63965.0	16760.7
合作经营	Cooperative Operation	67515.3	59082.5	8432.8
独资经营	Foreign Funded Enterprises	52760.9	52760.9	
股 份 制	Share Holding	1413.0	1413.0	
其　他	Others	4000.0	4000.0	
按行业分	**Grouped by Sector**			
工　业	Industry	34765.9	33945.7	820.2
建 筑 业	Construction	454.8	454.8	
商业饮食业	Commerce and Catering	2451.2	2451.2	
居民服务业	Residential Services	151168.0	126794.7	24373.3
# 房地产业	Real Estate	91456.5	67673.0	23783.5
其他行业	Others	17575.0	17575.0	
按客商国别(地区)分	**Grouped by Country(Region) of Foreign Partner**			
香港地区	Hongkong	95506.5	83204.4	12302.1
台湾地区	Taiwan	7071.8	6876.8	195.0
日　本	Japan	31410.4	30801.2	609.2
泰　国	Thailand	3773.0	3773.0	
新 加 坡	Singapore	7372.7	5772.7	1600.0
法　国	France	1745.1	1745.1	
美　国	United States	12604.1	12249.1	355.0
德　国	Germany	8501.6	8470.9	30.7
新 西 兰	New Zealand	1434.6	1434.3	
韩　国	Korea	4613.6	4613.6	
英　国	United Kingdom	4493.2	3001.4	1491.8
奥 地 利	Austria	15.0	15.0	
加 拿 大	Canada	3034.1	3034.1	
其　他	Others	24839.2	16229.5	8609.7

注：包括对外借款及其他形式，全年实际利用外资28.7亿美元。

Note：Including foreign loans and other investments,amount of foreign capital actually used is USD 28.7million.

11-10 外商投资企业投产开业情况
STATISTICS FOR OPENING OF FOREIGN FUNDED ENTERPRISES

项目	Item	企业单位数(个) Number of Enterprises (unit)		企业职工人数(人) Number of Staff and Workers (person)	
		1998	1997	1998	1997
合计	**Total**	**5190**	**4979**	**395796**	**404889**
按投资方式分	**Grouped by Investment Manner**				
合资经营	Joint Venture	3931	3868	341744	359678
合作经营	Cooperative Operation	278	253	17226	12951
独资经营	Foreign Funded Enterprises	981	858	36826	32260
按行业分	**Grouped by Sector**				
农林牧渔水利业	Farming,Forestry,Animal Husbandry,Fishery and Water Conservancy	50	43	4393	5194
工业	Industry	3637	3642	292857	292856
运输邮电业	Transportation,Posts and Telecommunications	19	18	815	576
商业饮食业	Commerce and Catering	280	278	25095	22196
居民服务业	Residential Services	225	200	36351	53652
其他行业	Others	979	798	36285	30415
按客商国别(地区)分	**Grouped by Country(Region) of Foreign Partner**				
#香港地区	Hongkong	2134	2077	158496	152678
澳门地区	Macao	46	47	2704	2797
台湾地区	Taiwan	510	512	25353	24865
朝鲜民主主义人民共和国	Democratic People's Republic of Korea	11	15	291	386
日本	Japan	581	551	63388	61992
泰国	Thailand	51	49	5573	5783
新加坡	Singapore	187	175	13148	13210
印度尼西亚	Indinesia	9	9	388	443
法国	France	64	60	4647	4595
意大利	Italy	19	22	1376	1700
荷兰	The Holland	26	22	3711	2851
瑞典	Sweden	20	20	2140	2213
西班牙	Spain	11	10	353	375
美国	United States	775	718	63460	63228
德国	Germany	76	63	8581	26138
丹麦	Denmark	9	11	867	1527
菲律宾	Philippines	16	15	1416	1570
澳大利亚	Australia	73	72	3323	3160
新西兰	New Zealand	18	17	486	412
韩国	Korea	142	134	11124	11228
英国	United Kingdom	52	38	4193	4007
瑞士	Switzerland	20	15	3037	2432
奥地利	Austria	13	11	394	394
加拿大	Canada	98	91	4207	3247

11-11 对外承包工程和劳务合作
CONTRACTED PROJECTS AND LABOR SERVICES COOPERATION WITH FOREIGN COUNTRIES

地区	Region	签定合同份数(份) Number of Contracts (unit)		签定合同金额(万美元) Contracted Value (USD 10000)		营业额(万美元) Fulfilled Value (USD 10000)	
		1998	1997	1998	1997	1998	1997
合计	**Total**	**184**	**107**	**28520**	**35640**	**45812**	**29629**
对外承包工程	**Constructed Projects**	**37**	**28**	**21789**	**22242**	**39207**	**17160**
#斯里兰卡	Sri Lanka	2		2670		1440	
马来西亚	Malaysia	3	4	2374	2665	2504	2267
美国	United States						20
巴基斯坦	Pakistan	2	3	470	1987	3189	2638
新加坡	Singapore	2	2	5801	5638	6461	7237
对外劳务合作	**Labor Services**	**136**	**70**	**6234**	**12266**	**6077**	**11685**
#日本	Japan	21	17	186	706	241	350
香港地区	Hongkong	3	2	146	140	132	143
马来西亚	Malaysia		3		23	5	13
新加坡	Singapore	7	19	139	189	57	98
韩国	Korea					1	6
埃及	Egypt	2		4		1	
美国	United States	13	2	27	13	3	13
德国	Germany	3	2	9	4		4
塞浦路斯	Cyprus	5		34		5	7
尼日利亚	Nigeria	9	1	15	1	20	1
泰国	Thailand	4	4	1	4	7	14
巴林	Bahrain	1		14			2
澳门地区	Macao	5	2	17	206	212	89
沙特阿拉伯	Saudi Arabia	1		6			2
斯里兰卡	Sri Lanka	2		123		102	
以色列	Israel		2				24
波兰	Poland						
设计咨询	**Consulting Services for Designing**	**11**	**9**	**497**	**1132**	**528**	**784**

11-12 海外企业审批情况
STATISTICS ON EXAMINING AND APPROVING OF CONTRACTS OF OVERSEAS ENTERPRISES

项目	Item	审批项目数(个) Number of Projects Examined and Approved (unit) 1998	1997	# 中方投资金额(万美元) Investment by Chinese Partner(USD 10000) 1998	1997
合计	**Total**	**21**	**19**	**550.7**	**473.0**
按投资方式分	**Grouped by Investment Manner**				
合资经营	Joint Venture	6	7	78.5	150.2
合作经营	Cooperative Operation				
独资经营	Foreign Enterprises	15	12	472.3	322.8
按生产性、非生产性分	**Grouped by Production and Non-production**				
生产性企业	Productive Enterprises	1	1	9.0	74.0
非生产性企业	Non-productive Enterprises	20	18	541.7	399.0
按投资国别(地区)分	**Grouped by Country(Region) of Investment**				
美国	United States	4	4	160.8	188.0
澳大利亚	Australia	1	2	10.5	116.0
日本	Japan	1	1		9.8
巴基斯坦	Pakistan	1			
蒙古	Mongolia	1		9.0	
印度尼西亚	Indonesia	1		12.3	
俄罗斯	Russia	2	2	1.3	8.9
德国	Germany	2		38.5	
英国	United Kingdom	1		52.0	
荷兰	Holland	2	1	89.4	20.0
罗马尼亚	Romania	2		16.0	
匈牙利	Hungary	2	1	151.0	15.0
南非	the South Africa Republic	1		10.0	

11-13 外国企业及华侨、港澳地区企业驻京代表机构
REPRESENTATIVE OFFICES IN BEIJING OF FOREIGN,OVERSEAS CHINESE HONGKONG AND MACAO ENTERPRISES

项目	Item	数量(个) Number(unit) 1998	1997	构成(%) Composition(%) 1998	1997
总计	**Total**	**7083**	**6413**	**100**	**100**
#日本	Japan	720	715	10.2	11.1
港澳地区	Hongkong and Macao	2192	2026	31.0	31.6
美国	United States	1322	1176	18.7	18.3
德国	Germany	343	302	4.8	4.7
法国	France	199	173	2.8	2.7
英国	United Kingdom	188	169	2.7	2.6
意大利	Italy	144	130	2.0	2.0
瑞士	Switzerland	96	81	1.4	1.3
瑞典	Sweden	49	43	0.7	0.7
加拿大	Canada	184	156	2.6	2.4
澳大利亚	Australia	134	111	1.9	1.7
比利时	Belgium	43	39	0.6	0.6
新加坡	Singapore	287	254	4.1	4.0
荷兰	The Holland	85	70	1.2	1.1
奥地利	Austria	44	42	0.6	0.7

11-14 区县对外经济基本情况
FOREIGN ECONOMY OF DISTRICTS AND COUNTIES

项目	Item	合计 Total	城区 City Proper	近郊区 Near Suburbs	远郊区 Outer Suburbs	各县 Counties
利用外资	**Utilization of Foreign Capital**					
签约项目 (个)	Projects Signed (unit)	523	104	245	23	151
合同外资金额 (万美元)	Contracted Foreign Capital (USD 10000)	248043.4	200795.1	23372.1	1697.2	22179.0
外商实际投资额 (万美元)	Foreign Actual Investment (USD 10000)	134463.3	80990.3	20538.6	1056.2	31878.2
出口商品交货	**Export Delivery**					
交货总额 (万元)	Total Value (10000 yuan)	379187.5	914.9	28688.6	38304.7	311279.3
直接交货 (万元)	Direct Delivery (10000 yuan)	285392.8	560.9	25209.6	32780.1	226842.2
#交本市外贸收购 (万元)	Purchased by Local Foreign Trade (10000 yuan)	141158.3	560.9	22080.5	3323.0	115193.9
间接交货 (万元)	Indirect Delivery	93794.7	354.0	3479.0	5524.6	84437.1
旅游业	**Tourism**					
接待海外游客 (人次)	Foreign Tourists (person.time)	189718	76909	83107	347	29355

11-15 接待旅游人数
TOURISTS

单位：人次 (person.time)

项目 Item		1998	1997	项目 Item		1998	1997
合计	**Total**	**2200947**	**2298368**	法国	France	69413	65158
外国人	**Foreigner**	**1781800**	**1868570**	德国	Germany	112580	91305
#日本	Japan	435156	430439	意大利	Italy	43579	40205
菲律宾	Philippines	9698	11293	瑞典	Sweden	25074	23146
新加坡	Singapore	68228	82676	瑞士	Switzerland	18597	23879
泰国	Thailand	25542	31384	俄罗斯	Russia	61555	65207
印度尼西亚	Indonesia	10429	24884	澳大利亚	Australia	46473	43486
马来西亚	Malaysia	74084	111947	新西兰	New Zealand	8142	7664
蒙古	Mongolia	20223	11563	荷兰	The Holland	27775	25562
韩国	Korea	81825	193733	西班牙	Spain	12542	12890
印度	India	5696	6740	**华侨**	**Overseas Chinese**	**28352**	**26456**
美国	United States	231662	216813	**港澳台胞**	**Hongkong,Macao and Taiwan Chinese**	**390795**	**403342**
加拿大	Canada	47874	40762				
英国	United Kingdom	88054	90402				
				#台胞	Taiwan Chinese	141292	140115

11-16 旅游外汇收入
FOREIGN EXCHANGE EARNING FROM INTERNATIONAL TOURISM

单位：亿美元 (USD 100 million)

项目 Item		1998	1997	1998年为1997年% 1998 as % of 1997	项目 Item		1998	1997	1998年为1997年% 1998 as % of 1997
合计	**Total**	**23.8**	**22.5**	**106.1**	住宿	Accommodation	3.5	3.6	97.2
长途交通费	Long-distance Transportation Expenses	8.0	7.8	102.9	餐饮	Catering Service	2.1	2.1	99.1
					商品	Commodity	4.0	3.8	106.9
					邮政电讯	Posts and Telecommunications	1.1	0.9	117.0
#民航	Civil Aviation	7.3	5.5	132.8					
铁路	Railway	0.2	1.2	17.4	景点门票	Tickets of Tourism Spots	0.6	0.7	79.2
汽车	Motor Vehicles	0.1	0.9	12.4					
					文化娱乐	Culture and Entertainment	1.2	0.4	292.5
市内交通费	Local Transportation Expense	0.5	0.5	88.9					
					其他	Others	2.9	2.6	110.3

11-17 生产型"三资"企业按销售收入
ARRANGING IN SALES REVENUE OF PRODUCTIVE FOREIGN FUNDED ENTERPRISES

排名 No.	单位名称 Enterprise	排名 No.	单位名称 Enterprise
1	北京诺基亚移动通讯有限公司	26	北京博士伦眼睛护理公司
2	北京爱立信移动通信有限公司	27	四通松下电工有限公司
3	北大方正电子有限公司	28	北京统益油脂有限公司
4	北京国际交换系统有限公司	29	北京广东健力宝饮料有限公司
5	北京.松下彩色显象管公司	30	北京熊猫宝洁洗涤用品有限公司
6	北京吉普汽车有限公司	31	北京南顺油脂有限公司
7	中国惠普有限公司	32	北京健力宝太平洋包装有限公司
8	和德集团有限公司	33	北京亚洲双合盛五星啤酒有限公司
9	北京大发正大有限公司	34	北京统一食品有限公司
10	北京轻型汽车有限公司	35	北京爱森绿宝有限公司
11	北京JVC电子产业有限公司	36	北京顺美服装有限公司
12	ＵＴ斯达康（中国）有限公司	37	北京皇冠制罐有限公司
13	北京市松下通信设备有限公司	38	北京金万利油脂有限公司
14	首钢宝生带钢有限公司	39	北京天纬油泵油嘴股份有限公司
15	首钢日电电子有限公司	40	北京贝尔通信设备制造公司
16	北京可口可乐饮料有限公司	41	北京松下控制装置有限公司
17	北京松下电子部品有限公司	42	北京富特波尔容器有限公司
18	北京朗讯科技光缆有限公司	43	北京恒通食品有限公司
19	北京飞利浦有限公司	44	北京大旺食品有限公司
20	北京诺基亚航星通讯系统有限公司	45	北京诺华制药有限公司
21	北京巴布科克威尔科克斯有限公司	46	北京三环亚太啤酒有限公司
22	爱芬食品北京有限公司	47	北京索鸿电子有限公司
23	北京红牛饮料有限公司	48	中迅电梯有限公司北京电梯厂
24	北京恩布拉科雪花压缩机有限公司	49	北京乐金电子部品有限公司
25	北京利乐包包装有限公司	50	北京爱立信通信系统有限公司

11-18 非生产型"三资"企业按销售收入排序
ARRANGING IN SALES REVENUE OF NON-PRODUCTIVE FOREIGN FUNDED ENTERPRISES

排名 No.	单位名称 Enterprise	排名 No.	单位名称 Enterprise
1	国际商业机械中国有限公司	26	松下电器(中国)有限公司
2	北京华远房地产股份有限公司	27	北京香格里拉饭店
3	西门子(中国)有限公司	28	世华房地产
4	北京燕莎友谊商城有限公司	29	北京长富宫中心有限责任公司
5	爱立信(中国)有限公司	30	北京顺峰饮食娱乐有限公司
6	崇文新世界房地产发展有限公司	31	北京城信房地产开发经营有限公司
7	北京香江花园别墅房产开发有限公	32	北京亮马河大厦有限公司
8	北京裕京花园别墅有限公司	33	北京西单国际大厦开发有限公司
9	北京中贸联万客隆商业有限公司	34	北京新世纪饭店有限公司
10	丽都饭店有限公司	35	金远见电脑技术有限公司
11	北京麦当劳食品有限公司	36	东方艺术大厦有限公司
12	北京百盛轻工发展有限公司	37	北京新协房地产开发有限公司
13	北京燕莎中心有限公司	38	北京华糖洋华堂商业有限公司
14	北京贵友大厦有限公司	39	赛贝斯软件(中国)有限公司
15	王府饭店	40	北京城市宾馆有限公司
16	北京精信广告有限公司	41	北京市建国饭店公司
17	正大(中国)投资公司	42	中国国际金融有限公司
18	北京肯德基有限公司	43	梯安梯国际交通
19	北京长城饭店	44	北京西苑置地有限公司
20	北京京广中心有限公司	45	北京东直门国际公寓
21	宝隆洋行公司	46	北京国际俱乐部有限公司
22	北京中粮广场	47	北京市京伦饭店
23	甲骨文软件系统有限公司	48	保利大厦公司
24	港澳中心公司	49	微软（中国）有限公司
25	通标标准技术服务有限公司	50	北京新东安有限公司

11-19 北京市旅游住宿设施一览表
LIST OF ACCOMMODATION INSTALLATION FOR TOURISM
一、涉外饭店
HOTELS

星 级 Star Grade	饭 店 名 称 Hotel	地 址 Address	邮政编码 Postcode	电 话 Telephone
5	北京饭店	北京市东城区东长安街33号	100004	65137766
5	长城饭店	北京市朝阳区东三环北路10号	100026	65905566
5	长富宫中心	北京市朝阳区建国门外大街26号	100022	65125555
5	钓鱼台宾馆	北京市阜成路 2号	100830	68591188
5	港澳中心瑞士酒店	北京市东城区朝阳门北大街2号	100027	65012288
5	贵宾楼饭店	北京市东城区东长安街35号	100006	65137788
5	华侨大厦	北京市东城区王府井大街2号	100006	65136666
5	皇冠假日饭店	北京市东城区王府井大街48号	100006	65133388
5	京广中心	北京市朝阳区呼家楼	100020	65978888
5	凯宾斯基饭店	北京市朝阳区亮马桥路50号	100016	64653388
5	昆仑饭店	北京市朝阳区新源南路2号	100004	65903388
5	王府饭店	北京市东城区金鱼胡同8号	100006	65128899
5	希尔顿酒店	北京市朝阳区东三环北路东方路1号	100027	64662288
5	香格里拉饭店	北京市海淀区紫竹院路29号	100081	68412211
5	新世纪饭店	北京市海淀区首体南路6号	100044	68492001
5	中国大饭店	北京市建外大街1号	100004	65052266
4	大观园酒店	北京市宣武区南菜园88号	100054	63538899
4	德宝饭店	北京市西城德宝新园22号	100044	68318866
4	国都大饭店	北京市朝阳区首都机场南小天竺村	100621	64565588
4	国际饭店	北京市东城区建国门内大街9号	100005	65126688
4	国贸饭店	北京市建外大街1号	100004	65052277
4	海逸酒店	北京市朝阳区将台西路8号	100016	64362288
4	和平宾馆	北京市东城区金鱼胡同3号	100004	65128833
4	河南大厦	北京市朝阳区潘家园华威里28号	100021	67751188
4	华润饭店	北京市朝阳区建国路35号	100025	65572233
4	皇家大饭店	北京市朝阳区北三环东路甲6号	100028	64663388
4	建国饭店	北京市朝阳区建国门外大街5号	100020	65002233
4	金都假日饭店	北京市西城区阜外北礼士路98号	100037	68338822
4	金台饭店	北京市东城区地安门西大街38号	100035	63099111
4	京都信苑宾馆	北京市海淀区什坊院6号	100036	63901166
4	京伦饭店	北京市朝阳区建国门外大街3号	100020	65002266
4	凯莱大酒店	北京市朝阳区建国门南大街2号	100022	65158855
4	丽都假日饭店	北京市朝阳区首都机场路将台路口	100004	64376688
4	亮马河大厦	北京市朝阳区东三环北路8号	100004	65906688
4	民族饭店	北京市西城区复兴门内大街51号	100046	66014466
4	赛特饭店	北京市朝阳区建国门外大街22号	100004	65123388
4	首都大酒店	北京市东城区前门东大街3号	100006	65129988
4	天伦王朝饭店	北京市东城区王府井大街50号	100006	65138888
4	五洲大酒店	北京市朝阳区北四环东路8号	100101	64915588
4	西苑饭店	北京市海淀区三里河路1号	100044	68313388
4	香山饭店	北京市海淀区香山公园内	100093	62591166
4	新大都饭店	北京市西城区车公庄21号	100044	68319988
4	燕山大酒店	北京市海淀区海淀路甲138号	100086	62563388
4	友谊宾馆	北京市海淀区白石桥路3号	100873	68498888
4	渔阳饭店	北京市朝阳区新源西里中街18号	100027	64669988
4	兆龙饭店	北京市朝阳区工体北路2号	100027	65972299
4	中旅大厦	北京市朝阳区北三环东路2号	100028	64622288
4	中苑宾馆	北京市海淀区高粱桥斜街18号	100081	62178888
3	奥林匹克饭店	北京市海淀区白石桥52号	100081	62176688
3	保利大厦	北京市东城区东直门南大街14号	100027	65001188
3	宝灵城饭店	北京市海淀区志新路16号	100083	62326655
3	北人大酒店	北京市东三环南路48号	100022	67716600
3	北展宾馆	北京市西城区西直门外大街135号	100044	68316633
3	碧湖宾馆	北京市怀柔县湖光小区37号	101400	69625088
3	城市宾馆	北京市朝阳区工体东路4号	100027	65007799
3	崇文门饭店	北京市崇文区崇文门西大街2号	100062	65122211
3	大雁楼供电培训中心	北京市怀柔雁栖湖南岸西端	101407	69662569
3	东方饭店	北京市宣武区万明路11号	100050	63014466
3	二十一世纪饭店	北京市朝阳区亮马桥路40号	100016	64663311

注：北京旅游涉外饭店住宿设施共308家，其中五星级16家，四星级32家，三星级66家，二星级112家，一星级36家。

Note: There are 308 foreign hotels ,including 16 5-grade hotels,32 4-grade hotels,66 3-grade hotels, 112 2-grade hotels, 36 1-grade 46 hotels and hotels with no grade.

11-19 续表 1 continued

星级 Star Grade	饭店名称 Hotel	地址 Address	邮政编码 Postcode	电话 Telephone
3	方舟宾馆	北京市朝阳区枣营路甲3号	100026	65947733
3	丰泽园饭店	北京市宣武珠市口西大街83号	100050	63186688
3	光明饭店	北京市朝阳区小亮马桥路	100016	64678822
3	国门路大饭店	北京市朝阳区和平路2号	100015	64378866
3	和平里大酒店	北京市和平里北街16号	100013	64221866
3	鸿翔大厦	北京市海淀区龙翔路15号	100083	62013355
3	华北大酒店	北京市朝阳区鼓楼外大街 19号	100011	62028888
3	华都饭店	北京市朝阳区新源南路8号	100027	65971166
3	华风宾馆	北京市前门东大街5号	100006	65247311
3	黄河京都大酒店	北京市崇文区夕照寺中街29号	100061	67135588
3	皇苑大酒店	北京市海淀区西三环北路厂洼19号	100081	68413388
3	回龙观饭店	北京市昌平县回龙观	102208	62913931
3	建银大厦	北京市丰台区太平桥东里九号	100073	63266633
3	金朗大酒店	北京市东城区崇内大街75号	100005	65136688
3	金世纪大酒店	北京市朝阳东三环南路1号	100022	67782255
3	金叶大厦	北京市朝阳水碓子东里26号	100026	65013322
3	京都苑宾馆	北京市建国门南大街8号	100022	65291166
3	京闽饭店	北京市朝阳区十八里店周庄	100023	67326699
3	凯迪克大酒店	北京市朝阳北辰东路18号	100101	64921188
3	空港花园酒店	北京市首都机杨道口	100621	64563388
3	龙泉宾馆	北京市门头沟区水闸北路21号	102300	69843366
3	梅地亚中心	北京市海淀区复兴路乙11号	100038	68514422
3	栖湖饭店	北京市怀柔雁栖湖北岸	101408	69661188
3	奇然大酒店	北京市宣武区陶然亭路2号	100050	63532288
3	前门饭店	北京市宣武区永安路75号	100050	63016688
3	日坛宾馆	北京市朝阳区日坛路1号	100020	65125588
3	商务会馆	北京市丰台右安门外玉林里一号楼	100054	63292244
3	神路圆大酒店	北京市朝外大街甲77号	100020	65041188
3	顺成饭店	北京市西城区金融大街甲16号	100032	66216688
3	四环宾馆	北京市海淀区永定路100号	100039	68185599
3	松鹤大酒店	北京市东城区灯市口大街88号	100006	65138822
3	苏源锦江大厦	北京市宣武区广安门外大街3号	100055	63267788
3	台湾饭店	北京市东城区王府井金鱼胡同5号	100006	65136688
3	泰山饭店	北京市海淀区西三旗安宁北里8号	100085	62919988
3	天龙宾馆	北京市顺义县天竺镇龙山村	101300	64591331
3	天桥宾馆	北京市宣武区西经路11号	100050	63012266
3	天坛饭店	北京市崇文区体育馆路1号	100061	67112277
3	天兆大饭店	北京市朝阳区工体东路18号	100020	65080088
3	铁道大厦	北京市海淀区北蜂窝甲102号	100083	63229199
3	锡华海体酒店	北京市海淀区西苑操场15号	100080	62646688
3	新侨饭店	北京市东城区东交民巷2号	100004	65133366
3	新兴宾馆	北京市海淀区西三环中路17号	100036	68166688
3	亚洲大酒店	北京市东城区新中西街8号	100027	65007788
3	燕京饭店	北京市西城区复外大街19号	100045	68536688
3	燕翔饭店	北京市朝阳区将台路甲2号	100016	64376666
3	裕龙大酒店	北京市海淀区阜成路40号	100046	68415588
3	圆山大酒店	北京市西城区德外裕民东里20号	100029	62010033
3	越秀大饭店	北京市宣武区宣武门东大街24号	100051	63014499
3	云湖度假村	北京市密云水库内湖	101512	61021982
3	云岫山庄	北京市怀柔雁栖湖东侧	101408	69962338
3	职工之家	北京市西城区真武庙路一号	100045	68566688
3	中粮龙泉山庄	北京市门头沟区龙家雾山	102300	60811616
3	中土大厦	北京市海淀区北蜂窝6号	100038	63246666
3	重庆饭店	北京市朝阳区光熙门北里15号	100028	64228888
3	竹园宾馆	北京市西城区旧鼓楼大街小石桥24号	100009	64032229
2	爱华饭店	北京市崇文区天坛东里乙48号	100061	67112255
2	八达岭长城大酒店	北京市延庆县八达岭特区	102102	69121302
2	北外宾馆	北京市海淀区西三环北路19号	100081	68241166
2	北纬饭店	北京市宣武区西经路13号	100050	63012266
2	北苑宾馆	北京市朝阳安外北苑路5号	100012	64232266

11-19 续表 2 continued

星 级 Star Grade	饭 店 名 称 Hotel	地 址 Address	邮政编码 Postcode	电 话 Telephone
2	长征宾馆	北京市丰台区南大红门路1号	100076	68380138
2	畅春园饭店	北京市海淀区西苑草场5号	100080	62561177
2	成府饭店	北京市海淀北四环中路261号	100083	62329558
2	达园宾馆	北京市海淀区福缘门甲1号	100091	62554104
2	大都老楼	北京市西城区车公庄21号	100044	68319988
2	大兴宾馆	北京市大兴县黄村兴丰南大街	102600	69242356
2	大钟寺饭店	北京市海淀区北三环西路18号	100086	62253388
2	德胜饭店	北京市西城区北三环中路14号	100011	62024477
2	东方红叶大饭店	北京市海淀区北洼村路12号	100081	68412233
2	芳园宾馆	北京市东城区灯市口西街36号	100006	65137712
2	房山宾馆	北京市房山区东大街8号	102400	69312523
2	丰台饭店	北京市丰台区丰台镇北大街3号	100071	63811177
2	枫露皇苑军体俱乐部	北京市通县城关镇焦王庄西	101101	89597788
2	格兰云天大酒店	北京市西城区北新华街甲45号	100031	66071166
2	工体宾馆	北京市朝阳区工人体育场内	100027	65016655
2	国安宾馆	北京市朝阳区东大桥	100020	65007700
2	国泰饭店	北京市朝阳区建外永安西里	100022	65013366
2	国展宾馆	北京市朝阳区静安西街10号	100028	64639922
2	哈德门饭店	北京市崇文区崇外大街甲2号	100062	67112244
2	韩村河山庄	北京市房山东营乡韩村河	102400	80380080
2	韩京宾馆	北京市朝阳区芳草地西街8号	100020	65936688
2	豪威大厦	北京市海淀北太平庄路25号	100088	62041188
2	河北饭店	北京市东城区安内车辇店甲11号	100009	64015522
2	红螺园宾馆	北京市怀柔镇东四村	101400	60681355
2	猴王大酒店	北京市朝阳区安苑里1号院	100029	64917766
2	湖苑山庄	北京市怀柔湖光小区25号	101400	69624827
2	护国寺宾馆	北京市西城区护国寺街125号	100035	66180141
2	花园饭店	北京市海淀区花园东路30号	100083	62011188
2	华乐苑酒店	北京市朝阳区金台里2号	100026	65068822
2	华侨饭店	北京市东城区北新桥三条5号	100004	64016688
2	华园饭店	北京市朝阳区东三环霄云路28号	100027	64678661
2	惠华大厦	北京市海淀大街36号	100080	62545522
2	惠侨饭店	北京市朝阳区惠新东街19号	100101	64918811
2	惠天大饭店	北京市东城安德路丙61号	100011	64225577
2	机场宾馆	北京市朝阳区首都机场路	100621	64577788
2	蓟门饭店	北京市海淀区学院路黄亭子	100088	62012211
2	金平大酒店	北京市昌平政府街19号	102200	69709988
2	京都紫禁城饭店	北京市宣武区广安门南街48号	100054	63549955
2	京丰宾馆	北京市丰台区丰台路71号	100071	63812233
2	京华饭店	北京市丰台区永外西罗园南里	100077	67222211
2	京环宾馆	北京市怀柔县湖光小区23号楼	101400	69642827
2	京燕饭店	北京市石景山区石景山路29号	100043	68876261
2	康运宾馆	北京市朝阳区麦子店78号	100026	65955588
2	孔雀鑫朝酒店	北京市海淀区永定路24号	100039	68282244
2	蓝特宾馆	北京市朝阳区广和南里2条9号	100021	67747188
2	劳动大厦	北京市朝阳德外北沙滩大屯路甲1号	100101	64874433
2	乐游饭店	北京市朝阳区东三环南路13号	100021	67712266
2	礼士宾馆	北京市东城东四南大街礼士大街18号	100010	65220033
2	丽华饭店	北京市丰台区马家堡东路71号	100077	67211144
2	联华京谊宾馆	北京市通县城关镇西马庄	101100	60513665
2	六合饭店	北京市朝阳区工体北路春秀街	100027	64157766
2	六亭饭店	北京市昌平县昌平镇东环路	102200	89706661
2	龙都宾馆	北京市海淀区万泉河路小南庄400号	100080	62542277
2	龙山宾馆	北京市怀柔县龙山路2号	101400	69641501
2	龙潭饭店	北京市朝阳区潘家园南里15号	100021	67712244
2	龙源宾馆	北京市丰台区菜户营东街甲34号	100054	63468882
2	侣松园宾馆	北京市东城区板厂胡同22号	100009	64040436
2	明宫宾馆	北京市朝阳区西坝河西里16号	100028	64273355
2	牡丹宾馆	北京市海淀区花园东路31号	100083	62025544
2	南粤苑宾馆	北京市丰台区郑王坟1号	100071	63844466
2	盘峰宾馆	北京市平谷县旧城街13号	101200	69962200

11-19 续表 3 continued

星 级 Star Grade	饭 店 名 称 Hotel	地 址 Address	邮政编码 Postcode	电 话 Telephone
2	齐鲁饭店	北京市西城区地安门西大街103号	100009	66180966
2	清华园宾馆	北京市海淀区成府路45号	100083	62573355
2	求实饭店	北京市朝阳区安华西里1区13楼	100011	64263335
2	山湖宾馆	北京市怀柔县龙山路2号	101400	69646688
2	上园饭店	北京市海淀区高梁桥斜街40号	100044	62251166
2	盛唐饭店	北京市海淀区万泉庄王公坟2号	100080	62564433
2	实华饭店	北京市朝阳区西坝河东里14号	100028	64665522
2	实兴海特大厦	北京市石景山区苹果园北路海特花园	100041	68861188
2	双龙宾馆	北京石景山玉泉路63号	100040	68214445
2	双阳职工培训中心	北京市怀柔青春路41号	101400	69658982
2	顺义宾馆	北京市顺义县府前中街	101300	69444815
2	松麓饭店	北京市海淀区田村路8号	100039	68221133
2	太阳宫宾馆	北京市安外甘水桥甲1号	100011	64237722
2	檀州宾馆	北京市密云镇长安街1号	101500	69043772
2	陶然宾馆	北京市宣武区太平街15号	100050	63543366
2	天坛体育宾馆	北京市崇文区体育馆路10号	100061	67113388
2	天天假日饭店	北京市海淀区万寿路17号	100036	68151133
2	天驿宾馆	北京首都机场南平街1号	100621	64567711
2	通华苑饭店	北京市西城区北礼士路101号	100044	68331155
2	外事服务高中实习饭店	北京市西城区西单教育街1号	100031	66016663
2	万隆酒店	北京市宣武区广外鸭子桥6号	100055	63262211
2	万泉庄园	北京市海淀区志新东路5号	100083	62324499
2	万寿宾馆	北京市海淀区万寿路甲12号	100036	68214433
2	温阳饭店	北京市怀柔县府前西街4号	101400	69624381
2	文轩宾馆	北京市宣武区南新华街甲1号	100051	63022731
2	西郊宾馆	北京市海淀区学院路丁11号	100083	62322288
2	西直门宾馆	北京市西城区西直门内大街172号	100035	66184488
2	新风大酒店	北京市延庆东外大街11号	102100	69141849
2	新街口饭店	北京市西城新街口南大街44号	100035	66166661
2	燕化宾馆	北京市房山区燕山岗南路2号	102500	69344434
2	燕岭宾馆	北京市丰台区槐树岭4号	100072	63867788
2	雁鸣楼饭店	北京市怀柔雁栖湖北岸	101408	69661124
2	颐泉山庄宾馆	北京市海淀区黑山沪羊场1号	100094	62895772
2	银亚大厦	北京市石景山区玉泉西路甲1号	100039	68152288
2	樱花宾馆	北京市朝阳区惠新东街17号	100029	64934455
2	渔阳商务会馆	北京市密云县农机路7号	101500	69046688
2	宇翔园宾馆	北京市丰台区南苑机场侯机楼	100076	67992129
2	玉都饭店	北京市海淀区西八里庄北街1号	100036	68428882
2	远东饭店	北京市宣武区铁树斜街90号	100050	63018811
2	远方饭店	北京市朝阳区光熙门北里22号	100028	64225588
2	云翔宾馆	北京市丰台区马家堡路12号	100077	67215559
2	珠穆朗玛宾馆	北京市西城区鼓楼西大街149号	100009	64018822
2	紫玉饭店	北京市海淀区增光路55号	100037	68411188
2	紫薇宾馆	北京市石景山区石景山路40号	100043	68878031
2	芙蓉宾馆	北京市朝阳区八里堡	100025	65565388
2	昊园宾馆	北京市崇文区天坛东路甲9号	100061	67014499
1	百灵饭店	北京市朝阳区东直门外左家庄前街	100028	64667744
1	北海宾馆	北京市西城区地安门西大街141号	100009	66162229
1	北林宾馆	北京市海淀区清华东路	100083	62326633
1	大北宾馆	北京市朝阳区建外南郎家园甲1号	100022	65065511
1	大森林酒店	北京市西城北三环中路甲19号	100029	62051119
1	飞霞饭店	北京市宣武区西便门西里5号楼	100053	63012228
1	富国饭店	北京市西城区富国街2号	100034	66182255
1	国务院第二招待所	北京市西城区西直门南大街6号	100035	66186688
1	海南饭店	北京市海淀区海淀南路15号	100080	62565550
1	华夏宾馆	北京市朝阳区工体路北春秀路	100027	64162575
1	化工轻工贸易大厦	北京市东城区安外青年湖北里6号	100011	64214466
1	佳丽饭店	北京市朝阳区酒仙桥路乙21号	100016	64363399
1	建国门饭店	北京市朝阳建外大街建华南里	100022	65055577
1	建苑宾馆	北京市西城区六部口北新平5号	100031	66053161
1	金海宾馆	北京市平谷县金海湖管理处	101201	69992789
1	京信大厦	北京市朝阳东三环北路2号	100027	64663366

11-19 续表 4 continued

星 级 Star Grade	饭 店 名 称 Hotel	地 址 Address	邮政编码 Postcode	电 话 Telephone
1	景泰宾馆	北京市崇文区永外景泰西里65号	100075	67212837
1	流芳宾馆	北京市西城区德外裕民东里甲20号	100029	62042266
1	龙泉百花饭店	北京市门头沟区新桥大街35号	102300	69842010
1	梅苑饭店	北京市海淀区高梁桥路上园村	100081	62241115
1	射击宾馆	北京市石景山区福田寺甲3号	100041	68862277
1	神木宾馆	北京市朝阳区双井北里14号	100022	67713355
1	台胞体育宾馆	北京市海淀区上园村甲4号	100044	62251114
1	天寿山饭店	北京市昌平县十三陵胡庄	102200	89761606
1	通州宾馆	北京市通县多福巷38号	101100	69537799
1	万年青宾馆	北京市海淀区西三环北路25号	100081	68425154
1	望海楼宾馆	北京市海淀区玉渊潭公园内	100038	68514447
1	卧佛寺饭店	北京市海淀区西山卧佛寺公园内	100093	62591459
1	西单饭店	北京市西单大木仓北一巷	100032	66032381
1	西直门饭店	北京市西城区西外高粱桥斜街42号	100044	62257766
1	香山别墅	北京市海淀区香山公园内	100093	62591155
1	延庆宾馆	北京市延庆县东外大街50号	102100	69102611
1	御园饭店	北京市海淀区太平路甲18号	100039	68216688
1	中成宾馆	北京市丰台区刘家窑定安东里1号	100075	67626688
1	中关村酒店	北京市海淀区海淀路19号	100080	62565577
1	洲际华侨酒店	北京市西外大街新兴东路	100044	68313355
	宝辰饭店	北京市东城区建国门内甲18号	100005	65266688
	北体宾馆	北京市海淀体育大学	100084	62989000
	碧海山庄	北京市平谷金海湖旅游区内	101201	69991201
	翠宫饭店	北京市海淀区知春路76号	100086	62628888
	大望宾馆	北京市朝阳区西大望路23号	100022	67780339
	东方宾馆	北京市通州区车站路12号	101100	69546870
	东方花园饭店	北京市东城区东直门南大街6号	100027	64168866
	飞鹰宾馆	北京市宣武区西大街10号楼	100053	63171116
	枫苑饭店	北京市东城区东交民巷甲23号	100006	65243311
	贵阳饭店	北京市西城区三里河月坛南街	100045	68513377
	国际高尔夫迎宾馆	北京市昌平县十三陵水库北侧	102213	69762288
	国谊宾馆	北京市西城区文兴东街1号	100044	68316611
	海兴大酒店	北京市丰台区永外海户屯166号	100075	67218855
	杭州湾大酒店	北京市丰台区安乐林路10号	100075	67661133
	好园宾馆	北京市东城区史家胡同53号	100010	65125557
	华泰饭店	北京市朝阳区劲松东口	100021	67716688
	江苏大厦	北京市东城安外大街88号	100011	64271188
	金安皇都大酒店	北京市北京站东街6号	100005	65158630
	岭南饭店	北京市海淀区八里庄北洼路28号	100046	68412288
	民族文化宫	北京市西城区复兴门内大街49号	100031	66024433
	内蒙古宾馆	北京市东城区美术馆后街71号	100010	64014499
	诺林大酒店	北京市宣武区菜园北里29号	100053	63551188
	侨园饭店	北京市丰台区右外东滨河路	100054	63012244
	融泉宾馆	北京市丰台区西客站东配楼	100055	63981166
	三元宾馆	北京市朝阳区东直门外斜街9号	100028	64678288
	商海洲宾馆	北京市丰台区丰台路口188号	100071	63814455
	四海通宾馆	北京市朝阳区东直门外六公坟	100015	64376988
	天鹅饭店	北京市怀柔县迎宾中路17号	101400	69643390
	天瑞泓胤酒店	北京市东城区柏树胡同15号	100006	65266699
	铁路宾馆	北京市朝阳区建国门外永安西里9	100022	65002211
	王府井大饭店	北京市东城区王府井大街57号	100006	65221188
	西藏大厦	北京市朝阳区北四环东路118号	100029	64981133
	希赛迪大酒店	北京市昌平县沙河定泗路	102206	69735533
	杏园国医馆	北京市顺义后沙峪镇	101300	62321166
	翔云楼宾馆	北京市海淀区德外苇子坑安祥北里	100101	66756900
	颐和园旅游服务部	北京市海淀区颐和园公园内	100091	62881200
	宜琴饭店	北京市东城朝阳门内小牌坊胡同7号	100010	65138477
	银丰宾馆	北京市东城安德里北街25号	100011	62019911
	银河宾馆	北京市朝阳区三元桥北曙光西里	100028	64663336
	永安宾馆	北京市朝阳区农展馆北路甲5号	100026	65011188
	友好宾馆	北京市东城区后圆恩寺7号	100009	64031114
	玉雪饭店	北京市朝阳区安外慧中路19号	100101	64941068
	元远温泉宾馆	北京市朝阳区团结湖路9号楼	100026	65065553
	远洋酒店	北京市东城区东四南大街189号	100005	65228888
	云水山庄	北京市密云水库走马庄副坝	101512	69011288
	竹园听松楼饭店	北京市西城区旧鼓楼大街小石桥24	100009	64032229

11-19 续表 5 continued

二、涉外公寓

FOREIGN APARTMENT HOUSES

单位名称 Unit	地　　址 Address	邮政编码 Postcode	电　话 Telephone
朝阳公寓	北京市朝阳区农展馆北里2号	100026	64677119
东苑公寓	北京市朝阳区枣营路25号	100026	64678678
东直门国际公寓	北京市东城区东直门外大街35号	100027	64678221
国际汇园公寓	北京市朝阳区安外安立路8号	100101	64933456
国际网球中心	北京市崇文区天坛东路50号	100061	67142370
国泰饭店松榆公寓	北京市朝阳区松榆西里	100021	67331988
华墅渡假村	北京市朝阳区十八里店老君堂	100023	67383555
华乡公寓	北京市朝阳区高碑店北路6号	100025	65001133
华威大厦	北京市西城区西单北大街130号	100032	66028888
汇园公寓	北京市朝阳区北四环中路8号	100101	64992662
京城大厦	北京市朝阳区新源南路6号	100004	64660088
九花山公寓	北京市海淀区半壁街南路甲1号	100081	68414440
万春园	北京市海淀区圆明园管理处内	100084	62616611
万泉公寓	北京市海淀区西三环北路甲1号	100081	68415813
紫金宫饭店	北京市东城区南河沿华龙街	100006	65130088

注：涉外公寓共15家。

Note: Number of foreign apartment houses is fifteen.

11-19 续表 6 continued

三、涉外写字楼

FOREIGN OFFICE-BUILDINGS

单位名称 Unit	地　　址 Address	邮政编码 Postcode	电　话 Telephone
发展大厦	北京市朝阳区东三环北路5号	100004	65908811
光华园大厦	北京市朝阳区东三环北路38号	100020	65018816
国际大厦	北京市朝阳区建外大街19号	100004	65001159
国际会议中心	北京市朝阳区北辰东路8号	100101	64922328
国际俱乐部有限公司	北京市朝阳区建国门外大街21号	100020	65023975
国际贸易中心	北京市朝阳区建成国门外大街1号	100004	65052288
华鹏大厦	北京市朝阳区东三环北路19号	100020	65975168
汇宾大厦	北京市朝阳区北辰东路8号	100101	64993873
凯威大厦	北京市朝阳区雅宝路10号	100020	65942288
太丰惠中大厦	北京市宣武区珠市口西大街120号	100050	63186068
幸福大厦	北京市朝阳区顺源街5号	100027	64669805
亚太大厦	北京市朝阳区雅宝路8号	100020	65139988
紫金宾馆	北京市崇文区崇文门西大街9号	100005	65136655

注：涉外写字楼共13家

Note: Number of foreign office-buildings is thirteen.

11-20 国际旅行社名录
INTERNATIONAL TRAVEL SERVICES

旅行社 Travel Service	地址 Address	邮政编码 Postcode	电话 Telephone
安琪旅行社	建外大街28号	100006	65122441
奥利富国际旅行社	西城区南礼士路36号	100037	68038261
北辰国际旅游公司	朝阳区安慧里三区10号	100101	64910683
北方国际旅行社	建外大街28号	100022	65158844
北京北奥国际旅行社	朝阳区建外大街28号	100022	65150515
北京方达信国际旅行社	朝阳区南大街20号	100020	65032328
北京国际商旅有限公司	朝阳区枣营路3号	100026	65011122
北京海外旅游公司	朝阳区光华路7号汉威大厦5层	100004	65611639
北京华堂国际旅行社	朝阳区东直门外新源南路19号	100027	64675464
北京旅行社	朝阳区关东店二号	100020	65957163
北京青年旅行社	北辰东路8号	100101	64924729
北京森林国际旅行社	北三环中路甲3号	100029	62063276
北京天平国际旅行社	朝阳区宵云里4号楼	100016	64629589
北京文物国际旅行社	丰台区右安门外玉林里小区10号	100054	63292246
北京职工旅行社	海淀区复兴路甲22号	100036	68275409
北京中国国际旅行社	海淀区知春里甲99号	100086	62525070
北京中国旅行社	东城区北河沿大街95号	100006	65245846
北京中汇国际旅行社	西城区阜外大街甲6号	100037	68584488
长城旅行社	西城区南三里河南三区甲32号	100045	68531830
朝阳旅行社	建外大街28号	100022	65156166
德宝国际旅行社	东城区东皇城根北街16号	100010	64074616
东华国际旅行社	崇文区西花市大街75号	100062	67123393
方舟旅行社	新中街11号	100027	64160370
风情旅行社	东城区安外东河沿和平西街79号	100011	64289224
凤凰假期国际旅行社	东直门北新仓18号	100700	64063330
国际鸿基旅行社	日坛路北街4号	100028	65287902
国际旅行社总社	和平里北街16号	100013	68422372
国际体育旅游公司	宣武枣林南街119号	100053	63561888
国贸国际旅行社	东城区鼓楼大街中绦51号	100009	64005800
海峡旅行社	西城区车公庄大街21号	100044	68319988
海洋国际旅行社	西城区新康甲1号	100088	62059007
航天国际旅行社	前门西街248号	100051	67013270
和平国际旅游公司	崇文区天坛东里二号	100061	65114447
华都旅行社	朝外大街317号	100020	65523437
华龙国际旅行社	国安宾馆204室	100020	65007990
华商国际旅行社	崇文区广渠门忠实里四巷9号	100022	67744232
华闻国际旅行社	东城区台基厂2条8号	100005	65275574
华远旅游公司	东城区天安大厦中段512室	100003	65220978
环球商务国际旅行社	德外北三环东路19号	100029	62382690
环宇国际旅行社	朝阳区酒仙桥路乙21号	100016	64362145
江河国际旅行社	朝阳区新源南路8号	100027	65971166
金门旅行社	朝阳区雅宝路7号	100020	65005828
金色假期旅行社	朝阳区顺源里14楼	100027	64652880
金台旅游公司	朝阳区北四环东路99号	100101	64934002
金叶国际旅行社	朝阳区将台路甲2号	100016	64376581
金友旅行社	海淀区五塔寺24号	100081	62178804
康复旅行社	朝阳门南大街16楼	100020	65950935
康辉旅游社总社	复兴门外大街19号	100045	68537530
科学国际旅行社	北三环东路二号	100028	64642560
蓝天旅行社	东郊民巷丙23号	100054	65243388
联合国际旅行社	光华东里甲18楼	100020	65081166
龙门旅行社	东三环北路28号	100026	65926714
龙腾旅行社	朝阳区东三环北路19号	100020	65975285
龙燕旅行社	安外大街183号京宝大厦515室	100011	64256142
旅游学院旅行社	前门东大街23号	100006	65059735

11-20 续表 continued

旅行社 Travel Service	地址 Address	邮政编码 Postcode	电话 Telephone
茂发国际旅行社	朝阳区东三环南路21号	100071	67735911
民间国际旅游公司	东长安街16号	100740	65250388
明星国际旅行社	工体宾馆21台	100027	65854913
青年旅行社总社	安外大街甲88号	100011	64285970
瑞驰旅行社	建内大街9号	100005	65229555
赛特国际旅行社	王府井大街57号	100006	65221188
三峡国际旅行社	东城区南河沿大街23号	100006	65248972
森林国际旅行社	北京饭店写字楼6233室	100001	65137766
神农国际旅行社	复兴门内大街103号	100800	66011122
神州国际旅游公司	朝阳区农展馆南路京朝大厦8层	100026	65940858
四达国际旅行社	西城区文华胡同32号	100031	66072739
天安旅行社	海淀区海淀南路30号	100080	68748327
天鹅国际旅游公司	西城区成方街甲32号	100032	66055060
天马国际旅行社	西城区三里河东三巷三号	100820	68318866
同源国际旅行社	西城区宫门口西岔85号	100034	66165482
王府国际旅行社	东城区鼓楼西大街47号	100009	64014525
香山旅行社	三里河二区223楼三层	100045	68517974
协力国际旅行社	西城区护国寺大街52号	100035	66165845
新大都国际旅游公司	西城区西郊民巷21号	100031	63095406
新都国际旅行社	崇文区体育馆路4号	100061	67123141
新华旅游集团公司	东城区大华路华诚大厦407	100000	65275599
幸福国际旅行社	朝阳区白家庄路甲6号	100020	65034358
燕都旅行社	崇文区龙潭路甲3号	100061	67117700
燕京旅行社	东郊民巷10号院9号楼	100005	65279018
燕翔旅行社	宣武区白广路北口综合楼	100053	63203559
邮电国际旅行社	广安门南街甲12号	100053	63547532
有朋国际旅行社	广安门南街60号	100054	63557244
招商旅游公司	日坛路1号	100020	65125588
职工旅行社总社	京城大厦9层	100027	64662696
中包旅行社	东四南大街演乐胡同116号	100010	65263536
中北旅行社	西单横二条3号	100031	66087016
中城国际旅行社	和平里东街18号	100714	64229944
中电国际旅行社	地安门西大街57号	100009	65187631
中福国际旅行社	朝阳区幸福一村三巷五号	100027	64167284
中钢国际旅行社	西长安街18号	100031	66017755
中广国际旅行社	朝阳区惠新东街3号	100029	62355347
中国航空国际旅行社	复兴门大街45号	100801	66094356
中国虹桥旅行社	安贞西里4区23号楼	100029	64410863
中国华运旅行社	朝阳区水锥东里26号	100026	65013322
中国旅行社总社	朝阳区东三环北路2号	100027	64623946
中国民族旅行社	建外永安西里9号	100022	65002211
中国山水旅行社	朝阳区向军南里二巷	100020	65085796
中国太和旅行社	海淀区花园路15号	100088	62054353
中环国际旅行社	中关村科学院南路55号	100086	62571104
中佳国际合作旅行社	友谊宾馆二号楼一层	100873	68499139
中建红晴蜓旅行社	西城区德外北滨河路白孔雀内	100011	62045948
中侨旅行社	丰台六里桥北里甲1号	100073	63497722
中商国际旅行社	建外大街1号	100004	65052288
中卫国际旅行社	海淀区阜成路白堆子131号	100037	68475136
中信国安旅行社	复兴路乙12号	100814	63975588
中信旅游总公司	海淀区翠微中里16号	100036	68259321
中艺国际旅行社	团结湖南里5号	100026	65098036
中谊国际旅行社	复兴门外大街2号	100866	66091718
中远国际旅行社	宣武区西经露11号天坛宾馆334	100050	63023585
怡安旅行社	复兴门外大街1号	100860	68013344
鑫海国际旅行社	海淀区花园路44号	100083	82079211

11-21 国内旅行社名录
DOMESTIC TRAVEL SERVICES

旅行社 Travel Service	地址 Address	邮政编码 Postcode	电话 Telephone
奥之光云龙旅行社	东城区安德路丙61号	100011	64225577
百达旅游有限公司	东城大雅宝1号	100730	65255776
北达旅行社	东城安德里北街20号	100011	64256710
北斗旅行社	鼓楼东大街167号	100010	64018192
北京铁总旅行社	东城区老前局甲18号	100005	65120060
滨河旅行社	东内大街145号	100007	64078660
长运平旅行社	安内花园胡同29号	100009	64073917
诚信旅行社	东四7条114号	100007	64046819
崇文旅行社	潘家坡4号	100020	65531528
春秋旅行社	海淀区阜成路23号	100037	88131944
达美旅行社	东城区福祥胡同13号	100010	64058112
大公假日旅行社	东长安街14号	100071	65204672
钓鱼台旅游实业公司	东四十条100号	100007	64010386
东日旅行社	灯市口大街33号柏景大厦403	100006	65229713
东卫旅行社	崇内麻线胡同13号	100005	65141850
风光旅行社	西城区展览路12号	100044	68334948
高尔夫旅行社	海淀区萃微北里甲6号	100036	68257329
高立旅游公司	东城区朝内大街甲180号	100037	68315927
古都旅行社	景山后街11号	100009	64054915
光正旅行社	西城区百万庄大街26号	100037	68320738
国旅风光游览公司	西城真武庙1号	100045	68566688
海员旅行社	月坛北街甲1号	100037	68042729
海运旅行社	西城区民族宫南街36号	100031	66034421
韩村河旅行社	木樨地南里公安大学	100038	63404433
好运旅行社	八达处公园	100041	68874661
宏光旅行社	西城区职教实习楼	100030	66083976
虹桥旅行社	西城区展览路29号	100037	68317967
华航旅行社	西城区群力胡同2号	100035	66181704
华农旅行社	永定门东街东里2楼1层	100050	87285040
华强旅行社	永外松林街23号	100077	67213881
环京旅行社	崇文门西河沿甲211号	100051	67013236
惠龙腾旅行社	天坛东路红桥市场四层4319	100061	67717450
嘉华旅行社	永外大街101号	100075	67211122
假日旅行社	宣武区棕树斜街42号	100051	63084056
教师旅行社	呼家楼向军南里二巷5号	100026	65083482
金湖旅行社	崇文区体育路8号	100061	67128657
金辉旅行社	宣武区马连道6号	100055	63449537
金良旅行社	宣武区里仁街4号	100054	63542515
金融旅行社	宣武区德源寺前街11号	100052	63515996
金体育旅行社	宣武区红莲北里10号楼	100055	63451859
京华教育旅行社	西城区东中胡同33号	100031	66066098
京怀旅行社	宣武区福长街45号	100050	63046021
京列旅行社	宣武区广内顺河三巷三号	100053	63042478
京铁旅游公司	马连道北里甲4号	100055	63408310
京育旅行社	施家胡同4号	100051	63032696
经工之友旅行社	宣武区朱市口西街30号	100050	63016184
开鑫旅行社	宣武区长椿街甲18号	100053	63044390
科技旅行社	崇文区法华寺大街136号	100061	67149549
蓝宝石旅行社	宣武区广外车站东街9号	100053	63271540

11-21 续表 continued

旅行社 Travel Service	地址 Address	邮政编码 Postcode	电话 Telephone
蓝谷旅行社	朝阳区东三环北路4号	100027	64670822
乐平旅行社	安定门外安华西里3区15楼	100011	65293546
乐游假日旅行社	安外北苑2号	100012	64291831
联运旅行社	朝阳区望京中环南路1号	100015	64371038
良友旅行社	朝阳区农展馆内14楼招待所	100026	65925386
岭南迎宾旅行社	安外外馆街3号	100011	65293552
隆福旅行社	东城区和平里中街28号	100013	64213316
路通旅行社	丰台区石榴庄南里石榴庄小学旁	100075	67654916
绿洲旅行社	东直门外新源里14号	100027	64665138
美雅旅行社	建外大街17号	100020	65324360
梦幻旅行社	东板桥15号	100009	64041048
岷江之旅旅游有限公司	东长安街12号	100742	63081487
南华旅行社	朝阳区南湖渠	100015	64363632
轻舟旅游服务公司	团结湖路7号	100026	65821195
三叶旅行社	朝阳区下甸厂波村16号	100022	67716774
山野旅行社	复外真武庙二条四号	100045	68012152
商务旅行社	崇文西大街2号崇文门饭店0564	100062	64526709
商友旅行社	朝阳区亮马河路25号	100016	64369847
世知旅行社	西城区黄寺大街29号	100011	62018335
首都旅行社	朝阳区津松西口811楼	100021	67721865
首方旅行社	建外大街28号	100101	64974725
天地旅行社	朝阳区芳草地北巷4号楼301	100020	65910650
天地通旅行社	安定门外大屯232号	100010	67935840
天虹旅行社	建外永安东里米阳大厦五层	100022	65940423
通四方旅行社	永外大红门南路	100075	67218750
万方舟旅行社	丰台花乡郑王坟150号	100071	63810391
温泉保健旅行社	建外大街28号	100022	65250490
沃德兰四海旅游有限公司	丰台区草桥赵村店420号	100054	63569076
五环腾飞旅行社	丰台路口61号	100071	63860042
五联旅行社	丰台区右安门外玉林里1号楼	100000	63292244
希育翔旅行社	丰台育菲东里1号	100071	63842339
乡情旅行社	刘家窑北里11楼西二层2001	100075	67672652
新北旅行社	丰台区西局南街21号	100073	63850699
新华祥旅行社	石景山区古城大街西侧	100043	68842140
新泰隆旅行社	海淀区阜成路21号	100037	68439193
新闻旅行社	丰台区文体路5号	100071	67252759
银海旅行社	岭南饭店三层	100037	68412288
银河旅行社	海淀区知春大厦B座0303号	100086	62548182
友联旅行社	海淀区东北旺	100094	62584554
友商旅行社	西外大街135号	100044	68316677
职教旅行社	复兴路81号东院	100039	68163031
中成旅游公司	房山北关大街11号	102400	69312818
中纺旅行社	房山区良乡月华大街18号	102401	89358501
中旅现代旅行社	房山区东营乡韩村河村	102423	80380015
中山旅行社	小汤山医院	102211	69782048
中天旅行社	顺西路西侧	101300	69443900
中通旅行社	大兴县光兴南大街40号	102600	69249714
中亚旅行社	怀柔青春路北里24号	101400	69642387
中业旅游公司	密云滨河路2号	101500	69027175
中银燕旅行社	延庆县八达岭镇青龙桥	102102	69121034

主要统计指标解释

进出口总额 海关进出口总额指实际进、出我国关境并能引起我国境内物质资源增加或减少的进出口货物总金额。包括我国境内法人和其他组织以一般贸易、易货贸易、加工贸易、补偿贸易、寄售代销贸易等方式进出口的货物、租赁期一年及以上的租赁进出口货物、边境小额贸易货物、国际援助物资或捐赠品、保税区和保税仓库进出口货物等的金额合计。进出口总额用以观察一个国家在对外贸易方面的总规模。我国规定出口货物按离岸价格统计，进口货物按到岸价格统计。

利用外资 指我国各级政府、部门、企业和其他经济组织通过对外借款、吸收外商直接投资以及用其他方式筹措的境外现汇、设备、技术等。

对外借款 是我国利用外资的主要部分。包括我国通过外国政府贷款，国际金融组织贷款，外国银行商业贷款，出口信贷以及对外发行债券，股票等方式，从境外筹措的资金。

外商直接投资 是指外国企业和经济组织或个人（包括华侨、港澳台同胞以及我国在境外注册的企业）按我国有关政策、法规、用现汇、实物、技术等在我国境内开办外商独资企业、与我国境内的企业或经济组织共同举办中外合资经营企业、合作经营企业或合作开发资源的投资（包括外商投资收益的再投资）以及经政府有关部门批准的项目投资总额内，企业从境外借入的资金。

对外承包工程 包括各对外承包公司以招标议标承包方式承揽的下列业务（1）承包国外工程建设项目；（2）承包我国对外经援项目；（3）承包我国驻外机构的工程建设项目；（4）承包我国境内利用外资进行建设的工程项目；（5）与外国承包公司合营或联合承包工程项目时我国公司分包部分；（6）以服务成果向业主收费的技术服务项目（包括承担地形地貌测绘；地质资源勘探与普查；建设区域规划；提供设计文件、图纸、生产工艺技术资料和工程技术经济咨询；工程项目的可行性考察、研究和评估；进行技术指导和培训人员等）；（7）对外承包兼营的房屋开发业务。对外承包工程的营业额是以货币表现的本期内完成的对外承包工程的工作量，包括以前年度签定的合同和本年度新签定的合同在报告期完成的工作量。

对外劳务合作 指以收取工资的形式向业主承包商提供技术和劳动服务的活动。我国对外承包公司在境外开办的合营企业，中国公司同时又提供劳务的，其劳务部分也纳入劳务合作统计。劳务合作营业额按报告期内向雇主提交的结算数（包括工资、加班费和奖金等）统计。

旅游人数 指来我国参观、访问、旅行、探亲、访友、休养、考察、参加会议和从事经济、科技、文化、教育、体育、宗教等活动的外国人、华侨、港澳和台湾同胞的人数。不包括外国在我国的常住机构，如使领馆、通讯社、企业办事处的工作人员；来我国常驻的外国专家、留学生以及在岸逗留不过夜人员。

国际旅游（外汇）收入 指入境旅游的外国人、华侨、港澳台同胞在中国大陆旅游过程中发生的一切旅游支出，对于国家来说就是国际旅游（外汇）收入。

Explanatory Notes On Main Statistical Indicators

Total Imports and Exports at Customs refer to the value of commodities imported and exported across the boundary of China and cause increase or decrease of material resource within the boundaries of our country. It includes imports and exports in manner of general trade, barter trade, processing trade, compensation trade, consignment and commission agent trade, leasing commodities with renting period in one year and above, imports and exports in border trade, donations and gifts between governments, imported and exported goods in China from bonded warehouses. The indicator of the total imports and exports at customs can be used to observe the total size of external trade in a country . In accordance with the stipulation of the Chinese government, imports are calculated at CIF, while exports are calculated at FOB.

Utilization of Foreign Capital refers to foreign exchange, equipment and technology financed with foreign loans, foreign direct investment and other ways undertaken by the Chinese governments at all levels, by various departments, enterprises and other economic units.

Foreign Loans refers to funds borrowed from abroad, including loans of foreign governments, loans of international financial institutions, commercial loans of foreign banks, export credit, and funds raised via bonds and shares issued abroad. It is a major part of China's utilization of foreign capital.

Direct Investment by Foreign Enterprises refers to the investments in foreign enterprises, Sino-foreign joint ventures and Sino-foreign cooperative enterprises in China and in Sino-foreign co-operative exploration of resources in China by foreign enterprises, economic organizations or individuals (including overseas Chinese, compatriots from Hong Kong, Taiwan and Macao, and Chinese enterprises registered abroad) , following the relevant policies and laws of China. It includes the re-investment of the foreign parties with the return of the investment and the funds that enterprises borrow from abroad for the investment of projects approved by the relevant government department.

Overseas Projects Contracted refer to projects undertaken by Chinese contractors (project contracting companies) through bidding process, which include:

(1) overseas civil engineering construction projects financed by foreign investor;

(2) overseas projects financed by the Chinese government foreign-aid programs;

(3) construction projects of Chinese institutions functioning abroad;

(4) construction projects in China financed by foreign investment;

(5) sub-contracted projects to be taken by Chinese contractors through a joint umbrella project with foreign contractors;

(6) technical assistance projects charged from the foreign owners according to service results (such as topographic surveying, geological prospecting, development zone programming, provision of designing documents, blueprint, materials on production process, technical consultation, project feasibility studies and evaluation, personnel training , etc.) ;

(7) house development projects.

The business income from overseas projects contracted is the work volume of contracted projects completed in the reference period, including completed projects signed contracts in previous years.

Overseas Labor Service Co-operation refers to the activities of providing technology and labor services to employers or contractors and getting salaries and wages in return. Labor services providing by contractual joint ventures of Chinese international contracting corporations should be included in the statistics of overseas labor service co-operation. The business income of labor service co-operation is the total income of wages, salaries, over-time pay, bonuses and other remuneration received from the employers during the reference period.

Number of Tourists refers to the number of foreigners, overseas Chinese, and compatriots from Hong Kong, Macao and Taiwan coming to China for sightseeing, visits, tours, family reunions, vacations, international meetings and other activities concerning business, science and technology, culture, education, physical culture and religious, which does not include the number of employees of foreign institutions in China such as embassies, consulates, news agencies, the offices of corporations and enterprises and foreign experts and students residing in China, or the persons without staying over night in China.

Foreign Exchange Receipt from International Tourism refers to the total expenditures of the foreigners, overseas Chinese, compatriots from Hong Kong , Macao and Taiwan during their staying in the mainland of China.

1999

金融、保险

BANKING AND INSURANCE

城乡居民储蓄存款余额

Saving Deposit Balance in Urban and Rural Areas

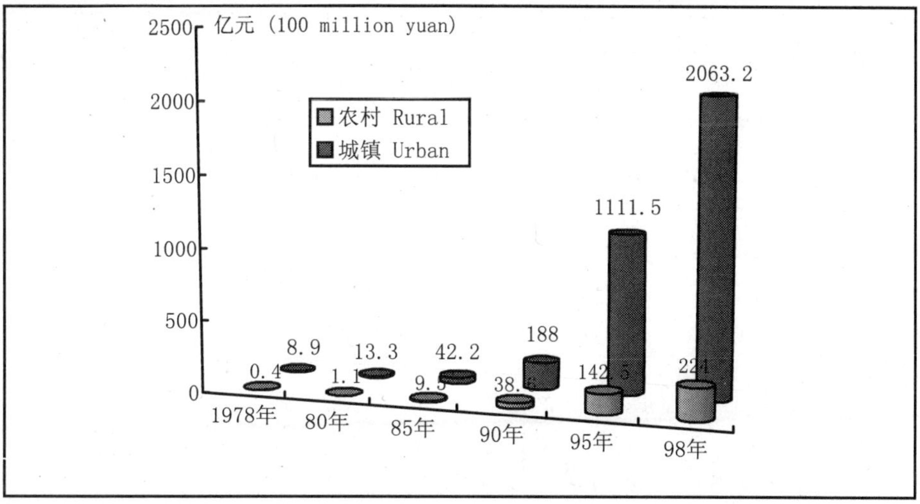

单位：亿元 (100 million yuan)		比年初增加额 Increase than Year-beginning	
	1998	1998	1997
地区金融机构存款余额 Deposits of Financial Institutions	6666.8	1263.2	871.1
地区金融机构贷款余额 Loans of Financial Institutions	3326.6	610.8	508

1998年城乡居民储蓄存款余额构成 （亿 元）

Saving Deposits Balance in Urban and Rural Aeras (100 million yuan)

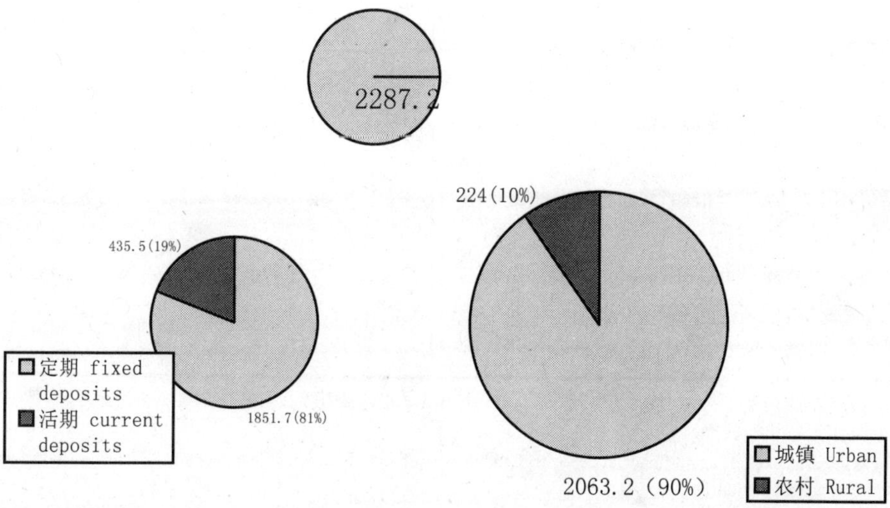

12-1 北京地区金融机构存贷款
DEPOSITS AND LOANS OF FINANCIAL INSTITUTIONS IN BEIJING

单位：万元 (10000 yuan)

项目	Item	1998年余额 Balance of 1998	比年初增减额(+、-) Increase or Decrease than Year-beginning	
			1998	1997
存款总计	**All Deposits**	**66668368**	**12631644**	**8710675**
全市各银行存款合计	**Total Deposits of Banks**	**62740154**	**12067272**	**8287537**
国家银行小计	National Banks	51560641	10266014	5496854
其他商业银行	Other Commercial Banks	11179513	1801258	2790683
信用合作机构存款	**Deposits of Credit Cooperatives**	**3600586**	**482072**	**459549**
农村信用社	Rural Credit Cooperatives	3600586	482072	459549
非银行金融机构存款	**Deposits of Non-bank Financial Institutions**	**327628**	**82300**	**-36411**
贷款总计	**All Loans**	**33265705**	**6107967**	**5079986**
全市各银行贷款合计	**Total Loans of Banks**	**31261511**	**5860469**	**4897112**
国家银行小计	National Banks	25453287	4720698	3351193
其他商业银行	Other Commercial Banks	5808224	1139771	1545919
信用合作机构贷款	**Loans of Credit Cooperatives**	**1693339**	**257854**	**165254**
农村信用社	Rural Credit Cooperatives	1693339	257854	165254
非银行金融机构贷款	**Deposits of Non-bank Financial Institutions**	**310855**	**-10356**	**17620**

注：本表各金融机构存款中，不包含其代理财政存款、汇出汇入款、委托及投资基金存款；各金融机构贷款中，包含代理金融机构贷款。

Note: All deposits exclude agent financial deposits,remittance, trust and investment-fund deposits;all loans include agent loans of financial institutions.

12-2 银行存款及贷款余额
DEPOSITS AND LOANS OF BANKS

项目	Item	绝对数(万元) Amount (10000 yuan)		1998年为1997年% 1998 as % of 1997	构成(%) Composition (%)	
		1998	1997		1998	1997
年末各项存款合计	**Deposits Balance (year-end)**	**62740154**	**50669842**	**123.8**	**100**	**100**
#地方存款	Local Deposits	49606422	41145092	120.6	79.1	81.2
# 地方工业企业存款	Industrial Enterprise	2887912	3036151	95.1	4.6	6.0
地方商业企业存款	Commercial Enterprise	2604718	2403513	108.4	4.2	4.7
#企业存款	Enterprise Deposits	36289291	29211539	124.2	57.8	57.7
# 工业存款	Industry	5646250	5319342	106.1	9.0	10.5
商业存款	Commerce	3262666	2971531	109.8	5.2	5.9
建筑业存款	Construction	2171962	1325401	163.9	3.5	2.6
城镇储蓄存款	Urban Savings Deposits	20631876	17709062	116.5	32.9	34.9
农业存款	Agricultural Deposits	266550	252358	105.6	0.4	0.5
信托存款	Trust Deposits	1731	2724	63.5		0.01
机关团体存款	Deposits of Government Organs and Bodies	2139696	1562975	136.9	3.4	3.1
年末各项贷款合计	**Loans Balance (year-end)**	**31261511**	**25444738**	**122.9**	**100**	**100**
#地方贷款	Local Loans	25712988	21209242	121.2	82.3	83.4
# 地方工业贷款	Industrial Enterprise	6309327	5386862	117.1	20.2	21.2
地方商业贷款	Commercial Enterprise	5433193	4931056	110.2	17.4	19.4
#短期贷款	Short-term Loans	20985647	18353500	114.3	67.1	72.1
# 工业贷款	Industry	8919232	7412815	120.3	28.5	29.1
商业贷款	Commerce	5892568	5632541	104.6	18.8	22.1
建筑业企业贷款	Construction	1383505	1000396	138.3	4.4	3.9
农业贷款	Agriculture	530789	477519	111.2	1.7	1.9
中长期贷款	Mid-term and Long-term Loans	7281840	5524730	131.8	23.3	21.7
# 基本建设贷款	Capital Construction	3001495	2297402	130.6	9.6	9.0
技术改造贷款	Technical Updates and Transformation	3844921	2749157	139.9	12.3	10.8
信托贷款	Trust Loans	1020	1129	90.3		

12-3 城乡居民储蓄存款余额
SAVINGS DEPOSIT BALANCE IN URBAN AND RURAL AREAS

项目	Item	绝对数(万元) Amount(10000 yuan) 1998	1997	1998年为1997年% 1998 as % of 1997	构成(%) Composition(%) 1998	1997
年末储蓄存款余额	**Savings Deposit Balance**	**22871883**	**19752621**	**115.8**	**100**	**100**
定　期	Fixed Deposits	18516975	16824687	110.1	81.0	85.2
活　期	Current Deposits	4354908	2927934	148.7	19.0	14.8
城镇居民存款	Urban Savings Deposit	20631876	17709062	116.5	90.2	89.7
农民存款	Rural Savings Deposit	2240007	2043559	109.6	9.8	10.4

12-4 银行、保险系统机构及人员
INSTITUTIONS AND PERSONNEL OF BANK AND INSURANCE SYSTEM

项目	Item	专业银行 Specialized Banks 机构(个) Institution(unit)	人员(人) Personnel(person)	保险公司 Insurance Company 机构(个) Institution(unit)	人员(人) Personnel(person)
全　市	**Total**	**2513**	**50795**	**98**	**5917**
城　区	City Propers	588	19622	32	3042
郊　区	Suburbs	1309	22634	42	2282
各　县	Counties	616	8539	24	593

注：专业银行中含农村金融体制改革办公室。

Note：Specialized bank included rural financial structural reforms office.

12-5 保险费收入
PREMIUMS INCOME

项目 Item		绝对数(万元) Amount (10000 yuan)		1998年为1997年% 1998 as % of 1997	构成(%) Composition(%)	
		1998	1997		1998	1997
国内保费总计	**Domestic Premiums**	**819012**	**796683**	**102.8**	**100**	**100**
财产险小计	**Property Insurance**	**217088**	**181021**	**119.9**	**26.5**	**22.7**
企业财产险	Enterprise Property	34904	30050	116.2	4.3	3.8
家庭财产险	Family Property	2925	3412	85.7	0.4	0.4
运输工具及责任险	Transportation Equipment and Responsibility	160636	132541	121.2	19.6	16.6
货物运输险	Freight Transport	9620	8573	112.2	1.2	1.1
农业险	Agricultural Insurance	154	198	77.8	0.02	0.02
其他财产险	Other Property	8849	6246	141.7	1.1	0.8
人身险小计	**Personal Insurance**	**601924**	**615662**	**97.8**	**73.49**	**77.28**
短期人身险	Short-term Insurance	25191	21668	116.3	3.1	2.7
养老年金	Pension Insurance	576733	593994	97.1	70.4	74.6
国外保费总计	**Oversease Premiums**	**24122**	**24105**	**100.1**	**100**	**100**
# 货物运输险	Freight Tranport Insurance	8609	7665	112.3	35.7	31.8
船舶险	Ship Insurance	13			0.1	
各种非水险	Non-water Insurance	5486	5661	96.9	22.7	23.5
飞机险	Airplane Insurance	9973	10720	93.0	41.3	44.5
航空人身险	Aviation Personal Insurance	41	59	69.5	0.2	0.2

12-6 金融市场交易量
FINANCIAL MARKET TRANSACTIONS

单位：万元 (10000 yuan)

项目 Item		1998	1997	1998年为1997年% 1998 as % of 1997
合　计	**Total**	**102415000**	**79344210.7**	**129.1**
国家债券	Treasury Bonds	12197900	6522224.7	187.0
股票交易	Stock Transactions	34263700	39009314.9	87.8
国债回购	Repurchase of Treasury Bonds	52156400	31925933.8	163.4
基　金	Funds	1870200		
其　他	Others	1926800	1886737.4	102.1

主要统计指标解释

信贷资金 国家银行用于发放贷款的资金叫信贷资金。中国人民银行信贷资金的来源有各项存款、对国际金融机构负债、流通中货币、银行自有资金及当年结益等。信贷资金的运用有各项贷款、黄金占款、外汇占款、财政借款及在国际金融机构中的资产等。

存款 企业、机关、团体或居民根据可以收回的原则，把货币资金存入银行或其他信用机构保管并取得一定利息的一种信用活动形式。根据存款对象的不同可划分为企业存款、财政存款、机关团体存款、基本建设存款、城镇储蓄存款、农村存款等科目。它是银行信贷资金的主要来源。

贷款 银行或其他信用机构根据必须归还的原则，按一定利率，为企业、个人等提供资金的一种信用活动形式。我国银行贷款分为流动资金贷款、固定资产贷款、城乡个体工商户贷款以及农业贷款等科目。

承保额 又叫保险金额。它是保险人对被保险人负提损失补偿或约定给负的金额。它是保险合同上的最高责任额，也是计算保费的依据。

保费 又叫保险费。是保险人根据保险合同的有关规定，为被保险人取得因约定危险事故发生所造成的经济损失补偿（或给付）权利，负给保险人的代价。包括财产险和人身险储金收入。

保险赔款 保险事故发生后，经查证确属保险责任范围以内的保险标的损失，保险人根据保险合同的规定履行赔偿义务，给予被保险人的款项叫做赔款。赔款可以分为已决赔款和未决赔款两种。

Explanatory Notes On Main Statistical Indicators

Credit Funds refer to the funds issued as loans by state banks. The sources of credit funds of the Peopls's Bank of China included deposits, liabilities to international financial institutions, currency in circulation, self-owned funds and current retained profits, etc. The credit funds can be used in forms of loan, gold, foreign exchange, government debt and assets in the international financial institutions.

Deposit is a form of credit by which enterprises,institutions,organization or residents can put money into banks and other credit institutions for safekeeping and interest earning under the principle of free withdrawal. According to different depositors,deposits are divided into enterprise deposits,treasury deposits, deposits of government organs and institutions,capital construction deposits, urban savings deposits, rural deposits and other deposits.Deposits are major sources of the credit funds of banks.

Loan is a form of credit by which banks and other credit institutions provide funds at certain interest rate to enterprises and individuals in the light of the principle of unconditional repayment. Loans from Chinese banks include circulating capital loans,fixed assets loans, loans to urban and rural individuals engaged in industrial and commercial business and agricultural loans.

Amount Insured refers to the amount of compensation for the loss or agreed sum of money to be paid by the insurer to the insured. It is maximum amount of liabilities written in the insurance contract and is also used as a basis to calculate the premium.

Premium is the fee paid by the insured based on a proportion of the benefit he or she may get from the insurance plus the insurance value. It includes the income from the deposit of property in surance and personal insurance.

Insurance Indemnity is the compensation paid by the insurer for an accident happening to the insured property or the insurance value paid for an accident happening to a person who has insured his life. It is further divided into settled and unsettled reparation.

物　价
PRICE INDEX

物　价　指　数　　Price Index

（上年=100　preceding year=100）

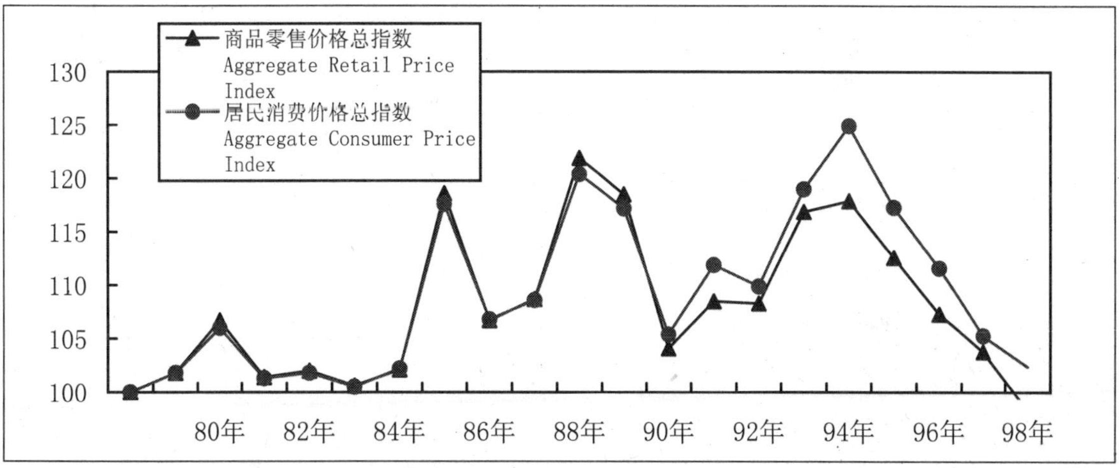

居民消费价格指数（上年=100）

Residence Consumer Price Index (preceding year=100)

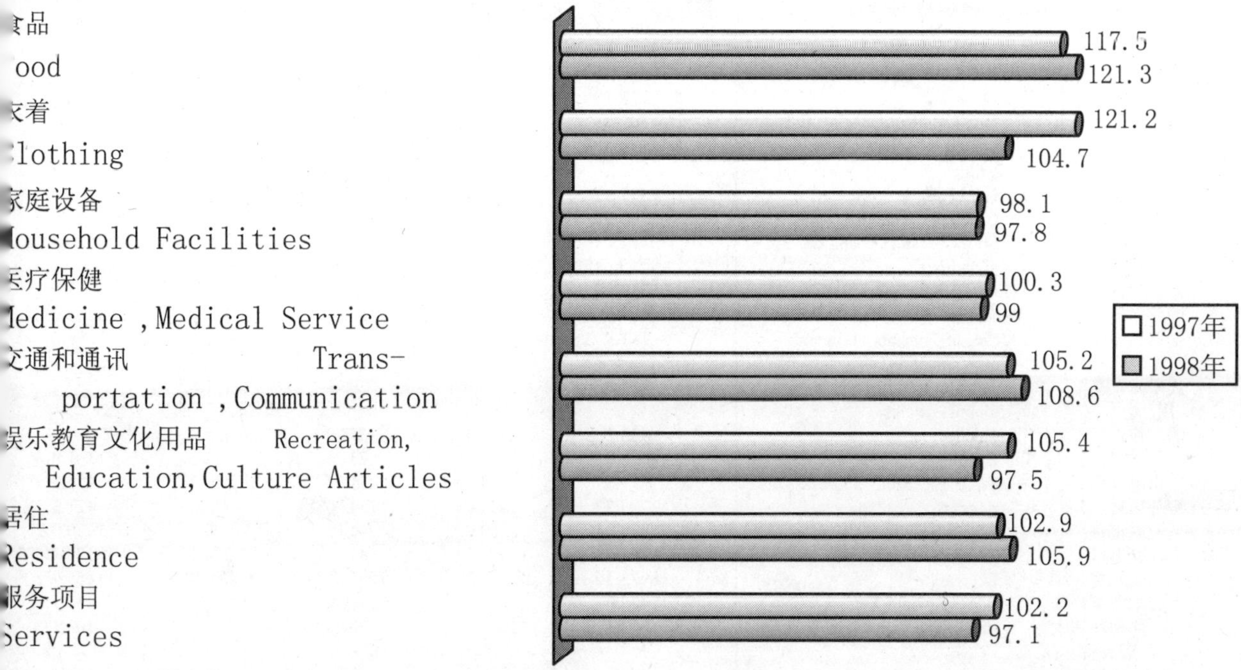

13-1 各种物价总指数
OVERALL PRICE INDICES

项目	Item	1978=100	1980=100	1985=100	1990=100	1997=100
居民消费价格总指数	Consumer Price Index of Residents	598.2	554.2	444.9	258.0	102.4
商品零售价格总指数	Retail Price Index	476.4	439.3	348.3	199.6	98.3
农副产品收购价格总指数	Farm and Sideline Products Purchasing Price Index	484.4	392.5	287.9	171.1	96.6
农业生产资料价格总指数	Means of Agricultural Production Price Index	372.2	381.3	338.4	203.9	102.6
郊区工业品零售价格总指数	Industrial Products of Suburb Retail Price Index	365.8	362.0	330.7	194.3	97.5
原材料、燃料、动力购进价格指数	Raw Material,Fuels and Motive Power Purchasing Price Index					98.1
工业品出厂价格总指数	Industrial Products Producer Price Index					95.1
城市农贸市场价格总指数	Urban Fair of Agriculture Price Index		352.0	278.8	157.2	93.9
固定资产投资额价格指数	Investment in Fixed Assets Price Index					100.8
建筑安装工程价格指数	Building Installation Price Index	476.2		340.7	275.3	101.4

13-2 居民消费价格指数
RESIDENTS CONSUMER PRICE INDICES

项目	Item	1978=100	1980=100	1985=100	1990=100	1997=100
总指数	**Aggregate Index**	**598.2**	**554.2**	**444.9**	**258.0**	**102.4**
食品类	Food	677.0	613.0	433.1	245.4	97.1
#粮食	Grain	719.0	719.0	691.2	487.2	96.4
油脂类	Oil	598.0	598.0	511.1	234.7	103.3
肉禽及其制品	Meat,Poultry and Related Products	688.4	557.1	409.7	239.1	93.2
水产品	Aquatic Products	1542.7	1096.0	437.2	172.2	94.8
菜类	Vegetable	1095.5	969.1	502.7	266.7	94.6
#鲜菜	Fresh Vegetable	1161.4	1016.5	479.7	252.7	93.9
干菜	Dried Vegetable	518.5	499.4	434.7	240.1	100.3
调味品	Flavoring	733.4	755.1	687.0	372.0	97.0
干鲜瓜果类	Dried and Fresh Melon and Fruits	707.2	660.9	363.2	181.3	90.8
衣着类	Clothing	371.8	380.3	402.0	227.6	105.9
服装	Garments	397.9	410.7	454.1	240.6	106.6
衣着材料	Clothing Material	268.2	269.2	304.8	189.7	100.0
鞋袜帽及其他衣着	Shoes,Socks,Hats and Other Clothing	374.2	379.7	357.1	221.9	106.7
家庭设备	Household Facilities	317.5	315.8	295.4	166.2	97.5
医疗保健	Medicine and Medical Services	483.2	444.2	361.1	197.0	108.6
交通和通讯工具	Means of Transportation and Communications	141.8	141.8	159.9	119.6	99.0
娱乐教育文化用品	Recreation,Education and Cultural Articles	217.4		205.9	111.8	97.8
居住	Residence	430.2	578.4	554.9	423.9	104.7
住房	Housing	466.8	737.7	731.8	517.6	101.0
水电燃料	Water,Electricity and Fuels	379.6	379.6	335.3	313.2	108.5
服务项目	Services	1736.7	1732.4	1542.0	745.8	121.3
#电讯费	Communication	569.0	569.0	440.5	299.7	100.0
交通费	Transportation	491.5	491.5	476.8	350.1	100.4
文娱费	Recreation	10975.2	10975.2	10059.5	4464.9	156.9
学杂保育费	Education and Nursery	1479.0	1479.0	1479.0	856.1	136.1
修理及其他服务费	Repair and Other Services	1057.1	1044.0	707.4	374.6	103.1
医疗保健服务	Medicine and Medical Service	1008.5	1008.5	1008.5	560.2	169.1

13-3 商品零售价格指数
RETAIL PRICE INDICES

项目	Item	1997=100	项目	Item	1997=100
商品零售价格指数	**Aggregate Index**	**98.3**	绸缎	Silk	101.8
食品类	Foods	96.9	其他纺织品	Other Textiles	99.9
粮食	Grain	96.4	中西药品类	Traditional Chinese and Western Medicines	108.6
油脂类	Oil	103.3	中药	Traditional Chinese Medicines	129.0
肉蛋禽	Meat,Egg and Poultry	94.4	西药	Western Medicine	96.0
水产品	Aquatic Products	94.8	医疗用品	Medicine and Medical Articles	100.0
鲜菜	Fresh Vegetable	94.8	化妆品类	Cosmetics	96.7
干菜	Dried Vegetable	102.6	书报杂志类	Book,Newspaper and Magazine	105.8
鲜果	Fresh Fruit	89.5	文化体育用品	Stationery and Sports Goods	98.1
干果	Nuts	96.2	文化用品	Stationery	97.9
其他食品类	Other Foods	99.7	体育用品	Sports Goods	102.0
饮食业	Catering	101.7	日用品类	Daily Use Articles	100.4
饮料烟酒类	Beverage,Tobacco and Liquor	99.3	一般日用品	Ordinary Daily Use Articles	98.3
饮料	Beverage	99.2	家具类	Furnitures	103.1
烟酒	Tobacco and Liquor	99.3	家用电器类	Household Appliances	94.7
服装鞋帽类	Garments,Shoes,Hats	106.4	首饰类	Jewelry	89.2
服装	Garments	106.6	燃料类	Fuels	100.4
鞋	Shoes	106.9	建筑装潢材料类	Building Decoration Materials	106.2
其他衣着	Other Clothing	103.2	机电产品类	Mechanical and Electrical Products	87.6
纺织品类	Textile	99.9			
棉布	Cotton Cloth	99.2			
棉花化纤混纺布	Blend Cloth	100.4			
化纤布	Chemical Fiber Cloth	99.3			
呢绒	Woolen Fabric	100.3			

13-4 居民货币购买力指数
MONETARY PURCHASING POWER OF RESIDENTS

基期 Base Period	1998	1997
1957=100	16.3	16.7
1965=100	16.9	17.3
1970=100	16.6	17.0
1975=100	16.6	17.0
1978=100	16.7	17.1
1980=100	18.1	18.5
1985=100	22.5	23.0
1990=100	38.8	39.7
以上年为100 Preceding Year=100	97.7	95.0

13-5 农贸市场农产品成交价格指数
TRANSACTION INDICES OF AGRICULTURAL PRODUCTS IN RURAL FREE MARKETS

项目	Item	1979=100	1985=100	1990=100	1997=100
总指数	**Aggregate Index**	**355.3**	**278.8**	**157.2**	**93.9**
粮食	Grain	339.5	346.3	190.8	94.1
油脂类	Oil	263.4	303.2	139.1	104.1
肉禽蛋	Meat,Poultry and Related Products	404.9	303.4	191.8	95.4
水产品	Aquatic Products	485.6	272.7	165.3	91.0
鲜菜	Fresh Vegetable	488.1	318.6	166.0	91.9
干菜	Dried Vegetable		294.7	143.8	97.7
干鲜果	Dried and Fresh Fruits	398.3	279.9	147.9	91.8

13-6 鲜菜零售价格指数
RETAIL PRICE INDICES OF FRESH VEGETABLE

项目	Item	1985=100	1990=100	1997=100
总指数	**Aggregate Index**	**479.7**	**252.7**	**93.9**
大白菜	Chinese Cabbage	814.4	700.9	90.3
元白菜	Cabbage	518.1	371.0	89.3
菠菜	Spinach	904.9	371.0	95.7
油菜	Rape	661.3	329.7	104.8
芹菜	Celery	533.0	288.5	122.7
韭菜	Chinese Chives	290.3	167.6	84.2
菜花	Cauliflower	315.6	165.8	95.1
生笋	Bamboo Shoot	478.7	312.0	97.0
黄瓜	Cucumber	485.3	211.3	98.6
冬瓜	Wax Gourd	787.2	324.0	98.5
西红柿	Tomato	507.8	205.4	89.8
茄子	Eggplant	409.4	206.1	97.7
青椒	Green Pepper	750.4	243.5	91.7
豆角	Fresh Kidney Beans	388.9	210.4	94.3
大葱	Scallion	510.1	304.8	73.9
大蒜	Garlic	464.9	340.6	84.0
萝卜	Radish	1178.1	424.0	97.5
胡萝卜	Carrot	1078.2	399.3	91.5

13-7 农副产品收购价格总指数
PURCHASING PRICE INDICES FOR FARM AND SIDELINES PRODUCTS

项目	Item	1978=100	1985=100	1990=100	1997=100
总指数	**Aggregate Index**	**453.4**	**287.9**	**171.1**	**93.6**
粮食类	Grain	333.3	228.8	146.2	96.1
经济作物类	Industrial Crops	564.9	337.7	145.1	107.5
畜禽产品类	Livestock Products,Poultry and Eggs	464.7	315.7	182.3	89.3
生猪	Pigs	618.0	420.6	212.8	90.7
鸡蛋	Chicken Eggs	320.9	222.4	134.2	92.6
干鲜果类	Dried and Fresh Fruits	539.9	303.6	194.9	82.8
鲜瓜果	Fresh Melons and Fruits	449.9	283.4	196.4	81.7
鲜果	Fresh Fruits	468.5	255.3	187.0	84.9
西瓜	Water Melon	306.5	223.5	142.0	76.5
鲜菜类	Fresh Vegetable	708.3	349.8	198.1	103.4
水产品类	Aquatic Products	581.5	204.5	131.3	104.3

13-8 郊区工业品零售价格指数
RETAIL PRICE INDICES OF INDUSTRIAL PRODUCTS IN SUBURBS

项目	Item	1978=100	1985=100	1990=100	1997=100
总指数	**Aggregate Index**	**365.8**	**330.7**	**194.3**	**97.5**
日用消费品	Daily Use Articles	356.5	330.2	191.5	96.7
食品类	Food	474.8	392.0	233.8	96.0
衣着类	Clothing	308.1	323.9	176.2	97.1
日用杂品类	Daily Use Sundries	258.5	246.8	150.8	98.1
农业生产资料	Agricultural Capital Goods	381.9	338.4	203.9	102.6
农业机械	Agricultural Machinery	299.5	287.0	180.3	100.0
化学肥料	Chemical Fertilizer	490.0	409.9	267.4	98.3
化学农药	Agricultural Chemicals	201.2	191.7	80.1	96.4
农机用油	Oil for Agricultural Machinery		372.0	302.9	99.5
种子	Seed		341.3	149.8	113.0
饲料	Forage		525.3	274.9	112.3

13-9 工农业产品综合比价指数
AGGREGATE PRICE PARITY INDEX OF INDUSTRIAL AND AGRICULTURAL PRODUCTS

基期 Base Period	农副产品收购价格总指数 Purchasing Price Indices of Farm and Sidelining Products	农村工业品零售价格总指数 Retail Price Index of Industrial Products in in Rural Area	工农业产品综合比价指数 Aggregate Parity Index of Industrial and Agricultural Products	
			以农产品指数为100 Agricultural Products Index=100	以工业品指数为100 Industrial Products Index=100
1957=100	556.6	349.5	62.8	159.3
1965=100	500.1	339.5	67.9	147.3
1970=100	499.3	360.6	72.2	138.5
1975=100	464.6	371.0	79.9	125.2
1978=100	453.4	365.8	80.7	124.0
1980=100	392.5	362.0	92.2	180.4
1985=100	287.9	330.7	114.9	87.1
1990=100	171.1	194.3	113.6	88.1
1995=100	88.2	103.6	117.5	85.1
1997=100	93.6	97.5	104.2	96.0

13-10 固定资产投资额价格指数
PRICE INDICES OF INVESTMENT IN FIXED ASSETS

项目	Item	1992=100	1993=100	1994=100	1997=100
总指数	**Aggregate Index**	**187.7**	**148.3**	**127.5**	**100.8**
建筑安装工程	Building Installation	210.8	160.8	134.2	101.4
设备、工器具购置	Purchase of Equipment, Tools and Instruments	147.5	128.3	125.7	100.5
其他费用	Others	160	131.1	106.1	99.5

注：按国家统计局的有关规定，固定资产投资额价格指数从1992年开始计算。

Note：According to rules of State Statistical Bureau, price indices of investment in fixed assets are counted from 1992.

13-11 建筑安装工程价格指数
PRICE INDICES OF BUILDING INSTALLATION

项目	Item	1978=100	1985=100	1990=100	1997=100
总指数	**Aggregate Index**	**476.2**	**340.7**	**275.3**	**101.4**
直接费用价格指数	Price Index of Direct Cost	599.0	378.6	306.7	101.3
人工费	Labor Cost	904.0	621.6	667.0	103.9
材料费用	Material Cost	518.6	365.7	263.7	100.5
其他费用价格指数	Price Index of Other Cost	324.5	233.9	185.7	102.0

13-12 建筑安装工程中主要材料费用价格指数
PRICE INDICES OF MAJOR MATERIALS IN BUILDING INSTALLATION

项目	Item	1978=100	1985=100	1990=100	1997=100
总指数	**Aggregate Index**	**518.6**	**365.7**	**263.7**	**100.5**
钢材	Rolled-steel Products	472.1	374.0	335.1	97.6
木材	Timber	837.4	431.6	315.3	98.2
水泥	Cement	706.1	502.5	320.2	99.7
地方材料	Local Materials	511.0	344.6	232.0	100.3
其他材料	Other Materials	535.6	380.3	267.9	106.7

主 要 统 计 指 标 解 释

零售价格指数 是反映城乡商品零售价格变动趋势的一种经济指数。零售价格的调整变动直接影响到城乡居民的生活支出和国家的财政收入，影响居民购买力和市场供需平衡，影响消费与积累的比例。因此，计算零售价格指数，可以从一个侧面对上述经济活动进行观察和分析。

居民消费价格指数 是反映一定时期内城乡居民所购买的生活消费品价格和服务项目价格变动趋势和程度的相对数。是综合了城市居民消费价格指数和农民消费价格指数计算取得。利用居民消费价格指数，可以观察和分析消费品的零售价格和服务价格变动对城乡居民实际生活费支出的影响程度。

农产品收购价格指数 是反映国有商业、集体商业、个体商业、外贸部门、国家机关、社会团体等各种经济类型的商业企业和有关部门收购农产品价格的变动趋势和程度的相对数。农产品收购价格指数可以观察和研究农产品价格总水平的变化情况，以及对农民货币收入的影响，作为制定和检查农产品价格政策的依据。计算指数所选的商品有 11 各大类、包括 276 种农副土特产品。采用加权倒数平均公式（即按报告期实际收购金额加权综合法）计算。

工业产品出厂价格指数 是反映全部工业产品出厂价格总水平的变动趋势和程度的相对数。其中包括工业企业售给商业、外贸、物资部门的产品外，还包括售给工业和其他部门的生产资料以及直接售给居民的生活消费品。通过工业生产价格指数能观察出厂价格变动对工业总产值的影响。

固定资产投资价格指数 是反映固定资产投资额价格变动趋势和程度的相对数。固定资产投资额是由建筑安装工程投资完成额、设备、工器具购置投资完成额和其他费用投资完成额三部分组成的。编制固定资产投资价格指数应首先分别编制上述三部分投资的价格指数，然后采用加权算术平均法求出固定资产投资价格总指数。

编制固定资产投资价格指数可以准确地反映固定资产投资中涉及的各类商品和取费项目价格变动趋势和变动幅度，消除按现价计算的固定资产投资指标中的价格变动因素，真实地反映固定资产投资的规模、速度、结构和效益，为国家科学地制定，检查固定资产投资计划并提高宏观调控水平，为完善国民经济核算体系提供科学的，可靠的依据。

原材料、燃料、动力购进价格指数 是反映全部工业原材料、燃料、动力购进价格总水平的变动趋势和程度的相对数。用其可以观察和研究工业企业原材料价格变动对生产的影响，以及企业对原材料涨价的消化能力和承受能力，为制订价格政策提供依据。

农贸市场农产品成交价格指数 是反映一定时期农贸市场农产品价格变动趋势和程度的相对数。编制农贸市场农产品成交价格指数，可以观察和分析农贸市场农产品价格变动及对农业生产和居民生活的影响程度。

Explanatory Notes On Main Statistical Indicators

Retail Price Index reflects the general trend in retail prices of commodities. The change and adjustment in retail prices directly affect the living expenditure of urban and rural residents, government revenue, purchasing power of residents and the equilibrium of market supply and demand, and the ratio of consumption to accumulation. Therefore, the calculation of retail price index is useful to analyze the relevant economic activities.

Consumer Price Index reflects the relative change in prices of consumer goods and services purchased by urban and rural residents, and is a composite index derived from the urban consumer price index and the rural consumer price index. Consumer price index can be used to analyze the impact of consumer price change on actual living expenditures of urban and rural residents.

Purchasing Price Index of Farm Products reflects the relative change in purchasing prices of farm products purchased by state-owned, collective-owned, and individual commercial enterprises, foreign trade sectors, government agencies, social organizations and other units of various types of ownership. It is used to observe the impact of change in purchasing prices of farm products on money income of peasants and is calculated with the method of weighted harmonic mean, taking the amount of purchases during a given period as the weight. Number of products involved in the current calculation totaled 276 in 11 categories.

Ex-factory Price Index of Industrial Products reflects the relative change in general ex-factory prices of all industrial products, including sales of industrial products to commercial enterprises, foreign trade sectors , materials supplying and distributing sectors as well as sales of production means to industry and other sectors and sales of consumer goods to residents. It can be used to analyze the impact of ex-factory prices on gross industrial output value.

Price Index of Investment in Fixed Asses reflects the change in prices of investment in fixed assets. The investment in fixed assets consists of three components, namely the investment in construction and installation, the investment in purchases of equipment and instrument, and the investment in other items. Price index of investment in fixed assets is calculated as the weighted arithmetic mean of the price indices of the three components.

Price index of investment in fixed asses reflects the change of price in various goods and services involved in investment in fixed assets and therefore can be used to observe the actual size, speed, structure, and efficiency of investment in fixed assets and provides reliable and rational data for government planning, management, decision making, and further improving the current national accounting system.

Purchase Price Index of Raw Materials, Fuel and Power reflects relative changes in the general purchase price of all industrial raw materials, fuel and power. The index can be used to study and analyze the impact of price changes of industrial raw materials of the production and enterprises capability to bear and digest the price increase of raw materials, so as to provide basis for the government to formulate price policies.

Market Price Index of Farm Product reflects the trend of price changes of farm products sold in farm product markets in a given period of time. Market price index of farm product can be used to study and analyze the price fluctuation of farm product

教育、文化

EDUCATION AND CULTURE

1998年平均每万人口在校学生数(人)
Average Number of Student Enrollment per 10000 Population (person)

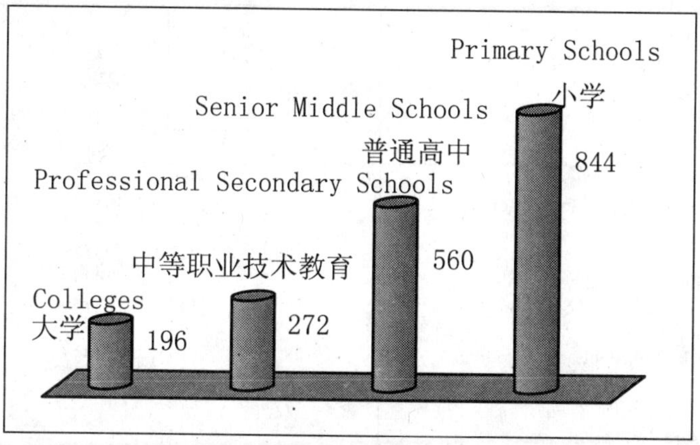

1998年	学校数（所） Number of Schools(unit)	在校学生数（人） Students Enrollment(person)
高等学校 Institutions of Higher Education	63	212984
中等职业技术教育 Professional Secondary Schools	434	295892
普通高中 Senior Middle Schools	282	145966
小学 Primary Schools	2511	919531

广播、电视、图书馆
Broadcasting, Television and Library

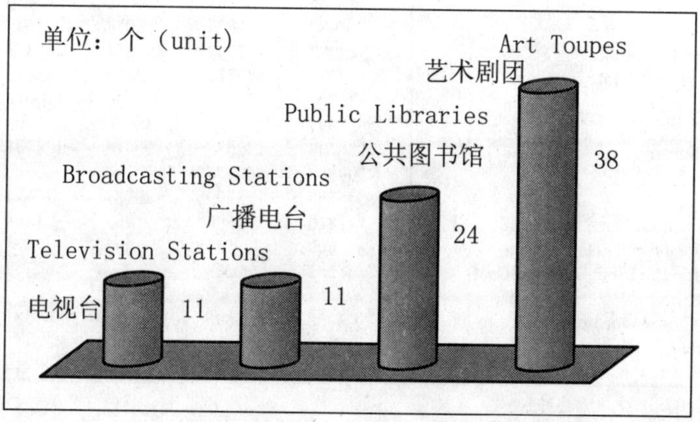

14-1 各类学校基本情况
BASIC STATISTICS FOR EDUCATION

单位：人 (person)

类别	Item	校数(所) Number of Schools (unit) 1998	1997	教职工数 Teachers,Staff and Workers 1998	1997	# 专任教师 Full-time Teachers 1998	1997
总计	**Total**	**3796**	**3950**	**284674**	**283569**	**164491**	**164515**
高等学校	**Institutions of Higher Education**	**63**	**65**	**101442**	**101206**	**36559**	**36541**
# 地方	Local	19	12	19956	15445	7618	5786
中等职业技术教育	**Professional Secondary Schools**	**434**	**424**	**35128**	**34801**	**17649**	**17124**
中等专业学校	Specialized Secondary Schools	118	118	14253	14526	6334	6442
技工学校	Secondary Technical Schools	143	132	7900	7693	3711	3589
职业学校	Vocational Schools	173	174	12975	12582	7604	7093
普通高中	**Senior Middle Schools**	**282**	**288**	**71849**	**71171**	**11412**	**10292**
城镇	Urban	265	270			10882	9767
农村	Rural	17	18			530	525
义务教育	**Compulsory Education**	**2981**	**3143**			**98044**	**99745**
初中	Junior Middle Schools	470	447			36242	37321
城镇	Urban	290	260			27512	28617
农村	Rural	180	187			8730	8704
小学	Primary Schools	2511	2696	74916	75125	61802	62424
城镇	Urban	1306	1487	52509	54620	42583	44877
农村	Rural	1205	1209	22407	20505	19219	17547
特殊教育	**Special Education**	**36**	**30**	**1339**	**1266**	**827**	**813**
工读学校	Schools for Juvenile Delinquents	6	6	414	374	183	190
盲聋哑学校	Schools for The Blind,Deaf and Deaf-Mutes	7	7	420	431	274	283
弱智儿童辅读学校(班)	Schools(Classes) for Less Intelligent Children	23	17	505	461	370	340
民办学校	**Non-state Owned Schools**	**83**	**54**	**4022**	**2372**	**2442**	**1358**

类别	Item	毕业生数 Graduates 1998	1997	招生数 New Students Enrollment 1998	1997	在校学生数 Students Enrollment 1998	1997
总计	**Total**	**492531**	**461896**	**473882**	**476348**	**2046766**	**2073003**
高等学校	**Institutions of Higher Education**	**49322**	**49973**	**62264**	**56884**	**212984**	**195842**
# 地方	Local	15230	11603	21449	14501	67342	43576
外国留学生	Foreign Students	5462	4081	6441	159536	9314	8193
中等职业技术教育	**Professional Secondary Schools**	**71734**	**59517**	**102808**	**100427**	**295892**	**265680**
中等专业学校	Specialized Secondary Schools	23078	18759	38003	36082	117965	104135
技工学校	Secondary Technical Schools	15491	13267	25215	23027	64879	53237
职业学校	Vocational Schools	33165	27491	39590	41318	113048	108308
普通高中	**Senior Middle Schools**	**39683**	**33010**	**52956**	**49566**	**145966**	**133461**
城镇	Urban	37703	31481	50898	47420	139886	127272
农村	Rural	1980	1529	2058	2146	6080	6189
义务教育	**Compulsory Education**	**329982**	**317740**	**254551**	**268103**	**1383468**	**1470070**
初中	Junior Middle Schools	173788	171717	154136	143872	463937	492747
城镇	Urban	135791	135188	115390	110072	354282	381115
农村	Rural	37997	36529	38746	33800	109655	111632
小学	Primary Schools	156194	146023	100415	124231	919531	977323
城镇	Urban	109868	107424	71134	86387	625668	694676
农村	Rural	46326	38599	29281	37844	293863	282647
特殊教育	**Special Education**	**1810**	**1656**	**1303**	**1368**	**8456**	**7950**
工读学校	Schools for Juvenile Delinquents	500	547	445	524	889	835
盲聋哑学校	Schools for The Blind,Deaf and Deaf-Mutes	252	219	273	257	1442	1315
弱智儿童辅读学校(班)	Schools(Classes) for Less Intelligent Children	1058	890	585	587	6125	5800
民办学校	**Non-state Owned Schools**	**6553**	**2994**	**17278**	**8414**	**38295**	**20964**

注：教职工数中，普通高中人数为初中和高中合计数。

Note: Number of teachers,staff and workers of senior middle schools includes those of junior and senior middle schools.

14-2 高等学校基本情况
BASIC STATISTICS FOR INSTITUTION OF HIGHER EDUCATION

单位：人 (person)

类别	Item	校数（所） Number of Schools (unit)	毕业生数 Graduates	招生数 New Students Enrollment	在校学生数 Students Enrollment	教职工数 Teachers, Staff and Workers	#专任教师 Full-time Teachers
总计	**Total**	**63**	**49322**	**62264**	**212984**	**101442**	**36559**
综合大学	Comprehensive Universities	3	6126	7650	25823	13534	4602
理工院校	Science and Engineering	20	21746	27617	97349	39800	13630
农业院校	Agriculture	2	2193	2618	8773	3570	1292
林业院校	Forestry	1	821	1086	3487	1258	393
医药院校	Medicine	6	1940	2193	9294	15564	5875
师范院校	Teacher Training	3	3663	4198	13507	6473	2564
语文院校	Literature	7	2797	3551	11205	5608	2331
财经院校	Economics and Finance	6	4295	5426	18944	5714	2198
政法院校	Politics and Law	4	3119	3951	10842	3872	1202
体育院校	Physical Culture	1	495	662	2337	918	376
艺术院校	Art	8	854	1290	4154	3241	1283
民族院校	National Colleges	1	908	782	3850	1776	730
短期职业大学	Short-Time Vocational Colleges	1	365	1240	3419	114	83
在总计中：	**Of Total:**						
市属院校	Municipal						
综合大学	Comprehensive Universities	1	2354	3576	11019	3233	1241
理工院校	Science and Engineering	7	6008	8006	26250	7599	2862
农业院校	Agriculture	1	347	611	1701	500	198
医药院校	Medicine	2	701	740	3019	1435	498
师范院校	Teacher Training	2	2414	2695	7917	3017	1211
语文院校	Literature	1	378	513	1274	269	107
财经院校	Economics and Finance	3	2472	3362	10947	3223	1184
政法院校	Politics and Law			356	627		
艺术院校	Art	1	191	350	1169	566	234
短期职业大学	Short-Time Vocational Colleges	1	365	1240	3419	114	83

14-3 高等学校分科学生数
NUMBER OF STUDENTS BY DEPARTMENTS IN INSTITUTIONS OF HIGHER EDUCATION

单位：人 (person)

学科	Item	毕业生数 Graduates	招生数 New Students Enrollment	在校学生数 Students Enrollment
总计	**Total**	**49322**	**62264**	**212984**
哲学	Philosophy	136	140	510
经济学	Economics	8840	10676	36991
法学	Law	3368	5271	14579
教育学	Education	2090	2578	7859
文学	Literature	6412	8083	25983
历史学	History	499	756	2364
理学	Science	3332	3903	14193
工学	Engineering	21495	27139	96540
农学	Agriculture	1015	1311	4084
医学	Medicine	2135	2407	9881

14-4 高等学校分科研究生数

NUMBER OF POSTGRADUATES BY DEPARTMENTS IN INSTITUTIONS OF HIGHER EDUCATION

单位：人 (person)

学科	Item	攻读博士学位研究生 Postgraduate for Doctor Degree 毕业生数 Graduates	招生数 New Students Enrollment	在学研究生数 Postgraduates Enrollment	攻读硕士学位研究生 Postgraduate for Master Degree 毕业生数 Graduates	招生数 New Students Enrollment	在学研究生数 Postgraduate Enrollment	研究生班研究生数 Postgraduates in Class
总计	**Total**	**2665**	**4311**	**12936**	**8380**	**11946**	**31805**	**132**
# 市属院校	Municipal	24	77	191	668	857	2354	
哲学	Philosophy	65	91	271	104	128	317	
经济学	Economics	211	341	987	952	1814	4521	
法学	Law	169	344	896	774	1375	3603	
教育学	Education	61	90	268	189	290	771	
# 体育学	Physical Culture	13	23	61	48	79	218	
文学	Literature	86	187	526	578	815	2100	132
# 艺术	Art	6	37	94	92	150	353	132
历史学	History	52	84	238	115	170	447	
理学	Science	704	960	2775	1055	1491	4019	
工学	Engineering	833	1663	5366	3935	4895	13377	
# 力学	Mechanics	53	78	308	115	131	390	
农学	Agriculture	130	178	462	193	275	735	
# 林学	Forestry	24	47	97	38	60	159	
医学	Medicine	354	373	1147	485	693	1915	

14-5 高等学校专任教师学历情况

EDUCATIONAL BACKGROUND OF FULL-TIME TEACHERS IN INSTITUTIONS OF HIGHER EDUCATION

单位：人 (person)

学历	Educational Background	总计 Total	正高级 Senior Title	副高级 Asso. Senior Title	中级 Middle Title	初级 Junior Title	其他 Others
合计	**Total**	**36559**	**6139**	**11529**	**12260**	**5325**	**1306**
研究生毕业	Postgraduate						
博士	Doctor Degree	4213	1022	1879	1122	112	78
硕士	Master Degree	11101	849	3031	4690	1992	539
未获博士硕士学位	Not Obtained Degrees	1233	401	395	391	30	16
本科毕业	Undergraduate						
学士	Bachelor	13047	1357	3087	4980	3025	598
研究生肄业	Not Pass the Postgraduate Study	154	20	53	71	9	1
未获学士学位	Not Obtained Degree	5744	2410	2663	579	60	32
专科毕业及本专科肄业两年及以上	Graduate from College for Professional Training and Undergraduate Study for Two Years above	843	43	349	347	88	16
本专科肄业未满两年	Undergraduate Study for Less than Two Years	224	37	72	80	9	26

14-6 中等专业学校基本情况
BASIC STATISTICS ON SPECIALIZED SECONDARY SCHOOLS

单位：人 (person)

类别 Item		校数(所) Number of Schools (unit)	毕业生数 Graduates	招生数 New Students Enrollment	在校学生数 Students Enrollment	教职工数 Teachers, Staff and Workers	#专任教师 Full-time Teachers
总计	**Total**	**118**	**23078**	**38003**	**117965**	**14253**	**6334**
中等技术学校	**Secondary Technical Schools**	**98**	**18606**	**36584**	**110765**	**11998**	**5275**
工业学校	Industry	32	11388	24153	71718	6154	2508
农业学校	Agriculture	1	795	1026	3161	339	129
林业学校	Forestry	1	108	192	618	94	35
医药学校	Medicine	37	2630	2803	10415	1878	907
财经学校	Economics and Finance	9	2088	5307	14438	1384	613
政法学校	Politics and Law	4	722	1447	4066	418	191
体育学校	Physical Culture	7	294	390	1182	619	224
艺术学校	Art	6	401	743	3523	1037	609
其他学校	Others	1	180	523	1644	75	59
中等师范学校	**Teacher Training Schools**	**20**	**4472**	**1419**	**7200**	**2255**	**1059**
# 幼儿师范	Kindergarten	1	266	192	613	142	56

14-7 中等专业学校专任教师学历
EDUCATIONAL BACKGROUND OF FULL-TIME TEACHERS IN SPECIALIZED SECONDARY SCHOOLS

单位：人 (person)

学历 Educational Background		中等专业学校 Secondary Specialized Schools		#中等专业技术学校 Secondary Technical Schools		# 中等专业师范学校 Teacher Training Schools	
		人数 Number of Persons	构成(%) Composition(%)	人数 Number of Persons	构成(%) Composition(%)	人数 Number of Persons	构成(%) Composition(%)
合计	**Total**	**6334**	**100**	**5275**	**83.3**	**1059**	**16.7**
本科毕业及以上	Undergraduate and the Level above	4711	74.4	3792	59.9	919	14.5
专科毕业和本专科肄业两年及以上	College for Professional Training and Undergraduate Study for Two Years above	1107	17.5	996	15.7	111	1.8
本专科肄业未满两年	Undergraduate Study for Less than Two Years	63	1	50	0.8	13	0.2
中专、高中毕业及以下	Specialized Secondary School,Senior Middle School and the Level Below	453	7.2	437	6.9	16	0.3

14-8 中等专业学校分学科学生数
NUMBER OF STUDENTS IN SPECIALIZED SECONDARY SCHOOLS BY FIELD OF STUDY

单位：人 (person)

学科	Item	毕业生数 Graduates 1998	1997	招生数 New Students Enrollment 1998	1997	在校学生数 Students Enrollment 1998	1997
总计	**Total**	**23078**	**18759**	**38003**	**36082**	**117965**	**104135**
工科	Engineering	8738	6642	17409	17112	52998	44884
农科	Agriculture	248	296	410	437	1426	1278
林科	Forestry	109	162	226	182	544	429
医药卫生	Medicine	2630	2267	2766	2770	10300	10232
财经	Economics and Finance	2848	1895	4128	5019	15670	14624
管理	Administration	2402	1327	8272	5554	18740	12990
政法	Politics and Law	722	283	1530	1026	4249	3455
艺术	Art	563	543	1374	1491	5437	4656
体育	Physical Culture	294	302	432	316	1267	1072
师范	Teacher Training	4524	5042	1456	2175	7334	10515
#幼儿师范专业	Kindergarten	422	320	208	270	825	970
特教师范专业	Special Education	38	39			41	79

14-9 普通中学分课程专任教师数
NUMBER OF FULL-TIME TEACHERS BY SUBJECTS OF REGULAR SECONDARY SCHOOLS

单位：人 (person)

学科	Item	合计 Total 1998	1997	高中 Senior Middle School 1998	1997	初中 Junior Middle School 1998	1997
总计	**Total**	**47654**	**47613**	**11412**	**10292**	**36242**	**37321**
政治	Politics	3296	3324	792	730	2504	2594
语文	Chinese	7493	7554	1670	1480	5823	6074
数学	Math	7688	7835	1742	1582	5946	6253
物理	Physics	3889	3854	1262	1104	2627	2750
化学	Chemical	2854	2777	1230	1080	1624	1697
生物	Biology	1777	1820	333	307	1444	1513
地理	Geography	1710	1684	324	303	1386	1381
历史	History	2257	2209	658	605	1599	1604
英语	English	7141	7172	1596	1434	5545	5738
俄语	Russian	1	3	1	3		
日语	Japanese	17	13	11	7	6	6
体育	Physical Education	2913	2914	708	649	2205	2265
生理卫生	Physiology	73	58	2	0	71	58
音乐	Music	1018	1000	120	104	898	896
美术	Art	939	935	95	72	844	863
计算机	Computer	725	559	279	241	446	318
职业劳动	Vocational labor	594	538	49	42	545	496
其他	Others	405	3364	70	549	335	2815

14-10 技工学校分专业学生数
NUMBER OF STUDENTS BY FIELD OF STUDY IN TECHNICAL SCHOOLS

单位：人 (person)

学科	Item	毕业生数 Graduates		招生数 New Students Enrollment		在校学生数 Students Enrollment	
		1998	1997	1998	1997	1998	1997
总计	**Total**	**15491**	**13267**	**25215**	**23027**	**64879**	**53237**
# 市属	Municipal	13430	11853	23013	21197	59417	48481
农、林、牧、渔业	Farming,Forestry,Animal Husbandry and Fishery	138	187	73	165	253	288
机械制造及加工业	Machinery Manufacturing and Processing	3150	2675	3575	3329	10460	7633
# 车工	Turner	1442	1009	1518	1338	4610	2788
钳工	Fitter	892	1288	1102	1132	3277	2961
铣工	Caster and Blacksmith	102	77	80	113	366	257
铸、锻工	Miller	290	161	100	221	199	343
铆、焊工	Riveter and Welder	424	140	775	525	2008	1284
地质矿产业	Geological and Mineral Industry	80		70		175	
冶金工业	Coal Mining and Processing	119	339	268	296	723	778
煤炭工业	Metallurgical Industry	90	80	90	140	219	390
电力工业	Electric Power Industry	341	235			338	304
石油工业	Petroleum Industry	207		74		501	
化学工业	Chemical Industry	486	446	343	547	1311	1381
有色金属工业	Nonferrous Metal Industry	232	143	841	643	1817	1208
轻工工业	Light Industry	1059	833	1887	1580	5320	3719
纺织工业	Textile Industry	975	937	1626	2742	4455	5773
电子、仪器、仪表	Electronic,Instruments and Meters	1346	941	2553	2313	6175	4983
电工、电气	Electrotechnics and Electric	582	552	1770	1076	3848	2608
医药、医疗	Medicine	464	356	479	591	984	1259
建材、建工、城建	Construction	907	876	1629	1292	3689	3029
交通运输	Transportation	1913	1172	1987	1802	5199	4684
邮电通讯	Post and Telecommunication	66			203	274	124
商业、饮食、旅游及服务业	Commerce,Catering Trade and Services	1877	2309	5480	4586	11377	9573
其他	Others	1459	1186	2470	1722	7761	5503

14-11 职业高中分科学生数
NUMBER OF STUDENTS BY FIELD OF STUDY IN VOCATIONAL SCHOOLS

单位：人 (person)

学科 Item		毕业生数 Graduates		招生数 New Students Enrollment		在校学生数 Students Enrollment	
		1998	1997	1998	1997	1998	1997
总计	**Total**	**33005**	**27491**	**39590**	**41158**	**112954**	**108148**
工科	Engineering	8839	8282	9526	10744	25537	29115
农科	Agriculture	194	270	132	590	299	1144
林科	Forestry	213	253	474	166	1254	554
医药	Medicine	684	528	1328	888	4025	2880
财经	Economics and Finance	5514	3872	4980	6014	17443	20544
管理	Administration	13860	11616	18238	18215	51125	42517
政法	Politics and Law	94	69	229	135	622	557
艺术	Art	2573	1734	3489	3064	8992	7343
体育	Physical Culture	175	36	359	166	968	260
师范	Teacher Training	859	831	835	1176	2689	3234

14-12 普通中学、职业中学、小学校舍情况
STATISTICS FOR SCHOOLHOUSES OF REGULAR SECONDARY SCHOOLS, VOCATIONAL SCHOOLS AND PRIMARY SCHOOLS

单位：万平方米 (10000 sq.m)

类别	Item	学校占地面积 Areas of Schools	校舍建筑面积 Floor Space of School-houses	教学及辅助用房 Teaching and Auxiliary Houses	行政办公用房 Administra-tive Houses	生活福利用房 Houses for Welfare and Life
合计	Total	**3977**	**1107**	**597**	**203**	**306**
城市	Urban	1181	601	317	115	168
县镇	Towns	1258	288	149	48	90
农村	Rural	1538	218	131	40	48
普通中学	**Regular Secondary Schools**	**1770**	**518**	**246**	**99**	**173**
城市	Urban	609	296	141	57	98
县镇	Towns	632	148	65	27	55
农村	Rural	529	74	40	15	20
职业中学	**Vocational Schools**	**303**	**115**	**58**	**22**	**34**
城市	Urban	136	82	42	18	21
县镇	Towns	98	23	10	3	10
农村	Rural	69	10	6	1	3
小学	**Primary Schools**	**1904**	**474**	**293**	**82**	**99**
城市	Urban	436	223	134	40	49
县镇	Towns	528	117	74	18	25
农村	Rural	940	134	85	24	25

14-13 普通中小学专任教师学历
EDUCATIONAL BACK OF FULL-TIME TEACHERS IN PRIMARY AND SECONDARY SCHOOLS

单位：人 (person)

学　历 Educational Background		高　中 Senior Middle Schools		初　中 Junior Middle Schools		小　学 Primary Schools	
		人　数 Number of Persons	构成(%) Composition(%)	人　数 Number of Persons	构成(%) Composition(%)	人　数 Number of Persons	构成(%) Composition(%)
总　计	**Total**	**11412**	**100**	**36242**	**100**	**61802**	**100**
本科毕业及以上	Undergraduate and The Level above	9323	81.7	14099	38.9	704	1.1
大专毕业	College for Professional Training	1948	17.1	18419	50.8	11409	18.5
中专毕业	Specialized Secondary School	95	0.8	2580	7.1	41728	67.5
高中及以下	Senior Middle School and the Level below	46	0.4	1144	3.2	7961	12.9

14-14 平均每万人口在校学生数
AVERAGE NUMBER OF STUDENT ENROLLMENT PER 10000 POPULATION

单位：人 (person)

类　别	Item	1998	1997
大　学	Colleges	195.6	181.0
中等职业教育	Professional Secondary Schools	271.7	245.6
普通中学	Regular Secondary Schools	560.0	578.8
小　学	Primary Schools	844.3	903.4

14-15 平均每一专任教师负担学生数
AVERAGE NUMBER OF STUDENTS INSTRUCTED BY A FULL-TIME TEACHER

单位：人 (person)

类　别	Item	1998	1997
大　学	Colleges	5.8	5.4
中等职业教育	Professional Secondary Schools	19.7	15.5
普通中学	Regular Secondary Schools	12.8	13.2
小　学	Primary Schools	14.9	15.7

14-16 小学学龄儿童入学率
ENROLLMENT RATE OF CHILDREN AT SCHOOL-AGE

单位：人 (person)

项目 Item		校内外学龄人口总数 Number of Children at School-age	# 女 Female	在校学龄人口总数 Number of Children at School-age in Schools	# 女 Female	入学率(%) Enrollment Rate(%)	# 女 Female
合计	**Total**	**873545**	**423211**	**873180**	**423026**	**99.96**	**99.96**
城市	Urban	377575	184007	377556	184000	99.99	100.00
县镇	Towns	222015	107197	221871	107112	99.94	99.92
农村	Rural	273955	132007	273753	131914	99.93	99.93

14-17 中、小学校外教育
AFTER-SCHOOL EDUCATION OF SECONDARY AND PRIMARY SCHOOLS

单位：人 (person)

项目 Item		单位数(个) Number of Units(unit)	活动小组数(个) Activities Groups(unit)	参加小组学生数 Students Join Groups	教职工人数 Staff and Workers	# 辅导员 Counselors	兼职辅导员 Part-time Counselors
总计	Total	1554	5617	85708	2836	2123	3079
少年宫	Children's Palace	17	1881	41418	965	515	274
少年科技馆(站)	Children's Scientific Museums (Centers)	9	381	11140	225	127	20
少年之家	Children's Home	37	872	16318	431	266	104
少年活动站	Children's Club	1491	2483	16832	1215	1215	2681

14-18 幼儿园基本情况
STATISTICS FOR KINDERGARTENS

单位：人 (person)

项目 Item		总计 Total	# 女 Female	城市 Urban	县镇 Towns	农村 Rural
园数 (所)	Number of Kindergartens (unit)	2662		730	510	1422
班数 (个)	Number of Classes (unit)	9109		4783	1677	2649
# 学前班	Preschool Classes	1135		387	173	575
在园幼儿数	Children Enrollment	245046	116434	134943	46772	63331
# 学前班	Preschool Classes	31885	14842	12327	4947	14611
教职工数	Teachers,Staff and Workers	30362	29010	22157	5100	3105
# 园长	Headmaster	2142	2090	1340	448	354
教师	Teachers	13841	13049	9347	2736	1758
保健员	Health Workers	1116	1113	881	156	79

14-19 各类成人教育毕业生、招生、在校学生数

NUMBER OF GRADUATES NEW STUDENTS ENROLLMENT AND STUDENTS ENROLLMENT OF ADULT EDUCATION

单位：人 (person)

类别	Item	校数(教学点)(所) Number of Schools(unit)	毕(结)业生数 Graduates	招生数 New Students Enrollment	在校学生数 Students Enrollment
高等教育	**Higher Education**		**59764**	**81253**	**227515**
广播电视大学	Radio and TV Universities	2	2058	1711	5261
职工高等学校	Schools for Staff and Workers	38	7516	11907	35160
管理干部学院	Management Colleges	30	7468	11165	23980
教育学院	Pedagogical Colleges	1	2374	1860	5805
独立函授学院	Independent Correspondence Colleges	2	734	465	2427
普通高校函授部	Correspondence Department Run by Institutions of Higher Education		25081	31778	95295
普通高校夜大学	Evening Universities Run by Institutions of Higher Education		9578	14915	44208
普通高校成人脱产班	Full Time Adult Class Run by Institutions of Higher Education		4955	7452	15379
中等专业教育	**Specialized Secondary Education**	**112**	**32274**	**16407**	**64678**
广播电视中专	Radio and TV Specialized Secondary Schools	1	9218	800	9810
职工中专学校	Specialized Secondary Schools for Staff and Workers	63	15022	9138	31006
干部中专学校	Specialized Secondary School for Cadres	8	905	1162	3001
农民中专学校	Specialized Secondary School for Peasants	16	4738	3010	12631
函授中专学校	Specialized Correspondence Secondary Schools	1	1586	1940	5520
教师进修学校	Teacher Training Schools	23	805	357	2710
中等文化教育	**Secondary Education**	**40**	**3507**	**3154**	**6347**
职工中学	Middle Schools for Staff and Workers	23	3183	2906	6023
农民中学	Middle Schools for Peasants	17	324	248	324

14-20 各类成人教育教职工数
NUMBER OF TEACHERS,STAFF AND WORKERS IN ADULT EDUCATION

单位：人 (person)

类别	Item	合计 Total 1998	1997	#专任教师 Full-time Teachers 1998	1997	#兼任教师 Part-time Teachers 1998	1997
高等教育	**Higher Education**	**20645**	**21833**	**8665**	**8874**	**4877**	**4349**
广播电视大学	Radio and TV Universities	1121	979	363	363	471	182
职工高等学校	School of Higher Education for Staff and Workers	10020	10235	4558	4645	2336	2348
管理干部学院	Management Colleges	6436	7473	2405	2645	292	318
教育学院	Pedagogical Colleges	566	578	231	238		
独立函授学院	Independent Correspondence Colleges	763	809	338	358	24	24
普通高校函授部、夜大学	Correspondence Department or Evening Universities Run by Institutions of Higher Education	1739	1759	770	625	1754	1477
中等专业教育	**Specialized Secondary Education**	**7069**	**7664**	**3188**	**3529**	**1922**	**2274**
广播电视中专	Radio and TV Specialized Secondary Schools	823	913	450	480	746	746
职工中专学校	Specialized Secondary Schools for Staff and Workers	2824	3354	1120	1393	675	766
干部中专学校	Specialized Secondary Schools for Cadres	474	441	120	138	96	134
农民中专学校	Specialized Secondary Schools for Peasants	878	910	403	424	384	614
函授中专学校	Specialized Correspondence Secondary Schools	204	204	97	97	14	14
教师进修学校	Teacher Training Schools	1866	1842	998	997	7	

14-21 民 办 学 校 基 本 情 况
STATISTICS FOR NON-STATE OWNED SCHOOLS

单位：人 (person)

类别		Item		1998	1997
普通中学		**Regular Secondary Schools**			
校　数	(个)	Number of Schools	(unit)	65	41
毕业生数		Number of Graduates		5486	2535
高　中		Senior Middle Schools		1813	1031
招生人数		New Students Enrollment		15419	7057
高　中		Senior Middle Schools		6038	4318
在校学生数		Students Enrollment		30788	16410
高　中		Senior Middle Schools		13005	8628
专任教师数		Full-time Teachers		1790	970
职业中学		**Vocational Secondary Schools**			
校　数	(个)	Number of Schools	(unit)	13	9
毕业生数		Number of Graduates		626	145
招生人数		New Students Enrollment		1241	839
在校学生数		Students Enrollment		2775	1425
专任教师数		Full-time Teachers		137	158
小　学		**Primary Schools**			
校　数	(个)	Number of Schools	(unit)	5	4
毕业生数		Number of Graduates		441	314
招生人数		New Students Enrollment		618	519
在校学生数		Students Enrollment		4732	3129
专任教师数		Full-time Teachers		515	559

14-22 公 共 图 书 馆
PUBLIC LIBRARIES

项　目 Item			总 计 Total	中央属 Central	市 属 Municipal	区县属 District and County
个　数	(个)Number	(unit)	24	1	2	21
从业人员	(人)Employment	(person)	2530	1541	237	752
总藏数	(万册、件)Total Collections	(10000 volumes)	2848	2135	302	411
# 图书	(万册、件) Books	(10000 volumes)	1246	628	235	383
建筑面积	(平方米)Floor Space of Building	(sq.m)	255579	163537	10492	81550
阅览座席	(个)Seats for Reading	(unit)	9093	2500	310	6283
外借人次	(万人次)Person-times of Lending	(10000)	189	23	10	156
外借册次	(万册次)Volume-times Lending	(10000)	433	69	21	343

14-23 档案事业基本情况
BASIC STATISTICS FOR ARCHIVES

项　目		Item		1998	1997
档案馆数	(个)	Number of Archives	**(unit)**	**20**	**22**
档案馆人数	(人)	**Number of Personal**	**(person)**	**571**	**488**
馆藏档案		Total Collections			
全　宗	(个)	Full-Records	(unit)	2066	1920
案　卷	(万卷)	Files	(10000 volumes)	240.2	234
案卷排架长度	(米)	Length of Shelf for Files	(meter)	29244	29952
建国前档案	(万卷)	Files of Pre-State-Founding	(10000 volumes)	81.4	81.4
建国后档案	(万卷)	Files of After-State-Founding	(10000 volumes)	158.8	152.6
照片档案	(张)	Photo Files	(picture)	159150	136442
音像档案	(盒)	Sounds and Pictures Files	(cassette)	5892	5988
资料	(万册)	Materials Collections	(10000 volumes)	22.1	22.4
开放档案	(万卷)	Opening Files	(10000 volumes)	84.9	54.3
馆内设备		**Facilities**			
缩微摄影机	(台)	Microcamera	(unit)	13	12
电子计算机	(台)	Computer	(unit)	176	144
复印机	(台)	Duplicator	(unit)	37	38
空调机	(台)	Air-Conditioner	(unit)	203	184
去湿机	(台)	Wet-Removing Machine	(unit)	74	64
档案馆建筑面积	**(平方米)**	**Floor Space of Archives**	**(sq.m)**	**67759**	**64147**
利用情况		**Utilization**			
利用档案	(卷件次)	Access to Files	(volume.time)	123527	238719
利用资料	(册份次)	Materials	(volume.time)	25161	15635
利用人次	(人次)	Users	(person.time)	27115	27659
编研资料	(万字)	Editing Materials	(10000 words)	408	480
机关档案工作情况		**Archives in Government Organs**			
档案室（处、科）	(个)	Department of Archives	(unit)	3623	3320
档案员	(人)	Archivists	(person)	30335	28973
案　卷	(万卷)	Files	(10000 volumes)	2144.6	1670.8
案卷排架长度	(米)	Length of Shelf for Files	(meter)	258812	238150
利用档案	(卷件次)	Access to Files	(volume.time)	1999877	1515767
利用人次	(人次)	Users	(perosn.time)	632988	534702
资　料	(万册)	Materials	(10000 volumes)	101.0	95.8

14-24 艺 术 剧 团
ART TROUPES

项目 Item		个数 (个) Number (unit)	从业人员 (人) Employment (person)	国内演出场次 (场) Domestic Performances	#农村 In Rural Areas	国内观众人数 (万人次) Domestic Spectator (10000 person. time)	总收入 (千元) Total Revenue (1000 yuan)	#演出收入 from Performances
总计	**Total**	**37**	**5388**	**8105**	**245**	**495**	**178234**	**33884**
按隶属关系分组	**Grouped by Administrative Relationship**							
中央属	Central	17	2710	1419	19	141	80053	17169
市属	Municipal	11	2309	5317	226	333	90729	13962
区县属	District and County	9	369	1369		21	7452	2753
按剧种分	**Grouped by Art Troupes**							
话剧、儿童剧团	Drama,Children's Play	5	1002	745		46	36298	2416
歌剧、舞剧、歌舞剧团	Opera,Dance Drama and Song and Dance Troupe	2	692	183	15	27	14129	4767
歌舞团、轻音乐团	Song and Dance Ensembles and Light Music Troupes	5	1418	1204		132	53526	17196
乐团	Philharmonic Troupes	4	784	399	5	39	33196	2688
文工团	Cultural Troupes	4	1078	604	300	70	30392	2351
戏曲剧团	Local Opera Troupes	12	1869	3207	146	159	59733	9058
# 京剧团	Local Beijing Opera Troupes	3	1103	1622	25	55	32338	6781
曲、杂、木、皮影剧团	Recitation and Ballad Troupe,Acrobatics and Circus Troupe,Puppet Show Troupe and Shadow Puppet Troupe	5	554	2884		149	20839	5926

注：因中铁建文工团改制，所以机构数含，其它指标均不含此单位情况。
Note: As China Railway Art Troupe reorganized, number of institutions includes it, but other indicators not includes the statistics of it.

14-25 电 影 摄 制 情 况
STATISTICS FOR FILM PRODUCTION

类别 Item		合计 Total		#长片 Long Film		#短片 Short Film	
		部 Film	本 Reel	部 Film	本 Reel	部 Film	本 Reel
合计	**Total**	**44**	**330**	**34**	**309**	**10**	**21**
故事片	Feature Film	17	149	17	149		
舞台艺术片	Stagecraft Film	8	77	8	77		
纪录片	Documentary Film	6	45	6	45		
科教片	Popular Science Film	10	21			10	21
译制片	Dubbed Film	3	38	3	38		
美术片	Puppet Film						

14-26 报纸出版情况
NEWSPAPER PUBLICATION

门类 Item		种数(种) Number of Publications	平均期印数(万份) Average Printed Copies Per Issue (10000)	总印数(万份) Total Printed Copies (10000)	总印张(千印张) Total Signatures (1000)
总计	**Total**	**247**	**3561.2**	**717019**	**13001409**
综合报	Comprehensive	46	1399.7	382110	6988359
专业报	Professional	201	2161.5	334909	6013050

14-27 杂志出版情况
MAGAZINES PUBLICATION

门类 Item		种数(种) Number of Publications	平均期印数(万册) Average Copies Per Issue (10000)	总印数(万册) Total Copies (10000)	总印张(千印张) Total Signatures (1000)
总计	**Total**	**2274**	**5797.1**	**72788.7**	**2654055.0**
综合	Comprehensive	129	876.6	11032.5	398751.0
哲学、社会科学	Philosophy and Social Sciences	545	2345.2	34002.0	1093425.3
自然科学技术	Natural Sciences and Technology	1254	1500.5	15699.2	704271.0
文化、教育	Culture and Education	191	599.8	6740.5	252338.8
文学、艺术	Literature and Art	101	238.1	2429.0	123776.0
少年儿童读物	Juvenile and Children's Books	16	176.8	2117.5	48601.0
画刊	Pictorial	38	60.0	768.0	32892.0

14-28 图书出版情况
BOOKS PUBLICATION

门类 Item		出版图书种数合计(种) Number of Publications (kind)	#新出 New Publications	总印数(万册、张) Total Copies (10000)	总印张(千印张) Total Signatures (1000)
总计	**Total**	**50155**	**31433**	**109477.4**	**8604677.9**
书籍合计	**Books**	**49553**	**30957**	**108515.4**	**8565208.9**
马列主义、毛泽东思想	Maxism-Leninism-Mao Zedong Thought	42	14	46.5	7877.3
哲学	Philosophy	518	304	509.5	61627.5
社会科学总论	General Social Sciences	611	494	525.0	71622.0
政治、法律	Politics and Law	3582	2723	6693.1	683184.1
军事	Military	272	253	263.0	28523.0
经济	Economics	4626	3530	5370.8	672821.7
文化、科学、教育、体育	Culture,Science,Education and Sports	11294	5733	63261.8	2856367.9
语言、文字	Languages	2326	1108	5486.0	856706.0
文学	Literature	5364	3983	5639.7	709629.9
艺术	Art	2201	1446	2230.3	173974.5
历史、地理	History and Geography	1847	1203	2799.4	217767.5
自然科学总论	General Natural Sciences	96	78	107.0	11949.3
数学科学、化学	Mathematics and Chemistry	1243	509	2012.5	244783.5
天文学、物理科学	Astronomy and Physics	430	378	153.0	14093.5
生物科学	Biology	311	196	167.0	24966.0
医药、卫生	Medicine and Health Care	2781	1761	2607.3	428221.1
农业科学	Agricultural Science	1716	998	1982.8	142800.6
工业技术	Industrial Technology	9140	5387	7499.2	1230028.0
交通运输	Transportation	392	280	499.6	60059.8
航空、航天	Aeronautics and Aerospace	45	45	11.0	1624.0
环境科学	Environmental Science	238	197	99.4	10571.7
综合性图书	General Books	478	337	551.2	56010.1
图片合计	**Pictures**	**602**	**476**	**962.0**	**39469.0**

14-29 电 视 台 情 况
BASIC STATISTICS ON TELEVISION STATIONS

项目		Item		1998 中央 Central	1998 地方 Local	1997 中央 Central	1997 地方 Local
基本情况		**Basic Statistics**					
电视台	(座)	Television Stations	(unit)	1	1	1	10
电视发射台、转播台	(座)	Transmission Stations and Relay Stations	(unit)	1	10	1	10
电视差转台	(座)	Transformation Stations	(unit)				
节目套数	(套)	Programs	(set)	8	12	8	12
平均每周播出时间 (按12月份第三周计算)	(时：分)	Program Hours Per Week (according to the third week of December)	(hour:minute)	1020:54	774:46	1008:30	777:00
播放节目情况		**Shows of TV Programs**					
自办节目时间	(时：分)	Self-Produced Programs	(hour:minute)	1021:54	673:46	1008:30	670:15
新闻节目	(时：分)	News Programs	(hour:minute)	177:10	103:05	147:54	94:10
专题节目	(时：分)	Special Topic Programs	(hour:minute)	317:59	104:46	343:22	108:05
教育节目	(时：分)	Educational Programs	(hour:minute)	28:45	47:14	31:15	48:40
文艺节目	(时：分)	Entertainment Programs	(hour:minute)	419:45	347:14	425:30	366:24
服务性节目	(时：分)	Service Programs	(hour:minute)	78:15	71:27	60:29	52:56

注：根据广电局精神，电视台数不包括区县电视台。
Note: Number of television stations excludes those of districts and counties.

14-30 广 播 电 台 情 况
BASIC STATISTICS ON BROADCASTING STATIONS

项目		Item		1998 中央 Central	1998 地方 Local	1997 中央 Central	1997 地方 Local
基本情况		**Basic Statistics**					
电　台	(座)	Broadcasting Stations	(unit)	2	1	2	9
发射台、转播台	(座)	Transmission Stations and Relay Stations	(unit)	5	10	5	9
节目套数	(套)	Programs	(set)	7	16	8	15
平均每日播音时间 (按12月份计算)	(时：分)	Program Hours Per Week (according to December)	(hour:minute)	320:00	174:40	295:30	156:03
播放节目情况		**Shows of TV Programs**					
自办节目时间	(时：分)	Self-Produced Programs	(hour:minute)	310:15	158:08	295:30	142:48
新闻节目	(时：分)	News Programs	(hour:minute)	85:10	14	74:46	14:35
专题节目	(时：分)	Special Topic Programs	(hour:minute)	89:05	28:15	109:00	27:00
教育节目	(时：分)	Educational Programs	(hour:minute)	26:30	19:05	6:30	16:47
文艺节目	(时：分)	Entertainment Programs	(hour:minute)	85:55	74:03	89:59	63:35
服务性节目	(时：分)	Service Programs	(hour:minute)	23:35	22:45	17:15	20:51

注：根据广电局精神，广播电台数不包括区县电台。
Note: Number of broadcasting stations excludes those of districts and counties.

14-31 文化产业活动单位情况
STATISTICS OF CULTURAL INDUSTRIAL UNITS

单位：个 (unit)

行业类别 Sector		合计 Total	按隶属关系分 Grouped by Administrative Relationship	
			地方属 Local	中央属 Central
合　　计	**Total**	**3664**	**2633**	**1031**
出版业	Publication	422	48	374
印刷业	Printing	237	159	78
图书报刊批发、零售业	Wholesale and Retail of Books and Newspapers	485	338	147
文化体育用品制造业	Stationery,Educational and Sports Goods Making	247	239	8
文化体育用品零售业	Retail of Stationery,Educational and Sports Goods	519	453	66
艺术业	Arts	86	45	41
文物保护业	Protection of Historical Relics	72	56	16
图书馆、档案馆	Libraries and Archives	42	28	14
群众文化业及其他文化业	Mass Culture and Others	173	141	32
广播电影电视业（含新闻）	Radio,Film and Television (including News)	143	95	48
体育	Sports	85	60	25
娱乐服务业	Recreational Services	269	243	26
摄影及扩印业	Photography and Large-printing	176	151	25
园林业	Parks	149	144	5
广告业	Advertisement	559	433	126

14-32 文化产业活动单位从业人员
EMPLOYMENT OF CULTURAL INDUSTRIAL UNITS

单位：人 (person)

行业类别 Sector		合计 Total	按隶属关系分 Grouped by Administrative Relationship	
			地方属 Local	中央属 Central
合　　计	**Total**	**223824**	**129142**	**94682**
出版业	Publication	36395	3747	32648
印刷业	Printing	29896	11224	18672
图书报刊批发、零售业	Wholesale and Retail of Books and Newspapers	11130	7166	3964
文化体育用品制造业	Stationery,Educational and Sports Goods Making	33335	33149	186
文化体育用品零售业	Retail of Stationery,Educational and Sports Goods	6713	5987	726
艺术业	Arts	10623	3589	7034
文物保护业	Protection of Historical Relics	5256	2053	3203
图书馆、档案馆	Libraries and Archives	4214	1432	2782
群众文化业及其他文化业	Mass Culture and Others	6589	5324	1265
广播电影电视业（含新闻）	Radio,Film and Television (including News)	21593	5836	15757
体育	Sports	8421	5359	3062
娱乐服务业	Recreational Services	13397	11900	1497
摄影及扩印业	Photography and Large-printing	4276	3562	714
园林业	Parks	21404	21187	217
广告业	Advertisement	10582	7627	2955

14-33 文化产业活动单位资产情况
ASSETS OF CULTURAL INDUSTRIAL UNITS

单位：万元 (10000 yuan)

行业类别	Sector	合计 Total	按隶属关系分 Grouped by Administrative Relationship 地方属 Local	中央属 Central
合计	**Total**	**2451432.2**	**957171.7**	**1494260.5**
出版业	Publication	460566.1	48121.2	412444.9
印刷业	Printing	249969.1	67986.6	181982.5
图书报刊批发、零售业	Wholesale and Retail of Books and Newspapers	68393.8	44035.1	24358.7
文化体育用品制造业	Stationery,Educational and Sports Goods Making	84786.6	84120.1	666.5
文化体育用品零售业	Retail of Stationery,Educational and Sports Goods	40190.1	35864.2	4325.9
艺术业	Arts	90997.5	18385.8	72611.7
文物保护业	Protection of Historical Relics	76871.1	51395.0	25476.1
图书馆、档案馆	Libraries and Archives	107806.0	17650.5	90155.5
群众文化业及其他文化业	Mass Culture and Others	108398.4	97515.8	10882.6
广播电影电视业（含新闻）	Radio,Film and Television (including News)	609830.9	127546.6	482284.3
体育	Sports	207982.1	82399.5	125582.6
娱乐服务业	Recreational Services	190850.4	166876.4	23974.0
摄影及扩印业	Photography and Large-printing	15232.9	8612.7	6620.2
园林业	Parks	73868.0	72135.8	1732.2
广告业	Advertisement	65689.2	34526.4	31162.8

14-34 文化产业活动单位创造增加值情况
VALUE ADDED OF CULTURAL INDUSTRIAL UNITS

行业类别	Sector	合计 (万元) Total (10000 yuan)	人均增加值 (元/人) Value Added Per Capita (yuan/person)
合计	**Total**	**879355.4**	**39288**
出版业	Publication	317453.2	87224
印刷业	Printing	69309.0	23183
图书报刊批发、零售业	Wholesale and Retail of Books and Newspapers	41229.3	37043
文化体育用品制造业	Stationery,Educational and Sports Goods Making	33040.6	9912
文化体育用品零售业	Retail of Stationery,Educational and Sports Goods	9671.0	14406
艺术业	Arts	23595.1	22211
文物保护业	Protection of Historical Relics	13340.1	25381
图书馆、档案馆	Libraries and Archives	15838.1	37584
群众文化业及其他文化业	Mass Culture and Others	51376.8	77974
广播电影电视业（含新闻）	Radio,Film and Television (including News)	162099.5	75070
体育	Sports	30832.7	36614
娱乐服务业	Recreational Services	2055.6	1534
摄影及扩印业	Photography and Large-printing	5907.7	13816
园林业	Parks	53310.7	24907
广告业	Advertisement	50296.0	47530

14-35 文化产业活动单位经营收入情况
OPERATING REVENUE OF CULTURAL INDUSTRIAL UNITS

单位：万元 (10000 yuan)

行业类别	Sector	合计 Total	按隶属关系分 Grouped by Administrative Relationship 地方属 Local	中央属 Central
合计	**Total**	**2842938.5**	**1121190.5**	**1721748.0**
出版业	Publication	828778.9	106757.4	722021.5
印刷业	Printing	129554.9	49409.4	80145.5
图书报刊批发、零售业	Wholesale and Retail of Books and Newspapers	348494.0	226701.1	121792.9
文化体育用品制造业	Stationery,Educational and Sports Goods Making	97613.6	96754.1	859.5
文化体育用品零售业	Retail of Stationery,Educational and Sports Goods	225253.3	202728.0	22525.3
艺术业	Arts	30830.4	6382.4	24448.0
文物保护业	Protection of Historical Relics	29356.1	7201.6	22154.5
图书馆、档案馆	Libraries and Archives	3884.5	844.0	3040.5
群众文化业及其他文化业	Mass Culture and Others	68715.4	58661.7	10053.7
广播电影电视业（含新闻）	Radio,Film and Television (including News)	664437.2	111577.0	552860.2
体育	Sports	48481.6	14714.1	33767.5
娱乐服务业	Recreational Services	82589.9	68243.2	14346.7
摄影及扩印业	Photography and Large-printing	20847.5	16772.8	4074.7
园林业	Parks	63221.1	62625.7	595.4
广告业	Advertisement	200880.1	91818.0	109062.1

14-36 文化产业活动单位人均营业收入情况
BUSINESS REVENUE PER CAPITA OF CULTURAL INDUSTRIAL UNITS

单位：元/人 (yuan/person)

行业类别	Sector	合计 Total	按隶属关系分 Grouped by Administrative Relationship 地方属 Local	中央属 Central
合计	**Total**	**127017**	**86818**	**182888**
出版业	Publication	227718	284914	221153
印刷业	Printing	43335	44021	42923
图书报刊批发、零售业	Wholesale and Retail of Books and Newspapers	313112	316357	307247
文化体育用品制造业	Stationery,Educational and Sports Goods Making	29283	29188	46210
文化体育用品零售业	Retail of Stationery,Educational and Sports Goods	335548	338614	310266
艺术业	Arts	29022	17783	34757
文物保护业	Protection of Historical Relics	55853	35078	69168
图书馆、档案馆	Libraries and Archives	9218	5894	10929
群众文化业及其他文化业	Mass Culture and Others	104288	110184	79476
广播电影电视业（含新闻）	Radio,Film and Television (including News)	307710	191187	350866
体育	Sports	57572	27457	110279
娱乐服务业	Recreational Services	61648	57347	95836
摄影及扩印业	Photography and Large-printing	48755	47088	234178
园林业	Parks	29537	29559	27438
广告业	Advertisement	189832	120385	369076

主 要 统 计 指 标 解 释

普通高等学校　指按照国家规定的设置标准和审批程序批准举办， 通过国家统一招生考试， 招收高中毕业生为主要培养对象， 实施高等教育的全日制大学、独立设置的学院和高等专科学校、短期职业大学。

成人高等学校　指按照国家有关规定审批， 招收通过全国成人高教统一招生考试的具有高中毕业或同等学历的在职从业人员，利用脱产、半脱产、业余或函授等多种形式对其实施高等学历教育， 培养高等教育专科或本科毕业水平的专门人才， 修业年限、课程设置和总学时数均按高等学历教育要求付诸实施的学校。包括广播电视大学、职工高等学校、农民高等学校、管理干部学院、教育学院、独立设置的函授学院等。

小学学龄儿童入学率　指调查范围内已入小学学习的学龄儿童占校内外学龄儿童总数（包括弱智儿童在内，但不包括聋哑儿童）的比重。计算公式：

$$小学学龄儿童入学率=\frac{已入学的小学学龄儿童数}{校内外小学学龄儿童总数}\times 100\%$$

艺术剧团　指从事戏曲、音乐、舞蹈、杂技等专业艺术表演，有独立帐户、实行独立核算的团体。不包括半工半艺和民间职业剧团。

艺术表演观众人数（人次）　指售票、包场演出或民族地区免费演出的艺术表演观众人次数。不包括彩排审查和内部观摩演出的观众人次数。

Explanatory Notes On Main Statistical Indicators

Regular Institutions of Higher Education refer to full-time universities, colleges, high professional schools and short-term professional universities set up according to the government standards and approval procedures, enrolling graduates from senior secondary schools through nation-wide unified examination and providing higher education courses and training.

Institutions of Higher Education for Adults refer to Radio and TV universities, staff colleges, peasants colleges, colleges for management cadres, educational colleges and independent correspondence colleges set up in line with relevant government policies, enrolling staff and workers with senior secondary school or equivalent education, and providing higher education courses in various forms of full-time, part-time, spare-time, or correspondence for adults. There are government regulations on various aspects for institutions of higher education for adults, such as the courses and total learning hours.

Enrollment Rate of School-Age Children refers to the proportion of primary school-age children enrolled at primary schools to the total number of primary school-age children both in and outside primary schools （including retarded children, but excluding blind, deaf and mute children）. The formula is:

$$\text{Enrollment Rate of School-age Children} = \frac{\text{Total school-age children in schools}}{\text{Total school-age children in and outside schools}} \times 100\%$$

Art Troupe refers to the troupe which is engaged in drama, opera, music, dance, acrobatics or other art performance, opens independent accounts in banks and has independent accounting system; excluding the troupes which are engaged partly in industrial or agricultural activities, partly in art performance or the non-governmental troupes.

Number of Spectators at Art Performance refers to the number of attendants at commercial shows, completely booked shows or free shows given in minority national areas, and does not include the number of spectators at rehearsals and internal shows.

1999

科 技

SCIENCE AND TECHNOLOGY

1998年专利申请及授权情况(项)
Patent Applications Examined and Certified(item)

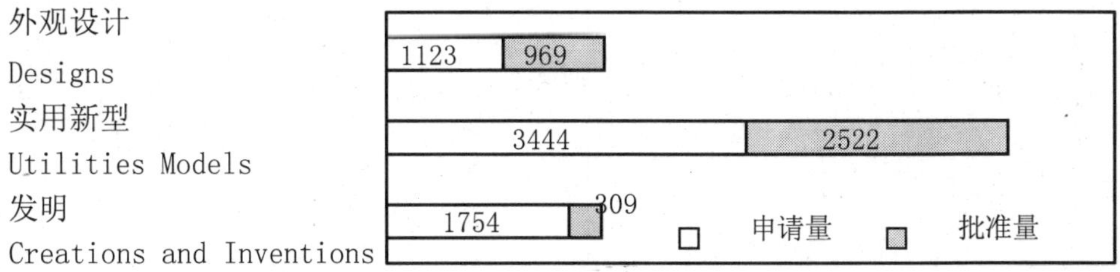

1998年国民经济各行业每万从业人员拥有专业技术人员(人)
Number of Scientific and Technical Personnel per 10000 Employment by Sectors of National Economy (person)

全 市	Total	2982
中 央	Central	3813
地 方	Local	2616

市属国有企事业单位专业技术人员（人）
Numbcr of Scientific and Teclmical Personnel in Local State-owend Enterprises and Institutions (person)

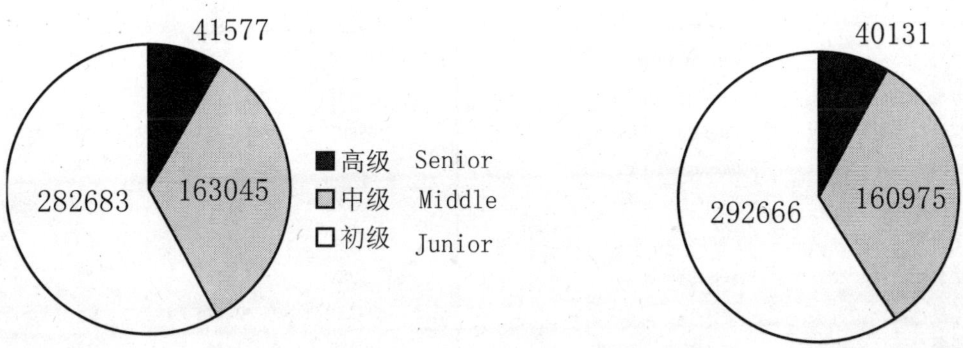

1998年　　　　1997年

15-1 国民经济各行业专业技术人员
NUMBER OF PROFESSIONAL TECHNICAL PERSONNEL BY SECTORS OF NATIONAL ECONOMY

单位：人 (person)

项目	Item	1998 全市 Total	1998 中央 Central	1998 地方 Local	1997 全市 Total
合计	**Total**	**1321559**	**516604**	**799645**	**1136750**
农、林、牧、渔业	Farming,Forestry,Animals Husbandry and Fishery	8337	931	7211	7760
采掘业	Excavation	3232	113	3109	1627
制造业	Manufacturing	224448	47409	176786	210300
电力、煤气及水的生产和供应业	Electricity,Gas and Water Production and Supply	8797	3148	5649	7472
建筑业	Construction	111948	32229	79575	96305
地质勘查业、水利管理业	Geological Prospecting and Water Conservancy	5608	3394	2204	4448
交通运输、仓储及邮电通讯业	Transportation,Storage,Posts and Telecommunications	37054	29515	7525	28600
批发和零售贸易、餐饮业	Wholesale,Retail and Catering	108146	32635	75362	81572
金融、保险业	Banking and Insurance	49347	46748	2599	51934
房地产业	Real Estate	21630	3350	18265	15181
社会服务业	Social Services	112580	31406	81055	74572
卫生、体育和社会福利业	Health Care,Sports and Social Welfare	92451	30119	61684	79928
卫生	Health Care	89959	29570	59742	77921
体育	Sports	1362	508	854	1115
社会福利保障业	Social Welfare	1130	41	1088	892
教育、文化艺术和广播电影电视业	Education,Culture and Arts and Radio,Film and Television	287586	101276	183993	256830
教育	Education	233776	57521	173938	215633
高等教育	Higher Education	67032	51219	15813	66749
中等教育	Secondary Education	84227	2913	81016	72956
初等教育	Primary Education	68524	800	65707	65008
文化艺术	Culture and Art	42379	34632	7747	32195
广播电影电视	Radio,Film and Television	11431	9123	2308	9002
科学研究和综合技术服务业	Scientific Research and Polytechnical Services	167807	117623	49746	161837
科学研究	Scientific Research	86837	79277	7560	103519
自然科学研究	Natural Science	56318	51284	5034	72178
社会科学研究	Social Science	5788	5517	271	5931
其他科学研究	Others	24731	22476	2255	25410
综合技术服务	Polytechnical Services	80970	38346	42186	58318
国家机关、政党机关和社会团体	Government Organs,Party Organs and Social Bodies	63544	25167	37730	44104
其他行业	Others	19044	11541	7152	14280

15-2 国民经济各行业每万从业人员拥有专业技术人员

NUMBER OF SCIENTIFIC AND TECHNICAL PERSONNEL PER 10000 EMPLOYMENT BY SECTORS OF NATIONAL ECONOMY

单位：人　　(person)

项　目	Item	1998 全市 Total	1998 中央 Central	1998 地方 Local	1997 全市 Total
合　计	**Total**	**2982**	**3813**	**2616**	**2380**
农、林、牧、渔业	Farming,Forestry,Animals Husbandry and Fishery	2406	5892	2240	1425
采掘业	Excavation	965	8626	935	399
制造业	Manufacturing	2083	2664	1968	1631
电力、煤气及水的生产和供应业	Electricity,Gas and Water Production and Supply	2093	2600	1888	1765
建筑业	Construction	2038	1751	2183	1549
地质勘查业、水利管理业	Geological Prospecting and Water Conservancy	3351	5432	2112	2814
交通运输、仓储及邮电通讯业	Transportation,Storage,Posts and Telecommunications	1831	2104	1215	1353
批发和零售贸易、餐饮业	Wholesale,Retail and Catering	2069	4348	1687	1426
金融、保险业	Banking and Insurance	6720	6860	4913	6898
房地产业	Real Estate	2306	2224	2322	2050
社会服务业	Social Services	2075	2715	1901	1457
卫生、体育和社会福利业	Health Care,Sports and Social Welfare	6723	7058	6573	5802
卫　生	Health Care	7210	7502	7076	6239
体　育	Sports	1632	1614	1643	1361
社会福利保障业	Social Welfare	2571	3832	2539	1914
教育、文化艺术和广播电影电视业	Education,Culture and Arts and Radio,Film and Television	6666	5910	7164	5953
教　育	Education	6898	5606	7459	6290
高等教育	Higher Education	5646	5661	5598	5389
中等教育	Secondary Education	7592	6330	7647	6616
初等教育	Primary Education	8689	8909	8687	7883
文化艺术	Culture and Art	5797	6320	4231	4650
广播电影电视	Radio,Film and Television	5883	6528	4231	4636
科学研究和综合技术服务业	Scientific Research and Polytechnical Services	5529	6439	4154	5346
科学研究	Scientific Research	6184	6235	5696	5827
自然科学研究	Natural Science	6134	6208	5468	5812
社会科学研究	Social Science	7142	7209	6009	5922
其他科学研究	Others	6105	6092	6238	5849
综合技术服务	Polytechnical Services	4966	6906	3964	4662
国家机关、政党机关和社会团体	Government Organs,Party Organs and Social Bodies	2053	1924	2148	1333
其他行业	Others	3119	3698	2513	2245

15-3 市属国有企事业单位专业技术人员
NUMBER OF SCIENTIFIC AND TECHNICAL PERSONNEL IN LOCAL STATE-OWNED ENTERPRISES AND INSTITUTIONS

单位：人 (person)

项目	Item	总计 Total	# 高级 Senior	# 中级 Middle	# 初级 Junior
总计	**Total**	**527920**	**41577**	**163045**	**282683**
工程技术人员	Engineering	128973	11080	38905	65433
农业技术人员	Agriculture	5784	269	1668	3448
科研实验人员	Scientific Research and Experimentation	3698	1046	1742	558
卫生技术人员	Health Care	69508	5152	17209	44760
教学人员	Teaching	168553	19372	65630	69927
高等教育	Higher Education	10160	3879	4155	1633
中专	Specialized Secondary Schools	10571	1338	3924	3399
中学	Secondary Schools	71709	14155	24996	25798
小学	Primary Schools	76113		32555	39097
民航人员	Aviation	8	1	4	3
船舶人员	Ship	3			2
经济人员	Economy	54223	1148	11423	36093
会计人员	Accountant	45308	462	6521	35186
统计人员	Statistician	9742	79	1982	7200
翻译人员	Translator	1356	65	673	516
图书档案人员	Librarian and Archivist	6498	235	2202	3711
新闻出版人员	News Publisher	3272	472	1232	1168
律师公证人员	Law and Notarization	307	13	88	130
播音人员	Broadcasting	161	12	44	76
工艺美术人员	Industrial Art	763	36	213	480
体育人员	Sports	844	147	330	306
艺术人员	Art	2536	477	1390	603
政工人员	Political Staff	26383	1511	11789	13083

15-4 科学研究机构及人员

SCIENTIFIC RESEARCH INSTITUTIONS AND PERSONNEL

项目	Item	机构（个）Institution (unit)	职工人数（人）Staff and Workers (person)	从事科技活动人员（人）Personnel Engaged in Scientific and Technological Activity (person)	# 大学毕业以上及具有高中级职称人员 Personnel at or above Undergraduate Level and Having Senior or Middle Title
合计	**Total**	**413**	**119762**	**73360**	**52829**
自然科学	**Natural Science**	**327**	**107377**	**64356**	**45884**
中央	Central	224	85976	54588	40059
地方	Local	103	21401	9768	5825
在自然科学研究机构中:	**Of Natural Scientific Research Institutions**				
农、林、牧、渔业	Farming,Forestry,Animals Husbandry and Fishery	26	4410	3101	2148
采掘业	Excavation	3	5011	3350	2152
制造业	Manufacturing	92	36155	18220	11666
电力、煤气及水的生产和供应业	Electricity,Gas and Water Production and Supply	4	1617	1125	818
建筑业	Construction	13	5039	3459	2526
地质勘查业、水利管理业	Geological Prospecting and Water Conservancy	12	2699	1982	1592
交通运输、仓储及邮电通信业	Transportation,Stock,Posts and Telecommunications	15	5588	3781	2993
房地产业	Real Estate	1	102	72	44
社会服务业	Social Services	13	1433	830	628
卫生、体育和社会福利业	Health Care,Sports and Social Welfares	41	16961	7822	4862
教育、文化艺术及广播电影电视业	Education,Culture,Art and Radio,Film and Television	9	774	574	399
科学研究和综合技术服务业	Scientific Research and Polytechnical Services	86	25049	18496	14970
国家机关、政党机关和社会团体	Government Organs,Party Organs and Social Bodies	8	1896	1076	739
其他行业	Others	4	643	468	347
社会科学	**Social Science**	**54**	**4997**	**4297**	**3529**
中央	Central	50	4337	3740	3084
地方	Local	4	660	557	445
在社会科学研究机构中:	**Of Social Scientific Research Institutions**				
管理学	Administration	2	175	147	130
马克思主义	Marxism	2	96	89	51
哲学	Philosophy	1	157	143	137
宗教学	Religion	1	77	74	67
语言学	Language	1	87	78	72
文学	Literature	3	287	270	261
艺术学	Art	2	617	501	296
历史学	History	4	416	380	346
考古学	Archeology	2	188	182	109
经济学	Economics	18	1385	1167	1012
政治学	Politics	3	116	101	89
法学	Law	3	196	176	153
社会学	Sociology	5	220	207	182
民族学	Ethnology	1	155	141	123
新闻学与传播学	News and Propagation	2	96	62	54
教育学	Education	3	657	543	411
统计学	Statistics	1	72	36	36
情报科学	**Intelligence Science**	**32**	**7388**	**4707**	**3416**

15-5 大中型工业企业技术开发机构和人员情况
INSTITUTIONS AND PERSONNEL OF TECHNOLOGICAL DEVELOPMENT IN LARGE AND MEDIUM INDUSTRIAL ENTERPRISES

项目	Item	企业数(个) Enterprises (unit)	技术开发机构数(个) Technological Development Institutions (unit)	企业从事技术开发人员(人) Personnel Engaged in Technological Development(person)	# 科学家和工程师 Scientists and Engineers
合计	**Total**	**511**	**285**	**37616**	**20354**
采掘业	**Excavation**	**6**	**4**	**301**	**191**
制造业	**Manufacturing**	**490**	**278**	**36337**	**19485**
食品加工业	Food Processing	26	4	146	102
食品制造业	Food Making	14	5	345	107
饮料制造业	Beverage Production	16	6	713	262
烟草加工业	Tobacco Processing	1	1	30	13
纺织业	Textile Industry	22	14	834	406
服装及其他纤维制品制造业	Garments and Other Fiber Products	17	5	77	6
皮革、毛皮、羽绒及其制品业	Leather,Furs,Down and Related Products	4	1	60	21
木材加工及竹、藤棕、草制品业	Timber Processing,Bamboo, Cane,Palm Fiber and Straw Products	2		10	6
家具制造业	Furniture Industry	1		13	6
造纸及纸制品业	Papermaking and Paper Products	7		142	100
印刷业、记录媒介的复制	Printing and Record Pressing	44	3	347	205
文教体育用品制造业	Stationery,Educational and Sports Goods	7		232	64
石油加工及炼焦业	Petroleum Processing and Coking Products	2	8	2392	1249
化学原料及化学制品制造业	Raw Chemical Materials and Chemical Products	23	15	1184	492
医药制造业	Medical and Pharmaceutical Products	13	10	635	275
化学纤维制造业	Chemical Fibers	5	2	59	41
橡胶制品业	Rubber Products	8	3	341	120
塑料制品业	Plastic Products	16	6	563	288
非金属矿物制品业	Nonmetal Mineral Products	34	20	1774	955
黑色金属冶炼及压延加工业	Smelting and Pressing of Ferrous Metals	3	3	2474	1423
有色金属冶炼及压延加工业	Smelting and Pressing of Nonferrous Metals	2	2	53	26
金属制品业	Metal Products	15	5	288	167
普通机械制造业	Ordinary Machinery	33	19	4031	2182
专用设备制造业	Special Purposes Equipment	33	25	2649	1463
交通运输设备制造业	Transportation Equipment	36	32	3730	2045
武器弹药制造业	Weapon and Ammunition	6	8	662	434
电气机械及器材制造业	Electric Equipment and Machinery	30	15	2238	1321
电子及通迅设备制造业	Electronic and Telecommunications	41	54	8740	4641
仪器仪表及文化、办公用机械制造业	Instrument,Meters,Cultural and Official Machinery	19	10	1446	989
其他制造业	Other Manufacturing	10	2	129	76
电力、煤气及水的生产和供应业	**Electricity,Gas and Water Production and Supply**	**15**	**3**	**978**	**678**
电力、蒸汽、热水的生产和供应业	Electricity,Steam and Hot Water Production and Supply	11	3	851	590
煤气生产和供应业	Gas Production and Supply	3		67	28
自来水的生产和供应业	Tap Water Production and Supply	1		60	60

15-6 大中型工业企业技术开发经费情况
FUND RAISING FOR TECHNOLOGICAL DEVELOPMENT IN LARGE AND MEDIUM INDUSTRIAL ENTERPRISES

单位：万元 (10000 yuan)

项目	Item	技术开发经费筹集 Funds of Technological Development	# 企业自筹 Self raising	技术开发经费支出 Expenses of Technological Development	# 用于开发新产品 New Products Development
合计	**Total**	**153459**	**116634**	**148891**	**60417**
采掘业	**Excavation**	**1176**	**1028**	**653**	**173**
制造业	**Manufacturing**	**149258**	**112815**	**146756**	**60229**
食品加工业	Food Processing	6246	6161	5174	2653
食品制造业	Food Making	197	112	393	79
饮料制造业	Beverage Production	3110	2629	3005	307
烟草加工业	Tobacco Processing	13	13	58	13
纺织业	Textile Industry	1982	1530	2351	1922
服装及其他纤维制品制造业	Garments and Other Fiber Products	324	304	314	121
皮革、毛皮、羽绒及其制品业	Leather,Furs,Down and Related Products	40	40	46	20
木材加工及竹、藤、棕、草制品业	Timber Processing,Bamboo, Cane,Palm Fiber and Straw Products	2	2	2	
家具制造业	Furniture Industry	10	10	10	
造纸及纸制品业	Papermaking and Paper Products	172	172	180	172
印刷业、记录媒介的复制	Printing and Record Pressing	1296	858	2105	327
文教体育用品制造业	Stationery,Educational and Sports Goods	582	507	561	163
石油加工及炼焦业	Petroleum Processing and Coking Products	10381	4980	10318	930
化学原料及化学制品制造业	Raw Chemical Materials and Chemical Products	4076	3077	4104	1703
医药制造业	Medical and Pharmaceutical Products	2562	1903	2489	608
化学纤维制造业	Chemical Fibers	80	58	58	
橡胶制品业	Rubber Products	561	521	551	502
塑料制品业	Plastic Products	1497	1182	1513	1341
非金属矿物制品业	Nonmetal Mineral Products	8788	3755	10687	2432
黑色金属冶炼及压延加工业	Smelting and Pressing of Ferrous Metals	15427	9338	14781	1384
有色金属冶炼及压延加工业	Smelting and Pressing of Nonferrous Metals	400	245	536	162
金属制品业	Metal Products	110	96	141	103
普通机械制造业	Ordinary Machinery	5772	5104	5574	2906
专用设备制造业	Special Purposes Equipment	6333	4793	6578	3077
交通运输设备制造业	Transportation Equipment	19181	16177	18184	10996
武器弹药制造业	Weapon and Ammunition	1507	137	1157	722
电气机械及器材制造业	Electric Equipment and Machinery	5766	4528	6017	4384
电子及通迅设备制造业	Electronic and Telecommunications	45855	40166	43544	19841
仪器、仪表及文化、办公用机械制造业	Instrument,Meters,Cultural and Official Machinery	5967	4103	5974	3030
其他制造业	Other Manufacturing	1021	314	351	331
电力、煤气及水的生产和供应业	**Electricity,Gas and Water Production and Supply**	**3025**	**2791**	**1482**	**15**
电力、蒸汽、热水的生产和供应业	Electricity,Steam and Hot Water Production and Supply	1771	1537	909	15
煤气生产和供应业	Gas Production and Supply	922	922	527	
自来水的生产和供应业	Tap Water Production and Supply	332	332	46	

15-7 技术合同签定及执行情况

CONCLUSION AND IMPLEMENTATION OF TECHNICAL CONTRACTS

项目	Item	签定合同数(项) Contracts Concluded (item)		合同金额(万元) Amount of Contracts (10000 yuan)	
		1998	1997	1998	1997
合计	**Total**	**20724**	**13866**	**815591.2**	**543191.7**
按合同类别分类	**Grouped by Type**				
技术开发合同	Technological Development	3609	2391	250149.9	206802.8
技术转让合同	Technology Transfer	3753	2735	158530.5	89878.0
技术咨询合同	Technical Consultation	1850	1630	36335.7	40369.6
技术服务合同	Technical Service	11512	7110	370575.1	206141.3
按合同卖方类别分类	**Grouped by Type of Seller**				
科研机构	Scientific Research Institutions	12647	8090	416830.4	291378.0
高等院校	Institutions of Higher Education	1911	511	49872.7	15122.4
工业企业	Industrial Enterprises	337	263	46862.1	13162.9
技术贸易机构	Technology Trade Institution	1839	1364	48734.1	50127.9
个人及个人合伙	Individual and Individual Partnership	88	254	2530.1	1551.4
其他	Others	3902	3384	250761.8	171849.1
按合同买方类别分类	**Grouped by Type of Buyer**				
工业企业	Industrial Enterprises	11067	6215	463984.4	250679.2
科研机构	Scientific Research Institutions	2533	1604	92689.7	67387.3
各级管理部门	Management Departments	1452	1261	86538.7	75974.9
技术贸易机构	Technology Trade Institution	1137	766	58441.8	38822.9
个人及个人合伙	Individual and Individual Partnership	734	388	1380.9	312.5
其他	Others	3801	3632	112555.7	110014.9
按服务社会经济目标分类	**Grouped by Social and Economic Service Objection**				
陆地、海洋和大气的开发与估价	Development and Appraisal of Lands,Seas and Atmosphere	62	83	9012.0	6112.2
民用宇宙空间	Civil Universal Space	278	65	7694.1	2424.5
农业、林业和渔业的发展	Development of Agriculture, Forestry and Fishery	694	273	27070.8	3869.1
促进工业的发展	Promoting Industrial Development	6607	5394	235423.7	201008.5
能源的生产、储存和分配	Production,Stockpile and Distribution of Energy	1566	584	68960.5	41199.0
交通、通讯事业的发展	Development of Transportation and Telecommunication	2131	1332	123677.3	80904.7
教育事业的发展	Development of Education	102	113	8236.1	1365.2
卫生事业的发展	Development of Health Care	957	601	21279.1	10830.8
社会发展和社会经济服务	Social Development and Economic Service	5493	3011	179582.6	74376.0
环境保护	Environmental Protextion	846	370	10010.6	9873.7
知识的全面发展	All-round Development of Knowledge	85	67	4258.5	1519.3
其他目标	Others	1689	1855	86485.2	83851.9
国防	National Defense	214	118	33900.7	25856.8
按技术流向分类	**Grouped by Spread Area**				
北京	Beijing	8684	6594	338420.6	275510.2
外地	Outside Beijing	12040	7272	477170.6	267681.5

15-8 科学技术协会及所属学会工作情况
BASIC STATISTICS OF SCIENCE AND TECHNOLOGY ASSOCIATION AND SUBORDINATE INSTITUTES

项目		Item		合计 Total	市科协 Municipal Science and Technology Association	市级学会 Institutes at Municipal Level
机构与人员		**Institutions and Personnel**				
机　构	(个)	Institutions	(unit)	147	1	146
人　员	(人)	Personnel	(person)	247466	54	247412
学术交流		**Academic Exchange**				
国内学术会议	(次)	Domestic Academic Meeting	(time)	574	8	566
参加人数	(人次)	Participants	(person.time)	44437	725	43712
交流论文	(篇)	Papers Presented	(article)	9100	264	8836
国际学术会议	(次)	International Academic Meeting	(time)	64	2	62
参加人数	(人次)	Participants	(person.time)	5814	300	5514
交流论文	(篇)	Papers Presented	(article)	1899	86	1813
民间科技交流		**Non-governmental Scientific and Technological Exchange**				
出国科学考察	(人次)	Scientific Visit abroad	(person.time)	119	80	39
出国参加国际会议	(人次)	Scientific Meeting abroad	(person.time)	120	27	93
出国参加技贸活动	(人次)	Technology Trade abroad	(person.time)	9	9	
外派科技研修生	(人次)	Study abroad	(person.time)	20	18	2
接待海外科技团组	(个)	Foreign Scientific and Technological Visit	(unit)	93	22	71
接待人次	(人次)	Participants	(person.time)	541	151	390
举办国际学术报告	(场)	International Academic Meeting	(unit)	121	13	108
听报告人次	(人次)	Participants	(person.time)	8643	1120	7523
科学普及		**Scientific Promoting**				
科普讲座	(次)	Lectures	(time)	402	70	332
参加人次	(人次)	Participants	(person.time)	143227	5364	137863
科普展览	(次)	Exhibitions	(time)	83	3	80
参观人次	(人次)	Participants	(person.time)	531510	103200	428310
科技培训		**Training Program**				
培训班数	(个)	Classes	(time)	374	56	318
培训人数	(人次)	Participants	(person.time)	25045	2536	22509
科技咨询服务		**Consultative Services**				
完成咨询合同	(项)	Contracts Completed	(item)	1299	652	647
咨询合同实现金额	(万元)	Contracts Revenue	(10000 yuan)	23160	22036	1124
无偿咨询项目	(项)	Free Consultative Project	(item)	1178	60	1118
决策合同	(项)	Contracts of Concluded	(item)	71	1	70
青少年科技活动		**Activity of Teenagers Science Technology**				
科技夏(冬)令营	(个)	Summer/Winter Science and Technology Camp	(time)	39	11	28
参加人数	(人次)	Participants	(person.time)	7144	814	6330
青少年科技竞赛	(个)	Science and Technology Competetions	(unit)	48	12	36
参加人数	(人次)	Participants	(person.time)	871135	653000	218135

15-9 专利申请及授权情况
PATENT APPLICATIONS EXAMINED AND CERTIFIED

单位：项 (item)

项目 Item		申请量 Total Applications Examined		批准量 Total Applications Certified	
		1998	1997	1998	1997
合计	**Total**	**6321**	**6313**	**3800**	**3327**
按种类分	**Grouped by Type**				
发明	Creations and Inventions	1754	1678	309	281
实用新型	Utility Models	3444	3667	2522	2340
外观设计	Designs	1123	968	969	706
按对象分	**Grouped by Applicator**				
工矿企业	Industrial and Mineral Enterprises	1252	1230	749	622
大专院校	Universities and Colleges	263	223	141	117
科研单位	Scientific Research Institution	547	636	373	381
机关团体	Government Organs and Associations	31	33	80	92
个人	Individuals	4228	4191	2457	2115

15-10 监督抽查北京地区产品质量情况(按企业规模分)
SPOT TEST SITUATION OF PRODUCTS QUALITY(BY SIZE OF ENTERPRISES)

企业规模 Size		抽查企业数(个) Number of Enterprises Spot Test (number)	合格企业数(个) Number of Passed Enterprises (number)	企业合格率(%) Passed Rate of Enterprises (%)	抽查产品种数(种) Kinds of Products Spot Test (number)	合格产品种数(种) Kinds of Passed Products (number)	产品合格率(%) Passed Rate of Products (%)
大型企业	Large	43	39	90.7	52	48	92.3
中型企业	Medium	91	76	83.5	116	101	87.1
小型企业	Small	269	185	68.8	341	251	73.6

15-11 计量器具检定情况
STATISTICS FOR MEASURING IMPLEMENTS TEST

单位：台、件、套 (unit)

地区 Region		合计 Total	长度 Length	温度 Temperature	力学 Mechanics	# 衡器 Weighing Apparatus	电学 Electricity	光学 Optics	声学 Acoustics	化学 Chemistry	电离辐射 Ionization Radiation	无线电 Radio	时间频率 Time Frequency	其他 Other
总计	**Total**	**691993**	**127669**	**27034**	**418224**	**68110**	**59324**	**2554**	**292**	**3355**	**852**	**1799**	**917**	**49973**
市属小计	**Municipal**	**188895**	**25775**	**1768**	**150829**	**630**	**3922**	**1321**	**240**	**2441**	**852**	**830**	**917**	
区县属小计	**District and County**	**503098**	**101894**	**25266**	**267395**	**67480**	**55402**	**1233**	**52**	**914**		**969**		**49973**
东城区	Dongcheng	46233	25279	77	17809	2422	2566							502
西城区	Xicheng	56781	28858	327	24295	4408	2509			373		419		
崇文区	Chongwen	16915	3442	562	11584	1310	1327							
宣武区	Xuanwu	35700	8258	13088	11202	2514	3152							
朝阳区	Chaoyang	70539	6427	2663	24954	6996	4512							31983
丰台区	Fengtai	21759	1813	541	18680	2378						140		585
石景山区	Shijingshan	8218	732	2115	5329	2542		42						
海淀区	Haidian	44665	3806	400	34966	7493	1786	1081		351		410		1865
门头沟区	Mentougou	15506	1178		13960		148							220
房山区	Fangshan	65774	4430	1493	16899	7679	31125							11827
通州区	Tongzhou	32553	5231	1318	22676	8314	3064							264
昌平县	Changping	21130	1300	450	19230	5207				150				
顺义县	Shunyi	15532	6029	974	7117	946	1412							
大兴县	Daxing	11496	821	281	7598	2017	80	59						2657
平谷县	Pinggu	9925	1028	450	7999	4624	330	26	52	40				
怀柔县	Huairou	10596	559		9599	1915	343	25						70
密云县	Miyun	16657	2352	406	10906	5566	2993							
延庆县	Yanqing	3119	351	121	2592	1149	55							

主 要 统 计 指 标 解 释

专业技术人员 指已取得专业技术职称，或大学、中专毕业，以及从工作实践中提拔， 从事研究、教学、生产的专业人员和在机关、企业、事业中从事管理工作的专业人员。

工程技术人员 指从事工程技术工作的专业技术人员，包括：高级工程师、工程师、助理工程师、技术员和未评定职称的技术人员。

农业技术人员 指从事农业技术工作的专业技术人员， 包括：高级农艺师、农艺师、助理农艺师、技术员和未评定职称的技术人员。

发明 指专利法及其实施细则所称的发明， 指对有关产品、方法或其改进所提出的新的技术方案。

实用新型 指专利法及其实施细则所称的实用新型，指对产品的形状、构造或者其结合所提出的适于实用的新的技术方案。

外观设计 指专利法及其实施细则所称的外观设计，指对产品的形状、图案、色彩或者其结合所作出的富有美感并适于工业上应用的新设计。

Explanatory Notes On Main Statistical Indicators

Professional and Technical Personnel refers to those professionals with technical titles, or those being graduated from colleges and specialized secondary schools, or those being promoted in practice and working on research, teaching and production , or the professionals doing administrative work in government agencies, enterprises and institutions.

Engineering Professionals refer to the persons who are engaged in engineering science and technology, including senior engineers, engineers, assistant engineers, technicians and technical personnel without professional titles.

Agricultural Professionals refer to the persons who are working on the science of agriculture, including senior agronomists, agronomists, assistant agronomists, technicians and technical personnel without professional titles.

Inventions refer to the inventions as specified by the patent law and its detailed rules and regulations for implementation, including the new technical proposals or modifications for products or the methods.

Utility Models refer to the utility models as specified by the patent law and its detailed rules and regulations for implementation, including the practical and new technical proposals on the shape and structure of the product or the combination of both .

External Form Design refer to the external form design specified by the patent law and its detailed rules and regulations for implementation, including the practical and new technical proposals on the structure, shape and color of the product or the combination of them.

1999

卫生、体育

HEALTH AND SPORTS

卫　　生　Health

		1998	1997
卫生事业机构 Health Care Institutions	（个） (unit)	5723	6577
床位 Beds	（张） (unit)	69095	67946
卫生技术人员 Medical Technical Personnel	（人） (person)	115976	119256
平均每千人拥有医生 Doctors per 1000 persons	（人） (person)	4.76	5.06

体　育　Sports

1998年		
创世界及纪录 World Records	（项） (item)	3
破全国纪录 National Records	（项） (item)	2

16-1 医疗卫生机构基本情况
BASIC STATISTICS FOR INSTITUTIONS OF PUBLIC HEALTH

项目 Item			1998	1997	构成(%) Composition(%) 1998	1997
卫生事业机构	**(个)Health Care Institutions**	**(unit)**	**5723**	**6577**	**100**	**100**
# 医 院	(个) Hospitals	(unit)	676	673	11.8	10.2
门诊部	(个) Clinics	(unit)	194	170	3.4	2.6
诊所、卫生保健所、医务室	(个) Clinics and Health Stations	(unit)	4613	5490	80.6	83.5
疗养院	(个) Sanitariums	(unit)	7	6	0.1	0.1
卫生防疫站	(个) Sanitation and Antiepidemic Stations	(unit)	22	22	0.4	0.3
妇幼保健所、站	(个) Maternity and Child Care Centers	(unit)	11	13	0.2	0.2
专科防治所、站	(个) Specialized Stations	(unit)	42	42	0.7	0.6
床 位	**(张)Beds**	**(unit)**	**69095**	**67946**	**100**	**100**
# 医 院	(张) Hospitals	(unit)	66954	65826	96.9	96.9
门诊部	(张) Clinics	(unit)	96	68	0.1	0.1
疗养院、所	(张) Sanitariums	(unit)	1219	1320	1.8	1.7
平均每千人拥有医院床位	(张) Hospital Beds per 1000 Population	(unit)	6.13	6.06		
卫生技术人员	**(人)Medical Technical Personnel**	**(person)**	**115976**	**119256**	**100**	**100**
医 生	(人) Doctors	(person)	51902	54909	44.8	46.0
护师(士)	(人) Senior and Junior Nurses	(person)	38883	38630	33.5	32.4
平均每千人拥有医生	(人) Doctors per 1000 Population	(person)	4.76	5.06		
平均每千人拥有护士	(人) Nurses per 1000 Population	(person)	3.56	3.56		

注：本表中医院包括县及县以上医院、其他医院和乡镇卫生院。（16-2、16-4表中医院不含乡镇卫生院）

Note：Hospitals of this table included those at county level and above，other hospitals and township hospitals. (hospitals of table 16-2、16-4 excluded township hospitals)

16-2 农村医疗卫生机构基本情况
HEALTH INSTITUTIONS IN RURAL AREA

项目 Item			1998	1997	构成(%) Composition(%) 1998	1997
卫生事业机构	**(个)Health Care Institutions**	**(unit)**	**1107**	**1587**	**100**	**100**
# 医 院	(个) Hospitals	(unit)	84	79	7.6	5.0
乡(镇)卫生院	(个) Township Hospitals	(unit)	157	166	14.2	10.5
床 位	**(张)Beds**	**(unit)**	**13845**	**13224**	**100**	**100**
# 医 院	(张) Hospitals	(unit)	11066	10566	79.9	79.7
乡(镇)卫生院	(张) Township Hospitals	(unit)	2229	2373	16.1	17.9
卫生技术人员	**(人)Medical Technical Personnel**	**(person)**	**19001**	**19167**	**100**	**100**
# 医 生	(人) Doctors	(person)	9534	9552	50.2	49.8
护师(士)	(人) Senior and Junior Nurses	(person)	5293	5142	27.9	26.8
乡村医生和卫生员	**(人)Doctors and Health Workers**	**(person)**	**5972**	**6132**	**100**	**100**
# 会接生的	(人) Midwife	(person)	604	678	10.1	11.1
乡村医生	(人) Doctors	(person)	5480	5327	91.8	86.9
卫生员	(人) Health Workers	(person)	492	805	8.2	13.1

16-3 全市各饮食单位食品卫生合格率情况
FOOD QUALIFIED RATE OF FOOD AND BEVERAGE DEALERS

单位：%　　(%)

地区	Region	合计 Total	生产加工业 Processing	批发零售业 Wholesale and Retail	饮食服务业 Catering Services	集体食堂 Canteen	食品摊贩 Food Street Pedlar
合计	**Total**	**85.8**	**90.5**	**92.9**	**83.1**	**88.1**	**83.6**
东城区	Dongcheng	94.3	88.5	93.5	90.5	95.5	98.9
西城区	Xicheng	71.7	100.0	82.4	65.9	79.9	66.3
崇文区	Chongwen	96.7	97.8	98.9	90.5	99.8	98.9
宣武区	Xuanwu	87.2	79.6	89.9	79.1	86.7	90.8
朝阳区	Chaoyang	89.8	76.3	86.5	80.6	85.7	92.0
丰台区	Fengtai	75.4	85.3	94.3	86.3	78.7	63.4
石景山区	Shijingshan	92.5	91.7	96.2	88.0	96.8	93.1
海淀区	Haidian	63.4	64.2	80.2	50.5	79.6	63.2
门头沟区	Mentougou	95.2	79.3	97.7	93.6	96.6	95.8
房山区	Fangshan	97.7	94.8	98.9	97.1	99.3	97.0
通州区	Tongzhou	95.7	95.0	96.9	94.1	96.7	94.6
昌平县	Changping	90.9	95.4	92.3	94.2	94.0	87.8
顺义县	Shunyi	98.7	95.4	99.1	99.1	97.8	99.0
大兴县	Daxing	92.9	95.5	92.0	93.8	95.5	91.6
平谷县	Pinggu	98.4	98.9	95.6	98.2	98.1	98.4
怀柔县	Huairou	91.8	94.6	92.1	88.1	94.5	93.1
密云县	Miyun	83.4	84.7	84.3	82.0	91.9	80.9
延庆县	Yanqing	86.8	78.4	93.0	83.3	86.2	82.3

16-4 全市医院基本情况
BASIC STATISTICS FOR HOSPITALS

项目	Item	医院数 (个) Hospitals (unit)	床位数 (张) Beds Workers (unit)	职工人数 (人) Staff and Workers (person)	#卫生技术人员 Medical Technical Personal	中医师 Doctors of Chinese Medicine	西医师 Junior of Western Medicine	中医士 Junior Doctors of Chinese Medicine
总计	**Total**	**449**	**63144**	**116470**	**86967**	**4229**	**27674**	**200**
县及县以上医院	**Hospitals at and above County Level**	**270**	**55976**	**105065**	**78265**	**3614**	**25052**	**123**
城市	Urban	208	45699	90897	67386	3092	21551	71
农村	Rural	62	10277	14168	10879	522	3501	52
其他医院	**Others**	**179**	**7168**	**11405**	**8702**	**615**	**2622**	**77**
在县及县以上医院中	**Of Hospitals at and above County Level**							
综合医院	Comprehensive Hospitals	193	34864	67699	50745	1250	17664	49
中医医院	Hospitals of Chinese Medicine	22	3844	8254	6227	1680	789	59
医学院校附属医院	Hospitals Attached to Medical College	9	4906	11085	8500	489	2605	
传染病院	Infectious Disease Hospitals	3	1034	1516	1125	12	307	
精神病院	Mental Hospitals	7	3881	2514	1749	16	403	1
结核病院	Tuberculosis Hospitals	1	533	589	432		120	
妇幼保健院	Hospitals for Maternity and Child Care	9	482	1261	1041	9	447	
妇产医院	Hospitals for Gynecology and Obstetrics	2	440	1056	726	6	158	1
儿童医院	Children's Hospitals	4	1030	2736	2087	34	662	
职业病院	Hospitals for Occupational Diseases	1	372	266	130	3	36	
肿瘤医院	Tumor Hospitals	3	1340	2168	1362	6	460	
康复医院	Recovery Hospital	5	885	1320	744	25	198	2
口腔医院	Stomatological Hospitals	1	80	645	449		210	
骨科医院	Hospitals of Orthopedics	2	360	679	488	23	158	3
整形医院	Plastically Hospitals	1	328	479	288	3	93	
中西医结合医院	Hospitals Which Integrate Traditional Chinese Therapeutics with tics in Practices	2	343	578	483	44	155	2
其他专科医院	Other Specialized Hospitals	5	1254	2220	1689	14	587	6

16-4 续表 continued

项 目 Item		西医士 Junior Doctors of Western Medicine	中西医结合医师 Doctors Who Integrate Traditional Chinese Therapeutics with Western Therapeutics in Practice	其他中医 Other Doctors of Chinese Me-	药 师 Pharmacists	检验师 Laboratory Technicians	助产士 Midwives	护师(士) Senior and Junior Nurses
总 计	**Total**	**2395**	**333**	**73**	**4955**	**2719**	**258**	**34827**
县及县以上医院	**Hospitals at and above County Level**	**1682**	**301**	**40**	**4307**	**2453**	**254**	**32373**
城 市	Urban	1157	293	19	3702	2141	217	27993
农 村	Rural	525	8	21	605	312	37	4380
其他医院	**Others**	**713**	**32**	**33**	**648**	**266**	**4**	**2454**
在县及县以上医院中	**Of Hospitals at and above County Level**							
综合医院	Comprehensive Hospitals	1286	53	11	2776	1696	117	21124
中医医院	Hospitals of Chinese Medicine	119	169	23	603	156	20	1975
医学院校附属医院	Hospitals Attached to Medical College	2	59	6	419	169	4	3470
传染病院	Infectious Disease Hospitals	9	1		56	97	13	517
精神病院	Mental Hospitals	20			60	33		1058
结核病院	Tuberculosis Hospitals				15	16		244
妇幼保健院	Hospitals for Maternity and Child Care	61	2		44	42	31	351
妇产医院	Hospitals for Gynecology and Obstetrics	71	1		13	23	64	313
儿童医院	Children's Hospitals	10	9		131	72		982
职业病院	Hospitals for Occupational Diseases	11			7	9		51
肿瘤医院	Tumor Hospitals	7	2		30	34		629
康复医院	Recovery Hospital	9	1		32	23		319
口腔医院	Stomatological Hospitals				13	8		129
骨科医院	Hospitals of Orthopedics	49			26	14	1	156
整形医院	Plastically Hospitals				6	4		145
中西医结合医院	Hospitals Which Integrate Traditional Chinese Therapeutics with tics in Practices	9	4		30	15	4	199
其他专科医院	Other Specialized Hospitals	19			46	42		711

16-5 医院、卫生院工作情况
WORKS OF HOSPITALS

项目 Item		机构数 (个) Institutions (unit)	诊疗人次数 (人次) Patients Treated (person.time)	#门诊 (人次) Out-patients (person.time)	健康检查人数 (人) Health Check (person)	平均开放病床数 (张) Beds in Use (unit)	入院人数 (人) In-patients (person)
合计	**Total**	**664**	**53453305**	**47437759**	**1545727**	**61799**	**761283**
县及县以上医院合计	**Hospitals at and above County Level**	**270**	**43054233**	**37928542**	**1010028**	**52367**	**653644**
卫生部门医院合计	Hospitals of Health Care Department	111	28448922	25295444	478051	34665	488864
综合医院	Comprehensive Hospitals	48	15627741	13491761	264616	17203	291395
# 县医院	Countyship Hospitals	18	3056083	2652749	74283	3790	86125
中医医院	Hospitals of Chinese Medicine	18	3402291	3166282	35492	3338	35284
医学院校附属医院	Hospitals Attached to Medical College	9	5361204	4830707	17924	4977	83319
传染病院	Infectious Disease Hospitals	3	135937	130079	1711	1021	6639
精神病院	Mental Hospitals	5	189598	186136	5445	2500	3679
结核病院	Tuberculosis Hospitals	1	37179	36504	370	578	2916
妇幼保健院	Hospitals for Maternity and Child Care	9	449840	405276	116612	425	12063
妇产医院	Hospitals for Gynecology and Obstetrics	2	293633	287645	1826	439	9060
儿童医院	Children's Hospitals	4	1855325	1720564	5580	918	17491
肿瘤医院	Tumor Hospitals	2	204920	197984	11466	1083	9992
康复医院	Recovery Hospitals	2	27972	24836	1500	374	589
口腔医院	Stomatological Hospitals	1	331587	322898		80	622
整形医院	Plastically Hospitals	1	18185	18032	139	328	2339
中西医结合医院	Hospitals Which Integrate Traditional Chinese Therapeutics with Western Therapeutics in Practices	1	274821	250130	12471	234	3568
其他专科医院	Other Specialized Hospitals	5	238689	226610	2899	1167	9908
工业及其他部门医院	Hospitals of Industry and Other Departments	150	13512841	11651488	498008	16143	151435
集体所有制医院	Collective-Owned Hospitals	9	1092470	981610	33969	1559	13345
其他医院合计	**Other Hospitals**	**168**	**4910231**	**4342578**	**215619**	**6088**	**39401**
卫生院合计	**Total Township Hospitals**	**226**	**5488841**	**5166639**	**320080**	**3344**	**68238**

16-5 续表 continued

项目	Item	出院人数(人) Leaving Hospital (person)	治愈率(%) Recovering Rate (%)	好转率(%) Mending Rate (%)	病死率(%) Rate of Death of Illness (%)	病床周转次数(次) Turnover Beds (times)	病床使用率(%) Utilization Rate (%)	出院者平均住院日(日) Average Hospitalization Period (day)
合计	**Total**	**745588**	**61.5**	**32.3**	**2.6**	**12.1**	**69.9**	**19.9**
县及县以上医院合计	**Hospitals at and above County Level**	**645041**	**61.0**	**32.5**	**2.7**	**12.3**	**73.7**	**20.9**
卫生部门医院合计	Hospitals of Health Care Department	482418	60.3	33.0	2.5	13.9	80.3	20.7
综合医院	Comprehensive Hospitals	285584	60.8	32.8	2.6	16.6	81.3	17.8
# 县医院	Countyship Hospitals	80512	64.0	30.7	1.7	21.2	72.2	12.0
中医医院	Hospitals of Chinese Medicine	34736	44.7	47.9	3.6	10.4	71.0	24.8
医学院校附属医院	Hospitals Attached to Medical College	83156	61.9	30.7	2.4	16.7	86.6	18.6
传染病院	Infectious Disease Hospitals	6635	59.6	28.6	6.1	6.5	53.7	30.5
精神病院	Mental Hospitals	3799	36.8	57.9	1.7	1.5	101.2	226.0
结核病院	Tuberculosis Hospitals	2961	21.6	50.5	6.2	5.1	71.3	52.9
妇幼保健院	Hospitals for Maternity and Child Care	12047	98.1	1.5	0.1	28.4	61.0	7.4
妇产医院	Hospitals for Gynecology and Obstetrics	9058	88.6	9.5	0.3	20.6	79.4	13.0
儿童医院	Children's Hospitals	17466	66.2	29.1	1.0	19.0	75.9	14.2
肿瘤医院	Tumor Hospitals	10004	52.4	35.7	3.2	9.2	96.7	36.6
康复医院	Recovery Hospitals	596	35.4	57.2	2.8	1.6	20.7	37.2
口腔医院	Stomatological Hospitals	623	87.5	12.3		7.8	44.1	20.8
整形医院	Plastically Hospitals	2359	92.7	7.0		7.2	54.7	28.2
中西医结合医院	Hospitals Which Integrate Traditional Chinese Therapeutics with Western Therapeutics in Practices	3517	54.6	40.6	2.2	15.0	77.2	18.7
其他专科医院	Other Specialized Hospitals	9877	44.1	46.9	3.1	8.5	72.8	31.6
工业及其他部门医院	Hospitals of Industry and Other Departments	149300	63.1	30.9	3.1	9.3	60.6	21.3
集体所有制医院	Collective-Owned Hospitals	13323	61.4	33.1	3.3	8.6	64.2	23.8
其他医院合计	**Other Hospitals**	**32544**	**47.8**	**42.4**	**5.1**	**5.4**	**51.2**	**25.9**
卫生院合计	**Total Township Hospitals**	**68003**	**72.4**	**25.5**	**0.3**	**20.3**	**43.3**	**7.1**

16-6 全市居民前十位死因顺位、死亡率及构成
DEATH RATE AND COMPOSITION OF 10 MAJOR DISEASE

顺 位 No.	死因名称	Cause of Death	死亡率 (1/10万) Death Rate (1/100 thousand)	构 成 (%) Composition (%)
	全 市	**Total**		
1	脑血管病	Cerebrovasular Disease	179.1	26.7
2	心脏病	Heart Trouble	151.2	22.6
3	恶性肿瘤	Malignant Tumour	116.6	17.4
4	呼吸系病	Respiratory Disease	85.9	12.8
5	损伤和中毒	Trauma and Toxicosis	37.9	5.7
6	内分泌、营养、代谢及免疫病	Internal System,Nutrition,Metabolite and Immunity Disease	20.0	3.0
7	消化系病	Gigestive Disease	17.1	2.6
8	泌尿生殖系病	Urinary Disease	10.5	1.6
9	神经系病	Neuropathy	5.9	0.9
10	传染病	Infection Disease	4.5	0.7
	市	**Districts**		
1	脑血管病	Cerebrovasular Disease	163.8	24.5
2	心脏病	Heart Trouble	161.1	24.1
3	恶性肿瘤	Malignant Tumour	130.4	19.5
4	呼吸系病	Respiratory Disease	79.9	12.0
5	损伤和中毒	Trauma and Toxicosis	29.9	4.5
6	内分泌、营养、代谢及免疫病	Internal System,Nutrition,Metabolite and Immunity Disease	23.1	3.5
7	消化系病	Gigestive Disease	19.6	2.9
8	泌尿生殖系病	Urinary Disease	11.0	1.6
9	传染病	Infection Disease	6.9	1.0
10	神经系病	Neuropathy	4.9	0.7
	县	**Counties**		
1	脑血管病	Cerebrovasular Disease	212.6	31.6
2	心脏病	Heart Trouble	129.7	19.3
3	呼吸系病	Respiratory Disease	98.9	14.7
4	恶性肿瘤	Malignant Tumour	86.2	12.8
5	损伤和中毒	Trauma and Toxicosis	55.4	8.2
6	内分泌、营养、代谢及免疫病	Internal System,Nutrition,Metabolite and Immunity Disease	13.1	1.9
7	消化系病	Gigestive Disease	11.5	1.7
8	泌尿生殖系病	Urinary Disease	9.3	1.4
9	传染病	Infection Disease	3.9	0.6
10	先天异常	Congenital Abnormality	3.5	0.5

16-7 全市0-6岁儿童系统管理情况
STATISTICS FOR SYSTEMATIC CARE OF CHILDREN AT AGE 0-6

地区 Region		0-6岁儿童数(人) Number of Children at Age 0-6 (person)	系统管理人数(人) Children under Systematic Care (person)	体检人数(人) Children Having Health Check (person)	0～2岁儿童佝偻病患病率(%) Suffering Rate from Rickets of Children at Age 0-2 (%)	0～2岁儿童贫血患病率(%) Suffering Rate from Amenia of Children at Age 0-2 (%)	3～6岁儿童贫血患病率(%) Suffering Rate from Amenia of Children at Age 3-6 (%)	0～6岁儿童系统管理覆盖率(%) Covering Rate of Systematic Care of Children at Age 0-6 (%)
合计	**Total**	**508086**	**460594**	**449754**	**1.01**	**5.25**	**1.91**	**95.63**
东城区	Dongcheng	21414	17773	17751	0.11	4.22	0.51	100
西城区	Xicheng	24762	21708	21642	0.04	5.76	0.72	99.28
崇文区	Chongwen	13597	12672	12649	0.04	11.57	2.54	100
宣武区	Xuanwu	10187	14896	14748	0.09	2.25	0.31	100
朝阳区	Chaoyang	54044	55539	55388	0.34	4.36	1.35	97
丰台区	Fengtai	26131	31923	31235	0.79	6.23	1.52	95.58
石景山区	Shijingshan	13248	13659	13351	0.61	4.43	0.94	99.01
海淀区	Haidian	101998	62862	61700	1.22	4.4	0.87	98.04
门头沟区	Mentougou	10943	8726	8653	3.88	12.77	4.38	83.7
房山区	Fangshan	42610	39228	39170	1.71	5.78	2.98	92.06
通州区	Tongzhou	29517	30688	27353	0.91	5.2	2.98	94.13
昌平县	Changping	21709	19039	19685	0.84	6.88	2.69	92.08
顺义县	Shunyi	23685	24043	23810	1.03	4.96	3.62	100
大兴县	Daxing	26983	29713	28955	0.81	2.15	1.19	99.95
平谷县	Pinggu	26609	23947	21981	1.26	5.42	3.64	94.26
怀柔县	Huairou	16701	14719	13766	0.75	11.53	3.58	96.44
密云县	Miyun	29282	24980	26519	1.92	1.97	1.58	85.31
延庆县	Yanqing	14666	14479	11398	3.66	9.64	3.6	91.44

16-8 全市婴儿、新生儿死亡率
DEATH RATE OF INFANT AND NEWBORN BABY

单位：‰ (‰)

地区 Region		婴儿死亡率 Death Rate of Infant		新生儿死亡率 Death Rate of Newborn Baby	
		1998	1997	1998	1997
合计	**Total**	**7.58**	**9.45**	**5.53**	**6.36**
区	District	9.07	10.49	6.46	6.75
县	County	5.75	8.05	4.39	5.83

16-9 农村改水情况
STATISTICS FOR WATER-CHANG IN RURAL AREA

项目 Item			1998	1997
农村总人口	(万人)Total Rural Population	(10000 persons)	373.4	373.4
# 女 性	(万人) Female	(10000 persons)		
已改水累计受益人口	(万人)Accumulative Population Benefited from Water-changing	(10000 persons)	372.5	372.2
# 女 性	(万人) Female	(10000 persons)		
饮用自来水	Using Tap Water			
现有水厂	(万座) Water Plants	(unit)	3828.0	3801.0
累计受益人口	(万人) Accumulative Benefited Population	(10000 persons)	365.3	363.7
饮用水压机井水	Using Motor-Pumped Water			
现有机井	(万台) Motor-Pumped Wells	(10000)	1.7	1.9
累计受益人口	(万人) Accumulative Benefited Population	(10000 persons)	5.4	6.1
其他形式	Others			
累计受益人口	(万人) Accumulative Benefited Population	(10000 persons)	1.9	2.3

16-10 举办运动会情况
SPORTS MEETINGS

项目 Item				1998	1997
举办县以上运动会次数	(次)	Sports Meetings above County Level(times)		2417	504
体委系统		Physical Culture and Sports Commissions		221	288
其他系统		Other Departments		2196	216
参加县以上运动会运动员人数	(人次)	Athletes Attending Sports Meetings above County Level	(person.time)	1009434	599617
体委系统		Physical Culture and Sports Commissions		240766	496723
其他系统		Other Departments		768668	102894
举办乡镇运动会次数	(次)	Sports Meetings at Town and Township Level	(times)	572	945
参加乡镇运动会运动员人数	(人次)	Athletes Attending Sports Meetings at Town and Township Level	(person.time)	107649	169569

16-11 分等级运动员情况
CERTIFIED ATHLETES

单位：人

(person)

项目 Item	合计 Total	国家级健将 National Master Athletes	运动健将 Master Athletes	一级 First Grade Athletes	二级 Second Grade Athletes	三级 Third Grade Athletes	少年级 Juvenile Grade Athletes
总 计 Total	**1784**	**4**	**51**	**243**	**1114**	**260**	**112**
# 女 性 Female	818	3	20	112	492	136	55

16-12　分等级教练员情况
CERTIFIED TRAINERS

单位：人　　　　(person)

项　　目 Item		合　计 Total Trainers	国家级教练 National Trainers	高级教练 Senior Trainers	一　级 First Grade Trainers	二　级 Second Grade Trainers	三　级 Third Grade Trainers
总　　计	**Total**	**576**	**3**	**107**	**238**	**216**	**12**
# 女　性	Female	169		21	69	76	3

16-13 分等级裁判员情况
CERTIFIED REFEREES

单位：人　　　　(person)

项　　目 Item		合　计 Total	国 家 级 National Referees	一　级 First Grade Referees	二　级 Second Grade Referees	三　级 Third Grade Referees
总　　计	**Total**	**1127**	**18**	**177**	**554**	**377**
# 女　性	Female	310	8	52	132	117

16-14 运动员获奖牌情况
STATISTICS ON MEDALS WON

单位：块　　　　(unit)

项　　目 Item		金　牌 Gold	银　牌 Silver	铜　牌 Bronze
合　计	**Total**	**79**	**61**	**45**
国际比赛	International Competitions	41	23	14
国内比赛	Domestic Competitions	38	38	31

16-15 北京市运动员获全国冠军名单
LIST OF NATIONAL CHAMPIONSHIPS WON BY ATHLETES OF BEIJING

比赛名称	Matches	大项名称	Item	小项名称 Item	姓名 Name
全国锦标赛	The National Championships	田径	Track and Field	男子跳高	周忠革
全国锦标赛	The National Championships	田径	Track and Field	男子跳远	许滨
全国锦标赛	The National Championships	田径	Track and Field	男子铅球	刘昊
全国锦标赛	The National Championships	田径	Track and Field	女子800米	张健
全国锦标赛	The National Championships	自行车	Cycling	男子公路个人计时赛40KM	汤学忠
全国锦标赛	The National Championships	自行车	Cycling	女子公路个人赛	王淑青
全国锦标赛	The National Championships	体操	Gymnastics	男子个人全能	张津京
全国锦标赛	The National Championships	体操	Gymnastics	男子单杠	张津京
全国锦标赛	The National Championships	体操	Gymnastics	女子团体	奎媛媛等七人
全国锦标赛	The National Championships	体操	Gymnastics	女子平衡木	孟菲
全国锦标赛	The National Championships	体操	Gymnastics	女子自由体操	孟菲
全国锦标赛	The National Championships	柔道	Judo	男子73公斤级	谢建华
全国锦标赛	The National Championships	游泳	Swimming	女子4x100米自由泳接力	
全国锦标赛	The National Championships	跳水	Diving	女子10米跳台	李娜
全国锦标赛	The National Championships	花样游泳	Figure Swimming	集体八人	李飞等10人
全国锦标赛	The National Championships	网球	Tennis	男子团体	李思 张宇 鲁凌 贾明
全国锦标赛	The National Championships	摔跤	Wrestling	自由式58公斤级	张帆
全国锦标赛	The National Championships	武术	Wushu	男子长拳全能	江邦军
全国锦标赛	The National Championships	武术	Wushu	男子太极拳全能	孔详东
全国锦标赛	The National Championships	武术	Wushu	女子长拳全能	刘青华
全国锦标赛	The National Championships	武术	Wushu	女子刀棍全能	王晓娜
全国锦标赛	The National Championships	武术	Wushu	女子枪剑全能	刘青华
全国甲级联赛	The National Grade A League Matches	棒球	Baseball	男子	王占鹏等18人
全国甲级联赛	The National Grade A League Matches	垒球	Softball	女子	徐健等18人
全国冠军赛	The National Tournament	田径	Track and Field	男子马拉松	战东林
全国冠军赛	The National Tournament	田径	Track and Field	男子跳高	周忠革
全国冠军赛	The National Tournament	田径	Track and Field	男子铅球	刘昊
全国冠军赛	The National Tournament	体操	Gymnastics	女子跳马	奎媛媛
全国冠军赛	The National Tournament	游泳	Swimming	女子50米自由泳	韩雪
全国冠军赛	The National Tournament	游泳	Swimming	女子100米自由泳	晁娜
全国冠军赛	The National Tournament	游泳	Swimming	女子100米蛙泳	韩雪
全国冠军赛	The National Tournament	花样游泳	Figure Swimming	集体	李飞等10人
全国冠军赛	The National Tournament	武术	Wushu	男子太极拳全能	孔详东
全国冠军赛	The National Tournament	武术	Wushu	女子长拳全能	刘青华
全国冠军赛	The National Tournament	武术	Wushu	女子刀棍全能	王晓娜
全国冠军赛	The National Tournament	跆拳道	Taiquan	男子67公斤级	宋喜江

主要统计指标解释

等级运动员人数 指经考核正式批准授予等级运动员称号的人数。运动员等级分为国际级运动健将、运动健将、一级运动员、二级运动员、三级运动员、少年级运动员。

等级裁判员人数 指经考核正式批准授予等级裁判员称号的人数。裁判员等级分为国际级裁判、国家级裁判、一级裁判、二级裁判、三级裁判。

卫生技术人员 指卫生机构支付工资的全部固定职工和合同制职工中现任职务为卫生技术工作的专业人员。包括中医师、西医师、中西医结合医师、护师、中药师、西药师、检验师、其他技师、中医士、西医士、护士、助产士、中药剂士、西药剂士、检验士、其他技士、其他中医、护理员、中药剂员、西药剂员、检验员，其他初级卫生技术人员。

Explanatory Notes On Main Statistical Indicators

Number of Athletes in Grades refers to the number of athletes who have been given titles through examination. The titles of athletes include international masters of sports, masters of sports, first-grade, second-grade and third-grade sportsmen and young athletes.

Number of Referees in Grades refers to the number of referees who have been given titles through examination. They are classified as international referees, national referees and referees of the first, second and third grades.

Medical Technical Personnel refers to all permanent medical staff and workers employed by medical institutions, including doctors of Chinese and Western medicine, doctors who integrate traditional Chinese therapeutics with Western therapeutics in practice, senior nurses, pharmacists of Chinese and Western medicine, laboratory specialists, other specialists, paramedics of Chinese and Western medicine, nurses, midwives, druggists in Chinese and Western medicine, laboratory technicians, other technicians, other practitioners of Chinese medicine , nursing attendants, pharmacological workers of Chinese and Western medicine, laboratory workers, and other primary medical personnel.

城市公用事业

URBAN PUBLIC UTILITIES

			1998	1997
	用电量 Electricity Consumption	（万千瓦小时） (10000 kwh)	2762080	2636078
	年末运营车辆 Operating Vehicles	（辆） (year-end, unit)	10819	10479
	桥梁 Bridges	（座） (unit)	715	693

公 共 交 通

Public Traffic

1998年

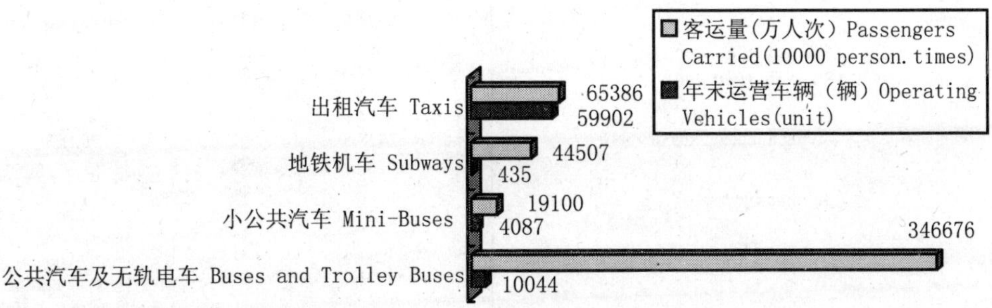

17-1 城 镇 建 设 用 地
URBAN CONSTRUCTION LAND

单位：公顷 (hectare)

项目	Item	全市 Total	城近郊区 City Proper and Near Suburbs	远郊区 Outer Suburbs	各县 Counties
合　　计	**Total**	**267**		**151**	**116**
商业服务业用地	Commerce and Services	35		33	2
工业用地	Industry	91		72	19
仓储用地	Stock	7		1	6
交通用地	Transportation	26		23	3
市政公用设施及绿化用地	Municipal Public Facilities and Green Areas	6			6
公共建筑用地	Public Construction	18		8	10
住宅用地	Residential Buildings	60		9	51
特殊用地	Special Purposes				
其他用地	Others	24		5	19

17-2 城 市 居 民 居 住 水 平
RESIDENTIAL CONDITIONS OF URBAN RESIDENTS

单位：万平方米 (10000 sq.m)

项目	Item	1998	#市区 City Proper and Near Suburbs	1997	#市区 City Proper and Near Suburbs
年末实有房屋建筑面积	Floor Space of Houses (year-end)	31019.2	25686.3	29294.1	24315.3
年末实有住宅建筑面积	Floor Space of Residential Buildings (year-end)	15794.0	13184.5	14817.3	12450.8
年末实有住宅居住面积	Living Space of Residential Building (year-end)	7428.5	6226.7	7021.3	5920.2
平均每人居住面积 (平方米)	Per Capita Living Space (sq.m)	10.03	9.87	9.66	9.49
年末实有住宅使用面积	Using Space of Residential Buildings (year-end)	11083.2	9356.1	10434.3	8859.3
平均每人使用面积 (平方米)	Per Capita Using Space (sq.m)	14.96	14.83	14.36	14.2

17-3 用　电　量（北京地区）
ELECTRICITY CONSUMPTION(BEIJING AREA)

单位：万千瓦小时　　(10000 kwh)

项目	Item	1998	1997	1998年为1997年% 1998as% of 1997
合　计	**Total**	**2762080**	**2636078**	**104.8**
农、林、牧、渔、水利业	**Farming,Forestry,Animals Husbandry, Fishery and Water Conservancy**	**108267**	**120444**	**89.9**
# 排灌	Irrigation and Drainage	62356	69606	89.6
工业	**Industry**	**1457149**	**1449129**	**100.6**
按轻重工业分	Grouped by Heavy and Light Industry			
轻工业	Light Industry	278785	274489	101.6
重工业	Heavy Industry	1178364	1174640	100.3
按行业分	Grouped by Sectors			
采掘业	Excavation	72226	73324	98.5
采矿业	Minerals Mining	47164	48366	97.5
制造业	Manufacturing	1384923	1375805	100.7
食品、饮料和烟草制造业	Food,Beverage and Tobacco Production	60802	57322	106.1
纺织业	Textile Industry	40751	43816	93.0
石油加工业	Petroleum Processing	104149	109022	95.5
炼焦、煤气及煤制品业	Coking,Gas and Coal Products	17438	16655	104.7
化学工业	Chemical Industry	170914	183985	92.9
建筑材料及其他非金属矿制品业	Construction Materials and Other Nonmetal Minerals Products	143981	136507	105.5
黑色金属冶练及压延加工业	Smelting and Pressing of Ferrous Metals	403551	405698	99.5
金属制品业	Metal Products	31506	32620	96.6
机械工业	Machinery Manufacturing	48938	49613	98.6
交通运输、电气、电子设备制造业	Transportations,Electric and Electronic Equipment Manufacturing	104749	100087	104.7
电力、蒸汽、热水生产和供应业	Electricity,Steam and Hot Water Production and Supply	108073	93356	115.8
自来水生产和供应	Tap Water Production and Supply	25062	24958	100.4
建筑业	**Construction**	**91336**	**80072**	**114.1**
地质普查和勘探业	**Geological Survey and Prospecting**	**1258**	**1054**	**119.4**
交通运输、邮电通信业	**Transportations,Posts and Telecommunications**	**90080**	**88516**	**101.8**
商业、公共饮食业、物资供销和仓储业	**Commerce,Catering,Capital Goods Distribution and Storage**	**237079**	**202158**	**117.3**
其他事业	**Others**	**482866**	**430046**	**112.3**
# 市内公共交通业	Municipal Public Transportation	5485	8935	61.4
# 路灯业	Road Lamps	7067	9123	77.5
城乡居民生活用电	**Electricity Consumption by Urban and Rural Households**	**294045**	**264659**	**111.1**
乡　村	Rural	73502	68018	108.1
城　市	Urban	220543	196641	112.2

17-4 供　　热
HEAT SUPPLY

项　　目 Item				1998	1997	1998年为1997年% 1998 as % of 1997
全市采暖面积合计		**Total Heating Area**		**9102.1**	**8398.7**	**108.4**
	(万平方米)		**(10000 sq.m)**			
集中供热		Central Heat Supply				
热力供应能力		Supply Capacity		9315.0	9315.0	100.0
	(百万千焦/小时)		(10^9 joule/hour)			
采暖单位	(户)	Heat Users	(unit)	2868.0	2745.0	104.5
采暖面积	(万平方米)	Heating Area	(10000 sq.m)	3645.8	3315.7	110.0
热力供应单位	(户)	Heat Suppler	(unit)	897.0	789.0	113.7
管道长度	(公里)	Length of Pipeline	(km)	227.0	220.1	103.1
销售量	(万百万千焦)	Volume Supplied	(10^13 joule)	1859.2	1778.6	104.5
小区集中供热		Central Heat Supply in Residential Districts				
采暖面积	(万平方米)	Heating Area	(10000 sq.m)	5232.9	4669.6	112.1
余热供热		Surplus Heat Supply				
采暖面积	(万平方米)	Heating Area	(10000 sq.m)	223.4	413.4	54.0

注：小区集中供热、联片供热、余热供热统计范围为市区10万平米以上的供热面积。

Note: Figures for central heat supply in residential districts,joint heat supply and surplus heat supply only include those who heating areas are more than 100000 sq.m.

17-5 供　　汽
STEAM SUPPLY

项　　目 Item				1998	1997	1998年为1997年% 1998 as % of 1997
蒸汽供应能力	(吨／小时)	Supply Capacity	(ton/hour)	850	850	100.0
用汽单位	(个)	Steam Users	(unit)	105	105	100.0
# 工　业	(个)	Industry	(unit)	98	92	106.5
管道长度	(公里)	Length of Pipeline	(km)	41.8	38.7	108.0
销售量	(万吨)	Volume Supplied	(10000 tons)	330.3	394.1	83.8
# 工　业	(万吨)	Industry	(10000 tons)	330.3	394.1	83.8

17-6 煤气、液化石油气及天然气
GAS,LIQUEFIED PETROLEUM GAS AND NATURAL GAS

项目		Item		1998	1997	1998年为1997年% 1998 as % of 1997
煤 气		**Gas**				
管道长度	(公里)	Length of Pipeline	(km)	1494.8	1811.1	82.5
供应量	(万立方米)	Gas Supply	(10000 cu.m)	84130	91450	92.0
# 公用局	(万立方米)	Public Utilities Bureau	(10000 cu.m)	81355	88234	92.2
销售量	(万立方米)	Gas Sale	(10000 cu.m)	68998	76429	90.3
# 工业用	(万立方米)	for Industrial Use	(10000 cu.m)	9994	9872	101.2
生活用	(万立方米)	for Living Use	(10000 cu.m)	58114	64983	89.4
# 公用局	(万立方米)	Public Utilities Bureau	(10000 cu.m)	55359	61770	89.6
用 户	(万户)	Consumer	(10000 households)	57.4	73.5	78.1
# 家庭用户	(万户)	Household	(10000 households)	57.1	73.1	78.1
液化石油气		**Liquefied Petroleum Gas**				
储气能力	(吨／罐)	Storage Capability	(ton/tank)	20905/81	26483/81	
# 公用局	(吨／罐)	Public Utilities Bureau	(ton/tank)	18000/49	22229/49	
供应站	(个)	Supply Units	(unit)	154	161	95.7
# 公用局	(个)	Public Utilities Bureau	(unit)	80	86	93.0
液化气钢瓶	(万个)	Tanks	(10000)	126.0	126.3	99.8
销售量	(吨)	Gas Sales	(ton)	174464	172879	100.9
# 工业用	(吨)	for Industrial Use	(ton)	2899	2795	103.7
生活用	(吨)	for Living Use	(ton)	168516	166599	101.2
# 公用局	(吨)	Public Utilities Bureau	(ton)	142957	143335	99.7
用 户	(万户)	Consumer	(10000 households)	118.4	117.7	100.6
# 家庭用户	(万户)	Household	(10000 households)	115.9	115.2	100.6
天然气		**Natural Gas**				
管道长度	(公里)	Length of Pipeline	(km)	2182	1489	146.5
供应量	(万立方米)	Gas Supply	(10000 cu.m)	37969	18365	206.7
# 公用局	(万立方米)	Public Utilities Bureau	(10000 cu.m)	37969	18365	206.7
销售量	(万立方米)	Gas Sales	(10000 cu.m)	32619	16565	196.9
# 工业用	(万立方米)	for Industrial Use	(10000 cu.m)	1876	2874	65.3
生活用	(万立方米)	for Living Use	(10000 cu.m)	29453	13691	215.1
# 公用局	(万立方米)	Public Utilities Bureau	(10000 cu.m)	29453	13691	215.1
用 户	(万户)	Consumer	(10000 households)	81.9	55.6	147.3
# 家庭用户	(万户)	Household	(10000 households)	81.4	54.7	148.8
居民燃气用户	**(万户)**	**Household with Access to Gas**	**(10000 households)**	**247.3**	**235.9**	**104.8**
气化率	(%)	Percentage of Population Using Gas	(%)	95.4	94.02	101.5

注：本表燃气气化率数字为年末燃气家庭用户占全部城市户数的百分比。

Note:Figure for percentage of population using gas refers to proportion of households using gas in total urban households.

17-7 自来水及自备水源
TAP WATER AND SELF-PROVIDED SOURCE OF WATER

项目		Item		1998	# 城近郊区 City Propers and Near Suburbs	1997	# 城近郊区 City Propers and Near Suburbs
自来水		**Tap Water**					
水厂	(个)	Water Plants	(unit)	24	13	24	13
生产能力	(万吨／日)	Production Capacity	(10000 tons/day)	330.3	266.0	301.8	249
管线长度	(公里)	Length of Pipelines	(km)	6989.3	5383.8	6338.8	5191.9
供水面积	(平方公里)	Area of Water Supply	(sq.m)	703.6	515.6	701.9	509.9
售水量	(万吨)	Sales in Volume	(10000 tons)	75968.5	65790.0	79045.8	65613.3
# 工业用	(万吨)	for Industrial Use	(10000 tons)	13944.9	11729.4	16471.1	11368.7
生活用	(万吨)	for Living Use	(10000 tons)	57032.0	50089.6	55950.2	48759
平均每人每日生活用水	(公斤)	Living Consumption Per Day	(kg)	238.2	256.2	229	250.5
自来水普及率	(%)	Percentage of Population Using Tap Water	(%)	100	100	100	100
自备水源		**Self-provided Source of Water**					
生产能力	(万吨／日)	Production Capacity	(10000 tons/day)	290.5	201.9	291.1	201
用水量	(万吨)	Consumption	(10000 tons)	47243.5	36050.8	44774.3	32078
生产用	(万吨)	Production	(10000 tons)	25543.5	17573.6	25151	16046
生活用	(万吨)	Living	(10000 tons)	21699.9	18477.2	19623.3	16032

17-8 节　　水
WATER SAVING

项目		Item		1998	1997	1998年为1997年% 1998 as % of 1997
节水量	(万吨)	Volume Saved	(10000 tons)	2107	2034	103.6
自来水	(万吨)	Tap Water	(10000 tons)	1555	1551	100.3
自备水井	(万吨)	Self-Provided Well	(10000 tons)	552	483	114.3
完成节水措施	(项)	Save Measures Completed	(item)	160	150	106.7

注：节水量中未包括河水节水量。
Note:Volume saved excluded river water.

17-9 公 共 交 通
PUBLIC TRAFFIC

项目		Item		1998	# 城近郊区 City Propers and Near Suburbs	1997	# 城近郊区 City Propers and Near Suburbs
年末营运车辆		**Operating Vehicles (year-end)**		**10819**	**9267**	**10479**	**8987**
公共汽车	(辆)	Buses	(unit)	9844	8292	9527	8035
# 小公共汽车	(辆)	Mini-Buses	(unit)	4102	2856	4087	2841
无轨电车	(辆)	Trolley Buses	(unit)	538	538	517	517
地铁机车	(辆)	Subways	(unit)	437	437	435	435
营业线路		**Operating Routes**					
条 数	(条)	Number	(line)	690	542	667	519
公共汽车	(条)	Buses	(line)	674	526	651	503
# 小公共汽车	(条)	Mini-Buses	(line)	340	200	340	200
无轨电车	(条)	Trolley Buses	(line)	14	14	14	14
地 铁	(条)	Subways	(line)	2	2	2	2
长 度	(公里)	Length	(km)	14929.2	11004.6	14010.5	10085.9
公共汽车	(公里)	Buses	(km)	14719.6	10795.0	13801.1	9876.5
# 小公共汽车	(公里)	Mini-Buses	(km)	6800	3000	6800	3000
无轨电车	(公里)	Trolley Buses	(km)	168	168	167.8	167.8
地 铁	(公里)	Subways	(km)	41.6	41.6	41.6	41.6
里程利用率		**Utilization Rate of Mileage**					
公共汽车	(%)	Buses	(%)	93.1	93.6	93.6	94.2
# 小公共汽车	(%)	Mini-Buses	(%)	87.9	86.7	87.9	86.7
无轨电车	(%)	Trolley Buses	(%)	99.6	99.6	99.4	99.4
地 铁	(%)	Subways	(%)	99.8	99.8	99.8	99.8
客运量	**(万人次)**	**Passengers Carried**	**(10000 person.times)**	**418824.9**	**408773.9**	**391182.2**	**381895.9**
按车种分		By Type of Vehicles					
公共汽车及无轨电车	(万人次)	Buses and Trolley Buses	(10000 person.times)	372494.2	362443.2	346675.7	337389.4
# 小公共汽车	(万人次)	Light Buses	(10000 person.times)	19100	15500	19100	15500
地 铁	(万人次)	Subways	(10000 person.times)	46330.7	46330.7	44506.5	44506.5
按购票方式分		By Ways of Payment					
普 票	(万人次)	Common	(10000 person.times)	122174.3	102967.6	101244.1	96914.1
月 票	(万人次)	Monthly	(10000 person.times)	305538.1	301266.1	285030.8	280596.5
包 车	(万人次)	Hire	(10000 person.times)	2931	2460	2728.6	2262
旅 游	(万人次)	Tourism	(10000 person.times)	863	849	904.5	892
免 费	(万人次)	Free of Charge	(10000 person.times)	1275	1231	1274.2	1231.3
售出月票	**(万张)**	**Monthly Ticket Sales**	**(10000)**	**1974.9**	**1974.9**	**1831.1**	**1801.5**
客运收入	**(万元)**	**Revenue of Passengers Traffic**	**(10000 yuan)**	**159542.1**	**150100.1**	**146146.8**	**136690.5**

17-10 客运出租汽车
TAXIS SERVICE

项目	Item		1998	1997	1998年为1997年% 1998 as % of 1997
出租汽车营运单位	**Operating Units**		**2175**	**2366**	**91.9**
国有单位 (个)	State-Owned	(unit)	381	426	89.4
集体单位 (个)	Collective-Owned	(unit)	542	757	71.6
个体户 (个)	Individuals	(unit)	1167	1166	100.1
中外合资 (个)	Joint Venture	(unit)	4	3	133.3
其他 (个)	Others	(unit)	81	14	578.6
营运车辆	**Operating Vehicles**		**61301**	**59902**	**102.3**
小轿车 (辆)	Cars	(unit)	54128	36636	147.7
微型面包车 (辆)	Minicoaches	(unit)	5152	21079	24.4
旅行车 (辆)	Wagon Cars	(unit)	968	1274	76.0
大轿车 (辆)	Coaches	(unit)	1053	913	115.3
客运量	**Passengers Carried**		**63817**	**65386**	**97.6**
小轿车 (万人次)	Cars	(10000 person.times)	54717	35045	156.1
微型面包车(万人次)	Minicoaches	(10000 person.times)	6855	28044	24.4
旅行车 (万人次)	Wagon Cars	(10000 person.times)	996	1147	86.8
大轿车 (万人次)	Coaches	(10000 person.times)	1249	1150	108.6
里程利用率	**Utilization Rate of Mileage**				
小轿车 (%)	Cars	(%)	67	68	98.5
微型面包车 (%)	Minicoaches	(%)	85	85	100.0
旅行车 (%)	Wagon Cars	(%)	85	85	100.0
大轿车 (%)	Coaches	(%)	87	85	102.4

17-11 交通管理设施
UTILITIES OF TRANSPORTATION ADMINISTRATION

项目	Item		1998	1997	1998年为1997年% 1998 as % of 1997
交通警岗 (个)	Police Boxes	(unit)	1089	912	119.4
灯岗 (个)	Lamp Posts	(unit)	208	304	68.4
巡逻岗 (个)	Patrol Posts	(unit)	881	608	144.9
信号灯 (座)	Traffic Lights	(unit)	482	460	104.8
# 自动信号灯 (座)	Automatic	(unit)	482	458	105.2
安全示意线 (公里)	Signal Lines for Safety	(km)	6463	6463	100.0
交通标志 (面)	Transportation Signal	(unit)	42784	40138	106.6
隔离墩 (套)	Separate Blocks	(set)	24732	24954	99.1
护栏 (米)	Protective Fences	(m)	168541	164082	102.7

17-12 道路及桥梁 ROADS AND BRIDGES

项目	Item	1998	# 城近郊区 City Proper and and Near Suburb	1997	# 城近郊区 City Proper and and Near Suburb
道路	Roads				
道路长度 (公里)	Length (km)	3720.9	3255.1	3637.6	3189.7
按质量分	By Quality				
# 高级	Senior	1667.8	1510.9	1722.9	1484.6
次高级	Secondary Senior	1446.5	1123.7	1371.3	1164.7
按车辆运行方式分	By Operating Ways of Vehicles				
# 快慢车分行路	Separate Routes of Quick and Slow Vehicles	381.1	267.0	354.4	251
道路面积 (万平方米)	Areas of Roads (10000 sq.m)	4214.2	3590.2	4060.8	3522.3
按质量分	By Quality				
# 高级	Senior	2680.3	2680.3	2694.2	2343.6
次高级	Secondary Senior	1248.0	1258.9	962.8	779.8
按车辆运行方式分	By Operating Ways of Vehicles				
# 快慢车分行路	Separate Routes of Quick and Slow	1113.9	848.0	1002.6	788
铺装步路 (万平方米)	Paved Roads (10000 sq.m)	574.9	444.3		
桥梁	Bridges				
城市桥梁 (座)	City Bridges (unit)	715	602	693	568
# 大型道路立交桥	Large Flyovers	138	113	140	113
行人过街天桥	Overpass	125	123	114	113
地下通道 (座/处)	**Underpass (unit/place)**	**167/126**	**167/126**	**162/121**	**136/95**

17-13 城市路灯设施 STREET LAMPS

项目	Item	1998	# 城近郊区 City Proper and and Near Suburb	1997	# 城近郊区 City Proper and and Near Suburb
路灯盏数 (盏)	**Number of Road Lamps (unit)**	**114917**	**89499**	**108211**	**84811**
白炽灯	Incandescent Lamps	7932	5507	7866	4883
汞灯	Mercury Lamps	57839	49164	56775	48518
钠灯	Sodium Lamps	49146	34828	43570	31410
线路长度 (公里)	**Length of Lines (km)**	**6414.9**	**3312.6**	**6458.9**	**3395.5**

17-14 城市园林绿化
GARDENS AND PLANTED AREAS

项目 Item	1998	# 城近郊区 City Proper and and Near Suburb	1997	# 城近郊区 City Proper and and Near Suburb
年末公共绿地面积 (公顷) Public Green Areas(year-end) (hectare)	6351	4945	5408	4257
平均每人占有公共绿地面积 (包括水面) (平方米) Per Capita Public Green Areas (including water surface) (sq.m)	8.97	8.18	7.8	7.2
城市绿化覆盖率 (%) Coverage of City Green Areas (%)	35.57	34.91	34.22	33.43
道路绿化总长度 (公里) Total Length of Green Roads (km)	2307	1844	2307	1844
年末实有树木 (万株) Trees(year-end) (10000)	4613	3590	4394	3419
# 本年新植 (万株) Newly Planted (10000)	257	207	294	219
全年出圃苗木 (万株) Total Nursery Stage (10000)	188	188	93	93
苗圃面积 (公顷) Areas of Nursery (hectare)	648	648	212.3	212.3
草坪面积 (万平方米) Areas of Lawn (10000 sq.m)	4219	3280	4001	3117
# 本年新植 (万平方米) Newly Planted (10000 sq.m)	272	216	378	179
公园 (个) Parks (unit)	116	94	115	93
公园(包括动物园)面积 (公顷) Parks(including zoos) (hectare)	4183	3847	4176	3840
全年游园人数 (万人次) Visitors to Parks and Zoos (10000 person.times)	9164	8707	9367	8989

17-15 城 市 排 水
DRAINAGE

项目 Item		1998	# 城近郊区 City Proper and and Near Suburb	1997	# 城近郊区 City Proper and and Near Suburb
下水道长度 (公里)	**Length of Sewer (km)**	**4645.6**	**3898.9**	**4343**	**3733**
雨水管 (公里)	Rain Pipes (km)	1346.5	1222.9	1257	1141
污水管 (公里)	Sewage Pipes (km)	1712.4	1557.1	1635	1491
雨污合流管 (公里)	Rain and Sewage Pipes (km)	1586.7	1118.9	1451	1101
污水处理	**Dispose of Sewage**				
处理厂 (个)	Disposal Plants (unit)	4	4	4	4
处理能力 (万吨/日)	Disposal Capability (10000 tons/day)	58.5	58.5	58.5	58.5
处理量 (万吨)	Disposed Volume (10000 tons)	22702	21170	22243	20112
处理率 (%)	Disposal Rate (%)	22.5	22.5	22.0	22.0
平均每日污水量 (万吨)	Daily Sewage (10000 tons)	276.4	258.2	276.5	250

17-16 城 市 环 境 卫 生
MUNICIPAL ENVIRONMENT AND SANITATION

项目 Item		1998	# 城近郊区 City Proper and and Near Suburb	1997	# 城近郊区 City Proper and and Near Suburb
工作量	**Work Load**				
清扫街道面积 (万平方米/日)	Area Cleaned (10000 sq.m/day)	5168	4308	4962	4126
清运垃圾 (万吨)	Garbage Disposal (10000 tons)	495.1	431.6	490	431
清运粪便 (万吨)	Night Soil Disposal (10000 tons)	295.6	269.9	279	253
环卫机械数量	**Number of Environmental Sanitation Equipment**	**3120**	**2733**	**2936**	**2579**
大中型扫尘车 (辆)	Large and Medium Road Sweepers (unit)	163	142	162	145
大中型洒水车 (辆)	Large and Medium Watering Cars (unit)	101	90	102	89
大中型垃圾车 (辆)	Large and Medium Dust-carts (unit)	1944	1681	1796	1572
真空吸粪车 (辆)	Vacuum Dung-drawer Carts (unit)	449	392	519	453
小型扫尘车 (辆)	Small Road Sweeper (unit)			8	6
其他环卫车辆 (辆)	Others (unit)	463	428	349	314
环卫设施	**Environmental Sanitation Facilities**				
垃圾台 (座)	Garbage Stages (unit)			32	
垃圾桶 (个)	Garbage Cans (unit)	11453	4655	35973	21971
果皮箱 (个)	Dustbins (unit)	10569	9087	12057	8828
公共厕所 (座)	Lavatories (unit)	6556	5825	6643	5568
密闭式集装箱垃圾站 (座)	Airtight Container Garbage Stations(unit)	745	709	1040	996

主 要 统 计 指 标 解 释

年底自来水生产能力 指城市供水设施取水、净水、送水、出厂输水干管等环节的综合生产能力，按设计能力（以四个环节中最薄弱环节为主）计算。在设计生产能力的基础上，经挖、革、改增加的生产能力，应按一次或数次增加的设计生产能力总和加原设计生产能力求得。

气化率 指使用燃气（包括人工煤气、液化石油气、天然气）的城市非农业人口数（不包括临时人口和流动人口）与城市非农业人口总数之比。计算公式：

$$气化率 = \frac{城市用气的非农业人口}{城市非农业人口总数} \times 100\%$$

城市桥梁 指城市范围内，修建在河道上的桥梁和道路与道路立交、道路跨越铁路的立交桥，以及人行天桥。包括永久性桥和半永久性桥，不包括临时性桥、铁路桥、涵洞。

城市下水道总长度 指汇集和排放污水、废水和雨水的管渠及其附属设施所组成的系统。长度按所有排水总管、干管、支管及检查井，联接井进出水口等长度之和计算，不包括雨水口至排水管道间的联接管、进户管及明渠。

城市污水日处理能力 指污水处理厂每昼夜处理污水量的设计能力。

营运线路长度 公共交通全部运营线路的长度之和。

公共绿地 指向公众开放的各级各类公园，小游园、街头绿地等，包括其范围内的水域。

Explanatory Notes On Main Statistical Indicators

Production Capacity of Tap Water at Year-end refers to the comprehensive production capacity such as water inflow, purification, conveyance and outflow of the trunk pipelines into account of the urban water-suppling construction, counted according to designed capacity(taking the weakest link of the above four as the principal one). The incremental capacity through innovation and reproduction on the bases of designed capacity, will be the sum of original designed capacity and incremental ones through one time or several times.

Length of Water Supply Pipelines at Year-end refers to the total length of all the pipelines between the water pumps and the users' water meters.

Percentage of Urban Gas Users refers to the ratio of the urban non-agricultural population using gas（including gas, liquefied petroleum gas and natural gas ）to the total of urban non-agricultural population （excluding temporary and mobile population）. The formula is:

$$\text{Percentage of Urban Gas Users} = \frac{\text{Urban gas users}}{\text{Urban Non-agricultural Population}} \times 100\%$$

Urban Bridges refer to bridges over river courses, great separated junctions and overpasses in urban areas, including permanent bridges and semi-permanent bridges, excluding temporary bridges, railway bridges and culverts.

Length of Urban Sewage Pipes refers to the total length of general drainage, trunks, branches and blind drainage, inspection wells, connection wells, inlets and outlets, etc.

Daily Disposal Capacity of Urban Sewage refers to the designed 24-hour capacity of sewage disposal at the sewage works.

Length of Routes in Operation refers to the sum length of all routes in operation of public traffic.

Public Green Area refers to green areas of various parks, amusement parks and green-land streets opened to the public, including waters within the above region.

1999

人民生活

PEOPLES LIVELIHOOD

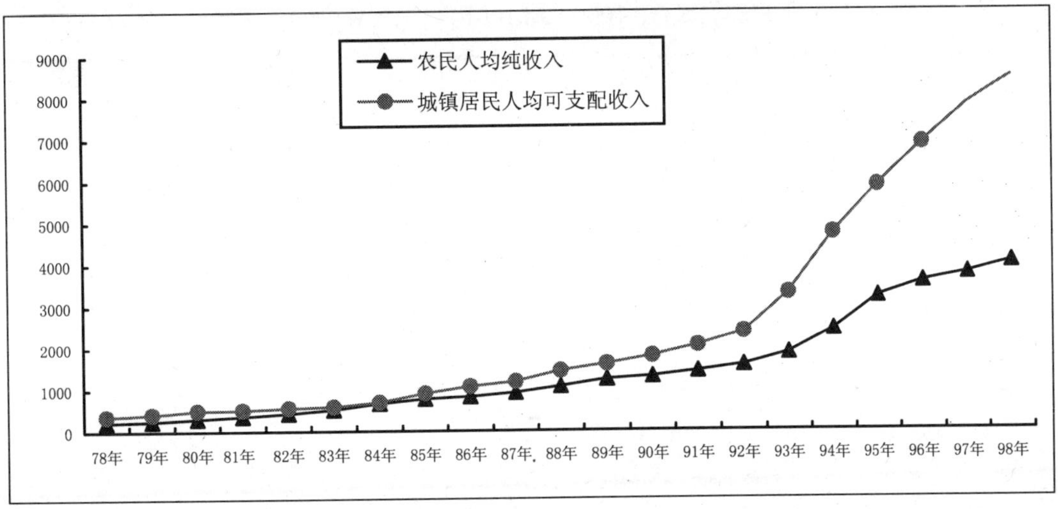

人均居住面积（平方米）
Per Capita Living Space(sq.m)

	1998	1978	1998年为1978年% 1998 as % of 1978
城镇(Urban)	14.86	4.55	326.6
农村(Rural)	27.64	9.25	298.8

1000户居民家庭平均每百户耐用消费品年末拥有量（1998年）
Per 100 Households year-end Possession of Durable Consumer Goods of 1000 Urban Households(1998)

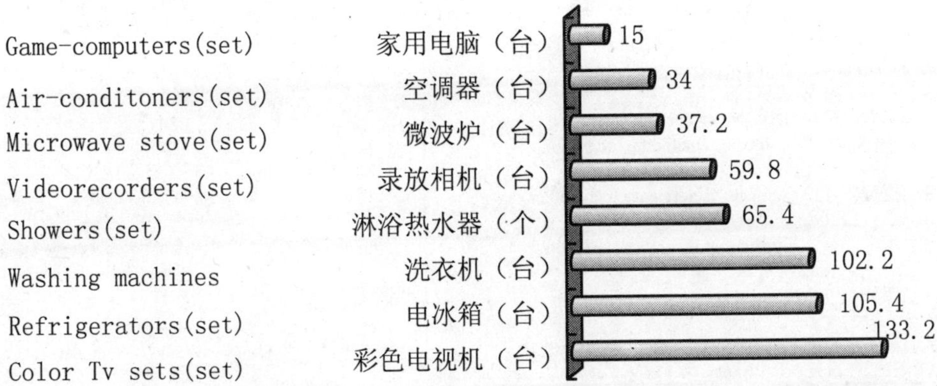

18-1 1000户居民家庭基本情况
BASIC STATISTICS OF 1000 SAMPLED URBAN HOUSEHOLDS

项目 Item			1998	1997	1998年为1997年% 1998 as % of 1997
调查户数	(户) Households Surveyed	(household)	1000	1000	
家庭人口数	(人) Persons of Households	(person)	3028.6	3057.3	99.1
平均每户人口	(人) Average Persons Per Household	(person)	3.03	3.06	99.0
就业人数	(人) Employees	(person)	1768.2	1766.8	100.1
平均每户就业人数	(人) Average Persons Per Household	(person)	1.77	1.77	100.0
平均就业面	(%) Percentage of Employment Per Household	(%)	58.4	57.7	101.3
平均每一就业者负担人口（包括就业者）	(人) Dependents Per Employee(Including the employee himself/herself)	(person)	1.40	1.43	97.9
离、退休人数	(人) Retirees	(person)	550.5	538.7	102.2
平均每一有收入者负担人口（包括有收入者）	(人) Dependents Per Person Having Income (Including the person himself/herself)	(person)	1.31	1.32	99.2
平均每人年可支配收入	(元) Annual Discretionary Income Per Capita	(yuan)	8472.0	7813.1	108.4
平均每人月可支配收入	(元) Monthly Discretionary Income Per Capita	(yuan)	706.0	651.1	108.4
平均每人年消费性支出	(元) Annual Living Expenditure Per Capita	(yuan)	6970.8	6531.8	106.7
平均每人月消费性支出	(元) Monthly Living Expenditure Per Capita	(yuan)	580.9	544.3	106.7

注：1.有收入者指就业者和16岁以上的、当月财产性收入、转移性收入和零星和劳动收入在50元以上的无职业者。

2.离、退休人数包括离、退休后再就业人员。

a) Persons having income refers to employees and unemployees over 16-year-old and month property-income,transfer-income and odd income totaled to more than 50 yuan.

b) Retirees include reemployees after retirement.

18-2 1000户居民家庭基本情况(按收入水平分)
BASIC STATISTICS OF 1000 SAMPLED URBAN HOUSEHOLDS(BY INCOME LEVEL)

项目 Item			全市合计 Total	低收入户 Low Income	中等偏下收入户 Medium-Low Income	中等收入户 Medium Income	中等偏上高收入户 Medium-High Income	高收入户 High Income
调查户数	(户) Households Surveyed	(household)	1000	200	200	200	200	200
家庭人口数	(人) Persons of Households	(person)	3028.6	671.14	636.5	603.5	583.98	533.52
平均每户人口	(人) Average Persons Per Household	(person)	3.0	3.4	3.2	3.0	2.9	2.7
就业人数	(人) Employee	(person)	1768.2	355.3	345.0	364.7	360.3	343.0
平均每户就业人数	(人) Average Employee Per Household	(person)	1.77	1.78	1.73	1.82	1.8	1.72
平均就业面	(%) Percentage of Employment Per Household	(%)	58.4	52.9	54.2	60.4	61.7	64.3
平均每一就业者负担人口(包括就业者)	(人) Dependents Per Employee(Including the employee himself)	(person)	1.40	1.60	1.51	1.37	1.33	1.21
离、退休人数	(人) Retirees	(person)	550.5	102.2	116.3	105.0	105.0	120.0
平均每一有收入者负担人口(包括有收入者)	(人) Dependents Per Person Having Income (Including the person himself/herself)	(person)	1.71	1.89	1.84	1.65	1.62	1.56
平均每人年可支配收入	(元) Annual Discretionary Income Per Capita	(yuan)	8472.0	4972.5	6622.8	7958.7	9651.4	14409.1
平均每人月可支配收入	(元) Monthly Discretionary Income Per Capita	(yuan)	706.0	414.4	551.9	663.2	804.3	1200.8
平均每人年消费性支出	(元) Annual Living Expenditure Per Capita	(yuan)	6970.8	4500.0	5700.3	6720.8	7882.7	10926.9
平均每人月消费性支出	(元) Monthly Living Expenditure Per Capita	(yuan)	580.9	375.0	475.0	560.1	656.9	910.6

18-3 1000户居民家庭每人每年现金收入
ANNUAL CASH INCOME PER CAPITA OF THE 1000 URBAN HOUSEHOLDS

单位：元　　　　(yuan)

项目	Item	总平均 Average	低收入户 Low Income	中等偏下收入户 Medium-Low Income	中等收入户 Medium Income	中等偏上收入户 Medium-High Income	高收入户 High Income	1998年为1997年% 1998 as % of 1997
现金收入	**Cash Income**	**10098.2**	**5450.4**	**7498.2**	**9490.2**	**11970.1**	**17725.8**	**115.5**
实际收入	Real Income	8520.6	5011.4	6664.7	8003.5	9711.8	14470.4	108.4
# 可支配收入	Discretionary Income	8472.0	4972.5	6622.8	7958.7	9651.4	14409.1	108.4
职工收入	Staff and Workers	5522.3	3385.1	4584.1	5488.6	6806.5	8067.1	103.8
个体经营劳动者收入	Individuals	57.2	72.8		76.9		146.2	149.3
离退休再就业人员收入	Reemployee after Retirement	295.4	66.1	170.7	234.4	334.9	736.3	120.5
其他就业者收入	Other Employee	7.5	10.1		8.6		20.2	70.1
其他劳动收入	Other Income from Work	209.8	123.7	112.1	190.3	175.7	494.2	125.3
财产性收入	Property Income	108.6	55.0	48.7	78.3	70.7	322.9	104.5
转移性收入	Transfer Income	2319.8	1298.5	1749.1	1926.4	2324.0	4683.5	117.4
离退休金	Pension	1925.3	1094.4	1487.1	1671.1	2015.4	3637.9	120.9
价格补贴	Subsidies for Price	18.2	13.6	17.7	12.2	10.3	40.2	79.2
赡养收入	Maintenance Income	92.3	36.8	119.2	35.2	67.7	222.5	105.6
赠送收入	Gift Income	121.6	57.6	48.7	91.0	52.0	400.8	134.8
亲友搭伙费	Poor Funds	65.2	20.4	20.7	43.4	74.6	189.0	91.9
记帐补贴	Subsidies of Account	43.3	38.5	40.9	41.4	50.9	46.3	99.3
出售财物收入	Proceeds from Sales of Belongings	4.8	8.9	1.0	4.2	5.7	4.1	61.8
其　他	Others	49.0	28.3	13.9	27.9	47.2	142.6	79.9
借贷收入	Credit Income	1577.6	439.1	833.4	1486.6	2258.3	3255.4	179.3

18-4 1000户居民家庭每人每年现金支出
ANNUAL CASH EXPENDITURES PER CAPITA OF THE 1000 URBAN HOUSEHOLDS

单位：元　　　　(yuan)

项目	Item	总平均 Average	低收入户 Low Income	中等偏下收入户 Medium-Low Income	中等收入户 Medium Income	中等偏上收入户 Medium-High Income	高收入户 High Income	1998年为1997年% 1998 as % of 1997
现金支出合计	**Total**	**9710.0**	**5220.9**	**7179.2**	**9078.8**	**11516.5**	**17159.4**	**119.5**
消费性支出	Living Expenditures	6970.8	4500.0	5700.3	6720.8	7882.7	10926.9	106.7
食　品	Food	2865.7	2297.6	2559.5	2898.7	3173.5	3580.6	100.4
衣　着	Clothing	713.7	396.8	594.0	717.2	919.2	1045.5	93.8
家庭设备用品及服务	Household Facilities,Articles and Services	794.1	347.7	515.8	542.6	993.1	1763.9	121.7
医疗保健	Medicine and Medical Services	347.9	180.3	315.1	394.7	357.7	530.6	116.9
交通通讯	Transportation and Communications	369.5	200.1	306.5	370.3	448.1	575.7	105.9
娱乐教育文化及服务	Recreation,Education and Cultural Service	964.2	590.5	805.2	1056.5	1067.8	1416.2	108.3
居　住	Residence	528.3	288.4	335.9	441.9	472.6	1211.9	148.5
杂项商品及服务	Miscellaneous Commodities and Services	387.4	198.8	268.4	299.0	450.7	802.5	104.2
非消费支出	Non-Living Expenditures	1246.0	285.5	635.1	1358.8	1950.2	2287.7	222.7
各种税金	Taxes	9.2	1.2	2.1	8.0	15.0	23.5	129.3
赡养支出	Support Expenditures	147.9	64.3	103.7	144.8	194.3	260.1	108.1
赠送支出	Gift Expenditures	324.6	140.0	216.8	383.2	401.8	534.3	132.3
购房与建房支出	Expenditures on Purchasing and Building Houses	717.8	63.2	286.9	789.5	1256.7	1384.5	557.0
其他非消费性支出	Others							
借贷支出	Credit Expenditures	1493.1	435.5	843.6	999.2	1683.7	3944.8	144.5

18-5 1000户居民家庭平均每人年消费性支出
ANNUAL LIVING EXPENDITURE PER CAPITA OF THE 1000 URBAN HOUSEHOLDS

单位：元 (yuan)

项目 Item		总平均 Average	低收入户 Low Income	中等偏下收入户 Medium-Low Income	中等收入户 Medium Income	中等偏上收入户 Medium-High Income	高收入户 High Income	1998年为1997年% 1998 as % of 1997
食品	**Food**	**2865.7**	**2297.6**	**2559.5**	**2898.7**	**3173.5**	**3580.6**	**100.4**
粮食	Grain	257.0	254.8	232.7	267.8	277.5	254.6	96.1
淀粉及薯类	Starches and Tuber	23.6	21.8	22.0	23.3	25.7	26.0	99.8
干豆类及豆制品	Bean and Bean Products	41.1	39.1	35.2	40.0	47.2	45.1	101.0
油脂	Oil	72.5	79.2	71.6	72.1	70.1	65.8	104.2
肉禽及其制品	Meat,Poultry and Related Products	590.6	495.4	524.7	573.4	665.6	733.4	95.6
蛋类	Eggs	78.5	71.7	71.2	79.1	84.2	87.8	95.4
水产品	Aquatic Products	128.2	91.2	112.6	105.9	148.3	196.3	98.6
菜类	Vegetables	233.5	204.2	220.6	233.3	255.9	260.4	89.5
调味品	Flavorings	57.0	49.4	52.1	57.0	62.0	66.2	101.1
糖类	Sugar	42.8	35.3	41.4	44.7	48.8	44.8	110.1
烟草类	Tabacco	91.0	83.6	90.6	88.3	76.0	119.9	96.3
酒和饮料类	Liquor and Beverages	180.1	141.9	150.2	193.0	203.6	224.1	104.5
干鲜瓜果类	Dried and Fresh Melons and Fruits	204.4	158.3	192.4	201.1	230.7	248.7	90.7
坚果及果仁	Nuts and Kernel	52.5	39.8	43.8	51.8	57.6	73.5	110.5
糕点	Cake	100.5	74.3	91.6	100.9	117.3	123.7	115.4
奶及奶制品	Milk and Dairy Products	113.3	71.7	103.9	104.1	126.3	173.0	112.3
其他食品	Other Food	100.7	56.1	79.3	103.3	134.0	141.8	106.6
在外用餐	Dinning Out	498.1	329.3	423.5	558.6	542.7	694.7	112.1
食品加工服务费	Food Processing Service	0.5	0.6	0.1	0.9	0.1	0.8	73.4
衣着	**Clothing**	**713.7**	**396.8**	**594.0**	**717.2**	**919.2**	**1045.5**	**93.8**
服装	Garments	455.9	251.2	347.5	458.0	597.1	702.4	97.0
衣着材料	Clothing Materials	55.2	22.6	53.3	58.5	78.1	69.6	72.5
鞋、袜、帽及其他衣着	Shoes,Hats,Socks and Other Clothing	178.1	113.1	174.4	178.7	202.7	239.4	94.6
衣着加工服务费	Tailoring and Laundering	24.6	9.9	18.8	22.0	41.4	34.2	100.0
家庭设备用品及服务	**Household Facilities, Articles and Services**	**794.1**	**347.7**	**515.8**	**542.6**	**993.1**	**1763.9**	**121.7**
耐用消费品	Durable Consumer Goods	517.7	220.8	313.7	288.2	623.3	1289.6	125.1
# 日用机电消费品	Daily Use Mechanical and Electrical Goods	271.9	114.2	165.6	182.1	287.3	697.3	98.4

18-5 续表 continued

单位：元 (yuan)

项目 Item		总平均 Average	低收入户 Low Income	中等偏下收入户 Medium-Low Income	中等收入户 Medium Income	中等偏上收入户 Medium-High Income	高收入户 High Income	1998年为1997年% 1998 as % of 1997
室内装饰品	Interior Decorations	21.3	4.4	9.9	20.2	23.7	53.4	128.1
床上用品	Bed Articles	26.0	10.5	24.5	30.5	25.5	43.7	91.1
家庭日用杂品	Daily Use Household Articles	173.5	99.3	139.9	151.5	241.0	257.0	114.8
家具材料	Furniture Materials	0.8	0.3	0.1	1.3	1.1	1.5	24.2
家庭服务	Household Services	54.7	12.4	27.7	51.0	78.7	118.7	141.7
医疗保健	**Medicine and Medical Services**	**347.9**	**180.3**	**315.1**	**394.7**	**357.7**	**530.6**	**116.9**
# 医药费	Medical Care Fee	254.8	149.4	260.6	301.8	226.9	354.2	130.6
交通和通讯	**Transportation and Communications**	**369.5**	**200.1**	**306.5**	**370.3**	**448.1**	**575.7**	**105.9**
交　通	Transportation	161.1	99.1	102.6	170.5	191.5	267.1	110.4
# 交通费	Transportation Fares	114.4	76.0	64.3	109.2	133.3	207.7	127.8
通　讯	Communications	208.4	101.0	203.9	199.8	256.6	308.6	142.8
# 电讯费	Telecommunication	150.9	81.1	124.3	154.0	184.6	232.8	137.3
娱乐、教育、文化服务	**Recreation,Education and Cultural Services**	**964.2**	**590.5**	**805.2**	**1056.5**	**1067.8**	**1416.2**	**108.3**
文娱用耐用消费品	Durable Consumer Goods for Recreational and Cultural Use	264.7	103.2	232.7	263.8	265.3	514.1	87.7
教　育	Education	459.7	345.7	372.0	573.5	502.1	530.4	138.3
# 学杂费	Tuition and Incidentals	288.5	216.2	239.1	394.8	295.9	318.6	143.4
托幼费	Child-care Fee	36.5	43.2	38.0	34.8	26.5	27.3	136.4
文化、娱乐	Recreation	239.8	141.6	200.5	219.2	300.4	371.7	93.7
# 书报杂志	Book,Newspaper and Magazine	70.7	40.0	71.6	65.1	89.9	93.7	97.6
居　住	**Residence**	**528.3**	**288.4**	**335.9**	**441.9**	**472.6**	**1211.9**	**148.5**
住　房	Housing	274.7	92.0	122.7	213.1	235.6	792.3	166.7
# 房　租	Rent	115.9	67.2	73.8	97.7	80.3	287.3	149.3
水电燃料	Water,Electricity and Fuels	235.8	186.7	205.9	208.3	223.6	377.2	123.6
杂项商品和服务	**Miscellaneous Commodities and Services**	**387.4**	**198.8**	**268.4**	**299.0**	**450.7**	**802.5**	**104.2**
个人消费	Personal Consumption	341.8	177.8	236.8	278.8	380.6	706.1	103.3
# 金银珠宝饰品	Golden, Silver and Jewelry Ornaments	26.5	15.7	10.5	26.5	37.6	46.8	86.1
旅　游	Tourism	137.1	46.6	67.0	81.9	127.4	412.0	116.6
理发、洗澡、美容	Hair-cut,Bath and Improving One's Looks	17.2	11.4	14.7	16.6	16.6	26.1	115.0
其他商品	Other Commodities	7.9	7.0	2.0	5.5	22.8	2.5	99.5
其他服务	Other Services	37.7	14.1	26.5	14.7	47.3	93.8	114.8

18-6 1000户居民家庭消费性支出构成
COMPOSITION OF LIVING EXPENDITURES OF THE 1000 HOUSEHOLDS

单位：%　　　　(%)

项目	Item	总平均 Average	低收入户 Low Income	中等偏下收入户 Medium-Low Income	中等收入户 Medium Income	中等偏上收入户 Medium-High Income	高收入户 High Income
消费性支出合计	**Total Living Expenditure**	**100**	**100**	**100**	**100**	**100**	**100**
食　品	Food	41.1	51.1	44.9	43.1	40.3	32.8
穿　着	Clothing	10.2	8.8	10.4	10.7	11.7	9.6
家庭用品及服务	Household Articles and Services	11.4	7.7	9.1	8.1	12.6	16.1
医疗保健	Medicine and Medical Services	5.0	4.0	5.5	5.9	4.5	4.9
交通通讯	Transportation and Communications	5.3	4.5	5.4	5.5	5.7	5.3
娱乐教育文化及服务	Recreation,Education and Cultural Services	13.8	13.1	14.1	15.7	13.6	13.0
居　住	Residence	7.6	6.4	5.9	6.6	6.0	11.1
杂项商品及服务	Miscellaneous Commodities and Services	5.6	4.4	4.7	4.5	5.7	7.3

18-7 1000户居民家庭平均每人年购买主要消费品支出
ANNUAL EXPENDITURE OF MAJOR CONSUMER GOODS PER CAPITA OF THE 1000 URBAN HOUSEHOLDS

单位：元　　　　(yuan)

项目	Item	总平均 Average	低收入户 Low Income	中等偏下收入户 Medium-Low Income	中等收入户 Medium Income	中等偏上收入户 Medium-High Income	高收入户 High Income	1998年为1997年% 1998 as % of 1997
粮　食	Grain	326.7	318.9	306.3	338.0	333.2	341.4	97.4
食用植物油	Edible Vegetable Oil	101.1	101.7	97.1	105.7	98.5	96.1	109.3
鲜　菜	Fresh Vegetables	298.8	244.1	274.0	315.6	328.9	343.9	92.5
猪肉及其制品	Pork and Related Products	468.1	367.1	410.5	474.2	519.5	599.6	101.8
牛羊肉及其制品	Beef,Mutton and Related Products	207.4	164.1	173.6	233.8	245.0	247.9	97.2
家　禽	Poultry	148.2	105.1	127.3	132.8	170.2	224.6	100.3
鲜　蛋	Fresh Eggs	97.1	84.5	85.0	103.8	104.0	110.7	100.0
水产品	Aquatic Products	178.8	117.2	152.6	155.3	208.2	286.8	103.5
食　糖	Sugar	15.2	14.4	13.4	14.6	17.9	15.4	102.7
卷　烟	Cigarettes	90.8	83.4	90.4	88.2	76.0	119.5	96.3
酒	Wine	76.9	61.5	66.2	86.1	79.0	99.6	109.3
茶　叶	Tea	39.8	32.2	32.6	45.8	45.7	43.4	103.7
鲜瓜果	Fresh Melons and Fruits	151.6	119.7	146.6	152.9	171.2	172.9	90.8
糖　果	Candy	15.5	12.3	14.8	12.5	19.3	19.4	116.4
糕　点	Cake	100.5	74.3	91.6	100.9	117.3	123.7	115.4
鲜　奶	Fresh Milk	58.0	39.6	53.2	49.2	69.2	85.7	112.9
棉　布	Cotton Cloth	8.0	3.0	8.4	10.8	8.3	10.3	75.7
棉化纤布	Blend Cloth with Cotton and Chemical Fabric	4.1	1.8	6.5	5.7	3.4	3.1	104.0
化纤布	Chemical Fabric Cloth	15.6	4.2	15.6	12.5	22.9	25.6	85.6
呢　绒	Woolen Fabric	11.0	1.9	7.9	11.2	19.3	16.6	66.4
绸　缎	Silk and Stains	3.1	1.1	3.0	3.6	3.6	4.9	47.1
毛皮大衣	Fur Coat	45.9	17.7	31.7	35.9	68.2	85.0	125.4
呢大衣	Woolen Coat	18.4	4.7	19.6	16.4	37.3	17.0	83.3
风雨衣	Raincoat	5.3	3.2	0.8	6.4	9.2	7.6	72.4
西　服	Western-style Clothes	27.1	14.4	10.7	35.3	36.9	45.6	134.0
毛线衣	Sweater	53.2	23.1	40.9	48.4	73.7	89.3	104.2
各式童装	Children Wear	33.3	25.9	37.7	43.1	28.9	34.7	100.6
毛　线	Knitting Wool	7.8	6.0	9.0	9.0	11.6	3.3	69.2
皮　鞋	Leather Shoes	91.8	52.4	87.5	93.4	93.7	144.5	98.5
旅游鞋	Travel Shoes	18.4	16.0	18.9	14.3	27.4	16.3	109.1

18-8 1000户居民家庭主要消费品平均每人年购买量
ANNUAL PURCHASES OF MAJOR CONSUMER GOODS PER CAPITA OF THE 1000 URBAN HOUSEHOLDS

项目 Item	总平均 Average	低收入户 Low Income	中等偏下收入户 Medium-Low Income	中等收入户 Medium Income	中等偏上收入户 Medium-High Income	高收入户 High Income	1998年为1997年% 1998 as % of 1997
粮食 (公斤) Food (kg)	82.3	86.4	77.9	84.9	84.2	77.1	99.2
食用植物油 (公斤) Edible Vegetable Oil (kg)	9.7	10.1	9.5	9.8	9.3	9.0	107.2
鲜菜 (公斤) Fresh Vegetable (kg)	173.6	146.4	161.4	185.4	189.4	190.6	90.4
猪肉及其制品 (公斤) Pork and Related Products (kg)	30.1	24.6	26.6	30.2	33.0	37.7	110.5
牛羊肉及其制品 (公斤) Beef Mutton and Related Products (kg)	12.3	10.0	10.4	14.0	14.5	14.2	96.7
家禽 (公斤) Poultry (kg)	9.5	7.3	8.2	9.0	10.8	13.0	105.5
鲜蛋 (公斤) Fresh Eggs (kg)	16.7	14.5	14.6	17.9	17.9	19.1	95.5
水产品 (公斤) Aquatic Products (kg)	12.8	9.8	12.1	11.4	13.9	17.8	109.6
食糖 (公斤) Sugar (kg)	2.6	2.4	2.2	2.5	2.9	2.6	103.2
卷烟 (盒) Cigarettes (case)	28.5	29.2	29.7	28.4	25.6	30.8	95.2
酒 (公斤) Wine (kg)	14.5	11.5	13.7	13.3	16.7	18.1	102.1
茶叶 (公斤) Tea (kg)	0.4	0.4	0.3	0.5	0.4	0.4	95.1
鲜瓜果 (公斤) Fresh Melons and Fruits (kg)	67.2	54.0	65.5	68.6	75.5	74.5	99.7
糖果 (公斤) Candy (kg)	0.6	0.5	0.6	0.5	0.7	0.7	111.3
糕点 (公斤) Cake (kg)	5.7	4.6	5.4	5.7	6.3	6.6	112.9
鲜奶 (公斤) Fresh Milk (kg)	16.9	11.4	15.7	14.4	20.4	24.7	106.6
棉布 (米) Cotton Cloth (m)	95.3	37.9	97.2	118.7	91.4	143.0	83.9
棉化纤布 (米) Cotton/Chemical Fabric Blend Cloth (m)	23.4	13.7	30.4	31.5	19.4	21.4	99.5
化纤布 (米) Chemical Fabric Cloth (m)	66.1	18.5	63.1	61.7	86.5	113.0	102.9
呢绒 (米) Woolen Fabric (m)	15.0	3.0	11.9	16.2	24.9	21.9	61.9
绸缎 (米) Silk and Stains (m)	8.2	2.2	7.6	7.0	11.9	13.5	54.5
毛皮大衣 (件) Fur Coat (unit)	3.3	1.8	2.2	2.3	4.5	6.4	114.6
呢大衣 (件) Woolen Coat (unit)	4.4	2.1	3.8	4.3	7.5	5.3	83.4
风雨衣 (件) Raincoat (unit)	3.4	2.7	0.9	3.3	6.5	3.8	79.3
西服 (件) Western-style Clothes (unit)	8.9	7.5	3.8	12.3	11.3	11.3	110.0
毛线衣 (件) Sweater (unit)	49.6	34.6	41.2	49.4	56.6	72.0	102.6
各式童装 (件) Children Wear (unit)	93.8	73.0	110.6	107.7	87.0	96.0	100.0
毛线 (公斤) Knitting Wool (kg)	11.0	9.4	13.7	11.2	16.6	3.5	76.3
皮鞋 (双) Leather Shoes (pair)	77.3	56.9	77.3	75.6	79.5	105.0	99.2
旅游鞋 (双) Travel Shoes (pair)	17.7	19.4	21.4	13.9	20.9	12.8	108.3

18-9 1000户居民家庭平均每百户耐用消费品年购买量
PER 100 HOUSEHOLDS ANNUAL PURCHASES OF DURABLE CONSUMER GOODS OF THE 1000 URBAN HOUSEHOLDS

项目 Item	总平均 Average	低收入户 Low Income	中等偏下收入户 Medium-Low Income	中等收入户 Medium Income	中等偏上收入户 Medium-High Income	高收入户 High Income	1998年为1997年% 1998 as % of 1997
毛皮大衣 (件)Fur coats (unit)	10	6	7	7	13	17	113.6
呢大衣 (件)Woolen Coats (unit)	13.4	7	12	13	22	14	82.7
地毯 (平方米)Carpets (sq.m)	4	4		6		10	142.9
组合家具 (套)Combined Furniture (set)	2.2	1		1	4	4	220.0
沙发床 (个)Bed with Mattress (unit)	3.2	2	3	3	3	5	66.7
沙发 (个)Sofas unit)	6.4	2	4	10	5	11	123.1
自行车 (辆)Bicycles (unit)	16.6	14	14	13	25	19	138.3
电风扇 (台)Electric Fans (set)	4.4	9	2	4	2	5	41.5
电冰箱 (台)Refrigerators (set)	5	3	2	4	6	10	104.2
冰柜 (台)Freezers (set)	0.4					2	50.0
洗衣机 (台)Washing Machines (set)	7	4	8	5	11	8	125.0
彩电 (台)Color TV Sets (set)	9.8	6	10	13	8	12	136.1
录放像机 (台)Videorecorders (set)	0.8			1	1	2	66.7
家用电脑 (台)Game-Computers (set)	2.4	1	1	3	1	6	80.0
组合音响 (套)Hi-Fi Systems (set)	0.4		1	1			25.0
收录机 (台)Recorders (set)							
照相机 (架)Cameras (set)	2	2	1	2	1	4	100.0
微波炉 (台)Microwave Stove (set)	8.6	9	8	9	8	10	93.5
空调器 (台)Air-Conditioners (set)	7	1	5	3	7	20	112.9
淋浴热水器 (个)Showers (set)	6.8	2	2	5	10	15	179.0
排油烟机 (台)Range Hoods (set)	3.2	2	2	2	3	7	145.5
吸尘器 (台)Dust Catcher (set)	0.2			1			50.0
电炊具 (台)Electric Cooking Appliances (set)	9.8	11	9	8	7	14	116.7

18-10 1000户居民家庭平均每百户耐用消费品年末拥有量
PER 100 HOUSEHOLDS ANNUAL PURCHASES OF DURABLE CONSUMER GOODS OF THE 1000 URBAN HOUSEHOLDS

项 目 Item			总平均 Average	低收入户 Low Income	中等偏下收入户 Medium-Low Income	中 等 收入户 Medium Income	中等偏上收入户 Medium-High Income	高收入户 High Income	1998年为1997年% 1998 as % of 1997
毛皮大衣	(件)Fur coats	(unit)	92	69	80	77	111	125	117.4
呢大衣	(件)Woolen Coats	(unit)	220	178	214	206	247	256	102.4
地 毯	(平方米)Carpets	(sq.m)	165	135	68	129	268	225	111.3
组合家具	(套)Combined Furniture	(set)	74.2	63	69	69	81	89	106.9
沙发床	(个)Bed with Mattress	(unit)	72.4	56	61	75	81	89	110.0
沙 发	(个)Sofas	(unit)	166	118	129	164	208	212	111.9
自行车	(辆)Bicycles	(unit)	221	232	223	225	218	208	105.5
电风扇	(台)Electric Fans	(set)	145	136	130	153	147	160	105.4
电冰箱	(台)Refrigerators	(set)	105.4	102	104	106	104	111	101.2
冰 柜	(台)Freezers	(set)	15.6	11	15	15	18	18	94.0
洗衣机	(台)Washing Machines	(set)	102.2	94	104	106	100	107	101.6
彩 电	(台)Color TV Sets	(set)	133.2	122	124	141	130	149	107.6
录放像机	(台)Videorecorders	(set)	59.8	52	52	58	69	68	106.8
家用电脑	(台)Game-Computers	(set)	15	9	17	15	10	24	123.0
组合音响	(套)Hi-Fi Systems	(set)	22.2	11	24	20	24	32	114.4
照相机	(架)Cameras	(set)	95.2	71	94	88	108	114	107.9
微波炉	(台)Microwave Stove	(set)	37.2	21	36	32	43	53	144.2
空调器	(台)Air-Conditioners	(set)	34	16	32	16	38	67	125.0
淋浴热水器	(个)Showers	(set)	65.4	39	54	60	79	94	112.0
排油烟机	(台)Range Hoods	(set)	59.4	36	46	60	70	85	105.3
吸尘器	(台)Dust Catcher	(set)	23.4	16	15	17	37	32	97.5
电炊具	(台)Electric Cooking Appliance	(set)	68.6	49	50	69	77	97	127.0
摩托车	(辆)Motorcycles	(unit)	3.8	3	1	4	4	7	90.5

18-11 2200户农民家庭基本情况
SAMPLING STATISTICS FOR 2200 RURAL HOUSEHOLDS

项目 Item	总平均 Average	按人均年纯收入水平分组 Grouped by Annual Net Income Per Capita				1998年为1997年% 1998 as % of 1997
		2000元以下 below 2000 yuan	2000～3500	3500～5000	5000元以上 above 5000 yuan	
调查户数 (户) Households Surveyed (household)	2200	394	691	523	592	100
常住人口 (人) Permanent Residents (person)	7991	1588	2629	1851	1923	98.9
平均每户 (人) Average Per Household (person)	3.63	4.03	3.8	3.54	3.25	98.9
整半劳动力 (个) Full-time and Part-time Labors (person)	5537	1045	1750	1313	1429	101.1
平均每户 (个) Average Per Household (person)	2.52	2.65	2.53	2.51	2.41	101.2
平均每一劳动力负担人口 (人) Dependents Per Labor Force (person)	1.44	1.52	1.5	1.41	1.35	98.0
学龄前儿童人数 (人) Number of Preschool Children (person)	225	60	87	49	29	94.5
6～11岁人口 (人) Persons at Age 6-11 (person)	588	132	206	122	128	87.4
# 在校人口 (人) at School (person)	546	119	193	112	122	86.5
12～14岁人口 (人) Persons at Age 12-14 (person)	459	90	165	100	104	92.2
# 在校人口 (人) at School (person)	458	89	165	100	104	92.7
15～17岁人口 (人) Persons at Age 15-17 (person)	417	69	152	99	97	103.0
# 在校人口 (人) at School (person)	409	67	148	99	95	102.5
家庭经营耕地面积 (公顷) Cultivated Land Area Runned by Households (hectare)	423.4	92.1	136.1	90.0	105.2	77.3
家庭经营山地面积 (公顷) Mountain Land Area Runned by Households (hectare)	97.8	44.0	35.4	11.3	7.1	136.8
人均生产性固定资产原值 (元) Original Value of Productive Fixed Assets Per Capita (yuan)	939.3	915.0	768.5	872.2	1257.5	122.4
人均住房面积 (平方米) Per Capita Living Space (sq.m)	27.6	23.4	25.9	29.4	31.8	100.9
人均总收入 (元) Per Capita Total Revenue (yuan)	4579.9	1911.3	3213.2	4608.9	8624.2	108.6
# 现金收入 (元) Cash Income (yuan)	4207.0	1634.7	2873.5	4274.2	8089.5	108.0
人均纯收入 (元) Net Income Per Capita (yuan)	4028.9	1468.4	2747.0	4129.2	7799.3	107.1
人均生活消费支出 (元) Per Capita Annual Living Expenditure (yuan)	2945.5	1547.7	2244.6	3120.6	4889.3	105.4
# 现金支出 (元) Cash Expenditures (yuan)	2789.3	1387.7	2066.6	2964.5	4766.3	105.5
职工人数 (人) Staff and Workers (person)	727	99	167	204	257	106.3
乡村企业从业人数 (人) Employees of Village Enterprises (person)	1137	135	343	292	367	93.0
平均每个劳动力创造纯收入 (元) Average Net Income Per Labor Force (yuan)	5467.4	2116.0	3908.4	5449.5	9843.7	103.7

18-12 2200户农民家庭平均每人年纯收入
ANNUAL NET INCOME PER CAPITA OF THE 2200 RURAL HOUSEHOLDS

单位：元 (yuan)

项目 Item		总平均 Average	按人均年纯收入水平分组 Grouped by Annual Net Income Per Capita				1998年为1997年% 1998 as % of 1997
			2000元以下 below 2000 yuan	2000～3500	3500～5000	5000元以上 above 5000 yuan	
合计	**Total**	**4028.9**	**1468.4**	**2747.0**	**4129.2**	**7799.3**	**107.1**
基本收入	**Basic Income**	**3788.4**	**1392.4**	**2601.6**	**3865.6**	**7315.0**	**106.1**
劳动者的报酬收入	Remuneration of Labors	2765.0	906.5	1861.3	2968.1	5339.6	106.9
在集体组织中劳动的报酬	from Collective Units	1150.6	375.2	730.6	1226.5	2292.0	125.2
在企业劳动得到的报酬	from Enterprises	1568.2	481.0	1081.4	1694.6	3009.7	94.8
在集体企业的劳动所得	Collective-owned	935.3	293.8	678.0	1006.6	1748.2	96.7
在个体企业的劳动所得	Individuals	155.6	51.7	103.0	156.9	212.1	166.5
在其他企业的劳动所得	Others	477.3	135.5	300.5	531.2	949.4	80.3
在其他单位劳动得到的报酬	from Other Units	46.2	50.3	49.2	47.1	38.0	349.7
家庭经营纯收入	Net Income from Family Business	1023.4	485.9	740.4	897.4	1975.4	103.9
从第一产业得到	Primary Industry	728.0	392.4	575.2	699.9	1241.0	95.0
从第二产业得到	Secondary Industry	26.2	-1.9	25.1	9.1	67.3	127.4
从第三产业得到	Tertiary Industry	269.2	95.5	140.1	188.4	667.0	136.0
转移性和财产性收入	**Transfer and Property Income**	**240.5**	**75.9**	**145.3**	**263.6**	**484.3**	**125.7**
在外人口寄、带回	Transferring from Family Members	9.6	6.3	6.4	11.3	15.0	94.1
农村外部亲友赠送	Gifts from Relatives and Friends	13.4	2.9	7.1	15.8	28.3	106.4
奖励收入	Rewards	20.7	5.0	8.6	31.2	40.2	65.2
财产性收入	Property Income	99.2	15.8	56.3	89.7	235.9	158.0

18-13 2200 户农民家庭平均每人年生活费支出

ANNUAL LIVING EXPENDITURES PER CAPITA OF THE 2200 RURAL HOUSEHOLDS

单位：元 (yuan)

项目	Item	总平均 Average	按人均年纯收入水平分组 Grouped by Annual Net Income Per Capita				1998年为1997年% 1998 as % of 1997
			2000元以下 below 2000 yuan	2000～3500	3500～5000	5000元以上 above 5000 yuan	
合计	**Total**	**2945.5**	**1547.7**	**2244.6**	**3120.6**	**4889.3**	**105.4**
食品支出	Food Expenditure	**1241.9**	**818.1**	**1054.2**	**1360.2**	**1734.5**	**99.5**
#主食	Staple Food	286.2	278.4	283.8	281.3	300.6	98.3
副食	Non-Staple Food	528.6	324.6	443.8	584.0	759.9	98.2
其他食品	Others	311.3	163.2	244.9	347.9	489.1	97.6
衣着支出	**Clothing Expenditure**	**262.1**	**108.0**	**176.3**	**291.2**	**478.5**	**94.9**
#服装支出	Garments	125.9	45.7	76.3	141.3	245.2	97.3
居住支出	**Residence**	**417.8**	**177.0**	**289.8**	**335.2**	**871.2**	**128.7**
#住房	Housing	317.8	125.8	204.6	218.2	726.8	145.4
燃料	Fuel	100.0	51.2	85.2	117.0	144.4	94.2
家庭设备用品及服务支出	**Household Facilities, Articles and Services**	**225.8**	**81.9**	**143.8**	**236.6**	**446.0**	**102.9**
#耐用消费品	Durable Consumer Goods	112.9	24.9	58.7	120.1	252.6	96.9
家庭日用杂品	Daily Use Household Articles	90.4	47.0	64.9	94.9	157.0	113.6
医疗保健支出	**Medicines and Medical Services**	**174.7**	**97.4**	**139.3**	**202.4**	**260.1**	**106.6**
交通和通讯支出	**Transportation and Communications**	**147.9**	**42.7**	**90.2**	**145.5**	**315.8**	**101.4**
#交通工具	Transportation Means	56.6	8.9	35.5	44.6	136.4	73.3
交通费	Transportation	18.6	8.7	10.5	22.1	34.3	121.0
邮电费	Posts and Telecommunications	30.4	11.8	16.5	39.4	56.3	147.4
文教娱乐用品及服务支出	**Cultural,Education and Recreation Articles and Services**	**384.4**	**199.8**	**299.4**	**446.2**	**593.5**	**124.8**
#文娱用机电消费品	Mechanical and Electric Consumer Goods of Culture and Recreation	82.1	23.9	39.0	97.4	174.5	162.1
书报杂志	Books,Newspapers and Magazines	5.2	1.7	3.1	6.0	10.3	121.6
学杂费	Tuition and Incidentals	245.6	157.9	231.9	282.8	301.0	118.7
文娱费	Recreation	12.6	2.8	4.6	14.4	30.1	101.6
其他商品及服务支出	**Other Commodity and Services**	**91.0**	**22.7**	**51.5**	**103.3**	**189.7**	**83.3**
#商品性支出	Commodity Expenditures	18.0	3.7	11.4	14.8	41.8	97.9

18-14 2200户农民家庭平均每人年粮食收支存情况
BROUGHT IN, SENT OUT AND INVENTORY OF GRAIN PER CAPITA OF THE 2200 HOUSEHOLDS

单位：公斤 (kg)

项目	Item	总平均 Average	按人均年纯收入水平分组 Grouped by Annual Net Income Per Capita 2000元以下 below 2000 yuan	2000～3500	3500～5000	5000元以上 above 5000 yuan	1998年为1997年% 1998 as % of 1997
年初粮食结存	**Grain Inventory (year-end)**	**205.0**	**196.1**	**214.8**	**240.6**	**164.7**	**83.6**
年内粮食收入	**Brought in within this Year**	**502.0**	**440.1**	**473.8**	**488.5**	**604.6**	**107.2**
从集体得到	From Collective	0.5	1.2	0.4		0.7	51.9
家庭经营生产	Household Production	412.9	347.1	392.9	405.2	502.1	107.4
购　入	Purchasing	86.4	91.3	78.9	80.9	97.7	107.4
# 从集市购入	From Free Market	38.3	39.0	32.2	38.6	46.0	112.1
其　他	Others	2.2	0.6	1.6	2.4	4.1	108.5
年内粮食支出	**Sent out within this Year**	**364.2**	**340.2**	**345.9**	**355.6**	**417.2**	**99.7**
生活用粮	Living Consumption	167.6	173.6	173.3	159.0	163.0	103.0
# 稻　谷	Rice	33.6	29.6	30.9	34.8	39.3	100.4
小　麦	Wheat	106.5	103.9	115.4	105.7	97.2	101.0
出售粮食	Selling	182.8	151.9	159.3	180.3	242.9	95.1
# 出售给国家	to Government	85.7	77.3	70.0	79.3	120.3	72.2
其　他	Others	13.8	14.7	13.3	16.3	11.3	131.7
年末粮食结存	**Grain Inventory (year-end)**	**342.8**	**296.0**	**342.7**	**373.4**	**352.1**	**98.6**
# 口　粮	Grain Ration	200.6	200.3	226.8	205.1	160.8	103.1
饲　料	Forage	4.7	4.2	4.4	4.7	5.6	131.4
种　籽	Seed	3.4	3.0	3.7	4.3	2.6	71.7

18-16 2200户农民家庭平均每百户耐用消费品拥有量
DURABLE CONSUMER GOODS POSSESSION PER 100 HOUSEHOLDS OF THE 2200 HOUSEHOLDS

项目 Item				总平均 Average	按人均年纯收入水平分组 Grouped by Annual Net Income Per Capita				1998年为1997年% 1998 as % of 1997
					2000元以下 below 2000 yuan	2000～3500	3500～5000	5000元以上 above 5000 yuan	
自行车	(辆)	Bicycles	(unit)	249	223	242	262	262	100.3
缝纫机	(架)	Sewing Machines	(unit)	70	71	68	72	69	102.7
钟	(只)	Clocks	(unit)	116	105	113	115	127	104.8
手　表	(只)	Wristwatches	(unit)	227	207	212	237	250	102.8
电风扇	(台)	Electric Fans	(set)	133	102	126	143	155	105.3
洗衣机	(台)	Washing Machines	(set)	85	70	83	89	94	101.6
电冰箱	(台)	Refrigerators	(set)	75	52	68	82	94	104.9
摩托车	(辆)	Motorcycles	(unit)	28	19	25	30	35	112.4
收音机	(台)	Radios	(set)	47	40	45	48	52	103.8
黑白电视机	(台)	Black and White TV Sets	(set)	39	52	40	38	29	90.7
彩色电视机	(台)	Color TV Sets	(set)	92	74	89	96	105	108.9
收录机	(台)	Recorders	(set)	58	48	56	61	64	100.0
照相机	(架)	Cameras	(set)	26	12	18	29	44	105.7
录相机	(台)	Videorecorders	(set)	15	6	9	18	27	107.7
抽油烟机	(台)	Range Hoods	(set)	15	8	8	17	27	120.7
吸尘器	(台)	Vacuum Cleaners	(set)	4	4	2	4	7	100.0
组合家具	(套)	Combined Furniture	(set)	49	42	42	51	60	105.9
沙　发	(个)	Sofas	(unit)	264	190	231	285	334	111.4
床	(个)	Beds	(unit)	201	156	187	223	229	102.0
大衣柜	(个)	Wardrobes	(unit)	103	95	104	102	109	103.6
写字台	(张)	Writing Desks	(unit)	103	90	99	110	110	104.0

主要统计指标解释

城镇居民家庭就业人口 指城镇居民从事社会劳动并取得劳动报酬或经营收入的人口。就业人口包括通过国家统筹规划和指导由劳动部门介绍就业，自愿组织起来就业和自谋职业等方式，在国有制、集体所有制、中外合资、中外合作、外资在华独资的企事业单位和私营企业单位工作或从事个体劳动的有固定性职业或临时性职业的人口。被聘用和留用的离退休人员也计入就业人口。本指标可以反映城镇居民的就业情况，是计算就业面、负担系数的重要资料。

城镇居民家庭全部收入 指被调查城镇居民家庭全部的实际现金收入，包括经常或固定的收入和一次性收入。不包括周转性收入，如提取银行存款、向亲友借入款、收回借出款以及其他各种暂收款。

城镇居民家庭可支配收入 指居民家庭在支付个人所得税后，所余下的实际收入。计算公式为：

可支配收入=实际收入－个人所得税－家庭副业生产支出－记帐补贴

城镇居民家庭消费性支出 指被调查的城镇居民家庭用于日常生活的全部支出，包括购买商品支出和文化生活、服务等非商品性支出。不包括罚没、丢失款和缴纳的各种税款（如个人所得税、牌照税、房产税等），也不包括个体劳动者经营过程中发生的各项费用。

农村居民家庭纯收入 指农村居民家庭总收入中，扣除从事生产和非生产经营费用支出、缴纳税款和上交承包集体任务金额以后剩余的，可直接用于进行生产性、非生产性建设投资、生活消费和积蓄的那一部分收入。它是反映农民家庭实际收入水平的综合性的主要指标。农民家庭纯收入，既包括从事生产性和非生产性的经营收入，又包括取自在外人口寄回带回和国家财政救济、各种补贴等非经营性收入；既包括货币收入，又包括自产自用的实物收入。但不包括向银行、信用社和向亲友借款等属于借贷性的收入。

农村居民家庭整半劳动力 指农村常住居民家庭成员中有劳动能力并经常参加实际劳动的人员。是生产的基本要素指标之一，是发展生产增加农民家庭收入的重要源泉。按规定，农村男 18 周岁至 50 周岁、女 18 周岁至 45 周岁为整劳动力；男 16 周岁至 17 周岁、51 周岁到 60 周岁，女 16 周岁到 17 周岁、46 周岁至 55 周岁为半劳动力。农民家庭整半劳动力既包括在上述规定劳动年龄内和在劳动年龄以外有劳动能力并经常参加实际劳动的男女整半劳动力；也包括农民家庭常住人员中属于职工的劳动力。但不包括在劳动年龄内已丧失劳动能力的人员。

农村居民家庭生活消费支出 指农村常住居民家庭年内用于日常生活的全部开支。它是用来反映和研究农民家庭实际生活消费水平高低的重要指标。农民家庭生活消费支出，包括用于吃、穿、住、烧、用等生活消费品开支和文化、生活服务费用开支两大部分。

Explanatory Notes On Main Statistical Indicators

Employed Population in Urban Households refers to urban residents engaged in certain work and receiving payment for their labor or income from their business operation, including those who work in state-owned or collective units, joint ventures, foreign-owned units and private units with permanent or temporary jobs, self-employed individuals and re-employed retirees. The indicator reflects the situation of urban employment and is the basic data for calculating employment rate and dependency ratio.

Total Income of Urban Households refers to the total actual cash income of the sample households, including regular or fixed income and occasional income. excluding temporary transferred income, such as withdrawal from bank deposits, borrowed money from relatives or friends, repayment of loans received and various temporary receipts of money.

Discretionary Income of Urban Households refers to the total actual income of households after individual income tax turned over.The formula：

Discretionary Income=Actual Income – Individual Income Tax – Expenditure of Sideline Production – Subsidies of Account

Expenditure on Consumption of Urban Households refers to total expenditure of the sample households on consumption in daily life, including expenditure on various commodities and non-commodity items, such as culture and service, etc., but excluding fines and confiscation, loss, tax payments（such as income tax, license tax, real estates tax, etc.）or various operating expenses in individual business.

Net Income of Rural Households refers to the total income of the permanent residents of the rural households with deduction of the operating expenses in productive and non-productive business, the tax payment and the payment to collective units for their contracted tasks. The net income can be used for investments in productive and non-productive construction, for consumption in daily life and for savings deposit. It is a comprehensive indicator to show the actual income level of the peasants' household, which includes not only the income from the productive and non-productive work, but also the transferred income, such as the money remitted or brought back by household members who are in other places, the government relief and various subsidies, not only the money income, but also the income in kind. But the money borrowed from banks, friends and relatives is excluded.

Full and half Labors of Rural Households refer to permanent residents of rural households who are able to work and actually engaged in social labor, which are factors of production and sources of rural household income. According to the relevant regulations, male aged 18-50 and female aged 18-45 are considered as full labors; male aged 16-17 and 51-60, female aged 16-17 and 46-55 are considered as half labors. Those who are not in the above age range but able to work and actually engaged in social labor are also considered as full or half labors.

Expenditure on Consumption of Rural Households refers to total expenditure of rural households on daily life , including expenses on food, clothing, housing , fuel, articles for daily use, and expenses on cultural life and services. This indicator is used to show the actual consumption level of peasants.

1999

社会福利、政法及其他

SOCICAL WELFARE，POLITICS，LAW AND OTHERS

历届律师资格考试情况（1988-1998）

Statistics for Lawyer Qualification Examination

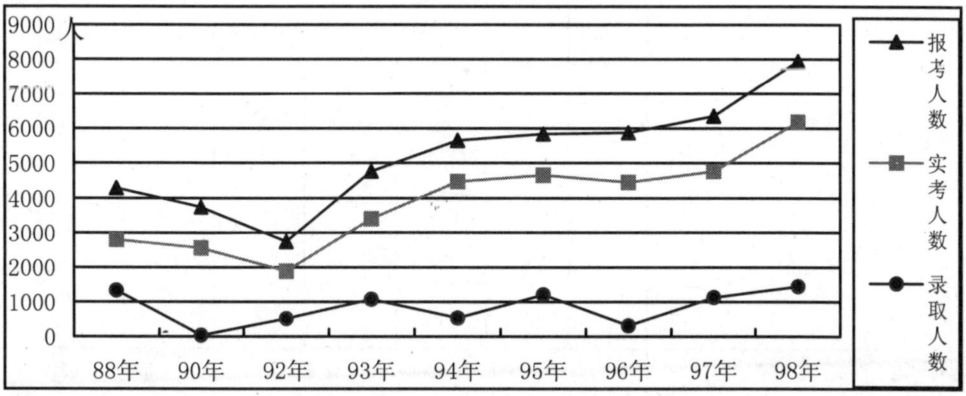

		1998	1997
离休、退休职工人数 Number of Retired and VCSR(person)	（人）	1555704	1442812
保险福利费用 Labour Insurance and Welfare Funds(10000 yuan)	（万元）		
在职职工 Staff and Workers at Posts		545084	480960
非在职职工 Staff and Workers off Posts		1411546	1182771

结 婚 登 记 情 况(对)

Basic Statistics for Marriage Registrations(couple)

1998年

84631

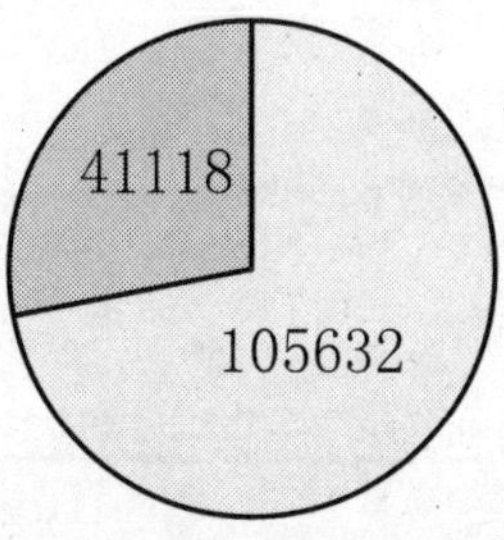

单位：人 person

□城市 Urban

■农村 Rural

1997年

83425

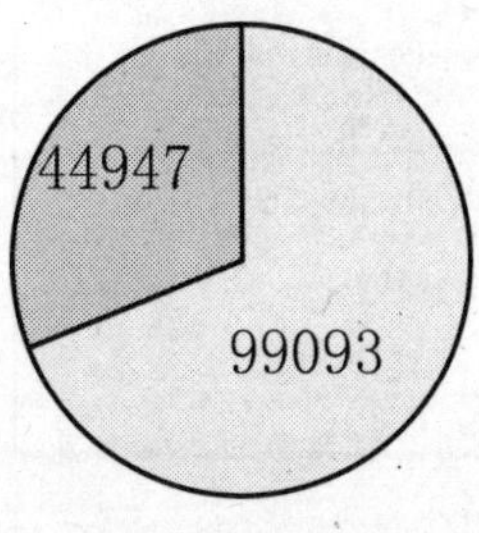

19-1 职工劳保福利费用

单位：万元

项目	Item	全市 Total	国有单位合计 State-Owned	农、林牧、渔业 Farming, Forestry, Animal Husbandry and Fishery	采掘业 Excavation	制造业 Manufacturing	电力煤气及水生产和供应业 Electricity, Gas and Water Production and Supply	建筑业 Construction	地质勘查业、水利管理业 Geological Prospecting and Water Conservancy
在职职工劳保福利费用	**Labor Insurance and Welfare Funds for Staff and Workers at Posts**	**545084**	**474656**	**8603**	**3236**	**94560**	**13043**	**30217**	**2485**
医疗卫生费	Medical Fare	365293	319936	5048	2033	69629	9199	20471	1602
丧葬、抚恤救济费	Funeral Expenses and Pensions for Family of the Deceased	5187	4668	96	379	1142	56	524	35
生活困难补助	Living Allowances	5779	5286	127	59	1162	45	380	13
文体宣传费	Expenses for Cultural Activities, Sports and Propaganda	20178	18287	207	224	3444	646	948	126
集体福利设施费	Collective Welfare Facilities	55738	49414	614	172	6627	2334	3581	371
计划生育补贴	Subsidies for Family Planning	7965	6994	114	35	1299	148	273	21
冬季取暖补贴	Heating Allowances	16891	13824	430	150	3033	178	854	56
其他	Others	68054	56247	1968	184	8226	438	3187	260
非在职职工保险福利费用	**Insurance and Welfare Funds for Staff and Workers off Posts**	**1411546**	**1194374**	**24787**	**23168**	**437797**	**21949**	**104675**	**5694**
离休工资	Wages for VCSR	100777	96122	907	1610	16587	859	4327	859
退休金	Pensions for Retired	948177	781024	17680	14631	330514	14624	69836	2984
退职生活费	Resignation Allowance	17853	7897	215	92	2634	225	836	15
医疗卫生费	Medical Care	247981	220583	4526	4388	70994	5650	20351	1406
其他	Others	96759	88747	1459	2447	17068	592	9325	430

LABOR INSURANCE AND WELFARE FUNDS FOR STAFF AND WORKERS

(10000 yuan)

交通运输仓储及邮电通信业 Transportation, Storage Post and Telecommunications	批发和零售贸易、餐饮业 Wholesale,Retail and Catering	金融、保险业 Banking and Insurance	房地产业 Real Estate	社会服务业 Social Services	卫生、体育和社会福利业 Health, Sports and Social Welfare	教育、文化艺术及广播电影电视业 Education, Culture, Arts,Radio Film and Television	科学研究和综合技术服务业 Scientific Research and Polytechnical Services	国家机关政党机关社会团体 Government Organs, Party Organs, and Social Bodies	其他行业 Others	集体所有制单位 Collective Owned	其它所有制单位 Others
65987	**39598**	**28916**	**6154**	**47819**	**8945**	**26606**	**57627**	**33662**	**7198**	**30413**	**40015**
45870	30813	16662	4774	35407	5082	16963	28595	23629	4159	22784	22574
390	234	72	23	290	113	340	423	491	60	286	234
538	430	100	33	684	72	400	671	520	55	299	191
2381	626	942	238	1766	700	1096	3608	1074	264	771	1119
3391	1606	2230	211	3965	1321	2349	17077	2436	1128	1205	5118
1167	455	915	76	418	169	354	861	592	97	560	411
1648	1548	538	192	1149	521	990	1155	1078	306	1718	1349
10602	3885	7457	609	4141	968	4115	5236	3843	1127	2790	9018
87857	**100439**	**15820**	**11548**	**58111**	**30794**	**90186**	**87787**	**80665**	**13098**	**194888**	**22284**
6652	6491	1394	411	4749	3988	11709	15629	19050	900	4022	633
60755	60173	5692	6234	32817	18797	55588	51978	34175	4547	150428	16724
1007	843	17	65	159	368	756	221	381	63	9781	175
10731	27566	6097	3599	15920	4603	12678	12931	15538	3606	23685	3713
8712	5366	2620	1239	4466	3039	9454	7027	11521	3982	6971	1040

19-2 离休、退休职工人数
NUMBER OF RETIRED AND VCSR

单位：人 (person)

行业	Sector	1998 合计 Total	1998 # 退休职工 Retired	1998 # 离休干部 VCSR	1997 合计 Total	1997 # 退休职工 Retired	1997 # 离休干部 VCSR
总计	**Total**	**1555704**	**1416383**	**91862**	**1442812**	**1304759**	**95708**
按隶属关系分	**Grouped by Administrative Relationship**						
中央单位	Central Units	322352	268865	48160	292771	235681	51467
地方单位	Local Units	1233352	1147518	43702	1150041	1069078	44241
按经济类型分	**Grouped by Ownership**						
国有经济	State-Owned	1232955	1124985	86942	1131925	1023917	89607
集体经济	Collective-Owned	294555	264443	4229	285849	257037	5392
其他经济类型	Others	28194	26955	691	25038	23805	709
在国有经济中：	**Of State-Owned Economy**						
农、林、牧、渔业	Farming,Forestry,Animal Husbandry and Fishery	32059	30543	993	31975	29554	2035
采掘业	Excavation	24061	22231	1531	23732	22828	650
制造业	Manufacturing	492608	470202	15058	448249	426415	14977
电力、煤气及水的生产和供应业	Electricity,Gas and Water Production and Supply	22868	21412	883	21261	19771	1030
建筑业	Construction	109653	103810	3742	93755	88598	3623
地质勘查业、水利管理业	Geological Prospecting and Water Conservancy	4491	3570	877	4125	2987	1089
交通运输、仓储及邮电通信业	Transportation,Storage, Posts and Telecommunications	100011	89898	8206	87713	78279	8023
批发、零售贸易、餐饮业	Wholesale,Retail and Catering	107799	99778	5591	101668	92625	7089
金融、保险业	Banking and Insurance	9289	8067	1195	6818	5882	920
房地产业	Real Estate	10425	9854	414	9421	8779	494
社会服务业	Social Services	62764	57473	4842	59613	53958	5003
卫生、体育和社会福利业	Health Care,Sports and Social Welfare	28689	24790	3120	26630	22360	3376
教育、文化艺术和广播电影电视业	Education,Culture,Arts, Radio,Film and Television	94680	79590	12462	102306	85291	14415
科学研究和综合技术服务业	Scientific Research and Polytechnical Services	63282	52429	10465	53222	41875	11111
国家机关、政党机关和社会团体	Government Organs,Party Organs and Social Bodies	62430	44615	16577	53506	37931	14691
其他行业	Others	7846	6723	985	7931	6784	1081

19-3 优抚、救济对象得到抚恤、补助、救济情况
STATISTICS FOR SPECIAL PENSIONS,ALLOWANCES AND RELIEF FUNDS

项目	Item	人数 (人) Number of Persons (person)	抚恤、补助、救济金额 (千元) Amount of Pensions, Subsidies and Relief Funds (1000 yuan)
烈属牺牲病故军人家属抚恤	Pensions for Members of Revolutionary Martyr's Family,Armymen Sacrificed and Died of Illness	3398	8736
革命伤残人员抚恤	Pensions for Disabled Veterans	12327	5474
复退军人生活补助	Living Allowances for Demobilized Soldiers	15211	42445
农村五保户定期救济补助	Register Relief for Rural Households with Five-guarantees	10428	22400
农村贫困户救济	Relief for Rural Poor Households	4413	8845
城镇散居孤老残幼救济	Relief for Urban Scattered Orphans and Widows,Disabled,the Old and the Youth	14444	7772
城镇贫困户定期救济	Register Relief for Urban Poor Households	27706	26885
精简退职老职工救济	Relief for Old Staff and Workers Reduced and Discharged	8250	12939
自然灾害救济 (人次)	Relief for Natural Calamity (person.time)	10.3	12465
临时救济困难户 (人次)	Temporary Relieves for Households with Living Difficulties (person.time)	79402	4130
离退休人员	VCSR and RRSW	30207	227516
# 离 休	VCSR	.2858	37149

19-4 优抚及主要救济对象情况
STATISTICS FOR PERSONS RECEIVING SPECIAL PENSIONS AND RELIEF

单位：人 (person)

项目	Item	人数 Number of Persons 1998	1997	1998年为1997年% 1998 as % of 1997
优抚对象合计	**Persons Receiving Special Pensions**	**289034**	**292640**	**98.8**
烈 属	Members of A Revolutionary Martyr's Family	17353	16265	106.7
牺牲、病故军人家属	Families of Soldiers Sacrificed or Died of Illness	2711	1664	162.9
现役军人家属	Servicemen's Families	137883	144010	95.7
革命伤残人员	Revolutionary Disabled	12327	13120	94.0
在乡复员军人	Demobilized Soldiers in Hometown	15015	15408	97.4
在乡退伍军人	Veterans in Hometown	103742	102169	101.5
在乡退伍军红军老战士	Demobilized Old Red Army Men in Hometown	3	4	75.0
主要救济对象	**Major Persons Receiving Special Relief**			
社会困难户人数	Households with Living Difficulties	65476	64548	101.4
社会散居孤老、残、幼	Scattered Orphans and Widows,Disabled the Old and the Youth	6264	5791	108.2
精简退职老职工	Old Staff and Workers Reduced and Discharged	8250	8434	97.8

19-5 社会福利事业情况
BASIC STATISTICS FOR SOCIAL WELFARE PROJECTS

项目		Item		1998	1997	1998年为1997年% 1998 as % of 1997
建立社会保障网络的乡镇	(个)	Town and Townships with Social Security Network	(unit)	178	199	89.4
社会福利企业	(个)	Social Welfare Enterprises	(unit)	2221	2322	95.7
# 民政部门办		Under the Civil Administration Department		185	179	103.4
职工人数	(人)	Staff and Workers	(person)	62683	65302	96.0
# 残疾职工		Disabled Persons		26940	28278	95.3
全年增加值	(万元)	Total Value Added	(10000 yuan)	1001630	780616	128.3
城镇社区服务设施	(个)	Urban Welfare Facilities	(unit)	1125	1328	84.7

19-6 城乡各种福利院情况
STATISTICS FOR URBAN AND RURAL WELFARE HOMES

项目		Item	合计 Total	光荣院 Homes for Disabled Veterans	社会福利院 Social Welfare Homes	儿童福利院 Welfare Homes for Children	精神病院 Mental Homes	敬老院 Homes for Old People
福利院单位数	(个)	Welfare Homes (unit)	297	10	5	1	2	279
职工人数	(人)	Staff and Workers (person)	3187	236	616	297	273	1765
床位数	(张)	Beds (bed)	13085	616	1113	997	632	9727
收养人数	(人)	Persons Adopted (person)	9210	507	1010	997	596	6100
# 自费	(人)	at One's Own Expense (person)	1031	12	656	19	344	
国家拨款	(千元)	Financial Allocation (1000 yuan)	50397	8555	22360	8790	5190	5502
集体资助	(千元)	Collective Donation (1000 yuan)	13454					13454

19-7 社会保险基金统筹情况
SOCIAL BLANKET INSURANCE FUNDS

项目	Item	退休(养老)基金统筹 Retirement Funds(Old-age)			失业保险基金统筹 Unemployment Insurance Funds		
		单位个数 (个) Number of Units (unit)	人数 (人) Number of Persons (person)	提取金额 (万元) Amount Drawn (10000 yuan)	单位个数 (个) Number of Units (unit)	人数 (人) Number of Persons (person)	提取金额 (万元) Amount Drawn (10000 yuan)
合计	**Total**	**18947**	**3516837**	**468917**	**13871**	**2229480**	**31056**
按登记注册类型分	**Grouped by Registered Type**						
国有	State-Owned	7699	2475398	346512	10513	1697537	26951
集体	Collective-Owned	4960	429429	45954	5246	264353	1427
其他	Others	6288	612010	76451	3112	267590	2678
按隶属关系划分	**Grouped by Administrative Relationship**						
中央单位	Central Units	1011	589189	32554	1151	266843	3581
地方单位	Local Units	17936	2927648	436363	17720	1962637	27475

19-8 婚姻登记情况
BASIC STATISTICS FOR MARRIAGE REGISTRATIONS

项目 Item				1998	1997	1998年为1997年% 1998 as % of 1997
登记结婚对数	**(对)**	**Registered Marriages**	**(couple)**	**84631**	**83425**	**101.4**
初婚人数	(人)	First Marriages	(person)	146750	144040	101.9
城市		Urban		105632	99093	106.6
男初婚人数		Male		54675	51394	106.4
#22-24岁		Age 22-24		6132	7450	82.3
25岁以上		Age 25 and above		48543	43944	110.5
女初婚人数		Female		50957	47699	106.8
#20-22岁		Age 20-22		4174	5010	83.3
23岁以上		Age 23 and above		46783	42689	109.6
农村		Rural		41118	44947	91.5
男初婚人数		Male		18121	20393	88.9
#22-24岁		Age 22-24		9272	11614	79.8
25岁以上		Age 25 and above		8849	8779	100.8
女初婚人数		Female		22997	24554	93.7
#20-22岁		Age 20-22		8153	8847	92.2
23岁以上		Age 23 and above		14844	15707	94.5
再婚人数	(人)	Remarriages	(person)	22512	22810	98.7
男性		Male		11835	11638	101.7
女性		Female		10677	11172	95.6
登记离婚对数	**(对)**	**Registered Divorces**	**(couple)**	**23683**	**22257**	**106.4**

19-9 律师工作
STATISTICS FOR LAWYERS

项目 Item				1998	1997	1998年为1997年% 1998 as % of 1997
律师事务所	(个)	Law Offices	(unit)	294	280	105.0
律师工作人员	(人)	Lawyers	(person)	4968	4480	110.9
专职律师		Full-time Lawyers		1915	2022	94.7
兼职律师		Part-time Lawyers		1122	1287	87.2
特邀律师		Lawyers Specially Invited		312	463	67.4
其他		Others		1619	708	228.7
聘请常年法律顾问的单位	(个)	Units with Permanent Legal Advisers	(unit)	4876	3703	131.7
民事代理	(件)	Civil Case	(case)	7868	5063	155.4
经济案件	(件)	Economic Case	(case)	6854	5354	128.0
行政案件	(件)	Administrative Case	(case)	162	134	120.9
刑事辩护	(件)	Criminal Defense	(case)	4867	4141	117.5
非诉讼法律事务	(件)	Off-court Case	(case)	12411	12589	98.6
解答法律咨询	(件)	Legal Advisory Services	(case)		14825	
代写法律事务文书	(件)	Legal Documents Written on Behalf of Clients	(case)		7617	

19-10 部分市属律师事务所主要业务情况
STATISTICS FOR MAJOR MUNICIPAL LAW OFFICES

律师事务所 Law Office	担任常年法律顾问(家) Acted as Permanent Legal Advisers (unit)	律协诉讼案件(件) Lawsuit Cases(case)			办理非诉讼法律事务(件) Off-court Case (case)
		刑 事 Criminal	民 事 Civil	经 济 Economic	
大成律师事务所	31	91	126	82	114
广盛律师事务所	19	3	4	53	14
中伦律师事务所	75	3	7	36	40
天元律师事务所	36	12	1	63	22
公诚律师事务所	18		2	10	190
北斗律师事务所	39	61	115	76	65
共和律师事务所	25	5	9	89	41
君屹律师事务所	4	2			46
君合律师事务所	27		2	72	333
陆通律师事务所	71	47	44	68	13
尚公律师事务所	1	2	9	14	11
金杜律师事务所	23		32	149	191
金通律师事务所	19	2	16	42	13
张涌涛律师事务所	16			46	36
浩天律师事务所	43	2	27	39	76
竞天律师事务所	8	2	6	63	63
海问律师事务所	15				111
嘉和律师事务所	76	18	77	123	285
隆安律师事务所	55	11	26	73	26

19-11 部分基层法律服务所主要工作情况
STATISTICS FOR MAJOR LAW SERVICE OFFICES AT BASIC-LEVEL

基层法律服务所 Basic-Level Law Service Office	担任常年法律顾问(家) Acted as Permanent Legal Advisers (unit)	民事代理(件) Civil Case (case)	代 写 法律文书(份) Legal Document Written on Behalf of Client (unit)	协办公证(件) Deal Notarization Jointly (case)	解 答 法律咨询(人次) Legal Advisory Services (person.time)
景山	16	42	60		550
双隆	10	53	60		631
华诚	26	89	67		158
陶然亭	10	34	37	243	3764
双桥	15	39	26	51	178
青龙桥	20	41	47	41	145
卢沟桥	11	29	93	3	178
农委	14	35	101		134
大峪	3	12	36		200
周口店	22	40	117	41	680
永顺	25	30	108	12	334
天竺	19	10	75	4	531
溪翁庄	17	25	67		489
夏各庄	29	11	68		253
沙河	42	71	157	17	363
黄村	18	75	120		320
永宁	16	21	98	2	2100
怀柔	15	34	73	9	227

19-12 历届律师资格考试情况
STATISTICS FOR LAWYER QUALIFICATION EXAMINATION

单位：人 (person)

项目 Item	报考人数 Number of Persons Registered	实考人数 Number of Persons Scattered	录取人数 Number of Persons Passed	录取人数占实考人数比例(%) Percentage of Passed in Persons Attended (%)
1988	4280	2782	1329	47.8
1990	3735	2549	46	1.8
1992	2732	1882	510	27.1
1993	4769	3400	1068	31.4
1994	5653	4480	533	11.9
1995	5842	4661	1204	25.8
1996	5873	4445	317	7.1
1997	6350	4760	1126	23.7
1998	7946	6188	1436	23.2

19-13 乡镇(街道)法律服务情况
STATISTICS FOR TOWNSHIP(URBAN SUBDISTRICT) LAW SERVICES

项目 Item				1998	1997	1998年为1997年% 1998 as % of 1997
法律服务所	(个)	Law Service Offices	(unit)	412	413	99.8
法律工作者	(人)	Law Personnel	(person)	2347	2377	98.7
调解纠纷	(件)	Disputes Mediated	(case)	9487	9541	99.4
法制宣传	(场次)	Law Propaganda	(performance)		11274	
协办公证	(件)	Deal Notarization Jointly	(case)	2950	2583	114.2
担任法律顾问	(家)	Act as Legal Advisers	(unit)	3406	3575	95.3
解答咨询	(人次)	Legal Advisory Services	(person.time)		101797	
代写法律文书	(份)	Legal Documents Written on Behalf of Client	(case)		24863	
民事代理	(件)	Civil Cases	(case)	15533	13398	115.9

19-14 法院行政案件收、结案情况
STATISTICS FOR ADMINISTRATIVE CASES ACCEPTED AND CLOSED BY COURT

单位：件 (case)

项目	Item	收案 Cases Accepted	结案 Cases Closed	#维持 Affirm	#撤销 Recall	#撤诉 Withdraw
合计	**Total**	**683**	**683**	**224**	**86**	**224**
公安	Security	90	96	28	7	35
工商	Industry and Commerce	24	28	5	7	10
卫生	Health Care	6	7	1	1	3
土地	Land	74	76	19	8	39
税务	Tax					
城建	Urban Construction	333	337	136	47	101
环保	Environmental Protection	7	5	1		2
林业	Forestry	2	1			1
专利	Patent	22	17	12	3	
民政	Civil Affairs	5	4			2
其他	Others	120	112	22	13	31

19-15 刑 事 案 件 情 况
STATISTICS FOR CRIMINAL CASES

单位：起 (case)

项目	Item	1998	1997	1998年为1997年% 1998 as % of 1997
刑事案件	**Criminal Cases**			
立 案	Cases Registered	72039	14068	512.1
破 案	Cases Solved	16519	11428	144.5
破案率	**Detection Rate**	**22.9**	**81.2**	**28.2**
# 重大案件	Important Cases			
立 案	Cases Registered	47446	8969	529.0
破 案	Cases Solved	8753	7013	124.8
破案率 (%)	Detection Rate (%)	18.4	78.2	23.5

注：1998年刑事案件与1997年统计口径不同，符合立案标准全都上报。

Note: Calculated standard of criminal cases of 1998 is different from 1997, those tally with the standard of cases registered are all reported.

19-16 法院刑事案件收、结案情况
STATISTICS FOR CRIMINAL CASES ACCEPTED AND CLOSED BY COURT

项目	Item	收案 (件) Cases Accepted (case)	结案 (件) Cases Closed (case)	排挤判决发生法律效力 Judgment with Legal Force	
				件数 (件) Number of Cases (case)	人数 (人) Number of Persons (person)
合 计	**Total**	**10884**	**10888**	**9346**	**13393**
危害国家安全罪	Offense against State Security	17	13	8	12
危害公共安全罪	Offense against Public Security	563	568	507	556
破坏社会主义市场经济秩序罪	Offense against the Socialist Market Economic Order	500	490	439	651
侵犯公民人身权利、民主权利罪	Infringement of Civil Personal Rights and Democratic Rights	2808	2788	2093	2560
侵犯财产罪	Infringement Property	5037	5058	4659	7341
妨害社会管理秩序罪	Interference with Public Function	1745	1763	1482	2086
危害国防利益罪	Offense against National Defense Interest	2	2	4	6
贪污贿赂罪	Corruption and Bribery Crime				
渎职罪	Malpraetice Duty	202	196	144	169
其 他	Others	10	10	10	12

19-17 法院民事案件收、结案情况
STATISTICS FOR CIVIL CASES ACCEPTED AND CLOSED BY COURT

单位：件 (case)

项目	Item	收案 Cases Accepted	结案 Cases Closed	# 调解 Mediation	# 判决 Judgment
合 计	**Total**	**66233**	**65752**	**22336**	**23559**
离 婚	Divorce	24678	24679	11449	5790
抚 育	Foster	2266	2261	990	734
继 承	Inherit	527	514	115	249
房 屋	House	7244	7124	1283	3423
相邻关系	Relation of Neighborhood	1323	1341	273	579
赔 偿	Compensation	7330	7255	1930	3597
债 务	Debt	17707	17562	5026	7005
著作权	Copyright	166	161	24	88
人身权	Personal Right	203	195	15	106
其 他	Others	4789	4660	1231	1988

19-18 法院经济纠纷案件收、结案情况
STATISTICS FOR ECONOMIC DISPUTE CASES ACCEPTED AND CLOSED BY COURT

单位：件 (case)

项目	Item	收案 Cases Accepted	结案 Cases Closed	# 调解 Mediation	# 判决 Judgment
合计	**Total**	**19827**	**19511**	**5787**	**6832**
购销合同	Purchases and Sales Contracts	8669	8728	2903	2757
加工承揽合同	Processing Contracts	1478	1501	480	479
借款合同	Debt Contracts	2089	1963	457	1036
企业承包经营合同	Contracts of Enterprises	608	609	110	246
联营合同	Joint Business Contracts	288	302	70	116
财产租赁合同	Property Leases Contracts	566	578	200	149
建筑工程承包合同	Construction Project Contracts	96	102	32	25
交通运输纠纷	Transportation Dispute	190	199	78	46
涉外、港澳、台经济纠纷	Foreign,Hongkong,Macao and Taiwan Economic Dispute				
其他	Others	5843	5529	1457	1978

19-19 检察机关办理各类案件情况
STATISTICS FOR CASES HANDLED BY PROCURATORIAL ORGAN

项目	Item	受案(受理) Cases Accepted 件 Case	受案(受理) Cases Accepted 人 Person	审结案合计 Cases Closed 件 Case	审结案合计 Cases Closed 人 Person	# 重特大案 Important Cases 人 Person
审查批捕	**Examine for Arrest**	**10154**	**15228**	**10223**	**14584**	**4167**
批准逮捕	Approve			9770	14016	
不批准逮捕	Disapprove			353	568	
审查起、免诉	**Examine for Sue**	**11241**	**16651**	**10399**	**15107**	
起诉	Sue			10286	14941	
不起诉	Immunity from Suit			113	166	
举报控告案件	Prosecution Cases	7330		7311		
申诉案件	Appeal Cases	290		258		
民事、行政检察	Civil and Administrative Procuratorial Work	1103				
民事案	Civil Cases	859				
知识产权案	Intellectual Property	15				
经济纠纷案	Economic Disputes	156				
行政案	Administrative Cases	73				

19-20 检察机关自侦经济、法纪案件情况
CASES SELF-INVESTIGATION OF ECONOMY,LAW AND DISCIPLINE BY PROCURATORIAL ORGAN

项目	Item	自侦经济案件 Self-investigate Economic Cases 合计 Total	# 贪污 Corruption	# 受贿 Accepting Bribes	# 行贿 Bribe	#挪用公款 Misappropriate Public Funds	自侦法纪案件 Self-Investigate Law and Discipline Cases
受案 (件)	**Cases Accepted** (case)	**1201**	**542**	**282**	**14**	**233**	**577**
立案 (件)	**Cases Registered** (case)	**262**	**121**	**47**	**4**	**74**	**9**
# 重特大案	Important Cases						1
5至10万元	50000-100000 Yuan	40	21	10		9	
10至50万元	100000-500000 Yuan	63	24	7	1	26	
50至100万元	500000-1000000 Yuan	10	4			5	
100万元以上	Over 1000000 Yuan	32	7	1		22	
结案	**Cases Closed**						
件数 (件)	Number of Cases (case)	331	129	61	11	83	19
人数 (人)	Number of Persons (person)	370	149	66	14	91	21
# 移送起诉	Hand over to Suit						
件数 (件)	Number of Cases (case)	253	103	49	4	71	13
人数 (人)	Number of Persons (person)	282	123	52	4	77	15
挽回经济损失 (万元)	**Retrieve Pecuniary Losses** (10000 yuan)	**33732.9**	**1904.8**	**964.0**		**10120.3**	

19-21 查处治安案件情况
STATISTICS FOR INVESTIGATING AND HANDLING PUBLIC ORDER CASES

项目	Item	查处(起) Investigating and Handling (case)	构成(%) Composition (%)
合计	**Total**	**140891**	**100**
扰乱工作、公共秩序	Disturb Working or Public Order	55395	39.3
结伙斗殴、寻衅滋事	Gang Fighting	1212	0.9
侮辱妇女及其他流氓活动	Insult Woman and Other Immoral Behavior	498	0.4
阻碍国家工作人员执行公务	Interference with Government Function	535	0.4
违反枪支管理规定	Violate Regulatory Regime for Firearms	152	0.1
违反爆炸物品管理规定	Violate Regulatory Regime for Explosive Goods	494	0.4
殴打他人	Beat up Others	9326	6.6
偷窃财物	Steal	11304	8.0
骗取、抢夺、敲诈勒索财物	Cheat,Rob and Extort Property	2114	1.5
哄抢公私财物	Rob Public Property	135	0.1
故意损坏公私财物	Damage Public and Private Properties Intentionally	382	0.3
伪造倒卖票券、证件	Forge,Resell Bill,Ticket and Credentials	1125	0.8
利用迷信扰乱秩序或骗财	Disturb Public Order or Defraud sb.of His Belongings by Superstitions	96	0.1
卖淫、嫖娼	Prostitution,Visit Prostitution	1692	1.2
赌　博	Gambling	1198	0.9
违反户口、居民身份证管理	Violate Regulations for Residence Cards or ID	27064	19.2
其　他	Others	28169	20.0

19-22 调解工作
MEDIATION

项目	Item	1998	1997	1998年为1997年% 1998 as % of 1997
专职司法助理员 (人)	Full-time Judicial Assistants (person)	645	639	100.9
人民调解委员会 (个)	People's Mediation Committees (unit)	12807	13330	96.1
调解人员 (万人)	Intermediators (10000 persons)	16.9	19.2	88.0
调解委员 (万人)	Members of the Mediation Institution (10000 persons)	5.7	6.1	93.4
调解各类纠纷 (万件)	Disputes Mediated (10000 cases)	13.5	12.3	109.8
防止民间纠纷激化 (件)	Prevent Intensification of Civil Disputes (case)	3160	2212	142.9
避免伤亡 (人)	Avoid Injuries and Deaths (person)		4365	

19-23 公　证　工　作
NOTARIZATIONS

项　目 Item			1998	1997	1998年为1997年% 1998 as % of 1997
公证处	(个) Notarial Offices	(unit)	24	24	100.0
公证人员	(人) Notarial Personnel	(person)	249	249	100.0
办理国内民事公证	(件) Notarized Domestic Civil Affairs	(case)	51826	28610	181.1
办理国内经济公证	(件) Notarized Domestic Economic Affairs	(case)	14045	10074	139.4
办理涉外公证	(件) Notarized Foreign Affairs	(case)	163147	163495	99.8

19-24 1998年全市公证办情况
STATISTICS FOR WORK OF NOTARIAL OFFICES

单位：件　　(case)

区　县	District and County	总办证量 Notarial Documents	国内民事 Domestic Civil Affairs	国内经济 Domestic Economic Affairs	涉外公证 Foreign Notary Affairs
东城区	Dongcheng	26276	12665	424	13187
西城区	Xicheng	11089	2513	24	8552
崇文区	Chongwen	4220	1512	281	2427
宣武区	Xuanwu	6155	2930	144	3081
朝阳区	Chaoyang	7398	2516	120	4762
丰台区	Fengtai	3934	1756	170	2008
石景山区	Shijingshan	5326	1896	43	3387
海淀区	Haidian	57162	6640	338	50184
门头沟区	Mentougou	1027	553	414	60
房山区	Fangshan	1625	512	808	305
通州区	Tongzhou	1768	1195	327	246
昌平县	Changping	849	500	119	230
顺义县	Shunyi	3107	2919	188	
大兴县	Daxing	762	604	92	66
平谷县	Pinggu	1933	112	1821	
怀柔县	Huairou	858	383	475	
密云县	Miyun	690	465	205	20
延庆县	Yanqing	536	374	135	27

19-25 国内公证文书分类
CLASSIFIED STATISTICS FOR DOMESTIC NOTARY DOCUMENTS

单位：件 (case)

项目	Item	民事公证数 Civil Notarization
收养	Adoption	398
解除收养	Dissolution of Adoption	9
继承权	Rights of Inheritance	2653
遗嘱	Testaments	470
产权	Property Rights	96
亲属关系	Kinship	47
死亡	Death Certificates	14
房屋买卖	House Purchase and Sale	1394
房屋租赁	House Leases	129
留学协议	Agreements on Studying Abroad	857
遗赠扶养协议	Agreements on Bequeath and Fostering	128
委托书	Certificate of Entrustment	3198
赠与书	Deed of Gift	4056
声明书	Declarations	1428
现场监督	Spot Supervision	7591
签名印鉴属实	True Signature	2083
文本相符	Confirmation of Copies to the Original	323
宅基地使用权	Using House Site Rights	1
证据保全	Evidence Preservation	443
拆迁协议	Dismantle,Move Agreement	490
计划生育	Family Planning Agreemen	2800
赡养协议	Support Agreements	172
合伙协议	Partnership Agreements	81
夫妻财产协议	Agreements on Estates by the Entirety	90
其他民事协议	Other Civil Agreements	6535
其他	Others	16340
合计	**Total**	**51826**

项目	Item	经济公证数 Economic Notarization
购销	Purchases and Sales	52
联营	Joint Business	16
拍卖	Actions	10
贷款	Loans	224
担保	Guarantees	27
招标投标	Bidding	47
科技协作	Scientific and Technological Cooperation	26
供用电	Electricity Supply or Use	
劳务合同	Labor Contracts	1264
建筑工程承包	Construction Projects Contracts	30
工商服务业承包	Contracts of Industry,Commerce and Services	7
农林牧副渔业承包	Contract of Farming,Forestry,Animal Husbandry, Sideline and Fishery	1806
乡镇企业承包	Contracts of Township Enterprises	73
财产租赁	Property Leases	459
企业租赁	Enterprise Leases	224
资产经营责任制	Asset Business Contracts	
还款协议	Agreements on Paying off Loans	1592
土地使用权出让转让	Selling and Transferring of Land Using Right	52
其他经济合同	Other Economic Contracts	4783
法人(代表人)资格	Identification of Institutional Units(Agent)	39
法人委托书	Trust Deeds of Institutional Units	1475
公司章程	Corporation Constitutions	4
执行许可证明	Operating Permits	21
提存	Drawings	3
抵押登记	Mortgage Registration	110
公司会议记录	Records of Corporation Conference	4
其他	Others	1697
合计	**Total**	**14045**

19-26 消 防 建 设 情 况
STATISTICS FOR FIRE FIGHTING

项 目 Item	1998	1997	1996	1995	1994	1993
消防队数 (队) Number of Fire Brigades	41	38	36	35	35	34
消防车辆 (辆) Number of Fire Engines (unit)	210	190	180	180	180	180
义务消防团 (个) Voluntary Fire Brigades (unit)			20	20	20	20
队数 (万个) Fire Bridges (10000)			3.9	3.9	3.9	3.9
人数 (万人) Persons (10000 persons)			77	77	77	77

19-27 火 灾 及 损 失
FIRE AND LOSSES

项 目 Item	数 量(起) Amount (unit)		直接经济损失(万 元) Direct Pecuniary Loss (10000 yuan)	
	1998	1997	1998	1997
总 计 Total	**4763**	**4324**	**4221.3**	**13137.2**
# 特大火灾 Extraordinarily Serious	2	2	2477.2	11730.5
重大火灾 Heavy	2	3	130.0	38.8
起火原因 Cause of Fire				
# 电 器 Electric Appliances	1346	1190	2618.9	12195.4
违反安全规定 Violate Safety Regulation	133	159	488.7	765.7
吸 烟 Smoking	715	684	145.3	86.0
生活用火不慎 Careless	1230	1061	170.7	182.0
玩 火 Play with Fire	178	181	13.7	17.2
伤 人 (人) Injuries (person)	**101**	**153**		
死 人 (人) Deaths (person)	**40**	**63**		

19-28 交通事故及损失
STATISTICS FOR TRAFFIC ACCIDENTS AND LOSSES

项目		Item		1998	1997	1998年为1997年% 1998 as % of 1997
总计	**(起)**	**Total**	**(case)**	**35778**	**25144**	**142.3**
伤人	(人)	Injuries	(person)	8464	5674	149.2
死亡	(人)	Deaths	(person)	1487	927	160.4
在总计中：机动车事故	**(起)**	**Of Total:Motor Vehicle Accident**	**(case)**	**33599**	**23615**	**142.3**
伤人	(人)	Injuries	(person)	6770	4403	153.8
死亡	(人)	Deaths	(person)	1031	705	146.2
直接经济损失	**(万元)**	**Direct Pecuniary Losses**	**(10000 yuan)**	**16454.6**	**13589.1**	**121.1**
每万辆机动车死亡	(人)	Deaths Per 10000 Motor Vehicles	(persons)	11.5	7.5	153.1

19-29 妇联组织状况
STATISTICS FOR WOMAN FEDERATION ORGANIZATIONS

单位：个，人 (unit,person)

项目	Item	1998	1997
区妇联数	Number of District Women Organizations	12	11
区妇联干部数	Cadres in District Women Organization Cadres	178	157
县妇联数	Number of County Women Organizations	6	7
县妇联干部数	Cadres in County Women Organization Cadres	55	64
乡妇联组织数	Number of Township Women Organizations	273	273
街妇联组织数	Number of Street Women Organizations	107	107
乡、街妇联干部数	Cadres of Township and Street Women Organization	456	466
城市基层妇代会组织数	Number of Urban Basic Women Congress	4988	4682
农村基层妇代会组织数	Number of Rural Basic Women Congress	4000	4278
机关及事业单位妇委会组织数	Number of Women Committees in Organs and Institutions	876	402
厂矿企业女职工委员会数	Number of Female Staff and Workers Committees in Industrial Enterprises	7683	7559
乡、镇企业妇委会组织数	Number of Women Committees in Township and Village Enterprises	1044	1044
各类妇女联谊组织数	Women Connection Organizations	14	14

19-30 工会组织及会员
LABOR UNIONS AND MEMBERS

项目	Item	基层工会委员会（个） Basic-level Labor Union(unit)		会员人数（人） Members(person)	
		1998	1997	1998	1997
总计	**Total**	**10662**	**10942**	**2467685**	**2551396**
按经济类型分	**Grouped by Ownership**				
国有单位	State-Owned Units	7907	8081	2043192	2131463
集体单位	Collective-Owned Units	1885	2056	216394	233230
私营经济	Private Business	43	67	1435	3158
个体经济	Individuals Business				
联营经济	Joint Owned Business	31	10	4143	2130
股份制经济	Share Holding Business	320	269	103217	71528
外商投资经济	Foreign Funded Business	283	411	75839	102288
港澳台投资经济	HongKong,Macao and Taiwan Funded Business	181	44	22742	6968
其他	Others	12	4	723	631
按国民经济部门分	**Grouped by Sector**				
农、林、牧、渔业	Farming,Forestry,Animal Husbandry and Fishery	339	398	35147	40995
采掘业	Excavation	24	43	38209	40329
制造业	Manufacturing	2068	2127	810172	873069
电力、煤气及水的生产和供应业	Electricity,Gas and Water Production and Supply	58	62	62357	64783
建筑业	Construction	522	556	216130	211108
地质勘探业、水利管理业	Geological Prospecting and Water Conservancy	72	68	13648	13887
交通运输业、仓储及邮电通信业	Transportion,Storage and Posts and Telecommunications	415	418	191245	195751
批发和零售贸易及餐饮业	Wholesale,Retail and Catering	2037	2097	271616	272135
金融、保险业	Banking and Insurance	312	271	52413	48664
房地产管理业	Real Estate	267	227	47650	43668
社会服务业	Social Services	866	900	204973	213927
卫生、体育和社会福利事业	Health Care,Sports and Social Welfares	510	555	86151	92612
教育、文化艺术和广播电影电视事业	Education,Culture,Arts,Radio,Film and Television	2263	2256	298204	281217
科学研究和综合技术服务事业	Scientific Research and Polytechnical Services	181	171	36870	27158
国家机关、政党机关和社会团体	Government Organs,Party Organs and Social Bodies	502	479	67218	68788
其他	Others	226	314	35682	63305

19-30 续表 continued

项 目 Item		基层工会委员会 (个) Basic-level Labor Union(unit)	会员人数 (人) Members(person)
总 计	**Total**	**10662**	**2467685**
按登记注册类型分	**Grouped by Registered Type**		
内资经济	Domestic Investment	10198	2369104
国有经济	State-owned	7907	2043192
集体经济	Collective-owned	1755	198730
股份有限公司	Share Holding Company	43	1435
有限责任公司	Limited-Liability Company	31	4143
股份合作企业	Share Holding Cooperative	132	54523
私营经济	Private Business	188	48694
联营经济	Joint-owned	130	17664
其他经济	Others	12	723
外商投资经济	Foreign Funded Business	283	75839
港澳台商投资经济	HongKong,Macao and Taiwan Funded Business	181	22742

19-31 职工民主管理情况
STATISTICS FOR WORKERS DEMOCRACY MANAGEMENT

项 目 Item		建立职工代表大会制的单位 (个) Units with Workers Congress System (unit)	召开职工代表大会情况 Workers Congress		
			召开职代会的单位 (个) Units Holded Workers Congress (unit)	提出提案 (项) Motions Put forward (item)	实现提案 (项) Motions Fulfilled (item)
总 计	**Total**	**8722**	**8346**	**66545**	**42232**
内资经济	Domestic Investment	8436	8080	65494	41601
国有经济	State-owned	6520	6262	55857	36908
集体经济	Collective-owned	1487	1406	5287	3048
股份有限公司	Share Holding Company	105	99	988	539
有限责任公司	Limited-Liability Company	145	142	2854	769
股份合作企业	Share Holding Cooperative	119	116	427	271
私营经济	Private Business	26	23	29	24
联营经济	Joint-owned	25	23	42	33
其他经济	Others	9	9	10	9
外商投资经济	Foreign Funded Business	172	158	652	341
港澳台商投资经济	HongKong,Macao and Taiwan Funded Business	114	108	399	290

19-32 职工民主参与情况
STATISTICS FOR WORKERS DEMOCRATIC PARTICIPATION

项 目 Item		1998	1997
本年度与同级政府、行政开过联席会议的单位 (个)	**Units Holded Joint Meeting with the Same Level Government in this Year (unit)**	**286**	**205**
全年议题提案 (件)	Motions Put forward (item)	1590	2059
解决处理提案 (件)	Motions Solved and Handled (item)	1038	1366
参加政府涉及职工利益的工作机构 (个)	**Joined Government Institutions Concerned Worker's Interests (unit)**	**157**	**87**
机构中参加工作的工会干部 (人)	Union Cadres Worked in Institutions (person)	245	89

19-33 《九十年代中国儿童发展规划纲要》监测统计资料(目标指标)

SUPERVISORY STATISTICS FOR 《PROGRAM OUTLINE OF CHINESE CHILDREN DEVELOPMENT IN 1990S》(OBJECT INDICATORS)

项目	Item	1990	1997	1998
婴儿死亡率 (‰)	Infant Death Rate (‰)	11.66	9.45	7.58
城市	Urban	11.15	10.49	9.07
农村	Rural	12.27	8.05	5.75
五岁以下儿童死亡率 (‰)	Death Rate of Children below 5-year-old (‰)	13.72	11.15	9.6
城市	Urban	13.06	12	11.08
农村	Rural	14.51	10	7.78
孕产妇死亡率 (1/10万)	Death Rate of Pregnant Woman and Lying-in Woman (10/million)	24.99	23.69	10.46
城市	Urban	20.92	25.25	10.87
农村	Rural	29.89	21.6	9.97
五岁以下儿童中重度营养不良患病率 (%)	Rate of Heavy Malnutrition of Children below 5-year-old (%)	2.44	1.06	0.78
城市	Urban	1.04	0.85	0.75
农村	Rural	3.49	1.41	0.83
年龄别体重	Weight by Stages of Age	2.44	1.06	0.78
年龄别身高	Height by Stages of Age		1.37	1.02
身高别体重	Weight by Stages of Height		0.53	0.47
缺水地区农村饮用水受益人口 (万人)	Population Benefited from Drinking Water in Rural Water Deficient Area (10000 persons)	62	74	74
城市污水处理率 (%)	Disposal Rate of Urban Sewage (%)	6.6	21.94	22.38
城市卫生厕所覆盖率 (%)	Covering Rate of Urban Toilet (%)	99.5	99.9	99.82
农村享有卫生厕所的人口比重 (%)	Rate of Rural Population Use Toilet (%)	8.54	62.6	71.2
学龄儿童入学率 (%)	Enrollment Rate of Children at School-age (%)	99.5	99.95	99.96
城市	Urban	99.7	99.98	99.97
农村	Rural	99.6	99.89	99.93
小学毕业率 (%)	Graduate Rate of Primary School (%)	99.2	99.87	99.81
小学巩固率 (%)	Stronging Rate of Primary School (%)	100.23	99.94	99.79
小学辍学率 (%)	Rate of Leaving off Study of Primary School (%)	-0.17	0.07	0.08
男	Male		0.11	0.13
女	Female		0.03	0.04
初中入学率 (%)	Enrollment Rate of Junior Middle School (%)	99.24	97.13	97.95
初中毕业率 (%)	Graduate Rate of Junior Middle School (%)	91.43	96.35	96
初中巩固率 (%)	Stronging Rate of Junior Middle School (%)	93.69	98.07	98.14
小学专任教师学历合格率 (%)	Qualified Rate of Educational Background of Full-time Teacher of Primary School (%)	89	96.42	97.34
3-6岁儿童入园率 (%)	Enrollment Rate of Kindergarten of Children at Age 3-6 (%)	71.2	80.2	81.9
城市	Urban	94.1		
农村	Rural	50.8		
青壮年文盲率 (%)	Illiteracy Rate of Young People (%)	1.6		
校外教育活动场所数 (个)	Number of Locations of After-school Education	1434	1782	1554
家长受教育率 (%)	Educated Rate of Parents (%)			97.3
科学育儿知识普及率 (%)	Spreading Rate of Raising Children with Scientific Method (%)	59.4	93.46	95.63
出生缺陷儿发生率 (‰)	Rate of Defect New-borns (‰)	7.36	8.56	9.53
城市	Urban	5.34	8.14	10.63
农村	Rural	6.34	9.25	8.52
婚前检查率 (%)	Rate of Pre-martial Check-up (%)	54.7	98.89	100
城市	Urban	77	102.08	101.82
农村	Rural	23.3	91.15	95.7
残疾儿童入学率 (%)	Enrollment Rate of Deformed Children (%)	64.15	95.18	97.24

19-34 《九十年代中国儿童发展规划纲要》监测统计资料(措施指标)
SUPERVISORY STATISTICS FOR 《PROGRAM OUTLINE OF CHINESE CHILDREN DEVELOPMENT IN 1990S》(MEASURE INDICATORS)

项目	Item	1990	1997	1998
人口自然增长率 (‰)	Natural Growth Rate of Population (‰)	6.62	1.89	0.03
节育手术并发症发生率 (1/万)	Rate of Complication from Birth Control Operation (1/ten thousand)	2.5	1.75	2.27
城市	Urban	3.5	1.93	2.68
农村	Rural	2.7	1.28	1.15
预算内卫生事业经费增长速度 (%)	Growth Rate of Budgetary Health Fund (%)			
妇幼保健费增长速度(卫生局系统) (%)	Growth Rate of Maternal and Child Hygiene Subsidies(Health Bureau System) (%)		3	-5
卫生防疫费增长速度(卫生局系统) (%)	Growth Rate of Epidemic Prevention Subsidies(Health Bureau System) (%)		37	8
新法接生率 (%)	Rate of Delivering Children with New Method (%)	99.7	100	100
城市	Urban	99.9	100	100
农村	Rural	99.6	100	100
孕产妇住院分娩率 (%)	Childbirth Rate of Pregnant Woman and Lying-in Woman in Hospital (%)	83.79	98.46	98.92
城市	Urban	99.9	98.98	99.22
农村	Rural	67.3	97.64	98.44
产后出血死亡率 (1/10万)	Death Rate of Birth Hemorrhage (10/million)	9.28	5.26	2.99
孕妇缺铁性贫血患病率 (%)	Rate of Iron-deficiency Anemia of Pregnant Woman (%)		4.99	6.94
城市	Urban		6.13	8.24
农村	Rural		2.81	4.47
母乳喂养率(0-4个月) (%)	Rate of Feeding on Mother Milk (0-4 months) (%)		74.86	90.3
城市	Urban	13.6	68.91	86.38
农村	Rural	67	82.77	95.46
七岁以下儿童保健复盖率 (%)	Health Protection Rate of Children below 7-year-old (%)	59.4	93.46	95.63
城市	Urban		93.83	96.6
农村	Rural	82.73	92.94	94.18
孕产妇保健复盖率 (%)	Covering Rate of Health Protection for Pregnant Woman and Lying-in Woman (%)		94.77	94.89
城市	Urban		94.86	94.78
农村	Rural		94.63	95.06
一岁以内儿童计划免疫"四苗"接种率 (%)	Inoculation Rate of Immunity Four-Vaccine of Children within 1-year-old (%)	98.73	99.5	99.76
卡介苗	BCG Vaccine	99.5	99.94	99.94
麻疹疫苗	Measles Vaccine	99.2	99.84	99.95
百白破三联制剂	Pertussis,Diphtheria and Tetanus Vaccine	99.1	99.79	99.87
脊髓灰质炎疫苗	Poliomyelitis Polio Vaccine	99.3	99.81	99.89
小儿脊髓灰质炎发病率 (1/10万)	Rate of Poliomyelitis Polio of Children (10/million)	0.04		
新生儿破伤风发病率 (‰)	Rate of Tetanus of New-borns (‰)	0.04	0.035	
新生儿破伤风死亡专率 (‰)	Death Rate of Tetanus of Newborns (‰)	0.5	1.51	
麻疹发病率 (1/10万)	Rate of Measles (10/million)	0.51	1.38	1.28
儿童腹泄发病率 (‰)	Rate of Diarrhea of Children (‰)		1.36	1.25
五岁以下儿童因腹泻死亡的人数比例 (%)	Proportion of Children below 5-year-old Died of Diarrhea (%)	4.46	4.53	1.78
急性呼吸道感染标准病例管理率 (%)	Managing Rate of Standard Case of Acute Infection of Respiratory Tract (%)		78.76	80.55
急性呼吸道感染临床管理率 (%)	Clinical Managing Rate of Acute Infection of Respiratory Tract (%)		70	93.69
五岁以下儿童因急性呼吸道感染死亡的人数 (人)	Number of Children below 5-year-old Died of Infection of Respiratory Tract (person)	92	77	45
地方性甲状腺肿大率 (%)	Rate of Local Goitre (%)	1.9	4.4	

19-35 全市市属律师事务所名录
LIST OF MUNICIPAL LAW OFFICES

所 名 Law Offices	电 话 Telephone	地 址 Address	邮编 Postcode	主任 Chairman
经济律师事务所	66014635	宣武门 西大街127号汇凯商苑4层	100031	王嘉本
华夏律师事务所	68870707	石景山路23号中础人厦205室	100043	谢建国
翱翔律师事务所	62367536	西城区德外大街34号德富宫宾馆	100011	万仲翔
北斗律师事务所	65936922/6 65073561	朝阳区六里屯北里1号(北京画院内)	100026	李永乐
北翔律师事务所	62172288-3902/11	海淀区白石桥路甲44号湖北宾馆九楼	100081	林子清
贝格律师事务所	64978208、64958968	北京市朝阳区亚运村北辰东路汇宾大厦916室	100101	李海彦
昌久律师事务所	66211663、66211885/9	西城区金融街27号投资广场A-902	100032	戴昌久
昌顺律师事务所	68311561	西城区百万庄大街19号写字楼2层	100037	冯林
长安律师事务所	65993388—80106	朝阳区朝外大街19号华普国际大厦801B	100020	王大成
大成律师事务所	68588091-96	西城区万通新世界广场B座22层	100007	彭雪峰
大地律师事务所	66211913~1915	西城区金融街27号投资广场B2103-2105	100032	梁人华
大理律师事务所	64273355-420/442	北京市朝阳区西坝河西里16号明宫宾馆420室	100028	李建玉
大正律师事务所	62352611/2	海淀区北太平庄花园路68号102室	100088	牛琳娜
当代律师事务所	68498061	海淀区白石桥路3号友谊宾馆迎宾楼1层	100873	王克义
地平线律师事务所	68498919	海淀区友谊宾馆雅园公寓63821室	100873	夏卫民
鼎铭律师事务所	66416688—8591~8599	宣武门西大街甲129号金隅大厦1818—1820室	100031	李杰
东友律师事务所	66058539	西城区灵镜胡同甲42号惠能大厦315室	100032	张予宪
方略律师事务所	64268138/42	东城区安德里北街乙21号奥星大厦 3层	100011	吴峥
公元律师事务所	68223559/3560	海淀区翠微路2号院印刷科贸世界	100036	张庆
共和律师事务所	64689106	朝阳区北三环东路8号静安中心9072室	100028	张建中
观韬律师事务所	68410567/68/69	海淀区车道沟1号滨河大厦12层	100089	韩德晶
国都律师事务所	63539935	宣武区陶然亭路2号奇然大酒店写字楼1230房间	100050	季力
国方律师事务所	62619988	海淀区知春路76号翠宫饭店写字楼610室	100086	丛培国
国信律师事务所	65978096/97/99	朝阳区京广中心商务楼十二层03号	100020	张自力
海斯律师事务所	62024455-3125/26	北三环中路38号金桥饭店125室	100088	杨新汉
海问律师事务所	64106920~6927	朝阳区东三环北路2号南银大厦1016室	100027	何斐
汉邦律师事务所	66055679、66054428	北京市西绒线胡同9号	100031	张康达
华通律师事务所	63542229-223/4/5	宣武区登莱胡同22号101-103室	100053	俞汉立
华洋律师事务所	63853885	丰台路口54号楼220室	100071	李法增
华宇律师事务所	67152889	崇文区广渠门内大街16#英奎斯写字楼	100062	葛传洪
华正律师事务所	64682850/2856	朝阳区左家庄前街1号百灵大厦A10层02号	100028	王洋
环中律师事务所	64200637/45	和平街北口甲12#北京基尔特中心 5006室	100013	孙卫宁
慧丰律师事务所	64411004	朝阳区安定门外皇姑坟1号安贞商务楼405室	100029	苗杰
嘉和律师事务所	65618880	朝阳区光华路7号汉威大厦 5A3室	100004	苏志鸿
金衡律师事务所	64987748	朝阳区小营路10号阳明国际公寓A--5D	100101	江明光
金桥律师事务所	68325012	北京市百万庄东大街甲2号	100037	李淑香
竞天律师事务所	65872200	朝阳区朝阳门外大街20号联合大厦1501、1504~1508室	100020	张绪生
凯源律师事务所	64929252 64937491	朝阳区北辰东路8号北京国际会议中心6019	100101	刘凝
力格律师事务所	68483244-46	海淀西三环北路11号华侨酒店写字楼B座二层	100081	邵国忠
隆海律师事务所	64411098	朝阳安外皇姑坟一号安贞商务写字楼317-319室	100029	王晶
明仁律师事务所	63969630	北京市复兴路甲14号华鹰大厦4座404室	100036	刘文荣
圣大律师事务所	67667676	丰台区芳诚园一区16号楼B座304号	100078	于君
双力律师事务所	65254131—1805	东城区东总布胡同5号办公大楼805、807室	100005	李翔
天安律师事务所	64040636-2105~08	东城区什锦花园23号	100007	郭凤武
天驰律师事务所	64283423~26	东城区安定门外大街208#三利大厦2017室	100011	刘延岭
天兆雨田律师事务所	65914739、65024689	朝阳区关东店南街2号新迪亚商务大厦1F101室	100020	于雷
通商律师事务所	65992255	朝阳区朝外大街19号华普国际大厦714室	100020	韩小京
通正律师事务所	65006430	建国门外大街19号国际大厦12C	100004	王宏林
同达律师事务所	65132136/34	东城区南河沿天安大厦519室	100006	刘红宇
万博律师事务所	64278199--510	东城区和平里东街民旺甲19号510室	100013	井宏林
威宇律师事务所	63409193	西城区莲花池东路甲3号北京3849信箱A座202室	100038	张巍
维义律师事务所	64617046	北京市朝阳区新源街19#楼	100027	孟庆龙
五环律师事务所	66081561、66081562	西城区宣武门西大街甲129号金隅大厦0816、0817室	100031	郝振刚
新纪元律师事务所	65542801/2/3/4	东城区朝阳门北大街8号富华大厦D座5层B室	100027	陈纪元
新世达律师事务所	66072346/7/8	西城区金融街37号百盛大厦809室	100032	赵秀峰
阳光律师事务所	67634679	北京市方庄小区方城园1区2楼首层	100078	王益民
正见永申律师事务所	64689128	北京市朝阳区北三环东路8号静安中心9071室	100026	于哮峰
中创律师事务所	62223419/20	西城区德胜门西大街68号	100035	柴志伟
中联律师事务所	66077680 66017755-3	北京市西长安街甲15#民航发展大厦二层	100031	袁曙宏
中业律师事务所	65229701~9708	东城区王府井大街33号柏景商业大厦 521室	100006	巩沙

19-35 续表1 continued

所　名 Law Offices	电　话 Telephone	地　　址 Address	邮编 Postcode	主任 Chairman
纵横律师事务所	63081044 63081335/39	东长安街42号(纺织总会)1335室	100742	沈志耕
安平城律师事务所	63022760/2823	宣武区珠市口大街120号太丰惠中大厦0327 室	100050	关安平
逢时律师事务所	67110422	北京市崇文区龙潭路3号	100061	王耀庭
光明律师事务所	65911546	朝阳区白家庄路3号物华庄园219室	100020	张卫华
汉华律师事务所	65541431-33	东城区朝阳门北大街8#富华大厦18层	100027	张晓维
衡石律师事务所	65031590	朝阳关东店2号广澳商务楼A座606室	100020	吴跃生
嘉华律师事务所	65925336/37	北京市朝阳区雅宝路10号凯威大厦603室	100020	魏蒂
嘉润律师事务所	65142061—2067	建外大街22号赛特大厦1701室	100004	安念念
剑锋律师事务所	65926720/21/23	朝阳区东三环北路52号博智大厦503室	100026	计剑峰
杰通律师事务所	62229101/9183	海淀区学院路41号法苑公寓3F	100088	唐国玺
金诚律师事务所	65263518	东城区建内大街8号中粮广场A座6层	100005	于德斌
金平律师事务所	64877783/84/85	北京市朝阳区北四环路北辰西路社科院1016室	100101	金莲淑
金通律师事务所	66417440/41	宣武门西大街金隅大厦1104—1106室	100031	张德荣
京都律师事务所	66213298/99	西城区金融街乙16号华实大厦5层	100032	田文昌
京融律师事务所	62624979/82	海淀区知春路46号二段楼1层2101室	100088	刘敬华
经纬律师事务所	84228867	和平里南街五区甲七号	100013	王以岭
明诚律师事务所	65872372~2375	朝阳区朝阳大街20号联合大厦703室	100020	梁祖杰
君合律师事务所	65134500	东城区和平宾馆19层	100004	巩军
君泽君律师事务所	64926458	北京市亚运村汇宾大厦B座1518.1520室	100101	金明
昆仑律师事务所	62569091、62644707	北京市海淀区倒座庙1号（民族翻译中心）	100080	陶雷
民言律师事务所	64974673	北京市朝阳区小营路亚运花园1号楼1D	100101	黄炎
清源律师事务所	62947533	朝阳区德清路千秋大厦	100085	黄志青
商海律师事务所	65283621	王府井大街99号世纪大厦A820室	100006	高晓风
尚公律师事务所	68587971/72/73/74	阜外大街2#万通新世界广场B座2201—2203室	100037	李尚公
时代律师事务所	65824176	朝阳区白家庄民航大院东里20号楼	100026	于宁
实现者律师事务所	62218489	海淀区西土城路25号中国政法大学图书馆三层西侧	100088	张丽萍
万象律师事务所	63842404	北京市丰台镇文体路11号	100071	梁建光
武石宋律师事务所	66184627　66184657	西城西内南草厂11号中发商务楼302室	100035	武利剑
益成律师事务所	65016677-32031/3	朝阳区朝阳门南大街14号外企服务公司C203室	100020	赵洪琛
中恒律师事务所	65235599—208~212	东城区东总布胡同弘通巷四号弘通写字楼	100005	阳志平
众朋律师事务所	64992616	朝阳区亚运村汇园公寓L座703室	100101	冯笑
众天律师事务所	64297862、64294898	朝阳区和平西街三川大厦208室	100013	苌宏亮
北方律师事务所	67111837	崇文区幸福大街甲28号	100061	刘鸿
博安律师事务所	64645969、64682846	朝阳区左家庄前街1号百灵大厦6层	100028	李安平
大众—旭业律师事务所	68021155—1101/2	西城区南礼士路13号中银写字楼110室	100045	
公诚律师事务所	65871145~1148	朝阳区朝外大街20号联合大厦1105室	100020	张宏久
浩天律师事务所	64634691	北京市朝阳区东三环北路甲2号京信大厦1132室	100027	马晓刚
华伦律师事务所	64282527	北京市朝阳区西坝河西里16号明宫宾馆218室	100028	刘子华
建诚律师事务所	63150588	北京市宣武区长椿街西里7号楼东楼201、202室	100053	李刚
建元律师事务所	66210763~66	西城区金融街23号平安大厦508室	100032	郭光
陆通联合律师事务所	65542883-86	朝阳门北大街8#富华大厦F座7--A	100020	刘红宇
融商律师事务所	65542823/24/25	东城区朝阳门北大街8号富华大厦A座302室	100027	杜宝成
商安律师事务所	68317708	西城区车公庄大街3号新华写字楼202室	100044	曾明
天鉴律师事务所	82611953	海淀区双榆树东里19号楼2层	100086	鲁晓风
万森律师事务所	64974342	北京市朝阳区安苑东里1区4号	100029	赵红革
喜马拉雅律师事务所	64980652	亚运村惠中里A区卧龙花园214楼103室	100010	索朗旺久
友邦律师事务所	66187607	北京市西城区西直门宾馆2号楼108室	100035	杨波
远望律师事务所	64003154	北京市朝内大街75号院2号楼	100010	何连水
岳成律师事务所	65542961	东城区朝阳门北大街8号富华大厦F座507室	100027	岳成
中盛律师事务所	68467083/4/6	北京市海淀区白石桥11号理工科技大厦2103室	100081	赵宏瑞
中洋律师事务所	65044005/6	朝阳区东三环北路36号朝阳剧场万业通写字楼203、205室	100026	王沐
中银律师事务所	66210709~12	西城区金融街23号平安大厦609室	100032	唐念龙
邦恒律师事务所	66985455	复兴路甲14号华鹰大厦312室	100036	吴志凡
金杜律师事务所	65541628/30/32/1155	东城区朝阳门北大街8号富华大厦c栋11层	100027	王俊峰
隆安律师事务所	65325588	朝阳区建国门外大街21号国际俱乐部238室	100020	李大中
明华律师事务所	67607082	丰台区方庄芳城园1区1号戊单元403室	100078	卢光耀
普华律师事务所	65097128~31	朝阳区团结湖南里甲5号京龙大厦908—910室	100026	刘守豹
齐致律师事务所	67085130~5133	崇文区打磨厂街宝鼎广场601室	100062	单卫红
商泰律师事务所	64052707--9	北京市东城区东四北大街343号长寿宫大厦7层	100010	郭华
实华律师事务所	64973261/62	朝阳区惠新东街8号1105室	100029	徐志远
天元律师事务所	68335690、68338606	西城区阜城门外大街17号大百科出版社808	100037	王立华

19-35 续表2 continued

所　名 Law Offices	电　话 Telephone	地　址 Address	邮编 Postcode	主任 Chairman
希望律师事务所	64280647	北京市东城区和平里五区甲19号楼	100013	赵湘
远东律师事务所	66706361	北京市海淀区复兴路83号院专修楼304、305室	100856	乔东升
正合律师事务所	68214433-8675	北京市万寿路甲12号万寿宾馆中宾楼673房间	100036	穆静
中伦律师事务所	64661648	北京市东三环北路甲二号京信大厦14层	100027	杨若寒
中润律师事务所	62053955、62384780	北京市西城区马甸南村双秀公园南区办公楼	100088	李世亮
中翔律师事务所	67654847	丰台区方庄芳城园1区2号楼	100078	张莲玉
广盛律师事务所	65913530/32	北京市建国路99号中服大厦25层2503室	100020	吴军
江川律师事务所	65992686-88	朝阳区朝阳门外大街19号华普国际大厦720室	10002	蒋京川
君屹律师事务所	65101247--52	北京市建国门内大街7号光华长安大厦209-210室	100005	刘屹
康信律师事务所	64215443	北京市和平里7区16号楼	100013	胡志强
律通律师事务所	68188437、68165784	海淀区王枫园宾馆B座305室	100039	李宝珠
吴栾赵阎律师事务所	68012986	西城区月坛北街甲1#吉百川写字楼	100037	吴以钢
正平律师事务所	65136511/2、65228815	北京市东城区史家胡同甲24号	100010	李炳成
中元律师事务所	64968738/62/8692	朝阳区小营路13号亚非大厦6001室	100101	康健
炜衡律师事务所	62005522—3162~3166	西城区北三环中路27号福尼特大厦435、436室	100029	张小炜
成师律师事务所	64311024	朝阳区将台路2号爱都大厦201、310室	100016	房金榲
海通律师事务所	65992378/79	朝阳区朝外大街19号华普国际大厦908室	100020	杨文贵
恒德律师事务所	64980527/28	朝阳区安外安定路1号	100029	徐蓬
瑞成律师事务所	65263291/3292	东城区东交民巷39号	100006	高国华
中诚律师事务所	68931230、68363948	海淀区首体南路2号228室	100044	陈平
中则律师事务所	62051321	朝阳区天星大厦812室	100029	董葭
惠中律师事务所	88140483	海淀区阜成路81号院1号楼3层	100036	吉达珠
天地和律师事务所	64680351/2/5	朝阳区小亮马桥东方东路6号御东商务楼507室	100027	舒玉晶
中济律师事务所	65126959	北京市东城区礼士胡同161号	100010	张志坚
周刘律师事务所	62375666	海淀区学院路丙39号L座	100083	刘玉明
威灵律师事务所	63182266--8611	宣武区西便门西里16号禾田大厦611室	100053	申杰
亿中律师事务所	68341839	北京市车公庄大街6号	100041	王明哲
翔龙律师事务所	67658972	北京市东铁匠营横七条三号	100075	吴宁
诚实律师事务所	69745577-5102	北京市昌平县中国政法大学外籍楼102室	102249	吴晓刚
现代律师事务所	65269454	北京市北京饭店1108室	100031	张洪涛
双城律师事务所	64662652	北京市东三环北路甲2号京信大厦主楼331室	100027	赵恒
民正律师事务所	66211612、66211613	西城区金融街27号投资广场B—21	100032	卞宜民
金台律师事务所	87289277	丰台区海户西里7区铭诚写字楼 314室	100077	王月圆
昌明律师事务所	64612505/06	朝阳区北三环东路2号中旅大厦2505室	100028	蒋五四
天时律师事务所	62005522-3005/6	西城区北三环东路27号福尼特大厦 605、606室	100029	杜金柱
国达律师事务所	62369935--9937	西城区黄寺大街23号大业商务俱乐部B座217室	100011	杨乐
中通律师事务所	65871043/1044/2243	朝阳区朝外大街20号联合大厦907室	100020	郑进峰
大都律师事务所	64430633/39	朝阳区安贞西里五区仟村商务大楼10层1005室	100029	杨月昆
大通—正达律师事务所	66417461/5/7	宣武门西大街金隅大厦14A12—A15	100031	谭[illegible]
世纪律师事务所	63954503/04	西客站莲花池东路肇麟大厦501室	100055	赵维光
海南方圆律师事务所北京分所	62379855	北太平庄双秀公园写字楼210室	100088	程建英
沈阳涉外经济律师事务所北京分所	62015588-429	北京市德外大街1号辽宁饭店4层	100088	张桂杰
新疆商务律师事务所北京分所	66094820	西城区复兴门内大街45#	100801	朱建文
开来律师事务所	64992318	亚运村汇园公寓K座9-318室	100101	开来
莫少平律师事务所	66058311	东城区中山公园水榭	100031	莫少平
谢朝华律师事务所	65978806	朝阳区呼家楼京广中心2901室	100020	谢朝华
国浩律师集团(北京)事务所	65051941	朝阳区光华路乙12号国贸中心咨询大楼13层	100020	张涌涛
徐玉光律师事务所	67128899—3820	崇文区光明路13号亿兴大厦西楼318室	100061	徐玉光
李文律师事务所	65923355	建国门外大街19号国际大厦2603室	100004	李文
步天律师事务所	68536688—6004/5	西城区复兴门外大街19号燕京饭店6004、6005室	100045	刘卫
城乡建设律师事务所	68017755--2423	南礼士路头条三号市建委南楼421室	100045	刘衡平
地石律师事务所	62511038　62511435	北京市海淀区人民大学院内	100872	孔庆云
法大律师事务所	62228810	北京市海淀区西土城路25号	100088	李梦福
法苑律师事务所	68582901	西城区白云观街北里6号法学会	100045	刘小力
光大律师事务所	62214370	海淀区西土城路25号	100088	刘金友
衡平律师事务所	66150594、66173246	北京市西城区丰盛胡同13号	100032	赵永林
华海律师事务所	64334485	酒仙桥路甲11号三峡大厦326室		
华坤律师事务所	68466395	北京市西三环北路56号计算机学院	100044	宋石民
华贸律师事务所	64942695 64974733	朝阳区小营东路12号亚运花园1号楼8B房间	100101	王晓川
汇明律师事务所	64411188—3025	朝阳区安贞西里五区仟村商务楼西门D—1层	100029	贾玉英
京工律师事务所	65252373	东城区灯市口大街100号	100006	焦延军

19-35 续表3 continued

所 名 Law Offices	电 话 Telephone	地 址 Address	邮编 Postcode	主任 Chairman
京颐律师事务所	62806401	海淀区大有庄100号	100091	李雅云
九州律师事务所	66051872	北京市西城区南长街头32号	100031	朱云
蓝盾律师事务所	63473081	西城区木樨地南里公安大学校内402号	100038	孟昭阳
奇鸣律师事务所	68323355-2476	西城区车公庄6号主楼503室	100044	赵奇
清华律师事务所	62773077	海淀区华业大厦1206室	100083	王承继
天京律师事务所	66186688-5305	西城区西直门南大街6号国务院二招5楼5310室	100035	朱天水
同和律师事务所	68498615/6	白石桥3号友谊宾馆4号楼40423、40424室	100873	刘东进
新达律师事务所	68224455-3603	北京市复兴路乙59号	100036	陈焕新
新元律师事务所	68904729、68904725	海淀区阜城路33号商学院	100037	刘淑莲
信义德律师事务所	62073679	西城区 北三环中路27号福尼特大厦615室	100029	王和
正大律师事务所	63047299	崇文区幸福大街26号南门	100061	许 藩
中北律师事务所		崇文区东大街4号楼6门1层	100051	
青山律师事务所	63032569	宣武区前门大街储子营9号	100050	田青云
求实律师事务所	64934751	朝阳区洼里南口大屯路商业房临7号|大屯路3号917大楼转	100101	涂斯春
四海律师事务所	65005783	北京市朝阳团结湖北区3条17楼2单元地下室	100026	李礼如
天宇律师事务所	65241973	北京市东城区东交民巷27号旁门	100006	仇明
正义律师事务所	65246275	北京市东交民巷西口正义律师事务所收	100006	井玉章
天中律师事务所	65992532/33/34/35	朝阳区朝外大街19号华普国际大厦829室	100020	金伊燕
天宁律师事务所	66169168	西城区黄城根北街1号万高写字楼	100034	刘子玉
中京律师事务所	62073620/21	西城区北三环中路27号福尼特大厦510室	100029	潘忠仁
力行律师事务所	68486201	海淀区西三环北路72号中经大厦228室	100037	李宪群
高朋律师事务所	65030460~0465	朝阳区东三环北路42号新东方写字楼	100020	胡莲萍
华一律师事务所	68486187/9、68486219	海淀区西三环北路72号中经大厦218室	100037	姚国斌
风清律师事务所	65911518	朝阳区白家庄路3号物华庄园107室	100020	卢亚文
华鹏律师事务所	62073040/6315	海淀区花园东路31号牡丹宾馆六层	100083	王京武
伟拓律师事务所	65011279/80	东直门南大街14号保利大厦568、574室		张建明
高问律师事务所	68095533	西城区阜外大街7号国投大厦407室	100037	高煜英
中瑞律师事务所	64689564/9566	朝阳区北三环东路8号静安中心2051室	100028	王淑焱
中仁律师事务所	68470048	海淀区白石桥11号理工科技大厦1102室	100081	邵长松
尚荣律师事务所	65869589/90/97	建国门外大街甲1号金之桥3层	100020	冯军
中基律师事务所	64661654/1853	东三环北路甲1号京信大厦14层1433室	100027	李洪积
国维律师事务所	82074750	朝阳区华严里1号	100029	陈秀改
怡丰律师事务所	64605596/7/8	朝阳区左家庄1号国门大厦A座3-G	100028	谢青
嘉维律师事务所	68284994、682786-612	海淀区复兴路24号嘉丰大厦6楼611—614室	100852	刘家生
至元律师事务所	65141388	东城区校蔚胡同5号文达写字楼206、207室	100730	汪贻祥
天钰衡律师事务所	67713256	朝阳区垂杨柳南街	100022	谷美荣
国联律师事务所	68363322—5007/8	西直门外大街6号中仪大厦540、540A、540B	100044	许涛
常春律师事务所 北京分所	64159547/9622	新中街乙12号紫铭大厦507室	100027	王峥
信达律师事务所 北京分所				刘凤良
建孚律师事务所	68244552	海淀区复兴路83号专修楼200室	100856	李景山
亦德律师事务所	66126027/6028	西城区新街口百花深处胡同16号居安文艺会馆201、202室	100035	张明
本杰律师事务所	62382211—6449	海淀区德胜门外东滨河路11号国旅发展大厦104室	100011	兰洋
思峰律师事务所	65101661/2/7/9	东城区建内大街7号光华长安大厦1座802室	100005	张玉栋
泽普律师事务所	65258999	东城区王府井大街99号世纪大厦A512A、A512B	100006	张彩萍
国地律师事务所	68305840、60/1/2	西城区车公庄大街乙1号富通大厦316室	100044	张长江
嘉安律师事务所	63957386/7387	复兴路12号思菲科技大厦B-210~212室	100038	郑爱利
道和律师事务所	62976005/7/8/9	海淀区上地信息中路20号新奥特大厦E-305、306室	100085	黄鹰
丰联律师事务所	64435181	朝阳区樱花西街8号北方安华大厦405室	100029	佟洁
元昊律师事务所	65235981	建国门内大街8号中粮广场B301室	100020	王汉军
中旭律师事务所	64920119	亚运村汇宾大厦1508室	100101	郝炼
格文律师事务所	65050627/1573/1910~1	朝阳区光华路乙12号经贸部咨询信息大楼八层	100020	姚晓明
开物律师事务所 北京分所	64289714	北京市朝阳区七圣路6号 沁园写字楼201-206室	100028	胡涛
河南学苑律师事务所北京分所	67126688-3201、3504	东花市大街221号东花市招待所201室	100062	赵贵训
众一律师事务所	67082605/2607/2608	崇文区东打磨厂街7号宝鼎广场501、502室	100062	梅慎实
威正律师事务所	88130266-2310	海淀区八宝庄小区11号楼2310室	100038	娄峻
泰德律师事务所	68498175/8197	海淀区友谊宾馆乡园62333/62334室	100873	赵要德

主要统计指标解释

社会福利事业单位 指为社会上丧失劳动能力、无依无靠、无生活来源的孤老残幼、家庭无力照管的老人、残疾儿童、精神病人和优抚对象、困难户、社区居民提供收养、帮助、服务的福利机构和福利设施。

社会福利企业 指以集中安置有一定劳动能力的残疾人就业为目的、带有社会福利性质的特殊企业的总称（残疾职工占生产人员10%以上）。

社会收养单位 指国有优抚（休）疗养院、福利院以及集体所有制和其他所有制的光荣院、敬老院事业单位的总称。

收养人数 指优抚(休)疗养院、福利院报告期末实际收养的优抚对象、社会“三无”对象和自费人员在院的总人数。

律师 指受聘参加律师事务所工作，提任法律顾问、刑（民）事代理人、刑事辩护人，办理非诉讼事件、解答法律询问，代写法律事务文书等主要从事律师业务的专职法律工作者和兼职律师。

公证人员 指在国家公证机关依法办理公证事务的司法人员。包括公证员、助理公证员和在公证处工作的其他人员。

办理公证文书 指公证处在一定时期内办结的公证文书件数。公证文书系按司法部规定或批准的格式制作。包括国内公证和涉外公证两部分。其中国内公证分为经济公证和民事法律关系公证两大类。

调解人员 指人民调解委员会担负调解民间一般民事纠纷和轻微违法行为所引起的纠纷的工作人员。包括调解委员会的委员和调解小组调解员。

调解民间纠纷 指调解委员会依照法律规定，根据自愿原则，用说服教育的方法调解民间发生的有关民事权利和义务的争执，促成当事双方达到协议和谅解，解决纠纷。包括婚姻家庭纠纷，财产权益纠纷等。不包括法院受理调解的民事案件数。

离休、退休、退职人员 指正式办理了离休、退休、退职手续，并享受相应的离休、退休、退职待遇的人员。

保险福利费用 指企业、事业、机关单位再工作以外实际支付给职工和离休、退休、退职人员个人以及用于集体的劳动保险和福利费用。

1. 职工保险福利费用具体包括：

（1）医疗卫生费 指实行公费医疗企业的职工及其供养的直系亲属的医疗费、医务经费、职工因工伤就医路费以及住院伙食补助费等；卫生部门开支的事业及机关单位职工的公费医疗经费；未参加公费医疗的企业、事业和机关单位职工的医疗费。

（2）丧葬抚恤救济费 指因职工死亡而支付的丧葬费、丧葬补助费和所遗供养直系亲属的抚恤费、救济费、生活补助费以及职工供养直系亲属死亡时的丧葬补助费等。

（3）生活困难补助 指对生活困难的职工实际支付的定期补助和临时性补助。

（4）文体宣传费 指企业、事业和机关单位实际支付的文体宣传费。不包括学习费。

（5）集体福利事业补贴费 指对职工浴室、理发室、洗衣房、哺乳室、托儿所等集体福利设施各项支出与收入相抵后的差额补助费。

（6）集体福利设施费 指按照国家规定开支的集体福利设施费用。如职工食堂炊事用具的购置费、修理费、职工宿舍的修缮费用。不包括由企业、事业和机关单位自筹经费开支的职工福利设施的基本建设费用。

（7）计划生育补贴 指发给职工独生子女的补贴费和保健营养费。

（8）其他 指上述费用以外，单位支付给职工的保险福利费。

2. 离休、退休、退职人员保险福利费用具体包括：

（1）离休金 指发给离休人员的工资和按1982年国务院发布的“关于老干部离职休养制度的几项规定”发给符合规定的离休干部相当于1-2个月标准工资的生活补贴和按有关文件规定提高离休人员的待遇所增加的费用及粮油价格补贴等。

（2）退休金 指按照国家有关规定发给退休人员的退休费和按有关文件规定提高退休人员的待遇所增加的费用及粮油价格补贴等。

（3）职工生活费 指按照1978年国务院《关于工人退休、退职的暂行办法》规定定期发给退职人员的生活费用和按有关文件规定提高退职人员的待遇所增加的费用及粮油价格补贴等。

（4）医疗卫生费　指离休、退休、退职人员的医疗费、住院费以及住院伙食补助等费用。

（5）护理费　指因工致残、饮食起居需人扶助的离休、退休人员的护理费以及因病不能自理的离休人员的护理费。

（6）生活补贴　指按照 1985 年国务院《关于发给离退休人员生活补贴费的通知》规定，发给离休、退休人员的生活补贴费。

（7）交通费补贴　指按月发给离休人员的交通费补贴。

（8）丧葬抚恤救济费　指离休、退休、退职人员死亡的丧葬费、丧葬补助费和所遗供养直系亲属的抚养费、救济费、生活补助费以及供养直系亲属死亡时的丧葬补助费等。

（9）其他　包括易地安置的离休、退休、退职人员的安家补助费；离休、退休、退职人员的生活困难补助费、书报费、洗理费、副食品价格补贴、房租价格补贴、水电补贴、少数民族补贴以及老干部活动经费开支的旅游费用等。

Explanatory Notes On Main Statistical Indicators

Social Welfare Institutions refer to institutions providing adoption,help and services to persons such as (1)those who have no kith and kin and can not support themselves, (2)the old,deformed children,mental patients with no cares of family (3)persons receiving special pensions or with living difficulties,etc.

Social Welfare Enterprises refer to special enterprises which centralized employing deformed man with ability to work （the proportion of deformed staff and workers to all production personnel above 10%）.

Adoption Units including state-owned sanatoriums for persons receiving special pensions,social welfare homes, collective-owned and other ownership homes for disable veterans and old people.

Number of People Adopted by Social Welfare Institutions refers to the number of persons receiving special pensions,those who have no ability to work,no dependent and no living source and persons at one's expenses taken in by social welfare institutions at the end of reported period.

Lawyers include full or part-time lawyers and full-time legal workers employed by law office to act as law advisers, agents in criminal or civil lawsuits, defenders in criminal lawsuits, or to handle non-litigious legal affairs, to advise on legal matters, or to write legal papers for others.

Notary Personnel refer to judicial officials of the state notary offices handling notarization work according to law. They include notaries, assistant notaries, and other people working for notary offices.

Notarized Documents refer to the notary documents finished by notary offices in a year. The notary documents are drawn up in accordance with the regulations of the Ministry of Justice, including domestic documents and foreign-related documents.

Domestic documents are divided into two major categories: documents on economy and documents on civil legal relations.

Mediators refer to workers in people's mediation committees responsible for mediating in civil disputes and cases of slight infraction of the law, including members of the mediation committees and mediators in mediation groups.

Mediation of Civil Disputes refers to mediation committees' work in mediating of civil disputes concerning civil rights and responsibilities through persuasion and education in accordance with the provisions of law on a voluntary basis, so as to solve disputes by helping the parties involved come to an agreement and understanding . The disputes include divorce cases and disputes over property ownership , but exclude the civil cases to be handled by the court.

Retired or Resigned Personnel refers to the persons who have formally gone through the formalities for their retirement or quitting work and enjoy the corresponding treatments.

Insurance and Welfare Funds refers to labor insurance and welfare fund paid by enterprises, organizations and institutions to their staff and workers as well as retired and quitted persons in addition to their wages and salaries.

1. Insurance and Welfare Funds for Staff and Workers include:

（1）Medical Care Allowance includes cost of medical care of staff and workers and their dependent family members covered by the medical care system of enterprises, traveling expenses of injured employees to hospital and their food subsidies during hospitalization; the cost of medical care of employees covered by the medical care system of institutions and organizations; the cost of medicine of employees in enterprises, institutions and organizations not covered by the medical care system.

（2）Funeral Expenses and Pensions for Family of the Deceased refer to funeral expenses of staff and workers, pensions and allowance for their dependent family members, as well as subsidies to funeral expenses of staff and workers' dependent family members.

(3) Allowance for Living refers to regular or temporary allowance to staff and workers with difficulties in making living.

(4) Expenses on Recreation, Sports and Publicity Activities refer to actual payment made by enterprises and institutions in recreational, sports and publicity activities, excluding training cost.

(5) Subsidies to Collective Welfare refer to the expenditures on making up the loss of welfare operations, such as public bathrooms, barber shops, laundries, nurseries and kindergartens.

(6) Expenses on Collective Welfare Facilities refer to expenditures on collective welfare facilities in line with state regulations, such as the purchase and repair of cooking utensils for canteens, and repair of living quarters of staff and workers, but excluding the expenses on welfare projects financed with self-raised funds.

(7) Family Planning Subsidy refers to subsidy of health allowance paid to staff and workers in one-child family.

(8) Others refer to other insurance and welfare funds paid to staff and workers.

2. Insurance and Welfare Funds for Retired and quitted Staff and Workers include:

(1) Merit Retirement Pensions refer to pensions and other subsidies paid to merit retired in line with relevant government documents.

(2) Retirement Pensions refer to pensions and other subsidies paid to retired staff and workers in line with the relevant government documents.

(3) Quitted Allowances for Living refer to living allowances and subsidies paid to quitted staff and workers in line with relevant government instructions.

(4) Expenses for Medical Care refer to the costs for medical treatment, hospitalization and food subsidies in hospitals for merit retired, retired and quitted staff and workers.

(5) Nursing Cost refers to cost for nursing retired or quitted staff and workers without ability to take care of themselves and need the help of nurses.

(6) Living Subsidy refers to living subsidy paid to merit retired and retired employees in line with the instructions in a 1985 State Council document.

(7) Traffic Subsidy refers to the traffic subsidy paid monthly to merit retired staff.

(8) Funeral Expenses and Pensions for Family of the Deceased refer to the funeral expenses of merit retired, retired and quitted staff and workers, pensions and allowances for their dependent family members, as well as subsidies to funeral expenses of their dependent family members.

(9) Others refer to other expenses, including moving and settlement allowance, living allowance for difficult families, book and newspaper allowance, subsidy for non-staple foods, allowance for bath and haircut, housing subsidy, water and electricity subsidy, special allowance for staff and workers of national minorities, travelling cost for senior retired staff, etc.

1999

服务业

SERVICE

固定资产原价构成
Composition of Original Value of Fixed Assets

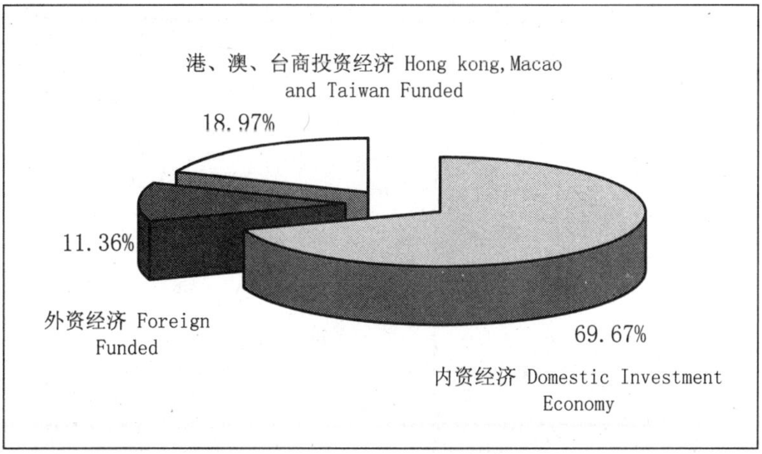

单位：亿元 100 million yuan	固定资产原价 Original Value of Fixed Assets	利润总额 Income Tax Payable	投资收益 Investment Income
总计 Total	1296.4	271.3	226
内资经济 Domestic Investment Economy	903.2	276.7	222.6
外商投资经济 Foreign Funded	147.3	0.5	3.24
港、澳、台商投资经济 Hong kong,Macao and Taiwan Funded	245.9	-5.8	0.18

主营业务收入构成
Composition of Revenue of Major Business

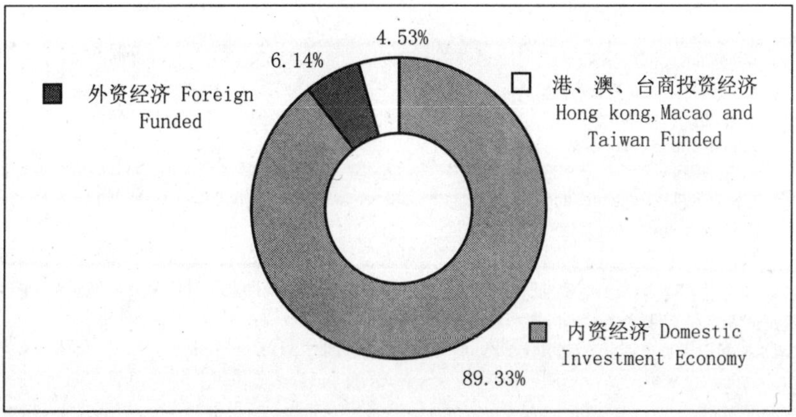

20-1 服务业企业财务状况

单位：千元

项目	Item	单位个数(个) Units (unit)	流动资产 合计 Total Circulating Assets	# 货币资金 Cash	# 应收帐款 Accounts Receivable	# 存货 Stock
合计	**Total**	**13296**	**1553374488**	**193358226**	**94121423**	**99527987**
按登记注册类型分	**Grouped by Registered Type**					
内资经济	Domestic Investment Economy	12039	1471697080	178698085	85469755	66285647
国有经济	State-owned	4496	1201765222	69342309	67569684	37487728
集体经济	Collective-owned	3008	48980869	26149803	2440446	2201286
联营经济	Joint Owned	289	5148896	1134382	538963	1530053
私营经济	Private Owned	1329	3105734	608154	374932	708674
股份合作企业	Share Holding Cooperative	865	24008724	16727879	582187	623875
股份有限公司	Share Holding Company	274	95995580	37917814	6141733	4107752
有限责任公司	Limited-Liability Company	1755	92215055	26794391	7808401	19440097
其他	Others	23	477000	23353	13409	186182
外商投资经济	Foreign Funded	700	38090326	8464522	5341545	10819411
港澳台商投资经济	Hongkong,Macao and Taiwan Funded	557	43587082	6195619	3310123	22422929
按国民经济行业分	**Grouped by Sector**					
金融业	Banking	96	1207631378	107643828	53609385	1742750
保险业	Insurance	9	26906273	18786639	298	1065
房地产业	Real Estate	758	138851142	13339356	10476187	77240584
公共服务业	Public Services	651	6815074	2429321	927125	1609842
居民服务业	Personal Services	736	869579	304084	214784	140193
旅馆业	Hotel	1179	11317040	4905356	1153781	1673742
旅游业	Tourism	222	3577625	923252	1261012	65753
交通运输辅助业	Logistic Support for Transportation	124	1694303	540704	458353	27534
仓储业	Storage	90	564031	126538	63307	46554
商业经纪与代理业	Commercial Brokerage and Agencies	50	7174427	3284655	1211023	556827
租赁服务业	Rental Services	154	3448766	569948	407890	113701
计算机应用服务业	Computer Application Services	1303	8593328	2223808	1389310	1966071
娱乐服务业	Entertainment Services	150	1882077	202451	155533	199342
信息咨询服务业	Consulting Services	2733	25561310	6400266	6811481	1106787
# 广告业	Advertisement	555	2568739	737241	647708	81703
其他社会服务业	Other Social Services	547	12835071	4129758	1789129	598561
卫生、体育和社会福利业	Health,Sports and Social Welfare	56	1090688	644138	284026	46117
教育文化艺术和广播电影电视业	Education,Culture,Arts, Radio,Film and Television	497	9132274	3620442	1009097	2195412
科学研究和综合技术服务业	Scientific Research and Polytechnical Services	3648	53930761	13686883	8937384	6098951
农林牧渔服务业	FFAF Services	97	350935	54468	153606	65228
地质勘察和水利管理业	Geological Prospecting and Water Conservancy	28	1885938	480348	235353	77232
其他	Others	168	29262468	9061983	3573359	3955741

注：服务业企业包括 (1)农林牧渔服务业；(2)地质勘察、水利管理业；(3)交通运输辅助业、其他交通运输业；(4)仓储业；(5)商业经纪与代理业；(6)金融、保险业；(7)房地产业；(8)社会服务业；(9) 卫生、体育和社会福利业；(10)教育、文化艺术及广播电影、电视业；(11)科学研究和综合技术服务业；(12)其他行业。

FINANCIAL INDICATORS FOR SERVICES ENTERPRISES

(1000 yuan)

长期 投资 Long-term Investment	固定资产 合计 Total Fixed Assets	固定资产 原价合计 Original Value of Fixed Assets	#生产 经营用 for Production Use	累计 折旧 Accumulative Depreciation	#本年 折旧 of this Year	无形及 递延资产 合计 Intangible and Deffered Assets	#无形 资产 Intangible	其他 资产 合计 Other Assets
332660183	112476824	129641804	72173045	37403750	6915835	24475500	13297664	948450797
316968533	83600517	90319161	51875692	24763623	4776496	17323592	8476753	944469092
247988129	65441542	69105965	40903461	18615623	3432964	11688909	6156495	932189268
16884202	5618742	7437347	3715160	2489370	473157	1447754	961430	226871
797092	1070520	1038721	681936	306340	57823	213735	39517	14969
479436	625760	692604	301045	164098	66672	392563	12914	72446
1137314	837264	978917	524141	636977	75758	342632	213961	194776
20545396	5743806	6087251	3066226	1376437	332477	1771394	523051	7659917
29069801	4244590	4952247	2668735	1166914	336101	1464963	568965	4110845
67163	18293	26109	14988	7864	1544	1642	420	0
14417045	11432611	14730467	9434595	4415486	893398	1867264	813186	2290611
1274605	17443696	24592176	10862758	8224641	1245941	5284644	4007725	1691094
212530403	14924881	15361641	5959266	3848323	850955	7469487	3920913	932878257
1075687	1496787	892964	469753	124026	52792	455100	6705	34918
10568289	19475350	23532806	10378151	5467712	981108	6632463	3915554	3448046
848179	9021164	12496779	10307149	4417929	772826	312736	221064	65234
142505	533298	631785	391087	208319	39470	93784	30323	45664
1461789	23416238	31450748	17688682	10629994	1473972	3953712	2036686	1290747
1772563	1825161	1659229	1036352	517128	87901	73202	36814	144356
725635	597800	746145	618512	185129	49135	70791	43282	91680
34197	730049	895109	316703	227005	27063	103402	75046	7134
2745891	1145159	1078062	812491	136383	35028	86411	60436	6949
240881	965297	1166941	743806	276217	69107	239755	42424	1466488
876957	1904622	2832475	1583906	1253016	307525	351864	244588	181215
81157	1399968	1904412	1425190	598621	123686	403451	125169	373658
23064846	5978785	5637586	3408486	1410390	389130	691740	215528	549093
331319	525952	655328	432530	206827	56393	70664	42489	38292
10916316	4047597	4079464	3005971	726431	211118	240054	97560	3356854
40998	969693	1033544	754463	213510	26835	130569	62672	24507
793984	6200198	6526492	3941377	1592166	301887	349469	250006	92896
15360149	11323971	11799843	6066859	3773730	969402	2541608	1795183	1624917
346956	195997	213478	124162	55497	6644	3745	907	5120
2460718	1347654	2225275	2013002	983542	20179	81485	10938	1127003
46572083	4977155	3477026	1127677	758682	120072	190672	105866	1636061

Note: Service enterprises include(a)FFAF services, (b)geographical prospecting and water conservancy, (c)logistic support for transportation and other transportation, (d)storage, (e)commercial brokerage and agencies, (f)banking and insurance, (g)real estate, (h)social services, (i)health,sports and social welfares, (j)education, culture,arts,radio,film and television, (k)scientific research and polytechnical services, (l)other services.

20-1 续表 1 continued

单位：千元

项目	Item	资产合计 Total Assets	流动负债合计 Total Circulating Liability	#短期借款 Short-term Loans	#应付帐款 Accounts Payable	长期负债合计 Total Long-term Liability
合计	**Total**	**3058865919**	**1927819977**	**277582240**	**110207447**	**632737911**
按登记注册类型分	**Grouped by Registered Type**					
内资经济	Domestic Investment Economy	2916019768	1864100398	261767066	98529980	599102797
国有经济	State-owned	2526015342	1603200899	226469045	79935332	548415353
集体经济	Collective-owned	74756855	54501716	2134903	4526462	12611911
联营经济	Joint Owned	7295669	4542018	878371	763114	902657
私营经济	Private Owned	4700181	2676710	361571	542337	789923
股份合作企业	Share Holding Cooperative	26558407	21622052	10024455	931681	2520333
股份有限公司	Share Holding Company	142361539	106779932	7263687	2914445	19658607
有限责任公司	Limited-Liability Company	133766813	70336734	14518949	8899384	14140846
其他	Others	564962	440337	116085	17225	63167
外商投资经济	Foreign Funded	70562474	28512426	7799142	5265584	14577627
港澳台商投资经济	Hongkong,Macao and Taiwan Funded	72283677	35207153	8016032	6411883	19057487
按国民经济行业分	**Grouped by Sector**					
金融业	Banking	2450887230	1663213025	217914337	62186895	510738804
保险业	Insurance	30061469	8203088		3337996	16514766
房地产业	Real Estate	183316830	113135007	23550331	14852842	24212204
公共服务业	Public Services	17165739	6720101	794028	2765515	831543
居民服务业	Personal Services	1703428	766065	87059	262462	69918
旅馆业	Hotel	42902315	15221418	3522591	2548029	15987206
旅游业	Tourism	7472633	3513975	872241	1049913	324450
交通运输辅助业	Logistic Support for Transportation	4165717	1597855	160746	796753	530451
仓储业	Storage	1494272	855865	488720	43564	149934
商业经纪与代理业	Commercial Brokerage and Agencies	11189885	6058250	942502	1612617	621739
租赁服务业	Rental Services	7616221	2841373	175020	767814	3489984
计算机应用服务业	Computer Application Services	12239206	6394819	1105475	1795777	1029158
娱乐服务业	Entertainment Services	4239546	2838481	941447	295693	488183
信息咨询服务业	Consulting Services	56207779	23220778	7927246	5693235	12706408
# 广告业	Advertisement	3563333	2256472	204438	683250	80484
其他社会服务业	Other Social Services	31596762	7993166	1723353	1381983	7325471
卫生、体育和社会福利业	Health,Sports and Social Welfare	2282884	1068102	39469	77199	150909
教育文化艺术和广播电影电视业	Education,Culture,Arts, Radio,Film and Television	16705421	5227392	607441	1486624	672258
科学研究和综合技术服务业	Scientific Research and Polytechnical Services	86458111	36248521	7770025	6632124	14477976
农林牧渔服务业	FFAF Services	907542	320765	135338	25703	182379
地质勘察和水利管理业	Geological Prospecting and Water Conservancy	6915644	1474823	793717	276269	1826470
其他	Others	83337285	20907108	8031154	2318440	20407700

20-1 续表 2 continued

(1000 yuan)

# 长期借款 Long-term Loans	负债合计 Total Liabilities	所有者权益合计 Ownership Interest	# 实收资本 Proceeds of Capital					
				#国家资本 State	#集体资本 Collective	#法人资本 Institutional Units	#个人资本 Individual	#港澳台资本 Hongkong, Macao and Taiwan
110185069	**2577147009**	**481718910**	**287392334**	**186012824**	**6523169**	**51058630**	**4418415**	**14085313**
84386977	2477940614	438079154	237127886	182513116	6032668	42137664	4352907	614437
67576966	2153733144	372282198	191081704	170778465	176663	18951397	23610	563556
994369	67334364	7422491	6161387	373693	4429922	685502	311272	3138
796341	5451529	1844140	1721963	658941	258691	778398	25732	
737787	3493722	1206459	1093120	3574	36370	199355	828906	11877
2262055	24151461	2406946	2012601	93760	385868	884032	612621	4653
1114281	126493336	15868203	12705898	2756913	336090	8415371	1045011	3119
10842011	96779514	36987299	22291165	7846950	405107	12171609	1502493	28094
63167	503544	61418	60048	820	3957	52000	3262	
11662932	44422029	26140445	30678115	1693788	289792	2656667	34800	3234517
14135160	54784366	17499311	19586333	1805920	200709	6264299	30708	10236359
27112011	2187759900	263127330	134988129	115718921	1068840	11990823	1248533	622252
	24717855	5343614	4100581	3600436		500000		145
16009172	139409742	43907088	32669814	8634833	596718	13354618	200560	7755196
346669	7555642	9610097	6089423	4895703	541653	449681	53646	72339
51406	849444	853984	680523	263911	152789	120244	36313	62629
13362269	31301502	11600813	18775143	6622616	685826	3662994	94716	2876693
234088	3842724	3629909	2193858	1626847	88472	218568	98591	4520
342172	2130400	2035317	1643640	412365	19873	1128491	7761	10377
80274	1007205	487067	496682	241512	92247	66958	358	55607
556963	6681941	4507944	3180007	2503004	7480	405828	1570	
2457269	6337137	1279084	1193174	248192	54816	447821	28596	116033
820978	7471539	4767667	3820203	1146484	586252	630243	353872	277734
463385	3474034	765512	1661060	177217	159110	419573	59294	458932
11253173	35951644	20256135	18198785	3647756	529908	6132949	1004902	437953
62496	2343353	1219980	1122588	403672	107649	256374	155508	18271
5793673	15329088	16267674	11507025	7676014	320643	894905	58593	268209
5570	1223500	1059384	409315	207630	19510	30404	9158	1504
511232	5904479	10800942	4543196	3035612	182839	505568	45347	607615
11691817	51064571	35393540	22997195	10739670	1142443	7416495	1115536	451021
128387	503273	404269	352123	92233	60655	196846	1069	
1514681	3301295	3614349	3121276	2614215	2011	505050		
17449880	41330094	42007191	14771182	11907653	211084	1980571		6554

单位：千元

20-1 续表 3 continued

项目	Item	#外商资本 Foreign	主营业务收入 Revenue of Major Business	营业成本 Operating Cost	营业费用 Operating Expenses	营业税金及附加 Operating Tax and Extra Charges
合计	**Total**	**20734152**	**300015695**	**243452966**	**21222847**	**6188887**
按登记注册类型分	**Grouped by Registered Type**					
内资经济	Domestic Investment Economy	201263	267991446	228836300	15868292	5039874
国有经济	State-owned	198496	219795345	193806753	10230123	3551913
集体经济	Collective-owned	815	9591539	6921998	1587664	348854
联营经济	Joint Owned	200	1547524	981211	164933	52048
私营经济	Private Owned	184	2760389	1764311	485685	71290
股份合作企业	Share Holding Cooperative		3904736	2918660	316937	106456
股份有限公司	Share Holding Company		15023632	11492827	1766820	483184
有限责任公司	Limited-Liability Company	1568	15327780	10927760	1308937	425053
其他	Others		40501	22780	7193	1076
外商投资经济	Foreign Funded	19488476	18433224	8832611	2515959	584369
港澳台商投资经济	Hongkong,Macao and Taiwan Funded	1044413	13591025	5784055	2838596	564644
按国民经济行业分	**Grouped by Sector**					
金融业	Banking	4038760	156710129	143717784	6912242	2688280
保险业	Insurance		18775650	19368574	599653	63660
房地产业	Real Estate	1992691	22712311	14136324	1989941	1127203
公共服务业	Public Services	33723	3642045	3265396	303807	239843
居民服务业	Personal Services	39735	1018941	464650	309317	38307
旅馆业	Hotel	1472727	12033927	2115687	4212241	589158
旅游业	Tourism	46667	4542486	3612816	310191	49340
交通运输辅助业	Logistic Support for Transportation	61940	893082	480601	127361	24534
仓储业	Storage	40000	528080	326117	101851	10493
商业经纪与代理业	Commercial Brokerage and Agencies	262125	1499541	1164856	67334	15925
租赁服务业	Rental Services	275987	920306	609697	134447	23611
计算机应用服务业	Computer Application Services	723470	8057873	6164877	630127	131057
娱乐服务业	Entertainment Services	385934	824200	170941	351806	54981
信息咨询服务业	Consulting Services	6155476	11969808	6554671	1634113	338512
# 广告业	Advertisement	65195	1971085	1039480	262396	91010
其他社会服务业	Other Social Services	2274120	4921468	2609197	1005031	164840
卫生、体育和社会福利业	Health,Sports and Social Welfare	140609	670310	382492	75975	6956
教育文化艺术和广播电影电视业	Education,Culture,Arts, Radio,Film and Television	53359	8332130	4600641	844298	215911
科学研究和综合技术服务业	Scientific Research and Polytechnical Services	2099987	30993162	24932432	1356909	312843
农林牧渔服务业	FFAF Services		149474	114645	9371	1558
地质勘察和水利管理业	Geological Prospecting and Water Conservancy		1737406	1368532	28512	18627
其他	Others	636842	9083366	7292036	218320	73248

20-1 续表 4 continued

(1000 yuan)

经营利润 Business Profits	其他业务利润 Profits of Other Business	管理费用 Overhead Expense	#税金 Taxes	#财产保险费 Premium of Property	#劳动待业保险 Premium for Employment	财务费用 Financial Expense	#利息支出 Interest Expenditure	营业利润 Operating Profits
29150995	**3375030**	**26027183**	**871840**	**187222**	**556958**	**4711335**	**8785930**	**1787507**
18246980	2895919	16385397	468452	123623	534594	2018916	7002154	2738586
12206556	2517651	11599053	396195	97824	460517	1244696	6418386	1880458
733023	75019	1236428	18208	11096	23319	147975	81228	-576361
349332	16538	293799	5172	1826	3263	31690	26197	40381
439103	11394	482811	3435	1333	712	10338	3361	-42652
562683	40238	322060	3941	1024	797	64957	33335	215904
1280801	83046	772997	13132	3739	21184	187873	171499	402977
2666030	148674	1670610	28361	6758	24780	327161	267958	816933
9452	3359	7639	8	23	22	4226	190	946
6500285	451637	6015453	168078	23592	12934	1096389	617472	-159920
4403730	27474	3626333	235310	40007	9430	1596030	1166304	-791159
3391823	990489	3717175	171707	8373	173851	-371032	5716920	1036169
-1256237	310925	453808	870	1351	1552	-174155	-174155	-1224965
5458843	297770	2993784	133618	45834	50316	1614326	1613690	1148503
-167001	58017	1100273	25160	13837	29804	44998	12672	-1254255
206667	18233	227780	2952	1119	14337	-897	-759	-1983
5116841	27471	4499798	233428	45510	84479	1793113	856887	-1148599
570139	4341	450436	28494	17218	33940	-9064	-20909	133108
260586	4233	234056	2189	1584	825	-25239	210	56002
89619	36325	132292	3766	1690	4102	29723	22588	-36071
251426	145119	272145	13095	9305	3818	-53136	-34493	177536
152551	11606	210438	6189	2052	1097	25344	12896	-71625
1131812	151941	1050837	13347	2063	4617	79717	17702	153199
246472	7773	412238	12781	1647	353	107133	31766	-265126
3442512	293786	3550837	101166	8014	10522	244873	143025	-59412
578199	8503	437986	3662	618	2548	-2334	-3695	151050
1142400	245457	995935	22597	5410	11250	81160	85912	310762
204887	1037	116587	945	454	163	-5306	-6315	94643
2671280	304471	1427557	49138	6871	55422	-63901	-22085	1612095
4390978	247174	3355735	38167	11693	60813	565696	227510	716721
23900	5601	31473	328	456	463	20672	18946	-22644
321735	7387	148332	819	321	2345	143425	215232	37365
1499762	205874	645667	11084	2420	12889	663885	68690	396084

20-1 续表 5 continued

单位：千元

项目	Item	投资收益 Investment Income	补贴收入 Subsidy Income	营业外收入 Out-business Income	营业外支出 Out-business Expenditure	利润总额 Total Profits
合计	**Total**	**22601268**	**2247890**	**1551787**	**1053922**	**27134530**
按登记注册类型分	**Grouped by Registered Type**					
内资经济	Domestic Investment Economy	22259554	2233937	1117257	680921	27668413
国有经济	State-owned	18528358	2215367	619888	453893	22790178
集体经济	Collective-owned	810833	3198	179325	55074	361921
联营经济	Joint Owned	20583	233	8138	11880	57455
私营经济	Private Owned	3202	122	3932	8430	-43826
股份合作企业	Share Holding Cooperative	83084	1454	12906	4518	308830
股份有限公司	Share Holding Company	1745919	3734	246706	103928	2295408
有限责任公司	Limited-Liability Company	1066693	9633	46334	42903	1896690
其他	Others	882	196	28	295	1757
外商投资经济	Foreign Funded	323893	1548	141269	260399	46391
港澳台商投资经济	Hongkong,Macao and Taiwan Funded	17821	12405	293261	112602	-580274
按国民经济行业分	**Grouped by Sector**					
金融业	Banking	17456948	542050	346984	274641	19107510
保险业	Insurance	668611		171029	6196	-391521
房地产业	Real Estate	437200	19751	143379	85883	1662950
公共服务业	Public Services	52138	1453734	69538	71564	249591
居民服务业	Personal Services	3506	100	24773	6508	19888
旅馆业	Hotel	67212	11180	298302	117282	-889187
旅游业	Tourism	64562	2291	17917	7983	209895
交通运输辅助业	Logistic Support for Transportation	78267	518	10355	2640	142502
仓储业	Storage	2972	6626	2133	1326	-25666
商业经纪与代理业	Commercial Brokerage and Agencies	83296	2732	7870	4283	267151
租赁服务业	Rental Services	10149		6792	11660	-66344
计算机应用服务业	Computer Application Services	56881	6846	43216	17466	242676
娱乐服务业	Entertainment Services	3099	499	19967	3801	-245362
信息咨询服务业	Consulting Services	447566	20176	52937	172477	288790
# 广告业	Advertisement	34994		15690	21631	180103
其他社会服务业	Other Social Services	616191	2765	36566	21963	944321
卫生、体育和社会福利业	Health,Sports and Social Welfare	702	1010	2400	694	98061
教育文化艺术和广播电影电视业	Education,Culture,Arts, Radio,Film and Television	49009	142588	67582	58566	1812708
科学研究和综合技术服务业	Scientific Research and Polytechnical Services	726422	12939	168406	130929	1493559
农林牧渔服务业	FFAF Services	24980	3163	6890	3564	8825
地质勘察和水利管理业	Geological Prospecting and Water Conservancy	15745	110	14031	3446	63805
其他	Others	1735812	18812	40720	51050	2140378

20-1 续表 6 continued

(1000 yuan)

应交所得税 Income Tax Payable	转作奖金的利润 Profits Distribut-ed as Bonus	提取盈余公积 Surplus Accu-mulation Funds Drawn	应付利润 Profits Payable	# 已分配股利 Divided Payment	未分配利润 Undis-tributed Profits	本年应付工资总额 Total Wages Payable in the Year	# 主营业务应付工资 Wage Payable of Major Business	本年应付福利费总额 Welfares Payable in the Year	# 主营业务应付福利费 of Major Business
9553885	**175019**	**3833763**	**2244190**	**663470**	**10860750**	**12086935**	**9451978**	**2127362**	**1645936**
8998718	115042	3748421	1439959	184208	16710654	9082736	6947243	1259986	928878
7670968	60414	2726491	734088	55042	14929852	6226189	4661039	857915	607914
118306	44113	145914	118360	34008	-529697	938447	757757	127887	103719
39983	950	15814	24694	16907	22138	134041	112592	16112	13250
18117	2690	13399	6093	20	-72002	270496	229298	30076	22611
51814	186	39970	7450	2520	162449	185650	132849	21272	13747
747789	424	559488	255240	59697	884503	567751	483701	108872	93726
351278	6265	247079	292447	15975	1319392	753647	564107	97466	73638
463		266	1587	39	-5981	6515	5900	386	273
166390	37188	33172	408175	184671	-1229096	1937906	1636510	494974	422883
388777	22789	52170	396056	294591	-4620808	1066293	868225	372402	294175
6535094	65938	1106718	696775	50046	15666460	1154214	753330	265272	152535
6849		5487			-3596438	116983	87998	12296	8457
665539	21656	247856	425709	171913	861239	1023694	863141	224872	169461
64777	1647	27731	53391	21934	91635	1360222	1206871	161386	146052
19009	455	16221	9447	323	-33758	223211	200939	25150	22711
203259	5078	7764	423616	264845	-4172425	1816604	1505850	489973	395712
69305	266	26409	7202	39	91565	193774	170256	25759	21618
39583	2	4316	21155	28037	182609	121185	110049	16900	14832
5382	1341	4387	2416	4	-37427	72810	61828	12357	10682
85262		63507	41494	15000	54521	70621	61060	9236	7608
11484	759	16435	8280	2400	-57339	64668	54092	13886	10403
79452	8197	66964	106172	64731	40645	536299	384629	98737	68492
-8212	11	2168	-874		-608675	164522	139364	43106	38708
236391	7560	100980	62401	1992	-465608	1254215	1132221	208259	191107
77533	6071	25012	33835	44	40496	152140	140229	22107	20570
178134	38970	245513	58530	20510	348255	1142961	740618	131233	96055
3429	803	97369	1426		5241	77063	58255	4744	3516
675622	9438	401799	50323	8354	1198445	606747	422454	89961	67153
284193	10917	467655	214972	12493	483663	1704470	1297546	244862	193737
239	814	7058	713		-5274	26925	16350	3078	2384
15636	1069	6550	17722		69178	44902	34873	5254	5049
383458	98	910876	43320	849	744238	310845	150254	41041	19664

1999

区县资料

STATISTICS FOR DISTRICTS AND COUNTIES

21-1 东城区、西城区国民经济主要指标
MAIN NATIONAL ECONOMIC INDICATORS FOR DONGCHENG AND XICHENG DISTRICTS

项目 Item	东城区 Dongcheng 1998	1997	1998年为1997年% 1998 as % of 1997	西城区 Xicheng 1998	1997	1998年为1997年% 1998 as % of 1997
综合 General Survey						
国内生产总值 (万元) Gross Domestic Product (10000 yuan)	234895	224988	104.4	353919	324662	109.0
第一产业 Primary Industry						
第二产业 Secondary Industry	27532	28858	95.4	26495	31484	84.2
第三产业 Tertiary Industry	207363	196130	105.7	327423	293178	111.7
财政收入 (万元) Fiscal Revenue (10000 yuan)	96318	82016	117.4	124571	110106	113.1
#各项税收 Taxes	85878.7	75133	114.3	102987	90225	114.1
财政支出 (万元) Fiscal Expenditure (10000 yuan)	118469	98765	120.0	139684	136377	102.4
#基本建设支出 Capital Construction	8390	7684	109.2	14444	14090	102.5
支援农业生产支出 Supporting Agriculture						
文教卫生事业费 Culture,Education and Health	34687	31801	109.1	40995	49726	82.4
人口和劳动力 **Population and Labor Force**						
总人口 (人) Total Population (person)	699752	717317	97.6	869006	877837	99.0
常住户籍人口 (人) Permanent Registered Population (person)	632533	642212	98.5	791595	804088	98.4
#非农业人口 Non-agriculture	632533	642212	98.5	791593	804088	98.4
男 Male	315550	320894	98.3	397054	400261	99.2
女 Female	316983	321318	98.7	394548	403827	97.7
出生率 (‰) Birth Rate (‰)	3.99	4.61		3.87	4.97	
死亡率 (‰) Death Rate (‰)	7.17	6.13		7.13	6.29	
自然增长率 (‰) Natural Growth Rate (‰)	-3.18	-1.52		-3.26	-1.32	
从业人员 (人) Employment (person)	120755	120346	100.3	115289	121467	94.9
按职工非职工分 Grouped by Staff and Workers or Non-staff-and-worker						
职工人数 (人) Staff and Worker (person)	115747	110796	104.5	110628	114221	96.9
#国有单位 State-owned	59085	59699	99.0	55581	63524	87.5
集体单位 Collective-owned	25891	27966	92.6	21023	27944	75.2
城镇个体劳动者 Urban and Rural Individuals	24119	22973	105.0	14388	14317	100.5
劳动工资 **Wages**						
工资总额 (万元) Total Wages (10000 yuan)	124190.1	110143.7	112.8	133423	122718	108.7
#国有单位 State-owned	71344.5	64981.1	109.8	72324	71531	101.1
集体单位 Collective-owned	19871	21097.7	94.2	18698	21627	86.5
职工平均工资 (元) Average Wage (yuan)	11265	10099	111.5	12079	11006	109.7
固定资产投资 **Investment in Fixed Assets**						
全社会固定资产投资 (万元) Total Investment in Fixed Assets (10000 yuan)	456580	240738	189.7	525194	351575	149.4
按建设性质分 Grouped by Type of Construction						
#基本建设投资 Capital Construction	33793	10408	324.7	47855	29774	160.7
更新改造投资 Innovation and Replacement	37207	6993	532.1	74514	36557	203.8
按经济类型分 Grouped by Ownership						
国有单位 (万元) State-owned (10000 yuan)	149906	101747	147.3	175001	136610	128.1
集体单位 (万元) Collective-owned (10000 yuan)	144			76		

21-1 续表 1 continued

项目 Item			东城区 Dongcheng 1998	1997	1998年为1997年% 1998 as % of 1997	西城区 Xicheng 1998	1997	1998年为1997年% 1998 as % of 1997
新增固定资产	(万元)	Incremental Fixed Assets (10000 yuan)	286816	98281	291.8	389769	312213	124.8
#国有单位		State-owned	74767	48793	153.2	52050	136823	38.0
集体单位		Collective-owned				76		
房屋施工面积	(万平方米)	Floor Space of Buildings Under Construction (10000 sq.m)	220.3	215.4	102.3	295.7	239.3	123.6
#国有单位		State-owned	77.4	89	87.0	78.4	106.2	73.8
集体单位		Collective-owned	0.15					
房屋竣工面积	(万平方米)	Floor Space of Buildings Completed (10000 sq.m)	53.4	23.9	223.4	56.6	81.3	69.6
#国有单位		State-owned	27.6	21.5	128.4	13.1	40.7	32.2
#住宅		Residence	18.3	13	140.8	6.2	19.6	31.6
#集体单位		Collective-owned						
#住宅		Residence						
工业		**Industry**						
全部工业企业单位数	(个)	Number of Enterprises (unit)	218	240	90.8	353	306	115.4
国有		State-owned	56	70	80.0	118	88	134.1
集体		Collective-owned	92	108	85.2	117	110	106.4
其他		Others	70	62	112.9	118	108	109.3
全部工业总产值(现价,万元)		Gross Output Value of Industry (at current prices,10000 yuan)	60809.9	55957	108.7	75306	68298	110.3
国有		State-owned	12543.7	10631.9	118.0	15609	16843	92.7
集体		Collective-owned	26704.3	24427.5	109.3	8322	8880	93.7
其他		Others	21561.9	20897.6	103.2	51375	42575	120.7
全部工业总产值(不变价,万元)		Gross Output Value of Industry (at constant prices,10000 yuan)	42495.8	40425.1	105.1	64621	58111	111.2
国有		State-owned	9606.8	9031.5	106.4	10090	11161	90.4
集体		Collective-owned	19447.1	19208.6	101.2	7092	7470	94.9
其他		Others	13441.9	12185	110.3	47440	39480	120.2
全部轻工业总产值(现价,万元)		Gross Output Value of Light Industry (at current prices,10000 yuan)	46506.9	44295.1	105.0	45535	47594	95.7
以农产品为原料		Using Farm Products as Raw Materials	40464.1	36433	111.1	31591	32558	97.0
以非农产品为原料		Using Non-farm Products as Raw Materials	6042.8	7862.1	76.9	13944	15036	92.7
全部重工业总产值(现价,万元)		Gross Output Value of Heavy Industry (at current prices,10000 yuan)	14303	11533.9	124.0	29771	20704	143.8
采掘工业		Excavation						
原料工业		Raw Materials Industry		25		2154	2475	87.0
制造工业		Manufacturing Industry	14303	11508.9	124.3	27617	18229	151.5
独立核算工业企业工业增加值	(万元)	Value Added of Enterprises with Independent Accounting system (10000 yuan)	12526.4	15349.5	81.6	26651	24259	109.9
独立核算工业企业平均职工人数	(人)	Average Number of Staff and Workers in Enterprises with Independent Accounting System (person)	6383	7771	82.1	8292	9340	88.8

21-1 续表 2 continued

项目	Item	东城区 Dongcheng 1998	1997	1998年为1997年% 1998 as % of 1997	西城区 Xicheng 1998	1997	1998年为1997年% 1998 as % of 1997
#国有	State-owned	1652	1876	88.1	2934	2724	107.7
集体	Collective-owned	3121	4362	71.5	2852	3760	75.9
独立核算工业企业总产值(现价,万元)	Gross Output Value of Enterprises with Independent Accounting System(at current prices, 10000 yuan)	44909.6	43230.1	103.9	75306	68298	110.3
#国有	State-owned	12128.5	10039.1	120.8	15609	16843	92.7
集体	Collective-owned	11219.2	12421.4	90.3	8322	8880	93.7
独立核算工业企业财务指标	Financial Indicators for Enterprises with Independent Accounting System						
产品销售收入 (万元)	Sales Revenue(10000yuan)	45075	43098.8	104.6	82408	75129	109.7
#国有	State-owned	11184.7	9724.8	115.0	15092	16367	92.2
产品销售成本 (万元)	Cost of Sales (10000yuan)	33555	32028	104.8	61283	56666	108.1
#国有	State-owned	7990.3	6574.5	121.5	12310	13029	94.5
固定资产原价 (万元)	Original Value of Fixed Assets (10000 yuan)	20039.8	19274.1	104.0	32302	27904	115.8
#国有	State-owned	4382.8	3614.3	121.3	8819	8927	98.8
固定资产净值 (万元)	Net Value of Fixed Assets (10000 yuan)	13891.2	13319.9	104.3	22151	17564	126.1
#国有	State-owned	3235.2	2329.2	138.9	6416	6033	106.3
全部流动资金年平均余额 (万元)	Annual Average Balance of Circulating Funds (10000 yuan)	47329.9	44791.1	105.7	96475	74214	130.0
#国有	State-owned	9867.4	9623.2	102.5	16108	14922	107.9
利润总额 (万元)	Total Profits (10000yuan)	442.5	2034	21.8	2614	2255	115.9
#国有	State-owned	1461.8	2017.4	72.3	896	1397	64.1
资金利税率 (%)	Ratio of Pre-tax Profits to Total Capital (%)	4.2	7.2		2.6	6.2	
产品销售率 (%)	Ratio of Sales Value to Gross Output Value (%)	97.5	95		92.9	95.4	
增加值率 (%)	Ratio of Added Value to Gross Output Value (%)	27.9	35.5		35	35	
独立核算工业企业全员劳动生产率 (元/人)	Overall Labor Productivity of Enterprises with Independent Accounting System (yuan/person)	19625	19752	99.4	90817	73124	124.2
#国有	State-owned	31477	28276	111.3	53199	61832	86.0
集体	Collective-owned	9171	9971	92.0	29179	23617	123.6
商业	**Commerce**						
社会消费品零售额 (万元)	Retail Sales of Consumer Goods (10000 yuan)	526483	496087	106.1	693817.5	606393	114.4
按经济类型分	Grouped by Ownership						
国有	State-owned	148538	171398	86.7	366335.6	376570	97.3
集体	Collective-owned	74603	69344	107.6	54117.8	49724	108.8
其他	Others	303342	255345	118.8	273364.1	180099	151.8
按类别分	Grouped by Type of Goods						
吃的商品 (万元)	Food (10000 yuan)	244638	249916	97.9	168597.7	167448	100.7

21-1 续表 3 continued

项目 Item		东城区 Dongcheng 1998	1997	1998年为1997年% 1998 as % of 1997	西城区 Xicheng 1998	1997	1998年为1997年% 1998 as % of 1997
穿的商品 (万元)	Clothing (10000 yuan)	69266	69778	99.3	164434.7	126865.3	129.6
用的商品 (万元)	Daily Used Articles (10000 yuan)	206796	173270	119.3	360785.1	291007.4	124.0
烧的商品 (万元)	Fuel (10000 yuan)	5783	3123	185.2			
网点数 (个)	Number of Outlets (unit)	14772	14387	102.7	12097	11970	101.1
商业	Wholesale and Retail	10533	10057	104.7	7910	8167	96.9
饮食业	Catering	2591	2419	107.1	2213	2117	104.5
服务业	Services	1648	1911	86.2	1896	1686	112.5
#宾馆、饭店	Hotels	112	119	94.1	78	47	166.0
营业人员 (人)	Personnel (person)	78713	72337	108.8	65335	52579	124.3
商业	Wholesale and Retail	50997	44869	113.7	41785	33871	123.4
饮食业	Catering Service	16201	15897	101.9	12080	13639	88.6
服务业	Services	11515	11571	99.5	8607	5069	169.8
#宾馆、饭店	Hotels	4684	3631	129.0	2863	1408	203.3
外经、外贸	**Foreign Economy and Trade**						
出口商品交货额 (万元)	Delivery Value of Exports (10000 yuan)				1730.6	2024.9	85.5
利用外资签订协议(合同)数 (个)	Number of Signed Agreements and Contracts of Foreign Capital to be Utilized (unit)	33	49	67.3	47	51	92.2
利用外资签订协议(合同)金额 (万美元)	Amount of Foreign Capital to be Utilized through Agreements and Contracts (USD 10000)	192997	8681	2223.2	3274.1	4441	73.7
实际利用外资 (万美元)	Amount of Foreign Capital Actually Used(USD 10000)	54323.5	16147	336.4	15520.7	19658	79.0
旅游人数 (人)	Number of Tourists (person)	22023	29967	73.5	23680000	15000000	157.9
教育	**Education**						
学校数 (个)	Number of Schools (unit)	113	109	103.7	138	145	95.2
小学	Primary Schools	66	66	100.0	81	87	93.1
普通中学	Regular Secondary Schools	33	30	110.0	45	42	107.1
中等专业教育	Specialized Secondary Schools	14	13	107.7	12	16	75.0
招生数 (人)	New Student Enrollment (person)	23023	23243	99.1	23688	23860	99.3
小学	Primary Schools	4940	5387	91.7	5060	5731	88.3
初级中等学校	Junior Secondary Schools	9336	9518	98.1	9901	9998	99.0
高级中等学校	Senior Secondary Schools	5376	4710	114.1	5283	4203	125.7
中等专业教育	Specialized Secondary Schools	3371	3628	92.9	3444	3928	87.7
在校学生 (人)	Student Enrollment (person)	96553	100857	95.7	79299	86984	91.2
小学	Primary Schools	41837	44803	93.4	47202	51652	91.4
初级中等学校	Junior Secondary Schools	29572	32277	91.6	32097	35332	90.8

注：东城区"旅游人数"指标仅包括海外旅游者人数。

Note: The data of number of tourists of Dongcheng District only includes that of overseas tourists.

21-1 续表 4 continued

项目 Item			东城区 Dongcheng 1998	1997	1998年为1997年% 1998 as % of 1997	西城区 Xicheng 1998	1997	1998年为1997年% 1998 as % of 1997
高级中等学校		Senior Secondary Schools	14303	12864	111.2	12550	14701	85.4
中等专业教育		Specialized Secondary Schools	10841	10913	99.3	10078	10509	95.9
毕业生	(人)	Graduates (person)	26764	25872	103.4	29577	30792	96.1
小学		Primary Schools	8547	8388	101.9	10363	10166	101.9
初级中等学校		Junior Secondary Schools	10790	11378	94.8	12057	13140	91.8
高级中等学校		Senior Secondary Schools	4166	3470	120.1	3857	4203	91.8
中等专业教育		Specialized Secondary Schools	3261	2636	123.7	3300	3283	100.5
达到"国家体育标准"学生数	(人)	Number of Students Come to the Standard for State Physical Training (person)	74335	88970	83.6	120341	109950	109.5
幼儿园、托儿所个数	(个)	Number of Kindergardens (unit)	71	80	88.8	98	103	95.1
幼儿入托数	(人)	New Enrollment (person)	10314	10944	94.2	13861	14274	97.1
文化		**Culture**						
文化馆、站	(个)	Cultural Centers (unit)	11	11	100.0	11	11	100.0
公共图书馆	(个)	Public Libraries (unit)	2	2	100.0	1	1	100.0
公共图书馆藏书	(万册)	Collection (10000 volume)	296.1	292.3	101.3	33.1	33.1	100.0
电影放映单位	(个)	Film Projection Units (unit)	6	6	100.0	15	15	100.0
区级以上重点文物保护单位	(个)	Cultural Relics Preserved at District Level and above (unit)	130	130	100.0	108	108	100.0
卫生		**Health**						
卫生机构数	(个)	Number of Health Institutions (unit)	84	70	120.0	747	747	100.0
#医院		Hospitals	30	27	111.1	26	26	100.0
卫生院		Clinics						
床位数	(张)	Number of Beds (unit)	6878	6754	101.8	7733	7613	101.6
#医院		Hospitals	6878	6754	101.8	7633	7610	100.3
卫生院		Clinics						
平均每千人拥有床位数	(张)	Average Number of Beds Per 1000 Persons (unit)	10.87	10.52	103.3	9.77	9.66	101.1
卫生技术人员	(人)	Medical Technical Personnel (person)	14237	13915	102.3	15323	15323	100.0
#医生		Doctors	5985	5948	100.6	6703	6703	100.0
城市公用		**Urban Public Utilities**						
区级以上公园	(个)	Parks at District Level and above (unit)	7	7	100.0	10	10	100.0
体育场馆	(个)	Stadiums and Gymnasiums (unit)	9	9	100.0	217	217	100.0
道路长度	(公里)	Length of Roads (km)	97	97	100.0	240.2	243.1	98.8

21-2 崇文区、宣武区国民经济主要指标
MAIN NATIONAL ECONOMIC INDICATORS FOR DONGCHENG AND XICHENG DISTRICTS

项目		Item	崇文区 Chongwen 1998	1997	1998年为1997年% 1998 as % of 1997	宣武区 Xuanwu 1998	1997	1998年为1997年% 1998 as % of 1997
综合		General Survey						
国内生产总值	(万元)	Gross Domestic Product (10000 yuan)	107668.6	105574	102.0	149151.2	133981.7	111.3
第一产业		Primary Industry						
第二产业		Secondary Industry	19595.6	12471.8	157.1	34865.3	29662.2	117.5
第三产业		Tertiary Industry	88073	93102.2	94.6	114285.9	104319.5	109.6
财政收入	(万元)	Fiscal Revenue (10000 yuan)	42168.8	35060.9	120.3	70750	60539	116.9
#各项税收		Taxes	33053.2	28346.9	116.6	56741	47684	119.0
财政支出	(万元)	Fiscal Expenditure (10000 yuan)	45303	38925.3	116.4	79844	67601	118.1
#基本建设支出		Capital Construction	1010	430	234.9	6539	6168	106.0
支援农业生产支出		Supporting Agriculture						
文教卫生事业费		Culture,Education and Health	16080	17518	91.8	24777	22097	112.1
人口和劳动力		**Population and Labor Force**						
总人口	(人)	Total Population (person)	461743	469948	98.3	593397	598507	99.1
常住户籍人口	(人)	Permanent Registered Population (person)	420540	430431	97.7	538567	543667	99.1
#非农业人口		Non-agriculture	420475	430367	97.7	538551	543650	99.1
男		Male	210264	215626	97.5	272022	274870	99.0
女		Female	210276	214741	97.9	266529	268780	99.2
出生率	(‰)	Birth Rate (‰)	3.26	4		3.6	4.1	
死亡率	(‰)	Death Rate (‰)	9.27	5.56		9.1	6.7	
自然增长率	(‰)	Natural Growth Rate (‰)	-6	-1.5		-5.5	-2.6	
从业人员	(人)	Employment (person)	59311	67826	87.4	59004	66217	89.1
按职工非职工分		Grouped by Staff and Workers or Non-staff-and-worker						
职工人数	(人)	Staff and Worker (person)	56727	64978	87.3	58390	60605	96.3
#国有单位		State-owned	32611	38817	84.0	34881	38457	90.7
集体单位		Collective-owned	15484	18968	81.6	16912	18891	89.5
城镇个体劳动者		Urban and Rural Individuals						
劳动工资		Wages						
工资总额	(万元)	Total Wages (10000 yuan)	55952.4	56080.1	99.8	62481.8	57597	108.5
#国有单位		State-owned	36465.3	37459.6	97.3	40860.2	40024.5	102.1
集体单位		Collective-owned	10382.8	12253.7	84.7	13530.3	12960.8	104.4
职工平均工资	(元)	Average Wage (yuan)	9863	8592	114.8	10881	9492	114.6
固定资产投资		**Investment in Fixed Assets**						
全社会固定资产投资	(万元)	Total Investment in Fixed Assets (10000 yuan)	169038	179049	94.4	320939	288553	111.2
按建设性质分		Grouped by Type of Construction						
#基本建设投资		Capital Construction	24387	14354	169.9	9899	81760	12.1
更新改造投资		Innovation and Replacement	569	24747	2.3	86200	7050	1222.7
按经济类型分		Grouped by Ownership						
国有单位	(万元)	State-owned (10000 yuan)	32527	48294	67.4	159983	204228	78.3

21-2 续表 1 continued

项目	Item	崇文区 Chongwen 1998	1997	1998年为1997年% 1998 as % of 1997	宣武区 Xuanwu 1998	1997	1998年为1997年% 1998 as % of 1997
集体单位 (万元)	Collective-owned (10000 yuan)	1672	1642	101.8	7344	9257	79.3
新增固定资产 (万元)	Incremental Fixed Assets (10000 yuan)	217220	160730	135.1	133624	104789	127.5
#国有单位	State-owned	12106	84907	14.3	67971	52653	129.1
集体单位	Collective-owned	569	90	632.2			
房屋施工面积 (万平方米)	Floor Space of Buildings Under Construction (10000 sq.m)	95.3	71.8	132.7	208.8	271.8	76.8
#国有单位	State-owned	29.6	41.9	70.6	110.1	180	61.2
集体单位	Collective-owned	3.9	6.6	59.1	17.9	34.4	52.0
房屋竣工面积 (万平方米)	Floor Space of Buildings Completed (10000 sq.m)	20.2	7.6	265.8	61.9	47.4	130.6
#国有单位	State-owned	3.4	7.4	45.9	27.6	27.5	100.4
#住宅	Residence	4.7	0.5	940.0	24	23.8	100.8
#集体单位	Collective-owned	3.8					
#住宅	Residence	3.5					
工业	**Industry**						
全部工业企业单位数 (个)	Number of Enterprises (unit)	170	191	89.0	230	212	108.5
#国有	State-owned	31	40	77.5	50	57	87.7
集体	Collective-owned	87	112	77.7	103	105	98.1
其他	Others						
全部工业总产值 (现价,万元)	Gross Output Value of Industry (at current prices,10000 yuan)	39953.6	32276.5	123.8	42913.1	30975.8	138.5
国有	State-owned	4189.3	3414.4	122.7	5381.4	4895.2	109.9
集体	Collective-owned	13155.1	16218.7	81.1	9133.7	10975.2	83.2
其他	Others	22609.2	12643.4	178.8	28398	15105.4	188.0
全部工业总产值 (不变价,万元)	Gross Output Value of Industry (at constant prices,10000 yuan)	32452	24603.3	131.9	42293	30880.5	137.0
国有	State-owned	3210.4	2485.6	129.2	5088.8	5278.3	96.4
集体	Collective-owned	10982	13196.5	83.2	9225.5	9331.7	98.9
其他	Others	18259.6	8921.2	204.7	27978.7	16270.5	172.0
全部轻工业总产值 (现价,万元)	Gross Output Value of Light Industry at current prices,10000 yuan)	30050.2	22710.6	132.3	37191.8	22412.5	165.9
以农产品为原料	Using Farm Products as Raw Materials	17608.1	15590.4	112.9	22884.3	16058.4	142.5
以非农产品为原料	Using Non-farm Products as Raw Materials	12442.1	7120.2	174.7	14307.5	6354.1	225.2
全部重工业总产值 (现价,万元)	Gross Output Value of Heavy Industry at current prices,10000 yuan)	9903.4	9565.9	103.5	5721.3	8563.3	66.8
采掘工业	Excavation						
原料工业	Raw Materials Industry	770.6	338.2	227.9	656.9	171.5	383.0
制造工业	Manufacturing Industry	9132.8	9227.7	99.0	5064.4	8391.8	60.3
独立核算工业企业工业增加值 (万元)	Value Added of Enterprises with Independent Accounting system (10000 yuan)	14528.8	12663.7	114.7	13978.8	5438	257.1
独立核算工业企业平均职工人数 (人)	Average Number of Staff and Workers in Enterprises with Independent Accounting System (person)	6066	6325	95.9	5515	5647	97.7

21-2 续表 2 continued

项目	Item	崇文区 Chongwen 1998	1997	1998年为1997年% 1998 as % of 1997	宣武区 Xuanwu 1998	1997	1998年为1997年% 1998 as % of 1997
#国有	State-owned	784	723	108.4	940	1046	89.9
集体	Collective-owned	3151	4232	74.5	2641	3307	79.9
独立核算工业企业总产值(现价,万元)	Gross Output Value of Enterprises with Independent Accounting System(at current prices, 10000 yuan)	39953.6	32276.5	123.8	42853.6	30975.8	138.3
#国有	State-owned	4189.3	3414.4	122.7	5321.9	4895.2	108.7
集体	Collective-owned	13155.1	16218.7	81.1	9133.7	10975.3	83.2
独立核算工业企业财务指标	Financial Indicators for Enterprises with Independent Accounting System						
产品销售收入 (万元)	Sales Revenue (10000yuan)	36950.6	40299.6	91.7	48915.7	37863.7	129.2
#国有	State-owned	4150.6	5010.2	82.8	5074.1	4913	103.3
产品销售成本 (万元)	Cost of Sales (10000yuan)	28387.8	31284.8	90.7	32745.7	28871	113.4
#国有	State-owned	3227	4039.5	79.9	4121.7	3958.5	104.1
固定资产原价 (万元)	Original Value of Fixed Assets (10000 yuan)	11967.9	14972.7	79.9	16662.3	13886.2	120.0
#国有	State-owned	804.6	732	109.9	2125.5	1759.9	120.8
固定资产净值 (万元)	Net Value of Fixed Assets (10000 yuan)	6614.1	8853	74.7	10576.7	8980.9	117.8
#国有	State-owned	442.3	383.2	115.4	1275.4	1071.2	119.1
全部流动资金年平均余额 (万元)	Annual Average Balance of Circulating Funds (10000 yuan)	33319.5	36589.5	91.1	21189.8	41369.2	51.2
#国有	State-owned	4453.9	3278.9	135.8	4378.3	3937.2	111.2
利润总额 (万元)	Total Profits (10000yuan)	1991.4	746.2	266.9	1832.2	-473.8	
#国有	State-owned	380.5	432.7	87.9	396.2	406.8	97.4
资金利税率 (%)	Ratio of Pre-tax Profits to Total Capital (%)	5.3	2.1		8.36		
产品销售率 (%)	Ratio of Sales Value to Gross Output Value (%)	98.3	98.2		100	100	100.0
增加值率 (%)	Ratio of Added Value to Gross Output Value (%)	39	39.2		32.6	17.6	
独立核算工业企业全员劳动生产率 (元/人)	Overall Labor Productivity of Enterprises with Independent Accounting System (yuan/person)	23951	20022	119.6	25346.8	9629.9	263.2
#国有	State-owned	18532	19267	96.2	19066	13282.1	143.5
集体	Collective-owned	15169	14962	101.4	9706	9721.2	99.8
商业	**Commerce**						
社会消费品零售额 (万元)	Retail Sales of Consumer Goods (10000 yuan)	331704	324253	102.3	359833	344994	104.3
按经济类型分	Grouped by Ownership						
国有	State-owned	58563	81898	71.5	66411	76897	86.4
集体	Collective-owned	16999	40924	41.5	104403	132075	79.0
其他	Others	132459	201431	65.8	189019	136022	140.0
按类别分	Grouped by Type of Goods						
吃的商品 (万元)	Food (10000 yuan)	172902	162773	106.2	137626	171875	80.1

21-2 续表 3 continued

项目 Item		崇文区 Chongwen 1998	1997	1998年为1997年% 1998 as % of 1997	宣武区 Xuanwu 1998	1997	1998年为1997年% 1998 as % of 1997
穿的商品 (万元)	Clothing (10000 yuan)	59200	61985	95.5	40942	24710	165.7
用的商品 (万元)	Daily Used Articles (10000 yuan)	97783	97148	100.7	178192	145685	122.3
烧的商品 (万元)	Fuel (10000 yuan)	1819	2347	77.5	3073	2724	112.8
网点数 (个)	Number of Outlets (unit)	7103	9562	74.3	10259	10368	98.9
商业	Wholesale and Retail	5090	7090	71.8	7995	7817	102.3
饮食业	Catering	708	755	93.8	1588	1446	109.8
服务业	Services	1305	1717	76.0	676	1105	61.2
#宾馆、饭店	Hotels	27	11	245.5	127		
营业人员 (人)	Personnel (person)	46295	56916	81.3	71378	68927	103.6
商业	Wholesale and Retail	34184	39546	86.4	38569	42415	90.9
饮食业	Catering Service	5141	3966	129.6	8186	8570	95.5
服务业	Services	6970	13404	52.0	24623	17942	137.2
#宾馆、饭店	Hotels	3125	1771	176.5	5531		
外经、外贸	**Foreign Economy and Trade**						
出口商品交货额 (万元)	Delivery Value of Exports (10000 yuan)	360.9	5.5	6561.8	197.1	222.7	88.5
利用外资签订协议(合同)数 (个)	Number of Signed Agreements and Contracts of Foreign Capital to be Utilized (unit)	15	15	100.0	11	17	64.7
利用外资签订协议(合同)金额 (万美元)	Amount of Foreign Capital to be Utilized through Agreements and Contracts (USD 10000)	10114.2	1807.2	559.7	107.7	7387.2	1.5
实际利用外资 (万美元)	Amount of Foreign Capital Actually Used (USD 10000)	13009.7	14133.7	92.0	639	367.3	174.0
旅游人数 (人)	Number of Tourists (person)	20228	31726	63.8	35889	43024	83.4
教育	**Education**						
学校数 (个)	Number of Schools (unit)	79	80	99.8	101	104	97.1
小学	Primary Schools	43	46	93.5	58	63	92.1
普通中学	Regular Secondary Schools	27	25	108.0	32	30	106.7
中等专业教育	Specialized Secondary Schools	9	9	100.0	11	11	100.0
招生数 (人)	New Student Enrollment (person)	13490	14097	96.7	15573	16125	96.6
小学	Primary Schools	2744	3256	84.3	3475	3854	90.2
初级中等学校	Junior Secondary Schools	5769	5949	97.0	6671	6926	96.3
高级中等学校	Senior Secondary Schools	2631	2441	107.8	2827	2638	107.2
中等专业教育	Specialized Secondary Schools	2346	2451	95.7	2600	2707	96.0
在校学生 (人)	Student Enrollment (person)	61916	67037	92.4	71283	76524	93.2
小学	Primary Schools	27750	30815	90.1	33011	36606	90.2
初级中等学校	Junior Secondary Schools	19145	21876	87.5	22175	25425	87.2

21-2 续表 4 continued

项目 Item			崇文区 Chongwen 1998	1997	1998年为1997年% 1998 as % of 1997	宣武区 Xuanwu 1998	1997	1998年为1997年% 1998 as % of 1997
高级中等学校		Senior Secondary Schools	7222	6667	108.3	7508	6416	117.0
中等专业教育		Specialized Secondary Schools	7799	7679	101.6	8589	8077	106.3
毕业生	(人)	Graduates (person)	18092	17436	103.8	19897	19508	102.0
小学		Primary Schools	5684	6009	94.6	6773	6934	97.7
初级中等学校		Junior Secondary Schools	8240	8014	102.8	9437	9586	98.4
高级中等学校		Senior Secondary Schools	2008	1500	133.9	1700	1587	107.1
中等专业教育		Specialized Secondary Schools	2160	1913	112.9	1987	1401	141.8
达到"国家体育标准"学生数	(人)	Number of Students Come to the Standard for State Physical Training (person)	55001	54861	100.3	56948	74076	76.9
幼儿园、托儿所个数	(个)	Number of Kindergardens (unit)	40	63	63.5	50	56	89.3
幼儿入托数	(人)	New Enrollment (person)	7072	8319	85.0	7525	8792	85.6
文化		**Culture**						
文化馆、站	(个)	Cultural Centers (unit)	10	9	111.1	9	9	100.0
公共图书馆	(个)	Public Libraries (unit)	1	1	100.0	1	1	100.0
公共图书馆藏书	(万册)	Collection (10000 volume)	38	36.5	104.1	23	23	100.0
电影放映单位	(个)	Film Projection Units (unit)	2	3	66.7	6	6	100.0
区级以上重点文物保护单位	(个)	Cultural Relics Preserved at District Level and above (unit)	21	21	100.0	38	38	100.0
卫生		**Health**						
卫生机构数	(个)	Number of Health Institutions (unit)	18	18	100.0	366	368	99.5
#医院		Hospitals	11	11	100.0	19	20	95.0
卫生院		Clinics						
床位数	(张)	Number of Beds (unit)	1730	1710	101.2	3981	3854	103.3
#医院		Hospitals	1730	1710	101.2	3981	3854	103.3
卫生院		Clinics						
平均每千人拥有床位数	(张)	Average Number of Beds Per 1000 Persons (unit)	4.1	4	102.5	7.4	7.1	104.2
卫生技术人员	(人)	Medical Technical Personnel (person)	4553	4599	99.0	7347	8577	85.7
#医生		Doctors	1517	1539	98.6	3102	3880	79.9
城市公用		**Urban Public Utilities**						
区级以上公园	(个)	Parks at District Level and above (unit)	4	4	100.0	4	4	100.0
体育场馆	(个)	Stadiums and Gymnasiums (unit)	6	6	100.0	2	2	100.0
道路长度	(公里)	Length of Roads (km)	176.37	176.37	100.0	113.9	118.3	96.3

21-3 朝阳区、丰台区国民经济主要指标
MAIN NATIONAL ECONOMIC INDICATORS FOR CHAOYANG AND FENGTAI DISTRICTS

项目		Item	朝阳区 Chaoyang 1998	朝阳区 Chaoyang 1997	朝阳区 Chaoyang 1998年为1997年% 1998 as % of 1997	丰台区 Fengtai 1998	丰台区 Fengtai 1997	丰台区 Fengtai 1998年为1997年% 1998 as % of 1997
综合		General Survey						
国内生产总值	(万元)	Gross Domestic Product (10000 yuan)	703017.3	625746.8	112.3	351959	300444	117.1
第一产业		Primary Industry	28377	30660	92.6	16199	19435	83.3
第二产业		Secondary Industry	177705.3	162729.8	109.2	118255	113501	104.2
第三产业		Tertiary Industry	496935	432357	114.9	217505	167508	129.8
财政收入	(万元)	Fiscal Revenue (10000 yuan)	173196	142396	121.6	63799	55773	114.4
#各项税收		Taxes	131147	132195	99.2	58719	49949	117.6
财政支出	(万元)	Fiscal Expenditure (10000 yuan)	190395	161925	117.6	87627	77141	113.6
#基本建设支出		Capital Construction	13550	9966	136.0	4960	7805	63.5
支援农业生产支出		Supporting Agriculture	8282	5868	141.1	853	1126	75.8
文教卫生事业费		Culture,Education and Health	61045	41927	145.6	24664	24773	99.6
人口和劳动力		**Population and Labor Force**						
总人口	(人)	Total Population (person)	1761500	1974507	89.2	1007611	982898	102.5
常住户籍人口	(人)	Permanent Registered Population (person)	1476931	1437509	102.7	794675	777433	102.2
#非农业人口		Non-agriculture	1280284	1233389	103.8	646355	626231	103.2
男		Male	752833	733509	102.6	404393	395473	102.3
女		Female	724098	704000	102.9	390282	381960	102.2
出生率	(‰)	Birth Rate (‰)	4.48	5.16		5.29	6.94	
死亡率	(‰)	Death Rate (‰)	4.76	5.6		8.49	5.51	
自然增长率	(‰)	Natural Growth Rate (‰)	-0.28	0.06		-3.2	1.43	
从业人员	(人)	Employment (person)	121451	120956	100.4	86562	80262	107.8
按产业分		Grouped by Industry						
第一产业		Primary Industry	391	234	167.1	336	294	114.3
第二产业		Secondary Industry	36786	32511	113.1	23373	27005	86.6
第三产业		Tertiary Industry	84274	88211	95.5	62853	52963	118.7
按职工非职工分		Grouped by Staff and Workers or Non-staff-and-worker						
职工人数		Staff and Worker	118312	114777	103.1	82956	77469	107.1
#国有单位		State-owned	73128	74028	98.8	43549	43566	99.6
集体单位		Collective-owned	38315	5575	687.3	15266	22843	66.8
城镇个体劳动者		Urban and Rural Individuals	42337	43615	97.1	11568	11675	99.1
劳动工资		**Wages**						
工资总额	(万元)	Total Wages (10000 yuan)	137888.7	122572.5	112.5	83499.4	69232.8	120.6
#国有单位		State-owned	97992	87798.1	111.6	48532.3	42834.4	113.3
集体单位		Collective-owned	30672	27767.3	110.5	10299	14677.1	70.2
职工平均工资	(元)	Average Wage (yuan)	11421	10512	108.6	10220	9303	109.9
固定资产投资		**Investment in Fixed Assets Assets**						
全社会固定资产投资	(万元)	Total Investment in Fixed Assets (10000 yuan)	284536	290412	98.0	82391	71212	115.7
按建设性质分		Grouped by Type of Construction						
#基本建设投资		Capital Construction	127804	283974	45.0	23683	17678	134.0
更新改造投资		Innovation and Replacement	559	1788	31.3			

21-3 续表 1 continued

项目	Item	朝阳区 Chaoyang 1998	朝阳区 Chaoyang 1997	朝阳区 Chaoyang 1998年为1997年% 1998 as % of 1997	丰台区 Fengtai 1998	丰台区 Fengtai 1997	丰台区 Fengtai 1998年为1997年% 1998 as % of 1997
按经济类型分	Grouped by Ownership						
国有单位 (万元)	State-owned(10000 yuan)	169681	168331	100.8	53373	48005	111.2
集体单位 (万元)	Collective-owned (10000 yuan)	4996	4650	107.4		1500	
新增固定资产 (万元)	Incremental Fixed Assets (10000 yuan)	210342	310229	67.8	79109	67204	117.7
#国有单位	State-owned	26701	169949	15.7	47859	26661	179.5
集体单位	Collective-owned					1500	
房屋施工面积 (万平方米)	Floor Space of Buildings Under Construction (10000 sq.m)	280.3	273.8	102.4	123.3	143.7	85.8
#国有单位	State-owned	108.2	133.7	80.9	98.5	117.4	83.9
集体单位	Collective-owned	2.2	7.9	27.8		0.8	
房屋竣工面积 (万平方米)	Floor Space of Buildings Completed (10000 sq.m)	67.8	65.1	104.1	39.5	34	116.2
#国有单位	State-owned	30.4	46.4	65.5	26.5	18.7	141.7
#住宅	Residence	13.2	31.3	42.2	16.7	10.7	156.1
#集体单位	Collective-owned		0.2			0.8	
#住宅	Residence						
农村经济	**Rural Economy**						
农村劳动力 (人)	Labor Force (person)	92651	87641	105.7	70258	70855	99.2
种植业	Planting	15629	15600	100.2	15603	15742	99.1
林业	Forestry	580	553	104.9	1700	1567	108.5
牧业	Animal Husbandry	1806	1563	115.5	1082	1006	107.6
渔业	Fishery	874	947	92.3	181	236	76.7
农村工业	Rural Industry	31209	33404	93.4	28941	30688	94.3
农村建筑业	Rural Construction	3669	3588	102.3	1813	1722	105.3
农村运输业	Rural Transportation	6332	5766	109.8	4764	4413	108.0
农村商、饮食业、服务业	Commerce,Catering and Services	8068	5443	148.2	16174	4823	335.4
耕地面积 (公顷)	Area under Cultivation (hectare)	13660	13720	99.6	6366.2	6823.4	93.3
农业机械总动力 (千瓦)	Total Power of Agricultural Machinery (kw)	261182	328364	79.5	171690	174921	98.2
化肥施用实物量 (吨)	Consumption of Chemical Fertilizers (ton)	13130	15975	82.2	5338.2	5480	97.4
化肥施用折纯量 (吨)	Consumption of Chemical Fertilizers(100%) (ton)	4311	5308	81.2	1742.8	1740	100.2
农村用电量 (万千瓦时)	Consumption of Electricity (10000 kwh)	32582	28664.2	113.7	25345.8	27646	91.7
农村国内生产总值 (万元)	Rural Gross Domestic Product (10000 yuan)	310902.1	234867.3	132.4	152127.2	161119.2	94.4
第一产业	Primary Industry	28311.3	36738.8	77.1	16552.3	19434.5	85.2
第二产业	Secondary Industry	116671.5	112893.1	103.3	57825	66316.2	87.2
第三产业	Tertiary Industry	165919.3	85235.4	194.7	77749.9	75368.5	103.2
农业总产值 (万元)	Gross Output Value of Agriculture (10000 yuan)	37147.7	36975.8	100.5	27608.9	29034.6	95.1
种植业	Planting	19365.3	18328.4	105.7	19162.5	16695.3	114.8
林业	Forestry	432.6	338.8	127.7	220.6	189.1	116.7
牧业	Animal Husbandry	12263.1	15041.9	81.5	7878.3	11815.5	66.7
渔业	Fishery	5086.8	3266.7	155.7	347.6	334.7	103.9
农作物总播种面积 (万公顷)	Sown Area of Farm Crops (10000 hectare)	1.2	1.9	63.2	0.81	0.84	96.4
粮食作物	Grain	1.2	1.3	92.3	0.34	0.36	94.4
经济作物	Industrial Crops				0.47	0.48	97.9
其他作物	Other Crops		0.6				

21-3 续表2 continued

项目	Item	朝阳区 Chaoyang 1998	1997	1998年为1997年% 1998 as % of 1997	丰台区 Fengtai 1998	1997	1998年为1997年% 1998 as % of 1997
农副产品产量	Yield of Farm and Side-line Crops						
粮食 (万吨)	Grain (10000 tons)	7.6	8		1.53	1.44	106.3
蔬菜 (吨)	Vegetable (ton)	182846	216313		190516	188793	100.9
干鲜果 (吨)	Dry and Fresh Fruits(ton)	980	1241		5814	5505	105.6
畜产品产量	Output of Livestock Products						
生猪出栏 (头)	Slaughtered Hogs (head)	304187	254312	119.6	100712	130980	76.9
商品猪 (头)	Commodity Hogs (head)		254235		100712	130869	77.0
猪牛羊肉 (吨)	Pork,Beef and Mutton(ton)	20756	16331	127.1	6470	8366	77.3
#猪肉	Pork	20165	15875	127.0	6402	8324	76.9
禽肉	Meat of Poultry (ton)	359	1510	23.8	1224	2842	43.1
禽蛋	Poultry Eggs (ton)	1584	7995	19.8	8213	13693	60.0
牲畜年底头数 (头)	Number of Livestock (year-end) (head)		200468				
大牲畜	Large Animals	3640	9930	36.7	1685	1692	99.6
猪	Hogs	178794	167136	107.0	60033	85186	70.5
羊	Goats and Sheep	17194	14500	118.6	7878	3832	205.6
水产品产量 (吨)	Output of Aquatic Product (ton)	6660	8220	81.0	649	812	79.9
农村集体经济收入 (万元)	Rural Collective Economic Revenue (10000 yuan)	1128116.6	1104330	102.2	843955	800057.1	105.0
农村集体经济利润总额 (万元)	Total Profits of Rural Collective Economy (10000 yuan)	76824.4	73590	104.4	76133	68054.9	112.0
国家税金	State Taxes	39847.3	37404	106.5	22497.5	21551	104.0
集体积累	Collective Accumulation	54001	53744	100.5	25337	26398	96.0
劳动所得	Income from Work	122514.3	109708	111.7			
乡镇企业单位数 (个)	Number of Township and Village Enterprise (unit)	1914	1986	96.4	1469	1502	97.8
乡镇企业人数 (人)	Number of Persons of Township and Village Enterprises (person)	91638	98319	93.2	63843	63207	101.0
乡镇企业纯利润 (万元)	Net Profit of Township and Village Enterprises (10000 yuan)	25978.5	17980	144.5	40922	46102	88.8
乡镇企业固定资产原价 (万元)	Original Value of Fixed Assets of Township and Village Enterprises (10000 yuan)	331937.8	271063	122.5	341583	330588	103.3
乡镇企业固定资产净值 (万元)	Net Value of Fixed Assets of Township and Village Enterprises (10000 yuan)	239321.2	196595	121.7	234863	232110	101.2
工业	**Industry**						
全部工业企业单位数 (个)	Number of Enterprises (unit)	2544	3561	71.4	939	987	95.1
国有	State-owned	215	216	99.5	87	73	119.2
集体	Collective-owned	1787	1793	99.7	694	786	88.3
其他	Others	542	1552	34.9	158	128	123.4
全部工业总产值 (现价,万元)	Gross Output Value of Industry (at current prices,10000 yuan)	549911.6	561116	98.0	411264	424678	96.8
国有	State-owned	18058.8	21016	85.9	27430	32744.1	83.8
集体	Collective-owned	304508.8	498096	61.1	208978	231616	90.0
其他	Others	227344	42004	541.2	174856	128759	135.8

21-3 续表 3 continued

项目	Item	朝阳区 Chaoyang 1998	1997	1998年为1997年% 1998 as % of 1997	丰台区 Fengtai 1998	1997	1998年为1997年% 1998 as % of 1997
全部工业总产值(90不变价,万元)	Gross Output Value of Industry (at constant price of 1990,10000yuan)	502409.5	506008	99.3	387725	417697	92.8
国有	State-owned	13727.8	17458	78.6	26424	28440.3	92.9
集体	Collective-owned	279827.3	446546	62.7	198710	224901	88.4
其他	Others	208854.4	42004	497.2	162591	132797	122.4
全部轻工业总产值(现价,万元)	Gross Output Value of Light Industry (at current prices,10000 yuan)	294869.2	275689.1	107.0	160632	172229	93.3
以农产品为原料	Using Farm Products as Raw Materials	226430.8	218910.7	103.4	105326	117606	89.6
以非农产品为原料	Using Non-farm Products as Raw Materials	68438.4	56778.4	120.5	55306	54623	101.3
全部重工业总产值(现价,万元)	Gross Output Value of Heavy Industry (at current prices,10000 yuan)	255042.4	219509.3	116.2	227093	245468	92.5
采掘工业	Mining and Quarrying				4131	2762	149.6
原料工业	Raw Materials Industry	26883.9	20363.8	132.0	37523	48747	76.9
制造工业	Manufacturing Industry	228158.5	199145.5	114.6	185439	193959	95.6
独立核算工业企业平均职工人数 (人)	Average Number of Staff and Workers in Enterprises with Independent Accounting System (person)	80625	63931	126.1	23163	27138	85.3
#国有	State-owned	3190	3613	88.3	3123	3753	83.2
集体	Collective-owned	56083	60318	93.0	8465	8685	97.4
独立核算工业企业总产值(现价,万元)	Gross Output Value of Enterprises with Independent Accounting System(at current prices, 10000 yuan)	549911.6	495198.4	111.0	216912	237106.5	91.5
#国有	State-owned	18058.8	21016	85.9	25642	32744.1	78.3
集体	Collective-owned	304508.8	295236.4	103.1	37806	40851.4	92.5
独立核算工业企业工业增加值 (万元)	Value Added of Enterprises with Independent Accounting system (10000 yuan)				62975	73329.3	85.9
独立核算工业企业财务指标	Financial Indicators for Enterprises with Independent Accounting System						
产品销售收入 (万元)	Sales Revenue (10000yuan)	543324.5	472232	115.1	205404	215389.7	95.4
#国有	State-owned	16690.2	18102	92.2	24475	33119.4	73.9
产品销售成本 (万元)	Cost of Sales (10000 yuan)	430233.3	385358	111.6	169402	166484.5	101.7
#国有	State-owned	13160	143888	9.1	19909	27140.2	73.4
固定资产原价 (万元)	Original Value of Fixed Assets (10000 yuan)		225181		133240	140539.2	94.8
#国有	State-owned		7669		6662	9255.7	72.0
固定资产净值 (万元)	Net Value of Fixed Assets (10000 yuan)	205208.6	153696	133.5	90976	112407.8	80.9
#国有	State-owned	5194.6	5361	96.9	4243	8688.5	48.8
全部流动资金年平均余额 (万元)	Annual Average Balance of Circulating Funds (10000 yuan)	452755.7	360432	125.6	208562	222666.1	93.7
#国有	State-owned	14850.6	13971	106.3	31825	35358.1	90.0
利润总额 (万元)	Total Profits (10000 yuan)	6312.2	8215	76.8	-1637	3374.1	
#国有	State-owned	795.7	1345	59.2	878	1913.2	45.9

21-3 续表 4 continued

项目	Item	朝阳区 Chaoyang 1998	1997	1998年为1997年% 1998 as % of 1997	丰台区 Fengtai 1998	1997	1998年为1997年% 1998 as % of 1997
资金利税率 (%)	Ratio of Pre-tax Profits to Total of Capital (%)				3	5.8	
产品销售率 (%)	Ratio of Sales Value to Gross Output Value (%)	92.96	93.98		95.2	89.1	
增加值率 (%)	Ratio of Added Value to Gross Output Value (%)	33.76	34.54		29	30.9	
独立核算工业企业全员劳动生产率 (元/人)	Overall Labor Productivity of Enterprises with Independent Accounting System (yuan/person)	23050	20124	114.5	22016	27021	81.5
#国有	State-owned	23058.9	27124	85.0	14259	28048	50.8
集体	Collective-owned	17813.8	25095	71.0	10487	11593	90.5
商业	**Commerce**						
社会消费品零售额 (万元)	Retail Sales of Consumer Goods (10000 yuan)	1158745	961270	120.5	549564	426135	129.0
按经济类型分	Grouped by Ownership						
国有	State-owned	410196	403733	101.6	102489	121420	84.4
集体	Collective-owned	177288	211479	83.8	75037	80129	93.6
其他	Others	571261	346058	165.1	372038	224586	165.7
按类别分	Grouped by Type of Goods						
吃的商品 (万元)	Food (10000 yuan)	272305	269156	101.2	242772	191195	127.0
穿的商品 (万元)	Clothing (10000 yuan)	121668	211479	57.5	62122	57091	108.8
用的商品 (万元)	Daily Used Articles (10000 yuan)	665120	451797	147.2	223536	159432	140.2
烧的商品 (万元)	Fuel (10000 yuan)	44032	28838	152.7	21134	18597	113.6
网点数 (个)	Number of Outlets (unit)	33066	39158	84.4			
商业	Wholesale and Retail	26926	33610	80.1			
饮食业	Catering	2758	2737	100.8			
服务业	Services	3382	2811	120.3			
#宾馆、饭店	Hotels						
营业人员 (人)	Personnel (person)	184708	117133	157.7			
商业	Wholesale and Retail	89469	78962	113.3			
饮食业	Catering	21241	12337	172.2			
服务业	Services	73998	25834	286.4			
#宾馆、饭店	Hotels						
外经、外贸	**Foreign Economy and Trade**						
出口商品交货额 (万元)	Delivery Value of Exports (10000 yuan)	22118.6	20653	107.1	2224.7	2722.4	81.7
利用外资签订协议(合同)数 (个)	Number of Signed Agreements and Contracts of Foreign Capital to be Utilized (unit)	93	105	88.6	35	50	70.0
利用外资签订协议(合同)金额 (万美元)	Amount of Foreign Capital to be Utilized through Agreements and Contracts (USD 10000)	9801.8	6634	147.8	8289.6	5396.1	153.6
实际利用外资 (万美元)	Amount of Foreign Capital Actually Used (USD 10000)	7764.6	7460	104.1	4496.8	598.9	750.8
旅游人数 (人)	Number of Tourists (person)						
教育	**Education**						
学校数 (个)	Number of Schools (unit)	324	355	91.3	173	184	94.0
小学	Primary Schools	220	229	96.1	122	125	97.6

21-3 续表 5 continued

项目	Item	朝阳区 Chaoyang 1998	朝阳区 Chaoyang 1997	1998年为1997年% 1998 as % of 1997	丰台区 Fengtai 1998	丰台区 Fengtai 1997	1998年为1997年% 1998 as % of 1997
普通中学	Regular Secondary School	76	98	77.6	50	58	86.2
中等专业教育	Specialized Secondary Schools	28	28	100.0	1	1	100.0
招生数 (人)	New Student Enrollment (person)	34945	39166	89.2	19398	19404	100.0
小学	Primary Schools	10278	13213	77.8	7541	8100	93.1
初级中等学校	Junior Secondary Schools	13918	15180	91.7	9140	8364	109.3
高级中等学校	Senior Secondary Schools	5254	5085	103.3	2637	2830	93.2
中等专业教育	Specialized Secondary Schools	5495	5688	96.6	80	110	72.7
在校学生 (人)	Student Enrollment (person)	163458	173965	94.0	101909	97113	104.9
小学	Primary Schools	88690	95819	92.6	58667	60837	96.4
初级中等学校	Junior Secondary Schools	44790	50631	88.5	35229	29067	121.2
高级中等学校	Senior Secondary Schools	14196	12470	113.8	7623	6686	114.0
中等专业教育	Specialized Secondary Schools	15782	15045	104.9	390	523	74.6
毕业生 (人)	Graduates (person)	41377	42510	97.3	22087	22472	98.3
小学	Primary Schools	15092	15180	99.4	9594	9432	101.7
初级中等学校	Junior Secondary Schools	18369	19418	94.6	10509	11019	95.4
高级中等学校	Senior Secondary Schools	3199	3051	104.9	1774	1774	100.0
中等专业教育	Specialized Secondary Schools	4717	4661	101.2	210	247	85.0
达到"国家体育标准"学生数 (人)	Number of Students Come to the Standard for State Physical Training (person)	101338	128514	78.9	80534	81492	98.8
幼儿园、托儿所个数 (个)	Number of Kindergardens (unit)				145	144	100.7
幼儿入托数 (人)	New Enrollment (person)				16138	17096	94.4
文化	**Culture**						
文化馆、站 (个)	Cultural Centers (unit)	43	43	100.0	17	17	100.0
公共图书馆 (个)	Public Libraries (unit)	1	1	100.0	1	1	100.0
公共图书馆藏书 (万册)	Collection (10000 volume)	44	41.3	106.5	20	20	100.0
电影放映单位 (个)	Film Projection Units (unit)	12	10	120.0	2	2	100.0
区级以上重点文物保护单位 (个)	Cultural Relics Preserved at District Level and above (unit)	13	13	100.0	20	22	90.9
卫生	**Health**						
卫生机构数 (个)	Number of Health Institutions (unit)	168	161	104.3	532	307	173.3
#医院	Hospitals	107	105	101.9	56	55	101.8
卫生院	Clinics						
床位数	Number of Beds (unit)	10213	9040	113.0	5324	5679	93.7
#医院	Hospitals	10187	8730	116.7	5324	5544	96.0
卫生院	Clinics						
平均每千人拥有床位数 (张)	Average Number of Beds Per 1000 Persons (unit)	6.9	6.3	109.5	6.8	7.3	93.2
卫生技术人员 (人)	Medical Technical Personnel (person)	15012	14796	101.5	8896	8989	99.0
#医生	Doctors (person)	6430	6321	101.7	3869	4158	93.0
城市公用	**Urban Public Utilities**						
区级以上公园 (个)	Parks at District Level and above (unit)	20	20	100.0	6	6	100.0
体育场馆 (个)	Stadiums and Gymnasiums (unit)	9	10	90.0	6	6	100.0
道路长度 (公里)	Length of Roads (km)	263.5	259	101.7		2	

21-4 石景山区、海淀区国民经济主要指标

MAIN NATIONAL ECONOMIC INDICATORS FOR SHIJINGSHAN AND HAIDIAN DISTRICTS

项目	Item	石景山区 Shijingshan 1998	1997	1998年为1997年% 1998 as % of 1997	海淀区 Haidian 1998	1997	1998年为1997年% 1998 as % of 1997
综合	General Survey						
国内生产总值 (万元)	Gross Domestic Product (10000 yuan)	98953	84407.2	117.2	1857424.9	1590962	116.7
第一产业	Primary Industry	1439.1	1928.2	74.6	21579.9	18160.7	118.8
第二产业	Secondary Industry	21289.8	17158.9	124.1	1063595	868783	122.4
第三产业	Tertiary Industry	76224.1	65320.1	116.7	772250	704019	109.7
财政收入 (万元)	Fiscal Revenue (10000 yuan)	26316	22239	118.3	172214	138507	124.3
#各项税收	Taxes	25738	21716	118.5	155828	130215	119.7
财政支出 (万元)	Fiscal Expenditure (10000 yuan)	48000	42118	114.0	259932	191410	135.8
#基本建设支出	Capital Construction	4348	2040	213.1	37313	32551	114.3
支援农业生产支出	Supporting Agriculture	209	545	38.3	4859	4304	112.9
文教卫生事业费	Culture,Education and Health	14391	10626	135.4	48035	47410	101.3
人口和劳动力	**Population and Labor Force**						
总人口 (人)	Total Population (person)	398541	390498	102.1			
常住户籍人口 (人)	Permanent Registered Population (person)	324230	318300	101.9	1526111	1493280	106.0
#非农业人口	Non-agriculture	308590	302495	102.0	1395802	1358430	102.8
男	Male	164194	161210	101.9	724393	768319	94.3
女	Female	144396	141285	102.2	671409	724961	92.6
出生率 (‰)	Birth Rate (‰)	4.6	5.8		5.99	5.76	
死亡率 (‰)	Death Rate (‰)	7	5.2		4.99	4.37	
自然增长率 (‰)	Natural Growth Rate (‰)	-2.4	0.6		0.12	1.36	
从业人员 (人)	Employment (person)	39710	36339	109.3			
按产业分	Grouped by Industry						
第一产业	Primary Industry				12239	13220	92.6
第二产业	Secondary Industry	10317	9015	114.4	50741	69131	73.4
第三产业	Tertiary Industry	29393	27324	107.6	221818	212915	104.2
按职工非职工分	Grouped by Staff and Workers or Non-staff-and-worker						
职工人数	Staff and Worker	38057	34676	109.8	233052	244006	95.5
#国有单位	State-owned	23027	24477	94.1	90029	104698	86.0
集体单位	Collective-owned	8740	6429	135.9	47139	62961	74.9
城镇个体劳动者	Urban and Rural Individuals				57154	33767	169.3
劳动工资	**Wages**						
工资总额 (万元)	Total Wages (10000 yuan)	41277	33919	121.7	326988.8	285229	114.6
#国有单位	State-owned	28905	25967	111.3	133228.9	124843.2	106.7
集体单位	Collective-owned	6133	4409	139.1	45296.5	45700.1	99.1
职工平均工资 (元)	Average Wage (yuan)	10872	10106	107.6	14277	12530	113.9
固定资产投资	**Investment in Fixed Assets Assets**						
全社会固定资产投资 (万元)	Total Investment in Fixed Assets (10000 yuan)	57890	49089	117.9	199620	124026	161.0
按建设性质分	Grouped by Type of Construction						
#基本建设投资	Capital Construction	22390	13901	161.1	161537	91917	175.7
更新改造投资	Innovation and Replacement	6613	834	792.9		16500	

21-4 续表1 continued

项目 Item	石景山区 Shijingshan			海淀区 Haidian		
	1998	1997	1998年为1997年% 1998 as % of 1997	1998	1997	1998年为1997年% 1998 as % of 1997
按经济类型分 Grouped by Ownership						
国有单位 (万元) State-owned(10000 yuan)	53989	38405	140.6	68661	59017	116.3
集体单位 (万元) Collective-owned (10000 yuan)	374	3723	10.0	38083	15609	244.0
新增固定资产 (万元) Incremental Fixed Assets (10000 yuan)	84023	41967	200.2	193218	44786	409.1
#国有单位 State-owned	74461	33527	222.1	82439	18227	452.3
集体单位 Collective-owned	4340	3306	131.3	48867	38	
房屋施工面积 (万平方米) Floor Space of Buildings Under Construction (10000 sq.m)	86.6	75	115.5	104.9	82.6	127.0
#国有单位 State-owned	78.4	62.9	124.6	57.6	45.5	126.6
集体单位 Collective-owned	2.7	5.1	52.9	19.1	17.5	109.1
房屋竣工面积 (万平方米) Floor Space of Buildings Completed (10000 sq.m)	36.2	25.5	142.0	40.3	11.8	341.5
#国有单位 State-owned	30.7	21.2	144.8	23.7	6.2	382.3
#住宅 Residence	14.9	16.3	91.4	5.2	0.9	577.8
#集体单位 Collective-owned	2.7	2.4	112.5	12.5	0	
#住宅 Residence	2.4	2.2	109.1	4.6		
农村经济 Rural Economy						
农村劳动力 (人) Labor Force (person)	7729	8212	94.1	57154	56277	101.6
种植业 Planting	736	627	117.4		9913	
林业 Forestry	120	109	110.1		479	
牧业 Animal Husbandry	284	301	94.4		1771	
渔业 Fishery	11	9	122.2		218	
农村工业 Rural Industry	3249	3663	88.7	23879	24654	96.9
农村建筑业 Rural Construction	97	111	87.4	2522	2607	96.7
农村运输业 Rural Transportation	390	444	87.8	1991	1609	123.7
农村商、饮食业、服务业 Commerce,Catering and Services	2842	788	360.7	5380	4949	108.7
耕地面积 (公顷) Area under Cultivation (hectare)	424.7	424.7	100.0	7311.6	8736	83.7
农业机械总动力 (千瓦) Total Power of Agricultural Machinery (kw)	46200	49392	93.5	155773	125000	124.6
化肥施用实物量 (吨) Consumption of Chemical Fertilizers (ton)	156.3	181	86.4	8951.6	8960.7	99.9
化肥施用折纯量 (吨) Consumption of Chemical Fertilizers(100%) (ton)	46.2	59.5	77.6	3071.8	2922.9	105.1
农村用电量 (万千瓦时) Consumption of Electricity (10000 kwh)	1683.1	1805.6	93.2	14860.3	15464.7	96.1
农村国内生产总值 (万元) Rural Gross Domestic Product (10000 yuan)	21099.7	18033.2	117.0	159532.4	136758.9	116.7
第一产业 Primary Industry	1920.7	1461.4	131.4	21579.9	18160.7	118.8
第二产业 Secondary Industry	7216.7	7358.4	98.1	52542	54004.6	97.3
第三产业 Tertiary Industry	11962.3	9213.4	129.8	85410.5	64593.6	132.2
农业总产值 (万元) Gross Output Value of Agriculture (10000 yuan)	4913.4	6397.4	76.8	50993.2	55509	91.9
种植业 Planting	1014.3	953.8	106.3	22988.9	22934	100.2
林业 Forestry	11	1.5	733.3	458.6	477.2	96.1
牧业 Animal Husbandry	3856.1	5416.1	71.2	25610.6	30450.2	84.1
渔业 Fishery	32	26	123.1	1935.1	1647.1	117.5
农作物总播种面积 (万公顷) Sown Area of Farm Crops (10000 hectare)	0.1	0.1	100.0	0.99	1.0	99.0
粮食作物 Grain				0.53	0.6	88.3
经济作物 Industrial Crops	0.1	0.1	100.0			
其他作物 Other Crops						

21-4 续表 2 continued

项 目 Item		石景山区 Shijingshan 1998	1997	1998年为1997年% 1998 as % of 1997	海淀区 Haidian 1998	1997	1998年为1997年% 1998 as % of 1997
农副产品产量	Yield of Farm and Side-line Crops						
粮食 (万吨)	Grain (10000 tons)				3.5	3.8	92.1
蔬菜 (吨)	Vegetable (ton)	9653	10068	95.9	157836	178349	88.5
干鲜果 (吨)	Dry and Fresh Fruits (ton)	852	1002	85.0	14844	17812	83.3
畜产品产量	Output of Livestock Products						
生猪出栏 (头)	Slaughtered Hogs (head)	27558	29811	92.4	170924	207587	82.3
商品猪 (头)	Commodity Hogs (head)	27558	29811	92.4	170924	207309	82.4
猪牛羊肉 (吨)	Pork,Beef and Mutton(ton)	1820	1875.8	97.0	10477	11134	94.1
#猪肉	Pork	1820	1837.5	99.0	10410	11069	94.0
禽肉	Meat of Poultry (ton)	283	462	61.3	1775	2264	78.4
禽蛋	Poultry Eggs (ton)	2254	4738	47.6	8419	12460	67.3
牲畜年底头数 (头)	Number of Livestock (year-end) (head)	11914	16337	72.9			
大牲畜	Large Animals	540	563	95.9	3559	4431	80.3
猪	Hogs	11374	15774	72.1	92448	112657	82.1
羊	Goats and Sheep				2543	2849	89.3
水产品产量 (吨)	Output of Aquatic Product (ton)	40	40	100.0	2584.5	2901.5	89.1
农村集体经济收入 (万元)	Rural Collective Economic Revenue (10000 yuan)				794818	803650	98.9
农村集体经济利润总额 (万元)	Total Profits of Rural Collective Economy (10000 yuan)				14778	12632	117.0
国家税金	State Taxes				20583	19300	106.6
集体积累	Collective Accumulation				36450	32434	112.4
劳动所得	Income from Work				63682	60142	105.9
乡镇企业单位数 (个)	Number of Township and Village Enterprise (unit)	256	295	86.8	1477	1327	111.3
乡镇企业人数 (人)	Number of Persons of Township and Village Enterprises (person)	9151	10132	90.3	53940	53117	101.5
乡镇企业纯利润 (万元)	Net Profit of Township and Village Enterprises (10000 yuan)	2545	1488	171.0	12236	10417	117.5
乡镇企业固定资产原价 (万元)	Original Value of Fixed Assets of Township and Village Enterprises (10000 yuan)	45403	53879	84.3	182153	161286	171.7
乡镇企业固定资产净值 (万元)	Net Value of Fixed Assets of Township and Village Enterprises (10000 yuan)	32255	37658	85.7	118682	106092	111.9
工业	**Industry**						
全部工业企业单位数 (个)	Number of Enterprises (unit)	288	289	99.7	1149	1302	88.3
国有	State-owned	45	51	88.2	174	218	79.8
集体	Collective-owned	150	153	98.0	629	837	79.8
其他	Others	93	85	109.4			
全部工业总产值 (现价,万元)	Gross Output Value of Industry (at current prices,10000 yuan)	73568.8	61211.1	120.2	3324840	2166837	147.1
国有	State-owned	1813.8	2696.5	67.3	2110791	1141370	184.9
集体	Collective-owned	32097.6	34005.8	94.4	264110.3	336428.3	78.5
其他	Others	39657.4	24508.8	161.8	949938.6	782072	121.5

21-4 续表 3 continued

项目	Item	石景山区 Shijingshan 1998	1997	1998年为1997年% 1998 as % of 1997	海淀区 Haidian 1998	1997	1998年为1997年% 1998 as % of 1997
全部工业总产值(90不变价,万元)	Gross Output Value of Industry (at constant price of 1990,10000yuan)	68642.3	58082	118.2	4703496.5	2735228.3	172.0
国有	State-owned	1778.2	2589.9	68.7	3510143.5	1691398	207.5
集体	Collective-owned	30020.4	33648.1	89.2	248738.3	324754.2	76.6
其他	Others	36843.7	21844	168.7	944615.7	719076.1	131.4
全部轻工业总产值(现价,万元)	Gross Output Value of Light Industry (at current prices,10000 yuan)	23720.7	26155.9	90.7	445642.4	562051.3	79.6
以农产品为原料	Using Farm Products as Raw Materials	18330.1	22066.7	83.1	270755	378059	71.6
以非农产品为原料	Using Non-farm Products as Raw Materials	5390.6	4089.2	131.8	174887.4	183992.3	95.1
全部重工业总产值(现价,万元)	Gross Output Value of Heavy Industry (at current prices,10000 yuan)	44836.6	19026.9	235.6	2879197.6	1697819	169.6
采掘工业	Mining and Quarrying	71.5			1099	2042.3	53.8
原料工业	Raw Materials Industry	6647	1819.4	365.3	93857.4	106742.8	87.9
制造工业	Manufacturing Industry	38158.1	17207.5	221.8	2784331.2	1541228	175.2
独立核算工业企业平均职工人数 (人)	Average Number of Staff and Workers in Enterprises with Independent Accounting System (person)	11237	10496	107.1	88605	86018	103.0
#国有	State-owned	752	875	85.9	21917	24540	89.3
集体	Collective-owned	7107	6962	102.1	34673	43222	80.2
独立核算工业企业总产值(现价,万元)	Gross Output Value of Enterprises with Independent Accounting System(at current prices, (10000 yuan)	73523.8	60969.3	120.6	3324840	2259870.3	147.1
#国有	State-owned	1813.8	2696.5	67.3	2110791.1	1141369	184.9
集体	Collective-owned	32052.6	34005.8	94.3	264110.3	243395.4	78.5
独立核算工业企业工业增加值 (万元)	Value Added of Enterprises with Independent Accounting system (10000 yuan)	27720.8			1045898.8	847188.1	123.5
独立核算工业企业财务指标	Financial Indicators for Enterprises with Independent Accounting System						
产品销售收入 (万元)	Sales Revenue (10000yuan)	74420.1	60669.1	122.7	3238554.3	2163643	143.7
#国有	State-owned	2084.6	2972.1	70.1	2013811.7	1128367	178.5
产品销售成本 (万元)	Cost of Sales (10000 yuan)	58174.2	45109.6	129.0	2525529.6	1698061	148.7
#国有	State-owned	1532.1	2462.8	62.2	1526130.5	920704.8	165.8
固定资产原价 (万元)	Original Value of Fixed Assets (10000 yuan)	50569.6	42857	118.0	829599	481163.8	157.9
#国有	State-owned	1712.6	1915.8	89.4	192741.1	200853.6	96.0
固定资产净值 (万元)	Net Value of Fixed Assets (10000 yuan)	36654	29632.2	123.7	597371.5	321923.6	185.6
#国有	State-owned	1383.2	1551.7	89.1	143594	130922.8	109.7
全部流动资金年平均余额 (万元)	Annual Average Balance of Circulating Funds (10000 yuan)	74397.3	59513.2	125.0	2741113.1	1991909	137.6
#国有	State-owned	2120.1	2507.8	84.5	1047272.5	749451.9	139.7
利润总额 (万元)	Total Profits (10000 yuan)	92.1	-2329.9		158954.2	139357.2	114.1
#国有	State-owned	-31.1	66.7		89391.4	78239.9	114.3

21-4 续表 4 continued

项目	Item	石景山区 Shijingshan 1998	1997	1998年为1997年% 1998 as % of 1997	海淀区 Haidian 1998	1997	1998年为1997年% 1998 as % of 1997
资金利税率 (%)	Ratio of Pre-tax Profits to Total of Capital (%)	0.4	-3.1		5.4	6.9	
产品销售率 (%)	Ratio of Sales Value to Gross Output Value (%)	96.3	95.8		96	98.2	
增加值率 (%)	Ratio of Added Value to Gross Output Value (%)	37.7	31		31.5	37.5	
独立核算工业企业全员劳动生产率 (元/人)	Overall Labor Productivity of Enterprises with Independent Accounting System (yuan/person)	24669	34570	71.4	118041	97511	121.1
#国有	State-owned	9121			310536	179189	173.3
集体	Collective-owned	11799			23393	31059	75.3
商业	**Commerce**						
社会消费品零售额 (万元)	Retail Sales of Consumer Goods (10000 yuan)	306219	241451	126.8	2388971	2060421	115.9
按经济类型分	Grouped by Ownership						
国有	State-owned	53213	76301	69.7	910209	877423	103.7
集体	Collective-owned	11848	8976	132.0	294548	477577	61.7
其他	Others	241158	156174	154.4	1184214	205421	167.8
按类别分	Grouped by Type of Goods						
吃的商品 (万元)	Food (10000 yuan)	160954	143414	112.2	417534	401137	104.1
穿的商品 (万元)	Clothing (10000 yuan)	14069	8961	157.0	108324	101554	106.7
用的商品 (万元)	Daily Used Articles (10000 yuan)	124027	86880	142.8	1842938	1388482	132.7
烧的商品 (万元)	Fuel (10000 yuan)	7169	2196	326.5	20775	9351	215.8
网点数 (个)	Number of Outlets (unit)	10583	10593	99.9			
商业	Wholesale and Retail	7625	7388	103.2	31005	30745	100.9
饮食业	Catering	815	959	85.0	3712	3386	109.6
服务业	Services	2143	2246	95.4	7398	6529	113.3
#宾馆、饭店	Hotels				41	40	102.5
营业人员 (人)	Personnel (person)	43175	37748	114.4	142971	123374	115.9
#商业	Wholesale and Retail	22317	16990	131.4	80598	74245	108.6
饮食业	Catering	3418	4431	77.1	20041	14062	142.5
服务业	Services	17440	16327	106.8	42332	35077	120.7
#宾馆、饭店	Hotels				16167	15039	107.5
外经、外贸	**Foreign Economy and Trade**						
出口商品交货额 (万元)	Delivery Value of Exports (10000 yuan)	5324.7	5591.4	95.2	190195.3	174031.8	109.3
利用外资签订协议(合同)数 (个)	Number of Signed Agreements and Contracts of Foreign Capital to be Utilized (unit)	10	10	100.0	122	133	91.7
利用外资签订协议(合同)金额 (万美元)	Amount of Foreign Capital to be Utilized through Agreements and Contracts (USD 10000)	300.2	458.5	65.5	19057.2	16563.9	115.1
实际利用外资 (万美元)	Amount of Foreign Capital Actually Used (USD 10000)	815	778	104.8	9077.6	7302	124.3
旅游人数 (人)	Number of Tourists (person)	4525612	4796481	94.4			
教育	**Education**						
学校数 (个)	Number of Schools (unit)	81	80	101.3	254	275	92.4
小学	Primary Schools	48	48	100.0	144	169	85.2

21-4 续表 5 continued

项目	Item	石景山区 Shijingshan 1998	1997	1998年为1997年% 1998 as % of 1997	海淀区 Haidian 1998	1997	1998年为1997年% 1998 as % of 1997
普通中学	Regular Secondary School	28	27	103.7	88	84	104.8
中等专业教育	Specialized Secondary Schools	5	5	100.0			
招生数 (人)	New Student Enrollment (person)	9130	9197	99.3			
小学	Primary Schools	2556	2736	93.4	14146	14374	98.4
初级中等学校	Junior Secondary Schools	3625	3518	103.0	16199	16488	98.2
高级中等学校	Senior Secondary Schools	1261	1082	116.5	10617	11243	94.4
中等专业教育	Specialized Secondary Schools	1688	1861	90.7			
在校学生 (人)	Student Enrollment (person)	41485	43917	94.5			
小学	Primary Schools	21367	22501	95.0	103746	104599	99.2
初级中等学校	Junior Secondary Schools	11622	13251	87.7	51377	55881	91.9
高级中等学校	Senior Secondary Schools	3589	3281	109.4	30796	28862	106.7
中等专业教育	Specialized Secondary Schools	4907	4884	100.5			
毕业生 (人)	Graduates (person)	11527	10867	106.1			
小学	Primary Schools	3640	3609	100.9	16093	15886	101.3
初级中等学校	Junior Secondary Schools	5314	5434	97.8	20873	20021	104.3
高级中等学校	Senior Secondary Schools	983	791	124.3	8430	7049	119.6
中等专业教育	Specialized Secondary Schools	1590	1033	153.9			
达到"国家体育标准"学生数 (人)	Number of Students Come to the Standard for State Physical Training (person)						
幼儿园、托儿所个数 (个)	Number of Kindergardens (unit)	53	75	70.7	233	243	95.9
幼儿入托数 (人)	New Enrollment (person)	2617	3114	84.0	42449	36538	116.2
文化	**Culture**						
文化馆、站 (个)	Cultural Centers (unit)	7	7	100.0	27	27	100.0
公共图书馆 (个)	Public Libraries (unit)	2	2	100.0	1	1	100.0
公共图书馆藏书 (万册)	Collection (10000 volume)	33.1	30	110.3	25	25	100.0
电影放映单位 (个)	Film Projection Units (unit)	1	1	100.0			
区级以上重点文物保护单位 (个)	Cultural Relics Preserved at District Level and above (unit)	2	2	100.0	39	39	100.0
卫生	**Health**						
卫生机构数 (个)	Number of Health Institutions (unit)	205	199	103.0	878	874	100.5
#医院	Hospitals	21	20	105.0	87	90	96.7
卫生院	Clinics	1	1	100.0	8	8	100.0
床位数	Number of Beds (unit)	3732	3948	94.5	9358	9954	94.0
#医院	Hospitals	3012	3258	92.4			
卫生院	Clinics	20	20	100.0	582	518	112.4
平均每千人拥有床位数 (张)	Average Number of Beds Per 1000 Persons (unit)	9.4	10.3	91.3	6.1	6.7	91.0
卫生技术人员 (人)	Medical Technical Personnel (person)	5289	5444	97.2	15008	16005	93.8
#医生	Doctors (person)	2338	2376	98.4	9988	7095	140.8
城市公用	**Urban Public Utilities**						
区级以上公园 (个)	Parks at District Level and Above (unit)	10	10	100.0	3	3	100.0
体育场馆 (个)	Stadiums and Gymnasiums (unit)	4	4	100.0	2	2	100.0
道路长度 (公里)	Length of Roads (km)	177.9	177.9	100.0	595	595	100.0

21-5 门头沟区、房山区国民经济主要指标
MAIN NATIONAL ECONOMIC INDICATORS FOR MENTOUGOU AND FANGSHAN DISTRICTS

项目 Item	门头沟区 Mentougou			房山区 Fanshan		
	1998	1997	1998年为1997年% 1998 as % of 1997	1998	1997	1998年为1997年% 1998 as % of 1997
综合 General Survey						
国内生产总值 (万元) Gross Domestic Product (10000 yuan)	142372.6	117246.2	121.4	667719.2	580491.8	115.0
第一产业 Primary Industry	4716.3	5161.2	91.4	67713.2	65006	104.2
第二产业 Secondary Industry	63298	52225.5	121.2	314986.8	273496.8	115.2
第三产业 Tertiary Industry	74358.3	59859.5	124.2	285019.2	241989	117.8
财政收入 (万元) Fiscal Revenue (10000 yuan)	14380	10073	142.8	55634	43913	126.7
#各项税收 Taxes	32062	23018	139.3	57717	54663	105.6
财政支出 (万元) Fiscal Expenditure (10000 yuan)	46413	37271	124.5	58734	52185	112.5
#基本建设支出 Capital Construction	1017	980	103.8	2227	991	224.7
支援农业生产支出 Supporting Agriculture	3496	2738	127.7	4915	4811	102.2
文教卫生事业费 Culture,Education and Health	11747	10702	109.8	20782	20353	102.1
人口和劳动力 **Population and Labor Force**						
总人口 (人) Total Population (person)	259107	267426	96.9	749978	752213	99.7
常住户籍人口 (人) Permanent Registered Population (person)	233088	238109	97.9	749978	752213	99.7
#非农业人口 Non-agriculture	148531	151234	98.2	262042	258431	101.4
男 Male	121740	124720	97.6	377884	379581	99.9
女 Female	111348	113389	98.2	372094	372632	99.9
出生率 (‰) Birth Rate (‰)	6.56	8.09		7.1	7.8	
死亡率 (‰) Death Rate (‰)	10.05	8.23		6.8	6.9	
自然增长率 (‰) Natural Growth Rate (‰)	-3.49	-0.14		0.3	0.9	
从业人员 (人) Employment (person)	91604	93138	98.4	278619	272676	102.2
按产业分 Grouped by Industry						
第一产业 Primary Industry	13529	13375	101.2	81787	82451	99.2
第二产业 Secondary Industry	25803	27446	94.0	94830	91932	103.2
第三产业 Tertiary Industry	52272	52317	99.9	102002	98293	103.8
按职工非职工分 Grouped by Staff and Workers or Non-staff-and-worker						
职工人数 Staff and Worker	41416	44398	93.3	49458	49183	100.6
#国有单位 State-owned	22178	22873	97.0	36399	36147	100.7
集体单位 Collective-owned	6631	9280	71.5	11167	12339	90.5
城镇个体劳动者 Urban and Rural Individuals	4658	4147	112.3	13500	13583	99.4
劳动工资 **Wages**						
工资总额 (万元) Total Wages (10000 yuan)	34532.5	32657.1	105.7	43433.4	38667.7	112.3
#国有单位 State-owned	21351.5	19815.4	107.8	35073.9	30835.2	113.7
集体单位 Collective-owned	4537.7	5952.2	76.2	7057.3	7334.8	96.2
职工平均工资 (元) Average Wage (yuan)	9146	8113	112.7	8708	7698	113.1
固定资产投资 **Investment in Fixed Assets**						
全社会固定资产投资 (万元) Total Investment in Fixed Assets (10000 yuan)	13018	23063	56.4	45299	39483.0	114.7
按建设性质分 Grouped by Type of Construction						
#基本建设投资 Capital Construction	9597	12378	77.5	10287	20280	50.7
更新改造投资 Innovation and Replacement	756	483	156.5	3578	4294	83.3

21-5 续表1 continued

项目 Item		门头沟区 Mentougou 1998	1997	1998年为1997年% 1998 as % of 1997	房山区 Fanshan 1998	1997	1998年为1997年% 1998 as % of 1997
按经济类型分	Grouped by Ownership						
国有单位 (万元)	State-owned(10000 yuan)	10939	13598	80.4	13865	24574	56.4
集体单位 (万元)	Collective-owned (10000 yuan)	742	3280	22.6	31434	12189	257.9
新增固定资产 (万元)	Incremental Fixed Assets (10000 yuan)	17510	7514	233.7	32264	23863	135.2
#国有单位	State-owned				13865	10016	138.4
集体单位	Collective-owned				18399	11477	160.3
房屋施工面积 (万平方米)	Floor Space of Buildings Under Construction (10000 sq.m)	25.5	19.1	133.0	54.1	43.1	125.5
#国有单位	State-owned				44.5	20.7	215.0
集体单位	Collective-owned				9.6	19.8	48.5
房屋竣工面积 (万平方米)	Floor Space of Buildings Completed (10000 sq.m)	14.0	7.1	196.5	18.5	25.8	71.7
#国有单位	State-owned				11.8	8.2	143.9
#住宅	Residence				9.3	5.9	157.6
#集体单位	Collective-owned				6.7	15.1	44.4
#住宅	Residence				2.2	6.7	32.8
农村经济	**Rural Economy**						
农村劳动力 (人)	Labor Force (person)	45530	44593	102.1	217501	223286	97.4
种植业	Planting	10237	10468	97.8	68081	69481	98.0
林业	Forestry	1495	1334	112.1	4538	5523	82.2
牧业	Animal Husbandry	1767	1547	114.2	8094	6312	128.2
渔业	Fishery	30	26	115.4	498	584	85.3
农村工业	Rural Industry	9688	9711	99.8	47284	51344	92.1
农村建筑业	Rural Construction	2028	1556	130.3	28502	27937	102.0
农村运输业	Rural Transportation	6246	5267	118.6	22431	21102	106.3
农村商、饮食业、服务业	Commerce,Catering and Services	3653	2551	143.2	38073	41003	92.9
耕地面积 (公顷)	Area under Cultivation (hectare)	2917.5	2830.5	103.1	39808.3	39792.6	100.0
农业机械总动力 (千瓦)	Total Power of Agricultural Machinery (kw)	109365	118627	92.2	689000	666806.0	103.3
化肥施用实物量 (吨)	Consumption of Chemical Fertilizers (ton)	1972.1	1376.6	143.3	51932.7	48003	108.2
化肥施用折纯量 (吨)	Consumption of Chemical Fertilizers(100%) (ton)	471.5	429.8	109.7	15454.8	14727.5	104.9
农村用电量 (万千瓦时)	Consumption of Electricity (10000 kwh)	5072.1	5365.9	94.5	25778.8	22717.6	113.5
农村国内生产总值 (万元)	Rural Gross Domestic Product (10000 yuan)	55240	46709.4	118.3	472399.2	456006.0	103.6
第一产业	Primary Industry	4920.7	5180	95.0	67713.2	65006	104.2
第二产业	Secondary Industry	23566.2	22106.9	106.6	223907.2	220000	101.8
第三产业	Tertiary Industry	26753.1	19422.5	137.7	180778.8	171000	105.7
农业总产值 (万元)	Gross Output Value of Agriculture (10000 yuan)	5733.5	6220.6	92.2	69681.9	65606.9	106.2
种植业	Planting	2097.2	2081.6	100.7	41468.4	39928.2	103.9
林业	Forestry	548.2	413.1	132.7	1362.1	1276.6	106.7
牧业	Animal Husbandry	2900.6	3572	81.2	25968.4	23639.1	109.9
渔业	Fishery	187.5	153.9	121.8	883	763	115.7
农作物总播种面积 (万公顷)	Sown Area of Farm Crops (10000 hectare)	0.488	0.482	101.2	5.8	5.9	98.3
粮食作物	Grain	0.401	0.391	102.6	5.4	5.4	100.0
经济作物	Industrial Crops				0.1	0.1	100.0
其他作物	Other Crops	0.087	0.091	95.6	0.3	0.5	60.0

21-5 续表2 continued

项目 Item		门头沟区 Mentougou 1998	1997	1998年为1997年% 1998 as % of 1997	房山区 Fanshan 1998	1997	1998年为1997年% 1998 as % of 1997
农副产品产量	Yield of Farm and Side-line Crops						
粮食 (万吨)	Grain (10000 tons)	0.9	0.5	180.0	29.8	29.1	102.4
蔬菜 (吨)	Vegetable (ton)	21293.8	28412	74.9	202449	200103	101.2
干鲜果 (吨)	Dry and Fresh Fruits (ton)	4886	3040	160.7	48027	41281	116.3
畜产品产量	Output of Livestock Products						
生猪出栏 (头)	Slaughtered Hogs (head)	38983	47864	81.4	276430	228212	121.1
商品猪 (头)	Commodity Hogs (head)		46854				
猪牛羊肉 (吨)	Pork,Beef and Mutton(ton)	3269	3492	93.6	22844	21658	105.5
#猪肉	Pork	2697	3123	86.4	20079	15879	126.5
禽肉	Meat of Poultry (ton)	187	127	147.2	4406	3302	133.4
禽蛋	Poultry Eggs (ton)	1704	2866	59.5	12962	14163	91.5
牲畜年底头数 (头)	Number of Livestock (year-end) (head)	99945	98521	101.4	416554	341905	121.8
大牲畜	Large Animals	2540	2753	92.3	13579	13042	104.1
猪	Hogs	28215	30706	91.9	180056	160772	112.0
羊	Goats and Sheep	69190	65062	106.3	222919	168091	132.6
水产品产量 (吨)	Output of Aquatic Product (ton)	350	343	102.0	2027.4	1951.6	103.7
农村集体经济收入 (万元)	Rural Collective Economic Revenue (10000 yuan)	109424	104344	104.9	752213.7	794688	94.7
农村集体经济利润总额 (万元)	Total Profits of Rural Collective Economy (10000 yuan)	5925	5786	102.4	40109.4	43980	91.2
国家税金	State Taxes	4181	4189	99.8	30594.6	27533	111.1
集体积累	Collective Accumulation	1761	1898	92.8	10675.4	12158	87.8
劳动所得	Income from Work	9342	9398	99.4	183241.4	166695	109.9
乡镇企业单位数 (个)	Number of Township and Village Enterprise (unit)	6720	5868	114.5	25728	24015	107.1
乡镇企业人数 (人)	Number of Persons of Township and Village Enterprises (person)	34172	30944	110.4	168502	170320	98.9
乡镇企业纯利润 (万元)	Net Profit of Township and Village Enterprises (10000 yuan)	15393	13492	114.1	85713	83018.8	103.2
乡镇企业固定资产原价 (万元)	Original Value of Fixed Assets of Township and Village Enterprises (10000 yuan)	39389	44988	87.6	249819	230119	108.6
乡镇企业固定资产净值 (万元)	Net Value of Fixed Assets of Township and Village Enterprises (10000 yuan)	27618	24272	113.8	187355	172647	108.5
工业	Industry						
全部工业企业单位数 (个)	Number of Enterprises (unit)	928	1042	89.1	3074	3106	99.0
国有	State-owned	29	40	72.5	23	23	100.0
集体	Collective-owned	442	498	88.8	1208	1450	83.3
其他	Others	457	504	90.7	1843	1633	112.9
全部工业总产值 (现价,万元)	Gross Output Value of Industry (at current prices,10000 yuan)	156054.3	143501.0	108.7	538898.8	534138.8	100.9
国有	State-owned	15878	17065.2	93.0	19452.7	22332.3	87.1
集体	Collective-owned	66046.2	72830.2	91.7	380664.1	423501.5	89.9
其他	Others	74130.1	53605.6	138.3	138782	88305	157.2

21-5 续表3 continued

项目	Item	门头沟区 Mentougou 1998	1997	1998年为1997年% 1998 as % of 1997	房山区 Fanshan 1998	1997	1998年为1997年% 1998 as % of 1997
全部工业总产值(90不变价,万元)	Gross Output Value of Industry (at constant price of 1990,10000yuan)	144661.3	133033.6	108.7	494227.1	470336.7	105.1
国有	State-owned	12634.2	20367.8	62.0	14480.5	16693.4	86.7
集体	Collective-owned	62899.8	57652.6	109.1	348109.7	365338.3	95.3
其他	Others	69127.3	55013.2	125.7	131636.9	88305	149.1
全部轻工业总产值(现价,万元)	Gross Output Value of Light Industry (at current prices,10000 yuan)	32348.5	30097.5	107.5	84898.7	79957.2	106.2
以农产品为原料	Using Farm Products as Raw Materials				56246	51737	108.7
以非农产品为原料	Using Non-farm Products as Raw Materials				28652.7	28220.2	101.5
全部重工业总产值(现价,万元)	Gross Output Value of Heavy Industry (at current prices,10000 yuan)	20628.1	21667.9	95.2	221615.1	211651.5	104.7
采掘工业	Mining and Quarrying				36931.6	32923.6	112.2
原料工业	Raw Materials Industry				57802.3	55029.4	105.0
制造工业	Manufacturing Industry				126881.2	123698.5	102.6
独立核算工业企业平均职工人数 (人)	Average Number of Staff and Workers in Enterprises with Independent Accounting System (person)	14908	16328	91.3	57939	56440	102.7
#国有	State-owned	2866	4244	67.5	9738	9407	103.5
集体	Collective-owned	6742	7018	96.1	43528	42330	102.8
独立核算工业企业总产值(现价,万元)	Gross Output Value of Enterprises with Independent Accounting System(at current prices, 10000 yuan)	107513.3	99735	107.8	306513.8	291608.8	105.1
#国有	State-owned	10470.2	17991.6	58.2	62946.1	61143.8	103.0
集体	Collective-owned	27629.3	22844.2	120.9	200621.4	192838.1	104.0
独立核算工业企业工业增加值 (万元)	Value Added of Enterprises with Independent Accounting system (10000 yuan)	33490.8	26662	125.6	99923.5	95647.7	104.5
独立核算工业企业财务指标	Financial Indicators for Enterprises with Independent Accounting System						
产品销售收入 (万元)	Sales Revenue(10000yuan)	80164.3	81353.2	98.5	281435.9	268091.9	105.0
#国有	State-owned	7306.7	14702.9	49.7	56653.1	51737	109.5
产品销售成本 (万元)	Cost of Sales(10000 yuan)	64187.7	65570.8	97.9	234819.3	225761.6	104.0
#国有	State-owned	6168.9	11778.6	52.4	44583.7	42330.3	105.3
固定资产原价 (万元)	Original Value of Fixed Assets (10000 yuan)	100748.2	110458	91.2	246101.1	235168.4	104.7
#国有	State-owned	16162.6	21167.9	76.4	67501.8	65847.1	102.5
固定资产净值 (万元)	Net Value of Fixed Assets (10000 yuan)	82818.2	76614.9	108.1	183123.8	174024.6	105.2
#国有	State-owned	12733.4	14275	89.2	40761.1	37626.9	108.3
全部流动资金年平均余额 (万元)	Annual Average Balance of Circulating Funds (10000 yuan)	96868.7	88117.6	109.9	224610.1	211651.5	106.1
#国有	State-owned	13958.1	22559.5	61.9	57708.7	56440.4	102.3
利润总额 (万元)	Total Profits (10000 yuan)	-3919.9	-5696.3		3596.2	3433.5	104.7
#国有	State-owned	-2032.7	-1366		-709.6	-810.6	

21-5 续表4 continued

项目		Item	门头沟区 Mentougou 1998	1997	1998年为1997年% 1998 as % of 1997	房山区 Fanshan 1998	1997	1998年为1997年% 1998 as % of 1997
资金利税率	(%)	Ratio of Pre-tax Profits to Total of Capital (%)	-1.5	-2.0			6.5	
产品销售率	(%)	Ratio of Sales Value to Gross Output Value (%)	97.7	90.8		94.4	92.9	
增加值率	(%)	Ratio of Added Value to Gross Output Value (%)	38.4	40.1		32.6	32.8	
独立核算工业企业全员劳动生产率	(元/人)	Overall Labor Productivity of Enterprises with Independent Accounting System (yuan/person)	16519	13533	122.1	13880	13416	103.5
#国有		State-owned	7967	9745	81.8	8786	11136.8	78.9
集体		Collective-owned	10892	9710	112.2	13335	15785.2	84.5
商业		**Commerce**						
社会消费品零售额	(万元)	Retail Sales of Consumer Goods (10000 yuan)	143717	113953	126.1	412074.7	380199.5	108.4
按经济类型分		Grouped by Ownership						
国有		State-owned	22480.3	48986	45.9	73443.5	134493	54.6
集体		Collective-owned	35764.7	28201.4	126.8	248523.9	93178.3	226.7
其他		Others	85472	36765.6	232.5	69666.7	138104.6	50.4
按类别分		Grouped by Type of Goods						
吃的商品	(万元)	Food (10000 yuan)	63137.9	42548.6	148.4	107828.8	92491.5	116.6
穿的商品	(万元)	Clothing (10000 yuan)	4391.9	8469.9	51.8	67667.8	61441.2	110.1
用的商品	(万元)	Daily Used Articles (10000 yuan)	71346.6	58090.2	122.8	199008	191912.5	103.7
烧的商品	(万元)	Fuel (10000 yuan)	4840.6	4844.3	99.9	37570.3	34354.3	109.4
网点数	(个)	Number of Outlets (unit)	6007	6832	87.9	9088	11538	78.8
商业		Wholesale and Retail	4750	5108	93.0	6518	7978	81.7
饮食业		Catering	545	671	81.2	1410	1804	78.2
服务业		Services	395	674	58.6	1150	1756	65.5
#宾馆、饭店		Hotels	14	4	350.0	63	62	101.6
营业人员	(人)	Personnel (person)	22431	31960	70.2	24995	35916	69.6
商业		Wholesale and Retail	16272	20200	80.5	20435	29365	69.6
饮食业		Catering	1828	2551	71.6	3725	5353	69.6
服务业		Services	3891	8562	45.4	3130	4498	69.6
#宾馆、饭店		Hotels	782	970	80.6	2602	2536	102.6
外经、外贸		**Foreign Economy and Trade**						
出口商品交货额	(万元)	Delivery Value of Exports (10000 yuan)	7662.2	7662.2	104.3	32091.7	25735.7	124.7
利用外资签订协议(合同)数	(个)	Number of Signed Agreements and Contracts of Foreign Capital to be Utilized (unit)	22	22	77.3	12	16	75.0
利用外资签订协议(合同)金额	(万美元)	Amount of Foreign Capital to be Utilized through Agreements and Contracts (USD 10000)	1032.9	1134.6	91.0	2152	489.2	439.9
实际利用外资	(万美元)	Amount of Foreign Capital Actually Used (USD 10000)	403.2	1313.3	30.7	2061	1688	122.1
旅游人数	(人)	Number of Tourists (person)	2615000	2085000	125.4	2502649	2522773	99.2
教育		**Education**						
学校数	(个)	Number of Schools (unit)	115	120	95.8	380	420	90.5
小学		Primary Schools	85	92	92.4	307	347	88.5

21-5 续表5 continued

项目	Item	门头沟区 Mentougou			房山区 Fanshan		
		1998	1997	1998年为1997年% 1998 as % of 1997	1998	1997	1998年为1997年% 1998 as % of 1997
普通中学	Regular Secondary School	24	22	109.0	65	64	101.6
中等专业教育	Specialized Secondary Schools	6	6	100.0	8	9	88.9
招生数 (人)	New Student Enrollment (person)	7651	7142	107.1	25522	28719	88.9
小学	Primary Schools	2266	2429	93.3	8596	11004	78.1
初级中等学校	Junior Secondary Schools	3751	3352	111.9	12923	12131	106.5
高级中等学校	Senior Secondary Schools	775	663	116.9	2619	3842	68.2
中等专业教育	Specialized Secondary Schools	859	698	123.1	1384	1742	79.4
在校学生 (人)	Student Enrollment (person)	33303	35291	94.4	136044	146574	92.8
小学	Primary Schools	18421	20285	90.8	85373	90445	94.4
初级中等学校	Junior Secondary Schools	10802	11357	95.1	39553	41006	96.5
高级中等学校	Senior Secondary Schools	2011	1819	110.5	6882	10814	96.6
中等专业教育	Specialized Secondary Schools	2069	1830	113.1	4236	4309	98.3
毕业生 (人)	Graduates (person)	8918	8361	106.7	29477	29682	99.3
小学	Primary Schools	3780	3333	113.4	13312	12561	106.0
初级中等学校	Junior Secondary Schools	4031	4103	98.2	12906	13019	99.1
高级中等学校	Senior Secondary Schools	553	449	123.2	2107	2903	72.6
中等专业教育	Specialized Secondary Schools	554	476	116.4	1152	1199	96.1
达到"国家体育标准"学生数 (人)	Number of Students Come to the Standard for State Physical Training (person)	27912	27201	102.6	127634	116787	109.3
幼儿园、托儿所个数 (个)	Number of Kindergardens (unit)	20	23	86.9	331	334	99.1
幼儿入托数 (人)	New Enrollment (person)	1830	2041	89.7	8080	8542	94.6
文化	**Culture**						
文化馆、站 (个)	Cultural Centers (unit)	15	15	100.0	15	15	100.0
公共图书馆 (个)	Public Libraries (unit)	1	1	100.0	1	1	100.0
公共图书馆藏书 (万册)	Collection (10000 volume)	21.6	21.6	100.0	7	6	116.7
电影放映单位 (个)	Film Projection Units (unit)	5	5	100.0	13	21	61.9
区级以上重点文物保护单位 (个)	Cultural Relics Preserved at District Level and above (unit)	74	59	125.4	68	68	100.0
卫生	**Health**						
卫生机构数 (个)	Number of Health Institutions (unit)	28	28	100.0	58	58	100.0
#医院	Hospitals	5	5	100.0	19	18	105.6
卫生院	Clinics	15	15	100.0	26	26	100.0
床位数	Number of Beds (unit)	724	726	99.7	3929	3810	103.1
#医院	Hospitals	621	621	100.0	3146	3312	95.0
卫生院	Clinics	103	105	98.1	565	498	113.5
平均每千人拥有床位数 (张)	Average Number of Beds Per 1000 Persons (unit)	3.1	3.0	103.3	5.2	5.1	107.0
卫生技术人员 (人)	Medical Technical Personnel (person)	1179	1187	99.3	5951	4778	124.6
#医生	Doctors (person)	581	622	93.4	4411	2080	212.1
城市公用	**Urban Public Utilities**						
区级以上公园 (个)	Parks at District Level and Above (unit)	4	4	100.0	6	6	100.0
体育场馆 (个)	Stadiums and Gymnasiums (unit)	2	2	100.0	259	256	101.2
道路长度 (公里)	Length of Roads (km)	448.5	364.1	100.5	1769.1	1649.5	107.3

21-6 昌平县、顺义县国民经济主要指标

MAIN NATIONAL ECONOMIC INDICATORS FOR CHANGPING AND SHUNYI COUNTIES

项目	Item	昌平县 Changping 1998	昌平县 Changping 1997	昌平县 Changping 1998年为1997年% 1998 as % of 1997	顺义县 Shunyi 1998	顺义县 Shunyi 1997	顺义县 Shunyi 1998年为1997年% 1998 as % of 1997
综合	**General Survey**						
国内生产总值 (万元)	Gross Domestic Product (10000 yuan)	455665.9	402583.8	113.2	690176.0	594108.8	116.2
第一产业	Primary Industry	45978.5	44816.4	102.6	147885.9	141426.7	104.6
第二产业	Secondary Industry	167855.2	148306.6	113.2	308607.7	250869.6	123.0
第三产业	Tertiary Industry	241823.2	209460.8	115.5	233682.4	201812.5	115.8
财政收入 (万元)	Fiscal Revenue (10000 yuan)	20377.0	16769.0	121.5	28423.0	24102.6	117.9
#各项税收	Taxes	18307.0	15562.0	117.6	26995.0	22832.2	118.2
财政支出 (万元)	Fiscal Expenditure (10000 yuan)	46541.0	37748.0	123.3	65375.0	52013.3	125.7
#基本建设支出	Capital Construction	861.0	740.0	116.4	4628.0	2072	223.4
支援农业生产支出	Supporting Agriculture	4217.0	3414.0	123.5	10911.0	4708	231.8
文教卫生事业费	Culture,Education and Health	13583.0	12437.0	109.2	21606.0	18042.2	119.8
人口和劳动力	**Population and Labor Force**						
总人口 (人)	Total Population (person)	459379	422518	108.7	539973.0	540394	99.9
常住户籍人口 (人)	Permanent Registered Population (person)	418775	419739	99.8	536913.0	536330	100.1
#非农业人口	Non-agriculture	165566	163338	101.4	103695.0	98995	104.7
男	Male	208863	209908	99.5	265973.0	266675	99.7
女	Female	209909	209831	100.0	274000.0	273719	100.1
出生率 (‰)	Birth Rate (‰)	7.1	8.4		7.57	7.55	
死亡率 (‰)	Death Rate (‰)	8.8	7.1		8.10	7.49	
自然增长率 (‰)	Natural Growth Rate (‰)	-1.7	1.3		-0.53	0.06	
从业人员 (人)	Employment (person)	170361	169162	100.7	270655.0	262933	102.9
按产业分	Grouped by Industry						
第一产业	Primary Industry	42117	37608	112.0	61961.0	59373	104.4
第二产业	Secondary Industry	54279	51447	105.5	99441.0	105176	94.5
第三产业	Tertiary Industry	73965	80107	92.3	109253.0	98384	111.0
按职工非职工分	Grouped by Staff and Workers or Non-staff-and-worker						
职工人数	Staff and Worker	67728	64029	105.8	64387.0	62729	102.6
#国有单位	State-owned	39429	36424	108.3	45723.0	42504	107.6
集体单位	Collective-owned	17452	21071	82.8	13143.0	16060	81.8
城镇个体劳动者	Urban and Rural Individuals	1054	2382	44.2	19240.0	9081	211.9
劳动工资	**Wages**						
工资总额 (万元)	Total Wages (10000 yuan)	55616.8	47823.0	116.3	57775.4	49382.5	117.0
#国有单位	State-owned	33460.3	28553.1	117.2	43217.3	35276.4	122.5
集体单位	Collective-owned	12409.0	13472.0	92.1	9110.7	11061.5	82.4
职工平均工资 (元)	Average Wage (yuan)	8390.0	7550.0	111.1	8978.2	7823	114.8
固定资产投资	**Investment in Fixed Assets Assets**						
全社会固定资产投资 (万元)	Total Investment in Fixed Assets (10000 yuan)	84669.4	74147.4	114.2	208000.0	161000	129.2
按建设性质分	Grouped by Type of Construction						
#基本建设投资	Capital Construction	71988.9	62599.9	115.0	108160.0	73000	148.2
更新改造投资	Innovation and Replacement	12680.5	11547.5	109.8	99840.0	88000	113.5

21-6 续表1 continued

项目	Item	昌平县 Changping 1998	1997	1998年为1997年% 1998 as % of 1997	顺义县 Shunyi 1998	1997	1998年为1997年% 1998 as % of 1997
按经济类型分	Grouped by Ownership						
国有单位 (万元)	State-owned (10000 yuan)	11508.0	9458.0	121.7	111000.0	120750	91.9
集体单位 (万元)	Collective-owned (10000 yuan)	72024.4	64689.4	111.3	74000	33810	218.9
新增固定资产 (万元)	Incremental Fixed Assets (10000 yuan)	57171.7	55777.0	102.5	137200	112700	121.7
#国有单位	State-owned	10327.0	8476.0	121.8	73260	84525	86.7
集体单位	Collective-owned	46844.7	47301.4	99.0	48840	23670	206.3
房屋施工面积 (万平方米)	Floor Space of Buildings Under Construction (10000 sq.m)	107.3	102.1	105.1	159	191	83.2
#国有单位	State-owned	19.5	24.8	78.6	68	130	52.3
集体单位	Collective-owned	87.8	77.3	113.6	62	44	140.9
房屋竣工面积 (万平方米)	Floor Space of Buildings Completed (10000 sq.m)	38.6	36.0	107.2	89	102.2	87.1
#国有单位	State-owned	7.6	7.7	98.7	45	68	66.2
#住宅	Residence	6.0	4.3	139.5	35	40.6	86.2
#集体单位	Collective-owned	31.0	28.3	109.5	24	17	141.2
#住宅	Residence	18.1	6.1	296.7	14	10	140.0
农村经济	**Rural Economy**						
农村劳动力 (人)	Labor Force (person)	102781	104089	98.7	187978	191123	98.4
种植业	Planting	32798	28873	113.6	45238	45958	98.4
林业	Forestry	3518	4341	81.0	2491	2560	97.3
牧业	Animal Husbandry	3999	3222	124.1	11262	7970	141.3
渔业	Fishery	668	595	112.3	1908	1994	95.7
农村工业	Rural Industry	20918	24025	87.1	57138	63224	90.4
农村建筑业	Rural Construction	6754	6102	110.7	14569	14773	98.6
农村运输业	Rural Transportation	9321	7808	119.4	11335	10325	109.8
农村商、饮食业、服务业	Commerce,Catering and Services	6462	5210	124.0	11370	7911	143.7
耕地面积 (公顷)	Area under Cultivation (hectare)	24456.9	24656.9	99.2	50650.0	50963.0	99.4
农业机械总动力 (千瓦)	Total Power of Agricultural Machinery (kw)	204000.0	271142.0	75.2	545438.0	567473.0	96.1
化肥施用实物量 (吨)	Consumption of Chemical Fertilizers (ton)	26907.0	30468.5	88.3	93033.4	95791.0	97.1
化肥施用折纯量 (吨)	Consumption of Chemical Fertilizers(100%) (ton)	9931.0	11287.9	88.0	34613.0	35155.0	98.5
农村用电量 (万千瓦时)	Consumption of Electricity (10000 kwh)	25584.0	21726.9	117.8	37779.5	30697.0	123.1
农村国内生产总值 (万元)	Rural Gross Domestic Product (10000 yuan)	242153.6	218557.9	110.8	408675.4	365869.4	111.7
第一产业	Primary Industry	45987.5	44816.4	102.6	146514.8	139020.2	105.4
第二产业	Secondary Industry	79006.1	71680.3	110.2	146136.6	135611.0	107.8
第三产业	Tertiary Industry	117160.0	102061.2	114.8	116024.0	91238.2	127.2
农业总产值 (万元)	Gross Output Value of Agriculture (10000 yuan)	115704.0	109731.2	105.4	204181.1	165189.0	123.6
种植业	Planting	46214.0	44618.1	103.6	75564.0	62968.2	120.0
林业	Forestry	2852.6	2554.5	111.7	1200.0	1149.1	104.4
牧业	Animal Husbandry	60303.6	56089.5	107.5	119372.9	94310.5	126.6
渔业	Fishery	6333.8	6469.1	97.9	8044.2	6761.2	119.0
农作物总播种面积 (万公顷)	Sown Area of Farm Crops (10000 hectare)	3.7	3.8	97.4	9.3	9.3	100.0
粮食作物	Grain	3.4	3.4	100.0	7.8	7.8	100.0
经济作物	Industrial Crops	...	...		1.4	1.4	100.0
其他作物	Other Crops	...	...		0.1	0.1	100.0

21-6 续表2 continued

项目	Item	昌平县 Changping			顺义县 Shunyi		
		1998	1997	1998年为1997年% 1998 as % of 1997	1998	1997	1998年为1997年% 1998 as % of 1997
农副产品产量	Yield of Farm and Sideline Crops						
粮食 (万吨)	Grain (10000 tons)	17.1	16.4	104.3	44.4	43.8	101.4
蔬菜 (吨)	Vegetable (ton)	104995.0	124237.0	84.5	839945.7	830444	101.1
干鲜果 (吨)	Dry and Fresh Fruits (ton)	50838.0	53963.0	94.2	41127.1	40683	101.1
畜产品产量	Output of Livestock Products						
生猪出栏 (头)	Slaughtered Hogs (head)	273996	276459	99.1	1199115	1026138	116.9
商品猪 (头)	Commodity Hogs (head)		272653		1199115	1025707	116.9
猪牛羊肉 (吨)	Pork,Beef and Mutton(ton)	17374.0	17059.2	101.8	112454.6	80856	139.1
#猪肉	Pork	14955.0	15238.5	98.1	100199.6	69457	144.3
禽肉	Meat of Poultry (ton)	15727.0	10861.8	144.8	68141.3	57841	117.8
禽蛋	Poultry Eggs (ton)	13077.0	17377.8	75.3	22789.2	24633	92.5
牲畜年底头数 (头)	Number of Livestock (year-end) (head)	245588	241557	101.7	915088	780833	117.2
大牲畜	Large Animals	18039	23527	76.7	31277	22712	137.7
猪	Hogs	168038	166464	100.9	769870	679550	113.3
羊	Goats and Sheep	59511	51566	115.4	97801	78571	124.5
水产品产量 (吨)	Output of Aquatic Product (ton)	8002.0	8226.6	97.3	16140	16008	100.8
农村集体经济收入 (万元)	Rural Collective Economic Revenue (10000 yuan)	345414.0	324633.0	106.4	1019446	964803	105.7
农村集体经济利润总额 (万元)	Total Profits of Rural Collective Economy (10000 yuan)	35302.0	25399.3	139.0	269349	248669	108.3
国家税金	State Taxes	18014.0	17311.0	104.1	14290	13031	109.7
集体积累	Collective Accumulation	12990.0	11325.0	114.7	22410	25124	89.2
劳动所得	Income from Work	101747.0	82034.0	124.0	193225	176626	109.4
乡镇企业单位数 (个)	Number of Township and Village Enterprise (unit)	1101	1232	89.4	1007	1092	92.2
乡镇企业人数 (人)	Number of Persons of Township and Village Enterprises (person)	48067	49015	98.1	86325	90370	95.5
乡镇企业纯利润 (万元)	Net Profit of Township and Village Enterprises (10000 yuan)	15227.0	11474.0	132.7	20535	20536	100.0
乡镇企业固定资产原价 (万元)	Original Value of Fixed Assets of Township and Village Enterprises (10000 yuan)	148945.0	140727.0	105.8	303957	297593	102.1
乡镇企业固定资产净值 (万元)	Net Value of Fixed Assets of Township and Village Enterprises (10000 yuan)	107748.0	102622.0	105.0	222223	225033	98.8
工业	**Industry**						
全部工业企业单位数 (个)	Number of Enterprises (unit)	1083	1509	71.8	2660	1956	136.0
国有	State-owned	47	60	78.3	83	122	68.0
集体	Collective-owned	780	1108	70.4	673	894	75.3
其他	Others	256	341	75.1	1904	940	202.6
全部工业总产值 (现价,万元)	Gross Output Value of Industry (at current prices,10000 yuan)	376876.7	360223.6	104.6	1094513.3	975508.8	112.2
国有	State-owned	34665.5	25518.2	135.8	297926.3	313872	94.9
集体	Collective-owned	195690.1	239495.7	81.7	323832.5	358072.2	90.4
其他	Others	146521.1	95209.7	153.9	472754.5	303564.6	155.7

21-6 续表3 continued

项目	Item	昌平县 Changping 1998	1997	1998年为1997年% 1998 as % of 1997	顺义县 Shunyi 1998	1997	1998年为1997年% 1998 as % of 1997
全部工业总产值(90不变价,万元)	Gross Output Value of Industry (at constant price of 1990,10000yuan)	358170.6	345654.7	103.6	962686.6	812676.1	118.5
国有	State-owned	27165.2	22860.4	118.8	205505.8	198553.8	103.5
集体	Collective-owned	190683.4	229083.4	83.2	298179.2	330750.3	90.2
其他	Others	140322.0	93710.9	149.7	459001.6	283372.0	162.0
全部轻工业总产值(现价,万元)	Gross Output Value of Light Industry (at current prices,10000 yuan)	193996.9	127706.7	151.9	679840.7	583294.4	116.6
以农产品为原料	Using Farm Products as Raw Materials	113193.2	82701.4	136.9	497707.0	449587.6	110.7
以非农产品为原料	Using Non-farm Products as Raw Materials	80803.7	45005.3	179.5	182710.2	133706.8	136.6
全部重工业总产值(现价,万元)	Gross Output Value of Heavy Industry (at current prices,10000 yuan)	164173.7	117156.3	140.1	334646.6	193557.5	172.9
采掘工业	Mining and Quarrying	6919.0	2898.8	238.7	2417.2	2705.4	89.3
原料工业	Raw Materials Industry	11948.8	7427.5	160.9	69926.8	54626.8	128.0
制造工业	Manufacturing Industry	145305.9	106830.0	136.0	263370.9	136225.3	193.3
独立核算工业企业平均职工人数 (人)	Average Number of Staff and Workers in Enterprises with Independent Accounting System (person)	53686	54569	98.4	104390	77605	134.5
#国有	State-owned	2447	3206	76.3	15464	14984	103.2
集体	Collective-owned	36962	24935	148.2	58977	38010	155.2
独立核算工业企业总产值(现价,万元)	Gross Output Value of Enterprises with Independent Accounting System(at current prices, 10000 yuan)	360692.8	290288.4	124.3	1020532	776851.9	131.4
#国有	State-owned	18972.6	25337.8	74.9	297926.3	306785.2	97.1
集体	Collective-owned	195199.1	171962.4	113.5	323832.5	218469	148.2
独立核算工业企业工业增加值 (万元)	Value Added of Enterprises with Independent Accounting system (10000 yuan)	123729.2	85203.8	145.2			
独立核算工业企业财务指标	Financial Indicators for Enterprises with Independent Accounting System						
产品销售收入 (万元)	Sales Revenue (10000yuan)	319612.9	261634.8	122.2	934105.4	723284	129.1
#国有	State-owned	21628.2	27538.8	78.5	282965.3	292791.4	96.6
产品销售成本 (万元)	Cost of Sales (10000 yuan)	257273.0	206976.4	124.3	739001.4	567690.6	130.2
#国有	State-owned	17653.9	22886.7	77.1	188900.1	209690.9	90.1
固定资产原价 (万元)	Original Value of Fixed Assets (10000 yuan)	259631.7	213264.6	121.7	714574.7	520506.2	137.3
#国有	State-owned	15535.6	21592.8	71.9	224361.7	179169.8	125.2
固定资产净值 (万元)	Net Value of Fixed Assets (10000 yuan)	180447.4	156602.6	115.2	532830.4	394428.2	135.1
#国有	State-owned	9969.4	16241.6	61.4	166255.8	120344.9	138.1
全部流动资金年平均余额 (万元)	Annual Average Balance of Circulating Funds (10000 yuan)	364520.8	262266.9	139.0	591836.6	446846.5	132.4
#国有	State-owned	17844.6	21750.6	82.0	157028.9	128261.8	122.4
利润总额 (万元)	Total Profits (10000 yuan)	10257.0	4551.8	225.3	47065.8	27914.2	168.6
#国有	State-owned	-141.9	-574.4		44559	30214.8	147.5

21-6 续表4 continued

项目	Item	昌平县 Changping 1998	昌平县 Changping 1997	昌平县 Changping 1998年为1997年% 1998 as % of 1997	顺义县 Shunyi 1998	顺义县 Shunyi 1997	顺义县 Shunyi 1998年为1997年% 1998 as % of 1997
资金利税率 (%)	Ratio of Pre-tax Profits to Total of Capital (%)	5.7	4.5		9.9	10.2	
产品销售率 (%)	Ratio of Sales Value to Gross Output Value (%)	91.5	84.1		92	96	
增加值率 (%)	Ratio of Added Value to Gross Output Value (%)	34.3	29.4		23.6	21.2	
独立核算工业企业全员劳动生产率 (元/人)	Overall Labor Productivity of Enterprises with Independent Accounting System (yuan/person)	23047.0	15614.0	147.6	29473	25588.7	115.2
#国有	State-owned	20587.0	15547.0	132.4	82088.6	67166.4	122.2
集体	Collective-owned	17589.0	13082.0	134.5	17150.1	15185.9	112.9
商业	**Commerce**						
社会消费品零售额 (万元)	Retail Sales of Consumer Goods (10000 yuan)	158686.0	149757.0	106.0	301749	272369	110.8
按经济类型分	Grouped by Ownership						
国有	State-owned	25829.0	32946.0	78.4	85025	65617	129.6
集体	Collective-owned	66946.0	54007.0	124.0	78467	87644	89.5
其他	Others	66911.0	65219.0	102.6	138257	119108	116.1
按类别分	Grouped by Type of Goods						
吃的商品 (万元)	Food (10000 yuan)	62788.0	46070.0	136.3	112808	98753	114.2
穿的商品 (万元)	Clothing (10000 yuan)	17072.0	16311.0	104.7	45729	41289	110.8
用的商品 (万元)	Daily Used Articles (10000 yuan)	66214.0	76844.0	86.2	111827	104955	106.5
烧的商品 (万元)	Fuel (10000 yuan)	12612.0	10532.0	119.7	31385	14073	223.0
网点数 (个)	Number of Outlets (unit)	7504	8375	89.6	5381	16011	
商业	Wholesale and Retail	4810	6773	71.0	3743	12035	
饮食业	Catering	869	731	118.9	633	1699	
服务业	Services	1791	867	206.6	1005	2277	
#宾馆、饭店	Hotels	3	4	75.0	9	5	180.0
营业人员 (人)	Personnel (person)	24748	23369	105.9	35109	36695	
商业	Wholesale and Retail	17677	19033	92.9	22311	23850	
饮食业	Catering	4061	3175	127.9	3933	3390	
服务业	Services	2740	1161	236.0	8865	9455	93.8
#宾馆、饭店	Hotels	415	379	109.5	2663	1141	233.4
外经、外贸	**Foreign Economy and Trade**						
出口商品交货额 (万元)	Delivery Value of Exports (10000 yuan)	39935.9	26219.1	152.3	189390.6	158985.7	119.1
利用外资签订协议(合同)数 (个)	Number of Signed Agreements and Contracts of Foreign Capital to be Utilized (unit)	18	27	66.7	40	39	102.6
利用外资签订协议(合同)金额 (万美元)	Amount of Foreign Capital to be Utilized through Agreements and Contracts (USD 10000)	6195.4	1136.9	544.9	6831.3	6751.5	101.2
实际利用外资 (万美元)	Amount of Foreign Capital Actually Used (USD 10000)	6741.4	2052.4	328.5	10257.6	10307	99.5
旅游人数 (人)	Number of Tourists (person)	9920000	9059000	109.5	700660	596402	117.5
教育	**Education**						
学校数 (个)	Number of Schools (unit)	190	199	95.5	202	207	97.6
小学	Primary Schools	147	156	94.2	161	166	97.0

21-6 续表5 continued

项目 Item			昌平县 Changping 1998	1997	1998年为1997年% 1998 as % of 1997	顺义县 Shunyi 1998	1997	1998年为1997年% 1998 as % of 1997
普通中学		Regular Secondary School	42	42	100.0	38	38	100.0
中等专业教育		Specialized Secondary Schools	1	1	100.0	3	3	100.0
招生数	(人)	New Student Enrollment (person)	13882	13577	102.2	20693	22795	90.8
小学		Primary Schools	3659	4073	89.8	5833	9742	59.9
初级中等学校		Junior Secondary Schools	6692	6094	109.8	11008	8911	123.5
高级中等学校		Senior Secondary Schools	3369	3205	105.1	2262	2375	95.2
中等专业教育		Specialized Secondary Schools	162	205	79.0	1590	1767	90.0
在校学生	(人)	Student Enrollment (person)	62890	66759	94.2	113950	117433	97.0
小学		Primary Schools	33571	36723	91.4	72954	78185	93.3
初级中等学校		Junior Secondary Schools	19576	20221	96.8	29917	35146	85.1
高级中等学校		Senior Secondary Schools	9084	8979	101.2	7163	6639	107.9
中等专业教育		Specialized Secondary Schools	659	836	78.8	3916	4102	95.5
毕业生	(人)	Graduates (person)	16455	15032	109.5	24487	21324	114.8
小学		Primary Schools	6714	6233	107.7	11083	9073	122.2
初级中等学校		Junior Secondary Schools	6801	6484	104.9	9715	9214	105.4
高级中等学校		Senior Secondary Schools	3069	1974	155.5	2041	1593	128.1
中等专业教育		Specialized Secondary Schools	339	341	99.4	1648	1444	114.1
达到"国家体育标准"学生数	(人)	Number of Students Come to the Standard for State Physical Training (person)	60986	65264	93.4	73246	113384	64.6
幼儿园、托儿所个数	(个)	Number of Kindergardens (unit)	184	173	106.4	134	164	81.7
幼儿入托数	(人)	New Enrollment (person)	9950	8954	111.1	9159	9934	92.2
文化		**Culture**						
文化馆、站	(个)	Cultural Centers (unit)	26	31	83.9	20	22	90.9
公共图书馆	(个)	Public Libraries (unit)	1	1	100.0	1	1	100.0
公共图书馆藏书	(万册)	Collection (10000 volume)	15.0	15.3	98.0	13.5	12.6	107.1
电影放映单位	(个)	Film Projection Units (unit)	50	52	96.2	28	22	127.3
区级以上重点文物保护单位	(个)	Cultural Relics Preserved at District Level and above (unit)	65	65	100.0	10	10	100.0
卫生		**Health**						
卫生机构数	(个)	Number of Health Institutions (unit)	149	121	123.1	46	44	104.5
#医院		Hospitals	15	11	136.4	11	10	110.0
卫生院		Clinics	26	26	100.0	26	26	100.0
床位数		Number of Beds (unit)	4556	4082	111.6	1706	1628	104.8
#医院		Hospitals	3767	3559	105.8	1324	1210	109.4
卫生院		Clinics	311	344	90.4	382	418	91.4
平均每千人拥有床位数	(张)	Average Number of Beds Per 1000 Persons (unit)	10.9	9.7	112.4	3.2	3	106.7
卫生技术人员	(人)	Medical Technical Personnel (person)	4000	3741	106.9	2706	2554	106.0
#医生		Doctors (person)	1744	1544	113.0	1333	1229	108.5
城市公用		**Urban Public Utilities**						
区级以上公园	(个)	Parks at District Level and Above (unit)	8	7	114.3	3	3	100.0
体育场馆	(个)	Stadiums and Gymnasiums (unit)	2	2	100.0	4	4	100.0
道路长度	(公里)	Length of Roads (km)	1370.0	1321.6	103.7	1438.4	1422.2	101.1

21-7 通州区、大兴县国民经济主要指标
MAIN NATIONAL ECONOMIC INDICATORS FOR TONGZHOU DISTRICT AND DAXING COUNTY

项目	Item	通州区 Tongzhou 1998	1997	1998年为1997年% 1998 as % of 1997	大兴县 Daxing 1998	1997	1998年为1997年% 1998 as % of 1997
综合	General Survey						
国内生产总值 (万元)	Gross Domestic Product (10000 yuan)	445273.8	403282.2	110.4	381726.0	344244.0	110.9
第一产业	Primary Industry	95698	80818.0	118.4	107804.0	106072.0	101.6
第二产业	Secondary Industry	139236.7	124676.7	111.7	112993.0	100525.0	112.4
第三产业	Tertiary Industry	210339.1	197787.5	106.3	160929.0	137627.0	116.9
财政收入 (万元)	Fiscal Revenue (10000 yuan)	23590	19051.0	123.8	21678.0	15036.0	144.2
#各项税收	Taxes	21025	12830.0	163.9	20319.0	13839.0	146.8
财政支出 (万元)	Fiscal Expenditure (10000 yuan)	45453	37089.0	122.6	47855.0	41287.0	115.9
#基本建设支出	Capital Construction	2403	808.0	297.4	1480.0	2049.0	72.2
支援农业生产支出	Supporting Agriculture	5118	2623.0	195.1	3559.0	5538.0	64.3
文教卫生事业费	Culture,Education and Health	13655	11265.0	121.2	17634.0	14727.0	119.7
人口和劳动力	**Population and Labor Force**						
总人口 (人)	Total Population (person)	626845	628326.0	99.8	601197.0	602278.0	99.8
常住户籍人口 (人)	Permanent Registered Population (person)	595890	596562.0	99.9	520858.0	521939.0	99.8
#非农业人口	Non-agriculture	175965	166938.0	105.4	143609.0	139637.0	102.8
男	Male	293806	294777.0	99.7	260752.0	261674.0	99.6
女	Female	301994	301245.0	100.2	260106.0	260265.0	99.9
出生率 (‰)	Birth Rate (‰)	5.63	6.87		6.7	7.6	88.2
死亡率 (‰)	Death Rate (‰)	6.6	6.86		6.5	6.9	94.2
自然增长率 (‰)	Natural Growth Rate (‰)	-0.97	0.01		0.2	0.7	28.6
从业人员 (人)	Employment (person)	236243	235025.0	100.5	254066.0	225425.0	112.7
按产业分	Grouped by Industry						
第一产业	Primary Industry	82193	76768.0	107.1	124914.0	122302.0	102.1
第二产业	Secondary Industry	75495	71678.0	105.3	61629.0	43690.0	141.1
第三产业	Tertiary Industry	78555	86579.0	90.7	67523.0	59433.0	113.6
按职工非职工分	Grouped by Staff and Workers or Non-staff-and-worker						
职工人数	Staff and Worker	49320	49617.0	99.4	73578.0	64440.0	114.2
#国有单位	State-owned	35017	35429.0	98.8	35408.0	30823.0	114.9
集体单位	Collective-owned	10250	10312.0	99.4	21377.0	23420.0	91.3
城镇个体劳动者	Urban and Rural Individuals	3606	4016.0	89.8	1376.0	1206.0	114.1
劳动工资	**Wages**						
工资总额 (万元)	Total Wages (10000 yuan)	42815	39387.5	108.7	61002.6	49170.0	124.1
#国有单位	State-owned	31492	29339.7	107.3	32211.0	25376.8	126.9
集体单位	Collective-owned	6704	6804.1	98.5	12933.9	14831.9	87.2
职工平均工资 (元)	Average Wage (yuan)	8571	7862.2	109.0	8439.0	7773.0	108.6
固定资产投资	**Investment in Fixed Assets Assets**						
全社会固定资产投资 (万元)	Total Investment in Fixed Assets (10000 yuan)	47957.1	39416.2	121.7	61294.0	49170.0	124.7
按建设性质分	Grouped by Type of Construction						
#基本建设投资	Capital Construction	34802.2	30280.0	114.9	58541.0	62721.3	93.3
更新改造投资	Innovation and Replacement	13154.9	9136.2	144.0	2753.0	1847.0	149.1

21-7 续表 1 continued

项目	Item	通州区 Tongzhou 1998	1997	1998年为1997年% 1998 as % of 1997	大兴县 Daxing 1998	1997	1998年为1997年% 1998 as % of 1997
按经济类型分	Grouped by Ownership						
国有单位 (万元)	State-owned(10000 yuan)	24618.1	19591.0	125.7	39387.0	17556.0	224.4
集体单位 (万元)	Collective-owned (10000 yuan)	12644.1	9431.2	134.1	13460.0	35028.3	38.4
新增固定资产 (万元)	Incremental Fixed Assets (10000 yuan)	44085.1	27953.2	157.7	69295.0	50749.8	136.5
#国有单位	State-owned	26858	13525	198.6	44142.0	11147.0	396.0
集体单位	Collective-owned	13260.1	3778.2	351.0	9955.0	32563.8	30.6
房屋施工面积 (万平方米)	Floor Space of Buildings Under Construction (10000 sq.m)	54	46.8	115.4	66.1	55.5	119.1
#国有单位	State-owned	29.5	27.9	105.7	38.3	26.2	146.2
集体单位	Collective-owned	16	6.7	238.8	10.1	17.1	59.1
房屋竣工面积 (万平方米)	Floor Space of Buildings Completed (10000 sq.m)	37.2	30.0	124.0	38.2	27.6	138.4
#国有单位	State-owned	18	13.6	132.4	22.3	12.2	182.8
#住宅	Residence	14.3	7.8	183.3	18.0	9.4	191.5
#集体单位	Collective-owned	13.2	5.7	231.6	9.3	11.9	78.2
#住宅	Residence	5.4	...		2.5	5.6	44.6
农村经济	**Rural Economy**						
农村劳动力 (人)	Labor Force (person)	183317	181392	101.1	179112	179723	99.7
种植业	Planting	70083	68448	102.4	114804	112059	102.4
林业	Forestry	1908	2000	95.4	4387	5382	81.5
牧业	Animal Husbandry	6928	3538	195.8	4635	3872	119.7
渔业	Fishery	2233	1950	114.5	507	494	102.6
农村工业	Rural Industry	48739	52920	92.1	21621	21875	98.8
农村建筑业	Rural Construction	13114	11544	113.6	5790	5152	112.4
农村运输业	Rural Transportation	9847	9213	106.9	6112	5461	111.9
农村商、饮食业、服务业	Commerce,Catering and Services	30465	31779	95.9	5603	5014	111.7
耕地面积 (公顷)	Area under Cultivation (hectare)	50907.7	51003.2	99.8	52435.6	52801.2	99.3
农业机械总动力 (千瓦)	Total Power of Agricultural Machinery (kw)	406506	431000	94.3	582000.0	452000.0	128.8
化肥施用实物量 (吨)	Consumption of Chemical Fertilizers (ton)	106457.4	117600.7	90.5	111965.3	112544.0	99.5
化肥施用折纯量 (吨)	Consumption of Chemical Fertilizers(100%) (ton)	37544.8	40146.6	93.5	34273.0	35092.7	97.7
农村用电量 (万千瓦时)	Consumption of Electricity (10000 kwh)	34719.6	27659.2	125.5	25449.3	22739.1	111.9
农村国内生产总值 (万元)	Rural Gross Domestic Product (10000 yuan)	296195.9	258975.1	114.4	284403.2	57589.9	493.8
第一产业	Primary Industry	95698	80818	118.4	107502.0	105987.8	101.4
第二产业	Secondary Industry	116776.4	103095.1	113.3	92562.7	77924.2	118.8
第三产业	Tertiary Industry	83721.5	75062	111.5	84338.5	73677.9	114.5
农业总产值 (万元)	Gross Output Value of Agriculture (10000 yuan)	107585	99991	107.6	140564.5	139217.3	101.0
种植业	Planting	68137	67059	101.6	98416.7	95819.4	102.7
林业	Forestry	653	542	120.5	1314.1	1364.2	96.3
牧业	Animal Husbandry	31560	26737	118.0	38616.4	39850.1	96.9
渔业	Fishery	7235	5641	128.3	2217.3	2183.6	101.5
农作物总播种面积 (万公顷)	Sown Area of Farm Crops (10000 hectare)	9.4	9.4	100.0	8.6	8.6	99.8
粮食作物	Grain	7.7	7.8	98.7	5.7	5.7	99.8
经济作物	Industrial Crops	0.2	0.2	100.0	0.4	0.4	97.5
其他作物	Other Crops	1.5	1.4	107.1	2.6	2.5	100.4

21-7 续表 2 continued

项目	Item	通州区 Tongzhou 1998	1997	1998年为1997年% 1998 as % of 1997	大兴县 Daxing 1998	1997	1998年为1997年% 1998 as % of 1997
农副产品产量	Yield of Farm and Sideline Crops						
粮食 (万吨)	Grain (10000 tons)	50.0	50.2	99.7	33.3	33.3	100.0
蔬菜 (吨)	Vegetable (ton)	753073.3	749612.0	100.5	929425.0	896028.0	103.7
干鲜果 (吨)	Dry and Fresh Fruits(ton	30963	24360.0	127.1	83413.0	82363.0	101.3
畜产品产量	Output of Livestock Products						
生猪出栏 (头)	Slaughtered Hogs (head)	394745	363053.0	108.7	357803.0	343539.0	104.2
商品猪 (头)	Commodity Hogs (head)	...	361946.0			342462.0	0.0
猪牛羊肉 (吨)	Pork,Beef and Mutton (ton)	31102	27298.0	113.9	25783.0	24392.0	105.7
#猪肉	Pork	27866	23897.0	116.6	22552.0	21543.0	104.7
禽肉	Meat of Poultry (ton)	7191	5168.0	139.1	8153.0	7579.0	107.6
禽蛋	Poultry Eggs (ton)	14116	15356.0	91.9	29220.0	40606.0	72.0
牲畜年底头数 (头)	Number of Livestock (year-end) (head)	348964	339631.0	102.7	407956.6	373556.0	109.2
大牲畜	Large Animals	18509	22566.0	82.0	20496.0	20692.0	99.1
猪	Hogs	237755	225395.0	105.5	238363.0	229679.0	103.8
羊	Goats and Sheep	92700	91670.0	101.1	143889.0	123185.0	116.8
水产品产量 (吨)	Output of Aquatic Product (ton)	11500	11200.0	102.7	5208.6	5279.0	98.7
农村集体经济收入 (万元)	Rural Collective Economic Revenue (10000 yuan)	390403	405408.0	96.3	476974.5	444626.0	107.3
农村集体经济利润总额 (万元)	Total Profits of Rural Collective Economy (10000 yuan)	27504	24472.0	112.4	41333.1	38379.0	107.7
国家税金	State Taxes	18246	16714.0	109.2	16983.4	14719.0	115.4
集体积累	Collective Accumulation	15559	14576.0	106.7	23017.5	18014.0	127.8
劳动所得	Income from Work	1080	1139.2	94.8	36772.8	36912.0	99.6
乡镇企业单位数 (个)	Number of Township and Village Enterprise (unit)	2832	2100.0	134.9	1427.0	2900.0	49.2
乡镇企业人数 (人)	Number of Persons of Township and Village Enterprises (person)	80252	80022.0	100.3	50457.0	59627.0	84.6
乡镇企业纯利润 (万元)	Net Profit of Township and Village Enterprises (10000 yuan)	21824	17745.0	123.0	26842.0	24940.0	107.6
乡镇企业固定资产原价 (万元)	Original Value of Fixed Assets of Township and Village Enterprises (10000 yuan)	301056	299301.0	100.6	206102.0	168234.0	122.5
乡镇企业固定资产净值 (万元)	Net Value of Fixed Assets of Township and Village Enterprises (10000 yuan)	221505	227222.0	97.5	158248.0	129943.0	121.8
工业	**Industry**						
全部工业企业单位数 (个)	Number of Enterprises (unit)	2507	2412.0	103.9	2125.0	2023.0	105.0
国有	State-owned	27	46.0	58.7	224.0	186.0	120.4
集体	Collective-owned	2155	1790.0	120.4	989.0	1200.0	82.4
其他	Others	325	576	56.4	912.0		
全部工业总产值 (现价,万元)	Gross Output Value of Industry (at current prices,10000 yuan)	490163	483631.1	101.4	501339.9	486706.8	103.0
国有	State-owned	30840.7	48132.1	64.1	67558.8	81506.9	82.9
集体	Collective-owned	312531	420006.3	74.4	199660.6	253476.8	78.8
其他	Others	146791.3	15492.7		234120.5	151723.1	154.3

21-7 续表 3 continued

项目	Item	通州区 Tongzhou 1998	1997	1998年为1997年% 1998 as % of 1997	大兴县 Daxing 1998	1997	1998年为1997年% 1998 as % of 1997
全部工业总产值(90不变价,万元)	Gross Output Value of Industry (at constant price of 1990,10000yuan)	475220.0	452019.1	105.1	475030.8	452221.4	105.0
国有	State-owned	23531.4	30144.6	78.1	52625.6	65739.8	80.1
集体	Collective-owned	311451.6	304407.1	102.3	196756.7	238920.2	82.4
其他	Others	140237.0	117467.4	119.4	225648.5		
全部轻工业总产值(现价,万元)	Gross Output Value of Light Industry (at current prices,10000 yuan)	90119.6	104933.6	85.9	280854.0	164000.5	171.3
以农产品为原料	Using Farm Products as Raw Materials	56244.6	71797.3	78.3	163469.7	107707.2	151.8
以非农产品为原料	Using Non-farm Products as Raw Materials	33875	33136.3	102.2	117384.3	56293.3	208.5
全部重工业总产值(现价,万元)	Gross Output Value of Heavy Industry (at current prices,10000 yuan)	74771.6	92293.2	81.0	220485.9	135749.9	162.4
采掘工业	Mining and Quarrying						
原料工业	Raw Materials Industry	13911	12585.7	110.5	37922.0	26642.3	142.3
制造工业	Manufacturing Industry	60860.6	79707.5	76.4	181508.1	109107.6	166.4
独立核算工业企业平均职工人数 (人)	Average Number of Staff and Workers in Enterprises with Independent Accounting System (person)	28184	34851	80.9	52737.0	33580.0	157.0
#国有	State-owned	5235	6472	80.9	10075.0	9069.0	111.1
集体	Collective-owned	14831	19536	75.9	24695.0	15178.0	162.7
独立核算工业企业总产值(现价,万元)	Gross Output Value of Enterprises with Independent Accounting System(at current prices, 10000 yuan)	164891.2	210285.9	78.4	493415.2	285048.1	173.1
#国有	State-owned	30840.7	44722.9	69.0	60957.3	71191.0	85.6
集体	Collective-owned	65870.4	102310.9	64.4	194409.1	80887.5	240.3
独立核算工业企业工业增加值 (万元)	Value Added of Enterprises with Independent Accounting system (10000 yuan)						
独立核算工业企业财务指标	Financial Indicators for Enterprises with Independent Accounting System						
产品销售收入 (万元)	Sales Revenue (10000yuan)	134141.8	164463.9	81.6	443925.2	260010.1	170.7
#国有	State-owned	22457.3	34130	65.8	57839.4	66343.1	87.2
产品销售成本 (万元)	Cost of Sales (10000 yuan)	106816.1	129310.9	82.6	354109.1	207806.4	170.4
#国有	State-owned	17866.6	31831.1	56.1	48096.7	54370.0	88.5
固定资产原价 (万元)	Original Value of Fixed Assets (10000 yuan)	155592.7	161699.4	96.2	296713.7	218363.0	135.9
#国有	State-owned	41801.8	39467.1	105.9	66683.3	90900.8	73.4
固定资产净值 (万元)	Net Value of Fixed Assets (10000 yuan)	108566	113834.4	95.4	227289.7	164368.7	138.3
#国有	State-owned	29624.2	25104.6	118.0	51577.6	72439.5	71.2
全部流动资金年平均余额 (万元)	Annual Average Balance of Circulating Funds (10000 yuan)	154314.9	181412.7	85.1	327202.0	206474.3	158.5
#国有	State-owned	28161.1	30456.2	92.5	52205.1	67820.1	77.0
利润总额 (万元)	Total Profits (10000 yuan)	476.2	409.7	116.2	14932.7	-8136.2	
#国有	State-owned	-15.0	-512.2		-105.1	-13748.7	

注：通州区轻、重工业总产值为乡及乡以上工业企业数。

Note: Data of gross output value of light and heavy industry of Tongzhou District refers to that of enterprises with independent accounting system at township level and above.

21-7 续表 4 continued

项目		Item	通州区 Tongzhou 1998	1997	1998年为1997年% 1998 as % of 1997	大兴县 Daxing 1998	1997	1998年为1997年% 1998 as % of 1997
资金利税率	(%)	Ratio of Pre-tax Profits to Total of Capital (%)	2.42	2.9		5.9	0.6	
产品销售率	(%)	Ratio of Sales Value to Gross Output Value (%)	90.65	93.3		91.5	91.2	
增加值率	(%)	Ratio of Added Value to Gross Output Value (%)	39.13	27.9		14.2	15.7	
独立核算工业企业全员劳动生产率	(元/人)	Overall Labor Productivity of Enterprises with Independent Accounting System (yuan/person)	15973	15151	105.4	18130.0	24926.0	72.7
#国有		State-owned	13976	14074	99.3			
集体		Collective-owned	15597	16080	97.0			
商业		**Commerce**						
社会消费品零售额	(万元)	Retail Sales of Consumer Goods (10000 yuan)	319921	306255	104.5	237173.0	224128.0	105.8
按经济类型分		Grouped by Ownership						
国有		State-owned	30728	34204	89.8	59111.0	68924.0	85.8
集体		Collective-owned	43089	114387	37.7	34612.0	57438.0	60.3
其他		Others	246104	157664	156.1	143450.0		
按类别分		Grouped by Type of Goods						
吃的商品	(万元)	Food (10000 yuan)	161165	139382	115.6	119370.0	120588.0	99.0
穿的商品	(万元)	Clothing (10000 yuan)	22900	26073	87.8	27244.0	24560.0	110.9
用的商品	(万元)	Daily Used Articles (10000 yuan)	129971	136419	95.3	76544.0	68312.0	112.1
烧的商品	(万元)	Fuel (10000 yuan)	5885	4831	121.8	14015.0	10668.0	131.4
网点数	(个)	Number of Outlets (unit)	11709	11537	101.5	14329.0	11411.0	125.6
商业		Wholesale and Retail	8322	8632	96.4	11531.0	8657.0	133.2
饮食业		Catering	1528	1478	103.4	1498.0	1550.0	96.6
服务业		Services	727	1407	51.7	1300.0	1204.0	108.0
#宾馆、饭店		Hotels	2	2	100.0	2.0	1.0	200.0
营业人员	(人)	Personnel (person)	24921	27195	91.6	27355.0	23547.0	116.2
商业		Wholesale and Retail	17818	21141	84.3	20634.0	18159.0	113.6
饮食业		Catering	3975	3523	112.8	4273.0	3683.0	116.0
服务业		Services	1438	2435	59.1	2448.0	1705.0	143.6
#宾馆、饭店		Hotels	612	651	94.0	564.0	231.0	244.2
外经、外贸		**Foreign Economy and Trade**						
出口商品交货额	(万元)	Delivery Value of Exports (10000 yuan)	50612.4	47417.8	106.7	46721.7	46117.2	101.3
利用外资签订协议(合同)数	(个)	Number of Signed Agreements and Contracts of Foreign Capital to be Utilized (unit)	34	31	109.7	31.0	39.0	79.5
利用外资签订协议(合同)金额	(万美元)	Amount of Foreign Capital to be Utilized through Agreements and Contracts (USD 10000)	2026.9	2042.9	99.2	2409.5	3361.3	71.7
实际利用外资	(万美元)	Amount of Foreign Capital Actually Used(USD 10000)	4123.1	3706.7	111.2	2709.1	2489.3	108.8
旅游人数	(人)	Number of Tourists (person)	1896500			339200	2050000	16.5
教育		**Education**						
学校数	(个)	Number of Schools (unit)	222	238	93.3	256.0	265.0	96.6
小学		Primary Schools	175	190	92.1	205.0	213.0	96.2

21-7 续表 5 continued

项目	Item	通州区 Tongzhou 1998	1997	1998年为1997年% 1998 as % of 1997	大兴县 Daxing 1998	1997	1998年为1997年% 1998 as % of 1997
普通中学	Regular Secondary School	43	44	97.7	46.0	46.0	100.0
中等专业教育	Specialized Secondary Schools	4	4	100.0	5.0	6.0	83.3
招生数 (人)	New Student Enrollment (person)	18718	21323	87.8	21702.0	20034.0	108.3
小学	Primary Schools	6805	10321	65.9	6469.0	9092.0	71.2
初级中等学校	Junior Secondary Schools	8882	8340	106.5	10400.0	8896.0	116.9
高级中等学校	Senior Secondary Schools	1923	1630	118.0	4280.0	1608.0	266.2
中等专业教育	Specialized Secondary Schools	1108	1032	107.4	553.0	438.0	126.3
在校学生 (人)	Student Enrollment (person)	100928	111461	90.6	106833.0	98624.0	108.3
小学	Primary Schools	65806	68354	96.3	66082.0	70422.0	93.8
初级中等学校	Junior Secondary Schools	27481	35832	76.7	28433.0	22748.0	125.0
高级中等学校	Senior Secondary Schools	5042	4701	107.3	10828.0	3866.0	280.1
中等专业教育	Specialized Secondary Schools	2599	2574	101.0	1490.0	1588.0	93.8
毕业生 (人)	Graduates (person)	23468	21370	109.8	22446.0	17934.0	125.2
小学	Primary Schools	9219	8646	106.6	10734.0	9104.0	117.9
初级中等学校	Junior Secondary Schools	11910	10741	110.9	8620.0	7796.0	110.6
高级中等学校	Senior Secondary Schools	1492	1221	122.2	2554.0	634.0	402.8
中等专业教育	Specialized Secondary Schools	847	762	111.2	538.0	400.0	134.5
达到"国家体育标准"学生数 (人)	Number of Students Come to the Standard for State Physical Training (person)	100456	105594	95.1			
幼儿园、托儿所个数 (个)	Number of Kindergartens (unit)	189	217	87.1	207.0	207.0	100.0
幼儿入托数 (人)	New Enrollment (person)	20598	24865	82.8	6357.0	7008.0	90.7
文化	**Culture**						
文化馆、站 (个)	Cultural Centers (unit)	19	19	100.0	22.0	22.0	100.0
公共图书馆 (个)	Public Libraries (unit)	1	1	100.0	1.0	1.0	100.0
公共图书馆藏书 (万册)	Collection (10000 volume)	15	13.9	107.9	11.0	11.0	100.0
电影放映单位 (个)	Film Projection Units (unit)	26	17	152.9	21.0	21.0	100.0
区级以上重点文物保护单位 (个)	Cultural Relics Preserved at District Level and above (unit)	25	25	100.0	15.0	15.0	100.0
卫生	**Health**						
卫生机构数 (个)	Number of Health Institutions (unit)	149	147	101.4	46.0	45.0	102.2
#医院	Hospitals	11	11	100.0	11.0	11.0	100.0
卫生院	Clinics	16	16	100.0	28.0	28.0	100.0
床位数	Number of Beds (unit)	1920	2037	94.3	1942.0	1838	105.7
#医院	Hospitals	1526	1634	93.4	1306.0	494.0	264.4
卫生院	Clinics	375	383	97.9	616.0	624.0	98.7
平均每千人拥有床位数 (张)	Average Number of Beds Per 1000 Persons (unit)	3.19	3.41	93.5	3.7	3.5	105.7
卫生技术人员 (人)	Medical Technical Personnel (person)	2883	3131	92.1	2450.0	2400.0	102.1
#医生	Doctors (person)	1421	1510	94.1	951.0	1162.0	81.8
城市公用	**Urban Public Utilities**						
区级以上公园 (个)	Parks at District Level and Above (unit)	1	1	100.0	2.0	2.0	100.0
体育场馆 (个)	Stadiums and Gymnasiums (unit)	1	1	100.0	2.0	2.0	100.0
道路长度 (公里)	Length of Roads (km)	1719.4	1702	101.0	1370.0	1350.0	101.5

21-8 平谷县、怀柔县国民经济主要指标
MAIN NATIONAL ECONOMIC INDICATORS FOR PINGGU AND HUAIROU COUNTIES

项目 Item	平谷县 Pinggu 1998	1997	1998年为1997年% 1998 as % of 1997	怀柔县 Huairou 1998	1997	1998年为1997年% 1998 as % of 1997
综合 General Survey						
国内生产总值 (万元) Gross Domestic Product (10000 yuan)	269820.4	246040.8	109.7	295864.3	269322.5	109.9
第一产业 Primary Industry	75290.8	73453.7	102.5	36680.5	35770.4	102.5
第二产业 Secondary Industry	98445.9	87083.8	113.0	153884.5	142733.9	107.8
第三产业 Tertiary Industry	96083.7	85503.3	112.4	105299.3	90818.2	115.9
财政收入 (万元) Fiscal Revenue (10000 yuan)	10711	9753	109.8	50398	41997	120.0
#各项税收 Taxes	10921	10507	103.9	49181	41298	119.1
财政支出 (万元) Fiscal Expenditure (10000 yuan)	50102	38339	130.7	64911	56413	115.1
#基本建设支出 Capital Construction	2146	1385	154.9	2560	1415	180.9
支援农业生产支出 Supporting Agriculture	4503	4680	96.2	6552	6042	108.4
文教卫生事业费 Culture,Education and Health	13084	11542	113.4	13345	11942	111.7
人口和劳动力 Population and Labor Force						
总人口 (人) Total Population (person)	395967	396746	99.8	264539	264101	100.2
常住户籍人口 (人) Permanent Registered Population (person)	388767	388720	100.0	262222	260762	100.6
#非农业人口 Non-agriculture	89162	83125	107.3	75320	71755	105.0
男 Male	47005	44159	106.4	134570	133051	101.1
女 Female	42157	38966	108.2	127652	127711	100.0
出生率 (‰) Birth Rate (‰)	5.61	7.41		7.42	9.97	
死亡率 (‰) Death Rate (‰)	5.56	6.65		8.47	6.54	
自然增长率 (‰) Natural Growth Rate (‰)	0.05	0.75		-1.05	3.43	
从业人员 (人) Employment (person)	193881	202124	95.9	142329	135643	104.9
按产业分 Grouped by Industry						
第一产业 Primary Industry	71816	68568	104.7	35540	31129	114.2
第二产业 Secondary Industry	66025	70906	93.1	53804	51683	104.1
第三产业 Tertiary Industry	56040	62650	89.4	52985	52831	100.3
按职工非职工分 Grouped by Staff and Workers or Non-staff-and-worker						
职工人数 Staff and Worker	47370	50887	93.1	43113	42985	100.3
#国有单位 State-owned	38023	40384	94.2	23532	30158	78.0
集体单位 Collective-owned	2650	3944	67.2	8962	9294	96.4
城镇个体劳动者 Urban and Rural Individuals	9409	11616	81.0	14328	13197	108.6
劳动工资 Wages						
工资总额 (万元) Total Wages (10000 yuan)	39321.7	37780	104.1	43469.9	39615.7	109.7
#国有单位 State-owned	33122.2	31602	104.8	24273.6	27304.8	88.9
集体单位 Collective-owned	853.4	1967.9	43.4	6642.3	6826.5	97.3
职工平均工资 (元) Average Wage (yuan)	8134	7268	111.9	9901	9177	107.9
固定资产投资 Investment in Fixed Assets Assets						
全社会固定资产投资 (万元) Total Investment in Fixed Assets (10000 yuan)	34124	42167	80.9	100649	87020	115.7
按建设性质分 Grouped by Type of Construction						
#基本建设投资 Capital Construction	25878	35094	73.7	89623	46401	193.1
更新改造投资 Innovation and Replacement	1530	1920	79.7	5600	20260	27.6

21-8 续表1 continued

项目 Item		平谷县 Pinggu 1998	1997	1998年为1997年% 1998 as % of 1997	怀柔县 Huairou 1998	1997	1998年为1997年% 1998 as % of 1997
按经济类型分	Grouped by Ownership						
国有单位 (万元)	State-owned(10000 yuan)	11585	10939	105.9	21766	22592	96.3
集体单位 (万元)	Collective-owned (10000 yuan)	11273	5333	211.4	40876	50814	80.4
新增固定资产 (万元)	Incremental Fixed Assets (10000 yuan)	29870	86997	34.3	64799	74359	87.1
#国有单位	State-owned	15206	9700	156.8	22636	16425	137.8
集体单位	Collective-owned	10572	195	5421.5	36487	54408	67.1
房屋施工面积 (万平方米)	Floor Space of Buildings Under Construction (10000 sq.m)	43.6	47.3	92.2	64.1	62	103.4
#国有单位	State-owned	20	25	80.0	19.6	15	130.7
集体单位	Collective-owned	13	4	325.0	37	47	78.7
房屋竣工面积 (万平方米)	Floor Space of Buildings Completed (10000 sq.m)	34.6	32	108.1	32.6	48.3	67.5
#国有单位	State-owned	16	11	145.5	11.9	13.4	88.8
#住宅	Residence	13	8	162.5	8.2	5.7	143.9
#集体单位	Collective-owned	9	4	225.0	19.2	34.9	55.0
#住宅	Residence	5	3.5	142.9	9.7	15	64.7
农村经济	**Rural Economy**						
农村劳动力 (人)	Labor Force (person)	139513	139337	100.1	81135	79461	102.1
种植业	Planting	62818	59648	105.3	24636	21967	112.2
林业	Forestry	2034	1950	104.3	7215	6279	114.9
牧业	Animal Husbandry	4372	4093	106.8	2892	2021	143.1
渔业	Fishery	1963	1970	99.6	349	353	98.9
农村工业	Rural Industry	32182	33444	96.2	13121	13734	95.5
农村建筑业	Rural Construction	11987	11869	101.0	5949	4250	140.0
农村运输业	Rural Transportation	4620	5478	84.3	5310	4258	124.7
农村商、饮食业、服务业	Commerce,Catering and Services	5063	4553	111.2	5070	3829	132.4
耕地面积 (公顷)	Area under Cultivation (hectare)	19117.3	19120.4	100.0	15403.4	15418.4	99.9
农业机械总动力 (千瓦)	Total Power of Agricultural Machinery (kw)	341630	326996	104.5	210753	212722	99.1
化肥施用实物量 (吨)	Consumption of Chemical Fertilizers (ton)	60500	57228	105.7	21937.4	21119.7	103.9
化肥施用折纯量 (吨)	Consumption of Chemical Fertilizers(100%) (ton)	19108	17375	110.0	8861.2	9984.8	88.7
农村用电量 (万千瓦时)	Consumption of Electricity (10000 kwh)	17821.4	17996.2	99.0	14416.7	12414.1	116.1
农村国内生产总值 (万元)	Rural Gross Domestic Product (10000 yuan)	165541.6	157155.4	105.3	190303.7	160157.2	118.8
第一产业	Primary Industry	61365	66055.3	92.9	36680.5	35692.8	102.8
第二产业	Secondary Industry	58017.1	53356.4	108.7	92355.1	74287.3	124.3
第三产业	Tertiary Industry	46159.5	37743.7	122.3	61268.1	50177.1	122.1
农业总产值 (万元)	Gross Output Value of Agriculture (10000 yuan)	81502.7	77460.7	105.2	43602.9	43385.6	100.5
种植业	Planting	44808.8	41700.4	107.5	21355.7	17439.9	122.5
林业	Forestry	1371.8	1319.8	103.9	3885.7	3699.8	105.0
牧业	Animal Husbandry	28236.1	28031.7	100.7	17086.5	21666.3	78.9
渔业	Fishery	7086	6408.8	110.6	1275	579.6	220.0
农作物总播种面积 (万公顷)	Sown Area of Farm Crops (10000 hectare)	3.5	3.5	100.0	2.35	2.38	98.7
粮食作物	Grain	2.7	2.7	100.0	2.09	2.09	100.0
经济作物	Industrial Crops	0.1	0.1	100.0	0.07	0.08	87.5
其他作物	Other Crops	0.7	0.7	100.0	0.19	0.21	90.5

21-8 续表 2 continued

项目 Item		平谷县 Pinggu 1998	1997	1998年为1997年% 1998 as % of 1997	怀柔县 Huairou 1998	1997	1998年为1997年% 1998 as % of 1997
农副产品产量	Yield of Farm and Sideline Crops						
粮食 (万吨)	Grain (10000 tons)	15.6	15.8	98.7	13.3	12.5	106.4
蔬菜 (吨)	Vegetable (ton)	296576	268606	110.4	50341	57649	87.3
干鲜果 (吨)	Dry and Fresh Fruits(ton	146147	137294	106.4	46178.9	43674	105.7
畜产品产量	Output of Livestock Products						
生猪出栏 (头)	Slaughtered Hogs (head)	228547	201581	113.4	192098	181487	105.8
商品猪 (头)	Commodity Hogs (head)		198287		176730	176406	100.2
猪牛羊肉 (吨)	Pork,Beef and Mutton(ton)	17173	17859	96.2	15725	15330	102.6
#猪肉	Pork	14550	14428	100.8	14152	13908	101.8
禽肉	Meat of Poultry (ton)	5777	5222	110.6	4805	9016	53.3
禽蛋	Poultry Eggs (ton)	28423	33179	85.7	8625	19907	43.3
牲畜年底头数 (头)	Number of Livestock (year-end) (head)	222042	212804	104.3	176516	175675	100.5
大牲畜	Large Animals	11089	12966	85.5	15111	15338	98.5
猪	Hogs	161681	150519	107.4	123481	123172	100.3
羊	Goats and Sheep	49272	49319	99.9	37924	37165	102.0
水产品产量 (吨)	Output of Aquatic Product (ton)	15449	14417.3	107.2	1602	1451	110.4
农村集体经济收入 (万元)	Rural Collective Economic Revenue (10000 yuan)	288232.4	282625.1	102.0	538575	457155	117.8
农村集体经济利润总额 (万元)	Total Profits of Rural Collective Economy (10000 yuan)	12102.8	11798.7	102.6	30495	27142	112.4
国家税金	State Taxes	13797.3	11378.2	121.3	18820	14471	130.1
集体积累	Collective Accumulation	4470.4	5181.2	86.3	13033	11271	115.6
劳动所得	Income from Work	21309.6	23428.5	91.0	14627	14371	101.8
乡镇企业单位数 (个)	Number of Township and Village Enterprise (unit)	798	835	95.6	730	734	99.5
乡镇企业人数 (人)	Number of Persons of Township and Village Enterprises (person)	50848	54135	93.9	39553	35363	111.8
乡镇企业纯利润 (万元)	Net Profit of Township and Village Enterprises (10000 yuan)	12846	7706	166.7	27900	21381	130.5
乡镇企业固定资产原价 (万元)	Original Value of Fixed Assets of Township and Village Enterprises (10000 yuan)	163041	141230	115.4	171430	152338	112.5
乡镇企业固定资产净值 (万元)	Net Value of Fixed Assets of Township and Village Enterprises (10000 yuan)	124882	110542	113.0	139661	124603	112.1
工业	**Industry**						
全部工业企业单位数 (个)	Number of Enterprises (unit)	285	279	102.2	679	773	87.8
国有	State-owned	69	68	101.5	55	29	189.7
集体	Collective-owned	139	142	97.9	464	689	67.3
其他	Others	77	69	111.6	160	55	290.9
全部工业总产值 (现价,万元)	Gross Output Value of Industry (at current prices,10000 yuan)	320901.5	249737.5	128.5	815513.7	679452.6	120.0
国有	State-owned	52649.1	69003.9	76.3	42896.6	88942	48.2
集体	Collective-owned	94601.6	68824.7	137.5	361774.8	406753.6	88.9
其他	Others	173650.8	111908.9	155.2	410842.3	183757	223.6

21-8 续表 3 continued

项目	Item	平谷县 Pinggu 1998	平谷县 Pinggu 1997	平谷县 Pinggu 1998年为1997年% 1998 as % of 1997	怀柔县 Huairou 1998	怀柔县 Huairou 1997	怀柔县 Huairou 1998年为1997年% 1998 as % of 1997
全部工业总产值(90不变价,万元)	Gross Output Value of Industry (at constant price of 1990,10000yuan)	311185.9	230759.8	134.9	832997.7	697570	119.4
国有	State-owned	58443.1	62722.8	93.2	44642	85447.6	52.2
集体	Collective-owned	92555.4	63450.7	145.9	351073.8	376407.1	93.3
其他	Others	160187.4	104586.3	153.2	437281.9	235715.3	185.5
全部轻工业总产值(现价,万元)	Gross Output Value of Light Industry (at current prices,10000 yuan)	198317.1	169821.5	116.8	542605.2	275148.5	197.2
以农产品为原料	Using Farm Products as Raw Materials	173072.3	126264.6	137.1	366797.2	185650.1	197.6
以非农产品为原料	Using Non-farm Products as Raw Materials	25244.8	43556.9	58.0	175808	89498.4	196.4
全部重工业总产值(现价,万元)	Gross Output Value of Heavy Industry (at current prices,10000 yuan)	122584.4	79916	153.4	270885.8	159396.5	169.9
采掘工业	Mining and Quarrying	3695.4	3400.7	108.7	25167.4	3690.6	681.9
原料工业	Raw Materials Industry	12099.9	7651.5	158.1	36229	43249.9	83.8
制造工业	Manufacturing Industry	106789.1	68863.8	155.1	209912.1	112456	186.7
独立核算工业企业平均职工人数 (人)	Average Number of Staff and Workers in Enterprises with Independent Accounting System (person)	37789	37904	99.7	42738	41645	102.6
#国有	State-owned	6422	9073	70.8	4344	6374	68.2
集体	Collective-owned	13905	11892	116.9	23923	18778	127.4
独立核算工业企业总产值(现价,万元)	Gross Output Value of Enterprises with Independent Accounting System(at current prices, 10000 yuan)	315480.7	246741.7	127.9	808513.7	686008.4	117.9
#国有	State-owned	47873.5	66340.4	72.2	35896.6	88942	40.4
集体	Collective-owned	93956.4	68492.4	137.2	361774.8	409725.2	88.3
独立核算工业企业工业增加值 (万元)	Value Added of Enterprises with Independent Accounting system (10000 yuan)	94481.4	76071.8	124.2	121597.2	112011.9	108.6
独立核算工业企业财务指标	Financial Indicators for Enterprises with Independent Accounting System						
产品销售收入 (万元)	Sales Revenue (10000yuan)	266659.8	206713.9	129.0	711525.3	425256.4	167.3
#国有	State-owned	39617.9	48239.9	82.1	32484	75341.3	43.1
产品销售成本 (万元)	Cost of Sales (10000 yuan)	214629	168810.1	127.1	572783.8	343924.6	166.5
#国有	State-owned	31270.7	39824.1	78.5	29173.1	63712.7	45.8
固定资产原价 (万元)	Original Value of Fixed Assets (10000 yuan)	274315.6	238011.9	115.3	386295.8	276933.3	139.5
#国有	State-owned	35695.9	37722.4	94.6	40560.8	48503.2	83.6
固定资产净值 (万元)	Net Value of Fixed Assets (10000 yuan)	219526.4	171395.2	128.1	332268.4	243464.6	136.5
#国有	State-owned	23425.5	28300.1	82.8	35122	42102.1	83.4
全部流动资金年平均余额 (万元)	Annual Average Balance of Circulating Funds (10000 yuan)	221119.2	200661.8	110.2	383435.2	267368.4	143.4
#国有	State-owned	34377.4	37863.3	90.8	29260.5	42760.9	68.4
利润总额 (万元)	Total Profits (10000 yuan)	9779.2	-1322.5		17831.8	-3447.6	
#国有	State-owned	1792.9	-131.4		-2764.2	2303.3	

21-8 续表 4 continued

项目 Item			平谷县 Pinggu			怀柔县 Huairou		
			1998	1997	1998年为1997年% 1998 as % of 1997	1998	1997	1998年为1997年% 1998 as % of 1997
资金利税率	(%)	Ratio of Pre-tax Profits to Total of Capital (%)	5.5	2.7		7.1	5.9	
产品销售率	(%)	Ratio of Sales Value to Gross Output Value (%)	93.9	92.5		96.8	93.21	
增加值率	(%)	Ratio of Added Value to Gross Output Value (%)	28.9	23.7		15	16.3	
独立核算工业企业全员劳动生产率	(元/人)	Overall Labor Productivity of Enterprises with Independent Accounting System (yuan/person)	25002	15354	162.8	191555	109634	174.7
#国有		State-owned	28975	22411	129.3	111105.4	134056	82.9
集体		Collective-owned	16742	10767	155.5	143006	89868	159.1
商业		**Commerce**						
社会消费品零售额	(万元)	Retail Sales of Consumer Goods (10000 yuan)	121958.9	113770	107.2	128162	126635	101.2
按经济类型分		Grouped by Ownership						
国有		State-owned	35915.2	35542	101.1	32345	34601	93.5
集体		Collective-owned	16950.7	21740	78.0	39959	65010	61.5
其他		Others	69093	56488	122.3	55858	27024	206.7
按类别分		Grouped by Type of Goods						
吃的商品	(万元)	Food (10000 yuan)	39911.4	41046	97.2	35962	42116	85.4
穿的商品	(万元)	Clothing (10000 yuan)	30855.6	28685	107.6	23407	18809	124.4
用的商品	(万元)	Daily Used Articles (10000 yuan)	40288.7	43209	93.2	63162	57019	110.8
烧的商品	(万元)	Fuel (10000 yuan)	10903.2	830	1313.6	5631	2184	257.8
网点数	(个)	Number of Outlets (unit)	7286	13486	54.0	8065	7326	110.1
商业		Wholesale and Retail	3897	7785	50.1	5824	5398	107.9
饮食业		Catering	706	2935	24.1	788	691	114.0
服务业		Services	710	1571	45.2	1453	1237	117.5
#宾馆、饭店		Hotels	21	8	262.5	31	30	103.3
营业人员	(人)	Personnel (person)	14898	19681	75.7	18050	19220	93.9
商业		Wholesale and Retail	8349	12138	68.8	12659	14539	87.1
饮食业		Catering	1186	3560	33.3	2722	2425	112.2
服务业		Services	999	1998	50.0	2669	2256	118.3
#宾馆、饭店		Hotels	1340	390	343.6	801	719	111.4
外经、外贸		**Foreign Economy and Trade**						
出口商品交货额	(万元)	Delivery Value of Exports (10000 yuan)	75668.8	71143.9	106.4	32266.8	28970.5	111.4
利用外资签订协议(合同)数	(个)	Number of Signed Agreements and Contracts of Foreign Capital to be Utilized (unit)	21	17	123.5	6	26	23.1
利用外资签订协议(合同)金额	(万美元)	Amount of Foreign Capital to be Utilized through Agreements and Contracts (USD 10000)	2177.1	1020	213.4	3200	3072.5	104.1
实际利用外资	(万美元)	Amount of Foreign Capital Actually Used(USD 10000)	2725	2080	131.0	1486.5	3715.5	40.0
旅游人数	(人)	Number of Tourists (person)	2615627	2201931	118.8	5000000	4670000	107.1
教育		**Education**						
学校数	(个)	Number of Schools (unit)	221	231	95.7	145	166	87.3
小学		Primary Schools	186	198	93.9	109	130	83.8

21-8 续表 5 continued

项目		Item	平谷县 Pinggu 1998	平谷县 Pinggu 1997	平谷县 Pinggu 1998年为1997年% 1998 as % of 1997	怀柔县 Huairou 1998	怀柔县 Huairou 1997	怀柔县 Huairou 1998年为1997年% 1998 as % of 1997
普通中学		Regular Secondary School	31	30	103.3	30	28	107.1
中等专业教育		Specialized Secondary Schools	4	3	133.3	1	3	33.3
招生数	(人)	New Student Enrollment (person)	16107	17443	92.3	10798	10585	102.0
小学		Primary Schools	5043	8187	61.6	3304	3616	91.4
初级中等学校		Junior Secondary Schools	8443	6754	125.0	4749	4069	116.7
高级中等学校		Senior Secondary Schools	1856	1714	108.3	1174	2203	53.3
中等专业教育		Specialized Secondary Schools	765	788	97.1	30	227	13.2
在校学生	(人)	Student Enrollment (person)	83449	86248	96.8	45792	48250	94.9
小学		Primary Schools	53924	57660	93.5	25191	27244	92.5
初级中等学校		Junior Secondary Schools	22487	21789	103.2	13280	13392	99.2
高级中等学校		Senior Secondary Schools	5114	5170	98.9	3226	5946	54.3
中等专业教育		Specialized Secondary Schools	1924	1629	118.1	158	718	22.0
毕业生	(人)	Graduates (person)	18387	15841	116.1	11823	10368	114.0
小学		Primary Schools	8575	6925	123.8	4827	4237	113.9
初级中等学校		Junior Secondary Schools	7473	7379	101.3	4857	4641	104.7
高级中等学校		Senior Secondary Schools	1857	1146	162.0	874	540	161.9
中等专业教育		Specialized Secondary Schools	482	391	123.3	175	52	336.5
达到"国家体育标准"学生数	(人)	Number of Students Come to the Standard for State Physical Training (person)	61442	68572	89.6	33476	41325	81.0
幼儿园、托儿所个数	(个)	Number of Kindergardens (unit)	320	320	100.0	138	132	104.5
幼儿入托数	(人)	New Enrollment (person)	12019	11870	101.3	5791	5513	105.0
文化		**Culture**						
文化馆、站	(个)	Cultural Centers (unit)	22	22	100.0	15	21	71.4
公共图书馆	(个)	Public Libraries (unit)	1	1	100.0	1	1	100.0
公共图书馆藏书	(万册)	Collection (10000 volume)	13.4	13.5	99.3	11	11	100.0
电影放映单位	(个)	Film Projection Units (unit)	11	12	91.7	51	55	92.7
区级以上重点文物保护单位	(个)	Cultural Relics Preserved at District Level and above (unit)	20	18	111.1	14	16	87.5
卫生		**Health**						
卫生机构数	(个)	Number of Health Institutions (unit)	75	100	75.0	429	417	102.9
#医院		Hospitals	5	6	83.3	9	8	112.5
卫生院		Clinics	20	20	100.0	11	17	64.7
床位数		Number of Beds (unit)	1029	999	103.0	893	884	101.0
#医院		Hospitals	670	660	101.5	844	824	102.4
卫生院		Clinics	279	294	94.9	49	58	84.5
平均每千人拥有床位数	(张)	Average Number of Beds Per 1000 Persons (unit)	2.6	2.6	100.0	3.4	3.4	100.0
卫生技术人员	(人)	Medical Technical Personnel (person)	1801	1862	96.7	1671	1323	126.3
#医生		Doctors (person)	865	925	93.5	753	718	104.9
城市公用		**Urban Public Utilities**						
区级以上公园	(个)	Parks at District Level and Above (unit)	1	1	100.0	8	7	114.3
体育场馆	(个)	Stadiums and Gymnasiums (unit)	1	1	100.0	4	4	100.0
道路长度	(公里)	Length of Roads (km)		824		79.38	79.38	100.0

21-9 密云县、延庆县国民经济主要指标

MAIN NATIONAL ECONOMIC INDICATORS FOR MIYUN AND YANQING COUNTIES

项目		Item	密云县 Miyun			延庆县 Yanqing		
			1998	1997	1998年为1997年% 1998 as % of 1997	1998	1997	1998年为1997年% 1998 as % of 1997
综合		**General Survey**						
国内生产总值	(万元)	Gross Domestic Product (10000 yuan)	259975.9	253656.5	102.5	166680.8	154964.9	107.6
第一产业		Primary Industry	60308.2	57136.3	105.6	69688.7	57578.3	121.0
第二产业		Secondary Industry	90581.4	104471.9	86.7	43029.9	42723.3	100.7
第三产业		Tertiary Industry	109086.3	92048.3	118.5	53962.2	54393.3	99.2
财政收入	(万元)	Fiscal Revenue (10000 yuan)	10480	8099	129.4	14990	10947	136.9
#各项税收		Taxes	11537	8139	141.7	9119	6172	147.7
财政支出	(万元)	Fiscal Expenditure (10000 yuan)	48768	45498	107.2	41678	35371	117.8
#基本建设支出		Capital Construction	1449	1195	121.3	1231	698	176.4
支援农业生产支出		Supporting Agriculture	5993	5747	104.3	3074	3245	94.7
文教卫生事业费		Culture,Education and Health	14145	14196	99.6	12410	10763	115.5
人口和劳动力		**Population and Labor Force**						
总人口	(人)	Total Population (person)	431654	429676	100.5	272017	271487	100.2
常住户籍人口	(人)	Permanent Registered Population (person)	425476	424263	100.3	269327	268957	100.1
#非农业人口		Non-agriculture	89216	85924	103.8	56143	54256	103.5
男		Male	214351	214288	100.0	138435	137260	100.9
女		Female	211125	209975	100.5	133582	131697	101.4
出生率	(‰)	Birth Rate (‰)	8.39	10.5		13.4	8.55	
死亡率	(‰)	Death Rate (‰)	3.93	6.9		7.03	6.74	
自然增长率	(‰)	Natural Growth Rate (‰)	4.46	3.61		6.34	1.81	
从业人员	(人)	Employment (person)	210987	213071	99.0	121446	122861	98.8
按产业分		Grouped by Industry						
第一产业		Primary Industry	72087	68775	104.8	47689	47094	101.3
第二产业		Secondary Industry	59200	62730	94.4	24739	27118	91.2
第三产业		Tertiary Industry	79700	81566	97.7	73757	48649	151.6
按职工非职工分		Grouped by Staff and Workers or Non-staff-and-worker						
职工人数		Staff and Worker	43572	41633	104.7	32217	33004	97.6
#国有单位		State-owned	31862	30594	104.1	24137	24633	98.0
集体单位		Collective-owned	3379	4151	81.4	6069	6593	92.0
城镇个体劳动者		Urban and Rural Individuals	12468	12842	97.1	10168	8740	116.3
劳动工资		Wages						
工资总额	(万元)	Total Wages (10000 yuan)	38218	33061	115.6	30151.9	25048.4	120.4
#国有单位		State-owned	30050	25285	118.8	23918.5	19897.8	120.2
集体单位		Collective-owned	1947	2527	77.0	4448.6	4351.4	102.2
职工平均工资	(元)	Average Wage (yuan)	8765	7807	112.3	8980	7696.9	116.6
固定资产投资		**Investment in Fixed Assets Assets**						
全社会固定资产投资	(万元)	Total Investment in Fixed Assets (10000 yuan)	60345	42997	140.3	19746	11986	165.1
按建设性质分		Grouped by Type of Construction						
#基本建设投资		Capital Construction	11556	41348	27.9	19471	11471	169.7
更新改造投资		Innovation and Replacement	1000	1649	60.6	275	515	53.3

21-9 续表 1 continued

项目 Item		密云县 Miyun 1998	1997	1998年为1997年% 1998 as % of 1997	延庆县 Yanqing 1998	1997	1998年为1997年% 1998 as % of 1997
按经济类型分	Grouped by Ownership						
国有单位 (万元)	State-owned(10000 yuan)	40683	36315	112.0	15291	8546	178.9
集体单位 (万元)	Collective-owned (10000 yuan)	6386	6682	95.6	4180	2410	173.4
新增固定资产 (万元)	Incremental Fixed Assets (10000 yuan)	53390	42928	124.4	12236	12786	95.7
#国有单位	State-owned	36688	36813	99.7	8643	9886	88.0
集体单位	Collective-owned	6256	6115	102.3	3593	2900	123.9
房屋施工面积 (万平方米)	Floor Space of Buildings Under Construction (10000 sq.m)	73	61.4	118.9	21.7	18.8	115.4
#国有单位	State-owned	47.7	50.2	95.0	15.8	11.9	132.8
集体单位	Collective-owned	10	11.2	89.3	5.9	5.7	101.7
房屋竣工面积 (万平方米)	Floor Space of Buildings Completed (10000 sq.m)	50.8	40.5	125.4	13.2	13.6	97.0
#国有单位	State-owned	27.5	30.7	89.6	8.3	7.4	112.2
#住宅	Residence	22.2	24.3	91.4	3.1	2.9	107.0
#集体单位	Collective-owned	8.4	9.8	85.7	4.9	5.7	86.0
#住宅	Residence	8.3	9.4	88.3	4.4	5.3	83.0
农村经济	**Rural Economy**						
农村劳动力 (人)	Labor Force (person)	156927	155867	100.7	88671	89857	98.7
种植业	Planting	54679	55955	97.7	40176	41696	96.4
林业	Forestry	7618	7169	106.3	2721	2780	97.9
牧业	Animal Husbandry	8277	4589	180.4	4036	2251	179.3
渔业	Fishery	991	1062	93.3	216	367	58.9
农村工业	Rural Industry	20432	21712	94.1	7946	10022	79.3
农村建筑业	Rural Construction	10912	9164	119.1	10038	7390	135.8
农村运输业	Rural Transportation	8188	7084	115.5	4685	4190	111.8
农村商、饮食业、服务业	Commerce,Catering and Services	6045	5929	102.0	18853	21161	89.0
耕地面积 (公顷)	Area under Cultivation (hectare)	23532.3	23489.6	100.2	32649.3	32591.3	100.2
农业机械总动力 (千瓦)	Total Power of Agricultural Machinery (kw)	292641	314834	93.0	191410	187311	102.2
化肥施用实物量 (吨)	Consumption of Chemical Fertilizers (ton)	45177	45247	99.8	39329	35976	109.3
化肥施用折纯量 (吨)	Consumption of Chemical Fertilizers(100%) (ton)	11400	11344	100.5	12042.1	10954.6	109.9
农村用电量 (万千瓦时)	Consumption of Electricity (10000 kwh)	9062.5	8765.8	103.4	5157.5	7706.4	66.9
农村国内生产总值 (万元)	Rural Gross Domestic Product (10000 yuan)	158072.2	147302.6	107.3	123894.9	109582.4	113.1
第一产业	Primary Industry	54016.5	50251.6	107.5	69688.7	61771.1	112.8
第二产业	Secondary Industry	50833.8	51698.5	98.3	27544.7	23560	116.9
第三产业	Tertiary Industry	53221.9	45352.5	117.4	26661.9	24251.3	109.9
农业总产值 (万元)	Gross Output Value of Agriculture (10000 yuan)	59650.9	53603.4	112.3	54712.24	52215.4	104.8
种植业	Planting	21982.2	23169.9	94.9	33620.28	27452.9	122.5
林业	Forestry	2128.2	1785	119.2	1388.19	2180.9	63.7
牧业	Animal Husbandry	29776.9	27306.3	109.0	18340.24	15458.4	118.6
渔业	Fishery	1529.8	1342.2	114.0	1363.53	1304.7	104.5
农作物总播种面积 (万公顷)	Sown Area of Farm Crops (10000 hectare)	3.2	3.3	97.0	3.1	2.5	124.0
粮食作物	Grain	2.5	2.5	100.0	2.5	2.5	100.0
经济作物	Industrial Crops	0.4	0.4	100.0	0.6	0.6	100.0
其他作物	Other Crops	0.3	0.4	75.0			

21-9 续表 2 continued

项目	Item	密云县 Miyun 1998	1997	1998年为1997年% 1998 as % of 1997	延庆县 Yanqing 1998	1997	1998年为1997年% 1998 as % of 1997
农副产品产量	Yield of Farm and Side-line Crops						
粮食 (万吨)	Grain (10000 tons)	13	11.1	117.1	17.7	13.7	129.2
蔬菜 (吨)	Vegetable (ton)	161349	166298	97.0	360962	355579	101.5
干鲜果 (吨)	Dry and Fresh Fruits(ton	55000	43100	127.6	32712	33455	97.8
畜产品产量	Output of Livestock Products						
生猪出栏 (头)	Slaughtered Hogs (head)	304893	282477	107.9	132106	122552	107.8
商品猪 (头)	Commodity Hogs (head)		275355		132106	119340	110.7
猪牛羊肉 (吨)	Pork,Beef and Mutton (ton)	24021	21817	110.1	11661	11526	101.1
#猪肉	Pork	21197	19291	109.9	9925	9123	108.8
禽肉	Meat of Poultry (ton)	11643	12248	95.1	5031	4503	111.7
禽蛋	Poultry Eggs (ton)	16267	17363	93.7	11179	11845	94.4
牲畜年底头数 (头)	Number of Livestock (year-end) (head)				152961	127043	120.4
大牲畜	Large Animals	23354	25840	90.4	22012	20992	104.9
猪	Hogs	212425	185157	114.7	82366	78167	105.8
羊	Goats and Sheep	108919	94950	114.7	48583	27884	174.2
水产品产量 (吨)	Output of Aquatic Product (ton)	3550	3203	110.8	2609	2513	103.8
农村集体经济收入 (万元)	Rural Collective Economic Revenue (10000 yuan)	428017	400065	107.0	136292	120183	113.4
农村集体经济利润总额 (万元)	Total Profits of Rural Collective Economy (10000 yuan)	1694.5	49721	3.4	7430.8	6314	117.7
国家税金	State Taxes	11160.7	10454.1	106.8	7701	7595	101.4
集体积累	Collective Accumulation		-661.6		2954	2461	120.0
劳动所得	Income from Work	98059.9	87254.1	112.4	70747	60495	116.9
乡镇企业单位数 (个)	Number of Township and Village Enterprise (unit)	8187	7841	104.4	2293	1015	225.9
乡镇企业人数 (人)	Number of Persons of Township and Village Enterprises (person)	52191	54776	95.3	30244	30229	100.1
乡镇企业纯利润 (万元)	Net Profit of Township and Village Enterprises (10000 yuan)	11995	11042.3	108.6	4438	3373	131.6
乡镇企业固定资产原价 (万元)	Original Value of Fixed Assets of Township and Village Enterprises (10000 yuan)	113347	115912.4	97.8	54687	48619	112.5
乡镇企业固定资产净值 (万元)	Net Value of Fixed Assets of Township and Village Enterprises (10000 yuan)	83259	86111.8	96.7	41575	36863	112.8
工业	**Industry**						
全部工业企业单位数 (个)	Number of Enterprises (unit)	1356	1418	95.6	214	190	112.6
国有	State-owned	22	24	91.7	24	27	88.9
集体	Collective-owned	312	378	82.5	145	124	116.9
其他	Others	1022	1016	100.6	47	39	120.5
全部工业总产值 (现价,万元)	Gross Output Value of Industry (at current prices,10000 yuan)	302851.3	322024	94.0	121374.6	118575.9	102.4
国有	State-owned	41375.4	44738.8	92.5	11628	20386.8	57.0
集体	Collective-owned	100565.2	115105.9	87.4	29953.8	32750.2	91.4
其他	Others	160910.7	162179.3	99.2	79792.8	65438.9	121.9

21-9 续表 3 continued

项目	Item	密云县 Miyun 1998	1997	1998年为1997年% 1998 as % of 1997	延庆县 Yanqing 1998	1997	1998年为1997年% 1998 as % of 1997
全部工业总产值(90不变价,万元)	Gross Output Value of Industry (at constant price of 1990,10000yuan)	269491.7	274213.7	98.3	115522.1	109541	105.5
国有	State-owned	27319.6	28716.8	95.1	7892.9	14526.2	45.7
集体	Collective-owned	90421.8	115105.9	78.6	28676.7	30695.4	93.4
其他	Others	151750.3	130391.8	116.4	78952.5	64319.4	122.8
全部轻工业总产值(现价,万元)	Gross Output Value of Light Industry (at current prices,10000 yuan)	148110.2	133811.7	110.7	74301.7	69859.9	106.4
以农产品为原料	Using Farm Products as Raw Materials	133035	122026.5	109.0	61667.2	55144.9	111.8
以非农产品为原料	Using Non-farm Products as Raw Materials	15075.2	11785.2	127.9	12634.5	14715	85.9
全部重工业总产值(现价,万元)	Gross Output Value of Heavy Industry (at current prices,10000 yuan)	69275.4	54039.3	128.2	41220.4	39681.1	103.8
采掘工业	Mining and Quarrying	21404.7	18891.2	113.3	408	1472.1	27.7
原料工业	Raw Materials Industry	9065.5	7984.1	113.5	5932	7622.5	77.8
制造工业	Manufacturing Industry	38805.2	27164	142.9	34880.4	30586.5	114.0
独立核算工业企业平均职工人数 (人)	Average Number of Staff and Workers in Enterprises with Independent Accounting System (person)	42293	40908	103.4	14221	14377	98.9
#国有	State-owned	7048	8237	85.6	2538	4429	57.3
集体	Collective-owned	23043	17155	134.3	6945	6478	107.2
独立核算工业企业总产值(现价,万元)	Gross Output Value of Enterprises with Independent Accounting System(at current prices, 10000 yuan)	217385.6	185405.6	117.2	58701	53773.3	109.2
#国有	State-owned	42022.9	44738.8	93.9	11628	17639.2	65.9
集体	Collective-owned	94936.5	51109.2	185.7	29953.8	21557.2	138.9
独立核算工业企业工业增加值 (万元)	Value Added of Enterprises with Independent Accounting system (10000 yuan)	66208.4	57482.3	115.2	22206.5	21307.2	104.2
独立核算工业企业财务指标	Financial Indicators for Enterprises with Independent Accounting System						
产品销售收入 (万元)	Sales Revenue(10000yuan)	189093.5	162565.7	116.3	52007.7	49481.8	105.1
#国有	State-owned	38931.1	42483.7	91.6	9693.3	16070.1	60.3
产品销售成本 (万元)	Cost of Sales (10000 yuan)	153290.1	135107.2	113.5	43256.5	43008	100.6
#国有	State-owned	31524.8	35495.4	88.8	7762.1	13943.4	55.7
固定资产原价 (万元)	Original Value of Fixed Assets (10000 yuan)	198019.9	168622.4	117.4	54519.6	53283.4	102.3
#国有	State-owned	50238.1	42856.7	117.2	14529.1	18253.5	79.6
固定资产净值 (万元)	Net Value of Fixed Assets (10000 yuan)	138090.8	123325	112.0	38467.4	36644.1	104.9
#国有	State-owned	31292.7	29162.2	107.3	9825.3	11602.3	84.7
全部流动资金年平均余额 (万元)	Annual Average Balance of Circulating Funds (10000 yuan)	184941.9	173979.4	106.3	54236.7	53874.8	100.7
#国有	State-owned	45051.7	45865.4	98.2	11383.7	16163.1	70.4
利润总额 (万元)	Total Profits (10000 yuan)	-10923.5	-8403.5		-1820	-4489.7	
#国有	State-owned	-2145.3	-1451.7		-1107.8	-2237.5	

21-9 续表 4 continued

项目 Item			密云县 Miyun			延庆县 Yanqing		
			1998	1997	1998年为1997年% 1998 as % of 1997	1998	1997	1998年为1997年% 1998 as % of 1997
资金利税率	(%)	Ratio of Pre-tax Profits to Total of Capital (%)	0.5	4.3		2.96		
产品销售率	(%)	Ratio of Sales Value to Gross Output Value (%)	94.1	96.9		83.2	91.4	
增加值率	(%)	Ratio of Added Value to Gross Output Value (%)	30	31		34.2	33.9	
独立核算工业企业全员劳动生产率	(元/人)	Overall Labor Productivity of Enterprises with Independent Accounting System (yuan/person)	51400	45323	113.4	41426	37402	110.8
#国有		State-owned	59624	54314	109.8	31098	39826	78.1
集体		Collective-owned	41200	29793	138.3	41291	33277	124.1
商业		**Commerce**						
社会消费品零售额	(万元)	Retail Sales of Consumer Goods (10000 yuan)	135258	122703	110.2	155695	147143	105.8
按经济类型分		Grouped by Ownership						
国有		State-owned	19590	26069	75.1	41569	47416	87.6
集体		Collective-owned	13437	10930	122.9	30429	41287	73.7
其他		Others	102231	85704	119.3	83697	58440	143.2
按类别分		Grouped by Type of Goods						
吃的商品	(万元)	Food (10000 yuan)	74889	75311	99.4	61698	55576	111.0
穿的商品	(万元)	Clothing (10000 yuan)	16082	14995	107.2	32840	33755	97.3
用的商品	(万元)	Daily Used Articles (10000 yuan)	38226	27558	138.7	55041	52149	105.5
烧的商品	(万元)	Fuel (10000 yuan)	6061	4839	125.3	6116	5663	108.0
网点数	(个)	Number of Outlets (unit)	8658	8779	96.6			
商业		Wholesale and Retail	6079	6441	94.4			
饮食业		Catering	872	793	110.0			
服务业		Services	1707	1545	110.5			
#宾馆、饭店		Hotels	115					
营业人员	(人)	Personnel (person)	18801	19081	95.5			
商业		Wholesale and Retail	13617	13874	98.1			
饮食业		Catering	1686	1602	105.2			
服务业		Services	3498	3605	97.0			
#宾馆、饭店		Hotels	1695					
外经、外贸		**Foreign Economy and Trade**						
出口商品交货额	(万元)	Delivery Value of Exports (10000 yuan)	41048.9	57170	71.8	13524.8	11069.5	122.2
利用外资签订协议(合同)数	(个)	Number of Signed Agreements and Contracts of Foreign Capital to be Utilized (unit)	16	12	133.3	6	11	54.5
利用外资签订协议(合同)金额	(万美元)	Amount of Foreign Capital to be Utilized through Agreements and Contracts (USD 10000)	2665.9	864.5	308.4	1301.3	1497.83	86.9
实际利用外资	(万美元)	Amount of Foreign Capital Actually Used (USD 10000)	1260.3	2025	62.2	92	113	81.4
旅游人数	(人)	Number of Tourists (person)	3600000	3120000	115.4	6246000	5764308	108.4
教育		**Education**						
学校数	(个)	Number of Schools (unit)	227	237	96.6	229	235	97.4
小学		Primary Schools	178	185	96.2	176	192	91.7

21-9 续表 5 continued

项目		Item	密云县 Miyun 1998	1997	1998年为1997年% 1998 as % of 1997	延庆县 Yanqing 1998	1997	1998年为1997年% 1998 as % of 1997
普通中学		Regular Secondary School	39	40	97.5	33	34	97.1
中等专业教育		Specialized Secondary Schools	2	2	100.0	20	9	222.2
招生数	(人)	New Student Enrollment (person)	13628	14873	91.6	11021	11146	98.9
小学		Primary Schools	4545	6530	69.6	3041	3811	79.8
初级中等学校		Junior Secondary Schools	6852	5932	115.5	5860	4487	130.6
高级中等学校		Senior Secondary Schools	1099	1069	102.8	1019	1820	56.0
中等专业教育		Specialized Secondary Schools	431	494	87.2	1101	1028	107.1
在校学生	(人)	Student Enrollment (person)	70132	71507	98.1	50726	52322	96.9
小学		Primary Schools	43465	45741	95.0	31366	34314	91.4
初级中等学校		Junior Secondary Schools	19688	21001	93.7	14096	12713	110.9
高级中等学校		Senior Secondary Schools	3261	3091	105.5	2767	2633	105.1
中等专业教育		Specialized Secondary Schools	1557	1674	93.0	2497	2662	93.8
毕业生	(人)	Graduates (person)	17130	16003	107.0	11089	10055	110.3
小学		Primary Schools	6986	6017	116.1	5879	4496	130.8
初级中等学校		Junior Secondary Schools	7583	7767	97.6	3736	3880	96.3
高级中等学校		Senior Secondary Schools	892	916	97.4	868	974	89.1
中等专业教育		Specialized Secondary Schools	818	549	149.0	606	705	86.0
达到"国家体育标准"学生数	(人)	Number of Students Come to the Standard for State Physical Training (person)	69474	70820	98.1	48403	35979	134.5
幼儿园、托儿所个数	(个)	Number of Kindergardens (unit)	245	235	104.3	61	61	100.0
幼儿入托数	(人)	New Enrollment (person)	10018	9642	103.9	5354	5188	103.0
文化		**Culture**						
文化馆、站	(个)	Cultural Centers (unit)	20	20	100.0	19	19	100.0
公共图书馆	(个)	Public Libraries (unit)	1	1	100.0	1	1	100.0
公共图书馆藏书	(万册)	Collection (10000 volume)	16	13	123.1	12.6	12.8	98.4
电影放映单位	(个)	Film Projection Units (unit)	22	22	100.0	15	15	100.0
区级以上重点文物保护单位	(个)	Cultural Relics Preserved at District Level and above (unit)	30	30	100.0	92	92	100.0
卫生		**Health**						
卫生机构数	(个)	Number of Health Institutions (unit)	32	33	97.0	32	54	59.3
#医院		Hospitals	8	7	114.0	6	4	150.0
卫生院		Clinics	17	17	100.0	17	24	70.8
床位数		Number of Beds (unit)	974	963	101.1	765	765	100.0
#医院		Hospitals	705	775	91.0	665	675	98.5
卫生院		Clinics	269	188	143.1	100	90	111.1
平均每千人拥有床位数	(张)	Average Number of Beds Per 1000 Persons (unit)	2.3	2.3	100.0	2.8	2.8	100.0
卫生技术人员	(人)	Medical Technical Personnel (person)	1773	1772	100.1	1220	1281	95.2
#医生		Doctors (person)	872	851	102.5	586	625	93.8
城市公用		**Urban Public Utilities**						
区级以上公园	(个)	Parks at District Level and Above (unit)	1	1	100.0	1	1	100.0
体育场馆	(个)	Stadiums and Gymnasiums (unit)	1	1	100.0	1	1	100.0
道路长度	(公里)	Length of Roads (km)	1173	1173	100.0	914	986	92.7

主要统计指标解释

国内生产总值 填报区县及以下单位创造的国内生产总值。不包括民航、铁路、及中央属、市属单位。

财政收入、财政支出 填报区县财政局提供的地方财政收支数字。

人口：填报公安局户籍人口按地域范围统计的数据。

从业人员：填报在区县及以下各单位中工作人员，包括在岗职工、聘用留用的离退休人员、外方和港澳台方人员以及人事档案关系保留在原单位的人员。

职工人数 填报区县及以下各单位职工人数，即在岗职工和不在岗职工。

工资总额 与“职工人数”同口径。

全社会固定资产投资 填报区县及以下各单位基本建设、更新改造、城镇集体单位投资及商品房投资。

工业增加值 填报区县及以下各独立核算工业企业进行的工业经济活动，不包括中央和市属各工业企业的经济活动。

轻、重工业总产值 为全部工业企业数据。

商业 填报区县及以下各商业活动单位数据。

外经、外贸 填报各区县外经委数据。

教育 用区县教育局数据，不包括成人教育。

文化 按地域统计。海淀区图书馆数和藏书应包括北京图书馆、东城区应包括首都图书馆。

卫生 填报各区县卫生局地域统计数据。

公园 按地域统计。

体育场馆 指专门用于体育训练、比赛和健身活动，有专人管理和一定投资的体育建筑设施。用于经营性和非经营性比赛训练和健身锻炼、长期闲置和临时被占用的体育场地均予统计，按地域统计。

道路长度 填报市政管理系统道路长度和公路局系统公路长度之和。

旅游人数 按地域统计（包括海外旅游者及国内旅游者）。

Explanatory Notes On Main Statistical Indicators

Gross Domestic Product refers to that created by units at district and county level and below, exclude units of civil aviation, railway and central , municipal units.

Fiscal Revenue or Expenditure refers to local fiscal revenue or expenditure provided by Bureau of Finance of district and county.

Population refers to registered statistics counted according to scope of region by Public Security Bureau.

Employment refers to those worked in units at district and county level and below, include staff and workers at their posts, retired and VCSR engaged and kept on, foreign, Hongkong, Macao and Taiwan employee and personnel who organizational afflication reserved in reformer units.

Staff and Workers refers to those at and off their posts in units at district and county level and below.

Total Wages the same account as “staff and workers”.

Total Investment in Fixed Assets include investment in capital construction, innovation, real estate and urban collective-owned investment of units at district and county level and below.

Value Added of Industry refers to that created by enterprises with independent accounting system at district and county level, exclude central and municipal industrial enterprises.

Gross Output Value of Light or Heavy Industry: refers to that created by all industrial enterprises .

Commerce refers to data of commercial units at district and county level and below.

Foreign Economy and Trade refers to data provide by Committee of Foreign Economics and Trade.

Education refers to data provided by Bureau of Education of district and county, exclude adult education.

Culture refers to data counted according to scope of region. Libraries and collections of Haidian District include Beijing Library, and those of Dongcheng District include Capital Library.

Health　refers to data counted according to scope of region by Health Bureau of district and county.

Parks　refers to data counted according to scope of region.

Stadiums and Gymnasiums　refers to data counted according to scope of region，　inculde physical construction with special managment and some investment specially used in training，match and body-building，also include long-time idle and temporarily occupied places used in managing or non-managing training，match and body-building.

Length of Roads　refers to the sum of length of roads of Municipal Managment System and Highway Bureau System.

Tourists　refers to data counted according to scope of region，　inculde foreign and domestic tourists.

1999

附 录

APPENDIX

附录1：历史资料

APPENDIX 1：HISTORICAL STATISTICS

附1-1 人 口 状 况

POPULATION

年 份 Year	年 底 总人口 (万人) Total Population (10000 persons)	按性别分 By Sex		按农业、非农业分 By Agriculture and Non-agriculture		人口 出生率 (‰) Birth Rate (‰)	人口 死亡率 (‰) Death Rate (‰)	人口自然 增长率 (‰) Natural Growth Rate (‰)
		男 Male	女 Female	农业人口 Agriculture	非农业人口 Non-agriculture			
1978	872	443	429	393	479	12.93	6.12	6.81
1979	897	455	442	387	510	13.67	5.92	7.75
1980	904	458	446	383	521	15.56	6.3	9.26
1981	919	466	453	386	533	16.93	6.02	10.91
1982	935	474	461	391	544	20.04	5.68	14.36
1983	950	483	467	393	557	15.63	5.49	10.14
1984	965	491	474	395	570	16.74	5.53	11.21
1985	981	500	481	395	586	15.45	5.75	9.7
1986	1028	524	504	407	621	15.82	4.47	11.35
1987	1047	525	522	410	637	17.29	5.4	11.89
1988	1061	534	527	411	650	14.43	5.08	9.35
1989	1075	538	537	431	664	12.84	5.53	7.49
1990	1086	545	541	413	673	13.04	5.75	7.23
1991	1094	547	547	411	683	8.03	5.82	2.21
1992	1102	554	548	410	692	9.22	6.11	3.11
1993	1112	559	553	405	707	9.35	6.16	3.19
1994	1125	564	561	400	725	8.96	5.76	3.2
1995	1251	627	624	436	815	7.92	5.12	2.8
1996	1259	639	620	430	829	8.02	5.34	2.68
1997	1240	629	611	414	826	7.91	6.02	1.89
1998	1246	631	615	408	838	6.0	5.3	0.7

注：1982-1989年数据是根据1982、1990年两年人口普查数据调整的，1990年以后数据是人口变动抽样调查数,其余年份数据为户籍统计数。

Note：Data from 1982 to 1989 were obtained from adjustment of cencus of 1982 and 1990,data after 1990 were those from sample survey of population changes,and data of other years were those of registered permanent population.

附1-2 按城乡分从业人员(年底数)

EMPLOYEE BY URBAN AND RURAL AREA(YEAR-END)

单位：万人 (10000 persons)

年份 Year	合 计 Total	城 镇 Urban	#国有经济单位 State-Owned	# 集体经济单位 Collective-Owned	#联营经济单位 Joint Owned	#股份制经济单位 Share Holding	#外商投资经济单位 Foreign Funded	# 港澳台投资经济单位 Hongkong, Macao and Taiwan Funded	# 个 体 Individuals	乡 村 Rural
1978	291.6	291.6	240.9	50.7						
1979	312.0	312.0	254.2	57.8						
1980	484.2	326.8	269.4	57.1					0.3	157.4
1981	511.7	345.2	283.1	61.3					0.8	166.5
1982	535.2	361.1	293.0	67.1					1.0	174.1
1983	552.0	373.8	303.4	68.5					1.9	178.2
1984	556.2	377.6	302.5	71.6			1.3		2.2	178.6
1985	558.7	384.8	308.1	72.6			1.6		2.5	173.9
1986	572.7	400.5	324.4	71.1			2.4		2.6	172.2
1987	580.3	408.4	331.8	70.7			2.8		3.1	171.9
1988	603.1	413.9	336.4	69.9	0.2		3.4		3.5	189.2
1989	593.9	424.0	343.8	67.4	3.4		3.7		5.6	169.9
1990	627.1	461.2	357.9	86.8	5.1		4.6		6.3	165.9
1991	634.0	477.2	367.8	89.0	0.5		7.7	0.2	7.2	156.8
1992	649.3	490.6	371.5	90.5	0.4		11.4	0.2	14.0	158.7
1993	627.8	481.4	362.3	79.7	2.8		11.0	6.4	14.0	146.4
1994	664.3	492.7	363.5	73.3	3.5	6.3	15.0	9.4	20.9	171.6
1995	665.3	492.7	358.1	72.1	3.7	8.0	17.4	10.4	21.9	172.6
1996	660.2	495.7	355.1	68.6	3.4	14.8	20.7	10.1	22.9	164.5
1997	655.8	498.8	354.7	68.5	3.2	19.3	21.2	10.2	21.2	157.1
1998	622.2	463.2	308.1	51.0	5.2	44.5	21.2	13.1		158.9

附1-3 从业人员和职工人数(年底数)

NUMBER OF EMPLOYEE,STAFF AND WORKERS(YEAR-END)

单位：万人 (10000 persons)

年 份 Year	从业人员 Employee	第一产业 Primary Industry	第二产业 Secondary Industry	第三产业 Tertiary Industry	职工人数 Staff and Workers	国有经济单 位 State-Owned	城镇集体经济单位 Urban Collective Owned	其 他 经济单位 Others
1978	444.1	125.9	177.9	140.3	291.6	240.9	50.7	
1979	470.5	121.4	195.2	153.9	311.9	254.2	57.7	
1980	484.2	118.0	207.3	158.9	326.5	269.4	57.1	
1981	511.7	117.2	220.4	174.1	344.4	283.1	61.3	
1982	535.2	115.1	228.6	191.5	360.1	293.0	67.1	
1983	552.0	117.1	240.2	194.7	371.9	303.4	68.5	
1984	566.5	106.7	246.5	213.3	375.4	302.5	71.6	1.3
1985	574.8	97.1	254.3	223.4	382.3	308.1	72.6	1.6
1986	590.0	93.3	260.8	235.9	397.9	324.4	71.1	2.4
1987	598.2	91.8	264.1	242.3	405.2	331.8	70.7	2.7
1988	584.1	88.4	267.6	228.1	410.4	336.4	69.9	4.1
1989	593.9	91.0	266.3	236.6	418.4	343.8	67.4	7.2
1990	627.1	90.7	281.6	254.8	454.9	357.9	86.8	10.2
1991	634.0	90.8	279.7	263.5	470.0	367.8	89.0	13.2
1992	649.3	84.5	281.6	283.2	476.6	371.5	90.5	14.6
1993	627.8	65.1	279.4	283.3	467.3	362.3	79.6	25.4
1994	664.3	73.2	272.2	318.9	471.8	363.5	73.4	34.9
1995	665.3	70.6	271.0	323.7	470.9	358.2	72.1	40.6
1996	660.2	72.5	260.1	327.6	460.6	349.0	64.8	46.8
1997	655.8	71.0	257.6	328.1	465.3	348.7	65.0	51.6
1998	622.2	71.5	226.0	324.7	450.1	321.7	50.8	77.6

附1-4 国民生产总值

GROSS NATIONAL PRODUCT

单位：亿元 (100 million yuan)

年份 Year	国民生产总值 Gross National Product	国内生产总值 Gross Domestic Product	第一产业 Primary Industry	第二产业 Secondary Industry	# 工业 Industry	# 建筑业 Construction	第三产业 Tertiary Industry	#运输邮电业 Transportation,Post and Telecommunication	# 商业 Commerce	人均国内生产总值(元) Per Capita Gross Domestic Product (yuan)
1978	108.84	108.84	5.63	77.43	70.22	7.21	25.78	7.00	8.28	1290
1979	120.11	120.11	5.17	85.18	77.37	7.81	29.76	6.55	8.79	1396
1980	139.07	139.07	6.07	95.79	86.94	8.85	37.21	6.96	11.01	1584
1981--1985	**950.95**	**950.95**	**62.46**	**589.30**	**515.41**	**73.89**	**299.19**	**48.08**	**80.80**	
1981	139.15	139.15	6.61	92.52	82.71	9.81	40.02	7.60	11.86	1558
1982	154.94	154.94	10.34	99.79	89.30	10.49	44.81	8.25	11.05	1704
1983	183.13	183.13	12.85	112.65	98.76	13.89	57.63	9.06	13.63	1979
1984	216.61	216.61	14.85	130.68	113.99	16.69	71.08	10.43	18.37	2306
1985	257.12	257.12	17.81	153.66	130.65	23.01	85.65	12.74	25.89	2702
1986--1990	**1978.58**	**1978.68**	**162.93**	**1084.23**	**917.29**	**166.94**	**731.52**	**94.39**	**172.89**	
1986	284.86	284.86	19.14	165.75	141.17	24.58	99.97	14.98	27.99	2953
1987	326.82	326.82	24.31	182.59	154.54	28.05	119.92	17.70	27.21	3336
1988	410.22	410.22	37.07	221.27	189.48	31.79	151.88	19.03	39.07	4124
1989	455.96	455.96	38.53	252.23	212.83	39.40	165.20	18.72	34.77	4509
1990	500.72	500.82	43.88	262.39	219.27	43.12	194.55	23.96	43.85	4878
1991--1995	**4650.47**	**4650.44**	**303.97**	**2167.24**	**1791.38**	**375.86**	**2179.23**	**247.74**	**586.26**	
1991	598.79	598.89	45.52	291.53	255.59	35.94	261.84	29.61	65.65	5782
1992	709.00	709.10	48.67	345.91	292.97	52.94	314.52	35.49	85.41	6804
1993	863.23	863.53	53.57	414.79	334.00	80.79	395.17	37.58	113.88	8239
1994	1084.33	1084.03	74.77	499.84	405.11	94.73	509.42	61.51	146.62	10261
1995	1395.12	1394.89	81.44	615.17	503.71	111.46	698.28	83.55	174.70	13085
1996	1616.03	1615.73	83.46	683.14	541.41	141.73	849.13	113.78	187.59	15044
1997	1810.49	1810.09	84.85	738.56	588.36	150.20	986.68	135.79	202.45	16735
1998	2011.77	2011.31	86.56	786.85	610.66	176.19	1137.90	154.45	207.33	18478

注：本表按当年价格计算。

Note：Data of this table is calculated at current prices.

附1-5 国民生产总值指数(1978=100)
INDEX OF GROSS NATIONAL PRODUCT(1978=100)

年 份 Year	国民生产总 值 Gross National Product	国内生产总 值 Gross Domestic Product	第一产业 Primary Industry	第二产业 Secondary Industry	# 工业 Industry	# 建筑业 Constru-ction	第三产业 Tertiary Industry	#运输邮电业 Transporta-tion,Post and Teleco-mmunication	# 商业 Commerce	人均国内生产总值(元) Per Capita Gross Domes-tic Product (yuan)
1978	100	100	100	100	100	100	100	100	100	100
1979	109.7	109.7	105	109.2	110.1	108.4	113.2	93.5	104.3	107.6
1980	122.6	122.6	114.8	120.2	121.2	119.6	134.1	96.7	124.5	117.8
1981	120.8	120.8	139.0	113.4	119.2	127.2	142.3	104.1	132.3	115.1
1982	129.7	129.7	157.6	116.9	123.0	141.3	167.5	117.5	151.7	121.4
1983	150.2	150.2	169.4	134.9	137.1	187.0	199.3	113.9	159.1	138.1
1984	176.7	176.5	180.9	157.8	158.6	222.1	242.4	130.1	210.5	159.9
1985	191.9	191.7	192.2	174.6	173.4	277.0	252.8	149.2	249.7	171.4
1986	209.0	208.8	192.4	178.9	178.2	278.1	320.3	152.1	255.4	184.3
1987	229.0	228.8	217.9	187.5	186.3	295.6	379.6	168.2	227.8	198.8
1988	258.3	258.1	242.3	213.0	210.5	314.9	424.0	166.7	268.9	220.9
1989	269.7	269.5	245.0	228.8	228.2	353.3	421.9	227.2	204.6	226.9
1990	284.3	284.0	253.3	231.1	232.5	337.7	480.9	241.3	244.9	235.5
1991	311.3	311.0	262.5	248.8	261.8	275.6	543.5	313.4	239.0	257.8
1992	347.4	347.1	270.3	279.0	288.8	346.4	611.4	344.4	283.5	286.0
1993	389.4	389.1	278.7	314.9	319.1	445.1	689.1	379.2	328.0	318.8
1994	442.0	441.6	286.0	360.9	362.2	537.7	783.5	471.0	359.5	359.0
1995	497.2	496.4	262.2	388.4	390.0	578.6	947.2	658.9	422.0	399.9
1996	543.0	542.0	254.4	417.1	413.8	659.0	1063.7	783.4	444.8	433.5
1997	595.1	594.1	256.9	450.9	449.8	692.6	1189.2	883.7	468.0	471.7
1998	653.4	652.3	260.8	494.2	488.9	790.9	1317.6	972.1	486.7	533.0

注：本表按可比价格计算。

Note: Data of this table are calculated at constant prices.

附1-6 国民生产总值指数(上年=100)
INDEX OF GROSS NATIONAL PRODUCT(PRECEDING YEAR=100)

年 份 Year	国民生产总值 Gross National Product	国内生产总值 Gross Domestic Product	第一产业 Primary Industry	第二产业 Secondary Industry	# 工 业 Industry	# 建筑业 Construction	第三产业 Tertiary Industry	#运输邮电业 Transportation,Post and Telecommunication	# 商业 Commerce	人均国内生产总值(元) Per Capita Gross Domestic Product (yuan)
1979	109.7	109.7	105.0	109.2	110.1	108.4	113.2	93.5	104.3	107.6
1980	111.8	111.8	109.3	110.1	110.1	110.3	118.5	103.4	119.4	109.5
1981	98.5	98.5	121.1	94.3	98.3	106.4	106.1	107.7	106.2	97.7
1982	107.4	107.4	113.4	103.1	103.2	111.1	117.7	112.8	114.7	105.5
1983	115.8	115.8	107.5	115.4	111.5	132.3	119.0	97.0	104.9	113.7
1984	117.6	117.5	106.8	117.0	115.7	118.8	121.6	114.2	132.3	115.8
1985	108.6	108.6	106.2	110.6	109.3	124.7	104.3	114.7	118.6	107.2
1986	108.9	108.9	100.1	102.5	102.8	100.4	126.7	101.9	102.3	107.5
1987	109.6	109.6	113.3	104.8	104.5	106.3	118.5	110.6	89.2	107.9
1988	112.8	112.8	111.2	113.6	113.0	106.5	111.7	99.1	118.0	111.1
1989	104.4	104.4	101.1	107.4	108.4	112.2	99.5	136.3	76.1	102.7
1990	105.4	105.4	103.4	101.0	101.9	95.6	114.0	106.2	119.7	103.8
1991	109.5	109.5	103.6	107.7	112.6	81.6	113.0	129.9	97.6	109.5
1992	111.6	111.6	103.0	112.1	110.3	125.7	112.5	109.9	118.6	110.9
1993	112.1	112.1	103.1	112.9	110.5	128.5	112.7	110.1	115.7	111.5
1994	113.5	113.5	102.6	114.6	113.5	120.8	113.7	124.2	109.6	112.6
1995	112.5	112.4	91.7	107.6	107.7	107.6	120.9	139.9	117.4	111.4
1996	109.2	109.2	97.0	107.4	106.1	113.9	112.3	118.9	105.4	108.4
1997	109.6	109.6	101.0	108.1	108.7	105.1	111.8	112.8	105.2	108.8
1998	109.8	109.8	101.5	109.6	108.7	114.2	110.8	110.0	104.0	113.0

注：本表按可比价格计算。
Note：Data of this table are calculated at constant prices.

附1-7 国 内 支 出 总 额
GROSS DOMESTIC EXPENDITUR

单位：亿元 (100 million yuan)

年 份 Year	国内支出总额 Gross Domestic Expenditure	最终消费 Final Consumption	居民消费 Residential Consumption	农 民 Peasant	非农业居民 Non-Peasant	政府消费 Government Consumption	资本形成总额 Total Capital Formation	固定资产 Fixed Assets	存 货 Stock
1978	108.84	40.98	30.47	7.32	23.15	10.51	31.67	24.84	6.83
1979	102.11	49.34	36.24	8.63	27.61	13.10	37.40	29.76	7.64
1980	139.07	57.44	44.35	10.53	33.82	13.09	43.69	35.63	8.06
1981--1985	**950.95**	**424.69**	**306.14**	**87.83**	**218.31**	**118.55**	**343.04**	**271.97**	**71.07**
1981	139.15	63.72	47.66	11.98	35.68	16.06	38.85	29.53	9.32
1982	154.94	71.22	51.24	13.64	37.60	19.98	34.43	26.10	8.33
1983	183.13	81.31	56.45	16.57	39.88	24.86	54.76	49.04	5.72
1984	216.61	96.14	67.65	21.05	46.60	28.49	78.57	68.60	9.97
1985	257.12	112.30	83.14	24.59	58.55	29.16	136.43	98.70	37.73
1986--1990	**1978.68**	**880.15**	**640.93**	**188.47**	**452.46**	**239.22**	**1218.96**	**925.87**	**293.09**
1986	284.86	125.16	92.40	26.10	66.30	32.76	156.33	129.75	26.58
1987	326.82	147.87	107.73	29.12	78.61	40.14	208.33	170.12	38.21
1988	410.22	178.49	131.98	37.25	94.73	46.51	250.01	197.79	52.22
1989	455.96	197.67	138.99	46.78	92.21	58.68	297.00	200.26	96.74
1990	500.82	230.96	169.83	49.22	120.61	61.13	307.29	227.95	79.34
1991--1995	**5274.68**	**1701.59**	**1177.92**	**276.13**	**901.79**	**523.87**	**3530.54**	**2119.49**	**1411.05**
1991	560.21	225.47	153.62	37.59	116.03	71.85	322.77	184.37	138.40
1992	681.43	262.97	177.08	40.11	136.97	85.89	423.71	200.98	222.73
1993	1019.55	310.28	207.21	52.95	154.26	103.07	625.15	326.82	298.33
1994	1318.60	396.29	264.55	66.95	197.60	131.74	902.63	519.01	383.62
1995	1694.89	506.58	375.46	78.53	296.93	131.32	1256.28	888.31	367.97
1996	1678.52	617.85	451.96	92.89	359.07	165.89	1107.06	922.48	184.58
1997	1870.93	703.36	492.88	97.25	395.63	210.48	1228.65	1001.73	226.92
1998	2046.31	809.82	563.62	109.26	454.36	246.20	1396.40	1171.90	224.50

注：本表按当年价格计算。
Note：Data of this table is calculated at current

附1-8 全社会固定资产投资
TOTAL INVESTMENT IN FIXED ASSETS

单位：亿元 (100 million yuan)

年 份 Year	固定资产投资总额 Total Investment in Fixed Assets	国有经济单位 State-Owned	#基本建设 Capital Construction	#更新改造 Innovation	集体经济单位 Collective Owned	#农村 Rural	其他经济单位 Others	个体经济 Individuals	#农村 Rural
1985	94.0	73.6	50.7	21.7	16.2	10.8		4.2	3.8
1986--1990	**724.1**	**609.6**	**378.2**	**201.3**	**83.1**	**49.1**		**31.4**	**27.5**
1986	106.2	88.7	54.2	33.4	13.3	6.4		4.2	4.0
1987	136.2	115.8	71.7	43.1	15.2	8.3		5.2	4.5
1988	163.0	133.2	87.7	43.6	21.4	13.7		8.4	7.6
1989	139.5	117.7	79.8	36.5	15.1	9.0		6.7	5.7
1990	179.2	154.2	84.8	44.7	18.1	11.7		6.9	5.7
1991--1995	**2358.7**	**1764.2**	**808.7**	**567.9**	**188.7**	**134.8**	**381.0**	**24.8**	**19.3**
1991	192.0	165.0	86.8	52.4	20.2	14.6		6.8	6.4
1992	266.0	230.1	114.9	79.2	27.3	19.8		8.6	7.4
1993	410.4	340.1	157.1	116.1	37.4	28.8	30.9	2.0	1.2
1994	648.8	514.8	229.2	179.2	44.6	33.7	86.3	3.1	2.0
1995	841.5	514.2	220.7	141.0	59.2	37.9	263.8	4.3	2.3
1996	876.9	545.7	241.8	156.4	57.6	41.1	268.8	4.8	2.5
1997	961.2	605.7	294.1	174.4	54.7	38.5	296.8	4.0	2.1
1998	1115.3	698.4	354.1	235.3	66.5	42.3	345.6	4.8	2.5

年份 Year	固定资产投资来源 Source of Investment in Fixed Assets 国家预算内投资 State Budgetary Investment	国内贷款 Domestic Loan	利用外资 Foreign Capital	自筹投资 Self-raised investment	其他投资 Other Investment	固定资产投资 Investment in Fixed Assets 第一产业 Primary Industry	第二产业 Secondary Industry	#工业 Industry	#能源工业 Energy	第三产业 Tertiary Industry	#运输邮电业 Transportation,Post and Telecommunications
1985	30.4	11.5	5.1	26.4	4.4	1.6	32.4	28.8	4.4	43.8	5.3
1986--1990	**184.9**	**90.3**	**69.1**	**245.6**	**39.5**	**9.4**	**218.8**	**209.1**	**43.1**	**384.2**	**47.7**
1986	33.0	17.0	4.6	37.4	2.5	1.5	41.4	38.8	5.5	51.6	6.6
1987	43.1	19.5	8.8	49.1	5.7	1.6	46.9	44.3	10.0	72.9	9.7
1988	37.4	18.2	22.3	62.3	9.2	2.0	48.8	47.2	9.9	87.9	7.8
1989	35.6	12.8	18.2	44.5	12.0	1.9	38.4	37.0	8.5	81.9	10.0
1990	35.8	22.8	15.2	52.3	10.1	2.4	43.3	41.8	9.2	89.9	13.6
1991--1995	**254.5**	**274.8**	**189.6**	**888.4**	**127.3**	**15.5**	**624.1**	**585.1**	**154.8**	**973.5**	**256.2**
1991	35.5	28.2	13.9	65.5	8.0	2.7	51.3	49.3	11.8	90.4	13.0
1992	42.2	40.1	14.9	109.9	9.6	3.9	82.9	80.2	22.0	114.2	28.4
1993	46.4	71.0	28.0	168.9	35.9	2.1	150.4	134.6	28.2	165.7	51.7
1994	62.5	70.9	87.8	283.7	44.8	3.7	185.8	175.9	40.2	318.4	81.2
1995	67.9	64.6	45.0	260.4	29.0	3.1	153.7	145.1	52.6	284.8	81.9
1996	73.1	71.1	53.8	265.7	39.8	2.8	174.9	167.3	69.8	319.7	99.5
1997	82.8	89.7	51.3	322.4	41.3	0.9	201.1	192.1	93.3	380.1	113.4
1998	93.9	108.4	41.2	382.9	43.0	1.5	201.7	192.6	96.2	479.7	169.8

注：1.全社会固定资产投资来源中,1985和1986年为固定资产投资完成额资金来源分组。

2.按资金来源和三次产业划分的固定资产投资不含房地产。

a) In source of total investment of fixed assets,data of 1985 and 1986 are grouped by source of investment completed.

b) Data of investment grouped by source of funds and three industry excluded real estate development.

附1-9 基 本 建 设 投 资 额
INVESTMENT IN CAPITAL CONSTRUCTION

年 份 Year	基本建设投资额 (万元) Investment (10000 yuan)	按隶属关系分 Grouped by Administrative Relationship		按建设性质分 Grouped by Type of Construction			新增固定资产 (万元) Incremental Fixed Assets (10000 yuan)	固定资产交付使用率 (%) Rate of Fixed Assets Put into Operation (%)
		中央 Central	地方 Local	新建 Newly-built	扩建、改建 Expanding, Replacement	其他 Others		
1978	198908	90498	108410				169148	85.0
1979	234741	124132	110609	107611	105561	21569	212111	90.4
1980	265185	139843	125342	123520	135064	6601	231715	87.4
1981--1985	**1672352**	**926161**	**746191**	**670739**	**827830**	**173783**	**1421535**	**85.0**
1981	238693	130589	108104	111150	121431	6112	309203	129.5
1982	259866	121116	138750	119196	130002	10668	199313	76.7
1983	271126	141087	130039	93471	172287	5368	236816	87.3
1984	360756	210516	150240	136480	161372	62904	360997	100.1
1985	541911	322853	219058	210442	242738	88731	315206	58.2
1986--1990	**4000931**	**2506444**	**1494487**	**1888490**	**1641503**	**470938**	**2662712**	**66.6**
1986	587030	358562	228468	249512	254774	82744	354264	60.3
1987	763286	494817	268469	297042	359192	107052	463887	60.8
1988	926549	590549	336000	454766	365721	106062	455230	49.1
1989	835661	521340	314321	419002	323336	93323	512484	61.3
1990	888405	541176	347229	468168	338480	81757	876847	98.7
1991--1995	**9314619**	**5081070**	**4233549**	**3940498**	**4651510**	**722611**	**5263959**	**56.5**
1991	902052	481844	420208	390091	412787	99174	779764	86.4
1992	1185313	646031	539282	458089	618029	109195	726984	61.3
1993	1726260	934439	791821	640690	962772	122798	805405	46.7
1994	2851219	1329286	1521933	1340373	1306164	204682	1386866	48.6
1995	2649775	1689470	960305	1111255	1351758	186762	1564940	59.1
1996	3138456	1892321	1246135	1213019	1675846	249591	2625211	83.6
1997	3743212	2233708	1509504	1250778	2124370	368064	2639688	70.5
1998	4155182	2506556	1648626	1196701	2559533	398948	3000077	72.2

附1-10 国有单位基本建设投资额
INVESTMENT IN CAPITAL CONSTRUCTION OF STATE-OWNED UNITS

年 份 Year	基本建设投资额 (亿元) Investment (100 million yuan)	按隶属关系分 Grouped by Administrative Relationship		按建设性质分 Grouped by Type of Construction			新增固定资产 (亿元) Incremental Fixed Assets (100 million yuan)	固定资产交付使用率 (%) Rate of Fixed Assets Put into Operation (%)
		中央 Central	地方 Local	新建 Newly-built	扩建、改建 Expanding, Replacement	其他 Others		
1981--1985	**160.2**						**132.6**	**82.8**
1981	23.4						24.9	106.4
1982	25.0	12.1	12.9				19.4	77.6
1983	26.4	14.1	12.3				23.2	87.9
1984	34.7	21.0	13.7	13.0	15.9	5.8	35.0	100.9
1985	50.7	32.3	18.4	18.8	23.9	8.0	30.1	59.4
1986--1990	**378.2**	**250.4**	**127.8**	**177.6**	**160.6**	**40.0**	**251.2**	**66.4**
1986	54.2	35.8	18.4	22.7	24.6	6.9	32.9	60.7
1987	71.7	49.5	22.2	26.8	35.5	9.4	43.7	60.9
1988	87.7	58.9	28.8	42.4	36.0	9.3	42.3	48.2
1989	79.8	52.1	27.7	40.1	31.7	8.0	48.3	60.5
1990	84.8	54.1	30.7	45.6	32.8	6.4	84.0	99.1
1991--1995	**808.7**	**480.8**	**327.9**				**457.9**	**56.6**
1991	86.8	48.2	38.6	38.1	40.4	8.3	75.6	87.1
1992	114.9	64.6	50.3	45.2	60.1	9.6	67.4	58.7
1993	157.1	89.7	67.4				53.5	34.1
1994	229.2	125.6	103.6				124.3	54.2
1995	220.7	152.7	68.0				137.1	62.1
1996	241.8	165.8	76.0				229.8	95.0
1997	294.1	193.0	101.1	64.5	194.0	35.6	221.0	75.1
1998	354.1	223.7	130.4	78.7	236.9	38.5	204.3	57.7

附1-11 更 新 改 造 投 资 额
INVESTMENT IN INNOVATIONS

年 份 Year	更新改造投资额 (万元) Investment (10000 yuan)	按隶属关系分 Grouped by Administrative Relationship		按建设性质分 Grouped by Type of Construction			新增固定资产 (万元) Incremental Fixed Assets (10000 yuan)	固定资产交付使用率 (%) Rate of Fixed Assets Put into Operation (%)
		中央 Central	地方 Local	新建 Newly-built	扩建、改建 Expanding, Replacement	其他 Others		
1980	66542						48089	72.3
1981--1985	**671784**						**479560**	**71.4**
1981	75545						56527	74.8
1982	84818	16044	68774				63785	75.2
1983	114327	26087	88240				88582	77.5
1984	161276	35069	126207	3354	138963	18959	110265	68.4
1985	235818	44706	191112	14281	208010	13527	160401	68.0
1986--1990	**2123897**	**331964**	**1791933**	**133715**	**1710681**	**279501**	**1511075**	**71.1**
1986	358357	57582	300775	26619	289075	42663	230940	64.4
1987	450629	79105	371524	11550	386744	52335	335159	74.4
1988	460025	66340	393685	29480	366311	64234	317796	69.1
1989	386827	58418	328409	26969	307067	52791	283194	73.2
1990	468059	70519	397540	39097	361484	67478	343986	73.5
1991--1995	**6178916**	**1888982**	**4289934**	**237180**	**5256320**	**685416**	**4378783**	**70.9**
1991	541624	86149	455475	11578	460759	69287	448861	82.9
1992	824518	169979	654539	17901	731095	75522	600487	72.8
1993	1218170	367869	850301	33269	1092674	92227	687026	56.4
1994	2022193	669408	1352785	36723	1855312	130158	1625303	80.4
1995	1572441	595577	976834	137709	1283375	151327	1017106	64.7
1996	1680479	636918	1043561	222645	1318904	138930	1553521	92.4
1997	1911525	894052	1017473	180134	1550027	181364	1301241	68.1
1998	2524288	1003398	1520890	437531	1822482	264275	1616523	64.0

附1-12 国有单位更新改造投资额
INVESTMENT IN INNOVATIONS OF STATE-OWNED UNITS

年 份 Year	更新改造投资额 (亿 元) Investment (100 million yuan)	按隶属关系分 Grouped by Administrative Relationship		按建设性质分 Grouped by Type of Construction			新增固定资产 (亿 元) Incremental Fixed Assets (100 million yuan)	固定资产交付使用率 (%) Rate of Fixed Assets Put into Operation (%)
		中央 Central	地方 Local	新建 Newly-built	扩建、改建 Expanding, Replacement	其他 Others		
1981--1985	**62.5**						**44.7**	**71.5**
1981	6.8						5.3	77.9
1982	7.9	1.6	6.3				5.9	74.7
1983	10.8	2.6	8.2				8.1	75.0
1984	15.3	3.5	11.8	0.3	13.2	1.8	10.3	67.3
1985	21.7	4.5	17.2	1.3	19.3	1.1	15.1	69.6
1986--1990	**201.3**	**33.2**	**168.1**	**12.8**	**163.1**	**25.4**	**143.2**	**71.1**
1986	33.4	5.7	27.7	2.4	27.1	3.9	21.9	65.6
1987	43.1	7.9	35.2	1.1	37.1	4.9	32.1	74.5
1988	43.6	6.6	37.0	2.8	34.9	5.9	29.5	67.7
1989	36.5	5.9	30.6	2.6	29.2	4.7	26.8	73.4
1990	44.7	7.1	37.6	3.9	34.8	6.0	32.9	73.6
1991--1995	**567.9**	**185.1**	**382.8**				**418.3**	**73.7**
1991	52.4	8.6	43.8	1.2	44.9	6.3	43.1	82.3
1992	79.2	17.0	62.2	1.8	70.5	6.9	57.8	73.0
1993	116.1	36.3	79.8				66.7	57.5
1994	179.2	65.9	113.3				154.9	86.4
1995	141.0	57.3	83.7				95.8	67.9
1996	156.4	61.8	94.6				138.4	88.5
1997	174.4	87.8	86.6	10.1	112.8	51.5	123.6	70.9
1998	235.3	98.4	136.9	41.6	170.4	23.3	151.1	64.2

附1-13 房地产投资额
INVESTMENT IN REAL ESTATE DEVELOPMENT

年份 Year	投资总额 (亿元) Total Investment (100 million yuan)	商品房屋施工面积 (万平方米) Floor Space of Commodity Buildings under Construction (10000 sq.m)	# 本年新开工面积 Construction of this Year	商品房屋竣工面积 (万平方米) Floor Space of Commodity Buildings under Construction (10000 sq.m)	商品房销售建筑面积 (万平方米) Floor Space of Commodity Buildings Sales (10000 sq.m)
1990	22.5	774.0	249.1	271.6	142.2
1991--1995	**568.4**	**7501.6**	**3022.6**	**2061.7**	**855.6**
1991	24.0	815.1	317.6	275.2	154.0
1992	33.7	1021.1	508.6	331.4	159.1
1993	58.4	1262.0	524.8	356.4	182.0
1994	99.5	1593.2	659.4	445.7	168.6
1995	352.8	2810.2	1012.2	653.0	191.9
1996	328.2	2824.6	578.7	663.4	215.3
1997	330.3	2869.6	848.4	682.3	290.9
1998	377.4	3499.1	1193.4	842.8	409.2

附1-14 地方财政收入
LOCAL FINANCIAL REVENUE AND EXPENDITURE

单位：亿元 (100 million yuan)

年份 Year	地方财政收入 Local Financial Revenue	#各项税收 Taxes	地方财政支出 Local Financial Expenditure	# 基本建设 Capital Construction	# 农业生产和农业事业费 Agricultural Production and Operating Expenses	# 文教科卫事业费 Culture,Education,Science and Health Expenses	# 教育事业费 Education	# 科学事业费 Scientific Research
1978	50.46	18.25	20.38	10.89	0.84	2.43	1.46	0.22
1979	47.75	19.41	20.06	10.07	0.86	2.94	1.77	0.24
1980	51.29	21.22	14.87	5.65	0.75	3.22	1.93	0.26
1981--1985	**234.27**	**149.21**	**111.40**	**39.75**	**4.69**	**24.82**	**14.04**	**1.64**
1981	49.12	22.47	14.85	5.95	0.71	3.65	2.15	0.29
1982	47.25	24.40	16.80	6.44	0.80	4.17	2.37	0.27
1983	39.84	26.45	19.61	6.47	0.83	4.63	2.65	0.36
1984	45.62	31.49	27.15	10.06	1.12	5.53	3.00	0.37
1985	52.44	44.40	32.99	10.83	1.23	6.84	3.87	0.37
1986--1990	**337.13**	**335.42**	**272.89**	**55.78**	**12.72**	**59.36**	**30.48**	**2.99**
1986	60.34	49.82	44.27	11.22	1.57	8.20	4.45	0.49
1987	63.62	55.16	49.67	10.47	1.91	9.21	4.79	0.58
1988	68.11	67.27	52.93	10.53	2.88	11.46	6.04	0.58
1989	71.05	79.30	59.50	11.70	3.15	13.67	7.00	0.57
1990	74.01	83.87	66.52	11.86	3.21	16.82	8.20	0.76
1991--1995	**456.48**	**586.35**	**473.64**	**51.07**	**22.74**	**131.86**	**73.30**	**7.36**
1991	77.02	92.02	67.98	9.35	3.67	17.58	9.41	1.01
1992	80.25	104.14	71.74	8.57	3.98	19.72	10.56	1.1
1993	84.10	136.77	80.99	10.35	4.33	24.08	13.10	1.3
1994	99.85	107.48	98.53	9.37	4.93	29.81	17.22	1.62
1995	115.26	145.94	154.40	13.43	5.83	40.67	23.01	2.34
1996	150.90	203.07	187.45	21.66	7.42	51.66	29.57	2.94
1997	209.91	239.13	262.20	24.89	9.85	63.83	35.97	3.74
1998	262.01	276.74	307.83	32.61	10.54	72.97	41.50	4.11

附1-15 国家银行各项存款年末余额
YEAR-END BALANCE OF DEPOSITS OF BANKS

单位：万元 (10000 yuan)

年 份 Year	合 计 Total	企业存款 Enterprises	财政存款 Financial	机关团体存 款 Government Organs and Bodies	城镇储蓄存 款 Urban Saving Deposits	农村存款 Rural
1978	1146580	527922	40273	389409	88991	46749
1979	1390517	649013	49342	463723	104400	57357
1980	1679891	834102	71486	566547	133310	67679
1981	2204737	1131870	65544	750606	157369	89070
1982	2792318	1432034	87904	974105	191882	105168
1983	3212851	1660027	85297	1087862	251065	128364
1984	3755220	2254153	129052	927955	321447	122081
1985	4109535	2454797	182064	890667	422447	137390
1986	5087562	3116297	165906	1027730	556249	179889
1987	6107619	3555956	150093	1335385	751854	205995
1988	6099142	3328559	97147	1180338	905519	295712
1989	7176132	3709770	259761	1218831	1337629	317000
1990	8689227	4293690	290365	1503878	1879081	297212
1991	11060952	5484293	333025	1879611	2498786	367665
1992	13095965	7005468	112779	1422621	3282099	534536
1993	16492164	8351199	142235	1551093	4824810	804791
1994	23111169	10377956	227561	2004247	7414350	932779
1995	30541198	16074288	359667	2116841	11034549	184283
1996	37818707	19705705	483317	2364532	15060889	199136
1997	51036605	29211539	381652	3303945	17709062	252358
1998	63691737	36289291	970772	5134092	20631876	266550

注：1997、1998年财政存款中包含中央财政存款。

Note: Financial deposits of 1997 and 1998 include central financial deposits.

附1-16 国家银行各项贷款年末余额
YEAR-END BALANCE OF LOANS OF BANKS

单位：万元 (10000 yuan)

年 份 Year	合 计 Total	工业生产企业贷款 Industrial Production	商 业企业贷款 Commerce	建 筑企业贷款 Construction	农业贷款 Agriculture	固定资产贷 款 Fixed Assets	短 期贷 款 Short-term	中长期贷 款 Mid,Long-term
1978	539078	214352	319239		5484	3		
1979	742332	216791	475507		6133	43901		
1980	873420	252528	495423	2198	7442	110685		
1981	912591	265718	517190	3624	8642	102540		
1982	1090686	346081	522596	10508	9479	178107		
1983	1494770	687371	552268	21486	14350	189486		
1984	1933724	774286	646218	76085	55606	304220		
1985	2534647	926420	697008	90789	61870	428020		
1986	3127010	1126873	814253	109423	96030	528287		
1987	3623937	1237457	896170	120812	126462	608207		
1988	4157237	1401628	1133718	162539	72292	753177	2777141	
1989	4870606	1740436	1407018	175324	99980	776477		
1990	5526782	2113813	1613340	187509	147878	946906	4159282	946906
1991	6326887	2407065	1810436	201089	193636	1159300	4724335	1159300
1992	7304636	2662278	2091350	218154	232829	1473004	5325684	1473004
1993	9715379	3372431	2519224	262157	271067	2344437	6713712	2344437
1994	10703251	3887403	1954192	284100	274209	3124624	7155394	3124624
1995	15605875	4643921	3592487	358327	339788	3563697	10159790	3563697
1996	18096848	5747916	4327060	483578	386784	3918864	12463119	3918864
1997	25444738	7412815	5632541	1000396	477519	5524730	18353500	5524730
1998	31261511	8919232	5892568	1383505	530789	7281840	20985647	7281840

附1-17 各种物价总指数
AGGREGATE PRICE INDICES

年 份 Year	商 品 零售价格 总指数 (上年=100) Aggregate Retail Price Index (preceding year=100)	居 民 消费价格 总指数 (上年=100) Aggregate Consumer Price Index (preceding year=100)	农副产品 收购价格 总指数 (上年=100) Purchasing Price Index of Farm and Sideline Products (preceding year=100)	农 业 生产资料 价格指数 (上年=100) Price Index of Agricultural Capital Goods (preceding year=100)	商 品 零售价格 总指数 (1978=100) Aggregate Retail Price Index (1978=100)	居 民 消费价格 总指数 (1978=100) Aggregate Consumer Price Index (1978=100)	农副产品 收购价格 总指数 (1978=100) Purchasing Price Index of Farm and Sideline Products (1978=100)	农 业 生产资料 价格指数 (1978=100) Price Index of Agricultural Capital Goods (1978=100)
1978	100.6	100.6			100.0	100.0	100.0	100.0
1979	101.8	101.8	109.5	100.0	101.5	101.4	109.5	100.0
1980	106.7	106.0	105.5	100.2	108.6	107.9	115.5	100.3
1981	101.4	101.3	109.4	100.1	110.2	109.2	126.4	100.3
1982	102.0	101.8	101.9	100.1	112.3	111.2	128.7	100.4
1983	100.6	100.5	101.8	101.6	113.0	111.8	131.0	102.0
1984	102.1	102.2	102.3	109.7	115.4	114.2	133.9	111.9
1985	118.6	117.6	117.6	100.9	136.8	134.4	157.5	112.9
1986	106.7	106.8	108.1	102.7	145.9	143.5	170.3	115.9
1987	108.7	108.6	116.1	110.8	158.6	155.8	197.6	128.4
1988	121.9	120.4	123.2	117.6	193.3	187.6	243.4	151.0
1989	118.5	117.2	106.8	121.5	229.1	219.9	260.0	183.5
1990	104.1	105.4	101.9	102.1	238.5	231.8	264.9	187.4
1991	108.5	111.9	101.7	102.5	258.8	259.4	269.4	192.1
1992	108.3	109.9	102.4	103.6	280.3	285.1	275.9	199.0
1993	116.9	119.0	107.0	109.1	327.7	339.3	295.2	217.1
1994	117.9	124.9	133.4	120.1	386.4	423.8	393.8	260.7
1995	112.6	117.3	130.6	133.2	435.1	497.1	514.3	347.3
1996	107.3	111.6	101.5	106.8	466.9	554.8	522.0	370.9
1997	103.8	105.3	92.8	100.4	484.6	584.2	484.4	372.2
1998	98.3	102.4	93.6	102.6	476.4	598.2	484.4	372.2

附1-18 职工工资总额和保险福利费
TOTAL WAGES,INSURANCE AND WELFARES OF STAFF AND WORKERS

年 份 Year	职 工 工资总额 (亿元) Total Wages (100 million yuan)	国有经济单 位 State-Owned	城镇集体经济单位 Urban Collective Owned	其他经济单 位 Others	职工保险福利费用总额 (亿元) Total Insurance and Welfares (100 million yuan)	国有经济单 位 State-Owned	城镇集体经济单位 Urban Collective Owned	其他经济单 位 Others
1978	18.7	16.2	2.5		2.6	2.6		
1979	22.4	19.4	3		3.1	3.1		
1980	26.9	23.3	3.6		4.3	4.3		
1981--1985	**183.7**	**153.7**	**29.6**	**0.4**	**39.5**	**39.5**		
1981	28.3	24.2	4.1		5.2	5.2		
1982	30.5	25.9	4.6		5.8	5.8		
1983	33.8	28.5	5.3		7.7	7.7		
1984	40.4	33.7	6.6	0.1	9.3	9.3		
1985	50.7	41.4	9	0.3	11.5	11.5		
1986--1990	**421.1**	**349.7**	**64.4**	**7**	**95.7**	**91.5**	**3.6**	**0.6**
1986	58	48.5	9.1	0.4	13.9	13.9		
1987	66.7	56	10.1	0.6	17	17		
1988	81.2	68.1	12.1	1	24.3	24.3		
1989	96.3	81	13.4	1.9	19.5	17.4	1.8	0.3
1990	118.9	96.1	19.7	3.1	21	18.9	1.8	0.3
1991--1995	**1198.1**	**950.3**	**156.6**	**91.2**	**156**	**138.9**	**10.9**	**6.2**
1991	132.2	106.1	21.5	4.6	25.3	22.6	2.1	0.6
1992	158.5	128.6	23.9	6	30.6	27.4	2.4	0.8
1993	218.9	176.6	28.5	13.8	36	32.2	2.5	1.3
1994	306.5	243.4	36.2	26.9	30.4	27	1.9	1.5
1995	382	295.6	46.5	39.9	33.7	29.7	2	2
1996	442.4	339.4	46.2	56.8	37.3	31.7	2.8	2.8
1997	514.8	383.6	53.8	77.4	48.1	41.6	2.8	3.7
1998	558.2	391.9	45	121.3	54.5	47.5	3	4

附1-19 职工平均工资及指数
AVERAGE WAGE AND INDEX OF STAFF AND WORKERS

年 份 Year	职 工 平均工资 (元) Average Wage (yuan)	国有经济单 位 State-Owned	城镇集体经济单位 Urban Collective Owned	其他经济单 位 Others	职工实际工资指数 (1978=100) Index of Actual Wage	国有经济单 位 State-Owned	城镇集体经济单位 Urban Collective Owned	其他经济单 位 Others
1978	673	703	471		100	100	100	100
1979	742	778	556		108.3	108.7	116	
1980	848	889	635		116.8	117.3	125	
1981	837	880	685		113.9	114.6	133.1	
1982	863	896	715		115.3	114.6	136.5	
1983	931	964	785		123.7	122.6	149	
1984	1086	1127	946	1170	141.3	140.3	175.8	
1985	1343	1367	1231	1768	148.5	144.7	194.5	112.5
1986	1488	1530	1287	2080	154.1	151.7	190.4	123.9
1987	1670	1712	1449	2267	159.3	156.3	197.5	124.4
1988	2000	2048	1738	2661	158.4	155.3	196.7	121.2
1989	2312	2366	1992	2761	156.2	153.1	192.3	107.3
1990	2653	2713	2334	3243	170.1	166.5	213.8	119.6
1991	2877	2937	2504	3713	164.8	161.1	205	122.3
1992	3402	3500	2828	4289	177.3	174.6	210.6	128.6
1993	4780	4920	3834	5469	209.3	206.3	239.9	137.8
1994	6540	6695	5009	8179	229.3	224.7	250.9	165
1995	8144	8237	6516	10278	243.4	235.7	278.3	176.7
1996	9579	9645	7133	13851	256.5	247.3	273	213.4
1997	11019	10917	8259	15370	280.2	265.6	300.2	224.9
1998	12285	11971	8800	15989	306.1	285.5	313.3	229.1

附1-20 居 民 生 活
PEOPLE'S LIVELIHOOD

年 份 Year	城镇居民家庭平均每人每年(元) Annual Per Capita of Urban Households(yuan)					农村居民家庭平均每人每年(元) Annual Per Capita of Rural Households(yuan)				
	全部收入 Total Income	可支配收入 Discretionary Income	可支配收入指数 (1978=100) Index of Discretionary Income (1978=100)	生活消费支出 Living Expenditures	#食品 Food	纯收入 Net Income	纯收入指数 (1978=100) Index of Net Income (1978=100)	总支出 Total Expenditures	生活消费支出 Living Expenditures	#食品 Food
1978	450.18	365.4	100	359.86	211.19	224.80	100	219	185.41	116.71
1979	491.54	414.95	111.57	408.66	236.73	249.99	110.9	235	204.65	131.06
1980	599.4	501.36	127.21	490.44	270.96	308.14	135.4	290	256.76	140.21
1981	619.57	514.14	128.79	511.43	295.05	361.40	158.5	351	307.19	160.63
1982	668.06	561.05	138.04	534.82	317.57	430.20	186.1	411	345.50	181.13
1983	716.6	590.47	144.48	574.06	337.74	519.48	225.1	499	384.41	193.82
1984	837.65	693.7	166.13	666.75	379.12	664.17	282.9	559	435.00	222.53
1985	1158.84	907.72	134.83	923.32	466.92	775.08	324	726	510.03	240.45
1986	1317.33	1067.52	203.52	1067.38	543.36	823.06	335.6	857	645.25	292.39
1987	1413.24	1181.87	207.47	1147.6	605.04	916.38	357.4	943	705.50	340.90
1988	1767.67	1436.97	209.33	1455.55	743.37	1062.61	368.8	1246	883.25	407.93
1989	1899.57	1787.08	198.51	1520.41	841.3	1230.65	376.8	1356	976.29	484.28
1990	2067.33	1787.08	210.82	1646.05	892.17	1297.09	384.8	1372	980.68	496.77
1991	2359.88	2040.43	215.25	1860.17	1016.8	1422.28	391.3	1585	1100.12	536.98
1992	2813.1	2363.68	226.87	2134.65	1126.27	1568.84	399.4	1684	1179.01	573.78
1993	3935.39	3296.04	265.89	2939.6	1404.66	1854.75	419.8	1714	1308.87	611.71
1994	5585.88	4731.24	305.51	4134.12	1919.04	2422.11	457.8	2175	1676.45	824.81
1995	6748.68	5868.36	322.92	5019.76	2436.48	3208.49	486.3	3080	2432.99	1206.00
1996	7945.78	6885.48	378.89	5729.45	2671.49	3562.73	509.8	3272	2655.5	1233.07
1997	8741.71	7813.11	365.86	6531.81	2854.35	3762.37	535.8	3379	2795.36	1248.42
1998	10098.23	8471.98	387.59	6970.83	2865.73	4028.86	571.7	3617	2945.45	1241.86

年 份 Year	每一城镇就业者负担人数(人) Dependents Per Urban Employee (person)	每一农村劳动力负担人数(人) Dependents Per Rural Labor Force (person)	城市人均居住面积(平方米) Urban Per Capita Living Space (sq.m)	农村人均住房面积(平方米) Rural Per Capita Living Space (sq.m)	城乡储蓄存款余额(亿元) Balance of Saving Deposits (100 million yuan)	城镇储蓄 Urban	农户储蓄 Rural	人均储蓄(元) Per Capita Saving Deposits (yuan)
1978	1.86	2.15	4.55	9.25	9.33	8.9	0.43	107.09
1979	1.83	2.16	4.57	9.67	11.07	10.44	0.63	123.04
1980	1.80	2.13	4.79	10.09	14.39	13.33	1.06	159.2
1981	1.72	2.13	5.08	12.35	17.39	15.74	1.65	189.23
1982	1.66	1.97	5.38	13.01	21.77	19.19	2.58	232.55
1983	1.65	1.82	5.68	14.09	29.81	25.11	4.7	312.49
1984	1.63	1.79	5.92	14.08	38.82	32.14	6.67	401.42
1985	1.66	1.64	6.17	16.37	51.7	42.24	9.45	522.7
1986	1.66	1.66	6.46	17.17	68.58	55.62	12.95	664.52
1987	1.65	1.64	6.82	18.38	92.98	75.19	17.79	871.38
1988	1.71	1.63	7.17	19.23	111.64	90.55	21.09	1032.98
1989	1.52	1.62	7.45	20.09	162.01	133.75	28.26	1597.76
1990	1.52	1.61	7.72	20.62	226.62	188.03	38.59	2208.73
1991	1.47	1.59	8.01	21.92	298.18	249.88	48.3	2878.21
1992	1.43	1.58	8.31	22.67	387.82	328.21	59.61	3721.93
1993	1.42	1.51	8.51	23.7	560.66	482.48	78.18	5349.78
1994	1.41	1.49	8.73	24.42	853.21	745.88	107.33	8079.62
1995	1.41	1.47	8.87	24.74	1253.95	1111.5	142.46	11757.61
1996	1.41	1.45	9.17	25.74	1706.98	1528.41	178.56	15839.09
1997	1.43	1.48	9.49	27.39	1975.23	1770.9	204.36	18196.8
1998	1.40	1.44	9.87	27.64	2287.19	2063.19	224	20954.54

附1-21 城镇居民家庭平均每百户主要耐用消费品拥有量
POSSESSION OF MAIN DURABLE CONSUMER GOODS OF PER 100 URBAN HOUSEHOLDS

年 份 Year	自行车 (辆) Bicycles (unit)	录放像机 (台) Videocorders (set)	淋浴热水器 (台) Showers (unit)	洗衣机 (台) Washing Machines (unit)	彩色电视机 (台) Color TV Sets (set)	黑白电视机 (台) Black and White (set)	收录机 (台) Recorders (set)	电冰箱 (台) Refrige-rators (unit)	照相机 (架) Cameras (set)
1978	135.8					19.2	0.6		7.5
1979	145.7			0.1		41.8	2.4		9.8
1980	150.9			1.9		65.8	9.5	0.3	11.4
1981	153.8			12.3	1.7	80.0	20.0	1.7	13.3
1982	166.5			18.8	1.7	84.8	28.0	2.7	17.2
1983	175.8			28.7	4.3	86.6	40.5	7.0	20.6
1984	183.0			42.3	8.0	86.5	51.5	15.3	29.1
1985	177.0			57.5	32.2	80.7	70.3	41.9	34.6
1986	193.9			75.9	50.9	69.2	80.1	61.5	47.4
1987	210.2			82.6	57.5	70.5	87.0	71.8	55.5
1988	193.7			86.0	69.7	57.8	91.8	81.2	59.6
1989	233.0	10.1		89.7	80.5	55.4	95.5	89.4	62.2
1990	228.3	19.9		93.2	90.9	51.2	99.6	96.4	66.5
1991	233.8	28.4		93.0	97.1	44.0	100.0	101.7	72.7
1992	229.2	41.7	17.0	96.1	101.4	39.5	104.1	101.3	77.2
1993	243.2	45.6	23.2	99.8	107.2	39.2	113.0	100.8	82.4
1994	246.8	49.8	38.8	102.8	111.8	37.4	107.8	104.4	85.4
1995	243.6	54.2	45.4	100.4	113.6	33.8	110.2	104.4	86.8
1996	249.0	57.8	52.0	101.4	119.2	30.8	113.8	105.4	87.2
1997	209.4	56.0	58.4	100.6	123.8		65.0	104.2	88.2
1998	221.0	59.8	65.4	102.2	133.2			105.4	95.2

附1-22 农民家庭平均每百户主要耐用消费品拥有量
POSSESSION OF MAIN DURABLE CONSUMER GOODS OF PER 100 RURAL HOUSEHOLDS

年 份 Year	自行车 (辆) Bicycles (unit)	缝纫机 (架) Sewing Machines (set)	手 表 (只) Watches (unit)	黑白电视机 (台) Black and White TV Sets (set)	彩色电视机 (台) Color TV Sets (set)	录音机 (台) Recorders (set)	照相机 (架) Cameras (set)	电风扇 (台) Electric Fans (unit)	洗衣机 (台) Washing Machines (unit)	电冰箱 (台) Refrige-rators (unit)
1978	109	36	46							
1979	98	32	67	1						
1980	123	39	103	5						
1981	135	46	136	14						
1982	141	50	169	33		2		11	2	
1983	167	55	192	41		7		17	6	
1984	187	58	211	57		14		28	15	1
1985	182	57	201	53	7	21	2	32	23	2
1986	191	56	211	59	12	28	4	42	39	5
1987	204	60	226	63	15	34	5	52	48	9
1988	218	61	231	66	20	41	7	61	56	14
1989	224	63	232	66	25	47	8	67	61	19
1990	235	65	243	65	29	47	8	73	63	23
1991	232	63	217	58	42	48	11	84	69	36
1992	245	64	229	60	46	50	14	92	73	40
1993	249	68	223	56	56	53	15	98	76	47
1994	254	69	239	54	65	59	17	109	80	53
1995	251	67	214	46	74	56	21	115	81	63
1996	250	68	217	44	79	58	21	117	83	67
1997	248	68	221	43	85	58	25	127	84	72
1998	249	70	227	39	92	58	26	133	85	75

附1-23 农业基本情况
BASIC STATISTICS FOR AGRICULTURE

年份 Year	农林牧渔业劳动力 (万人) Labors Force of Farming,Frcostry Animal Husbandry and Fishery (10000 persons)	年末实有耕地面积 (万公顷) Cultivated Area (year-end) (10000 hectare)	当年减少耕地面积 (万公顷) Decresae of Cultivated Area of this Year (10000 hectare)	播种面积 (万公顷) Sown Area (10000 hectare)	# 粮食作物 Grain Crops	# 经济作物 Cash Crops	造林面积 (万公顷) Afforestation Area (10000 hectare)	受灾面积 (万公顷) Disaster Area (10000 hectare)	成灾面积 (万公顷) Infested Area (10000 hectare)
1978	120.7	42.9	0.3	69.1	56.1	4.9	1.4		
1979	115.5	42.7	0.2	67.7	56	3.7	1.6		
1980	113.3	42.6	0.1	65.7	54.9	3.3	2.4		
1981	112.6	42.5	0.1	64.3	53	3.2	2.7		
1982	110.1	42.4	0.1	64.2	52.7	2.9	2.8		
1983	112.2	42.3	0.1	63.8	53	2.8	3.3	16.2	8.9
1984	101.1	42.2	0.1	63.3	52.3	2.7	3.2	18	14
1985	90.3	42.1	0.1	61.8	51.1	2.9	3	14	8
1986	86.1	41.9	0.2	60.5	49.9	2.4	1.4	7	3
1987	84.6	41.8	0.1	59.8	49.5	2	2	3	1
1988	80.9	41.6	0.2	59.5	48.8	1.9	1.6	11	5
1989	83.4	41.4	0.2	58.9	48.3	1.6	0.8	21	9
1990	82.5	41.3	0.1	59	48.4	1.6	4.1	17.8	8.7
1991	80.3	41.1	0.2	59	48.3	1.7	1.5	16.9	7.7
1992	74.6	40.9	0.2	58.6	47.7	1.7	1.5	3.8	0.8
1993	72.5	40.6	0.3	56.5	45.6	1.8	4.8	11.9	5.3
1994	68.7	40.2	0.4	55.1	43	1.7	5.5	19.3	4.6
1995	65.5	39.9	0.3	55.3	43.4	1.5	4.7	12.1	3.7
1996	66.9	34.4	0.3	53.8	42.7	1.4	4	12.3	5
1997	65.3	34.2	0.3	53.6	42.5	1.2	3.8		
1998	67.7	34.1	0.3	53.5	42.3	1.2	3.7		

注：1995、1996、1997年耕地面积由市土地局提供。

Note：Data of cultivated area of 1995 and 1996 are provided by Municipal Land Bureau.

附1-24 农 业 生 产 条 件
PRODUCTIVE CONDITIONS OF AGRICULTURE

年 份 Year	农用机械总动力 (万千瓦) Total Power of Agricultural Machinery (10000kw)	农用大中型拖拉机 (台) Large Medium Tractors (unit)	小型拖拉机 (台) Mini-Tractors (unit)	灌溉面积 (千公顷) Irrigated Area (1000 hectare)	化肥施用量 (万吨) Consumption of Chemical Fertilizers (10000 tons)	农村用电量 (万千瓦小时) Rural Electricity Consumption (10000 kwh)	农村居民家庭每户生产性固定资产 (元) Productive Fixed Assets Per Rural Households (yuan)	每公顷面积产量(公斤) Yield Per Hectare(kg) 粮食 Grain	棉花 Cotton	油料 Oilbearing Crops
1978	189.4	5568	23412	341.7	1.2	58802	5	3315	255	788
1979	212.2	6496	24724	340.8	1.1	59531	6.5	3090	278	855
1980	234.6	7705	24952	340.3	1.2	76753	8	3390	443	1118
1981	244.8	8284	23465	341.3	1.1	91843	10.9	3413	338	810
1982	242.2	9032	22843	339.3	1.2	96960	22.3	3518	503	953
1983	262.1	9855	22652	343.3	1.2	104608	95.3	3803	593	1065
1984	291.3	10859	26563	342.7	1.1	119287	163	4155	900	1500
1985	320.4	11319	35051	338.4	8.2	126830	394.3	4298	848	1928
1986	345.5	11664	37023	337.9	9.1	180640	419.2	4335	735	1530
1987	388.4	12170	37319	337.9	10	159450	444	4590	908	2085
1988	399.7	12596	45013	338.1	10.6	163986	549.7	4800	810	2055
1989	423.9	12344	47546	338.4	11.8	128414	543.3	4950	960	2220
1990	416.2	12844	47020	335.1	14.4	122711	595.6	5460	1035	2565
1991	384.8	12906	44610	328.7	14.4	111347	700.4	5787	885	2685
1992	399.8	12752	44525	331.1	14.4	143963	844.9	5907	1051	2760
1993	450.5	12701	44200	314.7	14.9	169911	951.6	6236	1043	3009
1994	459.2	12475	44500	323.4	19.8	172042	2194.6	6420	910	3051
1995	468.1	12228	42100	292.4	18.8	201731	2776.5	5985	825	2794
1996	468.4	12272	38200	301.9	18.9	275871	2394.2	5659	924	2741
1997	433.2	12088	30000	323.3	19.7	301655	2818.9	5594	1040	2736
1998	415.5	12032	30000	323.7	19.3	290859	3411.8	5660.6	854.4	2941.4

注：1.化肥施用量为折纯量。

2.农村居民家庭每户生产性固定资产为抽样调查数。

a) Consumption of chemical fertilizers are those converted into pure.

b) Data of productive fixed assets per rural household refers to those from sample survey.

附1-25 农林牧渔业总产值和指数

GROSS OUTPUT VALUE OF FARMING,FORESTRY,ANIMAL HUSBANDRY FISHERY AND THEIR INDEX

年 份 Year	农林牧渔业总产值 (亿元) Gross Output Value of Farming,Forestry, Animal Husbandry and Fishery (100 million yuan)	农 业 Farming	林 业 Forestry	牧 业 Animal Husbandry	渔 业 Fishery	农林牧渔业总产值指数 (1978=100) Index of Gross Output Value of FFAF (1978=100)	农 业 Farming	林 业 Forestry	牧 业 Animal Husbandry	渔 业 Fishery
1978	11.5	8.9	0.2	2.4	0.01	100	100	100	100	100
1979	12.3	8.8	0.2	3.3	0.02	99.1	95.8	87.5	108.5	200
1980	14.2	9.7	0.5	3.9	0.05	101.2	92.9	137.5	122	200
1981--1985	**98.2**	**63**	**4.2**	**30.1**	**0.8**					
1981	14.9	10.1	0.65	4.1	0.05	100.6	92.1	137.5	120.7	200
1982	16.7	11.2	0.7	4.7	0.05	108.5	96.3	137.5	140.2	200
1983	19.4	12.5	0.8	6	0.1	123.6	107.1	150	168.3	400
1984	22.2	14.4	0.9	6.7	0.2	137.6	120	150	182.9	600
1985	25.9	16.1	0.8	8.6	0.4	146.4	126.3	137.5	198.8	1200
1986--1990	**242.4**	**138.8**	**4.1**	**91.6**	**7.9**					
1986	28.1	17.2	0.8	9.4	0.7	147	125	125	202.4	1464.4
1987	34.4	20.3	0.8	12.3	1	160	134.2	137.5	224.4	2185.4
1988	52.6	31.4	0.9	18.6	1.7	179.4	140.8	125	278	2907.4
1989	60.4	34.2	0.7	23.3	2.2	198.2	151.3	112.5	324.4	3236.8
1990	70.2	39.0	0.9	28	2.3	210.3	154.2	125	348.8	3622.8
1991--1995	**567.9**	**291**	**11.2**	**244.6**	**21.1**					
1991	76.4	39.5	1.5	32.8	2.6	229.1	164.6	162.5	395.1	4211.4
1992	84.5	43.2	1.6	36.3	3.4	244.5	172.5	150	431.7	5092.8
1993	100.4	51.1	2.3	42.7	4.3	257.3	183.3	162.5	443.9	5887.7
1994	144.3	72.5	3.1	64	4.7	276.7	193.8	187.5	487.8	6131.4
1995	164.4	86.8	2.7	68.8	6.1	273.9	195.4	200	462.2	7500.8
1996	168.9	89.2	2.8	71.1	5.8	271.5	190	212.5	473.2	7000
1997	170.9	87	2.9	74.8	6.2	273.8	199.7	226.9	466.2	6522.4
1998	176.6	89.2	3.2	76.6	7.6	283	201.5	202.3	484.4	7374

注：绝对数按现价计算，指数按可比价计算。

Note：Value are calculated at current prices and index are calculated at constant prices.

附1-26 主要农业产品产量
OUTPUT OF MAJOR AGRICULTURAL PRODUCTS

年 份 Year	粮 食 (万吨) Grain (10000 tons)	# 谷物 Cereal	棉 花 (万吨) Cotton (10000 tons)	油 料 (万吨) Oilbearing Crops (10000 tons)	猪牛羊肉 (万吨) Pork,Beef and Mutton (10000 tons)	禽 蛋 (万吨) Poultry Eggs (10000 tons)	水产品 (万吨) Aquatic Products (10000 tons)	大牲畜年底头数 (万头) Large Animals (year-end) (10000 heads)	# 役畜 Draught Animals	猪年底头数 (万头) Hogs (year-end) (10000 heads)
1978	186	180.4	0.3	2.6	11.9	0.5	0.2	30.4	21.5	248.3
1979	172.8	168.4	0.1	2.6	13.2	1	0.3	29.2	20.4	246.7
1980	186	182.2	0.1	3.1	15.1	3.4	0.4	27.9	19.3	232.5
1981--1985	**1004.8**	**984.1**	**1.4**	**13.1**	**70.7**	**44.3**	**4**	**119.5**	**89.7**	**927**
1981	180.7	177.7	0.1	2.2	14.3	3.7	0.4	26.3	19.2	210.9
1982	185.5	182.5	0.1	2.3	14.1	5.4	0.4	24.9	18.2	206.4
1983	201.5	198.3	0.2	2.1	14.9	8.9	0.6	24.3	18.1	190.3
1984	217.4	211.5	0.6	2.6	13.9	12.2	1	22.8	17.6	161.8
1985	219.7	214.1	0.4	3.9	13.5	14.1	1.6	21.2	16.6	157.6
1986--1990	**1181.9**	**1154.1**	**1.4**	**15.2**	**77.3**	**103.8**	**18.8**	**115.2**	**82.7**	**805**
1986	216.5	211.2	0.2	3	13.3	14.7	2.2	21.9	16.6	145.6
1987	227	220.9	0.3	3.3	13	16.8	3	23.1	16.9	120.4
1988	234.6	229.2	0.3	3	13.4	21.8	3.9	23.1	16.3	145.3
1989	239.2	233.7	0.3	2.8	17.2	24.7	4.6	23.8	16.6	187.7
1990	264.6	259.1	0.3	3.1	20.4	25.8	5.1	23.3	16.3	206
1991--1995	**1381.6**	**1349.3**	**1.9**	**17.6**	**138**	**139.3**	**34.7**	**130.6**	**61.3**	**1276.5**
1991	279.7	274.7	0.3	3.3	24.8	25	5.6	27.9	15	241.7
1992	281.9	276.7	0.5	3.4	27.3	26.5	6.4	26.9	13.6	269.1
1993	284.1	278.2	0.4	3.8	28.2	28.1	7	26.2	12.8	252.2
1994	249.2	267	0.4	3.8	30.7	31.2	7.6	26.7	10.9	260.1
1995	259.8	252.7	0.3	3.3	27	28.5	8.1	22.9	9	253.4
1996	237.4	231.8	0.3	3	27.6	24.7	7.8	20.5	7.4	240
1997	237.5	232.3	0.2	2.7	27.9	23.8	7.7	19.7	6	241
1998	239.2	234	0.2	2.8	31.2	17.9	7.6	18.5	5.3	254.5

附1-27 每一农林牧渔业从业者农业生产量
PRODUCTION VOLUME PER EMPLOYEE OF FARMING,FORESTRY, ANIMAL HUSBANDRY AND FISHERY

年份 Year	农林牧渔业总产值 (元) Gross Output Value of Farming,Forestry, Animal Husbandry and Fishery (yuan)	粮食 (公斤) Grain (kg)	#谷物 Cereal	棉花 (公斤) Cotton (kg)	油料 (公斤) Oilbearing Crops (kg)	猪牛羊肉 (公斤) Pork,Beef and Mutton (kg)	禽蛋 (公斤) Poultry Eggs (kg)	水产品 (公斤) Aquatic Products (kg)
1978	977.9	1580.1	1529.3	2.9	22.2	101.1	4.6	1.5
1979	1066.7	1496.2	1458.3	0.6	22.2	114	8.5	2.4
1980	1248.9	1641.7	1608.1	0.8	27.3	133.2	29.6	3.6
1981	1318.8	1604.4	1577.7	0.6	19.8	127.1	32.7	3.8
1982	1512.3	1684.6	1657.5	0.9	20.7	128.3	51.1	3.4
1983	1729.1	1795.8	1767.1	1.8	18.3	132.6	79.2	4.9
1984	2146.4	2150	2092.4	5.6	26.2	137.5	120.9	10
1985	2823.9	2432.5	2370.5	4.8	43.6	149.3	156.1	17.6
1986	3228.8	2514.2	2453.3	2.5	35.4	155	170.6	25.6
1987	3995.3	2683.3	2610.9	3.1	38.7	153.1	198.4	35.5
1988	6415.3	2900	2833.6	3.4	37	166	269.1	48.2
1989	7146.3	2868.5	2801.6	3.1	34.1	205.8	296.3	55.2
1990	8400	3207.5	3140.5	4.2	37.5	247	312.4	61.9
1991	9402.2	3483.3	3421	4.3	40.9	309.1	311.5	69.4
1992	11166.2	3779.2	3708.9	6.5	45.6	366.5	355.1	86
1993	13848.3	3917.4	3837.8	5.9	52.2	389.1	387.7	96.9
1994	21004.4	4019.6	3886.2	5.4	55.2	447.4	453.8	111.1
1995	25099.2	3965.8	3858.3	4.2	50.2	412	435.7	122.9
1996	25232.6	3545.7	3465.4	3.8	44	411.6	368.8	117
1997	26152	3634.8	3556.1	3.4	41.8	426.8	363.9	117.3
1998	26076	3532.4	3454	2.7	41.9	460.8	264	129.1

附1-28 工 业 总 产 值
GROSS OUTPUT VALUE OF INDUSTRY

单位：亿元 (100 million yuan)

年 份 Year	工业总产值 Gross Output Value	# 国有工业 State-owned	# 集体工业 Collective-owned	# 乡及乡以上 at Township Level and above	轻工业 Light Industry	重工业 Heavy Industry	# 大中型工业 Large and Medium Industry
1984	276.2	217.27	54.14	276.2	117.99	158.22	178.66
1985	324.19	248.48	69.43	324.19	135.75	188.44	213.73
1986--1990	**2618.45**	**1491.4**	**516.39**	**2521.45**	**1070.73**	**1450.73**	**1741.65**
1986	344.95	268.2	68.8	344.95	144.34	200.61	237.43
1987	399.09	305.99	81.08	399.09	164.8	234.29	280.16
1988	508.69		104.06	508.69	218.16	290.53	354.45
1989	622.37	450.88	134.46	622.37	272.66	349.71	421.68
1990	743.35	466.33	127.99	646.35	270.77	375.59	447.93
1991--1995	**6866.31**	**3737.35**	**1139.43**	**5862.75**	**1952.32**	**3910.41**	**3799.15**
1991	880.79	527.78	146.53	757.05	309.08	447.96	526.02
1992	1085.37	627.84	170.07	915.5	326.31	589.19	625.27
1993	1513.59	797.13	227.78	1242.56	385.44	857.12	796.27
1994	1721.13	906.56	243.61	1456.85	460.06	996.79	915.45
1995	1665.43	878.04	351.44	1490.79	471.43	1019.35	936.14
1996	1853.34	887	277.38	1632.17	522.43	1109.74	987.48
1997	1963.83	960.04	179.76	1744.98	554.07	1190.91	958.61
1998	2027.02	863.46	301.14	1991.96	612.02	1379.94	1084.25

注：总产值按现价计算，乡及乡以上工业总产值从1998年开始调整为不含个体工业企业口径。（以下乡及乡以上口径变化与此相同）

Note：Gross output value is calculated at current prices,that at township level and above changed to that of enterprises except individual industry from 1998. (the followings have the same change)

附1-29 工业总产值指数(1978=100)
INDEX OF GROSS OUTPUT VALUE OF INDUSTRY(1978=100)

年 份 Year	工业总产值 Gross Output Value	# 国有工业 State-owned	# 集体工业 Collective-owned	# 乡及乡以上 at Township Level and above	轻工业 Light Industry	重工业 Heavy Industry	# 大中型工业 Large and Medium Industry
1978	100	100	100	100	100	100	100
1979	110.5	110.1	112.1	121.3	113.1	109.1	110.9
1980	121.3	118.6	134.3	122	134.9	113.9	118.5
1981--1985							
1981	112.1	119.5	139.8	123.3	154.5	106.4	121.2
1982	118.4	125.9	147.9	130.2	159.6	114.5	134.7
1983	129.7	136.3	170.4	142.7	171.9	127.2	151.4
1984	145.9	148.7	204.2	160.4	188.5	146.0	175.3
1985	159.2	158.4	240.2	175.1	204.7	159.9	199.1
1986--1990							
1986	166.6	167.0	242.4	183.2	214.9	166.9	212.1
1987	184.9	182.6	278.0	203.4	233.5	188.4	239.0
1988	216.6	207.0	337.9	238.2	280.5	216.3	274.8
1989	232.2	215.7	373.2	255.3	301.2	231.6	286.4
1990	257	215.7	396.3	268.3	312.2	245.9	297.7
1991--1995							
1991	398.1	230.3	447.2	299.1	340.9	278.3	329.7
1992	454.8	252.2	514.5	341.8	353.8	338.2	365.1
1993	516.1	277.9	651.4	413.8	418.4	415.0	381.0
1994	532.2	269.0	657.1	444.6	447.8	446.9	393.3
1995	569.5	290.4	665.9	494.1	432.3	533.6	472.6
1996	624.7	290.6	771.5	512.1	443.3	559.4	470.0
1997	694	325.9	485.9	574.1	487.0	628.5	442.3
1998	819.4	353.2	475.7	679.7	497.7	792.6	633.2

注：指数按可比价计算。

Note：Index are calculated at constant prices.(the following table is the same)

附1-30 工业总产值指数(上年=100)
INDEX OF GROSS OUTPUT VALUE OF INDUSTRY(PRECEDING YEAR=100)

年 份 Year	工 业 总 产 值 Gross Output Value	# 国有工业 State-owned	# 集体工业 Collective-owned	# 乡及乡以上 at Township Level and above			
					轻 工 业 Light Industry	重 工 业 Heavy Industry	# 大中型工业 Large and Medium Industry
1978	111.5	114.5	112.5	114.2	110.8	116.1	100.0
1979	111.2	110.1	112.1	110.5	113.1	109.1	110.9
1980	110.4	107.7	119.7	109.8	119.3	104.5	106.9
1981--1985							
1981	101.8	100.8	104.2	101.7	114.5	93.4	102.7
1982	106.1	105.4	105.8	105.6	103.3	107.6	111.2
1983	111.0	108.3	115.2	109.6	107.7	111.2	112.4
1984	113.8	109.1	119.9	112.4	109.6	114.7	115.7
1985	110.8	106.5	117.6	109.2	108.6	109.6	113.6
1986--1990							
1986	105.9	105.5	100.9	104.6	104.9	104.4	106.5
1987	113.4	109.3	114.7	111	108.7	112.8	112.7
1988	121.1	113.3	121.6	117.1	120.1	114.8	114.9
1989	109.0	104.2	110.4	107.2	107.4	107.1	104.2
1990	106.1	100.0	106.2	105.1	103.7	106.2	104.0
1991--1995							
1991	113.5	106.8	112.9	111.5	109.2	113.2	110.7
1992	118.0	109.5	115.0	114.3	103.8	121.5	110.7
1993	122.3	110.2	126.6	121.1	118.3	122.7	104.4
1994	104.2	96.8	100.9	107.4	107.0	107.7	103.2
1995	107.0	107.9	101.3	111.1	96.5	119.4	120.2
1996	109.7	103.8	126.1	109.2	109.7	109.7	102.5
1997	111.1	112.1	63	112.1	109.9	112.4	94.1
1998	118.1	108.4	97.9	118.4	102.2	126.1	142.4

附1-31 独立核算工业企业主要指标

MAIN INDICATORS FOR INDUSTRIAL ENTERPRISES WITH INDEPENDENT ACCOUNTING SYSTEM

年份 Year	平均职工人数(万人) Average Number of Staff and Workers (10000 persons)	总产值(现行价格)(万元) Gross Output Value (at current prices (10000 yuan)	固定资产原价(万元) Original Value of Fixed Assets (10000 yuan)	产品销售收入(万元) Sales Revenue (10000 yuan)	利税总额(万元) Total Pre-tax Profits (10000 yuan)	国有工业 State-owned				
						平均职工人数(万人) Average Number of Staff and Workers (10000 persons)	总产值(现行价格)(万元) Gross Output Value (at current prices (10000 yuan)	固定资产原价(万元) Original Value of Fixed Assets (10000 yuan)	产品销售收入(万元) Sales Revenue (10000 yuan)	利税总额(万元) Total Pre-tax Profits (10000 yuan)
1978	114.79	1654593	1305271	1098279		89	1397086	1211739	919313	435095
1979	116.79	1843056	1371335	1186497		92.3	1543621	1262408	984888	
1980	140.91	2061664	1495083	1987967	604177	95.3	1694298	1366890	1647908	520978
1981--1985		**12511777**	**9642045**	**12561630**	**3383077**		**9940322**	**8614039**	**10117128**	**2852798**
1981	152.9	2105591	1622035	2054862	599452	103.7	1716072	1474519	1693086	518716
1982	158.7	2205469	1750727	2183458	604372	107.6	1794192	1581902	1796342	521452
1983	161.98	2389253	1886857	2408893	642437	109.3	1918673	1693586	1961803	545140
1984	165.5	2702857	2045344	2728866	707360	109.4	2117273	1812660	2179349	589607
1985	165.63	3108607	2337082	3175551	829456	110.1	2394112	2051372	2486548	677883
1986--1990		**24483553**	**17321757**	**24054442**	**4825016**		**18108076**	**14798804**	**18384654**	**3925489**
1986	169.85	3365481	2627346	3385055	813979	111.5	2601751	2281006	2659067	676895
1987	170.52	3875977	3008917	3935004	885303	112.6	2970928	2604582	3065446	732447
1988	170.54	4956478	3412765	5032042	1081370	112.8	3695388	2949027	3835082	882479
1989		6026646	3890267	5597829	1087017		4352862	3294244	4258859	885038
1990	173.46	6258971	4382462	6104512	957347	115.4	4487147	3669945	4566200	748630
1991--1995		**57607603**	**44341698**	**57731437**	**8051832**		**35547109**	**35600600**	**37861701**	**5876833**
1991	172.39	7302060	5052285	7271529	1106009	112.2	5080426	4210383	5274088	837566
1992	175.48	8600195	5754181	8526860	1347058	116.3	5834134	4757957	6054470	1027279
1993	167.9	11666047	9986886	12822058	1811556	114.6	7598865	8471018	8977254	1379167
1994	179.5	15536585	9648050	13207344	1857476	109.9	8599364	7493956	7815491	1224709
1995	176.16	14502716	13900296	15903646	1929733	107.3	8434320	10667286	9740398	1408112
1996	166.63	15222854	16319878	15801389	1225314	97.7	8366714	12273744	9303959	762024
1997	157.52	17161951	18503218	17070867	1405499	91.2	9355501	14106270	9570024	878170
1998	167.11	19886587	22213387	20345380	1617338	70.25	8615543	13621321	9532486	823114

注：利税总额包括增值税。

Note：Total pre-tax profits included added value tax.

附1-32 独立核算工业企业效益指标

BENEFICIAL INDICATORS FOR INDUSTRIAL ENTERPRISES WITH INDEPENDENT ACCOUNTING SYSTEM

年份 Year	百元固定资产实现利税 (元) Pre-tax Profits/Fixed Assets (yuan)	资金利税率 (%) Pre-tax Profits/Total Assets (%)	产值利税率 (%) Pre-tax Profits/Gross Output Value (%)	百元销售收入实现利润 (元) After-tax Profits/Sales Revenue (yuan)	增加值劳动生产率 (元/人) Labor Productivity at Value Added (yuan/person)	国有工业 State-owned				
						百元固定资产实现利税(元) Pre-tax Profits/Fixed Assets (yuan)	资金利税率 (%) Pre-tax Profits/Total Assets (%)	产值利税率 (%) Pre-tax Profits/Gross Output Value (%)	百元销售收入实现利润(元) After-tax Profits/Sales Revenue (yuan)	增加值劳动生产率 (元/人) Labor Productivity at Value Added (yuan/person)
1978				33.76		35.91		31.14	34.71	
1979				34.92					36.24	
1980	40.42	38.5	29.31	22.79		38.11	38	20.75	23.65	
1981	36.96	34.7	28.47	21.45		35.18	34.4	30.23	22.53	
1982	34.52	32.6	27.4	20.15		32.96	32.5	29.06	21.16	
1983	34.05	34.8	26.89	19.48		32.19	34.7	28.41	20.27	
1984	34.58	35.3	26.17	18.51		32.53	35.33	27.85	19.24	
1985	35.49	35.47	26.68	17.3		33.05	35.34	28.31	17.68	
1986	30.98	28.13	24.19	15.48		29.68	30.79	26.02	16.11	
1987	29.42	29.98	22.84	14.5		28.12	28.85	24.65	15.21	
1988	31.69		21.82	13.94		29.92	30.38	23.88	14.64	
1989	27.94	25.03	18.04	11.4		26.87	25.95	20.33	11.79	
1990	21.84	19.21	15.3	8.02		20.4	19.33	16.68	7.72	
1991	21.89	19.5	15.15	8.02		19.89	19.07	16.49	7.7	
1992	23.41	16.46	15.66	8.77		21.59	16.98	17.61	8.92	
1993	18.14	12.37	15.53	8.54	24363	16.28	12.1	18.15	9.26	20197
1994	19.25	13.05	11.96	7.28	31294	16.34	12.78	14.24	7.73	25144
1995	13.89	9.92	13.31	5.36	26068	13.2	10.95	16.7	6.32	27241
1996	9.3	5.41	8.05	2.09	23445	7.88	5.19	9.11	1.82	19571
1997	9.36	5.44	8.19	2.37	28220	7.8	5.39	9.39	2.40	27534
1998	9.15	6.64	8.13	2.38	35033	7.69	5.10	9.55	2.31	36926

注：增加值劳动生产率按工业增加值计算。

Note：Labor productivity at value added is calculated by value added of industry.

附1-33 工业产品产量
OUTPUT OF INDUSTRIAL PRODUCTS

年 份 Year	布 (万米) Cloth (10000 m)	纱 (万吨) Yarn (10000 m)	机制纸及纸板 (万吨) Machine-made Paper and Paperboard (10000 tons)	合成洗涤剂 (万吨) Synthetic Detergents (10000 tons)	饮料酒 (万吨) Soft Drinking (10000 tons)	家用电冰箱 (万台) Household Refrige-rators (10000)	家用洗衣机 (万台) Household Washing Machines (10000)	电视机 (万台) TV Sets (10000)	# 彩色 Color TV Sets
1978	25436	5.35	12.10	2.07	8.44			3.87	0.02
1979	27297	5.78	13.90	2.23	9.86	2.01	0.70	12.52	0.30
1980	28940	6.45	14.00	2.43	11.62	2.58	5.83	27.97	1.16
1981--1985	**142080**	**34.54**	**86.90**	**18.94**	**87.27**	**41.55**	**211.73**	**262.28**	**79.47**
1981	28635	6.83	14.50	2.38	13.35	3.10	18.70	43.01	7.23
1982	29758	6.89	15.80	2.95	14.88	4.46	32.12	43.39	8.00
1983	30068	6.90	17.10	3.69	17.44	6.36	44.30	41.38	10.26
1984	27621	7.05	18.90	4.79	20.31	10.30	51.43	59.13	15.52
1985	25998	6.87	20.60	5.13	21.29	17.33	65.18	75.37	38.46
1986--1990	**153032**	**38.75**	**120.49**	**29.61**	**131.42**	**96.43**	**237.35**	**410.45**	**248.84**
1986	27503	7.37	21.90	5.75	21.51	18.11	70.00	67.51	34.20
1987	29738	7.71	24.10	5.43	22.72	19.38	57.69	85.13	48.45
1988	32262	8.13	23.30	5.66	23.93	23.57	58.03	92.88	57.91
1989	32271	7.87	25.78	6.37	28.70	24.70	31.90	88.86	57.55
1990	31258	7.67	25.41	6.40	34.56	10.67	19.73	76.07	50.73
1991--1995	**133994**	**38.61**	**116.45**	**38.15**	**347.26**	**27.02**	**81.69**	**369.89**	**299.38**
1991	31497	7.66	27.20	5.65	43.81	7.05	21.91	91.55	58.23
1992	29717	8.01	22.63	6.55	56.59	9.13	14.70	64.05	64.05
1993	26816	8.72	19.05	7.95	72.61	4.20	14.11	56.90	56.90
1994	21440	6.87	21.02	7.33	83.05	6.64	20.02	90.04	70.04
1995	24524	7.35	26.55	10.67	91.20		10.95	67.35	50.16
1996	22585	6.75	15.25	9.31	102.22	6.27	13.14	37.20	31.24
1997	25185	6.42	18.12	9.49	…	…	11.95	40.82	38.19
1998	21299	6.13	13.10	6.28		0.25	6.37	12.06	11.13

年 份 Year	原煤 (万吨) Coal (10000 tons)	发电量 (万千瓦时) Electricity (10000 kwh)	钢 (万吨) Steel (10000 tons)	成品钢材 (万吨) Rolled-steel (10000 tons)	水泥 (万吨) Cement (10000 tons)	硫酸 (万吨) Sulphuric Acid (10000 tons)	烧碱 (万吨) Caustic Soda (10000 tons)	化肥 (万吨) Chemical Fertilizer (10000 tons)	化学农药 (万吨) Chemical Pesticide
1978	818.7	990750	191.0	116.8	191.5	14.95	5.47	10.70	1.28
1979	811.1	1042870	196.5	137.5	196.9	14.05	6.68	12.01	1.08
1980	791.0	1065060	200.9	152.1	217.4	13.01	8.13	12.41	0.93
1981--1985	**4269.1**	**5101356**	**1114.2**	**907.9**	**1355.7**	**61.85**	**42.56**	**57.68**	**2.32**
1981	788.7	993071	190.3	149.5	225.7	13.02	7.81	12.19	0.76
1982	811.3	1003446	200.4	159.4	249.1	12.64	8.24	12.00	0.60
1983	840.5	1028826	214.1	177.9	270.8	15.20	8.41	13.04	0.41
1984	884.3	1038842	241.7	200.1	291.6	13.24	8.92	12.36	0.42
1985	944.3	1037171	267.7	221.0	318.5	7.75	9.18	8.09	0.13
1986--1990	**4745.3**	**5656282**	**1837.8**	**1556.7**	**1649.3**	**50.49**	**51.89**	**45.77**	**0.10**
1986	917.2	1043208	303.6	255.5	310.5	7.87	9.25	8.26	0.04
1987	899.8	1057493	335.5	283.4	319.6	11.86	9.61	9.02	
1988	906.0	1110758	369.0	314.9	334.3	13.07	11.04	9.53	0.02
1989	1016.8	1191269	386.0	327.9	345.9	10.64	11.26	9.74	0.02
1990	1005.5	1253554	443.7	375.0	339.0	7.05	10.73	9.22	0.02
1991--1995	**4851.0**	**6772732**	**3411.0**	**2613.9**	**2364.4**	**38.57**	**55.69**	**46.41**	**0.43**
1991	996.5	1318000	499.7	402.9	377.6	7.12	11.00	6.94	0.05
1992	1015.2	1423000	575.0	438.3	403.0	8.23	11.38	9.70	0.11
1993	835.4	1410900	702.7	525.3	477.9	3.96	11.23	9.61	0.14
1994	1008.5	1298718	828.7	617.6	531.7	9.29	10.76	9.57	0.10
1995	995.4	1322114	804.9	629.8	574.2	9.97	11.32	10.59	0.03
1996	1013.7	1415555	794.5	654.3	666.0	10.85		12.72	0.14
1997	1011.7	1464302	801.7	652.4	701.0	9.26	11.36	11.92	
1998	989.5	1566621	803.2	676.1	762.0	7.75	10.28	11.25	

附1-34 独立核算建筑业企业基本情况

BASIC STATISTICS FOR CONSTRUCTION ENTERPRISES WITH INDEPENDENT ALLOUNTING SYSTEM

年份 Year	建筑施工企业单位数(个) Construction Enterprises (unit)	建筑施工企业从业人员(万人) Employee (10000 persons)	建筑施工企业总产值(亿元) Gross Output Value (100 million yuan)	建筑施工企业全员劳动生产率(元/人) Overall Labor Productivity (yuan/person)	建筑施工企业工程优良品率(%) Rate of High Quality Projects (%)	建筑施工企业利润总额(万元) Total Profits (10000 yuan)
1978	64	25.4	10.5	4397	72.9	7017
1979	70	26.4	12.7	4680	67.9	9256
1980	71	27.8	14.7	5249	65.5	14543
1981	71	27	14.5	5264	65.9	15778
1982	91	30.7	17.3	5404	81.2	17169
1983	116	37.2	22.6	6128	68.3	25489
1984	2765	53	33.4	6345	45.3	32342
1985	2549	62.8	43.9	7197	31.8	39277
1986	2361	61.3	51.3	8702	56.3	33084
1987	2292	64.4	67	10832	61.3	41202
1988	1659	64.2	81.6	12992	58.2	38679
1989	1545	60	89	14539	53.8	38189
1990	994	60.2	94.7	16340	54.5	33762
1991	922	60.3	99.6	17031	47.7	27690
1992	976	62.7	122.6	19786	25	30984
1993	1098	75.9	210.7	27739	21.9	61432
1994	1259	73.4	301.5	41099	26.7	94385
1995	1332	82.6	370.7	44852	23.3	77857
1996	1292	82.5	468.1	56750	17.5	88896
1997	1297	80.3	519.2	64633	19.8	104320
1998	1482	75.6	624.7	73644	21.4	123744

注：1994年以后期末职工人数为计算劳产率的年平均人数；1996年以后全部指标不包括建筑业活动单位及四级以下施工企业。

Note: Data of number of staff and workers after 1994 refers to annual average number for calculating labor productivity; indicators after 1996 exclude construction units and enterprises below fourth grade.

附1-35 运输邮电业基本情况
TRANSPORTATON,POSTS AND TELECOMMUNICATIONS

年 份 Year	铁路里程 (公里) Railway Operating Length (km)	公路里程 (公里) Highway Operating Length (km)	客运量 (万人) Passenger Traffic (10000 persons)	#铁 路 Railway	#公 路 Highway	# 民 航 Civil Aviation	货运量 (万吨) Freight Traffic	# 铁 路 Railway	# 公 路 Highway
1978	699	6562		2264		46.5	7394.4	3370	4023
1979	700	7278		2504		53.2	7763.7	3485	4277
1980	707	7339		2762		58.4	7571	3356	4213
1981--1985				**17688**		**544**	**37500.1**	**15425**	**22061**
1981	858	7427		2982		70.7	6895.1	3046	3847
1982	858	7543		3205		78.8	7379.2	3065	4312
1983	860	2906		3546		78.3	7639.6	3152	4485
1984	864	8131		3877		169.1	7897.2	3133	4761
1985	876	8487		4078		147.1	7689	3029	4656
1986--1990			**38861.7**	**21290**	**16560**	**1011.7**	**74886**	**15522**	**59324**
1986	876	8849	7336.7	4106	3059	171.7	7994.3	3030	4958
1987	876	8956	7763.4	4418	3117	228.4	7985	3125	4852
1988	876	9124	8491.4	4782	3460	249.4	7598.1	3168	4421
1989	876	9218	7834.1	4214	3434	186.1	24918.8	3144	21767
1990	876	9648	7436.1	3770	3490	176.1	26389.8	3055	23326
1991--1995			**41315.9**	**21787**	**17370**	**2158.9**	**118991.4**	**15062**	**103852**
1991	876	10259	7649.2	4036	3378	235.2	26391.4	3051	23326
1992	875	10827	8158	4196	3593	369	26733.2	2983	23739
1993	875	11242	6887.2	4374	2141	372.2	3063.7	3048	26730
1994	875	11532	8537.5	3993	4008	536.5	30725.1	3006	27700
1995	875	11532	10084	5188	4250	646	32078	2974	29087
1996	922	11682	9798.9	4736	4395	668	32905.6	2851	29960
1997	923.5	12306	10383.8	4828.8	4902	653	32349.7	2883	29360
1998	923.5	12498	12419.4	4953.3	6704	762.1	30126.5	2563	27490

附1-35 续表1 continued

年 份 Year	# 民 航 Civil Aviation	旅 客 周转量 (万人公里) Passenger-Kilometers (10000 passenger-km)	# 铁 路 Railway	# 公路 Highway	# 民航 Civil Aviation	货 物 周转量 (万吨公里) Freight Ton-Kilometers (10000 ton-km)	# 铁 路 Railway	# 公 路 Highway	# 民 航 Civil Aviation
1978	1.4			59367				92247	
1979	1.7			64033				97616	
1980	2			73692				93899	
1981--1985	**14.1**							**437318**	
1981	2.1			81879				93254	
1982	2.2			90092				106767	24173
1983	2.6			103742				110118	26713
1984	3.2			113871				113871	20896
1985	4	1187072	473328	109184	604560	2128868	1992247	109184	27437
1986--1990	**40**	**6333894**	**2608550**	**629210**	**3076133**	**13732367**	**1007906**	**2496086**	**191715**
1986	6.3	1133620	496288	119065	518267	2579647	2133836	405645	28281
1987	8	1281763	534720	113735	613308	2802099	2282106	471393	37966
1988	9.1	1503508	588947	141625	772936	2896715	2344684	498391	42612
1989	7.8	1216981	521263	122435	573283	2765660	2179878	546022	38194
1990	8.8	1198022	467332	132350	598339	2688246	2067402	574635	44662
1991--1995	**77.4**	**8690002**	**2645880**	**842807**	**5201313**	**14180124**	**1382191**	**2797933**	**346841**
1991	14.4	1383465	506431	139041	737993	2938658	2230406	642200	65614
1992	11.2	1666810	531574	161735	973501	2799742	2153176	591187	54929
1993	15.7	1656130	551392	127461	977277	2458751	2303265	767790	73216
1994	19.1	1906718	547488	180030	1179199	3107722	2301941	725740	78142
1995	17	2076879	508995	234540	1333343	3231034	2393403	762027	74940
1996	17	2107834	459514	250488	1397832	3174846	2311011	784888	78595
1997	19	2154186	477538	261204	1415444	3127394	2263274	769190	94500
1998	22.4	2419787	505554	304592	1609641	2846652	1952602	783237	110470

附1-35 续表 2 continued

年 份 Year	民用汽车拥有量 (辆) Possession of Civil Motor Vehicles (unit)	# 公路部门 Highway Department	# 私人 Individuals	邮电局所 (处) Post and Telecommunications Offices (unit)	邮电业务总量 (万元) Revenue of Post and Telecommunications (10000 yuan)	市话交换机容量 (万门) City Switchboards Capacity (10000)	电话机拥有量 (部) Possession of Telephones (unit)	城 市 Urban	农 村 Rural
1978	77059			415	9050.6	26.2	87428	75597	11831
1979	89447			418	9986.8	31.5	93012	80365	12647
1980	103826			427	11403.7	35	99104	86057	13047
1981--1985									
1981	116360			427	12781.7	39	107310	94415	12895
1982	130332			437	13986.5	43.3	114908	101163	13745
1983	139756			450	15724	46.4	124907	111048	13859
1984	167028			472	18357.4	53.1	136481	123137	13344
1985	224272			479	22413.3	62.1	151861	138130	13731
1986--1990									
1986	266706			476	25347.7	69.6	178527	163377	15150
1987	272290	5983	7148	478	29282.3	83.8	209294	193865	15929
1988	312174			475	35478.5	101.6	238122	236389	1733
1989	353315	6195	24029	470	43922.3	119.9	277967	276234	1733
1990	384451			479	77205.6	136.2	332946	331188	1758
1991--1995									
1991				484	157417.7	165	394837	393046	1791
1992	341015	5813	48643	494	215768.9	193.9	479937	478024	1913
1993	416047	5298	66883	507	311251.3	226.2	664676	662449	2227
1994	481279	5280	85474	536	418773.9	303.5	1890224		
1995	577214	5237	127568	633	561296.4	369.3	2417207		
1996	614021		351835	681	729022.4	442	2923042		
1997	775946		540564	701	930136.7	546.4	3577825		
1998	890141		697707	728	1290966.5	686.8	5225253		

注：1.公路货运量1988年以前和1993年为交通运输部门数据。

2.铁路是北京市辖范围。

a) Data of freight traffic of highway before 1988 and 1993 were provided by transport department.

b) Railway refers to that within the jurisdiction of Beijing.

附1-36 社会消费品零售额
TOTAL RETAIL SALES OF CONSUMER GOODS

单位：亿元 (100 million yuan)

年 份 Year	社会消费品零售额 Retail Sales of Consumer Goods	按地区分 By Region			按经济类型分 By Ownership				
		市 City	县 County	县以下 Below County Level	国有经济 State-Owned	集体经济 Collective Owned	合营经济 Joint Owned	个体经济 Individuals	其他经济 Others
1978	44.2	34.5	5.3	4.4	37.2	7.0			
1979	52.2	41.6	5.8	4.8	44.2	7.9		0.1	
1980	61.3	49.3	6.6	5.4	49.1	11.8		0.4	
1981--1985	**455.3**	**364.0**	**48.3**	**43.0**	**301.7**	**143.5**	**1.0**	**9.1**	
1981	68.8	55.6	7.3	5.9	48.7	19.2	0.2	0.7	
1982	73.3	58.6	8.1	6.6	51.0	21.2	0.2	0.9	
1983	83.6	66.6	9.3	7.7	56.0	26.1	0.1	1.4	
1984	101.7	81.1	10.4	10.2	67.7	32.1	0.2	1.7	
1985	127.9	102.1	13.2	12.6	78.3	44.9	0.3	4.4	
1986--1990	**1131.8**	**943.0**	**103.4**	**85.4**	**617.7**	**401.1**	**6.4**	**106.7**	
1986	146.5	121.7	12.1	12.7	84.5	51.0	0.4	10.6	
1987	176.6	145.7	16.2	14.7	97.1	64.5	0.6	14.5	
1988	234.3	195.0	21.2	18.1	129.4	84.5	0.6	19.7	
1989	266.7	221.5	25.0	20.2	143.8	92.2	2.6	28.2	
1990	307.7	259.1	28.9	19.7	162.9	108.9	2.2	33.7	
1991--1995	**2813.6**	**2215.9**	**373.6**	**224.1**	**1332.7**	**792.6**	**76.3**	**530.3**	**81.7**
1991	357.8	301.2	33.4	23.2	191.8	122.9	2.6	40.5	
1992	430.0	360.2	41.1	28.7	230.6	139.6	3.3	56.5	
1993	531.8	430.9	60.6	40.3	273.0	162.5	8.1	88.2	
1994	667.0	525.1	90.6	51.3	299.3	171.2	23.1	152.3	21.1
1995	827.0	598.5	147.9	80.6	338.0	196.4	39.2	192.8	60.6
1996	923.7	664.5	95.6	163.6	314.8	217.3	70.5	241.8	79.3
1997	1051.5	808.3	88.2	155.0	368.8	247.9	83.4	236.5	114.9
1998	1195.2	952.5	77.0	165.7	344.8	231.5	114.3	243.0	261.6

年 份 Year	按行业分 By Sector				按类别分 By Category				农业生产资料零售额 Retail Sales of Agricultural Capital Goods	集市贸易成交额 Value of Country Fair Trade
	批发零售贸易业 Wholesale and Retail Sales	餐饮业 Catering	制造业 Manufacturing	其他行业 Others	食品类 Food	衣着类 Clothing	日用品类 Daily Use Articles	燃料类 Fuels		
1978	40.7	1.7	1.2	0.6	18.0	8.9	12.4	1.3	3.6	
1979	47.3	2.1	2.1	0.7	20.4	11.1	15.7	1.5	3.5	0.2
1980	53.5	2.7	3.5	1.6	24.4	12.9	18.8	1.6	3.6	0.7
1981--1985	**381.7**	**1.9**	**4.0**	**17.7**	**174.3**	**82.0**	**161.3**	**10.3**	**27.4**	**8.2**
1981	57.8	3.5	5.1	2.4	27.2	14.1	21.9	1.7	3.9	0.9
1982	61.4	3.7	5.5	2.7	28.9	13.3	24.2	1.7	5.2	1.1
1983	70.4	4.0	6.0	3.2	32.9	15.2	27.9	1.9	5.7	1.3
1984	85.6	4.7	7.8	3.6	38.1	18.0	37.0	2.2	6.4	1.5
1985	106.5	6.0	9.6	5.8	47.2	21.4	50.3	2.8	6.2	3.4
1986--1990	**906.7**	**70.7**	**64.5**	**89.9**	**451.8**	**152.4**	**447.9**	**24.1**	**55.6**	**71.1**
1986	119.3	8.1	8.9	10.2	57.4	21.6	57.1	3.3	7.1	6.4
1987	140.2	10.7	12.0	13.7	72.4	25.6	67.3	3.7	7.6	8.5
1988	186.4	16.1	13.9	17.9	92.0	33.0	93.9	4.1	11.3	14.1
1989	213.1	16.5	15.4	21.7	108.0	31.6	106.3	5.8	14.9	18.4
1990	247.7	19.3	14.3	26.4	122.0	40.6	123.3	7.2	14.6	23.6
1991--1995	**2079.3**	**215.5**	**119.8**	**399.0**	**1095.5**	**418.2**	**1195.0**	**64.9**	**4**	**514.9**
1991	286.2	22.9	16.8	31.9	138.6	47.1	146.6	7.7	17.8	31.0
1992	333.7	30.8	19.4	46.1	165.5	57.2	174.8	10.3	22.2	55.3
1993	393.0	44.6	28.7	65.5	192.0	84.0	241.5	14.3	17.6	83.4
1994	481.5	54.2	25.3	106.0	246.4	109.0	294.6	17.0	12.4	150.1
1995	584.9	63.0	29.6	149.5	353.0	120.9	337.5	15.6	13.4	195.1
1996	657.1	68.4	38.1	160.1	372.0	132.7	401.8	17.2	11.6	250.8
1997	709.4	72.5	56.3	213.3	389.7	140.6	492.2	29.0	9.5	285.3
1998	865.7	81.8	63.8	183.9	347.9	145.5	664.9	36.9	10.5	323.8

注：1993年以前是社会商品零售总额，1993年以后是社会消费品零售总额。

Note：Data before 1993 refers to total retail sales of commodity and data after 1993 refers to total retail sales of consumer goods.

附1-37 北京市对外经济贸易和国际旅游
FOREIGN ECONOMICS,TRADE AND TOURISM

年 份 Year	外贸部门进出口 总额 (万美元) Total Value of Imports and Exports (USD 10000)	# 出口 Exports	签订利用外资协议 项目 (个) Contracts Signed of Foreign Capital Utilization (unit)	# 对外借款 Foreign Loans	# 外商直接投资 Direct Foreign Investment	签订利用外资协议 金额 (万美元) Contracted Foreign Capital (USD10000)	对外借款 Foreign Loans	外商直接投资 Direct Foreign Investment	外商其他投资 Other Foreign Investment
1978	29751	28524							
1979	45036	41757							
1980	66280	59277							
1981--1985	**382296**	**308276**							
1981	70091	63230							
1982	68921	61339							
1983	69621	59009							
1984	76303	62623	55	2	31	13826	1600	11660	566
1985	97360	62075	108	1	83	40788	130	39649	1009
1986--1990	**940420**	**457112**	**853**	**58**	**709**	**171046**	**26952**	**138628**	**5467**
1986	166847	65252	85	2	63	55888	9700	41952	4236
1987	154470	78239	97	6	72	66515	3322	62414	779
1988	198846	99121	193	21	148	18533	4144	14202	187
1989	205162	102336	209	10	185	14252	5731	8372	149
1990	215095	112164	269	19	241	15859	4055	11688	116
1991--1995	**1999096**	**836561**	**10987**	**67**	**10911**	**1699801**	**168840**	**1530412**	**549**
1991	258632	123987	735	8	724	47995	19431	28488	76
1992	320171	152555	2231	23	2208	177274	30079	147195	
1993	420029	137056	3765	13	3752	664911	36987	627924	
1994	469339	195936	2688	13	2675	505300	52000	453300	
1995	530925	227027	1568	10	1552	304321	30344	273505	472
1996	539201	208624	868		868	179029		179029	
1997	557576	246503	798	8	790	171532	3429	168103	
1998	650536	282896	656	5	651	410567	890	409677	

年 份 Year	实际利用外资 金额 (万美元) Foreign Capital Actually Used (USD10000)	对外借款 Foreign Loans	外商直接投资 Direct Foreign Investment	外商其他投资 Other Foreign Invest-ment	对外承包工程和劳务合作 Constructed Projects and Labor Services Cooperation with Foreign Countries 合同数 (份) Contracts (unit)	合同金额 (万美元) Contracted (USD 10000)	完成营业额 (万美元) Fulfiled Value (USD 10000)	旅游外汇收入总额 (万美元) Tourism Foreign Exchange Earnings (USD 10000)
1978								10000
1979								9000
1980								12000
1981--1985								**94000**
1981								12000
1982								13000
1983					9	218.5	837.1	14000
1984					9	2801.5	1843.2	23000
1985					14	852.8	2083.1	32000
1986--1990					**331**	**7733.7**	**5108.9**	**280901**
1986					30	445.3	1535.5	46000
1987	17725.4	7146.6	9534.0	1044.8	37	548.6	697.6	55000
1988	61943.8	11524.4	50277.9	141.5	46	884.9	802.4	67000
1989	49506.8	17491	31845.9	169.9	113	2099.4	1017.5	47195
1990	40641.4	12743.5	27695.5	202.4	105	3755.5	1055.9	65706
1991--1995	**579524.3**	**168401.4**	**410896.0**	**226.9**	**586**	**79267.8**	**48984**	**735519**
1991	36798.1	12303.8	24481.8	12.5	114	3202.2	1896.8	85001
1992	52711.9	17710.8	34984.2	16.9	130	8887.6	3299.6	107286
1993	97619.8	30729.3	66693.0	197.5	117	36854	11442	124128
1994	194740.2	50280.2	144460.0		109	15521	18671	200904
1995	197654.3	57377.3	140277.0		116	15613	12789	218200
1996	225842.3	70552.3	155290.0		116	67688	43057	225200
1997	259161.8	73330.4	159286.4	26545.0	107	35640	29629	224800
1998	286973.4	57194.5	206414.9	23364.0	184	28520	45812	238400

注：进出口总额1986年至1998年为海关口径。

Note: Data of total value of imports and exports refers to customs from 1986 to 1998.

附1-38 教育基本情况
BASIC STATISTICS FOR EDUCATION

年份 Year	在校学生数(万人) Students Enrollment (10000 persons)				升学率(%) Rate of Entering Higher Grade Schools(%)		学龄儿童入学率(%) Enrollment Rate of Children at School-Age (%)	平均一专任教师负担学生数(人) Average Number of Students Instructed by a Professional Teacher(person)		
	合计 Total	高等学校 Institutions of Higher Education	普通中学 Regular Secondary Schools	小学 Primary Schools	初中毕业生 Graduates of Junior Middle Schools	小学毕业生 Graduates of Primary Schools		高等学校 Institutions of Higher Education	普通中学 Regular Secondary Schools	小学 Primary Schools
1978	208.1	4.9	109.5	93.7	79.7	102.6	99	2.4	19.9	20.7
1979	186.1	5.5	83.7	96.9	63	99.6	98.4	2.3	16.1	21.3
1980	173.5	6.4	71.9	95.2	80.3	99.5	98.7	2.6	14.5	21.7
1981	157.5	7.7	59.8	90	57.3	98.8	98.9	3.8	13.4	19.7
1982	144.6	7.2	51.9	85.5	58.6	97	98.9	3.2	12.3	19.5
1983	139.1	8.1	47.2	83.8	60.1	98.9	99	3	11.5	19.6
1984	137.4	9.1	52	76.3	61.2	98.7	99.3	3.3	13.2	18.2
1985	139.6	12	54.2	73.4	72.6	98.3	99.1	3.6	13.9	17.4
1986	156	13	56.5	74.9	77.1	97.8	99.49	3.6	13.9	17.4
1987	157.2	13.6	52.3	77.8	65.1	98.6	99.46	3.7	12.8	16.8
1988	160.3	14.5	46.9	85.1	64.3	98.5	99.5	4	11.4	17.6
1989	166	14.1	43.3	93.5	80.5	99.1	98.97	3.8	11	19.1
1990	168.7	14	40.9	99.6	81.8	99.3	99.47	3.9	10.1	18.6
1991	171.8	13.7	43.2	101.3	86.4	98.8	99.72	3.1	10.2	18
1992	176.2	14	47.7	100.2	88.5	99.6	99.65	4	11.3	17.4
1993	186.3	15.9	53.2	102.2	93.5	98.7	99.88	4.6	12.1	17.4
1994	196.1	17.5	58.4	102.5	86.7	99.4	99.92	4.9	13.1	16.9
1995	202.8	18.2	62.8	100.7	87.3	99.5	99.93	5.0	13.6	16.5
1996	207.9	19	64.9	100.0	88.1	99.3	99.93	5.2	13.7	16.1
1997	207.3	19.6	62.6	97.7	92.3	98.5	99.95	5.4	13.2	15.7
1998	204.7	21.3	61.0	92.0	92.2	98.7	99.96	5.8	12.8	14.9

附1-39 卫生情况和离退休退职人数
HEALTH AND NUMBER OF VCSR AND RRSW

年份 Year	医院数 (个) Hospital (unit)	医生数 (人) Doctors (person)	医院床位数 (万张) Beds (10000)	每千人拥有医生数 (人) Doctors Per 1000 Persons (person)	每千人拥有医院床位 (张) Beds Per 1000 Persons (bed)	离退休、退职人数 (万人) Number of VCSR and RRSW(10000 persons)	国有单位 State-Owned	城镇集体单位 Urban Collective Owned	其他单位 Others	在职职工与离退休退职人员之比 Ratio of Staff and Workers on Their Posts to VCSR and RRSW
1978	389	28435	26432	3.35	3.11					
1979	387	31842	26808	3.66	3.08					
1980	393	34365	28495	3.88	3.22					
1981	406	37886	29783	4.21	3.31					
1982	413	39385	30940	4.29	3.37					
1983	412	41216	32242	4.42	3.46					
1984	423	42112	34602	4.46	3.66					
1985	376	42498	38180	4.44	3.99					
1986	371	43403	40903	4.47	4.21					
1987	398	46007	44407	4.66	4.49					
1988	445	48216	48711	4.82	4.87					
1989	470	49361	51877	4.83	5.08	75.9	58.4	17.3	0.2	5.3
1990	512	50934	55474	4.93	5.37	81.9	64.2	17.5	0.2	5.3
1991	525	52309	58747	5.03	5.65	87.7	70.0	17.6	0.2	5.2
1992	535	53254	59833	5.1	5.73	94.1	75.8	18.1	0.2	5.1
1993	548	53906	62340	5.13	5.93	100.8	82.1	17.9	0.8	4.5
1994	629	53865	64416	5.07	6.07	110.5	86.6	23	0.9	4.3
1995	629	54114	64211	5.06	6	120.7	93.6	25.2	1.9	3.9
1996	405	54091	60997	5.02	6.02	133	103.5	27.1	2.4	3.5
1997	435	54909	61865	5.06	6.06	144.3	113.2	28.6	2.5	3.2
1998	449	51902	63144	4.76	6.13	155.6	123.3	29.5	2.8	2.9

注：1.最后一列以离退休、退职人数为1。

2.按卫生部指标解释，1996年医院数仅指县及县以上医院和其他医院，乡镇卫生院不再做为医院统计。

a) Data of last line are caculated according to number of VCSR and RRSW=1.

b) According to explanatory notes of health department,number of hospitals of 1996 included hospitals at county level and above and other hospitals,township hospitals were not calculated as hospitals any more.

附录2：各类开发区资料

APPENDIX 2：VARIOUS DEVELOPMENT ZONES

附2-1 各 类 开 发 区 基 本 情 况

BASIC STATISTICS FOR DEVELOPMENT ZONES

项目 Item			合计 Total	市属 Of City	区县属 Of Districts and Counties
开发区个数	(个)	Number of Development Zones (unit)	29	2	27
累计完成土地规划面积	(平方公里)	Accumulative Programmed Area (sq.km)	257.41	21.13	236.28
# 工业用地	(平方公里)	For Industrial Use (sq.km)	104.48	8.23	96.25
累计完成征用土地面积	(平方公里)	Accumulative Area of Requisitions Realized (sq.km)	46.94	8.46	38.48
累计"七通一平"土地开发施工面积	(平方公里)	Accumulative Area of Began Seven-through-One-Flat (sq.km)	35.56	7.95	27.61
累计完成"七通一平"土地开发面积	(平方公里)	Accumulative Area of Seven-through-One-Flat Realized (sq.km)	29.99	7.95	22.04
累计招商占用土地面积	(平方公里)	Accumulative Area Spared for Business (sq.km)	18.58	2.19	16.39
# 三资企业占用	(平方公里)	Foreign Funded Enterprises (sq.km)	6.65	1.46	5.19
累计招商个数	(个)	Accumulative Number of Hirer Leaseholder (unit)	1621	314	1307
累计项目总投资	(亿元)	Accumulative Investment (100 million yuan)	709.9	150.8	559.1
累计注册资本	(亿元)	Accumulative Registered Capital (100 million yuan)	364.9	100.5	264.4
# 外方	(亿元)	Foreign Partner (100 million yuan)	229.4	84.9	144.5
累计协议外资金额	(亿美元)	Accumulative Contracted Foreign Capital (USD10^9)	36.2	8.7	27.5
外商累计入资	(亿美元)	Accumulative Foreign Capital Inflow (USD 10^9)	25.4	7.2	18.2

说明：1.累计完成征用土地面积中包括原建成区面积。

2.表内"七通"指：上水、下水、煤气、热力、电力、通讯和道路通；"一平"指：场地自然平整。

3.表内"累计"指自开始至1998年末的累计数。

a) Accumulative requisition area of included original completed area.

b) Seven-through refers to water,drainage,gas,heat,electricity,communications and transportation,and one-flat refers to flat ground.

c) Accumulative data of this table refers to that from the beginning to the end of 1998.

附2-2 各类开发区主要指标完成情况

STATISTICS FOR FULFILLMENT OF MAJOR INDICATORS OF DEVELOPMENT ZONES

项目	Item	1998	1997	1998年为1997年% 1998 as % of 1997
自年初累计完成固定资产投资 (亿元)	Accumulative Investment in Fixed Assets from Year-beginning (100 million yuan)	65.9	59.7	110.0
自年初累计新增固定资产 (亿元)	Accumulative Incremental Fixed Assets from Year-beginning (100 million yuan)	26.3	18.9	139.0
自年初累计房屋建筑施工面积 (万平方米)	Accumulative Floor Space of Buildings under Construction from Year-beginning (10000 sq.m)	390.3	458.7	85.0
自年初累计房屋建筑竣工面积 (万平方米)	Accumulative Floor Space of Buildings Completed from Year-beginning (10000 sq.m)	108.2	64.4	168.0
自年初累计完成不变价增加值 (亿元)	Accumulative Value Added Completed from Year-beginning (at constant prices) (100 million yuan)	214.0	170.8	125.0
自年初累计实现销售收入 (亿元)	Accumulative Sales Revenue Completed from Year-beginning (100 million yuan)	689.0	482.0	143.0
自年初累计实现利润总额 (亿元)	Accumulative Total Profits Completed from Year-beginning (100 million yuan)	19.2	19.3	99.0
自年初累计应缴税金总额 (亿元)	Accumulative Total Taxes Turned Over from Year-beginning (100 million yuan)	27.3	18.4	148.0

附2-3 各类开发区一览表
DEVELOPMENT ZONES LIST

名 称 Name	通 讯 地 址 Address	主要负责人 Chairman	邮 编 Post Code	电 话 Telephone
北京经济技术开发区	北京经济技术开发区万源街4号	依锡群	100176	67881207
北京市王府井地区开发建设办公室	王府井大街99号世纪大厦A608室	刘晓晨	100006	65129999
北京西三旗高新建材城	海淀区德外西三旗东	蒋卫平	100085	82910873
北京市朝阳望京工业区	朝阳区南湖渠东湖大队甲3号	佟克克	100015	64374723
朝阳东部旅游经济开发区	朝阳区农展南路9号	张云翔	100026	65940942
北京新技术产业开发试验区海淀试验区	海淀大街1号	马 林	100080	62569636
北京新技术产业开发试验区丰台园区	丰台科学城富丰路4号	汪 洪	100070	63725608
北京八大处高科技园区	石景山苹果园北路海特花园实兴大厦	韩振北	100041	68863653
北京市门头沟石龙工业区	门头沟区石龙工业区	韩立宝	102300	69843664
北京良乡卫星城工业开发区	房山凯旋大街金光路2号	李建民	102401	39351867
北京市燕山东流水工业区	北京市燕山东流水工业区管委会	康振有	102500	69347332
北京大兴工业开发区	大兴县黄村康庄路口东	蔡连军	102600	69244179
北京埝坛工业区	大兴县黄村镇念坛村	刘中铁	102600	69245165
通州张家湾工业开发区	通州区张家湾镇	唐 钰	101113	69541700
北京永乐经济开发区	通州区永乐店小甸屯村南	赵桂栋	101105	69544479
北京次渠工业区	通州区次渠镇	杨 顺	101111	69502049
北京新技术产业开发试验区昌平园区	昌平科技园区超前路9号	洪起忠	102200	69709140
北京雁栖工业开发区	怀柔县雁栖工业开发区	崔玉明	101407	61668124
北京凤翔科技开发区	怀柔县杨宋镇	线继文	101400	61679488
北京怀柔农业经济开发区	怀柔县富乐小区北里26号	唐爱民	101400	69643427
北京中国乡镇企业城	海淀复兴路甲23号城乡华懋商厦14层	曹 林	101400	68298317
怀柔民营经济开发区	怀柔龙山宾馆北二楼万通公司	许 立	101400	60693701
平谷县滨河工业开发区	平谷县府前西大街22号	王新海	101200	69963791
平谷县兴谷经济开发区	平谷县城关镇府前街7号	李宝峰	101200	69964071
北京市密云县工业开发区	密云县鼓楼西大街21号	李永军	101500	69041550
北京林河工业开发区	顺义县林河工业区	张东生	101300	89493610
北京天竺空港工业区	顺义县天竺镇	李友生	101312	64565745
北京市延庆经济技术开发区	延庆县城东外大街15号	张德福	102100	69142562
北京八达岭经济开发区	延庆县城西大街2号	李志民	102100	69141563

附2-4 各类开发区招商、入资情况
STATISTICS ON HIRER LEASEHOLDER AND CAPITAL INFLOW OF DEVELOPMENT ZONES

名称 Name	自开始至报告期累计 Accumulative Number from Beginning					
	招商个数(个) Number of Hirer Leaseholder (unit)	项目总投资(万元) Total Investment (10000 yuan)	注册资本(万元) Registered Capital (10000 yuan)	# 外方 Foreign Partner	协议外资金额(万美元) Contracted Foreign Capital(USD 10000)	外商实际投资(万美元) Foreign Actual Investment (USD 10000)
北京经济技术开发区	294	1373168	915815	765837	77559	62971
北京市王府井地区开发建设办公室	25	1522075	354779	354779	142430	95080
北京西三旗高新建材城	20	135167	89634	83374	9004	8610
北京市朝阳望京工业区	22	231089	46505	17381	1715	1527
朝阳东部旅游经济开发区	6	210903	75032	75032	6191	4121
北京新技术产业开发试验区海淀试验区						
北京新技术产业开发试验区丰台园区	1001	215586	208705	80538	4686	4251
北京八大处高科技园区	525	175223	163931	41130	4503	3184
北京市门头沟石龙工业区	825	393391	335770	11999	7868	7649
北京良乡卫星城工业开发区	61	110974	15901	2413	317	322
北京市燕山东流水工业区	14	2456	1533	764	100	99
北京大兴工业开发区	120	154284	80847	35886	2132	2104
北京埝坛工业区						
通州张家湾工业开发区	28	75228	52027	31012	3905	3256
北京永乐经济开发区	4	29056	12613	9843	2895	588
北京次渠工业区	7	95200	67113	4382	644	193
北京市新技术产业开发试验区昌平园区	532	560000	286332	147573	12339	8406
北京雁栖工业开发区	75	129000	116000	109000	3462	3462
北京凤翔科技开发区	161	58000	26524	13380	2930	2350
北京怀柔农业经济开发区	26	12997	11022	4532	498	498
北京中国乡镇企业城	25	70954	46518	24600	5290	3500
怀柔民营经济开发区	40	86275	86275			
平谷县滨河工业开发区	187	102717	67299	20678	1724	1724
平谷县兴谷经济开发区	122	201646	90176	81104	14713	12443
北京市密云县工业开发区	37	281122	30911	21452	3454	3129
北京林河工业开发区	30	89254	35090	23428	2134	1529
北京天竺空港工业区	74	678708	354618	306013	49063	20795
北京市延庆经济技术开发区	175	48365	43314	21784	1536	1536
北京八达岭经济开发区	185	56505	34992	6382	778	778

附2-5 各类开发区投资、生产情况
INVESTMENT AND PRODUCTION OF DEVELOPMENT ZONES

单位：平方米、万元　　(sq.m, 10000 yuan)

名称 Name	自年初累计 Accumulative Amount from Year-beginning					
	完成固定资产投资 Investment in Fixed Assets	新增固定资产 Incremental Fixed Assets	房屋建筑施工面积 Floor Space of Buildings under Construction	房屋建筑竣工面积 Floor Space of Buildings Completed	完成产值 Gross Output Value Completed	完成销售收入 Sales Revenue Completed
北京经济技术开发区	111066	60012	616977	309493	315000	360000
北京市王府井地区开发建设办公室	245970	130	432403			55396
北京西三旗高新建材城	1920		85537		18467	20855
北京市朝阳望京工业区	77981	8048	1044634	76486	4084	4477
朝阳东部旅游经济开发区	302	40	3150	121		310
北京新技术产业开发试验区海淀试验区	103285	92671	641204	194287	3240200	4516600
北京新技术产业开发试验区丰台园区	11209	21457	168993	86881	146618	281540
北京八大处高科技园区	13122	10899	150804	54188	23524	105212
北京市门头沟石龙工业区	2933		34966	1086	149212	342700
北京良乡卫星城工业开发区	7086	4629	36378	26188	79657	85000
北京市燕山东流水工业区	2258	5	748	748	2256	1562
北京大兴工业开发区	12877	17759	157221	83228	29725	44282
北京埝坛工业区						
通州张家湾工业开发区	1600		16200		6132	7012
北京永乐经济开发区	350	250	3000	3000		
北京次渠工业区	2233	27	3550	3500	15498	12224
北京新技术产业开发试验区昌平园区	7382	5408	111378	27120	108000	140000
北京雁栖工业开发区					56800	46400
北京凤翔科技开发区	15000	1000	36000	36000	51000	78000
北京怀柔农业经济开发区	1140				1641	530
北京中国乡镇企业城	839	839			30244	25242
怀柔民营经济开发区					3850	750
平谷县滨河工业开发区	758	758	4201	4201	22463	22418
平谷县兴谷经济开发区	3000	3000	2000	2000	50401	53894
北京市密云县工业开发区	10540	2620	73527	56830	3478	3305
北京林河工业开发区	1826	947	11350	3550	7157	8064
北京天竺空港工业区	17160	29260	193000	81800	263573	244279
北京市延庆经济技术开发区	3548		31965	27000	47743	59881
北京八达岭经济开发区	3719	3368	43831	4600	53786	370000

附录 3：各类市场情况　APPENDIX 3：VARIOUS MARKETS

附3-1 房产交易情况
HOUSE PROPERTY BUSINESS

项目 Item		合计 Total 起 Case	间 Room	其中：楼房 Storied Building	建筑面积 (万平方米) Floor Space (10000 sq.m)	立契价 (万元) Contracted Price (10000 yuan)
合　计	**Total**	**112196**	**483148**	**474781**	**1188.21**	**2478679.04**
市房屋交易所	**Municipal Transaction Department of Houses**	**3009**	**43086**	**42193**	**65.81**	**589810.87**
区县交易所	**Transaction Department of District and County**	**109187**	**440062**	**432588**	**1122.4**	**1888868.17**
东城区	Dongcheng	2853	18100	16908	25.77	62165.81
西城区	Xicheng	4752	10945	10701	34.19	19326.62
崇文区	Chongwen	2819	10050	9483	31.43	132063.79
宣武区	Xuanwu	2962	13015	12825	31.52	86625.36
朝阳区	Chaoyang	20045	121065	121065	270.86	730518.53
丰台区	Fengtai	6381	38255	38128	85.49	199884.88
石景山区	Shijingshan	11607	43381	43374	92.39	76834.59
海淀区	Haidian	19103	65417	63476	184.06	231257.99
门头沟区	Mentougou	2139	8738	7815	18.68	17366.64
房山区	Fangshan	5151	14940	14649	42.53	33536.7
通州区	Tongzhou	8270	21528	21371	68.84	66570.57
昌平县	Changping	4205	9786	9713	26.31	17891.18
顺义县	Shunyi	4587	13738	13738	44.95	55746.62
大兴县	Daxing	5540	22050	21735	66.71	92620.95
平谷县	Pinggu	1597	4587	4378	13.8	7973.79
怀柔县	Huairou	2528	7307	7191	21.2	24535.82
密云县	Miyun	1281	4966	4381	29.04	13891.83
延庆县	Yanqing	3367	12194	11657	34.63	20056.5

附3-2 城乡集贸市场基本情况
URBAN AND RURAL FREE MARKET

单位：个 (unit)

项目	Item	全市 Total	城市 Urban	农村 Rural
集贸市场总数	**Number of Free Market**	**1034**	**799**	**235**
消费品综合市场	Mixed Markets of Consumer Goods	375	255	120
农副产品市场	Markets of Farm and Sideline Products	465	359	106
农副产品综合市场	Multiple Markets	437	334	103
农副产品专业市场	Specialized Markets	28	25	3
工业消费品市场	Markets of Industrial Consumer Goods	141	132	9
工业消费品综合市场	Multiple Markets	83	76	7
工业消费品专业市场	Specialized Markets	58	56	2
其他	Others	53	53	

附3-3 集市贸易成交额(按商品类别分)
TRANSACTION VALUE OF FREE MARKET(BY CATEGORY OF COMMODITY)

单位：万元 (10000 yuan)

项目	Item	全市 Total	城市 Urban	农村 Rural
成交总额	**Total Transaction Value**	**3237686**	**2649818**	**587868**
粮食类	Grain	244311	210472	33839
油脂油料类	Edible Vegetable Oil	229011	200153	28858
棉烟麻类	Cotton,Tobacco and Hemp Crops	1166	503	663
肉食禽蛋类	Meat,Poultry and Eggs	513944	382129	131815
水产品类	Aquatic Products	292946	248953	43993
蔬菜类	Vegetables	770779	649330	121449
干鲜果类	Dried and Fresh Fruits	280424	187751	92673
大牲畜类	Large Domestic Animals	1782	10	1772
家禽幼禽类	Young Poultry	2041	87	1954
工业品类	Industrial Products	664536	571597	92939
其他	Others	236746	198833	37913

附3-4 集 市 贸 易 成 交 额(按市场类型分)
TRANSACTION VALUE OF FREE MARKET(BY TYPE OF MARKET)

单位：万元 (10000 yuan)

项目	Item	全市 Total	城市 Urban	农村 Rural
成交总额	**Total Transaction Value**	**3237686**	**2649818**	**587868**
综合市场	Mixed Markets	1023674	796938	226736
农副产品市场	Markets of Farm and Sideline Products	1667228	1335598	331630
工业消费品市场	Markets of Industrial Consumer Goods	453388	433660	19728
其　他	Others	93396	83622	9774

附3-5 集 市 贸 易 成 交 量
TRANSACTION VOLUME OF FREE MARKET

单位：吨 (ton)

项目	Item	全市 Total	城市 Urban	农村 Rural
粮　食	Grain	854759	718973	135786
#大　米	Rice	426098	371955	54143
玉　米	Corn	27731	24566	3165
油脂油料类	Edible Vegetable Oil	180363	137943	42420
棉烟麻	Cotton,Tobacco and Hemp Crops	3620	3084	536
猪　肉	Pork	137733	88403	49330
牛　肉	Beef	46269	31642	14627
羊　肉	Mutton	47644	34710	12934
鲜　蛋	Poultry Eggs	91438	55561	35877
家　禽	Poultry	25903	21595	4308
水产品	Aquatic Products	161494	116743	44751
鲜　菜	Vegetables	4320917	3515480	805437
干鲜果	Dried and Fresh Fruits	1242673	824281	418392
家禽幼禽	Young Poultry	1570		1570

附3-6 集市贸易成交量占社会销售量比重
THE PROPORTION OF FREE MARKET VOLUME IN TOTAL SOCIAL SALES

单位：吨 (ton)

项目	Item	成交量 Transaction Volume	社会销售量 Total Sales Volume	成交量占社会销售量比重(%) Proportion(%)
粮　食	Grain	854759	1811690	47.2
油脂油料类	Edible Vegetable Oil	180363	294855	61.2
猪　肉	Pork	137733	245368	56.1
牛　肉	Beef	46269	50453	91.7
羊　肉	Mutton	47644	51289	92.9
鲜　蛋	Poultry Eggs	91438	95020	96.2
家　禽	Poultry	25903	36434	71.1
水产品	Aquatic Products	161494	269432	59.9
鲜　菜	Vegetables	4320917	4355275	99.2

附3-7 生产资料市场成交情况
STATISTICS FOR TRANSACTION IN CAPITAL GOODS MARKETS

项目 Item				1998	1997	1998年为1997年% 1998 as % of 1997
成交额	**(万元)**	**Transaction Value**	**(10000 yuan)**	**1462783**	**1084011**	**134.9**
成交量		**Transaction Volume**				
新、旧汽车	(辆)	New and Old Automobiles	(unit)	123432	90084	137.0
钢材	(吨)	Rolled Steel	(ton)	153509	117493	130.7
木材	(立方米)	Timber	(cu.m)	249434	247955	100.6
煤炭	(吨)	Coal	(ton)	5861	21083	27.8

附3-8 消费者投诉与处理
CONSUMER'S LAWSUITS AND HANDLING

单位：件 (case)

项目	Item	1998		1997	
		受理投诉件数 Cases Accepted	构成(%) Composition(%)	受理投诉件数 Cases Accepted	构成(%) Composition(%)
总计	**Total**	**13448**	**100**	**13782**	**100**
按行业分	**By Sector**				
家用电器类	Household Appliances	1299	9.7	1181	8.6
# 电视机	TV Sets	204	15.7	237	20.1
电冰箱	Refrigerators	98	7.5	125	10.6
洗衣机	Washing Machines	27	2.1	55	4.6
收录机	Recorders	85	6.5	77	6.5
家用机械类	Household Machines	750	5.6	947	6.9
# 照相机	Cameras	32	4.3	58	6.1
自行车	Bicycles	113	15.1	131	13.8
摩托车	Motorcycles	194	25.9	276	29.1
钟表	Clocks and Watches	103	13.7	173	18.3
日用百货类	Articles of Daily Use	4688	34.9	4841	35.1
# 家具	Furniture	614	13.1	853	17.6
服装	Garments	1255	26.8	1131	23.4
鞋	Shoes	2151	45.8	2219	45.8
化妆品	Cosmetics	167	3.6	91	1.9
食品	Food	1979	14.7	2430	17.6
药品	Medicine	78	0.6	154	1.1
服务	Services	2710	20.1	2316	16.8
农用资料	Materials for Agricultural Use	137	1	142	1
邮购	Mail-order	527	3.9	592	4.3
其他	Others	1280	9.5	1179	8.6
按内容分	**By Content**				
质量	Quality	9540	71	9880	71.7
价格	Price	584	4.3	572	4.2
虚假广告	False Advertisements	64	0.5	95	0.7
假冒伪劣商品	Counterfeit Goods	194	1.4	142	1
计量	Measure	895	6.6	1274	9.2
欺诈骗销	Cheating Sales	126	0.9	172	1.2
其他	Others	2045	15.3	1647	12

注：总解决率为98.7%。

Note：Total rate of settlement is 98.7%.

附3-9 私 营 企 业 户 数
NUMBER OF PRIVATE ENTERPRISES

单位：户 (unit)

项 目 Item		年末企业数合计 Total (year-end)		盈利企业 Profit-making Enterprises		亏损企业中减免税企业 Tax-Reduce Enterprise of Loss-making Enterprises	
		1998	1997	1998	1997	1998	1997
合 计	**Total**	**40420**	**18533**	**12034**	**4293**	**383**	**104**
农业企业	Agriculture	16		8			
工业企业	Industry	4057	2053	1550	496	24	15
施工房地产开发企业	Real Estate Development	603	241	226	62		
运输企业	Transportation	179	35	67	13		
商品流通企业	Commerce	22933	10748	7036	2427	101	18
旅游饮食及服务企业	Tourism,Catering and Services	10337	4754	2462	1140	131	19
金融企业	Banking						
其他企业	Others	2295	702	685	155	127	52

注：本资料由市地税局提供。(下表同)

Note：Data of this table is provided by Municipal Local Tax Bureau.(the following is the same)

附3-10 盈利私营企业主要指标
MAIN INDICATORS FOR PROFIT-MAKING PRIVATE ENTERPRISES

单位：千元 (1000 yuan)

项 目 Item		销售或营业收入 Sales Revenue		成本及费用 Cost and Expenses		利润总额 Total Profits		实缴所得税 Income Taxes	
		1998	1997	1998	1997	1998	1997	1998	1997
合 计	**Total**	**25045685**	**8338315**	**22003859**	**8760588**	**675923**	**261630**	**129319**	**49631**
农业企业	Agriculture	148		131					
工业企业	Industry	3586454	923237	3262217	833521	91540	48684	27508	13483
施工房地产开发企业	Real Estate Development	418754	124128	295031	114879	18856	7474	3754	2057
运输企业	Transportation	27696	8409	20269	7173	1023	124	299	186
商品流通企业	Commerce	17214088	5983356	15374099	5731746	238412	92646	60932	22758
旅游饮食及服务企业	Tourism,Catering and Services	1432362	694012	1144700	1580254	120501	32438	23888	6798
金融企业	Banking								
其他企业	Others	2366183	605173	1907412	493015	205591	80264	12938	4349

附录4：世界主要国家和地区统计资料

APPENDIX 4: STATISTICS OF MAJOR COUNTRIES AND TERRTORIES

附4-1 1996年世界主要国家和地区水资源使用情况

USE OF WATER RESOURCE IN MAJOR COUNTRIES AND TERRITORIES OF 1996

国家和地区	Country or Territory	水资源（立方米/人）Water Resource (cu.m/person)	水资源使用 Use				
			总量（十亿立方米）Total (1 billion cu.m)	占水资源的(%) Proportion (%)	用于农业(%) Agriculture (%)	用于工业(%) Industry (%)	家用(%) Household (%)
中国	China	2304	460	16.4	87	7	6
美国	United States	9270	467.3	19	42	45	13
日本	Japan	4350	90.8	16.6	50	33	17
德国	Germany	1172	46.3	48.2	20	70	11
英国	United Kingdom	1208	11.8	16.6	3	77	20
法国	France	3084	37.7	21	15	69	16
意大利	Italy	2778	56.2	35.3	59	27	14
加拿大	Canada	95097	45.1	1.6	12	70	18
澳大利亚	Australia	18731	14.6	4.3	33	2	65
波兰	Poland	1279	12.3	24.9	11	76	13
罗马尼亚	Romania	1637	26	70.3	59	33	8
保加利亚	Bulgaria	2154	13.9	77.2	22	76	3
印度	India	1957	380	20.5	93	4	3
印度尼西亚	Indonesia	12839	16.6	0.7	76	11	13
巴基斯坦	Pakistan	1858	155.6	62.7	96	2	2
泰国	Thailand	1833	31.9	29	90	6	4
菲律宾	Philippines	4492	29.5	9.1	61	21	18
马来西亚	Malaysia	22174	9.4	2.1	47	30	23
韩国	Korea Rep.	1451	27.6	41.8	46	35	19
尼日利亚	Nigeria	1929	3.6	1.6	54	15	31
巴西	Brazil	32163	36.5	0.7	59	19	22
墨西哥	Mexico	3836	77.6	21.7	86	8	6
阿根廷	Argentina	19705	27.6	4	73	18	9
孟加拉国	Bangladesh	11153	22.5	1.7	96	1	3
越南	Viet Nam	4990	28.9	7.7	78	9	13
阿尔及利亚	Algeria	483	4.5	32.4	60	15	25
南非	South Africa Rep.	1190	13.3	29.7	72	11	17
新西兰	New Zealand	89959	2	0.6	44	10	46

资料来源：世界银行《1998年世界发展指标》

Source: 1998 World Development Indicator of World Bank.

附4-2 世界主要国家和地区土地面积和森林覆盖情况
LAND AREA AND FOREST-COVERAGE IN MAJOR COUNTRIES AND TERRITORIES

国家和地区 Country or Territory		土地面积（千平方公里）Land Area (1000 sq.km)	森林覆盖 Forest-coverage		
			总面积（千平方公里）Total Area (1000 sq.km)	占土地面积（%）Proportion in Land Area(%)	年均砍伐率（%）Annual Felling Rate(%)
		1995	1996	1997	1990—1995
中国	China	9326.4	1333	14	0.1
美国	United States	9159.1	2125	23	-0.3
日本	Japan	376.5	251	67	0.1
德国	Germany	349.3	107	31	0
英国	United Kingdom	241.6	24	10	-0.5
法国	France	550.1	150	27	-1.1
意大利	Italy	294.1	65	22	-0.1
加拿大	Canada	9221	2446	27	-0.1
澳大利亚	Australia	7682.3	409	5	0
波兰	Poland	304.4	87	29	-0.1
匈牙利	Hungary	92.3	17	19	-0.5
罗马尼亚	Romania	230.3	62	27	0
保加利亚	Bulgaria	110.6	32	29	0
印度	India	2973.2	650	22	0
印度尼西亚	Indonesia	1811.6	1098	61	1
巴基斯坦	Pakistan	770.9	17	2	2.9
泰国	Thailand	510.9	116	23	2.6
菲律宾	Philippines	298.2	68	23	3.5
马来西亚	Malaysia	328.6	155	47	2.4
韩国	Korea Rep.	98.7	76	77	0.2
尼日利亚	Nigeria	910.8	138	15	0.9
埃及	Egypt	995.5	0	0	0
巴西	Brazil	8456.5	5511	65	0.5
墨西哥	Mexico	1908.7	554	29	0.9
阿根廷	Argentina	2736.7	339	12	0.3
孟加拉国	Bangladesh	130.2	10	8	0.8
越南	Viet Nam	325.5	91	28	1.4
阿尔及利亚	Algeria	2381.7	19	1	1.2
南非	South Africa Rep.	1221	85	7	0.2

资料来源：1998年《世界银行图表集》
Source: 1998 World Bank Collection of Chart.

附4-3 世界主要国家和地区水污染物质排放量

EMISSION OF WATER POLLUTION IN MAJOR COUNTRIES AND TERRITORIES

国家和地区 Country or Territory		每天排放量（千克/天）Emission Per Day (kg/day)		每人每天排放量（千克/天/人）Emission Per Capita Per Day (kg/day/person)	
		1980	1993	1980	1993
中国	China	3358203	5339072	0.14	0.15
美国	United States	2742993	2477830	0.14	0.15
日本	Japan	1456016	1548021	0.14	0.14
德国	Germany		1046176		0.12
英国	United Kingdom	964510	680865	0.15	0.16
法国	France	716285	609940	0.14	0.15
意大利	Italy	442712	353906	0.13	0.13
加拿大	Canada	330241	300071	0.18	0.18
澳大利亚	Australia	204333	173490	0.18	0.19
波兰	Poland	580869	365580	0.14	0.16
匈牙利	Hungary	201888	151311	0.15	0.18
罗马尼亚	Romania	352368	146154	0.12	0.08
保加利亚	Bulgaria	151016	111310	0.14	0.14
印度	India	1457474	1441293	0.21	0.2
印度尼西亚	Indonesia	214010	537142	0.22	0.19
巴基斯坦	Pakistan	75125		0.17	
泰国	Thailand	214426	256930	0.22	0.16
菲律宾	Philippines	182052	181714	0.19	0.19
马来西亚	Malaysia	77215	136055	0.15	0.12
韩国	Korea Rep.	281900	358610	0.14	0.13
尼日利亚	Nigeria	72082		0.17	
埃及	Egypt	169146	198373	0.19	0.19
巴西	Brazil	866790	855432	0.16	0.17
墨西哥	Mexico	130993	167335	0.22	0.18
阿根廷	Argentina	244711	179432	0.18	0.2
孟加拉国	Bangladesh	66713	171087	0.16	0.17
土耳其	Turkey	160173	168548	0.2	0.19
阿尔及利亚	Algeria	60290		0.19	
南非	South Africa Rep.	237599	251142	0.17	0.17

资料来源：世界银行《1998年世界发展指标》
Source: 1998 World Development Indicator of World Bank.

附4-4 1993年世界主要国家和地区水污染物质排放量的行业构成

SECTOR COMPOSITION OF WATER POLLUTION EMISSION IN MAJOR COUNTRIES AND TERRITORIES OF 1993

单位：%　　　　(%)

国家和地区 Country or Territory		初级金属 Primary Metals	纸和纸浆 Paper and Paper Pulp	化　工 Chemical Industry	食品和饮　料 Food and Beverage	石器、陶器和玻璃 Stoneware, Earthenware and Glass	纺 织 Textile	木 材 Timber	其 他 Others
中国	China	22	10	14	33.3	0.4	11.5	0.4	8.3
美国	United States	8.3	32.7	9.5	28.2	0.1	7.8	2.4	10.8
日本	Japan	9.9	22	8.8	36.5	0.2	7.9	1.9	12.8
德国	Germany	15.6	15.3	15.1	27.9	0.2	6.4	2	17.6
英国	United Kingdom	8.9	24.7	10.1	37.1	0.2	7.2	1.7	10
法国	France	11.9	20.7	11	37	0.2	6.7	1.8	10.8
意大利	Italy	17	16.1	10.5	25.8	0.3	16.1	2.1	12.1
加拿大	Canada	10.1	30.1	8.7	34.5	0.1	5.9	3.3	7.3
澳大利亚	Australia	12.4	22.7	6.8	43.4	0.2	5.3	2.8	6.4
波兰	Poland	13.4	6.6	7.7	48.4	0.3	12.5	2.4	8.7
匈牙利	Hungary	9.9	7.6	8.1	54.9	0.2	10.8	1.8	6.8
罗马尼亚	Romania		16.1	2.9	1.8		41.4	11.3	26.6
保加利亚	Bulgaria	11.5	6.2	16.2	42.1	0.3	14.8	2	6.9
印度	India	15.6	8.1	7.3	50.9	0.2	12.9	0.3	4.8
印度尼西亚	Indonesia		7.8	10.4	58.9	0.2	15.4	4.8	2.6
泰国	Thailand	6.3	7.6	6.8	46.4	0.3	26.4	1.9	4.3
科威特	Kuwait	2.5	16.1	11.4	47.9	0.4	12.4	3.7	5.5
菲律宾	Philippines	4.1	8.1	6.9	52.9	0.1	21.4	3.7	2.7
马来西亚	Malaysia	6.8	14.3	15.2	31.8	0.2	11.1	7.6	13.1
韩国	Korea Rep.	12.8	15.4	11.2	25.8	0.3	20.8	1.5	12.2
土耳其	Turkey	15.8	8	7	46.6	0.3	26.4	1.9	4.3
埃及	Egypt	11.7	7.1	9.1	50.5	0.3	17.5	0.5	3.5
巴西	Brazil	10.4	13.5	9.1	45.8	0.3	11.5	3	6.4
墨西哥	Mexico	11	9.8	12.6	51.9	0.3	7.6	0.5	6.4
阿根廷	Argentina	7.7	11.8	7.7	57.4	0.3	8.6	1.5	5.1
突尼斯	Tunisia	5.6	5.6	5.1	62.7	0.8	17.4	0.7	2.1
新西兰	New Zealand	4.6	20.4	5.3	56.5	0.1	6.4	2.5	4.3
南非	South Africa Rep.	12.7	16.7	9.5	41.3	0.2	11	2.7	5.9

资料来源：世界银行《1998年世界发展指标》

Source: 1998 World Development Indicator of World Bank.

附4-5 世界主要国家和地区能源生产和使用情况

PRODUCTION AND CONSUMPTION OF ENERGY IN MAJOR COUNTRIES AND TERRITORIES

单位：千公吨油当量 (1000 ktns oil equivalent)

国家和地区	Country or Territory	能源生产 Production	能源使用 Consumption	能源使用年均增长率（%）Annual Growth Rate of Consumption (%)	人均能源使用（千克油当量）Consumpeion Per Capita (kg oil equivalent)	人均能源使用年均增长率（%）Annual Growth Rate of Consumption Per Capita (%)
		1995	1995	1980--1995	1995	1980--1995
中国	China	866556	850521	5.1	707	3.7
美国	United States	1655644	2078265	1.3	7905	0.3
日本	Japan	99468	497231	2.8	3964	2.3
德国	Germany	142712	339287	-0.2	4156	-0.5
英国	United Kingdom	254967	221911	1	3786	0.7
法国	France	126866	241322	2.1	4150	1.6
意大利	Italy	28645	161360	1.4	2821	1.3
加拿大	Canada	350629	233328	1.6	7879	0.3
澳大利亚	Australia	186625	94200	2.2	5215	0.7
波兰	Poland	94666	94472	-2	2448	-2.5
匈牙利	Hungary	13295	25103	-1	2454	-0.7
罗马尼亚	Romania	30008	44026	-2.9	1941	-3.1
保加利亚	Bulgaria	9810	22878	-2.5	2724	-2.1
印度	India	196941	241291	6.5	260	4.4
印度尼西亚	Indonesia	169325	85785	8.9	442	7
泰国	Thailand	19430	52125	11.1	878	9.4
巴基斯坦	Pakistan	18612	31536	7	243	3.8
菲律宾	Philippines	6006	21542	3.6	307	0.9
马来西亚	Malaysia	62385	33252	9.8	1655	7
韩国	Korea Rep.	20570	145099	9.6	3225	8.4
越南	Viet Nam	13808	7694	4.1	104	1.8
埃及	Egypt	59287	34678	5.4	596	2.9
巴西	Brazil	73172	122928	4.2	772	2.3
墨西哥	Mexico	201957	133371	2.2	1456	0
阿根廷	Argentina	66055	53016	1.9	1525	0.5
阿尔及利亚	Algeria	109257	24346	4.2	866	1.4
新西兰	New Zealand	12436	15409	3.9	4290	3.1
南非	South Africa Rep.	116160	88882	1.8	2405	-0.2

资料来源：世界银行《1998年世界发展指标》

Source: 1998 World Development Indicator of World Bank.

附4-6 世界主要国家人均工业二氧化碳排放量

EMISSION OF INDUSTRIAL CARBON DIOXIDE PER CAPITA IN MAJOR COUNTRIES AND TERRITORIES

单位：吨 (ton)

国家和地区	Country or Territory	1985	1988	1989	1990	1991	1992	1993	1994	1995	1996
孟加拉国	Bangladesh	0.1	0.1	0.1	0.1	0.1	0.1	0.1	0.1	0.2	0.2
美国	United States	19.9	18.5	20	20.1	18.9	19	19.1	18.9	20.6	20.8
日本	Japan	7.8	7.4	8	8	8.5	8.6	8.8	8.5	8.9	9
德国	Germany						11	10.4	10.4	9.9	10.2
英国	United Kingdom	10.4	9.9	9.9	10	9.8	9.8	9.6	9.4	9.3	9.3
法国	France	9	6.8	5.7	6.2	6.2	6.4	6.1	6	5.6	5.8
意大利	Italy	6.6	6.3	6.6	6.9	7	7.2	7.1	6.9	6.8	7.2
加拿大	Canada	17.1	15.2	15.6	15.9	14.7	14.4	14.9	14.6	14.9	14.7
澳大利亚	Australia	13.8	14.2	14.6	15.2	14.8	14.9	14.8	15.6	15.4	16
波兰	Poland	12.8	12	11.8	11.2	9	8.9	8.8	9.2	8.8	8.8
俄罗斯	Russia							13	12.6	10.8	12.3
罗马尼亚	Romania	8.6	8.3	9	9.1	6.6	6	5.2	5.4	5	5.3
保加利亚	Bulgaria	8.5	9.8	9.5	9.5	8.9	6.8	6.2	8	6.3	6.7
印度	India	0.5	0.6	0.7	0.8	0.8	0.8	0.9	0.9	0.9	1
印度尼西亚	Indonesia	0.6	0.8	0.7	0.7	1.2	1.2	1.3	1.4	1.5	1.5
泰国	Thailand	0.9	1	1.2	1.4	1.7	2	2.2	2.4	2.7	2.9
巴基斯坦	Pakistan	0.4	0.5	0.5	0.6	0.6	0.6	0.6	0.6	0.7	0.7
菲律宾	Philippines	0.8	0.5	0.7	0.7	0.7	0.7	0.8	0.7	0.7	0.9
马来西亚	Malaysia	2	2.3	2.5	2.8	3.1	3.7	4.2	4.7	4.7	5.3
韩国	Korea Rep.	3.3	4.1	4.8	5.1	5.6	6.2	6.6	6.9	7.5	8.3
越南	Viet Nam	0.3	0.4	0.4	0.3	0.4	0.3	0.3	0.4	0.4	0.
埃及	Egypt	1.1	1.4	1.5	1.4	1.4	1.4	1.4	1.6	1.5	1.6
巴西	Brazil	1.5	1.3	1.4	1.4	1.3	1.4	1.4	1.4	1.5	1.6
墨西哥	Mexico	3.8	3.8	3.6	3.6	3.8	3.9	4	3.9	4.1	3.9
阿根廷	Argentina	3.8	3.2	3.8	3.6	3.4	3.5	3.5	3.6	3.8	3.7
新加坡	Singapore	13.2	12.2	12.7	13.7	14.8	15.7	16.9	17.7	27.1	21.3
新西兰	New Zealand	5.6	6.6	7.4	7.7	7.2	7.4	7.8	7.3	7.6	7.6
南非	South Africa Rep.	7.8	9	9.1	8.9	8.6	8.6	8.3	7.8	8.3	8.3
尼日利亚	Nigeria	1	0.8	0.8	0.8	1	0.9	1.1	1.1	0.9	0.8

资料来源：世界银行《1998年世界发展指标》

Source: 1998 World Development Indicator of World Bank.

附4-7 世界主要国家和地区科学与技术统计

STATISTICS FOR SCIENCE AND TECHNOLOGY OF MAJOR COUNTRIES AND TERRITORIES

国家和地区 Country or Territory		R&D			高科技出口 Export of Highly Science and Technology	
		每百万人中科学家和工程师人数（人） Number of Scientists and Engineers Per 1 Million Persons (person)	每百万人中技术人员数（人） Number of Technical Personnel 1 Million Persons (person)	R&D支出占GNP% the Expenses in GNP (%)	出口额（百万美元） Value (USD 1 million)	占制造业出口% the Proportion in Manufacturing (%)
		1981--1992			1995	
中国	China				24393	19
孟加拉国	Bangladesh				4	
美国	United States	3873		2.9	181233	43
日本	Japan	5677	869	3	165972	39
委内瑞拉	Venezuela				377	14
英国	United Kingdom			2.1	79256	41
法国	France	2267	2972	2.4	67152	31
意大利	Italy	1366	742	1.3	32496	16
加拿大	Canada	2322	978	1.6	27648	23
澳大利亚	Australia	2477	943	1.4	5802	41
波兰	Poland	1083	1380	0.9	1688	10
西班牙	Spanish	956	299	0.9	11834	17
罗马尼亚	Romania	1220	492	0.7	355	8
印度	India	151	114	0.8		
印度尼西亚	Indonesia	181		0.2	3615	16
泰国	Thailand	173	51	0.2	14826	36
巴基斯坦	Pakistan	54	76	0.9		
菲律宾	Philippines	90	35	0.1	2986	42
马来西亚	Malaysia	87	88	0.4	37072	67
韩国	Korea Rep.	2636	317	2.8	47805	42
土耳其	Turkey	209	23	0.8	1289	8
埃及	Egypt	458	340	1	89	6
巴西	Brazil	391		0.4	4021	16
墨西哥	Mexico	266	399	0.2	21438	35
阿根廷	Argentina	350	197	0.3	1126	16
新加坡	Singapore	2512	1524	1.1	69249	70
新西兰	New Zealand	1555	785	0.9	405	11
南非	South Africa Rep.	319	132	1	1879	15
尼日利亚	Nigeria	15	69	0.1		

资料来源：世界银行《1997年世界发展指标》。

Source: 1998 World Development Indicator of World Bank.

附4-8 1995年世界主要国家和地区信息指标统计

STATISTICS FOR INFORMATION OF MAJOR COUNTRIES AND TERRITORIES OF 1995

单位：每千人拥有量 (volume/1000 persons)

国家和地区 Country or Territory		电视机 TV Sets	移动电话 Mobilphone	传真机 Fax	个人计算机 PC	网络用户 Net Consumers
中国	China	250	3.0	0.2	2.2	0.09
孟加拉国	Bangladesh	7	…	…		
美国	United States	776	128.4	53.9	328	313.16
日本	Japan	619	81.5	48.1	152.5	39.65
委内瑞拉	Venezuela	180	18.0	0.8	16.7	
英国	United Kingdom	612	98.0	30.8	186.2	99.01
法国	France	579	23.8	32.7	134.3	32.69
意大利	Italy	436	67.4	3.5	83.7	19.97
加拿大	Canada	647	86.5	18.1	192.5	143.33
澳大利亚	Australia	641	127.7	26.3	275.8	220.15
波兰	Poland	408	1.9	0.8	28.5	9.95
西班牙	Spanish	490	24.1	5.5	81.6	15.93
罗马尼亚	Romania	201	0.4	0.9	5.3	1.20
印度	India	61	0.1	0.1	1.3	0.02
印度尼西亚	Indonesia	147	1.1	0.4	3.7	0.27
泰国	Thailand	221	18.5	1.0	15.3	1.08
巴基斯坦	Pakistan	22	0.3	1.2	1.2	0.03
菲律宾	Philippines	121	7.3	0.5	11.4	0.46
马来西亚	Malaysia	231	43.4	3.0	39.7	4.24
韩国	Korea Rep.	115	36.6	8.4	120.8	10.70
土耳其	Turkey	240	7.0	1.6	12.5	1.25
埃及	Egypt	126	0.1	0.4	3.4	0.14
巴西	Brazil	278	8.0	1.3	13	2.90
墨西哥	Mexico	192	7.0	2.1	26.1	2.21
阿根廷	Argentina	347	9.9	1.4	24.6	2.72
尼日利亚	Nigeria	38	0.1		4.1	…
新西兰	New Zealand	508	108.0	18.1	222.7	216.81
南非	South Africa Rep.	101	12.9	1.8	26.5	20.10
蒙古	Mongolia	59	…	0.9	0.2	0.04
缅甸	Burma	76	…	…		

注：网络用户数为1996年数据。

资料来源：世界银行《1997年世界发展指标》。

Note: Data of net consumers refers to that of 1996.

Source: 1998 World Development Indicator of World Bank.

附4-9 世界主要国家和地区的财富值及构成
WEALTH AND COMPOSITION OF MAJOR COUNTRIES AND TERRITORIES

国家和地区 Country or Territory		人均财富估计值（美元/人） Estimated Value of Wealth Per Capita (US$/person)	财富来源（美元/人） Source of Wealth(US$/person)			财富来源构成（%） Composition of Source(%)		
			人力资源 Human Resources	生产资产 Production Assets	自然资本 Natural Capital	人力资源 Human Resources	生产资产 Production Assets	自然资本 Natural Capital
中国	China	6600	5100	1010	530	77	17	8
孟加拉国	Bangladesh	3100	2400	430	220	79	14	7
美国	United States	421000	250480	66650	104280	59	16	25
日本	Japan	565000	455030	99640	10530	81	18	2
委内瑞拉	Venezuela	58000	22530	14710	20980	39	25	36
英国	United Kingdom	324000	267570	45990	10040	83	14	3
法国	France	413000	317650	68320	27360	77	17	7
意大利	Italy	373000	305610	54720	13010	82	15	3
加拿大	Canada	704000	154820	60900	488120	22	9	69
澳大利亚	Australia	835000	177740	62540	594650	21	7	71
波兰	Poland	50000	28130	6440	15660	56	13	31
西班牙	Spanish	268000	208160	34180	25290	78	13	9
罗马尼亚	Romania	17000	11940	2920	2170	70	17	13
印度	India	4300	2740	1080	480	64	25	11
印度尼西亚	Indonesia	12000	6870	2080	3440	55	17	28
泰国	Thailand	34000	27310	3700	3700	81	11	8
朝鲜	Democratic People's Rep. of Korea	30000	23150	5060	2040	77	17	7
菲律宾	Philippines	15000	10770	2470	1360	74	17	9
马来西亚	Malaysia	56000	32860	8900	14050	59	16	2
韩国	Korea Rep.	123000	107810	12580	2130	88	10	2
土耳其	Turkey	34000	24170	5080	4320	72	15	13
埃及	Egypt	10600	8030	2190	370	76	21	4
巴西	Brazil	47000	17390	8740	20990	37	19	45
墨西哥	Mexico	74000	53540	8190	12100	73	11	16
阿根廷	Argentina	120000	46760	11910	61490	39	10	51
尼日利亚	Nigeria	4100	730	2230	1160	18	54	28
新西兰	New Zealand	212000	82580	48340	81230	39	23	38
南非	South Africa Rep.	61000	24240	8410	28240	40	14	46
南斯拉夫	Yugoslavia F.R.	71000	12840	38020	19760	18	54	28
缅甸	Burma	14000	9500	2590	2380	66	18	16
澳门	Macao	105000	87890	16580	780	84	16	4
新加坡	Singapore	306000	259440	46590	130	85	15	
香港特区	Hongkong	302000	267150	34790	140	88	12	

附4-10 人均个人消费表（按1987年固定美元计算）
PRIVATE CONSUMPTION PER CAPITA(CONSTANT 1987 US$)

年度 Year	澳大利亚 Australia	巴西 Brazil	加拿大 Canada	智利 Chile	中国 China	芬兰 Finland	法国 France	香港 Hongkong	美国 USA	英国 Britain	瑞典 Sweden
1966	4919	606	5143	1137	45	5005	5493	1842	7770	4602	7240
1967	5125	646	5252	1063	44	5082	5728	1832	7916	4686	7349
1968	5299	694	5392	1084	40	5063	5912	1506	8257	4794	7607
1969	5497	699	5600	1139	46	5610	6219	1623	8483	4802	7891
1970	5615	786	5633	1123	51	6058	6426	1781	8599	4926	8090
1971	5651	871	5879	1240	51	6146	6680	1979	8784	5055	8042
1972	5857	947	6219	1268	52	6627	6948	2079	9186	5351	8294
1973	6082	1036	6570	1146	54	6982	7260	2309	8520	5632	8492
1974	6140	1138	6827	1185	54	7068	7300	2214	9383	5549	8753
1975	6265	1102	7014	768	56	7260	7474	2238	9484	5531	8963
1976	6358	1212	7371	821	53	7300	7807	2361	9886	5558	9302
1977	6398	1255	7511	947	56	7207	7985	2718	10171	5542	9172
1978	6547	1253	7689	1026	60	7358	8244	3138	10483	5839	9081
1979	6651	1332	7833	1158	64	7707	8456	3171	10618	6087	9280
1980	6839	1385	7902	1161	71	7850	8514	3502	10527	6075	9188
1981	7008	1269	7985	1296	75	7921	8640	3702	10584	6079	9132
1982	6978	1281	7682	1048	77	8262	8890	3832	10586	6141	9178
1983	7067	1227	7869	967	85	8466	8931	4062	10964	6412	8952
1984	7235	1248	8159	1001	97	8686	8991	4225	11400	6527	9075
1985	7404	1261	8500	975	114	8973	9169	4336	11807	6756	9305
1986	7345	1345	8779	1008	113	9302	9488	4626	12128	7197	9693
1987	7530	1303	9039	1063	123	9756	9718	5040	12376	7558	10100
1988	7739	1261	9319	1119	138	10220	9990	5414	12748	8105	10300
1989	7936	1254	9453	1215	142	10633	10195	5540	12929	8336	10351
1990	7876	1232	9402	1199	140	10577	10416	5837	13004	8357	10229
1991	8009	1246	9141	1284	147	10139	10498	6286	12780	8140	10254
1992	8165	1159	9127	1409	170	9591	10580	6701	13003	8105	10051
1993	8311	1239	9145	1498	188	9269	10543	7075	13245	8277	9687
1994	8593	1314	9312	1539	204	9403	10640	7405	13544	8459	9790
1995	8847	1439	9324	1693	214	9726	10794	7312	13760	8598	9809
1996			9436	1838		10023	10998	7463	13977	8830	9943

附4-10 续表 continued

年度 Year	印度 India	印尼 Indonesia	意大利 Italy	日本 Japan	韩国 Korea Rep	马来西亚 Malaysia	荷兰 Netherlands	新西兰 New Zealand	新加坡 Singapore	泰国 Thailand
1966	157	102	3812	5074	561	584	5465	5862	1443	296
1967	162	109	4063	5550	577	574	5697	5522	1542	316
1968	163	118	4247	6003	616	568	6009	5478	1667	338
1969	165	121	4501	6489	645	589	6409	5667	1772	345
1970	167	118	1818	6891	697	594	6798	5898	1958	348
1971	167	120	4967	7177	766	615	6939	5854	2151	344
1972	164	115	5116	7713	770	631	7110	6164	2308	355
1973	165	118	5419	8323	844	670	7334	6563	2495	374
1974	161	137	5586	8158	879	713	7546	6673	2636	382
1975	167	147	5593	8382	909	693	7726	6488	2666	391
1976	168	147	5846	8562	983	715	8072	6227	2751	411
1977	177	147	6006	8822	1017	770	8393	6008	2843	432
1978	183	165	6158	9202	1100	830	8705	6113	2967	448
1979	174	171	6563	9717	1202	899	8845	6108	3074	470
1980	185	173	6956	9743	1159	989	8742	6085	3172	485
1981	189	237	7048	9814	1192	1014	8425	6147	3259	486
1982	191	238	7123	10172	1259	1021	8348	5994	3324	487
1983	201	255	7168	10440	1349	1026	8395	6101	3424	514
1984	204	266	7344	10647	1410	1064	8462	6278	3543	528
1985	207	278	7570	10933	1503	1039	8659	6327	3456	528
1986	213	278	7886	11247	1625	910	8835	6577	3558	538
1987	216	277	8227	11663	1730	904	9020	6688	3848	575
1988	225	262	8597	12228	1864	1023	9037	6776	4290	615
1989	230	275	8901	12757	2064	1122	9296	6772	4569	673
1990	234	311	9113	13270	2239	1237	9622	6690	4812	747
1991	233	325	9350	13561	2431	1322	9842	6473	4986	782
1992	239	339	9458	13808	2564	1350	10019	6426	5213	830
1993	245	361	9108	13935	2686	1386	10053	6629	5664	891
1994	252	372	9186	14154	2856	1448	10208	6835	5888	956
1995	263	402	9279	14381	3067	1613	10369	7023	6081	1024
1996	276	432	9296	14746	3215	1646	·	7211	6446	1076

附4-11 人均GDP表（以购买力平价标准，按国际美元现价计算）

GDP PER CAPITA(PURCHASING-POWER-PARITY, CURRENT INTERNATIONAL $)

年度 Year	澳大利亚 Australia	巴西 Brazil	加拿大 Canada	智利 Chile	中国 China	芬兰 Finland	法国 France	香港 Hongkong	美国 USA	英国 Britain
1980	8844	3598	10425	3927	500	8392	9717	6620	12624	8322
1981	9487	3578	11354	4300	540	9054	10396	7570	13535	8729
1982	9221	3573	10995	3863	589	9417	10734	7750	13267	8978
1983	9772	3398	11337	3707	638	9697	10862	8180	13655	9327
1984	10649	3679	12523	4136	766	10423	11492	9270	15087	10053
1985	11518	4109	13725	4602	908	11329	12317	9660	16324	10952
1986	12562	4731	15176	5176	1060	12507	13615	11460	17968	12338
1987	14176	5217	16981	5878	1261	14123	15085	13940	19945	14025
1988	15387	5417	18630	6546	1471	15641	16624	15820	21734	15551
1989	15603	5506	18765	7101	1509	16506	17188	16070	22225	15858
1990	15438	5390	18662	7255	1556	16640	17747	16770	22527	16067
1991	15738	5023	18639	7831	1726	15824	18313	17980	22698	16138
1992	16766	5268	19336	8876	2049	15849	19228	19760	24083	16707
1993	17824	5415	19938	9525	2365	15948	19323	21060	24961	17389
1994	18782	5730	20937	9908	2695	16902	20185	22200	26153	18360
1995	19862	5983	21811	11162	3072	18086	21168	23490	27323	19321
1996	20596	6491	22104	12013	3364	18837	21585	24260	28023	19917

附4-11 续表 continued

年度 Year	印度 India	印尼 Indonesia	意大利 Italy	日本 Japan	韩国 Korea Rep	马来西亚 Malaysia	荷兰 Netherlands	新西兰 New Zealand	新加坡 Singapore	泰国 Thailand
1980	519	897	8668	8533	2442	3174	8935	8386	6151	1472
1981	570	1003	9250	9290	2720	3533	9389	9254	7035	1605
1982	582	1009	9411	9628	2867	3690	9359	9448	7475	1680
1983	623	1085	9602	9869	3184	3842	9569	9633	8028	1773
1984	664	1198	10328	10692	3618	4204	10321	10494	8968	1922
1985	724	1285	11215	11718	4025	4285	11181	11119	9159	2096
1986	795	1440	12471	12953	4812	4586	12359	12260	9979	2357
1987	887	1622	13984	14614	5794	5097	13555	13316	11756	2758
1988	1022	1803	15387	16379	6770	5710	14642	13968	13656	3252
1989	1063	1937	15837	17128	7139	6080	15256	14026	14710	3596
1990	1116	2096	16364	18176	7836	6588	15978	14004	15890	4000
1991	1139	2300	17024	19355	8720	7177	16689	14062	17178	4370
1992	1231	2543	17852	20365	9477	7901	17660	14695	18679	4867
1993	1290	2734	17987	20828	10162	8546	18079	15883	20674	5326
1994	1392	2950	18708	21305	11150	9297	18943	16647	22880	5827
1995	1515	3230	19829	22177	12355	10261	19838	17472	25158	6493
1996	1606	3456	20139	23158	13193	10905	20503	17758	26680	6873

附录5：香港特别行政区主要社会经济指标

APPENDIX 5：MAIN SOCIAL AND ECONOMIC INDICATORS OF HONGKONG

项　目		Item		1995	1996	1997	1998
年中人口数	（万人）	Mid-year Population	(10000 persons)	615.6	631.1	650.2	668.7
出生率	（‰）	Birth Rate	(‰)	11.2	10	9.1	7.9
死亡率	（‰）	Death Rate	(‰)	5.1	5.1	4.9	4.8
自然增长率	（‰）	Natural Growth Rate	(‰)	6.1	4.9	3.0	2.8
平均期望寿命	（岁）	Life Expectancy at Birth	(age)				
男		Male		76	76.3	76.8	76.9
女		Female		81.5	81.8	82.2	82.3
劳动力总人数	（万人）	Active Population Total	(10000 persons)	300.07	309.38	333.0	343.4
男		Male		184.05	188.69	201.6	207.8
女		Female		116.02	120.7	131.4	135.6
失业人数	（万人）	Unemployed	(10000 persons)	9.56	8.61	7.7	20.1
失业率	（%）	Unemployment Rate	(%)	3.2	2.8	2.2	4.7
国内生产总值		Gross Domestic Product					
以当时市价计算	（亿港元）	At Current Market Prices	(HK$100 million)	10771	11919	13441	12892
以固定市价计算	（亿港元）	At Constant Market Prices (1990=100)	(HK$100 million)	7558	7898	8313	7887
人均国内生产总值		Per Capita GDP					
以当时市价计算	（港元）	At Current Market Prices	(HK$)	174972	188859	206718	192785
以固定市价计算	（港元）	At Constant Market Prices (1990=100)	(HK$)	122778	125139	127854	117938
国内生产总值部门构成	(%)	Composition of GDP by Kind of Activity	(%)				
农业和渔业		Agriculture and Fishery		0.1	0.1	0.1	
采矿业		Mining and Quarrying					
制造业		Manufacturing		8.3	7.3	6.5	
电、煤气、水		Electricity,Gas and Water		2.3	2.4	2.3	
建筑业		Construction		5.4	5.8	5.8	
商业、饭店、旅馆		Whole Sale,Retail Sale and Hotels		26.6	26.7	26.1	
运输、仓储、通信		Transport,Storage and Communications		10.1	9.8	9.3	
金融、保险、不动产和产业服务		Financing,Insurance, Real Estate and Business Services		24.4	25.1	26.5	
房屋所有权		Ownership of Premises		13.3	13.1	13.0	
社会团体和个人服务		Community,Social and Personal Services		17.3	17.6	17.4	
制造业生产指数		Indices of Manufacturing Production Industry		126.2	121.5	120.6	110.0
商品进出口贸易总额	（亿港元）	Total Imports and Exports	(HK$100 million)				
商品进口额		Imports		14911.2	15355.8	16151	14291
商品出口额		Domestic Exports		2316.6	2121.6	2114	1885
商品转口额		Re-exports		11124.7	11857.6	12445	11592

附录5 续表 continued

项目		Item		1995	1996	1997	1998
政府财政收支	（十亿港元）	Government Revenue and Expenditure	(HK$1 billion)				
总收入		Total Revenue		153.2	173.9	208.4	275.2
总支出		Total Expenditure		155.9	151.9	173.6	194.2
消费者物价指数	(%)	Consumer Price Indices	(%)	101.8	107.9	105.8	102.8
电力耗用	（兆焦耳）	Electricity Consumption	(terajoules)				
住宅		Domestic				28937	32793
商业		Commercial				67849	73857
工业		Industrial				18965	18489
街灯		Street lighting				322	307
出口往中国内地		Export to the mainland of China				2014	2197
总计		Total				118088	127643
抵港及离港旅客人数	（千人次）	Number of Passengers	(1000 person.times)				
抵港		to Hongkong				52780	57742
离港		off Hongkong				52764	57745
公共道路长度	（公里）	Length of Roads	(km)			1831	1865
公共交通乘客人数	（百万人次）	Number of Passengers of Public Traffic	(1 million person.times)			3963	3925
按种类划分的领牌车辆数字	（千辆）	Vehicles grouped by Type	(1000)				
私家车		Individuals				315	318
电单车（包括机动三轮车）		Motorcycles				24	23
的士		Taxi				18	18
公共及私家巴士		Public and Private Mini-bus				11	12
公共及私家小型巴士		Public and Private Bus				7	7
货车		Trucks				118	115
特别用途车辆（*少于0.5）		Special-use(*<0.5)				*	*
政府车辆		of Government				8	7
总计		Total				500	501
按主要死亡原因划分的死亡人数及死亡率		Number Deaths and Death Rate by Death Cause					
恶性肿瘤死亡人数	（人）	Malignant Tumour	(person)			10373	10567
死亡率	（人/每十万名人口）	Death Rate	(1/100 ten thousand persons)			159.5	158.0
心脏病死亡人数	（人）	Heart Trouble	(person)			4806	4896
死亡率	（人/每十万名人口）	Death Rate	(1/100 ten thousand persons)			73.9	73.2
肺炎死亡人数	（人）	Pneumonia	(person)			4100	4177
死亡率	（人/每十万名人口）	Death Rate	(1/100 ten thousand persons)			63.1	62.5
脑血管疾病死亡人数	（人）	Cerebrovasular disease	(person)			3026	3083
死亡率	（人/每十万名人口）	Death Rate	(1/100 ten thousand persons)			46.5	46.1
受伤及中毒死亡人数	（人）	Injured and Poisoned	(person)			1908	1944
死亡率	（人/每十万名人口）	Death Rate	(1/100 ten thousand persons)			29.3	29.1
婴儿死亡率（按每千名出生登记活产婴儿计算）	（‰）	Death Rate of New-borns (according to 1000 New-borns registered)	（‰）			4.0	3.2

附录6：澳门地区主要社会经济指标

APPENDIX 6：MAIN SOCIAL AND ECONOMIC INDICATORS OF MACAO

项目	Item	1995	1996	1997	1998
人口总数 (万人)	Population Total (10000 persons)	41.5	41.6	42.2	43.0
失业率 (%)	Unemployment Rate (%)	3.4	4.3	3.2	4.6
国内生产总值 (百万美元)	Gross Domestic Product (USD 1 million)	7441.4	7311.8	7330.7	
人均国内生产总值 (美元)	GDP Per Capita ($)	18181.0	17600.0	17498.0	
实质本地增长率 (%)	Real Local Growth Rate (%)	3.6	-0.5	-0.1	
通胀率 (%)	Inflation Rate (%)	8.6	4.8	3.5	0.2
对外贸易 (百万元澳门币)	Foreign Trade (1 million MDP)				
出口总值(离岸价格)	Export Value(FOB)	16259.9	15898.5	17129.2	17083.6
本地产品出口	Local Products		13375.8	15048.1	14903.8
再出口	Re-export		2522.7	2081.0	2179.8
进口总值(到岸价格)	Import Value(CIF)	16506.0	15930.7	16603.4	15596.4
贸易差额	Balance of Trade Value	-246.1	-32.2	525.8	1487.2
出口/进口 (%)	Export/Import (%)	98.5	99.8	103.2	109.5
旅游指标	Tourism				
入境旅客 (千人)	Foreign Tourists (1000 persons)	7752.5	8151.1	7000.4	6948.5
酒店住客数目 (千人)	Visitors in Hotels (1000 persons)	2400.9	2636.7	2124.9	2080.8
留宿时间 (晚数)	Staying Time (night)	1.3	1.3	1.3	1.4
房间入住率 (%)	Living Rate of Rooms (%)	60.1	64.1	52.1	53.1
五星、四星及三星酒店	5,4 and 3 stars Hotels	63.6	68.3	55.7	56.8
酒店客房供应数目 (房间)	Number of Guest Rooms (room)	7796.0	7724.0	8324.0	8320.0
五星、四星及三星酒店	5,4 and 3 stars Hotels	6641.0	6615.0	7231.0	7232.0
能源指标	Energy				
电力	Electricity				
本地净生产电量 (百万千瓦小时)	Local Net Production (1 million kwh)	1119.5	1217.5	1248.1	1377.0
供应电量 (百万千瓦小时)	Supply (1 million kwh)	1261.8	1341.2	1404.9	1514.7
平均价格 (澳门币/千瓦小时)	Average Price (MDP/kwh)	1.0	1.0	1.1	1.1
进口燃料价值 (百万澳门币)	Fuels Value Imported (1 million MDP)	690.7	870.6	911.4	826.4
占进口总值% (%)	the Proportion in Import (%)	4.2	5.5	5.5	5.3
消费物价指数 (%)	Consumer Price Indices (%)	94.8	99.4	102.8	103.0
（九五年七月至九六年六月=100）	(July,1995--June,1996=100)				
粮食及不含酒精饮品	Grain and Soft Drink	95.8	100.1	103.7	104.3
衣履	Clothing	93.1	98.8	100.4	101.4
维修及住屋开支	Repairs and Residence	95.6	100.8	107.8	109.2
烟酒	Tabacco and Liquor	96.7	101.6	102.0	105.5
家居用品	Daily Use Articles	96.7	99.0	99.9	98.9
药物及医疗	Medicines and Medical Services	99.1	104.9	107.5	109.2
交通及通讯	Transportation and Communications	100.1	101.5	103.1	100.0
教育文化及休闲	Education,Culture and Recreation	89.3	96.1	102.4	104.7
其他物品及服务	Others	90.6	95.9	97.6	94.5
中央政府收支状况 (百万元澳门币)	Revenue and Expenditure of Central Government				
总收益	Total Revenue		14711.3	15000.6	10723.1
总支出	Total Expenditure		14687.1	14240.7	10680.4
财政结余	Balance		24.2	759.9	42.7
货币汇率	Exchange Rate				
（每百外币兑澳门元）	(Patacas to 100 unit of foreign currency)				
美元	USD	796.8	796.6	797.5	797.9
马克	DEM	557	529.5	460.6	454.2
英镑	GBP	1257.7	1244.1	1306.9	1322.4
法国法郎	FEF	159.9	155.8	136.8	135.5
欧洲货币单位	ECU	1031	997.6	901.9	896.1
日元	JPY	8.526	7.326	6.601	6.131
人民币	RMB	95.4	95.8	96.2	96.4
综合货币概况(期末数值） (百万元澳门币)	Currency				
货币供应（M2）	Supply(M2)	69284	74744	78354	86210
流通货币	Circulation	1280	1427	1518	1548
活期及储蓄存款	Current and Saving Deposits	17730	19012	17435	18617
预先通知及定期存款	Advance Noticed and Fixed Deposits	50274	54306	59401	66045
本地信贷	Local Credit	41613	44309	48738	48000
公共	Public	141	86	115	139
机构及私人	Institutions and Individuals	41472	44223	48622	47862
净对外资产	Net Foreign Assets	39257	43207	42820	52882
货币及汇兑监理署	Monetary authority	17978	19202	20223	19657
其他金融机构	Other Banking Institutions	21278	24005	22598	33225